THE ROUGH GUIDE TO
SCOTLAND

KU-073-049

This elev
Greg D
Norm

C016345012

ROUGH
GUIDES

Contents

Introduction to
Scotland

Clichéd images of Scotland abound – postcards of wee Highland terriers, glittering lochs, infinite variations on tartan and whisky – and they drive many Scots apoplectic. Yet Scotland has a habit of delivering on its classic images. In some parts ruined castles really do perch on every other hilltop, in summer the glens do indeed turn purple with heather, and you'll be unlucky not to catch sight of a breathless bagpiper while you're up here. Sure, the roads can be wiggly and the drizzle can be oppressive. But there's something intoxicating about these patriotic, Tolkien-esque lands that will have you yearning for more.

The complexity of Scotland can be hard to unravel: somewhere deep in its genes a generous dose of romantic **Celtic** hedonism blends (somehow) with stern **Calvinist** prudence. It's a country where the losers of battles (and football games) are more romanticized than the winners. The country's major contribution to medieval warfare was the chaotic charge of the half-naked Highlander, yet in modern times it has given the world steam power, the television and penicillin. Chefs throughout Europe rhapsodize over Scottish langoustine and Aberdeen Angus beef, while back at home there is still a solid market for deep-fried pizza.

Naturally, the tourist industry tends to play up the heritage, but beyond the nostalgia lies a modern, dynamic nation. **Oil** and **nanotechnology** now matter more to the Scottish economy than fishing or Harris tweed, and the **video gaming** industry continues to prosper. Edinburgh still has its medieval Royal Mile, but just as many folk are drawn by its **nightclubs** and modern **restaurants**, while out in the Hebrides, the locals are more likely to be building websites than shearing sheep. Even the Highland huntin' shootin' fishin' set are outnumbered these days by **mountain bikers** and wide-eyed whale-watchers. The ceilidh remains an important part of the Highlands social scene, although large-scale **outdoor music festivals** draw in revellers from around the world.

ABOVE GLEN COE **RIGHT** T IN THE PARK

Scotland will never be able to cut its geographical and historic ties with the "auld enemy", England, south of the border, although relations between these two countries are as complicated as ever. In the 2014 **independence referendum** Scots voted to remain part of the United Kingdom by a margin of 55.3 percent to 44.7 percent Despite this result, the nationalist movement continued to build momentum, with the SNP recording a historic landslide victory in the **2015 UK general election**, taking 56 of 59 seats; they had won just four in 2010.

In contrast, thanks to ancient links with Ireland, Scandinavia, France and the Netherlands, Scots are generally enthusiastic about the **European Union**, which – up until the 2016 **EU membership referendum** result – had poured large sums of money into infrastructure and cultural projects, particularly in the Highlands and Islands. While the UK as a whole defied pollsters by voting to leave the EU, 62 percent of the Scottish population and all 32 councils opted to remain. Whether this will lead to a second Scottish independence referendum, as First Minister **Nicola Sturgeon** desires, remains uncertain. But one thing's for sure: Scots are likely to continue to view matters south of the border with a mixture of exaggerated disdain and well-hidden envy. Open hostility is rare, but ask for a "full English breakfast" and you'll quickly be put right.

Where to go

Even if you're planning a short visit, it's perfectly possible to combine a stay in either Edinburgh or Glasgow with a brief foray into the Highlands. With more time, a greater variety of **landscapes** in Scotland is available, but there's no escaping the fact that travel in the more remote regions of Scotland takes time and money, even with your own

SCOTLAND

N

0   miles   50

ATLANTIC OCEAN

Unst
Yell
Fetlar
Shetland
Lerwick

Foula

Fair Isle

Sanday

Westray
Rousay
Orkney
Kirkwall
Stromness
Hoy

John O'Groats
Wick
Thurso
Helmsdale
A9
A836

North Rona

Sula Sgeir

Cape Wrath

Ullapool
A835
Gairloch

The Minch

Lewis
Stornoway

Harris
Western Isles

Flannan Isles

North Uist

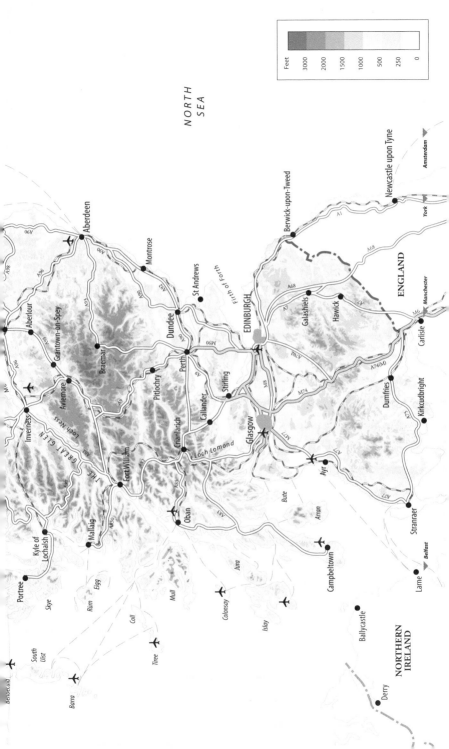

FACT FILE

- Scotland contains over **31,460 lochs**, and of its **790 islands**, 130 are inhabited.

- The **national animal** of Scotland is not sheep, Highland cattle, or even a loch-dwelling monster. It is in fact the unicorn, and has been since the twelfth century.

- Scotland itself has a **population** of around 5.4 million. However, nearly 28 million **Americans** define themselves as having Scottish ancestry. Famous names with Scots blood include Ben Affleck, Jack Daniel (of whisky fame), Kim Kardashian, Marilyn Monroe and Michael Phelps.

- The **shortest scheduled flight in the world** links Westray to Papa Westray in the Orkney Islands. At just one-and-a-half miles in length, the flight can take under two minutes with a tailwind.

- Never mind Nessie, **midges** are the real monsters of the Highlands. These tiny summer blood-suckers bite hardest from mid-May to August in calm cloudy conditions, especially at dawn and dusk. There's even a Midge Forecast (**w** midgeforecast .co.uk).

transport. If you plan to spend most of your time in the countryside, concentrate on just one or two areas for a more rewarding visit.

The initial focus for many visitors to Scotland is the capital, **Edinburgh**, a dramatically handsome and engaging city famous for its castle and historic Old Town. Come in August and you'll find the city transformed by the Edinburgh Festival, the largest arts festival in the world. An hour's travel to the west, the country's biggest city, **Glasgow**, is quite different in character. Once a sprawling industrial metropolis, it now has a lively social and cultural life to match its impressive architectural heritage. Other urban centres are inevitably overshadowed by the big two, although the transformation from industrial grey to cultural colour is injecting life into **Dundee**, while there's a defiant separateness to **Aberdeen**, with its silvery granite architecture and port. Other centres serve more as transport or service hubs to the emptier landscapes beyond, though some contain compelling attractions such as the wonderful castle in **Stirling** or the Burns' monuments in **Ayr**.

You don't have to travel far north of the Glasgow–Edinburgh axis to find the first hints of **Highland** landscape, a divide marked by the Highland Boundary Fault, which cuts across central Scotland. The lochs, hills and wooded glens of the **Trossachs** and **Loch Lomond** are the most easily reached and correspondingly busier. Further north, **Perthshire** and the Grampian hills of **Angus** and **Deeside** show the Scottish countryside at its richest, with colourful woodlands and long glens rising up to distinctive mountain peaks. South of Inverness the **Cairngorm** massif hints at the raw wilderness Scotland still provides, which is at its most spectacular in the north and western Highlands. To get to the far north you'll have to cross the **Great Glen**, an ancient geological fissure which cuts right across the country from Ben Nevis to **Loch Ness**, a moody stretch of water rather choked with tourists hoping for a glimpse of its monster. Arguably, Scotland's most memorable scenery is to be found on the jagged west coast, stretching from **Argyll** all the way north to **Wester Ross** and the sugarloaf hills of **Assynt**.

Not all of central and northern Scotland is rugged Highlands, however. The east coast in particular mixes fertile farmland with pretty stone-built fishing villages and

FROM TOP UPPER LOCH TORRIDON, WESTER ROSS (P.452); CITY CHAMBERS, GLASGOW (P.182)

golf courses – none more famous than that at the university town of **St Andrews**, the spiritual home of the game. Elsewhere, the whisky trail of **Speyside** and the castles and Pictish stones of the **northeast** provide themes for exploration, while in the southern part of the country, the rolling hills and ruined abbeys of the **Borders** offer a refreshingly untouristy vision of rural Scotland.

The splendour of the Highlands would be bare without the **islands** off the west and north coasts. Assorted in size, flavour and accessibility, the long chain of rocky Hebrides which necklace Scotland's Atlantic shoreline includes **Mull** and its nearby pilgrimage centre of **Iona**; **Islay** and **Jura**, famous for their wildlife and whisky; **Skye**, the most visited of the Hebrides, where the snow-tipped peaks of the Cuillin rise above deep sea lochs; and the **Western Isles**, an elongated archipelago that is the country's last bastion of Gaelic language and culture. Off the north coast, **Orkney** and **Shetland**, both with a rich Norse heritage, differ both from each other and quite distinctly from mainland Scotland in dialect and culture – far-flung islands buffeted by wind and sea that offer some of the country's wildest scenery, finest birdwatching and best archeological sites.

MUNRO-BAGGING

As the Inuit have dozens of words for snow, so a **hill** is rarely just a hill in Scotland. Depending on where you are, what it's shaped like and how high it is, a hill might be a ben, a mount, a law, a pen, a brae or even a pap (and that's without talking about the Gaelic *beinn*, *cnoc*, *creag*, *meall*, *sgurr* or *stob*). Even more confusing are "**Munros**". These are the Scottish hills over 3000ft high, defined by a list first drawn up by one Sir Hugh Munro in 1891. You "bag" a Munro by walking to the top of it, and once you've bagged all **284** you can call yourself a Munroist and let your chiropodist retire in peace. Actually, Munro-bagging at heart is less about conquering than appreciating the great Scottish outdoors. And if you do meet Sir Hugh's challenge, you can then start on the "Corbetts" (hills 2500–2999ft high) and "Donalds" (hills 2000–2499ft high).

Author Picks

Scotland has its poster places: Edinburgh's Royal Mile or Eilean Donan castle, for example. But the cherished memories of a country are usually more personal discoveries. Here are those of Rough Guides' authors as they travelled down every lane and supped in every pub in the cause of researching this Guide.

Mill on the Clyde Glasgow's prosperity wasn't just built on iron and ships. In the late eighteenth century, the Utopian mill village of New Lanark (p.219) inspired the Cooperative movement and introduced adult education.

Seafood sensation Look for the wooden shack in Crail harbour (p.310), select your lobster (caught that day), and have it cooked to order. Seafood doesn't get fresher than this.

Subculture Release your inner bohemian in the caverns beneath Edinburgh's South Bridge, rediscovered after two hundred lost years and turned into entertainments venue *The Caves* (p.97).

Skye crafts The mountains are marvellous, but Skye also appeals for its crafts; tanneries, weavers, brewers and all (p.487).

Stonehaven This coastal town (p.373), best known for its annual folk festival, is also near Scotland's finest medieval ruin, Dunottar Castle.

North Coast 500 This road trip around the northernmost reaches of Scotland covers some of the most spectacularly rugged scenery in the British Isles (p.440).

Beaver Trial Beavers are back in Scotland after a four-hundred-year absence, and the Beaver Trial at Knapdale (p.259) is a rare opportunity to seek out these hard-working creatures in the wild – the 60ft-long dam is a feat of engineering.

Flying visit The trip in an eight-seater plane to North Ronaldsay, Orkney (p.554), is worth it to see seaweed-eating sheep, even without a night at the ecofriendly bird observatory.

> Our author recommendations don't end here. We've flagged up our favourite places – a perfectly sited hotel, an atmospheric café, a special restaurant – throughout the Guide, highlighted with the ★ symbol.

FROM TOP DUNNOTTAR CASTLE (P.373); LOBSTER CREELS, CRAIL (P.310); NEW LIGHTHOUSE, NORTH RONALDSAY (P.555)

THE WEATHER

"There's no such thing as bad weather, only inadequate clothing", the poet laureate Ted Hughes is alleged to have said when asked why he liked holidaying on Scotland's west coast. For those who don't share Hughes' attitude, the **weather** is probably the single biggest factor to put you off visiting Scotland. It's not that it's always bad, it's just that it is **unpredictable**: you could just as easily enjoy a week of fabulous sunshine in early April while the rest of the UK was sodden as suffer a week of low-lying fog and drizzle in high summer.

No surprise then that six of the ten wettest counties in the UK are here. The reason is location: almost every **low pressure system** that barrels east out of the North Atlantic passes over Scotland, often forced north by the Azores' high pressure system. The good news is that such systems tend to blow over rapidly. Out in the islands, they say you can get all four seasons in a day. And even if the weather's not necessarily good, it's generally interesting – often exhilarating or dramatic, and certainly photogenic. And when the **sun** finally comes out all is forgiven. A week spent in thick mist is transformed when the clouds lift to reveal a majestic mountain range or a group of islands far offshore.

When to go

Scottish comedian Billy Connolly once said "there are two seasons in Scotland: June and winter". While the country is partial to a spot of unseasonal drizzle, the busy **summer** months – June, July and August – are generally warm and, most importantly, long, with daylight lingering until 9pm or till 10pm further north. **August** in Edinburgh is Festival time, which dominates everything in the city and means accommodation gets booked up very early. Elsewhere, events such as Highland Games, folk festivals or sporting events – most of which take place in the summer months – can tie up accommodation, though normally only in a fairly concentrated local area. If you're out and about in the countryside throughout the summer, you won't be able to avoid the clouds of small biting **midges**, which can be a real annoyance on still days, particularly around dusk.

May and **September** throw up weather every bit as good as, if not better than, the months of high summer. You're less likely to encounter crowds or struggle to find somewhere to stay, and the mild temperatures combined with the changing colours of nature mean both are great for outdoor activities, particularly hiking. The caveat is that September is prime **stalking season** for deer, which can affect access to some parts of the Highlands for hiking, fishing or riding a mountain bike.

The **spring** and **autumn** months of April and October bracket the tourist season for many parts of rural Scotland. A large number of attractions, tourist offices and guesthouses often open for business on the Easter weekend and shut up shop after the school half-term in mid-October. If places do stay open through the winter, it's normally with reduced opening hours; this is the best time to pick up deals at hotels and guesthouses. Note too that in more remote spots public transport will often operate on a reduced winter timetable.

Winter days, from November to March, occasionally crisp and bright, are often cold, gloomy and all too short, although Hogmanay and New Year has traditionally been a time to visit Scotland for partying and warm hospitality – something which improves as the weather worsens. While even tourist hotspots such as Edinburgh are notably quieter during winter, a fall of snow in the Highlands will prompt plenty of activity around the ski resorts.

AVERAGE DAILY TEMPERATURES AND MONTHLY RAINFALL

	Jan	Feb	March	April	May	June	July	Aug	Sept	Oct	Nov	Dec
EDINBURGH												
Max/min (°C)	7/1	8/1	10/3	12/4	15/7	17/10	19/12	19/11	17/9	13/7	10/4	7/1
Max/min (°F)	45/34	46/34	50/37	53/39	59/44	63/50	66/53	66/52	63/48	55/44	50/39	45/34
Rainfall (mm)	68	47	52	41	49	61	65	60	64	76	62	61
FORT WILLIAM												
Max/min (°C)	6/0	6/-1	7/1	10/2	14/4	16/7	17/10	17/9	15/7	11/5	8/2	6/1
Max/min (°F)	42/32	42/30	45/34	50/36	57/40	60/45	63/49	62/49	59/45	52/41	46/36	52/34
Rainfall (mm)	248	175	184	97	85	77	89	107	140	202	206	201
LERWICK												
Max/min (°C)	6/2	6/2	6/2	8/4	10/5	12/8	14/10	14/10	13/9	10/6	8/4	6/2
Max/min (°F)	43/35	43/35	43/35	46/38	51/42	54/46	58/40	58/50	55/48	51/43	46/39	43/35
Rainfall (mm)	143	121	125	71	53	58	67	84	106	142	146	143
TIREE												
Max/min (°C)	8/3	8/3	9/4	10/5	13/7	15/10	16/11	16/11	15/10	13/8	10/6	8/4
Max/min (°F)	46/38	46/38	48/39	51/41	55/45	59/49	61/52	61/52	59/49	55/46	49/43	46/39
Rainfall (mm)	138	101	103	73	60	66	80	107	112	150	136	132
WICK												
Max/min (°C)	6/1	6/1	8/2	10/4	11/5	14/8	16/10	16/10	14/9	12/6	9/4	7/1
Max/min (°F)	43/34	43/34	46/36	49/38	53/42	57/46	60/50	60/50	57/47	53/43	47/38	44/34
Rainfall (mm)	72	64	67	50	49	53	62	65	74	95	90	75

29

things not to miss

It's not possible to see everything that Scotland has to offer on a short trip – and we don't suggest you try. What follows, in no particular order, is a selective taste of the country's highlights: compelling sights, vibrant festivals and some of the most spectacular scenic wonders in Europe. All highlights have a page reference to take you straight into the Guide, where you can find out more.

1 EDINBURGH SKYLINE
Page 79
From Calton Hill, the Old Town appears as an unforgettable vista of tightly packed tenements and spires that rise to the immense castle.

2 HOGMANAY
Page 39
New Year celebrations, with whisky, dancing and fireworks staving off the midwinter chill.

3 CALEDONIAN FOREST
Page 425
Among the gnarled survivors of the great ancient forests you'll find one of Scotland's largest populations of the elusive red squirrel.

4 LOCH NESS
Page 407
Take the old road around the east shores to escape the caravanning crowds, and find tiny lochans and pretty pubs like the *Dores Inn*.

5 WHISKY
Page 35
Single malts have never been more varied or so innovative, and you'll find hundreds of varieties in Scotland's pubs. Good luck.

6 RHINNS OF GALLOWAY
Page 153

Famous for its balmy gulf-stream-fed microclimate, the southwest is a sanctuary for exotic plants, with six botanic gardens to discover.

7 ROSSLYN CHAPEL
Page 108

This richly decorated cathedral-like masterpiece is a testament to the skills of its medieval sculptors.

8 ISLAY
Page 266

Endless pretty villages and bays, wonderfully varied wildlife, and no fewer than eight whisky distilleries.

9 AILSA CRAIG
Page 168

Conspicuous, muffin-shaped hump just off the Ayrshire coast that's home to one of the world's largest colonies of gannets.

10 EIGG
Page 499

Perfect example of a tiny Hebridean island with a golden beach to lie on, a hill to climb and stunning views across to Rùm.

11 KNOYDART PENINSULA
Page 446

No matter whether you arrive by boat or on foot, the sense of dropping off the radar is the same in one of Britain's last wilderness regions.

10

11

12 BIKING AT GLENTRESS
Page 131

7stanes has seven forest centres with adrenaline-pumping downhill biking for all levels.

13 THE CUILLIN RANGE
Page 490

The most spectacular mountain range on the west coast: superb to see, breathtaking (literally) to climb.

14 THE CAIRNGORM MOUNTAINS
Page 425

Natural splendour and terrific outdoor activities abound here.

15 STAFFA AND THE TRESHNISH ISLES
Page 244

View the basalt columns of Fingal's Cave from the sea, then picnic beside the puffins on the Isle of Lunga.

16 SOUTH HARRIS BEACHES
Page 515

Take your pick of deserted golden beaches in South Harris, or further south in the Uists.

17 GLASGOW NIGHTLIFE
Page 211

Go for a proper pub crawl through the West End or experience the edgier nightlife around Glasgow Green.

18 WEST HIGHLAND WAY
Page 401

Ninety-six miles, five days, one utterly spectacular walk from Glasgow to Fort William.

12

13

14

15

16

17

18

19

20

21

22

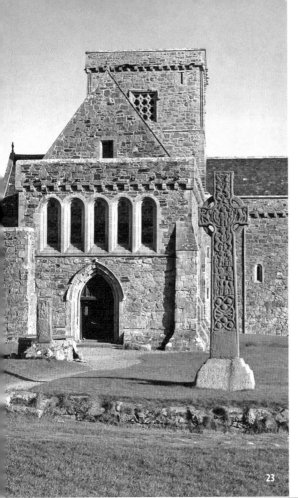

19 TOBERMORY
Page 240
The main town on the beautiful island of Mull, and Scotland's most picturesque fishing port.

20 JARLSHOF, SHETLAND
Page 568
An exceptional archeological site taking in Bronze Age, Iron Age, Pictish, Viking and medieval remains.

21 WHALE-WATCHING, MULL
Page 241
Look out for minke and killer whales in the abundant waters around Mull.

22 AUGUST FESTIVALS IN EDINBURGH
Page 101
Actors, comedians, artists, writers and celebs converge en masse for the world's biggest arts gathering.

23 IONA
Page 246
The home of Celtic Christian spirituality, an island of pilgrimage today as in antiquity.

24 FOOD ON SKYE
Pages 491 & 493
Skye is Scotland's foodie capital, from slap-up lobster and chips at *The Oyster Shed* to dining in the kitchen at *The Three Chimneys*.

25 CRAIL
Page 310

Fife's picture-perfect harbour town, home to small fishing vessels, caught-that-morning seafood and easel-toting artists.

26 STIRLING CASTLE
Page 280

The grandest castle in Scotland, with a commanding outlook over the Highlands and Lowlands.

27 GLEN COE
Page 404

Scotland's most spectacular glen puts Munro summits, glacial valleys and cool waterfalls within day-trip distance of Fort William.

28 CALLANISH, LEWIS
Page 512

Prehistoric standing stones that occupy a serene setting in the Western Isles.

29 CEILIDHS
Page 460

The ultimate Highland get-together, full of music, singing and dancing like there's no tomorrow.

Itineraries

The following itineraries plot routes through Scotland in all its variety, from the royal castles of Edinburgh to the blackhouses of the Western Isles, the putting greens of St Andrews and the Cuillin mountains' jagged ridges. Whether you're after a whistle-stop week, a fortnight of utter escapism or you're looking for an excuse to discover some of the finest tastes in Scotland, they will point the way.

A SCOTLAND PRIMER

Ten days isn't enough time to do the entire nation justice, yet this tour offers tasters of contemporary culture, heritage, Highland scenery and even island life.

❶ **Edinburgh** The capital deserves two days of any visit. Must-sees include the cobbled streets and castle of the Old Town, the view from Calton Hill, and perhaps the Museum of Scotland, or a pub like *Bow Bar* if it rains. **See p.52**

❷ **Fife** So close to Edinburgh, so different in atmosphere, Fife has some highlights of Scottish culture: lovely Culross village; a novice-friendly putting green at St Andrews; and fresh lobster for lunch in Crail. **See p.302**

❸ **Stirling and the Trossachs** One of Scotland's most iconic castles is reason enough to visit Stirling. It's also the gateway for walks and bike rides in the Trossachs, a sort of Highlands-lite, and beyond them, the much-mythologized Loch Lomond. **See p.276**

❹ **Gigha** Subtropical gardens, golden beaches and life in the slow lane – Gigha is the perfect island introduction to the Hebrides. **See p.262**

❺ **Glasgow** We bookend the route with the great rival to Edinburgh. Vibrant, modern Glasgow is all about the arts – don't miss the Glasgow School of Art – and nightlife that is glam and gritty by turns. **See p.178**

A TASTE OF SCOTLAND

A whistle-stop tour around the regional culinary highlights of Scotland – you'll have no trouble finding porridge, broth, cullen skink and haggis, neeps and tatties wherever you go.

❶ **Edinburgh** With both Michelin-starred restaurants and fine old drinking holes, foodies have never had it so good here. Highlights include *Wedgwood* and *The Kitchin*. **See p.91 & p.94**

❷ **Abroath** "A world-class delicacy" is how chef and writer Rick Stein describes the humble haddock after it's been smoke-cured here, and who are we to argue? Head to the harbour and take your pick from the family-run smokehouses. **See p.351**

❸ **Speyside** Welcome to the heartland of whisky country, nutured by pure cold water and a gentle climate. Of the fifty distilleries in the area, eight are on an official Malt Whisky Trail, from famous names like Glenfiddich and Glenlivet to wee distilleries like Strathisla. **See p.431**

❹ **Skye** Small gourmet restaurants like *Three Chimneys* and *Loch Bay* are reason enough to visit Skye. Expect innovative menus of super-fresh produce. **See p.493**

❺ **Islay** Peat and smoke define Islay single malts, heavy pungent whiskies compared to

- - - - - - - A SCOTLAND PRIMER
- - - - - - - A TASTE OF SCOTLAND
- - - - - - - TWO WEEKS ON THE ISLANDS

ATLANTIC
OCEAN

NORTH
SEA

NORTHERN
IRELAND

ENGLAND

the lighter honeys and vanilla in Speyside. Laphroaig, Lagavulin and Bowmore are the big hitters, and all eight offer tours. **See p.267**

❻ Loch Fyne Fine dining without the fuss in the most famous seafood restaurant in Scotland, the *Loch Fyne Oyster Bar and Restaurant*. Expect local oysters, langoustine, scallops and superb fish. **See p.231**

TWO WEEKS ON THE ISLANDS

While Orkney and Shetland deserve a dedicated trip, the west coast islands seem tailor-made to explore by ferry. Who needs Greece?

❶ Mull Embark from one of the Highlands' loveliest fishing ports, Tobermory, for one of its best wildlife adventures – whale-watching – and visit nearby Iona, its atmosphere steeped in thousands of years as a pilgrimage destination. **See p.237**

❷ Barra A pip-squeak among the Western Isles where clear bays, white beaches and impressive

mountains deliver a concentrated dose of Hebridean magic. **See p.524**

❸ The Uists Trout-fishing doesn't get much more fun than in the half-drowned lochs of North Uist. **See p.517**

❹ Lewis and Harris The conjoined twins of the Hebrides deserve several days of a trip. Visit for astonishing beaches like Luskentyre, mysterious standing stones at Callanish and to journey back a century in the restored village of Garenin. **See p.507 & p.514**

❺ Skye Skip back to Skye to tackle the Cuillin ridge, the must-do mountain route of any trail-junkie, or discover Loch Coruisk by boat, then settle into one of the island's many excellent hotels. **See p.484**

❻ The Small Isles So, what do you feel like doing today: sampling genuine island life on Eigg; discovering a barmy baronial manor on Rum; or spotting birdlife on strolls around tiny Muck? From Mallaig they're all just across the water. **See p.497**

UNST BUS STOP

Basics

Getting there

The quickest, easiest and cheapest way to get to Scotland is by plane. Scotland has three main international airports: Glasgow, Edinburgh and Aberdeen. Glasgow handles most long-haul flights, though all three have a reasonable spread of European connections, as does Glasgow Prestwick Airport, a hub for the budget airline Ryanair.

With most airlines nowadays, how much you pay depends on how far in advance you book and how much **demand** there is during that period – generally speaking, the earlier you book, the cheaper the prices. That said, it's worth looking out for sales, which often start 10–12 weeks before the departure date.

If you're coming from elsewhere in Britain, from Ireland or even northwest Europe, you can reach Scotland easily enough by **train**, **bus** or **ferry** – it probably won't work out cheaper or faster than flying, but it's undoubtedly better for the environment.

From England and Wales

If you're ultimately heading out to the Highlands and Islands, **flying** is the quickest way to travel. Airfares are most competitive on popular routes such as London or Birmingham to Edinburgh and Glasgow, which can cost as little as £30 return (journey time around 1hr). Once you add on the cost of transport to the airport and flying with **luggage** (many budget airlines charge for all but the smallest cabin bags), the savings compared with doing the same journey overland can be minimal.

Flying with airlines such as British Airways (Ⓦba .com), Ryanair (Ⓦryanair.com) and easyJet (Ⓦeasyjet.com) may be quick, but coach and train fares can be pretty competitive if you book in advance. Return **train** fares to Glasgow can cost as little as £30 from Manchester (3hr 30min) or £60 from London (4hr 45min), with the very cheapest tickets going on sale twelve weeks in advance. A more flexible or last-minute fare will cost two or three times the amount. Another option is the overnight **Caledonian Sleeper** (Ⓦsleeper.scot) from London Euston (Mon–Fri & Sun; journey time to Glasgow around 8hr); again, if you book in advance (up to twelve months), single overnight fares cost around £50, with no saving on return fares. The **coach** takes much longer than the train (around 9hr one-way), but can cost significantly less, with a London or Birmingham to Glasgow return starting for as little as £20.

From Ireland

Travel from Ireland is quickest by plane, with **airfares** from either Belfast or Dublin to Glasgow from as little as €45 return; try Aer Lingus (Ⓦaerlingus.com) and Ryanair (Ⓦryanair.com), both based in Ireland. Though P&O no longer runs its Larne to Troon service, there remain good **ferry** links with Northern Ireland via Cairnryan, with up to seven sea crossings daily (2hr; single passenger without car from £27; with car from £74). Stena Line also operates up to six services daily from Belfast to Cairnryan (2hr 15min; single passenger without car from £20; with car from £79).

From mainland Europe

Ferries run by DFDS Seaways (Ⓦdfdsseaways.co.uk) sail overnight from Amsterdam to Newcastle (daily; 16–17hr), less than an hour's drive south of the Scottish border. Return fares for single passengers start at £130, which includes an overnight berth (around £150 extra with a small car). A much quicker (and usually cheaper) alternative is to fly with one of Europe's big budget carriers, such as easyJet (Ⓦeasyjet.com), Ryanair (Ⓦryanair.com), Norwegian (Ⓦnorwegian.com) or Jet2 (Ⓦjet2.com).

From the US and Canada

If you fly nonstop to Scotland from **North America**, you'll arrive in either Glasgow or Edinburgh. The majority of cheap fares, however, route through Amsterdam, London, Manchester, Dublin or Paris. To reach any other Scottish airport, you'll definitely need to go via London, Glasgow or Edinburgh.

Figure on six to seven hours' flight time nonstop from the **east coast** of the US to Glasgow, or seven hours to London plus an extra hour and a quarter from London to Glasgow or Edinburgh (not including stopover time). Add three or four hours more for travel from the **west coast**.

United (Ⓦunited.com) flies direct from Newark Liberty International Airport in New York to Glasgow, with return fares (including taxes) from around $950. Air Canada (Ⓦaircanada.com) has direct flights to Edinburgh from Toronto; return fares for nonstop flights (including taxes) cost around $800.

From Australia and New Zealand

Flight time from **Australia** and **New Zealand** to Scotland is at least 22 hours. There is a wide variety of routes, with those touching down in Southeast Asia the quickest and cheapest on average. To reach

Scotland, you usually have to change planes either in **London** – the most popular choice – or in another European gateway such as Paris or Amsterdam. Given the length of the journey involved, you might be better off including a night's stopover in your itinerary.

The cheapest scheduled flights to London are usually to be found on one of the Asian airlines, such as Malaysia Airlines (Ⓦ malaysiaairlines.com) or Thai Airways (Ⓦ thaiair.com). Average **return fares** (including taxes) from eastern Australian cities to London are around Aus$1500–2000. Fares from Perth or Darwin cost around Aus$100 less. Return fares from Auckland to London range between NZ$2000 and NZ$3000 depending on the season, route and carrier.

From South Africa

There are **no direct flights** from South Africa to Scotland, so you must change planes en route. The quickest and cheapest route to take is via **London**, with flight time around eleven hours, usually overnight. **Return fares** from Cape Town to London are around ZAR10,000; try British Airways (Ⓦ ba .com), South African Airways (Ⓦ flysaa.com) or Virgin Atlantic (Ⓦ virgin-atlantic.com). You'll save money if you buy the next leg of your journey to Scotland separately, through one of the budget airlines.

AGENTS AND OPERATORS

North South Travel UK ☏ 01245 608 291, Ⓦ northsouthtravel .co.uk. Friendly, competitive travel agency, offering discounted fares worldwide. Profits are used to support projects in the developing world, especially the promotion of sustainable tourism.

STA Travel UK ☏ 0333 321 0099, US ☏ 1800 781 4040, Australia ☏ 134 782, New Zealand ☏ 0800 474 400, South Africa ☏ 0861 781 781, Ⓦ statravel.co.uk. Worldwide specialists in independent travel; also student IDs, travel insurance, car rental, rail passes, and more. Good discounts for students and under-26s.

Trailfinders UK ☏ 0207 368 1200, Ireland ☏ 021 464 8800 Ⓦ trailfinders.com. One of the best-informed and most efficient agents for independent travellers.

Travel CUTS Canada ☏ 1800 667 2887, US ☏ 1800 592 2887, Ⓦ travelcuts.com. Canadian youth and student travel firm.

USIT Ireland ☏ 01 602 1906, Australia ☏ 1800 092 499 Ⓦ usit.ie. Ireland's main student and youth travel specialists.

RAIL AND BUS CONTACTS

Caledonian Sleeper Ⓦ sleeper.scot. Sleeper train to Glasgow, Edinburgh, Aberdeen, Inverness and Fort William.

Man in Seat 61 Ⓦ seat61.com. The best train information website on the internet.

National Express ☏ 08717 818178, Ⓦ nationalexpress.com. Coaches to Scotland.

ScotRail Ⓦ scotrail.co.uk. Scotland's principal domestic operator, with full route and timetable info.

Trainline Ⓦ trainline.com. The best site for cheap tickets, with popular mobile app.

Traveline Scotland Ⓦ travelinescotland.com. Excellent Scotland-wide journey planner, connected to the latest bus and train timetables.

Virgin Ⓦ virgintrains.co.uk. Main operator from London to Scotland on both the East and West Coast routes.

FERRY COMPANIES

DFDS Seaways UK ☏ 0871 522 9955, International ☏ +44 330 333 0245, Ⓦ dfdsseaways.co.uk.

P&O Ferries UK 0800 130 0030, Ireland ☏ +353 1 686 9467, Ⓦ poferries.com.

Stena Line UK ☏ 0844 770 7070, Ⓦ stenaline.co.uk.

Getting around

The majority of Scots live in the central belt, with Glasgow in the west and Edinburgh in the east. Public transport in this region is efficient and most places are easily accessible by train and bus. Further south and north it can be a different story: off the main routes, public transport services are few and far between, particularly in more remote parts of the Highlands and Islands. With careful planning, however, practically everywhere is accessible, and the scenery is usually adequate compensation for a long journey.

By train

Scotland has a modest **rail network**, at its densest in the central belt, skeletal in the Highlands, and nonexistent in the Islands. The successful 2015 reopening of part of the historic Waverley Route to the Borders, however, proves that there's both the political will and public appetite for full-scale reversals of the infamous Beeching closures of the 1960s, and reopening the whole line (as far as Carlisle) hasn't been ruled out. ScotRail (Ⓦ scotrail .co.uk) runs the majority of train services, reaching all the major towns – sometimes on lines rated among the great scenic routes of the world.

You can buy train **tickets** at most stations, but if the ticket office is closed, or the automatic machine isn't working, you may buy your ticket on board from the inspector using cash or a credit card. Those eligible for a national rail pass (Ⓦ railcard.co.uk; £30) can obtain discounted tickets, with up to a third off most fares. These include the **16–25 Railcard**, for full-time students and those aged between 16 and 25, the **Two Together Railcard** for two named people aged over 16 travelling together, and the **Senior Railcard** for people over 60. Alternatively, a **Family & Friends Railcard** entitles up to four adults and up to four children to a reduction. There's also the new Club 50 (£15) scheme, offering discounted travel for those aged fifty and over, though its introduction has proved controversial.

In addition, ScotRail offers several regional passes. The most flexible is the **Spirit of Scotland Travelpass**, which gives unlimited train travel within Scotland. It's also valid on all CalMac ferries and on various buses in the remoter regions. The pass costs £134 for four days' travel in an eight-day period, or £179.70 for eight days' travel in a fifteen-day period. The **Highland Rover** allows unlimited train travel within the Highlands; it costs £81.50 for four out of eight consecutive days. Lastly, there's a **Central Scotland Rover**, which gives unlimited train travel on lines between Glasgow and Edinburgh; it costs £36.30 for three out of seven consecutive days.

On most ScotRail routes **bicycles** are carried free, but since there are only between two and six bike spaces available, it's a good idea to reserve ahead, and this is a requirement on longer journeys.

By coach and bus

All of Scotland's major towns and cities are served by a few long-distance bus services, known across Britain as **coaches**. Scotland's main long-distance operator is **Scottish Citylink** (☎08712 663333, ⓦcitylink.co.uk). On the whole, coaches are cheaper than trains and, as a result, are very popular, so for longer journeys it's advisable to book ahead.

There are various **discounts** on offer for those with children, those under 26 or over 60, and full-time students (contact Scottish Citylink for

more details), and you can also buy an **Explorer Pass**, which gives unlimited travel throughout Scotland (£41/3 days out of 5; £62/5 days out of 10; £93/8 days out of 16). **Local bus services** are run by a bewildering array of companies, many of which change routes and timetables frequently. Local tourist offices can provide free timetables or you can contact **Traveline Scotland** (☎0871 200 2233, ⓦtravelinescotland.com), which provides a reliable service both online and by phone. There is also a free app available for download.

Some remote parts of Scotland are only served by **postbuses**, vehicles carrying mail and a handful of fare-paying passengers. They set off early in the morning, usually around 8am and, though sociable, can be excruciatingly slow. You can view routes and timetables on the **Royal Mail website** (☎03457 740740, ⓦroyalmail.com/postbus). Sadly, the Western Isles routes were discontinued in March 2016.

By car

In order to **drive** in Scotland you need a current full driving licence. If you're bringing your own vehicle into the country you should also carry your vehicle registration, insurance and ownership documents at all times.

In Scotland, as in the rest of the UK, you **drive on the left**. Speed limits are 20–40mph in built-up areas, 70mph on motorways and dual carriageways (freeways) and 60mph on most other roads. Though many built-up areas (including Edinburgh) are increasingly moving towards 20mph, with speed bumps popping up all over the place, as a rule, assume that in any area with street lighting the limit is 30mph.

In the Highlands and Islands, there are still plenty of **single-track roads** with passing places; in addition to allowing oncoming traffic to pass at

---

MINIBUS TOURS

Minibus tours that operate out of Edinburgh (and Glasgow) and head off into the Highlands are popular with backpackers who want a quick taste of Scotland. Aimed at the youth market, they adopt an upbeat and irreverent approach to sightseeing, as well as offering a good opportunity to get to know fellow travellers.

The current leading operator, **Haggis** (☎01315 579393, ⓦhaggisadventures.com), has bright yellow minibuses setting off daily on whistle-stop tours lasting between one and ten days, in the company of a live-wire guide. A three-day trip from Edinburgh to Skye via Loch Ness costs £119 (food and accommodation not included).

Several other companies offer similar packages, including **Macbackpackers** (☎01315 589900, ⓦmacbackpackers.com), which runs tours linking up their own hostels round the country. The popular **Rabbie's** tours (☎01312 263133, ⓦrabbies.com) don't aim quite so squarely at the backpacker market and have a mellower outlook.

these points, you should also let cars behind you overtake. These roads can be frustrating but take care and stay alert for vehicles coming in the opposite direction, which may have been hidden by bends or dips in the road. In more remote regions, the roads are dotted with sheep (and occasionally even cattle), which are entirely oblivious to cars, so slow down and edge your way past; should you kill or injure one, it is your duty to inform the local farmer.

The AA (☎08008 87766, ⊕theaa.com), RAC (☎08008 28282, ⊕rac.co.uk) and Green Flag (☎08000 510636, ⊕greenflag.com) all operate 24-hour **emergency breakdown** services. You may be entitled to free assistance through a reciprocal arrangement with a motoring organization in your home country. If not, you can make use of these emergency services by joining at the roadside, but you will incur a hefty surcharge. In remote areas, you may have a long wait for assistance.

Be aware that a new drink driving limit set in 2014 (50 milligrams of alcohol per 100 millilitres of blood), bringing Scotland in line with much of Europe, means that even one pint of beer or glass of wine could leave you on the wrong side of the law.

Car rental

Car rental in Scotland is cheaper than it used to be thanks to online advance deals with comparison sites such as ⊕holidayautos.co.uk. The most economical cars can be rented for as little as £110 a week. Walk-in prices are more expensive at £20–50 per day, or around £130–200 a week. The major chains are confined mostly to the big cities, so it may be cheaper to use small **local agencies** – we've highlighted some in the Guide. With all rentals it's worth checking the terms and conditions carefully; some rentals only allow you to drive a limited number of miles before paying extra.

Automatics are rare at the lower end of the price scale – if you want one, you should book well ahead. **Camper vans** are another option; rates start at around £400 a week in the high season, but you'll save on accommodation (try ⊕bunkcampers.com, who have depots in London, Glasgow and Edinburgh). Few companies will rent to drivers with less than one year's experience and most will only rent to people over 21 or 25 and under 70 or 75 years of age.

Though **fuel** in Scotland has been expensive over the last decade, the current rock-bottom oil price means much cheaper prices at the pump, for now. At the time of writing petrol (gasoline) and diesel can be found for just over £1 per litre, though with such a volatile market prices are likely to continue fluctuating wildly. Note also that prices increase the further

you travel from the central belt, with the Highlands and Islands being considerably more expensive, albeit offset to some degree by government subsidies.

By ferry

Scotland has more than sixty inhabited islands, and nearly fifty of them have scheduled **ferry** links. Most ferries carry cars and vans, and, if you're driving, the vast majority can – and should – be booked in advance; there's usually a window of four to six months. There's no need to book if you're travelling on foot; simply buy your ticket at the port office or on board.

Caledonian MacBrayne aka CalMac has a virtual monopoly on services on the River Clyde and to the Hebrides, sailing to 22 islands and 4 peninsulas. They aren't quick – no catamarans or fast ferries – but with the recent introduction of the Scottish Government-sponsored RET (Road Equivalent Tariff) scheme, fares have been slashed. The ferry from Mallaig to Skye, for example, now costs £2.80 for foot passengers and £9.40 for cars. If you're taking more than one ferry, or aiming for a specific island grouping, you can also make significant savings with an **Island Hopscotch** ticket (there are 19 different variations to choose between). Given the notoriously fickle west coast weather, especially in winter, it's probably worth downloading the CalMac Service Status app.

Car ferries to **Orkney and Shetland** are run by NorthLink Ferries. Pentland Ferries also run a car ferry to Orkney, and John O'Groats Ferries run a summer-only passenger service to Orkney. The various Orkney islands are linked to each other by Orkney Ferries; Shetland's inter-island ferries are mostly council-run so the local tourist board (⊕shetland.gov.uk/ferries) is your best bet for information. There are also numerous **small operators** round the Scottish coast that run fast RIB taxi services, day-excursion trips, and even the odd scheduled service; their contact details are given in the relevant chapters of this Guide.

FERRY COMPANIES

CalMac ☎ 08000 665000, ⊕ calmac.co.uk
John O'Groats Ferries ☎ 01955 611353, ⊕ jogferry.co.uk
NorthLink Ferries ☎ 08456 000449, ⊕ northlinkferries.co.uk
Orkney Ferries ☎ 01856 872044, ⊕ orkneyferries.co.uk
Pentland Ferries ☎ 08006 888998, ⊕ pentlandferries.co.uk

By plane

Apart from the three major **airports** of Glasgow, Edinburgh and Aberdeen, Scotland has numerous minor airports around the Scottish Highlands and

Islands, some of which are little more than gravel airstrips. Airfares fluctuate enormously depending on demand – if you book early enough you can fly from Glasgow to Islay for £53 one-way, but leave it to the last minute and it could cost you more than twice that. Most flights within Scotland are operated by **flybe** (**W**flybe.com), or its franchise partner **Loganair** (**W**loganair.co.uk). The latter have recently teamed up with Scotrail to offer a flat rail transfer fare of £20 to anywhere in Scotland with connecting flights. For inter-island flights in Shetland, you need to book through **Directflight** (**☎**01595 840246; **W**directflight .co.uk/shetland). Competition emerges from time to time, with **Eastern Airways** (**W**easternairways .com) currently offering flights from Aberdeen to Stornoway and Wick.

Accommodation

In common with the rest of Britain, Scotland is expensive, but in terms of accommodation, budget travellers are relatively well catered for, with numerous hostels, campsites and bunkhouses. Those with money to spend will relish the more expensive country-house hotels. In the middle ground, however, the standard of many B&Bs, guesthouses and hotels can be disappointing. Welcoming, comfortable, well-run places do, of course, exist in all parts of the country – and you'll find the best ones listed in this Guide.

Star ratings

VisitScotland, the country's tourist board, operates a system for grading accommodation, which is updated annually. However, not every establishment participates, and you shouldn't assume that a particular B&B is no good simply because it's not on VisitScotland's lists. The tourist board uses star awards, from one to five, which are supposed to reflect the quality of welcome, service and hospitality – though it's pretty clear that places without en-suite toilets, a TV in every room, matching fabrics or packets of shortbread on the sideboard are likely to be marked down.

Booking accommodation

If you decide not to book online, most **tourist offices** will help you find accommodation and **book a room** directly, for which they normally

---

ACCOMMODATION ALTERNATIVES

Useful websites that provide alternatives to standard hotel and hostel accommodation.
CouchSurfing **W**couchsurfing.org.
Vacation Rentals by Owner **W**vrbo.com.
Airbnb **W**airbnb.com.
onefinestay **W**onefinestay.com.

charge a small fee. If you take advantage of this service, it's worth being clear as to what kind of place you'd prefer, as the tourist office quite often selects something quite randomly across the whole range of their membership. Bear in mind, too, that outside the main towns and cities many places are only open for the **tourist season** (Easter to Oct): you'll always find somewhere to stay outside this period, but the choice may be limited.

Hotels

Hotels come in all shapes and sizes. At the **upper end** of the market, they can be huge country houses and converted castles offering a very exclusive and opulent experience. Most will have a licensed bar and offer both breakfast and dinner, and often lunch as well. In the cities the increasing prevalence of modern **budget hotels** run by national (and international) chains may not win any prizes for aesthetics or variety, but they are competitively priced and for the most part meet criteria for clean, smart, serviceable accommodation.

Guesthouses and B&Bs

Guesthouses and B&Bs offer the widest and most diverse range of accommodation. VisitScotland uses the term "**guesthouse**" for a commercial venture that has four or more rooms, at least some of which are en suite, reserving "**B&B**" for a predominantly private family home that has only a few rooms to let. In reality, however, most places offer en-suite facilities, and the different names often reflect the pretensions of the owners and the cost of the rooms more than differences in service: in general, guesthouses cost more than B&Bs.

Similarly priced are **inns** (in other words, pubs), or their modern equivalent, "restaurants with rooms". These will often have only a handful of rooms, but their emphasis on creating an all-round convivial atmosphere as well as serving top-quality food often makes them worth seeking out.

A surprising number of guesthouses and B&Bs still have decor that consists of heavy chintz and floral designs, but a good location, and the chance to get an insight into the local way of life, can be some compensation. Many B&Bs, even the pricier ones, have only a few rooms, so **advance booking** is recommended, especially in the Islands.

Hostels

There's an ever-increasing number of **hostels** in Scotland to cater for travellers – youthful or otherwise – who are unable or unwilling to pay the rates charged by hotels, guesthouses and B&Bs. Most hostels are clean and comfortable, sometimes offering **doubles** and even **singles** as well as **dormitory accommodation**. Others concentrate more on keeping the price as low as possible, simply providing a roof over your head and a few basic facilities. Whatever type of hostel you stay in, expect to pay £8–20 per night.

The **Scottish Youth Hostels Association** (Ⓦsyha .org.uk), referred to throughout the Guide as "SYHA hostels", run the longest-established hostels in the Highlands and Islands. While these places sometimes occupy handsome buildings, many retain an institutionalized air. Bunk-bed accommodation in single-sex dormitories, lights out before midnight and no smoking/no alcohol policies are the norm outside the big cities. Breakfast is not normally included in the price, though most hostels have self-catering facilities.

If you're not a **member** of one of the hostelling organizations affiliated to **Hostelling International** (HI), you can pay your £15 joining fee (£6/under-25s) at most hostels. **Advance booking** is recommended, and essential at Easter, Christmas and from May to August. You can book online, in person or by phone.

There are also loads of **independent hostels** (sometimes known as "bunkhouses") across Scotland. These are usually laidback places with no membership, fewer rules, mixed dorms and no curfew. You can find most of them in the annually updated *Independent Hostel Guide* (Ⓦindependent hostelguide.co.uk). Many of them are also affiliated to Scottish Independent Hostels (Ⓦhostel-scotland .co.uk), which has a programme of inspection and lists members on its website.

Camping

There are hundreds of **caravan and camping parks** around Scotland, most of which are open from April to October. The majority of sites charge about £10–15 for two people with a car to pitch a tent, and are usually well equipped, with shops, a restaurant, a bar and, occasionally, sports facilities. Most of these, however, are aimed principally at **caravans**, trailers and motorhomes, and generally don't offer the tranquil atmosphere and independence that those travelling with just a tent are seeking.

That said, peaceful and **informal sites** do exist, and are described throughout this Guide, though they are few and far between. Many **hostels** allow camping, and farmers will usually let folk camp on their land for free or for a nominal sum. In this Guide, we've listed **the price for a pitch** (ie one tent for two people, plus a car) wherever possible. Where campsites charge per person, we've listed prices in that format instead.

Scotland's relaxed land access laws allow **wild camping** in open country. The basic rule is "leave no trace", but for a guide to good practice, visit Ⓦoutdooraccess-scotland.com. The great majority of **caravans** are permanently moored nose to tail in the vicinity of some of Scotland's finest scenery; others are positioned singly in back gardens or amid farmland. Some can be booked for self-catering, and with prices starting at around £100 a week, this can work out as one of the cheapest options if you're travelling with kids.

If you're planning to do a lot of camping at official camping and caravanning sites, it might be worthwhile joining the **Camping and Caravanning Club** (Ⓦcampingandcaravanningclub.co.uk). Membership costs £37 for the digital option and £43 for paper (with hard copies of the monthly magazine and campsite directory), entitling you to up to thirty percent discount at CCC sites. Those coming from abroad can get the same benefits by buying an international camping carnet, available from home motoring organizations or a CCC equivalent.

Self-catering accommodation

A huge proportion of visitors to Scotland opt for **self-catering** accommodation, booking a cottage or apartment for a week and often saving themselves a considerable amount of money by doing so. In many

---

5 CAMPSITES NOT TO MISS

Comrie Croft Near Crieff. See p.328.
Red Squirrel Glen Coe. See p.406.
Ardnamurchan Campsite Ormsaigbeg. See p.442.
Badrallach Badrallach. See p.447.
Camusdarach Campsite Camusdarach. See p.445.

cases, the minimum rental period is still one week, and therefore not a valid option if you're aiming to tour round the country, though increasingly, with the rise of websites like ⓦairbnb, owners are becoming more flexible. The least you can expect to pay in the high season is around £250 per week for a place sleeping four, but something special, or somewhere in a popular tourist area, might cost £500 or more. Such is the number and variety of self-catering places on offer that we've mentioned very few in the Guide. A good source of information is **VisitScotland**'s self-catering website (ⓦvisitscotland.com/accommodation/self-catering), updated frequently and listing thousands of properties. Alternatively, you could try one of the websites listed below.

HOLIDAY RENTAL AGENCIES

Cottages and Castles ☎ 01738 451610, ⓦ cottages-and-castles .co.uk. A range of self-catering properties, mostly in mainland Scotland.

Cottages4you ☎ 03454 986900, ⓦ cottages4you.co.uk. Hundreds of reasonably priced properties all over Scotland.

Ecosse Unique ☎ 01835 822277, ⓦ uniquescotland.com. Carefully selected cottages across mainland Scotland, plus a few in the Hebrides and Orkney.

Landmark Trust ☎ 01628 825925, ⓦ landmarktrust.org.uk. A very select number of historical properties, often in prime locations.

LHH ☎ 01381 610496, ⓦ lhhscotland.com. Attractive homes across Scotland, including mansions, castles and villas.

Mackay's Holidays ☎ 01237 426725, ⓦ mackaysholidays.com. A whole range of properties in every corner of mainland Scotland (plus Skye and Orkney), from chalets and town apartments to remote stone-built cottages.

National Trust for Scotland ☎ 01314 580200, ⓦ nts.org.uk. The NTS lets around forty of its converted historic cottages and houses, and also offers working conservation holidays.

Scottish Country Cottages ☎ 03452 680801, ⓦ scottish -country-cottages.co.uk. Superior cottages with lots of character, scattered across the Scottish mainland plus some of the Inner Hebrides.

Campus accommodation

A different and generally cheaper self-catering option, especially if you're staying a week or more in one of the cities, is **campus accommodation**. The universities of Glasgow, Strathclyde, Edinburgh, Stirling, St Andrews and Dundee all open their halls of residence to short-term visitors during the summer break, and some also offer rooms during the Easter and Christmas holidays. Accommodation varies from tiny single rooms in long, lonely corridors to relatively comfortable places in small, shared apartments. Prices start at around £30 per night for a single room, not always including breakfast. All the useful university details are given in the Guide.

Food and drink

While Scotland isn't exactly known for its culinary heritage, the country's eating habits are changing, and from the cities to some of the furthest islands, you can often eat extremely well, with a strong emphasis on fresh, local and organic produce.

Scottish **fish and shellfish** is the envy of Europe, with a vast array of different types of fish, prawns, lobsters, mussels, oysters, crabs and scallops found around the extensive coastline. The prevalence of fish-farming, now a significant industry in the Highlands and Islands, means that the once-treasured salmon is now widespread and relatively inexpensive. Both salmon and trout, another commonly farmed fish, are frequently served cold with bread and butter.

Scottish-reared **beef** is often delicious, especially the Aberdeen Angus breed, though Highland cattle are also rated for their depth of flavour. **Venison**, the meat of the red deer, is also popular – low in cholesterol and very tasty, it's served roasted or in casseroles, and is often cooked with juniper and red wine. Other forms of **game** include grouse, which when cooked properly is strong, dark and succulent; pheasant, a lighter meat; and the less commonly served, but still tasty, pigeon and rabbit.

In rural Scotland, attitudes towards **vegetarianism** are still some way behind the big cities. While almost all pubs and restaurants will have at least one or two vegetarian options on their menus, they're too often lazily predictable and overpriced. Veggies – and vegans for that matter – will nevertheless find plenty of great food on offer in Edinburgh and Glasgow.

Breakfast

In most hotels and B&Bs you'll be offered a **Scottish breakfast**, similar to its English counterpart of sausage, bacon and egg, but typically with the addition of black pudding (blood sausage) and potato scones. Porridge is another likely option, as is fish in the form of kippers, smoked haddock or even kedgeree. Scotland's staple dish, like England's, is **tea**, drunk strong and with milk, though **coffee** is just as readily available everywhere. However, while smart coffee shops are now a familiar feature in the cities, execrable versions of espresso and cappuccino, as well as instant coffee, are still all too familiar.

Lunches and snacks

The most common lunchtime fare in Scotland remains the **sandwich**. A bowl or cup of hearty **soup**

CLASSIC SCOTTISH DISHES

Arbroath smokies Powerful smoked haddock (see p.351).
Cullen skink Rich soup made from smoked haddock, potatoes and cream (p.385).
Haggis Flavoursome sausage meat (spiced liver, offal, oatmeal and onion) cooked inside a bag made from a sheep's stomach. Tasty and satisfying, particularly when eaten with its traditional accompaniments, "bashed neeps" (mashed turnips) and "chappit tatties" (mashed potatoes).
Porridge A breakfast staple, this is properly made with oatmeal and water, and cooked with a pinch of salt. Some prefer to add milk and honey, fruit or sugar to sweeten.
Scots broth Hearty soup made with stock (usually mutton), vegetables and barley.

is a typical accompaniment, particularly in winter. A **pub lunch** is often an attractive alternative. Bar menus generally have standard filling but unambitious options including soup, sandwiches, scampi and chips, or steak pie and chips, with vegetarians suffering from a paucity of choice. That said, some bar food is freshly prepared and filling, equalling the à la carte dishes served in adjacent hotel restaurants. Pubs or hotel bars are among the cheapest options when it comes to eating out – in the smallest villages, these might be your only option.

Restaurants are often, though not always, open at lunchtimes, when they tend to be less busy and generally offer a shorter and cheaper menu compared with their evening service. For morning or afternoon snacks, as well as light lunches, **tearooms** are a common feature; you will often find decent home baking on offer.

As for **fast food**, chip shops, or **chippies**, abound, the best often found in coastal towns within sight of the fishing boats. Deep-fried battered fish is the standard choice – when served with chips it's known as a "fish supper", even if eaten at lunchtime – though everything from hamburgers to haggis suppers is normally on offer, all deep-fried, of course. Scotland is even credited with inventing the **deep-fried Mars bar**, the definitive badge of a nation with the worst heart disease statistics in Western Europe. For alternative fast food, major towns feature all the usual pizza, burger and baked potato outlets, as well as Chinese, Mexican and Indian takeaways.

Evening meals

There's no doubt that, as with the rest of the UK, eating out in Scotland is **expensive**; our restaurant listings include a mix of high-quality and budget establishments. Wine in restaurants is marked up strongly, so you'll often pay £15 for a bottle selling for £5 in the shops; house wines generally start around the £10 mark.

If you're travelling in more remote parts of Scotland, or staying at a B&B or guesthouse in the countryside, ask advice about nearby options for your **evening meal**. Many B&Bs and guesthouses will cook you dinner, but you must book ahead and indicate any dietary requirements.

As for **restaurants**, standards vary enormously, but independent restaurants using good-quality local produce are now found all over Scotland. Less predictable are hotel restaurants, many of which also serve non-residents. Some can be very ordinary despite the highfalutin descriptions on the à la carte menu. You could easily end up paying £30–40 a head for a meal with wine.

In central Scotland (particularly in Edinburgh and Glasgow), and increasingly beyond, you'll find a range of **international cuisines** including Japanese, Thai, Caribbean and Turkish, as well as the more common Indian, Chinese and Italian establishments. Glasgow is one of Britain's curry capitals, while Edinburgh's restaurant scene is consistently lively, its seafood and vegetarian restaurants a particular strength.

Among traditional **desserts**, "clootie dumpling" is a sweet, stodgy fruit pudding bound in a cloth and cooked for hours, while Cranachan, made with toasted oatmeal steeped in whisky and folded into whipped cream flavoured with fresh raspberries, or the similar Atholl Brose, are considered more refined.

Food shopping

Most Scots get their supplies from supermarkets, but you're increasingly likely to come across good

MEAL TIMES

In many parts of Scotland outside the cities, inflexible **meal times** mean that you'll have to keep an eye on your watch if you don't want to miss out on eating. B&Bs and hotels frequently serve breakfast only until 9am, lunch is usually over by 2pm, and, despite the long summer evenings, pub and hotel kitchens often stop serving dinner as early as 8pm.

delis, farm shops and specialist **food shops**. Many stock local produce alongside imported delicacies, as well as organic fruit and veg, specialist drinks such as locally brewed beer, freshly baked bread, and sandwiches and other snacks to take away. Look out too for **farmers' markets** (W scottish farmersmarkets.co.uk), which generally take place on Saturday and Sunday mornings; local farmers and small producers, from pig farmers to cheesemakers and small smokeries, set up stalls to sell their specialist lines.

Scotland is notorious for its sweet tooth, and **cakes and puddings** are taken very seriously. Bakers with extensive displays of iced buns, cakes and cream-filled pastries are a typical feature of any Scottish high street, while home-made shortbread, scones or tablet (a hard, crystalline form of fudge) are considered great treats. In the summer, Scottish berries, in particular raspberries and strawberries, are particularly tasty.

You'll also find a number of specialist cheese shops, while many restaurants serve only **Scottish cheeses** after dinner. Look out for Isle of Mull, a tangy farmhouse cheddar; Dunsyre Blue, a Scottish Dolcelatte; or farmhouse Dunlop, the local version of cheddar.

Drinking

As in the rest of Britain, Scottish **pubs**, which originated as travellers' hostelries and coaching inns, are the main social focal points of any community. Pubs in Scotland vary hugely, from old-fashioned inns with open fires and a convivial atmosphere, to raucous theme pubs with loud music and satellite TV. Out in the islands, pubs are few and far between, with most drinking taking place in the local hotel bar. In Edinburgh and Glasgow you'll find traditional pubs supplemented by upbeat, trendy café-bars.

Pub **opening hours** are generally 11am to 11pm, but in the cities and towns, or anywhere where there is demand, places stay open much later. Whatever time the pub closes, "last orders" will be called by the bar staff about fifteen minutes before closing time to allow a bit of "drinking-up time". In general, you have to be 16 to enter a pub unaccompanied, though some places are relaxed about people bringing children in, or have special family rooms and beer gardens where the kids can run free. The legal drinking age is 18. As with the rest of the UK, **smoking** is not allowed in any pubs, bars or restaurants. Note that often-restrictive local byelaws govern alcohol consumption in public places, though enforcement varies.

Whisky

Whisky – *uisge beatha*, or the "water of life" in Gaelic – has been produced in Scotland since the fifteenth century, but only really took off after the 1780 tax on claret made wine too expensive for most people. The taxman soon caught up with whisky, however, and drove the stills underground. Today, many distilleries operate on the site of simple cottages that once distilled the stuff illegally.

MAKING MALT WHISKY

Malt whisky is made by soaking barley in **steeps** (water cisterns) for two or three days until it swells, after which it is left to germinate for around seven days, during which the starch in the barley seed is converted into soluble sugars – this process is known as **malting**. The malted barley or "green malt" is then dried in a **kiln** over a furnace, which can be oil-fired, peat-fired or, more often than not, a combination of the two.

Only a few distilleries still do their own malting and kilning in the traditional pagoda-style kilns; the rest simply have their malted barley delivered from an industrial maltings. The first process in most distilleries is therefore **milling**, which grinds the malted barley into "grist". Next comes the **mashing**, during which the grist is infused in hot water in mashtuns, producing a sugary concoction called "wort". After cooling, the wort passes into the washbacks, traditionally made of wood, where it is fermented with yeast for two to three days. During **fermentation**, the sugar is converted into alcohol, producing a brown foaming liquid known as "wash".

Distillation now takes place, not once but twice: the wash is steam-heated, and the vapours siphoned off and condensed as a spirit. This is the point at which the whisky is poured into oak casks – usually ones which have already been used to store bourbon or sherry – and left to age for a minimum of three years.

The average **maturation** period for a single malt whisky, however, is ten years; and the longer it matures, the more expensive it is, because two percent evaporates each year. Unlike wine, as soon as the whisky is bottled, maturation ceases.

Despite the dominance of blended whiskies such as Johnnie Walker, Bell's, Teacher's and The Famous Grouse, **single malt whisky** is infinitely superior and, as a result, a great deal more expensive. Single malts vary in character enormously depending on the amount of peat used for drying the barley, the water used for mashing and the type of oak cask used in the maturing process. Malt whisky is best drunk with a splash of water to release its distinctive flavours.

Beer

Traditional Scottish beer is a thick, dark ale known as **heavy**, served at room temperature in pints or half-pints, with a full head. Quite different in taste from English "bitter", heavy is a more robust, sweeter beer with less of an edge. All of the big-name breweries – McEwan's, Tennent's, Bellhaven and Caledonian – produce a reasonable selection of heavies. However, if you really want to discover Scottish beer, look out for the products of small **local breweries** such as Cairngorm, Cromarty, the Black Isle, Arran, Fyne Ales, Isle of Skye, Orkney or Valhalla. Look out, too, for Froach, available mostly in bottles, a delicious, lighter-coloured ale made from heather according to an ancient recipe. The Aberdeenshire-based Brewdog have taken both the Scottish and international markets by storm in recent years with hard-nosed marketing and an ever-expanding range of often eye-wateringly strong concoctions.

Water and soft drinks

Scotland produces a prodigious amount of **mineral water**, much of which is exported – tap water is chill, clean and perfectly palatable in most parts of the country, including the areas of the Highlands and Islands where it's tinged the colour of weak tea by peat in the ground. Locally produced **Irn-Bru**, a fizzy orange, sickly sweet concoction, has been known to outsell Coke and Pepsi in Scotland.

The media

Many Scots see the UK's "national media" as London-based and London-biased, and prefer to listen to Scottish radio programmes, read Scottish newspapers, and – albeit to a much lesser extent – watch Scottish TV. Local papers are also avidly consumed, with the weekly papers in places like Orkney and Shetland read by virtually the entire adult population.

The press

The Scottish press has traditionally centred on two serious **dailies** – The Scotsman, now published in tabloid format and based in Edinburgh, and The Herald, a broadsheet published in Glasgow. Both offer good coverage of the current issues affecting Scotland, along with British and foreign news, sport, arts and lifestyle pages. They've recently been joined by The National, a serious, low-priced left-wing and pro-independence daily launched in 2014. A rare success in an era of dwindling circulations, the paper has filled a glaring gap in the market and provided an alternative voice for just under half of the population who voted in favour of independace in the referendum. Scotland's biggest-selling dailies nevertheless remain the downmarket Daily Record, a tabloid from the same stable as the Daily Mirror, and the local edition of The Sun. Most of the main UK newspapers do produce specific Scottish editions, although the "quality" press, ranging between the right-wing Daily Telegraph and the left-of-centre Guardian, are justifiably seen in Scotland as being London papers.

The provincial daily press in Scotland is more widely read than its English counterpart, with the two biggest-selling **regional titles** being Aberdeen's famously parochial Press and Journal, read in the northeast, Orkney and Shetland, and the right-wing Dundee Courier, mostly sold in Perth, Angus, Tayside and Fife. The weekly Oban Times gives an insight into life in the Highlands and Islands, but is staid compared with the radical, campaigning weekly West Highland Free Press, printed on Skye; both carry articles in Gaelic as well as English. Further north, the lively Shetland Times and sedate Orcadian are essential weekly reads.

Many national **Sunday newspapers** have a Scottish edition, although Scotland has its own offerings – Scotland on Sunday, from the Scotsman stable, and the Sunday Herald (the only newspaper to come out in support of independence prior to the referendum), complementing its eponymous daily. Far more fun and widely read is the anachronistic Sunday Post, published by Dundee's D.C. Thomson publishing group. It's a wholesome paper, uniquely Scottish, and has changed little since the 1950s, since which time its two long-running cartoon strips, Oor Wullie and The Broons, have acquired cult status.

TV and radio

In Scotland there are six main (sometimes called "terrestrial") **TV channels**: state-owned BBC1, BBC2

BURNS NIGHT

To celebrate the birthday of the country's best-known poet, Rabbie Burns (1759–1796), Scots all over the world gather together for a **Burns Supper** on January 25. Strictly speaking, a piper should greet the guests until everyone is seated ready to hear the first bit of Burns's poetry, *The Selkirk Grace*.

At this point the star attraction of the evening, the **haggis**, is piped in on a silver platter, after which someone reads out Burns's *Ode to a Haggis*, beginning with the immortal line, "*Fair fa' your honest, sonsie face/Great chieftain o' the pudding-race!*". During the **recitation**, the reader raises a knife ("*His knife see Rustic-labour dight*"), pierces the haggis, allowing the tasty gore to spill out ("*trenching its gushing entrails*"), and then toasts the haggis with the final line ("*Gie her a Haggis!*"). After everyone has tucked into their **haggis, tatties and neeps**, someone gives a paean to the life of Burns along with more of his poetry. A male guest then has to give a speech in which women are praised (often ironically) through selective quotations from Burns, ending in a Toast to the Lassies. This is followed by a (usually scathing) reply from one of the Lassies, again through judicious use of Burns's quotes. Finally, there's a stirring rendition of Burns's poem, *Auld Lang Syne*, to the familiar tune.

and the Gaelic-language BBC Alba, and three commercial channels: STV, Channel 4 and Channel 5. **BBC Scotland** produces news programmes and a regular crop of local-interest lifestyle, current affairs, drama and comedy shows which slot into the schedules of the BBC channels. The vast majority of homes receive dozens of additional TV channels and radio stations through digital services like Freeview and Sky.

The **BBC radio** network broadcasts six main FM stations in Scotland, five of which are national stations originating largely from London: Radio 1 (youth-focused, playing pop and dance music), Radio 2 (mainstream pop, rock and light music), Radio 3 (classical music), Radio 4 (current affairs, arts and drama) and Radio 5 Live (sports, news and live discussions and phone-ins). Only the award-winning BBC Radio Scotland offers a Scottish perspective on news, politics, arts, music, travel and sport, as well as providing a Gaelic network in the Highlands with local programmes in Shetland, Orkney and the Borders. Note that in large areas of the Highlands and Islands, some or all of these stations are impossible to receive.

A web of local **commercial radio** stations helps to fill in the gaps, mostly mixing rock and pop music with news bulletins, but a few tiny community-based stations such as Lochbroom FM in Ullapool – a place famed for its daily midge count – transmit documentaries and discussions on local issues. The most populated areas of Scotland also receive UK-wide commercial stations such as Classic FM, Virgin Radio and TalkSport. With a DAB **digital radio**, you can get all the main stations crackle-free, along with special interest and smaller-scale stations.

Events and spectator sports

Scotland offers a huge range of cultural and heritage-themed events as well as a packed sporting calendar. Many tourists will home straight in on the Highland Games and other tartan-draped theatricals, but there's more to Scotland than this: numerous regional celebrations perpetuate ancient customs, and the Edinburgh Festival is an arts celebration unrivalled in size and variety in the world. A few of the smaller, more obscure events (particularly those with a pagan bent) do not always welcome the casual visitor. The tourist board publishes a weighty list of all Scottish events on its website (Ⓦvisitscotland.com).

Events calendar

DEC–JAN

Dec 31 and Jan 1 Hogmanay and Ne'er Day. Traditionally more important to the Scots than Christmas, the occasion is known for the custom of "first-footing" (see box, p.39). More popular these days are huge and highly organized street parties, most notably in Edinburgh (Ⓦ edinburgh shogmanay.com), but also in Aberdeen, Glasgow and other centres.

Jan 1 Stonehaven fireball ceremony. Locals swing fireballs on long sticks to welcome New Year and ward off evil spirits. Also Kirkwall Boys' and Men's Ba' Games, Orkney: mass, drunken football game through the streets of the town, with the castle and the harbour the respective goals. As a grand finale the players jump into the harbour.

Jan 11 Burning of the Clavie, Burghead, Moray Ⓦ hogmanay.net /events/burghead. A burning tar barrel is carried through the town and then rolled down Doorie Hill. Charred fragments of the Clavie offer protection against the evil eye.

Mid- to late Jan Celtic Connections, Glasgow ⓦ celticconnections .com. A major celebration of Celtic, folk, country and world music held in venues across the city.

Last Tues in Jan Up-Helly-Aa, Lerwick, Shetland ⓦ uphellyaa.org. Norse fire festival culminating in the burning of a specially built Viking longship. Visitors will need an invite from one of the locals, or you can buy a ticket for the Town Hall celebrations.

Jan 25 Burns Night. Scots worldwide get stuck into haggis, whisky and vowel-grinding poetry to commemorate Scotland's greatest poet, Robert Burns (see boxes, p.37 & p.165).

FEB–MARCH

Feb Scottish Curling Championship ⓦ royalcaledoniancurlingclub .org. Held in a different (indoor) venue each year.

Feb–March Six Nations Rugby tournament ⓦ rbs6nations.com. Tournament between Scotland, England, Wales, Ireland, France and Italy. Scotland's home games are played at Murrayfield stadium in Edinburgh.

March 1 Whuppity Scourie, Lanark. Local children race round the church beating each other with home-made paper weapons in a representation (it's thought) of the chasing away of winter or the warding off of evil spirits.

APRIL–MAY

April Scottish Grand National, Ayr ⓦ ayr-racecourse.co.uk. Not quite as testing as the English equivalent steeplechase, but an important event in the Scottish racing calendar. Also **Rugby Sevens** (seven-a-side tournaments; ⓦ melrose7s.com) in the Borders and the entertaining and inclusive **Edinburgh Science Festival** (ⓦ sciencefestival.co.uk).

April 6 Tartan Day. Over-hyped celebration of ancestry by North Americans of Scottish descent on the anniversary of the Declaration of Arbroath in 1320. Ignored by most Scots in Scotland, other than journalists.

Early May Spirit of Speyside Scotch Whisky Festival ⓦ spiritofspeyside.com. Four-day binge with pipe bands, gigs and dancing as well as distillery crawls. The **Shetland Folk Festival** (ⓦ shetlandfolkfestival.com) is one of the liveliest and most entertaining of Scotland's round of folk festivals.

May Scottish FA Cup Final. Scotland's premier football event, played in Glasgow.

Late May Atholl Highlanders Parade at Blair Castle, Perthshire ⓦ blair-castle.co.uk. The annual parade and inspection of Britain's last private army by their colonel-in-chief, the Duke of Atholl, on the eve of their Highland Games. Also **Burns an' a' That** (ⓦ burnsfestival.com), a modern celebration of Rabbie Burns, including gigs by contemporary pop acts.

JUNE–JULY

June–Aug Riding of the Marches in border towns such as Hawick, Selkirk, Jedburgh, Langholm and Lauder. The Ridings originated to check the boundaries of common land owned by the town and also to commemorate warfare between the Scots and the English.

June Beginning of the Highland Games season across the Highlands, northeast and Argyll. Also, the **St Magnus Festival**, Orkney (ⓦ stmagnusfestival.com), is a classical and folk music, drama, dance and literature festival celebrating the islands. The **Edinburgh**

International Film Festival (ⓦ edfilmfest.org.uk) runs from mid-June for ten days.

Late June Royal Highland Agricultural Show, at Ingliston near Edinburgh ⓦ royalhighlandshow.org. Old wooden boats and fishing craft gather for the **Traditional Boat Festival** at Portsoy on the Moray Firth coast (ⓦ stbfportsoy.com). **Glasgow Jazz Festival** (ⓦ jazzfest .co.uk).

Early July T in the Park, Strathallan Castle, Perthshire ⓦ tinthepark.com. Scotland's biggest outdoor music event, with a star-studded line-up of contemporary bands. At the opposite end of the music festival sprectrum is the **Kelburn Garden Party** (ⓦ kelburngardenparty.com), an intimate boutique affair in gorgeous surroundings near Largs. The **Scottish Open Golf Championship** is held each year at Loch Lomond golf course, just before the **British Open** tournament, which is played in Scotland at least every alternate year.

Late July The Wickerman Festival, near Kirkcudbright ⓦ thewickermanfestival.co.uk. Long-established, family-friendly alternative music festival in Dumfries and Galloway.

AUG–SEPT

Early Aug Belladrum Tartan Heart Festival, near Inverness ⓦ tartanheartfestival.co.uk. One of Scotland's most scenic and fastest-growing music shindigs; family friendly as well.

Aug Edinburgh Festival ⓦ edinburghfestivals.com. One of the world's great arts jamborees (see p.100). The **Edinburgh Military Tattoo** (ⓦ edintattoo.co.uk) features floodlit massed pipe bands and drums on the castle esplanade. There's also the **World Pipe Band Championship** in Glasgow (ⓦ seeglasgow.com/piping), and plenty more Highland Games.

Early Sept Shinty's Camanachd Cup Final ⓦ shinty.com. The climax of the season for Scotland's own stick-and-ball game, normally held in one of the main Highland towns. Also various food festivals and events under the banner of **Scottish Food and Drink Fortnight** (ⓦ scottishfoodanddrinkfortnight.co.uk).

Late Sept Doors Open Day ⓦ doorsopendays.org.uk. The one weekend a year when many public and private buildings are open to the public; actual dates vary. Also Dufftown's **Autumn Speyside Whisky Festival** (ⓦ spiritofspeyside.com), and the **Scottish Book Town Festival** in Wigtown (ⓦ wigtown-booktown.co.uk).

OCT–NOV

Oct Tiree Wave Classic ⓦ tireewaveclassic.co.uk. Annual event attracting windsurfers from around the world to the breezy Hebridean island.

Mid-Oct The National Mod ⓦ acgmod.org/nationalmod/. Held over nine days at a different venue each year, the Mod is a competitive festival and features all aspects of Gaelic performing arts.

Nov 30 St Andrew's Day. Celebrating Scotland's patron saint. The town of St Andrews hosts a week of events leading up to it (ⓦ standrews week.co.uk).

Highland Games

Despite their name, **Highland Games** are held all over Scotland between May and mid-September,

HOGMANAY

When hardline Scottish Protestant clerics in the sixteenth century abolished Christmas for being a Catholic mass, the Scots, not wanting to miss out on a mid-winter knees-up, instead put their energy into greeting the New Year, or **Hogmanay**. Houses were cleaned from top to bottom, debts were paid and quarrels made up, and, after the bells of midnight were rung, great store was laid by welcoming good luck into your house. Though it's a dying custom, this still takes the form of the tradition of "**first-footing**" – visiting your neighbours and bearing gifts. The ideal first-foot is a tall dark-haired male carrying a bottle of whisky; women or redheads, on the other hand, bring bad luck – though, to be honest, no one carrying a bottle of whisky tends to be turned away these days, whatever the colour of their hair. All this neighbourly greeting means a fair bit of partying, and no one is expected to go to work the next day, or, indeed, the day after that. Even today, January 1 is a public holiday in the rest of the UK, but only in Scotland does the holiday extend to the next day too.

varying in size and in the range of events they offer. The Games probably originated in the fourteenth century as a means of recruiting the best fighting men for the clan chiefs, and were popularized by **Queen Victoria** to encourage the traditional dress, music, games and dance of the Highlands; indeed, various royals still attend the Games at Braemar.

Apart from **Braemar**, the most famous games take place at **Oban** and **Cowal**, but the smaller events are often more fun – like a sort of Highland version of a school sports day. There's money to be won, too, so the Games are usually pretty competitive. The most distinctive events are known as the "heavies" – tossing the caber (pronounced "kabber"), putting the stone, and tossing the weight over the bar – all of which require prodigious strength and skill, and the wearing of a kilt. Tossing the caber is the most spectacular, when the athlete must lift an entire tree trunk up, cupping it in his hands, before running with it and attempting to heave it end over end. Just as important as the sporting events are the **piping** competitions – for individuals and bands – and **dancing** competitions, where you'll see girls as young as 3 tripping the quick, intricate steps of dances such as the Highland Fling.

Football

Football (soccer) is far and away Scotland's most popular spectator sport. The national team (accompanied by its distinctive and vocal supporters, known as the "Tartan Army") is a source of pride and frustration for Scots everywhere. Once a regular at World Cups where they were involved in some memorable matches against the likes of Holland and Brazil, Scotland have failed to qualify for an international tournament since 1998.

The national domestic league established in 1874 is one of the oldest in the world and holds many

European attendance records (with attendances still among the highest per head of population in Europe), but sadly today most of the teams that play in it are little known beyond the boundaries of Scotland. The exceptions are the two massive Glasgow teams that have long dominated the Scottish scene, **Rangers** and **Celtic** (see box, p.202) – known collectively as the "Old Firm". The infamous, sectarian-tainted, and occasionally violent, rivalry between these two is one of the least attractive aspects of Scottish life. Rangers were also at the heart of one of the biggest news stories in recent Scottish history when labyrinthine financial problems ultimately led to their liquidation in 2012, with the business and assets sold to a new company and the remains of the team forced to climb their way back from the former Third Division. Now finally back in the Premiership (⬦spfl.co.uk), they're sure – along with a resurgent Aberdeen – to make coming seasons slightly less predictable than of late.

Moreover, with Scottish football now operating in a severely restricted financial environment, the balance is increasingly tipping back in favour of home-grown young players over expensive imports, which should, in the long run, benefit the national team.

The **season** begins in early August and ends in mid-May, with matches on Saturday afternoons at 3pm (noon–1pm for televised games), and also often on Sunday afternoons and Tuesday or Wednesday evenings. Standard tickets cost around £25 for big games and can be purchased from club websites.

Rugby

Although **rugby** has always lived under the shadow of football in Scotland, it ranks as one of the country's major sports. Weekends when the national team is playing a home international at Murrayfield stadium in Edinburgh are colourful occasions, with kilted masses filling the capital's pubs and lining the streets leading to the ground. Internationals take place in late winter, when Scotland takes on the other "home nations", along with France and Italy, in the annual **Six Nations** tournament (see p.38), although there are always fixtures in the autumn against international touring teams such as New Zealand, Australia and South Africa. Tickets for big games are hard to come by; contact the **Scottish Rugby Union** (☎01313 465000, **W** sru.org.uk).

The area where the **domestic rugby** tradition runs deepest is in the Borders, where towns such as Hawick, Kelso and Galashiels can be gripped by the fortunes of their local team on a Saturday afternoon. The Borders are also the home of **seven-a-side rugby**, an abridged version of the game that was invented in Melrose in the 1890s and is now played around the world, most notably at the glamorous annual event in Hong Kong. The **Melrose Sevens** is still the biggest tournament of the year in Scotland (see p.122), although you'll find events at one or other of the Border towns through the spring, most going on right through an afternoon and invoking a festival atmosphere in the large crowd.

Shinty

Played throughout Scotland but with particular strongholds in the West Highlands and Strathspey, the game of **shinty** (the Gaelic *sinteag* means "leap") arrived from Ireland around 1500 years ago. Until the latter part of the nineteenth century, it was played on an informal basis and teams from neighbouring villages had to come to an agreement about rules before matches could begin. However, in 1893, the **Camanachd Association** – the Gaelic word for shinty is *camanachd* – was set up to formalize the rules, and the first Camanachd Cup Final was held in Inverness in 1896. Today, shinty is still fairly close to its Gaelic roots, like the Irish game of hurling, with each team having twelve players including a goalkeeper and each goal counting for a point. The game, which bears similarities to an undisciplined version of hockey, isn't for the faint-hearted; it's played at a furious pace, with sticks – called camans or cammocks – flying alarmingly in all directions. Support is enthusiastic and vocal, and if you're in the Highlands during the season, which runs from March to October, it's well worth trying to catch a match: check with tourist offices or the local paper, or go to **W** shinty.com.

Curling

The one winter sport which enjoys a strong Scottish identity is **curling** (**W** royalcaledoniancurlingclub .org), occasionally still played on a frozen outdoor rink, or "pond", though most commonly these days seen at indoor ice rinks. The game, which involves gently sliding smooth-bottomed 18kg discs of granite called "stones" across the ice towards a target circle, is said to have been invented in Scotland, although its earliest representation is in a sixteenth-century Flemish painting. Played by two teams of four, it's a highly tactical and skilful sport, enlivened by team members using brushes to sweep the ice furiously in front of a moving stone to help it travel further and straighter. If you're interested in seeing curling being played, go along to the ice rink in places such as Perth, Pitlochry or Inverness on a winter evening.

Outdoor activities

Scotland boasts a landscape that, weather conditions apart, is extremely attractive for outdoor pursuits at all levels of fitness and ambition, and legislation enacted by the Scottish Parliament has ensured a right of access to hills, mountains, lochs and rivers. Within striking distance of its cities are two national parks, remote wilderness areas and vast stretches of glens and moorland, while sea-kayakers, sailors and surfers can enjoy excellent conditions along the rugged but beautiful coastline.

Walking and climbing

The whole of Scotland offers superb opportunities for **walking**, with some of the finest areas in the ownership of bodies such as the National Trust for Scotland and the John Muir Trust (**W** jmt.org); both permit year-round access. Bear in mind, though, that restrictions may be in place during lambing and deerstalking seasons. See **W** outdooraccess-scotland .com for information about **hiking safely** during the stalking season. In addition, the green signposts of the Scottish Rights of Way Society point to established paths and routes all over the country.

There are several **long-distance footpaths**, such as the well-known West Highland Way (see box, p.401), which take between three and seven days to walk, though you can, of course, just do a section of them. Paths are generally well signposted and well supported, with a range of services from bunkhouses to baggage-carrying services.

Numerous short walks (from accessible towns and villages) and several major walks are touched on in this Guide. However, you should only use our notes as general outlines, and always in conjunction with a good map. Where possible, we have given details of the best maps to use – in most cases one of the excellent and reliable **Ordnance Survey** (OS) series (see p.47), usually available from local tourist offices, which, along with outdoor shops, can also supply other local maps, safety advice and guidebooks/leaflets.

For relatively gentle walking in the company of knowledgeable locals, look out for guided walks offered by rangers at many National Trust for Scotland, Forestry Commission and Scottish Natural Heritage sites. These often focus on local **wildlife**, and the best can lead to some special sightings, such as a badger's sett or a golden eagle's eyrie.

WALKING INFORMATION

Ⓦ **outdooraccess-scotland.com** All you need to know about the Scottish Outdoor Access Code, plus daily information for hill walkers about deerstalking activities (July–Oct).

Ⓦ **walking.visitscotland.com** Official site from VisitScotland, with good lists of operators, information on long-distance footpaths, and details of deerstalking restrictions and contact phone numbers.
Ⓦ **wildlife.visitscotland.com** Highlights the fauna and flora you may spot on a walk.

WALKING CLUBS AND ASSOCIATIONS

Mountain Bothies Association Ⓦ mountainbothies.org.uk. Charity dedicated to maintaining huts and shelters in the Scottish Highlands.
Mountaineering Council of Scotland Ⓦ mcofs.org.uk. The representative body for all mountain activities, with detailed information on access and conservation issues.
Ramblers Association Scotland Ⓦ ramblers.org.uk/scotland. Campaigning organization with network of local groups, and news on events and issues.
Scottish Mountaineering Club Ⓦ smc.org.uk. The largest mountaineering club in the country. A well-respected organization which publishes a popular series of mountain guidebooks.

WALKING TOUR OPERATORS

Adventure Scotland ☎ 01479 811411, Ⓦ adventure-scotland .com. Highly experienced operator providing a wide range of courses and one-day adventures, from telemark skiing to climbing, kayaking and biking.
C-N-Do Scotland ☎ 01786 445703, Ⓦ cndoscotland.com. Scotland's longest-established operator, offering Munro-bagging for novices and experts with qualified leaders.

MIDGES AND TICKS

Despite being only a fraction of an inch long, and enjoying a life span on the wing of just a few weeks, the **midge** (genus: *Culicoides*) – a tiny biting fly prevalent in the Highlands (mainly the west coast) and Islands – is considered to be second only to the weather as the major deterrent to tourism in Scotland. There are more than thirty varieties of midge, though only half of these bite humans. Ninety percent of all midge bites are down to the female *Culicoides impunctatus* or **Highland midge** (the male does not bite), which has two sets of jaws sporting twenty teeth each; she needs a good meal of blood in order to produce eggs.

These persistent creatures can be a nuisance, but some people also have a violent allergic reaction to midge bites. The easiest way to avoid midges is to visit in the winter, since they only appear between April and October. Midges also favour still, damp, overcast or shady conditions and are at their meanest around sunrise and sunset, when clouds of them can descend on an otherwise idyllic spot. Direct sunlight, heavy rain, noise and smoke discourage them to some degree, though wind is the most effective means of dispersing them. If they appear, cover up exposed skin and get your hands on some kind of repellent. Recommendations include Autan, Eureka!, Jungle Formula (widely available from pharmacists) and the herbal remedy citronella. An alternative to repellents for protecting your face, especially if you're walking or camping, is a **midge net**, which is a little like a beekeeper's hat; though they appear ridiculous at first, you're unlikely to care as long as they work. The latest deployment in the battle against the midge is a gas-powered machine called a "midge magnet" which sucks up the wee beasties and is supposed to be able to clear up to up to an acre; the most basic unit costs between £400 and £500, but there's been a healthy take-up by pubs with beer gardens and by campsite owners.

A huge rise in confirmed cases of Lyme disease in recent years means that extra care should be taken to avoid **ticks** if you're walking through long grass or bracken. These tiny parasites, no bigger than a pin head, bury themselves into your skin; the medically favoured way of extracting them is to pull them out carefully with small tweezers or a tick removal device. If flu-like symptoms persist after a tick bite, you should see a doctor immediately.

G2 Outdoor ☎ 01479 811008, ⓦ g2outdoor.co.uk. Personable, highly qualified adventure specialists offering gorge scrambling, hillwalking, rock climbing, canoeing and telemark skiing in the Cairngorms.

Glenmore Lodge ☎ 01479 861256, ⓦ glenmorelodge.org.uk. Based within the Cairngorm National Park, and internationally recognized as a leader in outdoor skills and leadership training.

Hebridean Pursuits ☎ 01631 720002, ⓦ hebrideanpursuits .co.uk. Offers hillwalking and rock climbing in the Hebrides and West Highlands, as well as surf-kayaking and sailing trips.

Nae Limits ☎ 01796 482600, ⓦ naelimits.co.uk. This excellent Perthshire-based operator offers everything from wet'n'wild rafting to bug canyoning and cliff jumping.

North-West Frontiers ☎ 01997 421474, ⓦ nwfrontiers.com. Based in Ullapool, offering guided mountain trips with small groups in the northwest Highlands, Hebrides and even the Shetland Islands.

Rua Reidh Lighthouse Holidays ☎ 01445 771263, ⓦ ruareidh .co.uk. From its spectacular northwest location, this company offers guided walks highlighting wildlife, rock-climbing courses and week-long treks into the Torridon hills.

Vertical Descents ☎ 01397 747111, ⓦ verticaldescents.com. Ideally located for the Glencoe and Fort William area. Activities and courses include canyoning, "funyakking" (a type of rafting) and climbing.

Walkabout Scotland ☎ 01312 432664, ⓦ walkaboutscotland .com. A great way to get a taste of hiking in Scotland, from exploring Ben Lomond to the Isle of Arran. Guided day and weekend walking trips from Edinburgh with all transport included.

Wilderness Scotland ☎ 01479 420020, ⓦ wildernessscotland .com. Guided, self-guided and customized adventure holidays that focus on exploring the remote and unspoiled parts of Scotland by foot, bike, sea-kayak, yacht and even on skis.

Winter sports

Skiing and **snowboarding** take place at five different locations in Scotland – Glen Coe, the Nevis Range beside Fort William, Glen Shee, the Lecht and the Cairngorms near Aviemore. The resorts can go for months on end through the winter with insufficient snow, then see the approach roads suddenly made impassable by a glut of the stuff. When the conditions are good, Scotland's **ski resorts** have piste and off-piste areas that will challenge even the most accomplished alpine or cross-country skier.

Expect to pay up to £35 for a standard day-pass at one of the resorts, around £25 for a half-day pass (usually available from noon) or around £110 for a four-day pass; rental of skis or snowboard comes in at around £30 per day, with reductions for multi-day rentals. At weekends, in good weather with decent snow, expect the slopes to be packed with trippers from the central belt, although midweek usually sees queues dissolving. For a comprehensive rundown of all the resorts, including ticket prices and conditions, visit ⓦ ski.visitscotland.com.

Cross-country skiing (along with the related telemark or Nordic skiing) is becoming increasingly popular in the hills around Braemar near Glenshee and the Cairngorms. The best way to get started or to find out about good routes is to contact an outdoor pursuits company that offers telemark or Nordic rental and instruction; in the Aviemore area try Adventure Scotland or G2 Outdoor (see p.425). Also check out the Huntly Nordic and Outdoor Centre in Huntly, Aberdeenshire (☎ 01466 794428, ⓦ nordicski.co.uk/hnoc). For equipment rental, sales or advice for Nordic and ski mountaineering equipment, contact Mountain Spirit (☎ 01479 811788, ⓦ mountainspirit.co.uk), located at the southern entrance to Aviemore village.

Pony trekking and horseriding

There are approximately sixty pony trekking or riding centres across the country, most approved by either the Trekking and Riding Society of Scotland (TRSS; ⓦ ridinginscotland.com) or the British Horse Society (BHS; ⓦ bhs.org.uk). As a rule, any centre will offer the option of **pony trekking**, **hacking** and **trail riding**. In addition, a network of special horse-and-rider B&Bs means you can ride independently on your own horse. The **Buccleuch Country Ride**, a three- to four-day, 57-mile-long route using private tracks, open country and quiet bridleways was the first route of its kind to be opened in Scotland. For more information about this, and the B&B network for riders, contact the Scottish Borders Tourist Board, or visit ⓦ southof scotlandcountrysidetrails.co.uk/buccleuch.php, where you'll find a link to an OS-based route map.

Cycling and mountain biking

Cycle touring is a great way to see some of the remoter parts of Scotland and navigate city streets (especially in Edinburgh). You'll find cycle shops in towns but few dedicated cycle lanes. In the countryside it can be tricky finding spare parts unless you are near one of Scotland's purpose-built mountain-bike trail centres.

Scotland is now regarded as one of the world's top destinations for **off-road mountain biking**. The Forestry Commission has established more than 1150 miles of excellent off-road routes. These are detailed in numerous "Cycling in the Forest" leaflets, available from the Commission's Forest Enterprise offices (see opposite). Alternatively, get hold of the *Scottish Mountain Biking Guide* from tourist information centres. Some of the tougher routes are best attempted on full suspension mountain bikes, although the easier (blue/green) trails can be ridden on a standard mountain or road bike. Pocket Mountains also publish a series of compact cycling guides to the country (Ⓦ pocketmountains.com).

For up-to-date information on long-distance routes, including **The Great Glen Cycle Way**, along with a list of publications detailing specific routes, contact the cyclists' campaigning group Sustrans (Ⓦ sustrans.co.uk), as well as the other organizations listed here.

Another option is to shell out on a cycling holiday package. Britain's biggest cycling organization, Cycling UK (formerly the **Cycle Touring Club**; Ⓦ cyclinguk.org), provides lists of tour operators and rental outlets in Scotland, and supplies members with touring and technical advice, as well as insurance. Visit Scotland's "Cycling in Scotland" brochure is worth getting hold of, with practical advice and suggestions for itineraries around the country. The tourist board's "Cyclists Welcome" scheme gives guesthouses and B&Bs around the country a chance to advertise that they're cyclist-friendly, and able to provide an overnight laundry service, a late meal or a packed lunch.

Transporting your bike **by train** is a good way of getting to the interesting parts of Scotland without a lot of hard pedalling. Bikes are allowed free on mainline East Coast and ScotRail trains, but you need to book the space as far in advance as possible. Train stations in all of Scotland's cities and many large towns have now signed up to the Bike & Go scheme (Ⓦ bikeandgo.co.uk), whereby, for an annual membership fee of £10, you can simply jump off the train and rent a bike (£3.80/24hr; up to 72hr). Bus and coach companies, including National Express and Scottish Citylink, rarely accept cycles unless they are dismantled and boxed. You'll find **bike rental** facilities in large towns and tourist centres; expect to pay around £20 per day, or more for top-notch mountain bikes. Most outlets also give good discounts for multi-day rents.

CYCLING INFORMATION

Cycle Scotland ☎ 01315 565560, Ⓦ cyclescotland.co.uk. Fully customized cycle tours at all levels, with accommodation ranging from campsites to country-house hotels, and a good range of bikes available for rent, from tandems to children's bikes.

Cycling UK ☎ 01483 238301, Ⓦ cyclinguk.org. Britain's largest cycling organization, and a good source of general advice; their handbook has lists of cyclist-friendly B&Bs and cafés in Scotland. Annual membership £43.

Forestry Commission ☎ 0300 0676156, Ⓦ forestry.gov.uk /mtbscotland. The best source of information on Scotland's extensive network of forest trails – ideal for mountain biking at all levels of ability.

Full On Adventure ☎ 01479 420123, Ⓦ fullonadventure.co.uk. Specialists in fully guided mountain-bike tours of the Cairngorms and Strathspey.

Highland Wildcat Trails Ⓦ highlandwildcat.com. Scotland's most northerly dedicated mountain-bike centre, complete with one of the country's longest downhill tracks.

Nevis Range Ⓦ ridefortwilliam.co.uk. Information on all the trails around Fort William, including the home of Scotland's World Cup downhill and cross-country tracks at Nevis Range.

North Sea Cycle Route Ⓦ northsea-cycle.com. Signposted 3875mile route round seven countries fringing the North Sea, including 775 miles in Scotland along the east coast, and in Orkney and Shetland.

Spokes ☎ 01313 132114, Ⓦ spokes.org.uk. Active Edinburgh cycle campaign group with plenty of good links, and news on events and cycle-friendly developments.

WolfTrax Mountain Bike Centre ☎ 01528 544786, Ⓦ forestry .gov.uk/wolftrax. This Central Highland bike centre near Newtonmore has almost 22 miles of routes for every standard of rider.

Air sports

Scotland has its fair share of fine sunny days, when it's hard to beat scanning majestic mountain peaks,

---

STAYING SAFE IN THE HILLS

Due to rapid weather changes, the **mountains** are potentially extremely **dangerous** and should be treated with respect. Every year, in every season, climbers and walkers lose their lives in the Scottish hills.

- Wear sturdy, ankle-supporting **footwear** and wear or carry with you warm, brightly coloured and **waterproof** layered clothing, even for what appears to be an easy expedition in apparently settled weather.
- Always carry adequate **maps**, a **compass** (which you should know how to use), food, water and a whistle. If it's sunny, make sure you use **sun protection**.
- Check the **weather forecast** before you go. If the weather looks as if it's closing in, get down from the mountain fast.
- Always **leave word** with someone of your route and what time you expect to return, and remember to contact the person again to let them know that you are back.
- In an emergency, call **mountain rescue** on ☎ 999.

lochs and endless forests from the air. Whether you're a willing novice or an expert **paraglider** or **skydiver**, there are centres just outside Glasgow, Edinburgh and Perth that will cater to your needs. There are also opportunities to try ballooning and gliding.

AIR SPORTS INFORMATION

British Gliding Association ☎ 01162 892956, Ⓦ gliding.co.uk. Governing body for gliding enthusiasts and schools across the UK with information on where to find clubs in Scotland.

Cloudbusters ☎ 07899 878509, Ⓦ cloudbusters.co.uk. Highly reputable paragliding school that runs taster and fully accredited paragliding courses in the Lanarkshire hills outside Glasgow every weekend. Full day's training £130.

Flying Fever ☎ 01770 303899, Ⓦ flyingfever.net. Based on the stunning Isle of Arran, forty miles southwest of Glasgow. From March to October, fully accredited paragliding courses and tandem flights cost £140.

Skydive St Andrews ☎ 01592 882400, Ⓦ skydivestandrews .co.uk. Year-round, highly professional, fully accredited parachute school that offers tandem, solo "static" line and "accelerated free-fall courses" over the Fife countryside. Tandem jump £270.

Skydive Strathallan ☎ 07774 686161, Ⓦ skydivestrathallan .co.uk. Located just outside Auchterarder, this non-commercial school operates year-round. Tandem jump £280.

Golf

There are more than four hundred golf courses in Scotland, where the game is less elitist and more accessible than anywhere else in the world. **Golf** in its present form took shape in the fifteenth century on the dunes of Scotland's east coast, and today you'll find some of the oldest courses in the world on these coastal sites, known as "links". It's often possible to turn up and play, though it's sensible to phone ahead; booking is essential for the championship courses.

Public courses are owned by the local council, while **private courses** belong to a club. You can play on both – occasionally the private courses require that you are a **member** of another club, however, and the odd one asks for introductions from a member, but these rules are often waived for overseas visitors and all you need to do is pay a one-off fee. The cost of a round will set you back around £20 on a small nine-hole course, around £70 on many good-quality eighteen-hole courses, and well into three figures on the championship courses.

St Andrews is the top destination for golfers: it's the home of the Royal and Ancient Golf Club, the body that regulates the rules of the game. Go to Ⓦ scotlands-golf-courses.com for contacts, score-cards and maps of signature holes for most of the

main courses. If you're coming to Scotland primarily to play golf, it's worth shelling out for one of the various multi-course passes or packages available, which gives you access to a number of courses in any one region. There's more information at Ⓦ scottishgolf.com and Ⓦ visitscotland.com/golf.

Fishing

Scotland's serrated **coastline** – with the deep sea lochs of the west, the firths of the east and the myriad offshore islands – ranks among the cleanest coasts in Europe. Combine this with an abundance of salmon, sea trout, brown trout and pike, acres of open space and easy access, and you have a wonderful location for game-, coarse- or sea-fishing.

No licence is needed to fish in Scotland, although nearly all land is privately owned and its fishing therefore controlled by a landlord/lady or his/her agent. Permission, however, is usually easy to obtain: permits can be bought at local tackle shops, rural post offices or through fishing clubs in the area – if in doubt, ask at the nearest tourist office. Salmon and sea trout have strict **seasons**, which usually stretch from late August to late February. Individual tourist offices will know the precise dates, or see the information and booking website Ⓦ fishpal.com.

Watersports

Opportunities for **sailing** around Scotland are outstanding. However, even in summer the full force of the North Atlantic can be felt, and changeable conditions combined with tricky tides and rocky shores demand good sailing and navigational skills. Yacht charters are available from various ports, either bareboat or in yachts run by a skipper and crew; contact Sail Scotland (Ⓦ sailscotland.co.uk) or the Association of Scottish Yacht Charterers (Ⓦ asyc .co.uk). An alternative way to enjoy Scotland under sail is to spend a week at a sailing school. Many schools, as well as small boat rental operations dotted along the coast, will rent sailing dinghies by the hour or day, as well as **windsurfing boards**.

Scotland's top spots for windsurfing and **kitesurfing** are Troon on the Ayrshire coast, St Andrews and Tiree. The latter is renowned for its beaches and waves and has an excellent surf, windsurfing and kitesurfing school, Suds Surf (Ⓦ surfschoolscotland.co.uk).

In recent years **sea-kayaking** has witnessed an explosion in popularity, with a host of operators offering sea-kayaking lessons and expeditions across the country. Canoe Scotland (Ⓦcanoe scotland.org) offers useful advice, while Glenmore Lodge (Ⓦglenmorelodge.org.uk), Uist Outdoor Centre (Ⓦseakayakouterhebrides.co.uk) and Skyak Adventures (Ⓦskyakadventures.com) are highly reputable for training and tours.

Surfing

In addition to sea-kayaking, Scotland is fast gaining a reputation as a **surfing** destination. However, the northern coastline lies on the same latitude as Alaska, so the water temperature is very low: even in midsummer it rarely exceeds 15°C; in autumn can drop to as low as 7°C. The one vital accessory, therefore, is a good **wet suit** (ideally a 5/3mm steamer), wet-suit boots and, outside summer, gloves and a hood, too.

Many of the best surf spots are surrounded by stunning scenery, and you'd be unlucky to share the waves with other surfers. However, this isolation – combined with the cold water and big, powerful waves – means that many of the best locations can only be enjoyed by experienced surfers. If you're a beginner, consider a **lesson** with a qualified coach such as Craig "Suds" Sutherland at Wild Diamond Watersports in Tiree (☎07793 063849, Ⓦsurfschoolscotland.co.uk).

Surf shops rent or sell equipment and provide good information about local breaks and events on the surfing scene. Two further sources of information are *Surfing Britain and Ireland* by Nelson/Taylor (Footprint; £14.99), which details breaks around Scotland, and the Surfing Great Britain website (Ⓦsurfinggb.com).

SURF SHOPS AND SCHOOLS

Coast to Coast Surf School Station Rd, Dunbar ☎07971 990361, Ⓦc2csurfschool.com. Year-round surfing lessons and surf safaris across Scotland.

Boardwise 4 Lady Lawson St, Edinburgh ☎01312 295887, Ⓦboardwise.com. Surf gear, clothes and short-term rental (board and wet suit £25/day).

Clan Surf 45 Hyndland St, Partick, Glasgow ☎01413 396523, Ⓦclanskates.co.uk. Combined surf, skate and snowboard shop. Lessons also available.

Granite Reef 45 The Green, Aberdeen ☎01224 252752, Ⓦgranite reef.co.uk. Sales, rental and boards available to try before you buy.

Tempest Surf Thurso harbour, Thurso ☎01847 892500, Ⓦcafetempest.co.uk. Surfing lessons, a shop and a café that may tempt you to remain snug indoors.

Suds Surf School Isle of Tiree ☎07793 063849, Ⓦsurfschoolscotland.co.uk. Professional instruction and rental for surfing, windsurfing, kitesurfing and kayaking.

Travel essentials

Costs

Scotland is a relatively **expensive** place to visit, with travel, food and accommodation costs higher than the EU average, though this has been balanced out with a plunging pound in the wake of the Brexit vote. Given Scotland's – and the UK's – unstable political and economic climate, costs are likely to continue fluctuating for the foreseeable future. The minimum expenditure for a couple travelling on public transport, self-catering and camping, is in the region of £35 each a day, rising to around £60 per person a day if you're staying at hostels and eating the odd meal out. Staying at budget B&Bs, eating at unpretentious restaurants and visiting the odd tourist attraction, means spending at least £75 each per day. If you're renting a car, staying in comfortable B&Bs or hotels and eating well, you should reckon on at least £100 a day per person.

Crime and personal safety

For the most part the Scottish **police** are approach-able and helpful to visitors. If you're lost in a major town, asking a police officer is generally the quickest way to get help. As with any country, Scotland's major towns and cities have their danger spots, but these tend to be inner-city housing estates where no tourist has any reason to roam. The chief urban risk is **pickpocketing**, so carry only as much money as you need, and keep all bags and pockets fastened. Out in the Highlands and Islands, crime levels are very low. Should you have anything stolen or be involved in some incident that requires reporting, contact the local police station (dial ☎101 from any location); ☎999 (or ☎112) should only be used in emergencies – in other words, if someone is in immediate danger or a crime is taking place.

Discounts

Most attractions in Scotland offer **concessions** for senior citizens, the unemployed, full-time students and children under 16, with under-5s being admitted free almost everywhere – proof of eligi-bility will be required in most cases. Family tickets are often available for those travelling with kids.

Once obtained, **youth/student ID cards** soon pay for themselves in savings. Full-time students are eligible for the International Student Identity Card or **ISIC** (Ⓦisiccard.com), which costs £12 and entitles the bearer to special air, rail and bus fares, and discounts at museums, theatres and other attractions. If you're not a student, but you're 25 or younger, you can get an International Youth Travel Card or **IYTC**, which costs the same as the ISIC and carries the same benefits.

Electricity

The current in Scotland is the **EU standard** of approximately 230v AC. All sockets are designed for British three-pin plugs, which are totally different from the rest of the EU. Adaptors are widely available at airports and electronics stores.

Emergencies

For **police**, **fire** and **ambulance** services phone ☎999.

Entry requirements

Citizens of all European countries – except Albania, Bosnia and Herzegovina, Macedonia, Montenegro, Serbia and all the former Soviet republics (other than the Baltic states) – can enter Britain with just a **passport**, for up to three months (and indefinitely if you're from the EU). Americans, Canadians, Australians, New Zealanders and citizens of many Latin American and Caribbean countries can stay for up to six months, providing they have a return ticket and adequate funds to cover their stay. Citizens of most other countries require a **visa**, obtainable from the British consulate or mission office in the country of application.

Note that visa regulations are subject to frequent changes, and given the recent vote to leave the EU, will almost certainly change in future, so it's always wise to contact the nearest British embassy or high commission before you travel. If you visit Ⓦukvisas.gov.uk, you can download the full range of **application forms** and information leaflets, and find out the contact details of your nearest embassy or consulate, as well as the rules regarding visa extensions. In addition, an independent charity, the Immigration Advisory Service or IAS (Ⓦiasuk .org), offers free and confidential advice to anyone applying for entry clearance into the UK.

LGBT travellers

Both Glasgow and Edinburgh have reasonably prominent **LGBT** communities, with a well-established network of bars, cafés, nightclubs, support groups and events. In **Edinburgh**, the area around Broughton Street is the heart of the city's "pink triangle", while in **Glasgow** the scene is mostly found in the Merchant City area; our entertainment listings for both cities include a number of gay bars and clubs. Elsewhere in Scotland, there are one or two gay bars in both Aberdeen and Dundee, and support and advice groups dotted around the country. Details for these, and many other aspects of the LGBT scene in Scotland, can be found in the monthly *Scotsgay* newspaper, versions of which can be downloaded for free online (Ⓦscotsgay.co.uk).

Health

Pharmacists (known as chemists in Scotland) can dispense only a limited range of drugs without a doctor's prescription. Most pharmacies are open standard shop hours, though there are also late-night branches in large cities and at 24-hour supermarkets.

If your condition is serious enough, you can turn up at the Accident and Emergency (A&E) department of local **hospitals** for complaints that require immediate attention. Obviously, if it's

---

HISTORIC ENVIRONMENT SCOTLAND AND NATIONAL TRUST FOR SCOTLAND

Many of Scotland's most treasured sights – from castles and country houses to islands, gardens and tracts of protected landscape – come under the control of the privately run **National Trust for Scotland** (Ⓦnts.org.uk) or the state-run **Historic Environment Scotland** (Ⓦhistoricenvironment.scot); we've quoted "**NTS**" or "**HES**" respectively for each site reviewed in this Guide. Both organizations charge an admission fee for most places, and these can be quite high, especially for the more grandiose NTS estates.

If you think you'll be visiting more than half a dozen NTS properties, or more than a dozen HES ones, it's worth taking **annual membership**, which costs around £47 (HES) or £48 (NTS), and allows free admission to their properties. In addition, both the NTS and HES offer short-term passes: the NTS has the **Discover Ticket**, which costs £26.50 for an adult ticket lasting three days, and £73 for a family ticket lasting fourteen days; and HES's **Explorer Pass**, ranging from £30 for three days (out of five) to £80 for seven days (out of fourteen) for a family.

an absolute emergency, ring for an ambulance (❶999). These services are free to all.

Insurance

Even though EU health-care privileges apply in the UK for now (the situation could well change after the UK leaves the EU), it's a good idea to take out **travel insurance** before travelling to cover against theft, loss and illness or injury. For non-EU citizens, it's worth checking whether you are already covered before you buy a new policy. If you need to take out insurance, you might want to consider the travel insurance deal we offer (see box above).

Internet

Wi-fi is available at most B&Bs and hostels, even in the Highlands and Islands. If you don't have your own smartphone, laptop or tablet, the tourist office should be able to help – sometimes they will have an access point – and public libraries often provide cheap or free access. Network coverage for 3G and 4G is good in cities and the central belt but patchy to non-existent in the Highlands, Islands and Borders.

Laundry

Coin-operated **laundries** are still found in a few Scottish cities and towns, but are becoming less and less common. A wash followed by a spin or tumble dry costs about £3.50; a "service wash" (having your laundry done for you in a few hours) costs about £2 extra. In the more remote regions of Scotland, you'll have to rely on hostel and campsite laundry facilities.

Mail

A stamp for a **first-class letter** to anywhere in the British Isles currently costs 64p and should arrive the next day; second-class letters cost 55p, taking three days. Note that there are now size restrictions:

letters over 240 x 165 x 5mm are designated as "Large letters" and are correspondingly more expensive to send. Prices to Europe and the rest of the world vary depending on the size of the item and how quickly you would like it delivered. To get an idea of how much you'll need to spend, or for general postal info, check the Royal Mail website (Ⓦroyalmail.com/price-finder).

Note that in many parts of the Highlands and Islands there will only be one or two mail collections each day, often at lunchtime or even earlier. **Stamps** can be bought at post office counters or from newsagents, supermarkets and local shops, although they usually only sell books of four, ten or twelve stamps.

Most **post offices** are open Monday to Friday 9am–5.30pm and Saturday 9am–12.30pm. In small communities you'll find post office counters operating out of a shop, shed or even a private house, and these will often keep extremely **restricted hours**.

Maps

The most comprehensive maps of Scotland are produced by the **Ordnance Survey** or OS (Ⓦordnancesurvey.co.uk), renowned for their accuracy and clarity. If you're planning a walk of more than a couple of hours in duration, or intend to walk in the Scottish hills at all, it is strongly recommended that you carry the relevant OS map and familiarize yourself with how to navigate using it. Scotland is covered by 85 maps in the 1:50,000 (pink) **Landranger** series which shows enough detail to be useful for most walkers and cyclists. There's more detail still in the full-colour 1:25,000 (orange) **Explorer** series, which covers Scotland in around 170 maps. All OS maps now also come with a smartphone download. The full range is only available at a few big-city stores or online, although in any walking district of Scotland you'll find the relevant maps in local shops or tourist offices.

Virtually every service station in Scotland stocks at least one large-format **road atlas**, covering all of

Britain at around three miles to one inch, and generally including larger-scale plans of major towns. For getting between major towns and cities a sat nav or GPS-enabled smartphone is hard to beat, but you'll have less luck in rural areas, where landmarks and even entire roads can be positioned incorrectly, leading to long and sometimes expensive detours.

Money

The basic unit of **currency** in the UK is the pound sterling (£), divided into 100 pence (p). Coins come in denominations of 1p, 2p, 5p, 10p, 20p, 50p, £1 and £2. Bank of England £5, £10, £20 and £50 banknotes are legal tender in Scotland; in addition the **Bank of Scotland** (HBOS), the **Royal Bank of Scotland** (RBS) and the **Clydesdale Bank** issue their own banknotes in all the same denominations, plus a £100 note. All Scottish notes are legal tender throughout the UK, no matter what shopkeepers south of the border might say. In general, few people use £50 or £100 notes, and shopkeepers are likely to treat them with suspicion; fear of forgeries is widespread. At the time of going to press, £1 was worth around $1.20, €1.10, Can$1.60, Aus$1.60 and NZ$1.70. For the most up-to-date exchange rates, check the useful website ⓦ xe.com.

Credit/debit cards are by far the most convenient way to carry your money, and most hotels, shops and restaurants in Scotland accept the major brand cards. In every sizeable town in Scotland, and in some surprisingly small places too, you'll find a branch of at least one of the big Scottish high-street **banks**, usually with an **ATM** attached. However, on some islands, and in remoter parts, you may find there is only a **mobile bank** that runs to a timetable (usually available from the local post office). General **banking hours** are Monday to Friday from 9 or 9.30am to 4 or 5pm, though some branches are open until slightly later on Thursdays. Post offices charge **no commission**, have longer opening hours, and are therefore often a good place to change money and cheques. Lost or stolen credit/debit cards should be reported to the police and the following numbers: MasterCard ⓣ 0800 964 767; Visa ⓣ 0800 891 725.

Opening hours and public holidays

Traditional **shop hours** in Scotland are Monday to Saturday 9am to 5.30 or 6pm. In the bigger towns and cities, many places now stay open on Sundays and late at night on Thursdays or Fridays. Large supermarkets typically stay open till 8pm or 10pm and a few manage 24-hour opening (excluding Sunday). However, there are also plenty of towns and villages where you'll find precious little open on a Sunday, with many small towns also retaining an "**early closing day**" – often Wednesday – when shops close at 1pm. In the Highlands and Islands you'll find precious few attractions open outside the tourist season (Easter to Oct), though ruins, parks and gardens are normally accessible year-round. Note that last entry can be an hour (or more) before the published closing time.

Phones

Public **payphones** are still occasionally found in the Highlands and Islands, though with the ubiquity of mobile phones, they're seldom used.

If you're taking your **mobile phone/cellphone** with you to Scotland, check with your service provider whether your phone will work abroad and what the call charges will be. The cost of calls within the EU has decreased significantly within recent years, with roaming charges set to be abolished entirely by 2017. Again, though, the Brexit vote has thrown into doubt how any new law in this regard will affect the UK. Calls to destinations further afield, however, are still unregulated and can be prohibitively expensive. Unless you have a tri-band phone, it's unlikely that a mobile bought for use in the **US** will work outside the States and vice versa. Mobiles in **Australia** and **New Zealand** generally use the same system as the UK so should work fine. All the main UK networks cover the Highlands and Islands, though you'll still find many places in among the hills or out on the islands where there's no signal at all. If you're having trouble with **reception**, ask a local where the strongest signals are.

Beware of premium-rate numbers, which are common for pre-recorded information services – and usually have the prefix ⓣ 09.

PUBLIC HOLIDAYS

Official **bank holidays** in Scotland operate on: January 1 and 2; Good Friday; the first and last Monday in May; the last Monday in August; St Andrew's Day (Nov 30), Christmas Day (Dec 25); and Boxing Day (Dec 26). In addition, all Scottish towns have one-day holidays in spring, summer and autumn – dates vary from place to place but normally fall on a Monday. While many local shops and businesses close on these days, few tourist-related businesses observe the holidays, particularly in summer.

Time

Greenwich Mean Time (GMT) – equivalent to Co-ordinated Universal Time (UTC) – is used from the end of October to the end of March; for the rest of the year the country switches to **British Summer Time** (BST), one hour ahead of GMT.

Tipping

There are no fixed rules for **tipping**. If you think you've received good service, particularly in restaurants or cafés, you may want to leave a tip of ten percent of the total bill (unless service has already been included). It's not normal, however, to leave tips in pubs, although bar staff are sometimes offered drinks, which they may accept in the form of money. The only other occasions when you'll be expected to tip are in hairdressers, taxis and smart hotels, where porters, bellboys and table waiters rely on being tipped to bump up their often dismal wages.

Tourist information

The official tourist board is known as **VisitScotland** (🆆visitscotland.com) and they run **tourist offices** (often called Visitor Information Centres, or even "VICs") in virtually every Scottish town. Opening hours are often fiendishly complex and often change at short notice.

As well as being stacked full of souvenirs and other gifts, most TICs have a decent selection of leaflets, displays, maps and books relating to the local area. The staff are usually helpful and will do their best to help with enquiries about accommodation, local transport, attractions and restaurants, although it's worth being aware that they're sometimes reluctant to divulge information about local attractions or accommodation options that are not paid-up members of the Tourist Board, and a number of perfectly decent guesthouses and the like choose not to pay the fees.

Travellers with disabilities

Scottish attitudes towards travellers with **disabilities** still lag behind advances towards independence made in North America and Australia. Access to many public buildings has improved, with legislation ensuring that all new buildings have appropriate facilities. Some hotels and a handful of B&Bs have one or two adapted rooms, usually on the ground floor and with step-free showers, grab rails and wider doorways. It's worth keeping in mind, however, that installing ramps, lifts, wide doorways and disabled toilets is impossible in many of Scotland's older and historic buildings.

Most **trains** in Scotland have wheelchair lifts, and assistance is, in theory, available at all manned stations – see 🆆scotrail.co.uk/plan-your-journey/accessible-travel. Wheelchair-users (alone or with a companion) and blind or partially sighted people (with a companion only) are automatically given thirty to fifty percent reductions on train fares, and people with other disabilities are eligible for the **Disabled Persons Railcard** (£20/year; 🆆disabledpersons-railcard.co.uk), which gives a third off most tickets. There are no bus discounts for disabled tourists. **Car rental** firm Avis will fit their cars (generally automatics only) with hand controls for free as long as you give them a few days' notice.

For more information and advice contact the disability charity Capability Scotland (☎0131 313 5510, 🆆capability-scotland.org.uk).

Working in Scotland

All Swiss nationals and EEA citizens can work in Scotland without a permit, though Bulgarian, Croatian and Romanian nationals may need to apply for permission. Other nationals need a **work permit** in order to work legally in the UK, with eligibility worked out on a points-based system. There are exceptions to the above rules, and these are constantly changing, so for the latest regulations visit 🆆gov.uk/government/organisations/uk-visas-and-immigration.

CALLING HOME FROM ABROAD

To make an international call, dial the international access code (in Scotland it's 00), then the destination's country code, before the rest of the number. Note that the initial zero is omitted from the area code when dialling Ireland, Australia and New Zealand from abroad.

Australia international access code + 61
New Zealand international access code + 64
US and Canada international access code + 1

Ireland international access code + 353
South Africa international access code + 27

Edinburgh and the Lothians

EDINBURGH CASTLE AND CITY SKYLINE

1

Edinburgh and the Lothians

Venerable, dramatic Edinburgh, the showcase capital of Scotland, is a historic, cosmopolitan and cultured city. The setting is wonderfully striking: perched on a series of extinct volcanoes and rocky crags which rise from the generally flat landscape of the Lothians, with the sheltered shoreline of the Firth of Forth to the north. "My own Romantic town", Sir Walter Scott called it, although it was another native author, Robert Louis Stevenson, who perhaps best captured the feel of his "precipitous city", declaring that "No situation could be more commanding for the head of a kingdom; none better chosen for noble prospects."

The centre has two distinct parts: the unrelentingly medieval **Old Town**, with its tortuous alleys and tightly packed closes, and the dignified, eighteenth-century Grecian-style **New Town**. Dividing the two are **Princes Street Gardens**, which runs roughly east–west under the shadow of **Edinburgh Castle**.

Set on the hill that rolls down from the fairy-tale Castle to the royal **Palace of Holyroodhouse**, the Old Town preserves all the key landmarks from its role as a historic capital, augmented by the dramatic and unusual **Scottish Parliament building**, opposite the palace. A few hundred yards away, a tantalizing glimpse of the wild beauty of Scotland's scenery can be had in **Holyrood Park**, an extensive area of open countryside dominated by **Arthur's Seat**, the largest and most impressive of the city's volcanoes.

Among Edinburgh's many museums, the exciting **National Museum of Scotland** houses ten thousand of Scotland's most precious artefacts, while the **National Gallery of Scotland** and its offshoot, the **Scottish National Gallery of Modern Art**, have two of Britain's finest collections of paintings.

In August, around a million visitors flock to the city for the **Edinburgh Festival**, in fact a series of separate festivals that make up the largest arts extravaganza in the world. On a less elevated theme, the city's distinctive pubs, allied to its brewing and distilling traditions, make it a great **drinking** city. Its four **universities**, plus several colleges, mean that there is a youthful presence for most of the year. Beyond the city centre, the most lively area is **Leith**, the city's medieval port, now a culinary hotspot with a series of great bars and upmarket seafood restaurants.

The wider rural hinterland of Edinburgh, known as the **Lothians**, mixes rolling countryside and attractive country towns with some impressive historic ruins. In East Lothian, blustery clifftop paths lead to the romantic battlements of **Tantallon Castle**, while nearby North Berwick, home of the **Scottish Seabird Centre**, looks out to the gannet-covered Bass Rock. The most famous sight in Midlothian is the mysterious fifteenth-century **Rosslyn Chapel**, while West Lothian boasts the towering, roofless **Linlithgow Palace**, thirty minutes from Edinburgh by train. To the northwest of the

THE EDINBURGH FESTIVAL FRINGE

Highlights

❶ The Old Town The evocative heart of the historic city, with its tenements, closes, courtyards, ghosts and catacombs cheek-by-jowl with many of Scotland's most important buildings. **See p.58**

❷ Edinburgh Castle Vertiginously sited upon an imposing volcanic plug, the Castle dominates Scotland's capital, its ancient battlements protecting the Crown Jewels. **See p.58**

❸ Scottish Parliament Enric Miralles' quirky yet thrilling design is a dramatic modern presence in Holyrood's historic royal precinct. **See p.70**

❹ Holyrood Park Wild moors, sheer cliffs and an 800ft-high peak (Arthur's Seat), all slap in the middle of the city. **See p.71**

❺ Café Royal Circle Bar In a city filled with fine drinking spots, there are few finer pubs in which to sample a pint of "Heavy" – a medium-strength Scottish cask ale; order six oysters (once the city's staple food) to complete the experience. **See p.95**

❻ The Edinburgh Festival The world's biggest arts gathering transforms the city every August: bewildering, inspiring, exhausting and endlessly entertaining. **See p.100**

❼ Rosslyn Chapel This impeccably preserved, cathedral-like Gothic masterwork boasts some of the finest examples of medieval stone craft in the world. **See p.108**

HIGHLIGHTS ARE MARKED ON THE MAP ON P.54 AND PP.60–61

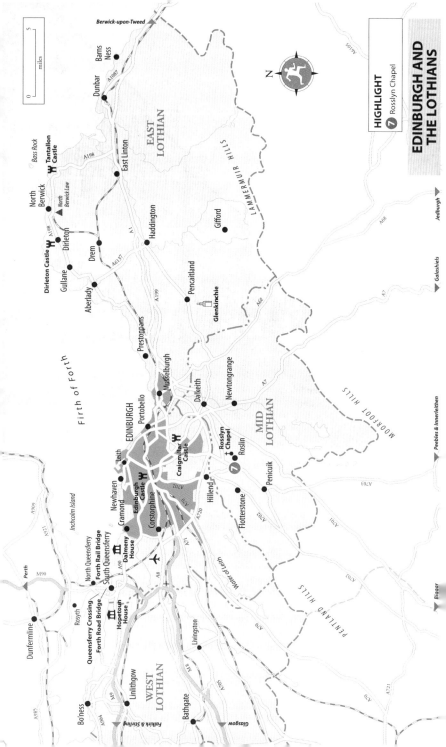

city, the dramatic steel geometry of the Forth Rail Bridge is best seen by walking across the parallel road bridge, starting at **South Queensferry**.

Brief history

It was during the **Dark Ages** that the name Edinburgh – at least in its early forms of Dunedin or Din Eidyn ("fort of Eidyn") – first appeared. The strategic fort atop the Castle Rock volcano served as Scotland's **southernmost border post** until 1018, when King Malcolm I established the River Tweed as the permanent frontier. In the reign of Malcolm Canmore in the late eleventh century the Castle became one of the main seats of the court, and the town, which was given privileged status as a **royal burgh**, began to grow.

Scotland's new capital

Robert the Bruce granted Edinburgh a **new charter** in 1329, giving it jurisdiction over the nearby port of Leith, and during the following century the prosperity brought by foreign trade enabled the newly fortified city to establish itself as the permanent **capital of Scotland**.

Under King James IV, the city enjoyed a short but brilliant **Renaissance era**, which saw not only the construction of a new palace alongside Holyrood Abbey, but also the granting of a **royal charter** to the College of Surgeons, the earliest in the city's long line of academic and professional bodies.

Turbulent Age of Reformation

Edinburgh's Renaissance period came to an abrupt end in 1513 with the calamitous defeat by the English at the **Battle of Flodden**, which led to several decades of political instability. In the 1540s King Henry VIII's attempt to force a royal union with Scotland led to the sack of Edinburgh, prompting the Scots to turn to France: French troops arrived to defend the city, while the young queen Mary was dispatched to Paris as the promised bride of the Dauphin, later (briefly) François II of France. While the French occupiers succeeded in removing the English threat, they themselves antagonized the locals, who had become increasingly sympathetic to the ideals of the **Reformation**. When the radical preacher **John Knox** (see box, p.68) returned from exile in 1555, he quickly won over the city to his Calvinist message.

James VI's rule saw the foundation of the University of Edinburgh in 1582, but following the **Union of the Crowns** in 1603 the city was totally upstaged by London. In 1633 Charles I visited Edinburgh for his coronation, but soon afterwards precipitated a crisis by introducing episcopacy to the Church of Scotland, in the process making Edinburgh a bishopric for the first time. Fifty years of religious turmoil followed, culminating in the triumph of **Presbyterianism**.

Acts of Union

The **Union of the Parliaments** of 1707 dealt a further blow to Edinburgh's political prestige, though by guaranteeing the preservation of the Church of Scotland and the legal and educational systems the acts ensured that the city was never relegated to a purely provincial role. Indeed, the second half of the eighteenth century saw Edinburgh achieve the height of its intellectual influence, led by natives such as David Hume and Adam Smith. Around the same time, the city began to expand beyond its medieval boundaries, laying out the **New Town**, a masterpiece of the Neoclassical style.

Victorian Edinburgh

Industrialization affected Edinburgh less than any other major city in the nation, and it never lost its white-collar character. Through the Victorian era Edinburgh cemented its role as a conservative bastion of the establishment, controlling Scotland's legal, ecclesiastical and education systems. Indeed, the city underwent an enormous **urban expansion** in the course of the nineteenth century, annexing, among many other small burghs, the large port of Leith.

1

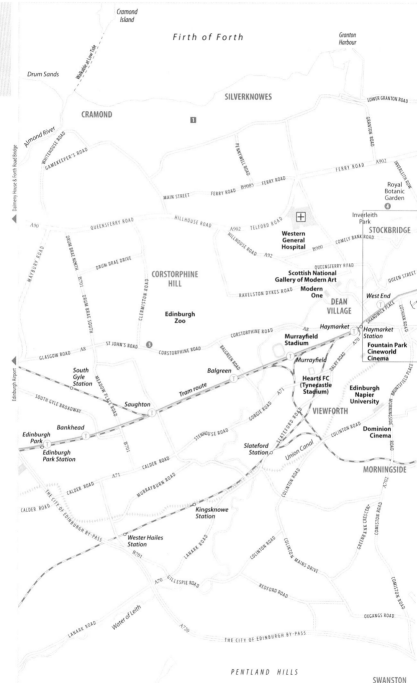

Firth of Forth

Cramond Island

Granton Harbour

Drum Sands

Walkable at Low Tide

SILVERKNOWES

LOWER GRANTON ROAD

CRAMOND

1

Almond River

WHITEHOUSE ROAD

GAMEKEEPER'S ROAD

PENNYWELL ROAD

GRANTON ROAD

INVERLEITH ROW

FERRY ROAD   A902

Royal Botanic Garden   4

Dalmeny House & Forth Road Bridge

A90

QUEENSFERRY ROAD

MAIN STREET   FERRY ROAD   B9085   FERRY ROAD

HILLHOUSE ROAD

TELFORD ROAD

A902

Inverleith Park

STOCKBRIDGE

MAYBURY ROAD

DRUM BRAE NORTH

DRUM BRAE DRIVE

CLERMISTON ROAD

DRUM BRAE SOUTH

CORSTORPHINE HILL

HILLHOUSE ROAD   A92

⊞ **Western General Hospital**

B900   COMELY BANK ROAD

QUEENSFERRY ROAD

QUEEN STREET

Scottish National Gallery of Modern Art Modern One

RAVELSTON DYKES ROAD

West End   7

DEAN VILLAGE

Edinburgh Zoo

CORSTORPHINE ROAD

A8   *Haymarket*

Murrayfield Stadium

Haymarket Station

SHANDWICK PLACE

LOTHIAN ROAD

GLASGOW ROAD   A8

ST JOHN'S ROAD   5

CORSTORPHINE ROAD

BALGREEN ROAD

A70

Fountain Park Cineworld Cinema

Balgreen

Murrayfield

DALRY ROAD

South Gyle Station

MEADOW PLACE ROAD

Tram route

Saughton

A71

Hearts FC (Tynecastle Stadium)

Edinburgh Napier University

BRUNTSFIELD PLACE

SOUTH GYLE BROADWAY

GORGIE ROAD

VIEWFORTH

MORNINGSIDE ROAD

Dominion Cinema

Edinburgh Park

Bankhead

B701

STENHOUSE ROAD

COLINTON ROAD

Edinburgh Park Station

CALDER ROAD

Slateford Station

Union Canal

MORNINGSIDE

A71   MURRAYBURN ROAD

COLINTON ROAD

A702

THE CITY OF EDINBURGH BY-PASS

CALDER ROAD

Kingsknowe Station

LANARK ROAD

COLINTON ROAD

COLINTON MAINS DRIVE

GREENBANK CRESCENT

COMISTON ROAD

COMISTON ROAD

Wester Hailes Station

B701

A70   GILLESPIE ROAD

REDFORD ROAD

OXGANGS ROAD

LANARK ROAD   *Water of Leith*   A720

THE CITY OF EDINBURGH BY-PASS

PENTLAND HILLS

SWANSTON

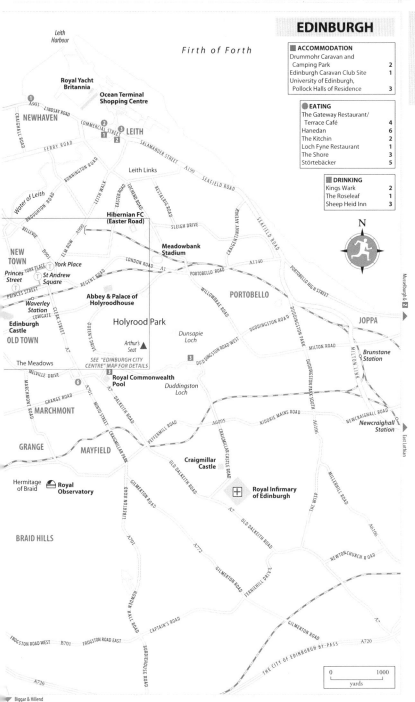

EDINBURGH

■ ACCOMMODATION
Drummohr Caravan and Camping Park	2
Edinburgh Caravan Club Site	1
University of Edinburgh, Pollock Halls of Residence	3

● EATING
The Gateway Restaurant/ Terrace Café	4
Hanedan	6
The Kitchin	2
Loch Fyne Restaurant	1
The Shore	3
Störtebäcker	5

■ DRINKING
Kings Wark	2
The Roseleaf	1
Sheep Heid Inn	3

1

The twentieth century and beyond

In 1947 Edinburgh was chosen to host the great **International Festival** which served as a symbol of the new peaceful European order; despite some hiccups, it has flourished ever since, in the process helping to make tourism a mainstay of the local economy. During the 1980s Glasgow, previously the poor relation but always a tenacious rival, began to challenge the city's status as a cultural centre, and it took the re-establishment of a devolved Scottish **Parliament** in 1999 for Edinburgh to reassert its status in a meaningful way. With debates, decisions and demonstrations about crucial aspects of the government of Scotland taking place in Edinburgh, there was a marked upturn in the perceived importance of the city, augmented by notable achievements in scientific research and the arts. The city's financial sector burgeoned, with the Royal Bank of Scotland becoming the second-largest banking group in the UK in the early years of the new century. Its near collapse, however, and subsequent bail-out by the government during the 2008 economic crisis dented not just the city's self-confidence, but also the arguments that Scotland has the stability and economic prowess to prosper as an independent country. Undeterred, the governing Scottish National Party (SNP) forged ahead with the 2014 Independence referendum that saw their cause soar in popularity towards the latter part of the campaign. In a last-minute effort to quell voter defections, the pro-UK British government attempted to appease the Scottish electorate with a raft of further devolved powers and the country voted to remain. In light of the 2016 "Brexit" referendum result, where Britain voted to leave the European Union against the wishes of the majority of Scottish voters, another Independence referendum in the near future seems inevitable.

The Old Town

The **OLD TOWN**, although only about a mile long and 400yds wide, represented the total extent of the twin burghs of Edinburgh and Canongate for the first 650 years of their existence, and its general appearance and character remain indubitably medieval. Containing the majority of the city's most famous tourist sights, it makes by far the best starting point for your explorations.

In addition to the obvious goals of the **Castle** and the **Palace of Holyroodhouse** at either end of the famous **Royal Mile**, you'll find scores of historic buildings along the length of the street. Inevitably, much of the Old Town is sacrificed to hard-sell tourism, and can be uncomfortably crowded throughout the summer, especially during the Festival. Yet the area remains at the heart of Edinburgh, with important daily business being conducted in the law courts, city chambers and, of course, the new **Scottish Parliament**, which is housed in a radical and controversial collection of buildings at the foot of the Royal Mile. It's well worth extending your explorations to the area immediately to the south of the Royal Mile, and in particular to the engaging **National Museum of Scotland**.

The Old Town is compact enough to allow a brief glance at the highlights in the course of a single day, but a thorough visit requires several days. No matter how pressed you are, make sure that you spare time for the wonderfully varied scenery and breathtaking vantage points of **Holyrood Park**, an extensive tract of open countryside on the eastern edge of the Old Town that includes Arthur's Seat, the peak of which rises so distinctively in the midst of the city.

The Castle

Castlehill • Daily: April–Sept 9.30am–6pm; Oct–March 9.30am–5pm (last entry 1hr before closing) • £16.50; guided tours (every 15min–1hr; 30min) free; audio tours £3.50 if bought as part of the entrance fee (pick up near Portcullis Gate); HES • ☎ 0131 225 9846, ⓦ edinburghcastle.gov.uk

The history of Edinburgh, and indeed of Scotland, is tightly wrapped up with its **Castle**, which dominates the city from a lofty seat atop an extinct volcanic rock. It requires no

1

great imaginative feat to comprehend the strategic importance that underpinned the Castle's, and hence Edinburgh's, pre-eminence in Scotland. From Princes Street, the north side rears high above an almost sheer rock face; the southern side is equally formidable and the western, where the rock rises in terraces, only marginally less so. Would-be attackers, like modern tourists, were forced to approach the Castle from the narrow ridge to the east on which the Royal Mile runs down to Holyrood.

The disparate styles of the fortifications reflect the change in its role from defensive citadel to national monument, and today, as well as attracting more paying visitors than anywhere else in the country, the Castle is still a **military barracks** and home to Scotland's **Crown Jewels**.

Brief history

Although Castlehill has been a defensive settlement since the Bronze Age, the oldest surviving part of the Castle complex is from the twelfth century. Nothing remains from its period as a seat of the Scottish court in the reign of Malcolm Canmore, having been lost to (and subsequently recaptured from) the English on several occasions. The return of King David II from captivity introduced a modicum of political stability and thereafter it gradually developed into Scotland's premier castle, with the dual function of fortress and royal palace. It last saw action in 1745, when Bonnie Prince Charlie's forces, fresh from their victory at Prestonpans, made a half-hearted attempt to storm it. Subsequent advances in weapon technology diminished the Castle's importance, but under the influence of the Romantic movement it came to be seen as a great national monument.

The Esplanade

Castlehill, top end of the Royal Mile • Free

The Castle is entered via the **Esplanade**, a parade ground laid out in the eighteenth century and enclosed a hundred years later by ornamental walls. For most of the year it acts as a coach park, though in the summer months huge grandstands are erected for the Edinburgh Military Tattoo (see p.103), which takes place every night during August, coinciding with the Edinburgh Festival. A shameless and spectacular pageant of swinging kilts and massed pipe bands, the tattoo makes full use of its dramatic setting.

Various memorials are dotted around the Esplanade, including an equestrian **statue of Field Marshal Earl Haig**, the controversial Edinburgh-born commander of the British forces in World War I, and the pretty Art Nouveau **Witches' Fountain** commemorating the three hundred or more women burnt at this spot on charges of sorcery, the last of whom died in 1722. Rising up to one side of the Esplanade are the higgledy-piggledy pink-and-white turrets and high gables of **Ramsay Gardens**, surely some of the most picturesque city-centre apartment buildings in the world. Most date from the 1890s and are the vision of Patrick Geddes, a pioneer of the modern town-planning movement.

The lower defences

Edinburgh Castle has a single entrance, a 10ft-wide opening in the **gatehouse**, one of many Romantic-style additions made in the 1880s. Rearing up behind is the most distinctive and impressive feature of the Castle's silhouette, the sixteenth-century **Half Moon Battery**, which marks the outer limit of the actual defences. Once through the gatehouse, you'll find the main ticket office on your right, with an information centre alongside. Continue uphill along Lower Ward, showing your ticket at the **Portcullis Gate**, a handsome Renaissance gateway of the same period as the battery above, marred by the addition of a nineteenth-century upper storey equipped with anachronistic arrow slits. Beyond this wide main path is known as Middle Ward, with the six-gun **Argyle Battery** to the right. Further west on **Mill's Mount Battery**, a well-known Edinburgh ritual takes place – the daily firing of the **one o'clock gun**. Originally designed for the benefit of ships in the Firth of Forth, these days it's an enjoyable ceremony for visitors to watch and a useful time signal for city-centre office workers.

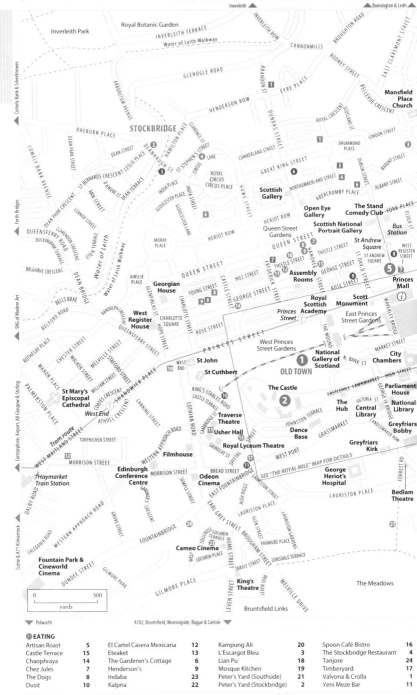

1

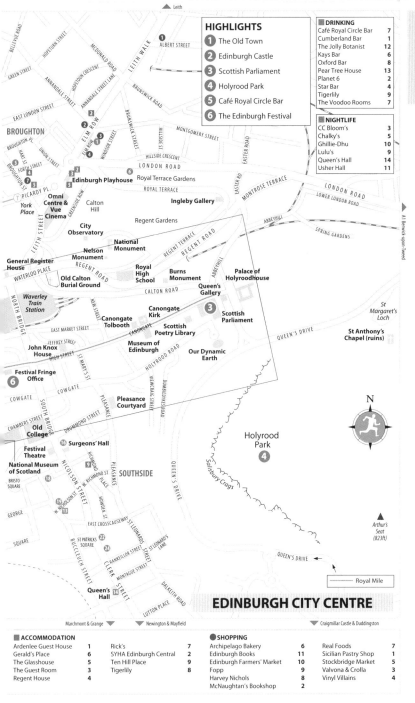

HIGHLIGHTS

1. The Old Town
2. Edinburgh Castle
3. Scottish Parliament
4. Holyrood Park
5. Café Royal Circle Bar
6. The Edinburgh Festival

DRINKING
Café Royal Circle Bar	7
Cumberland Bar	1
The Jolly Botanist	12
Kays Bar	6
Oxford Bar	8
Pear Tree House	13
Planet 6	2
Star Bar	4
Tigerlily	9
The Voodoo Rooms	7

NIGHTLIFE
CC Bloom's	3
Chalky's	5
Ghillie-Dhu	10
Lulu's	9
Queen's Hall	14
Usher Hall	11

EDINBURGH CITY CENTRE

N

Arthur's Seat (823ft)

——— Royal Mile

Marchmont & Grange ▼ Newington & Mayfield ▼ Craigmillar Castle & Duddingston ▼

ACCOMMODATION
Ardenlee Guest House	1
Gerald's Place	6
The Glasshouse	5
The Guest Room	3
Regent House	4
Rick's	7
SYHA Edinburgh Central	2
Ten Hill Place	9
Tigerlily	8

SHOPPING
Archipelago Bakery	6
Edinburgh Books	11
Edinburgh Farmers' Market	10
Fopp	9
Harvey Nichols	8
McNaughton's Bookshop	2
Real Foods	7
Sicilian Pastry Shop	1
Stockbridge Market	5
Valvona & Crolla	3
Vinyl Villains	4

1

There's an interesting little exhibition about the history of the firing of the gun in a room immediately below Mill's Mount Battery.

National War Museum of Scotland
Entry included in Castle entry fee

Located in the old hospital buildings, down a ramp between the café-restaurant immediately behind the one o'clock gun and the Governor's House, the **National War Museum of Scotland** covers the last four hundred years of Scottish military history. Scots have been fighting for much longer than that, of course, but the slant of the museum is very definitely towards the soldiers who fought for the Union, rather than against it (or against themselves). While the various rooms are packed with uniforms, medals, paintings of heroic actions and plenty of interesting memorabilia, the museum manages to convey a reflective, human tone. Just as delicate is the job of showing no favouritism to any of the Scottish regiments, each of which has strong traditions more forcefully paraded in the various regimental museums found in regions of Scotland – the Royal Scots and the Scots Dragoon Guards, for instance, both have displays in other parts of Edinburgh Castle.

St Margaret's Chapel
Near the highest point of the citadel is tiny **St Margaret's Chapel**, the oldest surviving building in the Castle, and probably in Edinburgh. Although once believed to have been built by the saint herself, and mooted as the site of her death in 1093, its architectural style suggests that it actually dates from about thirty years later.

Mons Meg
The battlements in front of the chapel offer the best of all the Castle's panoramic views. Here you'll see the famous fifteenth-century siege gun, **Mons Meg**, which could fire a 500lb stone nearly two miles. It last saw active service in the 1540s, and was thereafter used occasionally as a ceremonial saluting gun before being moved to the Tower of London in 1754. Such was Meg's emblematic value that Sir Walter Scott persuaded George IV to return it for his 1822 state visit to Scotland.

Continuing eastwards, you skirt the top of the Forewall and Half Moon Batteries, passing the 110ft-high **Castle Well** en route to Crown Square.

Crown Square
Crown Square, the historic heart of the Castle, is the most important and secure section of the entire complex. The square's eastern side is occupied by the **Palace**, a surprisingly unassuming edifice begun in the 1430s which owes its Renaissance appearance to King James IV – though it was remodelled for Mary, Queen of Scots and her consort Henry, Lord Darnley, whose entwined initials (MAH), together with the date 1566, can be seen above one of the doorways. This gives access to a few historic rooms, the most interesting of which is the tiny panelled bedchamber at the extreme southeastern corner, where Mary gave birth to James VI.

A section of the Palace houses a detailed audiovisual presentation on the nation's **Crown Jewels**, properly known as the **Honours of Scotland** and one of the most potent images of Scotland's nationhood; the originals are housed in the Crown Room at the very end of the display. James V's jewel-encrusted **crown** incorporates the gold circlet worn by Robert the Bruce and is topped by an enamelled orb and cross. The glass case containing the Honours has been rearranged to create space for the incongruously plain **Stone of Destiny** (see box opposite).

On the south side of Crown Square is James IV's hammer beam-ceilinged **Great Hall**, used for meetings of the Scottish Parliament until 1639, while opposite this on the north side is the serene Hall of Honour housing the **Scottish National War Memorial**, created in 1927 by the architect Sir Robert Lorimer and 200 Scottish artists and craftsmen.

THE STONE OF DESTINY

Legend has it that the **Stone of Destiny** (also called the Stone of Scone) was "Jacob's Pillow", on which he dreamed of the ladder of angels from earth to heaven. Its real history is obscure, but it is known to have been moved from Ireland to Dunadd by missionaries, and thence to Dunstaffnage, from where Kenneth MacAlpine, king of the Dalriada Scots, brought it to the abbey at Scone, near Perth, in 838. There it remained for almost five hundred years, used as a **coronation throne** on which all kings of Scotland were crowned.

In 1296 Edward I stole what he believed to be the Stone and installed it at **Westminster Abbey**, where, apart from a brief interlude in 1950 when it was removed by Scottish nationalists and hidden in Arbroath for several months, it remained for seven hundred years. All this changed in December 1996 when, after a ceremony-laden journey from London, the Stone returned to Scotland, in one of the doomed attempts by the Conservative government to convince the Scottish people that the Union was a good thing. Much to the annoyance of the people of Perth and the curators of Scone Palace (see p.324), and the general indifference of the people of Scotland, the Stone was placed in **Edinburgh Castle**.

However, speculation surrounds the **authenticity** of the Stone, for the original is said to have been intricately carved, while the one seen today is a plain block of sandstone. Many believe that the canny monks at Scone palmed this off onto the English king (some say that it's nothing more sacred than the cover for a medieval septic tank), and that the real Stone of Destiny lies hidden in an underground chamber, its whereabouts a mystery to all but the chosen few.

The rest of the complex

From Crown Square, you can descend to the **Vaults**, a series of cavernous chambers erected by James IV to provide a level surface for the buildings above. They were later used as a prison for captured foreign nationals, who bequeathed a rich legacy of graffiti. Directly opposite the entrance to the Vaults is the **Military Prison**, built in 1842, when the design and function of jails was a major topic of public debate. The cells, designed for solitary confinement, are less forbidding than might be expected.

The Royal Mile

The **Royal Mile**, the main thoroughfare linking the Castle to Holyrood Palace, was described by Daniel Defoe in 1724, as "the largest, longest and finest street for buildings and number of inhabitants, not in Britain only, but in the world". It is divided into four separate streets (**Castlehill**, **Lawnmarket**, **High Street** and **Canongate**, west to east respectively) – from which, branching out in a herringbone pattern, is a series of tightly packed **closes** and steep **lanes** entered via archways known as "pends". Hosting an architectural feast of styles from lofty rubblestone tenements and merchant houses to grand post-sixteenth-century sandstone structures built on medieval foundations – often resulting in hidden subterranean vaults and closes – The Royal Mile caters well to the hordes of tourists who gravitate towards it.

Scotch Whisky Experience

354 Castlehill • Daily: April–Aug 10am–6pm; Sept–March 10am–5pm • tours from £14.50 • ☎ 0131 220 0441, ⓦ scotchwhiskyexperience.co.uk

The **Scotch Whisky Experience** mimics the kind of tours offered at distilleries in the Highlands, and while it can't match the authenticity of the real thing, the centre does offer a thorough introduction to the "water of life" (*uisge beatha* in Gaelic), with tours featuring an entertaining tutorial on the specialized art of whisky "nosing", a gimmicky ride in a moving "barrel" car, a peek at the world's largest whisky collection and a tasting. On the ground floor, a well-stocked shop gives an idea of the sheer range and diversity of the drink, while downstairs there's a pleasant whisky bar and restaurant, *Amber* (see p.91).

1

ROSE STREET · FREDERICK STREET · HANOVER STREET · ROSE STREET · S ST DAVID ST · ST ANDREW'S ST

ROSE STREET SOUTH LN. · ROSE ST SOUTH LN. · ROSE ST SOUTH LN. · MEUSE LANE

Princes Street

Tram route

P R I N C E S   S T R E E T

PRINCES STREET

N

Royal Scottish Academy

Scott Monument

East Princes Street Gardens

Ross Bandstand

THE MOUND · WAVERLEY BRIDGE

NORTH BRIDGE

Waverley Train Station

West Princes Street Gardens

National Gallery of Scotland

MARKET STREET

Fruitmark Gallery

MARKET STREET

MARY KING'S CLOSE

FLESHMARKET CLOSE

COCKBURN STREET

NORTH BRIDGE

Edinburgh Castle

RAMSAY LANE · N · BANK ST · ST GILES St

Writers' Museum

MILNE'S CT · JAMES CT · MAKARS CT

BANK ST

City Chambers

Camera Obscura

Gladstone's Land

High Kirk of St Giles

CASTLE ESPLANADE

Witches' Fountain

CASTLEHILL

LAWNMARKET · HIGH STREET

HIGH STREET

Scotch Whisky Experience

The Hub

Heart of Midlothian

Fringe Office

Tron Kirk

ADVOCATE'S CLOSE · STEVENLAW'S CLOSE · BLAIR STREET

NIDDRY STREET

JOHNSTON TERRACE

CASTLE WYND

VICTORIA STREET

Parliament House

PARLIAMENT SQUARE

Mercat Cross

FISHMARKET CLOSE

SOUTH BRIDGE

W BOW

GEORGE IV BRIDGE

GRASSMARKET SQUARE

COWGATE

COWGATE

CANDLEMAKER ROW

MERCHANTS STREET

Greyfriars Bobby Statue

Greyfriars Kirk

CHAMBERS STREET

National Museum of Scotland

Old College

INFIRMARY STREET

● SHOPPING	
Blackwell's	6
Coda	3
I.J. Mellis	4
Tiso	1
Underground Solu'shun	2
Wm Armstrong	5

THE ROYAL MILE

Camera Obscura and World of Illusions

549 Castlehill • Daily: April–June, Sept & Oct 9.30am–7pm; July & Aug 9.30am–9pm; Nov–March 10am–6pm • £14.50 • ☎ 0131 226 3709, ⊛ camera-obscura.co.uk

Edinburgh's **Camera Obscura** has been a tourist attraction since 1853. Housed in the domed black-and-white turret on the roof, the "camera" consists of a small, darkened room with a white wooden table onto which a periscope reflects live images of prominent buildings and folk walking on the streets below. Today, the camera is somewhat overshadowed by "**World of Illusions**", a labyrinth of family-friendly exhibits of visual trickery – many of them playfully interactive – in the floors below.

The Hub

348 Castlehill • Daily 10am–5pm • ☎ 0131 473 2000, ⊛ thehub-edinburgh.com

The imposing black church at the foot of Castlehill is **The Hub**, also known as "Edinburgh's Festival Centre". It's open year-round, providing performance, rehearsal and exhibition space, a ticket centre and a café. The building itself was constructed in 1845 to designs by James Gillespie Graham and Augustus Pugin, one of the architects of the Houses of Parliament in London – a connection obvious from the superb neo-Gothic detailing and the sheer presence of the building, whose spire is the highest in Edinburgh.

Gladstone's Land

477B Lawnmarket • Daily: April–Oct 10am–5pm • £7; NTS • ☎ 0131 458 0200, ⊛ nts.org.uk

Doing its best to maintain its dignity among a sea of cheap tartan gifts and discounted woolly jumpers, **Gladstone's Land** is the Royal Mile's best surviving example of a typical seventeenth-century tenement. The tall, narrow building would have been home to various families living in cramped conditions: the well-to-do Gledstanes, who built it in 1620, are thought to have occupied the third floor. The National Trust for Scotland has carefully restored the rooms, filling them with period furnishings and fittings. The arcaded and wooden-fronted ground floor is home to a reconstructed cloth shop; pass

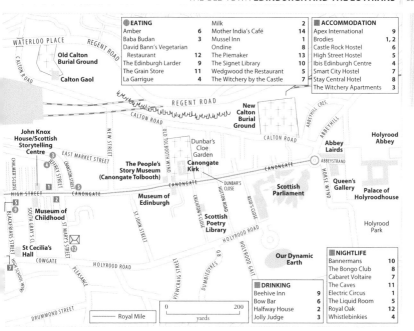

■ EATING					■ ACCOMMODATION	
Amber	6	Milk	2	Apex International	9
Baba Budan	3	Mother India's Café	14	Brodies	1, 2
David Bann's Vegetarian		Mussel Inn	1	Castle Rock Hostel	6
Restaurant	12	Ondine	8	High Street Hostel	5
The Edinburgh Larder	9	The Piemaker	13	Ibis Edinburgh Centre	4
The Grain Store	11	The Signet Library	10	Smart City Hostel	7
La Garrigue	4	Wedgwood the Restaurant	5	Stay Central Hotel	8
		The Witchery by the Castle	7	The Witchery Apartments	

■ NIGHTLIFE	
Bannermans	10
The Bongo Club	8
Cabaret Voltaire	7
The Caves	11
Electric Circus	1
The Liquid Room	5
Royal Oak	12
Whistlebinkies	4

■ DRINKING	
Beehive Inn	9
Bow Bar	6
Halfway House	2
Jolly Judge	3

through this and you encounter a warren of tight little staircases, tiny rooms, creaking floorboards and peek-hole windows. The finest room, on the first floor immediately above the arcade, has a marvellous painted ceiling and some fine old dark furniture.

Writers' Museum

Lady Stairs Close, Lawnmarket • Wed–Sat 10am–5pm, Sun noon–5pm • Free • ☎ 0131 529 4901, ⓦ edinburghmuseums.org.uk

Situated within the seventeenth-century Lady Stair's House, the **Writers' Museum** is dedicated to Scotland's three greatest literary lions: Sir Walter Scott, Robert Louis Stevenson and Robert Burns. The house itself holds as much interest as the slightly lacklustre collection of portraits, manuscripts and knick-knacks that make up the museum, its tight, winding stairs and poky, wood-panelled rooms offering a flavour of the medieval Old Town.

The Heart of Midlothian

Parliament Square, High St

The pattern set in the cobblestones near the main entrance to St Giles is known as the **Heart of Midlothian**, a nickname for the Edinburgh Tolbooth, which stood on this spot and was regarded as the heart of the city. The prison attached to the Tolbooth was immortalized in Sir Walter Scott's novel *Heart of Midlothian*, and you may still see locals spitting on the cobblestone heart, a continuation of the tradition of spitting on the door of the prison to ward off the evil contained therein.

High Kirk of St Giles

High St • May–Sept Mon–Fri 9am–7pm, Sat 9am–5pm, Sun 1–5pm; Oct–April Mon–Sat 9am–5pm, Sun 1–5pm • Free • ☎ 0131 226 0674, ⓦ stgilescathedral.org.uk

The **High Kirk of St Giles** is the original parish church of medieval Edinburgh, from where John Knox (see box, p.68) launched and directed the Scottish Reformation. St Giles is often referred to as a cathedral, although it has only been the seat of a bishop

1

on two brief and unhappy occasions in the seventeenth century. According to one of the city's best-known legends, the attempt in 1637 to introduce the English Prayer Book, and thus episcopal government, so incensed a humble stallholder named Jenny Geddes that she hurled her stool at the preacher, prompting the rest of the congregation to chase the offending clergy out of the building. A tablet in the north aisle marks the spot from where she let rip.

The spire and interior

The resplendent **crown spire** of the kirk is formed from eight flying buttresses and dates back to 1485, while **inside**, the four massive piers supporting the tower were part of a Norman church built here around 1120. In the nineteenth century, St Giles was adorned with a whole series of funerary monuments on the model of London's Westminster Abbey; around the same time it acquired several attractive Pre-Raphaelite stained-glass windows designed by Edward Burne-Jones and William Morris. A more recent addition was the great **west window**, whose dedication to Rabbie Burns in 1985 caused enormous controversy – as a hardened drinker and womanizer, the national bard was far from being an upholder of accepted Presbyterian values. Look out, too, for an elegant bronze relief of Robert Louis Stevenson on the south side of the church.

Thistle Chapel

At the southeastern corner of St Giles, the **Thistle Chapel** was built by Sir Robert Lorimer in 1911 as the private chapel of the sixteen knights of the Most Noble Order of the Thistle, the highest chivalric order in Scotland. Based on St George's Chapel in Windsor, it's an exquisite piece of craftsmanship, with an elaborate ribbed vault, huge drooping bosses and extravagantly ornate stalls showing off Lorimer's bold Arts and Crafts styling.

Mary King's Close

2 Warriston's Close, High St • April–Oct daily 10am–9pm; Nov–March Mon–Thurs & Sun 10am–5pm, Fri & Sat 10am–9pm • Tours (every 15min; 1hr) £14.50 • ☎ 0131 225 0672, ⓦ realmarykingsclose.com

When work on the Royal Exchange, known as the City Chambers, began in 1753, the existing tenements that overlooked **Mary King's Close** were only partially demolished to make way for the new building being constructed on top of them. The process left large sections of the houses, together with the old closes that ran alongside them, intact but entirely enclosed within the basement and cellars of the City Chambers. You can visit this rather spooky subterranean "lost city" on **tours** led by costumed actors, who take you round the cold stone shells of the houses where various scenes from the Close's history have been re-created. As you'd expect, blood, plague, pestilence and ghostly apparitions are to the fore, though there is an acknowledgement of the more prosaic side of medieval life in the archeological evidence of an urban cow byre. The tour ends with a stroll up the remarkably well-preserved close itself.

Museum of Childhood

42 High St • Mon–Sat 10am–5pm, Sun noon–5pm • Free • ☎ 0131 529 4142, ⓦ edinburghmuseums.org.uk

Harking back to simpler times, the **Museum of Childhood** hosts a joyful collection of toys, clothes, dolls and bikes that kids used to cherish before the advent of plastic. Over the five small exhibition spaces there's a surprisingly large amount to see here, including a beautiful model railway scene and some fancy old Victorian dollhouses.

The Scottish Storytelling Centre and John Knox House

43–45 High St • Mon–Sat 10am–6pm, also Sun noon–6pm in July & Aug • John Knox House £5; Storytelling Centre free • ☎ 0131 556 9579, ⓦ tracscotland.org/scottish-storytelling-centre

There are two distinct parts to the **Scottish Storytelling Centre**. One half is a stylish contemporary development containing an excellent café, the Netherbow Theatre and

FROM TOP ARTHUR'S SEAT (P.72); THE GRASSMARKET (P.72) >

1

JOHN KNOX

Protestant reformer **John Knox** has been credited with, or blamed for, the distinctive national characteristic of rather gloomy reserve that emerged from the Calvinist Reformation and which has cast its shadow right up to the present. Little is known about Knox's early years: he was born between 1505 and 1514 in East Lothian, and trained for the priesthood at St Andrews University. Ordained in 1540, Knox then served as a private tutor, in league with Scotland's first significant Protestant leader, **George Wishart**. After Wishart was burnt at the stake for heresy in 1546, Knox became involved with the group who had carried out the revenge murder of the Scottish primate, Cardinal David Beaton, subsequently taking over his castle in St Andrews. The following year this was captured by the French, and Knox was carted off to work as a galley slave.

He was freed in 1548, as a result of the intervention of the English, who invited him to play an evangelizing role in the spread of their own Reformation. When Mary Tudor, a Catholic, acceded to the English throne in 1553, Knox fled to the Continent to avoid becoming embroiled in the religious turmoil, ending up as minister to the English-speaking community in Geneva, which was then in the grip of the theocratic government of the Frenchman **Jean Calvin**.

When Knox was allowed to return to Scotland in 1555, he took over as spiritual leader of the Reformation, becoming minister of St Giles in Edinburgh, where he gained a reputation as a charismatic preacher. The establishment of Protestantism as the official religion of Scotland in 1560 was dependent on the forging of an alliance with **Elizabeth I**, which Knox himself rigorously championed: the swift deployment of English troops against the French garrison in Edinburgh dealt a fatal blow to Franco–Spanish hopes of re-establishing Catholicism in both Scotland and England. Although the return of **Mary, Queen of Scots** the following year placed a Catholic monarch on the Scottish throne, Knox was reputedly always able to retain the upper hand in his famous disputes with her.

Before his death in 1572, Knox began mapping out the organization of the **Scots Kirk**, sweeping away all vestiges of episcopal control and giving lay people a role of unprecedented importance. He also proposed a nationwide education system, to be compulsory for the very young and free for the poor, though lack of funds meant this could not be implemented in full. His final legacy was the posthumously published *History of the Reformation of Religion in the Realm of Scotland*, a justification of his life's work.

an airy **Storytelling Court** with a small permanent exhibition about Scottish stories from ancient folk tales to *Harry Potter*. By contrast, **John Knox House** next door – but part of the same complex – is a fifteenth-century stone-and-timber building which, with its distinctive external staircase, overhanging upper storeys and busy pantile roof, is a classic example of the Royal Mile in its medieval heyday. Inside, the house is all low doorways, uneven floors and ornate wooden panelling; it contains a series of displays about Knox (see box above), the minister who led the Reformation in Scotland and established Calvinist Presbyterianism as the dominant religious force in the country. Regular performances and events, often aimed at a younger audience, take place in the centre, particularly during the Festival. To get to the lovely, quiet **garden** behind the centre, head down Trunk's Close, a few doors uphill from John Knox House.

The People's Story Museum

Canongate Tolbooth, 163 Canongate • Mon–Sat 10am–5pm, also Sun noon–5pm in Aug • Free • ☎ 0131 529 4057, ⓦ edinburghmuseums.org.uk

Dominated by a turreted steeple and an odd external box clock, the late sixteenth-century **Canongate Tolbooth** has served both as the headquarters of the burgh administration and as a prison. It now houses **The People's Story Museum**, which contains a series of display cases, dense information boards and rather old-fashioned tableaux dedicated to the everyday life and work of Edinburgh's population down the centuries. This isn't one of Edinburgh's essential museums, but it does have a down-to-earth reality often missing from places dedicated to high culture or famous historical characters.

Museum of Edinburgh

142–146 Canongate • Mon–Sat 10am–5pm, also Sun noon–5pm in Aug • Free • ☎ 0131 529 4143, ⓦ edinburghmuseums.org.uk

The **Museum of Edinburgh** houses the city's principal collection devoted to local history, though the museum is as interesting for the labyrinthine network of wood-panelled rooms within as for its rather quirky array of artefacts. These do, however, include a number of items of real historical significance, in particular the **National Convention**, the petition for religious freedom drawn up on a deerskin parchment in 1638, and the original plans for the layout of the New Town drawn by James Craig (see p.75), chosen by the city council after a competition in 1767.

Scottish Poetry Library

5 Crighton's Close, Canongate • Tues, Wed & Fri 10am–5pm, Thurs 10am–7pm, Sat 10am–4pm • Free • ☎ 0131 557 2876, ⓦ scottishpoetrylibrary.org.uk

A small island of modern architectural eloquence amid a cacophony of large-scale developments, the **Scottish Poetry Library**'s attractive design harmoniously combines brick, oak, glass, Caithness stone and blue ceramic tiles while incorporating a section of an old city wall. Inside you'll encounter Scotland's most comprehensive collection of native poetry, and visitors are free to read the books, periodicals and leaflets found on the shelves, or listen to recordings of poetry in the nation's three tongues, Lowland Scots, Scots Gaelic and English.

Holyrood

At the foot of Canongate lies **Holyrood**, for centuries known as Edinburgh's royal quarter, with its ruined thirteenth-century **abbey** and the **Palace of Holyroodhouse**, the Queen's official Edinburgh residence. In recent years, however, the area has been transformed by the addition of Enric Miralles' dazzling but highly controversial new **Scottish Parliament**, which was deliberately landscaped to mimic the cliffs and ridges of Edinburgh's most dramatic natural feature, the nearby **Holyrood Park**, and its slumbering peak, Arthur's Seat.

The Palace of Holyroodhouse

Canongate • Daily: April–Oct 9.30am–6pm; Nov–March 9.30am–4.30pm; last admission 1hr 30min before closing (note that the palace is closed to visitors when the Queen is in residence; check the website for advance notice) • £12; entry includes an audio tour; HES • ☎ 0303 123 7306, ⓦ historicenvironment.scot

In its present form, the **Palace of Holyroodhouse** is largely a seventeenth-century creation, planned for Charles II. However, the tower house of the old palace (the sole survivor of a fire during Oliver Cromwell's occupation) built for James V in 1532 was skilfully incorporated to form the northwestern block of today's building, with a virtual mirror image of it erected as a counterbalance at the other end.

Tours of the palace move through a series of royal **reception rooms** featuring some outstanding encrusted plasterwork, each more impressive than the last – an idea Charles II had picked up from his cousin Louis XIV's Versailles – while on the northern side of the internal quadrangle, the **Great Gallery** extends almost the full length of the palace and is dominated by portraits of 96 Scottish kings, painted by

THE WORLD'S END BURGH

Canongate, the final leg of the Royal Mile, was for over seven hundred years a burgh in its own right that was entered through the now demolished gatehouse known as **Netherbow Port**. Some of the town's poorer residents couldn't afford the toll to pass through and spent their whole lives in Edinburgh – inspiration for the name of the *World's End* pub found by the Port site. Look for the brass plates - sunk into the road outside the pub - that mark the outline of the old gatehouse.

1

Jacob de Wet in 1684 to illustrate the lineage of Stewart royalty. The result is unintentionally hilarious, as it is clear that the artist's imagination was taxed to bursting point by the need to paint so many different facial types without having an inkling as to what the subjects actually looked like.

As you move into the oldest part of the palace, known as **James V's tower**, the formal, ceremonial tone gives way to dark medieval history, with a tight spiral staircase leading to the chambers used by **Mary, Queen of Scots**. These contain various relics, including jewellery, associated with the queen, though the most compelling viewing is a tiny supper room, from where in 1566 Mary's Italian secretary, **David Rizzio**, was dragged by conspirators, who included her jealous husband, Lord Darnley, to the outer chamber and stabbed 56 times; a brass plaque on the wall points out what are rather optimistically identified as the bloodstains on the wooden floor.

Holyrood Abbey

Free as part of palace tour

Standing beside the palace are the evocative ruins of **Holyrood Abbey**, some of which date back to the thirteenth century. Various invading armies paid little respect to the building over the years, and although it was patched up for Charles I's coronation in 1633 it was gutted in 1688 by an anti-Catholic mob. The roof finally tumbled down in 1768, but the melancholy scene has inspired artists down the years, among them Felix Mendelssohn, who in 1829 wrote: "Everything is in ruins and mouldering … I believe I have found the beginning of my Scottish Symphony there today." Adjacent to the abbey are the formal palace gardens, open to visitors during the summer months and offering some pleasant strolls.

Queen's Gallery

Canongate • Daily: April–Oct 9.30am–6pm; Nov–March 9.30am–4.30pm, last admission 1hr before closing • £6.70 or £16.90 for joint entry with Holyroodhouse • ☎ 0303 123 7306, Ⓦ royalcollection.org.uk

Essentially an adjunct to the Palace of Holyroodhouse, the **Queen's Gallery** is located in the shell of a former church directly between the palace and the Parliament. With just two principal viewing rooms, it's a compact space, but has an appealing contemporary

EDINBURGH'S CONTROVERSIAL PARLIAMENT

Made up of various linked elements rather than one single building, the unique design of the new **Scottish Parliament** complex was the vision of Catalan architect **Enric Miralles**, whose death in 2000, halfway through the building process, caused more than a few ripples of uncertainty as to whether the famously whimsical designer had in fact set down his final draft. Initial estimates for the cost of the building were tentatively put at £40 million; by the time the Queen cut the ribbon in October 2004, the final bill was over £400 million. A major public inquiry into the overspend blamed costing failures early in the project and criticized the spendthrift attitude of politicians and civil servants alike, yet the building is still an impressive – if imperfect – testament to the ambition of Miralles. While locals still mutter over the cost and the oddness of the design, the building has won over the majority of the general architectural community, scooping numerous prizes including, in 2005, the most prestigious in Britain, the Royal Institute of British Architects (RIBA) **Stirling Prize**. Among the most memorable features of the building are the fanciful motifs and odd architectural signatures running through the design, including the anvil-shaped panels which clad the exterior and the extraordinary windows of the offices shaped like the profile of a mountain or a section of the Forth Rail Bridge.

The stark concrete of the building's interior may not be to all tastes, but while some parts of the design are undoubtedly experimental and over-elaborate, there are moments where grace and boldness convene, exemplified by the **Garden Lobby**: an airy, bright meeting place in the heart of the campus with a fascinating roof of glass panels forming the shape of an upturned boat.

style which manages to remain sympathetic to the older elements of the building. It's used to display changing exhibitions from the **Royal Collection**, a vast array of art treasures held by the Queen on behalf of the British nation. Because the pieces are otherwise exhibited only during the limited openings of Buckingham Palace and Windsor Castle, the exhibitions here tend to draw quite a lot of interest. Recent displays have included an oil sketch of the newly crowned Queen Victoria aged eighteen by celebrated Scottish artist, David Wilkie.

The Scottish Parliament

Horse Wynd • Daily 10am–5pm • Free guided tours (1hr); booking is recommended (access is limited to lobby and debating chamber if unguided); free crèche • ☎ 0800 092 7500, ⓦ visitparliament.scot

For all its grandeur, Holyrood Palace is in danger of being upstaged by the striking buildings that make up the new **Scottish Parliament**. The most controversial public building to be erected in Scotland since World War II, it houses the country's directly elected assembly, which was reintroduced into the British political scene in 1999 – Scotland's parliament was abolished in 1707, when it joined the English assembly at Westminster as part of the Union of the two nations.

There's free access into the building's **entrance lobby**, where you'll find a small exhibition providing some historical, political and architectural background. If Parliament is in session, it's normally possible to watch proceedings in the **debating chamber** from the public gallery, though you have to get a pass from the front desk in the lobby. To see the rest of the interior properly you'll need to join one of the regular **guided tours**, highly recommended to better appreciate the quality, detailed features and unique vision of the building's design. Special tours dedicated to the architecture of the building and its collection of contemporary Scottish art also take place, but much less frequently – check the website for details.

Our Dynamic Earth

112 Holyrood Rd • April–June, Sept & Oct daily 10am–5.30pm; July & Aug daily 10am–6pm; Nov–March Wed–Sun 10am–5.30pm; last entry 1hr 30min before closing • adults £12.50; children £7.95 • ☎ 0131 550 7800, ⓦ dynamicearth.co.uk

Beneath a pincushion of white metal struts that make it look like a miniature version of London's Millennium Dome, **Our Dynamic Earth** is a hi-tech attraction based on the wonders of the natural world and aimed at families with kids between 5 and 15. Although James Hutton, the Edinburgh-born "Father of Geology", lived nearby in the eighteenth century, there are few specific links to Edinburgh or Scotland. Galleries cover the formation of the earth and continents with crashing sound effects and a shaking floor, while the calmer grandeur of glaciers and oceans is explored through magnificent large-screen landscape footage; further on, the polar regions – complete with a real iceberg – and tropical jungles are imaginatively re-created, with interactive computer screens and special effects at every turn. The tour is rounded off with a "smellivized" 4D cinema experience complete with moving furniture, a chilly blast of snow and a whiff of rhino poo.

Holyrood Park

Accessed from the foot of the Royal Mile • Always open • Coming by bus, take the #35 in the direction of the Old Town from Waverley Bridge

A natural wilderness in the very heart of the modern city, **Holyrood Park** is one of Edinburgh's greatest assets. Packed into an area no more than five miles in diameter is an amazing variety of landscapes – hills, crags, moorland, marshes, glens, lochs and fields – representing something of a microcosm of Scotland's scenery. While old photographs of the park show crops growing and sheep grazing, it's now used mostly by walkers, joggers, cyclists and other outdoor enthusiasts. A single tarred road, **Queen's Drive**, loops through the park, enabling many of its features to be seen by car, although you need to get out and stroll around to appreciate it fully.

1

Salisbury Crags

The amber hue of the setting sun's reflection on **Salisbury Crags**' sheer cliff face makes an enticing backdrop to an evening stroll. An easy hour-long circular route begins across the road from Holyroodhouse; the path nicknamed the "Radical Road" winds southwards around the foot of the crags for a little under a mile before you have the opportunity to hike north through the glen separating the Salisbury Crags and Arthur's Seat and back to your starting point.

Arthur's Seat

The usual starting point for the ascent of **Arthur's Seat**, which at 823ft above sea level towers over Edinburgh's numerous high points, is Dunsapie Loch, reached by following the tarred Queen's Drive in a clockwise direction from the palace gates (30–40min walk). Part of a volcano which last saw action 350 million years ago, its connections to the legendary king are fairly sketchy: the name is likely to be a corruption of the Gaelic *Ard-na-said*, or "height of arrows". From Dunsapie Loch it's a twenty-minute climb up grassy slopes to the rocky summit. On a clear day, the views might just stretch to the English border and the Atlantic Ocean; more realistically, the landmarks that dominate are Fife, a few Highland peaks and, of course, Edinburgh laid out on all sides.

The Grassmarket

Just south of the Castle

Used as the city's cattle market from 1477 to 1911, the **Grassmarket** is an open, partly cobbled area, which despite being girdled by tall tenements offers an unexpected view north up to the precipitous walls of the Castle. Come springtime, it's often sunny enough for cafés to put tables and chairs along the pavement; however, such Continental aspirations are a bit of a diversion as the Grassmarket is best remembered as the location of Edinburgh's public gallows – the spot is marked by a tiny garden. The notorious serial killers William Burke and William Hare had their lair in a now-vanished close just off the western end of the Grassmarket, and for a long time before its relatively recent gentrification there was a seamy edge to the place, with brothels, drinking dens and shelters for down-and-outs.

The Grassmarket's two-sided character is still on view, with stag and hen parties carousing between the area's pubs of an evening, while by day you can admire the architectural quirks and a series of interesting shops, in particular the string of offbeat,

THE CONNOLLY CONNECTION

Among Edinburgh's multitude of famous and infamous sons, one of the most obscure – and perhaps most unlikely – remains James Connolly, commander-in-chief of the Easter 1916 rising which eventually led to the formation of the Irish Republic. With no monument save for a small plaque at the foot of George IV Bridge in the Cowgate, few among Edinburgh's tourist hordes are likely aware that Connolly was born and raised there in the bowels of Edinburgh's Old Town. A pivotal figure in emerging socialist and trade union movements in Scotland, Ireland and beyond, including Keir Hardie's Independent Labour Party (a forerunner of the contemporary Labour Party), Connolly came to believe that armed insurrection was the only way to free Ireland from the British Empire, and his prominent role in the rising ultimately led to execution by firing squad (infamously while badly wounded and tied to a chair). While the uprising resulted in heavy casualties on both sides, as well as many civilian deaths, and the independent state that eventually emerged wasn't the socialist utopia he'd dreamed of, his vision of freedom and equality for all has remained an inspiration to many, not least John Lennon, who quoted Connolly's writings on female emancipation as a cue for "Woman is the Nigger of the World".

independent boutiques on curving **Victoria Street**, an unusual two-tier thoroughfare, with arcaded shops below and a pedestrian terrace above.

The Bridges

Leading eastwards from the Grassmarket is the **Cowgate**, one of Edinburgh's oldest surviving streets. It was also once one of the city's most prestigious addresses, but the construction of the great **viaducts** of George IV Bridge and South Bridge entombed it below street level, condemning it to decay and neglect and leading the nineteenth-century writer, Alexander Smith, to declare: "the condition of the inhabitants is as little known to respectable Edinburgh as are the habits of moles, earthworms, and the mining population." Various nightclubs and Festival venues have established themselves here – on Friday and Saturday nights the street heaves with revellers – but it remains a slightly insalubrious spot.

High above the crestfallen Cowgate, both bridges give the curious impression that you're on ground level thanks to the terraced buildings that rise up in line with the elevated streets. The lowermost **South Bridge**, leading off from halfway down the High Street, is unpleasantly congested with buses and garishly untempered retailers, although it does provide a decent selection of cheap café-restaurants.

By contrast, **George IV Bridge** to the west – built in the 1830s – is a sight to behold with its appealing melange of neo-French Renaissance and Neoclassical architecture.

At the southern end of the bridge, tourists invariably cluster around the tiny bronze statue of a Skye terrier called Greyfriars Bobby (see box below), while across the road, Chambers Street links the southernmost ends of the two bridges where you'll find the unmissable National Museum of Scotland (see p.74).

Greyfriars Kirk

1 Greyfriars • April–Oct Mon–Fri 10.30am–4.30pm, Sat 11am–2pm; Winter visits can be arranged by phone • Free • ☎ 0131 225 1900, Ⓦ greyfriarskirk.com

Greyfriars Kirk was built in 1620 on land that had belonged to a Franciscan convent, though little of the original late Gothic-style building remains. A fire in the mid-nineteenth century led to significant rebuilding and the installation of the first **organ** in a Presbyterian church in Scotland; today's magnificent instrument, by Peter Collins, arrived in 1990.

Outside, the kirkyard has a fine collection of seventeenth-century gravestones and mausoleums including the grave mourned over by the world-famous canine, Greyfriars Bobby. Visited regularly by ghost tours (see p.88), the kirkyard was known for **grave-robbing** as freshly interred bodies were exhumed and sold to the nearby medical school (a crime taken to a higher level by the notorious Burke and Hare, who bypassed the graveyards by simply murdering the victims they'd then sell on for dissection). More significantly, the kirkyard was the setting, in 1638, for the signing of the **National**

GREYFRIARS BOBBY

The small statue of **Greyfriars Bobby** at the junction of George IV Bridge and Candlemaker Row must rank as one of Edinburgh's more mawkish tourist attractions. Bobby was a **Skye terrier** acquired as a working dog by a police constable named John Gray. When Gray died in 1858, Bobby was found a few days later sitting on his grave, a vigil he maintained until his death fourteen years later. In the process, he became an Edinburgh celebrity, fed and cared for by locals who gave him a special collar to prevent him being impounded as a stray. The statue was modelled from life and erected soon after his death. Bobby's legendary dedication easily lent itself to children's books and was eventually picked up by Disney, whose 1960 feature film hammed up the story and ensured that streams of tourists have paid their respects ever since.

1

Covenant, a dramatic act of defiance by the Presbyterian Scots against the attempts of Charles I to impose an episcopal form of worship on the country. In an undemocratic age, thousands of townsfolk as well as important nobles signed the original at Greyfriars; copies were then made and sent around the country, with some three hundred thousand names being added.

National Museum of Scotland

Chambers St • Daily 10am–5pm • Free • Guided tours at 11am, 1 & 3pm (1hr; free) • ☎ 0131 247 4041, ⊛ nms.ac.uk

The **National Museum of Scotland** is essentially two distinct museums, internally connected to each other: the unorthodox **modern sandstone building** on the corner of George IV Bridge houses collections of Scottish heritage, while the much older **Venetian-style palace** offers a more global perspective. Inside, the wealth of exhibits is enough to occupy days of your time, but as entry is free you'll be able to dip in and out at leisure or during rain showers. Parents will also find the place a useful sanctuary since there are numerous child-friendly rooms, interactive exhibits and cafés.

The old building

Modelled on the former Crystal Palace in London, and with a spectacular cast-iron interior, the old building packs in a bedazzling array of artefacts, covering natural history, world culture, geology and technology. The exhibits are housed over three levels surrounding the **Grand Gallery**, a huge central atrium whose beautiful limestone floor turns out to be teeming with fossils, predominantly ammonites. One stand-out exhibit, by the main concourse, is the gruesome **Millennium Clock Tower**, a jumble of cogs, chains and wheels modelled in the form of a Gothic cathedral, with gargoyles and sinister-looking figurines representing characters from twentieth-century politics.

The **Natural World gallery** is particularly fine, too, inhabiting all tiers of the museum's eastern end with numerous re-created animals hanging top to bottom from the rafters and a fearsome T-rex skeleton at the entrance.

The new building

Given its confusing and unconventional layout, you might want to pick up a free map before tackling the new building's **Scottish galleries**, which detail the history of Scotland from its geological formation through to the present day. In between, there's a wealth of remarkably well-preserved medieval exhibits – religious, regal and day-to-day objects – on display in the **Kingdom of the Scots**, including the exquisitely idiosyncratic **Lewis chessmen**. Moving forward in time, **Scotland Transformed** offers an insight into the Union of Crowns and the crushed Jacobite rebellion, leading up to the Industrial Revolution – evoked by an unmissable life-size working model of a steam-driven Newcomen Atmospheric Engine. Designed in 1712, it foreshadows Scotland's role as covered in the next section, **Industry and Empire**, where you can see a full-size steam locomotive, the *Ellesmere*, highlighting the fact that in the nineteenth century Scotland was building more railway engines than anywhere else in the world.

Surgeons' Hall Museum

Nicolson St, between nos. 14 & 16 • Daily 10am–5pm • £6 • ☎ 0131 527 1711, ⊛ museum.rcsed.ac.uk

Surgeons' Hall, the former headquarters of the Royal College of Surgeons, is a handsome iconic temple with a stately columned facade, built by William Playfair (1789–1857), one of Edinburgh's greatest architects. Housed round the back is one of the city's most unusual and morbidly compelling museums. In the eighteenth and nineteenth centuries, Edinburgh was a leading centre of medical and anatomical research, nurturing world-famous pioneers such as James Young Simpson, founder of anaesthesia, and Joseph Lister, the father of modern surgery. The **history of surgery**

takes up one part of the museum, with intriguing exhibits ranging from early surgical tools to a pocketbook covered with the leathered skin of serial killer William Burke (see p.72). Another room has an array of gruesome instruments illustrating the history of dentistry, while the third and most remarkable part of the museum, the elegant **Playfair Hall**, contains an array of specimens and jars from the college's anatomical and pathological collections dating back to the eighteenth century.

The New Town

The **NEW TOWN**, itself well over two hundred years old, stands in total contrast to the Old Town: the layout is symmetrical, the streets are broad and straight, and most of the buildings are Neoclassical. Originally intended to be residential, the entire area, right down to the names of its streets, is something of a celebration of the Union, which was then generally regarded as a proud development in Scotland's history. Today, the New Town's main streets form the bustling hub of the city's commercial, retail and business life, dominated by shops, banks and offices.

In many ways, the layout of the greater New Town is its own most remarkable sight, an extraordinary grouping of squares, circuses, terraces, crescents and parks with a few set pieces such as **Register House**, the north frontage of **Charlotte Square** and the assemblage of curiosities on and around **Calton Hill**. However, it also contains assorted Victorian additions, notably the **Scott Monument** on Princes Street, the **Royal Botanic Garden** on its northern fringe, as well as two of the city's most important public collections – the **National Gallery of Scotland** and, further afield, the **Scottish National Gallery of Modern Art**.

Brief history

The existence of the New Town is chiefly due to the vision of **George Drummond**, who made schemes for the expansion of the city soon after becoming Lord Provost in 1725. Work began on the draining of the Nor' Loch below the Castle in 1759, a task that was to last some sixty years. The North Bridge, linking the Old Town with the main road leading to the port of Leith, was built between 1763 and 1772 and, in 1766, following a public competition, a plan for the New Town by 22-year-old architect **James Craig** was chosen. Its gridiron pattern was perfectly matched to the site: central **George Street**, flanked by showpiece squares, was laid out along the main ridge, with parallel **Princes Street** and **Queen Street** on either side below, and two smaller streets, Thistle Street and Rose Street, in between the three major thoroughfares providing coach houses, artisans' dwellings and shops. Princes and Queen streets were built up on one side only, so as not to block the spectacular views of the Old Town and Fife respectively. Architects were accordingly afforded a wonderful opportunity to play with vistas and spatial relationships, particularly well exploited by Robert Adam, who contributed extensively to the later phases of the work. The First New Town, as the area covered by Craig's plan came to be known, received a whole series of extensions in the early decades of the nineteenth century, all carefully in harmony with the Neoclassical idiom.

Princes Street

Although only allocated a subsidiary role in the original plan of the New Town, **Princes Street** had developed into Edinburgh's principal thoroughfare by the middle of the nineteenth century, a role it has retained ever since. Its unobstructed **views** across to the Castle and the Old Town are undeniably magnificent. Indeed, without the views, Princes Street would lose much of its appeal; its northern side, dominated by large outlets of the familiar national chains, is almost always crowded with shoppers, and

1

few of the original eighteenth-century buildings remain. Across the road, the southern side looks down onto the basin of Princes Street Gardens which is bisected midway by a direct route into the heart of the Old Town known as the **Mound**, formed in the 1780s by dumping piles of earth and other waste brought from the New Town's building plots.

General Register House

2 Princes St • Mon–Fri 9am–4.30pm • £15 day pass • ☎ 0131 535 1314, ⓦ nrscotland.gov.uk

Designed in 1774 by Robert Adam, the **General Register House** is the most distinguished building on Princes Street. Today it's home to the **Scotland's People Centre**, a dedicated family history unit which acts as a single point of access for those researching genealogical records. Visitors can pore over a mixed archive of records ranging from national censuses, criminal records and, stretching back to 1553, old parish registers of births, marriages and deaths. A large database complements the physical records and there are a number of computers for public use if you don't have your own. Part of the appeal of embarking on some research is the opportunity to spend time in the elegant interior, centred on a glorious rotunda, lavishly decorated with plasterwork and antique-style medallions.

Princes Street Gardens

Dawn to dusk • Free

It's hard to imagine that the Princes Street Gardens which flank nearly the entire length of Princes Street were once the stagnant, foul-smelling Nor' Loch into which the effluent of the Old Town flowed for centuries. The railway has since replaced the water and today a sunken cutting carries the main lines out of Waverley Station to the west and north. The gardens, split into east and west sections, were originally the private domain of Princes Street residents and their well-placed acquaintances, only becoming a public park in 1876. These days, the swathes of green lawn, colourful flower beds and mature trees are a green lung for the city centre: on sunny days local office workers appear in their droves at lunchtime, while in the run-up to Christmas the gardens' eastern section is home to a German Market, a towering Ferris wheel and a number of other appealingly lit rides. The larger and more verdant western section has a floral clock and the Ross Bandstand, a popular Festival venue.

Scott Monument

East Princes Street Gardens • April–Sept daily 10am–7pm; Oct–March daily 10am–4pm • £5 • ☎ 0131 529 4068, ⓦ edinburghmuseums.org.uk

Facing the Victorian shopping emporium Jenners, and set within East Princes Street Gardens, the 200ft-high **Scott Monument** was erected in memory of prolific author and patriot Sir Walter Scott within a few years of his death. The largest monument in the world to a man of letters, the architecture is closely modelled on Scott's beloved Melrose Abbey (see p.122), and the rich sculptural decoration shows sixteen Scottish writers and sixty-four characters from Scott's famous *Waverley* novels. On the central plinth at the base of the monument is a **statue** of Scott with his deerhound Maida, carved from a thirty-ton block of Carrara marble.

Inside, a tightly winding spiral staircase climbs 287 steps to a narrow platform near the top: from here, you can enjoy some inspiring – if vertiginous – vistas of the city below and hills and firths beyond.

National Gallery of Scotland

The Mound, Princes St • Daily 10am–5pm (until 6pm in Aug & until 7pm Thurs year-round) • Free; entrance charge for some temporary exhibitions • ☎ 0131 624 6200, ⓦ nationalgalleries.org

Built as a "temple to the fine arts" in 1850, the **National Gallery of Scotland** houses Scotland's premier collection of pre-twentieth-century **European art** in the larger of two

THE NATIONAL GALLERIES' COLLECTION 1

The **National Gallery of Scotland** is just one part of the national art collection housed around Edinburgh. Other works of the **National Galleries' collection** are on display at the **Scottish National Portrait Gallery** (see p.79) and the **Scottish National Gallery of Modern Art** (see p.80), housed in two neighbouring buildings, Modern One and Modern Two. A **free bus service** connects the National Gallery of Scotland with Modern One and Two (outbound: daily 11am–4pm, every hour on the hour except 1pm; return: 11.30am, 12.30pm, 2.30pm, 3.30pm & 5pm).

grand Neoclassical buildings found at the foot of the Mound (the other building houses the **Royal Scottish Academy**, which mostly holds temporary exhibitions).

Though by no means as vast as national collections found elsewhere in Europe, it does include a clutch of exquisite Old Masters and some superb Impressionist works. Benefiting greatly from being a manageable size, its series of elegant octagonal rooms is enlivened by imaginative displays and a pleasantly unrushed atmosphere.

On the ground floor the rooms have been restored to their 1850s appearance with pictures hung closely together on claret-coloured walls, often on two levels, and intermingled with sculptures and objets d'art to produce a deliberately cluttered effect. As a result some lesser works, which would otherwise languish in the vaults, are on display, a good 15ft up. The **layout** is broadly chronological, starting in the upper rooms above the gallery's entrance on the Mound and continuing clockwise around the ground floor.

Early works

Among the Gallery's most valuable treasures are **Hugo van der Goes**' *Trinity Panels*, on a long-term loan from the Queen. Painted in the mid-fifteenth century, they were commissioned by Provost Edward Bonkil for the Holy Trinity Collegiate Church, which was later demolished to make way for Edinburgh's Waverley Station. Bonkil can be seen amid the company of organ-playing angels in the finest and best preserved of the four panels, while on the reverse sides are portraits of James III, his son (the future James IV) and Queen Margaret of Denmark. The panels are turned by the gallery every half-hour.

European highlights

Poussin's *Seven Sacraments* are proudly displayed in their own room, the floor and central octagonal bench of which repeat some of the works' motifs. The series marks the first attempt to portray scenes from the life of Jesus realistically, rather than through images dictated by artistic conventions. **Rubens'** *The Feast of Herod*, enlivened by meticulous restoration, is an archetypal example of his sumptuously grand manner, its gory subject matter overshadowed by the gaudy depiction of the delights of the table. Among the canvases by **Rembrandt** are a poignant *Self-Portrait Aged 51* and the ripely suggestive *Woman in Bed*, which is thought to represent the biblical figure of Sarah on her wedding night, waiting for her husband Tobias to put the devil to flight. *Christ in the House of Martha and Mary* is the largest and probably the earliest of the thirty or so surviving paintings by **Vermeer**.

Scottish and English works

On the face of it, the gallery's Scottish collection, ambitiously covering the entire gamut from seventeenth-century portraiture to the Arts and Crafts movement, is a bit of an anticlimax. There are, however, a few significant works displayed within a broad European context. Both **Gavin Hamilton**'s *Achilles Mourning the Death of Patroclus*, painted in Rome, and Arts and Crafts painter **Robert Burns**'s *Diana and her Nymphs* are finer examples of arresting Scottish art.

1

One of the most popular portraits in the gallery is the immediately recognizable painting of a lesser-known pastor, *Reverend Robert Walker Skating on Duddingston Loch*, by Henry Raeburn.

George Street

Running parallel to Princes Street, **George Street** was designed to be the centrepiece of the First New Town, joining two grand squares (St Andrew Square and Charlotte Square). These days, the street is rapidly changing its role from a thoroughfare of august financial institutions to a highbrow version of Princes Street, where the big deals are done in designer-label shops.

St Andrew Square

Lying at the eastern end of George Street is the smartly landscaped **St Andrew Square**, whose centre is marked by the **Melville Monument**, a towering column topped by a statue of Lord Melville, Pitt the Younger's Navy Treasurer. Around the edge of the square you'll find Edinburgh's bus station, the city's swankiest shopping arcade, Multrees Walk, and a handsome eighteenth-century town mansion, designed by Sir William Chambers. Still the ceremonial headquarters of the Royal Bank of Scotland, the palatial mid-nineteenth-century banking hall is a symbol of the success of the New Town.

Charlotte Square

At the western end of George Street is **Charlotte Square**, designed by Robert Adam in 1791, a year before his death. For the most part, his plans were faithfully implemented, an exception being the domed and porticoed church of St George, simplified on grounds of expense. Generally regarded as the epitome of the New Town's elegant simplicity, the square was once the most exclusive residential address in Edinburgh, and though much of it is now occupied by offices, the imperious dignity of the architecture is still clear to see. Indeed, the north side, the finest of Adam's designs, is once again the city's premier address, with the official residence of the First Minister of the Scottish Government at no. 6 (Bute House), the Edinburgh equivalent of 10 Downing Street.

Georgian House

7 Charlotte Square • March daily 11am–4pm; April–June, Sept & Oct daily 10am–5pm; July & Aug daily 10am–6pm; Nov daily 11am–4pm; early Dec Thurs–Sun 11am–4pm; • £7; NTS • ☎ 0131 458 0200, ⓦ nts.org.uk

Restored by the National Trust for Scotland, the interior of this residential townhouse provides a revealing sense of well-to-do New Town living in the early nineteenth century. Though a little stuffy and lifeless, the rooms are impressively decked out in period **furniture** – look for the working barrel organ which plays a selection of Scottish airs – and hung with fine **paintings**, including portraits by Ramsay and Raeburn, seventeenth-century Dutch cabinet pictures and the beautiful *Marriage of the Virgin* by El Greco's teacher, the Italian miniaturist Giulio Clovio. In the basement you can see the original wine cellar, lined with roughly made bins, and a **kitchen** complete with an open fire for roasting and a separate oven for baking; video reconstructions of life below and above stairs are shown in a nearby room.

Queen Street

The last of the New Town's three main streets and the least tarnished by post Georgian development. **Queen Street**'s southern side is occupied mostly by offices, while across the road there's a huge private residents' garden. There are few individual attractions here, with the exception of the **Scottish National Portrait Gallery** at the eastern end, just to the north of St Andrew Square.

Scottish National Portrait Gallery

1 Queen St • Daily 10am–5pm (until 6pm in Aug, and until 7pm Thurs year-round) • Free • ☎ 0131 624 6200, ⓦ nationalgalleries.org

Housed in a fantastic Gothic Revivalist palace in red sandstone, the **Scottish National Portrait Gallery** makes an extravagant contrast to the New Town's prevailing Neoclassicism. The exterior of the building is encrusted with statues of national heroes, a theme reiterated in the stunning two-storey entrance hall by William Hole's tapestry-like **frieze** and **mural**, carefully restored in the building's revamp.

The gallery's **collection** extends to over thirty thousand images with seventeen exhibition spaces exploring the differing characteristics of Scotland as a nation and a people. Inevitably oil paintings of the likes of Mary, Queen of Scots and Robert Burns form the backbone of the collection, but there's a lot to be said for the contemporary portraits that often show a country in cultural flux.

Recent temporary instalments have included Calum Colvin's homage to the Jacobite Rebellion three hundred years on from the first uprising. Alongside, an exhibition tells the story of the 6th Earl of Mar, John Erskine, the man responsible for initiating the rebellion.

Calton Hill

Edinburgh's enduring tag as the "Athens of the North" is nowhere better earned than on **Calton Hill**, the volcanic crag which rises up above the eastern end of Princes Street. Numerous architects homed in on it as a showcase for their most ambitious and grandiose buildings and monuments, the presence of which emphasizes Calton's aloof air and sense of detachment. It's also one of the best viewpoints from which to appreciate the city as a whole, with its tightly knitted suburbs, landmark Old and New Town buildings and the sea beyond.

Calton Gaol

Waterloo Place • No public access

Many visitors arriving into Waverley Station at Calton Hill's southern drop imagine the picturesque castellated building hard up against rock to be Edinburgh Castle itself. In fact, it's the only surviving part of the **Calton Gaol**, once Edinburgh's main prison where former serial killer William Burke spent his final hours before being executed on Lawnmarket. Most of the prison was demolished in the 1930s to make way for the looming Art Deco St Andrew's House, which is today occupied by civil servants.

Old Calton Burial Ground

Waterloo Place • Open 24hr • Free

On Calton Hill's southern slopes, tucked behind a line of high, dark, forbidding walls, the picturesque assembly of mausoleums and gravestones of **Old Calton Burial Ground**, some at a jaunty angle and others weathered with age, makes for an absorbing wander. Notable among the monuments are the cylindrical memorial by Robert Adam to the philosopher David Hume, one of Edinburgh's greatest sons, and a piercing obelisk commemorating various political martyrs.

Nelson Monument

Calton Hill • April–Sept Mon–Sat 10am–7pm, Sun noon–5pm; Oct–March Mon–Sat 10am–3pm • £5 • ☎ 0131 556 2716, ⓦ edinburghmuseums.org.uk

Robert Louis Stevenson reckoned that Calton Hill was the best place to view Edinburgh, "since you can see the Castle, which you lose from the Castle, and Arthur's Seat, which you cannot see from Arthur's Seat". Though the panoramas from ground level are spectacular enough, those from the top of the **Nelson Monument**, perched near the summit of Calton Hill, are even better. Each day at 1pm a white ball drops down a mast at the top of the monument; this, together with the one o'clock gun fired from

1

the Castle battlements (see p.59), once provided a daily check for the mariners of Leith, who needed accurate chronometers to ensure reliable navigation at sea.

National Monument

Summit of Calton Hill

The **National Monument** is often referred to as "Edinburgh's Disgrace", yet many locals admire this unfinished and somewhat ungainly attempt to replicate the Parthenon atop Calton Hill. Begun as a memorial to the dead of the Napoleonic Wars, the project's shortage of funds led architect William Playfair to ensure that even with just twelve of the massive columns completed, the folly would still serve as a striking landmark.

City Observatory

Summit of Calton Hill

Designed by William Playfair in 1818, the **City Observatory** is the largest of the buildings at the summit of Calton Hill. Because of pollution and the advent of street lighting, which impaired views of the stars, the observatory proper had to be relocated to Blackford Hill before the end of the nineteenth century, but the equipment here continues to be used by students. At the corner of the curtain walls is the castellated Observatory House, one of the few surviving buildings by James Craig, designer of the New Town.

The Water of Leith

Slicing a diagonal cleft from the Pentland hills southwest of town, the **Water of Leith** twists and churns, carrying its peaty, golden-brown burden towards The Shore, Leith's (and now Edinburgh's) attractive old harbour. En route, although comfortably bypassing the city's Old Town, the river trundles by old villages that once depended on its power to drive mills. Nature abounds: swans and mallards are commonly sighted under the canopy, while otters, mink and kingfishers make sporadic appearances. The satellite attractions of the **Scottish National Gallery of Modern Art** near Dean Village and the **Royal Botanic Gardens** beside Stockbridge make a good draw from the river's edge. Downstream, the river's final twist opens wide as the boats and gourmet restaurants of Leith's harbour come into view. **The Shore** possesses two of Edinburgh's five Michelin-starred establishments while the wealth of quaint trad-pubs, cafés and floating restaurants on offer makes this the ideal finishing point for a **walk** along the river.

Scottish National Gallery of Modern Art

75 Belford Rd • Daily 10am–5pm (until 6pm in Aug) • Free; entrance charge for some temporary exhibitions • ☏ 0131 624 6200, ⓦ nationalgalleries.org • A free bus service connects the National Gallery of Scotland with the Modern One and Two galleries (outbound: daily 11am–4pm, every hour on the hour except 1pm; return: 11.30am, 12.30pm, 2.30pm, 3.30pm & 5pm)

Set in spacious parkland at the far northwestern fringe of the New Town, just west of quaint, riverside Dean Village, **The Scottish National Gallery of Modern Art** was the first collection in Britain devoted solely to post nineteenth-century painting and sculpture. The Gallery is housed in two impressive Neoclassical buildings – **Modern One** and

WATER OF LEITH WALKWAY

The Water of Leith flows in a northeasterly direction from the Pentland Hills to The Shore in Leith, over a distance of 24 miles. Following the final twelve miles of the river's course is the **Water of Leith Walkway**, making for a lovely riverside walk – a popular seven-mile stretch is from Colinton Village in the southwest (bus #10 from Princes St) to The Shore. For more information or to download a map, see ⓦ www.waterofleith.org.uk.

Modern Two – while its grounds serve as a **sculpture park**, featuring works by Richard Long, Henry Moore, Rachel Whiteread and, most strikingly, Charles Jencks, whose prize-winning *Landform*, a swirling mix of ponds and grassy mounds, dominates the area in front of Modern One.

The art collection here has a strong Scottish contingent, with a particularly fine body of works from the early twentieth-century **Colourists** – a term attributed to the Scots-born painters of the era who spent enough time in France to soak up some post-Impressionist ideas and blend them with Scottish painting traditions. Fluid paint handling and vivid colours characterize the works you're likely to encounter from the leading figures of the movement, such as Samuel Peploe, John Duncan Fergusson and Leslie Hunter. The collection's **international works** from the same period feature crowd-pleasing names like Matisse and Picasso, while Hockney, Warhol and Freud form the backbone of a solid postwar catalogue.

More recently the gallery has picked up a considerable collection of **contemporary** material from living British exponents of modern art such as Damien Hirst and Tracey Emin.

Modern One

The more cutting-edge of the two sister galleries, **Modern One** draws on the Gallery's enviable collection to bolster the themes of the temporary exhibits on show.

The building is divided into 22 exhibition spaces spread over two floors, with a good mix of audiovisual and sculpture art complementing the main exhibition, while on the ground floor there's a café with sun terrace and a well-stocked book and gift shop.

Modern Two

Just across Belford Road from Modern One, **Modern Two**, originally an orphanage, has been dramatically refurbished specifically to make room for the work of Edinburgh-born sculptor **Sir Eduardo Paolozzi**, described by some as the father of Pop Art. The collection, partly a gift from the artist himself, who died in 2005, includes some three thousand sculptures, two thousand prints and drawings and three thousand books.

There's an awesome introduction to Paolozzi's work in the form of the huge *Vulcan*, a half-man, half-machine which squeezes into the Great Hall immediately opposite the main entrance – view it both from ground level and the head-height balcony to appreciate the sheer scale of the piece. No less indicative of Paolozzi's dynamic creative talents are the rooms to the right of the main entrance, where his London studio has been expertly re-created, right down to the clutter of half-finished casts, toys and empty pots of glue. Elsewhere in the gallery, a selection of his sculptures and drawings is exhibited in a more traditional manner. The rooms upstairs are normally given over to special and touring exhibitions, which usually carry an entrance charge.

Dean Village

From Princes St, take bus #19, #37 or #113 and alight before Dean Bridge; Dean Village is a 10min walk down Miller Row, the lane immediately before the bridge

Less than half a mile from Princes Street's west end is the old milling community of **Dean Village**, one of central Edinburgh's most picturesque yet unexpected corners, its atmosphere of decay arrested by the conversion of numerous granaries and tall mill buildings into designer flats. Nestling close to the river, with steep banks rising up on both sides, the Victorian community has a self-contained air, its surviving features including a school, clock tower and communal drying green. High above Dean Village, **Dean Bridge**, a bravura feat of 1830s engineering by Thomas Telford, carries the main road over 100ft above the river.

1

Stockbridge

Bus #24, #29 or #42 from Princes St

Between the New Town and the Botanic Gardens, the busy suburb of **Stockbridge** grew up around the Water of Leith ford (and its seventeenth-century bridge) over which cattle were driven to market in Edinburgh. The hamlet was essentially gobbled up in the expansion of the New Town, but a few charming buildings and an independent character prevail in the district today. The area is a popular quarter for young professionals who can't afford the property prices in the New Town proper, and as a result there's a good crop of bars, boutiques and places to eat along both Raeburn Place, the main road, and St Stephen's Street, long one of Edinburgh's more offbeat side streets.

The Royal Botanic Garden

Arboretum Place • Daily: March–Sept 10am–6pm; Feb & Oct 10am–5pm; Nov–Jan 10am–4pm (note that glasshouses close 1hr before garden) • Garden free; glasshouses £5.50; guided tours £5 (tours last 1hr and leave from the John Hope Gateway at 11am and 2pm April–Oct) • ☎ 0131 248 2909, 🖰 rbge.org.uk • Take bus #23, #27 or #28 from The Mound

Just beyond the northern boundaries of the New Town is the seventy-acre site of the **Royal Botanic Garden**. Filled with mature trees and a huge variety of native and exotic plants and flowers, the "Botanics" (as they're commonly called) are most popular simply as a place to stroll and lounge around on the grass. The main entrance is the West Gate on Arboretum Place, through the contemporary, eco-designed John Hope Gateway, where you'll find interpretation areas, information, exhibitions, a shop and restaurant. Towards the eastern side of the gardens, a series of ten **glasshouses**, including a soaring 1850s **Palm House**, shows off a steamy array of palms, ferns, orchids, cycads and aquatic plants, including some huge circular water lilies. Elsewhere, different themes are highlighted: the large Chinese-style garden, for example, has a bubbling waterfall and the world's biggest collection of Asian wild plants outside China, while in the northwest corner there's a Scottish native woodland which very effectively evokes the wild unkemptness of parts of the Scottish Highlands and west coast. **Art** is also a strong theme within the Botanics, with a gallery showing changing contemporary exhibitions in the attractive eighteenth-century **Inverleith House** at the centre of the gardens. Scattered all around are a number of outdoor sculptures, including a giant pine cone by landscape artist Andy Goldsworthy and the striking stainless-steel east gate, designed in the form of stylized rhododendrons. Parts of the garden are also notable for their great vistas: the lawns near Inverleith House offer one of the city's best views of the Castle and Old Town's steeples and monuments.

Leith

Bus #16 or #22 eastbound from Princes St

Although **LEITH** is generally known as the port of Edinburgh, it developed independently of the city up the hill, its history bound up in the hard graft of fishing, shipbuilding and trade. The presence of sailors, merchants and continental traders also gave the place a cosmopolitan – if slightly rough – edge, which is still obvious today. While specific attractions are few, Leith is an intriguing place to explore, worth visiting not just for the contrasts to central Edinburgh, but also for its nautical air and the excellent eating and drinking scene, which majors on seafood but includes haute cuisine and well-worn, friendly pubs.

Leith's initial revival from down-and-out port to des-res waterfront began in the 1980s around the area known as The Shore, the old harbour at the mouth of the Water of Leith. Until recently, the massive dock areas beyond were being transformed at a rate of knots, with landmark developments including a vast building housing civil servants from the Scottish Executive, and Ocean Terminal, a shopping and entertainment complex, beside which the former **Royal Yacht Britannia** has settled into her retirement.

1

The Shore

The best way to absorb Leith's history and seafaring connections is to take a stroll along **The Shore**, a tenement-lined road running alongside the Water of Leith. Until the mid-nineteenth century this was a bustling and cosmopolitan **harbour**, visited by ships from all over the world, but as vessels became increasingly large, they moored up at custom-built docks built beyond the original quays; these days, only a handful of boats are permanently moored here. Instead, the focus is on the numerous **pubs and restaurants** that line the street, many of which spill tables and chairs out onto the cobbled pavement on sunny days. And the dining here is good; within a few hundred yards of each other Leith has two Michelin-starred restaurants in *The Kitchin* (see p.94) and *Martin Wishart*. The historic buildings along this stretch include the imposing Neoclassical **Custom House**, still used as offices for the harbour authority (and not open to the public); the round **signal tower**, which was originally constructed as a windmill; and the turrets and towers of the **Sailors' Home**, built in Scots Baronial style in the 1880s as a dosshouse for seafarers.

Royal Yacht Britannia

Ocean Terminal • Daily: April–Sept 9.30am–4.30pm; Oct 9.30am–4pm; Nov–March 10am–3.30pm • £15 • ☎ 0131 555 5566,
Ⓦ royalyachtbritannia.co.uk • Bus #11, #22 or #34 from Princes St; otherwise jump on one of the tour buses that leave from Waverley Bridge

A little to the west of The Shore, moored alongside **Ocean Terminal**, a huge shopping and entertainment centre designed by Terence Conran, is one of the world's most famous ships, the **Royal Yacht Britannia**. Launched in 1953 at John Brown's shipyard on Clydeside, *Britannia* was used by the royal family for 44 years for state visits, diplomatic functions and royal holidays. Leith acquired the vessel following decommission in 1997, against the wishes of many of the royal family, who felt that scuttling would have been a more dignified end. Alongside *Britannia*, the sleek former royal sailing yacht, *Bloodhound*, is also on view (Sept–June).

Visits to *Britannia* begin in the **visitor centre**, on the second floor of Ocean Terminal, where royal holiday snaps and video clips of the ship's most famous moments, which included the 1983 evacuation of Aden and the British handover of Hong Kong in 1997, are shown. An audio handset is then handed out and you're allowed to roam around the yacht: the **bridge**, the **engine room**, the **officers' mess** and a large part of the **state apartments**, including the cabins used by the Queen and the Duke of Edinburgh. The ship has been kept largely as it was when in service, with a well-preserved 1950s dowdiness that the audio-guide loyally attributes to the Queen's good taste and astute frugality in the lean post-war years. Certainly, the atmosphere is a far cry from the opulent splendour that many expect.

The guide's commentary also reveals quirkier aspects of *Britannia*'s history: a full Marine Band was always part of the three-hundred-strong crew; hand signals were used by the sailors to communicate orders as shouting was forbidden; and a special solid mahogany rail was built onto the royal bridge to allow the Queen to stand on deck as the ship came into port, without fear of a gust of wind lifting the royal skirt.

Greater Edinburgh

There's a great deal to be discovered in **Greater Edinburgh**, beyond the compact city centre. The attractive coastal suburbs of **Crammond**, **Newhaven** and **Portobello** are all popular at weekends when the sun shines. The pick of the historical destinations includes the imposing fifteenth-century **Craigmillar Castle** on the south side of the city and the sleepy medieval village of **Duddingston**, with its ancient pub, on the far side of Arthur's Seat. On the opposite side of town is **Edinburgh Zoo**, one of the city's best-loved attractions and home to the country's only pandas.

1

Newhaven

2 miles north of the centre of town • Bus #11 or #16 eastbound from Princes St

The old village (now suburb) of **Newhaven** was established by James IV at the start of the sixteenth century as an alternative shipbuilding centre to Leith: his massive warship, the *Great Michael*, capable of carrying 120 gunners, three hundred mariners and a thousand troops, and said to have used up all the trees in Fife, was built here. Newhaven has also been a ferry station and an important fishing centre, landing some six million oysters a year at the height of its success in the 1860s. Today, the chief pleasure is a stroll around the stone **harbour**, which still has a pleasantly salty feel, with a handful of boats tied up alongside or resting gently on the tidal mud.

Portobello

3 miles east of the centre of town • Bus #15 or #26 eastbound from Princes St

Among Edinburgh's least expected assets is its **beach**, a mile-long stretch of golden sand, most of which falls within **Portobello**, the suburb to the east of Arthur's Seat. Seeing a bit of a resurgence following the removal of some down-at-heel amusement

ROBERT LOUIS STEVENSON

Though **Robert Louis Stevenson** (1850–94) is sometimes dismissed for his straight-up writing style, he was one of the best-loved writers of his generation, and one whose novels, short stories, travelogues and essays remain enormously popular over a century after his death.

Born in Edinburgh into a distinguished family of lighthouse engineers, Stevenson was a sickly child, with a solitary childhood dominated by his governess, Alison "Cummie" Cunningham, who regaled him with tales drawn from Calvinist folklore. Sent to the university to study engineering, Stevenson rebelled against his upbringing by spending much of his time in the low-life howffs and brothels of the city. He later switched his studies to law, and although called to the bar in 1875, by then he had decided to channel his energies into literature: while still a student, he had already made his mark as an **essayist**, and eventually had more than a hundred essays published, ranging from light-hearted whimsy to trenchant political analysis.

Stevenson's other early successes included the **travelogue** *Travels with a Donkey in the Cevennes*, kaleidoscopic jottings based on his journeys in France, where he went to escape Scotland's weather, which was damaging his health. It was there that he met Fanny Osbourne, an American ten years his senior, who was estranged from her husband and had two children in tow. His voyage to join her in San Francisco formed the basis for his most important factual work, *The Amateur Emigrant*, a vivid first-hand account of the great nineteenth-century European migration to the United States. Having married the now-divorced Fanny, Stevenson began an elusive search for an agreeable climate that led to Switzerland, the French Riviera and the Scottish Highlands.

He belatedly turned to the novel, achieving immediate acclaim in 1881 for **Treasure Island**, a moralistic adventure yarn that began as an entertainment for his stepson and future collaborator, Lloyd Osbourne. In 1886 his most famous short story, **Strange Case of Dr Jekyll and Mr Hyde** (despite its nominal London setting) offered a vivid evocation of Edinburgh's Old Town: an allegory of its dual personality of prosperity and squalor, and an analysis of its Calvinistic preoccupations with guilt and damnation. The same year saw the publication of the historical romance **Kidnapped**, an adventure novel which exemplified Stevenson's view that literature should seek above all to entertain.

In 1887 Stevenson left Britain for good, travelling first to the United States where he began one of his most ambitious novels, *The Master of Ballantrae*. A year later, he set sail for the South Seas, and eventually settled in **Samoa**; his last works include a number of stories with a local setting, such as the grimly realistic *The Ebb Tide* and *The Beach of Falesà*. However, Scotland continued to be his main inspiration: he wrote *Catriona* as a sequel to *Kidnapped*, and was at work on two more novels with Scottish settings, *St Ives* and *Weir of Hermiston*, a dark story of father and son confrontation, at the time of his sudden death from a brain haemorrhage in 1894. He was buried on the top of Mount Vaea overlooking the Pacific Ocean.

arcades, it retains a certain faded charm from its heyday thanks to some attractive Victorian buildings and its delightful promenade. On hot summer weekends the beach can be a mass of swimmers, sunbathers, surfers and pleasure boats, while the rest of the year it makes for a pleasant stroll in between café stops.

Edinburgh Zoo

134 Corstorphine Rd, 3 miles west of the centre of town • Daily: April–Sept 9am–6pm; March & Oct 9am–5pm; Nov–Feb 9am–4.30pm • £17/person; family tickets £53.50 (if bought online) • ☎ 0131 334 9171, ⓦ edinburghzoo.org.uk • Bus #12, #26 or #31 westbound from Princes St

Set on an eighty-acre site on the slopes of Corstorphine Hill, **Edinburgh Zoo** has transformed itself in recent years into a modern and highly successful conservation and recreation park – one of the city's most popular attractions. Appealingly set in the midst of a botanic garden, the new enclosures offer plenty of opportunities for up-close animal encounters, and the heralded arrival of two **giant pandas** in 2012 bolstered the zoo's already impressive collection. Other highlights include the 2.15pm **Penguin Parade**, the **Budongo Trail** – a huge modern chimpanzee enclosure with intimate viewing positions – and the several walk-through enclosures where you might come face to face with a curious Saki monkey or a wallaby. Given the zoo's steep incline, you may want to hop on the regular free Hilltop Safari bus to the top of the hill and work your way back down. The zoo is big enough to warrant a full day's exploration so you may want to pick up a picnic from the nearby artisan German baker shop, *Störtebäcker* (see p.100), prior to entry.

Duddingston

2.5 miles southeast of the centre of town • Bus #42 south from Waverley Bridge

The beautiful conservation village of **Duddingston**, at the opposite end of Arthur's Seat from the centre, is attractively set on the shores of **Duddingston Loch** – best known as the setting for Henry Raeburn's *Reverend Robert Walker Skating on Duddingston Loch*, on show at the National Gallery (see p.78). Most visitors come here for a stiff drink at the *Sheep Heid Inn* (see p.96) after a hike over Arthur's Seat.

Cramond

5 miles northwest of the centre of town • Bus #41 westbound from central Princes St • For tide times, either check the notice board on shore or look for tide times for Leith on the BBC weather website

The enduring image of **Cramond** – a picturesque village by the Firth of Forth – is of step-gabled whitewashed houses rising uphill from the waterfront, though it also has the foundations of a Roman fort, as well as a tower house, church, inn and mansion, all from the seventeenth century. The best reason to come here is to enjoy a stroll around and a bit of fresh air. The **walk** along the wide promenade that follows the shoreline offers great views of the Forth; or head out across the causeway to the uninhabited bird sanctuary of **Cramond Island** – though be aware that the causeway disappears as high tide approaches and can leave you stranded if you get your timings wrong. Aim to get to and from the island in the two hours either side of low tide. Inland of Cramond, there's another pleasant walk along a tree-lined path leading upstream along the River Almond, past former mills and their adjoining cottages towards the sixteenth-century Old Cramond Bridge. These walks should take around an hour each.

Craigmillar Castle

Craigmillar Castle Rd, 5 miles southeast of the centre • April–Sept daily 9.30am–5.30pm; Oct daily 9.30am–4.30am; Nov–March Sat–Wed 10am–4pm • £5.50; HES • ☎ 0131 661 4445, ⓦ historicenvironment.scot • Take bus #8, #33 or #49 from North Bridge to Edinburgh Royal Infirmary, from where the castle is a 10min walk along a signposted footpath

1

Situated amid a small tranche of green belt, **Craigmillar Castle** offers an atmospheric, untrammelled contrast to packed Edinburgh Castle in the city centre. Before Queen Victoria set her heart on Balmoral, Craigmillar was considered her royal castle north of the border – which is hard to imagine now, given its proximity to the ugly council housing scheme of Craigmillar, one of Edinburgh's most deprived districts. That said, the immediate setting feels very rural and Craigmillar Castle enjoys splendid views back to Arthur's Seat and Edinburgh Castle. The oldest part of the complex is the L-shaped **tower house**, which dates back to the early 1400s – this remains substantially intact, and the **great hall**, with its resplendent late Gothic chimneypiece, is in good enough shape to be rented out for functions. The tower house was surrounded in the 1500s by a quadrangular wall with cylindrical corner towers and was used on occasion by Mary, Queen of Scots. It was abandoned to its picturesque decay in the mid-eighteenth century, and today the peaceful ruins and their adjoining grassy lawns make a great place to explore – and kids, in particular, love having the run of their very own castle.

The Pentland Hills

For Hillend, 6 miles south of the centre, take bus #4 or #15 westbound from Princes St; to get to Swanston, 5 miles south of the centre, take bus #16 westbound from Princes St or #27 southbound from The Mound to Oxgangs Rd, from where you can walk along Swanston Rd

The **Pentland Hills**, a chain some eighteen miles long and five wide, dominate most views south of Edinburgh and offer walkers and mountain bikers a thrilling taste of wild Scottish countryside just beyond the suburbs.

The simplest way to get a taste of the scenery of the Pentlands is to set off from the car park by the ski centre at **Hillend**, at the northeast end of the range; take the path up the right-hand side of the dry ski slopes, turning left shortly after crossing a stile to reach a prominent point with outstanding views over Edinburgh and Fife. If you're feeling energetic, go higher up where the vistas get even better. An alternative entry point to the Pentland Hills is **Swanston**, a short distance northwest of Hillend. It's an unspoiled, highly exclusive hamlet of whitewashed thatched-roof dwellings separated from the rest of the city by almost a mile of farmland; **Robert Louis Stevenson** (see box, p.84) spent his boyhood summers in Swanston Cottage, the largest of the houses, immortalizing it in the novel *St Ives*.

ARRIVAL AND DEPARTURE   EDINBURGH

BY PLANE

Edinburgh International Airport Edinburgh's airport (☎0844 448 8833, ⓦedinburghairport.com) is at Turnhouse, 6 miles west of the city centre, just off the A8.

Getting to/from the city centre Airlink #100 shuttle buses connect the airport with Waverley Rail Station in the centre of town (30min; £4.50; ☎0131 554 4494, ⓦflybybus.com), with services every 10–15min between 4am and midnight; a night bus #N22 takes over between midnight and 4am, running every 30min. The tram service also goes to the centre of town every 10–15min, running between 6am and 11pm and stopping at Murrayfield Stadium en route (38min; £5; ☎0131 555 6363, ⓦedinburghtrams.com). Otherwise, a metered taxi will charge around £20–24 to go between the airport and the town centre, while fixed-price taxis (£33 to the city centre) are offered by Airport Transfers Direct (☎0131 272 8222,

ⓦairport-transfers-direct.com) – you can pre-book larger vehicles if required.

BY TRAIN

Conveniently situated at the eastern end of Princes St, right in the heart of the city, Waverley Station (☎0845 748 4950, ⓦnationalrail.co.uk) is the arrival point for all mainline trains. There's a second mainline train stop, Haymarket Station, just under 2 miles west on the lines from Waverley to Glasgow, Fife and the Highlands, although this is only really of use if you're staying nearby.

Destinations Aberdeen (hourly; 2hr 20min); Birmingham (hourly; 5hr); Dunbar (8 daily; 30min); Dundee (hourly; 1hr 45min); Falkirk (every 15min; 25min); Fort William (3 daily, change at Glasgow; 4hr 55min); Galashiels (every 30min; 50min); Glasgow (every 15–30min; 50min); Inverness (6 daily direct; 3hr 50min); London (hourly; 4hr 30min); Manchester (3 daily; 4hr); Newcastle upon Tyne (hourly;

1hr 30min); North Berwick (hourly; 30min); Oban (2–3 daily, change at Glasgow; 4hr 10min); Perth (6 daily; 1hr 15min); Stirling (every 30min; 45min); York (hourly; 2hr 30min).

BY BUS
The bus and coach terminal for intercity services is located on the east side of St Andrew Square, a 2min walk from Waverley Station.

Destinations Aberdeen (hourly; 3hr 50min); Birmingham (2–3 daily; 6hr 50min); Dundee (hourly; 1hr 45min–2hr); Glasgow (every 15min; 1hr 10min); Inverness (hourly; 3hr 30min–4hr 30min); London (10 daily; 7hr 50min); Newcastle upon Tyne (5 daily; 2hr 45min); Perth (hourly; 1hr 20min).

GETTING AROUND

Although Edinburgh occupies a large area relative to its population – fewer than half a million people – most places worth visiting lie within the compact city centre, which is easily explored **on foot**. Most public transport services terminate on or pass through or near **Princes St**, the city's main thoroughfare, which divides the Old Town from the New Town, with the main **bus station** located just north of here on St Andrew Square.

BY BUS AND TRAM
Transport for Edinburgh The city is generally well served by buses; the white and maroon ones operated by Lothian Buses (ticket offices at 31 Waverley Bridge, 9 Clifton Terrace or 27 Hanover St; 9am–6pm; ☎ 0131 555 6363, ⓦ transportforedinburgh.com) and one solitary tram line connecting the airport with the centre via a few key stops. Note that all buses referred to in the text are run by Lothian unless otherwise stated. Usefully, every bus stop displays diagrams indicating which services pass by and the routes they take. A good investment, especially if you're staying away from the centre or want to explore the suburbs, is the £18 "Ridacard" pass allowing a week's unlimited travel on Lothian and tram services. Lothian also offer a day ticket allowing unlimited travel on bus or tram for £4, or you can pay £1.60 for any single journey. Tickets can be bought as you board the bus (exact change needed), whereas tram tickets must be purchased from the ticket machines prior to boarding.
First Edinburgh The predominantly white, single-decker buses of First Edinburgh (☎ 01224 650 100, ⓦ firstgroup .com) run services on a number of the main routes through town, but are better for outlying towns and villages. They have their own system of tickets and day tickets, similar in structure to Lothian Buses. Most services depart from or near the main bus station at St Andrew Square.
Art Gallery Bus A free service (see p.77) connects the National Gallery of Scotland with the Modern One and Two galleries.

BY TAXI
Edinburgh is well endowed with taxi ranks, and you can also hail black cabs on the street. Costs are reasonable – from the city centre to Leith, for example, costs around £8. All taxis are metered and the price structure is set by the council with evening and weekend rides costing £1 more than during the week. Companies include Computer Cabs (☎ 0131 272 8001, ⓦ comcab-edinburgh.co.uk), Central Taxis (☎ 0131 229 2468, ⓦ taxis-edinburgh.co.uk) and City Cabs (☎ 0131 228 1211, ⓦ citycabs.co.uk). Uber users will have little trouble finding a ride as the city is comprehensively covered.

BY CAR
Edinburgh is a relatively uncongested city (except during the August festivals) with just a few traffic jam hot spots, namely the main arterial routes to the centre and also the city bypass, particularly at the A7 intersection. Parking is very expensive and controlled areas stretch far out into the suburbs. Most on-street parking regulations don't apply on Sundays or after 6.30pm Mon–Sat and after 5.30pm Mon–Fri a little further out from the centre.
Car rental There are a few car rental desks in Waverley train station which arrange for customers to be shuttled to collect cars from nearby depots. Also in the centre of town try Hertz at 10 Picardy Place (☎ 0843 309 3026, ⓦ hertz .co.uk), or Avis, 24 East London St (☎ 0844 544 6059, ⓦ avis.co.uk). In addition, all the main rental companies have desks at the airport.

BY BIKE
Although hilly, Edinburgh is a reasonably bike-friendly city, with several cycle paths, particularly in the university areas south of the centre. The local cycling action group, Spokes (☎ 0131 313 2114, ⓦ spokes.org.uk), publishes an excellent map of the city with recommended cycle routes; pick up a copy at the tourist office.
Bike rental Available from Biketrax, 11–13 Lochrin Place, Tollcross (£17/day then £13 for additional days; ☎ 0131 228 6633, ⓦ biketrax.co.uk), and Edinburgh Cycle Hire, 29 Blackfriars St (from £20/day; ☎ 0131 556 5560, ⓦ cyclescotland.co.uk).

INFORMATION

Main tourist office Princes Mall, 3 Princes St, near the northern entrance to the train station (July–Sept Mon–Sat 9am–7pm, Sun 10am–7pm; Oct–June Mon–Sat 9am–5pm, Sun 10am–5pm; ☎ 0131 473 3868, ⓦ edinburgh.org).

1

Although inevitably hectic at the height of the season, it's reasonably efficient, with scores of free leaflets and a bank of computers available for free web surfing.

Airport tourist office At the far end of Arrivals in the direction of the trams (daily: 9.30am–7.30pm; ☎ 0131 473 3690, ⓦ edinburghairport.com). A smaller affair than its town-centre counterpart but has a shop and useful free maps.

TOURS

BUS TOURS

Open-top, hop-on, hop-off bus tours are big business in Edinburgh. All cost the same (currently £15/person) and depart from Waverley Bridge; see ⓦ edinburghtour.com for more info. Recommended companies include MacTours, which uses a fleet of vintage buses and a live guide, and Majestic Tour, ideal for seeing the harder-to-reach sites like the Royal Yacht Britannia (see p.83) and the Royal Botanic Garden (see p.82).

WALKING TOURS

Several companies offer walking tours, many of which depart from the central section of the Royal Mile near the High Kirk of St Giles, or further uphill on the High Street's Mercat Cross. Advance booking is recommended during peak season. The following companies are worth singling out.

Auld Reekie Tours ☎ 0131 557 4700, ⓦ auldreekie tours.com. Departs from The Tron Kirk, 122 High St, daily at noon, 2pm, 3pm (Sat only), 4pm, 6pm, 8pm & 10pm; fewer tours outside high season (£12). With a friendly mixture of ghost stories, town history and other jovial banter, the tours focus on Edinburgh's narrow closes and vaults, one of which contains a torture exhibition.

Edinburgh Literary Pub Tour ☎ 0800 169 7410, ⓦ edinburghliterarypubtour.co.uk. Mixing a pub crawl with extracts from local authors acted out along the way, this tour is a fun way to explore Edinburgh's fine drinking establishments. While being introduced to the scenes, characters and words of the major figures of Scottish literature, including Burns, Scott and MacDiarmid, you'll have the opportunity to nip in for a swift ale at each stop. Tours depart from outside the *Beehive Inn*, Grassmarket (see p.95), at 7.30pm: Jan–March Fri & Sun; April & Oct Thurs–Sun; May–Sept daily; Nov & Dec Fri; £14, or £12 online.

Mercat Tours ☎ 0131 225 5445, ⓦ mercattours.com. Offers a wide range of history and ghost tours from Mercat Cross, High St (£12–16); some depart late in the evening and include a candlelit poke around the underground vaults of Blair St.

ACCOMMODATION

As befits its status as a busy tourist city and important commercial centre, Edinburgh has a greater choice of **accommodation** than anywhere in Britain outside London. Hotels, hostels and rental apartments are essentially the only options you'll find right in the heart of the city, but within relatively easy reach of the centre the choice of guesthouses, B&Bs, campus accommodation and even **campsites** broadens considerably.

ESSENTIALS

Rates Room rates are significantly higher in Edinburgh than elsewhere in Scotland, with double rooms starting at around £80 a night. Budget hotel chains offer the best value if you want basic accommodation right in the centre, while £120–150 will get you something more stylish. Self-catering apartments – of which there are many in Edinburgh – are often the most economical option, especially if you're travelling in a group.

Reservations It's worth making advance reservations at any time of year, and is essential for stays during the Festival and around Hogmanay, when places can get booked out months in advance. Note that Visit Scotland (☎ 0131 472 2222, ⓦ visitscotland.com) operates a booking centre for accommodation in Edinburgh (and the rest of Scotland).

Access Bear in mind that many of the guesthouses and small hotels are located in Georgian and Victorian townhouses, over three or more floors, and usually have no lift, so are not ideal for those with restricted mobility.

OLD TOWN

Accommodation in the Old Town offers a well-balanced mix to cater for all budgets, although in recent years the number of five-star hotels being built has rapidly increased. There's a choice of backpacking hostels tucked in among the gloomier alleys, while mid-range accommodation – mostly branded hotel chains and self-catering apartments – tends to sit just off the main drag.

HOTELS

★**Apex International** 31–35 Grassmarket ☎ 0131 300 3456, ⓦ apexhotels.co.uk; map pp.64–65. This

TOP 5 BUDGET ACCOMMODATION OPTIONS

Castle Rock Hostel See opposite
Gerald's Place See p.90
High Street Hostel See opposite
Ibis Edinburgh Centre See opposite
Stay Central Hotel See opposite

ex-university building turned 175-bed business-oriented hotel has comfortable rooms, some with unencumbered views to the Castle and balconies that peer down onto the happening Grassmarket below. Up top there's a double rosette rooftop restaurant with a dramatic skyline view – especially impressive after dark – while downstairs you'll find a small pool and gym. £148

Ibis Edinburgh Centre 6 Hunter Square ☎ 0131 619 2800, ⓦ accorhotels.com; map pp.64–65. Probably the best-located chain hotel cheapie in the Old Town, within sight of the Royal Mile; rooms are modern and comfortable, but there are few facilities other than a rather plain bar. It's not really a problem with so many bars and cafés directly outside. £109

Stay Central Hotel 139 Cowgate ☎ 0131 622 6801, ⓦ staycentral.co.uk; map pp.64–65. An economical option if you are travelling in a large group, this neoteric hotel has lots of rooms that sleep up to six. Be sure to ask for a room at the back to avoid the noise of the revellers rising up from the late-opening pub next door. Doubles £140; dorms £42

Ten Hill Place 10 Hill Place ☎ 0131 662 2080, ⓦ tenhillplace.com; map pp.60–61. A contemporary hotel owned by the historic Royal College of Surgeons, with 78 sleek and smartly styled bedrooms, all run according to an environmentally conscious policy. The upper floors have a great view of the Salisbury Crags. £145

GUESTHOUSES

★**The Witchery Apartments** Castlehill ☎ 0131 225 5613, ⓦ thewitchery.com; map pp.64–65. Nine riotously indulgent suites grouped around the famously spooky restaurant just downhill from the Castle; expect antique furniture, big leather armchairs, tapestry-draped beds, oak panelling and huge roll-top baths, as well as ultra-modern sound systems and complimentary bottles of champagne. Top of the range, unique and memorable. £325

HOSTELS

Brodies 93 High St ☎ 0131 556 2223, ⓦ brodieshostels .co.uk; map pp.64–65. Extending over two buildings – the other being across the road at no. 12 – *Brodies* offers a few clean but poorly sound-proofed double rooms, some smelly dorms sleeping up to ten, and limited communal areas. Doubles £65; dorms £13

★**Castle Rock Hostel** 15 Johnston Terrace ☎ 0131 225 9666, ⓦ castlerockedinburgh.com; map pp.64–65. Tucked below the Castle ramparts, with two hundred or so beds arranged in large, bright dorms, as well as triple and quad rooms and some doubles. The communal areas include a games room with pool and table tennis and a sunny patio. Doubles £45; dorms £11

High Street Hostel 8 Blackfriars St ☎ 0131 557 3984, ⓦ highstreethostel.com; map pp.64–65. Lively and popular hostel in an attractive sixteenth-century building just off the Royal Mile with dorms of up to eighteen beds and twin rooms. The communal facilities include a kitchen, a quiet room and a large party dining lounge with piano and pool table. Twins £54; dorms £12

Smart City Hostel 50 Blackfriars St ☎ 0131 524 1989, ⓦ smartcityhostels.com; map pp.64–65. An upmarket hostel just off the Royal Mile, with twin rooms or dorms accommodating up to twelve guests. The café serves good-value food and breakfasts, and there is a late-night bar exclusively for residents plus a little courtyard with tables. Twins £125; dorms £27

CAMPUS ACCOMMODATION

★**University of Edinburgh, Pollock Halls of Residence** 18 Holyrood Park Rd, Newington ☎ 0131 651 2007, ⓦ edinburghfirst.com; map pp.56–57. Unquestionably the best setting of any of the city's university accommodation, right beside Holyrood Park, just southeast of the Old Town. It provides single rooms, doubles and self-catering flats, mostly available Easter & June to mid-Sept, though some rooms are available year-round. Singles £48; doubles £112.50; flats per week £525

NEW TOWN

Most of the New Town's accommodation is made up of townhouses converted into independent guesthouses and boutique hotels rather than purpose-built hotels. The dominant Georgian architecture means elegant large rooms, high ceilings and loftier prices, but there are a few exceptions to be found.

HOTELS

★**The Glasshouse** 2 Greenside Place, Broughton ☎ 0131 525 8200, ⓦ theglasshousehotel.co.uk; map pp.60–61. Incorporating the castellated facade of the former Lady Glenorchy's Church, this ultra-hip hotel has 65 chichi rooms with push-button curtains and sliding doors opening onto a huge, lush roof garden scattered with Philippe Starck furniture. Perfect if you're in town for an indulgent weekend. £174

Regent House 3 Forth St, Broughton ☎ 0131 556 1616, ⓦ regenthousehotel.co.uk; map pp.60–61. A good-value small hotel over four floors that makes up for its lack of glamour with a great location, right in the heart of Broughton on a quiet side street. Some rooms are big enough to accommodate three to five people. £89

GUESTHOUSES

Ardenlee Guest House 9 Eyre Place ☎ 0131 556 2838, ⓦ www.ardenleeguesthouse.com; map pp.60–61. Welcoming guesthouse at the foot of the New Town, with original Victorian features and nine reasonably spacious

1

rooms, seven of which are en suite and some suitable for families. A two-bed Georgian apartment (£150) is also available, close by at 3 Eyre Place. **£120**

★**Gerald's Place** 21b Abercromby Place ☎0131 558 7017, ⓦgeraldsplace.com; map pp.60–61. A homely taste of New Town life at an upmarket but wonderfully hospitable and comfy basement B&B. The rustic decor is tasteful, with some fine artwork and old books to catch your eye, while the breakfasts are generous, with many home-made components. **£119**

★**The Guest Room** 31a Nelson St ☎0131 556 4798, ⓦtheguestroom.co.uk; map pp.60–61. A notably unobtrusive B&B offering two spacious rooms with a choice of courtyard or garden views. Start the day with a breakfast tray of berries, porridge and freshly squeezed orange. **£95**

Rick's 55a Frederick St ☎0131 622 7800, ⓦricks edinburgh.co.uk; map pp.60–61. Ten much-sought-after rooms at the back of the popular New Town bar and restaurant. Beautifully styled with beds fitted with walnut headboards and plush fabrics, they look out onto a cobbled lane behind. **£124**

Tigerlily 125 George St ☎0131 225 5005, ⓦtigerlilyedinburgh.co.uk; map pp.60–61. A glitzy boutique hotel, bar and restaurant that epitomizes the excess of twenty-first-century George St. A classic Georgian townhouse transformed into a flamboyant design extravaganza; indulgent pink or black bedroom suites are kitted out with pre-loaded iPods, decadent fabrics, and some even have a real fire. **£220**

HOSTELS

SYHA Edinburgh Central 9 Haddington Place ☎0131 524 2090, ⓦsyha.org.uk; map pp.60–61. In a handy location at the top of Leith Walk (a 5min stroll from the centre), this five-star hostel has single, double and triple private rooms as well as eight-bed dorms with en-suite facilities. There is a reasonably priced bistro in addition to self-catering kitchen facilities. Private rooms **£70**; dorms **£22**

CAMPING

There are only a couple of established campsites within half an hour's travel of central Edinburgh.

Drummohr Caravan and Camping Park Levenhall, Musselburgh, on the B1348 ☎0131 665 6867, ⓦdrummohr.org; map pp.56–57. A large, pleasant site on the eastern edge of Musselburgh, a coastal satellite town to the east of Edinburgh, with excellent transport connections to the city centre. As well as the usual pitches, there are a few "bothies" (basic wooden huts that sleep four) and the more luxurious lodges that sleep eight. Bothies **£30**; lodges **£150**; camping per pitch **£20**

Edinburgh Caravan Club Site 35 Marine Drive, Silverknowes, 5 miles northwest of the centre ☎0131 312 6874, ⓦcaravanclub.co.uk; map pp.56–57. Caravan-dominated site in a pleasant location close to the shoreline, though there's little else here. Cramond village is a 10min walk west along the shore and has a pub and cafés. Per pitch **£12**

EATING

The last decade has seen a marked upsurge in style, sophistication and good taste in Edinburgh's restaurants and cafés. **Café culture** has hit the centre of the city, with tables spilling onto the pavements in the summer, and this has been matched by the rise of a clutch of original, upmarket and stylish **restaurants**, many identifying their cuisine as modern Scottish and championing top-quality local meat, game and fish. With four establishments holding **Michelin stars**, Edinburgh can justifiably claim third place behind London and Birmingham in the UK's fine-dining pecking order. As well as the wide choice offered in the Old Town and New Town, there are some great **neighbourhood** restaurants and cafés outside the centre – for example, in and around **Stockbridge**, on the northern fringe of the New Town; the student area encompassing **Southside**, south of the Old Town; and particularly in the **Shore of Leith**, the city's most inviting gastro hub. Just west of the Old Town, in the area around **Lothian Road**, you'll also find a good choice of economical pre-theatre menus.

THE OLD TOWN

There's a wide choice of restaurants and diners to suit all budgets and it doesn't take too much investigative work to track down places of character tucked away down the lanes and closes of the Old Town. In summer, this is the busiest part of town, so it's advisable to book a table for an evening meal.

CAFÉS

Baba Budan East Market St ☎07753 742550, ⓦbababudan.coffee; map pp.64–65. Billing itself as a "Donutterie", this new addition to Edinburgh's

unstoppable café culture is housed in one of the numerous recently converted arches between the station and the Royal Mile. The doughnuts here are crispy fresh on the outside and light in the middle with some appealing fillings to choose from, like raspberry cream or chocolate marshmallow at £2 each. Mon–Fri 7.30am–5pm, Sat–Sun 10.30am–4.30pm.

★**The Edinburgh Larder** 15 Blackfriars St ☎0131 556 6922, ⓦedinburghlarder.co.uk; map pp.64–65. Just off the Royal Mile, this overwhelmingly popular café dishes up top-quality breakfasts, cream teas and lunches if you can get a seat. Care is taken to ensure ingredients are in season and sourced from local producers. Begin with the veggie breakfast for £7.50 with haggis, home-made beans, mushrooms and egg and return later for a £7 soup and sandwich combo. Sept–Feb Mon–Fri 8am–5pm, Sat & Sun 9am–5pm, March–July daily 8am–5pm; Aug daily 7am–10pm.

The Signet Library Parliament Square ☎0131 225 0651, ⓦedinburghlarder.co.uk; map pp.64–65. Eye-wateringly expensive afternoon teas with mouth-wateringly tasty cakes and savoury bites. A giant gourmet leap above the egg and cress sandwiches of norm, here it's beef wellington pie, confit duck alongside blueberry éclairs and, naturally, scones. Silver service in these prestigious surroundings comes at a price: £30 per person. Mon–Fri 1–7pm, Sun 11am–7pm.

Milk Fruitmarket Gallery, 45 Market St ☎0131 226 8195, ⓦfruitmarket.co.uk; map pp.64–65. This attractive café feels like an extension of the gallery space, its airy, reflective ambience enhanced by the wall of glass onto the street. Lots of colourful, modern and healthy brunch options here like avocado and za'atar with poached egg on toast for £5.50. Nice cakes and expensive coffee too. Mon–Sat 10am–5.30pm, Sun 10am–4.30pm.

RESTAURANTS

Amber 354 Castlehill ☎0131 477 8477, ⓦamber -restaurant.co.uk; map pp.64–65. Connected to the major tourist attraction, The Scotch Whisky Experience (see p.63), this contemporary-styled restaurant offers the chance to explore the nation's cuisine with £2.15 Scottish tapas and a "whisky sommelier" on hand to suggest accompanying drams for each. For something more substantial there's an à la carte menu based around Scottish produce like the lamb rump with seasonal accompaniments for £19. Mon–Thurs & Sun 10am–8.30pm, Fri & Sat noon–9pm.

★**David Bann's Vegetarian Restaurant** 56–58 St Mary's St ☎0131 556 5888, ⓦdavidbann.com; map pp.64–65. Fine dining, vegetarian style, with a tried and tested menu. There are a few unconventional dishes offered here, such as their pulse-packed chilli pancakes with chocolate sauce – a savoury dish – and the parsnip, apple and blue cheese mousse served with roast tatties, for around £12. Mon–Thurs noon–9.45pm, Fri noon–10.15pm, Sat 11am–10.15pm, Sun 11am–9.45pm.

The Grain Store 30 Victoria St ☎0131 225 7635, ⓦgrainstore-restaurant.co.uk; map pp.64–65. This unpretentious restaurant is a relaxing haven amid the bustle of the Old Town, combining top-quality modern Scottish and French cuisines. Lunches (three courses for £16) offer the likes of mullet with mussel veloute, while the evening's £17 truffle gnocchi with Jerusalem artichoke is by far the cheapest on the à la carte menu. Daily noon–2pm & 6–9.45pm.

TOP 5 MUST-TRY RESTAURANTS

Tanjore See p.74
El Cartel Casera Mexicana See p.92
The Gardener's Cottage See p.92
Lian Pu See p.94
Wedgwood the Restaurant See p.91

La Garrigue 31 Jeffrey St ☎0131 557 3032, ⓦlagarrigue.co.uk; map pp.64–65. A double AA rosette-awarded bistro, with a menu and wine list dedicated to the produce and traditions of the Languedoc region of France. Dishes such as the cassoulet or rabbit with aubergine caviar are unmistakably authentic and delivered with a high degree of finesse. The two-course lunch (£14.50) and five-course dinner (£35) menus offer consistent quality and value for money. Daily noon–2.30pm & 6–9.30pm.

Mother India's Café 3–5 Infirmary St ☎0131 524 9801, ⓦmotherindiascafeedinburgh.co.uk; map pp.64–65. Tapas with a twist, so the restaurant slogan goes; the twist being that the food is Indian not Spanish. Although modern in concept, the menu won't trouble seasoned curry connoisseurs, with classics like daal makni and chicken tikka on offer (dishes £4–6). Mon–Wed noon–2pm & 5–10.30pm, Thurs noon–10.30pm, Fri & Sat noon–11pm, Sun noon–10pm.

★**Ondine** 2 George IV Bridge ☎0131 226 1888, ⓦondinerestaurant.co.uk; map pp.64–65. Dedicated seafood restaurant from Edinburgh-born Roy Brett, once Rick Stein's main chef in Padstow, turning out sublime dishes using native shellfish and fish from sustainable sources. Two-course lunch and pre-theatre menus cost £22. Mon–Sat noon–3pm & 5.30–10pm.

The Piemaker 38 South Bridge ☎0131 558 1728, ⓦthepiemaker.co.uk; map pp.64–65. Possibly the cheapest place to fill up in town, this is more of a pie shop with some bar stools than a true restaurant. However, the range of pies from carnivore to vegan plus a few sweet ones is mightily impressive, as are the prices at around £2 each. Nov–Feb Mon–Fri 9am–7pm, Sat 10am–11pm, Sun 10.30am–7pm; March–Oct Mon–Wed 9am–7pm, Thurs & Fri 9am–11pm, Sat 10am–11pm, Sun 10.30–7pm.

★**Spoon Café Bistro** 6a Nicholson St ☎0131 623 1752, ⓦspoonedinburgh.co.uk; map pp.60–61. A homely, first-floor room with quirky, retro fittings serving reliably rustic two- and three-course menus with punchy flavours from £14. For late risers, the brunch menu is not to be missed, with healthy fruity and yoghurt choices or decadent fry-ups and waffles with bacon. Under a different name, this was the café where J.K. Rowling first penned *Harry Potter*. Mon–Sat 10am–11pm, Sun noon–5pm.

★**Wedgwood the Restaurant** 267 Canongate

1

☎0131 558 8737, ⓦwedgwoodtherestaurant.co.uk; map pp.64–65. This small but reputable fine-dining restaurant with in-house forager creatively plates all the best of Scotland's land, rivers and seas. There's so much choice on the à la carte menu that they offer "deciding time" – canapés and champagne – while you peruse the menu. The mains here begin at £16, although the £15 lunch deal is the best value, all with seasonal freshness guaranteed. Mon–Sat noon–3pm & 6–10pm.

The Witchery by the Castle 352 Castlehill ☎0131 225 5613, ⓦthewitchery.com; map pp.64–65. An upmarket restaurant that only Edinburgh could create, set in magnificently over-the-top medieval surroundings full of Gothic wood panelling and heavy stonework, all a mere broomstick-hop from the Castle. The à la carte menu is as ostentatious as the surroundings with wallet-draining lobster and lamb wellington on offer; however, there are good-value set menus from £20 for two courses. Daily noon–11.30pm.

NEW TOWN

For the flashier end of the restaurant scene, the New Town and its western fringe, known as the West End, are the happening parts of town. Many nationwide chains have restaurants on and around Princes and George streets, but it's worth exploring a little further afield to areas such as Broughton Street to find more authentic, home-grown places.

CAFÉS

★**Artisan Roast** 57 Broughton St ☎07526 236 615, ⓦartisanroast.co.uk; map pp.60–61. If you're into the black stuff, this is the must-visit coffee shop in Edinburgh. A seemingly unstoppable force in the connoisseur coffee roasters' market, *Artisan Roast's* sweet, nutty brews are found in independent cafés all over town these days, but this narrow, grungy shop with hessian beans bags for decor and obligatorily bearded baristas is where their revolution started. Mon–Thurs 8am–7.30pm, Fri 8am–6.30pm, Sat–Sun 9am–6.30pm.

Eteaket 41a Frederick St ☎0131 226 2982, ⓦeteaket .co.uk; map pp.60–61. The best of the tea boutiques in the city centre, with a restrained but contemporary decor scheme and tables outside. There's an extensive menu of good-quality loose-leaf teas (mostly £2.70 a cup), some decent nibbles plus, for the adventurous, tea cocktails such as Earl Grey G&T for £6. Daily 9am–6pm.

★**Valvona & Crolla** 19 Elm Row, Leith Walk ☎0131 556 6066, ⓦvalvonacrolla.com; map pp.60–61. The café-bistro hidden at the back of what is arguably Britain's finest Italian deli serves authentic Italian pizzas for around £11 as well as delicious pastries, breakfasts and expensive à la carte meals as well as offering a cracking selection of wines. The best advert for the café is the walk through the shop – which has food stacked from floor to ceiling, with display cabinets full of sublime Italian olives, meats and cheeses imported directly from Milan. Mon–Thurs 8.30am–5.30pm, Fri & Sat 8am–6pm, Sun 10.30am–4.30pm.

RESTAURANTS

Chaophraya 33 Castle St ☎0131 226 7614, ⓦchaophraya.co.uk; map pp.60–61. Thai restaurant housed in one of Edinburgh's most glamorous dining spaces with a rooftop location that gives diners who sit in the "Glassbox" section a near 360-degree view of the city. The menu is stunning too, and reasonably priced; if you go veggie, there's a set meal for £25 and just £13 for midweek lunch. Otherwise try the £10 crispy pork belly or pass on the food altogether and have a drink on the convivial roof terrace. Mon–Sat noon–10.30pm, Sun noon–10pm.

Chez Jules 109 Hanover St ☎0131 226 6992, ⓦchezjulesbistro.com; map pp.60–61. Run by the former boss of the once mighty Pierre Victoire bistro chain. The formula is much the same: cheap and generous set menus, good table wine and an informal setting. Your two-course lunch (£7.90) might include French onion soup and beef bourguignon with fries. Mon–Thurs & Sun noon–11pm, Fri & Sat noon–midnight.

★**The Dogs** 110 Hanover St ☎0131 220 1208, ⓦthedogsonline.co.uk; map pp.60–61. Scottish gastro-pub cooking taken to a whole new level with confident use of traditional ingredients paired with modern flavours such as the shredded lamb and skirlie (oats and onions fried in lard) with pomegranate and almonds for £12. Mon–Fri noon–2.30pm & 6–10pm, Sat noon–4pm & 5–10pm, Sun noon–4pm & 6–10pm.

Dusit 49a Thistle St ☎0131 220 6846, ⓦdusit.co.uk; map pp.60–61. Bold Thai flavours delivered with uncustomary refinement, it's little wonder this wee restaurant is consistently the talk of the town. There are many of the usual suspects on the menu like pad Thai (£11), but the overriding genius of this place is its adventurous spirit; the Thai spice version of duck à l'orange, using marmalade and Cointreau, for £16 is inspired. Mon–Sat noon–3pm & 6–11pm, Sun noon–11pm.

★**El Cartel Casera Mexicana** 64 Thistle St ☎0131 226 7171, ⓦelcartelmexicana.co.uk; map pp.60–61. Mexican *antojitos* (tapas-sized street food) served with funky margaritas in a cool setting that draws heavily from the Día de los Muertos festival. Tacos, street corn and quesadillas feature on the menu as you might expect, but there's some rarer oddities there too, like the plantain nachos or *tlacoyo* (thick, filled corn bread). Dishes range from £4 to £8.50. Mon–Thurs & Sun noon–10pm, Sat noon–midnight.

★**The Gardener's Cottage** 1 Royal Terrace Gardens, London Rd ☎0131 558 1221, ⓦthegardenerscottage .co; map pp.60–61. In an achingly beautiful little cottage, uniquely sited in a parkland setting, it's incredible to think you're steps away from the city's beating heart. Dining is intimate, in two small rooms with communal long tables, while the open kitchen is stamp-sized. There's no choice, just seven outstanding courses of Scottish design for £40, featuring seasonal ingredients such as wild garlic or rhubarb in spring or chanterelles in autumn. Wed–Mon noon–2.30pm & 5–10pm.

Henderson's 94 Hanover St ☎ 0131 225 2131, ⓦ hendersonsofedinburgh.co.uk; map pp.60–61. Over the past fifty years Henderson's has evolved from a veggie canteen into a gourmet institution and arts centre. At street level there's a deli and bakery with a vegan bistro around the corner, while the canteen below still bashes out a superb feast of salads and hot comfort food, buffet style, where you can fill up for around £10. Mon–Thurs 8am–9pm, Fri–Sat 8am–9.30pm, Sun 10.30–3.30pm.

L'Escargot Bleu 56 Broughton St ☎ 0131 557 1600, ⓦ lescargotbleu.co.uk; map pp.60–61. A big step on from the rustic, no-frills French bistro of yesteryear, here classic French country cooking is brought to bear on a range of locally sourced produce, as in the black pudding and gizzard pie. Two-course pre-theatre or lunch menus are a snip at £13. Mon–Thurs noon–2.30pm & 5.30–10pm, Fri & Sat noon–3pm & 5.30–10.30pm.

Mussel Inn 61–00 Rose St ☎ 0843 289 2481 ⓦ mussel -inn.com; map pp.64–65. Offering an honest lunchtime platter of moules-frites and a perfectly quaffable glass of vin du table for under £8, it's no surprise there's a demand to get in here. Their close ties to west-coast shellfish farmers help ensure that the journey from sea to plate is short and swift. Check the website for special deals. Mon–Thurs noon–3pm & 5.30–10pm, Fri & Sat noon–10pm, Sun 12.30–10pm.

Yeni Meze Bar 73 Hanover St ☎ 0131 225 5755, ⓦ yenirestaurant.com; map pp.60–61. Specializing in lamb kofte and *imam bayildi* (baked aubergine dish), this is ultimately a Turkish restaurant that draws in additional dishes from around the Med like their Italian arancini. The best way to tackle the vast menu is to go for the £15 banquet and see the delights that keep arriving. Mon–Sat noon–9.30pm.

STOCKBRIDGE AND AROUND

On the northern fringe of the New Town, Stockbridge is home to many of the city's young professionals and consequently has more than its fair share of fine cafés and restaurants.

CAFÉS

The Gateway Restaurant/Terrace Café Royal Botanic Garden, Arboretum Place ☎ 0131 552 2674; map pp.56–57. At the West Gate of the Botanics, the John Hope Gateway Centre has tables and a terrace overlooking the gardens on its upper floor, serving cream tea for £9.50 as well as full breakfasts and posh lunches for around £9 with many ingredients grown in the gardens. A few hundred yards beyond, the busy *Terrace Café* serves coffees, snacks and less formal lunches, with lots of outdoor tables and kid-friendly options. Daily: March–Sept 10am–6pm; Feb & Oct 10am–5pm; Nov–Jan 10am–4pm.

★**Peter's Yard** 3 Deanhaugh St ☎ 0131 332 2901, ⓦ petersyard.com; map pp.60–61. Another side to the Continental baking scene, this time a Swedish sourdough outfit with the ovens on view and baskets of delicious, crusty loaves out front. They also sell delicate cardamom pastries to go with their satisfyingly nutty coffees for around £5, while most popular around mealtimes is the vibrant sourdough pizza at £10. Mon–Fri 8am–9pm, Sat & Sun 9am–9pm.

RESTAURANTS

The Stockbridge Restaurant 54 St Stephen St ☎ 0131 226 6766, ⓦ thestockbridgerestaurant.co.uk; map pp.60–61. It's hard to believe swanky St Stephen's St used to be one of Edinburgh's worst slums. This basement restaurant sums up how far things have come with its fine linen, silverware and fancy platters, while the blackened stone walls and candlelit hearth give it a slightly bohemian atmosphere. Save for one veggie option, featuring the ubiquitous butternut squash, it's meat, game and fish all the way, but the quality is exceptional and affordable; set menus begin at £27. Tues–Sat 7–9.30pm, Sun 7–9pm.

LOTHIAN ROAD & TOLCROSS
RESTAURANTS

Lothian Road's twin role as Edinburgh's theatre and financial districts has seen money pour into the area in recent times. It still has a rough element on a Friday night thanks to its various late-night bars hosting drinks promotions. However, gentrification is in full swing and consequently there's a decent selection of sophisticated, lively places to eat and drink, plus good-value pre- and post-theatre deals.

Castle Terrace 33–35 Castle Terrace ☎ 0131 229 1222, ⓦ castleterracerestaurant.com; map pp.60–61. Sister restaurant to the highly successful *The Kitchin* (see p.94), bringing high-level French cooking to bear on high-quality Scottish produce. Chef-patron Dominic Jack's philosophy is "nature to plate", but clearly there's some magic in between, presumably conjured over his years as sous chef to three-starred Alain Solivérès. If your budget will stretch, head straight for the £65 or £75 tasting menus, otherwise try the three-course lunch at £29.50. Tues–Sat noon–2pm & 6.30–10pm.

★**Indaba** 3 Lochrin Terrace ☎ 0131 221 1554, ⓦ edindaba.co.uk; map pp.60–61. An unlikely combination of South African and northern Spanish

1

cuisine, this modest side-street restaurant delivers some of the best tapas in town. The South African contributions are predominantly meaty, like the dried boerewors for £4, a thin chewy sausage with spices, while the Spanish plates are vibrantly colourful. There's also a Scottish tapa on the menu, made from vegetarian haggis. Mon–Thurs 5–9.30pm, Fri–Sat 5–10pm.

Kampung Ali 97–101 Fountainbridge ☎0131 228 5069, ☯kampungali.com; map pp.60–61. If you can reserve judgement beyond the ghastly yellow exterior and the frankly bizarre decor inside, you're in for an authentic Malay treat here. There are two stand-out dishes not to be missed: firstly the *laksa* – a traditional Malaysian dish somewhere between a coconut curry and a noodle soup – deep, sweet and sour flavours and spicy hot; then there's the sticky, melt-in-your-mouth spicy aubergine main for £8. Mon & Wed–Fri noon–2.30pm & 5–11pm, Sat–Sun noon–11pm.

★**Timberyard** 10 Cambridge St ☎0131 221 1222, ☯timberyard.co; map pp.60–61. This swanky yet somehow rustic old workshop makes for a genial atmosphere with its shared, candlelit indoor benches and sunny courtyard garden. The food focuses on high-quality Scottish produce, some of it home-grown or smoked on site; much of the rest is sourced from local foragers or farmers directly. As a result, unlikely bedfellows like halibut, wild leeks and elderberries come together harmoniously on one plate as part of a four-course £55 menu. Tues–Sat noon–2pm & 5.30–9.30pm.

SOUTHSIDE

As the student quarter of the city, the Southside boasts plenty of good-value eating, but it's also an area where more progressive and interesting restaurants can establish themselves on the fringe of the more expensive city centre.

CAFÉS

★**Peter's Yard** 27 Simpson Loan, Southside ☎0131 228 5876, ☯petersyard.com map pp.60–61. Southside branch of the popular independent café-bakery, specializing in cardamom buns, sourdough loaves and Nordic crispbread, all baked to perfection in house. Mon–Fri 7.30am–7pm, Sat & Sun 9am–7pm.

RESTAURANTS

Hanedan 41 West Preston St ☎0131 667 4242, ☯hanedan.co.uk; map pp.56–57. Not the roomiest of restaurants but that's partly down to the unrelenting popularity of this authentic Turkish gem. There are plenty of the usual meze choices and skewered meats on offer, but the charcoal grilled sardines at £9.50 are not to be missed when available. Tues–Sun noon–3pm & 5.30–10.30pm.

Kalpna 2–3 St Patrick Square ☎0131 667 9890, ☯kalpnarestaurant.com; map pp.60–61. Outstanding vegetarian family restaurant that's been serving authentic Gujarati dishes in town for over 25 years. Four *thaalis* (£13–15), including a vegan option, stand alongside the main menu for those keen to sample a range of dishes, while the lunch buffet is an "all you can eat" for £8. Daily noon–2pm & 5.30–10.30pm.

★**Lian Pu** 14 Marshall St ☎0131 662 8895, ☯lianpu .co.uk; map pp.60–61. Thoroughly hip restaurant among Edinburgh's surging Chinese student community, thanks to its true home-from-home cooking and palatable prices. The place retains a canteen, fast-food atmosphere despite the addition of contemporary soft furnishings and some interesting pictures of old China. Try the tofu noodle stir-fry for £6.70 with a side order of the deeply savoury spicy shredded cabbage. Daily noon–10pm.

Mosque Kitchen Edinburgh Central Mosque, 50 Potterrow (entrance on West Nicholson St) ☎0131 667 4035, ☯edmosque.com; map pp.60–61. Out of the many "curry in a hurry" establishments that are cropping up around the Nicholson St area, this is a true veteran. Tagged onto the mosque, this very basic canteen has for years been dishing out fragrant rice and curry (around £5) to be eaten outside under a large awning. Daily 11.30am–8pm; closed Fri 12.50–1.50pm for prayer.

★**Tanjore** 6–8 Clerk St ☎0131 478 6518, ☯tanjore .co.uk; map pp.60–61. South Indian cuisine's finest ambassador on these shores, drawing in all the regional standards including *vadai* (crunchy lentil doughnuts), *idli* (rice and lentil cake) and *sambar* – a distinctly rich, savoury curry with fragrant, bitter-sweet curry leaves. The freshly made *dosai* (lentil and rice crêpes) are among the lightest and crispiest you'll ever taste and come with a wide variety of fillings for around £7. Mon–Fri noon–2.30pm & 5–10pm, Sat–Sun noon–3.30pm & 5–10pm.

LEITH AND THE SHORE

The area around the cobbled Shore of Leith, along the edge of the Water of Leith just as it reaches the sea, is the best-known dining quarter in Edinburgh, and lives up to its billing with good-quality, laidback seafood bistros and a concentration of Michelin stars.

RESTAURANTS

★**The Kitchin** 78 Commercial Quay ☎0131 555 1755, ☯thekitchin.com; map pp.56–57. Opened in 2006 by celebrity chef Tom Kitchin and the winner – less than six months later – of a Michelin star, the motto here is "from nature to plate", a philosophy that ensures the freshest ingredients, particularly well demonstrated on their "Celebration of the Season" menu that might include hand-dived Orkney scallops or west-coast spider crabs. Menus range from £29.50 (lunch) to £80 (tasting). Tues–Thurs 12.15–2.30pm & 6.30–10pm, Fri–Sat 12.15–2.30pm & 6.30–10.30pm.

★**The Shore** 3 Shore ☎0131 553 5080, ⓦfishersbistros.co.uk; map pp.56–57. Tasteful, well-lived-in bar/restaurant with huge mirrors, wood panelling and aproned waiters who serve up good sea and land food from £11.50. Live jazz, folk and hubbub float through from the adjoining bar where you'll find a wide selection of snacks on offer, including smoked trout and herb croquettes and deep-fried camembert at £4.50 each. Mon–Sat noon–1am, Sun 12.30pm–1am.

GREATER EDINBURGH

RESTAURANTS

Loch Fyne Restaurant 25 Pier Place, Newhaven Harbour ☎0131 559 3900, ⓦlochfyneseafoodandgrill .co.uk; map pp.56–57. A fantastic location by Newhaven's fish market and harbour for this chain with strong connections to Scotland's west coast. The menu's pretty exciting, with such delights as the langoustine and salmon ravioli in a creamy seafood broth or squid with salt and Szechuan peppercorn. Evening three-course set menus from £18. Mon–Thurs 11.30am–10pm, Fri 11.30am–10.30pm, Sat 9am–11pm, Sun 9am–10pm.

DRINKING

Many of Edinburgh's **pubs**, especially in the Old Town, have histories that stretch back centuries, while others, particularly in the New Town, are unaltered Victorian or Edwardian period pieces. Add a plentiful supply of trendy, modern **bars**, and there's enough to cater for all tastes. The standard licensing hours are 11am–11pm (noon–11pm on Sun), but many places stay open later, and, during the Festival especially, you won't have a problem finding a bar open till at least 1am. Edinburgh has a long history of beer-making, though only one significant working brewery remains in the city itself, the small **Caledonian Brewery** in the western reaches of town. Owned by multinational Scottish & Newcastle, it still uses old techniques and equipment to produce some of the best specialist beers in Britain, including its popular Deuchars IPA. If you fancy a pub crawl, a fun way to explore Edinburgh's pubs is to take a **Literary Pub Tour** (see p.88).

THE ROYAL MILE AND AROUND

Beehive Inn 18–20 Grassmarket ☎0131 225 7171, ⓦtaylor-walker.co.uk; map pp.64–65. One of the few family-friendly pubs in the centre with an even scarcer beer garden out back. Inside it's a beautiful early Victorian building with high-backed red leather seating and corniced ceilings in each of its three rooms. Out front is the regular starting point for the Literary Pub Tour. Mon–Sat 9am–1am, Sun 12.30pm–1am.

Bow Bar 80 West Bow ☎0131 226 7667, ⓦthebowbar.co.uk; map pp.64–65. Wonderful old wood-panelled bar and one of the nicest, most convivial drinking spots in the city centre, although it can get uncomfortably busy at weekends. Choose from among nearly 150 whiskies or a changing selection of first-rate Scottish and English cask beers. Mon–Sat noon–midnight, Sun noon–11.30pm.

Halfway House 24 Fleshmarket Close ☎0131 225 7101; map pp.64–65. Edinburgh's smallest pub, found halfway up the steep, narrow close between the train station and the Royal Mile, is a good place to stop and catch your breath. Lots of real ales and a few simple bar meals on offer, like cullen skink for £5. Mon–Sat 11am–11pm, Sun 12.30am–11pm.

★**Jolly Judge** 7 James Court ☎0131 225 2669, ⓦjollyjudge.co.uk; map pp.64–65. Atmospheric, low-ceilinged bar in a close just down from the Castle which features in the Literary Pub Crawl. Cosy in winter and pleasant outside in summer. Mon & Fri–Sat noon–midnight, Tues–Thurs noon–11pm, Sun 12.30–11pm.

NEW TOWN

Café Royal Circle Bar 17 West Register St ☎0131 556 1884, ⓦcaferoyaledinburgh.co.uk; map pp.60–61. Worth a visit just for its Victorian decor, notably the huge elliptical island bar and tiled portraits of renowned inventors. The menu is appropriately swanky too, with a wide choice of champagnes and oysters (£10 for six), while real ale fans will not be disappointed by the native selection. Mon–Wed 11am–11pm, Thurs 11am–midnight, Fri–Sat 11am–1pm, Sun 12.30–11pm.

★**Cumberland Bar** 1–3 Cumberland St ☎0131 558 3134, ⓦcumberlandbar.co.uk; map pp.60–61. This lovely old pub is just far enough off the beaten track to remain off the radar to the weekend's pub-crawling masses. Its other great assets are its willow-shaded beer garden and fantastic assortment of cask ales. Mon–Wed noon–midnight, Thurs–Sat noon–1pm, Sun 11am–midnight.

★**Kays Bar** 39 Jamaica St ☎0131 225 1858, ⓦkaysbar .co.uk; map pp.60–61. Tucked away in a New Town side street, this former Georgian coaching house was remodelled in the Victorian era as a wine and spirit merchant. Thankfully it has retained its Victorian charm and now operates as a cosy little pub serving real ale and plenty of whiskies. Mon–Thurs 11am–midnight, Fri & Sat 11am–1pm, Sun 12.30pm–11pm.

Oxford Bar 8 Young St ☎0131 539 7119, ⓦoxfordbar .co.uk; map pp.60–61. This is an unpretentious, unspoilt, no-nonsense city bar – which is why local crime writer Ian Rankin and his Inspector Rebus like it so much. Fans duly make the pilgrimage, but fortunately not all the regulars

1

have been scared off. Mon–Thurs 11am–midnight, Fri & Sat 11am–1am, Sun 12.30–11pm.

Star Bar 1 Northumberland Pl ☎0131 558 2874; map pp.60–61. A veritable antidote to the smart cocktail purveyors that comprise much of the New Town's drinking scene. Reassuringly down to earth and so well hidden it's seldom stumbled upon by tourists. A dark, unpretentiously decorated pub with a dartboard and well-stocked juke box, its greatest asset, however, is its south-facing beer garden. Daily 11am–1am.

Tigerlily 125 George St ☎0131 225 5005, ⓦtigerlilyedinburgh.co.uk; map pp.60–61. The daddy of all George St's decadent destination bars, where the locals come to see and be seen. Can be tons of fun – but only if you're wearing the right clothes. Daily 8am–1am.

The Voodoo Rooms 19a West Register St ☎0131 556 7060, ⓦthevoodoorooms.com; map pp.60–61. Glamorous gilt and plush booths attract a dressed-up crowd, especially at the weekend. Frequent live music, performance and club nights, including Edinburgh's legendary Vegas! Mon–Thurs 4pm–1am, Fri–Sun noon–1am.

GAY BAR

Planet 6 Baxter's Place, New Town ☎0131 556 5551; map pp.60–61. Loud and outrageous bar beside the Playhouse Theatre, with DJs at weekends and regular drinks promotions making it a popular meeting point. Daily 1pm–1am.

OUTSIDE THE CITY CENTRE

The Jolly Botanist 256–260 Morrison St, Haymarket ☎0131 228 5596, ⓦthejollybotanist.co.uk; map pp.60–61. Riding on the back of gin drinking's phenomenal comeback, this new bar has made a name for itself for its range of eclectic liquor sourced from micro-distilleries

around the globe. The neo-Victorian decor completes the vibe if you can ignore the flat-screen TV on the wall. Sun–Thurs 10am–midnight, Fri & Sat 10am–1am.

Kings Wark 36 Shore, Leith ☎0131 554 9260; map pp.56–57. Real ale in a restored fifteenth-century pub with attached restaurant right in the heart of Leith's old port. Its picturesque interior of stone walls and corniced ceilings gives an ambience that's little changed since the days of the old sea dogs telling tales at the bar. Sun–Thurs noon–11pm, Fri & Sat noon–midnight, Sun 11am–11pm.

★**Pear Tree House** 36 West Nicolson St, Southside ☎0131 667 7533, ⓦpear-tree-house.co.uk; map pp.60–61. Fine bar in an eighteenth-century house with two beautiful old pear trees trained on its west wall. Its greatest asset, however, is its large courtyard – one of central Edinburgh's very few beer gardens. In summer there are live bands and barbecues outside, weather permitting. Mon–Thurs 11am–11.45pm, Fri & Sat 11am–12.45am, Sun 12.30–11.45pm.

The Roseleaf 23–24 Sandport Place, Leith ☎0131 476 5268, ⓦroseleaf.co.uk; map pp.56–57. Chintzy-cool local that's a little off the beaten track but worth the trip for the pot-tails alone – funky cocktails served in vintage teapots at around £10 for two people. Daily 10am–1am.

★**Sheep Heid Inn** 43 The Causeway, Duddingston ☎0131 661 7974, ⓦthesheepheidedinburgh.co.uk; map pp.56–57. Laying claim to be the city's oldest licensed premise and one-time rural watering hole to Bonnie Prince Charlie, this pub retains many of its historical charms, including an antique skittle alley (rentable for £20) through the back. In winter there are open fires and comfy chairs, while in summer, punters gravitate to the courtyard garden. Mon–Thurs 11am–11pm, Fri & Sat 11am–midnight, Sun 12.30–11pm.

NIGHTLIFE

Inevitably, Edinburgh's **nightlife** is at its best during the Festival (see p.100), which can make the other 48 weeks of the year seem like an anticlimax. However, while it lacks Glasgow's clout, Edinburgh's **club scene** can be enormously enjoyable, with a mix of mainstream discos offering pop and dance music and left-field clubs with a dressed-down vibe and a wide range of themed nights, usually rotating on a monthly or fortnightly basis. Most of the city-centre clubs stay open till around 3am. Meanwhile, you can normally hear **live jazz**, **folk** and **rock** every evening in one or other of the city's pubs. For the really big rock events, ad hoc places – such as the Castle Esplanade or Murrayfield Stadium – are pressed into service.

LISTINGS INFO

The best way to find out about clubs, music and anything else that's going on is to pick up a copy of *The List* (ⓦlist .co.uk), a fortnightly magazine covering both Edinburgh and Glasgow. Alternatively, get hold of *The Skinny* (ⓦtheskinny.co.uk), a free culture magazine with frequent arts, music and events listings found in trendy bars and cafés around town. Information on nightclubs can also be

found on posters and the flyers distributed to most of the pre-club bars around town.

CLUBS

The Bongo Club 66 Cowgate, Old Town ☎0131 558 8844, ⓦthebongoclub.co.uk; map pp.64–65. Legendary Edinburgh club and arts venue; its line-up is eclectic but always worth checking out. Look out for the monthly dub and reggae Messenger Sound System. (Entry £3–7). Daily 1pm–3am.

Cabaret Voltaire 36 Blair St, Old Town ☎0131 247 4704, ⓦ thecabaretvoltaire.com; map pp.64–65. Atmospheric nightclub in the Old Town's subterranean vaults, playing host to some of the city's best and cheapest (entry £4–7) underground electronic music as well as live rock bands. Club nights Tues–Sat 11pm–3am.

Electric Circus 36–39 Market St, Old Town ☎0131 226 4224, ⓦ theelectriccircus.biz; map pp.64–65. Offers a host of private karaoke rooms (£10–100/room), and puts on burlesque and live music with an indie slant. Clubs here, like Magic Nostalgic and Beep Beep, Yeah!, tend to follow an unashamedly retro vibe. Sun–Thurs 4pm–1am, Fri & Sat 2pm–3am.

Lulu's 125b George St, New Town ☎0131 225 5005, ⓦ luluedinburgh.co.uk; map pp.60–61. Sultry subterranean nightspot beneath restaurant *Tigerlily*. A place to see and be seen; Monaco's Prince Albert and Zara Phillips join the tally of A-listers who have pulled shapes on the sound-responsive disco light floor. Sun–Thurs 10pm–3am, Fri & Sat 9pm–3am.

LGBT CLUBS

Edinburgh has a dynamic LGBT culture, for years centred round the top of Leith Walk and Broughton Street, where the first gay and lesbian centre appeared in the 1970s. Since the early 1990s, more and more gay enterprises, especially cafés and nightclubs, have moved into this area, now dubbed the "Pink Triangle".

CC Bloom's 23–24 Greenside Place, New Town ☎0131 556 9331, ⓦ ccbloomsedinburgh.com; map pp.60–61. Edinburgh's most enduring gay bar, with a big dancefloor, stonking rhythms, a young, friendly crowd and free entry all night. Daily 11am–3am.

Chalky's 4 Picardy Place, New Town ☎0131 558 7538, ⓦ chalkysedinburgh.co.uk; map pp.60–61. Stylish bar and club catering to a dressed-up crowd. Highlights on the nightly club menu include Cabaret Thursday and Fired Up, an unabashed rotation of anthemic dancefloor fillers. Tues–Sun 11pm–3am.

LIVE MUSIC VENUES

Bannermans 212 Cowgate, Old Town ☎0131 556 3254, ⓦ bannermanslive.co.uk; map pp.64–65. A subterranean labyrinth of caves and musky warrens located at the base of South Bridge; the most atmospheric joint in town in which to discover local indie bands hoping for a big break. Mon–Sat noon–1am, Sun 12.30pm–1am.

★**The Caves** 8–12 Niddry St, Old Town ☎0131 557 8989, ⓦ thecavesedinburgh.com; map pp.64–65. Housed in a labyrinth of arches rediscovered after a hundred years, this bohemian multi-functional venue has the city's most staggeringly atmospheric setting. As well as live music and occasional club nights it's also used for private functions and weddings. Consequently there's little consistency as to when public nights are on, so keep an eye on their website. 7pm–1am.

Ghillie-Dhu Rutland Place, New Town ☎0131 222 9930, ⓦ ghillie-dhu.co.uk; map pp.60–61. Housed in a rather fancy auditorium just off Princes St, Ghillie-Dhu (a male fairy from Scottish folklore) wholeheartedly embraces Scotland's traditional musical heritage. A rotation of accomplished folk groups plays throughout the week (free entry), culminating in Friday and Saturday's jovial ceilidh nights (£5 entry). Daily 10am–3am.

The Liquid Room 9c Victoria St, Old Town ☎0131 225 2564, ⓦ liquidroom.com; map pp.64–65. Open every evening, this small venue is frequented by local acts and touring indie bands as well as a variety of alternating club nights geared towards student patronage. Club nights most Wed, Fri & Sat 10.30pm–3am.

Queen's Hall 85–89 Clerk St, Southside ☎0131 668 2019, ⓦ thequeenshall.net; map pp.60–61. Converted Georgian church which now operates as a concert hall; it's used principally by the Scottish Chamber Orchestra and

HOGMANAY

Hogmanay's meaning is, put simply, the last day of the year, but in reality it's all about celebrating the beginning of a new one. The best way to do so is to join one of the street parties that are held in the middle of towns and cities, often centred around a prominent clock face which rings out "the bells" at midnight. These days, the largest New Year's Eve street party in Europe takes place in Edinburgh, with around eighty thousand people enjoying the culmination of a week-long series of events. On the night itself, stages are set up in different parts of the city centre, with big-name rock groups and local ceilidh bands playing to the increasingly inebriated masses. The high point of the evening is, of course, midnight, when hundreds of tons of fireworks are let off into the night sky above the Castle, and revellers begin to chorus "**Auld Lang Syne**", an old Scottish tune with lyrics by Robert Burns, Scotland's national poet. For information about celebrations in Edinburgh, and how to get hold of **tickets** for the street party, visit the Fringe Office at 180 High St (☎0844 573 8455; tickets go on sale in July) or go to ⓦ edinburghshogmanay.org.

1

Scottish Ensemble, but is also much favoured by jazz, blues and folk groups. Box office Mon–Sat 10am–5.15pm.
Royal Oak 1 Infirmary St, Old Town ☎ 0131 557 2976, ⓦ royal-oak-folk.com; map pp.64–65. Traditional Scottish pub hosting daily informal folk sessions performed by locals. On Sundays there's the "Wee Folk Club" (£5 entry) where they bring in soloists or groups from around the country and beyond. Mon–Sat 11.30am–2am, Sun 12.30pm–2am.
Usher Hall Lothian Rd ☎ 0131 228 1155, ⓦ usherhall .co.uk; map pp.60–61. Reopened after a major refurbishment with a strikingly contemporary extension,

Edinburgh's main civic concert hall frequently features choral and symphony concerts, as well as legends of country, jazz, world and pop. The upper-circle seats are cheapest and have the best acoustics. Box office Mon–Sat 10am–5.30pm and evenings when there is a concert on.
Whistlebinkies 4–6 South Bridge, Old Town ☎ 0131 557 5114; map pp.64–65. One of the most reliable places to find live music every night of the week and often afternoons too. On the whole it's local indie bands or rock and pop covers, though there are some folk evenings as well. Daily 11.30am–3am.

ENTERTAINMENT

Edinburgh has permanent venues large enough to host touring **orchestras** and **ballet** companies, while elsewhere you can uncover a lively **comedy** club and a couple of excellent art-house **cinemas**.

THEATRE AND DANCE
Assembly Rooms 54 George St, New Town ☎ 0131 220 4348, ⓦ assemblyroomsedinburgh.co.uk. This complex of small and large halls is used all year, but really comes into its own during the Fringe, featuring large-scale drama productions and mainstream comedy.
Edinburgh Playhouse 18–22 Greenside Place ☎ 0131 524 3333, ⓦ playhousetheatre.com. The largest theatre in Britain with a capacity of over three thousand. Opened in the 1920s as a cinema, it's now used largely for extended runs of popular musicals and occasional music concerts.
Festival Theatre 13–29 Nicolson St, Southside ☎ 0131 529 6000, ⓦ edtheatres.com/festival. The largest stage in Britain, principally used for Scottish Opera and Scottish Ballet's appearances in the capital, but also for everything from the children's shows like *Mary Poppins* to orchestral jazz.
King's Theatre 2 Leven St, Tollcross ☎ 0131 529 6000, ⓦ edtheatres.com/kings. Majoring in pantomime, touring West End plays and the occasional major drama or opera performance, this stately Edwardian civic theatre, with its bold Neoclassical frontage, is a masterpiece of its era. The interior is surprisingly luxurious, with marble staircases, carved mahogany doors and a sumptuously regal auditorium.
Royal Lyceum Theatre 30 Grindlay St, Lothian Rd ☎ 0131 248 4848, ⓦ lyceum.org.uk. A fine, moderately compact, Victorian civic theatre with its stage overlooked by three curved tiers orbiting the ornate ceiling's glittering chandelier. The leading venue for mainstream drama, the theatre commissions around seven plays annually as well as hosting travelling productions.
Traverse Theatre 10 Cambridge St, Lothian Rd ☎ 0131 228 1404, ⓦ traverse.co.uk. One of Britain's premier venues for new plays and avant-garde drama from around

the world, going from strength to strength in its custom-built home beside the Usher Hall. Also has a lively and popular bar.

COMEDY
The Stand Comedy Club 5 York Place, New Town ☎ 0131 558 7272, ⓦ thestand.co.uk. The city's undisputed top comedy spot, with different acts on every night and some of the UK's top comics headlining at the weekends. Be sure to arrive early to secure a good table for the evening. Entry ranges from £2 midweek to £16 at weekends.

CINEMAS
Cameo 38 Home St, Tollcross ☎ 0871 902 5723, ⓦ picturehouses.com. A treasure of an art-house cinema with a cosy wee bar – opened by Sean Connery – attached; screens more challenging mainstream releases and cult late-nighters in its traditional and intimate auditoria. Tarantino's been here and thinks it's great.
Dominion Cinema Newbattle Terrace ☎ 0131 447 4771, ⓦ dominioncinemas.net. Just south of the centre, this lovely Art Deco cinema generally sticks to the blockbusters. The smaller screens have lovers' sofas and footstools.
Filmhouse 88 Lothian Rd ☎ 0131 228 2688, ⓦ filmhousecinema.com. Three screens showing an eclectic programme of independent, art-house and classic films. The box office doubles as a DVD shop with an excellent range of arty titles, while through the back the café-bar is a hangout for the city's film buffs and serves healthy, light meals for around £6.
Odeon 118 Lothian Rd ☎ 0333 006 7777, ⓦ odeon .co.uk. This central four-screen cinema shows the latest Hollywood releases, including those available in 3D. It sells the same awful food as the multiplexes but with fewer films on offer.

Vue Omni Centre, Greenside Place, New Town ☎ 0871 224 0240, ⓦ myvue.com. The most central of the big multiscreen venues, this modern glass-fronted cinema shows all the latest mainstream releases including the 3D ones. On Sundays at 9.45am they do a Mini Mornings showing for just £2, usually featuring an animation released a few months prior.

SHOPPING

Despite the relentless advance of the big chains, it's still possible to track down some appealing and unusual shops in central Edinburgh. **Princes Street**, one of Britain's most famous shopping streets, is all but dominated by standard chain outlets. More upmarket shops and boutiques are to be found on and around parallel **George Street**, including an upscale shopping area on the east side of St Andrew Square. There's nothing compelling about central Edinburgh's two big shopping malls, **Princes Mall** and the **St James Centre**, the latter of which is set for demolition. For more original outlets, head for **Cockburn Street**, south of Waverley Station, a hub for trendy clothes and record shops, while on **Victoria Street** and in and around the **Grassmarket** you'll find an eclectic range of antiques, crafts, food and bookshops. Along and around the **Royal Mile**, meanwhile, several distinctly offbeat places sit among the tacky souvenir sellers.

BOOKS

Blackwell's 53–62 South Bridge, Southside ☎ 0131 622 8222, ⓦ blackwell.co.uk; map pp.64–65. Sited near the university, this rambling, multi-floored bookseller has a strong – although far from exclusive – focus on academic tomes. You'll also find many volumes and travel guides relating to Scotland. Mon–Tues & Thurs–Fri 9am–8pm, Wed 9.30am–8pm, Sat 9am–6pm, Sun noon–6pm.

Edinburgh Books 147 West Port, Old Town ☎ 0131 229 4431, ⓦ edinburghbooks.net; map pp.60–61. Edinburgh's largest secondhand bookseller is a quirky place: overlooked by a bust of a water buffalo, patrons shuffle through the narrow corridors of teetering bookcases unnervingly stuffed to the ceiling. Just when you think you've seen it all you find a further warren of rooms downstairs in the basement. Mon–Sat 10am–6pm.

McNaughtan's Bookshop 3a–4a Haddington Place, Leith Walk ☎ 0131 556 5897, ⓦ mcnaughtans bookshop.com; map pp.60–61. Probably Edinburgh's oldest purveyor of antiquarian literature, this shop aims for quality over quantity, consequently feeling more spacious than its counterparts. Housed in a beautiful old basement, there's also a contemporary art exhibition space. Tues–Sat 11am–5pm.

CLOTHES

In the town centre, Princes Street – particularly its east end and the Princes Mall next to Waverley train station – are where you'll find the biggest names in clothing retail. For more exclusive retailers and expensive designer labels aim for George Street and Multrees Walk next to the bus station.

Wm Armstrong 83 Grassmarket, Old Town ☎ 0131 220 5557, ⓦ armstrongsvintage.co.uk; map pp.64–65. A real treasure trove of vintage and retro fashion, this small chain is like a museum; stuffed to the gunwales with items encompassing everything from pre-war civvies to the static-inducing nylon-wear of the 1970s. Mon–Thurs 10am–5.30pm, Fri & Sat 10am–6pm, Sun noon–6pm.

FOOD SHOPS

Edinburgh has plenty of good delis and specialist food retailers, particularly down Broughton Street or through the main parts of Stockbridge or Bruntsfield, where you're most likely to find small artisan shops, good delis and traditional butchers and fishmongers.

Archipelago Bakery 39 Dundas St, New Town ☎ 07932 462715, ⓦ archipelagobakery.co.uk; map pp.60–61. Serving up some of Edinburgh's crustiest loaves, you can sit and drink coffee here while marvelling at the mouth-watering breads, pies and pastries thrust out of the ovens in view. Daily Mon–Wed 9am–5pm.

Harvey Nichols St Andrew Square, New Town ☎ 0131 524 8388, ⓦ harveynichols.com; map pp.60–61. Harvey Nichols' top-floor food hall is at the cutting edge of foodie fads with its mind-numbing array of ingredients you never thought you needed, but do now, like black venus rice or lobster oil. Don't miss the ice-cream counter selling jam doughnut ice cream. Mon–Wed 10am–6pm, Thurs 10am–8pm, Fri & Sat 10am–7pm, Sun 11am–6pm.

I.J. Mellis Cheesemonger 30a Victoria St, Old Town ☎ 0131 226 6215 ⓦ mellischeese.co.uk; map pp.64–65. Founded in 1993, Mellis' Old Town shop is charmingly kitted out in a Victorian style and well stocked with expertly conditioned farmhouse and artisan cheeses from Britain, Ireland and, to a lesser extent, the Continent. The Mellis brand is expanding fast and there are shops cropping up in affluent high streets Scotland-wide. Mon–Wed 9.30am–6.30pm, Thurs–Sat 9am–7pm, Sun 11am–5pm.

Real Foods 37 Broughton St, New Town ☎ 0131 557 1911, ⓦ realfoods.co.uk; map pp.60–61. Edinburgh's

1

long-standing supermarket for wholefoods, organic produce and niche products that can't be found elsewhere in town. The range here is vast, making it a must for those with special diets or an interest in discovering new and curious foods. Mon–Fri 8am–9pm, Sat 9am–6.30pm, Sun 10am–6pm.

Sicilian Pastry Shop 14–16 Albert St, Leith ☎0131 554 7417; map pp.60–61. A brilliant little family shop selling sweet and colourful cakes, mostly Sicilian in style – featuring lots of cream. Not really a café but they do sell a good strong espresso here, too. Mon–Fri 8am–5pm, Sat 8am–4pm.

★ **Störtebäcker** 38 St John's Rd, Corstorphine, 3 miles west of the centre ☎07752 186564, ⓦstortebacker .co.uk; map pp.56–57. Surely the world's smallest bakery, housed in "The Wee Shop" with standing room for just two people and a veritable bounty of outstanding home-made sourdoughs, cakes, pastries and tarts. Loosely translated as "harassed baker", this is the brainchild of two German friends with a passion for pastries and the recipes from their native country. Tues–Wed 9am–2pm, Fri & Sat 9am–2pm.

Valvona & Crolla 19 Elm Row, Leith Walk ☎0131 556 6066, ⓦvalvonacrolla.co.uk; map pp.60–61. Open the door to this most venerated of Edinburgh's delis and you're instantly welcomed by a glorious odour reminiscent of Italian markets. Indeed, it is from the markets of Milan that much of the fine produce here directly originates. Mon–Thurs 8.30am–6pm, Fri & Sat 8am–6.30pm, Sun 10am–5pm.

MARKETS

Edinburgh's climate doesn't cultivate a strong outdoor market culture but in recent years there's been a re-emergence of farmers' markets as an antidote to the supermarket dominance of the city's grocery pound.

Edinburgh Farmers' Market Castle Terrace, Lothian Rd ☎0131 220 8580, ⓦedinburghfarmersmarket.com; map pp.60–61. Run by the council, the majority of this market's stallholders must be primary producers, selling what they grow. The rigidity of this policy may have somewhat stifled its success as there's an oversupply of vacuum-packed meat and fish; however, you'll always find some interesting cottage-industry produce here. Sat 9am–2pm.

Stockbridge Market Kerr St, Stockbridge ⓦstock bridgemarket.com; map pp.60–61. Recently expanded across three new sites in Grassmarket (Sat), Fountainbridge (Fri) and Leith (Sat), the sky's the limit for the capital's favourite foodie market. Even with the belligerent Scottish

climate, there's somehow an international buzz as scores of locals and tourists dine out on paella or African samosas, or wash a German pastry down with a coffee served out of the back of a VW camper. Sun 10am–5pm.

MUSIC

Coda 12 Bank St, Old Town ☎0131 622 7246, ⓦcodamusic.co.uk; map pp.64–65. Just steps from the touristic Royal Mile it's unsurprising to find a record shop with a focus on Scottish music, but Coda's range goes far deeper than the whiny "Bagpipes Plays the Beatles" records that you might find in tacky gift shops nearby. The passion in Coda's collection is for contemporary folk and roots music. Daily 9.30am–5.30pm.

Fopp 3–15 Rose St, New Town ☎0131 243 0870, ⓦfopp.com; map pp.60–61. One-time hugely successful Scottish indie record chain, since swallowed by its mainstream rival HMV, not that you'd notice. You'll find a wide range of mostly indie titles and classic albums on CD being sold cheaper than anywhere else. Mon–Wed & Sat 9am–6pm, Thurs 9am–7pm, Fri 9am–6.30pm, Sun 11am–6pm.

Underground Solu'shun 9 Cockburn St, Old Town ☎0131 226 2242, ⓦundergroundsolushn.com; map pp.64–65. The only surviving dance and electronic music specialist in town, selling records mostly in vinyl format and DJ-oriented hardware. There's a lot of house and techno here, but they also dabble in disco, funk and soul. Mon–Wed, Fri & Sat 10am–6pm, Thurs 10am–7pm, Sun noon–6pm.

Vinyl Villains 5 Elm Row, Leith Walk ☎0131 558 1170, ⓦvinyl-villains.co.uk; map pp.60–61. An ancient but struggling Edinburgh institution selling some new but mostly secondhand records as well as T-shirts and collectable music-related ephemera. The racks are mostly filled with Sixties and Seventies rock LPs and singles, but no genre or era is excluded entirely. Mon–Fri 10.30am–6pm, Sat 10.30am–5.30pm, Sun 1–5pm.

OUTDOOR GEAR

There's a concentration of useful stores specializing in outdoor gear on Rose St in the New Town and round the corner on Frederick St.

Tiso 123–125 Rose St ☎0131 225 8369, ⓦtiso.com; map pp.64–65. A department store for the outdoors; spread over four floors, with maps, knowledgeable staff and all you could need in Scotland's vast wilderness. Mon, Tues, Fri & Sat 9.30am–5.30pm, Wed 10am–5.30pm, Thurs 9.30am–7.30pm, Sun 11am–5pm.

THE EDINBURGH FESTIVAL

August's **Edinburgh Festival** is actually an umbrella term encompassing several different festivals taking place at around the same time in the city. The principal events are the **Edinburgh International Festival** and the much larger

Edinburgh Festival Fringe, but there are also **Book, Jazz and Blues** and **Art** festivals, among others, as well as the **Military Tattoo** on the Castle Esplanade.

1

PROGRAMMES, LISTINGS AND INFORMATION

As well as the official Edinburgh Festivals website (ⓦ edinburghfestivals.co.uk), each festival produces its own programme well in advance. During August, various publications give information about what's on and what's good – best of these is *The Scotsman* newspaper's daily supplement, but also worthwhile are *The Guide*, published daily by the Fringe Office; weekly *The List*; and *Fest*, best of the freebie newspapers available around town.

THE EDINBURGH INTERNATIONAL FESTIVAL

The original Edinburgh Festival, sometimes called the "Official Festival", was conceived in 1947 as a celebration of pan-European culture in the postwar era. Initially dominated by opera, other elements such as top-grade theatre, ballet, dance and classical music were gradually introduced, and it's still very much a highbrow event, its high production values and serious approach offering an antidote to the Fringe's slapdash vigour.

International Festival Box Office The Hub, Castlehill, Old Town ☎ 0131 473 2000, ⓦ eif.co.uk. This is the year-round headquarters and box office for the Edinburgh

International Festival, which generally runs for most of August, culminating in a ticketed Fireworks Concert based in Princes Street Gardens but visible from all over the city. Performances take place at the city's larger venues such as the Usher Hall and the Festival Theatre, and, while ticket prices can run to over £90, it is possible to see even the big productions for as little as £10 if you're prepared to sit at the back.

The Fireworks Concert Princes Street Gardens ☎ 0131 473 2000, ⓦ eif.co.uk. Tickets for the Fireworks Concert (£13.50 standing, £30 seated) sell out well in advance; however, a few extra tickets are released for sale at 10am at the Hub, Castlehill, on the day before the show. The concert begins on the last day of the festival at 9pm.

THE EDINBURGH FESTIVAL FRINGE

The Edinburgh Festival Fringe is easily the world's largest arts gathering, and dealing with the logistics of it all can be bewildering. We set out the basics below, but as dates, venues and acts change from one year to the next, be prepared for the unexpected. The Fringe starts and finishes on the same days as the International Festival, kicking off in early August and ending on the last weekend of the month.

THE FRINGE

Following decades of war, economic turmoil and racial intolerance, a few wise civic leaders were offered an opportunity to create a festival that would celebrate diversity and "provide a platform for the flowering of the human spirit". When a handful of theatre companies turned up uninvited to the International Festival's 1947 inauguration, the seeds of the Fringe festival were unintentionally sown. In the following years more and more performers began showing up, culminating in the formation of the **Festival Fringe Society** in 1958. A charitable union, it provided unbiased assistance to artists and companies who wished to perform in Edinburgh during August. Today it still provides the same service, but on a much grander scale. Even standing alone, the **Edinburgh Festival Fringe** is now easily the world's largest arts gathering. Each year sees over thirty thousand performances from some seven hundred companies, with more than twelve thousand participants from all over the world. There's something in the region of 1500 shows every day, round the clock, in two hundred venues around the city. While the headlining names at the International Festival reinforce the Festival's cultural credibility, it is the dynamism, spontaneity and sheer exuberance of the Fringe that dominate Edinburgh every August, giving the city its unique atmosphere. These days, the most prominent and ubiquitous aspect of the Fringe is **comedy**, having overtaken theatre as the largest genre in 2008. As well as sell-out audiences and quotable reviews, most of the comedy acts are chasing the **Foster's Edinburgh Comedy Award**, given to the outstanding stand-up or comedy cabaret. At the same time, the Fringe's **theatre** programme shows no signs of dying out, with hundreds of brand-new works airing alongside offbeat classics and familiar Shakespearean tragedies. The venues are often as imaginative as the shows themselves – play-parks, restaurants and even parked cars have all been used to stage plays. The Fringe also offers fine musicals, dance, children's shows, exhibitions, lectures and music.

1

BOOKING TICKETS FOR THE FRINGE

Festival Fringe Office 180 High St, Old Town ☎0131 226 0000, ⓦedfringe.com. The full Fringe programme is usually available in June from the Festival Fringe Office. Online and telephone bookings for shows can be made immediately after its release, while during the Festival, tickets are sold at the Fringe Office, as well as online or at venues. Ticket prices for most Fringe shows start at £6, and average from £10 to £15 at the main venues, with the best-known acts going for even more; there are often cheap deals on the opening weekend. Performances are staged around the clock, with most scheduled to run for an hour. A downloadable app is available from the edfringe website where you can find shows and book tickets, including those from the Half Price Hut (see below). During the Festival daily 10am–9pm.

Half Price Hut Mound Precinct, beside the National Gallery of Scotland. This is the place to head for bargains, where Fringe shows that are struggling to woo audiences cut their prices in half. There's a downloadable app available from iTunes linked from the edfringe.com website. During the Festival daily 10am–9pm.

FRINGE VENUES

While the Fringe is famous for its tiny and unexpected auditoria, most of the venue spaces across the city are colonized by the four dominant Fringe companies – Assembly, Pleasance, Gilded Balloon and Underbelly. If you're new to the Fringe, these are all safe bets for decent shows and a bit of star-spotting.

The Assembly Rooms 54 George St, New Town ☎0131 220 4348, ⓦassemblyroomsedinburgh.co.uk. Provides a slick, grand setting for top-of-the-range drama and big-name music and comedy acts. Crowds spill out of here onto the temporarily pedestrianized George St where there are makeshift beer gardens.

Gilded Balloon Teviot Row House, Bristo Square, Southside ☎0131 622 6552, ⓦgildedballoon.co.uk. Basing its operations in a Fringe hot spot housed in a beautiful Victorian building designed to look like a sixteenth-century palace, this is the most elegant of the main Old Town venues. It's predominantly mainstream comedy here, although they don't shy away from championing emerging talent. Shows continue into the wee small hours with their raucous Late n Live show at 1am and 5am.

Pleasance Courtyard 60 The Pleasance, Old Town ☎0131 556 6550, ⓦpleasance.co.uk. The atmosphere in the courtyard surrounded by the sixteen auditoria here has a slightly chaotic feel thanks to its busy courtyard bars and kids' zone. Indoors you'll find offbeat comedy mixing with whimsical appearances by panellists on Radio 4 game shows.

Pleasance Dome Potterrow, Bristo Square, Southside ☎0131 556 6650, ⓦpleasance.co.uk. Located in one of Edinburgh University's student unions, there are four small auditoria here, all accessed from the sky-lit dome room.

The Underbelly Bristo Square, Southside ☎0844 545 8252, ⓦunderbelly.co.uk. Underbelly's giant, inflatable upside-down cow – the Udderbelly – is a makeshift performance space that is one of the Fringe's most unusual and eye-catching venues. The company provides further shows down in their oppressive Cowgate building.

EDINBURGH INTERNATIONAL BOOK FESTIVAL

Edinburgh International Book Festival Ticket office at Charlotte Square, New Town ☎0845 373 5888, ⓦedbookfest.co.uk. The world's largest celebration of the written word is held in a tented village in Charlotte Square during the last two weeks of Aug. It offers talks, readings and signings by a star-studded line-up of visiting authors, as well as panel discussions and workshops. Well-known Scottish authors such as Ian Rankin and Alexander McCall-Smith are good for an appearance most years, while visitors from a bit further afield have included Paul Merton, Louis de Bernières, Marilynne Robinson, George Monbiot and Salman Rushdie. In addition, there's a dedicated programme of children's activities, debates, writing workshops and book-related events, an on-site café and, of course, a bookshop. Tickets (generally £10–15) often sell out quickly, particularly for the big-name events.

EDINBURGH JAZZ AND BLUES FESTIVAL

The Edinburgh Jazz and Blues Festival Ticket office at The Hub, 348 Castlehill, Old Town ☎0131 473 2000, ⓦedinburghjazzfestival.com. Easing the city into the festival spirit, the Edinburgh Jazz and Blues Festival runs for two weeks from mid-July with a full programme of gigs in many different locations. Scotland's own varied and vibrant jazz scene is always fully represented, and atmospheric late-night clubs complement major concerts given by international stars. Past visitors have included B.B. King, Bill Wyman, Dizzy Gillespie, Dave Brubeck, Van Morrison, Carol Kidd and The Blues Band. Highlights include the nightly Jam Sessions and a colourful New Orleans-style Mardi Gras and street parade. Tickets range in price from £5 for small pub gigs to £25 for a seat in a big venue.

EDINBURGH ART FESTIVAL

Edinburgh Art Festival ⓦedinburghartfestival .com or ⓦnationalgalleries.org/tickets. A relative newcomer on the scene, August's Edinburgh Art Festival has quickly established itself as an important addition to the festivals portfolio. This is due, in large part, to the ambition and diversity of its programme, which has included high-profile exhibitions by internationally renowned contemporary artists such as Tracey Emin, Douglas Gordon and Ron Mueck, as well as retrospectives of work by pioneering twentieth-century artists including sculptor Eva Hesse, photographer Robert Mapplethorpe, pop artists Gilbert and George and elder statesmen of Scottish painting Alan Davie and John Bellany. Virtually every art gallery in the city participates in the festival, from small private concerns to blockbuster shows at the National Galleries of Scotland's five venues. Most exhibitions are free, though entry to the National Galleries' exhibitions costs £7–10.

THE MILITARY TATTOO

The Military Tattoo Tattoo Office, 32 Market St, Old Town ☎0131 225 1188, ⓦedintattoo.co.uk. Staged in the spectacular stadium of the Edinburgh Castle Esplanade, the Military Tattoo is an unashamed display of pomp and military pride. The programme of choreographed drills, massed pipe bands, historical tableaux, energetic battle re-enactments, national dancing and pyrotechnics has been a feature of the Festival for over half a century, its emotional climax provided by a lone piper on the Castle battlements. Followed by a quick fireworks display, it's a successful formula barely tampered with over the years. Tickets (£25–66 depending on seat location, plus a £5 booking fee if bought online) need to be booked well in advance, and it's advisable to take a cushion and rainwear.

1

EDINBURGH'S OTHER FESTIVALS AND EVENTS

Science Festival From Easter for two weeks ☎0844 557 2686, ⓦsciencefestival.co.uk. Incorporates hands-on children's events as well as numerous lectures on a vast array of subjects.

Beltane Night of April 30 ☻festival@beltane.org, ⓦbeltane.org. An ancient Celtic fire festival, held on Calton Hill, celebrating the arrival of spring. Has a New Age feel to it, with lots of painted flesh, beating drums and huge bonfires. Tickets cost £10.

Imaginate Festival Late May ☎0131 225 8050, ⓦimaginate.org.uk. Low-key children's festival with readings, magicians, drama and puppetry.

International Film Festival Second half of June ☎0131 228 4051, ⓦedfilmfest.org.uk. With a programme crammed with premieres, film shorts and retrospectives, this is the perfect Hollywood antidote. That said, you still see the occasional film star getting the red

carpet treatment outside the festival's main hub at The Filmhouse on Lothian Rd.

Edinburgh's Christmas Dec ☎0844 545 8252, ⓦedinburghschristmas.com. Growing exponentially every year, Edinburgh's Christmas draws together various seasonal events, most prominently the installation of a huge Ferris wheel beside the Scott Monument and the 60,000-bulb Street of Lights – a free, synchronized light show – on the Royal Mile. There's also outdoor skating, fairground rides and a German Christmas market.

Edinburgh's Hogmanay The Festival Fringe Office, 180 High St ☎0844 573 8455 ⓦedinburghshogmanay .org. One of the world's largest New Year street parties, involving torchlight processions, folk and rock concerts, ceilidhs and fireworks galore (see box, p.97). Box office opens early December.

SPORTS

SPECTATOR SPORTS
FOOTBALL

Heart of Midlothian FC McLeod St, off Gorgie Rd ☎0333 043 1874, ⓦheartsfc.co.uk. Edinburgh's oldest football club dating back to 1874, Heart of Midlothian or "Hearts" play in the west of Edinburgh in their 17,000-capacity Tynecastle Stadium.

Hibernian FC 12 Albion Place, off Easter Rd ☎0131 661 2159, ⓦhibernianfc.co.uk. Hearts arch rivals Hibernian FC or "Hibs" was founded in 1875 by Irish immigrants. Based at the 20,000-capacity Easter Road Stadium, northeast of the centre, their support tends to come from Leith and its surrounding areas.

RUGBY

Murrayfield Roseburn St ☎0131 346 5000, ⓦscottishrugby.org. The home of Scottish rugby, this huge stadium plays host to 6 Nations games in

February and March and occasional friendlies, plus the odd rock concert.

SPORTS FACILITIES
CLIMBING

Edinburgh International Climbing Arena South Platt Hill, Ratho ☎0131 333 6333, ⓦeica-ratho.co.uk. Immense indoor climbing facility built into the shell of an old quarry just west of the city beyond the airport. There's a huge choice of climbs to challenge climbers of all levels, plus bouldering practice and a vertiginous aerial assault challenge. Costs £10.80 plus equipment rental. Mon–Fri 8am–10pm, Sat–Sun 9am–6pm.

SNOWSPORTS

Midlothian Snowsports Biggar Rd (buses #4 & #15 from Princes St) ☎0131 445 4433, ⓦmidlothian.gov .uk. Sited just south of the city limits in the Pentland Hills

1

(see p.86), the extensive dry slope here makes for an excellent year-round ski and snowboard facility. Costs £12 for first hour then £5.50/hr plus equipment rental. Mon–Fri 9.30am–9pm, Sat–Sun 9.30am–7pm.

SWIMMING
Royal Commonwealth Pool 21 Dalkeith Rd ☎0131 667 7211, ⓦedinburghleisure.co.uk. Huge, recently renovated facility with three pools: for diving, for kids and a 50m pool for general swimming. Mon–Fri 5.30am–10pm, Sat 5.30am–8pm, Sun 7.30am–8pm.

TENNIS
There are free tennis courts available at The Meadows near Buccleuch St and in Inverleith Park across the road from the Royal Botanic Gardens (see map pp.60–61).

DIRECTORY

Banks and exchange All the major UK banks have branches in central Edinburgh, with ATMs and currency exchange; the main concentrations are in the area between Hanover St and St Andrew Square in the east end of the central New Town. Post offices will exchange currency and there are also currency exchange outlets in Waverley Station. To change money after hours, try one of the upmarket hotels – but expect a hefty commission charge.
Hospitals and clinics The Hospital Royal Infirmary, Little France (☎0131 536 1000), has a 24hr casualty department, and the Royal Hospital for Sick Children, 9 Sciennes Rd, Marchmont (☎0131 536 1000), has a casualty department for children, although this is expected to close and move to the Royal Infirmary in late 2017. Western General, Crewe Rd North (☎0131 537 1000), provides a minor injuries clinic 8am–9pm. NHS24 (☎111, ⓦnhs24.com) offers 24hr health advice and clinical assessment over the phone or online.
Left luggage Waverley train station has a counter charging £12 per item per day (daily 7am–11pm; ☎0208 090 9937). The Bus Station is far more reasonable, at £5 to £10 per day depending on bag size (daily 24hr ☎0131 555 6363).
Police Lothian and Borders Police (☎999, or ☎101 for non-emergencies) have stations at 2 Gayfield Square and 188 High St.
Post office 33 Forrest Rd (Mon–Fri 8.30am–6pm, Sat 9am–5.30pm; ☎0845 722 3344).

East Lothian

East Lothian consists of the coastal strip and hinterland immediately east of Edinburgh, bounded by the Firth of Forth to the north and the Lammermuir Hills to the south. All of it is within easy day-trip range from the capital, though there are places you can stay overnight if you're keen to explore it properly. Often mocked as the "home counties" of Edinburgh, there's no denying its well-ordered feel, with prosperous farms and large estate houses dominating the scenery.

The most immediately attractive part of the area is the coastline, extending from the town of Musselburgh, all but joined onto Edinburgh, round to the harbour town of **Dunbar**, birthplace of the famous naturalist John Muir. There's something for most tastes here, including wide sandy beaches, the enjoyable Seabird Centre at **North Berwick** and the nearby castles of **Dirleton** and **Tantallon**, the latter set in a vertiginous clifftop location. Inland, at the foot of the Lammermuirs, is the county town of **Haddington**, a pleasant enough place, though the attraction nearby of **Glenkinchie**, Edinburgh's "local" whisky distillery by Pentcaitland, is likely to be a stronger draw.

North Berwick and around

NORTH BERWICK, 25 miles east of Edinburgh, has a great deal of charm and a somewhat faded, old-fashioned air, its guesthouses and hotels extending along the shore in all their Victorian and Edwardian sobriety. The town's small harbour is set on a headland which cleaves two crescents of sand, providing the town with an attractive coastal setting, though it is the two nearby volcanic heaps, the offshore **Bass Rock** and 613ft-high **North Berwick Law**, which are the town's defining physical features.

CLOCKWISE FROM TOP LEFT NATIONAL GALLERY OF SCOTLAND (P.76); EDINBURGH FRINGE FESTIVAL (P.101); THE SCOTTISH PARLIAMENT (P.70); CAFÉ ROYAL CIRCLE BAR (P.95) >

1

Scottish Seabird Centre

The Harbour • Feb, March, Sept & Oct Mon–Fri 10am–5pm, Sat & Sun 10am–5.30pm; April–Aug daily 10am–6pm; Nov–Jan Mon–Fri 10am–4pm, Sat & Sun 10am–5pm • £8.95 • ☎ 01620 890202, ⓦ seabird.org • Boat trips April–Oct daily (times vary; prices range from £10 to £125 depending on itinerary)

Housed in an attractively designed new building by the harbour, the **Scottish Seabird Centre** offers access to the gannets and puffins that thrive on the rocky outcrops in the sea before North Berwick. There are live links from the centre to cameras mounted on the islands which show close-up pictures of the birds in their nesting grounds. At the risk of getting wet (and cold), you can hop aboard one of the thrilling speedboat rides to the islands – weather permitting. Trips range from a thirty-minute puffin-spotting jaunt to a five-hour trip with time on the Bass Rock itself. Contact the Seabird Centre to find out what boat tours are available on any given day.

Dirleton Castle

2.5 miles west of North Berwick, signposted off the A198 • April–Sept daily 9.30am–5.30pm; Oct–March daily 10am–4pm • £5.50; HES • ☎ 01620 850330, ⓦ historicenvironment.scot • Reached in 15min from North Berwick on the Edinburgh bus (First Bus #124; every 30min)

The genteel hamlet of Dirleton huddles around the romantic thirteenth-century ruins of **Dirleton Castle**, which saw action in the Wars of Scottish Independence. It was later rendered militarily defunct after a besiegement by Oliver Cromwell's army to flush out bandits. Today it's an attractive relic, largely intact, with restored Victorian gardens making for a popular wedding venue.

Tantallon Castle

3 miles east of North Berwick on the A198 • Daily: April–Sept 9.30am–5.30pm; Oct–March 10am–4pm • £5.50; HES • ☎ 01620 892727, ⓦ historicenvironment.scot • From North Berwick take the Dunbar bus (Eves Coaches #120; Mon–Sat 6 daily, 2 on Sun; 6min), or you can walk there from town along the cliffs in around an hour

The melodramatic ruins of **Tantallon Castle** stand on the precipitous cliffs facing the Bass Rock. With a sheer drop down to the sea on three sides and a sequence of moats and ditches on the fourth, the desolate invincibility of this fourteenth-century stronghold is daunting, especially when the wind howls over the remaining battlements and the surf crashes on the rocks far below.

ARRIVAL AND DEPARTURE   NORTH BERWICK AND AROUND

By train North Berwick is served by an hourly train from Edinburgh Waverley (33min). From the station it's a 10min walk east to the town centre.

By bus First Group #124, #X24 and #X25 from Edinburgh's bus station (every 30min; 1hr 35min) run along the coast

and stop on High St, North Berwick.

By car From Edinburgh take the A1 (London Rd) and turn onto the A198 at Tranent. From here, it's a further 13 miles to North Berwick.

ACCOMMODATION AND EATING

The Glebe House B&B Law Rd, North Berwick ☎ 01620 892608, ⓦ glebehouse-nb.co.uk. A grand eighteenth-century manse in secluded grounds 100 yards inland but still overlooking the sea. With decor befitting of its period, the rooms are spacious yet homely, and at breakfast you can opt for a Scottish fry-up – although there are healthier choices too. **£130**

★ **Osteria** 71 High St, North Berwick ☎ 01620 890589, ⓦ osteria-no1.co.uk. Run by a highly successful father and daughter team; this is one of the country's top Italian restaurants. Expect bold flavours, vibrant colours and a level of finesse little seen outside the main cities. Prices hover around £8 for *primi* courses, while the *secondi piatti* rise steeply from £15. Booking recommended. Tues–Sat 12.30–2pm & 6–10pm, and July–Aug Mon 6–10pm.

Dunbar

Thirty miles east of the capital lies the coastal town of **DUNBAR**, with its delightfully intricate double harbour set beside the shattered remains of a once-mighty castle. Its local industry is fishing but the more affluent residents are commuters who take advantage of the town's station on the main London to Edinburgh train line. Dunbar's High Street is graced by several grand old stone buildings, one of which is the birthplace of nineteenth-century explorer and naturalist, **John Muir**, whose name is also given to the attractive **country park** neighbouring the town. You can get to the park on an easy three-mile walk west of the harbour, along a rugged stretch of coast to the sands of Belhaven Bay.

John Muir Birthplace

126 High St • April–Oct Mon–Sat 10am–5pm, Sun 1–5pm; Nov–March same hours but closed Mon & Tues • Free • ☎ 01368 865899, ⓦ jmbt.org.uk

More famous abroad than in his native Scotland, John Muir (1838–1914) was a tireless campaigner for the protection of the natural world and played an integral role in the creation of the United States' national parks system. The **John Muir Birthplace** was born out of demand from the many Americans visiting Dunbar in the hope of learning more about Muir's early life and childhood inspirations. The three-storey whitewashed tenement describes itself as an interpretative centre rather than a museum, and while it engagingly tells the story of Muir's passage from childhood to pioneer, there are few historical artefacts on show.

ARRIVAL AND DEPARTURE   DUNBAR

By train Dunbar is served by trains from Edinburgh Waverley (every 30min; 20min). From the station it's a 5min walk north to the high street.
By bus Three buses (#X6, #X8 & #253) depart from Edinburgh's bus station (every 30min) to Dunbar High St;

the quickest is the #253 (1hr).
By car From Edinburgh take the A1 (London Rd) and turn onto the A199 3 miles after East Linton, after which Dunbar is a 5min drive.

EATING

The Creel Restaurant 25 Lamer St, near the old harbour ☎ 01368 863279, ⓦ creelrestaurant.co.uk. Run by a former chef to Rick Stein, this restaurant knows a thing or two about seafood. Championing locally sourced food, this is a great place to tuck into posh fish (battered using

the local Belhaven beer) and chips or, if you prefer something more exotic, lemon sole with a spicy Spanish salsa. The lunch menu is best value at £16.50 for two courses. Wed 6.30–9pm, Thurs–Sat noon–2.30pm & 6.30–9pm, Sun noon–2.30pm.

Haddington and around

Sitting on the banks of the River Tyne with the hulking mass of **St Mary's Church**, Scotland's largest parish church, rising tall near its centre, this is one of Scotland's most respectable county towns. Other than a stroll along the riverbank or through the seventeenth-century medicinal gardens of **St Mary's Pleasance** on Sidegate, there's not much to detain you in the town unless you arrive on the last Saturday of the month for the **farmers' market**.

Just four miles south of town, the pretty hamlet of **Gifford**, with its eighteenth-century estate cottages flanked by a trim whitewashed church and a couple of good pubs, makes for a good last stop before the godforsaken wilderness of the Lammermuir Hills.

Glenkinchie Distillery

7 miles southwest of Haddington on the A6093 • Easter–Oct Mon–Sat 10am–5pm, Sun noon–5pm; Nov–Feb daily 10am–4pm, March–Oct daily 10am–5pm; last tour 1hr before closing • £8 • ☎ 01875 342012

The **Glenkinchie Distillery** is the closest place to Edinburgh where malt whisky is made. Here, of course, they emphasize the qualities that set Glenkinchie, a lighter, drier malt, apart from the peaty, smoky whiskies of the north and west. On display is a pleasant little exhibition featuring some quaint distilling relics, which enhance the factory tour experience almost as much as the free dram at the end.

1

Midlothian

Immediately south of Edinburgh lies the old county of **Midlothian**, once called Edinburghshire. It's one of the hilliest parts of the Central Lowlands, with the Pentland chain running down its western side and the Moorfoots defining its boundary with the Borders to the south. Though predominantly rural, it contains a belt of former mining communities that are still struggling to come to terms with the decline of the industry. Such charms as it has are mostly low-key, with the exception of the riotously ornate chapel at **Roslin**. An otherwise nondescript place, the village has two unusual claims to fame: it was near here, at the Roslin Institute, that the **world's first cloned sheep**, Dolly, was created in 1997; and it's home to the mysterious, richly decorated late Gothic **Rosslyn Chapel**.

Rosslyn Chapel

Chapel Loan, Roslin, 7 miles south of Edinburgh just off the A701 • April–Sept Mon–Sat 9.30am–6pm, Sun noon–4.45pm; Oct–March Mon–Sat 9.30am–4.30pm, Sun noon–4.45pm • £9 • ☎ 0131 440 2159, ⓦ rosslynchapel.com • Bus #15 (every 30min; 40min) westbound from Princes St in Edinburgh

Revered for its sublime **stone carvings** – some of the finest in the world – and subject of intrigue and mystery with its alleged Crusader connections, Rosslyn is more cathedral-like than chapel in its dimensions. It was intended to be a huge collegiate church dedicated to St Matthew, but construction halted soon after the founder's death in 1484, and the vestry built onto the facade nearly four hundred years later is the sole subsequent addition. After a long period of neglect, a massive fifteen-year restoration project has recently been completed.

Rosslyn's **exterior** bristles with pinnacles, gargoyles, flying buttresses and canopies, while **inside** the stonework is, if anything, even more intricate. The **foliage carving** is particularly outstanding, with botanically accurate depictions of over a dozen different leaves and plants. Among them are cacti and Indian corn, compounding the legend that the founder's grandfather, the daring sea adventurer Prince Henry of Orkney, did

LEGENDS OF ROSSLYN CHAPEL

Rosslyn Chapel is famous for its exquisite carvings – but almost as compelling are the fascinating **legends** associated with this mysterious building, and the many secrets said to lurk within the cracks and crannies of its skilfully engraved stone.

The greatest and most original carving to grace Rosslyn Chapel is the extraordinary knotted **Apprentice Pillar** at the southeastern corner of the Lady Chapel. According to local legend, the pillar was carved by an apprentice during the absence of the master mason, who **killed** him in a fit of jealousy on seeing the finished work. A tiny head of a man with a slashed forehead, set at the apex of the ceiling at the far northwestern corner of the building, is popularly supposed to represent the apprentice, his murderer the corresponding head at the opposite side.

The imagery of carvings such as the floriated **cross and five-pointed star**, together with the history of the family, the St Clairs of Rosslyn, which owns the chapel, leaves little doubt about its links to the **Knights Templar** and **Freemasonry**. Two members of the St Clair family, for example, were allegedly grand masters of the Prieuré de Sion, the shadowy order linked to the Templars, while the Masonic connection was said to have saved the chapel from the armies of Oliver Cromwell, himself a Freemason, which destroyed the surrounding area but spared Rosslyn.

More intriguing still are claims that, because of such connections, Rosslyn Chapel has been the repository for items such as the lost Scrolls of Solomon's Temple in Jerusalem, the true Stone of Scone and, most famously, the **Holy Grail**.

The chapel is regularly drawn into conspiracy theories on these themes, most famously through Dan Brown's 2003 bestseller **The Da Vinci Code**; the chapel's appearance in the film of the same name precipitated a huge surge in visitor numbers, detracting a little from the mysterious air of the place.

indeed set foot in the New World a century before Columbus. The rich and subtle **figurative sculptures** have given Rosslyn the nickname of "a Bible in stone", though they're more allegorical than literal, with portrayals of the Dance of Death, the Seven Acts of Mercy and the Seven Deadly Sins.

West Lothian

To many, **West Lothian** is a poor relative to the rich, rolling farmland of East and Midlothian, with a landscape dominated by motorways, industrial estates and giant hillocks of ochre-coloured mine waste called "bings". However, in the ruined royal palace at **Linlithgow**, the area boasts one of Scotland's more magnificent ruins. Not too far away, the village of **South Queensferry** lies under the considerable shadow of the Forth rail and road bridges, though it's an interesting enough place in its own right, with a historic high street and the notable stately homes **Dalmeny** and **Hopetoun** nearby. It's also the starting point for boat trips out to **Inchcolm Island**, home to a beautifully preserved medieval abbey.

Linlithgow

Roughly equidistant between Falkirk and the outskirts of Edinburgh, the ancient burgh of **Linlithgow** has largely kept its medieval layout. Sadly, development since the 1960s has stripped it of some fine buildings, in particular close to the **Town Hall** and **Cross** (the former marketplace) on the long High Street – the town does, however, preserve some notable gems, including its ruined palace and an ancient church.

Linlithgow Palace

Kirkgate • Daily: April–Sept 9.30am–5.30pm; Oct–March 10am–4pm • £5.50; HES • ☎ 01506 842896, ⓦ historicenvironment.scot

Hidden from the main road, **Linlithgow Palace** is a splendid fifteenth-century ruin romantically set on the edge of Linlithgow Loch. The pile is associated with some of Scotland's best-known historical figures, including **Mary, Queen of Scots**, who was born here on December 8, 1542 and became queen six days later. A royal manor house is believed to have existed on this site since the time of David I, though James I began construction of the present palace, a process that continued through two centuries and the reign of no fewer than eight monarchs. From the top of the northwest tower, Queen Margaret looked out in vain for the return of James IV from the field of Flodden in 1513 – indeed, the views from her bower, six giddy storeys up from the ground, are exceptional. The ornate octagonal **fountain** in the inner courtyard, with its wonderfully intricate figures and medallion heads, flowed with wine for the wedding of James V and Mary of Guise.

This is a great place to take children: the elegant, bare rooms echo with footsteps and there's a labyrinthine network of spiral staircases and endless nooks and crannies. The galleried **Great Hall** is magnificent, as is the adjoining kitchen, which has a truly cavernous fireplace.

St Michael's Church

Kirkgate • Mon–Sat: April–Sept 9.30am–5.30pm; Oct–March 9.30am–4.30pm • Free • ☎ 01506 842188, ⓦ stmichaelsparish.org.uk

St Michael's Church, adjacent to Linlithgow Palace, is one of Scotland's largest pre-Reformation churches, consecrated in the thirteenth century. The present building was completed two hundred years later, with the exception of the hugely incongruous aluminium spire, tacked on in 1964. Inside, it's a soaring Gothic masterwork with a layout typical of the time; huge stone arches and pillars combine to divide the outer aisles from the nave, above which the impressive vaulted ceiling draws the eye forward to the chancel.

1

Linlithgow Canal Centre

Manse Rd Basin, 100yds southwest of Linlithgow's train station • Boat trips (from £4) depart every half hour between 2pm and 4pm at weekends Easter–Sept, daily July & Aug; self-drive boat hire from £80 • ☎ 01506 671215, ⓦ lucs.org.uk

The **Linlithgow Canal Centre** sits on the banks of the tranquil **Union Canal**, the 31-mile-long waterway that runs from Fountainbridge, near the heart of Edinburgh, through Linlithgow and west to Falkirk, where it meets the Forth & Clyde Canal linking the capital with Glasgow; the two canals are connected by the Falkirk Wheel (see p.288). The Canal Centre runs a couple of regular **narrow-boat trips** through town or east towards the Avon Aqueduct – Scotland's largest – as well as the occasional foray onto the Forth & Clyde via the Falkirk Wheel. Along the way, the guide will tell of the near two-hundred-year history of the canals and serve tea and biscuits too.

ARRIVAL AND DEPARTURE
LINLITHGOW

By train Linlithgow is on the main train routes from Edinburgh to both Glasgow Queen St (4 trains hourly) and Stirling (2 trains hourly); the journey from Edinburgh takes

20min and the train station lies at the southern end of town. **By car** 19 miles west of Edinburgh, Linlithgow is just off the M9 road to Stirling.

EATING

Livingston's Restaurant 52 High St, a minute's walk northwest of the station ☎ 01506 846565, ⓦ livingroom-livingstons.co.uk. Part housed in the original stable building for Linlithgow Palace, this award-winning family business is split over three stylish rooms,

two of which look onto a pleasant enclosed garden. The cuisine is heavily French-influenced but there are flashes of inspired originality like the smoked pigeon with morels and a radish and raspberry dressing; part of the £37 two-course menu. Tues–Sat noon–2pm & 6–9pm.

South Queensferry

Eight miles northwest of Edinburgh city centre, the small town of **South Queensferry** (also known as Queensferry) is best known today for its location at the southern end of the three mighty **Forth bridges** (see p.315). Named after the saintly wife of King Malcolm Canmore, Margaret, who would often use the ferry here to travel between the royal palaces in Dunfermline and Edinburgh, it's an attractive settlement tightly packed with old buildings, most of which date from the seventeenth and eighteenth centuries. Only one row of houses separates the cobbled High Street from the water; through the gaps there's a great perspective of the bridges, an old stone harbour and a curved, pebbly beach, the scene each New Year's Day of the teeth-chattering "Loony Dook", when a gaggle of hungover locals charges into the sea for the quickest of dips.

Queensferry Museum

53 High St • Mon & Thurs–Sat 10am–1pm & 2.15–5pm, Sun noon–5pm • Free • ☎ 0131 331 5545, ⓦ edinburghmuseums.org.uk

The tiny **Queensferry Museum** contains photos and relics of the town's history showing its importance as a ferry port. The most interesting item on show is the **Burry Man costume**, part of a unique Queensferry tradition designed to ward off evil spirits. Still worn around town on the first Friday of August every year, the Burry man suits are cotton with over ten thousand sticky "burrs" – burdock seed cases – attached from head to toe. You'll also find details on the building of the first two bridges.

ARRIVAL AND DEPARTURE
SOUTH QUEENSFERRY

By train From Edinburgh Waverley take the train to Dalmeny (every 30min; 20min). From there it's a mile to town: head west on Station Rd then turn right on The Loan. **By bus** Regular buses (3 hourly) connect Edinburgh's bus

station with Hopetoun Rd at the heart of South Queensferry within 40min. **By car** South Queensferry is signposted off the M90 motorway on the south end of the Forth Rd Bridge.

EATING AND DRINKING

The Boathouse 19b High St ☎ 0131 331 5429, ⓦ theboathouse-sq.co.uk. With incredible Rail Bridge views it's little wonder this seafood restaurant – with tagged-on bistro and cocktail bar – is so popular. The dishes are pretty simple; just two or three luxurious ingredients delicately forming a jus, oil or sauce to complement the catch of the day. Two-course lunches are a little steep at £18 in the restaurant, but the bistro has some enticing sandwiches, like their steak and onion ciabatta with chips for around £7. Daily 10am–11.30pm.

1

Dalmeny House

Dalmeny Estate, 3 miles east of South Queensferry • June & July Mon–Wed & Sun guided tours at 2.15pm & 3.30pm • £10 • ☎ 0131 331 1888, Ⓦ dalmeny.co.uk • Arriving on foot from South Queensferry, follow the High St eastwards for 1.5 miles until you reach the estate entrance; by car follow signposts from the A90 near South Queensferry

Set on a two-thousand-acre estate, **Dalmeny House** may not be the prettiest mansion you'll encounter in Scotland, but the quality of the items on show within makes it a fascinating place to visit. As well as some of the finest Baroque and Neoclassical **furniture** produced for Louis XIV, Louis XV and Louis XVI in the hundred years before the French Revolution, there's also a valuable selection of memorabilia relating to Napoleon Bonaparte. The **art** collection is surprisingly strong too, with a very rare set of **tapestries** made from cartoons by Goya, and portraits by Raeburn, Reynolds, Gainsborough and Lawrence.

Hopetoun House

3 miles west of South Queensferry • Easter–Sept daily 10.30am–5pm • House and grounds £9.85, grounds only £4.55 • Free tour daily at 2pm • ☎ 0131 331 2451, Ⓦ hopetoun.co.uk • Arriving from South Queenferry on foot, follow the coastline westwards for 3 miles; by car take the M90 turn-off onto the A904, from where it's signposted

Sitting in its own extensive estate on the south shore of the Forth, **Hopetoun House** is one of the most impressive stately homes in Scotland. The original house was built at the turn of the eighteenth century for the first earl of Hopetoun by Sir William Bruce, the architect of Edinburgh's Holyroodhouse. A couple of decades later, William Adam carried out an enormous extension, engulfing the structure with a curvaceous main facade and two projecting wings – superb examples of Roman Baroque pomp and swagger. Hopetoun's **architecture** is undoubtedly its most compelling feature, but the **furnishings** aren't completely overwhelmed, with some impressive seventeenth-century tapestries, Meissen porcelain and portraits by Gainsborough, Ramsay and Raeburn. The house's **grounds** include a regal driveway and some lovely walks along woodland trails and the banks of the Forth.

Inchcolm Island

From South Queensferry's Hawes Pier, just west of the rail bridge, a couple of ferry services head out to **Inchcolm Island**, located about five miles northeast of South Queensferry near the Fife shore. The island is home to the best-preserved medieval **abbey** in Scotland, founded in 1235 after King Alexander I was storm-bound on the island and took refuge in a hermit's cell. Although the structure as a whole is half-ruined today, the tower, octagonal chapterhouse and echoing cloisters are intact and well worth exploring. The hour and a half you're given ashore by the boat timetables also allows time for a picnic on the abbey's lawns or the chance to explore Inchcolm's old military fortifications and extensive bird-nesting grounds.

ARRIVAL AND DEPARTURE | **INCHCOLM ISLAND**

BY BOAT
From South Queensferry There are regular crossings from Hawes Pier between April and Oct on the *Maid of the Forth* (times vary, more regular in high season; £18.50; 45min each way; ☎ 0131 331 5000, Ⓦ maidoftheforth.co.uk).

From Edinburgh From Waverley Bridge, *Forth Belle* makes two to five sailings each day between mid-Feb and Oct (£20 including bus from Edinburgh, landing fee on the island £5.50 extra; 45min each way; ☎ 0870 118 1866, Ⓦ forthtours.com).

The Borders

FIDDLE PLAYER AT A BORDERS FESTIVAL

The Borders

Sandwiched between the Cheviot Hills on the English border and the Pentland, Moorfoot and Lammermuir hills south of Edinburgh, the Borders is a region made up of the old shire counties of Berwick, Roxburgh, Selkirk and Peebles. Travelling from the bleak moorland of neighbouring Northumberland, you'll be struck by the green lushness of Tweeddale, whose river is the pivotal feature of the region's geography. Yet the Borders also incorporate some of the barren stretches of the Southern Uplands, with their bare, rounded peaks and weather-beaten heathery hills.

Tweeddale is the Borders at its best, with the finest section between **Melrose** and **Peebles**, where you'll find a string of attractions, from the eccentricities of Sir Walter Scott's mansion at **Abbotsford** to the intriguing Jacobite past of **Traquair House**, plus a clutch of ruined abbeys. The valley widens to the east to form the **Merse** basin, an area of rich arable lands that features a series of grand stately homes, principally **Floors Castle**, **Manderston**, **Paxton** and **Mellerstain House**, all featuring the Neoclassical work of the Adam family.

To the west, the Borders have a wilder aspect, where a series of four narrow valleys lead, up to the border with Dumfriesshire. North of the Tweed, the bleak **Lammermuir Hills** form the southern edge of Lothian and are a favourite haunt of Edinburgh-based ramblers, while further east in **Berwickshire**, especially around **St Abb's Head**, the coastline becomes more rugged, its dramatic cliffs and rocky outcrops harbouring a series of desolate ruined castles.

Brief history

The Borders' most famous sights are its **ruined abbeys**, founded under King David I (1124–53), whose policy of encouraging the monastic orders had little to do with spirituality. The monks of Kelso, Melrose, Jedburgh and Dryburgh were the frontiersmen of David's kingdom, helping advance his authority in areas of doubtful allegiance. This period of relative stability was interrupted in 1296 by the Wars of Independence with England.

From the first half of the sixteenth century until the Act of Union, the Borders again experienced turbulent times, bloodily fought over by the English and the Scots, and plagued by endless clan warfare and Reivers' raids (see p.123). Consequently, the countryside is strewn with ruined castles and keeps, while each major town celebrates its agitated past in the **Common Ridings**, when locals – especially the "callants" (young men) – dressed in period costume ride out to check the burgh boundaries. It's a boisterous, macho business, performed with pride and matched only by the local love of **rugby union**, which reaches a crescendo with the **Melrose Sevens** tournament in April.

GETTING AROUND AND INFORMATION   THE BORDERS

By bus and train There are two train lines in the Borders: one follows the A7 southeast from Edinburgh to Galashiels; the other runs along the east coast between Edinburgh and Berwick-upon-Tweed without stopping in the Borders at

MELROSE ABBEY

Highlights

❶ St Abb's Head Easily accessible, spectacular coastal scenery with sea stacks, sheer cliffs and nesting seabirds galore, all found at the point where Scotland collided with its southern neighbour over four hundred million years ago. **See p.117**

❷ Melrose Abbey The vast Border abbey with the best-preserved sculptural detail set within the most charming of the Border towns. Look out for the burial plot of Robert the Bruce's heart. **See p.122**

❸ Walking around Peebles The banks of the Tweed are at their most scenic around Peebles, and you can walk to medieval Neidpath Castle or the lovely Kailzie Gardens. **See p.129**

❹ Dawyck Botanic Garden Take an exotic hike around one of the world's finest arboreta, with seventeenth-century origins and links to the great, global plant-hunting expeditions. **See p.129**

❺ Traquair House A romantic, castellated former hunting lodge of royalty dating back to the eleventh century. Explore the house and extensive grounds then sink a dark and spicy Jacobite ale made here at the in-house brewery. **See p.130**

❻ Biking at Glentress and Innerleithen Eight adrenaline-pumping downhill trails through thick forest, this is the place for exhilarating off-road biking, with runs to suit all levels. **See p.131**

HIGHLIGHTS ARE MARKED ON THE MAP ON P.116

all. Travelling around by bus can take some planning, although there is a good network of bus routes linking the key towns and smaller villages – pick up timetables from the local tourist offices.

Tourist information ⓦ scot-borders.co.uk. For a bus network map, see ⓦ firstgroup.com.

Eyemouth and around

2

The history of **EYEMOUTH**, the only settlement of any size on the Borders' coastline, is forever tied up with the sea. Its long, slender harbour remains very much the focus of activity, its waters packed with deep-sea and inshore fleets and its quay strewn with tatters of old net, discarded fish and fish crates.

Eyemouth Maritime Centre

Harbour Rd • April–Oct Mon–Sat 10am–5pm, Sun 10am–4pm • Free • ⓣ 01890 751020, ⓦ worldofboats.org/emc

Housed in a unique waterside structure designed to look like an eighteenth-century frigate, the **Eyemouth Maritime Centre** displays an outstanding array of old sailing craft including a small, seven-man whaling boat containing a hand-held harpoon.

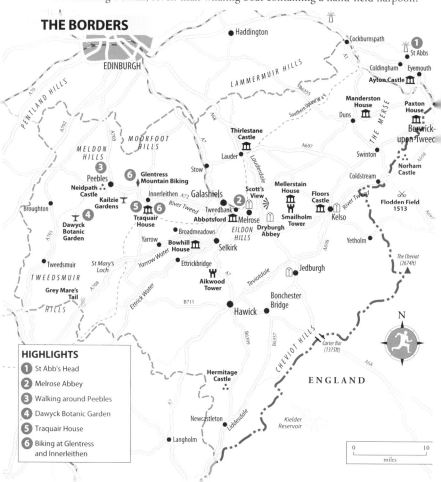

THE BORDERS

HIGHLIGHTS

1 St Abb's Head
2 Melrose Abbey
3 Walking around Peebles
4 Dawyck Botanic Garden
5 Traquair House
6 Biking at Glentress and Innerleithen

There's also an interesting exhibition of photographs and ephemera once owned by the Scottish men who braved the south Atlantic to hunt whales from the turn of the twentieth century onwards.

Eyemouth Museum

Auld Kirk, Manse Rd · Easter–Oct Mon–Sat 10am–4pm, Sun noon–4pm · £3.50 ☎ 01890 751701, ⍟ eyemouthmuseum.org

Documenting the life and times of this small fishing community, the **Eyemouth Museum** focuses in particular on the 1881 disaster when a freak storm took the lives of 189 men, including 129 from Eyemouth, a tragedy of extraordinary proportions for a place of this size. A 15ft tapestry commemorating the event hangs in the museum along with old social and industrial memorabilia relating to farming and fishing. The museum doubles as a **tourist information centre**.

2

St Abb's Head

4 miles northwest of Eyemouth; from just outside the village of St Abbs, take the only single track north and continue to the end of the road · Reserve always open · Parking £2; NTS · ☎ 0131 4580200; ⍟ nts.org.uk

Perhaps not suited for those without a head for heights, **St Abb's Head** rises 300ft out of the sea, its sheer cliffs providing a nesting place for great numbers of kittiwakes, guillemots, razorbills and other seabirds. Either side of the small valley you'll see different coloured rock marking a geological divide: grey sedimentary to the west and red volcanic to the east. From the car park, an easily followed, mile-long walking trail ends at the Stevensons' lighthouse, but you only need to take it for half a mile before being rewarded with a spectacular view of the Berwickshire coast.

Paxton House

10 miles south of Eyemouth; 5 miles west of Berwick-upon-Tweed on the B6461 · **House** Mid-March to Oct daily 10am–5pm (tours 10.30am, noon, 2pm & 3.30pm; 1hr) · £8.50 · **Gardens and grounds** Daily 10am–sunset · £3.50 · ☎ 01289 386291, ⍟ paxtonhouse.co.uk · #32 bus (Mon–Fri 3 daily, Sat 4 buses; 17min) from Berwick-upon-Tweed

Overlooking the River Tweed, **Paxton House** is a perfectly proportioned Palladian mansion built for Patrick Home of Billie. It was a desperate and unsuccessful attempt to woo his Prussian lover, Sophie de Brandt, lady-in-waiting to Queen Elizabeth Christine, wife of Frederick the Great. Forced to return home on the murder of his mother – apparently, the butler did it – he began building Paxton in 1758 but gradually lost interest in the project as the reality that he would never see his lover again set in. Patrick never moved in and sold it unfinished to his cousin for £15,000.

The interior features a stunning collection of Chippendale furniture, commissioned by the cousin to whom Patrick sold the house on the death of Sophie. The other highlight is the **Picture Gallery**, completed in the 1810s, with its rich Neoclassical plasterwork and changing display of works from the National Gallery of Scotland. The **grounds**, laid out by an assistant of Capability Brown, include gentle footpaths, a croquet lawn, an army-built adventure playground, a tearoom, Highland cattle, Shetland ponies, a Victorian boathouse housing a salmon-netting museum, and a hide, from where you can spy on red squirrels and woodpeckers.

Manderston House

1 mile east of Duns, signposted off the A6105 · **House** May to Sept Thurs & Sun 1.30–5pm · £10 · **Gardens** Thurs & Sun 11.30am–dusk · £6 · ☎ 01361 883450, ⍟ manderston.co.uk · Bus #60 from Galashiels, Melrose, Berwick-upon-Tweed and Tweedmouth (Mon–Fri 9 daily; Sat–Sun 5 daily)

Manderston House encapsulates high-class living in late Victorian and Edwardian

2

Britain. Between 1871 and 1905, the Miller family spent most of their herring and hemp fortune on turning their Georgian home into a prestigious country house. It's certainly a staggering sight, from the intricate plasterwork ceilings to the inlaid marble floor in the hall and the extravagant silver staircase. The whole is sumptuously furnished with trappings worthy of a man who had just married into the aristocracy: James Miller married Eveline Curzon, the daughter of Lord Scarsdale, in 1893. Manderston is currently the home of Lord and Lady Palmer, of Huntley & Palmers biscuits fame – hence the Biscuit Tin Museum in the house. The extensive **gardens** are noted for their courtyard stables (where the café is situated), cloistered marble dairy, mock tower house, rhododendrons and azaleas.

ARRIVAL AND INFORMATION

By bus Buses to Eyemouth stop in Albert St, one block south of the main shopping thoroughfare.
Destinations Berwick-upon-Tweed (hourly; 20min); Edinburgh (Mon–Sat 7 buses, Sun 3 buses; 2hr);

EYEMOUTH AND AROUND

St Abbs (hourly; 15min).
Tourist office The tourist office is in Eyemouth Museum, Auld Kirk, Manse Rd (Easter–Oct Mon–Sat 10am–4pm, Sun noon–4pm; ☎ 01890 751701).

ACCOMMODATION AND EATING

★**Giacopazzi's** 20 Harbour Rd ☎ 01890 750317, ⓦ giacopazzis.co.uk. There's no mistaking from the man-sized ice-cream models outside this shop that Giacopazzi's are tremendously proud of their gelati. Made daily, the ice cream is, for many, a reason alone to come to Eyemouth; they do a good fish dinner too, for £13.50 (or £6.50 takeaway).

Sun–Thurs 9am–8.30pm, Fri–Sat 9am–9.30pm.
Hillcrest Bed and Breakfast Coldingham Rd ☎ 01890 752993, ⓦ bedandbreakfasteyemouth.co.uk. A short saunter inland from the harbour, this sparklingly clean B&B is nothing flashy but has very comfortable beds and does excellent cooked breakfasts. **£80**

The Tweed valley

Rising in the hills far to the west, the **River Tweed** snakes its way across the Borders until it reaches the North Sea at Berwick-upon-Tweed, most of its final stretch forming the boundary between Scotland and England. This is the area known as the **Merse** (from the

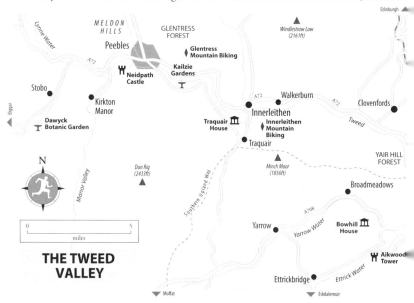

THE TWEED VALLEY

Old English for marsh), a flat landscape of rich farmland and wooded riverbanks where the occasional military ruin serves as a reminder of more violent days. The **Border abbeys** – perhaps the best reason for visiting the region – also lie in ruins, not because of the Reformation, but because they were burnt to the ground by the English, for whom the lower Tweed was the obvious point at which to cross the border into Scotland.

The lower Tweed has just one town of note, **Kelso**, a busy agricultural centre, with a couple of stately homes close by and a ruined abbey, the latter easily upstaged by those at **Melrose** and **Dryburgh**, further upstream. Melrose makes a great base for exploring the middle reaches of the Tweed valley. The rich, forested scenery inspired Sir Walter Scott, whose own purpose-built creation, **Abbotsford**, stands a few miles outside Melrose. Perhaps fortunately, Scott died before the textile boom turned his beloved **Selkirk** and **Galashiels** into mill towns. The Tweed is at its most beguiling in the stretch between Melrose and the pleasant country town of **Peebles**, when it winds through the hills past numerous stately homes, most notably **Traquair House**. Public transport is no problem, with frequent buses travelling along the valley. Just west of Peebles, the Tweed curves south towards Tweedsmuir, from where it's just a few miles further to Moffat in Dumfries and Galloway.

2

Kelso and around

Sir Walter Scott (see p.127) once referred to **KELSO** as the "the most beautiful, if not the most romantic village in Scotland." While its aesthetic powers may have diminished somewhat since Scott's days, this place retains a somewhat jaded charm thanks to its historical buildings and its position at the confluence of the Tweed and Teviot. Today's Kelso grew up in the shadow of its now-ruined Benedictine abbey, which had brought prosperity to the town until the Reformation. The town is now centred on **The Square**, an unusually large cobbled expanse a short distance from the abbey and presided over by the elegant honey-hued **Town Hall**. To one side stands the imposing *Cross Keys Hotel*, with its distinctive rooftop balustrade, and a supporting chorus of three-storey eighteenth- and nineteenth-century pastel buildings on every side. Leaving The Square along Roxburgh Street, take the alley down to the **Cobby Riverside Walk**, where a brief stroll leads to Floors Castle.

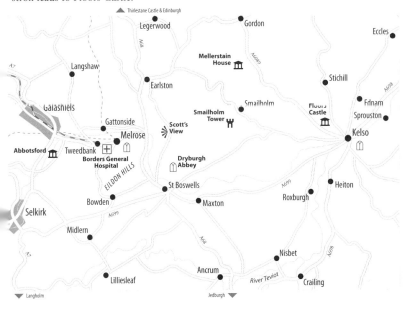

2

Kelso Abbey

Bridge St • Daily dawn–dusk • Free; HES • ☎ 0131 6688081, ⓦ historicenvironment.scot

Once the richest and most powerful abbey in the Borders, **Kelso Abbey** was savaged by the English three times in the sixteenth century: the last (and by far the worst) assault was part of the "Rough Wooing" (see p.585). Such was the extent of the devastation – further compounded by the Reformation – that less survives of Kelso than any of the other Border abbeys. Nevertheless, at first sight it looks pretty impressive, with the heavy Norman west end of the abbey church almost entirely intact. Beyond, little remains, though it is possible to make out the two transepts and towers that gave the abbey the shape of a double cross, unique in Scotland.

Floors Castle

1 mile northwest of Kelso; from the square, follow Roxburgh St to the entrance gate on the outskirts of town, or walk from town centre along Cobby Riverside Walk • Daily: Easter–April 10.30am–4pm, May–Sept daily 10.30am–5pm, Oct 11am–4pm • £12.50; garden and grounds only £8.50 • ☎ 01573 223333, ⓦ roxburgh.net

From Kelso's handsome bridge over the Tweed, you can easily make out the pepper-pot turrets and castellations of **Floors Castle**, the country's largest inhabited building. Designed by William Adam in the 1720s for the first Duke of Roxburghe, the interior still demonstrates his uncluttered style, despite some Victorian modifications, while the superb views from the windows give the place an airy feel. Floors remains the home of the Duke of Roxburghe – his imperious features can be seen in a variety of portraits and photos around the house – so you get to see only ten rooms and the basement. In 1903, the eighth duke married Mary Goelet, the wealthiest heiress in America at the time, and the **paintings**, by Matisse, Augustus John and Odilon Redon, as well as the Brussels and Gobelin **tapestries** she carried off from her family home, are now the castle's highlights. There's an above-average **café**, and you can wander down to the Tweed and see the holly tree that marks the spot where James II was killed by an exploding cannon during the siege of Roxburgh Castle. His son, also James, was crowned James III at the age of 9 at Kelso Abbey.

Mellerstain House

6 miles northwest of Kelso signposted off the A6089 • May–Sept Fri–Mon 12.30–5pm (gardens open 11.30am) • £8.50; gardens only £5 • ☎ 01573 410225, ⓦ mellerstain.com

Mellerstain House represents the very finest of the Adam family's work: William designed the wings in 1725, and his son Robert the main mansion house fifty years later. Inside, it has an elegant, domestic air, lacking in pomposity. Robert Adam's love of columns, delicate roundels and friezes culminates in a stunning sequence of

KELSO FESTIVALS AND EVENTS

Held between Duns and Kelso over three days from the end of May, the **Jim Clark Rally** (ⓦ jimclarkrally.org) is mainland Britain's only on-road rally, and the five races are a major event on the sporting calendar; one popular position from which to watch is nearer to Duns at the Langton splash, where the cars soak spectators by belting through a large puddle.

In Springwood Park during one weekend in mid-June, the **Border Union Dog Show** (ⓦ buas.org/dogs), a canine festival and Crufts qualifier, takes place. Over a hundred horse-riders in period regalia canter cross-country from Kelso to Yetholm and back for the **Civic Week Sat** (ⓦ kelso.bordernet.co.uk/civic-week), a Borders tradition in mid-July. Prior to the ride there are week-long festivities including a ceilidh, fireworks and a torch-lit procession. During October to May at Golf Course Road just north of town, the **Kelso Races** (ⓦ kelso-races.co.uk; £13 entry) feature a small-jump horse-racing circuit with race meets mostly at weekends.

On the last Saturday of each month Kelso hosts a small but appealing farmers' market in the main square with a range of stalls selling fantastic picnic fodder, like artisan goat's cheese and crusty bread.

plaster-moulded, pastel-shaded ceilings, which still preserve the original colours; the **library** is the architectural highlight, with four unusual long panels in plaster relief of classical scenes relegating the books to second place. Perhaps the most intriguing Adam creation is the bathroom in the basement, the only one known to have been designed by him. Notable among the paintings are works by Constable, Gainsborough, Ramsay and Veronese. The house remains the home of the Earl of Haddington, descendant of the Baillie family who acquired the estate in 1642. After the tour you can wander the formal Edwardian gardens, which slope down to the lake, or venture further afield to the Fairy Glen. There's also a children's play area and an excellent tearoom.

2

Smailholm Tower

Sandyknowe Farm; signposted from Smailholm village and 7 miles west of Kelso • April–Sept daily 9.30am–5.30pm • £4.50; HES • ☎ 0131 6688081, ⓦ historicenvironment.scot

Perched alone on a remote rocky outcrop, craggy and evocative **Smailholm Tower** inspired Walter Scott, and conjures up the era of Reivers' raids and border skirmishes. The fifteenth-century tower was designed to withstand sudden attack: the rough rubble walls are 6ft thick and both the entrance – once guarded by a heavy door plus an iron yett (gate) – and the windows are disproportionately small. Inside, make your way up to the roof, where two narrow **wall-walks**, jammed against the barrel-vaulted roof and the crow-stepped gables, provide panoramic views. On the north side the watchman's seat has also survived, stuck against the chimney stack for warmth and with a recess for a lantern.

KELSO AND AROUND

ARRIVAL AND INFORMATION

By bus Buses arrive at the covered stop on Horsemarket, the road leading off from The Square.

Destinations Berwick-upon-Tweed (Mon–Sat 8 daily, 5 on Sun; 50min); Galashiels (Mon–Sat 8 daily, 5 on Sun; 50min); Hawick (Mon–Sat 9 daily; 55min); Jedburgh (Mon–Sat 9 daily; 25min); Melrose (Mon–Sat 8 daily; 5 on Sun; 30min).

Tourist office In a room on the town hall's ground floor in The Square (Easter–June & Sept–Oct Mon–Sat 10am–4pm; July & Aug daily 10am–5pm; ☎ 01573 223464, ⓦ visitkelso.com).

ACCOMMODATION, EATING AND DRINKING

Cobbles Inn 7 Bowmont St ☎ 01573 223548, ⓦ thecobbleskelso.co.uk. This pub has a formidable reputation locally, not just for real ales (supplied by the proprietor's own brewery, Tempest) but also for its top-notch gastro-cuisine. Leaning towards red meat and game, the dinner menu reflects the produce of the region, with dishes like wild wood pigeon, served with black pudding and a blackcurrant and honey gel, part of a four-course £45 menu. Less formal bar meals are also available, including fish and chips for £11. Mon–Thurs 11.30am–11pm, Fri–Sat 11am–late, Sun noon–11pm.

Duncan House Chalkheugh Terrace ☎ 07980 809774, ⓦ duncanhouse.co.uk. Ideally sited, overlooking the Tweed and beyond to Floors Castle, this guesthouse is tastefully presented with period furnishings to match its roomy Georgian dimensions. Ornate open fires, a black lab and a friendly host make for a homely stay. **£75**

★**The Old Priory** Woodmarket ☎ 01573 223030, ⓦ theoldpriorykelso.com. Just off The Square, this is a beautifully furnished Georgian townhouse, full of lived-in character, and with a lush garden out back. There are two double rooms, the best of which overlooks the garden, as well as a two-room connected family suite. **£85**

★**Rutherfords Micropub** 38 The Square ☎ 07803 208460, ⓦ rutherfordsmicropub.co.uk. Fiercely proud of its status as Scotland's "first micropub", the ethos here is all about back-to-basics drinking. No TVs or fruit machines here; it's just quality craft ales poured straight from the cask, artisan gin on tap and hand-made pork pies. Mon 4–9pm, Sun & Tues–Thurs noon–9pm, Fri–Sat noon–10pm.

SHOPPING

Kelso Pottery The Knowes; across the graveyard from Kelso Abbey to the east ☎ 01573 224027. Run by Ian and Elizabeth Hird, who use differing colours of local clay to make a variety of objects, including "Time Tablets", using patterns from other countries, all wrapped in dried local vegetation and fired in their large outdoor pit kiln. Tues–Sat 10am–5pm.

Melrose and around

Tucked in between the Tweed and the gorse-backed Eildon Hills, minuscule **MELROSE** is one of the most appealing towns in the Borders. Centred on its busy little market square, its narrow streets are trimmed by a harmonious ensemble of styles, from pretty little cottages and tweedy shops to high-standing Georgian and Victorian facades. Its chief draw is its ruined **abbey**, by far the finest of the Border abbeys, but it's also perfectly positioned for exploring the Tweed valley. Most of the year it's a sleepy little town, but as the birthplace in 1883 of the **Rugby Sevens** (seven-a-side games; see box below), it swarms during Sevens Week (second week in April) and during the **Borders Book Festival** in mid-June.

Melrose Abbey

Abbey St • Daily: April–Sept 9.30am–5.30pm; Oct–March 10am–4pm • £5.50; HES • ☎ 0131 6688081, ⓦ historicenvironment.scot

The pink- and red-tinted stone ruins of **Melrose Abbey** soar above their riverside surroundings. Founded in 1136 by King David I, Melrose was the first Cistercian settlement in Scotland and grew rich selling wool and hides to Flanders, but its prosperity was fragile: the English repeatedly razed Melrose, most viciously under Richard II in 1385 and the Earl of Hertford in 1545. Most of the present remains date from the intervening period, when extensive rebuilding abandoned the original Cistercian austerity for an elaborate, Gothic style inspired by the abbeys of northern England.

The site is dominated by the **Abbey Church**, which has lost its west front, and whose nave is reduced to the elegant window arches and chapels of the south aisle. Amazingly, the stone **pulpitum** (screen), separating the choir monks from their lay brothers, is preserved. Beyond, the **presbytery** has its magnificent perpendicular window, lierne vaulting and ceiling bosses intact, with the most intricate of curly kale carving on the supporting columns, while in the **south transept**, another fine fifteenth-century window sprouts yet more delicate, foliate tracery. This kind of finely carved detail is repeated everywhere you look. Outside, the exterior sculpture is even more impressive: crouching figures holding scrolls bearing inscriptions such as "He suffered because he willed it". Elsewhere, look for the numerous mischievous **gargoyles**, from peculiar crouching beasts to the pig playing the bagpipes on the roof on the south side of the nave.

Commendator's House

The paltry ruins of Melrose's abbey continue across Cloisters Road where they edge on to the **Commendator's House** (same hours as the abbey), a lovely red-sandstone building converted into a private house in 1590 by the abbey's last commendator, and now housing a modest collection of ecclesiastical bric-a-brac. Beyond the house is the mill-lade, where water used to flow in order to power the abbey's mills; it was also diverted to flush the monks' latrines.

Priorwood Garden

Abbey St • Easter–Oct Mon–Sat 10am–5pm, Sun 1–5pm; Nov & Dec Mon–Sat 10am–4pm; Jan–Easter Tues–Sat 11am–4pm • Free; NTS • ☎ 0131 4580200, ⓦ nts.org.uk

As well as the kempt flower and herb borders, **Priorwood Garden** features a heritage

---

RUGBY SEVENS

With a surprisingly long lineage, **seven-a-side rugby** was initially conceived by a pair of Melrose butchers in 1883 as a fundraiser for their local club and quickly became a regional obsession. Nowadays, all the main Borders towns (and a few beyond) take on a kind of carnival atmosphere as they take turns to host one of ten all-day **tournaments** between April and May, with twelve teams competing for the Kings of the Sevens crown. See ⓦ kingsofthesevens.net.

THE BORDER REIVERS

From the thirteenth to the early seventeenth centuries, the wild, inhospitable border country stretching from the Solway Firth in the west to the Tweed valley in the east, well away from the power bases of both the Scottish and English monarchs, was overrun by outlaws known as the **Border Reivers**, *reive* being a Scots word for plunder. As George MacDonald Fraser put it in his book *The Steel Bonnets*, "The great border tribes of both Scotland and England feuded continuously among themselves. Robbery and blackmail were everyday professions; raiding, arson, kidnapping, murder and extortion were an accepted part of the social system." This, then, was no cross-border dispute, but an open struggle for power among Borders folk. Those who "shook loose the Border" included people from all walks of life – agricultural labourers, gentleman farmers, smallholders, even peers of the realm – for whom theft, raiding, tracking and ambush became second nature.

2

The source of this behaviour was the destruction and devastation wrought upon the region by virtually continual warfare between England and Scotland, and the "slash and burn" policy of the era. With many residents no longer able to find sustenance from the land, crime became the only way to survive. Cattle-rustling, blackmail and kidnapping led to an anarchical mindset, where feuding families would habitually wreak havoc and devastation on each other.

The legacy of the Border Reivers can still be seen today in the region's fortified farms and churches; in the **Common Riding** traditions of many border towns; in the great family names such as Armstrong, Graham, Kerr and Nixon, which once filled the hearts of Borderers with dread; and in the language – the words "blackmail" (first used to describe the protection money paid by farmers to the local clan chiefs) and "bereaved" (originally referred to being robbed) have their roots in the mayhem of this period.

apple orchard, beautifully set within the garden's walled confines with Melrose Abbey standing tall beyond. Unique for its focus on growing flowers for drying, the shop here sells some of the produce that you'll see in the drying area en route to the garden.

Harmony Garden

St Mary's Rd • Jan–Easter Mon–Sat 10am–5pm; Easter–Oct Mon–Sat 10am–5pm, Sun 1–5pm; Nov–Dec Mon–Sat 10am–4pm • Free; NTS • ☎ 0131 4580200, ⓦ nts.org.uk

More of a pleasant picnic spot than an exotic botanical experience, **Harmony Garden** is as memorable for its setting as for its plants. Its roomy croquet lawn lies before the garden's Georgian villa while the borders and vegetable plots form a seductive foreground to the abbey and Eildon Hills, which rise beyond the garden walls.

Dryburgh Abbey

Dryburgh village; 6 miles southeast of Melrose, off the B6356 • Daily: April–Sept 9.30am–5.30pm; Oct–March 10am–4pm • £5.50; HES • ☎ 0131 6688081, ⓦ historicenvironment.scot

Hidden away in a U-bend in the Tweed, the remains of **Dryburgh Abbey** occupy an idyllic position against a hilly backdrop, with ancient cedars, redwoods, beech and lime trees and wide lawns flattering the pinkish-red hues of the stonework. The Premonstratensians, or White Canons, founded the abbey in the twelfth century, but they were never as successful – or apparently as devout – as their Cistercian neighbours in Melrose. Their chronicles detail interminable disputes about land and money: one story relates how a fourteenth-century canon called Marcus flattened the abbot with his fist.

The romantic setting is second to none, but the ruins of the **Abbey Church** are much less substantial than, say, at Melrose or Jedburgh. Virtually nothing survives of the nave, but the transepts have fared better, their chapels now serving as private burial grounds for, among others, **Sir Walter Scott** and Field Marshal Haig.

THE HEART OF ROBERT THE BRUCE

Legend has it that the heart of **Robert I** is buried at Melrose Abbey (his body having been buried at Dunfermline Abbey), and in 1997, when a heart cask was publicly exhumed, this theory received an unexpected boost. However, the burial location was not in accordance with Bruce's own wishes. In 1329, the dying king told his friend, Sir James Douglas, to carry his heart on a Crusade to the Holy Land in fulfilment of an old vow: "Seeing therefore, that my body cannot go to achieve what my heart desires, I will send my heart instead of my body, to accomplish my vow." Douglas tried his best, but was killed fighting the Moors in Spain – and Bruce's heart ended up in Melrose. A commemorative stone laid in 1998 marks its current resting place in the chapterhouse, north of the sacristy.

Scott's View

Drivers and cyclists should approach the abbey via the much-visited **Scott's View**, to the north on the B6356, overlooking the Tweed valley, where the writer and his friends often picnicked and where Scott's horse stopped out of habit during the writer's own funeral procession. The scene inspired J.M.W. Turner's *Melrose* (1831), now on display in the National Gallery of Scotland (see p.76).

Abbotsford

B6360, 2 miles west of Melrose • Daily: April–Oct 10am–5pm, Nov–March 10am–4pm • £8.95 • ☎ 01896 752043, ⓦ scottsabbotsford.co.uk

A stately home designed to satisfy the romantic inclinations of Sir Walter Scott, **Abbotsford** was home to the writer from 1812 until his death twenty years later. Built on the site of a farmhouse Scott bought and subsequently demolished, Abbotsford (as Scott chose to call it) took twelve years to evolve, with the fanciful turrets and castellations of the Scots Baronial exterior incorporating copies of medieval originals: the entrance porch imitates that of Linlithgow Palace and the screen wall in the garden echoes Melrose Abbey's cloister. Scott was proud of his *folie de grandeur*, writing to a friend, "It is a kind of conundrum castle to be sure [which] pleases a fantastic person in style and manner." That said, it was undoubtedly one of the chief causes of Scott's subsequent bankruptcy.

Despite all the exterior pomp, the interior is surprisingly small and poky, with just six rooms open for viewing on the upper floor. Visitors start in the wood-panelled **study**, with its small writing desk made of salvage from the Spanish Armada at which Scott churned out the Waverley novels at a furious rate. The heavy wood-panelled **library** contains Scott's collection of more than nine thousand rare books and an extraordinary assortment of memorabilia, the centrepiece of which is Napoleon's pen case and blotting book. Also here are Rob Roy's purse and *skene dhu* (knife), a lock of Nelson's hair – and of Bonnie Prince Charlie's – plus the latter's *quaich* (drinking cup), Flora Macdonald's pocketbook, the inlaid pearl crucifix that accompanied Mary, Queen of Scots, to the scaffold and even a piece of oatcake found in the pocket of a dead Highlander at Culloden. You can also see Henry Raeburn's famous portrait of Scott in the **drawing room**, and all sorts of weapons – notably Rob Roy's sword, dagger and gun – in the **armoury**. In the barbaric-looking **entrance hall**, hung with elk and wild cattle skulls, and spoils gathered from the battlefield of Waterloo by Scott himself, is a model of the skull of Robert the Bruce and some of Scott's dandyish clothes.

Thirlestane Castle

B6362, Lauder • May–Sept Tues, Wed, Thurs & Sun 10am–3pm (grounds open until 5pm); guided tours only • £8; grounds only £3.50 • ☎ 01578 722430, ⓦ thirlestanecastle.co.uk • Take the signposted footpath from the main square in Lauder

Located ten miles north of Melrose is **Thirlestane Castle**, an imposing Scots

2

WALKING IN THE EILDON HILLS

Ordnance Survey Explorer map 338

From the centre of Melrose, it's a vigorous three mile walk to the top of the **Eildon Hills**, whose triple volcanic peaks are the Central Borders' most distinctive landmark. The tourist office sells a leaflet detailing the hike, which begins about 90yds south of, and up the hill from, the Market Square, along the B6359 to Lilliesleaf.

The hills have been associated with all sorts of legends, beginning with tales of their creation by the wizard-cum-alchemist Michael Scott (1175–1230) who, in the words of Sir Walter Scott, "cleft the Eildon Hills in three". It was here that the mystic **Thomas the Rhymer** received the gift of prophecy from the Faerie Queen, and Arthur and his knights are reckoned to lie asleep deep within the hills, victims of a powerful spell. The ancient Celts, who revered the number three, also considered the site a holy place and maintained their settlements on the slopes long after the Romans' departure.

Melrose is also the starting point for the popular **St Cuthbert's Way**, a sixty-mile walk which finishes at Lindisfarne (Holy Island) on the Northumbrian coast. The tourist office can give details of the walk, though the trail is well marked by yellow arrows from the abbey up over the Eildons to the pretty village of **Bowden**, where you can make a detour to see a twelfth-century kirk, half a mile down the hill from the square, and browse secondhand books and get a fine home-made tea at *The Old School*.

Baronial pile with reddish turrets and castellated towers. Begun by John Maitland in the late sixteenth century, when he became Lord Chancellor of Scotland, and still owned by the family, the castle's somewhat undistinguished interior is redeemed by the extravagant plasterwork of the Restoration ceilings and a wealth of domestic detail from the Victorian period, including a wonderland of children's toys. There's also an adventure playground for those with children, and a woodland walk.

ARRIVAL AND INFORMATION   MELROSE AND AROUND

By bus Buses to Melrose stop in Buccleuch St, a few paces from the abbey ruins and the tourist office opposite. Destinations Berwick-upon-Tweed (Mon–Sat 8 daily, 6 on Sun; 1hr 10min); Duns (Mon–Sat 8 daily, 6 on Sun; 50min); Edinburgh (Mon–Sat every 30min, Sun hourly; 2hr 20min); Galashiels (Mon–Sat every 30min, Sun hourly; 20min); Kelso (Mon–Sat 8 daily, 5 on Sun; 30min); Jedburgh (school days only, 1 daily; 40min); Peebles (Mon–Sat every 30min, Sun hourly; 1hr 10min); Selkirk (Mon–Sat hourly, 3 on Sun; 20min).

Tourist office A good source of walking maps is found at the tourist office at Abbey House, Abbey St, opposite the entrance to the Abbey (Easter–Oct, Mon–Sat 10am–5pm, Sun 1–5pm; 01896 820178).

ACCOMMODATION

Braidwood Buccleuch St 01896 822488, braidwoodmelrose.co.uk. A comfortable, early Victorian cottage guesthouse ideally sited between the town centre and its abbey. Cheaper rooms have private facilities in the hall or £5 extra gets you an en-suite upgrade. **£65**

Dunfermline House 3 Buccleuch St 01896 822411, dunfermlinehouse.co.uk. Standard townhouse B&B with en-suite rooms that look on to the garden or across to the abbey. The decor here might be a bit 1980s in style but everything's clean and in good order. **£65**

Gibson Caravan Park Gibson Park; off the B6374 just west of the centre 01896 822969, caravanclub.co.uk. This lovely, central little campsite opposite the rugby ground caters mostly to caravans although tents are welcome too. Open all year. Pitch **£11**, per person **£8.50**

★Old Bank House 27 Buccleuch St 01896 823712, oldbankhousemelrose.co.uk. Tastefully furnished Victorian B&B with charming hosts and three pristinely maintained and comfy en-suite rooms. The fine Scottish or vegetarian cooked breakfasts are served on Spode crockery in the old bank manager's office. **£65**

Townhouse Market Square 01896 822645, thetownhousemelrose.co.uk. Upmarket, central hotel with tasteful, modern decor and generously proportioned en-suite rooms that come in single, double and family sizes (£17 extra). Avoid the street-facing suites to ensure a peaceful night's sleep. **£132**

EATING AND DRINKING

★ **Abbey Fine Wines & The Cellar Coffee Shop** Abbey St ☎01896 823224, ⓦabbeyfinewines.co.uk. Stocking the finest range of wines and spirits in the Borders, there are always bottles opened and ready for sampling here. You can pick any bottle you fancy and enjoy it in the café at the back of the shop with their £11 speciality cheese platter. Mon–Sat 9.30am–4.30pm; shop closes 5.30pm.

Hoebridge Inn Hoebridge Rd East, Gattonside; 500yds past Melrose Abbey and across the old suspension bridge ☎01896 823082, ⓦthehoebridgeinn.com. Once a bobbin mill, this restaurant retains a timeless charm thanks to its deep rubble walls and simple furnishings. Its menu offers some classic French-style choices using Scots produce such as duck breast with cauliflower purée and blackcurrant jus for £17. Wed–Sat 5.30pm–9.30pm.

Marmion's Brasserie Buccleuch St ☎01896 822245, ⓦmarmionsbrasserie.co.uk. While this popular all-day bistro might have overdone it a bit with pine cladding, it still manages to conjure up a peppy atmosphere of an evening. The menu offers plenty of choice: dependable meat dishes as well as a surprisingly adventurous selection of vegetarian mains like the cauliflower and leek open lasagne for £12.50. Mon–Sat 9am–9pm.

Ship Inn East Port ☎01896 822190, ⓦshipinnmelrose .co.uk. The liveliest pub in town, especially on certain Saturday afternoons when Melrose rugby supporters file in before and after the games. While it could certainly do with some redecoration, its saving grace is the beer garden out back. Mon–Thurs 11am–11pm, Fri–Sat 11am–1am, Sun noon–11pm.

ENTERTAINMENT

The Wynd 7 The Wynd, Buccleuch St ☎01896 820028, ⓦsites.google.com/site/thewyndtheatre. Melrose's very own pint-sized theatre, tucked away down an alleyway, north off the main square, shows films and puts on classic, jazz and folk concerts as well as live drama. Box office Tues & Thurs 11am–1pm.

SIR WALTER SCOTT

Walter Scott (1771–1832) was born to a solidly bourgeois family in Edinburgh. Crippled by polio, he was sent by his parents to recuperate at his grandfather's farm in Smailholm, where the boy's imagination was fired by his relatives' tales of derring-do, the violent history of the Borders retold amid the rugged landscape that he spent long summer days exploring. Throughout the 1790s he transcribed hundreds of old Border ballads, publishing a three-volume collection entitled *Minstrelsy of the Scottish Borders* in 1802. An instant success, *Minstrelsy* was followed by Scott's own *Lay of the Last Minstrel*, a narrative poem whose strong story and rose-tinted regionalism proved very popular.

More **poetry** was to come, most successfully *Marmion* (1808) and *The Lady of the Lake* (1810), not to mention an eighteen-volume edition of the works of John Dryden and nineteen volumes of Jonathan Swift. However, despite having two paid jobs, one as **Sheriff-Depute** of Selkirkshire, the other as clerk to the Court of Session in Edinburgh, his finances remained shaky.

From 1813, Scott was writing to pay the bills and poured out a veritable flood of **historical novels** using his extensive knowledge of Scottish history and folklore. He produced his best work within the space of ten years: *Waverley* (1814), *The Antiquary* (1816), *Rob Roy* and *The Heart of Midlothian* (both 1818), as well as two notable novels set in England, *Ivanhoe* (1819) and *Kenilworth* (1821). In 1824 he returned to Scottish tales with *Redgauntlet*, the last of his quality work. As Scott's financial problems increased, the quality of his writing deteriorated, and the effort broke his health. His last years were plagued by illness, and in 1832 he died at Abbotsford and was buried at Dryburgh Abbey (see p.123).

Although Scott's interests were diverse, his historical novels focused mostly on the Jacobites, whose loyalty to the Stewarts had riven Scotland since the "Glorious Revolution" of 1688. That the nation was prepared to be entertained by such tales was essentially a matter of timing: by the 1760s it was clear that the Jacobite cause was lost for good and Scotland, emerging from its isolated medievalism, had been firmly welded into the United Kingdom. Thus its turbulent history and independent spirit were safely in the past, and ripe for romancing – as shown by the arrival of King George IV in Edinburgh during 1822 decked out in Highland dress. Yet for Sir Walter the romance was tinged with a genuine sense of loss. Loyal to the Hanoverians, he still grieved for Bonnie Prince Charlie; he welcomed a commercial Scotland but lamented the passing of feudal ties, and so his heroes are transitional, fighting men of action superseded by bourgeois figures searching for a clear identity.

Galashiels

In a tour of the region, it's hard to avoid going through "Gala", a hard-working textile town four miles west of Melrose whose grey-green workers' terraces spread along the valley of the Gala Water near its junction with the Tweed. Hopes for a return to prosperous times were given a much-needed boost after the 2015 opening of the Borders Railway, re-linking Gala with Edinburgh after a 45-year hiatus. Its main street runs parallel with the river, the southern end cheered by a melodramatic equestrian statue of a Border Reiver above the town's war memorial. The long-demolished New Gala House, a mansion that stood at the top of the town, was taken over during World War II by Edinburgh girls' school, **St Trinnean's**; the artist Ronald Searle met two of the pupils in 1941, inspiration for the unruly schoolgirls in his St Trinian's novels.

ARRIVAL AND INFORMATION   GALASHIELS

By train The train station is just east of the town centre, across the river beside the A7.

Destination Edinburgh (Mon–Sat every 30min, Sun 1 hourly; 50min).

By bus The region's principal bus station is just east of the town centre, across the river and near the train station.

Destinations Edinburgh (Mon–Sat every 30min, Sun 1 hourly; 2hr); Peebles (Mon–Sat 2 hourly, 1 on Sun; 40min); Hawick (Mon–Sat 2 hourly, 1 on Sun; 35min);

Jedburgh (Mon–Fri 1 daily; 50min); Kelso (Mon–Sat 8–10 daily, 5 on Sun; 55min); Langholm (Mon–Sat 2 hourly, 1 on Sun; 1hr 15min); Melrose (Mon–Sat 2 hourly, 1 on Sun; 20min); Selkirk (Mon–Sat 2 hourly, 1 on Sun; 15min).

Tourist information There's no tourist office in town, but there are plenty of leaflets at the library (Lawyers Brae, south of the river; Mon, Wed & Fri 9.30am–5pm, Tues and Thurs 9.30am–7pm, Sat 9am–12.30pm; ☎01896 664170).

Peebles and around

Fast, wide, tree-lined and fringed with grassy banks, the Tweed looks at its best at **PEEBLES**, a handsome royal burgh that sits on the north bank, 22 miles due south of the capital. The town has a genteel, relaxed air, its wide, handsome High Street bordered by houses in a medley of architectural styles, mostly dating from Victorian times. A steady stream of day-trippers from the capital, as well as the large population of commuter locals, makes this an affluent place; consequently, there are plenty of enticing shops, restaurants and tearooms.

Nearby, hills, drove roads and a disused railway line make this a perfect starting point for easy-going treks into the lush green landscape. Upstream from Peebles the Tweed gradually narrows as the hills tighten up on either side and settlements become small and sparse. Lush fields and deciduous trees thrive in the valley floor while the surrounding high peaks offer a foreboding blanket of heather interrupted frequently by over-regular spruce plantations.

Old Parish Church

High St • Daily 10am–4pm • Free • ☎01721 723986, ⓦ topcop.org.uk

The soaring crown spire of the **Old Parish Church** rises up at the western end of the High Street and, inside, the church has some unusual features such as the elegant oak, bronze and engraved-glass entrance screen and 22 modern oil paintings illustrating the Scriptures. Suspended from the ceiling are tattered Napoleonic flags, emblems of 1816, the year the Peebleshire Militia disbanded.

Tweeddale Museum and Gallery

Chambers Institute, High St • Mon–Fri 10.30am–12.30pm & 1–4pm, Sat 9.30am–12.30pm • Free • ☎01721 724820, ⓦ scotborders.gov.uk

Housed in the Chambers Institute, presented to the town by local worthy William Chambers in 1859, the **Tweeddale Museum and Gallery** is dedicated to the enlightenment of his neighbours. The benefactor stuffed the place with casts of the

WALKS AROUND PEEBLES

Ordnance Survey Explorer maps 337 and 338

A series of footpaths snakes through the rough-edged burns, bare peaks and deep wooded hills of the surrounding Peebles. The five-mile **Sware Trail** is one of the easiest and most scenic, weaving west along the north bank of the river and looping back to the south. On the way, it passes **Neidpath Castle**, a gaunt medieval tower house perched high above the river on a rocky bluff. The walk also goes by the splendid skew rail bridge, part of the Glasgow line, which was finished in 1850 and closed in 1969. Other, longer footpaths follow the old drove roads, like the thirteen-mile haul to **St Mary's Loch** or the fourteen-mile route to Selkirk via Traquair House (see p.130). For either of these, you'll need an Ordnance Survey map, a compass and proper hiking gear, while for a more gentle stroll there's a three-mile amble downstream on the Tweed's southern banks which takes you to the privately owned **Kailzie Gardens.**

2

world's most famous sculptures and, although most were lost long ago, today's "Secret Room", once the Museum Room, contains two handsome friezes: one a copy of the Elgin Marbles taken from the Parthenon; the other of the Triumph of Alexander, originally cast in 1812 to honour Napoleon.

Dawyck Botanic Garden

Stobo, 8 miles southwest of Peebles on the B712 • Daily: Feb & Nov 10am–4pm; March & Oct 10am–5pm; April–Sept 10am–6pm • £6.50 • ☎ 01721 760254, ⓦ rbge.org.uk

An outstation of the Royal Botanic Garden in Edinburgh, the masterpiece of seventeenth-century horticultural passion and creativity that is **Dawyck Botanic Garden** ranks among the world's finest arboreta. Hosting species from climatically similar corners of the globe, the 62-acre garden was the culmination of early plant-hunting expeditions, particularly those by David Douglas (of Douglas fir fame). One of the best times to visit is in spring, when, as you enter the garden through the ultra-modern visitor centre, you're welcomed by the feast that is the Azalea Walk in full bloom. Over the brow of the hill, 300-year-old redwoods tower over a gushing burn that feeds the roots of gigantic gunnera plants. In autumn, sorbis and acers mount a flaring foliage of reds, oranges and yellows.

Kailzie Gardens

3 miles east of Peebles on the B7062 • Daily: April–Oct 10am–5pm; Nov–March dawn–dusk • ☎ 01721 720007, ⓦ kailziegardens.com • £5 (less in winter)

Kailzie Gardens encompasses fifteen acres of pleasant, partly formal gardens including a burnside walk, a fishable pond, a delightful walled garden (not open winter), and a pleasant wood-panelled tearoom. In the dedicated viewing hut, you can watch live CCTV pictures of the ospreys that have been successfully introduced into the nearby forest.

Robert Smail's & Sons Printing Works

High St, Innerleithen, 7 miles east of Peebles on the A72 • Easter–Oct Fri–Sat & Mon 11am–5pm, Sun 1–5pm; tours last 1hr • £6.50; NTS • ☎ 0131 4580200, ⓦ nts.org.uk

Little changed since its establishment in 1866, **Robert Smail's Printing Works** is now a living, working museum, offering an enjoyable insight into the world of Victorian printing. Originally powered by watermill, the great machines' huge belts and flywheels are now electrically powered, about the only concession to progress here. Tours also take in the case room upstairs where you get the chance to set and print your own block. Most fascinating of all, however, is the archive of every single job the Smails printed for nearly a hundred years as well as wage books, ledgers and other ephemera.

Traquair House

7 miles southeast of Peebles on the B7062 • Daily: Easter–Sept 11am–5pm; Oct 11am–4pm; Nov Sat & Sun 11am–3pm • £8.70; grounds only £4.50 • ☎ 01896 830323, ⓦ traquair.co.uk

Peeping out from the trees just south of Innerleithen, **Traquair House** is the oldest continuously inhabited house in Scotland, with the present line of owners – the Maxwell Stuarts – having lived here since 1491. The first laird of Traquair inherited an elementary fortified tower, which his powerful descendants gradually converted into a mansion that was visited, it is said, by 27 monarchs, including Mary, Queen of Scots.

Traquair's main appeal is in its ancient shape and structure. The whitewashed facade is strikingly handsome, with narrow windows and trim turrets surrounding the tiniest of front doors. Inside, you can see the original vaulted cellars, where locals once hid their cattle from raiders, and the twisting main staircase as well as the earlier medieval version, later a secret escape route for persecuted Catholics until the Emancipation Act freed things up in 1829. Of the furniture and fittings, it's not any particular piece that impresses, but rather the accumulation of family possessions and revealing letters that give a real insight into the Maxwell Stuarts' revolving-door fortunes and eccentricities. In the **museum room** is a wealth of treasures, including a rosary and crucifix owned by Mary, Queen of Scots and the cloak worn by the earl of Nithsdale during his dramatic escape from the Tower of London, where he was under sentence of death for his part in the Jacobite Rising of 1715. The earl was saved by his wife who got his jailers drunk and smuggled him out disguised as a maid in spite of his red beard.

It's worth sparing time for the surrounding **gardens**, where you'll find a **hedge maze**, several craft workshops and the **Traquair House Brewery** dating back to 1566, which was revived in 1965 and claims to be the only British brewery that still ferments totally in oak. You can learn about the brewery and taste the ales in the Brewery Shop.

There's also an attractive café serving above-average snacks in an estate cottage on the redundant avenue, which leads to the locked **Bear Gates**; Bonnie Prince Charlie departed the house through the gates, and the then-owner promised to keep them locked until a Stuart should ascend the throne.

ARRIVAL AND INFORMATION

PEEBLES AND AROUND

By bus The bus terminal is next to the main car park just north of the eastern end of the main shopping street.
Destinations Edinburgh (2 hourly, 1 on Sun; 1hr); Galashiels (2 hourly, 1 on Sun; 40min); Melrose (2 hourly, 1 on Sun; 1hr).
Tourist office A well-stocked tourist office is in the High

St (Easter to mid-June & Sept to mid-Dec Mon–Sat 9am–5pm, Sun 11am–4pm; mid-Dec to Easter Mon–Fri 9am–5pm, Sat 9am–4pm; mid-June to Aug Mon–Sat 9am–5.30pm, Sun 11am–4pm; ☎ 01721 728095), with 24hr virtual tourist information available by way of a touch-screen tablet stuck onto the shop window.

ACCOMMODATION

Glentress Forest Lodges The Peel Gateway, entrance to Glentress, 2 miles east of Peebles on the A72 ☎ 01721 721007, ⓦ glentressforestlodges.co.uk. Like sections of upturned boat hulls, these simple but attractive wooden huts are arranged in clusters, somehow resembling a prehistoric settlement. The accommodation is basic; some benches to sit/sleep on, a door and a window, but there's also a communal kitchen and a generous firewood supply. Sleeps five at a push. **£46**

Green Tree Hotel 41 Eastgate ☎ 01721 720582, ⓦ greentreehotel.com. An economical option in the heart of town, between the bus station and the High St,

with a choice of singles, doubles and family rooms. All are perfectly comfortable with simple decor and come with en suite and breakfast included. **£80**

Kingsmuir House Springhill Rd ☎ 01721 724413 ⓦ kingsmuirhouse.co.uk. Dating from the 1850s, this generously proportioned villa offers two exemplary guest rooms with well-coordinated decor and traditional furnishings; just 2min from the main drag and overlooking Victoria Park across the Tweed from the centre. **£140**

Rosetta Holiday Park Rosetta Rd ☎ 01721 720770, ⓦ www.rosettaholidaypark.com. The only campsite in

MOUNTAIN BIKING IN GLENTRESS FOREST AND INNERLEITHEN

Glentress Forest, two miles east of Peebles on the A72, has some of the best opportunities for mountain biking in Scotland. Not only are there five superb, carefully crafted, purpose-built trails, colour-coded for difficulty, there's a fantastic bike centre at the entrance to the forest called the **Peel Gateway**. This is a great place for mountain bikers, with changing rooms and showers, a café and a shop filled with spares as well as bike rental from Alpine Bikes. If you fancy staying several days it's worth checking out the timber wigwams (see opposite) near the entrance. There are more trails just a few miles southeast of Glentress near **Innerleithen**, geared towards more advanced riders, with bike rental available in Innerleithen. Glentress and Innerleithen are collectively one of seven forest biking centres in southern Scotland, known collectively as the **7stanes** (⟨W⟩7stanesmountainbiking.com).

BIKE RENTAL

Bike hire can be pricey hereabouts, ranging from £20 to £80 per day although child bikes are just £15. Alpine Bikes have two centres in the area, one is based in a disused church on Peebles Rd, **Innerleithen** (Mon–Fri 9.30am–5.30pm, Sat & Sun 9am–5.30pm; ⟨T⟩01896 830880, ⟨W⟩alpinebikes.com) and the other at the Peel Gateway at the entrance to **Glentress Forest**, two miles east of Peebles on the A72 (Mon–Fri 9.30am–6pm, Sat–Sun 9am–6pm; ⟨T⟩01721 724522, ⟨W⟩tweedvalley bikehire.com).

Peebles not next to a main road, it's peacefully set on the northwest edge of town, surrounded by mature woods, with hike-able drove roads up the Meldon Hills starting almost from the site entrance. There's a bar that serves food in the evenings, and, for kids, a TV/pool room as well as a walled playground. April–Oct. Per pitch £12

Traquair 7 miles east of Peebles, on the B7062 ⟨T⟩01896 830323, ⟨W⟩traquair.co.uk. Most visitors come here as a day-trip from Peebles, but if you're really taken by the place, you can stay in one of its three double guest rooms, exquisitely decked out with antiques and four-posters, on a bed-and-breakfast basis. £190

EATING AND DRINKING

★**Bridge Inn** 72 Port Brae ⟨T⟩01721 720589. With its attractive mock-Tudor, dormer frontage, this traditional pub cuts a fine figure in the Peebles skyline. Inside, its classic decor and cosy seating arrangements complement the wide range of real ales and whiskies on offer while out back there's a sunny terrace looking on to the river. Mon–Wed 11am–midnight, Thurs–Sat 11am–1am, Sun noon–midnight.

Coltman's Deli & Kitchen 71–73 High St ⟨T⟩01721 720405, ⟨W⟩coltmans.co.uk. Passing through the narrow alley next to their immaculate deli, you'll find yourself at *Coltman's*, Peebles' most sophisticated dining experience. While most of the ingredients are seasonal and sourced locally, the cuisine thinks globally with imagination and originality. Fish enthusiasts might try the loin of coley with chorizo then move on to the brioche bread-and-butter pudding with marmalade ice cream; part of the two-course, £23 set menu. Sun–Wed 10am–5pm, Thurs–Sat 10am–10pm.

★**Leaven Deli** 6 Newby Court, just off the High St near the tourist office ⟨T⟩01721 721088, ⟨W⟩leavendelipeebles.wix.com/leavendeli. Hidden in a tiny courtyard just off the main drag, this not-for-profit social enterprise offers up fresh loaves, artisan cheeses and a few deli treats as well as light lunches and coffees that can be enjoyed in the sun trap outside. Mon–Sat 8.30am–5pm.

Osso 43 Eastgate ⟨T⟩01721 724477, ⟨W⟩ossorestaurant .com. Contemporary restaurant, just east of the Eastgate theatre, that does fancy lunches like their French toast with bacon and maple syrup for £7, and moves into more creative territory in the evening with dishes like crab and cheddar tart with fennel salad and chips for £15. Daily 10am–4.30pm, Tues–Sat 6–9pm.

The Prince of India 84–86 High St ⟨T⟩01721 724455, ⟨W⟩princeofindiarestaurant.com. Long-established and thriving Indian restaurant with a wide choice of robust curries, many with unashamedly liberal spicing. With mains ranging from £10–16, it's a tad more expensive than your average curry house but well worth forking out for. Daily 5pm & 11.30pm.

ENTERTAINMENT

Eastgate Theatre and Arts Centre Eastgate ⟨T⟩01721 725777, ⟨W⟩eastgatearts.com. This former church east of High St has been converted into a modern arts space with an eclectic programme of world, folk and light orchestral music as well as theatre, dance and cinema performances. Art exhibitions are, naturally, here too, sited beside the in-house café. Box office: Mon–Sat 10am–5pm.

Yarrow Water valley

Cutting through the hills southeast of Peebles is the **Yarrow Water valley**, with a river system that, along with the Ettrick Water, fed the once prosperous mills of Selkirk. First stop upstream is **Bowhill House**, a part Georgian, part Victorian stately home with one of the finest private art collections in the county and a pleasant lakeside walk. For more strenuous exercise, head three miles west on the A708 to the parking area at Yarrowford, a starting point for some of the Borders' finest hikes. From here, you can reach the hilltop cairns of **The Three Brethren** (1530ft), whose summit offers excellent views over this remote corner of the Borders. You can also link up with stretches of the Southern Upland Way by heading east down through Yair Hill Forest, or by following an old drove road west to the Cheese Well at Minchmoor and ending up at Traquair House near Innerleithen (see p.130).

St Mary's Loch and Loch of the Lowes

Sixteen miles west of Selkirk on the A708 lies the Yarrow's source, a pair of icy lakes: **St Mary's Loch**, and its diminutive neighbour, **Loch of the Lowes**, separated by a slender isthmus – home to the Tibbie Shiels Inn – and magnificently set beneath the surrounding hills. This spot was popular with the nineteenth-century Scottish literati, especially Walter Scott and James Hogg, the "Shepherd Poet of Ettrick", who eulogized "the bosom of the lonely Lowes".

For a short and enjoyable walk, follow the path from the inn along the east side of St Mary's Loch into the forest. Eventually this meets up with the Southern Upland Way from where you can head across the moors north to Traquair House or south to the valley of the **Ettrick Water**, both strenuous hikes that require an Ordnance Survey map, a compass and proper clothing.

Grey Mare's Tail Waterfall

If you're continuing west along the A708 into Dumfries and Galloway, don't miss the 200ft **Grey Mare's Tail Waterfall** (NTS), four miles southwest of Loch of the Lowes, which tumbles down a rocky crevasse as you descend into Dumfriesshire. The base of the falls is approached by a precipitous footpath along the left side of the stream, a ten-minute clamber each way from the road.

Bowhill House

3 miles west of Selkirk on the A708 • **House** Tours only Easter, May & Aug bank holidays and all July Wed–Mon 11.30am, 12.30pm, 1.30pm & 2.30pm • **Estate** Easter–Sept Mon–Fri 10am–4pm, Sat–Sun 10am–5pm • House & Estate £10, Estate only £4.50 • ☏ 01750 22204, ⓦ bowhillhouse.co.uk

The property of the Duke of Buccleuch, a seriously wealthy man, the fine part Georgian, part Victorian mansion **Bowhill House** is well known for its art collection and connections to Sir Walter Scott, who visited regularly. There's a room dedicated to the writer, with Henry Raeburn's 1826 portrait of Scott on display alongside various artefacts relating to the author. Other famous painters' works are on display here too, including portraits by Reynolds, Gainsborough and a Canaletto cityscape, while the drawing room has Boulle furniture, Meissen tableware plus paintings by Ruysdael, Leandro Bassano and Claude Lorraine.

The adjoining estate is criss-crossed by scenic paths that loop around a pair of forest-fringed lakes. The grounds also shelter the Bowhill Theatre, a seventy-seat auditorium housed in what was once the estate's cold storage larder with productions ranging from musical comedies to children's fables. Details of plays are listed on the website.

Jedburgh

Just ten miles north of the English border, **JEDBURGH** nestles in the lush valley of Jed Water near its confluence with the Teviot out on the edge of the wild Cheviot Hills. During the interminable wars between England and Scotland, Jedburgh was the quintessential frontier town, a heavily garrisoned royal burgh incorporating a mighty castle and abbey. Though the castle was destroyed by the Scots in 1409 to keep it out of the hands of the English, its memory has been kept alive by stories. In 1285, for example, King Alexander III was celebrating his wedding feast in the great hall when a ghostly apparition predicted his untimely death and a bloody civil war; sure enough, he died in a hunting accident shortly afterwards and chaos ensued. Today, Jedburgh is the first place of any size that you come to on the A68 if crossing over Carter Bar from England, and as such gets quite a bit of passing tourist trade. The ruined **abbey** is the main event, though a stroll round the old town centre is a pleasant way to while away an hour or so.

2

Jedburgh Abbey

Abbey Bridge End • Daily: April–Sept 9.30am–5.30pm, Oct–March 10am–4pm • £5.50; HES • ☎ 01316 688081, ⓦ historicenvironment.scot

Despite its ruinous state, **Jedburgh Abbey** still dominates the town, particularly when approached from the south. Founded in the twelfth century as an Augustinian priory by King David I, it's the best preserved of all the Border abbeys, its vast church towering over a sloping site right in the centre of town, beside Jed Water. The abbey was burnt and badly damaged on a number of occasions, but by far the worst destruction was inflicted by the English in the 1540s. By this time, the contemplative way of life had already fallen prey to corruption and only a few canons remained living in the ruins of the abbey, until it was finally closed in 1560. The abbey church remained the parish kirk for another three centuries and as a result has survived particularly intact.

All that remains of the conventual buildings where the canons lived are the foundations and basic ground plan, but then Jedburgh's chief glory is really its **Abbey Church**, which remains splendidly preserved. As you enter via the west door, the three-storey nave's perfectly proportioned parade of columns and arches lies before you, a fine example of the transition from Romanesque to Gothic design, with pointed window arches surmounted by the round-headed arches of the triforium, which, in turn, support the lancet windows of the clerestory. Be sure you climb up the narrow staircase in the west front to the balcony overlooking the nave, where you can contemplate how the place must have looked all decked out for the marriage of Alexander III to Yolande de Dreux in 1285.

Jedburgh Castle Jail

Castlegate; a 5min walk signposted from the main square • Easter–Oct Mon–Sat 10am–4.30pm, Sun 1–4pm • Free • ☎ 01835 863254, ⓦ museumsgalleriesscotland.org.uk

An impressive castellated nineteenth-century pile, **Jedburgh Castle Jail**, as its name suggests, was built on the site of the old royal castle. As well as detailed information about Jedburgh's history, there's a fascinating insight into conditions in jail, deportations, crime and punishment. The cells themselves are, for the period, remarkably comfortable, reflecting the influence of reformer John Howard.

Mary, Queen of Scots House

Queen St • March–Nov Mon–Sat 10am–4.30pm, Sun noon–4.30pm • Free • ☎ 01835 863331, ⓦ marie-stuart.co.uk

Despite the name, it's unlikely that Mary actually stayed in the sixteenth-century house

2

JEDBURGH FESTIVALS

Jedburgh is at its busiest during the town's two main festivals. The **Common Riding**, or Callants' Festival, takes place from late June to early July, when the young people of the town mount up and ride out to check the burgh boundaries, a reminder of more troubled days when Jedburgh was subject to English raids. In similar spirit, early February sees the day-long **Jedburgh Hand Ba'** game, an all-male affair between the "uppies" (those born above Market Place) and the "doonies" (those born below). The aim of the game is to get a hay-stuffed leather ball – originally representing the head of an Englishman – from one end of town to the other.

known as **Mary, Queen of Scots House**, though she did visit the town in 1566 for the Assizes. The attempt to unravel her complex life is cursory, the redeeming features being a copy of her death mask and one of the few surviving portraits of the Earl of Bothwell, her third husband.

ARRIVAL AND INFORMATION   JEDBURGH

By bus Buses pick up and drop off by the car park on Canongate near the town centre.

Destinations Edinburgh (Mon–Sat 7 daily, 5 on Sat, 4 on Sun; 1hr 50min); Galashiels (Mon–Sat hourly, 6 on Sun; 45min); Hawick (Mon–Fri 8 daily, 6 on Sat; 25min); Kelso (Mon–Fri 8 daily, 3 on Sat; 25min); Melrose (Mon–Sat hourly, 6 on Sun; 30min).

Tourist office On Murray's Green across the road from the Abbey; stocks the Jedburgh Town Trail leaflet (Easter to mid-June & Sept–Oct Mon–Sat 9am–5pm, Sun 10am–4pm; mid-June to Aug Mon–Sat 9am–5.30pm, Sun 10am–5pm; Nov to Easter Mon–Sat 9am–4pm; ☎ 01835 863170, ⟨w⟩ jedburgh.org.uk).

ACCOMMODATION

Jedwater Caravan Park 4 miles south of Jedburgh, signposted off the A68 ☎ 01835 840219, ⟨w⟩ jedwater .co.uk. The cheaper and more secluded choice of two campsites nearby, with a pleasant riverside setting. It's a family-orientated site, sizeable enough to have a shop, a decent play park and a few cute farm animals. March–Oct. Per pitch **£22**

Meadhon House 48 Castlegate ☎ 01835 862504, ⟨w⟩ meadhon.co.uk. Pronounced "mawn", this is the

finest of several B&Bs among Castlegate's pleasant and antique row of houses, with tasteful en-suite rooms. **£68**

Willow Court The Friars; from Market Place follow Exchange St and take the first right into Friarsgate ☎ 01835 863702, ⟨w⟩ willowcourtjedburgh.co.uk. This five-star B&B, a 2min walk from the centre, has three frill-packed en suites offering the highest level of comfort in Jedburgh. **£80**

EATING AND DRINKING

Border Meringues Unit 1, Old Station Yard, Edinburgh Rd; 0.5 mile north of the Abbey opposite the Shell garage ☎ 01835 863383, ⟨w⟩ border-meringues.co.uk. An unlikely setting for a café/cake shop in an anonymous industrial estate building on the outskirts of town, but locals go out of their way for this place. There is all manner of cakes and tray bakes here, with prices starting at £2. Mon–Sat 10.30am–4.30pm.

★ **The Capon Tree Town House** 61 High St ☎ 01835

869596, ⟨w⟩ thecapontree.com. Part fine dining restaurant, part wine bar, this place conjures up the best plates in town from breakfast to supper. The lunch menu is made up of crowd-pleasers like posh fish and chips for £11, while the evening menu plays around with the classics like the Dijon crusted lamb with mint jus and a black pudding mash for £18.50. Tues–Thurs 10am–11pm, Fri–Sat 10am–1am, Sun noon–4pm.

Hawick and around

Despite being a busy, working mill town, **HAWICK** (pronounced "hoyk") has a surprising number of visitors, the majority of whom come in search of bargains from its woollen knitwear factory outlets. Its textiles industry has been the mainstay of the economy for the last few hundred years, but the town's true heyday came with the advent of steam power which saw a rapid expansion from the town's fifty or so watermills and the formation of knitwear brands like Pringle, Lyle & Scott and Peter Scott. Much of the Victorian architecture here reflects the prosperity of this period, particularly the Scots Baronial town hall halfway down the high street. The town's pre-industrial fortunes were not so good, though one exception is a skirmish in 1514 when the local Hawick callants (boys) defeated a small English force and captured their banner, an event immortalized by the statue at the end of the high street.

Hermitage Castle

2

16 miles south of Hawick, signposted off the B6399 • April–Sept daily 9.30am–5.30pm • £4.50; HES • ☎ 0131 6688081, ⓦ historicenvironment.scot

Bleak and forbidding, **Hermitage Castle** is bedevilled by all sorts of horrifying legends: one owner, William Douglas, starved his prisoners to death, while Lord de Soulis, another occupant, engaged the help of demons to fortify the castle in defiance of the king, Robert the Bruce, who had him boiled to death. From the outside, the castle remains an imposing structure, its heavy walls topped by stepped gables and a tidy corbelled parapet. However, the apparent homogeneity is deceptive: certain features were invented during a Victorian restoration, a confusing supplement to the ad hoc alterations that had already transformed the fourteenth-century original. The ruinous interior is a bit of a letdown, but look out for the tight Gothic doorways and gruesome dungeon.

ARRIVAL AND INFORMATION

HAWICK AND AROUND

By bus The main bus stand is just north of the centre in Mart St.

Destinations Edinburgh (Mon–Sat half-hourly, Sun hourly; 2hr 5min); Galashiels (Mon–Sat half-hourly, Sun hourly; 40min); Jedburgh (Mon–Fri 8 daily, 6 on Sat; 25min); Kelso (Mon–Fri 8 daily, 3 on Sat; 25min); Langholm (Mon–Sat hourly, 4 on Sun; 40min); Selkirk (Mon–Sat half-

hourly, Sun hourly; 20min).

Tourist office The tourist office is in Tower Mill, a converted watermill housing a cinema and a good café-bar at the southern end of High St (Mon & Wed 10am–5.30pm, Tues & Thurs 10am–6.15pm, Fri–Sat 10am–7.15pm, Sun noon–2.45pm; ☎ 01450 373993).

EATING

Turnbull's The Horse Monument, 4 Oliver Place ☎ 01450 372020, ⓦ turnbullshop.com. A family business since 1855, this characterful deli/café is an essential stop if you're in Hawick. As well as serving light lunches (from

around £5) and the town's best coffee, beautifully packaged, old-fashioned products are on sale such as the shop's own blended whisky and peppermint sweets known as Hawick Balls. Mon–Sat 9.30am–5pm, Sun 11am–4pm.

Dumfries and Galloway

CAERLAVEROCK CASTLE

Dumfries and Galloway

Scotland's southwest corner, now known as Dumfries and Galloway, is a region set apart, with few people bothering to exit the main Carlisle–Glasgow motorway that runs through the county. Yet the area has stately homes, deserted hills and ruined abbeys to compete with the best of the Borders. It also has something the Borders don't have, and that's the Solway coast, a long, indented coastline of sheltered sandy coves that's been dubbed the "Scottish Riviera" – an exaggeration perhaps, but it's certainly Scotland's warmest, southernmost stretch of coastline.

3

Dumfries is the region's main settlement, a market town by the **River Nith** originally founded as a royal burgh in 1186. Today it's a must for those on the trail of **Robert Burns**, who spent the last part of his life here. More compelling is the nearby coast, overlooking the Solway Firth, the shallow estuary wedged between Scotland and England, famed for its wildlife and for the nearby red-sandstone ruins of **Caerlaverock Castle** and **Sweetheart Abbey**. Edged by tidal marsh and mudbank, much of the Solway shoreline is flat and eerily remote, but there are also some fine rocky bays sheltering beneath wooded hills, most notably along the **Colvend coast**. Further along the coast is **Kirkcudbright**, once a bustling port thronged with sailing ships, later an artists' retreat and now a tranquil, well-preserved little eighteenth- and early nineteenth-century town. Like Kirkcudbright, **Threave Garden** and **Threave Castle**, just outside Castle Douglas, are popular with – but not crowded by – tourists.

Contrasting with the essentially gentle landscape of the Solway coast is the brooding presence of the **Galloway Hills** to the north, their beautiful moors, mountains, lakes and rivers centred on the 235 square miles of the **Galloway Forest Park**, a hillwalking and mountain-biking paradise that deserves to be better known than it is. As you continue west into what used to be Wigtownshire, the landscape becomes flatter and more relentlessly agricultural. The main points of interest here are the attractive seaport of **Portpatrick** on the hammer-headed Rhinns of Galloway and the **Mull of Galloway**, Scotland's southernmost point and a nesting site for thousands of seabirds.

The combination of rolling landscape and quiet back roads makes the region good for **cyclists**: five of the **7stanes** (Ⓦ scotland.forestry.gov.uk/activities) purpose-built mountain-bike routes are in the forested hills of Dumfries and Galloway. This is also rewarding **walking** country, featuring the **Southern Upland Way** (Ⓦ www.southern uplandway.gov.uk), a 212-mile coast-to-coast hike from Portpatrick in the west to Cockburnspath in the east.

Brief history

The region has a fascinatingly diverse heritage. Originally inhabited by southern Picts, it has at various times been overrun by Romans, Anglo-Saxons from Northumberland and Celts from Ireland: the name Galloway means the "land of the stranger Gaels". It was an unruly land, where independent chieftains maintained close contacts with the Vikings rather than the Scots, right up until medieval times. Gradually, this autonomy

KIRKCUDBRIGHT

Highlights

❶ Caerlaverock Castle One of Scotland's most photogenic moated castles, beside a superb site for waterfowl and waders. **See p.144**

❷ Crawick Multiverse Charles Jencks's otherworldly landscape of sculptured hills and standing stones, representing humanity's connection with the Universe. **See p.146**

❸ Kirkcudbright One-time artists' colony, and the best-looking town in the "Scottish Riviera". See p.147

❹ Threave Garden and Threave Castle The perfect day-trip from Castle Douglas: azaleas and rhododendrons to die for and a medieval castle on an island. **See p.149 & p.150**

❺ Galloway Forest Park Go mountain biking along remote forest tracks, or hiking on the Southern Upland Way. **See p.152**

❻ Logan Botanic Garden Scotland's most exotic garden, where tree ferns, palms and eucalyptus flourish in the southwest's balmy climate. **See p.154**

❼ Mull of Galloway Picture-postcard headland, with a Stevenson lighthouse, cliffs full of seabirds and views across the Irish Sea. **See p.155**

HIGHLIGHTS ARE MARKED ON THE MAP ON P.140

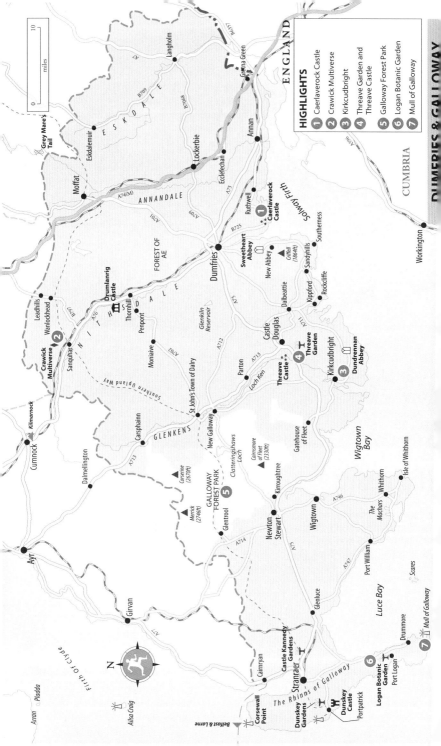

ENGLAND

CUMBRIA

HIGHLIGHTS

1. Caerlaverock Castle
2. Crawick Multiverse
3. Kirkcudbright
4. Threave Garden and Threave Castle
5. Galloway Forest Park
6. Logan Botanic Garden
7. Mull of Galloway

N

0   10
miles

Solway Firth

Workington

Gretna Green
Annan
Ruthwell
Southerness
Sandyhills
Kippford
Rockcliffe

Caerlaverock Castle ①

Sweetheart Abbey
New Abbey
Criffel (1864ft)

Dumfries

Langholm
Eskdalemuir
ESKDALE
Grey Mare's Tail
Moffat
Lockerbie
Ecclefechan
ANNANDALE
FOREST OF AE
B709
B7068
B7076
A7
A74(M)
A709
A701
A75

Dalbeattie
Castle Douglas
Threave Garden ④
Threave Castle
Kirkcudbright ③
Dundrennan Abbey

Leadhills
Wanlockhead
Crawick Multiverse ②
Sanquhar
Drumlanrig Castle
Thornhill
Penpont
Moniaive
NITHSDALE
Glenkiln Reservoir
A76
A702
A712
A713

St John's Town of Dalry
Parton
Loch Ken
Southern Upland Way
New Galloway
GLENKENS
Carsphairn
Dalmellington
Cumnock
Kilmarnock

Gatehouse of Fleet
Clatteringshaws Loch
Cairnsmore of Fleet (2330ft)
Kirroughtree
GALLOWAY FOREST PARK ⑤
Corserine (2670ft)
Merrick (2746ft)
Glentrool

Wigtown Bay
Newton Stewart
Wigtown
Whithorn
The Machars
Isle of Whithorn
A714
A746
A75
A747

Port William

Ayr
Girvan
Firth of Clyde
Arran
Pladda
Ailsa Craig
A77
A713

Glenluce
Luce Bay
Scares
Drummore
Castle Kennedy Gardens
Stranraer
Cairnryan
The Rhinns of Galloway
Corsewall Point
Dunskey Gardens
Dunskey Castle
Portpatrick
Logan Botanic Garden ⑥
Port Logan
Mull of Galloway ⑦
Belfast & Larne

GRETNA GREEN MARRIAGES

Up until 1754 English couples could buy a quick and secret wedding at London's Fleet Prison, bribing imprisoned clerics with small amounts of money. The **Hardwicke Marriage Act** brought an end to this seedy wheeze, enforcing the requirement of a licence and a church ceremony. However, in Scotland, a marriage declaration made before two witnesses remained legal. The consequences of this difference in the law verged on farce: hundreds of runaway couples dashed north to Scotland, their weddings witnessed by just about anyone who came to hand – ferrymen, farmers, tollgate keepers and even self-styled "priests" who set up their own "marriage houses".

Gretna Green, due to its position beside the border on the main turnpike road to Edinburgh, became the most popular destination for the fugitives. In their rush, many people tied the knot at the first place to hand after dismounting from the stagecoach, which happened to be a **blacksmith's shop** situated at the crossroads, though the better-off maintained class distinctions, heading for the staging post at Gretna Hall. The association with blacksmiths was strengthened by one of the first "priests", the redoubtable Joseph Paisley, a 25-stone Goliath who – in business from 1754 to 1812 – gave a certain style to the ceremony by straightening a horseshoe, a show of strength rather than a symbolic act. His melodramatic feat led to stories of Gretna Green weddings being performed over the blacksmith's **anvil**, and later "priests" were more than happy to act out the rumour. Gretna Green boomed until the marriage laws were further amended in 1856, but some businesses continued right up to 1940, when marriage by declaration was made illegal.

The only marriages that take place in Gretna Green nowadays, however, are for couples taken in by the "romance" of the name – more than 4000 annually – and English couples under 18, who want to get married without the permission of their parents (ⓦ gretnaweddings.com).

3

was whittled away, and the area was swallowed up by the Scottish Crown, though Galloway continued to be a fiercely independent region, typified by local hero Robert the Bruce. Later, it became a stronghold of the Covenanters, and suffered terribly during the "Killing Times" following the Restoration, when the government forces came to impose Episcopalianism. From around the seventeenth century, the ports of the Solway coast prospered with the expansion of local shipping routes over to Ireland. The region subsequently experienced economic decline as trade routes changed, turning busy ports into sleepy backwaters.

ARRIVAL AND DEPARTURE   DUMFRIES AND GALLOWAY

By train Three train lines run through Dumfries and Galloway. One tracks the A74 motorway between Carlisle and Glasgow, while another heads up Nithsdale via Dumfries and a third stretches from Glasgow to Stranraer in the far southwest.

By ferry Two companies provide services between

Northern Ireland and Cairnryan, 6 miles north of Stranraer with 4–8 daily bus connections from Cairnryan to Stranraer and Ayr: StenaLine serves Belfast (5–6 crossings daily; 2hr 15min; ☎ 08447 707070, ⓦ stenaline.co.uk) and P&O Ferries has services to Larne (5–7 crossings daily; 2hr; ☎ 0800 130 0030, ⓦ poferries.com).

GETTING AROUND AND INFORMATION

By bus The main bus company for the region is Stagecoach West (☎ 01292 613500, ⓦ stagecoachbus.com), servicing all the main towns and villages but of little use for the Galloway Forest Park.

Tourist information The website ⓦ visitdumfries andgalloway.co.uk is a good resource for in-depth information and ideas, particularly for families and walking enthusiasts.

Dumfries

Situated on the wide banks of the River Nith, a short distance inland from the Solway Firth, **DUMFRIES** is by far the largest town in southwest Scotland, with a population of more than thirty thousand. Long known as the "Queen of the South" (as is its football club), it flourished as a medieval seaport and trading centre, its success attracting the attention of many English armies. Despite this, it went on to prosper, with its light industries and port supplying the agricultural hinterland. The town planners of the 1960s badly damaged its appearance, but many of the warm red-sandstone buildings that distinguish Dumfries from other places in the southwest survive. The town is second only to Ayr for its associations with **Robert Burns** (see p.165), who spent the last five years of his life here employed as an excise man. Consequently a number of sights in Dumfries pay homage to the great poet, including his home, his statue, Burns House, his pub, the *Globe Inn*, and his final resting place in a mausoleum beside St Michael's Church.

Globe Inn

56 High St • Mon–Wed 10am–11pm, Thurs 10am–midnight, Fri–Sat 10am–1am, Sun 11.30am–midnight • Free • ☎ 01387 252335, ⊛ globeinndumfries.co.uk

If you're on Burns's trail, make sure you duck down the alleyway to the seventeenth-century **Globe Inn**, just past the ornate red and gold Victorian fountain. Burns had a fling with Annie Park, a barmaid in this pub, and the resultant child was taken into the Burns household by his long-suffering wife, Jean Armour. Beyond the main bar you can enter the beautifully panelled snug and sit in the very chair used by the poet – although if you do, by tradition you'll be expected to recite a Burns poem or else buy everyone in the bar a drink.

Burns House

Burns St • April–Sept Mon–Sat 10am–5pm, Sun 2–5pm; Oct–March Tues–Sat 10am–1pm & 2–5pm • Free • ☎ 01387 255297

In the simple sandstone building now known as **Burns House**, Robert Burns died of rheumatic heart disease in 1796 aged 37, a few days before the birth of his last

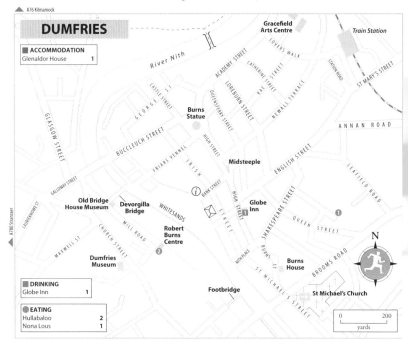

son, Maxwell. He lived here for his last three years, though his wife, Jean Armour, stayed on until her own death, some 38 years later. Inside, there's a collection of Burns memorabilia – manuscripts, letters, his copper kettle, nutmeg grater and the like – while one of the bedroom windows bears his signature, scratched with his diamond ring.

St Michael's Church

As a member of the Dumfries Volunteers, Burns was given a military funeral, before being buried nearby in a simple grave by **St Michael's Church**, a large red-sandstone church on St Michael's Street, built in 1745. In 1815 his body was dug up and moved across the graveyard to a purpose-built **mausoleum**, a bright white Neoclassical eyesore that houses a statue of him being accosted by the poetic Muse. The graveyard features several tombstones of the poet's friends, a number of them inscribed with wonderfully verbose epitaphs.

Robert Burns Centre

Mill Rd • April–Sept Mon–Sat 10am–5pm, Sun 2–5pm; Oct–March Tues–Sat 10am–1pm & 2–5pm; films Tues–Sat from 3.45pm • Free • ☎ 01387 264808, ⓦ rbcft.co.uk

In a converted watermill on the western banks of the Nith, the **Robert Burns Centre**, or RBC, has a straightforward exhibition on the poet's years in Dumfries, although the most interesting item on display here is the scale model of the town from the 1790s. There's a good audiovisual presentation on Burns in the small cinema, which also shows predominantly art-house films in the evenings.

Dumfries Museum

The Observatory, Rotchell Rd • April–Sept Mon–Sat 10am–5pm, Sun 2–5pm; Oct–March Tues–Sat 10am–1pm & 2–5pm; camera obscura open weather permitting • Free; camera obscura £2.70 • ☎ 01387 253374

On the hill west of the Nith stands the **Dumfries Museum**, from which there are great views over the town. The museum is housed partly in an eighteenth-century windmill, which was converted into the town's observatory in the 1830s and features the world's oldest working **camera obscura** on its top floor, well worth a visit on a clear day when the views are projected inside to maximum effect. On the floors below, the focus is on local history and prehistory, with a good collection of tools and weaponry from the region's earliest peoples as well as some impressive carved masonry from the era of the first Christians.

ARRIVAL AND INFORMATION   DUMFRIES

By train Dumfries train station is a 5min walk east of the town centre.
Destinations Carlisle (Mon–Sat every 1–2hr, 5 on Sun; 40min); Glasgow Central (Mon–Sat every 1–2hr, 2 on Sun; 1hr 45min); Sanquhar (Mon–Sat every 1–2hr, 2 on Sun; 25min).
By bus Most buses stop off at Whitesands beside the River Nith.
Destinations Kirkcudbright, with a coordinated change at

Castle Douglas (Mon–Sat hourly, 3 on Sun; 1hr 20min), Moffat (Mon–Sat hourly, Sun every 1–2hr; 40min); New Abbey (Mon–Sat hourly, 6 on Sun; 15min); Stranraer (Mon–Sat every 2hr, 2 on Sun; 2hr 15min).
Tourist office 64 Whitesands (Easter to mid-June & Sept–Oct Mon–Sat 9.30am–5pm, Sun 11am–4pm; mid-June to Aug Mon–Sat 9.30am–5.30pm, Sun 11am–4pm; Oct–Easter Mon–Fri 9.30am–4.30pm; ☎ 01387 253862).

ACCOMMODATION

Glenaldor House 5 Victoria Terrace ☎ 01387 264248, ⓦ glenaldorhouse.co.uk. A light and bright Victorian house near the station with four comfortably spacious en-suite bedrooms. Wake up to a customized cooked breakfast offered alongside a buffet with healthy cereal options, pastries and jams. **£65**

EATING

Hullabaloo Robert Burns Centre, Mill Rd ☎01387 259679, ⓦhullabaloorestaurant.co.uk. A casual restaurant on the top floor of a restored old watermill that also houses the Burns Centre and art cinema. The menus offer an unusually wide and creative choice for vegetarians, like the aubergine schnitzel with fire-roasted peppers, or the (in-house) oak-smoked goat's cheese with pickles and salad, both at £10.95. Tues–Sat noon–3pm & 5.30–9.30pm, Sun noon–4.45pm, Mon noon–3pm; Oct–Easter closed Sun.

★**Nona Lous** Old St Andrews Primary School, Brooke St ☎07989 031491. Located in a converted primary school among arts and beauty-related businesses, this thoroughly hip tearoom bakes stunningly attractive cakes and a few pastries too. Old crockery and knitted tea and cup cosies give the place a personal touch. Light breakfasts and lunches including sandwiches from £2.50. Mon–Wed 10am–5pm, Thurs–Fri 10am–5.30pm, Sat 10am–4pm.

DRINKING

Globe Inn 56 High St ☎01387 252335, ⓦglobe inndumfries.co.uk. The Robert Burns connection certainly pulls in the punters in this pub, but is by no means the only reason to visit. It's a rare example of traditional pub authenticity with its attractive wood panelling and ornate cornices. There's a good selection of food here, but for the full Burns experience aim for the haggis, neeps and tatties at £6. Mon–Wed 10am–11pm, Thurs 10am–midnight, Fri–Sat 10am–1am, Sun 11.30am–midnight.

Around Dumfries

Southeast of Dumfries, the medieval ruins of **Caerlaverock Castle** are simply magnificent, as is the adjacent nature reserve and the early Christian cross at nearby **Ruthwell**. On the west bank of the Nith estuary, the star attraction is **Sweetheart Abbey**, the best preserved of the trio of Cistercian abbeys in Dumfries and Galloway.

Caerlaverock Castle

8 miles southeast of Dumfries along the B725 • Daily: April–Sept 9.30am–5.30pm; Oct–March 10am–4pm • £5.50; HES • ☎01387 770244, ⓦhistoricenvironment.scot • #D6A bus from Great King St in Dumfries (5 buses Mon–Sat, 2 on Sun; 22min)

Picture-perfect **Caerlaverock Castle**, a moated ruin, was built in the late thirteenth century out of the rich local red sandstone and preserves a mighty double-towered gatehouse. During the siege of 1300 by Edward I, a contemporary bard commented: "In shape it was like a shield, for it had but three sides round it, with a tower at each corner." Caerlaverock sustained further damage in 1312, this time from the Scots, and again in 1356–57 from the English, forcing numerous rebuilding programmes. The most surprising addition lies inside, where you're confronted by the ornate Renaissance facade of the **Nithsdale Lodging**, erected in the 1630s by the first earl of Nithsdale. Just six years later the earl and his garrison were forced to surrender after a thirteen-week siege and bombardment by the Covenanters, who proceeded to wreck the place. It was never inhabited again.

Caerlaverock Castle makes a good family day out, with a siege-engine playground, a tearoom and an exhibition and video on the siege of 1300, where kids can create their own heraldry. Waymarked walks in the neighbouring **Caerlaverock Wetland Centre** – an area of salt marsh and mud flats abutting the Solway Firth – include one leading to the earthworks of the castle that preceded Caerlaverock; en route, listen out for the rare natterjack toad.

Ruthwell Church

7 miles east of Caerlaverock

The modest country church at **RUTHWELL** houses the remarkable 18ft **Ruthwell Cross**, an extraordinary early Christian monument from the early or mid-eighth century when Galloway was ruled by the Northumbrians. The cross was considered idolatrous during the Reformation, smashed and buried, and only finally reassembled in the nineteenth century. The decoration reveals a strikingly sophisticated style and iconography, probably derived from the eastern Mediterranean. The main inscriptions are in Latin, but running round the edge is a poem written in the Northumbrian dialect in runic figures. However, it's the biblical carvings on the main face that really catch the eye – notably Mary Magdalene washing the feet of Jesus.

Sweetheart Abbey

Main St, New Abbey • April–Sept daily 9.30am–5.30pm; Oct–March Sat–Wed 10am–4pm • £4.50; HES • ☎ 01387 850397, ⓦ historicenvironment.scot • Bus #372 from Dumfries every 2hr Mon–Sat, 3 on Sun; 15min

The last of the Cistercian abbeys to be founded in Scotland, in 1273, **Sweetheart Abbey** is dominated by the red sandstone abbey church, intact minus its roof. Standing in the grassy nave, flanked by giant compound piers supporting early Gothic arches, and above them a triforium, it's easy to imagine what the completed church must have looked like. The central square tower is a massive, brutal structure, but the elaborate tracery in some of the windows and flamboyant corbelling below the central tower clearly mark a change from the austere simplicity of earlier Cistercian foundations. Sweetheart Abbey takes its unusual name from its founder, Devorgilla de Balliol, Lady of Galloway. She carried the embalmed heart of her husband, John Balliol (after whom Balliol College, Oxford, is named) around with her for the remaining 22 years of her life – she is buried, with the casket, in the presbytery.

ACCOMMODATION AND EATING

AROUND DUMFRIES

Abbey Cottage 26 Main St, New Abbey ☎ 01387 850377, ⓦ abbeycottagetearoom.com. Enjoying an unrivalled view over Sweetheart Abbey, this tearoom with terrace is renowned for its quality home-made cakes and even sells its own cake-related cookbook. If you're stopping for lunch, expect to pay around £7.50 for home-made soup and a sandwich. Daily 10am–5pm.

Caerlaverock Wetland Centre Eastpark Farm, 8 miles southeast of Dumfries along the B725 ☎ 01387 770200, ⓦ wwt.org.uk/wetland-centres/caerlaverock /plan-your-visit/accommodation. This farmhouse, run by the Wildfowl and Wetlands Trust and with its own attached observation tower, is in the heart of a remote, nature-rich

wetland. There are five bedrooms – some en suite – and a shared lounge, kitchen and laundry room. £64

★ **Marthrown of Mabie** Mabie Forest ☎ 01387 247900, ⓦ marthrownofmabie.com. Deep in the heart of the forest this remote encampment offers tipis and yurts (each sleeping four), a bunkhouse and, most magical of all, a beautifully thatched, replica Iron Age roundhouse with a central log fire for cooking and warmth. There's a wood-fired hot tub and sauna as well as meals provided at the bunkhouse. Also in the forest are superb purpose-built mountain-biking trails run by the 7stanes (see ⓦ 7stanesmountainbiking.com). Roundhouse per person £17.50; tipis £60; yurts £160; bunkhouse per person £19.50

Nithsdale

North of Dumfries, the A76 and the railway line to Kilmarnock travel the length of **Nithsdale**, whose gentle slopes and old forests hide one major attraction: the many-turreted seventeenth-century mansion of **Drumlanrig Castle** near **Thornhill**, just one of three substantial country seats owned by the duke of Buccleuch. At the opposite end of the class system were the miners who worked the lead mines in the neighbouring Lowther Hills, to the east, now commemorated in the intriguing **Museum of Lead Mining** in Wanlockhead.

Wanlockhead

From the Nith Valley 24 miles north of Dumfries, **WANLOCKHEAD** is six miles northeast up the striking Mennock Pass. Exposed in its remote and windswept position at a lofty 1500ft, this is the highest village in Scotland.

Museum of Lead Mining

Toll Brae, Wanlockhead • Daily: Easter–June & Sept 11am–4.30pm, July–Sept 10am–4.30pm • £8.25 • ☎ 01659 74387, ⓦ leadminingmuseum.co.uk

A visit to the **Museum of Lead Mining** starts with a brief foray into the main exhibition where the miners' lives and working conditions are described with the aid of a few mannequin-enhanced historic scenes. From there you don a hard hat and go on a guided tour of the underground **Lochnell Mine**, resurfacing for a tour of a **miner's cottage** from the 1740s and then one from a hundred years or so later. Also well worth a look is the remarkable eighteenth-century **Miners' Library**, whose 3000-plus volumes were purchased from the voluntary subscriptions of its members. At the end of the visit you can try your hand at gold panning – a sure-fire hit if you have children in tow.

ARRIVAL AND DEPARTURE   WANLOCKHEAD

By bus Buses run from Sanquhar (4 daily: Mon–Sat; 15min), which is well served by buses from Dumfries.

Crawick Multiverse

Sanquhar, 27 miles north of Dumfries signposted from the A76 • Sept–June daily 10am–4pm, July–Aug daily 10am–6pm • £5 • ☎ 01659 50242, ⓦ crawickmultiverse.co.uk • Regular trains between Dumfries and Glasgow Central stop at Sanquhar, 1 mile south of the park.

Renowned landscape artist Charles Jencks' tangible vision of the Universe – or indeed multiverse – is splayed across the site of a 55-acre former coal pit. Hike up sculptured hills that spiral up to giant standing stones – representing the Milky Way's destined collision with Andromeda – or follow the Comet Walk that elliptically surrounds the main amphitheatre. While Jenck's subject matter may have been otherworldly, there's an unmistakable familiarity to the place, like a homage to those Paganistic cultures that looked up into space and were inspired to build Stonehenge and the like. Indeed, the summer solstice is celebrated here with a festival featuring fire displays, music and arts performances.

Drumlanrig Castle

Thornhill, 18 miles north of Dumfries signposted from the A76 • **House** All holiday weekends from Easter–May & July–Aug 11am–5pm; guided tours only • £10 • **Country park and gardens only** Easter–Sept daily 10am–5pm • £6 • ☎ 01848 331555, ⓦ drumlanrig.com • Bus stop 1.5 miles' walk; services from Dumfries (every 1 to 2hr; 45min) and from Ayr (Mon–Sat 5 buses, Sun 2 buses; 1hr 20min)

Stately **Drumlanrig Castle** is not a true castle but the grandiose home of the supremely wealthy Duke of Buccleuch and Queensberry. Approached by an impressive driveway that sweeps along an avenue of lime trees, the seventeenth-century sandstone "Pink Palace" bristles with cupolas, turrets and towers. The highlights of the richly furnished interior are the **paintings** by the great masters, most notably Rembrandt, Van Dyck, Holbein and Gainsborough.

Drumlanrig offers a host of other attractions, including formal **gardens** and a forested **country park**. Before you go for a stroll round the gardens, pick up the tree trail leaflet, which points out significant trees, such as the red oak planted by Neil Armstrong; seek out the Victorian **Heather Hut**. The old stableyard beside the castle contains a visitor centre, a few shops, the inevitable tearoom and a useful **bike rental** outlet (£7/hr), as the park is crisscrossed by footpaths and cycle routes. A **cycle museum** boasts a replica of the first-ever pedal bike, invented in 1839 by local boy Kirkpatrick MacMillan.

The Colvend coast

The **Colvend coast**, twenty miles or so southwest of Dumfries, is probably one of the finest stretches of coastline along the so-called "Scottish Riviera". The best approach is via the A710, which heads south through New Abbey, before cutting across a handsome landscape of rolling farmland to the aptly named **Sandyhills.** A scenic five-mile coastal path runs from there past the cliffs of Castlehill Point and through the pleasant estuary villages of **Rockcliffe** and **Kippford**.

Sandyhills

Little more than a scattering of houses dotted around a wide, sandy bay, **SANDYHILLS**, 18 miles southwest of Dumfries, looks across the tidal mud flats of the Solway Firth to the Lake District beyond. There are some dramatic coves a short walk west of the bay, while inland the hills undulate gently with farmland interspersed with clutches of forest and small lochs.

ARRIVAL AND DEPARTURE | SANDYHILLS

By bus Buses from Dumfries (6 daily, Mon–Sat, 4 on Sun; 55min) and Rockcliffe (5 daily, Mon–Sat, 4 on Sun; 10min).

ACCOMMODATION

Craigbittern Main Rd ☎ 01387 780247, ⓦ craigbittern cottage.co.uk. An attractive two-bedroom, stone cottage a short walk away from the sandy beach. Inside, the decor is mostly modern although the owners have retained the ceiling beams. The building is set back from the road and looks out to the Solway Firth; available for rent by the week. Per week **£450**

Rockcliffe and Kippford

A village on the Urr estuary twenty miles southwest of Dumfries, **ROCKCLIFFE** shelters peacefully between wooded hills and its beautiful rocky, sand and shell bay. For vehicles, Rockcliffe is a dead end, but it's the start of a pleasant half-hour walk along the Jubilee Path to neighbouring **KIPPFORD**, a tiny, lively yachting centre strung out along the east bank of the estuary. En route, the path passes the Celtic hillfort of the **Mote of Mark**, a useful craggy viewpoint. At low tide you can walk over the Rough Firth causeway from the shore below across the mud flats to **Rough Island**, a humpy bird sanctuary owned by the National Trust for Scotland – it's out of bounds in May and June when terns and oystercatchers are nesting.

ARRIVAL AND DEPARTURE | ROCKCLIFFE AND KIPPFORD

By bus Buses stop at the road's end next to the bay and serve Dumfries (Mon–Sat 3 daily, 4 on Sun; 1hr 5min) and Kippford (Mon–Sat 5 daily, 4 on Sun; 10min).

ACCOMMODATION AND EATING

The Mariner Hotel Opposite Kippford harbour ☎ 01556 620206, ⓦ themariner-kippford.co.uk. With its greatest asset being the large beer garden out back with a terrific play area for the kids, this is the best place in town to sink a cold one. The food is nothing special – typical pub grub like fish and chips for £10.50 – but it is available all day at weekends and for lunch and dinner daily midweek.

Sun–Thurs 11am–10pm, Fri–Sat 11am–11pm.
★**Roughfirth House** Roughfirth, Kippford ☎ 01556 620330, ⓦ kippford.com. Halfway between Kippford and Rockcliffe accessed by a private cul-de-sac from Kippford, this B&B has an en-suite double and a two-bedroomed family suite with sun lounge overlooking the waterfront. Doubles **£105**; family suite **£130**

Kirkcudbright and around

Hugging the muddy banks of the River Dee ten miles southwest of Castle Douglas, **KIRKCUDBRIGHT** – pronounced "kir-coo-bree" – is the only major town along the Solway coast to have retained a working harbour. In addition, it has a ruined castle and the most attractive of town centres, a charming medley of simple two-storey cottages with medieval pends, Georgian villas and Victorian townhouses, all built in a mixture of sandstone, granite and brick, and attractively painted. Not surprisingly, Kirkcudbright became something of a magnet for Scottish artists from the late nineteenth century onwards.

MacLellan's Castle

Castle St · April–Sept Mon–Sat 9.30am–5.30pm · £4.50; HES · ☎ 01557 331856, ⓦ historicenvironment.scot

The most striking sight in Kirkcudbright is **MacLellan's Castle**, a pink-flecked sixteenth-century tower house that sits at one end of the High Street, by the harbourside. Part fortified keep and part spacious mansion, the castle was built in the 1570s for the Provost of Kirkcudbright, Sir Thomas MacLellan of Bombie, when a degree of law and order permitted the aristocracy to relax its defensive preoccupations and satisfy its desire for comfort. As a consequence, chimneys replaced battlements and windows begin at the ground floor. Nevertheless, the walls remain impressively thick and there is a handful of wide-mouthed gun loops. The interior is well preserved, from the kitchen and vaulted storerooms in the basement, to the warren of well-appointed domestic apartments above. MacLellan's son, Robert, amassed so many debts that on his death in 1639, the house had to be sold off, and from then on it was more or less abandoned.

Broughton House

12 High St · Easter–Oct daily noon–5pm; also Feb & March garden only Mon–Fri 11am–4pm · £6.50, garden free; NTS · ☎ 01557 330437, ⓦ nts.org.uk

This smart Georgian townhouse, set back from, and elevated above, the surrounding terraces, is the former home of the artist **Edward Hornel** (1863–1933). An important member of the late nineteenth-century Scottish art scene, he spent his childhood a few doors down the street, and returned in 1900 to establish an artists' colony in Kirkcudbright with some of the "Glasgow Boys" (see box, p.196). Hornel bought Broughton House in 1901 and added a studio and a glass-roofed, mahogany-panelled gallery at the back of the house. The gallery, now filled with the mannered and rather formulaic paintings of girls at play that he churned out in the latter part of his career, also features a scaled-down plaster cast of some of the Elgin Marbles. A trip to Japan in 1893 imbued Hornel with a life-long affection for the country, and his surprisingly large, densely packed, wonderful jewel-box **gardens** have a strong Japanese influence.

Stewartry Museum

6 St Mary St · Mon–Sat 11am–5pm, Sun 2–5pm · Free · ☎ 01557 331643

An extraordinary collection, not to be missed: the **Stewartry Museum** has cabinets crammed with anything from glass bottles, weaving equipment, pipes, pictures and postcards to stuffed birds, pickled fish and the tricorn hats once worn by town officials. There are also examples of book jackets designed by Jessie M. King and E.A. Taylor.

KIRKCUDBRIGHT'S FESTIVALS

Kirkcudbright was the location of much of the cult 1970s film, *The Wicker Man*, and is the nearest town for **The Wickerman Festival** (ⓦ thewickermanfestival.co.uk), southwest Scotland's biggest music festival, on the third weekend in July, during which a giant Wicker Man is torched. The town also has a much smaller **jazz festival** (ⓦ kirkcudbrightjazzfestival .co.uk) in mid-June, with a strong emphasis on Dixieland as well as a host of other **summer festivities** (ⓦ kirkcudbright.co.uk) culminating in a military tattoo and fireworks display at the end of August.

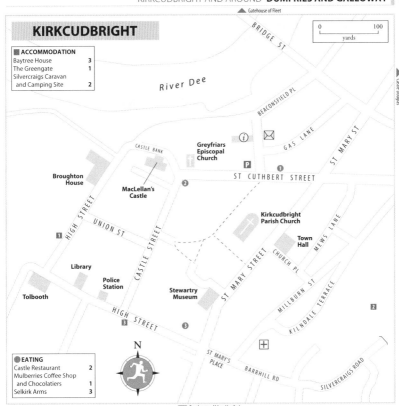

KIRKCUDBRIGHT

■ ACCOMMODATION
Baytree House	3
The Greengate	1
Silvercraigs Caravan and Camping Site	2

● EATING
Castle Restaurant	2
Mulberries Coffee Shop and Chocolatiers	1
Selkirk Arms	3

Dundrennan Abbey

Dundrennan, 6 miles southeast of Kirkcudbright • April–Sept daily 9.30am–5.30pm • £4.50; HES • ☎ 01557 500262, ⓦ historicenvironment.scot • Bus #505 connects Dundrennan with Kirkcudbright (Mon–Sat 6 daily; 10min)

Founded in 1142, Dundrennan was the mother house of the local Cistercian abbeys of Sweetheart and Glenluce, and was clearly the grandest of the lot, even though it's now reduced to just its transepts. The chief treasures of the abbey are the chapterhouse's finely carved cusped portal, and the medieval effigy of a tonsured abbot in the northwest corner of the nave; he was murdered – hence the faded dagger in his chest – and the figure being trampled at his feet is thought to be his assassin, in the process of being disembowelled.

Threave Garden

2 miles southwest of Castle Douglas • March–Oct daily 10am–5pm, Nov–Feb 11am–3pm; Threave House can be visited on a guided tour Easter–Oct Wed–Fri & Sun 11.30am–1.30pm • £7.50; house and garden £12.50; NTS • ☎ 01556 502575, ⓦ nts.org.uk

The premier horticultural sight in Dumfries and Galloway, **Threave Garden** is a pleasant mile-long walk or cycle south of Castle Douglas, along the shores of Loch Carlingwark. The garden features a magnificent spread of flowers and woodland across sixty acres, subdivided into more than a dozen areas, from the old-fashioned herbaceous borders of the Walled Garden to the brilliant banks of rhododendrons in the Woodland Garden and the ranks of primula, astilbe and gentian in the Peat Garden. In springtime, thousands of visitors turn up for the flowering of more than two hundred types of daffodil.

Threave is also home to the School of Practical Gardening, whose postgraduate students occupy one floor of **Threave House**, a hulking Scots Baronial mansion built by the Gordon family in 1872, and now restored to its 1938 condition.

Threave Castle

2 miles west of Castle Douglas, off the A75 · Daily: April–Sept 10am–4.30pm, Oct 10am–3.30pm · £4.50; HES · ☎ 07711 223101, ⓦ historicenvironment.scot

A visit to **Threave Castle** begins with a ten-minute walk from the car park to the River Dee, where you ring a brass bell for the boat to take you over to the flat and grassy island on which the stern-looking castle stands.

Built in around 1370 for one of the Black Douglases, Archibald the Grim, first Lord of Galloway and third Earl of Douglas, the fortress was among the first of its kind, a sturdy, rectangular structure completed shortly after the War of Independence. The rickety curtain wall to the south and east is all that remains of the **artillery fortifications**, hurriedly constructed in the 1450s by the ninth earl in a desperate – and unsuccessful – attempt to defend the castle against James II's newfangled cannon. The castle was partially dismantled in the 1640s, but enough remains of the interior to make out its general plan.

ARRIVAL AND INFORMATION

KIRKCUDBRIGHT AND AROUND

By bus Buses to Kirkcudbright stop by the harbour car park, near the tourist office.
Destinations Dumfries, with a coordinated change at Castle Douglas (Mon–Sat hourly, 3 on Sun; 1hr 20min); Gatehouse of Fleet (Mon–Sat 8 buses; 17min).

Tourist office Harbour Square (Feb–March & Nov Mon–Sat 11am–4pm; April–June & Sept–Oct Mon–Sat 10am–5pm, Sun 11am–3pm; July & Aug Mon–Sat 9.30am–6pm, Sun 10am–5pm; ☎ 01557 330494, ⓦ kirkcudbright.co.uk).

ACCOMMODATION

Baytree House 110 High St ☎ 01557 330824, ⓦ baytreekirkcudbright.co.uk. An old-fashioned Georgian B&B with four spacious rooms and a drawing room for use by guests. There's also a self-catering garden studio for two with its own conservatory and garden (minimum stay usually three days). Doubles **£84**; apartment per week **£375**

★**The Greengate** 46 High St ☎ 01557 331895, ⓦ thegreengate.co.uk. Once the home of the illustrator Jessie M. King, this attractive, creaky old B&B offers more privacy than your average guesthouse. There's only

one double room for rent, with its own lounge and reception room with log fire and antique furniture. You can also visit the artist owners' studio or take a stroll round the garden. **£80**

Silvercraigs Caravan and Camping Site Silvercraigs Rd ☎ 07824 528482. Centrally located overlooking town, a small, no-frills campsite run by the council. It mostly caters to caravans and motorhomes but it's possible to pitch a tent here too. The facilities on offer include electric connection, a playground and self-service laundry. Easter–Oct. Per pitch **£11.50**; per caravan **£20.50**

EATING

★**Castle Restaurant** 5 Castle St ☎ 01557 330569, ⓦ thecastlerestaurant.net. An intimate contribution to Kirkcudbright's restaurant scene, offering Scots-French cuisine in tasteful, homely surroundings overlooking the castle. The changing menu offers generally good value, with dishes like mussels with chilli and tomato for £9, rising to £16.50 for fillet medallions with a rich peppercorn sauce – although the wine list is less palatably priced. Occasional music nights. Book ahead. Mon–Sat 6–9pm. On request, open for lunches any day or Sunday dinner.

Mulberries Coffee Shop and Chocolatiers 11 St Cuthbert St ☎ 01557 330961. The town's finest coffee,

cakes and chocolates are served in this cosy little café near the harbour car park. They also do excellent burger evenings (all home-made and around £10) on the last Friday of the month – a hugely popular sideline that requires advance booking. Mon–Wed & Fri–Sat 10am–6pm, Thurs 10am–7pm, Sun 11am–6pm.

Selkirk Arms 125 High St ☎ 01557 330402. One of the town's more economical dining options, with bistro and restaurant. Its wide-ranging menu covers gastropub grub fish and chips at £12 to posh nosh like roast suckling pig with baked apples for £15. Daily noon–2pm & 6–9pm.

OPPOSITE MULL OF GALLOWAY LIGHTHOUSE (P.155) >

Galloway Forest Park and around

The strange thing about Galloway is that, while the area around the coast is all rolling farmland, stately homes, sandy coves and estuarine mud flats, you only have to head north ten or twenty miles and you're transported to the entirely different landscape of the Galloway Hills, an environment of glassy lochs, wooded hills and bare, rounded peaks. Much of this landscape is now incorporated into the **Galloway Forest Park**, Britain's largest forest park, which stretches all the way from the southern part of Ayrshire right down to Gatehouse of Fleet, laid out on land owned by the Forestry Commission. Few people live here, but the park is a major draw for hikers and mountain bikers. Accommodation is sparse in the park itself: use **Newton Stewart**, to the southwest, as a base.

ARRIVAL AND DEPARTURE — GALLOWAY FOREST PARK AND AROUND

3

By bus No buses run along the park's only road (the Queen's Way/A712), so if you don't have transport you either need to approach the park from New Galloway to the east or Newton Stewart to the southwest.

Destinations from New Galloway Castle Douglas (Mon–Sat 6 daily; 30min); Dumfries (Mon–Sat 2 daily; 1hr).

Destinations from Newton Stewart Dumfries (Mon–Sat every 1–2hr, 2 on Sun; 1hr 30min); Stranraer (Mon–Sat hourly, 4 on Sun; 45min); Wigtown (Mon–Sat hourly, 6 on Sun; 15min).

INFORMATION

Tourist office Dashwood Square, Newton Stewart (April–June & Oct Mon–Sat 9.30am–4pm, July–Sept Mon–Sat 9.30am–4.30pm, Sun 11am–3pm; T 01671 402431, W newtonstewart.org).

Galloway Forest Park Office 26 Main St, St John's Town of Dalry (Mon–Thurs 8am–5pm, Fri 8am–4.30pm; T 01671 402420, W gallowayforestpark.com).

Visitor centres By Clatteringshaws Loch (T 01644 402165), at Glentrool (T 01671 840302), and at Kirroughtree (T 01671 420285). Times vary but are generally daily 10am–5pm. Each has a tearoom, several waymarked walks and lots of information on activities and events.

HIKING, BIKING AND STARGAZING: GALLOWAY FOREST PARK

Both Glentrool and Kirroughtree have mountain-bike trails, which form part of southern Scotland's outstanding mountain-biking facilities, known as the **7stanes** (W 7stanes.co.uk). Of the two, **Kirroughtree**, three miles east of Newton Stewart, is by far the most varied and fun, with lots of exciting single-track trails for all abilities and good bike-rental facilities.

Hikers are better off heading for **Glentrool**, at the western edge of the park, about ten miles north of Newton Stewart, where a narrow lane twists the five miles over to **Loch Trool**. On the north side of the loch the **Bruce Stone**, near the lovely Buchan Waterfall, marks the spot where Robert the Bruce ambushed an English force in 1307 after routing the main body of the army at Solway Moss. From here, you can follow the Gariland Burn to Loch Neldricken and Loch Enoch, with their silver granite sands, and then on to the Devil's Bowling Green, strewn with hundreds of erratic boulders left by the retreating glaciers. Alternatively, you can head for the Range of the Awful Hand, whose five peaks include the **Merrick** (2746ft), the highest hill in southern Scotland.

The only surfaced road to cross the park is the desolate twenty-mile stretch of the A712 between Newton Stewart and New Galloway, known as the **Queen's Way**. About seven miles east of Newton Stewart, at the **Grey Mare's Tail Bridge**, there are various forest trails, all delving into the pine forests beside the road, crossing gorges, waterfalls and burns. There's also a **Wild Goat Park** and, a mile or so further up the road, a **Red Deer Range**. A few more miles on, you'll come to **Clatteringshaws Loch**, a reservoir surrounded by pine forest, and connected with the Southern Upland Way on its north side. Heading southeast from Clatteringshaws is the **Raiders Road**, a ten-mile-long toll road that shadows the River Dee, with some great waterfalls and pools for swimming in.

The park has been formally designated a "dark sky park", with designated spots for astronomy (see W forestry.gov.uk/darkskygalloway).

WATERSPORTS IN GALLOWAY FOREST PARK

Loch Ken on the eastern edge of the Galloway Forest Park is a hub for water activities. **Loch Ken Water Ski and Wakeboard School** (Loch Ken Marina, Parton ☏ 01644 470333, ⓦ skilochken.co.uk) on the eastern side of the loch, halfway down, can give an hour's ski tuition for £110 or a shot on a towed banana boat for £10. For other watersports head for the **Galloway Activity Centre** (Loch Ken, on the A713 ☏ 01556 503011, ⓦ lochken.co.uk) where you can kayak for £17 an hour or have half a day's windsurfing for £39.50.

ACCOMMODATION AND EATING

Wild camping is permitted within the Galloway Forest Park but otherwise most accommodation options are limited to in and around Newton Stewart and New Galloway on the park's western and eastern fringes.

Creebridge House Hotel Creebridge, Newton Stewart ☏ 01671 402121, ⓦ creebridge.co.uk. The town's most luxurious hotel is this eighteenth-century former hunting lodge, with extensive grounds. It's also a welcoming spot for a pint of local real ale; the chef's signature dish is the bitter-sweet barbary duck breast, which comes with ratatouille fondant potato for £16. Food served noon–2pm & 6–9pm. £112

Galloway Activity Centre Loch Ken, on the A713, near New Galloway ☏ 01556 502011, ⓦ lochken.co.uk.

As well as hosting a wide variety of land- and water-based activities, this company also offers a range of accommodation, including a private lochside cabin with heating and electricity or a Mongolian yurt with a central wood stove. The café caters for non-residents and sells cakes, tray bakes and light lunches. Guests can also eat here in the evenings by arrangement for £10.50. Café April–May & Sept–Oct Sat–Sun 9am–5pm, June–Aug daily 9am–5pm. Cabin for two £38; yurt for six £87

3

Wigtown

Seven miles south of Newton Stewart, **WIGTOWN** is tiny yet was once the county town of Wigtownshire. Despite its modest size, it has a remarkable main square, a vast, triangular-shaped affair, its layout unchanged since medieval times. Over the last decade or so Wigtown has reinvented itself as "Scotland's National Book Town", with several **bookshops** occupying some of the houses lining the square, and more elsewhere; the town hosts a high-profile autumn book festival (ⓦ wigtownbookfestival.com).

ARRIVAL AND DEPARTURE   WIGTOWN

By bus Buses stop on the main square and services run to Newton Stewart (Mon–Sat hourly, 6 on Sun; 15min) and Stranraer (Mon–Sat 2 daily; 1hr 30min).

EATING AND DRINKING

★**Craft** 30 South Main St ☏ 01988 403236, ⓦ craft restaurant.co.uk. Small, attractive bar and restaurant that takes its food and drink seriously, with microbrewery ales on the pumps and hearty artisan burgers for around £10. Look out for the Highland beef pastrami toasted sandwich that crops up in the specials. It's an uncharacteristically youthful place for the area, with regular live music and a sunny beer garden. Thurs–Sun noon–10pm, Wed 4–10pm.

The Rhinns of Galloway

The hilly, hammer-shaped peninsula at the westernmost point of the Solway coast, known as the **Rhinns of Galloway**, encompasses two contrasting towns: the old seafaring port of **Portpatrick** and the dishevelled port of **Stranraer**, which is struggling with the loss of its regular ferry services to Northern Ireland in 2011 (these now depart from Cairnryan seven miles north). At either end of the peninsula are two lighthouses: one stands above **Corsewall Point**, and now houses a luxury hotel, the other stands on the

Mull of Galloway, a windswept headland at the southwest tip of Scotland, which is home to a vast array of nesting seabirds.

The Gulf Stream dominates the climate here and subtropical plants grow in abundance throughout the area's gardens, linked by the signposted official garden route (Ⓦscotlandsgardenroute.co.uk). Each has its own personality, with colourful seasonal displays and palm trees, and many have coastal views. If you only have time to visit two, aim for Castle Kennedy Gardens and Logan.

Castle Kennedy Gardens

Castle Kennedy, 3 miles east of Stranraer • Feb–March Sat–Sun 10am–5pm; April–Oct daily 10am–5pm • £5.50 • ☎ 01776 702024, Ⓦ castlekennedygardens.co.uk

The approach to **Castle Kennedy Gardens** passes along a tree-lined avenue that frames the ruined medieval fortress of Castle Kennedy beyond, and then across a palm-fringed canal. The castle forms the centrepiece of the gardens, on a hill squeezed between two lochs, though its ruins can no longer be visited. The 75-acre landscaped gardens stretch west as far as nearby Lochinch Castle, seat of the earl of Stair (and also inaccessible), via a giant lily pond and a stupendous avenue of monkey puzzle trees.

Portpatrick

Situated roughly halfway along the west shore of the Rhinns, **PORTPATRICK** has an attractive pastel-painted seafront wrapped around a small rocky bay, sheltered by cliffs. Until the mid-nineteenth century Portpatrick was a thriving seaport, serving as a major embarkation point for Ireland, with coal, cotton and British troops heading in one direction, Ulster cattle and linen in the other. Nowadays, minus its railway, it's a quiet, comely resort enjoyed for its rugged scenery, sea angling and gentle hikes.

ARRIVAL AND DEPARTURE   PORTPATRICK

By bus Buses leave from South Crescent next to the sandy bay for Ayr (8 daily, 4 on Sun; 1hr 30min) and Stranraer (hourly; 25min).

ACCOMMODATION

Castle Bay Holiday Park 0.5 miles south of Portpatrick ☎ 01776 810462, Ⓦ castlebayholidaypark.co.uk. Near the cliff's edge next to Dunskey Castle a short walk south of town, with two-bedroom static homes available to rent by the week. The caravans are reasonably well equipped and there's a little play park in the grounds. Caravans per week **£350**

★ **Rickwood House Hotel** Heugh Rd ☎ 01776 810270, Ⓦ portpatrick.me.uk. Set back from the harbour, with contemporarily furnished en-suite rooms with views of the sea and, weather permitting, the sunset. Guests can take a drink in the conservatory where there's a small library of books, or have a good soak in the garden hot tub. **£95**

EATING AND DRINKING

Campbell's Restaurant 1 South Crescent ☎ 01776 810314, Ⓦ campbellsrestaurant.co.uk. Pleasantly located overlooking the town's crescent-shaped sandy bay, this modern bistro churns out some superb seafood dishes. There's a wide selection from fish soup to Cajun salmon but your best bet is to stick with the catch of the day; grilled or, if you're feeling flush, the lobster for £28. Sun–Thurs noon–10pm, Fri–Sat noon–11pm.

The Crown 9 North Crescent ☎ 01776 810261, Ⓦ crown portpatrick.com. Right on the seafront, this cosy inn is a good bet for fresh seafood, hand-pulled ales and live music in front of an open fire. For a light lunch try the cullen skink (smoked haddock soup) for £6 or the delightful seafood pancake gratin for £14. Sun–Thurs 11am–midnight, Fri–Sat till 1pm.

Logan Botanic Garden

2 miles north of Port Logan • Feb to mid-March Sun only 10am–5pm; mid-March to Oct daily 10am–5pm • £6.50 • ☎ 01776 860231, Ⓦ rbge.org.uk • Bus #407 from Stranraer stops at Port Logan (Mon–Sat 6 daily; 30min), then a 2-mile walk north

---

WALKS AROUND PORTPATRICK

Ordnance Survey Explorer map 309

For a spectacular one-mile circular stroll from Portpatrick along the sea cliffs to the shattered ruins of **Dunskey Castle**, follow the coastline south from the harbour until you reach the steps leading up to the cliffs. The route up to the castle, a sixteenth-century L-shaped tower house, is quite vertiginous in places, but the way back via the disused railway is less hair-raising.

An easy four-mile circular walk takes you north from Main Street to **Dunskey Gardens**. From there head southwest following the stream down Dunskey Glen to the coast to link up with the **Southern Upland Way**, which takes you back to the quayside.

An outpost of Edinburgh's Royal Botanic Garden, **Logan Botanic Garden** is a marvellously exotic place where the mild air brought by the Gulf Stream supports an eye-opening abundance of tree ferns and palm trees. Check out the primeval giant Brazilian rhubarb in the Gunnera Bog, take a wander in the woods to the south, and head for the enormous walled gardens, where you'll find a water garden, a peat garden (the first ever), and a massive 20ft-high beech hedge.

Mull of Galloway

Right at the southern tip of the Rhinns peninsula, the isolated **Mull of Galloway** is well worth the ride and really feels like the end of the road. From this precipitous headland on a clear day you can see the Isle of Man and the coasts of Ireland and England. The southernmost point in Scotland, it's a favourite nesting spot for guillemots, razorbills, kittiwakes, shags, fulmars and even a few puffins; skeins of gannets fish here, too, from their gannetry on the Scares, clearly visible to the east. The headland is also an RSPB reserve – good for spotting linnets and twite – with a **visitor centre** in a building near the **lighthouse**.

Mull of Galloway Lighthouse

Mull of Galloway • Easter–June & Sept–Oct Sat–Sun 10am–4pm; July & Aug daily 10am–4pm • £2.50 • ☎ 01776 840554, Ⓦ mull-of-galloway.co.uk

Sited 325ft above sea level at the southern end of the Rhinns peninsula, the **Mull of Galloway Lighthouse**, built by Robert Stevenson, was manned from 1830 until as recently as 1988. Today there's a small museum with old photos and running videos, but it's the heady view from the top that impresses the most.

ARRIVAL AND INFORMATION   MULL OF GALLOWAY

By bus The nearest bus stop is 4 miles north at Drummore, with services to Port Logan (Mon–Sat 5 daily; 10min) and Stranraer (Mon–Sat 6 daily; 40min).

Information Next to the lighthouse, the RSPB Visitor Centre (April to mid-Oct daily 10am–4pm; ☎ 01988 402130, Ⓦ rspb.org.uk) provides a wealth of material about local bird, plant and marine life, and has live images of bird colonies nesting on the cliffs. Outside there's a couple of short nature trails.

EATING

Gallie Craig Just south of the lighthouse ☎ 01776 840558, Ⓦ galliecraig.co.uk. Perched on the cliff edge, roofed with turf and with a panoramic glass wall and terrace looking out to the sea, Scotland's most southerly building provides armchair birdwatching while you enjoy some coffee and cake for around a fiver. If you're stopping for lunch there are also some reasonably priced light meals here too like soups and toasties, some of which are suitable for vegetarians. Feb–Easter Sat–Wed 11am–4pm, Easter–Oct daily 10am–5.30pm, Nov Sat–Sun 11am–4pm.

Ayrshire
and Arran

HIKER ON GOAT FELL, ARRAN

Ayrshire and Arran

The rolling hills and rich soil of Ayrshire make for prime farming country, etched with a patchwork of lush fields and hedgerows. The region's real draw, however, is its coastline, thanks to its wide, flat, sandy beaches, while its endless, fantastic golfing possibilities (including several championship links courses) attract golfers from all over the world. The county town is Ayr, which draws a healthy number of visitors thanks to its associations with Robert Burns, who was born in nearby Alloway. The real highlight here, though, is Arran, often described as "Scotland in miniature", thanks to its highland/lowland divide and abundance of man-made and natural heritage.

Fifty miles from top to bottom, the largely unblemished **South Ayrshire coastline**, between Ayr and Stranraer, offers several appealing possibilities: notably **Culzean Castle**, Robert Adam's cliffside Neoclassical mansion, and the little-visited but wonderful medieval ruins of **Crossraguel Abbey**. Out in the Firth of Clyde stands **Ailsa Craig**, the giant muffin-shaped island, which is home to the world's second-largest gannetry. Back inland, **Dumfries House** is one of the finest eighteenth-century stately homes in Britain.

The disparate **North Ayrshire coastline**, whose towns once benefited from the industrialization of Glasgow, offers fewer incentives to visit. That said, **Irvine**, home to the terrific Scottish Maritime Museum, and **Largs**, the area's liveliest seaside resort, from where you can catch a ferry across to **Great Cumbrae**, both merit a portion of your time.

Without doubt the most alluring destination in Ayrshire is the **Isle of Arran**, its jagged outline visible across the Firth of Clyde from the entire length of the Ayrshire coast. The beautiful, barren north of the island is a great place to get a quick taste of the Highlands, while the southern half contains the island's largest settlements, including the capital, **Brodick**, and bulk of attractions.

GETTING AROUND   **AYRSHIRE AND ARRAN**

By bus All the towns along the coast are well served by buses from Glasgow, with a regular express service (#X77) to Ayr.
By train Ayr, Largs and Irvine are all served by frequent trains from Glasgow Central; the line to Ayr continues down the coast to Stranraer.
By ferry to Arran CalMac (☎0800 066 5000, ⊛calmac .co.uk) operate ferries to Brodick, on Arran (5–8 daily, 55min), from Ardrossan, 23 miles north of Ayr.

Ayr and around

With a population of around fifty thousand, **AYR** is by far the largest town on the Firth of Clyde coast. It was an important seaport and trading centre for many centuries, rivalling Glasgow in size and significance right up until the late seventeenth century. In recognition, Cromwell made it a centre for his administration and built an enormous fortress here, long since destroyed. With the relative decline of its seaborne trade, Ayr

---

Horse racing in Ayr p.163
On the Burns trail p.164
Robert Burns p.165
Golf in Ayr p.167

The Battle of Largs p.169
Arran Golf Pass p.173
Goat Fell p.174

CULZEAN CASTLE

Highlights

❶ Alloway The village where poet Robert Burns was born, and the best of many Burns pilgrimage spots in the region. **See p.163**

❷ Dumfries House An eighteenth-century architectural masterpiece, designed by the Adam brothers and decked out by Thomas Chippendale. **See p.166**

❸ Culzean Castle Stately home with a fabulous cliff-edge setting, surrounded by acres of gardens and woods reaching down to the shore. **See p.167**

❹ Ailsa Craig Watch baby gannets learn the art of flying and diving for fish on this distinctive island mountain some nine miles offshore. **See p.168**

❺ Goat Fell, Arran Spectacular views over north Arran's craggy mountain range and the Firth of Clyde. **See p.174**

❻ Isle of Arran Distillery, Lochranza Take a tour and have a dram at one of Scotland's smallest distilleries. **See p.175**

HIGHLIGHTS ARE MARKED ON THE MAP ON P.160

reinvented itself in the nineteenth century as an administrative centre and a popular resort for middle-class Victorians – aided by the opening of the Glasgow-to-Ayr train line in 1840, which brought in the first major influx of holiday-makers. While there are few real sights in town to detain you, its prestigious **racecourse** pulls in huge crowds, there's superb **golf** all around, and the local tourist industry continues to do steady business out of the fact that Robert Burns was born in the neighbouring village of **Alloway** (see p.163).

HIGHLIGHTS

1 Alloway
2 Dumfries House
3 Culzean Castle
4 Ailsa Craig
5 Goat Fell, Arran
6 Isle of Arran Distillery, Lochranza

AYRSHIRE & ARRAN

Auld Brig and Auld Kirk

Auld Kirk Blackfriar's Walk • Feb–June & Sept–Nov Tues 1–2pm; July & Aug Sat 10.30am–12.30pm • Free • ☎ 01292 262938, ⓦ auldkirk.org

One of the oldest stone bridges in Scotland, Ayr's wonderfully crooked, four-arched **Auld Brig** was built during the reign of James IV (1488–1513), having replaced an earlier, thirteenth-century wooden one. Thankfully, it survived the threat of demolition in the early twentieth century, thanks largely to Burns's poem *The Brigs of Ayr*, as the plaque halfway along the bridge acknowledges.

A short stroll upstream from the Auld Brig stands the town's much-restored **Auld Kirk**, which Burns attended as a young boy. At the lych gate, look out for the coffin-shaped mortsafe (heavy grating) on the walls; placed over newly dug graves, these mortsafes were an early nineteenth-century security system, meant to deter body snatchers at a time when bodies were swiftly bought up by medical schools, with no questions asked.

Citadel and St John's Tower

All you can see of Cromwell's zigzag **Citadel**, built to the west of the town centre in the 1650s, is a small section of the old walls – the area was built over, for the most part, in Victorian times, but is still known locally as "the Fort". The best-preserved section of the fortifications lies on South Harbour Street, though the one surviving corbelled corner turret is, in fact, a Victorian addition known as **Miller's Folly** after its eccentric former owner.

Another survivor from the distant past is **St John's Tower**, near Bruce Crescent, which stands on its own in a well-kept walled garden at the heart of the old citadel, and is all that remains of the medieval church where the Scottish parliament met after the Battle of Bannockburn in 1315 to decide the royal succession. Although a spiral staircase links the five floors (vault, three rooms and bell chamber), it's not possible to access the interior.

Wellington Square and Esplanade

The epitome of Ayr's main Georgian and Regency residential development, and the town's showpiece, is **Wellington Square**, whose first occupants were "Gentlemen of Rich Fortune and Retired Army Officers"; its trim gardens and terraces are overlooked by the **County Buildings**, a vast, imposing Palladian pile from 1820.

Esplanade and Low Green

Unless the weather's fantastic, you'll find only the hardiest types taking a stroll along Ayr's bleak, long **Esplanade** and beach, which look out to the Isle of Arran. The one building of note is the distinctive whitewashed **Ayr Pavilion**, built in 1911, with its four tall corner towers; it's known locally as "the Piv" and now houses the suitably tacky Pirate Pete's Family Entertainment Centre. You're far better off directing the kids to the superb adventure playground next door.

The pavilion sits on the edge of **Low Green**, a lovely expanse of grass that was originally used as common grazing land. As well as being a great spot for a bracing walk, and, if it's not too windy, a picnic, it's also where tens of thousands of people congregate in early September for the **Scottish International Airshow**, with spectacular flying displays along the seafront.

ARRIVAL AND INFORMATION

AYR AND AROUND

By train Ayr train station is 10min walk southeast of the town centre on Station Rd.

Destinations Girvan (Mon–Sat hourly, 5 on Sun; 30min); Glasgow Central (every 20min; 50min–1hr 15min); Irvine (every 20min; 20min); Stranraer (Mon–Sat 7 daily, 5 on Sun; 1hr 25min).

By bus The bus station is smack-bang in the centre of town at the corner of Sandgate and Fullarton St. Note that express bus #X77 to Glasgow's Buchanan station departs from Douglas St, opposite the bus station.

Destinations Ardrossan (Mon–Sat every 30min, Sun 6; 55min); Culzean Castle (Mon–Sat hourly, Sun every 2hr;

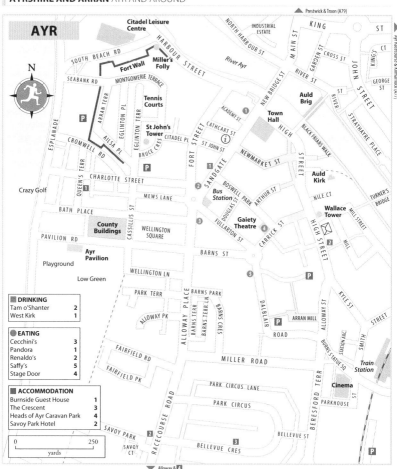

4

▣ DRINKING
Tam o'Shanter	2
West Kirk	1

● EATING
Cecchini's	3
Pandora	1
Renaldo's	2
Saffy's	5
Stage Door	4

▣ ACCOMMODATION
Burnside Guest House	1
The Crescent	3
Heads of Ayr Caravan Park	4
Savoy Park Hotel	2

30min); Girvan, for Ailsa Craig (Mon–Sat every 30min, Sun hourly; 1hr); Glasgow (Mon–Sat every 30min, Sun hourly; 55min); Irvine (every 30min; 30min); Largs (Mon–Sat every 30min, 5 on Sun; 1hr 25min); Stranraer (Mon–Sat 7 daily, 4 on Sun; 2hr); Wemyss Bay (Mon–Sat every 30min, 5 on Sun; 1hr 40min).

Tourist office 22 Sandgate (Easter–Sept Mon–Sat 9am–5pm, Sun 10am–5pm; Oct–Easter closed Sun;

☎01292 290300, ⓦayrshire-arran.com). Packed with local and regional info, the tourist office can also help with accommodation, which is a particularly useful service during big horse-racing meetings. Outside, take a look up at the plaque, which denotes that this is one of the oldest buildings in town and the birthplace, in 1756, of road engineer John McAdam, who invented the process known as "macadamization", hence the word tarmac.

ACCOMMODATION

Guesthouses dominate in Ayr, with plenty clustered in the streets between the town centre and the Esplanade, and a few smarter places to be found in the leafy streets to the south of the town centre. There are no hostels in town, though there are a couple of **campsites** in the vicinity.

Burnside Guest House 14 Queen's Terrace ☎01292 263912, ⓦtheburnsideguesthouse.co.uk. The pick of the many guesthouses along this street, the six extremely comfortable, tastefully designed rooms (including a single and a family room) come with restored wooden furnishings, wicker chairs and old-fashioned clocks and lamps. **£60**

HORSE RACING IN AYR

Horse racing in Ayr dates back to the seventeenth century, though Ayr's present **racecourse** (Ⓦ ayr-racecourse.co.uk) staged its first race in 1907. Today it ranks as Scotland's premier course, staging both flat and national hunt (jump) races, including Scotland's two most prestigious outings; the **Scottish Grand National** in April and the **Gold Cup** in September.

The Crescent 26 Bellevue Crescent ☎ 01292 287329, Ⓦ 26crescent.co.uk. Spacious and cosy Victorian house with five distinctively furnished rooms (one a four-poster suite), though Laura Ashley-style wallpaper, curtains and the like dominate. A cracking breakfast is served in the elegant dining room. **£85**

Heads of Ayr Caravan Park Dunure Rd ☎ 01292 442269, Ⓦ headsofayr-caravanpark.co.uk. Some 3 miles south of town along the coastal A719, beside the popular Heads of Ayr Farm Park, this caravan site also has pitches for tents. March–Oct. Per pitch **£22.50**

Savoy Park Hotel 16 Racecourse Rd ☎ 01292 266112, Ⓦ savoypark.com. A splendid red sandstone Scots Baronial building which, though a little lacking in atmosphere (and often geared towards weddings), does possess extremely well-appointed rooms. The public rooms are suitably grand, too, and there's a lovely garden complete with gazebo and swings. **£75**

EATING

Cecchini's 72 Fort St ☎ 01292 263607, Ⓦ cecchinisayr .co.uk. A cut above your average pizza and pasta joint, cool *Cecchini's* has an enticing range of mains, such as borlotti casserole (beans with thickly chopped Italian sausage on a bed of mash; £8.95), and *spezzatino* (Scotch beef cooked with red wine and tomatoes; £13.95), as well as any number of terrific value daily deals. Mon–Sat 10am–10pm, Sun 10am–9pm.

Pandora 32 New Bridge St ☎ 01292 289919, Ⓦ pandoracoffeehouse.co.uk. Stylish, dark wood-panelled coffee house offering great caffeine fixes alongside light snacks like soups, baguettes and crêpes (£5.95). The poached egg and toasted bagel breakfasts (served until noon) are a good shout too. Mon–Sat 7.30am–6pm, Sun 10am–5pm.

Renaldo's 98 Sandgate ☎ 01292 265956, Ⓦ renaldo's .co.uk. Cheery *Renaldo's* is renowned for its authentic Italian ice cream (£1.70 a tub), all of which is made on the premises, with flavours ranging from the sublime (pistachio, strawberries and cream) to the ridiculous (Irn-Bru). Mon–Sat 9am–9pm, Sun 11am–9pm.

Saffy's 2 Dalblair Rd ☎ 01292 288598, Ⓦ saffys-ayr .co.uk. There's certainly nothing fancy about the exterior, but the interior – mixed-up furniture and wall-mounted artwork – is most comforting, as is the food; the specials are more appealing than the regular menu, so expect fish stew with tomato, orange and chilli, or spiced Shetland salmon with curry cream (£11.95). Well-priced two-course lunch (noon–2.30pm; £12.50) and dinner (5–6.30pm; £13.50) menus. Tues–Sat 10am–2.30pm & 5–9pm, Sun noon–8pm.

Stage Door 12 Carrick St ☎ 01292 280444, Ⓦ stagedoorcafe.co.uk. Sharing the same space as the theatre box office, this simple but perennially busy restaurant offers favourably priced dishes like peppered chicken and haggis burger, and Parma ham-wrapped monkfish tail (£7.95) to tempt you in. The two-course express lunch menu is good value at £10.95. Daily 10am–11pm.

DRINKING

Tam o' Shanter 230 High St ☎ 01292 611684. So-named after the eponymous Burns character, this cosy, thatched inn, dating from 1749, receives a steady flow of locals throughout the day, here for a bit of banter while supping on a pint of the local real ale, from the Ayr Brewing Company. Open mic night on Wednesdays. Daily 11am–midnight.

West Kirk 58a Sandgate ☎ 01292 880416. For a quiet pint of real ale, or a craft beer, head to this music-free Wetherspoon church-to-pub conversion, with wooden balconies held up by pistachio-coloured fluted pillars. Daily 8am–midnight.

Alloway

ALLOWAY, formerly a small village but now on the southern outskirts of Ayr, is the birthplace of Robert Burns (1759–96), Scotland's national poet. Today it is totally dominated by all things Burnsiana, all of which is gathered under the umbrella of the **Robert Burns Birthplace Museum**. Note that the entrance fee applies only to the museum and cottage, and tickets are valid for three consecutive days meaning you can visit as many times as you wish during this period; the other sights are free to visit and have no set opening times.

ON THE BURNS TRAIL

As well as the numerous attractions associated with Robert Burns in **Alloway**, two more places that resonate with Burns fans can be found not too far from Ayr; six miles northeast of Ayr is **The Bachelors' Club** (Easter–Sept Fri–Tues 1–5pm; £3.50; NTS), a wee thatched house in the tiny village of Tarbolton. It was here in the upstairs room that the 20-year-old Burns attended dancing classes, set up a debating society and became a Freemason. In Kirkoswald, fourteen miles southwest of Ayr, is **Souter Johnnie's Cottage** (Easter–Sept Mon, Tues, Fri–Sun 11.30am–5pm; free; NTS), once the home of John Davidson, Burns's boon companion and the original inspiration for Souter (cobbler) Johnnie in *Tam o' Shanter*. The main building is now an art gallery, while the restored alehouse to the rear houses brilliant, life-size sandstone figures of Johnnie, Tam, the innkeeper and his wife. In the graveyard across the road are the graves of John Davidson and Tam, as well as those of Burns' grandparents and his headmaster; a plate on the gate denotes their whereabouts. Inside the roofless kirk is the font reputedly used for the christening of Robert the Bruce in 1274, though the event itself actually took place at Crossraguel (see p.166).

Burns Museum

Murdoch's Lone • Daily: April–Sept 10am–5.30pm; Oct–March 10am–5pm • £9 (including entrance to cottage); NTS • ☎ 01292 443 700, ⓦ burnsmuseum.org.uk

The centrepiece of the Birthplace Museum is the **museum** itself, a voluminous and illuminating exhibition that should satisfy even the most ardent Burns fan. Inevitably, the main focus is on his extraordinary literary accomplishments – look out for four skilfully carved wooden friezes depicting the key scenes in *Tam o' Shanter*, and a marvellous chair made from the Kilmarnock printing press, which produced the first edition of *Poems, Chiefly in the Scottish Dialect* in 1786; it, too, features some wonderful carvings, including a bas-relief of the Brig o' Doon and, on the armrest, two dogs (Luath and Caesar from *The Twa Dogs*); above is a photo of Muhammad Ali (a man who wasn't averse to a rhyme or two himself) sitting in this very chair in 1965. Elsewhere, the beautifully presented glass cabinets are stuffed with memorabilia pertaining to other, lesser known, aspects of his life, such as the pistol he used as an exciseman, and the apron he wore at Masonic meetings in Dumfries. In addition, you can view his parlour chair and desk, the wedding ring belonging to his wife, Jean Armour, and dozens of books and letters dedicated to friends and family.

Burns Monument and Brig o' Doon

Heading through the carefully manicured garden behind the museum, you can't miss the **Burns Monument**, a striking, slightly ludicrous Neoclassical rotunda, topped by a scalloped cornice and a miniature copper-gilt baldachin. Climb to the top for views over to the **Brig o' Doon**, the picturesque thirteenth-century hump-backed bridge over which Tam is forced to flee for his life. In the nearby **Statue House**, admire some eighteenth-century stone statues of Tam, Soutar and Nanse, which are, in fact, portraits of Burns's friends.

Alloway Kirk

Across the road from the museum is the plain, roofless ruin of the sixteenth-century **Alloway Kirk**, setting for much of *Tam o' Shanter*; Tam, having got drunk in Ayr, passes "by Alloway's auld haunted kirk" and stumbles across a riotous witches' dance. All that remains inside are a pair of iron mortsafes. The Kirk is also where Robert's father, William, and his sister, Isabella Burns Begg, are buried. His father's grave is prominently located at the entrance to the church; the mournful epitaph on the back of the headstone was penned by Burns.

Burns Cottage

Greenfield Avenue • Daily: April–Sept 10am–5.30pm; Oct–March 10am–5pm • £9 (including entrance to Burns Museum); NTS •
☎ 01292 443 700, ⓦ burnsmuseum.org.uk

Standing opposite the village post office is the **Burns Cottage**, birthplace of the poet and his home for the first seven years of his life. Built by his father, William, the low, whitewashed, thatched cottage was where animals and people lived under the same roof, with a separate section for grain storage – something that was quite modern in its day. Much altered over the years, there's not an awful lot to see inside, but you can nevertheless gain an impression of what the place must have been like when Burns, the first of seven children, was born in the box-bed in the only room in the house.

ARRIVAL AND DEPARTURE
ALLOWAY

By bus The #X77 from Glasgow (via Ayr) drops off at the museum (2–3 daily), while bus #361 (hourly) departs from Carrick St in Ayr and drops off at Burns Cottage.

ROBERT BURNS

The first of seven children, **Robert Burns**, the national poet of Scotland, was born in Alloway on January 25, 1759. His father, William, was a tenant farmer at Mount Oliphant, near Alloway, moving to Lochlie Farm, Tarbolton, eleven years later. A series of bad harvests and the demands of the landlord's estate manager bankrupted the family, and William died almost penniless in 1784. These events had a profound effect on Robert, leaving him with an antipathy towards political authority and a hatred of the land-owning classes.

With the death of his father, Robert became head of the family and they moved again, this time to a farm at Mossgiel, near Mauchline. Burns had already begun writing **poetry** and **prose** at Lochlie, recording incidental thoughts in his *First Commonplace Book*, but it was here at Mossgiel that he began to write in earnest, and his first volume, *Poems, Chiefly in the Scottish Dialect*, was published in Kilmarnock in 1786. The book proved immensely popular, with the satirical trilogy *Holy Willie's Prayer*, *The Holy Fair* and *Address to the Devil* attracting particular attention. The object of Burns's poetic scorn was the kirk, whose ministers had obliged him to appear in church to be publicly condemned for **fornication**.

Burns spent the winter of 1786–87 in the capital, lionized by the literary establishment. Despite his success, however, he felt trapped, unable to make enough money from writing to leave **farming**. He was also in a political snare, fraternizing with the elite, but with radical views and pseudo-Jacobite nationalist sympathies that constantly landed him in trouble. His frequent recourse was to play the part of the unlettered ploughman-poet, the noble savage who might be excused his impetuous outbursts and hectic womanizing.

He had, however, made useful contacts in **Edinburgh** and as a consequence was recruited to collect, write and rearrange two volumes of songs set to traditional Scottish tunes. These volumes, James Johnson's *Scots Musical Museum* and George Thomson's *Select Scottish Airs*, contain the bulk of his **songwriting**, and it's on them that Burns's international reputation rests, with works like *Auld Lang Syne*, *Scots, Wha Hae*, *Coming Through the Rye* and *Green Grow the Rushes, O*. At this time, too, though **poetry** now took second place, he produced two excellent poems: *Tam o' Shanter* and a republican tract, *A Man's a Man for a' That*.

Burns often boasted of his sexual conquests, and he fathered several illegitimate children, but in 1788, he eventually married **Jean Armour**, a stonemason's daughter from Mauchline, with whom he already had two children, and moved to Ellisland Farm, near Dumfries. The following year he was appointed excise officer and could at last leave farming, moving to Dumfries in 1791. Burns's years of comfort were short-lived, however. His years of labour on the farm, allied to a rheumatic fever, damaged his heart, and he died in Dumfries on July 21, 1796, aged 37.

Burns's work, inspired by his sexual conquests, and he fathered several illegitimate children, but in 1788, he eventually married **romantic nationalism** and tinged with a wry wit, has made him a potent symbol of "Scottishness". Ignoring the anglophile preferences of the Edinburgh elite, he wrote in Scots vernacular about the country he loved: an exuberant celebration that filled a need in a nation culturally colonized by England. Today, Burns Clubs all over the world mark every anniversary of the poet's birthday with the **Burns Supper**, complete with Scottish totems – haggis, piper and whisky bottle – and a ritual recital of Burns's *Ode to a Haggis*.

4

4

Dumfries House

Outside Cumnock, 14 miles east of Ayr off the A70 • April–Oct daily 10.45am–3.30pm; Nov–March Sat & Sun only, same times; pre-booked guided tours only • £9 • ☎ 01290 425959, ⓦ dumfries-house.org.uk • Bus #42 (hourly) from Ayr to Cumnock

A handsome Palladian villa, **Dumfries House** was commissioned by the fifth earl of Dumfries, a widower who wanted to remarry and ensure that he had an heir for the family estate. The house, the first major early commission for the Adam brothers, was conceived as a honey trap to lure a potential wife, and, judging by the portrait of the ageing, gouty earl in the Pink Drawing Room, he needed all the help he could get. Such was the earl's urgency, the house was built and decked out relatively swiftly – between 1756 and 1760 – meaning its Rococo decorative scheme is in perfect harmony with the graceful sandstone exterior. The earl secured a wife but died without producing an heir; the family subsequently turned their attention to creating **Mount Stuart** (see p.229), leaving Dumfries House to be looked after by a series of housekeepers. The recent story of the house is as remarkable as its past: the building and its contents were all up for sale in 2007, and some of the furniture had begun its journey south to Christie's when Prince Charles and a hastily assembled trust intervened to make a heritage "save".

Chief among the treasures is an outstanding collection of **Chippendale furniture**, some ordered direct from Thomas himself, and some created from his "Director" (book of designs) and augmented by local craftsmen with Scottish saltires. Among the 57 Chippendale pieces on display (which amounts to around ten percent of his entire oeuvre) is a truly spectacular, one-of-a-kind rosewood bookcase, reputedly now worth around £20 million; elsewhere, card tables, gilded mirrors, a study table with draws on all four sides, and a gorgeous, blue stretch silk bed lie in wait. Otherwise, the family symbols of the wyvern (small dragon) and the thistle recur in inventive and playful touches, and exotic Oriental motifs crop up in the fanciful Adam plasterwork ceilings, tapestry fire screens and gilded pier glasses. Among the many other highlights is a rare, eighteenth-century Grand Orrery, a mechanical model of the solar system, this one featuring an exquisite ivory globe.

The grounds

Following Prince Charles' intervention, the whole estate, with its sweet-smelling pines, ponds and streams, has continued to undergo a remarkable transformation; a few paces from the house is the Adam-designed **Avenue Bridge**, an elegant, triple-arched structure, across which lies a beautifully landscaped **arboretum**, lined with red gravel walkways and an abundance of woodland flowers and shrubs. Completing this fabulous ensemble is a five-acre **walled garden**, with neatly laid out plots of flowers, herbs and vegetables, stepped terraces and greenhouses.

Crossraguel Abbey

A77, 2 miles south of Maybole • April–Sept daily 9.30am–5.30pm • £4.50; HES • ☎ 01655 883113, ⓦ historicenvironment.scot

The substantial remains of **Crossraguel Abbey** provide a lovely antidote to the hordes that pile into Culzean. A Cluniac monastery – one of only two in Scotland – it was founded in 1250, though most of what you see here dates from the late fourteenth century following extensive damage during the wars with England.

At the heart of the complex is the **abbey church**, which has ornate carvings over the piscina and sedilia, though it's not as impressive as the fifteenth-century **sacristy**, which has kept its vaulted ceiling and its decorative capitals, corbels and bosses, embellished with squirrels, lions, a triple-faced head and a green man. Next door, off the cloisters, is the similarly intact, though less decorative, **chapterhouse**. The **tower house**, tacked onto the eastern end of the complex, was built in the early sixteenth century as luxury accommodation for William Kennedy, the last abbot to reside here, between 1520 and 1547; in keeping with the abbot's high status in the outside world, it clearly illustrates the corruption of the monastic ideal that spurred the Reformation. On the opposite side of the abbey, the **gatehouse** is equally grand, and has been restored so that you can climb right up to the cap house and walk out onto the battlements.

Visible in one corner of the complex is a beehive-shaped **dovecote**, complete with well-preserved nesting boxes. This was a crucial part of the abbey's economy, as the monks not only ate the doves but also relied on them for eggs.

Culzean Castle

A719, 4km west of Maybole • **Castle** Easter–Oct daily 10.30am–5pm • £15.50; NTS • **Country park** Daily 9.30am–dusk • £10.50 • ☎ 01655 884455, ⓦ culzeanexperience.org • Bus #60 from Ayr

Sitting on the edge of a sheer cliff, looking out over the Firth of Clyde to Arran, Culzean Castle couldn't have a more impressive situation. Given its strategic position, it's hardly surprising that the Kennedy family maintained a castle at Culzean (pronounced "cullane") from the twelfth century onwards. The current castle is actually a grand, late eighteenth-century stately home, designed by the Scottish Neoclassical architect **Robert Adam** for the tenth earl of Cassillis (pronounced "cassles"), as the Kennedys had by then become.

From the **visitor centre** in the modernized Home Farm buildings, where you can watch an audiovisual show on the house, it's a few minutes' walk through Adam's mock-ruined arch to the **castle** itself, which overlooks the pristine lawn and herbaceous borders of the Fountain Court on one side, with the high sea cliffs on the other. Begun in 1777, Culzean's exterior preserves a medieval aspect, with its arrow slits and battlements; the interior, however, exemplifies the delicate, harmonious Neoclassical designs that Adam loved – look out for the dolphins and swans (emblems of the Kennedy family) and the rams' heads (Adam's own favourite motif). The most brilliantly conceived work by Adam is the **Oval Staircase**, where tiers of classical columns lead up to a huge glazed cupola allowing light to stream down. After admiring the portrait of Napoleon by Lefèvre, you pass through to the impressive circular **Saloon**, whose symmetrical flourishes deliberately contrast with the natural land and seascapes dramatically on view through the windows. One of the last rooms you come to (though it's closed off by perspex) is the still fully furnished office used by General Eisenhower (including a beaten leather chair, his phone and some family photos); one of the conditions stipulated by the Kennedys before handing over the castle to the National Trust in 1945 was that Eisenhower be gifted use of the top-floor apartments, in recognition of America's support during World War II; in the event, he visited Culzean four times, including once during his second term of presidency.

It's worth leaving enough time for an exploration of the 500-acre **country park**, the highlights of which are the walled garden, with its stone and glass orangery, stone grotto and fruit houses, and the Swan Pond, abundant with waterfowl. Close by is Adventure Cove, a vast wooden playground with all manner of climbing equipment for kids to get lost in.

4

GOLF IN AYR

Few parts of Scotland can boast as many world-class **golf courses** as this stretch of the Ayrshire coast, with two in particular – **Royal Troon** (ⓦ royaltroon.co.uk), ten miles north of Ayr, and **Turnberry** (ⓦ turnberry.co.uk), sixteen smiles south of Ayr – ranking among the world's most prestigious. Both courses are on the British Open roster, with Troon the last of these two great courses to stage the event, in 2016. A round at either course will cost you a small fortune (about £150), but there are half a dozen or so far more affordable places to play throughout the region; check out ⓦ golfsouthayrshire.com.

Ailsa Craig

As you travel along the South Ayrshire coast, the giant muffin-shaped island of **Ailsa Craig** is an intriguing presence on the horizon, stranded as it is in the middle of the Firth of Clyde. The island's name means "Fairy Rock" in Gaelic, though it was a less than enchanting place for the persecuted Catholics who escaped here during the Reformation. The island's granite has long been used for making what many consider to be the finest curling stones – a company in nearby Mauchline still has exclusive rights and sporadically collects a few boulders. In the late nineteenth century, 29 people lived on the island, either working in the quarry or at the Stevenson lighthouse.

With its volcanic, columnar cliffs and 1114ft summit, Ailsa Craig is now a **bird sanctuary** that's home to some 40,000 gannets, plus thousands of other seabirds. Trips to the island depart from **Girvan**, 21 miles south of Ayr. The best time to make the trip is at the end of May and in June when the fledglings are trying to fly. It takes about an hour to reach the island, after which you get enough time to walk up to the summit of the rock and watch the birds, weather permitting.

TOURS AILSA CRAIG

Boat tours Several companies in Girvan offer cruises round the island, but only Mark McCrindle is licensed to land (☎01465 713219 or ☎07773 794358, ⓦailsacraig .org.uk). The exact timings and prices depend on the length of trip, tides and weather, but, generally speaking these take place between April and September with either one or two trips each day (£20/3hr). Booking ahead is essential.

4 Irvine

IRVINE, twelve miles north of Ayr, was once the principal port for trade between Glasgow and Ireland, and later for coal from Kilmarnock. Those halcyon days are long gone, and the town, sadly, has little now to commend it. That said, it does possess one of the region's finest museums, and for that reason alone, it is worth a visit.

Scottish Maritime Museum

6 Gottries Rd • Daily 10am–5pm, Tues till 6.30pm • £7.50 • ☎01294 278283, ⓦscottishmaritimemuseum.org

Irvine's one major draw is the **Scottish Maritime Museum**, which is spread across several locations down at the town's carefully restored old harbour. The main exhibition is held inside the **Linthouse Engine Shop**, a magnificent late nineteenth-century hangar-like building held up with massive iron girders, moved here brick by brick from Govan in 1991. As well as superbly documenting the many marvellous feats of engineering, courtesy of engines and turbines galore, it's the spectacular array of vessels that really catches the eye, such as the rusting hull (minus bow) of the **SS Rifle**, the earliest surviving example of a pre-fabricated screw steamer; this one was laid up in 1930, before sinking and then being raised in 1990. There's also an ingeniously crafted parachuted airborne lifeboat – named the **Uffa Fox** after its creator – designed to be dropped close to airmen forced to ditch at sea. Inevitably though, some vessels recall tales of disaster, such as the **RNLI TGB**, which capsized in 1969 while attempting a rescue at Longhope in the Orkneys, leading to the loss of all eight crew members. More mysterious is the story of Kenneth Kerr and his 13ft glass-fibre dinghy, **Bass Conqueror**. In October 1980, while on his second attempt to row across the Atlantic in the smallest ever boat, Kerr ran into difficulties somewhere off the Irish coast and all radio contact was lost. The dinghy was found near Stavanger several months later, but Kerr was never found.

Moored at the **pontoons** on Harbour Street is the **MV Kyles**, a coaster built in 1872, which you can board, alongside a couple of other vessels, namely the **MV Spartan**, a "puffer" boat, and the **SY Carola**, the oldest seagoing steam yacht in the country – though these last two are due to be moved to the car park. Three times a day there are free guided tours of MV *Kyles*, in conjunction with the nearby **Shipyard Worker's**

Tenement Flat, which has been restored to something like its appearance in 1910, when a family of six to eight would have occupied its two rooms and scullery.

Largs

Nineteen miles north of Irvine, tucked in between the hills and the sea, **LARGS** remains the most traditional of Ayrshire's family resorts, its guesthouses and B&Bs spreading out behind an elongated seaside promenade. Despite the obvious tack along parts of the seafront, the town does have a couple of worthwhile sites, and is also where ferries depart for the short hop across the water to Great Cumbrae.

Skelmorlie Aisle

Manse Court • June–Aug Mon–Sat 2–5pm; keys available from the museum next door • Free • ☏ 01475 687081

Largs' one real gem is **Skelmorlie Aisle**, a slice of the Renaissance hidden away beside the old graveyard off Main Street – to get there, enter the yard opposite WHSmith. Once the north transept of a larger church (long since gone), and now standing alone in the graveyard, the aisle was converted in 1636 into a **mausoleum** by Sir Robert Montgomerie, a local bigwig, in memory of his wife who died in a horseriding accident. Carved by Scottish masons following Italian patterns, the tomb is decorated with Montgomerie's coat of arms as well as symbols of mortality such as the skull, winged hourglass and inverted torch. Up above, the intricate paintwork of the barrel-vaulted ceiling includes the signs of the zodiac, biblical figures and texts.

Vikingar!

Greenock Rd, 5min walk north of the pier • Feb & Nov Sat & Sun 11.30am–2.30pm; March daily 11.30am–1.30pm; April–June daily 10.30am–2.30pm; July & Aug daily 10.30am–3.30pm; Sept & Oct daily 10.30am–2.30pm • £4.50 • ☏ 01475 689777, ⓦ kaleisure.com

The Battle of Largs provides a historical link for **Vikingar!**, a light-hearted Viking-themed museum housed in a purpose-built leisure complex that also includes a swimming pool and theatre. Led by your very own Viking (in a manner of sorts), you first enter a mock-up Norwegian longhouse, which variously functioned as a living space, bedroom, kitchen and barn – you get to try on various bits of armoury too, if you so wish; thereafter you head into the Hall of the Gods (or Valhalla), featuring impressively carved wooden friezes of four of the gods, before finishing with a big-screen presentation re-creating the famous battle.

Kelburn Castle and Country Centre

Fairlie, 2 miles south of Largs • Easter–Oct daily 10am–6pm; castle tours July & Aug daily 2pm • £9; castle tours £2; pony rides £3; playbarn £1.50 • ☏ 01475 568685, ⓦ kelburnestate.com

The Battle of Largs is commemorated by the distinctive **Pencil Monument** in Fairlie, a modern obelisk a mile south of town, close to the marina, and opposite the **Kelburn Castle and Country Centre**, seat of the earls of Glasgow (aka the Boyle family) since the twelfth century. The castle itself is no great shakes inside and can only be seen by guided tour. Much more enticing are the **grounds**, which feature a steep gorge and waterfall, 1000-year-old yew trees, an Adam monument and some lovely gardens.

THE BATTLE OF LARGS

Largs' chief historical claim to fame is the **Battle of Largs**, which took place in 1263. The battle was forced on King Haakon's Vikings when their longships were blown ashore by a gale. The invaders were attacked by the Scots and, although both sides claimed victory, the Norwegians retreated north and abandoned their territorial claims to the Hebrides three years later. The battle is celebrated in the hugely entertaining, week-long **Viking Festival** (ⓦ largsvikingfestival .com) at the end of August/beginning of September, with music, dancing and fireworks. The highlights are the burning of the Viking Longship and a re-enactment of the famous skirmish.

There's also plenty for kids to do, including a small adventure course, a secret forest playground, animal farm and pets' corner, a playbarn, and pony rides in the paddock.

ARRIVAL AND DEPARTURE
LARGS

By train The train station is on Main St, from where it's a 5min walk to the pier and seafront.
Destinations Glasgow Central (hourly; 1hr).
By bus The bus station is on Main St, next door to the train station.
Destinations Ayr (Mon–Sat every 30min, 5 on Sun; 1hr 25min); Glasgow (every 20–30min; 1hr 30min).

ACCOMMODATION AND EATING

Nardini's 2 Greenock Rd ☎01475 675000, ⓦnardinis .co.uk. Locally renowned Italian restaurant and ice-cream parlour housed in a wonderful L-shaped Art Deco building on the Promenade, just north of the pier. The freshly caught fish and home-made pasta are terrific, though the Tea Time Special (fish and chips, ice cream and a pot of tea; 6–8pm) for £7.95 is a real steal. Daily noon–11pm; ice-cream parlour 10am–9pm.

Old Rectory 2 Aubery Crescent ☎01475 674405, ⓦoldrectorylargs.co.uk. Formerly the home of the ministers of the neighbouring Episcopal Church, this accomplished seafront guesthouse at the northern end of town has just three rooms (two double and a twin), all of which are exquisitely furnished with period pieces and have excellent views over to Cumbrae and Arran. £75

South Whittlieburn Farm Brisbane Glen Rd ☎01475 675881, ✉largsbandb@southwhittlieburn farm.freeserve.co.uk. Situated on a working sheep farm in a peaceful glen about 3 miles northeast of town, this is a great option if you're up for a genuine rural retreat; although primarily a (small) caravan and camping site, they also do excellent B&B in the farmhouse. Per pitch £14; doubles £65

St Leonard's Guest House 9 Irvine Rd ☎01475 673318, ⓦstleonardsguesthouse.com. Located just down the hill as you come into Largs on the road from Ayr, this comely guesthouse offers six modestly sized but extremely comfortable rooms (doubles and twins), and a cracking breakfast. £75

Great Cumbrae

Immediately offshore from Largs lies **Great Cumbrae**, a plump, hilly and wonderfully peaceful little island roughly four miles long and half as wide. The most popular activity here is **cycling**, a circuit of the island taking no more than two hours even at a very leisurely pace, while there are a couple of good red sandstone beaches on the west coast overlooking Bute. The only settlement of any size is **Millport**, which curves around a lovely wide bay on the south coast, overlooking the privately owned neighbouring island of Wee Cumbrae.

Garrison House and the Museum of the Cumbraes

Glasgow St • Mon 1–5pm, Tues 1–7.30pm, Fri 10am–1pm & 2–5pm, Sat 10am–noon • Free • ☎01475 530742, ⓦgarrisonhousecumbrae.com

Millport's seafront is one long parade of Victorian seaside villas and terraces, interrupted only by **The Garrison**, a distinctive old barracks building with castellated gables, and the one-time summer retreat of the Earls of Glasgow. Although its main function is now as a library, it also houses the small but illuminating **Museum of the Cumbraes**, which documents life on Cumbrae through the years; the main focus is on some of the characters who have shaped the island's development, such as G.F. Boyle, provost of Millport for 22 years, and local entrepreneur John Kennedy, who ran a highly successful lemonade business in Fintry Bay in the early twentieth century. The exhibition also recalls how smuggling and tourism have influenced island life, though the most prominent exhibit here is the lamp and dick from the Wee Cumbrae lighthouse, the first one to be built on the Clyde, in 1757, and where it remains to this day. There's a delightful courtyard café here, too.

Cathedral of Argyll & the Isles

College St • Daily 8.30am–6pm; concerts July–Sept Sun 3pm • Free

Hidden from view in the woods above the town is the Episcopal **Cathedral of Argyll &**

the Isles, completed in 1851 to a design by William Butterfield, one of the leading High Victorian Gothic architects. The cathedral's most striking feature is a stone screen with cross supported by chunky granite pillars, but otherwise it's pretty modest by Butterfield standards, with only the polychromatic tiling in the chancel giving any hint of his usual exuberance. However, it does have the distinction of being Britain's smallest cathedral, with seating for just a hundred or so worshippers.

Robertson Museum & Aquarium

Near Millport • July–Sept Mon–Fri 9am–4.30pm, Sat 10am–4pm; Oct–June Mon–Fri 9am–12.15pm & 2–4.15pm • £2 • ☎ 01475 530581

Just out of Millport, to the east, overlooking the Hunterston nuclear power station and iron-ore terminal back on the mainland, is the Field Studies Council, one part of which contains the **Robertson Museum & Aquarium**; so-named after the esteemed nineteenth-century naturalist, David Robertson, it holds a laudably ecological exhibition on the local marine environment, a mock-up of the Ark (Millport's original marine station), and an aquarium displaying all manner of local marine life. On the waterfront opposite the museum, a plaque on a large stone marks the spot where the *Scotia* landed upon the return of the 1902–04 Scottish National Antarctic Expedition.

ARRIVAL AND GETTING AROUND   GREAT CUMBRAE

By ferry The CalMac ferry from Largs (every 15min in summer; £3.20 return/person, £12.20/car) takes just 10min to reach the island's northeast tip, with a connecting bus to Millport.

Bike rental On Your Bike, 27 Stuart St (☎ 01475 530300, ⓦ onyourbikemillport.com; £4.60/2hr, £6/day), also does repairs and rents out single and double kayaks (£10/hr; £20/hr).

ACTIVITIES

National Centre Cumbrae Near the ferry terminal on the northeast of the island ☎ 01475 530757, ⓦ nationalcentrecumbrae.org.uk. Scotland's national watersports centre offers courses in just about every conceivable waterbound activity, including sea-kayaking, windsurfing, powerboating and dinghy sailing; most of these activities cost around £50 for the day.

ACCOMMODATION AND EATING

College of the Holy Spirit College St ☎ 01475 530353, ⓦ cumbraeguesthouse.co.uk. If you fancy stopping over, make a beeline for the delightfully tranquil Anglican retreat house adjacent to the cathedral, which has a mix of twins, double and family rooms, some en suite. The library and common rooms are available to guests too. **£80**

Ritz Café 26 Stuart St ☎ 01475 530459. If you don't fancy fish and chips, head to the fabulous *Ritz Café*, which has been in business since 1906, doling out home-made ice cream, marshmallow ices, toasties and Millport Rock, among other goodies. Daily 10am–11pm.

Isle of Arran

Shaped like a kidney bean and occupying centre stage in the Firth of Clyde, **Arran** is the most southerly (and therefore the most accessible) of all the Scottish islands. The Highland–Lowland dividing line passes right through its centre – hence the cliché about it being like "Scotland in miniature" – leaving the northern half sparsely populated, mountainous and bleak, while the lush southern half enjoys a much milder climate. The population of around five thousand tends to stick to the southeastern quarter of the island, leaving the west and the north relatively undisturbed.

There are two big crowd-pullers on Arran: **geology** and **golf**. The former has fascinated rock-obsessed students since Sir James Hutton came here in the late eighteenth century to confirm his theories of uniformitarianism. A hundred years later, Sir Archibald Geikie's investigations were a landmark in the study of Arran's geology, and the island remains a popular destination for university and school field trips. As for golf, Arran boasts seven courses, including three of the eighteen-hole variety at Brodick, Lamlash and Whiting Bay, and a unique twelve-hole course at Shiskine, near Blackwaterfoot.

Although **tourism** is now by far its most important industry, Arran, at twenty miles in length, is large enough to have a life of its own. While the island's post-1745 history, including the Clearances (set in motion by the local lairds, the Hamiltons), is as

4

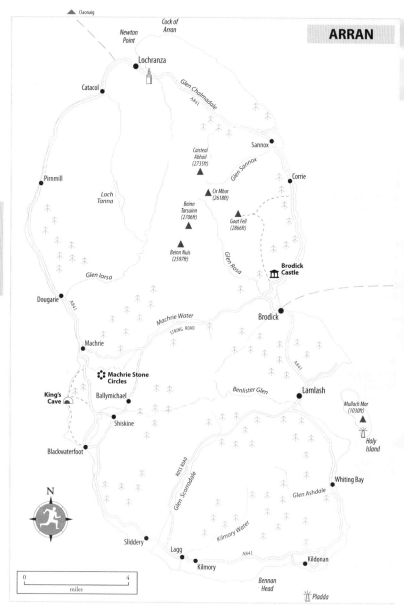

ARRAN

Claonaig
Newton Point
Cock of Arran
Lochranza
Catacol
Glen Chalmadale
A841
Caisteal Abhail (273ft)
Sannox
Glen Sannox
Corrie
Pirnmill
Loch Tanna
Cir Mhor (2618ft)
Beinn Tarsuinn (2706ft)
Goat Fell (2866ft)
Beinn Nuis (2597ft)
Glen Rosa
Brodick Castle
Glen Iorsa
Dougarie
A841
Machrie Water
STRING ROAD
Brodick
Machrie
Machrie Stone Circles
King's Cave
Ballymichael
Benlister Glen
Lamlash
Mullach Mor (1030ft)
Holy Island
Shiskine
A841
Blackwaterfoot
N
ROSS ROAD
Glen Scorrodale
Whiting Bay
Glen Ashdale
Sliddery
Lagg
Kilmory Water
A841
Kildonan
Kilmory
Bennan Head
Pladda

0   4
miles

depressing as elsewhere in the Highlands, in recent years Arran's population has actually increased, in contrast with more remote islands.

ARRIVAL AND GETTING AROUND

ISLE OF ARRAN

By ferry CalMac (📀 calmac.co.uk) operate two year-round ferry services: one from Ardrossan in Ayrshire to Brodick (April–Oct 6–8 daily; 55min), and a smaller ferry from Claonaig on the Kintyre peninsula to Lochranza in the north (April–Oct 8–9 daily; 30min).

By bus Transport on Arran itself is pretty good: daily buses circle the island (Brodick tourist office has timetables) while the Arran Day Rider (£5.60) allows you to hop on and off as you please. Buses also link in with the two ferry services.

Brodick

The resort of **BRODICK** (from the Norse *breidr vik*, "broad bay") is a place of only moderate charm, but it does have a grand setting in a wide, sandy bay set against a backdrop of granite mountains. Its development as a tourist resort was held back for a long time by its elitist owners, the dukes of Hamilton, though nowadays, as the island's capital and main communication hub, Brodick is by far the busiest town on Arran.

The town's shops and guesthouses are spread out along the south side of the bay, along with the tourist office and the CalMac pier. Its tourist sights, meanwhile, are clustered on the west and north side of the bay, a couple of miles from the ferry terminal.

Arran Heritage Museum

Rosaburn • April–Oct daily 10.30am–4.30pm • £4 • ☎ 01770 302636, 📀 arranmuseum.co.uk

Up along the road to the castle, the intermittently interesting **Arran Heritage Museum** is housed in a whitewashed eighteenth-century crofter's farm, and contains an old smiddy and a twee Victorian cottage with box-bed and range. In the old stables, the main exhibition considers the island's intriguing geological and archeological heritage – the most notable exhibit is an incredibly well-preserved early Bronze Age cist grave, complete with intact food vessel – while another section recalls the island's prominent wartime role, as testified by the dozen or so air crashes here during the course of World War II.

Brodick Castle

2.5 miles north of town, just off the A841 • **Castle** Daily April–Sept 11am–4pm • £12.50; NTS • **Gardens** Daily 9.30am–dusk • £7 • ☎ 01770 302202

Former seat of the duke of Hamilton, **Brodick Castle** is set on a steep bank on the north side of Brodick Bay. The bulk of the castle was built in the nineteenth century, giving it a domestic rather than a military look, and the interior is decidedly dour in tone, though there are a few gems to look out for. Don't miss the portrait of the eleventh duke's faithful piper, who injured his throat on a grouse bone, was warned never to pipe again, but did so and died. There are also a handful of sketches by Gainsborough in the boudoir. Probably the most atmospheric room is the copper-filled Victorian kitchen, which conjures up a vision of the sweated and sweating labour required to feed the folk upstairs.

Much more attractive are the walled **gardens** and extensive grounds, a treasury of exotic plants, trees and rhododendrons, which command a superb view across the bay. There's an adventure playground for kids, but the whole area is a natural playground, with waterfalls, a giant pitcher plant that swallows thousands of midges daily, and a

---

ARRAN GOLF PASS

The **Arran Golf Pass** (📀 golfonarran.com) currently costs £99, which is remarkable value given that it entitles you to a round on each of the island's seven courses; three 18-hole and three 9-hole courses, as well as the superb 12-hole course at Shiskine. You can buy the pass online or at any of the seven clubs.

4

> **GOAT FELL**
>
> Arran's most accessible peak is also the island's highest, **Goat Fell** (2866ft) – take your pick from the Gaelic, *goath*, meaning "windy", or the Norse, *geit-fjall*, "goat mountain" – which can be ascended in around four hours from Brodick or around five hours from Corrie, though it's a strenuous hike whichever way you do it; the latter route is, though, tougher.

maze of paths. Buried in the grounds is a bizarre Bavarian-style **summerhouse** lined entirely with pine cones; it's one of three built by the eleventh duke to make his wife, Princess Marie of Baden, feel at home.

ARRIVAL AND INFORMATION
BRODICK

By bus The main bus station is by the ferry terminal. Destinations Blackwaterfoot (Mon–Sat 8–10 daily, 4 on Sun; 30min); Lamlash (Mon–Sat hourly, 6 on Sun; 10–15min); Lochranza (Mon–Sat 7 daily, 4 on Sun; 45min).

Tourist office By the CalMac pier (April–Sept Mon–Sat 9am–5pm, Sun 10am–5pm; Oct–March Mon–Sat 10am–4pm; ☎ 01770 303774, ⍟ visitarran.com).

ACCCOMMODATION

★ **Brodick Bunkhouse** Shore Rd ☎ 01770 302897, ⍟ brodickbunkhouse.co.uk. Sparkling new bunkhouse offering brightly painted three- and six-bed dorms with spacious bunks (some are triple-height) made from wood sourced from the local sawmill; all rooms have sinks, though the wet rooms are as stylish as the dorms, and there's an honesty breakfast bar. There's no reception; you'll be emailed the code to let yourself in. **£25**

Douglas Hotel Shore Rd ☎ 01770 302968, ⍟ thedouglashotel.co.uk. Virtually opposite the ferry terminal, this large and handsome sandstone building offers some of the most comfortable accommodation on the island, with a selection of bright, modern and tidily furnished rooms, in a mostly grey-checked tartan flavour, many of which have sea-facing views. **£90**

Glen Rosa 2 miles from town off the B880 to Blackwaterfoot ☎ 07985 566004, ✉ glenrosacamping @hotmail.com. Very basic, almost wild, campsite (no showers and cold water only) enjoys a wonderful setting beside a burn, with superb views across the glen. Campfires are allowed too. There's no reception; the owner will pitch up at some point and collect your money. Per person **£4**

Glenartney Guest House Mayish Rd ☎ 01770 302220, ⍟ glenartney-arran.co.uk. Tucked away just uphill from the post office, this is the pick of the town's guesthouses, with a dozen or so immaculately presented, albeit not overly spacious, rooms. Two homely lounges and an evening bar enhance the Glenartney's charms, while you can expect a spectacular breakfast to see you on your way. **£86**

EATING AND DRINKING

Brodick Bar and Brasserie Alma Rd ☎ 01770 302169, ⍟ brodickbar.co.uk. There's decent fare on offer at this big, family-orientated restaurant opposite the post office. Chalked up on a huge board, the diverse menu features lots of fish and meaty treats (baked halibut with asparagus, honey-glazed belly of pork and bean casserole), while the home-made thin-crust pizzas (£10) are worth a punt. Mon–Sat noon–2.30pm & 5.30–10pm.

Creelers Home Farm ☎ 01770 302810, ⍟ creelers .co.uk. Located out on the road towards the castle, *Creelers* is the place to come on Arran for seafood; steamed halibut with squat lobster tails (£23) is typical of the dinner menu,

while the cheaper lunch menu features the likes of salt and pepper fried squid with chips (£7.95). You can bring your own bottle too (£3 corkage). Easter–Oct Tues–Sat noon– 2.30pm & 6–10pm.

Fiddlers' Shore Rd ☎ 01770 302579, ⍟ fiddlersmusic bar.com. The fabulous music bar, with acoustic performances nightly at 7.30pm (2.30pm on Sundays), is actually more restaurant than drinking den, offering succulent dishes like chargrilled swordfish steak, and Texan spiced black and blue burger (£12.95). Diners are given preference (and keep their table for the evening), but if you just fancy a pint, pop along after 9pm. Daily 9am–midnight.

Lamlash and around

With its distinctive Edwardian architecture and mild climate, **LAMLASH**, four miles south of Brodick, epitomizes the sedate charm of southeast Arran. Lamlash Bay has, in its time, sheltered King Haakon's fleet, in 1263, and, more recently, served as a naval base during both world wars.

Holy Island

The Holy Island boat runs May–Sept daily and more or less hourly, though it's subject to cancellations in windy weather • £12 return •
☎ 01770 700463, 🌐 holyisland.org

The best reason for coming to Lamlash is to visit the slug-shaped hump of **Holy Island**, where a group of **Tibetan Buddhists** have established a retreat. Providing you don't dawdle, it's possible to scramble up to the top of Mullach Mór (1030ft), the island's highest point, and still catch the last boat back. En route, you might well bump into the island's most numerous residents: feral goats, Eriskay ponies, Soay sheep and rabbits.

ACCOMMODATION AND EATING
LAMLASH AND AROUND

Drift Inn Shore Rd ☎ 01770 600608, 🌐 driftinnarran .com. Ignore the undistinguished exterior: the food at this seafront pub – mussels in chilli sauce, or Arran venison haunch with hazelnut risotto (£15.50) – make it worth a visit. Convivial beer garden. Daily noon–11pm.

Glenisle Hotel Shore Rd ☎ 01770 600559, 🌐 glenislehotel.com. High-end option, with thirteen

gorgeous rooms, each painted and furnished in colours that reflect those of the island itself; around half the rooms have a sea view. Terrific bistro too. **£145**

Lilybank Shore Rd ☎ 01770 600230, 🌐 lilybank-arran .co.uk. This sunny roadside B&B is a typically welcoming island guesthouse, offering seven floral, pastel-coloured rooms, four of which overlook the bay. **£80**

Lochranza

The ruined castle that occupies the mud flats of the surrounding bay and the brooding north-facing slopes of the mountains that frame it make for one of the most spectacular ensembles on the island, yet **LOCHRANZA**, despite being the only place of any size in this sparsely populated area, attracts far fewer visitors than Arran's southern resorts.

4

Arran distillery

South end of the village • March–Oct daily 10am–5.30pm, Nov–Feb 10.30am–4pm; first tour 10.15am (11am in winter), then every 90min • £7.50 • ☎ 01770 830264, 🌐 arranwhisky.com

One of the island's most popular tourist attractions these days is the **Arran distillery**, distinguished by its pagoda-style roofs at the south end of the village. Established as recently as 1995 – the first on the island since 1837 – this modern distillery produces the relatively little-known, fourteen-year-old single Arran malt. The tour itself is an entertaining and slick affair, beginning with an audiovisual presentation in a mock-up crofter's cottage, before you are led through the distillery; two tastings are included.

ACCOMMODATION
LOCHRANZA

Apple Lodge 500m from the distillery on the main through road ☎ 01770 830229, 🌐 applelodgegearran .co.uk. The old village manse accommodates four beautifully conceived rooms decked out with colourful embroidery and paintings, and an abundance of antique furnishings; one contains a superb four-poster bed. Closed mid-Dec to mid-Jan. **£80**

Lochranza Camping By the golf course ☎ 01770 830273, 🌐 arran-campsite.com. Relaxed and scenically placed campsite where red deer come to graze in the early

evening. Aside from pitches, there are three, two-man pods, each with heating and lighting, while facilities include modern shower blocks, laundry and a camper's lounge. March–Oct. Per pitch **£18**; pods **£60**

SYHA Lochranza Near the castle, en route to the ferry terminal ☎ 01770 830631, 🌐 syha.org.uk. Friendly and well-equipped SYHA hostel with three- to eight-bed dorms, plus doubles, most of which overlook the bay. Breakfast £4.95, packed lunch £5.95. April–Oct, sometimes open weekends winter. Dorms **£22**; doubles **£58**

EATING AND DRINKING

Sandwich Station Opposite the CalMac slipway ☎ 07810 796248, 🌐 thesandwichstation.com. Hot breakfast rolls, panini and soups, plus hot drinks and smoothies. Perfect if you need a bite before hopping aboard the ferry. March–Oct Mon–Sat 9am–5pm.

Stags Pavilion ☎ 01770 830600, 🌐 stagspavilion.com.

Popular restaurant set in an attractive pavilion at the entrance to the campsite, with sumptuous dishes like slow-roasted honey shoulder of Arran lamb (£12.75), and blackberry crème brûlée. No licence, but bring your own bottle (no corkage fee). Reservations advised. Mon, Tues & Thurs 5.30–10pm; Fri–Sun 11am–2.30pm & 5.30–10pm.

Glasgow and the Clyde

CLYDE AUDITORIUM

5

Glasgow and the Clyde

Rejuvenated, upbeat Glasgow, Scotland's largest city, changed irrevocably in 1990 when it energetically embraced its status as European City of Culture. Set on the banks of the mighty River Clyde, this former industrial giant can seem less than enticing as you approach, and many of its outer suburbs remain seriously deprived. However, after a little time exploring, visitors will find a city that is, in its own idiosyncratic way, a cultured and dynamic place well worth getting to know.

GLASGOW has much to offer, including some of the most imaginative museums and galleries in Britain – among them the voluminous **Kelvingrove Art Gallery and Museum**, and the Zaha Hadid-designed **Riverside Museum** – nearly all of which are free. Glasgow's **architecture** is some of the most striking in the UK, from the restored eighteenth-century warehouses of the **Merchant City** to the hulking Victorian prosperity of **George Square**. Most distinctive of all is the work of local luminary Charles Rennie Mackintosh, whose elegantly streamlined Art Nouveau designs appear all over the city, reaching their apotheosis in the stunning **Glasgow School of Art**, currently being restored after a devastating fire in 2014. Development of the old shipyards of the Clyde, notably in the space-age shapes of the **Glasgow Science Centre**, hint at yet another string to the city's bow: combining design with innovation. The metropolis also boasts thriving live-music venues, busy theatres, concert halls and an opera house. Moreover, Glasgow has undergone a dramatic culinary renaissance in recent years, and eating out here is a real joy, as is frequenting one of the city's many new craft coffee houses. Above all, the feature that best defines the individualism and peculiar attraction of the city is its **people** – something acknowledged in the city's newly acquired marketing slogan, "Glasgow Makes People" – whether rough-edged comedians on the football terraces or style-obsessed youth hitting the designer bars.

Despite all the upbeat hype, Glasgow's gentrification has passed by deprived inner-city areas such as the **East End**, home of the **Barras market** and some staunchly change-resistant pubs. Indeed, even in the more fashionable quarters of Glasgow, there's a gritty edge that's never far away, reinforcing a peculiar mix of grime and glitz that the city seems to have patented.

Glasgow is the obvious base from which to explore the **Clyde Valley and coast**, made easily accessible by a reliable train service. Chief among the draws is the remarkable eighteenth-century **New Lanark** mills and workers' village, a World Heritage Site, while other day-trips might take you to Charles Rennie Mackintosh's **Hill House** in Helensburgh or on a boat heading "doon the watter" towards the scenic Argyll **sea lochs**, past the old shipbuilding centres on the Clyde estuary.

Brief history

Glasgow's earliest history, like so much else in this surprisingly romantic city, is obscured in a swirl of myth. The city's name is said to derive from the Celtic *Glas-cu*,

GLASGOW CATHEDRAL

Highlights

❶ **Necropolis** Elegantly crumbling graveyard on a city-centre hill behind the ancient cathedral, with great views. **See p.188**

❷ **Rennie Mackintosh architecture** The visionary architect left an extraordinary legacy, manifest in masterpieces such as the Glasgow School of Art and Scotland Street School. **See p.191 & p.200**

❸ **Kelvingrove Art Gallery and Museum** Splendid civic collection of art and artefacts in a Gothic red-sandstone palace in the city's lively West End. **See p.194**

❹ **Clydeside** The river that made Glasgow: walk or cycle along it, take a boat on it, cross a bridge over it, or get a view of it from the superb Riverside Museum. **See p.198**

❺ **Craft coffee** Get your caffeine kicks with a double shot of espresso in one of the city's cool new artisan coffee houses, such as *Laboratorio* or *Spitfire*. **See p.206 & p.207**

❻ **"Glesga" nightlife** Sample the glamour and the grit with a gin and tonic at *Gin 71* followed by a pint of heavy at the *Horseshoe Bar*. **See p.211 & p.212**

❼ **New Lanark** A fascinating eighteenth-century planned mill village set in a dramatic gorge. **See p.219**

HIGHLIGHTS ARE MARKED ON THE MAP ON P.180

which loosely translates as "the dear, green place" – a tag that the tourist board is keen to exploit as an antidote to the sooty images of popular imagination. It is generally agreed that the first settlers arrived in the sixth century to join Christian missionary **Kentigern** – later to become St Mungo – in his newly founded monastery on the banks of the tiny Molendinar Burn.

The growth of the city

William the Lionheart gave the town an official charter in 1175, after which it continued to grow in importance, peaking in the mid-fifteenth century when the **university** – the second in Scotland after St Andrews – was founded on Kentigern's site. This led to the establishment of an archbishopric, and city status, in 1492, and, due to its situation on a large, navigable river, Glasgow soon expanded into a major industrial **port**.

The first cargo of tobacco from Virginia offloaded in Glasgow in 1674, and the 1707 Act of Union between Scotland and England – despite demonstrations against it in Glasgow – led to a boom in trade with the colonies until American independence. Following the **Industrial Revolution** and James Watt's innovations in steam power, coal from the abundant seams of Lanarkshire fuelled the ironworks all around the Clyde, which were worked by the cheap hands of the Highlanders and, later, those fleeing the Irish potato famine of the 1840s.

Victorian Glasgow

The **Victorian age** transformed Glasgow beyond recognition. The population mushroomed from 77,000 in 1801 to nearly 800,000 at the end of the century, and new tenement blocks swept into the suburbs in an attempt to cope with the choking influxes of people. Two vast and stately **International Exhibitions** were held in 1888 and 1901 to showcase the city and its industries to the outside world, necessitating the construction of huge civic monoliths such as the Kelvingrove Art Gallery and the Council Chambers in George Square. At this time Glasgow revelled in the title of the "Second City of the Empire", an unexpected epithet for a place that rarely acknowledges second place in anything.

The shipbuilding era

By the turn of the twentieth century, Glasgow's industries had been honed into one massive **shipbuilding** culture. Everything from tugboats to transatlantic liners was fashioned out of sheet metal in the yards that straddled the Clyde from Gourock to Rutherglen.

In the harsh economic climate of the 1930s, however, unemployment spiralled, and Glasgow could do little to counter its popular image as a city dominated by inebriate violence and (having absorbed vast numbers of Irish emigrants) sectarian tensions. The **Gorbals** area in particular became notorious as one of the worst slums in Europe.

Renaissance

Shipbuilding, and many associated industries, died away almost completely in the 1960s and 1970s, leaving the city depressed, jobless and directionless. Then, in the 1980s, the self-promotion began, starting with the upbeat "Glasgow's Miles Better" campaign in 1983, and snowballing towards the 1988 Garden Festival and the year-long party as European City of Culture in 1990. Further prestige came in 1999 when Glasgow was designated UK City of Architecture and Design, followed in 2002 by hosting the Champions' League Final, and then the staging of the **Commonwealth Games** in 2014. These various titles have helped to reinforce the impression that Glasgow, despite its many problems, has successfully broken the industrial shackles of the past and evolved into a city of stature and confidence.

5

George Square and around

The imposing architecture of **George Square** reflects the confidence of Glasgow's Victorian age. The wide-open plaza almost has a continental airiness about it, although there isn't much subtlety about the 80ft column rising up at its centre, which is topped by a statue of Sir Walter Scott. Haphazardly dotted around the great writer's plinth are a number of dignified statues of assorted luminaries, ranging from Queen Victoria to Scots heroes such as James Watt and Rabbie Burns.

City Chambers

George Square • Guided tours Mon–Fri 10.30am & 2.30pm • Free • ☎ 0141 287 4018 • Buchanan Street underground

The florid splendour of the **City Chambers**, opened by Queen Victoria in 1888, occupies the entire eastern end of George Square. Built from wealth gained by colonial trade and heavy industry, it epitomizes the aspirations and optimism of late Victorian city elders. Its intricately detailed facade includes high-minded **friezes** typical of the era: the four nations which then comprised the United Kingdom at the feet of the throned queen, the British colonies and allegorical figures representing Religion, Virtue and Knowledge. The only way to see the labyrinthine interior is to join a **guided tour**, which begins at the bottom of a magnificent Italian marble stairwell; the highlight of the tour (which may be restricted owing to council business) is a visit to the council chamber, richly furnished in Spanish dark mahogany and embossed leather. If you want to see the chamber in full swing, it's possible to attend one of the council meetings, which are held roughly every six weeks on a Thursday.

The Gallery of Modern Art

Royal Exchange Square • Mon–Wed & Sat 10am–5pm, Thurs 10am–8pm, Fri & Sun 11am–5pm • Free • ☎ 0141 287 3050, ⓦ glasgowlife.org.uk • Buchanan Street underground

The focal point of **Royal Exchange Square** is the graceful mansion built in 1775 for tobacco lord William Cunninghame. This was the most ostentatious of the Glasgow merchants' homes and, having served as the city's Royal Exchange and central library, it now houses the **Gallery of Modern Art**. Alas, GoMA hasn't really lived up to the potential of the building itself, or the location, though as it's free it does merit a quick visit. The mirrored reception area leads you straight into the spacious ground-floor gallery, a striking room with rows of Corinthian pillars and huge windows. This is one of the four galleries housed here, each one typically staging two or three exhibitions a year; the basement, meanwhile, is home to one of the city's two tourist offices, a library and café.

Buchanan Street

Buchanan Street runs north–south one block west of George Square, defining Glasgow's main shopping district. At the southern end of the street is the **Princes Square** shopping centre, hollowed out of the innards of a soft sandstone building. The interior, all recherché Art Deco and ornate ironwork, has lots of pricey fashionable shops, set to a soothing background of classical music. Glaswegians' voracious appetite for shopping is fed further at the northern end of Buchanan Street, just beyond the underground station, in the vast **Buchanan Galleries** shopping centre, stuffed with the more predictable raft of chain stores. Just below the Royal Concert Hall is a statue of **Donald Dewar**, Scotland's First Minister until his untimely death in 2000.

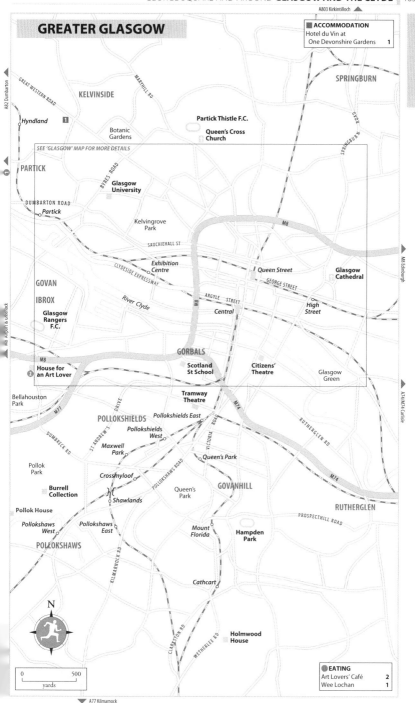

GREATER GLASGOW

5

A803 Kirkintilloch

ACCOMMODATION
Hotel du Vin at
One Devonshire Gardens **1**

A82 Dumbarton

GREAT WESTERN ROAD

MARYHILL RD

KELVINSIDE

SPRINGBURN

SPRINGBURN RD

Hydland **1**

Botanic
Gardens

Partick Thistle F.C.

**Queen's Cross
Church**

SEE 'GLASGOW' MAP FOR MORE DETAILS

PARTICK

BYRES ROAD

**Glasgow
University**

DUMBARTON ROAD

Partick

Kelvingrove
Park

SAUCHIEHALL ST

M8

CLYDESIDE EXPRESSWAY

**Exhibition
Centre**

Queen Street

GEORGE STREET

**Glasgow
Cathedral**

GOVAN

IBROX

River Clyde

ARGYLE STREET

M8

Central

**High
Street**

M8 Edinburgh

A8 Airport & Greenock

**Glasgow
Rangers
F.C.**

GORBALS

M8

**House for
an Art Lover** **2**

**Scotland
St School**

**Citizens'
Theatre**

Glasgow
Green

A74/M74 Carlisle

Bellahouston
Park

M77

**Tramway
Theatre**

M74

POLLOKSHIELDS Pollokshields East

ST ANDREW'S DRIVE

**Pollokshields
West**

VICTORIA ROAD

RUTHERGLEN RD

DUMBRECK RD

*Maxwell
Park*

POLLOKSHAWS ROAD

Queen's Park

M74

Pollok
Park

Crossmyloof

Queen's
Park

GOVANHILL

RUTHERGLEN

**Burrell
Collection**

Shawlands

PROSPECTHILL ROAD

Pollok House

*Pollokshaws
West*

*Pollokshaws
East*

*Mount
Florida*

**Hampden
Park**

POLLOKSHAWS

KILMARNOCK RD

Cathcart

CLARKSTON RD

WETHERLEE RD

**Holmwood
House**

N

0   500
yards

EATING
Art Lovers' Café   **2**
Wee Lochan   **1**

A77 Kilmarnock

5

■ NIGHTLIFE	
Barrowland	9
O2 Academy	12
Queen Margaret Union	2

■ DRINKING	
Bon Accord	7
Brewdog	6
Clutha Vaults	10
Dram!	5
Drygate	8
Lismore Lounge	4
Oran Mor	1
Stravaigin	3
West Brewing Company	11

A82 Dumbarton

Botanic Gardens

Kibble Palace

GREAT WESTERN ROAD

WOODSIDE ROAD

MARYHILL ROAD

Hillhead

GREAT GEORGE ST

HILLHEAD ST

BANK STREET

OTAGO STREET

NORTH WOODSIDE ROAD

Kelvinbridge

GIBSON STREET

Cottier Theatre

Grosvenor

BYRES ROAD

Hunterian Art Gallery & Mackintosh House

UNIVERSITY AVENUE

Glasgow University

WEST END

The Stand Comedy Club

Kelvinhall

DUMBARTON ROAD

Hunterian Museum

CHURCH ST

DUMBARTON ROAD

Partick

BENALDER ST

Kelvingrove Park

River Kelvin

KELVIN WAY

PARK QUAD

WOODLANDS ROAD

KINNOCH TERR

PARK CIRCUS

PARK TERR

WOODLANDS TERR

WOODSIDE CRES

FERRY ROAD

Kelvin Hall

ARGYLE STREET

Kelvingrove Art Gallery & Museum

SAUCHIEHALL STREET

GRAY ST

KELVINGROVE ST

ARGYLE STREET

BERKELEY STREET

Riverside Museum

Govan Ferry

The Tall Ship at Glasgow Harbour

KELVINHAUGH STREET

Exhibition Centre Station

CLYDESIDE EXPRESSWAY

ST VINCENT STREET

Mitchell Library

Govan

GOVAN ROAD

Scottish Exhibition and Conference Centre & Clyde Auditorium

Glasgow Tower

Quay for P.S. Waverley

MILLENNIUM BRIDGE

The "Armadillo"

BELLS BRIDGE

SSE Hydro

Finnieston Crane

FINNIESTON STREET

ELLIOT STREET

LANCEFIELD STREET

HYDE PARK STREET

GOVAN

Glasgow Science Centre

Pacific Quay

IMAX Theatre

BBC Scotland

CLYDE ARC

River Clyde

LANCEFIELD QUAY

ANDERSON QUAY

PACIFIC DRIVE

GOVAN ROAD

Ibrox

WHITEFIELD ROAD

Glasgow Rangers Football Club

Cessnock

PAISLEY ROAD WEST

PAISLEY ROAD

Kinning Park

0   300
yards

A737 Paisley

GLASGOW

M8, Airport & Greenock

M77, Burrell Collection & Pollok Park

M8

Shields Road

SCOTLAND STREET

Scotland Street School Museum

The Lighthouse

11 Mitchell Lane • Mon–Sat 10.30am–5pm, Sun noon–5pm • Free • ☎ 0141 276 5365, ⓦ thelighthouse.co.uk • St Enoch underground

A spectacularly converted Charles Rennie Mackintosh building, **the Lighthouse** has found new life as Scotland's **Centre for Design and Architecture**. The 1895 building was Mackintosh's first public commission, and housed the offices of the *Glasgow Herald* newspaper until 1980, before remaining derelict until 1999; despite glass and

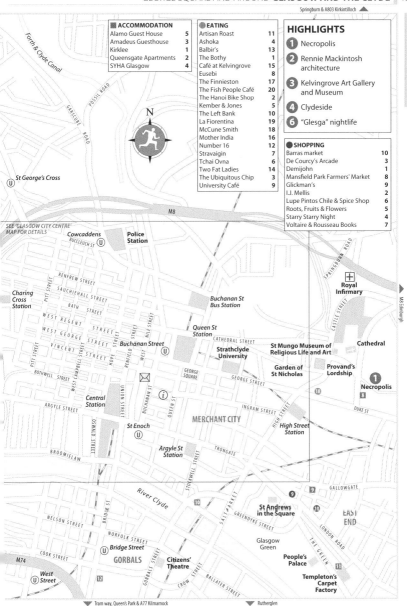

■ ACCOMMODATION	
Alamo Guest House	5
Amadeus Guesthouse	3
Kirklee	1
Queensgate Apartments	2
SYHA Glasgow	4

● EATING	
Artisan Roast	11
Ashoka	4
Balbir's	13
The Bothy	1
Café at Kelvingrove	15
Eusebi	8
The Finnieston	17
The Fish People Café	20
The Hanoi Bike Shop	2
Kember & Jones	5
The Left Bank	10
La Fiorentina	19
McCune Smith	18
Mother India	16
Number 16	12
Stravaigin	7
Tchai Ovna	6
Two Fat Ladies	14
The Ubiquitous Chip	3
University Café	9

HIGHLIGHTS

1 Necropolis

2 Rennie Mackintosh architecture

3 Kelvingrove Art Gallery and Museum

4 Clydeside

5 "Glesga" nightlife

● SHOPPING	
Barras market	10
De Courcy's Arcade	3
Demijohn	1
Mansfield Park Farmers' Market	8
Glickman's	9
I.J. Mellis	2
Lupe Pintos Chile & Spice Shop	6
Roots, Fruits & Flowers	5
Starry Starry Night	4
Voltaire & Rousseau Books	7

sandstone additions, it retains many original features, including the distinctive tower from which the building takes its name.

The building's star attraction is the superb **Mackintosh Interpretation Centre** up on the third floor. It's an illuminating trawl through the great man's work, with plans, photographs, models and video displays exploring many of the themes behind his buildings and interiors; here too are some original items, including an armchair

5

designed for the director's room at the School of Art and a gorgeous cabinet for the manager's office at the *Herald*. Elsewhere, paintings and book cover designs further demonstrate Mackintosh's outstanding versatility. The sixth-floor viewing platform and the Lighthouse Tower itself give fantastic views out over the city skyline, while the ground-floor shop offers a fine selection of Mackintosh-inspired goodies (see p.215).

The Merchant City

The grid of streets that lie immediately east of the City Chambers is known as the **Merchant City**, an area of eighteenth-century warehouses and homes once bustling with cotton, tobacco and sugar traders. In the last two decades the area has been sandblasted and swabbed clean with greater enthusiasm and municipal money than any other part of Glasgow in an attempt to bring residents back into the city centre; the resulting designer shops, stylish bars and bijou cafés give the area a pervasive air of sophistication and chic.

Trades Hall

Glassford St • Mon–Fri 9am–5pm • Free • ☎ 0141 552 2418, ⓦ tradeshallglasgow.co.uk • St Enoch underground

Passing the delicate white spire of **Hutcheson Hall**, an early nineteenth-century building designed by Scottish architect David Hamilton, you come to the Robert Adam-designed **Trades Hall**, easily distinguished by its neat green copper dome. Purpose-built in 1794, it still functions as the headquarters of the Glasgow trade guilds. These include corporations of Bakers, Hammermen, Gardeners and Weavers, among others, although today they have limited connections to their respective trades and act as charitably minded associations. The former civic pride and status of the guilds is still evident, however, from the rich assortment of carvings and stained-glass windows, with a lively pictorial representation of the different trades in the silk frieze around the walls of the first-floor grand hall. Visitors are free to look around the building, and access is only restricted if there is a function taking place.

Trongate 103

Trongate 103 • Tues–Sat 10am–5pm, Sun noon–5pm; open Thurs till 9pm Feb–Dec • Free • ☎ 0141 276 8380, ⓦ trongate103.com • St Enoch underground

Behind a sleek glass frontage among otherwise nondescript and downmarket shops on Trongate you'll find **Trongate 103**, a sparkling, six-storey arts centre exhibiting printmaking, contemporary photography, video work and ceramics in airy light-filled spaces. Formerly a tannery, clothes factory and air-raid shelter, among other things, this B-listed Edwardian building dating from 1902 today houses a number of organizations, including the Glasgow Print Studio, Street Level Photoworks and Transmission Gallery.

Sharmanka Kinetic Gallery

Trongate 103 • Wed & Fri 3pm, Thurs & Sun 3pm & 7pm, Sat 3pm & 4.15pm • 45min (3pm & 4.15pm), 70min (7pm) show £6/8 • ☎ 0141 552 7080, ⓦ sharmanka.com • St Enoch underground

Trongate 103 is home to Glasgow's most unusual attraction. Founded by Russian émigrés Eduard Bersudsky and Tatyana Jakovskaya, the **Sharmanka Kinetic Gallery** is like a mad inventor's magical workshop, with dozens of allegorical contraptions made from old wheels, levers, lights, carved wooden figures and scrap metal that spark into life during performances. A unique art form, Sharmanka (Russian for "barrel organ" or "hurdy-gurdy") is at once hypnotic, playful and deeply poignant, with its mechanical sculptures, or "kinemats", imprisoned in their relentless routine, while choreographed lighting draws you from one part of the show to the next and rather sinister fairground-style music plays in the background.

The East End

East of Glasgow Cross, down Gallowgate beyond the train lines, lies the **East End**, the district that perhaps most closely corresponds to the old perception of Glasgow. Hemmed in by Glasgow Green to the south and the old university to the west, this densely packed industrial area essentially created the city's wealth. The Depression caused the closure of many factories, leaving communities stranded in an industrial wasteland. Today, isolated pubs, tatty shops and cafés sit amid this dereliction, in sharp contrast to the gloss of the Merchant City only a few blocks to the west. You're definitely off the tourist trail, but unless you're here after dark it's not as threatening as it may feel, and there's no doubt that the area offers a rich flavour of working-class Glasgow.

Glasgow Green

Between London Road and the River Clyde are the wide and tree-lined spaces of **Glasgow Green**. Reputedly the oldest public park in Britain, the Green has been common land since at least 1480, when it was first mentioned in records. Glaswegians hold it very dear, considering it to be an immortal link between themselves and their ancestors, for whom a stroll on the Green was a favourite Sunday afternoon jaunt. Various memorials are dotted around the lawns: an Adams triumphant arch rescued from the demolished Assembly Rooms on Ingram Street, with panels featuring The Three Graces and Apollo with his lyre; the 146ft-high **Nelson Monument**; and a stern monument extolling the evils of drink and the glory of God that was erected by the nineteenth-century **Temperance movement**.

The People's Palace

Glasgow Green • Tues–Thurs & Sat 10am–5pm, Fri & Sun 11am–5pm; Winter Gardens daily 10am–5pm • Free • ☎ 0141 276 0788, Ⓦ glasgowlife.org.uk • St Enoch underground

Glasgow Green's most conspicuous building is **The People's Palace**, which houses a wonderfully haphazard evocation of the city's history. This squat, red-sandstone Victorian building, with a vast semicircular glasshouse tacked on the back, was purpose-built as a museum back in 1898 – almost a century before the rest of the country caught on to the fashion for social history collections. Many of the displays are designed to instil a warm glow in the memories of locals: indeed, the museum is refreshingly unpretentious, even if it feels a little tired.

Throughout, various themes with a particular resonance in Glasgow are explored, including alcohol – look out for the Drunk's Barrow in which the most inebriated were carted off to jail for the night – and crime and punishment, where you'll find the bell from the notorious Duke Street Prison, which rang when someone was hanged on the Green, and an assortment of beautifully painted batons. On a more cheerful note, the section on the Barras recalls evenings of dancing and merriment at the nearby Barrowland Ballroom and there's some guidance to understanding "the Patter" – Glaswegians' idiosyncratic version of the Queen's English. There's also a reconstruction of a "single-end" or one-roomed house, a typical setting for the daily life of hundreds of thousands of Glasgow people through the years. For all this, though, the star exhibit is Billy Connolly's pair of big banana boots.

The Victorian glasshouse at the back of the palace contains the **Winter Gardens**, which has assorted tropical plants and shrubs, a water garden and a café. Directly in front of the palace stands the ornate terracotta **Doulton Fountain** – originally designed for the

5

1888 Glasgow Exhibition in Kelvingrove Park – which rises like a wedding cake to a pinnacle where Queen Victoria oversees her Empire.

Templeton's Carpet Factory

On the northeast side of the Green, just beyond the People's Palace, it's worth taking a look at the extraordinary **Templeton's Carpet Factory**, a massive brick and moulded terracotta edifice of turrets, arched windows, mosaic-style patterns and castellated grandeur designed in the style of the Doge's Palace in Venice and built in 1892. It has been converted into apartments, but also houses the West Brewing Company's excellent *bier halle* and microbrewery (see p.212). Opposite the factory, you can still see lines of **Victorian washing poles**, recalling the days when the Green was very much a public space in daily use.

Glasgow Cathedral and around

Castle St • April–Sept Mon–Sat 9.30am–5.30pm, Sun 1–5pm; Oct–March Mon–Sat 10am–4pm, Sun 1–4pm • Free • ☎ 0141 552 8198, ⓦ glasgowcathedral.org.uk • Buchanan Street underground

Built in 1136, destroyed in 1192 and partially rebuilt soon after, stumpy-spired **Glasgow Cathedral** was not completed until the late fifteenth century, with the final reconstruction of the chapterhouse and the aisle designed by Robert Blacader, the city's first archbishop. Thanks to the intervention of the city guilds, it is the only Scottish mainland cathedral to have escaped the hands of religious reformers in the sixteenth century. The cathedral is dedicated to the city's patron saint and reputed founder, St Mungo, otherwise known as St Kentigern.

Because of the sloping ground on which it is built, at its east end the cathedral is effectively on two levels, the crypt being part of the lower church. Either side of the nave, the narrow **aisles** are illuminated by vivid stained-glass windows, most of which date from the last century. Threadbare Union flags and military pennants hang listlessly beneath them, serving as a reminder that the cathedral is very much a part of the Unionist Protestant tradition. Beyond the nave, the **choir** is hidden from view by the curtained stone pulpit, making the interior feel a great deal smaller than might be expected from the outside. In the choir's northeastern corner, a small door leads into the gloomy **sacristy**, in which Glasgow University was founded over five hundred years ago. Wooden boards mounted on the walls detail the alternating Roman Catholic and Protestant clergy of the cathedral, testimony to the turbulence and fluctuations of the Church in Scotland.

Two sets of steps from the nave lead down into the **lower church**, where you'll see the dark and musty **chapel** surrounding the tomb of St Mungo, though the saint's relics were removed in the late Middle Ages, their whereabouts unknown. The chapel itself is one of the most glorious examples of medieval architecture in Scotland, best seen in the delicate fan vaulting rising up from the thicket of cool stone columns.

The Necropolis

Rising up behind the cathedral, the atmospheric **Necropolis** is a grassy mound covered in a fantastic assortment of crumbling and tumbling gravestones, ornate urns, gloomy catacombs and Neoclassical temples. Inspired by the Père Lachaise cemetery in Paris, this garden of death was established in 1832, and it quickly became a fitting spot for the great and the good of wealthy nineteenth-century Glasgow to indulge their vanity; some 50,000 burials have taken place since the first one, and there are 3,500 monuments. Various paths lead through the rows of eroding, neglected graves, and from the summit, next to the column topped with an indignant John Knox, there are superb **views** of the cathedral below and the city beyond.

St Mungo Museum of Religious Life and Art

2 Castle St • Tues–Thurs & Sat 10am–5pm, Fri & Sun 11am–5pm • Free • ☎ 0141 276 1629, ⓦ glasgowlife.org.uk • Buchanan Street underground

The **St Mungo Museum of Religious Life and Art**, housed in a rather bland late twentieth-century pastiche of a Scots medieval townhouse, is not nearly as bland as its title might suggest. Focusing on objects, beliefs and art from Christianity, Buddhism, Judaism, Islam, Hinduism and Sikhism, the most enlightening of the museum's three galleries is the Gallery of Religious Art, whose stand-out objects are a rare Kalabari Screen – an ancestral funerary screen from Nigeria comprising three wood-carved figures – and a fabulous bronze sculpture of a dancing Shiva, the Hindu god. The Religion in Scotland Gallery, meanwhile, offers up a rich collection of photographs, papers and archive material looking at religion in Glasgow, the zealotry of the nineteenth-century Temperance movement and Christian missionaries, notably local boy David Livingstone, whose telescope, map and bible used on expeditions in Africa are exhibited here. Outside is a permanent dry-stone Zen Buddhist garden.

Provand's Lordship

3 Castle St • Tues–Thurs & Sat 10am–5pm, Fri & Sun 11am–5pm • Free • ☎ 0141 276 1625, ⓦ glasgowlife.org.uk • Buchanan Street underground

The oldest house in the city, the **Provand's Lordship** dates from 1471 and has been used as an ecclesiastical residence and an inn, among other things. A warren of rooms, the house is of more appeal from an architectural perspective, unless you've an interest in seventeenth-century period furniture, that is. As a reminder of the manse's earthier history, the upper floor contains pictures of assorted low-life characters such as the notorious drunkards and prostitutes of eighteenth- and nineteenth-century Glasgow; one of the most infamous, and represented here, was Hawkie, a street beggar and political street entertainer.

Behind the Provand's Lordship lies the small **Garden of St Nicholas**, a herb garden contrasting medieval and Renaissance aesthetics and approaches to medicine. The cloistered walkway that surrounds it is an unattractive feature, save for the so-called Tontine heads, thirteen keystones removed from the old, eighteenth-century Tontine Hotel which once stood in Trongate; carved in wonderfully expressive poses, they remain remarkably well preserved given their age.

Sauchiehall Street and around

Glasgow's most famous street, **Sauchiehall Street**, runs in a straight line west from the northern end of Buchanan Street, past some unexciting shopping malls to a few of the city's most interesting sights, including Mackintosh's reconstructed **Willow Tea Rooms** and his masterpiece, the **Glasgow School of Art**. Close by, the touching **Tenement House** is well worth a visit.

Willow Tea Rooms

217 Sauchiehall St • Mon–Sat 9am–5pm, Sun 10.30am–5pm • Free • ☎ 0141 332 0521, ⓦ willowtearooms.co.uk • Cowcaddens underground

Charles Rennie Mackintosh fans should head for the **Willow Tea Rooms**, which were originally created for Kate Cranston – one of the architect's few contemporary supporters in the city – in 1903. Taking inspiration from the word *Sauchiehall*, which means "avenue of willow", he chose the willow leaf as a theme to unify the whole structure, from the tables to the mirrors and the ironwork. The motif is most apparent in the stylized linear panels of the bow window, which continues into the intimate dining room as if to surround the sitter, like a willow grove. These elongated forms

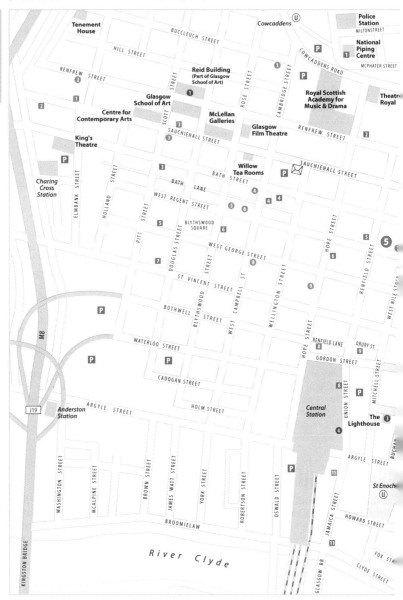

were used to enhance the small space and demonstrate Mackintosh's superb ability to fuse function with decoration. Closed for more than fifty years, the faithfully re-created tearooms reopened in 1983, but, in 2016, they closed again pending a major refurbishment expected to last until at least 2018. In the meantime, the Willow Tea Rooms have been re-created at the nearby Watt Brothers store on the corner of Sauchiehall Street and Hope Street.

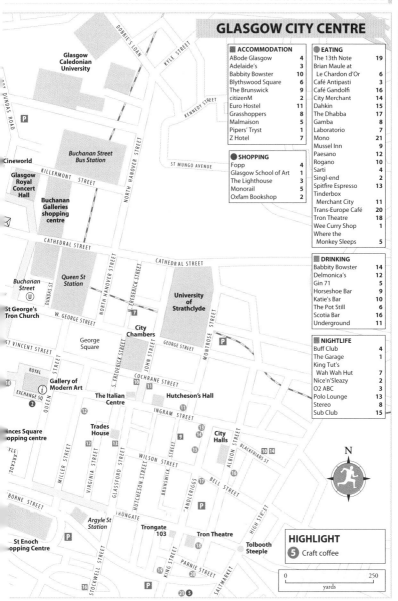

GLASGOW CITY CENTRE

■ ACCOMMODATION	
ABode Glasgow	4
Adelaide's	3
Babbity Bowster	10
Blythswood Square	6
The Brunswick	9
citizenM	2
Euro Hostel	11
Grasshoppers	8
Malmaison	5
Pipers' Tryst	1
Z Hotel	7

● SHOPPING	
Fopp	4
Glasgow School of Art	1
The Lighthouse	3
Monorail	5
Oxfam Bookshop	2

● EATING	
The 13th Note	19
Brian Maule at	
Le Chardon d'Or	6
Café Antipasti	3
Café Gandolfi	16
City Merchant	14
Dakhin	15
The Dhabba	17
Gamba	8
Laboratorio	7
Mono	21
Mussel Inn	9
Paesano	12
Rogano	10
Sarti	4
Singl-end	2
Spitfire Espresso	13
Tinderbox	
Merchant City	11
Trans-Europe Café	20
Tron Theatre	18
Wee Curry Shop	1
Where the	
Monkey Sleeps	5

■ DRINKING	
Babbity Bowster	14
Delmonica's	12
Gin 71	5
Horseshoe Bar	9
Katie's Bar	10
The Pot Still	6
Scotia Bar	16
Underground	11

■ NIGHTLIFE	
Buff Club	4
The Garage	1
King Tut's	
Wah Wah Hut	7
Nice'n'Sleazy	2
O2 ABC	3
Polo Lounge	13
Stereo	8
Sub Club	15

HIGHLIGHT

5 Craft coffee

N

0 ——————— 250
yards

The Glasgow School of Art

167 Renfrew St • Window on Mackintosh Visitor Centre daily 10am–4.30pm; guided tours daily: April–Sept 11am, 1pm & 3pm; Oct–March 11am & 3pm; booking advised • Guided tours £9.75 • ☎ 0141 353 4526, ⓦ www.gsa.ac.uk • Cowcaddens underground

Rising above Sauchiehall Street to the north is one of the city centre's steepest hills, with Dalhousie and Scott streets veering up to Renfrew Street, where you'll find Charles Rennie Mackintosh's **Glasgow School of Art** at number 167 – one of the most prestigious

5

art schools in the UK. Tragically, in May 2014, a fire – which started in the basement – took hold in the west wing, destroying studios, archival stores and, worst of all, the library. Currently enveloped in scaffolding, the restoration work, which is expected to cost anything up to £30 million, is not due to be complete until 2018 at the earliest.

The Glasgow School of Art was actually founded in 1845, occupying two previous sites before moving here in 1897. Widely considered to be the pinnacle of Mackintosh's work, the school is a characteristically angular building of warm sandstone that, due to financial constraints, had to be constructed in two stretches (1897–99 and 1907–09). There's a clear change in the architect's style from the mock-Baronial east wing to the softer lines of the western half.

Despite the fact that the building is inaccessible during the period of restoration, the popular, student-led **guided tours** are still very worthwhile. These begin inside the big glass **Reid Building** directly opposite the Art School, which, ironically, was finished just one month prior to the fire. For now then, tours concentrate on the exterior, and in particular the east and north facades, the latter distinguished by beautiful wrought-iron brackets and railings, and the iconic square light box above the entrance. Back over in the Reid building, the tour concludes in the **Furniture Gallery**, which shelters an Aladdin's cave of Mackintosh's original designs – numerous tall-backed chairs, a semicircular settle designed for the Willow Tea Rooms, a chest of drawers with

CHARLES RENNIE MACKINTOSH

The work of the architect **Charles Rennie Mackintosh** (1868–1928) has come to be synonymous with the image of Glasgow. Historians may disagree over whether his work was a forerunner of the modernist movement or merely the sunset of Victorianism, but he undoubtedly created buildings of great beauty, idiosyncratically fusing Scots Baronial with Gothic, Art Nouveau and modern design. Though the bulk of his work was conceived at the turn of the twentieth century, since the 1970s Mackintosh's ideas have become particularly fashionable, giving rise to a certain amount of ersatz "**Mockintosh**" in his home city, with his distinctive lettering and design features used time and again by shops, pubs and businesses. Fortunately, there are also plenty of examples of the genuine article, making the city something of a pilgrimage centre for art and design students from all over the world.

Mackintosh's big break came in 1896, when he won the competition to design a new home for the **Glasgow School of Art** (see p.191). This is his most famous work, but a number of smaller buildings created during his tenure with the architects Honeyman and Keppie, which began in 1889, document the development of his style. One of his earliest commissions was for a new building to house the *Glasgow Herald* on Mitchell Lane, off Argyle Street. A massive tower rises up from the corner, giving the building its popular name of **The Lighthouse**; it now houses the Mackintosh Interpretation Centre (see p.185).

In the 1890s Glasgow went wild for tearooms, where the middle classes could play billiards and chess, read in the library or merely chat. The imposing Miss Cranston, who dominated the Glasgow teashop scene, commissioned Mackintosh to plan the interiors for her growing business. Over the next twenty years he designed articles from teaspoons to furniture and, finally, as in the case of the **Willow Tea Rooms** (see p.189), the structure itself.

The spectre of limited budgets was to haunt Mackintosh throughout his career, and he never had the chance to design and construct with complete freedom. However, these constraints didn't manage to dull his creativity, as demonstrated by the **Scotland Street School** of 1904, just south of the river (see p.200). It is his most symmetrical work, with a whimsical nod to history in the Scots Baronial conical tower roofs and sandstone building material. Mackintosh's forceful personality and originality did not endear him to construction workers: he would frequently change his mind or add details at the last minute, often overstretching a budget. This lost him the support of local builders and architects and prompted him to move to Suffolk in 1914 to escape the "philistines" of Glasgow and to re-evaluate his achievements. Indeed, the building that arguably displays Mackintosh at his most flamboyant was one he never saw built, the **House for an Art Lover** (see p.201), constructed in Bellahouston Park in 1996, 95 years after the plans were submitted to a German architectural competition.

highlighted silver panels, and a fine Kimono-shaped bookcase from Windyhill; there are also a couple of pieces by his wife, Margaret, notably a magnificent gesso panel.

Venue for the school's design courses, the Reid Building is also home to the **Window on Mackintosh Visitor Centre**, an enlightening timeline tracing the work of the school's students, featuring many original items such as a copper mantel clock, and a canvas skirt with block pattern print, plus drawers stuffed with plans, programmes and flyers.

The Tenement House

145 Buccleuch St • April–June & Sept–Oct daily 1–5pm; July & Aug Mon–Sat 11am–5pm, Sun 1–5pm • £6.50; NTS • ☎ 0141 333 0183 • Cowcaddens underground

For a snapshot of life in Glasgow in the late nineteenth and early twentieth centuries, pay a visit to the fascinating **Tenement House**. Glasgow's tenements were originally conceived as a convenient way to house the influx of workers to the city in the late 1800s, though it didn't take long for the wealthy middle classes to realize their potential. Rising three to five storeys, they have two or three apartments per floor; important rooms are picked out with bay windows, middle storeys are emphasized by architraves or decorated panels below sill or above lintel, and street junctions are given importance by swelling bay windows, turrets and domes. Indeed, tenement flats were home for the vast majority of Glaswegians for much of the twentieth century, and as such developed a culture and vocabulary all of their own: the "hurley", for example, was the bed on castors which was kept below the box-bed in an alcove off the kitchen.

This is a typical tenement block still lived in on most floors, except for the ground and first floors, where you can see the respectable if cramped home of **Agnes Toward**, who moved here with her mother in 1911, changing nothing and throwing very little out until she was hospitalized in 1965, where she remained until her death in 1975. Thereafter, it was inhabited for seven years by Anne Davidson, niece of Sam Davidson, Miss Toward's church elder.

On the ground floor, there's a fascinating display on the development of the humble tenement block as the bedrock of urban Scottish housing, with a poignant display of relics – ration books, letters, bills, holiday snaps and so forth – from Miss Toward's life. Upstairs, you have to ring the doorbell to enter the flat, whose four rooms give every impression of still being inhabited; the cluttered kitchen features a superb cast-iron range, cupboards crammed with utensils (one has a full jar of jam from 1929) and a box-bed, which would sleep up to five children. Elsewhere, there are framed religious tracts, a sewing machine and a walnut and rose piano, which it is believed both Miss Toward and her mother played. The only major change since Miss Toward left has been the reinstallation of the flickering **gas lamps** she would have used in the early days.

National Piping Centre

30–34 McPhater St • Museum: Mon–Thurs 9am–7pm, Fri 9am–5pm, Sat 9am–1pm • £4.50 • ☎ 0141 353 0220, ⓦ thepipingcentre.co.uk • Cowcaddens underground

Equipped with rehearsal rooms, performance halls, conference centre, accommodation (see p.205), museum and a café, the **National Piping Centre** prides itself on being an international centre for the promotion of the bagpipe. For the casual visitor, the single-room **museum** is of most interest, with a fascinating collection of instruments and related artefacts from the fourteenth century to the present day, including great Highland pipes, small pipes, reed pipes and bellows. Of the older exhibits, the most noteworthy is a stock-and-horn (sheep bone) belonging to Robert Burns and a stunning late seventeenth-century pipe made from lignum-vitae belonging to Iain Dall Mackay, the "Blind Piper of Gairloch"; believed to be the only one of its kind left in existence, the pipe's return from Nova Scotia in 2010, after several generations in the family, was certainly not without controversy. Less well known is the popularity of

5

bagpipes throughout Europe during the medieval period, as evidenced here by the presence of a *chalumeau* (French chamber pipe) and a *gaita* from Spain, among others. You can even have a go yourself on a chanter, a practice pipe.

The West End

The urbane **West End** seems a world away from Glasgow's industrial image and the hustle and bustle of the city centre. In the 1800s the city's wealthy merchants established huge estates away from the soot and grime of city life, and in 1870 the ancient university was moved from its cramped home near the cathedral to a spacious new site overlooking the River Kelvin. Elegant housing swiftly followed, the Kelvingrove Art Gallery and Museum was built to house the 1888 International Exhibition, and, in 1896, the Glasgow District Subway – today's underground – started its circuitous shuffle from here to the city centre.

The hub of life in this part of Glasgow is **Byres Road**, running between Great Western Road and Dumbarton Road past Hillhead underground station. Shops, restaurants, cafés, some enticing pubs and hordes of roving young people, including thousands of students, give the area a sense of style and vitality. Glowing red-sandstone tenements and graceful terraces provide a suitably stylish backdrop to this cosmopolitan district.

The main sights straddle the banks of the River Kelvin, which meanders through the gracious acres of the **Botanic Gardens** and the slopes, trees and statues of **Kelvingrove Park**. Overlooked by the Gothic towers and turrets of **Glasgow University**, which also houses the marvellous **Hunterian Museum**, Kelvingrove Park is home to the pride of Glasgow's civic collection of art and artefacts, **Kelvingrove Art Gallery and Museum**.

Kelvingrove Art Gallery and Museum

Argyle St • Mon–Thurs & Sat 10am–5pm, Fri & Sun 11am–5pm • Free • ☎ 0141 276 9599, ⊕ glasgowlife.org.uk • Kelvin Hall underground

Founded on donations from the city's Victorian industrialists and opened at an international fair held in 1901, the huge, red sandstone fantasy castle of Kelvingrove Art Gallery and Museum is a brash statement of Glasgow's nineteenth-century self-confidence. Intricate and ambitious both in its riotous outside detailing and within, where a superb galleried main hall running the length of the building gives way to attractive upper balconies and small, interlinked display galleries, Kelvingrove offers an impressive and inviting setting for the engaging display of art and artefacts within. There are recitals on the giant ornate organ in the Centre Hall at 1pm (3pm on Sundays).

The displays are organized under two principal headings: **Life**, in the western half of the building, encompassing archeology, local history and stuffed animals, and **Expression**, in the eastern half, which houses much of the superb art collection. However, it does occasionally feel a little muddled, which has led to accusations that the museum is somewhat ill-defined – in any case, there's much to absorb, and a repeat visit may be in order. Highlights from the Life exhibition include ancient Egyptian relics and, from the Scotland's First People gallery, a logboat from Loch Glashan in Argyll.

Inevitably though, it's the **paintings** that draw the biggest crowds, the most famous of which is Salvador Dalí's radically foreshortened *Christ of St John of the Cross*, located in a separate room on the South Balcony. The focus of huge controversy when it was purchased by the city in 1952 for what was regarded as the vast sum of £8200, it has become an icon of the collection and essential viewing on any visit here. Other favourites include Rembrandt's calm *A Man in Armour*, Van Gogh's *The Blute-Fin Windmill*, and a portrait of Glasgow art dealer Alexander Reid (with whom he once briefly shared a flat in Paris), and a very strong French presence, with at least one painting apiece by big hitters Monet, Gauguin, Pissarro, Cézanne and Renoir. You can

FROM TOP THE BOTANIC GARDENS (P.198); KELVINGROVE ART GALLERY AND MUSEUM (ABOVE) >

5

also acquaint yourself with significant **Scottish art** including works by the Glasgow Boys and the Scottish Colourists (see box below), the latter heavily influenced by the French school, as demonstrated in wildly colourful pieces like *Landscape* and *Laggan Farm Buildings near Dalbeattie* by Peploe. There's also a special section of paintings, furniture and murals devoted to Charles Rennie Mackintosh and the "**Glasgow Style**" that he and his contemporaries inspired.

Glasgow University

University Ave • University Visitor Centre & Shop Mon–Sat 9.30am–5pm, Sun 11am–4pm; guided tours Thurs–Sun at 2pm • £10 • ☎ 0141 330 5360, ⬥ src.glasgow.ac.uk/tours • Kelvin Hall/Hillhead underground

Dominating the West End skyline, the gloomy turreted tower of **Glasgow University**, designed by Sir George Gilbert Scott in the mid-nineteenth century, overlooks the glades edging the River Kelvin; the university itself was founded in 1451, which ranks it as the fourth oldest in the English-speaking world, and was originally located near the cathedral on High Street. Access to the main buildings and museums is from University Avenue, running east from Byres Road. In the dark neo-Gothic pile under

THE GLASGOW BOYS AND THE COLOURISTS

In the 1870s a group of Glasgow-based painters formed a loose association that was to imbue Scottish art with a contemporary European flavour far ahead of the rest of Britain. Dominated by five men – Guthrie, Lavery, Henry, Hornel and Crawhall – **The Glasgow Boys** came from very different backgrounds, but all violently rejected the eighteenth-century sentimental renditions of Scottish history peopled by "poor but happy" families. They began to experiment with colour, liberally splashing paint across the canvas. The content and concerns of the paintings, often showing peasant life and work, were as offensive to the art establishment as their style.

Sir James Guthrie, taking inspiration from the *plein-air* painting of the Impressionists, spent his summers in the countryside. Typical of his finest work during the 1880s, *A Highland Funeral* (in the Kelvingrove collection, see p.194) was hugely influential for the rest of the group, who found inspiration in its restrained emotional content, colour and unaffected realism. It persuaded **Sir John Lavery**, then studying in France, to return to Glasgow. Lavery was eventually to become an internationally popular society portraitist, his subtle use of paint revealing his debt to Whistler, but his earlier work, depicting the middle class at play, is filled with fresh colour and figures in motion.

Rather than a realistic aesthetic, an interest in colour and decoration united the work of friends **George Henry** and **E.A. Hornel**. The predominance of colour, pattern and design in Henry's *Galloway Landscape*, for example, is remarkable, while their joint work *The Druids*, in thickly applied impasto, is full of Celtic symbolism; both are part of the Kelvingrove collection. In 1893 the two artists set off for Japan, funded by Alexander Reid and later William Burrell, where their vibrant tone and texture took Scottish painting to the forefront of European trends.

Newcastle-born **Joseph Crawhall** was a reserved and quiet individual who combined superb draughtsmanship and simplicity of line with a photographic memory to create watercolours of an outstanding naturalism and freshness.

THE SCOTTISH COLOURISTS

The Glasgow Boys school had reached its height by 1900 and did not outlast World War I, but they inspired the next generation of Edinburgh painters, who became known as the "**Colourists**". Samuel John Peploe, John Duncan Fergusson, George Leslie Hunter and Francis Cadell shared an understanding that the manipulation of colour was the heart and soul of a good painting. All took inspiration from the avant-garde of late nineteenth-century Paris as well as the landscapes of southern France. **J.D. Fergusson**, in particular, immersed himself in the progressive Parisian scene, rubbing shoulders with writers and artists including Picasso. The influence of **post-Impressionists** such as Matisse and Cézanne is obvious in the work of all four, with their seascapes, society portraits and still lifes bursting with fluidity, unconventionality and, above all, manipulation of colour and shape.

the tower you'll find the **University Visitor Centre & Shop** which is where student-led guided tours of the campus begin; no buildings are entered; instead the tour focuses on the university's history, taking in the grounds, notable statues, tombstones and the like.

Hunterian Museum

University Ave • Tues–Sat 10am–5pm, Sun 11am–4pm • Free • ☎ 0141 330 4221, ⓦ gla.ac.uk/hunterian • Kelvin Hall/Hillhead underground

Located in the same building as the Visitor Centre is the **Hunterian Museum**, Scotland's oldest public museum, dating back to 1807. The collection was donated to the university by ex-student William Hunter (1718–83), a pathologist and anatomist, whose eclectic tastes form the basis of a diverting zoological and archeological jaunt. The most fascinating – and gruesome – exhibits pertain to obstetrics, a discipline in which Hunter was pre-eminent, having published, in 1774, *The Anatomy of the Human Gravid Uterus*, an illustrated text on pregnancy; alongside the book is a womb with a foetus that died at five months, as well as a crude-looking assortment of implements, including wooden forceps. On a lighter note, keep an eye out for a superb ceremonial Maori knife inlaid with shark's teeth from Captain Cook's third voyage, and the world's smallest dinosaur footprint. Upstairs is Lord Kelvin's exhaustive collection of scientific instruments, one of the most notable objects being a gas discharge tube presented to him by Nikola Tesla, the leading physicist of the time.

The Hunterian's most outstanding spectacle, however, is the exhibition entitled *The Antonine Wall: Rome's Final Frontier*; the shorter counterpart to Hadrian's Wall further south, this highly developed wall was built around 142 AD and ran from Clyde to the Firth of Forth (see p.288). On display are sixteen distance slabs (it's thought that there were nineteen), carved stones that document the work of the legions, alongside funerary monuments and sculptural stones, a quite unique ensemble from the Roman Empire.

The Hunterian Art Gallery

University Ave • Tues–Sat 10am–5pm, Sun 11am–4pm • Free • ☎ 0141 330 4221, ⓦ gla.ac.uk/hunterian • Kelvin Hall/Hillhead underground

Across University Avenue is Hunter's more frequently visited bequest, the **Hunterian Art Gallery**, best known for its wonderful works by **James Abbott McNeill Whistler**: only Washington DC has a larger collection. Whistler's portraits of women give his subjects a resolute strength in addition to their occasionally winsome qualities: look out especially for the trio of full-length portraits, *Harmony of Flesh Colour*, *Black, Pink and Gold: The Tulip* and *Red and Black: The Fan*, as well as his dreamy night-time visions of the Thames. Whistler's most important piece, however, is *The Rich and Poor Peacock*, a decorative mural designed for Frederick Leyland's Peacock Room in London, which supposedly symbolized the fractious relationship between artist and client.

The gallery's other major collection is of nineteenth- and twentieth-century Scottish art, including the quasi-Impressionist Scottish landscapes of **William McTaggart**, a forerunner of the **Glasgow Boys** movement, itself represented here by Hornel, Henry (keep an eye out for the striking *The Hedge Cutter*) and Paterson, whose lovely *Moniaive* is suggestive of southern France but is in fact south of Glasgow near Dumfries. Taking the aims of this group one step further were the **Scottish Colourists**; the monumental dancing figures of J.D. Fergusson's *Les Eus* preside over a small collection of work by this group, including Hunter, Peploe and Cadell, who left a vibrant legacy of thickly textured, colourful landscapes and portraits, a fine example being Hunter's bold *Houseboats: Loch Lomond*.

A small selection of **French Impressionism** includes works by Boudin and Pissarro, with Corot's soothing *Distant View of Corbeil* being a highlight from the Barbizon school.

Mackintosh House

2 Hillhead St • Tues–Sat 10am–5pm, Sun 11am–4pm; tours every 30min • £5 • ☎ 0141 330 4221, ⓦ gla.ac.uk/hunterian

A side gallery off the Hunterian leads to the **Mackintosh House**, an assemblage of the

5

interior of the now-demolished Glasgow home of Margaret MacDonald and Charles Rennie Mackintosh. The house can only be visited on a guided tour, which, at just thirty minutes, is far too short. Passing the original front door, which was deliberately placed ten feet off the ground for maximum light effect, you are led into an exquisitely cool interior that contains more than sixty pieces of Mackintosh furniture on three floors, many featuring his signature leaf and rose motifs. The first room is the dining room, complete with three-dimensional fireplace and a half a dozen chairs considered so futuristic that they have been used in episodes of *Babylon 5* and *Dr Who*. The studio drawing room – a startlingly modern design for that period – contains Mackintosh's ebony writing desk, while the standout items in the white-painted oak bedroom are a pair of stunning dove wardrobes and a slimming mirror. There are also plenty of contributions from his wife, not least several impressive gesso panels.

The Botanic Gardens

730 Great Western Rd • Botanic Gardens: daily 7am–dusk; glasshouses: 10am–6pm, till 4.15pm in winter • Free • ☎ 0141 276 1614, ⓦ glasgowbotanicgardens.com • Hillhead underground

For a spot of peace and tranquillity, pop into Glasgow's exotic and lush **Botanic Gardens**, which date back to 1817. The best-known glasshouse here, the hulking, domed **Kibble Palace**, was built in 1863 for wealthy landowner John Kibble's estate on the shores of Loch Long, where it stood for ten years before he decided to transport it into Glasgow, drawing it up the Clyde on a vast raft pulled by a steamer. For over two decades it was used not as a greenhouse but as a Victorian pleasure palace, before the gardens' owners put a stop to the drunken revels that wreaked havoc with the lawns and plant beds. Today the palace is more sedate, housing the magnificent **National Collection of Ferns** with samples from around the world, though Australasia has the lion's share. Nearby, the **Main Range Glasshouse** is home to lurid flowers and plants luxuriating in the humidity, including stunning orchids, cacti, palms and tropical fruit; the annual Orchid Fair is held in mid-May.

In addition to the area around the main glasshouses, there are some beautifully remote paths in the gardens that weave along the closely wooded banks of the deep-set River Kelvin, linking up with the walkway that runs alongside the river all the way down to Dumbarton Road, near its confluence with the Clyde; en route you'll find a rose garden and a children's garden and, beyond here, the **arboretum**, replete with birch, fir and pine trees. After all that walking, pop into the teahouse for a cuppa.

Clydeside

"The **Clyde** made Glasgow and Glasgow made the Clyde" runs an old saw, full of sentimentality for the days when the river was the world's premier shipbuilding centre, and when its industry lent an innovation and confidence which made Glasgow the second city of the British Empire. Despite the hardships that heavy industry brought, every Glaswegian would follow the progress of the skeleton ships under construction in the riverside yards, cheering them on their way down the Clyde as they were launched. The last of the great liners to be built on **Clydeside** was the *QE2* in 1967, yet such events are hard to visualize today, with the banks of the river all but devoid of any industry: shipbuilding is now restricted to a couple of barely viable yards, as derelict warehouses, crumbling docks and overgrown wastelands crowd the river's flanks.

Following a flurry of construction in the last few years, Clydeside has once again become a focus of attention. Striking constructions such as the titanium-clad **Clyde Auditorium** (aka the "Armadillo"), the creatively lit **Clyde Arc** (known as "the squinty bridge"), and, most recently, the enormous **SSE Hydro** centre (sadly without a nickname),

5

have become icons of the city's forward-thinking image. On the opposite side stands the box-like home of **BBC Scotland** and the curvaceous **Glasgow Science Centre.**

Its shipbuilding heritage has not been forgotten though, with the **Tall Ship Glenlee**, located next to the superb **Riverside Museum**, and the **Finnieston Crane**, retained as an icon of shipbuilding days.

The Riverside Museum

Riverside Museum 100 Pointhouse Place • Mon–Thurs & Sat 10am–5pm, Fri & Sun 11am–5pm • Free • **Tall Ship** Daily 10am–5pm • Free • ☎ 0141 287 2720, ⓦ glasgowlife.org.uk • Partick underground; the #100 Riversider bus runs every 30min from George Square via the Kelvingrove Art Gallery

The wave-like titanium-clad building on the north bank of the river houses the magnificent **Riverside Museum**, Scotland's old Museum of Transport and Travel. Designed by the late Zaha Hadid, and a recent winner of the prestigious European Museum of the Year award, its cathedral-like interior is home to a huge, dramatically displayed collection of trains, boats, trams, bikes and cars, and the intricate models on which full-scale ships were based. Of the many fine trams on show, look out for the no. 1088, boasting a beautiful, upholstered leather interior, brass fittings and stained-glass windows, though for sheer spectacle, nothing comes close to the formidable South African Class 15F locomotive, which is testament to the engineering prowess of the North British Locomotive Company in Glasgow, once the largest loco manufacturer in Europe.

On the two-wheeled front, there's the bike that Graham Obree twice broke the one-hour world record on, plus his skins from the 1996 Olympics; a speedway bike belonging to World War II pilot George Pinkerton (who, it is alleged, got the first kill in the Battle of Britain); and the motorbike ridden by Ewan McGregor during his 22,000-mile road trip through eighteen countries in 2004, recorded in the television documentary *Long Way Round*. The one disappointment is the Wall of Cars, the vehicles mounted on shelves several levels high, meaning that you don't actually get to see them properly. Elsewhere, interactive exhibits provide engaging background on the city's social fabric, with walk-through streets incorporating real interiors from Glasgow shops and cafés.

Berthed alongside the museum is **The Tall Ship**, a square-rigger called *Glenlee*. A 245ft-long, three-masted barque launched on the river in 1896, she circumnavigated the globe four times before being put to use as a sail training vessel – it's now one of only five large sailing vessels built on Clydeside that are still afloat. Here too is the **Clyde Ride**, a rigid inflatable that offers breakneck trips along the river (£10 for 20min).

The Glasgow Science Centre

Science Mall 50 Pacific Quay • Daily 10am–5pm • £11 • **Glasgow Tower** April–Nov (11am–5pm) • £6.50 • ☎ 0141 420 5000, ⓦ glasgowsciencecentre.org • Cessnock or Ibrox underground

The south bank of the river is dominated by three space-age, titanium-clad constructions which make up the **Glasgow Science Centre**, the largest of which is the curvaceous, wedge-shaped **Science Mall**. Behind the vast glass wall that faces the river are four floors of interactive exhibits ranging from lift-your-own-weight pulleys to high-tech thermograms. Described as "hands-on info-tainment for the genome generation", it's like all your most enjoyable school science experiments packed into one building, with in-house boffins demonstrating chemical reactions, and pensioners and toddlers alike captivated by cockroach colonies and jigsaw puzzles of human organs. The centre covers almost every aspect of science, from simple optical illusions to cutting-edge computer technology, including a section on moral and environmental issues. Within the mall, an impressive planetarium and 3D virtual science theatre put on shows throughout the day. Alongside the Science Mall is the bubble-like **IMAX theatre** (see p.214).

Also on the site of the Glasgow Science Centre is the 417ft-high **Glasgow Tower**, the tallest freestanding structure in Scotland, built with an aerofoil-like construction to allow it to rotate to face into the prevailing wind. Glass lifts ascend to the viewing cabin at the top, offering terrific panoramic views of central Glasgow.

The Southside

The section of Glasgow south of the Clyde is generally described as the **Southside**, though within this area there are a number of districts with recognizable names, including the notoriously deprived **Gorbals** and **Govan**, which are sprinkled with new developments but still obviously derelict and tatty in many parts. There's little reason to venture here unless you're making your way to one of the revived architectural gems of Charles Rennie Mackintosh – the **Scotland Street School** and the **House for an Art Lover**, or the famously innovative **Citizens' Theatre** (see p.213).

As you move further south, inner-city decay fades into altogether gentler and more salubrious suburbs, including **Queen's Park**, home to Scotland's national football stadium, **Hampden Park**; Pollokshaws and the rural landscape of **Pollok Park**, which contains two of Glasgow's major museums, the **Burrell Collection** and **Pollok House** (though the former is closed until at least 2019); and Cathcart, location of Alexander "Greek" Thomson's **Holmwood House**.

Scotland Street School Museum

225 Scotland St • Tues–Thurs & Sat 10am–5pm, Fri & Sun 11am–5pm • Free • ☎ 0141 287 0500, ⓦ glasgowlife.org.uk • Shields Road underground

The wonderfully designed **Scotland Street School Museum** is another of the city's Charles Rennie Mackintosh treasures, and the one to head for if time is limited. This was Mackintosh's second commission for the School Board and the last individual building he designed in Glasgow. The school opened in 1906, before finally closing in 1979. Throughout its period of construction, there were frequent clashes between Mackintosh and the governors, the former favouring a distinctly more ornamental style, not least with regard to the tiling scheme; in the event, Mackintosh was forced to back down. The most immediately striking elements are the twin towers (one of Mackintosh's favoured design features), one an entrance for boys, the other for girls. Entering via the light-filled Drill Hall and its superb geometrically patterned, green- and white-tiled columns, you continue up to the mezzanine, where blue tiles are employed along with leaded pane windows.

There are reconstructed classrooms from the Victorian era – which would cater for up to seventy pupils – World War II, and the 50s and 60s, when forty-five pupils was the norm; indeed, if you visit on a weekday during term time, you're quite likely to stumble on a period lesson, local schoolkids struggling with their ink blotters, gas masks and archly unsympathetic teachers, the faint smell of antiseptic conjuring up memories of scuffed knees and playground tantrums. One room is given over to exhibiting Mackintosh's designs, while another fondly recalls the school's history, with books, photos, and a rather grand roll-top desk belonging to William Davidson, the first headmaster. In addition there are changing rooms, a primitive domestic science room and re-creations of the school matron's sanatorium and a janitor's lair.

House for an Art Lover

10 Dumbreck Rd, Bellahouston Park • Daily 10am–5pm, though it's best to call ahead as the building is often used for public functions • £4.50 • ☎ 0141 353 4770, ⊕ houseforanartlover.co.uk • Dumbreck station

Tucked just inside Bellahouston Park is Charles Rennie Mackintosh's **House for an Art Lover**. Designed in 1901 for a German competition, it wasn't until 1987 that civil engineer Graham Roxburgh conceived the idea of building the house (he just happened to be running past the site one day), and it eventually opened in 1996; however, few original drawings for the house remained, so its design was largely based on other Mackintosh buildings. It's all quintessential Mackintosh, the exquisitely stylish and original nature of the design making it hard to imagine it suffering the wear and tear of day-to-day life.

The house is entered via the **Main Hall**, a deliberately grand, high space where massive windows cast a cool light upon an area designed for large parties. In the **Margaret Macdonald Room**, there's a film giving a detailed account of the building's history, before you pass into the delicate **Oval Room**, intended for women to retire to after dinner; not only is the room itself oval, but so is everything within it, such as the windows, stained-glass ceiling light and chair motifs. Next door, the dazzling white **Music Room** has bow windows opening out to a large balcony, though the garden view is marred by an artificial ski slope; designed to symbolize a forest glade, features here include floor-to-ceiling pillars, teardrop leaves, clusters of lanterns, and rose stencils above the hearth – the room's most theatrical piece, though, is a piano enclosed within a four-poster bed. In complete contrast, the **Dining Room** is decorated with darkened stained wood and enhanced by some beautiful gesso tiles. While here, it'd be remiss not to have a bite to eat or something to drink in the lovely ground-floor **café** (see p.211).

Hampden Park

Mount Florida • Mon–Sat 10am–5pm, Sun 11am–5pm; tour times 11am, 12.30pm, 2pm & 3pm • Museum £6, guided tour £8; combined £12 • ☎ 0141 616 6139, ⊕ scottishfootballmuseum.org.uk • Trains from Central station to Mount Florida

Just east of leafy Queen's Park, the floodlights and giant stands of Scotland's national football stadium, **Hampden Park**, loom over the surrounding suburban tenements and terraces. Home of Queen's Park Football Club, the fact that it's the venue for Scotland's international fixtures and major cup finals makes it a place of pilgrimage for the country's football fans. Regular **guided tours** offer the chance to see the changing rooms and warm-up areas before climbing the stairs for the obligatory lifting of the cup.

Also here is the engaging **Scottish Football Museum**, which has extensive collections of memorabilia, video clips and displays covering almost every aspect of the game. While the standard of Scottish football might not be up to much these days, it has rated some fine players over the years, as demonstrated in the **Hall of Fame**, which honours the likes of Denis Law, Jimmy Johnstone and Kenny Dalglish.

Pollok House

2060 Pollokshaws Rd • Daily 10am–5pm • April–Oct £6.50, Nov–March free; café and gardens free year-round; NTS • ☎ 0141 616 6410 • Train to Pollokshaws West station (not to be confused with Pollokshields West)

Lovely eighteenth-century **Pollok House** was the manor of the Pollok Park estate and once home of the Maxwell family, local lords and owners of most of southern Glasgow until well into the last century. Designed by **William Adam** in the mid-1700s, the house

5

FOOTBALL IN GLASGOW

Football is one of Glasgow's great passions – and one of its great blights. While the city can claim to be one of Europe's premier footballing centres, it's known above all for one of the most bitter rivalries in any sport, that between **Celtic** and **Rangers**. The latter climbed back to the premiership in 2016, four years after being demoted to the fourth (bottom) tier following liquidation. Two of the largest clubs in Britain, with weekly crowds regularly topping 50,000, the Old Firm, as they're collectively known, have dominated Scottish football for a century, lavishing vast sums of money on foreign talent (albeit much less so in recent years) in an often frantic effort both to outdo each other and to keep up with the top English and European teams.

The roots of Celtic, who play at **Celtic Park** in the eastern district of Parkhead, lie in the city's immigrant Irish and Catholic population, while Rangers, based at **Ibrox Park** in Govan on the Southside, have traditionally drawn support from local Protestants. As a result, sporting rivalries have been enmeshed in a sectarian divide that many argue would not have remained so long, nor so deep, had it been divorced from the footballing scene. While large-scale violence on the terraces and streets has not been seen for some time – thanks in large measure to canny policing – Old Firm matches often seethe with bitter passions, and sectarian-related assaults do still occur in parts of the city.

However, there is a less intense side to the game in Glasgow, and watching one of the smaller clubs – who actively distance themselves from the Old Firm – offers the best chances of experiencing the more down-to-earth side of Glaswegian football. **Partick Thistle**, who play at Firhill Stadium in the West End, complete the trio of current Glaswegian premiership teams, while both **Queen's Park**, residents of Hampden, and **St Mirren**, the Paisley team, plod along in the lower reaches of the Scottish league.

THE TEAMS

Celtic Celtic Park, Parkhead (☎0871 226 1888, ⓦcelticfc.net).
Partick Thistle Firhill Stadium (☎0141 579 1971, ⓦptfc.co.uk).
Queen's Park Hampden (☎0141 632 1275,

ⓦqueensparkfc.co.uk).
Rangers Ibrox Park, Govan (☎0871 702 1972, ⓦrangers.co.uk).
St Mirren Paisley (☎0141 840 6130, ⓦsaintmirren.net).

---

is typical of its age: graciously light and sturdily built, it looks out onto pristine raked and parterre gardens. Appropriately, the house is now under the management of the National Trust for Scotland, as it was in the upstairs smoking room in 1931 that the then-owner, Sir John Stirling Maxwell, held the first meetings with the Eighth Duke of Atholl and Lord Colquhoun of Luss that led to the formation of the NTS. The Trust has made a deliberate effort to return the house to the layout and style it enjoyed when the Stirling Maxwells were living here in the 1920s and 1930s. As a result, the **paintings** range from Spanish masterpieces – among them two El Greco portraits and works by Murillo and Goya – in the morning room and some splendid Dutch hunting scenes in the dining room to Sir John's own worthy but noticeably amateur efforts, which line the upstairs corridors.

Generally, though, the rooms have the flavour of a well-to-do but unstuffy country house, with the odd piece of attractive furniture and some pleasant rooms, but little that can be described as outstanding. The servants' quarters downstairs, however, do capture the imagination – the virtually untouched labyrinth of tiled Victorian parlours and corridors includes a **tearoom** in the old kitchen. Free tours of the house are available from the front desk, or you can wander around at your own pace.

Holmwood House

61–63 Netherlee Rd • April–Oct Thurs–Mon noon–5pm • £6.50; NTS • ☎0141 571 0184 • Train to Cathcart station, from where it's a 15min walk, or buses #4 and #6

Holmwood House is the finest domestic design by rediscovered Glasgow architect

5

Alexander "Greek" Thomson. A commission by James Couper, co-owner of a paper mill on the nearby River Carth, the house shows off Thomson's bold classical concepts, with exterior pillars on two levels and a raised main door, as well as his detailed and highly imaginative interiors. One room upstairs is given over to a series of displays about Thomson and the history of the house. Also on the upper floor is the **drawing room** – look for the white marble fireplace and the night-time star decorations on the ceiling, which contrast with a black marble fireplace and sunburst decorations in the **parlour** immediately underneath on the downstairs level, which also features a delightful round bay window. Across the corridor, the **dining room** has a frieze of scenes from the *Iliad*, along with a skylight at the back of the room designed to allow the Greek gods to peer down on the feasts being consumed inside. One unusual feature not designed by Thomson is the small hatch cut in the interconnecting door between the dining room and the butler's pantry; the house was last occupied by a sisterhood of nuns, who used the dining room as a chapel and created the small hatch for use as a confessional.

ARRIVAL AND DEPARTURE

GLASGOW

BY PLANE

Glasgow International Airport Abbotsinch, 8 miles southwest of the city (☎ 0844 481 5555, ⓦ glasgowairport .com).

Getting to/from the city centre The 24hr Glasgow Shuttle bus (every 10–15min; £7, open return £9.50) runs to the Buchanan St bus station, also stopping at Bothwell St/Hope St and Queen St train station; tickets can be purchased from the Visit Scotland information desk (see p.204) or on the bus. Taxis charge around £22 to the city centre.

BY TRAIN

Central station Above Argyle St, one of the city's main shopping thoroughfares, Central station (☎ 0845 748 4950, ⓦ nationalrail.co.uk) is the terminus for trains to Ayrshire and the Clyde coast, as well as nearly all trains from England. The walk between Glasgow Central and Queen St station takes less than 10min; otherwise, bus #398 from the front entrance on Gordon St shuttles every 10min to Queen St.

Destinations Ardrossan for Arran ferry (every 20–30min; 40–50min); Ayr (every 20–30min; 50min); Birmingham (hourly; 4 6hr); Blantyre (every 15 30min; 20min); Carlisle (every 40–60min; 1hr 10min); East Kilbride (hourly; 30min); Gourock (every 20–30min; 45min); Greenock (every 20–30min; 40min); Lanark (every 20–30min; 50min); Largs (hourly; 1hr); London Euston (hourly; 4hr 30min); Paisley (every 10min; 10min); Queens Park (every 15min; 6min); Wemyss Bay (hourly; 50min).

Queen Street Station Corner of George Square. Terminus for trains serving Edinburgh and the north.

Destinations Aberdeen (6 daily; 3hr 10min); Aviemore (3 daily; 3hr 10min); Balloch (every 30min; 45min); Dumbarton (every 15min; 35min); Dundee (hourly; 1hr 20min); Edinburgh (every 15min; 1hr 10min); Fort William (Mon–Sat 3 daily, 2 on Sun; 3hr 50min); Helensburgh (every 30min; 45min); Inverness (Mon–Sat 6 daily, 3 on Sun; 3hr 45min); Mallaig (Mon–Sat 3 daily, 2 on Sun; 5hr 15min); Milngavie (every 30min; 25min); Oban (Mon–Sat 5 daily, 3 on Sun; 3hr 10min); Perth (hourly; 1hr); Stirling (every 20min; 25–40min).

BY BUS

Buchanan Street Station This is the arrival point for regional and intercity coaches.

Citylink coaches Connects major Scottish cities including Aberdeen, Dundee, Edinburgh, Fort William, Inverness, Oban and Perth (☎ 0871 266 3333, ⓦ citylink.co.uk).

Destinations Aberdeen (hourly; 3hr); Campbeltown (5 daily; 4hr 15min); Dundee (twice hourly; 1hr 50min); Edinburgh (every 15min, 1hr 10min); Fort William (4 daily; 3hr); Glen Coe (4 daily; 2hr 30min); Inverness (4 daily; 3hr 20min); Kyle of Lochalsh (3 daily; 5–6hr); Loch Lomond (hourly; 45min); Oban (5 daily; 3hr); Perth (hourly; 1hr–1hr 40min); Portree (3 daily; 6–7hr); Stirling (hourly; 45min).

GETTING AROUND

ON FOOT

Walking is the best way of exploring any one part of the city. However, as the main sights are scattered – the West End, for example, is a good 30min walk from the centre – you'll probably need to use the comprehensive public transport system, which includes an underground network. If you're travelling beyond the city centre or the West End, or to the main sights on the Southside, you may need to use the bus and train networks. For information on all transport within the city and further afield, call Traveline or check online (☎ 0871 200 2233, ⓦ travelinescotland.com); otherwise, you can get information and pick up timetables at the Travel Centre (Mon–Sat 6.30am–10.30pm, Sun 7am–10.30pm) in Buchanan St bus station.

5

PASSES

Various public transport passes are available if you plan to do lots of travelling on one day or are in the city for more than a few days.

Roundabout Glasgow For train and underground travel the Roundabout Glasgow ticket gives unlimited travel for a day (Mon–Fri after 9am, all day Sat & Sun; £6.30).

Zonecards The simplest of a complicated system of Zonecards, covering train, underground, buses and ferries, costs around £18.50 and gives travel for a week in central Glasgow, including all the attractions on the Southside.

BY UNDERGROUND

The best way to get between the city centre and the West End is to use the underground (Mon–Sat 6.30am–11.45pm, Sun 10am–6.15pm), whose stations are marked with a large orange U. Affectionately known as the "Clockwork Orange" (there's only one, circular, route and the trains are a garish bright orange), the service is extremely easy to use. There's a flat fare of £1.40, or you can buy a day ticket for £4.

Stations The main stations are Buchanan St, near George Square and connected to Queen St train station by a moving walkway, and St Enoch, at the junction of Buchanan St pedestrian precinct and Argyle St. Hillhead station is bang in the heart of the West End, near the university.

BY TRAIN

Surburban trains The suburban train network is swift and convenient. Suburbs south of the Clyde are connected to Central station, either at the mainline station or the subterranean low-level station, while trains from Queen St (which also has mainline and low-level stations) head into the northeast suburbs.

Cross-city lines There are two grim but functional cross-city lines: the one running through Central station connects to southeastern districts as far out as Lanark, while the Queen St line links to the East End and points east. Trains on both lines go through Partick station, near the West End, which is also an underground stop; beyond Partick, the trains are an excellent way to link to points west and northwest of Glasgow, including Milngavie (for the start of the West Highland Way), Dumbarton and Helensburgh.

BY BUS

Buchanan Street bus station Glasgow's main bus terminus (daily 6am–11pm; ☎0141 333 3708), north of Sauchiehall St and opposite the Royal Concert Hall. As well as intercity buses, this is where local city services depart from.

First Glasgow Serves Glasgow, Edinburgh, central Scotland, the Borders and Aberdeen (☎0141 423 6600, ⊛firstgroup.com/greater-glasgow). A flat fare costs £2 and a FirstDay pass, allowing unlimited travel throughout Glasgow, costs £4.50; tickets can be purchased on the bus (have the exact change ready).

BY TAXI

You can hail a black taxi from anywhere in the city centre, day or night. There are also taxi ranks at Central and Queen St train stations and Buchanan St bus station. Expect to pay around £6–7 for a journey from the city centre to the West End. Uber users will have little trouble finding a ride as the city is comprehensively covered.

Taxis Glasgow Taxi Ltd (☎0141 429 7070, ⊛glasgowtaxis .co.uk), Hampden Cabs (☎0141 332 5050, ⊛hampdencabs.co.uk), West End Radio Cars (☎0141 954 2000, ⊛westendradiocars.co.uk).

BY CAR

The M8 motorway runs right through the heart of Glasgow, making the city centre very accessible by car; once you're there, however, the grid of one-way streets and pedestrian precincts can be frustrating to navigate. You'll find plenty of parking meters as well as car parks dotted all around the centre.

Car rental Arnold Clark, multiple branches (☎0141 301 1820); Avis & Budget, 70 Lancefield St (☎0844 544 6064); Hertz, 138 Hydepark St (☎0843 309 3032). All the main rental companies have desks at the airport.

BY FERRY

Govan Ferry The Govan ferry (July to mid-Sept; free) runs between the pontoon at Water Row and the Kelvin Harbour landing stage linking the Riverside Museum with Govan.

INFORMATION AND TOURS

Tourist office The tourist office has moved location on numerous occasions in recent years, but there are currently two branches: one in the basement of the Gallery of Modern Art (Mon–Wed & Sat 10am–4.45pm, Thurs 10am–6.45pm, Fri & Sun 11am–4.45pm; ⊛peoplemakeglasgow.com) and another inside the Kelvingrove Museum (Mon–Thurs & Sat 10am–4.45pm, Fri & Sun 11am–4.45pm). There's also a Visit Scotland desk in the domestic arrivals hall at the airport (Mon–Sat 7.30am–5pm, Sun 8am–3.30pm;

☎0141 848 4440, ⊛visitscotland.com).

City Sightseeing Open-top, hop-on, hop-off bus tours (daily: May–Sept 9.30am–6.30pm, Oct–April 9.30am–4.30pm; one day £13, two days £15; ☎0141 204 0444, ⊛citysightseeingglasgow.co.uk) leave every 10min (every 30mins in winter) from George Square on a continuous circuit of all the major attractions in the city centre and West End, allowing you to get on and off as you please.

ACCOMMODATION

Glasgow has plentiful accommodation, and while many hotels are business-oriented, this means that you can often negotiate good deals at weekends. There are an increasing number of fashionable (though fairly priced) design hotels, while the majority of the best guesthouses and B&Bs can be found in the **West End**. There's also a reasonable, though not particularly exciting, spread of hostels across the city.

CITY CENTRE
HOTELS AND GUESTHOUSES

ABode Glasgow 129 Bath St ☎0141 221 6789, ⓦabodeglasgow.co.uk; map pp.190–191. A classy hotel that delights on many levels, from the warm welcome and original cage lift, to the rooms themselves, of which there are four categories, ranging from "Comfortable" to "Fabulous"; the main difference between them is size and the odd extra (for example, Nespresso machines), though nearly all feature black and white, or colour, print wallpaper, picture frame headboards and tartan spreads, while a few rooms retain the original wood-panelled walls and stained-glass windows. **£80**

Adelaide's 209 Bath St ☎0141 248 4970, ⓦadelaides .co.uk; map pp.190–191. Eight brightly coloured and well-furnished rooms (some good for families) in a beautifully restored church building, run by pleasant staff as part of a broad-thinking, approachable Baptist church community. Continental breakfast included. **£75**

Babbity Bowster 16–18 Blackfriars St, off High St ☎0141 552 5055, ⓦbabbitybowster.com; map pp.190–191. Best known as a pub (see p.211), *Babbity Bowster* also features six plain but serviceable rooms that provide visitors with a great, and decently priced, Merchant City location; a simple breakfast is included. **£70**

Blythswood Square 11 Blythswood Square ☎0141 248 5888, ⓦtownhousecompany.com; map pp.190–191. Fronting one of the city's loveliest squares, this swish but respectful conversion of the landmark Georgian Royal Scottish Automobile Club offers magnificently appointed rooms, featuring Spanish cut marble, Harris tweed and Egyptian cotton. There's also a luxury spa. **£180**

The Brunswick 106 Brunswick St ☎0141 552 0001, ⓦbrunswickhotel.co.uk, map pp.190 191. A small, independent designer hotel in the heart of the Merchant City offering eighteen fashionable and individually coloured rooms with minimalist furniture; the "Compact" rooms (which really are compact) are a bargain at just £50 per night, while those standard rooms on the higher levels

---

TOP 5 BOUTIQUE HOTELS

ABode Glasgow See above
Blythswood Square See above
citizenM See above
**Hotel du Vin at One Devonshire
   Gardens** See p.206
Z Hotel See above

---

are less prone to the traffic noise; smart restaurant/bar to boot. **£65**

citizenM 60 Renfrew St ☎0141 404 9485, ⓦcitizenm .com; map pp.190–191. This modern European chain offers a luxury experience that won't break the bank; check in via computer then head to your room to enjoy the innovative mood lighting, hip decor and rain shower. After that, you could do a lot worse than hang around in the cool CanteenM, a homely breakfast bar-cum-lounge area that's open round the clock – indeed, you're quite likely to spend more time in this hotel than out of it. **£64**

★**Grasshoppers** 87 Union St ☎0141 222 2666, ⓦgrasshoppersglasgow.com; map pp.190–191. Occupying the sixth (top) floor of the former Caledonian Railway Company building, the ground-floor entrance is somewhat unprepossessing, but don't let that put you off. This medium-sized hotel is a real gem, from the artwork-lined corridors to the rooms themselves, which manifest an understatedly cool, urban feel: oak flooring, bespoke, Scandinavian-style furnishings and pod-like bathrooms. The service, meanwhile, is second to none. **£78**

Malmaison 278 West George St ☎0141 572 1000, ⓦmalmaison.com; map pp.190–191. Glasgow's version of this sleek, chic hotel group, the austere Grecian-temple frontage masks a superbly comfortable designer hotel whose rooms are dominated by various shades of greys and purples, and come with deep, inviting beds and big fluffy pillows. **£95**

Pipers' Tryst 30–34 McPhater St ☎0141 353 5551, ⓦthepipingcentre.co.uk; map pp.190–191. Attached to the National Piping Centre (see p.193), and despite its location on a main thoroughfare, the eight decently sized rooms are fully soundproofed, with decor that is firmly on the side of cheery tartan; tremendously helpful staff and a wholesome breakfast on your way out. **£104**

★**Z Hotel** 36 North Frederick St ☎0141 212 4550, ⓦthezhotels.com; map pp.190–191. The handsome, sandstone facade of this former printworks conceals small but fabulously sleek rooms, minimally furnished (there are few tables and chairs to speak of, and TVs are embedded in the wall), with sparkling wet rooms boxed off by glass partitions; each evening between 5 and 8pm there's a free buffet, including a glass of wine, while the good-humoured, unfailingly helpful staff conspire to make this a terrific place to spend a night or two. **£75**

HOSTELS AND CAMPUS ACCOMMODATION

Euro Hostel 318 Clyde St ☎0845 539 9956, ⓦeurohostels.co.uk; map pp.190–191. This enormous,

5

TOP 5 BUDGET STAYS

Adelaide's See p.205
Alamo Guest House See below
Amadeus Guesthouse See below
Babbity Bowster See p.205
SYHA Hostel See below

seven-storey hostel can feel a bit impersonal given its size, though its location facing the Clyde means that many rooms have great views. A mix of en-suite rooms (sleeping anything from two to fourteen) and suites, the latter with a small lounge/TV area; there's also a self-catering kitchen, laundry and adjoining bar, which is where breakfast (£5) is taken. Dorms **£12**, suites per person **£14**, doubles **£50**

University of Glasgow ☎0141 330 4116, ⑩cvso .co.uk. Low-priced, self-catering accommodation in single rooms only, which are mostly in the West End. June to early Sept. **£26**

THE WEST END

HOTELS AND GUESTHOUSES

Alamo Guest House 46 Gray St ☎0141 339 2395, ⑩alamoguesthouse.com; map pp.184–185. Good-value, family-run boarding house next to Kelvingrove Park, with ten rooms, each one completely different in size and character, variously featuring stucco plasterwork, French oak beds, slate-tile sinks and cast-iron chandeliers, or perhaps a freestanding tub. **£70**

★**Amadeus Guesthouse** 411 North Woodside Rd ☎0141 339 8257, ⑩amadeusguesthouse.co.uk; map pp.184–185. Handily located near Great Western Rd opposite the deep green gully of the River Kelvin, this welcoming – and family-friendly – Victorian townhouse offers stylish, generously sized en-suite rooms. **£80**

Hotel du Vin at One Devonshire Gardens 1 Devonshire Gardens, Great Western Rd ☎0141 378

0385, ⑩hotelduvin.com; map p.183. Glasgow's most exclusive and exquisite small hotel, set in a handsome row of converted townhouses a 10min walk up the Great Western Rd from the Botanic Gardens; rooms typically feature large open-plan seating areas, Bose sound systems and monsoon power showers, and there's further decadence courtesy of the cigar shack and whisky bar. **£140**

Kirklee 11 Kensington Gate ☎0141 334 5555, ⑩kirkleehotel.co.uk; map pp.184–185. Quirky and highly patterned West End B&B in a red-brick Edwardian townhouse, with antique furniture, lush fabrics and walls crammed with paintings and etchings; guests are free to use the lounge with its carved fire mantel and views across extensive gardens. **£85**

HOSTEL

SYHA Glasgow 7–8 Park Terrace ☎0141 332 3004, ⑩syha.org.uk; map pp.184–185. Popular but surprisingly low-key hostel located in a wonderful townhouse in one of the West End's grandest terraces. All the dorms (singles up to eight-bed) are en suite, while other facilities include common area, self-catering kitchen and laundry. It's a 10min walk south of Kelvinbridge underground station, while bus #4 or #4A from the city centre leaves you with a short stroll west up Woodlands Rd. Evening meals are also available; breakfast £4.95. Dorms **£24**, doubles **£68**

SELF-CATERING

Queensgate Apartments 107 Dowanhill St ☎0141 339 1615, ⑩queensgateapartments.com; map pp.184–185. Two attractive and cosy flats in traditional West End tenement buildings. One sleeps four in two bedrooms and has a gleaming wood-panelled hall and a lovely patio garden; the other sleeps two and also has a patio garden. Four-person apartment per week **£690**, two-person apartment per week **£490**

EATING

Glasgow's restaurant scene has improved dramatically over the past few years and can now hold its own with the best cities in Britain. Originally brought up on the culinary skills of the long-established **Italian** community and later waves of **Indian** and **Chinese** immigrants – indeed, the city has some of the best Indian restaurants in the UK – there's been a more studied move towards the use of great **Scottish produce**, and many menus now contain a seasonal and modern Scottish component, offering a new take on the country's culinary traditions. Although there's a decent spread of cafés and restaurants throughout the city centre, there's a fantastic concentration of places in the West End, particularly along Argyle St, Byres Rd and Gibson St. Note that many restaurants have excellent **set lunch**, pre-theatre or early dining deals.

CITY CENTRE AND THE MERCHANT CITY

CAFÉS

★**Laboratorio** 93 West Nile St ☎0141 353 1111; map pp.190–191. The "Lab", as it's more popularly known, is a terrific little bolt-hole with cement board walls and recycled wood panelling, and super-friendly baristas who really do know their beans; there's typically a single-origin

espresso and a guest espresso on the go at any one time. Sit-down and takeaway. Mon–Fri 7.30am–5.30pm, Sat 9am–5pm, Sun 11am–5.30pm.

★**McCune Smith** 3–5 Duke St ☎0141 548 1114, ⑩mccunesmith.co.uk; map pp.184–185. Named after the nineteenth-century physician and abolitionist – and Glasgow's first African-American student – this sparkling café is a welcome addition to the East End. Enjoy superb coffee along with an "enlightened" sandwich, each one conceived after a figure from the Scottish Enlightenment, for example New York pastrami, after McCune, and hot smoked salmon, after Thomas Campbell. Mon–Fri 8am–4pm, Sat 9am–5pm.

Singl-end 265 Renfrew St ☎ 0141 353 1277, ⊛ singl -end.co.uk; map pp.190–191. An engaging, below-street-level café and bakehouse with pretty, blue shuttered windows and, inside, blue-painted steel girders and glass-topped tables laden with postcards and photos of Glasgow. This is a great spot to kick back with a cup of coffee and a slice of apple and olive oil cake, or something more substantial like spicy baked eggs with toasted sourdough bread. Mon–Fri 9am–5pm, Sat & Sun 10am–5pm.

Spitfire Espresso 127 Candleriggs St ☎ 07578 250105; map pp.190–191. Another fine addition to the city's roster of artisan coffee houses, this cool, light and airy space, with marine-blue painted walls and window frames, offers a short but enticing coffee menu – using Gunnerbean coffee from Colombia and Brazil – alongside a delicious all-day egg menu, among other treats. Mon–Sat 8am–6pm, Sun 10am–3pm.

Tinderbox Merchant City 118 Ingram St ☎ 0141 552 6907; map pp.190–191. Colourful, labyrinthine coffee house serving half a dozen varieties of strong espressos, as well as good fresh sarnies and cakes. Mon–Sat 7.15am–10pm, Sun 8am–10pm.

★ **Trans-Europe Café** 25 Parnie St ☎ 0141 552 7999, ⊛ transeuropecafe.co.uk; map pp.190–191. Named after the legendary Kraftwerk album, this fun, railway-style diner – with 80s-style bus seating – takes culinary inspiration from various European capitals, hence gourmet sandwiches like the Madrid (chorizo sausage, pesto and mozzarella) and the Monte Carlo (tuna melt with cheddar and mayonnaise; £6.95). On weekend evenings they serve bistro-style fare. Mon–Wed & Sun 10am–5pm, Thurs–Sat 10am–10pm.

Tron Theatre Chisholm St, off Trongate ☎ 0141 552 8587, ⊛ tron.co.uk; map pp.190–191. Arty hangout of this well-respected theatre (see p.214) that's especially popular with writers and theatrical types, who happily frequent both the contemporary street-side café-bar and the pleasantly careworn Victorian pub further inside. Mon–Sat 10am–late, Sun 11am–6pm.

Where the Monkey Sleeps 182 West Regent St ☎ 0141 226 3406, ⊛ monkeysleeps.com; map pp.190–191. Owned by graduates of the nearby Glasgow School of Art who acquired their barista skills between classes, this hip home-grown café features freshly prepared sandwiches and salads, and the espressos are superb. Mon–Fri 7am–3pm.

RESTAURANTS

The 13th Note 50–60 King St ☎ 0141 553 1638, ⊛ 13thnote.co.uk; map pp.190–191. Vegetarian and vegan food with Greek and other Mediterranean influences

TOP 5 BUDGET EATS   5

The 13th Note See below
The Hanoi Bike Shop See p.210
Trans-Europe Café See below
University Café See p.208
Wee Curry Shop See p.208

in one of Glasgow's hipper restaurants and experimental indie music haunts on arty King St. Mains, such as lemongrass and ginger risotto cakes, and halloumi with red pepper kebabs, all around £7/8. Daily noon–midnight.

Brian Maule at Le Chardon d'Or 176 West Regent St ☎ 0141 248 3801, ⊛ brianmaule.com; map pp.190–191. Owner-chef Maule, who worked with the Roux brothers at *Le Gavroche* in London, turns out fancy but unpretentious French-influenced food along the lines of assiette of pork with creamed potatoes and truffle jus (£26). Mon–Sat noon–3pm & 5–10pm.

Café Antipasti 305 Sauchiehall St ☎ 0141 332 9002, ⊛ antipasti.co.uk; map pp.190–191. A busy and bright Italian bistro with a handsome wood interior, serving tasty and well-priced stone-baked pizzas and pasta dishes; the two-course pre-theatre menu is just £10.95. Mon–Fri noon–10pm, Sat & Sun 10am–10pm.

Café Gandolfi 64 Albion St ☎ 0141 552 6813, ⊛ cafegandolfi.com; map pp.190–191. Designed with distinctive wooden furniture from the Tim Stead workshop, *Gandolfi* serves up a wonderful selection of Scottish-inspired dishes, such as Stornoway black pudding, peat-smoked salmon, and haggis-stuffed pork belly (£18). The snappy little attic bar offers the same food plus a cracking little pizza menu; great gin card too. Café 8am–midnight, bar 11am–midnight.

City Merchant 97 Candleriggs ☎ 0141 553 1577, ⊛ citymerchant.co.uk; map pp.190–191. Warm, classy brasserie that blazed the Merchant City trail and is still going very strong. Offers plenty of fresh Scottish produce, from Ayrshire lamb to the house speciality: collops of fillet steak with oatmeal-encrusted haggis in a whisky jus. Well-priced lunch (£11.50) and pre-theatre menus (£12.50). Mon–Sat noon–10.30pm.

Dakhin 89 Candleriggs ☎ 0141 553 2585, ⊛ dakhin.com; map pp.190–191. Roomy first-floor restaurant specializing in South Indian cuisine – you won't find *naan* here, but instead lots of clean and fresh-tasting dishes like grilled lamb in a ginger and coconut marinade, though the *dosas* (£15) are well worth considering – and the entire menu is gluten-free. Mon–Fri noon–2pm & 5–11pm, Sat & Sun 1–11pm.

The Dhabba 44 Candleriggs ☎ 0141 553 1249, ⊛ thedhabba.com; map pp.190–191. Sister restaurant to *Dakhin*, this is not your typical Glasgow curry house. Prices are higher and portions are smaller, but the menu has some truly interesting options and uses fresh ingredients that

5

place it steps above most others. The tandoor dishes are cooked with North Indian spices in a clay oven, for example whole black bream with carom and tandoori masalas (£18). Mon–Fri noon–2pm, 5–11pm, Sat & Sun 1–11pm.

★**Gamba** 225a West George St ☎0141 572 0899, ⓦgamba.co.uk; map pp.190–191. Continental contemporary sophistication prevails in this super basement restaurant where fish is king: once you've devoured the signature fish soup (Portland crabmeat and prawn dumplings), perhaps try some crisp-fried red mullet and crayfish tails with melon and goat's cheese (£18.50). A beautifully refined interior and outstanding service. The three-course lunch menu is terrific value at £22. Mon–Sat noon–2.30pm & 5–10pm, Sun 5–9pm.

Mono 12 King's Court ☎0141 553 2400, ⓦmonocafe bar.com; map pp.190–191. This unassuming, multifunctional venue combines a fully vegan restaurant, Fairtrade food shop, bar and indie CD shop (see p.216). Mains such as Malaysian *nasi goreing* and porcini risotto cost around £8, and there's a superb selection of craft beers and organic wines. Regular gigs (alternative, rock) too. Mon–Thurs & Sun 11am–11pm, Fri & Sat 11am–1am.

Mussel Inn 157 Hope St ☎0141 572 1405, ⓦmussel -inn.com; map pp.190–191. This busy, buzzy restaurant, with high ceilings and aquamarine-painted walls, concentrates on simply prepared pots of fresh mussels, grilled or chilled oysters, queen scallops (£8.80) and other delights from the sea. For the £7.95 lunchtime quickie, you get a bowl of flavoured mussels or seafood chowder, salad or fries, and a drink. Mon–Fri noon–2.30pm & 5–10pm, Sat noon–10pm, Sun 12.30–10pm.

★**Paesano** 94 Miller St ☎0141 258 5565, ⓦpaesanopizza.co.uk; map pp.190–191. In a city bursting with great Italian restaurants, this authentic Neapolitan pizzeria is a real standout. Rustled up in wood-fired ovens made in Naples, there are eight different pizzas to choose from (£6–8), each one made using a hybrid yeast and sourdough recipe and with the freshest ingredients from Campania. Daily noon–midnight.

Rogano 11 Exchange Place ☎0141 248 4055, ⓦrogano glasgow.com; map pp.190–191. A Glasgow institution since 1935, this Art Deco fish restaurant replicates the style of the Queen Mary ocean liner, which was launched that same year. It's wearing its age well and the food is still top drawer, from the legendary fish soup to dishes like fillet of sea bream with black olive polenta and Provençal sauce; *Café Rogano*, in the basement, is slightly cheaper, but, better still, park yourself down at the bar and indulge in some oysters (six for £11). Daily noon–10.30pm.

Sarti 133 Wellington St, 121 Bath St & 42 Renfield St ☎0141 204 0440, ⓦfratelli-sarti.co.uk; map pp.190–191. The Sarti brothers' flagship Italian café and restaurant remains as authentic and as popular as ever, with pizzas and

primi piatti for around £12; the breakfast club (8–11am) is great fun. The slightly more formal dining space is accessed from the Bath St entrance. Mon–Thurs 8am–10pm, Fri & Sat 8am–10.30pm, Sun noon–10pm.

Wee Curry Shop 7 Buccleuch St ☎0141 353 0777, ⓦweecurryshopglasgow.co.uk; map pp.190–191. Tiny but welcoming place near the Glasgow Film Theatre and Sauchiehall St shops (there's also a branch in the West End on Ashton Lane), serving home-made bargain meals to compete with the best in town; the haggis pakora (£6.20) and butter chicken (£10.90) are favourites. BYOB. Mon–Thurs noon–2.30pm & 5–10.30pm, Fri & Sat noon–11pm, Sun 1–10.30pm.

THE WEST END

CAFÉS

Artisan Roast 15 Gibson St ☎07864 984253, ⓦartisan roast.co.uk; map pp.184–185. One of the trendiest offerings in this style-conscious city, this modern espresso café offers a delicious array of caffeine fixes, brewed various ways, for example Aeropress, Chemex and French Press. Mon–Sat 8am–6.30pm, Sun 8.30am–6.30pm.

Café at Kelvingrove Kelvingrove Museum ☎0141 353 8040, ⓦglasgowlife.org.uk; map pp.184–185. An elegant modern space within Glasgow's Victorian palazzo, the café has long windows looking out onto verdant Kelvingrove Park. Serves breakfast, light lunches such as cullen skink (£4.95), and more substantial dishes like beef and heather ale casserole (£7.95). Afternoon tea includes hot salmon sandwiches, scones and clotted cream (2–4pm; £8.95). Mon–Thurs & Sat 10am–4pm, Fri & Sun 11am–4pm.

Kember & Jones 134 Byres Rd ☎0141 337 3851, ⓦkemberandjones.co.uk; map pp.184–185. This stylish café and deli more than holds its own in the ultra-competitive Byres Rd area, thanks to its freshly made salads, sandwiches, and irresistible cakes and pastries. Better still, they roast their own coffee, most enjoyable with a warm waffle breakfast. Mon–Fri 8am–10pm, Sat 9am–10pm, Sun 9am–6pm.

Tchai Ovna 42 Otago Lane ☎0141 357 4524, ⓦtchaiovna.com; map pp.184–185. Situated down a cobbled lane, this low-key bohemian hangout delights with its haphazardly arranged furnishings – low tables with floor cushions, garden benches, rugs and paper lanterns – and dozens of teas from around the world. Daily 11am–11pm.

University Café 87 Byres Rd ☎0141 339 5217; pp.184–185. This institution dates from the 1910s and has been adored by several generations of students and West End residents, with its formica tables in snug booths, etched glass partitions and cinema-style pull-down seating. The favourites here are fish'n'chips or mince'n'tatties, rounded off with an ice-cream wafer

FROM TOP STAINED GLASS, HOUSE FOR AN ART LOVER (P.201); CAFÉ GANDOLFI (P.207) >

5

sandwich – you won't spend more than a tenner per head. Mon–Thurs 9am–10pm, Fri & Sat 9am–10.30pm, Sun 10am–10pm.

RESTAURANTS

Ashoka 19 Ashton Lane ☎0141 337 1115, ⓦashokarestaurants.com; map pp.184–185. Lively and moderately priced curry house, which has franchises across the west of Scotland; all offer consistent quality. Other *Ashoka* restaurants are at 1284 Argyle St (☎0141 339 3371), and on the Southside at 268 Clarkston Rd (☎0141 637 0711). Mon–Thurs noon–midnight, Fri & Sat noon–1am, Sun 5pm–midnight.

Balbir's 7 Church St ☎0141 339 7711, ⓦbalibirs.co.uk; map pp.184–185. Owner Balbir Singh Sumal is one of the city's long-standing curry kings, and this quite startling-looking restaurant – with its capacious, darkened interior – reflects his wholesome approach to affordable Indian cuisine. Mon–Thurs & Sun 5–10.30pm, Fri & Sat 5–11pm.

The Bothy 11 Ruthven Lane ☎0141 334 4040, ⓦbothyglasgow.co.uk; map pp.184–185. Set in a lovely 1870s stone mansion, cosy inside and with bench seating in the cobbled yard outside. The emphasis here is firmly on Scottish flavours, for example whisky anster risotto (£11), and beer-battered Scrabster haddock with chunky chips and mushy peas (£13). Recommended. Mon–Fri noon–midnight, Sat & Sun 10am–midnight.

★**Eusebi** 152 Park Rd ☎0141 648 999, ⓦeusebideli .com; map pp.184–185. Cheery, family-run enterprise that has been doling out a veritable cornucopia of foodie treats for nigh on forty years: pasta straight out of the *pastaficio*, cured meats from the *salumeria* and delectable-looking cannoli in the cabinets. With its floor-to-ceiling windows and bold red and white livery, *Eusebi* has a great feel to it too. Daily 7am–10pm.

The Finnieston 1125 Argyle St ☎0141 222 2884, ⓦthefinniestonbar.com; map pp.184–185. The West End's burgeoning culinary reputation has been further enhanced by this snappy neighbourhood restaurant where seafood reigns supreme – indeed, you could do a lot worse than opt for the day's market fish (£16.95), perhaps with a side of pickled fennel and roast squash, and a roast shallot and pink peppercorn butter sauce. Even if you're not eating here, the gin cocktail bar is worth rolling up for. Daily noon–1am.

TOP 5 FINE DINING

Brian Maule at Le Chardon d'Or see p.207
The Finnieston see above
Gamba see p.208
Number 16 see above
Stravaigin see above

★**The Hanoi Bike Shop** Ruthven Lane ☎0141 334 7165, ⓦhanoibikeshop.co.uk; map pp.184–185. This enthusiastically run Vietnamese place just off the busy Byres Rd might not have much to do with bicycles (though there are wheels on the walls), but it is just the ticket for a quick hit of freshly prepared street food, for example sesame chicken livers, black pepper tofu or chilli glazed pork, and all very reasonably priced at between £6–8. Colourful, casual and a lot of fun. Mon–Thurs noon–11pm, Fri noon–12.30am, Sat 11am–12.30pm, Sun 11am–11pm.

The Left Bank 33–35 Gibson St ☎0141 339 5969, ⓦtheleftbank.co.uk; map pp.184–185. Part bar and part bistro, this neighbourhood gaff, adjacent to the university, dishes up wholesome, rustic food in a chic modern setting; the brunch and breakfast menus are firm favourites, especially the Lebanese breakfast (£6.75). Mon–Fri 9am–midnight, Sat & Sun 10am–midnight.

Mother India 28 Westminster Terrace, off Sauchiehall St ☎0141 221 1663, ⓦmotherindia.co.uk; map pp.184–185. Still setting the standard for Indian cuisine in Glasgow, there's fine home cooking to be enjoyed here, with some original specials (ginger crab and prawn dosa) alongside old favourites (monkfish kebab, lamb pasanda), all at affordable prices. Surroundings are elegant but laidback. Mon–Thurs 5.30–10.30pm, Fri & Sat noon–11pm, Sun noon–10pm.

Number 16 16 Byres Rd ☎0141 339 2544, ⓦnumber16.co.uk; map pp.184–185. Intimate, wood-beamed establishment covering two floors, with daily menus of Scottish produce, from seared fillet of Shetland mackerel with beetroot gazpacho (£6.95) to roast haunch of Highland venison (£19.50). Three-course menu for £18.95. Mon–Sun noon–2.30pm & 5.30–10pm, Sun 1–3pm & 5.30–9pm.

★**Stravaigin** 28–30 Gibson St ☎0141 334 2665 ⓦstravaigin.co.uk; map pp.184–185. This gorgeous basement restaurant and hip street-level café-bar combination offers exciting dining utilizing a host of unexpected ingredients, resulting in unusual and wildly inventive combinations such as pork neck and truffle dumplings with pig's cheek bacon, apple and crème fraîche (£17.95). Look out, too, for the occasional "wild food" night. Restaurant Mon–Fri 5–11pm, Sat 11am–11pm, Sun 11am–10pm; café-bar Mon–Fri 9am–1am, Sat & Sun 11am–1am.

Two Fat Ladies 88 Dumbarton Rd ☎0141 339 1944, ⓦtwofatladiesrestaurant.com; map pp.184–185. The original Two Fat Ladies branch (there are three) has been doing the business in the West End for some 25 years, and remains highly regarded for its mussel, langoustine and scallop dishes (£14–20); the interior, with its jet-black walls, crushed-velvet seating and candle-topped tables looks fabulous. And if you didn't guess, the place is named after the number in the address – think bingo parlance. Mon–Sat noon–3pm & 5.30–10.30pm, Sun 1– 9pm.

The Ubiquitous Chip 12 Ashton Lane ☎0141 334 5007, ⓦubiquitouschip.co.uk; map pp.184–185. Opened in 1971, the *Chip* led the way in headlining high-end modern Scottish cuisine, and it's still going strong today. There's fine dining in the foliage-entwined courtyard or more informal brasserie fare upstairs, but either way, expect mouth-watering plates like grilled kohlrabi with duck egg yolk and forest mushrooms, and Galloway roe deer with squash, smoked potato and hazelnuts (£26). Mon–Sat noon–2.30pm & 5–11pm, Sun 12.30–3pm & 5–11pm.

Wee Lochan 340 Crow Rd ☎0141 338 6606, ⓦan -lochan.com; map p.183. If you want the best in fresh, unadulterated west-coast Scottish fish (mains such as gin-cured salmon, and pan-fried sea bass with braised monkfish cheeks cost around £18), there are few better places in Glasgow, although it is off the beaten track, in the Jordanhill district. Mon–Thurs 11am–11pm, Fri & Sat 11am–midnight, Sun 11am–10pm.

THE SOUTHSIDE
RESTAURANTS
Art Lovers' Café House for an Art Lover (see p.201), Bellahouston Park ☎0141 353 4770, ⓦhousearan artlover.co.uk; map p.183. Whether you're visiting the

house or not, the dining room in this showcase house is well worth making the effort to get to; both light lunches and full meals are served, for example a smoked salmon bagel with caper berries (£4.50), and rump of lamb with pickled wild mushrooms (£11.25); afternoon tea (£8.95) is served 2–4pm. Lovely garden views too. Daily 10am–5pm (lunch served noon–4pm).

★**The Fish People Café** 350a Scotland St ☎0141 429 8787, ⓦthefishpeoplecafe.co.uk; map pp.184–185. Ignore the wholly unappealing and, quite frankly, peculiar, location (right outside the subway station on a dismal main road): this fish restaurant is top drawer. Take your pick from any number of excellent dishes, like roast stone bass with grilled asparagus and Stornoway black pudding (£18.50), or just perch yourself up at the marble-topped bar with a bowl of Cumbrae rock oysters. Tues–Thurs noon–9pm, Fri & Sat noon–10pm, Sun noon–8.45pm.

La Fiorentina 2 Paisley Rd West ☎0141 420 1585, ⓦla-fiorentina.com; map pp.184–185. A critics' favourite that also tops popular surveys, this Tuscan-oriented restaurant has become an institution. The highly creditable, and lengthy, menu features the like of smoked salmon pasta parcels with ricotta and crayfish sauce, and veal medallions with wild mushrooms and pancetta (£15.95). Tues–Fri noon–2.30pm & 5.30–10.30pm, Sat noon–10.15pm, Sun 1–8.30pm.

DRINKING

Many drinking dens in Glasgow's city centre, the adjoining Merchant City and buzzy West End are places to experience real local bonhomie. The city's mythical tough-guy image was once linked to its **pubs**, mistakenly believed by a few to be no-go areas for visitors. Today, however, the city is much changed, and windowless, nicotine-stained working-men's taverns are much harder to find than airy modern **bars** (except in neighbourhoods that you're unlikely to visit). If you tire of trendy bars, set out for the slightly edgier district near the Clyde and Glasgow Green, where the local spit-and-sawdust establishments offer a welcome change. A **pub crawl** through either the West End or city centre is easily done on foot; decent pubs are more widely scattered across the Southside, but you'll still find a handful of pleasant spots, ranging from stylish hangouts to historic locals.

CITY CENTRE AND THE MERCHANT CITY
Babbity Bowster 16–18 Blackfriars St, off High St ☎0141 552 5055, ⓦbabbitybowster.com; map p.190–191. Named after an eighteenth-century wedding dance, this lively, fuss-free pub offers an assortment of colourful local characters, and features music on Wednesdays and Saturdays (gypsy jazz), as well s spontaneous folk sessions at other times. Mon–Sat 11am–midnight, Sun 12.30pm–midnight.

Clutha Vaults 167 Stockwell St ☎0141 552 7520; map p.184–185. The scene of a tragic helicopter accident in 2013, the original part of this iconic live music venue remains closed, but is operating out of the (now covered) beer garden; there's still live music most nights, including the popular Glasgow Unsigned on Thursdays. Daily noon–midnight.

Drygate 85 Drygate ☎0141 212 8815, ⓦdrygate.com; map pp.184–185. Injecting a welcome dollop of life into the East End, this small but progressive brewery has a ground-floor restaurant and bar – manifesting shiny steel and cast concrete – and an upstairs beer hall leading to a rooftop terrace. Five of its own craft beers on tap plus a dozen or so guest ales, and a regular programme of live music and comedy. Well worth the short trek out from the city centre. Daily 11am–midnight. Brewery tours, which include several tastings, are on Sundays at noon & 5pm (£10).

★**Gin 71** 71 Renfield St ☎0141 353 2959, ⓦgin71 .com; map pp.190–191. The night-time incarnation of *Cup Tea Lounge*, this gorgeous, glamorous gin bar occupies the old Bank of India building, hence the lavishly coloured tiles and dazzling mosaic flooring. There are gins of every

5

persuasion here – 71 in fact: fruity, floral, citrus, spiced, you name it, and all with superb tasting notes. But if it's all still too confusing, have a cheeky bash at a gin flight (three gins for £15). Mon–Thurs & Sun 6–11pm, Fri & Sat till midnight.

Horseshoe Bar 17 Drury St ⊕ 0141 248 6368, ⓦ horseshoebar.co.uk; map pp.190–191. A must for pub aficionados, this original "Gin Palace", from 1894, has the longest continuous bar in the UK; it's no less renowned for its nightly karaoke sessions, which take place upstairs and are hosted by Raymond. Mon–Sat 10.30am–midnight, Sun 12.30pm–midnight.

The Pot Still 154 Hope St ⊕ 0141 333 0980; map pp.190–191. Whisky galore! In excess of seven hundred different single malts are to be found in this warm and very traditional pub, which also offers a decent real ale selection. Daily 11am–midnight.

Scotia Bar 112 Stockwell St ⊕ 0141 552 8681, ⓦ scotiabar.net; map pp.190–191. Dating from 1792, which (allegedly) makes it the city's oldest pub, this happily careworn place has a cracking atmosphere, thanks in no small part to its programme of semi-pro live folk, blues and rock sessions, typically on Friday evenings and Sunday afternoons at 5pm. Mon–Sat 11am–midnight, Sun 12.30–midnight.

West Brewing Company Templeton's Carpet Factory, Glasgow Green ⊕ 0141 550 0135, ⓦ westonthegreen .com; map pp.184–185. Housed inside the old Templeton building, this place is fashioned after a Bavarian beer hall and brews its own excellent Munich-style lager, free of additives and preservatives, the most popular of which is the cool and crisp St Mungo. Mon–Thurs & Sun 11am–11pm, Fri & Sat 11am–midnight.

LGBT BARS

Delmonica's 68 Virginia St ⊕ 0141 552 4803, ⓦ delmonicas.co.uk; map pp.190–191. One of Glasgow's liveliest and largest gay bars, in a popular area with a mixed, hedonistic crowd, and nightly entertainment and events. Mon–Sat noon–midnight, Sun 12.30pm–midnight.

Katie's Bar 17 John St ⊕ 0141 237 3030, ⓦ glasgow -katiesbar.co.uk; map pp.190–191. The city's hottest gay bar, with an easy-going vibe and staging an event most nights. Daily noon–midnight.

Underground 6a John St ⊕ 0141 553 2456, ⓦ underground-glasgow.com; map pp.190–191. This welcoming, low-key basement bar is geared more towards the art of conversation than dance, although

Tuesdays (karaoke) and Saturdays (Drag Queen) see things perk up a bit; welcomes men and women. Daily noon–midnight.

THE WEST END

Bon Accord 153 North St ⓦ bonaccordweb.co.uk; map pp.184–185. Located at the eastern edge of the West End, this pub began the real-ale revival in Glasgow, and often hosts beer festivals. Mon–Sat 11am–midnight, Sun 12.30pm–midnight.

★**Brewdog** 1397 Argyle St ⊕ 0141 334 7175, ⓦ brewdog.com; map pp.184–185. Dedicated, and quite brilliant, craft beer bar with fourteen ales on tap (around half of which are Brewdog's own creations), plus dozens more bottled possibilities; tricky choices await, therefore, but if you're completely stumped, try guzzling a beer flight (£5.70 for four "third" pints). There's a terrific punk-ethos about the place and it's popular with all-comers. Daily noon–midnight.

Dram! 232 Woodlands Rd ⊕ 0141 332 1622, ⓦ dramglasgow.co.uk; map pp.184–185. The name suggests whisky, and indeed that's one of this big bar's main draws, but there's much more besides, including a healthy selection of craft beers and a regular programme of events, such as folk and Celtic music, comedy and quiz nights. Mon–Fri noon–midnight, Sat & Sun 11am–midnight.

Lismore Lounge 206 Dumbarton Rd ⊕ 0141 576 0102; map pp.184–185. Decorated with specially commissioned stained-glass panels depicting the Highland Clearances, this bar is a meeting point for the local Gaels, who come here to chat, relax and listen to impromptu music sessions. Daily 11am–midnight.

★**Oran Mor** Byres Rd, at Great Western Rd ⊕ 0141 357 6200, ⓦ oran-mor.co.uk; map pp.184–185. Capacious bar, club venue and performance-space auditorium (plus two different dining rooms), all within the tastefully restored Kelvinside parish church; perhaps the best reason to visit, though, is for the perennially popular *A Play, A Pie and A Pint* lunchtime theatre programme (Mon–Sat £12.50). Mon–Wed 9am–2am, Thurs–Sat 9am–3am, Sun 11am–3am.

Stravaigin 28–30 Gibson St ⊕ 0141 334 2665, ⓦ stravaigin.co.uk; map pp.184–185. Above the expensive restaurant of the same name (see p.210) is this lively and amiable café-cum-bar, harbouring decent ales, an extensive wine selection and top-notch food. Mon–Fri 9am–1am, Sat & Sun 11am–1am.

NIGHTLIFE

The liveliest area for nightlife remains the **West End**, with students mixing with locals around Byres Rd, as well as in the nearby Woodlands and Kelvingrove districts. The city's **clubbing** scene is also rated among the best in the UK, attracting top DJs from around the world and also breeding a good deal of local talent. Establishments are pretty mixed and an **underground scene** thrives, while some mega-clubs in this designer-label-conscious city insist on **dress codes**

Opening hours hover between 11pm to 3am, though some stay open until 5am. **Cover charges** are variable: expect to pay around £5 during the week and up to £25 at the weekend. Glasgow has long had one of the most exciting **music** scenes in the UK – indeed, the city has produced some of the finest bands in the UK, such as Franz Ferdinand, Primal Scream and Mogwai – and on any given night you can catch a raft of top-class gigs.

INFORMATION AND TICKETS

For detailed listings on what's on, check out *The List* (ⓦ list .co.uk), which also covers Edinburgh, or visit ⓦ theskinny .co.uk.

Tickets Scotland 237 Argyle St, under Central station's platforms ☎ 0141 204 5151, ⓦ tickets-scotland.com. Sells tickets for theatre productions and big concerts. Mon–Wed, Fri & Sat 9am–6pm, Thurs 9am–7pm, Sun 11.30am–5.30pm.

CLUBS

Buff Club 142 Bath Lane ☎ 0141 248 1777, ⓦ the buffclub.com; map pp.190–191. The playlist of vintage disco, funk and northern soul here draws an eclectic crowd of clubbers. Mon & Tues, Thurs–Sat 11pm–3am.

The Garage 490 Sauchiehall St ☎ 0141 332 1120, ⓦ garageglasgow.co.uk; map pp.190–191. Medium-sized, indie-oriented student club that also hosts gigs across the rock'n'roll spectrum. Daily 11pm–3am.

Nice'n'Sleazy 421 Sauchiehall St ☎ 0141 333 0900, ⓦ nicensleazy.com; map pp.190–191. Don't be put off by the name – this Glasgow institution is a great venue with DJs on the decks most nights, playing everything from garage and punk to indie and techno; it also hosts the occasional alternative and indie-oriented act in the performance space below the funky bar. Daily. Check website for event details.

Polo Lounge 84 Wilson St, off Glassford St ☎ 0141 553 1221, ⓦ pologlasgow.co.uk; map pp.190–191. Original Victorian decor – marble tiles and open fires – and a gentleman's club atmosphere upstairs, with a dark, pounding nightclub underneath that attracts a gay-friendly crowd. Daily 10pm–3am.

Sub Club 22 Jamaica St ☎ 0141 248 4600, ⓦ subclub .co.uk; map pp.190–191. Near-legendary venue and base for the noteworthy Optimo club night as well as Saturday night's Subculture, this is the home for house and techno lovers in the west of Scotland. Tues–Sun 11pm–3am.

LIVE MUSIC VENUES

O2 ABC 300 Sauchiehall St ☎ 0141 332 2232, ⓦ academymusicgroup.com; map pp.190–191. More proof that Glasgow's a gig-hungry town, this medium-sized hall offers an intimate setting in which to see well-established bands. Excellent club nights too.

O2 Academy 121 Eglinton St ☎ 0141 332 2232, ⓦ academymusicgroup.com; map pp.184–185. Sister venue to ABC, and with capacity for 2500, the city's principal mid-sized venue is much like any other in this chain – though there's always a cracking atmosphere.

Barrowland 244 Gallowgate ☎ 0141 552 4601, ⓦ glasgow-barrowland.com; map pp.184–185. Legendary East End ballroom accommodating around two thousand people, it hosts big-time acts who return to it as their favourite venue in Scotland, as well as bands on the rise.

The Garage 490 Sauchiehall St ☎ 0141 332 1120, ⓦ garageglasgow.co.uk; map pp.190–191. Vast nightclub with a number of music-themed rooms, but which also converts into a small-to-medium-sized venue.

King Tut's Wah Wah Hut 272a St Vincent St ☎ 0141 221 5279, ⓦ kingtuts.co.uk; map pp.190–191. Renowned as the place where Oasis were discovered, and still with one of the city's best live music programmes. Also has a good bar with an excellent jukebox.

Queen Margaret Union 22 University Gardens ☎ 0141 339 9784, ⓦ qmunion.org.uk; map pp.184–185. Hosts indie and dance-oriented acts, including the occasional big name, plus the always enjoyable Unplugged Open Mic night on Tuesdays.

Stereo 22–28 Renfield Lane ☎ 0141 222 2254, ⓦ stereocafebar.com; map pp.190–191. Housed inside the Mackintosh-designed former *Daily Record* office, this cool café-cum-bar is now the place to track down up-and-coming local bands. Mon–Thurs & Sun noon–midnight, Fri & Sat till 3am.

ENTERTAINMENT

Glasgow is no slouch when it comes to the performing arts scene: it's home to Scottish Opera, Scottish Ballet, the Royal Scottish National Orchestra, and the BBC Scottish Symphony Orchestra. All told, the city's cultural programme offers a range of **music**, from contemporary to heavyweight classical, plus **dance** and **theatre** (both mainstream and experimental performance art). Most of the larger theatres, cinema multiplexes and concert halls are in the city centre; the West End is home to one or two venues, while the Southside has the Citizens', a much-loved theatre noted for cutting-edge drama.

THEATRES AND COMEDY VENUES

Citizens' Theatre 119 Gorbals St ☎ 0141 429 0022, ⓦ citz.co.uk. The "Citz" has evolved from its 1960s working-class roots into one of the most respected and

innovative contemporary theatres in Britain; it's also home to the well-regarded Vanishing Point theatre company. Offers three stages, concession rates for students and free preview nights.

5

Cottier Theatre 93–95 Hyndland St ☎0141 357 4000, ☯cottiers.com. This performance space in the old Dowanhill church hosts touring shows, dance performances and gigs. An adjoining bar with beer garden is a favourite on warm summer evenings.

King's Theatre 297 Bath St ☎0844 871 7648, ☯atgtickets.com. This theatre has gorgeous interiors within an imposing red-sandstone Victorian building; the programme is good quality, if safely mainstream.

The Stand 333 Woodlands Rd ☎0141 212 3389, ☯thestand.co.uk. Sister to the first-rate comedy club in Edinburgh, booking local, national and international acts, with gigs on most nights of the week.

Theatre Royal 282 Hope St ☎0844 871 7648, ☯glasgow theatreroyal.org.uk. Glasgow's oldest playhouse, dating from 1867, is the opulent home of the Scottish Opera. It also plays regular host to visiting theatre groups, including the Royal Shakespeare Company, as well as orchestras.

Tramway 25 Albert Drive, off Pollokshaws Rd ☎0845 330 3501, ☯tramway.org. Based in a converted tram terminus, this is a superb contemporary art, theatre and dance space; its lofty proportions qualified it as the only suitable UK venue for Peter Brook's famous production of the *Mahabharata* in 1998, while in 2015 it hosted the Turner Prize.

Tron Theatre 63 Trongate ☎0141 552 4267, ☯tron .co.uk. Critically acclaimed venue staging a varied repertoire of some mainstream, as well as more challenging, productions from leading local companies. Also has folk music performances and Sunday jazz in the theatre's Victorian bar.

CONCERT HALLS

City Halls Candleriggs ☎0141 353 8000, ☯glasgow concerthalls.com. Completely renovated Victorian halls, this Merchant City venue is home to the BBC Scottish Symphony Orchestra and hosts many of the annual Celtic Connections concerts. The adjoining Old Fruitmarket, with its cast-iron columns and balcony, is a fabulously atmospheric space, hosting mainly jazz and contemporary music events.

Glasgow Royal Concert Hall 2 Sauchiehall St ☎0141 353 8000, ☯glasgowconcerthalls.com. One of Glasgow's less memorable modern buildings, though with great acoustics, this is the venue for big-name touring orchestras and the home of the Royal Scottish National Orchestra. Also features major rock and r'n'b stars. Box office Mon–Sat 10am–6pm.

St Andrews in the Square 1 St Andrew's Square ☎0141 559 5902, ☯standrewsinthesquare.com. Hidden away in the East End, this a magnificent temple-like Georgian church, topped with a slender tower. It is now the Centre for Traditional Scottish Music, Song and Dance.

SSE Hydro Finnieston Quay ☎0844 395 4000, ☯thesse hydro.com. Part of the Scottish Exhibition and Conference centre, this vast 12,500-capacity arena, which opened in 2013, is Glasgow's – and Scotland's – premier concert venue, hosting the very biggest names in the world.

CINEMAS

Cineworld 7 Renfrew St ☎0871 200 2000, ☯cineworld .co.uk/glasgow. Gigantic multistorey cinema with first-run Hollywood mainstream movies, plus a few art and independent films.

Glasgow Film Theatre 12 Rose St ☎0141 332 6353, ☯glasgowfilm.org. Dedicated art, independent and repertory cinema house in an Art Deco building; it's also home to the Glasgow Film Festival in February. The in-house Café Cosmo is an excellent place for pre-show drinks.

Grosvenor 24 Ashton Lane ☎0845 166 6002, ☯grosvenorwestend.co.uk. Renovated two-screen West End film house with a bar, and sofas you can reserve for screenings of mostly mainstream films.

IMAX Theatre Glasgow Science Centre, 50 Pacific Quay ☎0141 420 5000, ☯glasgowsciencecentre.org. Shows 3D and super-screen documentaries and features.

GLASGOW'S FESTIVAL YEAR

Glasgow offers a terrific year-round roster of festivals: kicking things off in February is the **Glasgow Film Festival** (☯visitgff.glasgowfilm.org) offering up premieres of both mainstream and independent movies from both home and abroad. Next up in March, the three-week-long **Glasgow International Comedy Festival** (☯glasgowcomedyfestival.com) is Europe's largest, while April sees the **Glasgow Restaurant Festival** (☯glasgowrestaurantfestival .co.uk), a two-week celebration of all that's great about the city's cuisine, and the biennial (even-numbered years) **Glasgow International Festival of Visual Art** (☯glasgow international.org), which brings together local and international artists in dozens of city-wide spaces, from shop fronts to market stands. Music takes over in June with the **Glasgow International Jazz Festival** (☯jazzfest.co.uk) at various venues including the Old Fruitmarket in Merchant City. This area is also the location for the eponymous **Merchant City Festival** (☯merchantcityfestival.com) in July, nine days of colourful street art, music, theatre, food and drink and loads more. The city's main LGBT event is the **Glasgay!** (☯outspokenarts.org) in October/November, covering the whole spectrum of artistic genres.

SHOPPING

5

Glasgow's **shopping** is among the best in the UK, after London. While the city's gritty industrial reputation doesn't appear to fit with its status as an oasis of retail therapy, Glaswegians have long enjoyed dressing up to go out. The main area for spending in the city centre is formed by the Z-shaped and mostly pedestrianized route of **Argyle**, **Buchanan** and **Sauchiehall streets**. Along the way you'll find **Princes Square**, the city's poshest mall (see p.182), plus major department stores and branches of high-end chains. **The Buchanan Galleries**, a bland complex built around John Lewis, features some high-fashion budget stores; more interesting is the Parisian-style Victorian **Argyle Arcade**, specializing in antique and contemporary jewellery. Otherwise, make for the **Merchant City** or the **West End**, which have more individual offerings – the latter features quirky vintage and one-off fashion boutiques and is the only district in the city with antiquarian **bookshops**.

ARTS AND CRAFTS

Glasgow School of Art Reid Building, 164 Renfrew St ☎0141 353 4526, ⊛gsashop.co.uk; map pp.190–191. A showcase for the work of both established GSA talent and art school graduates, with jewellery, homeware, textiles and accessories. The shop also commissions the art school's students, staff and graduates to create new products inspired by Mackintosh's work. Daily 10am–4.30pm.

The Lighthouse 11 Mitchell Lane ☎0141 276 5336, ⊛thelighthouse.co.uk; map pp.190–191. Well stocked with tasteful gifts and original design items, from furniture to lighting and accessories, much of it Mackintosh-inspired. Mon–Sat 10.30am–5pm, Sun noon–5pm.

BOOKS

Oxfam Bookshop 5 Royal Exchange Square ☎0141 248 9176; map pp.190–191. Small, but incredibly well-stocked secondhand bookshop near the GOMA, with fiction, crime, history, cookery and Scottish sections. Daily 10am–5pm.

Voltaire & Rousseau Books 18 Otago Lane ☎0141 611 8764, ⊛voltaire-rousseau.co.uk; map pp.184–185. This bookshop, which has been going for over forty years, really has to be seen to be believed; secondhand books of every persuasion, including many rare titles, piled high on shelves and floors with barely an inch to move. Mon–Sat 10am–6pm.

FASHION

Fashionistas with money to burn should head for the chichi and pricey Italian Centre in the Merchant City for some imported glamour, where you'll find lots of designer names under one (Neoclassical) roof. By far the best option for more affordable and stylish gear is the West End, specifically Byres Rd and the cluster of vintage stores on Ruthven Lane.

VINTAGE

De Courcy's Arcade 5 Cresswell Lane ☎0141 334 8211; map pp.184–185. Features an appealing collection of cute boutiques and vintage stores selling upcycled and preloved furniture, clothing and accessories; there's also a vinyl shop and a wonderful retro teashop serving tea and cupcakes. Mon–Sat 10am–6pm, Sun noon–5pm.

Starry Starry Night 19 Dowanside Lane, near Byres Rd ☎0141 337 1837, ⊛starrystarrynightvintage.co.uk; map pp.184–185. Stocks vintage clothing, textiles and accessories, including some antique pieces such as top hats; it also incorporates Bethsy Gray's handmade silver jewellery store. Mon–Sat 10am–5.30pm, Sun 11am–5pm.

FOOD AND DRINK

Demijohn 382 Byres Rd ☎0141 337 3600, ⊛demijohn .org; map pp.184–185. A quirky foodie attraction, this delightful shop is lined with demijohns of olive oil, vinegar, gin, whisky and wine; the brandy, gin and whisky racks make for fabulous gifts. Mon–Sat 10am–6pm, Sun 11.30am–5pm.

Glickman's 157 London Rd ☎0141 552 0880, ⊛glickmans.co.uk; map pp.184–185. Fulfil all your sweet-toothed fantasies in this wonderfully old-fashioned East End confectioner's that's been around since 1903; specialities are cream tablets and macaroon cakes, but there's loads more to feast on. Wed–Sun 10am–4pm.

I.J. Mellis 492 Great Western Rd ☎0141 339 8998, ⊛mellischeese.co.uk; map pp.184–185. Superb cheesemonger specializing in farmhouse cheeses from the British Isles, though they also stock a selection of the best from the Continent; there's also a terrific charcuterie. Mon–Fri 9am–7pm, Sat 9am–6pm, Sun 11am–6pm.

Lupe Pintos Chile & Spice Shop 313 Great Western Rd ☎0141 334 5444, ⊛lupepintos.com; map pp.184–185. Those looking for Mexican, Spanish, American and Asian treats shouldn't miss this crazily colourful store. Mon–Wed & Sat 10am–6pm, Thurs & Fri 10am–7pm, Sun 12.30pm–5.30pm.

Roots, Fruits & Flowers 451–457 Great Western Rd ☎0141 334 3530, ⊛rootsfruitsandflowers.com; map pp.184–185. Fabulous fruit and veg merchant with shelves piled high with breads, jams and olives, among other things; they also specialize in products for vegans, vegetarians and coeliacs. On-site deli and florist's too. Mon–Sat 7.30am–7pm, Sun 9am–7.30pm.

MARKETS

Barras market 244 Gallowgate ⊛glasgow -barrowland.com; map pp.184–185. Red iron gates

5

announce the official entrance, but boundaries are breached as the stalls – selling household goods, bric-a-brac, secondhand clothes and records (none of it of particularly high quality) – spill out into the surrounding cobbled streets. It's a little tired these days, but the fast-talking traders, lively atmosphere and entertaining vignettes of Glasgow life make it an offbeat diversion from shopping-mall banality. Sat & Sun 10am–5pm.

Mansfield Park Farmers' Market Just off Dumbarton Rd; map pp.184–185. The countryside comes to Glasgow, with around 35 vendors selling fine Scottish produce and tempting snacks. Second & fourth Sat 10am–2pm.

MUSIC

Fopp 19 Union St ☎ 0141 285 7190, ⓦ fopp.com; map pp.190–191. This small UK-wide chain really is the business when it comes to cheap CDs, but they've also got a fantastic collection of vinyl. Mon–Sat 9.30am–6pm, Sun 11am–5.30pm.

Monorail Inside Mono café bar (see p.208), 97 King St, Kings Court ☎ 0141 552 9458, ⓦ monorailmusic.com; map pp.190–191. Indie record store with close links to the local music community, offering a big range of contemporary CDs, eclectic vinyl, secondhand stock and reissues; good choice of world music too. Mon–Sat 11am–7pm, Sun noon–7pm.

DIRECTORY

Hospital There is a 24hr A&E at the Royal Infirmary, 84 Castle St near Glasgow Cathedral (☎ 0141 211 4000).

Left luggage Buchanan St bus station has left-luggage facilities (£5/24hr), and there are lockers at Central and Queen St train stations.

Police Police Scotland, Glasgow City Centre Office,

50 Stewart St. For emergencies, dial ☎ 999.

Post office General information (☎ 0345 611 2970). 135 West Nile St (Mon–Sat 9am–5.30pm); 177 Sauchiehall St (Mon–Sat 9am–5.30pm, Sun 10.30am–2.30pm); 59 Glassford St (Mon–Sat 8.30am–5.30pm).

The Clyde

The **RIVER CLYDE** is the dominant physical feature of Glasgow and its environs, an area that comprises the largest urban concentration in Scotland, with almost two million people living in a hinterland of satellite towns. West of the city, regular trains and the M8 motorway dip down from the southern bank of the Clyde to **Paisley**, where the distinctive cloth pattern gained its name, before heading back up to the edge of the river again as it broadens into the **Firth of Clyde**. Here you have **Wemyss Bay**, jumping-off point for the lochs and hills of Argyll, and Helensburgh, birthplace of architect Charles Rennie Mackintosh and the site of one of his greatest buildings, the **Hill House**.

As you head southeast out of Glasgow, the industrial landscape of the **Clyde Valley** eventually gives way to far more attractive scenery of gorges and towering castles, and is also home to a couple of interesting museums. Here eighteenth-century philanthropists built their model workers' community around the mills of **New Lanark**, and the spectacular Falls of Clyde, a mile upstream.

Paisley

Founded in the twelfth century as a monastic settlement around an abbey, **PAISLEY** expanded rapidly after the eighteenth century as a linen-manufacturing town, specializing in the production of highly fashionable imitation Kashmiri shawls. The town quickly eclipsed other British centres producing the cloth, eventually lending its name to the swirling pine-cone design; these days, it more than merits a visit, courtesy of its quite superb abbey and a museum packed with an array of terrifically varied exhibits.

Paisley Abbey

Abbey Close • Mon–Sat 10am–3.30pm, guided tours Tues & Thurs 2pm • Free • ☎ 0141 889 7654, ⓦ paisleyabbey.org.uk

Paisley Abbey was established by Cluniac monks in 1163, and became an abbey in 1219, before being massively overhauled in the Victorian age. Inside the squat grey building, the elongated choir – the longest of any medieval abbey in Scotland – is illuminated by jewel-coloured stained glass from a variety of ages and styles. Elsewhere, take a look inside the St Mirin chapel, whose superb, though incomplete, frieze depicts the life of the saint, to whom the original priory was dedicated. The abbey's oldest monument, meanwhile, is the tenth-century Celtic cross of St Barochan, located under the Wallace Memorial window. Finally, don't miss the exhibition in the sacristy, which displays finds from a section of the monastery's **Medieval Drain**, an arched tunnel dating from the fourteenth century that was discovered in 1990; among the extraordinary items recovered are copper alloy tweezers, a bone die, and a fragment of lead slate with script.

Paisley Museum and Art Gallery

High St • Tues–Sat 11am–4pm, Sun 2–5pm • Free • ☏ 0141 618 2598

Housed inside an attractive civic building, **Paisley Museum and Art Gallery** embraces several extremely engaging collections, from archeology and natural history to local history. In the latter, local tragedies dominate, specifically a boat sign and some newspaper cuttings from the Paisley Canal disaster of 1810, in which a barge capsized, killing 85 people; and the Glen Cinema fire in 1929, which resulted in the deaths of 71 children. Most people, though, come to see the **Shawl Gallery**, which traces the familiar pine-cone (or teardrop) pattern from its simple beginnings to elaborate later incarnations. The **Upper Gallery** houses a small art collection including works by Glasgow Boys Hornel, Guthrie and Lavery (see p.196), as well as paintings by local artist and playwright John Byrne.

ARRIVAL AND DEPARTURE   PAISLEY

By train Regular trains from Glasgow Central run to Paisley's Gilmour St station in the centre of town, and they're a faster, more convenient option than buses.
By bus McGills bus #38 departs from Renfield St in Glasgow every 15min. Bus #757 departs from Paisley's Gilmour St (stand 7) every 10–15min for Glasgow International Airport, two miles north of the town.

Greenock and around

Newark Castle: Castle Rd • April–Sept daily 9.30am–5.30pm • £4.50; HES • ☏ 01475 741858

Twenty-five miles west of Glasgow, **GREENOCK** was the site of the first dock on the Clyde, founded in 1711, and the community has grown on the back of shipping ever since. To get there, you'll pass through **Port Glasgow**, a small fishing village until 1688, when the burghers of Glasgow bought it and developed it as their main harbour. Right on the banks of the river stands the sturdy fifteenth-century **Newark Castle**, which originally dates from 1478 and the time of the Maxwells; its present, largely Renaissance, form was implemented by Sir Peter Maxwell just over a century later.

In Greenock itself, the finest building is the Neoclassical **Custom House** on the dockside, splendidly located looking out over the river. It was from here that tens of thousands of nineteenth-century emigrants departed for the New World.

McLean Museum and Art Gallery

15 Kelly St • Mon–Sat 10am–5pm • Free • ☏ 01475 715624

The **McLean Museum and Art Gallery** contains pictures and contemporary records of the life and achievements of Greenock-born James Watt, a prominent eighteenth-century industrialist and pioneer of steam power, as well as featuring exhibits on the shipbuilding industry and other local trades. The small **art gallery** on the ground floor contains work by Glasgow Boys Hornel and Guthrie plus Colourists Fergusson, Cadell and Peploe (see box, p.196).

5

By train Trains run from Glasgow Central to Greenock Central (every 20–30min; 30min).

By bus Served by regular McGill's buses (#901, #906 and #907) from Glasgow's Buchanan St station.

Boat tours Clyde Cruises (☎01475 721281, ⓦclydecruises.com) operates from Victoria Harbour, a few minutes from Central station; it runs various trips between April and September, including a sail down the Clyde to Glasgow (2hr 45min; £18), and a cruise to Loch Long and Loch Goil (3–4hr; £26).

GOUROCK

By ferry CalMac (☎0800 066 5000, ⓦcalmac.co.uk) and the more frequent Western Ferries (☎01369 704452, ⓦwestern-ferries.co.uk) ply the 20min route across the Firth of Clyde from Gourock (two miles west of Greenock) to Dunoon on the Cowal peninsula (£4.40; car plus passenger £16.80), while a passenger-only ferry runs from Gourock to Kilcreggan on the north bank of the Clyde (Mon–Sat 13 daily; £2.60 single; ⓦspt.co.uk/kilcreggan-ferry).

Hill House

Upper Colquhoun St, Helensburgh, 20 miles northwest of Glasgow • April–Oct daily 11.30–5pm • £10.50; NTS • ☎01436 673900 • Train to Helensburgh Central, from where it's a 20min uphill walk; alternatively, take a taxi (£5) from the station

In 1902, Charles Rennie Mackintosh was commissioned by the Glaswegian publisher Walter Blackie to design the **Hill House** in Helensburgh. Without doubt the best surviving example of Mackintosh's domestic architecture, the house is stamped with his very personal, elegant interpretation of Art Nouveau – right down to the light fittings and fire irons. Various upstairs rooms are given over to interpretative displays on the architect's use of light, colour, form and texture, while changing exhibitions on contemporary domestic design from around Britain are a testament to Mackintosh's ongoing influence and inspiration. After exploring the house, head for the **tearoom** in the kitchen quarters, or wander round the beautifully laid-out **gardens**.

The Clyde Valley

The journey southeast of Glasgow into Lanarkshire, while mostly following the course of the **CLYDE VALLEY** upstream, is dominated by endless suburbs, industrial parks and wide strips of concrete highway. The principal road here is the M74, though you'll have to get off the motorway to find the main points of interest. Less than ten miles from central Glasgow, **Bothwell Castle** lies about a mile north of Blantyre, and five miles west of here, on the outskirts of the new town of East Kilbride, the **National Museum of Rural Life** offers an in-depth look at the history of agriculture in Scotland.

From here, the Clyde winds through lush market gardens and orchards before passing beneath the sturdy little town of Lanark, the best base from which to explore the valley; **New Lanark**, on the riverbank, is a remarkable eighteenth-century planned village.

Bothwell Castle

A mile or so north of Blantyre • April–Sept daily 9.30am–5.30pm; Oct–March Sat–Wed 10am–4pm • £4.50; HES • ☎01698 816894 • First Bus #255 from Glasgow (Buchanan St) will drop you off on the Bothwell Rd near the entrance; by car, approach from the B7071 Bothwell–Uddingston road.

Bothwell Castle is one of Scotland's most dramatic citadels, its great red sandstone bulk looming high above a loop in the Clyde. The oldest, and most impressive, section is the solid cylindrical donjon built by the Moray family in the late thirteenth century to protect themselves against the English king, Edward I, during the Scottish Wars of Independence; Edward only succeeded in capturing it after ordering the construction of a massive siege engine. Elsewhere throughout the stronghold, you can explore the prison tower and peek inside the fourteenth-century chapel.

National Museum of Rural Life

East Kilbride, 7 miles southeast of Glasgow • Daily 10am–5pm • £7; NTS • ☎ 0300 123 6789 • First Bus #31 from Glasgow's St Enoch Centre to East Kilbride takes you past the museum (Stewartfield Way); you can also get a train from Glasgow Central, and then take a taxi for the final 3 miles

An unexpected union of historic farm and modern museum, the **National Museum of Rural Life** documents some three centuries of farming life. From the museum, a tractor and trailer shuttles visitors the half-mile up to the eighteenth-century **farmhouse**, which is furnished as it would have been in the 1950s. As a working farm, there's plenty to entertain the kids, including cattle, sheep, pigs and hens, while harvesting and haymaking are further activities, depending upon the season.

New Lanark

1 mile below Lanark town on Braxfield Rd

The first sight of **NEW LANARK**, hidden away down in the gorge, is unforgettable: large broken curving walls of honeyed warehouses and tenements, built in Palladian style, are lined up along the turbulent river's edge. The community was founded by David Dale and Richard Arkwright in 1785 to harness the power of the Clyde waterfalls in their **cotton-spinning industry**, but it was Dale's son-in-law, Robert Owen, who revolutionized the social side of the experiment in 1798, creating a "village of unity". Believing the welfare of the workers to be crucial to industrial success, Owen built adult educational facilities, the world's first day nursery and playground, and schools in which dancing and music were obligatory and there was no punishment or reward. The spinning centre closed in 1968, before the whole site was granted World Heritage status in 2001.

New Lanark Visitor Centre

New Lanark • Daily April–Oct 10am–5pm; Nov–March 10am–4pm • Passport ticket £9.50 • ☎ 01555 661345, ⓦ newlanark.org

While you're free to wander around the village, which is still partially residential, to get into any of the **exhibitions** you need to buy a passport ticket. The Neoclassical building that now houses the visitor reception was opened by Owen in 1816 under the utopian title of **The Institute for the Formation of Character**. The multitude of fascinating on-site attractions includes the **Annie McCleod Experience**, an "immersive" ride which whisks visitors on a chairlift through a social history of the village through the eyes of the eponymous millworker, reconstructed **Millworker's Houses** from both the 1820s and the 1930s, the **Historic Classroom**, and the stunningly designed **Roof Garden**, complete with water features and animal sculptures. You can also poke around the domestic kitchen, study and living areas of **Robert Owen's House**, which contains his desk.

Beyond the visitor centre, a riverside path leads you the mile or so to the **Falls of the Clyde**, where the river plunges 90ft in three tumultuous stages.

ARRIVAL AND INFORMATION

NEW LANARK

By train Trains run from Glasgow Central to Lanark (every 30min; 50min); from there either walk (it's 1.5 miles away) or take one of the hourly buses, which depart from next to the train station.

Tourist office In the Horsemarket, 100yds west of the station (May–Sept daily 10am–5pm; Oct–April Mon–Fri 10am–5pm; ☎ 01555 668249).

ACCOMMODATION AND EATING

New Lanark Mill Wee Row, Rosedale St ☎ 01555 667200, ⓦ newlanarkhotel.co.uk. A four-star hotel converted from an eighteenth-century mill building, holding accomplished rooms with lovely views and bags of character; there's also a swimming pool and sauna, as well as the very creditable *Mill One* restaurant. **£99**

Wee Row Hostel Rosedale St ☎ 01555 666710, ⓦ newlanarkhostel.co.uk. At the heart of the New Lanark complex, this lovely hostel is located within a restored mill-workers' tenement row, with two-, three- and four-bed rooms, all with river views; self-catering kitchen and laundry available. April–Oct. Dorms **£14**; doubles **£65**

Argyll and Bute

IONA

6

Argyll and Bute

Cut off for centuries from the rest of Scotland by the mountains and sea lochs that characterize the region, Argyll remains remote, its scatter of offshore islands forming part of the Inner Hebridean archipelago (the remaining Hebrides are dealt with in Chapters 13 & 14). Geographically as well as culturally, this is a transitional area between Highland and Lowland, boasting a rich variety of scenery, from lush, subtropical gardens warmed by the Gulf Stream to flat and treeless islands on the edge of the Atlantic; it's these islands that are the real magnet here, with their magnificent wildlife, endless walking possibilities and some of the world's finest whiskies. It's in the folds and twists of the countryside, the interplay of land and water and the views out to the islands that the strengths and beauties of mainland Argyll lie, though there is also one area of man-made sights you shouldn't miss, which is the cluster of Celtic and prehistoric relics in mid-Argyll near Kilmartin.

Much of mainland Argyll is comprised of remote peninsulas separated by a series of long sea lochs. The first peninsula you come to from Glasgow is **Cowal**, cut off from the rest of Argyll by a set of mountains including the Arrochar Alps. Nestling in one of Cowal's sea lochs is the **Isle of Bute**, whose capital, Rothesay, is probably the most appealing of the old Clyde steamer resorts. **Kintyre**, the long finger of land that stretches south towards Ireland, is less visually dramatic than Cowal, though it does provide a stepping stone for several Hebridean islands, as well as Arran (see p.171). North of here, **Inveraray**, picturesquely set upon the shores of Loch Fyne, has a superb jail museum to detain you, while further north still, **Oban** is comfortably the largest town in Argyll, as well as its chief ferry port.

Of the islands covered in this chapter, mountainous **Mull** is the most visited, though it is large enough to absorb the crowds, many of whom are only passing through en route to the tiny isle of **Iona**, a centre of Christian culture since the sixth century, or to visit **Tobermory**, the island's impossibly picturesque port (aka "Balamory"). **Islay**, best known for its distinctive malt whiskies, is fairly quiet even in the height of summer, as is neighbouring **Jura**, which offers excellent walking opportunities. And, for those seeking further solitude, there's the island of **Colonsay**, with its beautiful golden sands, and the windswept islands of **Tiree** and **Coll**, which also have great beaches and enjoy more sunny days than anywhere else in Scotland.

ARRIVAL AND GETTING AROUND   ARGYLL AND BUTE

By train The one main train line in the region runs from Glasgow up to Oban, though it takes in very few places covered in this chapter.

By bus Buses serve most major mainland settlements, with fairly regular services on weekdays, though usually much-reduced service at weekends. There's a good service

Highlights

Mount Stuart, Bute Explore this
architecturally overblown mansion set in
magnificent grounds. **See p.229**

Tobermory, Mull Archetypal picturesque
fishing village, with colourful houses
arranged around a sheltered harbour.
See p.240

Boat trip to Staffa and the Treshnish Isles
Take the boat to see the "basalt cathedral" of
Fingal's Cave, and then picnic amid the puffins
on Lunga. **See p.241**

Golden beaches Kiloran Bay on Colonsay is
one of the most perfect sandy beaches in Argyll,
but there are plenty more on Islay, Coll and
Tiree. **See p.253**

❺ **Knapdale** Explore ancient Atlantic woodland,
lochs and coastline in one of Scotland's
least-known but most alluring spots. **See p.258**

❻ **Whisky distilleries, Islay** With eight
beautifully sited distilleries to choose from, Islay is
the ultimate whisky lover's destination. **See p.267**

❼ **Corryvreckan Whirlpool** Get rocking and
rolling in one of the UK's great natural
phenomena. **See p.273**

HIGHLIGHTS ARE MARKED ON THE MAP ON PP.224–225

ARGYLL & BUTE

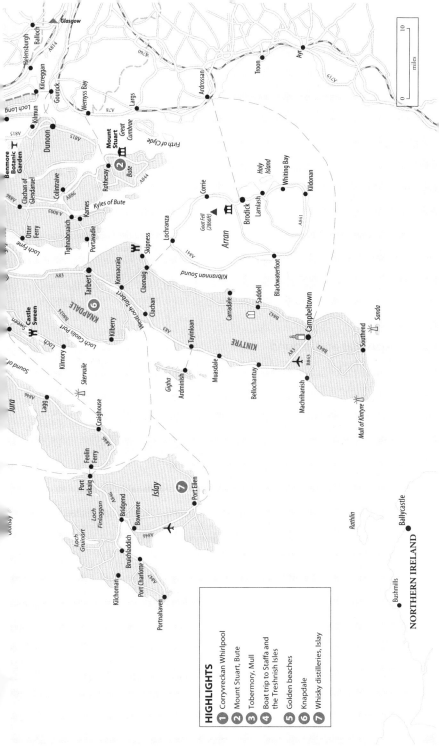

HIGHLIGHTS

1. Corryvreckan Whirlpool
2. Mount Stuart, Bute
3. Tobermory, Mull
4. Boat trip to Staffa and the Treshnish Isles
5. Golden beaches
6. Knapdale
7. Whisky distilleries, Islay

Glasgow

Balloch
Helensburgh
Balloch
Kilcreggan
Gourock
Wemyss Bay
Largs
Troon
Ayr
Ardrossan

Kilmun
Dunoon
Benmore Botanic Garden
Clachan of Glendaruel
Colintraive
Rothesay
Mount Stuart
Bute
Kyles of Bute
Tighnabruaich
Kames
Portavadie
Otter Ferry

Loch Long
Loch Fyne

Firth of Clyde
Great Cumbrae
Holy Island
Corrie
Whiting Bay
Kildonan
Brodick
Goat Fell (2866ft)
Arran
Lamlash
Lochranza
Blackwaterfoot
Kilbrannan Sound

Tarbert
Skipness
Kennacraig
Claonaig
Clachan
Skipness
Carradale
Saddell
Campbeltown
Southend
Sanda
Mull of Kintyre
Machrihanish
Bellochantuy
Tayinloan
Muasdale
KINTYRE

Castle Sween
Loch Sween
KNAPDALE
Kilberry
Kilmory
Loch Caolis Port
West Loch Tarbert

Skervuile
Jura
Lagg
Feolin Ferry
Craighouse
Port Askaig
Gigha
Ardminish

Sound of Jura

Loch Gruinart
Loch Finlaggan
Bridgend
Bowmore
Bruichladdich
Port Charlotte
Kilchoman
Portnahaven
Islay
Port Ellen

Rathlin
Bushmills
Ballycastle
NORTHERN IRELAND

0   10   miles

from Glasgow down to Campbeltown via Arrochar, Inveraray and Tarbert. Most of the islands have at least a handful of daily buses too.

By car If you're planning to take a car across to one of the islands, it's essential that you book both your outward and return journeys as early as possible, as the ferries get booked up early, especially in summer.

By ferry CalMac (T 0800 066 5000, W calmac.co.uk) operates a comprehensive timetable of ferries between the islands, though this is reduced during the winter months; information on individual ferry crossings is given in the relevant town accounts.

Cowal

The claw-shaped **COWAL** peninsula, formed by Loch Fyne and Loch Long, has been a popular destination since the nineteenth century when rapid steamer connections brought hordes of Glaswegian holidaymakers to its shores. It's still quickest to reach Cowal by ferry across the Clyde – by car, it's a long, though exhilarating, drive through some rich Highland scenery in order to reach the same spot.

Beyond the old-fashioned coastal towns such as **Dunoon**, the largest settlement in the area, the Cowal landscape is extremely rich and varied, ranging from the Munros of the north to the gentle, low-lying coastline of the southwest. One way to explore it is to follow the 57-mile **Cowal Way** (W cowalway.co.uk), a terrifically scenic, often rugged, waymarked long-distance footpath between Portvadie and Inveruglas. The western edge of Cowal is marked by the long, narrow Loch Fyne, famous for both its kippers (smoked herrings) and oysters.

Arrochar and around

Approaching by road from Glasgow, the entry point to Cowal is **ARROCHAR**, at the head of Loch Long. The village itself is ordinary enough, but the area has the peninsula's most grandiose scenery, including the ambitiously named **Arrochar Alps**, whose peaks offer some of the best climbing in Argyll: Ben Ime (3318ft) is the tallest range, while Ben Arthur or "**The Cobbler**" (2891ft), named after the anvil-like rock formation at its summit, is the most distinctive. If you head west from Arrochar to Inveraray or the rest of Cowal, you can climb **Glen Croe**, a strategic hill pass whose saddle is called – for obvious reasons – **Rest-and-be-Thankful**.

Ardkinglas Woodland Garden and House

Just off the A83, behind the village of Cairndow • **Garden** Daily dawn–dusk • £5 • **House** April–Oct, visits by guided tour only, every Fri 2pm • £7.50 • T 01499 600261, W ardkinglas.com

The wonderful **Ardkinglas Woodland Garden** contains exotic rhododendrons, azaleas, hydrangeas and a superb collection of conifers, including five so-called Champion Trees – those deemed to be the tallest or broadest examples of their kind within Britain; indeed, the garden is home to what is still the tallest tree in the British Isles, a Grand Fir introduced by David Douglas in 1830 and now standing at a mighty 210ft. Look out, too, for the magnificent Silver Fir (159ft), typically found in Central Europe. You can pick up a *Woodland Garden Map* at the entrance to guide you around.

In the southern part of the gardens stands **Ardkinglas House**, a particularly handsome Scottish Baronial mansion, built in 1907 by Robert Lorimer for the Noble family; the house was, technologically, fairly advanced for its time, and included a goods lift, central heating and the latest sanitary fittings, much of which remains unaltered to this day.

ARRIVAL AND DEPARTURE — ARROCHAR AND AROUND

By train Arrochar and Tarbet train station is a mile or so east of town, just off the A83 to Tarbet.

Destinations Glasgow (Mon–Sat 5–6 daily, Sun 3 daily; 1hr 20min).

By bus Buses stop just on the A814 near Church Rd.

Destinations Glasgow (6 daily; 1hr 10min); Inveraray (6 daily; 35min).

ACCOMMODATION AND EATING

Fascadail Church Rd, Arrochar ☎ 01301 702344, ⓦ fascadail.com. A Victorian guesthouse set within its own grounds in the quieter southern part of the village, with five colourfully furnished and superbly equipped rooms. Enjoy breakfast in the dining room with glorious views across the garden. **£75**

Village Inn Shore Rd, Arrochar ☎ 01301 702279. If you need a bite to eat, or just fancy a pint, head for this delightful hostelry a short walk south of the Fascadail, which has tables outside overlooking the loch as well as a cosy real-ale bar. Mon–Thurs 11am–11pm, Fri–Sun 11am–midnight.

Benmore Botanic Garden

A815, 6 miles north of Dunoon • Daily: March & Oct 10am–5pm; April–Sept 10am–6pm • £6.50 • ☎ 01369 706261, ⓦ rbge.org.uk • Buses #484 and #486 from Dunoon

Serenely pitched amid lush mountain scenery at the foot of Loch Eck, **Benmore Botanic Garden** is an offshoot of Edinburgh's Royal Botanic Garden. It's a beautifully laid-out garden occupying 120 acres of lush hillside, the mild, moist climate allowing a vast range of unusual plants to grow here, with different sections devoted to rainforest species native to places as exotic as China, Chile and Bhutan. The garden boasts 300 species of rhododendron and a memorably striking avenue of great redwoods, planted in 1863 and now over 150ft high. You can also wander through a Victorian **fernery**, as impressive for its architectural features – notably a fine vaulted entrance, grotto and pool – as for the plants housed within. And look out, too, for "Puck's Hut", designed by the prolific Scottish architect Sir Robert Lorimer, in honour of Sir Isaac Bayley Balfour, who did much to raise awareness of the Royal Botanic Garden Edinburgh. Clad in various timbers and tiled with red cedar, it originally stood in Puck's Glen in the Eachaig Valley, hence the name.

Isle of Bute

The island of **BUTE** is in many ways simply an extension of the Cowal peninsula, from which it is separated by the narrow Kyles of Bute. Thanks to its mild climate and its ferry link with Wemyss Bay, Bute has been a popular holiday and convalescence spot for Clydesiders for over a century. In its heyday in the 1880s, thirty steamers a day would call in at the island's capital, **Rothesay**, which still rates as the most attractive seaside resort on the Clyde, although it does feel a little weary in places these days. The most compelling reason to visit Bute, however, is the chance to amble around **Mount Stuart**, one of Scotland's most singular aristocratic piles.

Bute's inhabitants live around the two wide bays on the island's east coast, which resembles one long seaside promenade. To escape the crowds head for the sparsely populated west coast, which, in any case, has the sandiest beaches. The best of these, six miles south of Rothesay, are **Kilchattan Bay**, which has a lovely arc of sand overlooked by a row of grand Victorian houses and, further up the west coast, **Ettrick Bay**.

ARRIVAL AND DEPARTURE ISLE OF BUTE

By ferry Two CalMac ferry services operate from the mainland to Bute; the main crossing is from Wemyss Bay to Rothesay, and the other is the very short crossing at the northern tip of

the island, from Colintraive, in Cowal, to Rhubodach. Destinations Colintraive–Rhubodach (every 30min; 5min); Wemyss Bay–Rothesay (every 45–60min; 35min).

Rothesay

Bute's only town, **ROTHESAY** is a handsome Victorian resort, set in a wide, sweeping bay, backed by green hills, with a classic palm-tree promenade and 1920s pagoda-style pavilion originally built to house the Winter Gardens. Many of the buildings could use a lick of paint or two, but despite this, the town retains a certain well-worn charm.

BUTE FESTIVALS

Bute stages a trio of terrific annual events; namely, the long-standing **Bute Jazz Festival** (ⓦbutejazz.com) over the May Bank Holiday, which always draws some class international artists; **Bute Fest** (ⓦbutefest.co.uk) on the last weekend of July, featuring well-established pop, rock and folk acts; and finally, its own **Highland Games** (ⓦbutehighlandgames.org) on the Saturday of the third weekend of August – this ends in a grand parade through town.

6

Pavilion toilets

The Pier • Daily: Easter–Sept 8am–7.45pm; Oct–Easter 9am–4.45pm • 30p

Rothesay's **Victorian toilets**, built in 1899 by Twyfords, are a feast of marble, ceramics and brass so ornate that they're now one of the town's most celebrated sights. The Victorians didn't make provision for ladies' conveniences, so the women's half is a modern add-on, but if the coast is clear the attendant (attired in a neat burgundy waistcoat) will allow ladies a tour of the gents; it's clad in colourfully painted ceramic tiles and mosaics, and stars an impressive central stand with six urinals – never has the call of nature seemed so attractive.

Rothesay Castle

Castle Hill St • April–Sept daily 9.30am–5.30pm; Oct–March Mon–Wed, Sat & Sun 10am–4pm • £4.50; HES • ☎01700 502691, ⓦhistoricenvironment.scot

Incongruously located amid the town's backstreets stand the militarily useless, but architecturally impressive, moated ruins of **Rothesay Castle**. Built around the twelfth century, it was twice captured by the Norwegians, firstly in 1230, then in 1263; such vulnerability was the reasoning behind the unusual, almost circular, curtain wall, with its four big drum towers, only one of which remains fully intact. Look upwards inside the tower and you'll see a superbly preserved dovecot (with nesting boxes), which was a seventeenth-century addition. The wall was actually heightened in the early sixteenth century – the line is clearly identifiable in the stonework; the earlier, lower half comprises light ashlar, the upper half is darker and of rougher hew.

Ascog Hall Gardens

Ascog, a mile or so east of Rothesay • Easter–Oct daily 10am–5pm • £5 • ☎01700 503461, ⓦascogfernery.com

The **Ascog Hall Gardens** is chiefly notable for its highly unusual **Victorian fernery**, a beautiful, dank place, sunk into the ground, and featuring ferns from all over the world. This one fairly recently replaced the original fernery dating from around 1870, its red, weathered sandstone walls, shade and humidity ideal conditions for cultivating these plants. The gardens themselves are a delight, featuring a truly exotic array of flowers, such as rhododendrons, wild orchids and a stunning array of blue poppies; look out, too, for the magnificent Chilean firetree. The best time to visit is spring when the aforementioned flowers are in full bloom.

ARRIVAL AND DEPARTURE   ROTHESAY

By ferry The CalMac terminal is smack-bang in the middle of the Esplanade.
Destinations Wemyss Bay (every 45–60min; 35min).
By bus The main point for bus departures and arrivals is

Guildford Square, opposite the ferry terminal.
Destinations Kilchattan Bay (Mon–Sat hourly, 3 on Sun; 30min); Mount Stuart (Mon–Sat hourly; 15min); Rhubodach (Mon–Sat 2–3 daily; 20min).

ACTIVITIES AND INFORMATION

Bike rental The Bike Shed, 23–25 East Princes St (Mon–Sat 9.30am–5.30pm; ☎01700 505515, ⓦbikeshedbute .co.uk) has great-value bike rental (£6/5hr, £10/day) and also does repairs and servicing.
Tourist office Inside the Winter Gardens on Victoria St

(April–June & Sept–Oct daily 10am–5pm, July & Aug daily 9.30am–5.30pm, Nov–March Mon–Sat 10am–4pm, Sun 11am–3pm; ☎01700 502151, ⓦvisitbute.com). Also located here is the "Discovery Centre", which has some well-presented displays on the life and times of Bute.

ACCOMMODATION

Boat House 15 Battery Place ☎ 01700 502696, ⓦ the boathouse-bute.co.uk. Chic and utterly contemporary guesthouse with five self-contained suites furnished in cool pinks, greys and blacks and offering all the modern conveniences you could wish for. Each suite – all of which have sea views – sleeps between two and four and offers a kitchen-cum-dining room; breakfast ingredients (bread, jam, coffee, cereal) are also provided. <u>£80</u>

Bute Backpackers 36 Argyle St ☎ 01700 501876, ⓦ butebackpackers.co.uk. Conveniently located a 5min walk along the seafront towards Port Bannatyne, the island's sole hostel offers reasonably furnished two- to six-bed rooms, with shared shower facilities. Breakfast is not included but there's a large kitchen for general use. Dorm <u>£20</u>; Double <u>£50</u>

EATING

Harry Haws 23–25 High St ☎ 01700 505857, ⓦ harryhaws.com. Wholesome, warming food is the deal here, such as home-made crab cakes, boar burger with black pudding, and fish and chips with vinegar pea mash (£9). The interior, meanwhile, offers up some lovely, homely touches, notably framed black-and-white photos of locals and visitors to Rothesay over the years. Daily noon–9pm.

Musicker 11 High St ☎ 01700 502287, ⓦ musicker.co uk. Funky café-cum-music retailer just across from the castle, with delicious coffee and cakes, decent veggie snacks and even better music, courtesy of the rather ace jukebox and occasional jam session. Mon–Sat 10am–5pm.

Squat Lobster The Harbour ☎ 07884 290996. Housed in a mid-nineteenth-century hut that used to be a refuge for horse cabbies, this super chippie next to the putting green doles out freshly caught fish of the day as well as mussels, whelks, langoustines, and the eponymous squat lobster, served with garlic butter (£5.95). Daily noon–8pm, though opening times are erratic.

6

Mount Stuart

4 miles south of Rothesay • **Grounds** Daily 10am–6pm • £6.50 • **House and grounds** April–Oct daily noon–4pm • £11.50 • ☎ 01700 503877, ⓦ mountstuart.com

Bute's most compelling sight is **Mount Stuart**, a huge, fantasy Gothic mansion set amid acres of lush woodland gardens overlooking the Firth of Clyde, and ancestral home of the seventh marquess of Bute, also known as Johnny Bute (or, in his Formula One racing days, as Johnny Dumfries). The building was created by the marvellously eccentric third marquess and architect Robert Rowand Anderson after a fire in 1877 destroyed the family seat. With little regard for expense, the marquess shipped in tons of Italian marble, built a railway line to transport it down the coast and employed craftsmen who had worked with William Burges on the marquess's other medieval concoction, Cardiff Castle.

The *pièce de résistance* is the columned **Marble Hall**, its vaulted ceiling and twelve stained-glass windows decorated with the signs of the zodiac, reflecting the marquess's taste for mysticism; during World War I, the hall was used as a makeshift medical centre, some lovely photos of which you can see in the courtyard toilets. He was equally fond of animal and plant imagery; hence you'll find birds feeding on berries in the dining-room frieze and monkeys reading (and tearing up) books and scrolls in the library. Look out also for the unusual heraldic ceiling in the drawing room. After all the heavy furnishings, there's aesthetic relief in the vast **Marble Chapel**, built entirely out of dazzling white Carrara marble, with a magnificent Cosmati floor pattern. Upstairs, the highlight is the **Horoscope Room**, so named after the fine astrological ceiling, though do seek out the wall panels carved with occasionally amusing friezes, such as a frog playing a lute. Beyond the adjacent observatory/conservatory, you walk out onto the balcony, offering superlative views across the water, before descending a tight spiral staircase to a stunning basement pool, apparently the first house in the world to have a heated pool, though sadly it's no longer in use.

There are a number of fine **walks** to be had within the vast grounds, ranging from a 15-minute stroll down through the woods to the seashore, to a more vigorous, two-hour walk taking in the **Wee Garden** and **Calvary Pond** (the latter located at the head of a small burn).

Mount Stuart restaurant Second floor of visitor centre, Mount Stuart ☎ 01700 505276, Ⓦ mountstuart.com. The on-site restaurant is certainly worth making a trek to even if you're not visiting the estate. The majority of ingredients are sourced from the estate's Kitchen Garden, resulting in scrumptious dishes like smoked pork belly, sweet paprika and cumin cabbage (£6.95); the three-course Sunday roast (£19) is a belter too. Thurs–Sun 11am–3pm. There are also coffee shops at both the visitor centre (daily 10am–5pm) and in the courtyard of the house itself (daily 10.30am–4pm).

Inveraray

The traditional county town of Argyll, and a classic example of an eighteenth-century planned town, **INVERARAY** was built in the 1770s by the Duke of Argyll in order to distance his newly rebuilt castle from the hoi polloi in the town, and to establish a commercial and legal centre for the region. Inveraray has changed very little since and remains an absolute set piece of Scottish Georgian architecture, with a truly memorable setting, the brilliant white arches of Front Street reflected in the still waters of Loch Fyne.

Despite its picture-book location, there's not much more to Inveraray than its distinctive **Main Street** (perpendicular to Front Street), flanked by whitewashed terraces, which are characterized by black window casements. At the top of the street, the road divides to circumnavigate the town's Neoclassical **church**: originally the southern half served the Gaelic-speaking community, while the northern half served those who spoke English.

Inveraray Jail

Church Square • Daily: April–Oct 9.30am–6pm; Nov–March 10am–5pm • £10.95 • ☎ 01499 302381, Ⓦ inverarayjail.co.uk

Inveraray's most enjoyable attraction is **Inveraray Jail**, comprising an attractive Georgian courthouse and two grim prison blocks that, in their day, were the principal ones in Argyll. Originally built in 1820, the prison blocks ceased to function in 1889, though the courthouse continued in one form or another until 1954. The jail is now a thoroughly enjoyable museum, which graphically recounts prison conditions from medieval times to the twentieth century.

Following a trawl through some of the region's most notorious crimes, you get to listen to a **re-enactment** of a trial of the period, staged in the original semicircular courthouse of some 170 years ago. More fascinating, though, are the prisons themselves; the Old Prison housed all convicts – men, women, children, the insane – until 1849 when the New Prison was built, whose twelve cells held male prisoners only. In the courtyard stands the minute "**Airing Yards**", two caged cells where the prisoners got to exercise for an hour a day, though they were forbidden to talk to each other.

Inveraray Castle

A 10min walk north of Main Street • April–Oct daily 10am–5.45pm • £10 • ☎ 01499 302203, Ⓦ inveraray-castle.com

Inveraray Castle remains the family home of the Duke of Argyll, the present (thirteenth) incumbent being Duke Torquhil Ian Campbell. Built in 1745, it was given a touch of the Loire in the nineteenth century with the addition of dormer windows and conical corner spires. In truth, the interior is fairly dull, save for a pair of Beauvais tapestries in the drawing room, and the armoury hall, whose displays of weaponry – supplied to the Campbells by the British government to put down the Jacobites – rise through several storeys. Otherwise, look out for the small exhibition on Rob Roy, complete with his belt, sporran and dirk handle.

ARRIVAL AND INFORMATION

By bus Buses stop on Front St, opposite the tourist office. Destinations Dunoon (3 daily; 1hr 10min); Glasgow (4–6 daily; 2hr); Oban (4 daily; 1hr 5min); Tarbert (2–3 daily; 1hr 30min).

INVERARAY

Tourist office Front Street (daily: April–June & Sept–Oct 10am–5pm; July & Aug 9am–6pm; Nov–March 10am–4pm; ☎01499 302063, ⓦinveraray-argyll .com).

ACCOMMODATION

Loch Fyne Hotel Shore Rd ☎01499 302980, ⓦcrerarhotels.com. Refined spa hotel out on the road to Lochgilphead offering the full complement of spa facilities (pool, hot tub, steam room and jacuzzi), in addition to a supremely comfortable range of rooms, many with a tartan theme. **£110**

★**Newton Hall** Shore Rd ☎01499 302484, ⓦnewtonhallguesthouse.co.uk. This former church now accommodates an outstanding ensemble of seven rooms. Each one is named after an Argyll Island and has been conceived in a completely different style, though they're all

possessed of strikingly bold colours and cool, modern furnishings; a couple of rooms have even retained Gothic-style church windows, through which there are splendid views across the loch. **£70**

SYHA Inveraray Dalmally Rd ☎0870 004 1125, ⓦsyha.org.uk. Small, low-key hostel in a low, wood-and-stone chalet-type building a short walk up the A819 to Oban (just beyond the petrol station). Twin and quad rooms, all with shared shower facilities, as well as a lounge and kitchen for communal use. Breakfast £3.50. Easter to Oct. Dorms **£17**

EATING AND DRINKING

George Hotel Main St East ☎01499 302111, ⓦthe georgehotel.co.uk. The rambling, and very convivial, restaurant/bar of the *George* feels like a proper pub with its flagstone flooring, log fires, and dimly lit nooks and crannies in which to linger over a pint; the food is surprisingly accomplished too, such as pork belly cured in Loch Fyne whisky with pickled cabbage, though there are of course the classic pub standards, like gammon steak with Scottish cheddar sauce and chips (£10). Daily 11am–11pm.

★**Loch Fyne Oyster Bar and Shop** On the A83, 2 miles north of Cairndow and 8 miles east of Inveraray ☎01499 600482, ⓦlochfyne.com. On the shores of Loch Fyne is the famous *Loch Fyne Oyster Bar*, which spawned the Loch Fyne chain of restaurants. The food is utterly delicious and beautifully thought out, from Makar

gin-cured salmon (£9) to whole sea bream curry (£20). The restaurant itself oozes class, though it's anything but stuffy, but more fun is the superb marble-topped oyster bar where you can tuck into oysters (6 for £12), clams, cockles and heaps of other tasty wet stuff. The gorgeous on-site shop/ deli is a great place to assemble a gourmet picnic. Reservations advised. Restaurant daily 9am–10pm; shop Mon–Sat 9am–6pm, Sun 10am–5pm.

Samphire 6a Arkland ☎01499 302321, ⓦsamphire seafood.com. Smart yet informal restaurant whose dazzling seafood menu features flamboyantly prepared dishes like pancetta-wrapped loin of hake with roasted pepper butter bean and chorizo ragout (£15.95), or you might just like to plump for some lightly grilled west coast oysters with Isle of Mull cheddar and baby spinach (£2.30 each). Closed Jan. Tues–Sat noon–2.30pm & 5–9pm.

Oban and around

The solidly Victorian resort of **OBAN** enjoys a superb setting – the island of Kerrera to the southwest providing its bay with a natural shelter – distinguished by a bizarre granite amphitheatre, dramatically lit at night, on the hilltop above the town. Despite a population of just 8000, it's by far the largest port in northwest Scotland, the second-largest town in Argyll and the main departure point for ferries to the Hebrides. Although Oban is not blessed with a particularly stunning array of sights, there's more than enough to keep you entertained for a day or so, and it's one of the best places in Scotland to eat fresh seafood.

McCaig's Tower

Apart from the setting and views, the only truly remarkable sight in Oban is the town's landmark, **McCaig's Tower**, a stiff ten-minute climb from the quayside. Built in imitation of Rome's Colosseum, it was the brainchild of a local businessman a century

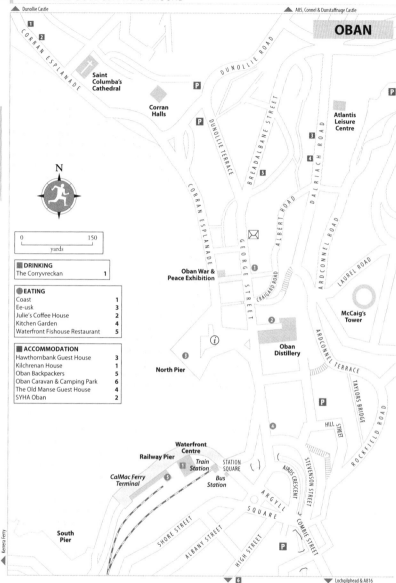

△ Dunollie Castle

△ A85, Connel & Dunstaffnage Castle

OBAN

N

0 ——————— 150
yards

■ **DRINKING**
The Corryvreckan   1

● **EATING**
Coast	1
Ee-usk	3
Julie's Coffee House	2
Kitchen Garden	4
Waterfront Fishouse Restaurant	5

■ **ACCOMMODATION**
Hawthornbank Guest House	3
Kilchrenan House	1
Oban Backpackers	5
Oban Caravan & Camping Park	6
The Old Manse Guest House	4
SYHA Oban	2

Saint Columba's Cathedral

Corran Halls

Atlantis Leisure Centre

Oban War & Peace Exhibition

McCaig's Tower

Oban Distillery

North Pier

Waterfront Centre

Railway Pier

Train Station

STATION SQUARE

Bus Station

CalMac Ferry Terminal

South Pier

Kerrera Ferry ◁

▽ Lochgilphead & A816

ago, who had the twin aims of alleviating off-season unemployment among the local stonemasons and creating a museum, art gallery and chapel. Originally, the plan was to add a 95ft central tower, but work never progressed further than the exterior granite walls before McCaig died. In his will, McCaig gave instructions for the lancet windows to be filled with bronze statues of the family, though no such work was ever undertaken. Instead, the folly has been turned into a sort of walled garden, which is a popular rendezvous for Oban's youth after dark, but for the rest of the time simply provides a wonderful seaward panorama, particularly at sunset.

Oban Distillery

Stafford St • Jan & Feb daily 12.30–4.30pm; March–June & Oct–Nov daily 9.30am–5pm; July–Sept Mon–Fri 9.30am–7.30pm, Sat & Sun 9.30am–5pm, Dec daily noon–4.30pm; last tour 1hr 15min before closing • £8 • ☎ 01631 572004, ⊕ discovering-distilleries.com

Oban Distillery is one of Scotland's oldest, founded in 1794 by the Stevenson brothers, and today it produces in excess of a million bottles a year of its lightly peaty malt, which is acknowledged to be a touch easier on the palate than many other whiskies produced hereabouts. The excellent 45-minute guided tours take in the Mash House, with four massive Scandinavian larch washbacks, and the Still House, with its beautifully proportioned copper stills – the tours ends, as is the custom, with a generous dram.

6

Oban War and Peace Exhibition

Corran Esplanade • May–Oct Mon–Thurs 10am–6pm, Fri–Sun 10am–4pm; March, April & Nov daily 10am–4pm • Free • ☎ 01631 570007, ⊕ obanmuseum.org.uk

Housed in the old *Oban Times* building beside the Art Deco *Regent Hotel* on the Esplanade, the charming **War and Peace Exhibition** is stuffed full of local (and not so local) memorabilia – bizarrely, even a chunk of the Berlin Wall has ended up here. Overall though, the emphasis is on the wartime role of the area around Oban, when it operated as a flying-boat base, mustering point for Atlantic convoys, and as a training centre for the D-Day landings. Also on display are bits of cargo (including a ladder) washed ashore from the Dutch cargo steamer, the *Breda*, which was attacked in nearby Ardmucknish Bay in 1940. It's now a popular site for wreck diving.

ARRIVAL AND DEPARTURE

OBAN AND AROUND

By plane Tiny Oban Airport is six miles north of town in North Connel (☎ 01631 572910, ⊕ obanand theislesairports.com); the nearest train station to the airport is Connel Ferry, or take bus #405 from Oban to Barcaldine.

Destinations Coll (Mon & Wed 2 daily, Fri & Sun 1 daily; 30min); Colonsay (Tues & Thurs 2 daily); Islay (Tues & Thurs 2 daily; 40min); Tiree (Mon & Wed 2 daily; 1hr).

By train The train station is on Railway Pier.

Destinations Glasgow, Queen St (4 daily; 3hr 15min).

By bus On Station Rd, adjacent to the train station.

Destinations Appin (Mon–Sat 2–3 daily; 45min); Connel

(Mon–Sat hourly; 10–15min); Cruachan (5 daily; 30min); Fort William (3 daily; 1hr 30min); Glasgow (5 daily; 3hr); Inveraray (4 daily; 1hr 10min); Kilmartin (Mon–Fri 5 daily, Sat 2 daily; 1hr 15min).

By ferry The CalMac terminal (☎ 01631 566688, ⊕ calmac .co.uk) is on Railway Pier, close to both the train and bus stations.

Destinations Achnacroish, Lismore (Mon–Sat 4 daily, 2 on Sun; 55min); Castlebay, Barra (daily except Wed; 4hr 45min); Coll (daily except Wed & Fri; 2hr 40min); Colonsay (daily; 2hr 15min); Craignure, Mull (9 daily; 50min); Tiree (1 daily; 3hr 40min).

INFORMATION, ACTIVITIES AND TOURS

Tourist office 3 North Pier (April, May, Sept & Oct Mon–Sat 9am–5pm, Sun 10am 5pm; June daily 9am–6pm, July & Aug daily 9am–7pm; Nov–March 10am–5pm; ☎ 01631 563122, ⊕ oban.org.uk).

Bike rental Oban Cycles, 87 George St (Tues–Sat 10am–5pm; ☎ 01631 566033, ⊕ obancyclescotland.com), rents bikes (£25/day) and also does repairs and servicing.

Diving If you fancy something a little more vigorous, head to

the Puffin Dive Centre, based a mile south of Oban at Port Gallanach (☎ 01631 566088, ⊕ puffin.org.uk), where you can take the plunge with a fully qualified instructor (£90/2hr).

Wildlife-watching tours The best of the wildlife-watching companies hereabouts is Coastal Connection, based on Oban Pier (☎ 01631 565833, ⊕ coastal -connection.co.uk), who offer 2–5hr trips (£30–40) spotting bird and sea life.

ACCOMMODATION

Oban is positively heaving with **hotels** and **B&Bs**, most of them reasonably priced and many within easy walking distance of the quayside. Unlikely as it is, if you're struggling to find a place, note that there are stacks more guesthouses in Connel, five miles north.

Hawthornbank Guest House Dalriach Rd ☎ 01631 562041, ⊕ hawthornbank.co.uk. Decent, traditional guesthouse in the lower backstreets of Oban, just across the road from the leisure centre. Its seven immaculately

6

kept rooms, one of which has a four-poster bed, come complete with mahogany antique furnishings and a small seating area with coffee table. March–Oct. **£70**

Kilchrenan House Corran Esplanade ☎01631 562663, ⓦkilchrenanhouse.co.uk. A bright and hospitable home located near the cathedral, with fourteen rooms, variously furnished with antique furnishings, leather armchairs and tartan sofas to go alongside the tremendous sea views. March–Oct. **£70**

Oban Backpackers Breadalbane St ☎01631 562107, ⓦobanbackpackers.com. Large, friendly and colourful hostel with a range of differently sized dorms, the largest accommodating twelve beds. The big, open lounge-dining area has mismatched sofas, a pool table and a real fire. Breakfast £2. Dorms **£17.50**

★**The Old Manse Guest House** Dalraich Rd ☎01631 564886, ⓦobanguesthouse.co.uk. There are few more welcoming places in town than this spotlessly clean Victorian villa whose five rooms (two with sea views) offer thoughtful touches all round, including CD players, complimentary sherry, and a great selection of toiletries. The breakfast is top-notch too. Mid-Feb to Oct. **£92**

SYHA Oban Corran Esplanade ☎01631 562025, ⓦsyha.org.uk. Occupying a super seafront position in a converted Victorian house, this hostel hardly sparkles with character, but the two- to six-bed en-suite rooms are kept to a very high standard. The only downside is that it's a fair trek with a backpack from the ferry terminal. Breakfast £4.95. Doubles **£47**; dorms **£20**

CAMPSITE

Oban Caravan & Camping Park Gallanach Rd ☎01631 562425, ⓦobancaravanpark.com. Two miles southwest of Oban up a pretty glen, this is a huge, well-equipped site with lots of camping space and great views across to Kerrera, with a good chance of a breeze to blow the midges away; there are also a handful of cool pods, with a small kitchen area, that sleep two to four people. Facilities include a self-catering kitchen, TV/games lounge, BBQs and on-site shop. April to mid-Oct. Per pitch **£16**; pods from **£45**

EATING

Oban rates as one of the finest places in Scotland to eat **fresh seafood**, with a handful of highly commendable seafood **restaurants** to choose from, not to mention several superb fish-and-chip shops. Moreover, if you're on the go, or just need a quick bite while waiting for the ferry, you'll find a cluster of excellent seafood **stalls** down by the harbour.

Coast 104 George St ☎01631 569900, ⓦcoastoban .com. A slick place with a metropolitan atmosphere, serving acclaimed and original fish dishes like pan-fried fillet of red gurnard with anchovy and parsley fritters (£17.50) and Oban whisky cured hot smoked salmon. As you'd expect from one of the town's classiest outfits, the atmosphere and service are first-rate. Mon–Sat noon–2.30pm & 5.30–10pm, Sun 5.30–9.30pm.

Ee-usk North Pier ☎01631 565666, ⓦeeusk.com. Salmon mousse, sea bass with creamed leeks and savoury mash, and glistening seafood platters (£19.95 for two) are typical offerings in this bright and breezy waterfront restaurant that makes the most of the uninterrupted harbour views. Children are not allowed in the evenings. Daily noon–3pm & 5.45–10pm.

Julie's Coffee House 33 Stafford St ☎01631 565952. The pick of the many cafés hereabouts, this is a warm, friendly local with super home-baked treats – from panini to peanut butter and chocolate cheesecake – and tasty coffee. Tues–Sat 10am–5pm, also Mon in July & Aug.

Kitchen Garden 14 George St ☎01631 566332, ⓦkitchengardenoban.co.uk. Impressive, central deli with a licensed café up on the mezzanine offering breakfast rolls, filled toasted croissants, and sweet and savoury scones, among other delicious things at good prices. Mon–Sat 9am–5.30pm, Sun 10am–4.30pm.

★**Oban Fish and Chips** 116 George St ☎01631 567000, ⓦobanfishandchipshop.co.uk. A cut above your average chippie, with some surprisingly sophisticated food like battered salt and pepper squid with chilli jam (£12.50) to go alongside the stock fish and chips; good ice cream too, and there's seating available. Daily 11am–11pm.

Original Green Shack Railway Pier. Long-standing and hugely popular seafood shack serving langoustine sandwiches, scallops in hot garlic butter (£6.95), mussels in white wine (£3.95), oysters, prawns, cockles and much much more. Wooden benches available for seating. Mon–Fri & Sun 10am–6pm, Sat 10am–8pm.

Waterfront Fishouse Restaurant 1 Railway Pier ☎01631 563110, ⓦwaterfrontfishouse.co.uk. Despite the unprepossessing exterior, this is a great place rustling up impressive dishes primarily using scallops (chargrilled Isle of Mull scallops with a parmesan and basil mash langoustine (crispy tails) and the best of the daily catch; alternatively, have yourself three oysters (natural, grilled or deep-fried) with a choice of dressings for £5.75. The two-course lunch and early evening menu is a steal at £13.95. Try and bag a sea-facing table. Daily noon–2pm & 5.30–10pm.

DRINKING

The Corryvreckan The Waterfront Centre ☎01631 568910. Although it looks and feels just like the Wetherspoons it is, this barn of a place is the town's social hub and occupies a terrific harbourfront spot; the £2.75 coffee (free refills) and cake deal is just the job before a ferry crossing. Daily 7am–midnight.

Isle of Kerrera

One of the best places to escape from the crowds in Oban is the low-lying island of **KERRERA**, which shelters Oban Bay from the worst of the westerly winds. Measuring just five miles by two, the island is easily explored on foot. The island's most prominent landmark is the **Hutcheson's Monument**, commemorating David Hutcheson, one of the Victorian founders of what is now Caledonian MacBrayne. The most appealing vistas, however, are from Kerrera's highest point, **Càrn Breugach** (620ft), over to Mull, the Slate Islands, Lismore, Jura and beyond.

The ferry lands roughly halfway down the east coast, at the north end of **Horseshoe Bay**, where King Alexander II died in 1249. If the weather's good and you feel like lazing by the sea, head for the island's finest sandy beach, **Slatrach Bay**, on the west coast, one mile northwest of the ferry jetty. Otherwise, there's a very rewarding trail down to the clifftop ruin of **Gylen Castle** and back to the ferry via Drove Road.

6

ARRIVAL AND DEPARTURE ISLE OF KERRERA

By ferry The passenger and bicycle ferry crosses regularly (summer 8.40am & 10.30am, then every 30min until the last crossing at 5.55pm; winter every 90min; ☎01631 563665, ⊛ kerrera-ferry.co.uk; £4.50 return) through the day from the mainland 2miles down the Gallanach road from Oban. In summer, bus #431 from Oban train station connects with the ferry once a day.
Destinations Gallanach (every 30min; 10min).

ACCOMMODATION AND EATING

Kerrera Bunkhouse Lower Gylen ☎01631 566367, ⊛ kerrerabunkhouse.co.uk. Located in a lovely spot a 15min walk from the ferry, this converted eighteenth-century stable building has seven beds, a bell tent with double bed and wood-burning stove, and a cowshed living space for rent by the evening. Bed per person £15; bell tent (April–Sept) £45

Kerrera Teagarden Lower Gylen, next to the bunkhouse ☎01631 566367. Given that Kerrera has no shop, you may well find yourself at this delightful café where you can eat home-made veggie snacks, cakes and coffee. Easter–Sept daily 10.30am–4.30pm.

Appin

Seventeen miles north of Oban is **Appin**, best known as the setting for Robert Louis Stevenson's *Kidnapped*, a fictionalized account of the "Appin Murder" of 1752, when Colin Campbell was shot in the back, allegedly by one of the disenfranchised Stewart clan. The name Appin derives from the Gaelic *abthaine*, meaning "lands belonging to the abbey", in this case the one on the island of Lismore, which is linked to the peninsula by passenger ferry from **Port Appin**.

Port Appin and Castle Stalker

Castle Stalker A828, near Port Appin • Visits by tour only, March–Oct • £20 • ☎01631 740315, ⊛ castlestalker.com

One of Argyll's most picturesque spots, **Port Appin** is a pretty little fishing village at the peninsula's westernmost tip, overlooking a host of tiny little islands dotted around Loch Linnhe, with Lismore and the mountains of Morvern and Mull in the background.

Framed magnificently as you wind along the single-track road to Port Appin is one of Argyll's most romantic ruined castles, the much-photographed sixteenth-century ruins of **Castle Stalker**. Privately owned, the castle can only be visited on a pre-booked tour, which departs from the boathouse and last for around two hours. Otherwise, there is a footpath from the *Castle Stalker View* café that winds down to a point some 200 yards from the castle, affording some cracking photo opportunities.

By ferry Ferries to Lismore depart from a small jetty at the southernmost point of the village, by the *Pierhouse Hotel*.

Destinations Lismore (hourly; 10min).

ACCOMMODATION AND EATING

Castle Stalker View Overlooking Castle Stalker ☎01631 730444, ⌨ castlestalkerview.co.uk. In a tiptop position overlooking Castle Stalker, this large, light-filled café makes for a super little pit stop, serving up fluffy jacket spuds with unusual fillings like crayfish tails or haggis (£7.95), and a mouthwatering selection of baked goodies. Mid-Feb to Oct daily 9.30am–5pm; Nov & Dec Thurs–Sun 10am–4pm.

Pierhouse Hotel Just a few paces from the jetty ☎01631 730302, ⌨ pierhousehotel.co.uk. Perched on the waterfront, the whitewashed Pierhouse has twelve sumptuously furnished rooms decorated in cool beige and mocha tones, half of which have unrivalled loch views. The hotel's sparkling seafood restaurant is highly rated in these parts too. **£145**

Isle of Lismore

Lying in the middle of Loch Linnhe, to the north of Oban, and barely rising above a hillock, the narrow island of **LISMORE** (around ten miles long and a mile wide) offers wonderful gentle walking and cycling opportunities, with unrivalled views – in fine weather – across to the mountains of Morvern, Lochaber and Mull. Legend has it that saints Columba and Moluag both fancied the skinny island as a **missionary base**, but as they raced towards it Moluag cut off his finger and threw it ashore ahead of Columba, claiming the land for himself. Of Moluag's sixth-century foundation nothing remains, but from 1236 until 1507 the island served as the seat of the **bishop of Argyll**. Lismore is one of the most fertile of the Inner Hebrides – its name derives from the Gaelic *lios mór*, meaning "great garden" – and before the Clearances (see p.591) it supported nearly 1400 inhabitants; the population today is around 150. The island's main settlement, and landing spot for the ferry, is Achnacroish.

Ionad Naomh Moluag

500yds west of Achnacroish • April–Oct daily 11am–4pm • £3.50 • ☎01631 760030, ⌨ lismoregaelicheritagecentre.org

To get to grips with the history of the island and its Gaelic culture, follow the signs to the Heritage Centre, **Ionad Naomh Moluag**, a turf-roofed, timber-clad building with a permanent exhibition on Lismore, a reference library, a gift shop and a café with an outdoor terrace. Your ticket also covers entry to the nearby restored nineteenth-century cottar's (landless tenant's) cottage, **Taigh Iseabal Dhaibh**, with its traditionally built stone walls, birch roof timbers and thatched roof.

Cathedral of Moluag and around

In **CLACHAN**, two and a half miles north of Achnacroish, you'll find the diminutive, whitewashed fourteenth-century **Cathedral of St Moluag**, whose choir was reduced in height and converted into the parish church in 1749. Due east of the church – head north up the road and take the turning signposted on the right – the circular **Tirefour Broch**, over two thousand years old, occupies a commanding position and has walls almost 10ft thick in places.

By ferry Two ferries serve Lismore: a small CalMac car ferry from Oban to Achnacroish (Mon–Sat 4 daily, 2 on Sun; 55min), roughly halfway along the eastern coastline; and a

shorter passenger- and bicycle-only crossing from Port Appin to Point, the island's north point (hourly; 10min).

GETTING AROUND AND INFORMATION

Bike rental Bike rental is available from Lismore Bikes (☎01631 760204; £15/day), who will deliver to the ferry upon request.

Information In the absence of a tourist office, the website ⌨ isleoflismore.com has some useful information.

ACCOMMODATION AND EATING

Bachuil ☎ 0845 4900 562, ⓦ bachuil.co.uk. Accommodation on the island is extremely limited, but this gorgeous, whitewashed country house, just north of Clachan and home of the Barons of Bachuil, has three extremely well-appointed rooms. Two-course evening meals are served for a very reasonable £20 per person. **£120**

Loch Awe

Legend has it that **Loch Awe**, twenty miles east of Oban, was created by a witch and inhabited by a monster even more gruesome than the one at Loch Ness. At more than 25 miles in length, Loch Awe is actually the longest stretch of fresh water in the country, but most travellers only encounter the loch's north end as they speed along its shores by car or train on the way to or from Oban.

Kilchurn Castle

Several tiny islands on the loch sport picturesque ruins, including the fifteenth-century ruins of **Kilchurn Castle**, strategically situated on a rocky spit (once an island) at the head of the loch; to visit the castle, you can approach by foot from the A85 to the east. The castle is essentially a shell, but its watery setting and imposing outlines make it well worth a detour.

Cruachan Power Station

A85, 19 miles east of Oban • Easter–Oct: daily 9.30am–4.45pm; Nov–March: Mon–Fri 10am–3.45pm • Tours £7 • ☎ 0141 614 9105, ⓦ visitcruachan.co.uk

The main attraction on the shores of Loch Awe is none too picturesque. **Cruachan Power Station** is actually constructed inside mighty Ben Cruachan (3693ft), which looms over the head of Loch Awe; it was built in 1965 as part of the hydroelectric network that generates around ten percent of Scotland's electricity. Thirty-minute guided tours set off every half-hour from the **visitor centre** by the loch, taking you to a viewing platform above the generating room deep inside the "hollow mountain", a 91yd-long cavern big enough to contain the Tower of London. The whole experience of visiting an industrial complex hidden within a mountain is very James Bond, and it certainly pulls in the tour coaches. Even if you don't partake in a tour, the visitor centre offers some thoroughgoing and interesting explanations of the workings of the power station and renewable energy projects, and an interactive play area for kids, while the adjoining café has marvellous loch views.

Isle of Mull and around

The second largest of the Inner Hebrides, **MULL** is by far the most accessible: just forty minutes from Oban by ferry. As so often, first impressions largely depend on the weather – it is the wettest of the Hebrides (and that's saying something) – for without the sun the large tracts of moorland, particularly around the island's highest peak, Ben More (3169ft), can appear bleak and unwelcoming. There are, however, areas of more gentle pastoral scenery around **Dervaig** in the north, and the indented west coast varies from the sandy beaches around **Calgary** to the cliffs of Loch na Keal. The most common mistake is to try and "do" the island in a day or two: flogging up the main

---

MULL FESTIVALS

Mull stages a terrific triple-header of festivals, the first of which is the **Mendelssohn on Mull Festival** (ⓦ mendelsshononmull.com) at the beginning of July, a week of world-class chamber music commemorating the composer's visit here in 1829. Also in July (usually the third weekend) is the **Mull Highland Games**, and then, in October, the **Mull Rally** (ⓦ mullrally .org), a major racing event around the island's fantastically winding roads.

6

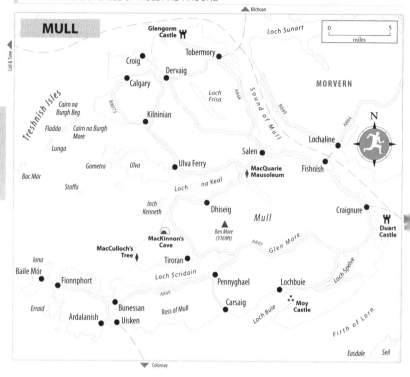

road to the picturesque capital of **Tobermory**, then covering the fifty-odd miles between there and Fionnphort, in order to visit **Iona**. Mull is a place that will grow on you only if you have the time and patience to explore.

Historically, crofting, whisky distilling and fishing supported the islanders (*Muileachs*), but the population – which peaked at 10,000 – decreased dramatically in the late nineteenth century due to the Clearances and the 1846 potato famine. On Mull, it is a trend that has been reversed, mostly owing to the large influx of settlers from elsewhere in the country, which has brought the current population up to more than 2800. One of the main reasons for this resurgence is, of course, tourism – more than half a million visitors come here each year. As good a reason as any to visit Mull, and one of the main reasons why many do so, is to view the abundant **wildlife**, with the magnificent white-tailed eagles the major draw, followed by whale and dolphin watching.

ARRIVAL AND DEPARTURE
ISLE OF MULL AND AROUND

By ferry Craignure is the main ferry terminal, with a frequent daily car ferry link to Oban, though booking ahead on this route is strongly advised. A smaller and less expensive car ferry crosses daily from Lochaline on the Morvern peninsula (see p.441) to Fishnish, six miles northwest of Craignure. Another even smaller car ferry connects Kilchoan on the Ardnamurchan peninsula (see p.442) with Tobermory, the island's capital.

GETTING AROUND

By bus The two main bus routes are the #95 (#495) between Craignure and Tobermory, and the #96 (#496) between Craignure and Fionnphort, with a third route (#494) from Tobermory to Dervaig and Calgary.
By car The majority of the island's roads are single-track, with passing places, which can slow journeys down considerably; greater concentration is required too.
By bike Between Easter and October there are bikes for rent at the tourist office in Craignure (£15/day).

Craignure and around

CRAIGNURE is little more than a scattering of cottages, though there is a small shop, a bar, some toilets and a CalMac ticket and **tourist office** situated opposite the pier. However, there is plenty of accommodation here, as well as a few places to eat and drink, so it is a useful place to base yourself.

Duart Castle

A848, 3 miles south of Craignure • April Sun–Thurs 11am–4pm; May to mid-Oct daily 10.30am–5pm • £6 • ☏ 01680 812309, ⓦ duartcastle.com

Perched on a rocky promontory sticking out into the Sound of Mull, and buffeted by winds and weather, **Duart Castle** makes for a striking landmark viewed from the Oban–Craignure ferry. Duart was headquarters of the once-powerful MacLean clan from the thirteenth century, but was burnt down by the Campbells and confiscated after the 1745 rebellion. In 1911, the 26th clan chief, Fitzroy MacLean – not to be confused with the Scottish writer of the same name – managed to buy it back and restore it, and he remained here until his death, in 1936, at the ripe old age of 101 – look out for the wonderful black-and-white photos of MacLean on his 100th birthday, still looking remarkably fit even then. The banqueting room showcases some superb exhibits, particularly items belonging to Fitzroy from his time serving in the 13th Light Dragoons and 13th Hussars; keep an eye out for his dirk, passport and fob watch used during the Crimean War. Among the many gifts on display is a dazzling silver cup presented to Fitzroy from the former French president Giscard d'Estaing.

In the upstairs exhibition room you can also learn about the world scout movement; in 1959, Charles MacLean (the 27th clan chief) became Chief Scout, a role he performed with some distinction until 1971. From here, climb up to the ramparts for superlative views of the island and beyond; on a clear day, you can just make out the summit of Ben Nevis. Sir Lachlan, the current clan chief, lives in the castle annexe and you're quite likely to see him mingling among visitors. After your visit, head to the castle's pretty, barn-like tearoom, where there's an impressive array of home-made cakes on offer.

ARRIVAL AND INFORMATION

CRAIGNURE AND AROUND

By ferry The ferry terminal dominates the centre of the village, with the CalMac office located directly opposite, in the same building as the tourist office.
Destinations Oban (9 daily; 50min).

By bus Buses pick up and drop off by the main road by the ferry terminal.
Destinations Fionnphort (Mon–Sat 3–5 daily, 1 on Sun;

1hr 10min); Fishnish (2–3 daily; 15min); Salen (4–6 daily; 25min); Tobermory (4–6 daily; 45min).

Tourist office Opposite the ferry terminal in shared premises with CalMac (April–June, Sept & Oct daily 9am–5pm; July & Aug daily 9am–7.30pm; Nov–March Mon–Sat 9am–5pm, Sun 10am–noon & 2–5pm; ☏ 01680 812377).

ACCOMMODATION AND EATING

★**Craignure Bunkhouse** 350yds up the road towards Fionnphort ☏ 01680 812043, ⓦ craignure-bunkhouse .co.uk. Super-smart eco-designed hostel accommodating four en-suite bunk rooms, each with four or six beds, plus a large, homely lounge with woodburner, sofas and a library of books. A self-catering kitchen, laundry and drying room complete this excellent ensemble. Bed £20

Craignure Inn 400yds up the road towards Fionnphort ☏ 01680 812305, ⓦ craignure-inn.co.uk. A 2min stroll from the ferry terminal, this eighteenth-century whitewashed inn, frequented by locals and tourists alike, is a snug little place to hole up in, be it for a pint in the bar or a meal in the adjoining restaurant; venison loin saddle (£14.95) is a popular dish. Daily 11.30am–11pm.

Old Mill Cottage Lochdonhead ☏ 01680 812442, ⓦ oldmillmull.com. A sensitively converted mill 3 miles south on the A849, having three rooms with thick-set wood furnishings and nice touches; they also provide attractive self-catering accommodation for four in the old smiddy. Buses to Fionnphort stop on the road outside. April–Oct. £80

Shieling Holidays Half a mile from the ferry terminal on the road to Fionnphort ☏ 01680 812496, ⓦ shielingholidays.co.uk. Set above a shingle beach, this tidy campsite also offers cool accommodation in the form of "shielings" (large, sometimes furnished, hard-top tents – think downmarket glamping), sleeping between two and six people; some are en-suite. There are bikes for rent too. March–Oct. Per pitch £18.50; shielings from £37

6

Tobermory

Mull's chief town, **TOBERMORY**, at the northern tip of the island, is easily the most attractive fishing port on the west coast of Scotland, its clusters of brightly coloured houses and boats sheltering in a bay backed by a steep bluff. Founded in 1788 by the British Society for Encouraging Fisheries, it never really took off as a fishing port and only survived due to the steady influx of crofters evicted from other parts of the island during the Clearances. It is now the most important, and by far the most vibrant, settlement on Mull, and if you've got young kids, you'll instantly recognize it as the place where *Balamory* was filmed.

The harbour – known as **Main Street** – is one long parade of multicoloured hotels, guesthouses, restaurants and shops, and you could happily spend an hour or so meandering around. The rest of the upper town, laid out on a classic grid plan, merits a stroll too, if only for the great views over the bay.

Mull Museum

Main St • Easter to mid-Oct Mon–Fri 10am–4pm, Sat 10am–1pm • Free • ☎ 01688 301100, ☻ mullmuseum.org.uk

A good wet-weather retreat is the **Mull Museum**, essentially a tiny room packed with fascinating local information and artefacts. Among these is a handful of objects salvaged from the *San Juan de Sicilia*, a ship from the Spanish Armada which sank in 1588 and now lies at the bottom of Tobermory harbour; even today, it remains subject to repeated salvage attempts by locals still, somewhat optimistically, seeking gold. During World War II, Tobermory was an important naval base, in particular as a centre for the training of Escort vessels, whose job it was to protect convoy ships from being attacked by U-boats. Leading the training was one Vice Admiral Gilbert Stephenson, whose prolific and strict regime (he trained up over nine hundred ships in just four years) earned him the moniker, "The Terror of Tobermory". Such was the Admiral's notoriety that he even had a beer named after him.

Tobermory Distillery

Ledaig car park • Mon–Fri 10am–5pm, Sat & Sun 10am–4pm; tours hourly • £8 • ☎ 01688 302647, ☻ tobermorydistillery.com

Founded in 1798, the minuscule **Tobermory Distillery** has had a chequered history, closing down three times since then, though today it's back in business and thriving thanks to its signature fifteen-year-old Tobermory and ten-year-old Ledaig malts. Although its tour is rather drab compared to most distilleries, you do get to see the four magnificent copper stills, as well as try a dram or two at the end.

Mull Aquarium

Harbour Building, Ledaig car park • April–Oct daily 9.30am–5pm • £5 (day ticket) • ☎ 01688 302876, ☻ mullaquarium.co.uk

An absolute delight, the small, community-owned **Mull Aquarium** is the first catch-and-release aquarium in Europe, meaning that all marine life – caught by local divers, fishermen and anyone else willing to head out to sea – is released back into the waters within four weeks. So, for example, you might get to see dogfish, jellyfish, sea scorpions or velvet swimming crabs in the half a dozen or so tanks, alongside all manner of other weird and wonderful creatures. There are touchpool stations, too, where demonstrations are given and visitors are encouraged to handle the creatures.

Glengorm Castle

5 miles northwest of Tobermory • Easter–Oct daily 10am–5pm; guided walks from £8 • ☎ 01688 302932, ☻ glengormcastle.co.uk

Lying along a dead-end single-track road, **Glengorm Castle** is a Scots Baronial pile overlooking the sea. Here too is an attractively converted steading, housing a delightful café, well-stocked farm shop and art gallery. The castle is not open to the public, but you can walk around their attractive walled garden or make for the longer forest, archeological and coastal trails; they also offer guided walks, though you need to book in advance. There's luxury accommodation available here too (see opposite).

WILDLIFE-WATCHING TRIPS FROM TOBERMORY

Although boat trips leave from several different places around Mull, Tobermory is as good a place as any from which to begin a **wildlife-watching tour**. Easily the best company is **Sea Life Surveys** (Easter–Oct; ☎01688 302916, ⓦsealifesurveys.com), who focus on seeking out the whales (minke and even killer whales are the most common), porpoises, dolphins and basking sharks that spend time in the waters around the Hebrides; their seven-hour whale-watching trips (£80) are not recommended for under-12s, though they do offer a five-hour whale-watch trip (adult £50, child £40), while their two-hour Ecocruz (adult £30, child £20) is much more family oriented and includes a visit to a seal colony. For more information on the local wildlife, pop into the **Hebridean Whale and Dolphin Trust visitor centre** at 28 Main St (☎01688 302620, ⓦhwdt.org), where you can also view a small exhibition.

6

ARRIVAL AND INFORMATION

TOBERMORY

By ferry The CalMac terminal is at the far end of Main St, in the northernmost part of the bay.
Destinations Kilchoan (5–7 daily; 35min).
By bus The bus station is in the town's main Ledaig car park, by the distillery.
Destinations Calgary (Mon–Fri 4 daily, Sat 2 daily; 45min); Craignure (4–6 daily; 45min); Dervaig (Mon–Fri 4 daily, Sat

2 daily; 25min); Fishnish (2–4 daily; 40min).
Tourist information Privately run Explore Mull, located in a cabin in the Ledaig car park (April–Oct daily 9am–6pm; ☎01688 302875, ⓦisle-of-mull.net), has tons of information, and also arranges accommodation and wildlife tours.

ACCOMMODATION

Glengorm Castle 5 miles northwest of Tobermory ☎01688 302321, ⓦglengormcastle.co.uk. Fairy-tale, rambling Baronial mansion in a superb, secluded setting, with incredible coastal views, lovely gardens and local walks. Guests get use of the castle's wood-panelled library and lounge, the five large bedrooms are full of splendid features and there are self-catering cottages available too. **£135**

★**Highland Cottage** Breadalbane St ☎01688 302030, ⓦhighlandcottage.co.uk. Super-luxurious B&B run by a very welcoming couple in a quiet street high above the harbour; the six modestly sized but gorgeously furnished rooms, each one named after an Argyll island, are fashioned with home comforts firmly in mind, such as shelves rammed with books. **£155**

★**Strongarbh House** Upper Tobermory ☎01688 302319, ⓦstrongarbh.com. Erstwhile bank, doctor's surgery and officers' mess, but now a fantastic and engagingly run B&B with four rooms that brilliantly combine elements of Victorian and modern; each room has an iPad for starters. There's also a library with books, newspapers and games, while complimentary tea and coffee, and cakes, are served daily between 4pm and 6pm. April–Oct. **£120**

SYHA Tobermory Main St ☎0870 004 1151, ⓦsyha .org.uk. Small, friendly and superbly located on the harbourfront, with two- to- five-bed rooms, plus shared shower facilities, very well-equipped kitchen, TV lounge and laundry facilities. Breakfast £4.95. Mid-March to mid-Oct. Doubles **£50**; dorms **£19**

Tobermory Hotel 53 Main St ☎01688 302091, ⓦthetobermoryhotel.com. Smallish, fairly smart hotel converted from three fishermen's cottages, hence the maze-like warren of variously configured, extremely cosy, rooms, some with coved ceilings, others with window seats, though most with a smattering of light tartan. April–Oct. **£120**

CAMPSITE

Tobermory Camping 1.5 miles uphill from Tobermory on the B8073 to Dervaig ☎01688 302624, ⓦtobermory -campsite.co.uk. Small, spruce campsite serenely situated in woodland; tents are pitched alongside the burn, and there are three little shepherd's huts each sleeping two and with cooking facilities. Buses from Tobermory to Calgary stop here. April–Oct. Pitch **£16**, shepherd's huts **£40**

EATING

An Tobar Argyll Terrace ☎01688 302211, ⓦantobar .co.uk. Housed in a converted Victorian schoolhouse at the top of Back Brae, this small but attractive café doubles up as the town's principal arts centre, with a strong and imaginative programme of visual art and live music, often attracting some stellar names. The café can also be

accessed via a very steep path from Main St. Mon–Sat 10am–5pm.
Café Fish The Pier ☎01688 301253, ⓦthecafefish .com. Stylish harbourfront restaurant above the Calmac office sporting an all-glass frontage with superb views. Fresh from their own boat, the day's catch is prominently

6

displayed in a large glass cabinet, which could mean anything from cracked crab claws with yuzo mayo to grilled gigha halibut with smoked pancetta and pea sauce (£21). Easter–Oct daily 11.30am–10pm.

Fisherman's Pier Fish & Chip Van Fisherman's Pier ☎01688 301109. The friendly proprietors of this venerable takeaway van serve up all the traditional fish suppers, though most venture here for their scrumptious scallops and chips (£9.50). Mon–Sat 12.30–9pm; June–Sept also Sun.

★**Highland Cottage** Breadalbane St ☎01688 302030, ⌨highlandcottage.co.uk. For a treat, look no further than this sublime guesthouse restaurant, which offers an evening four-course menu for £42.50, and which – once you've had a glass of fizz and some canapés – could feature anything from hot smoked with soused cucumber to roast loin of lamb with a haggis parcel and dauphinoise

potatoes, and ending with a lemon posset and home-made shortbread. Reservations only, hence there are no defined opening hours.

Isle of Mull Ice Cream Main St ☎07867 489853, ⌨isleofmullicecream.co.uk. Artisan ice-cream parlour doling out scrummy flavours like whisky marmalade, peanut and chocolate, and cherry (£2.25 for one scoop/£3.25 for two), alongside an equally original range of frozen yoghurts and sorbets. Daily 8am–5.30pm.

Tobermory Hotel 53 Main St ☎01688 302091, ⌨the tobermoryhotel.com. The *Tobermory Hotel*'s highly creditable restaurant conjures up tempting dishes like home-made crab cakes with lemongrass, chilli and roasted garlic mayonnaise, and grilled Isle of Mull langoustines (£23.95). There's a pleasant, warming atmosphere about the place and the service is first-rate. Daily 6–10pm, plus Sun 1–3pm.

DRINKING

MacGochan's Ledaig car park ☎01688 302350, ⌨macgochans-tobermory.co.uk. Heaving, hugely popular harbourside pub just a few paces from the distillery, with a terrific beer garden (albeit facing a car park), well-frequented restaurant-bar and occasional live music to liven things up further. Daily 11am–1am.

Mishnish Main St ☎01688 302009. Inside the hotel of the same name, the "Mish" has been the town's most popular local watering hole for aeons, with a couple of superb snugs rammed with maritime and musical paraphernalia, and regular evenings of live music, quizzes and loads of other happenings. Daily 11am–1am.

Dervaig

The gently undulating countryside west of Tobermory, beyond the freshwater Mishnish lochs, provides some of the most beguiling scenery on the island. Added to this, the road out west, the B8073, is exceptionally dramatic. The only village of any size on this side of the island is **DERVAIG**, which nestles beside narrow Loch Chumhainn, just eight miles southwest of Tobermory, distinguished by its unusual pencil-shaped church spire and single street of dinky whitewashed cottages and old corrugated-iron shacks. Dervaig has a shop, a bookshop/café and a wide choice of places to stay, eat and drink.

ACCOMMODATION AND EATING   DERVAIG

Am Birlinn Penmore ☎01688 400619, ⌨ambirlinn .com. The cross-country road from Dervaig takes you through Penmore where you'll find this striking wood-and-glass-clad building serving up meat and seafood of the highest order: oven-baked guinea fowl on pearl barley risotto with crispy pancetta and game reduction (£16.50) is one of the restaurant's typically flamboyant dishes. April–Oct Wed–Sun noon–2.30pm & 5–9pm; mid-July to Aug also Tues.

The Bellachroy Centre of village ☎01688 400314, ⌨thebellachroy.co.uk. Rugged early seventeenth-century inn with an attractive whitewashed interior, whose pull is its local real ales; the food is comforting rather than being anything particularly sophisticated, for example shepherd's pie with parsley mash (£12.95). Daily 8.30am–11pm.

Dervaig Village Hall Hostel Centre of village ☎01688 400491 or ☎07919 870664, ⌨mull-hostel-dervaig .co.uk. Somewhat peculiarly located inside the village hall though certainly none the worse for it, this clean and welcoming bunkhouse offers two bunkrooms, one sleeping six, the other four, each of which has its own wet room. Bedding is provided. There's also a self-catering kitchen, sitting room and washing machine. Breakfast not included. Dorms **£18**

Druimnacroish Hotel 2 miles out on the Salen road ☎01688 400274, ⌨druimnacroish.co.uk. Erstwhile farmhouse and mill, this lovely country house, pleasantly secreted away, has six amply sized and very reasonably priced rooms. Breakfast is taken in the conservatory overlooking the gardens and glen, and there's also a cosy lounge with an honesty bar. Easter–Oct. **£70**

Calgary

Some five miles beyond Dervaig is **CALGARY**, once a thriving crofting community, now a quiet glen which opens out onto Mull's finest sandy bay, backed by low-lying dunes and machair, with wonderful views over to Coll and Tiree. Aside from the beach, there's a super **woodland sculpture walk** that begins at the *Calgary Farmhouse* and winds gently down through the woods to the beach. It encompasses some twenty cleverly constructed pieces of artwork hewn from various materials; bronze, copper, steel, willow and so on – a little map (£1) outlining the trail is available from the farmhouse. For the record, the city of Calgary in Canada does indeed take its name from this little village, though it was not so named by Mull emigrants, but instead by one Colonel McLeod of the North West Mounted Police, who once holidayed here.

6

ACCOMMODATION AND EATING   CALGARY

Calgary Farmhouse Back up the road from the beach ☎01688 400256, ⌨calgary.co.uk. This delightful farmhouse provides glamorous self-catering accommodation in studio lofts sleeping between two and four people, as well as other properties scattered around he vicinity. The daytime café, serving light lunches and super baked treats, is well worth venturing to, as is the adjoining art gallery. Café: daily 10am–5pm. Three-day minimum stay **£180**

Camping Down by the beach itself, there's a spectacular and very popular spot for camping rough; the only facilities are the basic public toilets.

Isle of Ulva

ULVA's population peaked in the nineteenth century at a staggering 850, sustained by the huge quantities of kelp that were exported for glass and soap production. That was before the market for kelp collapsed and the 1846 potato famine hit, after which the remaining population was brutally evicted. Now privately owned, around fifteen people currently live here, and the island is littered with ruined crofts. It's great walking country, however, with several clearly marked paths crisscrossing the native woodland and the rocky heather moorland interior – and you're almost guaranteed to spot some of the abundant wildlife, particularly red deer, mountain hares and seals.

Heritage Centre and Sheila's Cottage

You can learn more about the history of the island from the exhibition inside the **Heritage Centre** (just up from the pier on Ulva) and, nearby, the thatched smiddy housing **Sheila's Cottage**, which has been restored to the period when islander Sheila MacFadyen lived there in the first half of the last century. Originally a milkmaid, Sheila later made her living by gathering and selling winkles to locals and visitors to the island.

ARRIVAL AND INFORMATION   ISLE OF ULVA

By car To get to Ulva, which lies just a hundred yards or so off the west coast of Mull, follow the signs for "Ulva Ferry" west from Salen or south from Calgary.

By bus From April to October, the Ulva Ferry Community bus runs a twice-daily service on Fridays, Saturdays and Sundays between Calgary and Salen, stopping at Ulva Ferry en route; this is, though, a request service so you must phone or text by 4pm the day before (☎07775 531301).

By ferry From Ulva Ferry, a small bicycle/passenger-only ferry (£5 return; bike 50p) is available on demand (Mon–Fri 9am–5pm; June–Aug also Sun; at other times by arrangement on ☎01688 500226).

Information The website ⌨isleofulva.com contains all you need to know about visiting the island.

ACCOMMODATI00ON AND EATING

Ballygown 3 miles from the ferry on the B8073 road towards Calgary ☎01688 500113, ⌨ballygownmull .co.uk. Enchanting, family-run cottage restaurant whereby you feel like you're eating in their lounge – come to think of it, you pretty much are. There are typically three choices each of a starter (£5), main (£10) and dessert (£5), which might be garlic prawns, ox cheeks in red wine, or sticky toffee and apple trifle, though it's the home-made haggis that most guests home in on. Unlicensed but you're welcome to bring your own booze. April–Oct Tues–Sun 5.30–10pm; Nov–March Fri–Sun 5.30–10pm.

The Boathouse Near the ferry slip on the Ulva side

☎ 01688 500241, ⊛ theboathouseulva.co.uk. Cheery, licensed tearoom serving a mouthwatering selection of seafood tempters like smoked mackerel pâté (£7.50), potted crab (£9.50) and Ulva oysters, alongside home-baked cakes and coffee. Easter–Sept Mon–Fri 9am–5pm; June–Aug also Sun.

Camping There's no accommodation here, but wild camping is permitted on the island, so long as it's not within sight of any dwelling and you stay no longer than one night in the same place.

Isle of Staffa and around

Five miles southwest of Ulva, **STAFFA** is one of the most romantic and dramatic of Scotland's many uninhabited islands. On its south side, the perpendicular rock face features an imposing series of black basalt columns, known as the Colonnade, which have been cut by the sea into cathedral-esque caverns – most notably **Fingal's Cave**. The Vikings knew about the island – the name derives from their word for "Island of Pillars" – but it wasn't until 1772 that it was "discovered" by the world. Turner painted it, Wordsworth explored it, but Mendelssohn's *Die Fingalshöhle* (the lovely "*Hebrides Overture*"), inspired by the sounds of the sea-wracked caves he heard on a visit here in 1829, did most to popularize the place – after which Queen Victoria gave her blessing, too. The polygonal basalt organ-pipes were created some sixty million years ago when a huge mass of molten basalt burst forth onto land and, as it cooled, solidified into hexagonal crystals. The same phenomenon produced the Giant's Causeway in Northern Ireland, and Celtic folk tales often link the two with rival giants Fionn mac Cumhail (Irish) and Fingal (Scottish) throwing rocks at each other across the Irish Sea.

Treshnish Isles

Northwest of Staffa lie the **Treshnish Isles**, an archipelago of uninhabited volcanic islets, none more than a mile or two across. The most distinctive is **Bac Mór**, shaped like a Puritan's hat and popularly dubbed the Dutchman's Cap. **Lunga**, the largest island, is a summer nesting place for hundreds of seabirds, in particular guillemots, razorbills and puffins; the last of these are far and away the star attraction, and, for many, the main reason for visiting. It's also a major breeding ground for seals. The two most northerly islands, **Cairn na Burgh More** and **Cairn na Burgh Beg**, have remains of ruined castles, the first of which served as a lookout post for the Lords of the Isles and was last garrisoned in the Civil War; Cairn na Burgh Beg hasn't been occupied since the 1715 Jacobite uprising.

TOURS | **ISLE OF STAFFA AND AROUND**

Boat tours From April to October several operators offer boat trips to Staffa and the Treshnish Isles. Long-established Turus Mara, a classy outfit based in Penmore (☎ 01688 400242, ⊛ turusmara.com), sets out from Ulva Ferry and charges £60 for a 6hr round trip to Staffa and the Treshnish Isles – typically including 1hr on Staff and 2hr on Lunga; as well as a 3.5hr trip just to Staffa (£30). There's also Staffa Trips (☎ 01681 700358, ⊛ staffatrips.co.uk) who charge £30 for passage from Iona and Fionnphort to Staffa on the *MB Iolaire*.

Ben More and around

From the southern shores of Loch na Keal, which almost splits Mull in two, rise the terraced slopes of **Ben More** (3169ft) – literally "big mountain" – a mighty extinct volcano, and the only Munro in the Hebrides outside of Skye. It's most easily climbed from Dhiseig, halfway along the loch's southern shores, though an alternative route is to climb up to the col between Beinn Fhada and A'Chioch, and approach via the mountain's eastern ridge. Further west along the shore the road carves through spectacular overhanging cliffs before heading south past the Gribun rocks, which face the tiny island of **Inch Kenneth**, where Unity Mitford lived until her death in 1948. There are great views out to Staffa and the Treshnish Isles as the road leaves the coast behind, climbing over the pass to Loch Scridain, where it eventually joins the equally dramatic Glen More road (A849) from Craignure.

If you're properly equipped for walking, you can also explore the **Ardmeanach peninsula**, to the west of the road. The area, which features a large sea cave and a fossilized tree, is NTS-owned, and there is a car park just before *Tioran House.*

Mull Eagle Watch

April–Sept • £8 • ☎ 01680 812556, ⊕ mulleaglewatch.com

The largest and heaviest bird of prey, the **white-tailed eagle** (or sea eagle) became an extinct species in the British Isles in 1916, but since a successful reintroduction programme from Norway in the late 1970s, the population has thrived, and today there are currently twenty pairs of breeding eagles on Mull. In association with the RSPB, ranger-led tours currently take place at two sites: the first is the Glen Seilisdeir hide, located a short way north of Loch Scridain in the Tioran forest, with another at West Ardhu near Dervaig – the rendezvous point is arranged at the time of booking and tours last around two hours. While a sighting is by no means guaranteed, the chances of seeing one, or more, of these magnificent birds are usually pretty good; eaglets typically hatch at the beginning of May, before fledging in August.

6

The Ross of Mull

Stretching for twenty miles west as far as Iona is Mull's rocky southernmost peninsula, the **Ross of Mull**, which, like much of Scotland, appears blissfully tranquil in good weather, and desolate and bleak in bad climes. Most visitors simply drive through the Ross en route to Iona, but if you have the time it's definitely worth considering exploring, or even staying in, this little-visited part of Mull.

Bunessan

BUNESSAN is the largest village on the peninsula, roughly two-thirds of the way along the Ross. Just before the *Argyll Arms Hotel*, a road leads up to **Ardalanish Weavers** (April–Oct daily 10am–5pm, Nov, Dec, Feb & March Mon–Fri 10am–4pm; free; ☎ 01681 700265, ⊕ ardalanish.com), where beautiful durable organic tweed is produced on Victorian looms originally from Torosay Castle. The tweed is snapped up by high-end high-street stores, and is used for the elegant couture collection displayed in the small shop; you can also buy other beautiful items here, such as scarves, rugs, wraps and blankets, though they don't come cheap. Otherwise, on weekdays, you're quite welcome to watch the girls at work in the mill. A couple of miles out of Bunessan is the wide expanse of **Ardalanish Bay**.

Fionnphort and around

The road along the Ross of Mull ends at **FIONNPHORT**, a small, not especially attractive settlement, but it does offer some handy accommodation as well as several places to eat, including the island's best restaurant; it's also where ferries ply the short route across to Iona. Around a mile and a half south of Fionnphort are the golden sands of **Fidden beach**, which looks out to the **Isle of Erraid**, where Robert Louis Stevenson is believed to have written *Kidnapped* while staying in one of the island's cottages; *Kidnapped*'s hero, David Balfour, is shipwrecked on the Torran Rocks, out to sea to the south of Erraid, beyond which lies the remarkable, stripy **Dubh Artach Lighthouse** (meaning "black stony ground" in Gaelic), built by Stevenson's father in 1867. In the book, Balfour spends a miserable time convinced that he's stranded on Erraid, which can, in fact, be reached across the sands on its eastern side at low tide.

ARRIVAL AND DEPARTURE   **THE ROSS OF MULL**

By bus Craignure, via Bunessan (Mon–Sat 4–5 daily, 1 on Sun; 1hr 10min).

By ferry The CalMac passenger ferry from Fionnphort to Iona is very frequent and takes just 10min (£3.30 return).

ACCOMMODATION AND EATING

UISKEN

Camping Uisken beach, two miles south of Bunessan, is a wonderful spot for wild camping, but ask permission first at *Uisken Croft* (☎ 01681 700307), just up the hill.

FIONNPHORT

Fidden Farm Campsite Knockvologan Rd, Fidden ☎ 01681 700427. This simple, getting away from it all campsite has a wonderful location, with direct access to Fidden beach. There's a Portakabin with toilets and showers, and, best of all, campfires are allowed. Easter–Oct. **£12**

★**Ninth Wave** Bruach Mhor ☎ 01681 700757, ⓦ ninthwaverestaurant.co.uk. For something a little special, head to this fabulous restaurant – in a renovated 200-year-old bothy – secreted away in wonderful rural isolation about a mile north of the village (it's well signposted). The owner catches and then serves up crab, lobster and other

fishy treats, while the veg is supplied from their own kitchen garden, resulting in fantastic dishes like pan-seared scallops with garden pernod spinach, crispy smoked ham and caviar. The wines (mostly organic), gins and cocktails are something special too. Three-course meal with coffee and chocolates is £46; reservations required. May–Oct Wed–Sun 7–11pm.

Seaview About 200yds up from the ferry terminal ☎ 01681 700235, ⓦ iona-bed-breakfast-mull.com. This conscientiously run sandstone Victorian villa has five somewhat boxy, but pretty and well-equipped, rooms adorned with splashes of artwork. They've also got bikes for rent. March to mid-Nov. **£80**

Staffa House 300yds up from the ferry terminal ☎ 01681 700677, ⓦ staffahouse.co.uk. Handsome whitewashed building, with four light and immaculately presented rooms, and a lovely glass conservatory for breakfast. Two-night minimum stay. March–Oct. **£76**

Isle of Iona

Less than a mile off the southwest tip of Mull, **IONA** – just three miles long and not much more than a mile wide – has been a place of pilgrimage for several centuries, and a place of Christian worship for more than 1400 years. For it was to this flat Hebridean island that St Columba fled from Ireland in 563 and established a monastery which was responsible for the conversion of more or less all of pagan Scotland as well as much of northern England. This history and the island's splendid isolation have lent it a peculiar religiosity; in the much-quoted words of Dr Johnson, who visited in 1773, "That man is little to be envied … whose piety would not grow warmer among the ruins of Iona."

Few of Iona's many day visitors get further than Baile Mór, the island's village, and the abbey, but it's perfectly possible to walk to the stunning sandy beaches and turquoise seas at the **north end** of the island, or up to the highest point, **Dún I**, a mere 328ft above sea level but with views on a clear day to Skye, Tiree and Jura. Alternatively, it takes about half an hour to walk over to the **machair**, or common grazing land, on the west side of Iona, which lies adjacent to the evocatively named Bay at the Back of the Ocean, a crescent of pebble and shell-strewn sand with a spouting cave to the south. Those with more time (2–3hr) might hike over to the **south** of the island, where Port a'Churaich ("Bay of the Coracle", also known as St Columba's Bay), the saint's traditional landing place on Iona, is filled with smooth round rocks and multicoloured pebbles and stones.

Baile Mór

The passenger ferry from Fionnphort drops you off at **BAILE MÓR** (literally "Large Village"), which is in fact little more than a single terrace of cottages facing the sea. You will, though, find the island's main hotel, restaurant and shop.

Augustinian nunnery

A short walk up from the jetty lie the extensive pink-granite ruins of the fourteenth-century **Augustinian nunnery**, disused since the Reformation, though it did continue to be used as a place of burial for women. A beautifully maintained garden now occupies the cloisters, and if nothing else the complex gives you an idea of the state of the present-day abbey before it was restored.

6

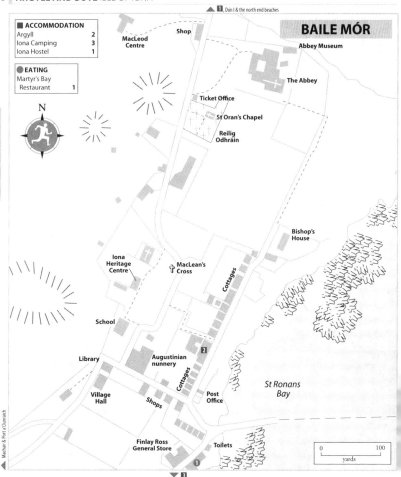

BAILE MÓR

ACCOMMODATION
Argyll	2
Iona Camping	3
Iona Hostel	1

EATING
| Martyr's Bay Restaurant | 1 |

Iona Heritage Centre

North of the Augustinian nunnery • Easter–Oct Mon–Sat 10.30am–5.15pm • £3 • ☎ 01681 700576, ⓦ ionaheritage.co.uk

In the island's former manse is the **Iona Heritage Centre**, with displays on the social history of the island over the last 200 years, including the Clearances, which nearly halved the island's population of 500 in the mid-nineteenth century. One of the more intriguing exhibits is part of the stern belonging to the *Guy Mannering*, a sailing packet on the New York to Liverpool route which sank in machair in 1865 – indeed, it was just one of twenty or so vessels believed to have been lost in waters hereabouts around that time. At a bend in the road, just south of the manse, stands the slender, fifteenth-century **MacLean's Cross**, a fine, late medieval example of the distinctive, flowing, three-leaved foliage of the Iona school.

Iona Abbey

A 5min walk up the road from the Heritage Centre • Daily: April–Sept 9.30am–5.30pm; Oct–March 9.30am–4.30pm; there are free daily guided tours of the abbey (the times are posted up at the ticket office) • £7.10; HES • ☎ 01681 700512, ⓦ historicenvironment.scot

Although no buildings remain from Columba's time, the present **Iona Abbey** dates from the arrival of the Benedictines in around 1200, though it was extensively rebuilt in the fifteenth and sixteenth centuries, and restored virtually wholesale last century.

St Oran's Chapel

Iona's oldest building, the plain-looking eleventh-century **St Oran's Chapel**, lies south of the abbey, on the right. Legend has it that the original chapel could only be completed through human sacrifice. Oran apparently volunteered to be buried alive, and was found to have survived the ordeal when the grave was opened a few days later. Declaring that he had seen hell and it wasn't all bad, he was promptly reinterred for blasphemy.

6

Reilig Odhráin

Oran's Chapel stands at the centre of Iona's sacred burial ground, **Reilig Odhráin** (Oran's Cemetery), which is said to contain the graves of sixty kings of Norway, Ireland, France and Scotland, including Duncan and Macbeth. The best of the early Christian gravestones and medieval effigies that once lay in the Reilig Odhráin have been removed to the Abbey Museum and to various other locations within the complex.

Street of the Dead

Approaching the abbey from the ticket office, you cross an exposed section of the evocative medieval **Street of the Dead**, whose giant pink-granite cobbles once stretched from the abbey, past St Oran's Chapel, to the village. Beside the road stands the most impressive of Iona's Celtic high crosses, the eighth-century **St Martin's Cross**, smothered with figural scenes – the Virgin and Child at the centre, Daniel in the lions' den, Abraham sacrificing Isaac, and David with musicians in the shaft below. The reverse side features Pictish serpent-and-boss decoration. Standing directly in front of the abbey are the base of **St Matthew's Cross** (the rest of which is in the Abbey Museum) and, to the left, a concrete cast of the eighth-century **St John's Cross**, decorated with serpent-and-boss and Celtic spiral ornamental panels. Before you enter the abbey, take a look inside **St Columba's Shrine**, a small steep-roofed chamber to the left of the main entrance. Columba is believed to have been buried either here or under the rocky mound to the west of the abbey, known as Tórr an Aba.

The Abbey

The **Abbey** itself has been simply and sensitively restored to incorporate the original elements. You can spot many of the medieval capitals in the south aisle of the choir

ST COLUMBA AND IONA

Legend has it that **St Columba** (Colum Cille), born in Donegal some time around 521, was a direct descendant of the semi-legendary Irish king, Niall of the Nine Hostages. A scholar and soldier priest, who founded numerous monasteries in Ireland, he is thought to have become involved in a bloody dispute with the king when he refused to hand over a copy of *St Jerome's Psalter*, copied illegally from the original owned by St Finian of Moville. This, in turn, provoked the Battle of Cúl Drebene (Cooldrumman) – also known as the **Battle of the Book** – at which Columba's forces won, though with the loss of over 3000 lives.

The story goes that, repenting this bloodshed, Columba went into exile with twelve other monks, eventually settling on **Iona** in 563, allegedly because it was the first island he encountered from which he couldn't see his homeland. The bottom line, however, is that we know very little about Columba, though he undoubtedly became something of a cult figure after his death in 597. He was posthumously credited with miraculous feats such as defeating the Loch Ness monster – it only had to hear his voice and it recoiled in terror – and casting out snakes (and, some say, frogs) from the island. He is also famously alleged to have banned women and cows from Iona, exiling them to **Eilean nam Ban** (Woman's Island), just north of Fionnphort, for, as he believed, "Where there is a cow there is a woman, and where there is a woman there is mischief".

6

and in the south transept, where the white marble effigies of the eighth Duke of Argyll and his wife, Ina, lie in a side chapel – an incongruous piece of Victorian pomp in an otherwise modest and tranquil place. The finest pre-Reformation effigy is that of John MacKinnon, the last abbot of Iona, who died around 1500, and now lies on the south side of the choir steps. For reasons of sanitation, the **cloisters** were placed, contrary to the norm, on the north side of the church (where running water was available); entirely reconstructed in the late 1950s, they now shelter lots of medieval grave slabs.

ARRIVAL, INFORMATION AND TOURS ISLE OF IONA

By ferry The CalMac passenger ferry from Fionnphort is very frequent and takes just 10min (£3.30 return, bicycles free).

Information In the absence of a tourist office, ⓦ welcometoiona.com is a useful resource.

Boat tours Mark Jardine's Alternative Boat Hire is based at

Lovedale Cottage, near the *Argyll Hotel* (☎01681 700537, ⓦ boattripsiona.com). The owner takes the lovely wooden gaff-rigged sailing boat *Birthe Marie* on short trips to some of the less-visited spots around the Sound of Iona and Erraid (Easter–Oct; 3hr trip £25). For details of trips across to Staffa, see p.244.

ACCOMMODATION

Argyll ☎01681 700334, ⓦ argyllhoteliona.co.uk. Inviting, stone-built hotel in the village's terrace of cottages overlooking the Sound of Iona, with 16 sweet, though somewhat boxy, rooms spread throughout a maze of corridors. The restaurant is first-class (for example, braised Mull beef cheek with roast shallots and wild garlic butter; £16), or you can sup a pint out on the trim, sea-facing lawn. Feb–Oct. **£99**

Iona Camping Cnoc-Oran ☎01681 700112, ⓦ ionacampsite.co.uk. Turn left at the jetty and it's a 20min walk to this super little campsite, which has a couple

of showers and toilets, firepits and BBQs. You can also rent tents and sleeping bags. Per person **£6.50**

Iona Hostel Lagandorain; follow the road past the abbey for half a mile ☎01681 700781, ⓦ ionahostel .co.uk. Terrific hostel located to the north of the island, with impeccable green credentials; five rooms sleeping two to six people, and there's a main living space filled with lovely wooden furniture and a wood-burning stove that has views out to the Treshnish Isles. They've also got a delightful shepherd's bothy tucked away on a rocky outcrop just behind the hostel. Dorms **£21**; bothy **£60**

EATING

Martyr's Bay Restaurant ☎01681 700382. A self-service canteen by day, a fully fledged restaurant come evening; either way, the tourist hordes invariably pack this

place out for steaks and seafood. Lunch meals like haddock and chips (£9.95) and baked potato with haggis are worth a punt too. Tues–Sat 11am–11pm, Sun & Mon 11am–9pm.

Isle of Coll

Roughly thirteen miles long and three miles wide, the fish-shaped rocky island of **COLL**, with a population of around a hundred, lies less than seven miles off the coast of Mull. For the most part, this remote island is low lying, treeless and exceptionally windy, with white sandy beaches and the highest sunshine records in Scotland. The majority of visitors to Coll (and Tiree) stay for a week in self-catering accommodation, though there are hotels and B&Bs on the islands, which should be booked in advance – as should the ferries.

Arinagour

The ferry docks at Coll's only real village, **ARINAGOUR**, whose whitewashed cottages line the western shore of Loch Eatharna, a popular safe anchorage for boats. Half the island's population lives in the village, and it's here you'll find the island's hotel and pub, post office, churches and a couple of shops. The island's petrol pump is also in Arinagour, and is run on a volunteer basis – effectively it's open when the ferry arrives.

The Breachacha castles

On the southwest coast there are two edifices, both confusingly known as **Breachacha Castle**, and both built by the MacLeans. The older, at the head of Loch Breachacha, is a fifteenth-century tower house with an additional curtain wall, now used by Project Trust overseas aid volunteers as a training centre. The less attractive "new castle", to the northwest, is made up of a central block built around 1750 and two side pavilions added a century later, now converted into holiday cottages. It was here that Dr Johnson and Boswell stayed in 1773 after a storm forced them to take refuge en route to Mull. Much of the surrounding area is now owned by the RSPB, in the hope of protecting the island's corncrakes, of which there are currently around 66 calling males; you're also likely to see white-fronted and barnacle geese, lapwing and redshank.

6

ARRIVAL AND DEPARTURE   ISLE OF COLL

By ferry Throughout the summer, the CalMac ferry from Oban calls daily at Coll (2hr 40min) and Tiree (3hr 40min).

Destinations Barra (Wed 1 daily; 4hr); Oban (daily except Tues & Wed; 2hr 40min).

ACCOMMODATION AND EATING

Coll Hotel Arinagour ☎ 01879 230334, ⓦ collhotel.com. Small, family-run hotel providing refined accommodation in six rooms, four of which overlook the bay; among the many lovely touches offered is a goodie basket with biscuits, tablet and water. The hotel also offers bike rental, and can do pick-ups/drop-offs to/from the ferry. Wild camping is also possible on the hill behind the hotel, but you should contact the hotel first; it's free, though a donation is appreciated. Creel-caught seafood forms the mainstay of a mouthwatering menu. Restaurant noon–2pm & 6–9pm. **£100**

Garden House Down a track on the left before the turn-off for the castle ☎ 01879 230374, ⓔ collcampsite @hotmail.com. There's very basic camping at this working farm in the shelter of what was formerly a walled garden,

with showers, toilets and a campers' room. April–Oct. Per pitch **£16**

Island Café Shore St ☎ 01879 230262. In the old harbour stores overlooking the bay, offering hot meals all day, though Sundays are most popular when they rustle up a superb two-course late lunch, comprising a roast and a dessert (£18), for which reservations are advised. Wed–Sat 11am–2pm & 5–9pm, Sun noon–6pm.

Tigh-na-Mara Arinagour Bay ☎ 01879 230354, ⓦ tighna mara.info. The "House by the Sea" is a modern guesthouse near the pier, with a selection of shared bathroom and en-suite rooms, the latter being £10 more expensive. Such is its location that there's a good chance you'll see some great wildlife while eating your breakfast. **£70**

Isle of Tiree

TIREE, as its Gaelic name *tir-iodh* (land of corn) suggests, was once known as the breadbasket of the Inner Hebrides, thanks to its acres of rich machair. Nowadays crofting and tourism are the main sources of income for the resident population of around 750. One of the most distinctive features of Tiree is its architecture, in particular the large numbers of "pudding" or "spotty" houses, where only the mortar is painted white. In addition, there are numerous "white houses" (*tigh geal*) and traditional "blackhouses" (*tigh dubh*). With no shortage of wind, Tiree's sandy beaches attract large numbers of windsurfers for the Tiree Wave Classic (ⓦ tireewaveclassic.co.uk) every October.

An Turas and Scarinish

An Iodhlann July & Aug Mon–Fri 11am–5pm; Sept–June Mon, Wed & Thurs 9am–1pm, Tues & Fri 11am–3.30pm • £3 • ☎ 01879 220793, ⓦ aniodhlann.org.uk

The ferry calls at Gott Bay Pier, now best known for **An Turas** (The Journey), Tiree's award-winning "shelter", a structure that consists of two parallel white walls connected via a black felt section to a glass box which punctures a stone dyke and frames a sea view. Just up the road from the pier is the village of **SCARINISH**, home to a post office, a supermarket, the butcher's and the bank, with a petrol pump back at the pier. Also in Scarinish you'll find **An Iodhlann** – "haystack" in Gaelic – the island's two-roomed archive, which has an enlightening exhibition on the islands' history, covering everything from the sea and settlers to saints and Vikings.

Hynish

The island's most intriguing sights lie in the bulging western half of the island, where Tiree's two landmark hills rise up. Below the higher of the two is **HYNISH** whose **harbour** was designed by Alan Stevenson – uncle of Robert Louis Stevenson – in the 1830s to transport building materials for the magnificent 157ft-tall **Skerryvore Lighthouse**, the tallest in the UK, which lies on a sea-swept reef some twelve miles southwest of Tiree. Up on the hill behind the harbour, beside the row of lighthouse keepers' houses, stands a stumpy granite signal tower, whose signals used to be the only contact the lighthouse keepers had with civilization.

Skerryvore Lighthouse Exhibition and the Treshnish Isles Exhibition

Lower Square • Easter to mid-Oct daily 9am–5pm • Free, but suggested £3 donation • ☎ 01879 220045, ⊛ hebrideantrust.org

Occupying a converted smithy, the **Skerryvore Lighthouse Exhibition** recalls the Herculean effort required to erect the lighthouse, alongside many intriguing items gathered along the way. A few paces along, in some converted cowsheds, the **Treshnish Isles Exhibition** documents the wonderfully diverse array of flora and fauna to be found on the Hebridean Trust-owned islands.

Ceann a'Mhara and around

A mile or so across the golden sands of Balephuil Bay is the spectacular headland of **Ceann a'Mhara** (pronounced "kenavara"), home to thousands of seabirds, including fulmars, kittiwakes, guillemots, razorbills, shags and cormorants, with gannets and terns feeding offshore.

Taigh Iain Mhoir

Taigh Iain Mhoir Sandaig • June–Sept Mon–Fri 2–4pm • Free

In the scattered west coast settlement of **SANDAIG**, to the north of Ceann a'Mhara, three thatched white houses in a row have been turned into the **Taigh Iain Mhoir**, which gives an insight into how the majority of islanders lived in the nineteenth century, thanks to a collection of old photographs and other memorabilia.

ARRIVAL AND DEPARTURE	ISLE OF TIREE
By plane Tiree Airport (☎ 01879 220456, ⊛ hial.co.uk) is around three miles west of Scarinish. Most hosts are happy to collect you upon arrival. Destinations Coll (Mon & Wed 1 daily; 15min); Glasgow (2 daily; 1hr); Oban (Mon & Wed 2 daily; 1hr). **By ferry** Throughout the summer, the CalMac ferry from	Oban calls daily at Coll (2hr 40min) and Tiree (3hr 40min). On Wednesdays (though the day may change) the ferry continues to Barra in the Western Isles, and calls in at Tiree on the way back, making a day-trip from Oban possible. Destinations Castlebay, Barra (Wed 1 daily; 2hr 45min); Oban (1 daily; 3hr 40min).

GETTING AROUND AND INFORMATION	
By minibus Tiree has a Ring'n'Ride minibus service (Mon–Sat 7am–6pm, Tues 7am–10pm; ☎ 01879 220419) that will take you anywhere on the island, though you should book in advance; costs vary between £1.25 and £3. **Bike/car rental** Based at Scarinish Pier, MacLennan	Motors (☎ 01879 220555, ⊛ maclennanmotors.com) offers both car (£48/day) and bike (£10/day) rental. They can also drop cars at the airport. **Information** In the absence of a tourist office ⊛ isleoftiree.com is a useful resource.

ACCOMMODATION	
Balinoe Camping Balinoe ☎ 01879 220399, ⊛ wilddiamond.co.uk. Located in the southwest of the	island, six miles from Scarinish, the island's only formal campsite is operated by Wild Diamond Watersports, and i

well equipped with showers, toilets, a self-catering kitchen and washing/drying facilities. Per pitch **£24**

Millhouse Hostel Near Loch Bhasapol, in the northwest of the island ☎ 01879 220892, ⓦ tireemillhouse.co.uk. This superbly converted early twentieth-century barn now accommodates a colourful hostel, with two dorms each sleeping six, a couple of doubles and a triple. The excellent open-plan kitchen/lounge opens up onto a patio where you

can kick back with a beer and listen to corncrakes while watching the sunset. Doubles **£44**; dorms **£19**

Scarinish Hotel Scarinish ☎ 01879 220308, ⓦ tiree scarinishhotel.com. Super location overlooking the old harbour offering ten pristine rooms (a couple with shared bathroom facilities), furnished in solid, if not spectacular, fashion. The Upper Deck lounge is a lovely spot to watch the comings and goings around the harbour. **£80**

6

Isle of Colonsay and around

Isolated between Mull and Islay, **COLONSAY** – measuring just eight miles by three – is nothing like as bleak and windswept as Coll or Tiree. Its craggy, heather-backed hills even support the occasional patch of woodland, plus a bewildering array of plant and birdlife, including wild goats and rabbits, and a very fine quasi-tropical garden. The current population of around a hundred is down from a pre-Clearance peak of nearly a thousand. With only one hotel and infrequent ferry links with the mainland, there's no fear of mass tourism taking over any time soon. The ferry terminal is at **SCALASAIG**, on the east coast, where there's a post office/shop, a petrol pump, a brewery, a café and the island's hotel.

Colonsay House

Two miles north of Scalasaig • Gardens: March–Sept Wed & Fri noon–5pm, Sat 2–5pm; the house itself is closed to the public • £2.50 • ☎ 01951 200316, ⓦ colonsayholidays.co.uk

Colonsay House was built in 1722 by Malcolm MacNeil, but in 1904 the island and house were bought by Lord Strathcona, who made his fortune building the Canadian Pacific Railway (and whose descendants still own the island). He was also responsible for the house's romantically dilapidated woodland **gardens**, home to one of the most extensive rhododendron collections anywhere in Scotland. The gardens also shelter the strange eighth-century **Riasg Buidhe Cross**, which is decorated with an unusually lifelike mug shot (possibly of a monk) – ask for directions from the tearoom.

The beaches

To the north of Colonsay House is the island's finest sandy beach, the breathtaking **Kiloran Bay**, where the breakers roll in from the Atlantic. There's another unspoilt sandy beach backed by dunes at Balnahard, two miles northeast along a rough track; en route, you might spot wild goats, choughs and even a golden eagle.

Isle of Oronsay

While on Colonsay, it's worth taking a day out to visit the **ISLE OF ORONSAY**, half a mile to the south, with its ruined Augustinian priory. The two islands are separated by "The Strand", a stretch of tidal mud flats, which act as a causeway for two hours either side of low tide (check locally for timings); you can drive over to the island at low tide, though most people park their cars and walk across. Legends (and etymology) link saints Columba and Oran with Colonsay and Oronsay, although the ruins only date back to the fourteenth century. You can, nevertheless, still make out the original church and tiny cloisters, abandoned since the Reformation and now roofless. The highlight, though, is the **Oronsay Cross**, a superb example of late medieval artistry from Iona which, along with thirty or so beautifully carved grave slabs, can be found in the restored side chapel. It takes about an hour to walk from the tip of Colonsay across The Strand to the priory (Wellington boots are a good idea).

ARRIVAL AND DEPARTURE

ISLE OF COLONSAY AND AROUND

By plane Colonsay airport is three miles west of Scalasaig (T 01951 200211, W hebrideanair.co.uk).

Destinations Islay (Tues & Thurs 1 daily; 20min); Oban (Tues & Thurs 2 daily; 25min).

By ferry CalMac ferries run from Oban and once a week from Kennacraig via Islay, when a day-trip is possible, giving you around six hours on the island. Ferries also make the trip from Port Askaig on Islay.

Destinations Kennacraig (Wed 1 daily; 3hr 40min); Oban (daily except Wed & Sat; 2hr 15min); Port Askaig (Wed & Sat 1 daily; 1hr 10min).

GETTING AROUND AND INFORMATION

By minibus There's no public transport, but a minibus meets the Wednesday ferry and takes folk on a tour of the island.

Bike rental Archie McConnell (T 01951 200355) rents bikes.

Website In the absence of a tourist office, W colonsay.org.uk is a useful resource.

ACCOMMODATION AND EATING

There are a couple of modern **B&Bs** to choose from, though most visitors rent **self-catering accommodation**, the majority of which is run by the estate. **Wild camping** is, of course, an option.

Backpacker's Lodge Overlooking Loch Fada about 2 miles from the ferry terminal T 01951 200211, W colonsayholidays.co.uk. The Colonsay Estate's very comfortable hostel consists of the house itself (a former gamekeeper's lodge), with lounge and real fire, and a bothy with three cabins, each sleeping two people and with a shower block outside. There's a well-equipped dining bothy too. Dorms £20; cabin £40

The Colonsay Scalasaig T 01951 200316, W colonsay holidays.co.uk. A cosy eighteenth-century inn at heart, and a short stroll from the pier, the island's only hotel has transformed itself into a really stylish, comfortable place to stay; handily, it also has a restaurant serving decent food (black bream with fennel salad; £16.95) and acts as the island's social centre. Daily noon–2.30pm & Sun 6–10pm. £105

★**The Colonsay Pantry** Above the pier in Scalasaig T 01951 200325, W thecolonsaypantry.co.uk. Delightful establishment offering both light refreshments (tea, coffee and cake) alongside substantial and scrumptious home cooking (smoked haddock scramble with chips costs £9.95). Monday is steak night and Wednesday fish night, but in any case, you must phone ahead for any evening meals. Mon & Wed–Sat 10am–8pm, Tues 10am–4.30pm, Sun 3–8pm

Mid-Argyll

MID-ARGYLL loosely describes the central wedge of land south of Oban and north of Kintyre. The highlights of this gently undulating scenery lie along the sharply indented and remote western coastline. Closest to Oban are the former slate mining settlements of Seil, Easdale and Luing, known collectively as the **Slate Islands**. Further south, the rich Bronze Age and Neolithic remains in the **Kilmartin Glen** comprise one of the most important prehistoric sites in Scotland. Separating Kilmartin Glen from the **Knapdale** peninsula is the **Crinan Canal**, a short cut for boats disinclined to round the Mull of Kintyre, which ends in the pint-sized, picturesque port of **Crinan**.

The Slate Islands

Eight miles south of Oban, a road heads off the A816 west to the minuscule **SLATE ISLANDS**, which at their peak in the mid-nineteenth century quarried over nine million slates annually. Today the old slate villages are sparsely populated, and an air of melancholy hangs over them, but their dramatic setting amid crashing waves makes for a rewarding day-trip.

Isle of Seil

The most northerly of the Slate Islands is **Seil**, a lush island separated from the mainland only by the thinnest of sea channels, which is spanned by the elegant single-arched humpback **Clachan Bridge**, built in 1793 and popularly known as the

"Bridge over the Atlantic". In spring, the bridge sprouts a splendid flourish of purple fairy foxglove, which makes for a quite lovely sight.

The main village on Seil is **ELLENABEICH**, its neat white terraces of workers' cottages crouching below black cliffs on the westernmost tip of the island. This was once the tiny island of Eilean a'Beithich (hence Ellenabeich), separated from the mainland by a slim sea channel until the intensive slate quarrying succeeded in silting it up. Confusingly, the village is often referred to by the same name as the nearby island of Easdale, since they formed an interdependent community based exclusively around the slate industry.

6

Slate Islands Heritage Centre

Ellenabeich • April–Oct daily 10.30am–1pm & 2–5pm • Free • Ⓦ slateislands.org.uk

The **Slate Islands Heritage Centre**, in one of the village's little white cottages, documents the lives and times of island folk in the form of old photographs and artefacts, though mostly the emphasis is inevitably on the local quarry workings, including a model of the slate quarry as it would have been in its heyday. Moreover, and in common with many of Argyll's heritage centres, there's a dedicated genealogical department here.

Isle of Easdale

Easdale (Ⓦ easdale.org) remains an island, though the few hundred yards that separate it from Ellenabeich have to be dredged to keep the channel open. Up until the eve of a great storm in 1881, Easdale supported an incredible 452 inhabitants, despite being less than a mile across at any one point. That night, waves engulfed the island and flooded the quarries and the island never really recovered.

With lots of wonderfully flat stones freely available, Easdale makes the perfect venue for the annual **World Stone Skimming Championships** (Ⓦ stoneskimming.com), held on the last Sunday of September. Just for the record, a legal skim qualifies as a stone that bounces twice – and if you fancy having a go, you can, as it's open to anyone.

Easdale Folk Museum

Near the main square, Easdale • April to mid-Oct 11am–4pm • £2.50 • ☎ 01852 300173, Ⓦ easdalemuseum.org

Many of the village's old workers' cottages now serve as holiday homes, and one is home to the interesting **Easdale Folk Museum**, near the main square, which has surprisingly expansive collections covering not just the local slate industry but also the island's social and military associations. It also sells a useful historical map of the island, and you can buy some interesting slate souvenirs in the shop.

Isle of Luing

Ⓦ isleofluing.co.uk

South of Seil, across the narrow, treacherous Cuan Sound, lies **Luing** – pronounced "Ling" – the largest of the Slate Islands, a long, thin, fertile island which once supported more than six hundred people, but now has a third of that. During the Clearances, the population was drastically reduced to make way for cattle; Luing is still renowned for its beef and for the chocolate-brown crossbreed named after it.

Cullipool, a mile or so southwest of the ferry slipway, is the main village, its whitewashed cottages (mostly built by the slate company) dotted along the shore facing Scarba and Mull. Luing's only other village, **Toberonochy**, lies on the more sheltered east coast, three miles southeast, and boasts the same distinctive white cottages, with red- or blue-painted door and window frames.

Atlantic Islands Centre

Cullipool • Easter–Oct Mon–Thurs 10am–5pm, Fri & Sat 10am–10pm, Sun noon–5pm; Nov–Easter daily 11am–4pm • Free • ☎ 01852 314096, Ⓦ atlanticislandscentre.com

Positioned near the waterfront, the **Atlantic Islands Centre** is an exciting new heritage centre comprising a couple of engaging exhibitions, art space and a terrific café (see below). On the ground floor, a series of colourful and informative wall panels documents the forces that have shaped life on this side of the Atlantic; here too is the original lens from the Fladda Lighthouse, which was used from its inception in 1860 until 1956, when it became one of the first lighthouses in Scotland to be automated. Upstairs, the **Living History Exhibition** traces the development of the island in tandem with the local slate industry; better still are the marvellous views of Scarba, the Garvellachs and the lighthouses on Fladda and Benahua.

6

GETTING AROUND AND TOURS   THE SLATE ISLANDS

By ferry The Cuan Ferry runs from Seil to Luing (every 30min; 5min; £2 return, car £8.10 return). The passenger-only ferry from Ellenabeich to the Isle of Easdale runs more or less on demand (press the buttons in the ferry shed or phone ☎01852 300559).

Boat tours Three, four- and five-hour wildlife and whale-watching cruises (£52–75), as well as high-adrenaline boat trips to the Corryvreckan Whirlpool, are offered by Sealife Adventures (☎01852 300203 or ☎01631 571010, ⓦsealife-adventures.com), whose pontoon is located just across the Clachan Bridge on Seil; depending upon the time of year, expect to see gannets, shags, kittiwakes, seals, dolphins, porpoises and sea eagles.

EATING AND DRINKING

Atlantic Islands Centre Café Cullipool ☎01852 314096, ⓦatlanticislandscentre.com. Lovely, airy café offering both great views and great food, for example a warm haggis wrap or Luing scallops with Stornoway black pudding (£12.95); or you could just opt for a cuppa and a chunk of home-made chocolate cake. Meals are also served on Friday and Saturday evenings, for which booking is advised. Easter–Oct Mon–Thurs 10am–5pm, Fri & Sat 10am–10pm, Sun 10am–5pm; Nov–Easter daily 11am–4pm.

Oyster Bar and Restaurant Ellenabeich ☎01852 300121, ⓦoysterbareasdale.com. For delicious seafood – mussels in white wine (£7.95), king prawns and sweet chilli (£9.95) – or just a pint of real ale, pop inside the snug wood-panelled bar of the *Oyster* on the way to or from the ferry. April–Oct daily 11am–10pm, Nov–March Thurs–Sat 6–10pm, Sun noon–6pm.

Puffer Bar 200yds from the Folk Museum ☎01852 300022, ⓦpufferbar.com. Should you wish to hang about, then you could do worse than visit the terrific *Puffer* restaurant and bar; the former serves the best of the day's fresh catch, while the latter is a convivial spot for a drink Mon–Sat 11am–1am, Sun 12.30–11pm.

Arduaine Garden

A816, 10 miles north Kilmartin • Daily 9.30am–dusk • £6.50; NTS • ☎01852 200366

A great spot at which to stop and have a picnic on the A816 from Oban to Lochgilphead is **Arduaine Garden**, overlooking Asknish Bay and the islands of Shuna, Luing, Scarba and Jura. The gardens, whose original foundations were laid in 1898, are stupendous, particularly in May and June, and have the feel of an intimate private garden, with immaculately mown lawns, lily-strewn ponds, mature woods and spectacular rhododendrons and azaleas. You can follow several pathways through the gardens, one of which is the woodland walk, which leads down to the lakeshore, where there's a good chance of spotting otters, sea eagles and hen harriers.

ACCOMMODATION AND EATING   ARDUAINE GARDEN

★**Loch Melfort Hotel** Adjacent to Arduaine Garden ☎01852 200233, ⓦlochmelfort.co.uk. This fine, privately run country-house hotel overlooking Asknish Bay offers a selection of beautifully appointed rooms, each with its own private patio or balcony; best of all, though, are the views, which are some of the finest in Scotland. The hotel's restaurant is outstanding (four-course *table d'hote* menu £42), while their sparky *Chartroom II Bistro* next door isn't half bad either; the seafood rates highly, as do the home-made burgers, for example wild venison or spiced chick pea and vegetable (£12.95). Moreover, every first and third Friday evening of the month, the bistro has live music. Daily 11am–10pm. **£160**

Kilmartin Glen and around

The chief sight on the road from Oban to Lochgilphead is **KILMARTIN GLEN**, the most important prehistoric site on the Scottish mainland. The most remarkable relic is the

linear cemetery, where several cairns are aligned for more than two miles to the south of the village of Kilmartin. These are thought to represent the successive burials of a ruling family or chieftains, but nobody can be sure. The best view of the cemetery's configuration is from the Bronze Age **Mid-Cairn**, but the Neolithic **South Cairn**, dating from around 3000 BC, is by far the oldest and the most impressive, with its large chambered tomb roofed by giant slabs.

Close to the South Cairn, the two **Temple Wood stone circles** appear to have been the architectural focus of burials in the area from Neolithic times to the Bronze Age. Visible to the south are the impressively cup-marked **Nether Largie standing stones** (no public access), the largest of which looms over 10ft high.

Cup- and ring-marked rocks are a recurrent feature of prehistoric sites in Kilmartin Glen and elsewhere in Argyll. There are many theories as to their origin: some see them as Pictish symbols, others as primitive solar calendars. The most extensive markings in the entire country are at **Achnabreck**, off the A816 towards Lochgilphead.

6

Kilmartin Museum

Kilmartin village • Daily: March–Oct 10am–5.30pm; Nov to Christmas 11am–4pm • £6 • ☎ 01546 510278, ⓦ kilmartin.org

Situated on high ground to the north of the Kilmartin cairns is the tiny village of **KILMARTIN**, an unremarkable place but home to the superb **Kilmartin Museum**, housed in the old manse adjacent to the village church. Not only can you learn about the various theories concerning prehistoric crannogs, henges and cairns, but you can practise polishing an axe, examine different types of wood, and listen to a variety of

6

weird and wonderful sounds (check out the Gaelic bird imitations). Among the many remarkable exhibits is an eagle bone flute, a bronze sword from Shuna, a carved slab from the Nether Largie north cairn, and decorated querns (stones used for making flour from grain) from Barnasluagan. At 2pm on Wednesdays, museum staff run a superb (free) two-hour guided walk of the cairns.

Carnasserie Castle

Commanding a high ridge a mile up the road towards Oban are the ruins of **Carnasserie Castle**. Built in the 1560s by Protestant reformer John Carswell – who published the first book to be printed in Scottish Gaelic (a translation of John Knox's *Book of Common Order*) – the castle is a good example of the transition between fully fortified castles and later mansion houses, and has several original finely carved stone fireplaces and doorways, as well as numerous gun-loops and shot holes. The reward for climbing the five-storey structure is a wonderful view of Kilmartin Glen dead straight ahead.

Mòine Mhór

To the south of Kilmartin, beyond the linear cemetery, lies the raised peat bog of **Mòine Mhór** (Great Moss), now a nature reserve and home to remarkable plant, insect and birdlife. To get a close look at the sphagnum moss and wetlands, head for the Tileworks Walk, just off the A816, which includes a short boardwalk over the bog.

Dunadd

Mòine Mhór is best known as home to the Iron Age fort of **Dunadd**, one of Scotland's most important Celtic sites, occupying a distinctive 176ft-high rocky knoll once surrounded by the sea but currently stranded beside the winding River Add. It was here that Fergus, the first king of Dalriada – which embraced much of what is now Argyll – established his royal seat, having arrived from Ireland in around 500 AD. Its strategic position, the craggy defences and the view from the top are all impressive, but it's the **stone carvings** (albeit now fibreglass copies) between the twin summits which make Dunadd so remarkable: several lines of inscription in Ogham (an ancient alphabet of Irish origin), the faint outline of a boar, a hollowed-out footprint and a small basin. The boar and the inscriptions are probably **Pictish**, since the fort was clearly occupied long before Fergus got there, but the footprint and basin have been interpreted as being part of the royal coronation rituals of the kings of Dalriada. It is thought that the Stone of Destiny was used at Dunadd before being moved to Scone Palace (see box, p.63).

ACCOMMODATION AND EATING   **KILMARTIN GLEN**

Dunchraigaig House 1 mile south of Kilmartin ☎ 01546 510396, ⊚ dunchraigaig.co.uk. This large detached Victorian house situated opposite the Ballymeanoch standing stones offers five spotless en-suite rooms with either woodland or Jura Island views, though its star attraction is the local pine marten, which appears at the feeding table most mornings for a bite to eat. The guests' breakfast, meanwhile, is usually something special, and is likely to include some home-made clootie dumpling. March–Nov. **£80**

Kilmartin Museum Café Kilmartin Museum ☎ 01546 510278. Looking out across to Glebe Cairn, this is a lovely spot at which to refuel after examining the local treasures, with the likes of wild venison burger (£8.95) and smoked salmon hoagies to feast on, as well as lots of delicious home-baked fare, not least a divine selection of cakes and buns. Daily March–Oct 10am–5.30pm; Nov to Christmas 11am–4pm

Knapdale and around

Forested **Knapdale** – from the Gaelic *cnap* (hill) and *dall* (field) – forms a buffer zone between the Kintyre peninsula and the rest of Argyll, bounded to the north by the Crinan Canal and to the south by West Loch Tarbert, and consisting of three progressively fatter fingers of land, separated by Loch Sween and Loch Caolisport. Knapdale is a little-visited area, which is surprising, as the ancient wooded landscape is among some of the most beautiful, and unique, in the country. Not only that, but

THE SCOTTISH BEAVER TRIAL

In 2009, a colony of beavers from Norway was introduced to Knapdale Forest as part of a five-year project by the **Scottish Beaver Trial** (ⓦ scottishbeavertrial.org.uk). The first beavers in the wilds of Scotland for over four hundred years, their arrival met with a rather mixed reaction, though their effect on the environment (and to a lesser degree the local economy) has been, and continues to be, closely monitored by an independent project team; the trial phase ended in 2016, but at the time of writing no decision had been made as to whether the beavers should remain.

From the interpretation centre at **Barnluasgan** (four miles west of Cairnbaan), it's a twenty-minute walk to Dubh Loch, where most of the beaver activity takes place. Here, there's a viewing platform and another rough path that cuts through to Loch Coille Bharr, the two lochs separated by a 60ft-long dam that took the beavers around four to five months to build – a quite remarkable feat of engineering. Either side of these two lochs, you'll also see their lodges, large and impressive tangles of severed branches, wood and mud. The best time to see these fascinating creatures is either at dawn or dusk, and though sightings are by no means guaranteed, there is a strong possibility that you will witness some beaver activity. Take along some binoculars, midge repellent and refreshments (you could be waiting a while), and don't bring dogs. You can follow the trail yourself or, alternatively, join one of the **free guided tours** that take place on Tuesday and Saturday evenings between June and September.

there is some spectacular wildlife to observe here as well, not least thanks to the recent reintroduction of beavers to the area (see box above).

Crinan Canal

The nine-mile-long **Crinan Canal** opened in 1801, linking Loch Fyne, at Ardrishaig south of Lochgilphead, with the Sound of Jura, thus cutting out the long and treacherous journey around the Mull of Kintyre. John Rennie's original design, although an impressive engineering feat, had numerous faults, and by 1816 Thomas Telford was called in to take charge of the renovations. The canal runs parallel to the sea for quite some way before cutting across the bottom of Mòine Mhór and hitting a flight of locks either side of **CAIRNBAAN** (there are fifteen in total). The walk along the towpath is utterly delightful (both picturesque and not too strenuous), though you could, of course, cycle too.

The most relaxing place from which to view the canal in action is **CRINAN**, the pretty little fishing port at the canal's western end. Crinan's tiny harbour is, for the moment at least, still home to a small fishing fleet; a quick burst up through Crinan Wood to the hill above the village will give you a bird's-eye view of the sea lock and its setting.

ACCOMMODATION AND EATING · CRINAN CANAL

CAIRNBAAN

Cairnbaan Hotel By lock no. 5 on the canal ☎ 01546 603668, ⓦ cairnbaan.com. Eighteenth-century coaching inn built at the same time as the canal, which it overlooks, with twelve very accomplished and well-designed rooms. The lively restaurant-cum-bar deservedly does well from lots of passing trade from the canal, with dishes such as pork belly with Stornoway black pudding, and smoked haddock on chive mash with Kintyre cheddar (£14.50). Otherwise, just grab a pint and watch the boats pass by. Daily 11am–10pm. **£85**

CRINAN

Crinan Hotel ☎ 01546 830261, ⓦ crinanhotel.com. Occupying an enviable position overlooking the harbour, this mildly eccentric family-run hotel has twenty superbly

conceived rooms (indeed, the hotel has its own gallery), each one named after a Scottish artist and featuring an original piece of work by that artist. All offer splendid loch views. **£220**

Crinan Seafood Bar Crinan Hotel ☎ 01546 830261. Reward yourself after the long canal-side walk with some steamed mussels or an Arbroath smokie (£13) washed down with a pint, at the same time as enjoying one of the most beautiful views in Scotland – especially at sunset, when the myriad islets and the distinctive Paps of Jura are reflected in the waters of the loch. Occupying the adjacent horse stables is the hotel's cheery coffee shop, serving bacon rolls, home-baked cakes, tea and coffee. Easter–Oct daily noon–12.30pm & 6–8.30pm. Café March–Oct daily 10am–5pm, Nov & Dec Sat & Sun 10am–4pm.

Kintyre

But for the mile-long isthmus between West Loch Tarbert and the much smaller East Loch Tarbert, the little-visited, sparsely populated peninsula of **KINTYRE** – from the Gaelic *ceann tìre*, "land's end" – would be an island. Indeed, in the eleventh century, when the Scottish king, Malcolm Canmore, allowed Magnus Barefoot, King of Norway, to lay claim to any island he could circumnavigate by boat, Magnus dragged his boat across the Tarbert isthmus and added the peninsula to his Hebridean kingdom. Despite its relative proximity to Scotland's central belt, Kintyre remains quiet and unfashionable; its main towns of **Tarbert** and **Campbeltown** have few obvious attractions, but that's part of their appeal.

Kintyre's bleak but often beautiful **west coast** ranks among the most exposed stretches of coastline in Argyll. Atlantic breakers pound the rocky shoreline, while the persistent westerly wind forces the trees against the hillside. However, when the weather's fine and the wind not too fierce, there are numerous deserted sandy beaches to enjoy, with great views over to Gigha, Islay, Jura and even Ireland. By way of contrast, the **east coast** of Kintyre is gentler than the west, sheltered from the Atlantic winds and in parts strikingly beautiful, with stunning views across to Arran.

ARRIVAL AND DEPARTURE   KINTYRE

By plane Campbeltown has an airport, with flights to and from Glasgow.

By bus There are regular daily buses from Glasgow to Campbeltown, via Tarbert and the west coast. Note that the bus service from Campbeltown only reaches as far as the fishing village of Carradale, some 13 miles up the coast.

By ferry Kintyre is well served with ferries: the main port is at Kennacraig, 5 miles south of Tarbert on the west coast, with ferries serving Port Askaig and Port Ellen on Islay. There are also ferries from Tarbert to Portavadie on the Cowal peninsula, from Claonaig to Lochranza on Arran, and a summer-only one from Campbeltown to Ardrossan.

Tarbert

A distinctive rocket-like church steeple heralds the fishing port of **TARBERT** (in Gaelic *An Tairbeart*, meaning "isthmus"), sheltering an attractive little bay backed by rugged hills. Tarbert's **herring industry** was mentioned in the Annals of Ulster as far back as 836 AD, though right now the local fishing industry is down to its lowest level ever. Ironically, it was local Tarbert fishermen who, in the 1830s, pioneered the method of herring fishing known as trawling, seining or ring-netting, which eventually wiped out the Loch Fyne herring stocks.

Tourism is now an increasingly important source of income, and though there's little of substance to see in Tarbert itself, it's a good hub, with excellent transport links, a decent stock of accommodation, and some highly commendable seafood restaurants. Moreover, it stages two prestigious annual events: the Scottish Series yacht races in late May, and the Tarbert Seafood Festival in early July when traditional boats also hit town.

ARRIVAL AND INFORMATION   TARBERT

By bus Buses stop in the centre of town on Campbeltown Rd and Barmore Rd.

Destinations Campbeltown (5 daily; 1hr 15min); Claonaig (Mon–Sat 3 daily; 30min); Glasgow (5 daily; 3hr 10min).

KINTYRE WAY

The best way to really appreciate Kintyre's remote but beguiling landscape is to tackle the **Kintyre Way** (Ⓦ kintyreway.com), which begins in Tarbert and zigzags its way for 100 miles down the peninsula to Southend. There are seven stages in all, mostly with moderate walking (one or two sections are more demanding), comprising hill paths, moorland, forest trails and coast. The website also has suggestions for accommodation at the end of each stage.

Kennacraig (5 daily; 15min); Kilberry (2 daily on schooldays; 40min); Skipness (Mon–Sat 3 daily; 35min); Tayinloan (Mon–Fri 3 daily; 30min).
By ferry The ferry terminal is on Pier Rd, a 10min walk along Harbour St.

Destinations Portavadie (hourly; 25min).
Tourist office Harbour St (April–June, Sept & Oct Mon–Sat 10am–5pm, Sun 11am–5pm; July & Aug Mon–Sat 9am–6pm, Sun 10am–5pm; Nov–March Tues–Sat 10am–2pm; ☎01880 820429, ⚲tarbertlochfyne.com).

ACCOMMODATION

★Anchor Hotel Harbour St ☎01880 820577, ⚲lochfyne-scotland.co.uk. While this smart, harbour-facing hotel itself has thirteen perfectly accomplished rooms, it's the barge across the road that you should be heading for; brilliantly converted into four luxury cabins, you wouldn't even know you were on the water were it not for the occasional gentle bob and swans gliding past your window at eye level. Cool, relaxing and a lot of fun. Rooms £120; cabins £220

Knap Guest House Campbeltown Rd ☎01880 820015, ⚲knapguesthouse.co.uk. Handsome Victorian townhouse with four pristine rooms leading

off a beautifully appointed lounge; each room manifests a curious mixture of traditional Scottish and Asian furnishings, which somehow works very well. A little tricky to find, it's opposite the Co-op. £75

Struan House Harbour St ☎01880 820190, ⚲struan.biz. Built in 1846 as a small hotel, this is now a charming six-roomed guesthouse with bespoke furnishings, grand wooden bedsteads, and some sweet little touches like bedside lamps, books and wall-mounted artwork. It's opposite the Harbour Authority building up towards the ferry terminal. £75

EATING AND DRINKING

Ca'Dora Harbour St ☎01880 820258. The pick of several cafés ranged along the seafront which, despite looking rather dull from the outside, pulls in the punters for its comfort food such as cottage pie, and battered haddock and chips (£9), though it's renowned, above all, for its ice cream. Daily 8am–9pm.

Seabed Restaurant Harbour St ☎01880 820577, ⚲lochfyne-scotland.co.uk. Complement your stay on the barge with dinner in the *Anchor Hotel's* inviting, cheerily staffed restaurant, which offers up accomplished dishes

such as Stornoway black pudding bon bons, and pan-seared seabass with chive mash and crayfish beurre blanc (£17.95). Daily noon–9.30pm.

★Starfish Castle St ☎01880 820733, ⚲starfishtarbert.com. Sparkling, informally run seafood restaurant where scallops are king, literally – a plate of these will set you back £18, as will the Starfish stew, comprising mussels, queen scallops and the catch of the day. Complete your meal with the crumble of the day. Mon–Thurs & Sun 6–10pm, Fri & Sat noon–2pm & 6–10pm.

Carradale and around

The village of **CARRADALE** itself is rather drab, but the tiny, very pretty harbour with its small fishing fleet, and the wide, sandy beach to the south, make up for it, while there is a handful of lovely places to stay and eat here too. On the road into town, the small **Network Centre** has bikes and all-terrain electric buggies to rent (daily 10am–4pm; ☎01583 431296; £14/5hr, £20/day), and there's good home baking to be had in the tearoom. The B842 ends fourteen miles north of Carradale at **CLAONAIG**, little more than a slipway for the small summer car ferry to Arran.

ARRIVAL AND DEPARTURE   CARRADALE AND AROUND

By ferry The ferry terminal is at Claonaig, fourteen miles north of Carradale.

Destinations Lochranza, Arran (8–9 daily; 30min).

ACCOMMODATION AND EATING

Ashbank Hotel Centre of village ☎01583 431650, ⚲ashbankhotel.com. A dinky little place in the heart of the village, with five boxy but comfy en-suite rooms – three with a sea view – and the Egyptian cotton bedding is something to savour. Breakfast is taken in the sweet little downstairs bar. £75

Carradale Bay Caravan Park Outside Carradale

village ☎01583 431665, ⚲carradalebay.com. The nearest campsite to town is the superbly equipped and well-sheltered Carradale Bay Caravan Park, right by, and with great access to, the sandy beach. Although it's predominantly a caravan site, there is a separate area to pitch tents. Easter–Oct. Per pitch £23

★Dunvalanree Port Righ Bay ☎01583 431226,

ⓦ dunvalanree.com. Imposing house overlooking the sheltered little bay of Port Righ, towards Carradale Point; the five rooms are of the highest order, with beautiful, bespoke beds, though for those on a tighter budget, a couple of cheaper rooms are available. The three-course *table d'hote* dinner costs just £23 extra, exceptional value given sumptuous dishes like seared scallops on pea mash with pancetta, and collops of Argyll venison with poached brambles and wild garlic pesto. The cost to non-guests is £28. Advance booking required. __£80__

Skipness

6

Heading north of the Claonaig ferry terminal, a dead-end road winds its way along the shore a few miles further north to the tiny village of **SKIPNESS** and the considerable ruins of the thirteenth-century **Skipness Castle** (open access; free). The castle's two surviving rooms form the base of the sixteenth-century tower; from here a slender spiral staircase leads to the roof and glorious views across the Kilbrannan Sound to Arran. To the right as you enter, the old latrine was converted into a dovecote, as evidenced by the holes in the walls on all sides.

There are also several gentle **walks** laid out in the nearby mixed woodland, up the glen, but the main reason people make the effort to visit Skipness is the wonderful *Skipness Seafood Cabin*.

ARRIVAL AND EATING   **SKIPNESS**

By bus Buses run between Skipness and Kennacraig via the ferry terminal at Claonaig (Mon–Sat 3 daily; 20min).

Skipness Seafood Cabin Below the castle ☎ 01880 760207, ⓦ theseafoodcabin.co.uk. Little more than a hut, the Cabin has been doling out fresh local seafood for years: hot smoked salmon or crab rolls (£5), fresh oysters, queenies (queen scallops), langoustine, mussels and home-baked cakes are just some of the treats. There are wooden tables and bench seating from which to admire the splendid views across to Arran. Whit Sunday to Sept 11am–7pm; closed Sat.

Isle of Gigha

Just six miles by one mile, **GIGHA** – pronounced "Geeya", with a hard "g" – is a low-lying, fertile island, with a population of around 150, just three miles off the west coast of Kintyre. The island's Ayrshire cattle produce over a quarter of a million gallons of milk a year to produce the island's distinctive (occasionally fruit-shaped) cheese. Like many of the smaller Hebrides, Gigha was bought and sold numerous times after its original lairds, the MacNeils, sold up, and was finally bought by the islanders themselves in 2002.

The real draw of Gigha, apart from the peace and quiet, is the white sandy beaches – including one at Ardminish, the island's only village – that dot the coastline. The ferry from Tayinloan deposits you at **ARDMINISH**, where you'll find the post office and shop, and the all-denomination island church, which has some interesting stained-glass windows. Although most visitors come to Gigha for the day, it's a great place to stay.

Achamore Gardens

1.5 miles south of Ardminish • Daily 9am–dusk • £6

The main attraction on Gigha is the **Achamore Gardens**, established by the first postwar owner, Sir James Horlick of hot-drink fame. Its spectacularly colourful displays of azaleas are best seen in early summer, but elsewhere, the rhododendrons merit seeking out, as does the walled garden, with its hugely diverse collection of plants, a bamboo maze, and a superb panorama across the island's west coast and beyond to Islay and Jura. At the heart of the complex stands Achamore House itself, though this is now privately owned and off-limits to visitors.

To the southwest of the gardens, the ruins of the thirteenth-century **St Catan's Chapel** are floored with weathered medieval gravestones; the ogham stone nearby is the only one of its kind in the west of Scotland.

ARRIVAL AND INFORMATION ISLE OF GIGHA

By ferry CalMac ferries depart more or less hourly from Tayinloan, 23 miles south of Tarbert, for the 20min crossing to Ardminish.

Gigha Boats Activity Centre Ardminish Bay (Easter–Sept daily 10am–6pm; ☎07876 506520, ⓦ gighaboatsactivitycentre.co.uk). Next to the ferry slip,

this is effectively the island's information point, but is mainly concerned with renting out bikes (£10/half day, £15/day), kayaks (£10/1hr), stand-up paddle-boards (£10/1hr) and rowing boats (£20/1hr). The website, ⓦ gigha.org.uk, is also a useful resource.

ACCOMMODATION AND EATING

The Boathouse Ardminish Bay ☎01583 505123, ⓦ boathousegigha.co.uk. Inside this low dark-stone building, perched above a white sandy bay, is a gorgeous little restaurant rustling up treats like dressed crab salad (£16), langoustine tails in garlic, and seared scallops with ginger, chilli and lime. April–Sept daily 11.30am–9pm.

Boathouse Camping On the grass adjacent to The Boathouse ☎01583 505123, ⓦ boathousegigha.co.uk.

This designated camping area, with just twenty pitches, has fantastic beach views. Facilities are limited to showers (£1) and toilets, though they sell some basic foodstuffs too. Booking ahead is advisable. Per pitch £9

Gigha Hotel ☎01583 505254, ⓦ gigha.org.uk. Just 200yds from the ferry terminal, this is the island's social hub and a very welcoming place to stay. Its twelve, largely pinewood-furnished rooms are inviting and spotlessly clean without being particularly exciting. £85

6

Machrihanish and around

The only major development along the entire west coast of Kintyre is **MACHRIHANISH**, at the southern end of Machrihanish Bay, the longest continuous stretch of sand in Argyll. There are two approaches to the **beach**: from Machrihanish itself, or from Westport, at the north end of the bay, where the A83 swings east towards Campbeltown; either way, the sea here is too dangerous for swimming. Machrihanish itself was once a thriving salt-producing and coal-mining centre – you can still see the miners' cottages at neighbouring Drumlemble – but now survives solely on tourism, in particular golf.

Machrihanish Golf Club and Machrihanish Dunes Golf Club

Machrihanish Golf Club Between the beach and Campbeltown Airport • Daily April–Oct £65; Nov–March £30 • ☎01586 810277, ⓦ machgolf.com **Machrihanish Dunes Golf Club** East of Campbeltown Airport • Daily April–Oct £75; Nov–March £40 • ☎01586 810000, ⓦ machrihanishdunes.com

Dominating the village of Machrihanish is the exposed 18-hole championship course of the **Machrihanish Golf Club**, between the beach and Campbeltown Airport on the nearby flat and fertile swathe of land known as the Laggan. One of Scotland's finest links courses (established in 1876), it plays out on a quite spectacular landscape, and is particularly notable for its first hole, which cuts across the Atlantic in dramatic fashion.

Established as recently as 2009, the sister course of Machrihanish golf course, the 18-hole **Machrihanish Dunes**, on the other side of the airport, is perhaps even more impressive. The course layout, including the tee and green positions, is dictated solely by the lie of the land.

ARRIVAL AND INFORMATION MACHRIHANISH

By bus Buses stop in the centre of the village near the golf club.

Destinations Campbeltown (Mon–Sat 7 daily; 20min).

ACCOMMODATION AND EATING

Machrihanish Holiday Park Machrihanish Village ☎01586 810366, ⓦ campkintyre.co.uk. Superbly located next to the fairways and with direct sea views, this large, fully equipped, family-run campsite has a terrific mix

of caravan and tent space, as well as heated wooden wigwams (sleeping three people) and fully fitted bell tents (sleeping two adults and two children). March–Oct. Per pitch £15; wigwams £40; bell tents (July & Aug only) £70

Old Clubhouse Pub Machrihanish Village ☎ 01586 810000. Overlooking the first tee, the erstwhile clubhouse is now a very agreeable village pub, frequented by golfers and locals alike, which means it's not nearly as pretentious as it might be. Good bar food and decent ales. Daily 11am–11pm.

Campbeltown

Set within a deep bay, sheltered by Davaar Island and the surrounding hills, **CAMPBELTOWN** is Kintyre's largest town with a population of around 5000. Originally known as Kinlochkilkerran (Ceann Loch Cill Chiaran), the town was renamed in the seventeenth century by the Earl of Argyll – a Campbell – when it became one of the main points for immigration from the Lowlands. As is evident from the architecture, Campbeltown's heyday was the Victorian era, when shipbuilding was going strong, coal was shipped by canal from Drumlemble, the fishing fleet was vast and Campbeltown Loch was said to be made of whisky. Nineteenth-century visitors to Campbeltown frequently found the place engulfed in a thick fog of pungent peat smoke from the town's 34 whisky distilleries. Today, only three distilleries are left to maintain this regional subgroup of single-malt whiskies.

If you're here on the third weekend of August, be prepared for the **Mull of Kintyre Music & Arts Festival** (Ⓦ mokfest.com), which pulls in some big-name rock bands, plus some good traditional Irish and Scottish ones.

Springbank distillery

55 Longrow, but sign-up at Cadenhead's whisky shop 30–32 Union St • Mon–Sat 10am & 1.30pm • £7 • ☎ 01586 551710, Ⓦ springbankwhisky.com

Whisky-lovers shouldn't miss a visit to the **Springbank distillery**, a deeply traditional, family-owned business (founded in 1828) that produces three different single malts; indeed, it's the only distillery in Scotland to carry out the full production process on one site, from the malting to the bottling. You first get to see the malting floor (Springbank is now one of only half a dozen or so distilleries in Scotland that still does its own malting), before continuing down to the peat stacks and kiln, which again is not something you normally see on a distillery tour. Having viewed the magnificent copper stills, the tour winds up inside the capacious warehouse, which stretches for 100yds or so. You actually sign up for the tour at **Cadenhead's** whisky shop on Union Street, which you then return to afterwards to collect your free miniature.

Burnet Building

St John St • Mon–Fri 9am–12.30pm & 1.30–5pm • Free • ☎ 01586 559017

Built as the town library in 1897, the **Burnett Building** is crowned by a distinctive lantern and decorated with four relief panels depicting the town's main industries at the time. The building harbours a very old-fashioned one-room local **museum**, with some intriguing finds such as a gold Viking arm ring and a gorgeous jet necklace, as well as a few pieces by the acclaimed landscape painter William McTaggart. Most people, though, are drawn to the **Linda McCartney Memorial Garden**, which you should approach from Shore Street. Here, you'll find a slightly ludicrous bronze statue of Linda holding a lamb, a piece commissioned by Paul McCartney, who spent many happy times with Linda and the kids on the farm he owns near Campbeltown.

Campbeltown Heritage Centre

Lorne St • April–Sept Mon–Sat 9am–5pm • £2 • ☎ 07733 485387, Ⓦ campbeltownheritagecentre.co.uk

The former Lorne Street Church, with its stripy bell-cote and pinnacles, has been cleverly converted into the intermittently interesting **Campbeltown Heritage Centre**. Due prominence is given to the town's once glittering industrial heritage, in particular the local fishing and whisky industries; going hand in hand with local malt production was a significant coopering industry, and at one stage there were more than sixty coopers in Campbeltown. By far the most prominent exhibit here, however, and occupying the spot where the main altar once stood, is a beautiful wooden skiff called "Yerda", dating from 1906. Look out, too, for the model of the Victorian harbourfront with the light railway running along Hall Street.

ARRIVAL AND INFORMATION — CAMPBELTOWN

By plane Campbeltown Airport (☏ 01586 553797, ☜ hial .co.uk) lies 3 miles west, towards Machrihanish.
Destinations Glasgow (Mon–Fri 2 daily; 40min).

By bus The town's main bus terminal is in front of the swimming pool on the Esplanade.
Destinations Carradale (Mon–Fri 5 daily, 4 on Sat; 45min); Glasgow (5 daily; 4hr 15min); Machrihanish (Mon–Sat 9 daily; 20min); Southend (Mon–Sat 6 daily; 25min); Tarbert (5 daily; 1hr 10min).

By ferry The ferry terminal is on the south side of the harbour, from where it's a 5min walk into the centre.
Destinations Ardrossan (Thurs, Fri & Sun 1 daily; 2hr 40min).

Tourist office Old Quay (April–June & Sept Mon–Sat 10am–5pm, Sun noon–4pm; July & Aug Mon–Sat 9am–6pm, Sun 11am–5pm; Oct–March Mon–Fri 10am–4pm; ☏ 01586 556162).

ACCOMMODATION

Ardshiel Hotel Kilkerran Rd ☏ 01586 552133, ☜ ardshiel.co.uk. A former whisky distiller's Victorian mansion situated on a lovely leafy square just a block or so back from the harbour front. The rooms are functional more than anything else. More impressive is the hotel's glamorous, grown-up whisky bar, stocking in excess of 700 malts, well worth a visit even if you're not staying here. **£85**

Campbeltown Backpackers Big Kiln ☏ 01586 551188, ☜ campbeltownbackpackers.co.uk. Occupying the old school house in the courtyard across from the heritage centre, this new, community-trust-run bunkhouse has sixteen firm, pine beds in two dormitories, a self-catering kitchen and small lounge. There's no reception as such, so if there's no one there, pop into the heritage centre; when that's closed just call

the number on the door. Dorms **£18**

Oatfield House 3 miles down the B842 ☏ 01586 551551, ☜ oatfield.org. A beautifully renovated whitewashed laird's house set in its own grounds on the road to Southend, retaining three rooms of some character and distinction. Guests are also free to avail themselves of the panelled dining room and parlour. **£80**

Royal Hotel Main St ☏ 0800 151 3701, ☜ machrihanishdunes.com. Owned by the golf club, this high-end hotel sits well with the recent redevelopment of the harbourfront area, and injects a big dollop of colour into this otherwise dull street. The supremely comfortable rooms are mostly furnished in bold tartan colour schemes, with deep armchairs, big beds with thick duvets and fluffy pillows, and a host of other neat touches. **£140**

EATING AND DRINKING

Black Sheep Pub Main St ☏ 0800 151 3701. The *Royal Hotel*'s pub is by far the most enjoyable watering hole in town, with seating arranged around a shiny, semi-circular bar, in addition to some outdoor tables overlooking the harbour. Some decent cask ales too. Daily noon–1am.

Café Bluebell 6 Hall St ☏ 01586 552800. Simple-looking but warm and welcoming café opposite the tourist office offering a terrific selection of light snacks (soups, sandwiches, sausage rolls), as well as a gut-busting all-day breakfast (£7.95). Tues–Sat 9am–4.30pm, Sun 11am–4pm.

Mull of Kintyre

Most people venture south of Campbeltown to make a pilgrimage to the **Mull of Kintyre**, made famous by the mawkish number-one hit by one time local resident Paul McCartney, with the help of the Campbeltown Pipe Band. It's also infamous as the site of the RAF's worst peacetime accident when, on June 2, 1994, a Chinook helicopter on its way from Belfast to Inverness crashed, killing all 29 on board. A small memorial can be found on the hillside, not far from the **Gap** (1150ft) – after which no vehicles are allowed. The Mull is the nearest Britain gets to Ireland, just twelve miles away, and the Irish coastline appears remarkably close on fine days. There's nothing specifically to see, but the trek down to the lighthouse, itself 300ft above the ocean waves, is challengingly tortuous.

Isle of Islay

The fertile, largely treeless island of **ISLAY** (pronounced "eye-la") is famous for one thing – single-malt **whisky**. The smoky, peaty, pungent quality of Islay whisky is unique, recognizable even to the untutored palate, and all eight of the island's distilleries will happily take visitors on a guided tour, ending with the customary tipple. Yet, despite the fame of its whiskies, Islay still remains relatively undiscovered, especially when compared with Arran, Mull or Skye, partly, perhaps, because of the two-hour ferry journey from Kennacraig on Kintyre. If you do make the effort, however, you'll be rewarded with a genuinely friendly welcome from islanders proud of their history, landscape and Gaelic culture.

In medieval times, Islay was the political centre of the Hebrides, with **Finlaggan**, near Port Askaig, the seat of the MacDonalds, Lords of the Isles. The picturesque, whitewashed villages you see on Islay today, however, date from the planned settlements founded by the Campbells in the late eighteenth and early nineteenth centuries. Apart from whisky and solitude, the other great draw is the **birdlife** – there's a real possibility

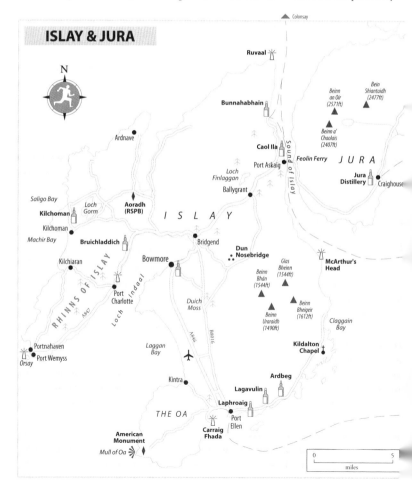

ISLAY WHISKY DISTILLERIES

It goes without saying that Islay's **whisky distilleries** are a major tourist attraction. Nowadays, every distillery offers guided tours, which usually last an hour and traditionally end with a generous dram, and occasionally a free glass. Most also offer more comprehensive tours with more tastings, and some even do warehouse tours. Phone ahead to make sure there's a tour running, as times do change frequently.

Ardbeg Port Ellen ☎01496 302244, ☜ardbeg.com. Ardbeg is traditionally considered the saltiest, peatiest malt on Islay, and that's saying something. Thoroughly overhauled and restored following its acquisition by Glenmorangie in 1997, it's a relatively small distillery by Islay's standards yet it has bags of character inside and out, and the tour is one of the best. Moreover, its café, the *Old Kiln*, is excellent. Tours £5; daily 11am & 3pm; Old Kiln Café April–Oct daily 10am–4.30pm; Nov–March Mon–Fri 10am–4.30pm.

Bowmore School St ☎01496 810441, ☜bowmore .com. Bowmore is the most touristy of the Islay distilleries, but it is by far the most central (with unrivalled disabled access), and also one of the few still doing its own malting and kilning. Tours £7; April–Sept Mon–Sat 9.30, 10.30 & 11.30am & 2.30 & 3.30pm, Sun 12.30 & 2pm; Oct–March Mon–Fri 10.30am & 3pm, Sat 9.30am.

Bruichladdich Bruichladdich ☎01496 850190, ☜bruichladdich.com. In the centre of the village of the same name, this independent distillery was rescued in 2001 by a group of whisky fanatics, but was bought out by Remy-Cointreau in 2012. Progressive and innovative, this is one distinctly cool distillery; moreover, they also produce the island's only gin, the scrumptious Botanist. Tours £5; April–Sept Mon–Fri 10.30, 11.30am & 1, 2 & 4pm, Sat & 1 & 2pm, Sun 1 & 2pm; Oct Mon–Sat 10, 11am & 1 & 3pm; Nov–March Mon–Fri 10, 11am & 2pm, Sat 10am & 2pm.

Bunnahabhain 4 miles north of Port Askaig ☎01496 840557, ☜bunnahabhain.com. A visit to Bunnahabhain (pronounced "Bunna-have-in") is really only for whisky obsessives. The road from Port Askaig is windy, the whisky the least characteristically Islay and the distillery itself only in production for a few months each year. Tours £7; April–Oct Mon–Sat 10am, 11.30am & 1, 2.30 & 4pm, Sun 11am & 12.30 & 2pm; Nov–March Mon–Sat 10am & 2pm, Sun noon & 2pm.

Caol Ila Port Askaig ☎01496 302760, ☜discovering -distilleries.com. Caol Ila (pronounced "Cull-eela"), just north of Port Askaig, is a modern distillery, the majority of whose lightly peaty malt goes into blended whiskies. Tours £6; March–Oct Mon–Fri 9.30am & 12.30 & 3.30pm, Sat 9.30am, Sun 10.30am; Nov–Feb Tues–Sat 10.30am.

Kilchoman Rockside Farm, Bruichladdich ☎01496 850011, ☜kilchomandistillery.com. Established in 2005 as the first new distillery on Islay for over a century, Kilchoman is a very welcoming, tiny, farm-based enterprise that grows its own barley, as well as distilling, maturing and bottling its whisky on site. Also, along with Ardbeg, this is the only distillery on the island with a café, and very lovely it is too, serving good coffee, plus home-made soup and baked goodies. Tours £6; April–Oct daily 10, 11.30am & 3.30pm; Nov–March Mon–Fri 10am & 3.30pm. Café Mon–Sat 10am–5pm.

Lagavulin Port Ellen ☎01496 302749, ☜discovering -distilleries.com. Enjoying a fabulous setting in the bay of the same name, Lagavulin – which marked two hundred years of production in 2016 – is probably the classic, all-round Islay malt, with lots of smoke and peat. Tours £6; April–Sept daily 9.30 & 11.30am & 3.30pm; March & Oct Mon–Fri 9.30am & 12.30pm, Sat & Sun 12.30pm; Nov–Feb daily 12.30pm.

Laphroaig Port Ellen ☎01496 302418, ☜laphroaig .com. This famous distillery, in another wonderful setting, celebrated its two-hundredth anniversary in 2015, and is another classic smoky, peaty Islay malt. The third of the island's distilleries to do its own malting, it also has a great little museum. Tours £6; March–Oct Mon–Fri 10.30am & 2 & 3.15pm; Nov–Feb 10am & 2pm.

of spotting a golden eagle, or the rare crow-like chough, and no chance of missing the white-fronted and barnacle geese that winter here in their thousands.

A great time to visit is late May for the **Feis Ile**, or Islay Festival of Malt and Music (☜islayfestival.com), with whisky tasting, piping recitals, folk dancing and other events celebrating the island's Gaelic roots.

ARRIVAL AND DEPARTURE
ISLE OF ISLAY

By plane Islay's airport (☎01496 302361, ☜hial.co.uk) is miles north of Port Ellen on the A846.

Destinations Colonsay (Tues & Thurs 1 daily; 20min);

Glasgow (Mon–Fri 2 daily, Sat 1 daily; 35min); Oban (Tues & Thurs 2 daily; 35min).

By ferry CalMac ferries from Kennacraig on Kintyre

6

connect with both Port Ellen and Port Askaig. There's also a ferry that makes the short trip across to Jura, and, between April and September, a passenger-only ferry between Craighouse and Tayvallich on the mainland.

GETTING AROUND

By bus The island's main bus route links Port Askaig with Bridgend, from where buses continue down to Port Ellen, via Bowmore, and Portnahaven, via Port Charlotte. There is no service in Sundays.

Car rental To save on ferry fares, it's worth considering car rental on the island itself – Islay Car Hire (☎ 01496 810544, ⓦ islaycarhire.com; from around £45/day) will deliver to both ferry terminals and the airport. If driving, there are filling stations at Port Askaig, Bowmore and Bridgend.

Port Ellen and around

Laid out as a planned village in 1821 by Walter Frederick Campbell, and named after his wife, **PORT ELLEN** is the chief port on Islay, with the island's largest fishing fleet, and main CalMac ferry terminal. The neat, whitewashed terraces that overlook the town's bay of golden sand are strikingly pretty, but the view is dominated by the village's modern maltings, whose powerful odours waft across the town.

The distilleries

As you head east out of Port Ellen, a dead-end road passes three **distilleries** in as many miles; however, a more relaxing – indeed, sensible – way of visiting them is to walk the new **three distilleries path**, which begins just outside Port Ellen and links all three. First up is **Laphroaig**, which, as every bottle tells you, is Gaelic for "the beautiful hollow by the bay", and, true enough, the whitewashed distillery is indeed in a gorgeous setting by the sea. Laphroaig also has the stamp of approval from Prince Charles, who famously paid a flying visit to the island in 1994, crashing an airplane of the Queen's Flight in the process.

A mile down the road lies **Lagavulin** distillery, beyond which stands **Dunyvaig Castle**, a romantic ruin on a promontory looking out to the tiny isle of Texa. Another mile further on, the traditional pagoda-style kiln roofs of **Ardbeg** distillery hove into view – in common with all Islay's distilleries, all three offer guided tours (see box, p.267).

Kildalton Chapel

Two miles down the track from Ardbeg and you eventually come to the simple thirteenth-century **Kildalton Chapel**, which has a wonderful eighth-century Celtic ringed cross made from the local "bluestone". The quality of the scenes matches any to be found on the crosses carved by the monks in Iona: the Virgin and Child are on the east face, with Cain murdering Abel to the left, David fighting the lion on the top, and Abraham sacrificing Isaac on the right; on the west side amid the serpent-and-boss work are four elephant-like beasts.

ARRIVAL AND DEPARTURE

PORT ELLEN AND AROUND

By ferry The ferry terminal is a 2min walk from the village's main through roads.
Destinations Kennacraig (3–4 daily; 2hr 20min).
By bus Buses pick up and drop off on Charlotte St in the centre of the village.
Destinations Bowmore (Mon–Sat 8 daily; 25min); Port Askaig (Mon–Sat 3 daily; 50min).

ACCOMMODATION AND EATING

Islay Hotel 18 Charlotte St ☎ 01496 300109, ⓦ theislayhotel.com. One of the finest hotels on the island, with thoroughly modern, sharp-looking rooms, and superbly equipped and very large bathrooms (two with whirlpool bathtub). The *Islay* is also Port Ellen's social hub, with a fine restaurant and a buzzy, more informal whisky bar. The former rustles up sublime dishes like pan-fried turbot with saffron potatoes and white wine cream sauce (£20), while at the latter you can grab a steak pie with creamy mash (£9.50) washed down with a micro-brewed beer. Restaurant: daily noon–2.30pm & 6–9pm; Bar: daily 11am–11pm. **£120**
★**Kintra Farm campsite** 3 miles northwest of Port Ellen ☎ 01496 302051, ⓦ kintrafarm.co.uk. Enjoying stunning situation at the southern tip of sandy Laggan Bay

among the grassy dunes, this is not far off wild camping at its best. Facilities are basic, but there are showers and running water as well as laundry. Once settled in, you're unlikely to bother exploring anywhere else. May–Sept. Per pitch **£16**

Lach Mhara The Oa ☎01496 302666, ⓦlach-mhara .co.uk. Enviably sited near the Carraig Fhada lighthouse, the

"Sea Duck" bed and breakfast offers as restful a stay as you could imagine; two comely, sea-facing rooms with glass doors that open up onto a patio, and underfloor heated bathrooms (not en-suite) set off from the rooms themselves. Breakfast is taken upstairs in the open-plan living area, which otherwise offers tremendous views across to Port Ellen. **£90**

Bowmore

On the north side of the monotonous peat bog of Duich Moss, and the south shore of the tidal Loch Indaal, lies **BOWMORE**, Islay's administrative capital, with a population of around 800. Dominated by the distillery, it's a striking place, laid out in 1768 on a grid plan rather like Inveraray, with the whitewashed terraces of Main Street climbing up the hill in a straight line from the loch to the town's crowning landmark, the **Round Church**, whose central tower looks uncannily like a lighthouse. Built in the round, so that the devil would have no corners in which to hide, it has a plain, wood-panelled interior, with a lovely tiered balcony and a big central mushroom pillar.

6

ARRIVAL AND DEPARTURE
BOWMORE

By bus Buses stop on the main square, which, strangely enough, is called The Square.
Destinations Port Askaig (Mon–Sat 5–6 daily; 25min);

Port Charlotte (Mon–Sat 6 daily; 25min); Port Ellen (Mon–Sat 9 daily; 25min); Portnahaven (Mon–Sat 6 daily; 50min).

GETTING AROUND AND INFORMATION

Bike rental Bike rental is available from the post office at the top of Main St (Mon–Fri 9am–5.30pm, Sat 9am–12.30pm; £10/day; ☎01496 850232).
Tourist office The Square, Main St (April–Sept Mon–Sat

9.30am–5.30pm, Sun noon–3pm; Oct–March Mon–Fri 10am–3pm; ☎01496 305165). The staff here can help you find accommodation anywhere on the island and also on Jura.

ACCOMMODATION AND EATING

Bowmore House Shore St ☎01496 810324, ⓦthebowmorehouse.co.uk. This grand-looking house, positioned on the main road entering the village, has five fabulous rooms exquisitely furnished in different styles, but all with plush carpets and plump beds, as well as sparkling bathrooms replete with luxury toiletries. There's a complimentary laundry service too. **£135**

Lambeth Guesthouse Jamieson St ☎01496 810597, ⓔlambethguesthouse@tiscali.co.uk. Just off Main St, this is a jovially run guesthouse with six modestly sized but

impeccably prepared en-suite rooms. A little tricky to find: it's next to the tiny filling station, the door being around to the side. **£96**

Harbour Inn The Square ☎01496 810330, ⓦharbour -inn.com. Smart, if unadventurously decorated, harbourside restaurant with lovely views, and serving sumptuous plates of food like black squid ink risotto with pickled crab meat (£19.50); scrummy oyster menu too. Alternatively, you can warm yourself by a peat fire in the adjoining pub, where they also do lunchtime bar snacks. Daily noon–2pm & 6–10pm.

Loch Gruinart

Between October and mid-April, it's impossible to miss the island's staggeringly large wintering population of **Greenland barnacle** and **white-fronted geese**. You can see the geese just about anywhere on the island – there are an estimated 5,000 white-fronted and 40,000 barnacles here (and rising) – with the largest concentrations in the fields between Bridgend and Ballygrant, and on the tidal mud flats and fields around **Loch Gruinart**. There's an RSPB-run **visitor centre** (seven miles north of Bridgend on the B8017; daily 10am–5pm; free; ☎01496 850505, ⓦrspb.org.uk/lochgruinart) at the nearby farm of Aoradh (pronounced "oorig"), with a scale model of the reserve and a sightings board, but you're better off getting yourself down to one of the two hides (both open access), just a couple of hundred yards apart from each other overlooking the salt flats and marshes at the head of the loch.

Kilchoman

Without doubt the best sandy beaches on Islay are to be found on the isolated northwest coast near the village of **KILCHOMAN**, in particular, the lovely golden beach of **Machir Bay**, which is backed by great white-sand dunes. The sea here has dangerous undercurrents, however, and is not safe to swim in (the same goes for the much smaller Saligo Bay, to the north), but the beaches are still lovely to walk across.

Port Charlotte

Founded in 1828 by Walter Frederick Campbell, and named after his mother, **PORT CHARLOTTE** was originally set up to provide housing facilities for the workers of the former Lochindaal distillery, which eventually closed in 1929. It's generally agreed to be Islay's prettiest village, its immaculate whitewashed cottages clustered round a sandy cove overlooking Loch Indaal.

Museum of Islay Life

Daal Terrace • April–Sept Mon–Fri 10.30am–4.30pm • £3.50 • ☎ 01496 850358, ⊛ islaymuseum.org

On the northern fringe of the village, in a whitewashed former chapel, the engaging **Museum of Islay Life** is crammed to bursting with local memorabilia. As well as tantalizing snippets about eighteenth-century illegal whisky distillers, there are some terrific photos and a good library of books about the island. Best of all, though, are the displays on the SS *Tuscania* and HMS *Otranto*, both of which were sunk in the waters hereabouts during World War I. Among the exhibits from the *Tuscania* is its bell, a bunk-side cabinet, and the notebook belonging to Sergeant Malcolm McNeill, in which he records the names and conditions of those who perished, including one, he writes rather grimly, "whose body is so much decayed that it is crumbling to pieces".

Islay Natural History Trust Visitor Centre

Main St • May–Sept Mon–Fri 10.30am–4.30pm • £3.50 • ☎ 01496 850288, ⊛ islaynaturalhistory.org

The **Islay Natural History Trust Visitor Centre**, housed in the former distillery warehouse, is well worth a visit for anyone interested in the island's fauna and flora. As well as an extensive library to browse, there's lots of hands-on stuff for kids: microscopes, a touch table full of natural goodies, a sea-water aquarium, a bug world and owl pellets to examine. Tickets are valid for a week, allowing you to go back and identify things you've seen on your travels. They also organize weekly nature rambles each Sunday between July and September (£4), which could be anything from rock-pooling to beachcombing.

ARRIVAL AND DEPARTURE

PORT CHARLOTTE

By bus Buses stop just outside the *Port Charlotte Hotel.*

Destinations Bowmore (Mon–Sat 6 daily; 25min); Port Wemyss (6 daily; 15min).

ACCOMMODATION AND EATING

Port Charlotte Hotel Main St ☎ 01496 850360, ⊛ portcharlottehotel.co.uk. Beautifully appointed whitewashed stone hotel right in the heart of the village overlooking the beach. A handful of the ten rooms have retained their original exposed stone walls, but they're all thoughtfully designed and decorated in bold but beautiful colours. The hotel restaurant is of a similarly high order, though it's much more fun to tuck into one of their seafood lunches out on the patio, for example pan-seared Islay scallops with pancetta and herb oil (£9.75). There's usually live music on Wednesday and Sunday evenings in the bar.

Restaurant 6.30–9pm; bar noon–11pm. **£210**

Port Mòr Campsite Just outside the village out on the road to Portnahaven ☎ 01496 850441, ⊛ islandofislay .co.uk. A community-run campsite with glorious sea views and tip-top facilities: modern shower block, laundry, café and a brilliant playground for the kids. March–Nov. Per pitch **£19**

SYHA Port Charlotte Main St ☎ 01496 850385, ⊛ syha.org.uk. Next door to the Natural History Trust Visitor Centre, Islay's only hostel is housed in an old bonded warehouse by the sea. It possesses a handy mix of double and triples all the way up to six-bed dorms, and each with shared bathroom facilities; there's also a large kitchen and common room. Breakfast £3.95. Mid-March to mid-Oct. Doubles **£45**; dorms **£18.50**

Yan's Kitchen Main St ☎ 01496 850230, ⓦ yanskitchen .co.uk. Opposite the museum in a former croft kitchen, this convivial place offers a clever mix of seafood, grilled meats (duck breast with Stornoway black pudding; £18) and tapas (garlic chicken in scallops, chorizo *con patatas*), the latter coming in at round £3.50 a pop. March–Oct Tues–Sat 10.30am–10pm, Sun 11am–10pm.

Portnahaven and Port Wemyss

6

The main coastal road on Islay culminates seven miles south of Port Charlotte at **PORTNAHAVEN**, a fishing and crofting community since the early nineteenth century. The familiar whitewashed cottages wrap themselves prettily around the steep banks of a deep bay where seals bask on the rocks in considerable numbers; in the distance, you can see Portnahaven's twin settlement, **PORT WEMYSS**, a mile south. The communities share a little whitewashed church, located above the bay in Portnahaven, with separate doors for residents of each village.

ARRIVAL AND DEPARTURE	PORTNAHAVEN AND PORT WEMYSS
By bus Buses make their way into the centre of both villages, dropping off first at Portnahaven.	Destinations Bowmore (Mon–Sat 6 daily; 50min); Port Charlotte (Mon–Sat 6 daily; 15min).

ACCOMMODATION AND EATING

Burnside B&B Shore St, Port Wemyss ☎ 01496 860296, ⓦ burnsidelodge.co.uk. Located just off the coastal path, this sweet little place offers three rooms (one en suite) of modest but tidy proportions. The friendly owner here also rustles up delectable home-baked goodies, in particular cupcakes and muffins; you can enjoy these, with a mug of tea, in the cosy residents' lounge or outside on one of the barrel seats looking across to Rhinns Point, below which seals bask on the shore. Food served April–Sept Fri–Mon 10.30am–4.30pm. **£95**

Loch Finlaggan

Just beyond Ballygrant, on the road to Port Askaig midway between Ballygrant and Port Askaig, a narrow road leads off north to **Loch Finlaggan**, site of a number of **prehistoric crannogs** (artificial islands) and, for four hundred years from the twelfth century, headquarters of the Lords of the Isles, semi-autonomous rulers of the Hebrides and Kintyre. The site is evocative enough, but there are, in truth, very few remains beyond the foundations. Remarkably, the palace that stood here appears to have been unfortified, a testament perhaps to the prosperity and stability of the islands in those days.

To the northeast of the loch, the **information centre** (April–Oct Mon–Sat 10.30am–4.15pm; £2) exhibits a number of extraordinary finds uncovered on the site, notably some twelfth-century leather soles and uppers, and a thirteenth-century cast bronze figure of Christ. From the centre, a path heads down to the site itself, which is dotted with interpretive panels. Duckboards allow you to walk out across the reed beds of the loch and explore the main crannog, **Eilean Mor**, where several carved gravestones are displayed under cover in the chapel, all of which seem to support the theory that the Lords of the Isles buried their wives and children there, while having themselves interred on Iona. Further out into the loch is another smaller crannog, **Eilean na Comhairle**, originally connected to Eilean Mor by a causeway, where the Lords of the Isles are thought to have held meetings of the Council of the Isles.

Port Askaig

Islay's other ferry connection with the mainland, and its sole link with Colonsay and Jura, is from **PORT ASKAIG**, a scattering of buildings which tumbles down a little cove by the narrowest section of the Sound of Islay or Caol Ila. There's next to nothing here, save for a hotel, shop and post office.

ARRIVAL AND TOURS

PORT ASKAIG

By ferry After Port Ellen, Port Askaig is the second of the island's main ferry terminals.
Destinations Colonsay (Wed & Sat 1 daily; 1hr 10min); Feolin ferry to Jura (Mon–Sat hourly, Sun 7 daily; 5min); Kennacraig (3–4 daily; 2hr 5min).
By bus Buses depart from a spot just up from the ferry

terminal.
Destinations Bowmore (Mon–Sat 5–6 daily; 25min); Port Ellen (3 daily; 50min).
Boat tours Based in Port Askaig, Islay Sea Safari (☎ 01496 840510, ⓦ islayseasafari.co.uk) offers high-adrenaline boat trips round the distilleries in a rigid inflatable.

ACCOMMODATION AND EATING

★**Ballygrant Inn** Ballygrant ☎ 01496 840277, ⓦ ballygrant-inn.co.uk. Incredibly hospitable, family-run affair, with seven immaculately kept rooms. Its restaurant is top-notch, serving the likes of Islay venison and red wine casserole (£13.95), though it's the brilliant bar, stocking some 400 whiskies and voted Scotland's Whisky Bar of 2015, that's the real draw; the half a dozen tasting menus (from £22) are far superior to anything offered in the distilleries, so a visit is very much the order of the day. Mon–Sat 11am–1am, Sun 12.30pm–midnight. **£80**
Kilmeny Farmhouse Ballygrant ☎ 01496 840668, ⓦ kilmeny.co.uk. Three miles south of Port Askaig, this whitewashed farmhouse is a place that richly deserves all the superlatives it regularly receives. Antique furnishings,

locally made fabrics and slipper baths feature in some or all of the four colour-coordinated rooms. You can expect to be well pampered for the duration of your stay, and the gourmet breakfast is a real treat, comprising, among other things, poached plums, Scottish pancake stack, and smoked Argyll salmon and scrambled eggs. March–Nov. **£138**
Persabus Farm 1.5km inland from Port Askaig ☎ 01496 840243, ⓦ persabus.co.uk. Out on the road to Bunnahabhain, one of the farm's outbuildings is now a delightful café-cum-pottery, where everything is handcrafted and fired on site – you can even have a go yourself, and while you're waiting for it to be set, partake in a fresh cup of coffee with a slice of scrummy home-made cake. Daily noon–4.30pm.

Isle of Jura

Twenty-eight miles long and eight miles wide, the long whale-shaped island of **JURA** is one of the wildest and most mountainous of the Inner Hebrides, its entire west coast uninhabited and inaccessible except to the dedicated walker. The distinctive **Paps of Jura**, so-called because of their smooth breast-like shape, seem to dominate every view off the west coast of Argyll, their glacial rounded tops covered in a light dusting of quartzite scree. The island's name is commonly thought to derive from the Norse *dyr-oe* (deer island) and, appropriately enough, the current deer population of 6000 outnumbers the 190 or so humans 33 to 1; other wildlife to look out for include mountain hares and eagles. With just one road, which sticks to the more sheltered eastern coast of the island, and only one hotel, a couple of B&Bs and some self-catering cottages, Jura is an ideal place to go for peace and quiet, and some great walking.

Craighouse

Anything that happens on Jura happens in the island's only real village, **CRAIGHOUSE**, eight miles up the road from Feolin Ferry. The village enjoys a sheltered setting, overlooking Knapdale on the mainland – so sheltered, in fact, that there are even a few palm trees thriving on the seafront. In terms of facilities, and things to see and do, there's a shop/post office, hotel and tearoom, plus the tiny **Isle of Jura distillery**.

Isle of Jura distillery

Opposite the Jura Hotel • Guided tours Mon–Fri 11am & 2pm, plus Sat April–Oct • £6 • ☎ 01496 820385, ⓦ jurawhisky.com

Established in 1810 by the Campbells, the **Isle of Jura distillery** has endured a somewhat chequered history. It went out of business in the early 1900s, before reopening in 1963 on the premises of the then derelict distillery. It now produces four distinctive single malts, with two notable success stories, the ten-year-old "Origin", and the sixteen-year-old "Diurachs' Own" – you'll get to sample one or both of these on one of the guided tours.

GEORGE ORWELL ON JURA

In April 1946, Eric Blair (better known by his pen name of **George Orwell**), intending to give himself "six months' quiet" in which to complete his latest novel, moved to a remote farmhouse called **Barnhill**, at the northern end of Jura, which he had visited for the first time the previous year. He appears to have relished the challenge of a spartan existence here with his adopted 3-year-old son Richard, and later his sister Avril; fishing almost every night, shooting rabbits, laying lobster pots and even attempting a little farming. The book Orwell was writing, under the working title *The Last Man in Europe*, was to become *1984* (the title was arrived at by simply reversing the last two digits of the year in which it was finished – 1948). During his time on Jura, however, Orwell was suffering badly from tuberculosis, and eventually he was forced to return to London, where he died in January 1950.

Barnhill, 23 miles north of Craighouse, is as remote today as it was in Orwell's day. The road deteriorates rapidly beyond Lealt, where vehicles must be left, leaving pilgrims a four-mile walk to the house itself. Alternatively, the Richardsons of Kinuachdrachd (☎07899 912116) can organize a taxi and guided walk, and also run a bunkhouse. Orwell wrote most of the book in the bedroom (top left window as you look at the house); the place is now a self-catering cottage (☎01786 850274). If you're keen on making the journey out to Barnhill, you might as well combine it with a trip to the nearby **Corryvreckan Whirlpool**, which lies between Jura and Scarba, to the north (see below). Orwell nearly drowned in the whirlpool during a fishing trip in August 1947, along with his three companions (including Richard): the outboard motor was washed away, and they had to row to a nearby island and wait for several hours before being rescued by a passing fisherman.

Corryvreckan Whirlpool

Between the islands of Scarba and Jura is the raging **Corryvreckan Whirlpool** (ⓦwhirlpool-scotland.co.uk), one of the world's most spectacular whirlpools – and supposedly the third largest – thought to be caused by a rocky pinnacle some 100ft below the sea. Exactly how the whirlpool appears depends on the tide and wind, but there's a potential tidal flow of over eight knots, which, when accompanied by gale-force winds, can create standing waves up to 15ft high. Inevitably there are numerous legends about the place – known as *coire bhreacain* (speckled cauldron) in Gaelic – concerning *Cailleach* (Hag), the Celtic storm goddess. From the land, the best place from which to view it is Carraig Mhor on the northern tip of Jura, though the best trips to the whirlpool – which can be quite spectacular, and hair-raising – depart from Seil (see p.256).

ARRIVAL AND DEPARTURE   ISLE OF JURA

By ferry The Feolin ferry from Port Askaig will not run if there's a strong northerly or southerly wind, so bring your toothbrush. If you're coming for a day-trip. Roughly six times a day, the Jura minibus (☎01496 820314) meets the car ferry from Port Askaig and goes up to Inverlussa via Craighouse – phone ahead to check times.
Destinations Port Askaig (Mon–Sat every 45–60min, Sun

7 daily; 5min; £3.95 return, car £14.95 return).
By passenger ferry Between April and September, there's also a passenger ferry service (☎07768 450000, ⓦjurapassengerferry.com; £20) from Tayvallich, on the Argyll mainland, to Craighouse; bikes can be carried too.
Destinations Tayvallich (Mon, Tues & Thurs–Sat 2 daily, Sun 1 daily; 1hr).

ACCOMMODATION AND EATING

The Antlers 100yds north of the distillery ☎01496 820496. Delightful bistro restaurant that serves up burgers, sandwiches and salads for lunch, and beautifully presented Jura lamb on the one evening it's open, for which you must book. Unlicensed, but you're welcome to bring your own corkage £3). Daily 10am–4pm, plus Fri 6.30–8.30pm.
Jura Hotel Craighouse ☎01496 820243, ⓦjura hotel.co.uk. The island's one and only hotel is not much

to look at from the outside, but it's warm and friendly within and the rooms are right up to the mark. Campers are welcome to pitch tents in the field fronting the hotel, and there's a shower block and laundry facilities round the back. Unsurprisingly, it's also the centre of the island's social scene, with a restaurant, lounge-bar and pub. Bar: daily 11am–11pm. Pitch £5 (showers £1); __£95__

6

Stirling, Loch Lomond and the Trossachs

WOODLANDS IN THE TROSSACHS

Stirling, Loch Lomond and the Trossachs

The central lowlands of Scotland were, for several centuries, the most strategically important area in the country. In 1250, a map of Britain was compiled by a monk of St Albans, which depicted Scotland as two separate land masses connected only by the thin band of Stirling Bridge; although this was a figurative interpretation, it is true that Stirling was once the only gateway from the fertile central belt to the rugged, mountainous north. For long periods of Scotland's history kings, queens, nobles, clan chiefs and soldiers wrestled for control of the area, and it's no surprise that today the landscape is littered with remnants of the past – well-preserved medieval towns and castles, royal residences and battle-sites.

7

Lying at the heart of Scotland, **Stirling** and its fine **castle**, from where you can see both snowcapped Highland peaks and Edinburgh, are unmissable for anyone wanting to grasp the complexities of Scottish history. The castle esplanade commands an impressive view of the surrounding area, including the rocket-like **National Wallace Monument**, a Victorian homage to a local hero.

To the south of the city, on the road to Edinburgh, lies **Falkirk**, its industrial heritage enlivened by the intriguing Falkirk Wheel; to the east, the gentle Ochil Hills run towards Fife. The highlight of the string of mostly drab towns at the foot of the Ochils is handsome **Dollar**, from where a path leads up the steep glen to dramatically perched Castle Campbell. The flat plain extending west, the **Carse of Stirling**, has the little-visited **Campsie Fells** on its southern edge and the fabled mountains, glens, lochs and forests of the **Trossachs**, stretching west from **Callander** to Loch Lomond, to the north. Here you'll find abundant opportunities for hiking and mountain biking, as well as sublime mountain scenery.

On the western side of the region, **Loch Lomond** is the largest – and most romanticized – stretch of fresh water in Scotland. At the heart of the Loch Lomond and the Trossachs National Park, the peerless scenery of the loch can be tainted by the sheer numbers of tourists and day-trippers who flock here in summer. It can get similarly clogged in parts of the neighbouring Trossachs, although there's much to appreciate once you break away from the main routes. The area is particularly good for **outdoor activities**: it's traversed by the **Glasgow–Loch Lomond–Killin cycleway**; the forest tracks are ideal for mountain biking; the mountains of the Trossachs provide great hiking; and the **West Highland Way**, Scotland's premier long-distance footpath, winds along the length of Loch Lomond up to Fort William in the Highlands.

GETTING AROUND AND INFORMATION   CENTRAL SCOTLAND

By train, bus, car or bike While Stirling, Falkirk and Perth are well served by trains from all over Scotland, the rest of the region is only accessible on sporadic local bus services so you may find it easier to have your own transport. Many people opt to explore the Trossachs by mountain bike. For a bus network map see ⓦ firstgroup.com.

Tourist information See ⓦ visitstirling.org.

The Antonine Wall p.288
Hiking and biking in the Trossachs p.296

Rob Roy p.297
Cruises on Loch Katrine p.298

FALKIRK WHEEL

Highlights

❶ **Stirling Castle** Impregnable, impressive and resonant with history. If you see only one castle in Scotland, make it this one. **See p.280**

❷ **A dram at Deanston Distillery** Deanston produce a relatively new, non-peaty whisky, which you can sample in the beautiful surroundings of a former mill village. **See p.287**

❸ **Falkirk Wheel** The most remarkable piece of modern engineering in Britain, this fascinating contraption lifts boats 100ft between two canals. **See p.288**

❹ **Inchcailloch** Putter out on a Loch Lomond mail boat to this tranquil wooded island at the heart of Scotland's first national park. **See p.292**

❺ **Mountain biking in the Trossachs** Cycle along a loch, ride a forest path or travel the National Cycle Network from Loch Lomond to Killin. **See p.296**

❻ **The Lake of Menteith** One of the loveliest stretches of water in the country, with fishing, swimming and boat trips to an island with a romantic ruined abbey. **See p.296**

❼ **Food at Brig o'Turk** This tiny Trossachs village has two enticing eating options: a wood-lined tearoom serving great cakes, and a gastro pub set in a rugged stone barn. **See p.298**

HIGHLIGHTS ARE MARKED ON THE MAP ON PP.278–279

Stirling

Straddling the River Forth a few miles upstream from the estuary at Kincardine, **STIRLING** appears at first glance like a smaller version of Edinburgh. With its crag-top castle, steep, cobbled streets and mixed community of locals, students and tourists, it's a fairly appealing city, though it definitely lacks the cosmopolitan edge of its near neighbours Edinburgh and Glasgow.

STIRLING, LOCH LOMOND & THE TROSSACHS

Stirling was the scene of some of the most significant developments in the evolution of the Scottish nation. It was here in 1297 that the Scots, under William Wallace, defeated the English at the **Battle of Stirling Bridge**, only to fight – and win again – under Robert the Bruce just a couple of miles away at the **Battle of Bannockburn** in 1314. Stirling enjoyed its golden age in the fifteenth to seventeenth centuries, most notably when its castle was the favoured residence of the Stuart monarchy and the setting for the coronation in 1543 of the young Mary, future Queen of Scots.

HIGHLIGHTS

1. Stirling Castle
2. A dram at Deanston Distillery
3. Falkirk Wheel
4. Inchcailloch
5. Mountain biking in the Trossachs
6. The Lake of Menteith
7. Food at Brig O'Turk

Today the city is best known for its **castle** and the lofty **National Wallace Monument**, a mammoth Victorian monolith high on Abbey Craig to the northeast.

Stirling Castle

Old Town • Daily: April–Sept 9.30am–6pm; Oct–March 9.30am–5pm • £14.50, includes entry to Argyll's Lodging (see p.282); audio-guide £3; car park £4; HES • ☎ 01786 450000, ⓦ stirlingcastle.gov.uk

Stirling Castle presented would-be invaders with a formidable challenge. Its impregnability is most daunting when you approach the town from the west, from where the sheer 250ft drop down the side of the crag is most obvious. The rock was first fortified during the Iron Age, though what you see now dates largely from the fifteenth and sixteenth centuries. On many levels, the main buildings are interspersed with delightful gardens and patches of lawn, while endless battlements, cannon ports, hidden staircases and other nooks and crannies make it thoroughly explorable and inspiring.

7

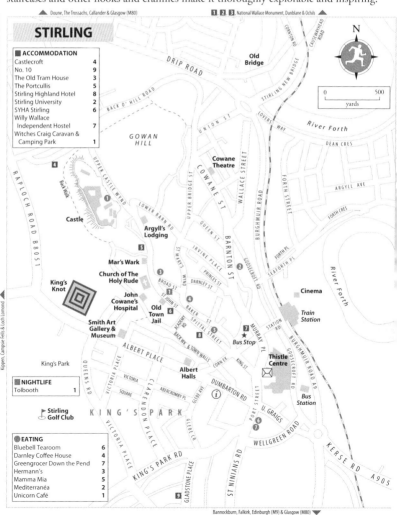

STIRLING

■ **ACCOMMODATION**
Castlecroft	4
No. 10	9
The Old Tram House	3
The Portcullis	5
Stirling Highland Hotel	8
Stirling University	2
SYHA Stirling	6
Willy Wallace Independent Hostel	7
Witches Craig Caravan & Camping Park	1

■ **NIGHTLIFE**
Tolbooth	1

● **EATING**
Bluebell Tearoom	6
Darnley Coffee House	4
Greengrocer Down the Pend	7
Hermann's	3
Mamma Mia	5
Mediterranéa	2
Unicorn Café	1

Doune, The Trossachs, Callander & Glasgow (M80)

National Wallace Monument, Dunblane & Ochils

N

0 — 500 yards

Old Bridge

DRIP ROAD

STIRLING NEW BRIDGE

LOVERS WAY

River Forth

BACK O' HILL ROAD

UNION ST

DEAN CRES

GOWAN HILL

UPPER CASTLE WYND

Castle

Back Walk

RAPLOCH ROAD B8051

King's Knot

Kippen, Campsie Fells & Loch Lomond

Mar's Wark
Church of The Holy Rude
John Cowane's Hospital
Smith Art Gallery & Museum
Old Town Jail

Argyll's Lodging

LOWER BARN RD
UPPER BRIDGE ST
COWANE ST
WALLACE STREET

Cowane Theatre

QUEEN ST
BARNTON ST
BURGHMUIR ROAD
FORTH STREET

ARGYLL AVE
FORTH CRES

IRVINE PLACE
ST MARYS WYND
BROAD ST
DARNLEY ST
PRINCES ST
GOOSECROFT

River Forth

Cinema

Train Station

Bus Stop

King's Park

ALBERT PLACE
Albert Halls
VICTORIA PLACE
SQUARE
ABERCROMBY PL
DUMBARTON RD
GLEBE AVE
CORN EX
KING ST

Thistle Centre

Bus Station

KING'S PARK

VICTORIA PLACE

KING'S PARK RD

GLADSTONE PLACE

ST NINIANS RD

WELLGREEN ROAD

GOOSECROFT RD A9

KERSE RD A905

Stirling Golf Club

For the chance to see the castle at night, look out for special **events** such as the Hogmanay (new year) party and concerts in the atmospheric Great Hall by luminaries such as the Scottish Chamber Orchestra.

The Great Hall
In the central part of the castle, the **Outer Close** is the first of two main courtyard areas. Looming over it is the magnificently restored **Great Hall**, dating from 1501–03 and used as a barracks by the British army until 1964. The building stands out across Stirling for its controversially bright, creamy yellow cladding, added in the 1990s after the discovery during renovations of a stretch of the original sixteenth-century limewash behind a bricked-up doorway. Inside, the hall has been restored to its original state as the finest medieval secular building in Scotland, complete with five gaping fireplaces and an impressive hammer beam ceiling of rough-hewn wood created from 35 oak trees.

The Palace
The exterior of the **Palace**, the largest building in the castle, dates from 1540–42 and is richly decorated with grotesque carved figures and Renaissance sculpture, including, in the left-hand corner, the glaring bearded figure of James V in the dress of a commoner. Inside in the royal apartments are the **Stirling Heads**, 56 elegantly carved oak medallions that once comprised the ceiling of the Presence Chamber, where visitors were presented to royalty. Now costumed actors play the role of various nobles, while specially commissioned furniture and tapestries – the result of an impressive fourteen-year research and weaving project – have returned the rooms to something like their appearance in the mid-sixteenth century.

7

Chapel Royal and the King's Old Building
On one side of the Inner Close, the steeply sloping upper courtyard of the castle, is the **Chapel Royal**, built in 1594 by James VI for the baptism of his son. Alongside, the **King's Old Building**, at the highest point in the castle, houses the museum of the Argyll and Sutherland Highlanders regiment, with its collection of well-polished silver and memorabilia.

Douglas Gardens
Go through a narrow passageway between the King's Old Building and the Chapel Royal to get to the **Douglas Gardens**, reputedly the place where the eighth earl of Douglas, suspected of treachery, was thrown to his death by James II in 1452. It's a lovely, quiet corner of the castle, with mature trees and battlements over which there are splendid views of the Highlands, as well as a bird's-eye view down to the **King's Knot**, a series of grassed octagonal mounds which in the seventeenth century were planted with box trees and ornamental hedges.

The Old Town
Stirling evolved from its castle, gradually spreading south and east onto the low-lying flood plain. At the centre of the original **Old Town**, Broad Street was the main thoroughfare, with St John Street running more or less parallel, and St Mary's Wynd forming part of the original route to Stirling Bridge below. Because Stirling is a compact town, sightseeing in the Old Town is best done on foot.

Town Walls
The old centre of Stirling is fortified behind the massive, whinstone boulders of the **town walls**, built in the mid-sixteenth century and intended to ward off the advances of Henry VIII, who had set his sights on the young Mary, Queen of Scots as a wife for his son, Edward. The walls now constitute some of the best-preserved town defences in

Scotland, and can be traced by following the path known as **Back Walk**. This walkway was built in the eighteenth century and in the upper reaches leads right under the castle, taut along the edge of the crag. It's a great way to take in the castle's setting, and gives panoramic views of the countryside.

Argyll's Lodging

At the top of Castle Wynd • Guided tour only; book on ☎ 01786 450000 • Entry included with ticket to Stirling Castle

Argyll's Lodging is a romantic Renaissance townhouse built by Sir William Alexander of Menstrie in the seventeenth century. Once the home of Alexander, the first earl of Stirling, it was later used as a military hospital and youth hostel. The oldest part of the building, with its low ceilings and tiny windows, is the Great Kitchen, whose enormous fireplace comes complete with a special recess for salt, while the Drawing Room, hung with lavishly decorated purple tapestries, contains the ninth earl's imposing chair of state.

Mar's Wark and Church of the Holy Rude

Down Castle Wynd and at the top of Broad Street, a richly decorated facade is about all that survives of **Mar's Wark**, a would-be palace that the first earl of Mar, regent of Scotland and hereditary Keeper of Stirling Castle, started in 1570. His dream house was never to be realized, however, for he died two years later and what had been built was left to ruin, its degeneration speeded up by extensive damage during the 1745 Jacobite rebellion.

Behind here is the **Church of the Holy Rude** (Easter–Sept daily 11am–4pm), the oldest parts of which, including the impressive oak hammer beam ceiling, date from the early fifteenth century.

John Cowane's Hospital

49 St John St • ☎ 01786 472247, Ⓦ cowanes.org.uk

Near the Church of the Holy Rude and on the edge of the crag, the rugged, whitewashed **John Cowane's Hospital** was built in 1649 as an almshouse for, at its founder John Cowane's request, "decayed [unsuccessful] members of the Guild of Merchants". Above the entrance, Cowane, a wealthy merchant himself, is commemorated in a painted statue that, it is said, comes alive at Hogmanay. The almshouse is currently closed for restoration, with plans to reopen it as an events and exhibition space.

Old Town Jail

St John St • July–Sept daily 10am–5pm • £6.50 • ☎ 01786 475019

A sweeping driveway leads from St John Street and up to the impressive **Old Town Jail**, built by Victorian prison reformers as an alternative to the depravity of the medieval Tolbooth. Subsequently used as a military jail, it was rescued from dereliction in 1994, with part of the building turned into offices and a substantial section used to create a (summer-only) visitor attraction. Telling the history of the building and prisons in general, tours are taken by actors, who enthusiastically change costumes and character a number of times; among the features of the jail they'll introduce you to is a working example of the dreaded crank, a lever that prisoners had to turn 14,400 times a day. Take the glass lift up to the prison roof to admire spectacular **views** across Stirling and the Forth Valley.

Opposite and just uphill from the entrance to the Old Town Jail on St John Street, look out for the **Boys' Club**, a 1929 conversion of the town's old butter market, with its encouraging little mottoes engraved above the door such as "Keep smiling" and "Quarrelling is taboo".

Tolbooth

Jail Wynd • Daily from 9am • See website for admission charges • ☎ 01786 274000, Ⓦ culturestirling.org/tolbooth

The town's original medieval prison is the **Tolbooth**, now an innovative music and arts centre. Originally built in 1705, the striking modern redevelopment received an architectural award as the UK's best public building. During the renovations a secret staircase was discovered, as was a complete skeleton, thought to have been that of the last man publicly hanged in Stirling. Inside there's access to a top-floor viewing platform looking out over the Old Town rooftops and a box office where you can find out about the centre's programme, which mostly centres on modern folk music (see p.285).

Mercat Cross and Darnley's House

On Broad Street, the town's former marketplace, the various historical buildings and monuments include the stone **Mercat Cross** (the unicorn on top is known, inexplicably, as "the puggy") and **Darnley's House**, where Mary, Queen of Scots' husband is believed to have lodged while she lorded it up in the castle; it now houses a coffee shop (see p.284).

The Lower Town and around

In the eighteenth and nineteenth centuries, as the threat of attack on Stirling decreased, the centre of commercial life crept down towards the River Forth, with the modern town growing on the edge of the plain over which the castle stands guard. By the time the two main streets of the Old Town merge into King Street, austere Victorian facades block the sun from the cobbled road. The fifteenth-century **Old Bridge** over the Forth lies to the north on the edge of the town centre. Although once the most important river crossing in Scotland, it now stands virtually forgotten, an incidental reminder of Stirling's former importance.

7

Smith Art Gallery and Museum

Dumbarton Rd • Tues–Sat 10.30am–5pm, Sun 2–5pm • Free • ☎ 01786 471917, ⓦ smithartgalleryandmuseum.co.uk

The **Smith Art Gallery and Museum** sits near the edge of town near the King's Knot. Founded in 1874 with a legacy from local painter and collector Thomas Stuart Smith, it attempts to balance the stories of kings and queens with more social and domestic history. The museum's collection includes the world's oldest known football, made out of a pig's bladder; found in the rafters of the Queen's Chamber in the castle, it is thought to date from the 1540s. The small art gallery includes changing displays of mostly local arts and crafts, contemporary art and photography, and there's a pleasant café.

The National Wallace Monument

1.5 miles north of the Old Town • Daily: April–June & Sept–Oct 10am–5pm; July & Aug 10am–6pm; Nov–March 10.30am–4pm • £9.99 • ☎ 01786 472140, ⓦ nationalwallacemonument.com • Served by various local buses including First's #63 from Murray Place

A mile and a half north of the Old Town, the prominent **National Wallace Monument** is a freestanding, five-storey tower built in the 1860s as a tribute to Sir William Wallace, the freedom fighter who led Scottish resistance to Edward I, the "Hammer of the Scots", in the late thirteenth century. The crag on which the monument is set was the scene of Wallace's greatest victory, when he sent his troops charging down the hillside onto the plain to defeat the English at the Battle of Stirling Bridge in 1297. An audio-tour handset (free) leads you round inside the tower, where you can find Wallace's long steel sword and the Hall of (Scottish) Heroes, a row of stern white marble busts featuring John Knox and Adam Smith. If you can manage the climb – up 246 spiral steps – to the top of the 220ft **tower**, you'll be rewarded with superb views across to Fife and Ben Lomond. There's a handy coffee shop at the car park level for refuelling.

ARRIVAL AND DEPARTURE	STIRLING
By train The train station is near the centre of town on Station Rd, a 2min walk from the bus station and a 5min walk from the town centre.	**Destinations** Aberdeen (hourly; 2hr 5min); Dundee (hourly; 55min); Edinburgh (every 30min; 1hr); Falkirk (every 30min; 30min); Glasgow Queen Street (every 20min; 25–40min);

Inverness (3–5 daily; 2hr 55min); Perth (hourly; 30min).

By bus The bus station is on Goosecroft Rd, within easy walking distance of the centre.

Destinations Aberfoyle (4 daily; 45min); Callander (every 40min–1hr; 45min); Dollar (every 2hr; 35min); Doune (every 40min–1hr; 25min); Dunblane (hourly; 20min); Dundee (hourly; 1hr 30min); Edinburgh (hourly; 1hr); Falkirk (hourly; 30min); Glasgow (hourly; 50min); Inverness (every 2hr; 3hr 20min); Perth (hourly; 40min); St Andrews (every 2hr; 1hr 55min).

INFORMATION

Tourist office The main tourist office is in the Old Town Jail in the historic part of town, towards the castle, on St John St (daily 10am–5pm; ☎01786 475019).

ACCOMMODATION

Castlecroft Ballengeich Rd ☎01786 474933, ⓦcastlecroft-uk.com. Modern guesthouse with six en-suite rooms on the site of the King's Stables just beneath the castle rock, with terrific views north and west, and a very friendly welcome. **£65**

No. 10 10 Gladstone Place ☎01786 472681, ⓦcameron-10.co.uk. Modernized Victorian home with neat, uncluttered decor providing friendly and pleasant B&B accommodation. It's close to the city centre, but on a quiet and elegant King's Park street. **£70**

The Old Tram House 42 Causewayhead Rd ☎01786 449774, ⓦcastlecroft-uk.com. Located near the Wallace Monument, this Victorian stone house features chintzy, cosy decor, lavish breakfasts (haggis optional) and a warm welcome. **£50**

The Portcullis Castle Wynd ☎01786 472290, ⓦtheportcullishotel.com. Traditional and slightly fusty hotel with four en-suite rooms in an imposing building dating from 1787 with a dramatic Old Town location adjacent to the castle. Old-fashioned bar, open log fire and beer garden. **£109**

Stirling Highland Hotel Spittal St ☎01786 272727, ⓦthehotelcollection.co.uk/hotels/stirling-highland-hotel. Upmarket if rather pretentiously genteel hotel in a handsome Victorian Gothic building that once housed Stirling High School and still maintains an observatory on the top floor. It is just 500yds from the castle and features comfortable rooms and leisure facilities. **£95**

SYHA Stirling St John St ☎01786 473442, ⓦsyha.org.uk. Situated at the top of the town (a strenuous trek with a backpack), in a converted church with an impressive 1824 Palladian facade. The small dorms all have en-suite showers and toilets, and facilities include a games room and internet access. Dorms **£13.50**; doubles **£34**

Willy Wallace Independent Hostel 77 Murray Place ☎01786 446773, ⓦwillywallacehostel.com. Located 100yds from the station in a Victorian building on a busy street, this is the liveliest (and noisiest) budget option in town, with a big common room (complete with wi-fi, guitar and piano), five dorms, a family room and a couple of double and twin rooms. Dorms **£12**; doubles **£36**

SELF-CATERING

Stirling University Bridge of Allan ☎01786 467141, ⓦwww.stir.ac.uk/about/short-breaks-and-vacations. Campus accommodation in halls of residence, wooden chalets and self-catering flats a couple of miles north of the town centre. The famously leafy and beautiful campus is served by regular buses from Murray Place in the town centre. Accommodation is available June to early Sept. Per person **£15**

CAMPING

★**Witches Craig Caravan & Camping Park** Blairlogie, 3 miles east of the centre off the A91 to St Andrews ☎01786 474947, ⓦwitchescraig.co.uk. A very attractive and multi-award-winning site tucked under the Ochil Hills. Take #62 bus from Stirling. April–Oct Per pitch **£20**

EATING

Bluebell Tea Room 1a Pitt Terrace ☎07580 914740, ⓦbluebelltearoom.com. Traditional Scottish afternoon tea (£12.95) is the thing to have in this bright little café: loose-leaf tea, fruit loaves and scones and delicious cakes. All options are available gluten-free. Mon–Sat 9am–5pm, Sun 11am–4pm.

Darnley Coffee House 18 Bow St (the continuation of Broad St) ☎01786 474468. A bit old-fashioned but with plenty of Old Town atmosphere and serving reasonably priced lunches, teas and home-made cakes in an impressive sixteenth-century barrel-vaulted interior. Snacks from round £6. Daily 11am–4pm.

Greengrocer Down the Pend 81 Port St ☎01786 479159. A handy coffee or lunch stop, this lively deli/caf tucked down a pend (passageway) in the centre of town serves delicious home-made soups for around £5, plus sharing platters, hearty sandwiches, scones and cakes. Mon–Sat 9am–5.30pm.

★**Hermann's** Mar Place House, 58 Broad St ☎01786 450632, ⓦhermanns-restaurant.co.uk. The classiest option in Stirling, Hermann's is set in the historic and stately Mar Place House towards the top of the Old Town with views of the Church of the Holy Rude. It operates brasserie-style at lunchtime and offers upmarket Austrian-Scottish dining such as *jäger schnitzel* (veal) or Scottish lamb with cheese potatoes in the evening (mains around £15). Daily noon–2.30pm & 6–11pm.

Mamma Mia 52 Spittal St ☏01786 446124, ⓦmammamiastirling.com. Set in an Old Town mansion, this is an irrepressibly friendly southern Italian restaurant, run by some boys from Bari. They specialize in seafood dishes such as *spaghetti alla pescatora* (£18.50) as well as Italian standards. Mon & Tues 5–11pm, Wed–Sat noon–3pm & 5–11pm, Sun noon–9pm.

Mediterránea 4 Viewfield Place ☏01786 478534, ⓦmediterranearestaurant.co.uk. Spanish tapas (from £4.25) and moderately priced pan-Mediterranean dishes (such as moussaka for £10.95) in an upbeat atmosphere. Daily 5.30–10pm.

Unicorn Café Stirling Castle ☏01786 450000, ⓦstirlingcastle.gov.uk/shop-eat/cafe. The castle's efficiently run café is a better-than-average spot for a simple soup (£4.75) and sandwich or coffee and cake. The rooftop terrace enjoys sweeping views. April–Sept 9.30am–6pm; Oct–March 9.30am–5pm.

NIGHTLIFE AND ENTERTAINMENT

MacRobert Arts Centre On the university campus at Bridge of Allan ☏01786 466666, ⓦmacrobertartscentre.org. Shows mainstream and art-house films, and hosts theatre, music and dance events. The campus itself is regularly voted the most beautiful in Scotland.

★**Tolbooth** Jail Wynd ☏01786 274000, ⓦculture stirling.org/tolbooth. By far the best option for a night out, the Tolbooth has a glamorous high-ceilinged bar (open only when there's an event on) and a folk-orientated live music programme, with occasional classical and jazz concerts. Open daily.

Around Stirling

Just on the outskirts of town is **Bannockburn**, one of the country's most significant battlefields, while the satellite town of **Bridge of Allan** offers more sedate attractions. North and west of Stirling are the historic draws of the cathedral at **Dunblane**, the imposing castle at **Doune** and the attractive settlements of the **Carse of Stirling**, while, on either side of the Forth, the county of **Clackmannanshire** lies at the foot of the **Ochil Hills**. A highlight of the semi-industrial hinterland to the east and south of the city is the massive **Falkirk Wheel**, a spectacular feat of modern engineering. Rugged ruined castles are the draw at both **Dollar** and **Loch Leven**.

Bannockburn Heritage Centre

.872, 2 miles south of Stirling city centre • Daily: March–Oct 9am–5.30pm; Nov–Feb 9am–5pm • ☏ 0844 493 2139, ⓦbattleof annockburn.com • £11.50 • #24, #52 or #57 bus from Stirling bus station or Murray Place

A couple of miles south of Stirling, all but surrounded by drab suburban housing, the **Bannockburn Heritage Centre** commemorates the most famous battle in Scottish history, when King Robert the Bruce won his mighty victory over the English at the **Battle of Bannockburn** on June 24, 1314. It was this battle, the climax of the Wars of Independence, which united the Scots under Bruce and led to independence from England, sealed by the Declaration of Arbroath (1320) and the Treaty of Northampton (1328).

The main focus of the visitor centre is a **3-D military game** for kids, and there is interactive material where you can listen to a range of accounts of the proceedings. The whole affair is over-reliant on digital technology, impressive though that is, and lacks the emotional punch of an actual site: most experts agree that the location of the visitor entre is not that of the real-life battle.

Dunblane

Small, attractive **DUNBLANE** has been an important ecclesiastical centre since the eventh century, when the Celts founded the church of St Blane here. The cathedral, raised in the highest terms by John Ruskin, stands serenely amid a clutch of d buildings.

Dunblane Cathedral

The Cross • April–Sept Mon–Sat 9.30am–12.30pm & 1.30–5pm, Sun 2–5pm; Oct–March Mon–Sat 9.30am–4pm, Sun 2–4pm • Free; HES • ☎ 01786 825388, ⓦ historicenvironment.scot

Dunblane Cathedral dates mainly from the thirteenth century, and restoration work carried out a century ago returned it to its Gothic splendour. Inside, note the delicate blue-purple stained glass, and the exquisitely carved pews, screen and choir stalls, all crafted in the early twentieth century. Memorials include a tenth-century Celtic cross-slab standing stone and a modern, four-sided standing stone commemorating the tragic shooting in 1996 of sixteen Dunblane schoolchildren and their teacher.

Dunblane Museum

The Cross • May to early Oct Mon–Sat 10.30am–4.30pm • Free • ☎ 01786 825691

The seventeenth-century Dean's House contains the small **Dunblane Museum**, which has exhibits on local history, memorabilia from the battle of Sherrifmuir, medieval coins and suchlike. There's also a display on Dunblane's favourite son, **Andy Murray**, who triumphantly won the men's singles at Wimbledon in 2013 and 2016, as well as Olympic gold medals in London 2012 and Rio 2016: you can see a signed tennis racquet, plus his Olympic cap and jacket from the London 2012 Olympics.

Leighton Library

61 High St • May–Sept Mon–Sat 11am–1pm • Donation requested • ☎ 01786 822296, ⓦ leightonlibrary.co.uk

The crow-stepped and whitewashed **Leighton Library**, established in 1684, is the oldest private lending library in Scotland and houses 4500 books in ninety languages, printed between 1500 and 1840. Visitors can browse through some of the country's rarest books, including a first edition of Sir Walter Scott's *Lady of the Lake*.

ARRIVAL AND DEPARTURE   **DUNBLANE**

By train Frequent trains connect Stirling with Dunblane (every 20min; 13min); the station is a 10min walk south of the city centre.

By bus Occasional buses (#47 and #C48 from Stirling bus station) make the journey five miles north of Stirling t Dunblane train station.

ACCOMMODATION AND DRINKING

Chimes House B&B Cathedral Square ☎ 01786 822481, ⓦ bedandbreakfast-scotland.co.uk. A friendly, old-fashioned B&B which overlooks the cathedral and offers pleasant en-suite doubles as well as a good Scottish breakfast. **£50**

Tappit Hen Kirk St ☎ 01786 825226, ⓦ thetappithen -dunblane.co.uk. This trad flower-bedecked pub right b the cathedral is a good place for a pint of real ale, and host regular folk music nights. Sun–Thurs 11am–midnigh Fri & Sat 11am–1am.

Doune

DOUNE, eight miles northwest of Stirling and three miles due west of Dunblane, is a sleepy village surrounding a medieval **castle**, a marvellous semi-ruin standing on a small hill in a bend of the River Teith.

Doune castle

A 5min walk south of Main St • Daily: April–Sept 9.30am–5.30pm; Oct–March 10am–4pm • £5.50; HES • ☎ 01786 841742, ⓦ historicenvironment.scot

Doune Castle's most prominent features are its mighty 95ft-high **gatehouse**, with its spacious vaulted rooms, and the **kitchens**, complete with medieval rubbish chute. Buil in the fourteenth century by Robert, Duke of Albany, it ended up in the hands of the second earl of Moray, James Stewart – son of James V and half-brother of Mary, Quee of Scots – who was murdered in 1592 and immortalized in the ballad *The Bonnie Earl of Moray*; it was also used as a prison by Bonnie Prince Charlie's army after the battle c Falkirk. The castle's greatest claim to fame today, however, is as the setting for the

1970s movie *Monty Python and the Holy Grail*, which attracts legions of Python fans – a selection of film souvenirs is available, including bottles of the local Holy Grail Ale.

Deanston Distillery

A84, 1 mile south of Doune • Daily 10am–5pm • Tours £9–35 • ☎ 01786 843010, ⓦ deanstonmalt.com

In the eighteenth century **Deanston** was a cotton mill staffed by Gaelic-speaking victims of the Clearances, and featured the biggest water wheel in Europe. Following the decline of the British cotton industry, the mill finally closed in 1965, but swiftly reopened as a **distillery**; the first single malt was created in 1982. True to its water-powered origins, Deanston is self-sufficient in hydroelectricity and even supplies a surplus to the national grid. The distillery is notable for its gleaming brass stills as well as for its non-peaty whisky, with notes of vanilla and honey. Barrels are stored in the vast 1825 weaving shed, and the old mill clock still keeps time. A range of **tours** is on offer; afterwards, take a short stroll up the road from the distillery to see the attractive purpose-built **mill village**.

ACCOMMODATION AND EATING   DOUNE

Buttercup Café 7 Main St ☎ 01786 842511, ⓦ buttercupcafe.co.uk. This bright and inviting village café does breakfast, lunches (everything from light salads to hearty steak sandwiches for £7.45) and afternoon tea (£9.95) served on a tiered stand. They offer a good selection of cakes and bakes, including gluten-free options. Mon–Fri 9am–4pm, Sat 9am–5pm, Sun 10am–4pm.

Glenardoch House Castle Rd ☎ 01786 841489, ⓦ glenardochhouse.com. An excellent eighteenth-century country-house B&B near the castle, which has two comfortable en-suite rooms and a beautiful riverside garden. May–Sept. **£80**

L'Angolino House 47 Main St ☎ 01786 841850. This little corner (*angolino*) of Doune is home to a rustic family-run Italian restaurant, dishing up home-made pasta and pizza. Welcoming and unpretentious vibe. Wed–Fri 5–9.15pm, Sat & Sun noon–2pm & 5–9.15pm.

SHOPPING

Scottish Antique & Arts Centre 1 mile west of Doune on the A84 ☎ 01786 841203, ⓦ scottish-antiques.com. Just outside the village of Doune, the "antiques village", as it's known locally, is a vast covered market selling high-quality memorabilia and furniture, notably some stunning Arts and Crafts pieces. There's a reasonable on-site café. Daily 10am–5pm.

The Carse of Stirling

West of Stirling, the wide flood plain of the Forth River is known as the Carse of Forth, or **Carse of Stirling**. This is beautifully lush farmland dramatically bounded on the south by the **Gargunnock** and **Fintry hills**, which gradually blend into the **Campsie Fells**. **Kippen**, a scenic village with strong Rob Roy associations, has a couple of good eating options. To the north, the Trossachs inevitably draw many visitors.

Flanders Moss nature reserve

Open access 24hr • Turn north off the A811 on the B822 towards Callander, and follow the signs

You can find out about the rich ecology and history of the carse's reclaimed marshland in the **Flanders Moss** nature reserve, where you walk through the peat bog on raised boardwalks, spotting dragonflies, damselflies, pond-skaters and green tiger beetles among the sphagnum moss, heather, cotton grass and bog rosemary. A 23ft timber viewing tower allows you to survey it all from above.

Drymen

At the western end of the Campsie Fells, all roads, including the West Highland Way (see box, p.401), meet at the small village of **DRYMEN**, an ancient ecclesiastical centre and stopover point for Highland drovers, which sits peacefully in the hills overlooking the winding Endrick Water as it nears Loch Lomond.

7

Glengoyne Distillery

Dumgoyne • Tours (from £9) on the hour daily: March–Nov 10am–4pm; Dec–Feb 11am–3pm • ☎ 01360 550254, ⓦ glengoyne.com

South of Drymen and not far from Killearn, picturesque **Glengoyne Distillery** features a pagoda roof and whitewashed buildings. Tours range from explorations of the building, or classes on matching whisky with chocolate, to a five-hour masterclass.

ARRIVAL AND DEPARTURE   CARSE OF STIRLING

By bus The hourly bus #12 from Stirling to Balfron goes through Gargunnock and Kippen.

ACCOMMODATION AND EATING

GARGUNNOCK

Gargunnock House 1 mile east of the village centre ☎ 01628 825925, ⓦ landmarktrust.org.uk. If you're in a group, consider a stay at this wonderful country house operated by the Landmark Trust. Behind the Georgian facade are elements of the original sixteenth-century tower house. The historic interiors are plush and beautifully preserved, and there's a piano once played, allegedly, by Chopin. Sleeps sixteen. Four nights from **£887**

KIPPEN

★**Inn at Kippen** Fore Rd ☎ 01786 870500, ⓦ the innatkippen.co.uk. A long, whitewashed sixteenth-century former coaching house, now housing a bar and an excellent restaurant. They dish up fabulous home-cooked dishes, many adaptable as dairy- and gluten-free; the meat, seafood and veg platters are superb (£10–15). There are four boutique-style en-suite rooms. Mon, Tues & Sun 9–11am & noon–8pm, Wed–Sat 9–11am & noon–9pm. **£85**

Woodhouse Just off the roundabout outside Kippen on the A811 ☎ 01786 870156, ⓦ thewoodhouse kippen.com. Buzzy, bright and irresistible self-styled diner with a wood-fired stove and an attached farm shop. Excellent soups, sandwiches, specials and baking (from £5) are all home-made, mostly with local ingredients. Mon–Fri 9am–5pm, Sat & Sun 10am–5pm.

DRYMEN

Clachan Inn Drymen Square ☎ 01360 660824 ⓦ clachaninndrymen.co.uk. Dating back to 1734, the inn is an atmospheric spot for a pint and offers a range of great simple pub grub such as scampi and burgers (from £7.50) Mon–Sat 11am–11pm, Sun 12.30pm–10.30pm; food served all day.

Winnock Hotel The Square ☎ 01360 660245, ⓦ winnoc hotel.com. In the village square, this flower-bedecked eighteenth-century coaching inn has fairly comfortable en-suite rooms. Look out for the ceilidh nights. **£74**

The Falkirk Wheel

Lime Rd, Tamfourhill • **Visitor centre** Daily 10am–5.30pm • Free • **Boat tours** Daily: April–Oct every 30min 10am–4.30pm; Nov–March hourly 10am–3pm • £12.50 • ☎ 0870 050 0208, ⓦ scottishcanals.co.uk/falkirk-wheel • Bus #3 from Falkirk town centre or walk along the Union Canal from Falkirk High train station (2.5 miles to the east)

The icon of an ambitious project to link Falkirk's two long-neglected canals is the remarkable **Falkirk Wheel**, opened in 2002 two miles west of Falkirk town centre. Looking more like a giant metal claw than a wheel, it was designed to solve the problem of the 115ft gap between the Union and Forth and Clyde canals. Back in the 1930s, before the canals went to rack and ruin, barges had to spend a day passing though eleven locks. To solve the problem, engineers designed the giant lift, which

THE ANTONINE WALL

Rough Castle, signposted off the B816 just west of Falkirk, is one of the forts set up at two-mile intervals to defend the entire length of the Roman **Antonine Wall**. The most northerly frontier of the Roman Empire, the wall was built in 142 AD, of turf rather than stone, and stretched for 37 miles right across the country from the Forth to the Clyde. Assailed by skirmishing Picts and the grim Scottish weather, it didn't take long for the Romans to abandon the wall and retreat to Hadrian's Wall, just south of Scotland's present border with England. The signposted site lies along the potholed back road, and though little more than a large grassy mound interpreted by a couple of information boards, the remains at Rough Castle are the best-preserved part of the wall, which has UNESCO World Heritage Site status.

scoops a boat in one claw and an equal weight of water in the other. The simple process of rotating the perfectly weighted claws and depositing the boat in the other canal is said to use only the same energy that it takes to boil eight kettles.

Boat tours take you from the visitor centre on a one-hour journey from the lower basin into the wheel, along the Union Canal for a short distance, then back down to the basin again via the wheel. The boat trip isn't essential if you just want to see the wheel in action, which can be done by **walking** around the basin and adjoining towpaths.

Dollar

Nestling in a fold of the Ochils on the northern bank of the small River Devon, where mountain waters rush off the hills, affluent **DOLLAR** is known for its Academy, founded in 1820 with a substantial bequest from local lad John MacNabb; its pupils and staff account for around a third of the town's population. The walk from town up the glen to moody Castle Campbell makes for a dramatic approach.

7

Castle Campbell
Castle Rd • April–Sept daily 9.30am–5.30pm; Oct–March Mon–Wed, Sat & Sun 10am–4pm • £5.50; HES • ☎ 01259 742408,
🌐 historicenvironment.scot

Above Dollar, the steep ravine of **Dollar Glen** is commanded by **Castle Campbell**, formerly, and unofficially, known as Castle Gloom – a fine and evocative tag but, prosaically, a derivation of "Gloume", an old Gaelic name. A one-and-a-half-mile-long road leads up from Dollar's main street, but becomes very narrow and steep and stops short of the castle, with only limited parking at the top. A series of marked **walks** leads up the glen, taking in mossy crags, rushing streams and, if you strike out on the three-hour hike to the top of Dollar Hill, great views.

ARRIVAL AND ACTIVITIES | DOLLAR

By bus The Stagecoach bus service #23 between Stirling and St Andrews travels along the A91 through the Hillfoot villages to Dollar.

Walking A map shows the walks on a board on the way up to the castle, though it's advisable to buy the relevant OS map (Explorer 366) if you're setting off for the longer hike.

ACCOMMODATION AND EATING

Café des Fleurs 44 Bridge St ☎ 01259 743699. Stylish little café/tearoom featuring impressive home baking: you might encounter a coconut and fresh lime cake, strawberry and white chocolate scones or mini red velvet sponges (£2.50). Daily 9am–5pm.

★ Kennels Cottage Dollarbeg ☎ 01259 742186,

🌐 guesthousescotland.co.uk. A great B&B located in an attractive whitewashed former gamekeeper's cottage at Dollarbeg, just south of Dollar. Their own chickens provide the breakfast eggs. They can arrange classic car rental as part of the deal. £80

Loch Leven

Without doubt the biggest attraction of **Kinross**, ten miles east of Dollar, is trout-filled **LOCH LEVEN**, signposted from the main street. The whole loch is a National Nature Reserve; it's a good place to see visiting geese. There's a reasonable **café** by the ferry ticket office.

Loch Leven Castle
Loch Leven • Daily: April–Sept 9.30am–4.15pm; Oct 10am–3.15pm • £5.50 including ferry trip; HES • ☎ 07778 040483,
🌐 historicenvironment.scot

From the shore a small ferry chugs over to an island on which stands the ruined fourteenth-century **Loch Leven Castle**, where Robert the Bruce established his exchequer and where Mary, Queen of Scots was imprisoned for eleven months in 1567–68. This isn't the only island fortress Mary spent time in; it's easy to imagine the isolation of the tragic queen, who is believed to have miscarried twins while here. She managed to charm the 18-year-old brother of the castle's owner, Sir William Douglas, into helping her escape: he stole the castle keys, secured a boat in which to row ashore, locked the castle gates behind them and threw the keys into the loch – from where they were retrieved three centuries later.

The classically proportioned pile you'll see on the boat trip is late seventeenth-century **Kinross House**, which was built and owned by the architect of Holyroodhouse in Edinburgh.

ARRIVAL AND DEPARTURE   LOCH LEVEN

By bus Bus #23 from Stirling stops in the centre of Kinross (6 daily; 55min). Here, it's a 15min walk to the loch shore.

Loch Lomond

7

The largest stretch of fresh water in Britain (23 miles long and up to five miles wide), **Loch Lomond** is the epitome of Scottish scenic splendour, thanks in large part to the ballad that fondly recalls its "bonnie, bonnie banks". The song was said to have been written by a Jacobite prisoner captured by the English, who, sure of his fate, wrote that his spirit would return to Scotland on the low road much faster than his living compatriots on the high road.

The **Loch Lomond and the Trossachs National Park** covers over seven hundred square miles of scenic territory from the shores of Loch Long in Cowal to Loch Earn and Loch Tay, on the southwest fringes of Perthshire. The centrepiece is undoubtedly Loch Lomond, and the most popular gateway is **Balloch**, the town at the loch's southern tip; with Glasgow city centre just nineteen miles away, both Balloch and the southwest side of the loch around **Luss** are often packed with day-trippers and tour coaches. Many of these continue up the **western side** of the loch, though the fast A82 road isn't ideal for tourists who wish to enjoy a leisurely drive.

Very different in tone, the verdant **eastern side** of the loch, abutting the Trossachs, operates at a different pace, with wooden ferryboats puttering out to a scattering of tree-covered islands off the village of **Balmaha**. If you're looking for a relatively easy climb with an impressive view over Loch Lomond, start at Balmaha for the ascent of **Conic Hill** (1175ft), a two- to three-hour round-trip walk through forest and open hillside. Much of the eastern shore can only be reached by boat or on foot, although the West Highland Way long-distance footpath (see box, p.401) and the distinctive peak of **Ben Lomond** ensure that even these parts are well traversed.

Balloch

The main settlement by Loch Lomond is **BALLOCH**, at the southwestern corner of the loch, where the water channels into the River Leven for its short journey south to the sea in the Firth of Clyde. Balloch has few redeeming features and is little more than a suburb of the factory town of Alexandria, but you might want to arrange a loch trip from here, or shop at the Loch Lomond stores complex. Across the river in the extensive mature grounds of **Balloch Castle Country Park**, there are shoreside and sylvan walks.

ARRIVAL AND DEPARTURE   BALLOCH

By train Balloch has a direct train connection with Glasgow Queen Street (every 30min; 50min). The station sits between the loch and the town centre.

By bus Regular buses connect Balloch with Balmaha (every 2hr; 25min) and Luss (hourly; 15min).

CLOCKWISE FROM TOP STIRLING CASTLE (P.280); CURLING, LAKE OF MENTEITH (P.296); TAPESTRY, STIRLING CASTLE (P.280)

INFORMATION AND ACTIVITIES

Tourist office The Old Station Building opposite the modern train station contains a tourist office (daily: June–Aug 9.30am–6pm; Sept–May 10am–5pm; ☎ 01389 753533).

Outdoor activities Based right beside Drumkinnon Tower on Ben Lomond Way, Can You Experience (☎ 01389 602576, ⓦ canyouexperience.com) rents out canoes, bikes,

fishing boats and pedalos. They also organize bushcraft classes, hikes and Highland games.

Loch trips Sweeney's Cruises, in the centre of town near the bridge (☎ 01389 752376, ⓦ www.sweeneys cruises.com), offers a choice of loch trips including a 2hr sailing to Luss.

ACCOMMODATION

Cameron House Loch Lomond, Alexandria ☎ 0871 222 4681, ⓦ cameronhouse.co.uk. The exclusive DeVere *Cameron House* resort just north of Balloch has its own spa and championship golf course as well as the area's best restaurant, an offshoot of Edinburgh's *Martin Wishart*. **£242**

Dumbain Farm Off Dumbain Crescent ☎ 01389 752263, ⓦ dumbainfarm.co.uk. Rambling whitewashed farm with converted outbuildings, containing bright and elegant rooms with TVs and tea- and coffee-making facilities. Trad Scottish breakfast, cooked on an Aga, with home-made jams and baking. **£70**

SHOPPING

Lomond Shores Ben Lomond Way, Balloch ☎ 01389 751031, ⓦ lochlomondshores.com. A "retail crescent" of shops including branches of Edinburgh's venerable

department store, Jenners, and of the city's best deli, Valvona & Crolla. The complex is a 10min walk from town along the lakeside path.

The eastern shore

The loch's tranquil **eastern shore** is far better for walking and appreciating its natural beauty than the overcrowded western side. It's the access point for climbing **Ben Lomond** and visiting **Inchcailloch** island, and where the minor road peters out at **Rowardennan** you can continue on foot to the village of **Inversnaid**.

Balmaha

The tiny lochside settlement of **BALMAHA** stands on the Highland Boundary Fault: if you stand on the viewpoint above the pier, you can see the fault line clearly marked by the series of woody islands that form giant stepping stones across the loch. Many of the loch's 37 **islands** are privately owned, and, rather quaintly, an old wooden mail boat still delivers post to four of them. Balmaha gets very busy in summer, not least with day-trippers on the West Highland Way.

Inchcailloch

Ferries from Balmaha (☎ 01360 870214, ⓦ balmahaboatyard.co.uk) operate daily 9am–5pm, with departures on demand; the journey takes 5min and costs £5 return

Owned by Scottish Natural Heritage, **Inchcailloch** is the closest island to Balmaha. A signposted two-mile **nature trail** loops around the island, which was extensively planted with oaks to provide bark for the local tanning industry. Along the way you'll encounter the ruins of a fourteenth-century nunnery and associated burial ground, and there's a picnic and camping site at Port Bawn on the southwestern side of the island, near a sandy beach. Until the mid-seventeenth century parishioners on the far (western) shore of Loch Lomond used to row across to Inchcailloch for Sunday services at the church linked to the nunnery. It's possible to make the short trip by **rowing boat** yourself; contact MacFarlane & Son to rent one (from £10/hr or £40/day; ☎ 01360 870214, ⓦ balmahaboatyard.co.uk), or use their on-demand ferry service (see above).

Rowardennan

Public transport ends at Balmaha, but another seven miles north through the woods brings you to the end of the road at **ROWARDENNAN**, a scattered settlement below Ben Lomond.

Ben Lomond

Ben Lomond (3192ft) is the most southerly of the "Munros" (see p.10) and one of the most popular mountains in Scotland, its commanding position above Loch Lomond affording amazing views of both the Highlands and Lowlands. The well-signposted route to the summit and back from Rowardennan takes five to six hours.

Inversnaid

Only walkers can continue north up the lochside from Rowardennan, where the only other settlement is seven miles north at **INVERSNAID**, made famous by a poem of the same name by Gerard Manley Hopkins about a frothing waterfall nearby ("This darksome burn, horseback brown/His rollrock highroad roaring down").

ARRIVAL AND DEPARTURE   THE EASTERN SHORE

By car or bus The dead-end B837 from Drymen (see p.287) will take you halfway up the east bank to Rowardennan, as far as you can get by car or bus (#309 from Balloch and Drymen runs to Balmaha every 2hr), while the West Highland Way sticks close to the shore for the entire length of the loch.

Ferry to Rowardennan Passenger ferries (Easter–Sept

2 daily; ☎01301 702356, ⍵ cruiselochlomond.co.uk) cross from Tarbert, on the west shore.

Ferry to Inversnaid It's also possible to get to or from Inversnaid by ferry (£4 one-way/£5 return), which crosses from Inveruglas, directly opposite on the western shore. You'll have to phone the *Inversnaid Hotel* (☎01887 386223) to make arrangements.

INFORMATION AND TOURS

National Park Centre The national park visitor centre is located beside the large car park in Balmaha (April–Sept daily 9.30am–4pm; ☎01389 722600, ⍵ lochlomond trossachs.org); it offers information about local forest walks and occasional wildlife workshops.

Boat tours It's possible to join the mail-boat cruise, which is run by MacFarlane & Son, from the jetty at Balmaha. The

timetable allows a one-hour stop on Inchmurrin Island, which has just ten permanent residents; it has the ruins of a monastery and castle, and food is served in the bar of the *Inchmurrin Hotel* (May–Oct Mon, Thurs & Sat 11.30am, returns 2pm; July & Aug daily 11.30am, returns 2pm; Oct–April Mon & Thurs 10.50am, returns noon; £9; ☎01360 870214, ⍵ balmahaboatyard.co.uk).

ACCOMMODATION AND EATING

BALMAHA

Balmaha B&B and Bunkhouse Balmaha House, Main St ☎01360 870218, ⍵ balmahahouse.co.uk. Welcoming West Highland Way accommodation located on the loch shore, with two B&B rooms, a well-equipped bunkhouse (£20/bed) and a self-catering chalet sleeping four (£80) which overlooks the bay. Doubles **£70**

Oak Tree Inn ☎01360 870357, ⍵ theoaktreeinn .co.uk. This well run inn is set back from the boatyard, and offers en-suite doubles and bunk-bed quads. There's also a convivial pub, where food is served all day, plus a coffee shop with ice-cream parlour. **£90**

Passfoot Cottage B&B ☎01360 870324, ⍵ www .passfoot.com. This friendly and appealing little option is housed in a whitewashed toll cottage, enjoying an idyllic location and lochside garden. Great for walks along the shore. **£80**

ROWARDENNAN

Cashel 3 miles south of Rowardennan ☎01360 870234. A lovely, secluded Forestry Commission campsite on the loch shore with a decent loo block. Campers can launch craft from here onto the loch, and Ben Lomond is just four miles away. April–Oct. Per pitch **£15**

Clansman Bar Rowardennan Hotel, on the lake shore ☎01360 870273, ⍵ rowardennanhotel.co.uk. Nightlife in the area centres on this hotel's bar, which features open fires, a beer garden and weekend live music. Closed weekdays out of season. Mon–Fri 11am–9pm, Sat 11am–11pm, Sun 11am–10pm.

SYHA Rowardennan Lodge A 15min walk north of the Rowardennan Hotel ☎01360 870259, ⍵ syha.org.uk. A wonderfully situated SYHA hostel in a classic turreted Scots Baronial lodge with lawns running down to the shore. March–Oct. Dorms **£16**

The western shore

Despite the roar of traffic hurtling along the upgraded A82, the **west shore** of Loch Lomond is an undeniably beautiful stretch of water. Ten miles north of attractive **Luss** is the small settlement of **TARBET**, where the West Highland **train** reaches the shoreline.

North of Tarbet, the A82 turns back into the narrow, winding road of old, making for slower but much more interesting driving. There's one more **train station** on Loch Lomond at Ardlui, at the mountain-framed head of the loch, but most travellers continue a couple of miles further north to **INVERARNAN**, where you'll find the *Drovers Inn* (see below), possibly the most idiosyncratic hotel in Scotland.

Luss

LUSS is the prettiest village in the region, with its prim, identical sandstone and slate cottages garlanded in rambling roses, and its narrow sand and pebble strand. However, its charms are no secret and its streets and beach can become crowded in summer. If you want to escape the hordes, pop into the parish **church**, a haven of peace with some fine Victorian stained-glass windows and a lovely ceiling made from Scots pine rafters.

ARRIVAL AND DEPARTURE   THE WESTERN SHORE

By bus Buses run from Tarbet to Loch Lomond's western shore (hourly; 10min).

INFORMATION AND TOURS

Tourist information You can pick up local information at the Luss Visitor Centre at the car park (daily 10am–5pm; ☎01436 860229) or the small tourist office on Harbour St in Tarbet (April–Oct daily; ☎01301 702260).
Boat tours At the pier over the road from the prominent

Tarbet Hotel you can hop on an hour-long loch cruise run by Cruise Loch Lomond (☎01301 702356, ⌨cruiseloch lomond.co.uk). The same operator also offers trips to Inversnaid and Rowardennan on the eastern side.

ACCOMMODATION AND EATING

LUSS
Coach House Loch Lomond Trading Company Ltd, Church Rd ☎01436 860341. A spruce and lively little tearoom with friendly tartan-wearing staff, serving a range of teas, cakes, ciabattas, Orkney ice cream and their own take on haggis (snacks from £5). Daily 10am–5pm.
Lodge on Loch Lomond Loch shore, immediately north of Luss ☎01436 860201, ⌨loch-lomond.co.uk. This modern lodge, just north of town, has a string of rooms with balconies and views over the loch, and serves decent meals in its restaurant, *Colquhoun's*. Mon–Sat

noon–5pm & 6–9.45pm, Sun 12.30–3.30pm & 6–9.45pm. **£124**

INVERARNAN
Drovers Inn By Ardlui, North Loch Lomond ☎0130 704234, ⌨thedroversinn.co.uk. The bar (self-proclaimed "pub of the year 1705") features a roaring fire, barmen dressed in kilts, weary hillwalkers sipping pints, and bearded musicians banging out folk songs. Down the creaking corridors, past moth-eaten stuffed animals, are a number of resolutely old-fashioned rooms. Mon–Sat 11am–11pm, Sun noon–11pm. **£75**

Crianlarich and Tyndrum

CRIANLARICH, some eight miles north of the head of Loch Lomond, is an important staging post on various transport routes, including the West Highland Railway which divides here, one branch heading due west towards Oban, the other continuing north over Rannoch Moor to Fort William. The West Highland Way long-distance footpath (see box, p.401) passes by. Otherwise, there's little reason to stop here, unless you're keen on tackling some of the steep-sided hills that rise up from the glen.

Five miles further north from here on the A82/A85, the village of **TYNDRUM** owes its existence to a minor (and very short-lived) nineteenth-century gold rush, but today supports little more than a busy service station and several characterless hotels.

ARRIVAL AND DEPARTURE   CRIANLARICH AND TYNDRUM

By train Crianlarich is well served by regular trains. Tyndrum has two train stations: the upper station serves

the scenic West Highland Line, while the lower has services to and from Crianlarich and the south.

Destinations from Crianlarich Fort William (3–4 daily Mon–Sat, 1–3 on Sun; 1hr 50min); Glasgow Queen Street (6–8 daily Mon–Sat, 1–3 on Sun; 1hr 50min); Oban (3–4 daily Mon–Sat, 1–3 on Sun; 1hr 15min). Destinations from Tyndrum Fort William (upper station 3–4 daily; 1hr 35min); Crianlarich (lower station 5 daily;

8min); Glasgow Queen Street (lower station 5 daily Mon–Sat, 1 on Sun; 2hr 5min).

By car At Tyndrum the road divides, with the A85 heading west to Oban, and the A82 heading for Fort William via Glen Coe.

ACCOMMODATION AND EATING

By The Way Hostel and Campsite Lower Station Rd, Tyndrum ✆ 01838 400333, ⊚ tyndrumbytheway.com. Right beside Tyndrum Lower railway station is a good campsite and small purpose-built bunkhouse; the cute wooden "hobbit houses" (£40) in the grounds sleep four and are self-catering. Hostel per person £18; camping per person £8

Real Food Café Main St, Tyndrum ✆ 01838 400 235, ⊚ therealfoodcafe.com. For a refreshingly different roadside dining experience, it's well worth trying the airy café on the main road serving fresh, fast food that's locally sourced and cooked to order, including fish and chips from £5.95. Mon–Thurs & Sun 9am–10pm, Fri 11am–10pm, Sat 7.30am–9pm.

7

The Trossachs

Often described as the Highlands in miniature, the **Trossachs** area boasts a magnificent diversity of scenery, with distinctive peaks, silvery lochs and mysterious, forest-covered slopes. Strictly speaking, the name "Trossachs", normally translated as either "bristly country" or "crossing place", originally referred only to the wooded glen between **Loch Katrine** and Loch Achray, but today it is usually taken as being the whole area from **Callander** right up to the eastern banks of Loch Lomond, with which it has been grouped as one of Scotland's national parks.

The Trossachs' high tourist profile was largely attributable in the early days to Sir Walter Scott, whose novels *Lady of the Lake* and *Rob Roy* were set in and around the area. According to one contemporary account, after Scott's *Lady of the Lake* was published in 1810, the number of carriages passing Loch Katrine rose from fifty the previous year to 270. Since then, neither the popularity nor beauty of the region has waned, and in high season it can be jam-packed. Autumn is a better time to come, when the hills are blanketed in rich, rusty colours and the crowds are thinner. In terms of where to stay, **Aberfoyle** has a rather dowdy air while **Callander** feels somewhat overrun, and you're often better off seeking out one of the guesthouses or B&Bs tucked away in secluded corners of the region.

GETTING AROUND   THE TROSSACHS

By bus First Group (✆ 01324 602200, ⊚ firstgroup.com) operates between Callander and Stirling; reduced service at weekends.

By bike There are two options for bike rental in the area. Wheelology, 4 Ancaster Square in Callander

(✆ 01877 331052, ⊚ cyclehirecallander.co.uk), and Wheels Cycling Centre on Invertrossachs Rd, 1.5 miles southwest of Callander (✆ 01877 331100, ⊚ scottish -cycling.com); the latter is the best option in the Trossachs.

Aberfoyle and around

Each summer the sleepy little town of **ABERFOYLE**, twenty miles west of Stirling, dusts itself down for its annual influx of tourists. Though of little appeal itself, Aberfoyle has an ideal position in the heart of the Trossachs, with **Loch Ard Forest** and **Queen Elizabeth Forest Park** stretching across to Ben Lomond and Loch Lomond to the west, Loch Katrine and Ben Venue to the northwest, and Ben Ledi to the northeast. Don't come here for lively nightlife or entertainment, but for a good, healthy blast of the outdoors.

HIKING AND BIKING IN THE TROSSACHS

The Trossachs are ideal for exploring on **foot** or on a **mountain bike**. This is partly because the terrain is slightly more benign than the Highlands proper, but much is due to the excellent management of the **Queen Elizabeth Forest Park**, a huge chunk of the national park that lies between Loch Lomond and Loch Lubnaig. The main visitor centre for the area, David Marshall Lodge (see below), is just outside Aberfoyle, and is well worth a visit.

For **hillwalkers**, as far as height goes, the prize peak is Ben Lomond (3192ft), best accessed from Rowardennan (see p.292). Other highlights include Ben Venue (2370ft) and Ben A'an (1520ft) on the shores of Loch Katrine, as well as Ben Ledi (2857ft), just northwest of Callander, which all offer relatively straightforward but very rewarding climbs and, on clear days, stunning views.

Walkers can also choose from any number of waymarked routes through the forests and along lochsides; pick up a map of these at the visitor centre. A great long-distance option is the 30-mile **Great Trossachs Path**, a series of linked routes along the lochs: it can also be cycled. **Bikers** are served by a network of forest paths and one of the more impressive stretches of the National Cycle Network, cutting through the region from Loch Lomond to Killin.

7

Lake of Menteith

About 4 miles east of Aberfoyle towards Doune

The **Lake of Menteith** is a superb fly-fishing centre and Scotland's only lake (as opposed to loch), so-named due to a historic mix-up with the word *laigh*, Scots for "low-lying ground", which applied to the whole area. There are also some secluded spots along the shore for picnics and swims. To rent fishing gear, contact the Lake of Menteith Fisheries (☎01877 385664, ⊛menteith-fisheries.co.uk; April–Oct).

Island of Inchmahome

Lake of Menteith • Daily: April–Sept 9.30am–4.30pm; Oct 9.30am–3.30pm • £5.50 including ferry; HES • ⊛ historicenvironment.scot

From the northern shore of the Lake of Menteith, you can take a little ferry out to the **Island of Inchmahome** to explore the ruined Augustinian abbey. Founded in 1238, **Inchmahome Priory** is the most beautiful island monastery in Scotland, its remains rising tall and graceful above the trees. The masons employed to build the priory are thought to be those who built Dunblane Cathedral (see p.286); certainly the western entrance there resembles that at Inchmahome. The nave of the church is roofless, but in the choir are preserved the graves of important families from the surrounding area. Most touching is a late thirteenth-century double effigy depicting Walter, the first Stewart earl of Menteith, and his countess, Mary, who, feet resting on lion-like animals, turn towards each other and embrace.

Five-year-old Mary, Queen of Scots was hidden at Inchmahome in 1547 before being taken to France, and there's a formal garden in the west of the island, known as Queen Mary's Bower, where she played, according to legend. Visible on a nearby but inaccessible islet is the ruined castle of **Inchtalla**, the home of the earls of Menteith in the sixteenth and seventeenth centuries.

Queen Elizabeth Forest Park

David Marshall Lodge visitor centre March–June, Sept & Oct daily 10am–5pm; July & Aug daily 10am–6pm; Nov & Dec daily 10am–4pm; Jan Sat & Sun 10am–4pm; Feb Thurs–Sun 10am–4pm • Car park £3 • ☎01877 382258

North of Aberfoyle, the A821 road to Loch Katrine winds its way into the **Queen Elizabeth Forest Park**, snaking up **Duke's Pass** (so-called because it once belonged to the duke of Montrose). You can walk or drive the short distance from Aberfoyle to the park's excellent **visitor centre** at David Marshall Lodge, where you can pick up maps of the walks and cycle routes in the forest, get background information on the area's flora and fauna or settle into the **café** with its splendid views out over the tree tops.

ROB ROY

A member of the outlawed Macgregor clan, **Rob Roy** was born in 1671 in Glengyle, just north of Loch Katrine, and lived for some time as a respectable cattle farmer and trader, supported by the powerful duke of Montrose. In 1712 Rob Roy absconded with £1000, some of it belonging to the duke. He took to the hills to live as a brigand, his feud with Montrose escalating after the duke repossessed Rob Roy's land and drove his wife from their house. He was present at the Battle of Sheriffmuir during the Jacobite uprising of 1715, ostensibly supporting the Jacobites but probably as an opportunist: the chaos would have made cattle-raiding easier. Eventually captured and sentenced to transportation, Rob Roy was pardoned and returned to **Balquhidder** (see p.299), where he remained until his death in 1734. His status as a local hero in the mould of Robin Hood should be tempered with the fact that he was without doubt a bandit and blackmailer. His life has been much romanticized, from Sir Walter Scott's 1818 novel **Rob Roy** to the 1995 film starring Liam Neeson, although the tale does serve well to dramatize the clash between the doomed clan culture of the Gaelic-speaking Highlanders and the organized feudal culture of lowland Scots, which effectively ended with the defeat of the Jacobites at Culloden in 1746. His **grave** in Balquhidder, a simple affair behind the ruined church, is mercifully free of the tartan trappings that plague parts of the Trossachs, predictably dubbed "Rob Roy Country" by the tourist board.

7

ARRIVAL AND INFORMATION

ABERFOYLE AND AROUND

ABERFOYLE

By bus Regular buses from Stirling pull into the car park on Aberfoyle's Main St.

Destinations Callander (late June to mid-Oct 4 Thurs–Tues; 25min); Port of Menteith (late June to mid-Oct 4 Thurs–Tues; 10min).

Tourist office The tourist office (April–Oct daily 10am–5pm; Nov–March Sat & Sun only; ☎ 08707 200604) has full details of local accommodation, sights and outdoor activities.

LAKE OF MENTEITH

By bus Take First Edinburgh bus #11 from Stirling to the Lake of Menteith (5 daily; 50min).

ACCOMMODATION AND EATING

ABERFOYLE

Trossachs Holiday Park 3 miles south of Aberfoyle ☎ 01877 382614, ⌨ trossachsholidays.co.uk. This excellent family-run 40-acre holiday park is fringed by oak and bluebell woods. Bikes available for rent. March–Oct. Per pitch £21

★ Wee Blether Tea Room 4 miles west of Aberfoyle on the shores of Loch Ard ☎ 01877 387337, ⌨ weeblethertearoom.co.uk. Excellent home baking and an idyllic loch location make this homely place a winner.

Soups, toasties, pies and lots of cakes; snacks such as "jacket tatties" cost around £6. April–Oct 10am–5pm.

LAKE OF MENTEITH

Lake of Menteith Hotel Port of Menteith ☎ 01877 385258, ⌨ lake-hotel.com. A beautiful place to stay, with an idyllic waterfront setting next to Port of Menteith's Victorian Gothic parish church, and also has a classy restaurant. £138

Loch Katrine

Heading down the northern side of the Duke's Pass, you come first to **Loch Achray**, tucked under Ben A'an. Look out across the loch for the small **Callander Kirk** in a lovely setting alone on a promontory. At the head of the loch a road follows the short distance through to the southern end of **Loch Katrine** at the foot of Ben Venue (2370ft).

Brig o'Turk and Loch Venachar

From Loch Katrine the A821 heads due east past the tiny village of **Brig o'Turk**, where there are a couple of excellent eating options. From here, carry on along the shores of **Loch Venachar**, where *Venacher Lochside* houses an attractive café and a **fishing centre** offering boat rental and fly-fishing tuition.

CRUISES ON LOCH KATRINE

The elegant Victorian **passenger steamer**, the SS *Sir Walter Scott* (April–Oct daily; £16 return; ☎ 01877 376315, ⓦ lochkatrine.com), has been plying the waters of Loch Katrine since 1900, chugging up to the wild country of Glengyle. It makes various **cruises** each day, stopping off at Stronachlachar; the shorter hour-long cruises (£13) don't make any stops. A popular combination is to rent a bike from the Katrinewheelz hut by the pier (£20/day; ☎ 01877 376366, ⓦ katrinewheelz.co.uk), take the steamer up to Stronachlachar, where the waterside *Pier Tearoom* is an excellent place for refreshments, then **cycle** back by way of the road around the north side of the loch.

EATING AND DRINKING

BRIG O'TURK AND LOCH VENACHAR

Brig o'Turk Tea-Room Glen Finglas Rd, Brig o'Turk ☎ 01877 376283, ⓦ brigoturktearoom.co.uk. This cosy, wooden-clad little spot is a good place to refresh after a walk or cycle. Good coffee and excellent home-made cakes dished up on retro crockery. Also serves appealing dinner options: try the beef goulash (£9.50). Easter–Sept daily except Wed 10am–9pm.

★ **Byre Inn** Just east of Brig o'Turk ☎ 01877 376292, ⓦ byreinn.co.uk. A tiny country pub and classy restaurant offering mains such as fillet of cod for £10.95 and set in an old stone barn with wooden pews; it's the starting point for waymarked walks to lochs Achray, Drunkie and Venachar. There's a boules/petanque piste outside. Daily noon–late; food served noon–3pm & 5.30–8pm.

Callander and around

CALLANDER, on the eastern edge of the Trossachs, sits on the banks of the River Teith at the southern end of the **Pass of Leny**, one of the key routes into the Highlands. Significantly larger than Aberfoyle, it suffers in high season for being right on the main tourist trail from Stirling through to the west Highlands, meaning the plethora of restaurants, tearooms and gift shops is always well served. Callander first came to fame during the "Scottish Enlightenment" of the eighteenth and nineteenth centuries, with the glowing reports of the Trossachs given by Sir Walter Scott and William Wordsworth. Development was given a further boost when Queen Victoria chose to visit, and then by the arrival of the train line – long since closed – in the 1860s.

North of Callander, you can walk or ride the scenic six-mile **Callander to Strathyre Cycleway** (Route 7), which forms part of the network of cycleways between the Highlands and Glasgow.

ARRIVAL AND DEPARTURE

CALLANDER AND AROUND

By bus Callander has bus connections with Loch Katrine (late June to mid-Oct 4 daily Thurs–Tues; 55min).

INFORMATION AND ACTIVITIES

Tourist office In a converted church at Ancaster Square (☎ 08707 200628; March–Oct daily).

Bike rental There's bike rental at Wheelology (☎ 0187 331052, ⓦ cyclehirecallander.co.uk), 4 Ancaster Square.

ACCOMMODATION

Arden House Bracklinn Rd ☎ 01877 330235, ⓦ ardenhouse.org.uk. A grand Victorian guesthouse in its own gardens with good views and woodland walks from the back door. They also have a self-catering studio in the grounds (from £50). April–Oct. **£80**

Callander Hostel 6 Bridgend ☎ 01877 331465, ⓦ callanderhostel.co.uk. Swish new hostel in a distinctive timbered building, with mountain views, a bistro, self-catering facilities and a BBQ area. Dorms **£25**; doubles **£60**

Callander Meadows 24 Main St ☎ 01877 33018? ⓦ callandermeadows.co.uk. Centrally locate accommodation in an attractive townhouse with thre comfortable en-suite rooms and a very good restaurar Full board available. **£75**

Roman Camp Country House Hotel 182 Main S ☎ 01877 330003, ⓦ romancamphotel.co.uk. Th town's most upmarket option is this turrete seventeenth-century hunting lodge set in riversic gardens. **£160**

EATING AND DRINKING

Lade Inn Kilmahog, 1 mile west of Callander ☎ 01877 330152, ⓦ theladeinn.com. Pub food such as beer-battered chicken goujons (£10.75) can be had at this convivial inn where the owners are keen on real ales; an on-site shop sells bottled beers. Mon–Thurs noon–11pm, Fri & Sat noon–1am, Sun 12.30pm–10.30pm; food served daily except Mon–Fri 2.30–5.30pm.

★ **Mhor Fish** 75–77 Main St ☎ 01877 330213, ⓦ mhor .net. Boasts a sustainable fish policy, daily specials and everything from snacks to bistro-style seafood dishes – and you can get fish suppers, burgers, pies and haggis to take away for around £12. Daily 10am–10pm.

Balquhidder

Beyond the northern end of Loch Lubnaig is tiny **BALQUHIDDER**, famed as the site of the **grave of Rob Roy** (see box, p.297), which is in the small yard behind the ruined church. His grave is marked by a rough stone carved with a sword, cross and a man with a dog.

ACCOMMODATION AND EATING   BALQUHIDDER

MHOR 84 Lochearnhead ☎ 01877 384622, ⓦ mhor .net/mhor-84-motel. Seven-room motel with a super-cool restaurant, serving excellent seafood dishes (mains £12–30). Live folk every Thurs. Daily noon–11pm. **£80**

★ **Monachyle Mhor** Loch Voil, 6 miles west of Balquhidder ☎ 01877 384622, ⓦ mhor.net/monachyle -mhor-hotel. This eighteenth-century farmhouse features chic rooms and a terrific restaurant (book ahead; set dinner £55). Expect locally sourced food, much of it from the family's farm and bakery, and tranquil views over Loch Voil. Daily noon–1.45pm & 7–9pm. **£195**

7

Fife

CULROSS PALACE

Fife

Barely fifty miles at its widest point, the ancient Kingdom of Fife, designated as such by the Picts in the fourth century, is a small area but one which has a distinct identity. It is inextricably linked with the waters that surround it on three sides – the Tay to the north, the Forth to the south, and the cold North Sea to the east. One of its most striking aspects is how it changes in character within a few miles, with a marked difference between the rural north and the semi-industrial south. Tourism and agriculture are the economic mainstays of the northeast corner of Fife, where the landscape varies from gentle hills in the rural hinterland to windswept cliffs, rocky bays and sandy beaches. Fishing still has a role, but ultimately it is to St Andrews, Scotland's oldest university town and the home of the world-famous Royal and Ancient Golf Club, that most visitors are drawn. Development here has been cautious, and both the town itself and the surrounding area retain an appealing and old-fashioned feel. South of St Andrews, the tiny stone harbours of the East Neuk fishing villages are a deeply appealing extension to any visit to this part of Fife.

Inland from St Andrews, the central Fife settlements of **Glenrothes**, an unremarkable post-war new town, and **Cupar**, a more interesting market town, are overshadowed by the absorbing village of **Falkland** with its impressive ruined palace. In the **south**, the closure of the coal mines over the last thirty years has left local communities floundering to regain a foothold, and the squeeze on the fishing industry may well lead to further decline. In the meantime, a number of the villages have capitalized on their appeal and welcomed tourism in a way that has enhanced rather than degraded their natural assets. The perfectly preserved town of **Culross** is the most notable of these; once a lively port that enjoyed a thriving trade with Holland, the Dutch influence is obvious here in its striking crow-step gabled houses that line the cobbled lanes.

Otherwise, southern Fife is dominated by the town of **Dunfermline**, a former capital of Scotland, and industrial **Kirkcaldy**, with the Forth rail and road bridges the most memorable sights of this stretch of coastline.

GETTING AROUND

By train The train line follows the coast as far north as Kirkcaldy where you can change for East Neuk bus connections. It then cuts inland towards Dundee, stopping en route at Cupar and Leuchars (from where buses run to St Andrews).

By bus The main bus operator in Fife is Stagecoach (ⓦ stagecoachbus.com), with a fleet servicing St Andrews, East Neuk and the rest of the coast as well as

the interior, with train connections at Kirkcaldy and Leuchars.

By car The main road into the region is the M90, which links the Forth Road Bridge northwest of Edinburgh with Perth. From just north of the bridge, you can join the 85-mile semicircular Coastal Tourist Route (signposted), taking in many of the highlights from the Forth to the Tay estuaries.

Golf in St Andrews p.305
The vision of St Rule p.307

The Fife Coastal Path p.309

HIMALAYAS PUTTING GREEN, ST ANDREWS

Highlights

❶ Himalayas putting green, St Andrews
The world's finest putting course right beside
the world's finest golf course, a snip at £3 a
round. **See p.308**

❷ The East Neuk After a bracing walk along
the Fife Coastal Path, try freshly cooked crab or
lobster from the wooden shack at Crail's historic
stone harbour, or dine in style at one of the
excellent seafood restaurants in the nearby
fishing towns. **See p.309**

❸ Falkland Palace Beautifully placed in a
well-preserved village beneath the Lomond
Hills, the former hunting retreat of the Stuart
kings is an atmospheric semi-ruin in gracious
gardens. **See p.314**

❹ Forth Rail Bridge One of the great
engineering wonders of the Victorian age, a
huge cantilever structure spanning the Firth
of Forth, floodlit to stunning effect at night.
See p.315

❺ Culross Scotland's best-preserved historic
village, all pantile roofs and cobbled wynds,
with its own palace and ruined medieval abbey.
See p.316

❻ Dunfermline Abbey and Palace Vast,
dramatic ruins of the former seat of the Kings
of Scotland and burial site of the legendary
Robert the Bruce. **See p.317**

HIGHLIGHTS ARE MARKED ON THE MAP ON P.304

St Andrews

Confident, poised and well groomed, if a little snooty, **ST ANDREWS** is Scotland's oldest **university town** and a pilgrimage centre for **golfers** from the world over, situated on a wide bay on the northeastern coast of Fife. Of all Scotland's universities, St Andrews is the one most often compared to Oxford or Cambridge, both for the dominance of gown over town and for the intimate, collegiate feel of the place. The university attracts a significant proportion of English students including, famously, Prince William, who spent four years studying here and met his bride to be, Kate Middleton. There's an open, airy feel here, encouraged by the long stretches of sand on either side of town and the acreage of golf links all around.

St Andrews is compact and easy to walk around. With its medieval layout intact, its three main streets, almost entirely consisting of listed buildings, run west to east past several of the original fifteenth-century university campuses towards the heavily ruined Gothic **cathedral**. There's little left of the town's **castle**, which sits on the promontory further north.

St Andrews Cathedral

North St • April–Sept daily 9.30am–5.30pm; Oct–March 10am–4pm; grounds year-round 9am–5.30pm • £4.50, joint ticket with castle £8; grounds free; HES • ☎ 01334 472563, ⓦ historicenvironment.scot

The ruin of the once-great **St Andrews Cathedral** gives only an idea of the importance of what was once the largest cathedral in Scotland. Though founded in 1160, it was

HIGHLIGHTS

1. Himalayas putting green, St Andrews
2. The East Neuk
3. Falkland Palace
4. Forth Rail Bridge
5. Culross
6. Dunfermline Abbey and Palace

GOLF IN ST ANDREWS

St Andrews **Royal and Ancient Golf Club** (or "R&A") is the international governing body for golf, and dates back to a meeting of 22 of the local gentry in 1754, who founded the Society of St Andrews Golfers, being "admirers of the ancient and healthful exercise of golf". The game itself has been played here since the fifteenth century. Those early days – highlighted in the British Golf Museum (see p.307) – were instrumental in establishing Scotland as the home of golf, for the rules were distinguished from those of the French game by the fact that participants had to manoeuvre the ball into a hole, rather than hit an above-ground target. It was not without its opponents, however – particularly James II who, in 1457, banned his subjects from playing since it was distracting them from archery practice.

The approach to St Andrews from the west runs adjacent to the famous **Old Course**, one of seven courses in the immediate vicinity of the town. The R&A's strictly private **clubhouse**, a stolid, square building dating from 1854, is at the eastern end of the Old Course overlooking both the eighteenth green and the long strand of the West Sands. The British Open Championship was first held here in 1873, having been inaugurated in 1860 at Prestwick in Ayrshire, and since then it has been held at St Andrews regularly, pulling in enormous crowds. Guided walks of the Old Course are available (see p.308), though any golf aficionado will savour a stroll around the immediate environs of the golf courses, where there are numerous golf shops, including a couple selling and repairing old-fashioned hickory-shafted clubs.

---

not finished and consecrated until 1318, in the presence of Robert the Bruce. On June 5, 1559, the Reformation took its toll, and supporters of John Knox, fresh from a rousing meeting, plundered the cathedral and left it to ruin. Stone was still being taken from the building for various local projects as late as the 1820s.

The cathedral site, above the harbour where the land drops to the sea, can be a blustery place, with the wind whistling through the great east window and down the stretch of turf that was once the central aisle. In front of the window a slab is all that remains of the high altar, where the relics of St Andrew were once enshrined. From the top of the **St Rule's Tower** (a climb of 150-odd steps), built as part of an abbey in 1130, there's a good view of the town and surroundings, and of the remains of the monastic buildings that made up the priory. Around the entire complex is a sturdy wall dating from the sixteenth century, over half a mile long and with three gateways.

Southwest of the cathedral enclosure lies **The Pends**, a huge fourteenth-century vaulted gatehouse that marked the main entrance to the priory, and from where the road leads down to the harbour.

St Andrews Castle

The Scores • Daily: April–Sept 9.30am–5.30pm, Oct–March 10am–4pm • £5.50, joint ticket with cathedral £8; HES • ☎ 01334 447169, ☻ historicenvironment.scot

With a drop to the sea on two sides and a moat on the inland side, **St Andrews Castle**, founded around 1200, was built as part of the palace of the bishops and archbishops of St Andrews. By consequence it was the scene of some fairly grim incidents at the time of the Reformation. There's not a great deal left, since the castle fell into ruin in the seventeenth century – most of what can be seen dates from a century earlier, apart from the fourteenth-century Fore Tower.

St Andrews Preservation Trust Museum and Garden

12 North St • Daily 2–5pm, only when exhibitions are on • Free • ☎ 01334 477629, ☻ standrewspreservationtrust.co.uk

A compact museum housed in a picturesque sixteenth-century cottage with a low wooden door and rubble stone facade, the **St Andrews Preservation Trust Museum** was originally home to four fishermen's families. Today you'll encounter inside a mock-up vintage grocers, a chemist and a gratifyingly generous array of antiquarian bric-a-brac.

ST ANDREWS

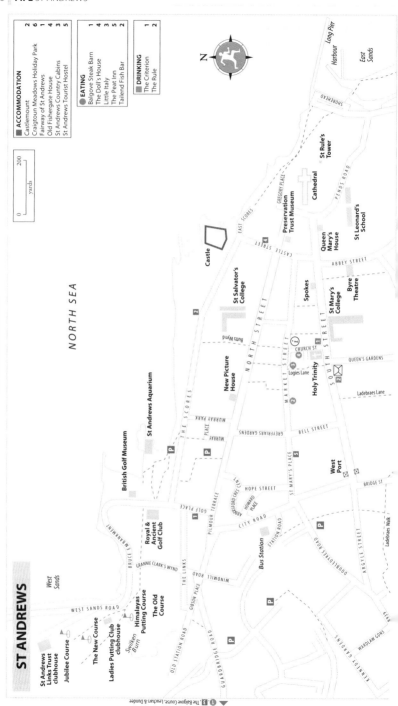

NORTH SEA

West Sands

St Andrews Links Trust clubhouse

Jubilee Course

The New Course

Ladies Putting Club clubhouse

Swilken Burn

Himalayas Putting Course

The Old Course

WEST SANDS ROAD

BRUCE EMBANKMENT

GRANNIE CLARK'S WYND

THE LINKS

British Golf Museum

St Andrews Aquarium

Royal & Ancient Golf Club

THE SCORES

Castle

EAST SCORES

GREGORY PLACE

Preservation Trust Museum

St Rule's Tower

Cathedral

PENDS ROAD

Harbour

Long Pier

East Sands

SHOREHEAD

CASTLE STREET

St Salvator's College

Queen Mary's House

St Leonard's School

ABBEY STREET

New Picture House

Butts Wynd

NORTH STREET

MARKET STREET

CHURCH ST

Logies Lane

Holy Trinity

Spokes

St Mary's College

Byre Theatre

SOUTH STREET

QUEEN'S GARDENS

Ladebraes Lane

MURRAY PARK

MURRAY PLACE

GREYFRIARS GARDENS

BELL STREET

GOLF PLACE

PILMOUR TERRACE

ABBOTSFORD CRES

HOWARD PLACE

HOPE STREET

CITY ROAD

ST MARY'S PLACE

West Port

BRIDGE ST

ARGYLE STREET

Ladebraes Walk

WINDMILL ROAD

STATION ROAD

Bus Station

OLD STATION ROAD

GIBSON PLACE

GUARDBRIDGE ROAD

DOUBLEDYKES ROAD

KENNEDY GARDENS

WARDLAW GDNS

A918

ACCOMMODATION

Castlemount	2
Craigtoun Meadows Holiday Park	6
Fairway of St Andrews	1
Old Fishergate House	4
St Andrews Country Cabins	3
St Andrews Tourist Hostel	5

● EATING

Balgove Steak Barn	1
The Doll's House	4
Little Italy	3
The Peat Inn	5
Tailend Fish Bar	2

■ DRINKING

The Criterion	1
The Rule	2

0 — 200 yards

N

8

▲ A91, The Balgove Course, Leuchars & Dundee

St Andrews University

ⓘ 01334 476161, Ⓦ st-andrews.ac.uk

Scattered around the town centre, **St Andrews University** is the oldest in Scotland. Founded in 1410 by Bishop Henry Wardlaw, the original building was on the site of the Old University Library and by the end of the Middle Ages three colleges had been built: **St Salvador's** (1450), **St Leonard's** (1512) on Pends Road and **St Mary's** (1538) on South Street. At the time of the Reformation, St Mary's became a seminary of Protestant theology, and today it houses the university's Faculty of Divinity.

British Golf Museum

Bruce Embankment • April–Oct Mon–Sat 9.30am–5pm, Sun 10am–5pm; Nov–March Mon–Sat 10am–4pm • £7 • ⓘ 01334 460046, Ⓦ britishgolfmuseum.co.uk

A collection of national importance, the **British Golf Museum** has pictures of golfing greats from Tom Morris to Tiger Woods, along with clubs, trophies and a variety of paraphernalia from the seventeenth century onwards. It's predominantly an attraction for golfing obsessives, but the museum is designed to be family friendly. You can try your hand with an old ball and putt on the museum's indoor green or get togged up in traditional golfing attire.

East and West Sands

St Andrews has two great beaches: the vast expanse of **West Sands**, just north of town, and the more compact **East Sands**, beside the harbour. The West Sands are best known from the opening sequences of the Oscar-winning film *Chariots of Fire*, and while they're still used by budding athletes, less energetic activities include sandcastle competitions, breathtaking dips in the North Sea, and birdwatching at the lonely north end. The blustery winds that are the scourge of golfers and walkers alike do at least make the beach a great place to fly a kite.

8

ARRIVAL AND DEPARTURE
ST ANDREWS

By train The nearest train station is at Leuchars on the Edinburgh–Dundee line, 5 miles northwest across the River Eden, from where regular buses make the 15min trip into town. When you buy your rail ticket to Leuchars, ask for a St Andrews rail-bus ticket that includes the bus fare.
Destinations Aberdeen (1–2 hourly; 1hr 30min); Dundee (1–2 hourly; 15min); Edinburgh (1–2 hourly; 1hr).

By bus The bus station is on City Rd at the west end of Market St.
Destinations Anstruther (2 hourly; 20–25min); Dundee (1–2 hourly; 35min); Edinburgh (1–2 hourly; 1hr 30min); Leuchars (1–2 hourly; 10min).

GETTING AROUND AND INFORMATION

Bike rental Spokes (37 South St, Mon–Sat 9am–5.30pm; ⓘ 01334 477835, Ⓦ spokescycles.net) offers bike rental for £20/day including locks and helmets.

Tourist office The good-sized tourist office is at 70 Market St (April–June & Sept–Oct Mon–Sat 9.15am–5pm, Sun 10am–5pm; Nov–March Mon–Sat 9.15am–5pm, closed Sun; July–Aug Mon–Sat 9.15am–6pm, Sun 10am–5pm; ⓘ 01382 472021, Ⓦ visitstandrews.com); free internet access.

THE VISION OF ST RULE

According to legend, St Andrews was founded, pretty much by accident, in the fourth century. **St Rule** – or Regulus – a custodian of the bones of St Andrew in Patras in southwestern Greece, had a vision in which an angel ordered him to carry five of the saint's bones to the western edge of the world, where he was to build a city in his honour. The conscientious courier set off, but was shipwrecked on the rocks close to the present harbour. Struggling ashore with his precious burden, he built a shrine to the saint on what subsequently became the site of the **cathedral**; St Andrew became Scotland's patron saint and the town its ecclesiastical capital.

TOURS AND ACTIVITIES

TOURS

Golf tours For a bracing introduction to the importance of golf to the town, the St Andrews Links Trust runs 50min guided walking tours of the Old Course before handing out a complimentary golf ball and novelty scorecard. Starts from outside the golf shop at the eighteenth hole of the Old Course, north of town (Easter–Sept daily at 11am & 2pm; £10; ☎01334 466666, ☻standrews.com).

GOLF

You can play any of the town's courses, all of which are administered by the St Andrews Links Trust. With the exception of the Balgove Course and Ladies Putting Club, all of the town's courses must be booked; this can be done through ☎01334 466666 or ☻standrews.org.uk. The main courses are on the north side of St Andrews; follow the brown "Golf" signposts off the A91.

Balgove Course The only nine-hole course in St Andrews is designed for families and beginners, and, unlike the others, you can just turn up and play. Green fees £8–15. Open daily all year: Easter–Sept open 7am–dusk; Oct–Easter open 8.40am–dusk.

Castle Course Built in 2008, the newest addition to the St Andrews Links has already gained a positive following in part thanks to its clifftop position and views to the town. However, putting here can be a bit frustrating as the greens are not as flat as you might expect for a modern course, and even experienced golfers can be heard cursing the design.

Green fees £60–120. Open daily all year: Easter–Sept open 7am–dusk; Oct–Easter open 8.40am–dusk.

The Himalayas (Ladies Putting Club) Officially named the Ladies Putting Club but more commonly referred to as The Himalayas, this course is open to the public without booking, and offers arguably the best golfing experience in St Andrews. Even if you can't tell a birdie from a bogey, it's a fantastically lumpy eighteen-holer in an ideal setting right next to the Old Course and the sea. You can have all the thrill of sinking a six-footer in golf's most famous location for a bargain price. Green fees £3. March Sat 11am–4pm, Sun noon–4pm; April–Sept Mon–Fri 10.30am–6.30pm, Sat 10.30am–6pm Sun noon–6.30pm; Oct daily 11am–3pm.

New Course Designed in 1895, this has some pretty bumpy putting greens and the fairways have hard ground and plenty of ball-swallowing bunkers to test any well-seasoned pro. Green fees £37–75. Open daily all year: Easter–Sept open 7am–dusk; Oct–Easter open 8.40am–dusk.

Old Course The oldest course in the world offers the amateur the chance to pit their game against the generations of golfing legends that have birdied and bogeyed their way round the eighteen windswept greens. Its popularity is unrelenting; to play here you must have a handicap certificate (24 for men/36 for women) and enter a ballot at least two days in advance. Green fees £85–175. Open daily all year: Easter–Sept open 7am–dusk; Oct–Easter open 8.40am–dusk.

ACCOMMODATION

There's no shortage of accommodation both in town and around, although average **prices** in all categories vie with Edinburgh's as the highest in Scotland. **Upmarket hotels** are thick on the ground, notably around the golf courses. There are plenty of **guesthouses**, though rooms often get booked up in the summer, when you should definitely book in advance.

Castlemount 2 The Scores ☎01334 475579, ☻castlemount.net. Charming old B&B romantically set overlooking the castle ruins and to the sea beyond. Within, there's a patchwork of bygone furniture and fabrics throughout, and en-suite rooms, some with four-poster beds. **£130**

Craigtoun Meadows Holiday Park 2 miles southwest of town signposted off the A915 ☎01334 475959, ☻craigtounmeadows.co.uk. Reasonably convenient for the centre of town, this site is well run and has a surprisingly good range of facilities, particularly for children. Camping per pitch **£20**; static caravan rental per week (mid-March to Oct) **£595**

Fairways of St Andrews 8A Golf Place ☎01334 479513, ☻fairwaysofstandrews.co.uk. One of the cheapest options in town, this small guesthouse has three contemporary en-suite rooms, the best of which has a balcony overlooking the golf courses. **£49**

★**Old Fishergate House** 35 North Castle St ☎01334 470874, ☻oldfishergatehouse.co.uk. Entered via a quaint cobbled pavement, this seventeenth-century townhouse is one of the more personal places to stay in town, with its books, pictures and antique furniture including an old piano. The en-suite rooms have wi-fi and TV. The obvious choice for traditionalists. **£115**

St Andrews Country Cabins Cuplahills Farm, 7 miles northwest of St Andrews, off the A914 ☎01334 870225, ☻standrewscountrycabins.co.uk. A surprisingly luxurious option for families and groups, these superb eco lodges sleep six in three contemporary bedrooms. There's a kitchen and lounge as well as an exterior deck and six playground. Minimum stay three nights. Per night up to six guests **£185**

St Andrews Tourist Hostel Inchape House, St Mary Place ☎01334 479911, ☻hostelworld.com. Handily placed backpacker hostel in a converted townhouse right above *The Grill House* restaurant, with plenty of dorm beds but no doubles. The cheapest option in town, but not the quietest. Dorms **£14**

EATING

St Andrews has no shortage of restaurants and cafés. Most are found on Market St, South St and the interlinking closes between the two.

★**Balgove Steak Barn** 1 mile northwest of St Andrews on the A91 ☎01334 898145, ⓦbalgove .com. Sited in an open former saw mill, mostly enclosed by stacked potato boxes and climbing plants, this ingenious fair-weather restaurant does a roaring trade thanks to its unorthodox set-up and gourmet comfort food. Beefburgers and mushroom burgers (£9 and £8 respectively) are grilled before your eyes on the huge cast-iron barbecue. Wash them down with local draught ales before visiting their fantastic sister farm shop/deli next door. May–Sept Thurs–Sun noon–8.30pm.

The Doll's House 3 Church Square ☎01334 477422, ⓦdollshouse-restaurant.co.uk. Stylish comfort food based around Scottish meat and fish, with a continental feel to the outdoor tables. There are a nice couple of pies to choose from – rabbit (£13) or celeriac and leek (£10) – as well as lighter options like tuna steak and Niçoise salad. Great breakfasts are served until midday too. Daily 10am–10pm.

Little Italy 2 Logies Lane ☎01334 479299. Ticks every

cliché in the book from the Marlon Brando pictures on the wall to the gaudy red and green decor, but the food and wine are reliably great and the atmosphere is always lively. Pizzas and pastas start at £9. Daily noon–11pm.

The Peat Inn 6 miles southwest of St Andrews, on the junction of the B940 and B941 ☎01334 840206, ⓦthepeatinn.co.uk. With a reputation as one of Scotland's gourmet hot spots for the past thirty years, *The Peat Inn* offers Michelin star-quality fine dining featuring top local produce in an intimate dining room. Menus range from a three-course set lunch (£19) to a six-course tasting menu (£70), with dishes like wood pigeon salad or crispy confit pork cheek. Tues–Sat 12.30–2pm & 6.30–9pm.

Tailend Fish Bar 130 Market St ☎01334 474070. A terrific and popular restaurant/takeaway dishing up fresh fish sourced from nearby Arbroath. Treat yourself to the famous – and now EU-protected – Arbroath Smokie (£7 takeaway or £11.50 eat in), a pungent haddock smoked in the traditional way, over hardwood chips. Daily 11.30am–10pm.

DRINKING

★**The Criterion** 99 South St ☎01334 474543. One of the town's more charming pubs; it's a sensitively preserved Victorian relic – well illuminated by its lofty windows – with good beers and whiskies and a vibrant atmosphere, particularly on live music nights. South-facing in aspect, the pavement tables are a particular draw on sunny afternoons and, for the peckish, they sell a range of "Cri" pies throughout the day. Sun–Wed 10am–midnight,

Thurs–Sat 10am–1am.

The Rule 116 South St ☎01334 473473, ⓦthe-rule .co.uk. A large, modern pub-diner with cheap grub (cooked breakfast is just £4) and a strong focus on noisy sports screenings. The one redeeming feature here is the generous sun-trapping beer garden to the rear. Mon–Wed 9am–midnight, Thurs 9am–1am, Fri–Sat 9am–2am, Sun 9am–11pm. Food served daily 9am–9pm.

The East Neuk

Extending south of St Andrews as far as Largo Bay, the **East Neuk** ("neuk" is Scots for "corner") is famous for its series of quaint fishing villages. Old cottages and merchants' houses huddle round stone-built harbours in groupings that are fallen upon with joy by artists and photographers. Their Flemish-influenced crow-stepped gables and red pantiled roofs indicate a history of strong trading links with the Low Countries. Inland, gently rolling hills provide some of the best farmland in Scotland, with quiet

THE FIFE COASTAL PATH

Taking in the East Neuk villages, The **Fife Coastal Path** (ⓦfifecoastalpath.co.uk) follows the shoreline for 117 miles between the Forth and Tay bridges, with useful bus services covering some sections. To sample Fife's remoter seafront try the five-mile tranche between Crail and Kingsbarns rounding the headland of Fife Ness. Buses between St Andrews and Crail stop at Kingsbarns, from where the path is well signposted. Another interesting section is from St Andrews south to Boarhills, just past the town's golf courses. It's an easy three-mile stretch passing by rocky bays where you'll see the Rock and Spindle, a twisting volcanic sea stack by the water's edge.

country lanes more redolent of parts of southern England than north of the border, although, not surprisingly, the area is dotted with windy **golf courses**.

Well patronized by holiday-makers and weekenders from the central belt, the East Neuk is particularly regarded for its arts and crafts and good food; the **restaurants** are well known for serving fresh seafood, often complemented by produce from the fertile Fife farmland.

Crail

CRAIL is the archetypally photogenic East Neuk fishing village, its maze of rough cobbled streets leading steeply down to a tiny stone-built harbour surrounded by piles of lobster creels, with fishermen's cottages tucked into every nook and cranny in the cliff. Beyond the harbour is a sand beach, and above are perched the grander merchants' houses, as well as the twelfth-century church, where John Knox (see box, p.68) once delivered a damning sermon rallying against the local fishermen for working on Sundays.

The village still has a working harbour, and if the boats have been out you can often buy fresh lobster and crab cooked to order from a small wooden shack right on the harbour edge.

Kingsbarns Distillery

2 miles north of Crail just off the A917 • Daily: Nov–Feb 11am–4pm, March & Oct 10am–5pm, April–Sept 10am–6pm • £10 • ☎ 01333 451300, ⓦ kingsbarnsdistillery.com

Scotland's newest distillery and set in a converted farm steading, the **Kingsbarns Distillery** opened for business in 2015 with its first drops of single malt expected to flow from 2018. The tour guide will proudly show off the beautiful hand-forged copper stills containing the spirit made from locally grown barley and the water pumped up from the aquifer below. The tour ends, as always, with a whisky tasting; the quality will improve over time as the spirit ages.

ARRIVAL AND INFORMATION | CRAIL

By bus Stopping on the High St, bus #95 runs hourly to St Andrews (25min) and Leven (for bus connection to Edinburgh; 1hr).

Tourist office The tourist office doubles with the Crail Museum and Heritage Centre (62 Marketgate; Easter–May & Oct Sat 11am–4pm, Sun 1.30–4pm; June–Sept Mon– Sat 11am–4pm, Sun 1.30–4pm; ☎ 01333 450869, ⓦ crailmuseum.org.uk) as a free village museum with displays on the village's close ties to the sea, farming and golf, as well as the local contribution to war efforts.

ACCOMMODATION

The Hazelton 29 Marketgate North ☎ 01333 450250, ⓦ thehazelton.co.uk. A pleasant and reasonably priced B&B peacefully located just off the High St. Rooms are well proportioned with high ceilings, en-suite shower rooms and a hospitality tray that includes home-made shortbread. **£70**

The Sauchope Links Park Balcomie Rd, on Crail's eastern fringe ☎ 01333 450460, ⓦ largoleisure.co.uk. A very pleasant campsite on the coast with caravans, lodges and more basic glamping domes for rent as well as the usual pitches. There's a grocery shop on site and recreation facilities include a heated pool (open June– Sept) and a games room. Per pitch **£17**

EATING

With a notable lack of places to sit down and eat, particularly in comparison with what's on offer elsewhere in the East Neuk, the village's businesses cater mostly for day-trippers. It's still possible to enjoy a good cooked lunch, usually involving seafood, but in the evening you'll be restricted to bar meals at one of the hotels.

Crail Harbour Gallery and Tearoom Shoregate ☎ 01333 451896, ⓦ crailharbourgallery.co.uk. Discreet café/gallery tucked into a cottage on the way down to the harbour, with low timbers, rough stone flooring and

terrace overlooking the Isle of May. Predominantly serving fresh coffee, cakes and toasted panini plus a few cooked meals including dressed crab for £12. Jan–Oct daily 10.30am–5pm.

★ **Reilly Shellfish** 34 Shoregate ☎ 01333 450476. The little wooden shack down at the harbour cooks the freshest takeaway lobster you're ever likely to find. Take your pick from the condemned crustaceans scuttling around the tank next to the shack (£11 a whole lobster). Tues–Sun noon–4pm.

SHOPPING

Crail Pottery 75 Nethergate ☎ 01333 451212, ⓦ crailpottery.com. An unmissable stop for its wide range of stoneware, terracotta pots and painted earthenware, hand-thrown on the wheel in the workshop. Mon–Fri 9am–5pm, Sat & Sun 10am–5pm.

Anstruther and around

The largest of the East Neuk fishing harbours, **ANSTRUTHER** retains an attractively old-fashioned air and no shortage of character in its houses and narrow streets. Life here mostly centres on or around its part-cobbled promenade, which separates the fish and chip shops, cafés and ice creameries of the cheerful Shore Street from the old harbour where small pleasure yachts vie for limited mooring space.

Scottish Fisheries Museum

East Shore, harbour • April–Sept Mon–Sat 10am–5.30pm, Sun 11am–5pm; Oct–March Mon–Sat 10am–4.30pm, Sun noon–4.30pm • £8 • ☎ 01333 310628, ⓦ scotfishmuseum.org

Set in an atmospheric complex of sixteenth- to nineteenth-century buildings with timber ceilings and wooden floors, the wonderfully unpretentious **Scottish Fisheries Museum** chronicles the history of the Scottish fishing and whaling industries with ingenious displays, including a whole series of exquisite model ships, built on site by a resident model-maker.

Isle of May

Boat trips Anstruther Harbour • Easter–Sept Mon–Sat one trip daily at varying times according to the tides; journey takes 50min each way and 2hr 30min spent on island • £25 • ☎ 07957 585200, ⓦ isleofmayferry.com

Located on the rugged **Isle of May**, several miles offshore from Anstruther, is a lighthouse erected in 1816 by Robert Louis Stevenson's grandfather, as well as the remains of Scotland's first lighthouse, built in 1636, which burnt coals as a beacon. The island is now a nature reserve and bird sanctuary. Between April and July the dramatic sea cliffs are covered with breeding kittiwakes, razorbills, guillemots and shags, while inland there are thousands of puffins and eider ducks. Boat-trippers should bring warm waterproof clothing and a picnic.

Scotland's Secret Bunker

4 miles north of Anstruther on the B940 signposted from the St Andrews road (B9131) • March–Oct daily 10am–5pm • £12 • ☎ 01333 310301, ⓦ secretbunker.co.uk

Scotland's Secret Bunker is as idiosyncratic a tourist attraction as you are likely to find. Long a top-secret part of the military establishment, the bunker was opened to the public in 1994 following its decommissioning at the end of the Cold War. Above ground is an innocent-looking farmhouse, although the various pieces of military hardware parked outside and the rows of barbed wire fencing hint that something more sinister is afoot. From the farmhouse, you walk down a long ramp to the bunker, which comprises a vast subterranean complex of operations rooms 100ft below ground and encased in 15ft of reinforced concrete. In the event of a nuclear war this was to have become Scotland's new administrative centre, with room for three hundred people; it has not been spruced up for tourists, and remains uncompromisingly spartan, with various rooms showing dormitories, radio rooms and James Bond-like control centres.

8

ARRIVAL AND DEPARTURE

ANSTRUTHER AND AROUND

By bus Buses stop at the harbour and serve Edinburgh (1–2 hourly; 2hr 15min) and St Andrews (hourly; 25min).

ACCOMMODATION AND EATING

★**Anstruther Fish Bar and Restaurant** 42–44 Shore St ☎01333 310518, ⓦanstrutherfishbar .co.uk. There's nowhere in Fife better to tuck into a haddock and chips (£6.30 takeaway/£8.65 eat-in) than Anstruther. The reputation of this restaurant has for years been far-reaching thanks to a close relationship between the shop and the quayside fish sellers. Daily 11.30am–10pm.

The Waterfront 20 Shore St ☎01333 312200,

ⓦanstruther-waterfront.co.uk. Overlooking the harbour, this restaurant with ten rooms offers modern and spacious en-suite comfort with a cooked breakfast included. Sadly, the rooms don't come with a view, but they're all the more peaceful for it. The restaurant spills out onto the pavement on balmier days and serves all meals from breakfast to dinner, with cream teas in between. From the wide seafood menu, go for the Fisherman's Pie at £8.50. Food served daily 8am–10pm. **£100**

Pittenweem and around

Despite its steady tourist influx, the pretty East Neuk village of **PITTENWEEM** thrives, as it always has done, on fishing, thanks to its deep harbour and busy fish market. With its sandy bay west of the port and fishermen's cottages lining the seafront and up into the high street, the village has become something of an artists' colony. An arts festival takes place every year in early August (ⓦpittenweemartsfestival.co.uk), with dozens of locals turning their houses into temporary galleries for the week.

Kellie Castle

3 miles northwest of Pittenweem on the B9171 • Easter–May & Sept Sat–Thurs 10.30–5pm; June–Aug daily 12.30–5pm; Oct Sat–Thurs 10.30–4.30pm • £9; NTS • Grounds year-round daily 9am–6pm (or dusk) • £10.50; NTS • ☎01333 720271, ⓦnts.org.uk

Kellie Castle has an unusual but harmonious mix of twin sixteenth-century towers linked by a seventeenth-century building. Abandoned in the early nineteenth century, it was rediscovered in 1878 by Professor James Lorimer, a distinguished political philosopher, who took on the castle as an "improving tenant". The wonderful, under-manicured **gardens**, where space is broken up by arches, alcoves and paths that weave between profuse herbaceous borders, were designed by the professor's son Robert, aged just 16.

8

ARRIVAL AND DEPARTURE

PITTENWEEM AND AROUND

By bus Buses stop at Viewforth Place (on the main road through town) for Edinburgh (1–2 hourly; 2hr 5min) and St

Andrews (2 hourly; 25–30min).

ACCOMMODATION AND EATING

Albert Cottage 15 Viewforth Place ☎01333 313973, ⓦalbertcottagefife.co.uk. Offering the best value for money in town, this welcoming B&B on the main thoroughfare has clean, colourful rooms and a hospitality tray. Guests can also make use of the sitting room and the pleasant rear garden. **£70**

West End Bar and Gantry 30–32 South Loan ☎01333 311587, ⓦwestendbarandgantry.co.uk.

A cosy old-fashioned local with a small selection of ales and a pretty beer garden housing a retired fishing vessel. Light lunches including soups and toasties are available, and, if you book, they do three-course evening meals on Saturdays for £14 a head that include a vegetarian option as well as fish and chips. Mon–Thurs 11.30am–midnight; Fri–Sat 11.30–1am; Sun 12.30pm–midnight.

Elie

Gathered round a curve of golden-brown sand twelve miles south of St Andrews, **ELIE** is a popular escape for middle-class Edinburgh families who come for the bracing air and golf courses. This was once a popular bathing spot; east of Elie bay stands a tower built as a summerhouse for Lady Janet Anstruther in the late eighteenth century, with a hanging room to allow her to bathe in a pool in the rocks below.

ARRIVAL AND DEPARTURE ELIE

By bus Buses stop on the High St for Edinburgh (1–2 hourly; 1hr 55min) and St Andrews (2 hourly; 35–40min).

ACTIVITIES

Elie Watersports Elie Harbour ☎01333 330962, ⓦeliewatersports.com. Elie's sheltered bay is understandably popular for watersports, and this is the place to come if you fancy a spin on a windsurfer (£20/hr), canoe (£14), sailing boat (£25) or even a fun pedal boat (£10/30min). June–Aug 10am–6pm.

ACCOMMODATION AND EATING

Ship Inn The Toft, by the harbour ☎01333 330246, ⓦshipinn.scot.com. The essential (and child-friendly) pub stop in Elie, the *Ship* has low timber ceilings and real fires, while the beer garden to the rear offers sweeping views over the golden sandy bay near the harbour. The bar meals offered here range from haddock crepe for £10 up to the £20 roast duck. On fair weather weekend days you can grab a £5 burger cooked on the garden barbecue. The pub also provides tasteful rooms, the best with views over the bay. Sun–Thurs 10.30am–11pm, Fri–Sat 10.30am–midnight. **£110**

Central Fife

With its undulating landscape of fertile arable land, **central Fife** has markedly fewer settlements than its coastline and consequently sees less of the region's tourism. Notable exceptions to this are **Hill of Tarvit**, one of the country's finest Edwardian mansion houses, and **Falkland Palace**, a medieval gem in the heart of Scotland's first conservation village. **Falkland** sits at the foot of the twin-peaked, heather-swathed **Lomond Hills** that provide a grandstand view of the region from the easily walked ridge between West Lomond (1696ft) and East Lomond (1378ft).

Falkland

On the eastern margins of the Lomond Hills regional park, ten miles north of Kirkcaldy, the conspicuously handsome small town of **FALKLAND** is a popular day-tripping destination thanks to its grand, medieval palace and narrow streets lined with well-preserved historic buildings.

Falkland Palace

East Port, Falkland • March–Oct Mon–Sat 11am–5pm, Sun noon–5pm • £12.50; NTS • ☎01337 857397, ⓦnts.org.uk

A hunting retreat to the Stewart kings for two hundred years, the construction of **Falkland Palace** began at the behest of James IV in 1500, and was completed and embellished by James V. Charles II stayed here in 1650 when he was in Scotland for his coronation, but after the Jacobite rising of 1715 and temporary occupation by Rob Roy the palace was abandoned, remaining so until the late nineteenth century when the keepership was acquired by the third marquess of Bute. He completely restored the palace, and today it is a stunning example of early Renaissance architecture, complete with corbelled parapet, mullioned windows, round towers and massive walls. Inside there's a stately drawing room, a Chapel Royal (still used for Mass) and a Tapestry Gallery, swathed with seventeenth-century Flemish hangings. Outside, the **gardens** have well-stocked herbaceous borders lining a pristine lawn. Look out for the high walls of the oldest real (or royal) tennis court in Britain – built in 1539 for James V and still in use.

ARRIVAL AND DEPARTURE FALKLAND

By bus Buses stop on New Rd, a few paces east of the palace.

Destinations Glenrothes (Mon–Sat 2 hourly, 7 on Sun; 20min); Perth (Mon–Sat hourly, 2 on Sun; 55min); St Andrews (Mon–Sat hourly, 5 on Sun; 1hr 30min).

ACCOMMODATION AND EATING

Covenanter Hotel The Square ☎01337 857163, ⓦcovenanterfalkland.co.uk. This traditional inn at the heart of the village has a cosy pub and a good-value restaurant serving unpretentious food from its all-day menu. The evening à la carte options include roast vegetable lasagne for a bargain £8.25 or herb roasted chicken with mash for £8.75. If you're staying over, the hotel offers wide en-suite rooms, big comfy beds and a full Scottish breakfast. Food served 11am–late. **£95**

Hill of Tarvit

Just off the A916, 2 miles south of the A91 at Cupar • **House** Easter–June & Sept–Oct Thurs–Mon 11am–4.30pm; July–Aug daily 11am–4.30pm • **Gardens** All year daily 9am–6pm or dusk • **Scotstarvit Tower** Keys available from the house Easter–Oct • £10.50; NTS • ☎01337 840319, ⓦnts.org.uk

Remodelled in 1906 by Sir Robert Lorimer from a late seventeenth-century building, **Hill of Tarvit** offers a rare insight into the lives of the wealthy from the turn of the twentieth century, with its central heating, telephones, plumbing and lighting – all state of the art at the time. This Edwardian mansion – formerly the home of the geographer and cartographer Sir John Scott – also contains an impressive collection of eighteenth-century Chippendale and French furniture, Dutch paintings, Chinese porcelain and a restored Edwardian laundry.

Three-quarters of a mile west of the present house and also on the estate, you can visit the five-storey, late sixteenth-century **Scotstarvit Tower**, a fine example of a Scots tower house.

| ARRIVAL AND DEPARTURE | HILL OF TARVIT | **8** |

By bus Buses stop at the Cupar entrance (A916) and serve Glenrothes (Mon–Sat hourly, 5 on Sun; 1hr) and St Andrews (Mon–Sat hourly, 5 on Sun; 1hr).

Western Fife

Fife's **south coast** curves sharply north at the mouth of the Firth of Forth, exposing the towns and villages to an icy east wind that somewhat undermines the sunshine image of the beaches. The highlight of the coast is one of the largest man-made structures in Scotland, the impressive **Forth Rail Bridge**, which joins Fife at **North Queensferry**.

East from here you'll find a straggle of Fife fishing communities such as **Aberdour** and **Kinghorn** which have depended on the sea for centuries, and now popular, although not especially attractive, holiday spots as well as being part of Edinburgh's commuter belt.

To the west of the bridge, the shorefront, blighted by industry and docklands, has one great surprise in the time-capsule village of **Culross**, with links from the sixth century to the dawn of the industrial revolution.

Inland, just north from the bridge, lies **Dunfermline**, Scotland's capital until the Union of the Crowns in 1603. This "auld, grey toun" is built on a hill, dominated by its abbey and ruined palace at the top.

The Forth Bridges

The cantilevered **Forth Rail Bridge**, built from 1883 to 1890 by Sir John Fowler and Benjamin Baker, ranks among the supreme achievements of Victorian engineering. Some fifty thousand tons of steel were used in the construction of a design that manages to express grace as well as might. Just upriver, the **Forth Road Bridge** is a suspension bridge that strikingly complements the older structure. Erected between 1958 and 1964, it finally killed off a 900-year-old route, and now attracts a heavy volume of traffic. A little further west is the **Queensferry Crossing**; the newest road bridge addition (due to open in 2017) and the world's longest cable-stayed bridge. For the best **view** of the rail bridge, make use of the pedestrian and cycle lane on the east side of the road bridge. For more on the bridge, head to the museum in South Queensferry (see p.110).

ARRIVAL AND DEPARTURE
THE FORTH BRIDGES

By train: Trains from Edinburgh cross the rail bridge, stopping a short walk from the bridge at North Queensferry (every 10min; 20min).

By car The A90 crosses the road bridge 10 miles west of Edinburgh. Exit the dual carriageway at North Queensferry.

Culross

CULROSS (pronounced "Coorus"), is the best-preserved seventeenth-century village in Scotland, thanks in large part to the work of the National Trust for Scotland, which has been renovating its palace and whitewashed, pantiled buildings since 1932. All cobbled streets and squat cottages with crow-stepped gables, as well as crooked passageways with names such as "Wee Causeway" and "Stinking Wynd", the royal burgh was first developed in the fifth century with the arrival of St Serf on the northern side of the Forth at Cuileann Ros. By the sixteenth and seventeenth centuries Culross was at the centre of the coal-mining industry and operated the world's first below-sea extractions while bailing out the water using a horse-driven Egyptian wheel system. The village's time-warp character brings in plentiful visitors, but its popularity by no means detracts from its charms.

Culross Palace

West Green • Easter–May & Sept Wed–Sun noon–5pm; June–Aug daily noon–5pm; Oct Wed–Sun noon–4pm; Gardens Easter–Oct noon–5pm • £10.50; NTS • ☎ 01383 880359, Ⓦ nts.org.uk

The most impressive building in the village, the ochre-coloured **Culross Palace** was built by wealthy coal merchant George Bruce in the late sixteenth century. It is not a true palace at all, but a grand and impressive house with lots of small rooms and connecting passageways. Inside, you follow the fixed route, taking in wonderful painted ceilings, pine panelling, antique furniture and curios, while outside, dormer windows and crow-stepped gables dominate the walled court in which the house stands. The garden is planted with grasses, herbs and vegetables of the period (some on sale), carefully grown from seed, while Dumpy hens roam free.

Culross Abbey

Kirk St, beyond Back Causeway, which is signposted from the main road • Always open • Free • ☎ 01383 880231

Founded by Cistercian monks on land given to the Church in 1217 by the earl of Fife, the nave of the original building of **Culross Abbey** is a ruin – a lawn studded with great stumps of columns. The choir of the abbey became the **parish church** in 1633; inside, wooden panels detail the donations given by eighteenth-century worthies to the parish poor, and a tenth-century Celtic cross in the north transept is a reminder of the abbey's origins. Many of the stones in the **graveyard** are eighteenth century, with symbols depicting the occupation of the person who is buried; the gravestone of a gardener has a crossed spade and rake as well as an hourglass with the sand run out.

ARRIVAL AND DEPARTURE
CULROSS

By bus Buses stop outside the palace for Stirling (Mon–Sat hourly; 50min) and Dunfermline (1–2 hourly; 30min).

EATING AND DRINKING

Red Lion Inn Low Causeway ☎ 01383 880225, Ⓦ redlionculross.co.uk. The only pub in the village and the only place for miles to serve food into the evening. Expect your standard pub menu with lots of meaty choices from sausages to steak pies, with mains hovering around the £10 mark. There are, however, a few more appealing vegetarian and salad dishes if you fancy something lighter. Daily noon–9pm.

Dunfermline

The former de facto capital of Scotland and royal seat of power established by Malcolm III in the mid-eleventh century, **DUNFERMLINE** made the significant contribution to medieval Scots politics until it was abandoned by James VI after the 1603 Union of the Crowns. Today the town's charm has been considerably eroded by twentieth-century development, and few visitors venture further than the outstanding ruined abbey and its small old town.

Dunfermline Abbey and Palace

Monastery St, 10min walk west of Dunfermline train station • April–Sept daily 9.30am–5.30pm; Oct–March Sat–Wed 10am–4pm • £4.50; HES • ☎ 01383 739026, ⊛ historicenvironment.scot

Dunfermline Abbey is a monolithic demonstration of stone workmanship from the Middle Ages, its oldest part attributable to Queen Margaret, who began building a Benedictine priory in 1072 (still visible beneath the nave of the present church). Her son, **David I**, raised the priory to the rank of abbey in the following century. In 1303, during the first of the **Wars of Independence**, most of the monastic buildings were destroyed by the English King Edward I's troops, who occupied the palace and had the church roof stripped of lead to provide ammunition for his army's catapults. **Robert the Bruce** helped rebuild the abbey and when he died of leprosy was buried here minus his heart, which was sent, unsuccessfully, on a pilgrimage to the Holy Land, only to be buried at Melrose Abbey (see p.122). Inside, the stained glass is impressive, and the thick columns are artfully carved with chevrons, spirals and arrowheads.

The guesthouse of Queen Margaret's Benedictine monastery, south of the abbey, became the **palace** in the sixteenth century under James VI, who gave both it and the abbey to his consort, Queen Anne of Denmark. Charles I, the last monarch to be born in Scotland, entered the world here in 1600. Today, all that is left of the palace is a long sandstone facade, especially impressive when silhouetted against the evening sky.

8

ARRIVAL AND INFORMATION

DUNFERMLINE

By train Trains stop at Dunfermline's train station, halfway down the long hill of St Margaret's Drive, southeast of the centre, with services to Edinburgh every 30min; 30min).

By bus The bus station is on Queen Anne St, a block north of High St.

Destinations Culross (1–2 hourly; 30min); Edinburgh (2 hourly; 1hr).

Tourist office Offering an accommodation booking service, the tourist office is at 1 High St (Mon–Sat 9.30am–5pm, mid-June to Aug Sun 11am–4.30pm; ☎ 01383 720999, ⊛ visitdunfermline.com).

EATING AND DRINKING

Khushi's 1 Canmore St ☎ 01383 737577, ⊛ khushis.com/dunfermline. Dunfermline branch of the Edinburgh-based restaurant charged with introducing curry to Scotland back in the 1940s. Today the original family members still have a watchful eye on the quality. All the favourites are on the menu, from chicken tikka to Goan fish curry. Lunch set menu costs £13. Mon–Sat noon–3pm & 5–10pm; Sun 1.30–10pm.

Perthshire

LOCH TUMMEL

9

Perthshire

Genteel, attractive Perthshire is, in many ways, the epitome of well-groomed rural Scotland. An area of gentle glens, mature woodland, rushing rivers and peaceful lochs, it's the long-established domain of Scotland's well-to-do country set. First settled over eight thousand years ago, it was ruled by the Romans and then the Picts before Celtic missionaries established themselves here, enjoying the amenable climate, fertile soil, and ideal location for defence and trade.

Occupying a strategic position at the mouth of the River Tay, the ancient town of **Perth** has as much claim as Stirling to be the gateway to the Highlands. Salmon, wool and, by the nineteenth century, whisky – Bell's, Dewar's and the Famous Grouse brands all hail from this area – were all exported from here. At nearby **Scone**, Kenneth MacAlpine established the capital of the kingdom of the Scots and the Picts in 846. When this settlement was washed away by floods in 1210, William the Lion founded Perth as a royal burgh and it stood as Scotland's capital until the mid-fifteenth century.

Rural Perthshire is dominated by the gathering mountains of the Highlands, topography that tolerates little development. There's plenty of good agricultural land, however, and the area is dotted with neat, confident towns and villages like **Crieff**, at the heart of the rolling Strathearn Valley, ancient **Dunkeld**, with its independent cafés and craft shops, and lovely ruined cathedral, and **Aberfeldy**, set deep amid farmland east of Loch Tay. Among the wealth of historical sites in Perthshire are splendid Baronial **Blair Castle**, north of Pitlochry, and the impressive Italianate gardens at **Drummond Castle** near Crieff.

North and west of Perth, **Highland Perthshire** begins to weave its charms: mighty woodlands blend with glassy waterways, most notably the River Tay, overlooked by **Ben Lawers**, the area's tallest peak. Further north, the countryside becomes more sparsely populated and ever more spectacular, and there is some wonderful walking country around **Pitlochry**, **Blair Atholl** and the wild expanses of **Rannoch Moor** to the west.

GETTING AROUND   **PERTHSHIRE**

By train The Perth to Inverness train line hugs the A9 road. There are also train services connecting Perth with Dundee and, in the south, Stirling.

By bus Direct, long-distance buses link Perthshire with Dundee, Inverness and Aberdeen. Local buses – albeit

often infrequent – connect towns like Perth with mo[re] remote areas.

By car Perthshire's most useful road is the A9, which cuts a line north from Perth to Inverness, passing Dunkeld an[d] Pitlochry.

Perth and around

Surrounded by fertile agricultural land and beautiful scenery, the market town of **PERTH** was Scotland's capital for several centuries. It has a long history of **livestock trading**, a tradition continued throughout the year, with regular Aberdeen Angus show[s] and sales from June to September, while its position at the heart of one of Scotland's richest food-production areas encouraged a regular **farmers' market** (see p.326).

BLAIR CASTLE

Highlights

The Fergusson Gallery A touch of Antibes in Perthshire: this Perth gallery celebrates the vibrant work of J.D. Fergusson and his dancer wife Margaret Morris. **See p.323**

Drummond Castle Gardens These terraced gardens near Crieff are a symmetrical marvel, leading into spacious parkland beyond. **See p.328**

Folk music Join in a session at the bar of the Taybank in the gorgeously preserved town of Dunkeld. **See p.330**

Pitlochry Festival Theatre A gleaming glassy building on the banks of the Tummel River, home to a long-established repertory company. **See p.335**

Blair Castle Observe the grand life of the Highland nobility, along with extensive parkland and the country's only private army. **See p.335**

Schiehallion Scale Perthshire's "fairy mountain" for the views over lochs, hills, glens and moors. **See p.336**

Rannoch Moor One of the most inaccessible places in Scotland, where hikers can discover a true sense of remote emptiness. **See p.337**

HIGHLIGHTS ARE MARKED ON THE MAP ON P.322

9

Perth's compact **centre** occupies a small patch on the west bank of the River Tay, flanked by two large areas of green parkland, known as the North and South Inch. The closure of the McEwens department store, which started trading in 1868, has been a blow to the city's economy and shopping prowess. The main shopping areas are **High Street** and **South Street**, as well as St John's shopping centre on King Edward Street. Opposite the entrance to the centre is the imposing **City Hall**, used by Scotland's politicians for party conferences. Perth is at its most attractive along **Tay Street**, with a succession of increasingly grand buildings along one side and the attractively landscaped riverside embankment on the other.

Brief history

During the reign of James I, Parliament met in Perth on several occasions, but its glory was short-lived: the king was murdered in the town's Dominican priory in 1437 by Sir Robert Graham, who was captured in the Highlands and tortured to death in Stirling. In May 1559, during the Reformation, John Knox preached a rousing sermon in St John's Kirk, which led to the destruction (by those Knox later condemned as "the rascal multitude") of the town's four monasteries – an event that quickened the pace of reform in Scotland. Despite

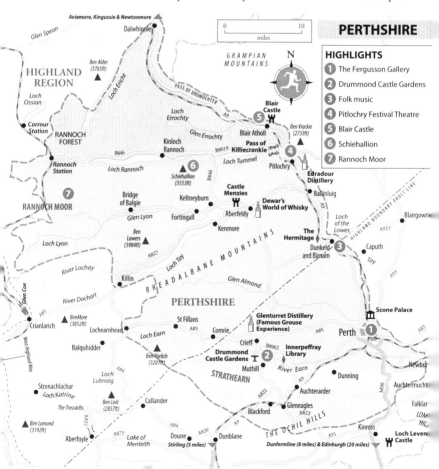

PERTHSHIRE

HIGHLIGHTS

1. The Fergusson Gallery
2. Drummond Castle Gardens
3. Folk music
4. Pitlochry Festival Theatre
5. Blair Castle
6. Schiehallion
7. Rannoch Moor

OUT AND ABOUT IN PERTHSHIRE

To many, Perthshire means a celebration of the great outdoors, with **activities** from gentle strolls through ancient oak forests to white-knuckle rides down frothing waterfalls. The variety of landscapes and their relative accessibility from the central belt has led to a significant number of operators being based in the area.

Rafting and other water activities Nae Limits, based in Ballinluig, near Pitlochry (☎01796 482600, ⓦnaelimits.co.uk), runs a varied programme of canyoning, whitewater rafting, river tubing and cliff-jumping that's sure to satisfy adrenaline junkies. Splash, in Aberfeldy (☎01887 829706, ⓦrafting .co.uk), offers rafting sessions on larger craft through the best rapids on the Tay at Grandtully, as well as accredited rafting courses.

Paintballing and quad biking As well as whitewater rafting, Splash can arrange other activities including paintballing and quad biking.
Safari In Dull, near Aberfeldy, Highland Safaris (☎01887 820071, ⓦhighlandsafaris.net) are a good bet if you'd like an introduction to wild Scotland, in which you're taken by 4WD vehicle to search for golden eagle eyries, stags and pine martens.

decline in the seventeenth century, the community expanded in the eighteenth century and has prospered ever since; today the whisky and insurance trades employ significant numbers.

St John's Kirk

31 St John St • May–Sept daily 10am–4pm; Sunday service begins at 9.30am • Free • ⓦst-johns-kirk.co.uk

Solid and attractive **St John's Kirk**, surrounded by cobbled lanes and cafés, was founded by David I in 1126. The present building dates from the fifteenth century and was restored in 1923–28 to house a war memorial chapel designed by Robert Lorimer. Perth was once known as "St John's Town", and the local football team takes the name **St Johnstone** rather than that of Perth.

The Fergusson Gallery

Marshall Place • Mon–Sat 10am–5pm; also Sun 1–4.30pm May–Aug • Free • ☎01738 783425, ⓦmuseumsgalleriesscotland.org.uk

On the corner of Tay Street and Marshall Place, the **Fergusson Gallery** is the town's one essential place to visit, located in a striking round Victorian water tower with a cast-iron dome. The gallery is home to an extensive collection of work by **J.D. Fergusson**, the foremost artist of the Scottish Colourist movement (see box, p.196). Born in Leith, he lived and worked for long periods in France, where he was greatly influenced by Impressionist and post-Impressionist artists. At the beginning of the twentieth century, Fergusson developed a more radical technique to paint some dramatic nudes such as the Matisse-inspired *At My Studio Window*, which mixes elements of an illuminated Celtic manuscript with his confident understanding of the female form. Look out, too, for *Eastre: Hymn to the Sun*, an exotic and radiant brass head inspired by his dancer wife and collaborator Margaret Morris.

Museum and Art Gallery

8 George St • Mon–Sat 10am–5pm; also Sun 1–5pm May–Oct • Free • ☎01738 632488, ⓦpkc.gov.uk

Housed in one of Perth's grandest buildings, the **Museum and Art Gallery** has exhibits on local history, art, natural history, archeology, glass and whisky, and gives a good overview of local life through the centuries. Among the exhibits is a Pictish cross slab, and there's a display on the discoveries at prehistoric Forteviot, including a rare dagger burial.

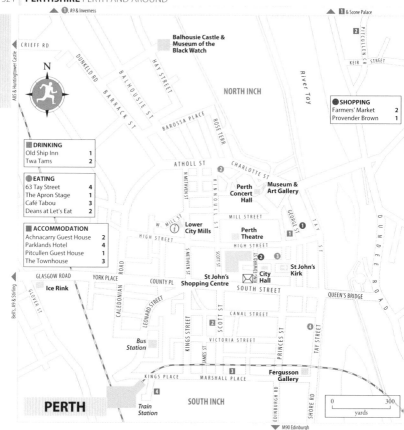

On the map:

Balhousie Castle & Museum of the Black Watch

CRIEFF RD

DUNKELD RD

BALHOUSIE ST

BARRACK ST

HAY STREET

NORTH INCH

BAROSSA PLACE

ROSE TERR

River Tay

SHOPPING
| Farmers' Market | 2 |
| Provender Brown | 1 |

DRINKING
| Old Ship Inn | 1 |
| Twa Tams | 2 |

ATHOLL ST

CHARLOTTE ST

Perth Concert Hall

Museum & Art Gallery

EATING
63 Tay Street	4
The Apron Stage	1
Café Tabou	3
Deans at Let's Eat	2

W. MILL ST

Lower City Mills

MILL STREET

Perth Theatre

GEORGE ST

ACCOMMODATION
Achnacarry Guest House	2
Parklands Hotel	4
Pitcullen Guest House	1
The Townhouse	3

HIGH STREET

HIGH STREET

ST EDWARD ST

St John's Kirk

City Hall

St John's Shopping Centre

SOUTH STREET

QUEEN'S BRIDGE

GLASGOW ROAD   YORK PLACE

Ice Rink

CALEDONIAN ROAD

COUNTY PL

CANAL STREET

KINGS STREET

SCOTT ST

VICTORIA STREET

PRINCES ST

TAY STREET

Bus Station

KINGS PLACE   MARSHALL PLACE

Fergusson Gallery

PERTH

Train Station

SOUTH INCH

EDINBURGH RD

SHORE RD

0   300
yards

M90 Edinburgh

Museum of the Black Watch

Hay St • Daily 9.30am–4.30pm • Free • ☎ 01738 638152, ⓦ theblackwatch.co.uk

North of the town centre, just off Hay Street and adjacent to the North Inch, fifteenth-century Balhousie Castle is home to the headquarters of the Black Watch regiment and the **Museum of the Black Watch**. The Black Watch – whose name refers to the dark colour of their tartan – was the local regiment until it was merged with other Scottish infantry battalions in 2006. The museum chronicles its history, dating back to 1740, through a good display of paintings, uniforms, documents, weapons and photographs.

Scone Palace

2 miles north of Perth on the A93 • Daily: May–Sept 9.30am–5pm; March, April & Oct 10am–4pm; grounds close 5.45pm • Palace and groun £11; grounds only £6.70 • ☎ 01738 552300, ⓦ scone-palace.co.uk • Take the #58 bus from Perth bus station, or bus #3 from South St

Almost as well known as Perth itself is **Scone** (pronounced "skoon"), one-time home of the Stone of Destiny and the first capital of a united Scotland. **Scone Palace** exudes graceful Scottish country living and there are some pleasant walks in the grounds that surround it. Owned and occupied by the Earl and Countess of Mansfield, whose family has held it for almost four centuries, the two-storey building on the eastern side of the Tay is more a home than a monument: the rooms, although full of antiques and lavish furnishings, feel lived-in and used.

Scone was once the capital of Pictavia, and it was here that Kenneth MacAlpine, first king of a united Scotland, brought the famous Coronation **Stone of Destiny**, or Stone of Scone, which is now to be found in Edinburgh Castle (see box, p.63). A replica of the (surprisingly small) stone can be found on Moot Hill, immediately opposite the palace. **Moot Hill**, as its name suggests, was the place where Scottish earls came to swear loyalty to their king and discuss the affairs of state in an early form of national parliament. In a symbolic gesture, oak trees from the estate were used in the construction of Scotland's parliament at Holyrood in Edinburgh.

Inside the palace, the library houses one of the foremost collections of **porcelain** in the world, with items by Meissen, Sèvres, Chelsea, Derby and Worcester.

Huntingtower Castle

3 miles northwest of Perth on the A85 • April–Sept daily 9.30am–5.30pm; Oct daily 9.30am–4.30pm; Nov–March Mon–Wed, Sat & Sun 9.30am–4.30pm • £4.50; HES • ☎ 01738 627231, ⓦ historicenvironment.scot • Catch bus #13 from South St to Perth Mart

Nothing like as grand as Scone Palace, but intriguing for its historical connections, is **Huntingtower Castle**. Two three-storey towers formed the original fifteenth- and sixteenth-century tower house, linked in the seventeenth century by a range to provide more room. Formerly known as Ruthven Castle, it was here that the Raid of Ruthven took place in 1582, when the 16-year-old James VI, at the request of William, fourth Earl of Ruthven, came to the castle only to be held captive by a group of conspirators demanding the dismissal of favoured royal advisers. The plot failed, and the young James was released ten months later. Today the castle's chief attractions are its splendid sixteenth-century painted ceilings in the east tower's main hall.

Stanley Mills

Stanley village, 8 miles north of Perth on the A9 • Daily: April–Sept 9.30am–5.30pm; Oct 10am–4pm • £5.50; HES • ☎ 01738 627 958, ⓦ historicenvironment.scot • Catch bus #34 from Mill St to Stanley

An unexpectedly grand complex of eighteenth-century red brick and pink sandstone buildings, **Stanley Mills** is dramatically backed by the wide Tay. Built to produce textiles, the complex has partly been converted into housing, but the museum section gives a vivid sense of the sights – and deafening sounds – of the working mill.

ARRIVAL AND DEPARTURE
PERTH AND AROUND

By train Perth connects with the main train lines north from Edinburgh and Glasgow; trains pull in at the station west of the centre, where Kings Place runs into Leonard St.

Destinations Aberdeen (hourly; 1hr 30min–1hr 50min); Blair Atholl (3–8 daily; 40min); Dundee (hourly; 25min); Dunkeld (5–8 daily; 20min); Edinburgh (every 1–2hr; 1hr 30min); Glasgow Queen Street (at least hourly; 1hr); Inverness (7–11 daily; 2hr); Pitlochry (7–11 daily; 30min); Stirling (roughly hourly; 30min).

By bus Perth is well connected by bus; the main bus station is just north of the railway station on the opposite side of Leonard St.

Destinations Aberfeldy (hourly; 1hr 25min); Crieff (hourly; 40min); Dundee (every 30min; 1hr 10min); Dunkeld (hourly; 30min); Edinburgh (hourly; 1hr 40min); Glasgow (hourly; 1hr 35min); Gleneagles (hourly; 25min); Inverness (every 2hr; 2hr 45min); Pitlochry (every 2hr; 45min); Stirling (hourly; 50min).

INFORMATION

Tourist office West Mill St (April–July & Sept–Oct Mon–Sat 9.30am–5pm, Sun 10.30am–3.30pm; Aug Mon–Sat 9.30am–6pm, Sun 10am–4.30pm; Nov–March Mon–Sat 9.30am–4.30pm; ☎ 01738 450600, ⓦ perthshire.co.uk).

ACCOMMODATION

Achnacarry Guest House 3 Pitcullen Crescent ☎ 01738 621421, ⓦ achnacarry.co.uk. Victorian B&B a 5min walk from the main drag, on the eastern side of the city. Family rooms (£80) make it a good option for those travelling with kids. **£60**

Parklands Hotel 2 St Leonards Bank ☎ 01738 622451, ⓦ theparklandshotel.com. Of the numerous central hotels in Perth, aim for this award-winning place close to

9

the train station, which has a touch of contemporary styling with flatscreen TVs and wi-fi in all rooms. It also has a good restaurant and bistro. **£110**

★**Pitcullen Guest House** 17 Pitcullen Crescent ☎01738 626506, ⓦpitcullen.co.uk. Swish, well-run B&B offering neatly styled en-suite rooms. Little extras like blackout blinds, in-room fridges and a map room make it a cut above others in the same price range. **£65**

The Townhouse 17 Marshall Place ☎01738 446179, ⓦthetownhouseperth.co.uk. Enjoying a leafy location on the South Inch Park, this lofty Georgian townhouse offers a pleasant peek at the genteel side of the city. Plush furnishings, all mod cons, home-made biscuits and helpful hosts. **£110**

EATING

63 Tay Street 63 Tay St ☎01738 441451, ⓦ63taystreet.com. At the top end of Perth's dining scene is this classy restaurant, serving modern Scottish food like Scrabster cod with red wine. The two-course dinner costs £23.50. Lunch: Thurs–Sat noon–2pm; pre-theatre menu: Tues–Fri 5.45–6.30pm; dinner: Tues–Sat 6.30–9pm.

★ **The Apron Stage** 5 King St, Stanley ☎01738 828888, ⓦapronstagerestaurant.co.uk. A rustic but surprisingly high-quality option 8 miles north of town in the village of Stanley, where you can visit the mills (see p.325). Beautifully presented and delicately flavoured dishes are rustled up in a tiny kitchen; beer-braised beef cheeks cost £15.95. Book in advance. Wed & Thurs

6–9.30pm, Fri & Sat 12.30–3pm & 5.50–9.30pm, Sun pre-booking required.

Café Tabou 4 St John's Place ☎01738 446698, ⓦcafetabou.co.uk. For moderately priced food try this buzzy café, with its menu of French classics and shellfish (from £12) – and pleasant street-side seating. Mon 10am–3pm, Tues–Thurs 10am–9.30pm, Fri & Sat 10am–9pm, Sun noon–3pm.

Deans at Let's Eat 77–79 Kinnoull St ☎01738 643377 ⓦletseatperth.co.uk. Serves indulgent dishes like loin of Ochil venison (for £19.95), in a relaxed space, with a focus on Scottish ingredients. Tues–Sat noon–2pm & 6.30–9.30pm.

DRINKING

Old Ship Inn Just off the high street on Skinnergate ☎01738 624929. The seventeenth-century *Old Ship Inn* serves real ale (pints from £2.70) and basic pub grub. Mon–Thurs 11am–11pm, Sat 11am–midnight, Sun 12.30–11pm.

Twa Tams 79 Scott St ☎01738 580948, ⓦtwatams-perth.co.uk. Has a good beer garden as well as regular live music, and also serves a range of cheap meals (two mains for £9.99 Mon–Thurs & Sun). Thurs–Sat 11am–midnight, Mon–Wed & Sun 11am–11.15pm.

ENTERTAINMENT

Perth Concert Hall 79 Scott St ☎01738 621031, ⓦhorsecross.co.uk/perth-concert-hall. Modern glassy

concert hall, hosting touring orchestras, opera and recitals as well as more mainstream fare.

SHOPPING

Farmers' Market King Edward St ☎01738 582159, ⓦperthfarmersmarket.co.uk. This market takes place on the first Saturday of every month, with around forty stalls selling local produce from home-baked cakes to freshly butchered venison. First Sat of the month 9am–2pm.

Provender Brown 23 George St ☎01738 587300, ⓦprovenderbrown.co.uk. Perth's best deli, where you can buy everything from Isle of Mull cheeses to Scottish craft beers (from £2.45 a bottle). Mon–Wed & Sat 9am–5pm, Thurs & Fri until 5.30pm.

Strathearn

STRATHEARN – the valley of the River Earn – stretches west of Perth for some forty miles to **Loch Earn**, a popular watersports spot located just to the north of the Trossachs. The Roman general Agricola was here around two thousand years ago, trying to establish a foothold in the Highlands; later the area was frequented by Bonnie Prince Charlie and Rob Roy, both bound up in the north–south struggle between Highlands and Lowlands. Today the main settlement in the valley is the well-heeled town of **Crieff**, which, despite its prosperous air, has some hints of the wilder Highland countryside close by, notably around the popular **Glenturret Distillery**.

Blackford

The village of **BLACKFORD**, just west of Gleneagles, is famous for its high-quality spring water. This, coupled with an abundance of locally produced barley, made Blackford the perfect place to brew beer, and in 1488 James IV demanded that ale made from the village's water be served at his coronation. These days the water is bottled and sold under the Highland Spring brand around the UK.

St Serf's

Dunning, 5 miles east of Auchterarder on the B8062 • April–Sept daily 9.30am–5.30pm; Oct–March access by arrangement • Free • ☎ 01764 684497

In the quiet village of Dunning is **St Serf's**, a rugged church with a Norman tower and arch, which houses the magnificent **Dupplin Cross**, reckoned to be the finest surviving carved Pictish stone. Dating from the early ninth century, it was made in honour of Constantine, the first king of the Picts, who also reigned over the Scots of Dalriada (Argyll). The combination of Pictish and Christian imagery – intricately carved Celtic-knot patterns, depictions of animals and warriors – illustrates the developing relationship between king and the Church.

Crieff and around

At the heart of Strathearn sits the old spa town of **CRIEFF**, in a lovely position on a south-facing slope of the Grampian foothills. Cattle drovers used to come to a market, or "tryst", here in the eighteenth century, but Crieff really came into its own with the arrival of the railway in 1856. Shortly after that, Morrison's Academy, a local private school, took in its first pupils, and in 1868 the grand *Crieff Hydro*, then known as the *Strathearn Hydropathic*, opened its doors to Victorian visitors seeking water-therapy cures. These days, Crieff values its respectability and has an array of fine Edwardian and Victorian houses, with a busy little centre that retains something of the atmosphere of the former spa town.

Famous Grouse Experience

At the Glenturret Distillery, 1 mile north of Crieff, just off the A85 to Comrie • Daily: March–Oct 10am–6pm; Nov–Feb 10am–5pm • £10 • ☎ 01764 656565, ⓦ thefamousgrouse.com • Catch any bus going to Crieff, Comrie or St Fillans and ask the driver to drop you at the bottom of the Glenturret Distillery road, from where it's a 5min walk

From Crieff, it's a short drive or a twenty-minute walk north to the **Famous Grouse Experience**, located at the venerable **Glenturret Distillery**. Glenturret is Scotland's **oldest distillery**, established in 1775, and still one of the more attractive, with whitewashed buildings and pagoda roofs situated beside a gurgling stream. In recent years it has become the home of the Famous Grouse blend. While the corporate edge may be hard to avoid, and the coach park is often full, this is one distillery that makes a decent effort to be family-friendly and to avoid much of the romanticized pomposity which comes with other parts of the malt whisky trail.

Innerpeffray Library

miles southeast of Crieff on the B8062 road to Auchterarder • March–Oct Wed–Sat 10am–12.45pm & 2–4.45pm, Sun 2–4pm; Nov–Feb phone for appointment • £7.50 • ☎ 01764 652819, ⓦ innerpeffraylibrary.co.uk

Little known but well worth a visit is the delightfully hidden **Innerpeffray Library**, situated in an attractive eighteenth-century building right by the River Earn. Beside an old stone chapel and schoolhouse, this serene and studious public library, founded in 1680, is the oldest in Scotland. It's a must for bibliophiles, its shelves containing some four thousand cloth and leather-bound books, mainly on theological and classical subjects, but also witchcraft and medicine. Among the rare Scottish books, there's a first edition of Samuel Johnson's *Journey to the Western Isles* (1775).

9

Drummond Castle Gardens

Near Muthill, 2 miles south of Crieff on the A822 • Daily: Easter weekend & June–Aug 11am–6pm; Sept & Oct 1–6pm • £5 • ☎ 01764 681433, ⓦ drummondcastlegardens.co.uk • Take bus #47 or #18 from Crieff towards Muthill, then walk 1.5 miles up the castle drive

Of all the attractions around Crieff, most impressive are the magnificent **Drummond Castle Gardens**. The approach, up a splendid avenue of beech trees, is pretty enough, but by crossing the courtyard of the castle to the grand terrace you can view the garden in all its symmetrical glory. It was begun as early as 1630 (the date of the tall central sundial), though the design of the French/Italianate parterre is Victorian: it depicts a St Andrew's cross and incorporates other images associated with the Drummonds, including two crowns and the wavy motif found on the family crest. Italian marble statues punctuate the long lines of the cross, and the overall effect is of exceptional harmony and grace. The castle itself is closed to visitors.

ARRIVAL AND INFORMATION

By bus Buses from/to Stirling (7 daily; 55min) stop on the high street, near the junction with Hill St.

Tourist office In the town hall on High St (April–June Mon–Sat 10am–4pm, Sun 10.30am–3.30pm; July & Aug Mon–Sat 10am–5pm, Sun 10.30am–3.30pm; Sept–March Mon–Sat 10.30am–3.30/4pm; ☎ 01764 652578).

CRIEFF AND AROUND

Visitor centre At the bottom of the hill, on Muthill Rd (daily 10am–4.30pm; ☎ 01764 653868, ⓦ crieff.co.uk). Incorporates a garden centre, an exhibition about cattle drovers and the Caithness Glass visitor centre and factory, which you can tour for free.

ACCOMMODATION

★**Barley Bree** 6 Willoughby St, Muthill ☎ 01764 681451, ⓦ barleybree.com. The obvious choice if you decide to stay in Muthill, a handsome eighteenth-century village with an ancient church. The rooms are chic and bright, and the French/Scottish cooking has a well-deserved reputation for quality. **£110**

Comrie Croft 4 miles west of Crieff, just off the A85 ☎ 01764 670140, ⓦ comriecroft.com. Largish bunkhouse/activity centre set on a farm halfway between Crieff and Comrie, with its own private fishing loch, mountain-bike rental and a network of paths and walks; you can also camp here in the woodland, either in your own tent or a Nordic kåta. Dorms **£20**; doubles **£60**; camping per person **£10**

Crieff Hydro North of the centre near Crieff Golf Course ☎ 01764 655555, ⓦ crieffhydro.com. The imposing *Crieff Hydro* is still the grandest place in town, despite the institutional atmosphere. It has splendid leisure facilities including a pool and stables. **£180**

Galvelmore House 5 Galvelmore St ☎ 01764 655721 ⓦ galvelmore.co.uk. A friendly B&B close to the main drag, with a lovely oak-panelled lounge that has a selection of board games. There's also a pretty two-bedroom self-catering apartment. **£68**

★**Gleneagles Hotel** Just west of Auchterarder, at the southern edge of Strathearn ☎ 0800 389 3737, ⓦ gleneagles.com. Iconic Gleneagles is famously home to three championship golf courses and enclosed in more than eight hundred acres of countryside. The resort has welcomed leaders and celebrities from every corner of the globe. **£350**

Knock Castle Drummond Terrace ☎ 01764 650088, ⓦ knockcastle.com. Built for a shipping tycoon in 1885, this grand home is now a luxurious retreat with an indulgent spa and a restaurant that has panoramic views over the Perthshire countryside. The snug ground-floor bar is also open to non-residents. **£129**

EATING AND DRINKING

★**Andrew Fairlie at Gleneagles** Gleneagles Hotel, just west of Auchterarder, at the southern edge of Strathearn ☎ 0800 389 3737, ⓦ andrewfairlie.co.uk. If staying the night at the hotel is beyond your means, consider eating at the main restaurant, the refreshingly unstuffy *Andrew Fairlie at Gleneagles* (tasting menu £125). It has two Michelin stars and is perhaps the finest restaurant in all of Scotland, with dynamic dishes like roast fillet of brill with seaweed butter. Mon–Sat 6.30–10pm.

★**Delivino** 6 King St ☎ 01764 655665, ⓦ delivino .co.uk. Just downhill from the tourist office, this swish Italian café serves antipasti, tapas, good pizzas (£7–8.50), coffee and cakes. It also has a small but selective wine list. Mon–Sat 9am–6pm, Sun noon–4pm.

Lounge 1–3 West High St ☎ 01764 65440, ⓦ loungeincrieff.co.uk. Cosy daytime hangout that mixes tearoom with tapas bar. Serves good breakfasts such as eggs Benedict (£8.50), plus soups and burgers. Daily 11am–9.30pm.

Yann's at Glenearn Glenearn House, Perth Rd ☎ 01764 650111, ⓦ yannsatglenearnhouse.com. A good bet locally for fine food, with French Alpine dishes (mains £14–20) from Yann's home province served in a bistro-style setting. There are attractive rooms here too. Wed–Fri 6–9pm, Sat & Sun noon–2pm & 6.30–9pm.

SHOPPING

Harrison's Fine Wines 1A Galvelmore St ☎ 01764 655016. The physical face of ⓦ winestore.co.uk, this shop stocks everything from Veuve Clicquot to vegan-friendly reds. There's also a sister shop in nearby Comrie. Mon–Sat 10am–8pm.

Strathearn Gallery 32 West High St ☎ 01764 656100, ⓦ strathearn-gallery.com. This small commercial gallery on the corner of Galvelmore St regularly hosts exhibitions that include ceramics, jewellery and landscape paintings. Mon–Sat 10am–5pm, Sun 1–5pm.

Loch Earn

At the western edge of Strathearn lies **Loch Earn**, a gently lapping Highland loch dramatically edged by rippling mountains. The A85 runs north along the loch shore from the village of **St Fillans**, at the eastern tip, to a slightly larger settlement, **Lochearnhead**, at the western end of the loch, where it meets the A84 linking the Trossachs to Crianlarich (see p.294). The wide tranquil expanse of Loch Earn is popular for **watersports**, particularly engine-based pursuits like waterskiing, powerboating and jet skiing.

ACCOMMODATION AND EATING | **LOCH EARN**

Four Seasons Hotel St Fillans, at the eastern end of the loch ☎ 01764 685333, ⓦ thefourseasonshotel.co.uk. A superb waterside location makes this hotel the area's best place to stay, and there are also half a dozen chalets (sleeping two) tucked behind the main building; it's a great place to organize loch-bound activities. The on-site bistro is a good spot for food, with mains for around £9. Daily noon–2.30pm & 6–9pm. Chalets **£108**; doubles **£122**

Lochearnhead Hotel Lochside, Lochearnhead ☎ 01567 830229, ⓦ lochearnhead-hotel.com. Cheerful hotel set back from the A85, with ten fresh-feeling en-suite bedrooms, some of which have views over the loch. There's also a bar selling evening meals. Daily 6–8pm. **£80**

Lochearn House Near the post office in Lochearnhead ☎ 01567 830380, ⓦ lochearnhouse.co.uk. The three double rooms at this small modern B&B are good value, and are well taken care of by a friendly retired couple. **£80**

Strath Tay and around

Heading due north from Perth, both the railway and main A9 trunk road carry much of the traffic heading into the Highlands, often speeding straight through some of Perthshire's most attractive countryside in its eagerness to get to the bleaker country to the north. Perthshire has been dubbed "**Big Tree Country**" by the tourist board in recognition of some magnificent woodland in the area, including a number of individual trees that rank among Europe's oldest and tallest specimens.

Many of these trees are found around the valley of the River Tay, which flows east towards the sea from attractive Loch Tay and is known as **STRATH TAY**. The loch is set among the high Breadalbane Mountains which include the striking peak of **Ben Lawers**, Perthshire's highest, and the hills that enclose the long, enchanting **Glen Lyon**. Studded around Loch Tay are the remains of crannogs – ancient dwellings built on man-made islands. Not far downriver is the prosperous small town of **Aberfeldy**; from here the Tay drifts southeast between the unspoilt twin villages of **Dunkeld** and **Birnam** before meandering its way past Perth.

Dunkeld

DUNKELD, twelve miles north of Perth on the A9, was proclaimed Scotland's ecclesiastical capital by Kenneth MacAlpine in 850. Its position at the southern

9

boundary of the Grampian Mountains made it a favoured meeting place for Highland and Lowland cultures, and the town is one of the area's most pleasant communities, with handsome whitewashed houses, appealing arts and crafts shops and a charming cathedral. Dunkeld sits just across the River Tay from its sister village, Birnam. The town is a great starting point for signposted river and forest walks, including a half-hour stroll to the **Hermitage**, a cluster of Georgian follies on the River Braan.

Dunkeld Cathedral

Cathedral St • Daily: April–Sept Mon–Sat 9.30am–6.30pm, Sun 2–4.30pm; Oct–March Mon–Sat 9.30am–4pm, Sun 2–4pm • Free • ☎ 01350 727249, ⓦ dunkeldcathedral.org.uk

Dunkeld's partly ruined **cathedral** is on the northern side of town, in an idyllic setting amid lawns and trees on the east bank of the Tay. As early as 570, missionaries from Iona built a wattle monastery here; construction on the current building began in the early twelfth century and continued throughout the next two hundred years, but it was more or less ruined at the time of the Reformation. The present structure consists of the fourteenth-century choir and the fifteenth-century nave; the choir, restored in 1600 (and several times since), now serves as the parish church, while the nave remains roofless apart from the clock tower. Inside, look out for the effigy of the **Wolf of Badenoch**, Robert II's son, who was born in 1343. The Wolf acquired his name and notoriety when, after being excommunicated for leaving his wife, he took his revenge by burning the towns of Forres and Elgin, and sacking the latter's cathedral.

ARRIVAL AND INFORMATION   DUNKELD

By train The nearest train station is in nearby Birnam (see opposite).

By bus Buses travelling to and from Perth (every 30min; 40min) and Inverness (5 daily; 2hr 30min) stop opposite the *Royal Dunkeld Hotel* on Atholl St, Dunkeld.

Tourist office The Visit Scotland information centre is on The Cross, in the middle of Dunkeld (April–June & Sept–Oct Mon–Sat 10am–4.30pm, Sun 11am–4pm; July & Aug Mon–Sat 9.30am–5.30pm, Sun 10.30am–5pm; Nov–March Fri–Sun 11am–4pm; ☎ 01350 727688).

ACCOMMODATION

The Bridge 10 Bridge St ☎ 01350 727068, ⓦ thebridge-dunkeld.co.uk. A soothingly decorated and extremely comfortable Georgian home located in the heart of Dunkeld. The hosts are warmly welcoming, and breakfast comes with local smoked salmon. **£80**

The Pend 5 Brae St ☎ 01350 727586, ⓦ thepend.com This elegantly furnished B&B is just off the main street in Dunkeld, with three large rooms that share a couple of bathrooms. Dinner is also available for residents. **£76**

EATING AND DRINKING

The Scottish Deli 1 Atholl St ☎ 01350 728028, ⓦ scottish-deli.com. Fill up on gourmet delights including artisan breads at this well-stocked deli, which also has its own wine room. There's also a counter selling sandwiches and salads for £4.50. Mon–Fri 9.30am–5.30pm, Sat 9am–5.30pm, Sun 10.30am–4.30pm.

★**The Taybank** Tay Terrace ☎ 01350 727340, ⓦ thetaybankdunkeld.com. A riverside beacon for music fans, who come for the regular live sessions in the conviv[ial] bar. It's a good, simple place to eat – they serve Scottish specialities such as stovies, made from beef and potatoes for £7.50. Mon–Thurs & Sun 11am–11pm, Fri & Sat 11am–midnight.

Birnam

Dunkeld is linked to its sister community, **BIRNAM**, by Thomas Telford's seven-arched bridge of 1809. This little village has a place in history thanks to Shakespeare, for it was on Dunsinane Hill, to the southeast of the village, that Macbeth declared: "I will not be afraid of death and bane/Till Birnam Forest come to Dunsinane". The **Birnam Oak**, a gnarly old character propped up by crutches, which can be seen on the waymarked riverside walk, is inevitably claimed to be a survivor of the infamous mobile forest.

Birnam Arts

Station Rd • Daily 10am–4.30pm • £3 • ☎ 01350 727674, ⓦ birnamarts.com

Just like Shakespeare, children's author Beatrix Potter drew inspiration from the Birnam area, recalling her childhood holidays here when penning the Peter Rabbit stories. A Potter-themed exhibition and garden can be found in impressive **Birnam Arts**, a lively theatre, café and arts and community centre.

ARRIVAL AND DEPARTURE   BIRNAM

By train The Dunkeld and Birnam train station, just south of the A9 in Birnam, is a stop on services to Inverness (8 daily; 1hr 50min) and Perth (10 daily; 20min).

By bus Direct bus services to Inverness (5 daily; 2hr 30min) and Perth (every 30min; 40min) leave from opposite the *Birnam Hotel* on Perth Rd.

ACCOMMODATION

Merryburn Hotel Station Rd ☎ 01350 727216, ⓦ merryburn.co.uk. An old ironmonger's shop converted into a small and inviting hotel, just across from Birnam

Arts. Many of the building's original Victorian features are still intact. **£80**

Aberfeldy and around

From Dunkeld the A9 runs north alongside the Tay for eight miles to Ballinluig, a tiny village marking the turn-off along the A827 to **ABERFELDY**, a prosperous settlement of large stone houses that acts as a service centre for the wider Loch Tay area. Aberfeldy sits at the point where the Urlar Burn – lined by the silver birch trees celebrated by Robert Burns in his poem *The Birks of Aberfeldy* – flows into the River Tay.

Wade's Bridge

In Aberfeldy the Tay is spanned by the humpbacked, four-arch **Wade's Bridge**, built by General Wade in 1733 during his efforts to control the unrest in the Highlands, and one of the general's more impressive pieces of work. Overlooking the bridge from the south end is the **Black Watch Monument**, depicting a pensive, kilted soldier; it was erected in 1887 to commemorate the first muster of the Highland regiment gathered as a peacekeeping force by Wade in 1740.

Dewar's World of Whisky

Half a mile east of Aberfeldy, just off the A827 • April–Oct Mon–Sat 10am–6pm, Sun noon–4pm; Nov–March Mon–Sat 10am–4pm • Tours from £17 • ☎ 01887 822010, ⓦ livetrue.dewars.com

The main set-piece attraction in Aberfeldy is **Dewar's World of Whisky**, at the Aberfeldy Distillery, which puts on an impressive show of describing the process of making whisky. A **Connoisseur Tour** (£27) is available for real aficionados, giving a more in-depth look around the distillery and a chance to taste (or "nose") the whisky at different stages in its life.

Castle Menzies

One mile west of Aberfeldy, across Wade's Bridge • Easter to late Oct Mon–Sat 10.30am–5pm, Sun 2–5pm • £6.50 • ☎ 01887 820982, ⓦ castlemenzies.org

One mile west of Aberfeldy, **Castle Menzies** is an imposing, Z-shaped, sixteenth-century tower house, which until the middle of the last century was the chief seat of the Clan Menzies (pronouced "Ming-iss"). With the demise of the family line, the castle was taken over by the Menzies Clan Society, which since 1971 has been involved in the ongoing process of restoring the building. Today much of the interior is on view, and most of it is refreshingly free of fixtures and fittings, displaying an austerity that is much more true to medieval life than the more ostentatiously opulent castles that you will find elsewhere in the country.

By bus Buses stop on Chapel St in Aberfeldy, near the junction with Dunkeld St (the A827), with regular services to Perth (up to 12 daily; 1hr 25min).

Tourist information The Square in the town centre (April–June, Sept & Oct Mon–Sat 10am–5pm, Sun 10.30am–3.30pm; July & Aug Mon–Sat 9.30am–5pm, Sun 10.30am–3.30pm; Nov–March Mon–Wed 10am–4pm; ☏ 01887 820276, ⊕ visitaberfeldy.co.uk). Good for advice on local accommodation and details of nearby walking trails.

ACTIVITIES

Land Rover trips A couple of miles west of Castle Menzies, near the hamlet with the unfortunate name of Dull (twinned with Boring, Oregon, USA), off the B846, Highland Safaris (☏ 01887 820071, ⊕ highlandsafaris.net) arranges Land Rover trips into the heather-clad hills nearby in search of eagles, red deer and grouse. At the lodge you can try your hand at gold and mineral panning (£5).

Outdoor activities and bike rental Dunolly Adventure Outdoors (☏ 01887 820298, ⊕ dunolly adventures.co.uk) on Taybridge Drive, close to the River Tay, offers kayaking, rafting and other activities, plus bike rental (£20/day).

ACCOMMODATION

★ **Coshieville House** 5.5 miles west of Aberfeldy along the B846 ☏ 01887 830319, ⊕ aberfeldybandb .com. In peaceful surroundings, this 300-year-old inn provides modern accommodation with nice touches like fresh flowers brightening up the communal areas. **£70**

Balnearn Guest House Crieff Rd ☏ 01887 820431 ⊕ balnearnhouse.co.uk. Stylish and unpretentious rooms close to the middle of town, with the added bonus of a drying room for your outdoor gear. **£65**

The Bunkhouse Glassie Farm, 3 miles from Aberfeldy along the winding track that starts near the footbridge ☏ 01887 820265, ⊕ thebunkhouse.co.uk. The closest bunkhouse to Aberfeldy has small rooms that share simple showers, plus two self-catering kitchens and a communal area with magnificent views over the town. Groups only at weekends. Dorms **£17**

EATING AND DRINKING

Ailean Chraggan Across Wade's Bridge in Weem ☏ 01887 820346. The long, regularly updated lunch and dinner menu at this hotel-restaurant includes plenty of fishy mains (£11–16). Daily noon–2pm & 5.30–8/9pm.

★ **The Watermill** Mill St ☏ 01887 822896, ⊕ aberfeldywatermill.com. Aberfeldy isn't short on cafés, but the best bet for a good cup of coffee, a bowl of lunchtime soup (£5) or afternoon tea is this relaxed superbly restored early nineteenth-century mill, with pretty riverside garden. There's also an inspiring bookshop Mon–Sat 10am–5pm, Sun 11am–5pm.

Loch Tay and around

Aberfeldy grew up around a crossing point on the River Tay, which leaves it six miles adrift of **Loch Tay**, a fourteen-mile-long stretch of fresh water connecting the western and eastern Highlands. Rising steeply above the loch's northern edge is Ben Lawers, the tenth-highest peak in Scotland, whose mineral-rich slopes support plant life more commonly seen in the Alps or Arctic.

Glen Lyon

North of Loch Tay, the mountains tumble down into **Glen Lyon** – at 34 miles long, the longest enclosed glen in Scotland – where, legend has it, the Celtic warrior Fingal built twelve castles. The narrow single-track road through the glen starts at **Keltneyburn**, near Kenmore, at the northern end of the loch, although a road does struggle over the hills to **Bridge of Balgie**, halfway down the glen. Either way, it's a long, winding journey.

Fortingall

A few miles on from Keltneyburn, the village of **FORTINGALL** is little more than a handful of pretty thatched cottages, though locals make much of their 5000-year-old yew tree – believed (by them at least) to be the oldest living thing in Europe. The venerable tree can be found in the churchyard, with a timeline nearby listing some of the events the yew has lived through. One of these, bizarrely, is the birth of Pontius Pilate, reputedly the son of a Roman officer stationed near Fortingall.

Ben Lawers

Dominating the northern side of Loch Tay is moody **Ben Lawers** (3984ft), Perthshire's highest mountain; from the top there are incredible views towards both the Atlantic and the North Sea. The ascent – which shouldn't be tackled unless you're properly equipped for Scottish hillwalking – takes around three hours from the NTS car park, which you can reach by following a winding, hilly road off the A827.

Killin

The mountains of **Breadalbane** (pronounced "bred-albin", from the Gaelic "braghaid Albin" meaning "high country of Scotland") loom over the southern end of Loch Tay. Glens Lochay and Dochart curve north and south respectively from the small town of **Killin**, right in the centre of which the River Dochart comes rushing down over the frothy **Falls of Dochart** before disgorging into Loch Tay. A short distance west of Killin the A827 meets the A85, linking the Trossachs with Crianlarich (see p.294), an important waypoint on the roads to Oban, Fort William and the west coast.

There's little to do in Killin itself, but it makes a convenient base for some of the area's best walks.

INFORMATION AND ACTIVITIES   KILLIN

Tourist office On the ground floor of the old watermill by the falls (April–Oct daily 10am–4pm; ☎ 01567 820527, ⌨ killin.net).

Outdoor activities The helpful and enthusiastic Killin Outdoor Centre and Mountain Shop on Main St (daily 8.45am–5.30pm; ☎ 01567 820652, ⌨ killinoutdoor.co.uk) rents out mountain bikes, canoes and tents.

ACCOMMODATION AND EATING

Bridge of Lochay Hotel Aberfeldy Rd ☎ 01567 820272, ⌨ bridgeoflochayhotel.com. Traditional old whitewashed inn serving above-average food including steak and ale pies (£9.95) and venison casserole (£12.95). Daily noon–9pm.

The Old Smiddy Main St ☎ 01567 820619, ⌨ theoldsmiddykillin.co.uk. Offers three neat B&B rooms near the centre of the town, two of which have views of the river. The bistro-style café downstairs is a popular spot for cakes and ice creams. **£56**

Highland Perthshire

North of the Tay Valley, **Highland Perthshire** doesn't discard its lush richness immediately, but there are clear indications of the more rugged, barren influences of the Highlands proper here. The principal settlements of **Pitlochry** and **Blair Atholl**, both just off the A9, are separated by the narrow gorge of Killiecrankie. Though there are reasons to stop in both places, inevitably the greater rewards are to be found further afield, most notably in the winding westward road along the shores of **Loch Tummel** and **Loch Rannoch** past the distinctive peak of **Schiehallion**, which eventually leads to the remote wilderness of **Rannoch Moor**.

Pitlochry

PITLOCHRY is undoubtedly a useful place to find somewhere to stay or eat en route to or from the Highlands. However, there's little charm to be found on its main street, with its crawling traffic and endless shops selling cut-price woollens and knobbly walking sticks to tourists, who use the town as a starting point for scenic hikes (see box, p.334). Far more appealing is the area south of the river, which is home to a renowned theatre and a serene botanical garden.

9

Edradour Distillery

2.5 miles east of Pitlochry on the A924 • Mid-April to Oct Mon–Sat 10am–5pm • £7.50 • ☎ 01796 472095, ⍟ edradour.com

The **Edradour Distillery** – Scotland's smallest – has an idyllic position, tucked into the hills east of Pitlochry. Although the tour of the distillery itself isn't out of the ordinary, the lack of industrialization and the fact that the whole traditional process is done on site give Edradour more personality than many of its rivals.

Explorers: the Scottish Plant Hunters' Garden

Across the river from the town centre, near the theatre • April–Oct daily 10am–5pm • £4, tours £1 extra • ☎ 01796 484600, ⍟ www.explorersgarden.com

If you want to escape the bustle of Pitlochry's main drag, it's worth having a wander around **Explorers: the Scottish Plant Hunters' Garden**, a garden and forest area that pays tribute to Scottish botanists and collectors who roamed the world in the eighteenth and nineteenth centuries in search of new plant species. An open-air amphitheatre in the grounds is sometimes used for outdoor performances.

Pitlochry Power Station and Dam

A short stroll upstream to the west of the theatre is the **Pitlochry Power Station and Dam**, a massive concrete wall that harnesses the water of artificial Loch Faskally, just north of the town, for hydroelectric power. Near the base of the dam there's a small observation cabin where you can take a peek at the underwater workings of Pitlochry's **salmon ladder**, a staircase of murky glass boxes through which you might see some nonplussed fish making their way upstream past the dam. An electronic counter shows how many of them have successfully completed the climb.

With parking available at the theatre, nearby, the dam makes a good starting point for a complete loop of the loch (around nine miles to the Pass of Killiecrankie and back).

ARRIVAL AND DEPARTURE   **PITLOCHRY**

By train Pitlochry is on the main train line to Inverness (every 1–2hr; 1hr 35min); trains stop at Perth en route (30min).

By bus Buses from/to Perth (every 1–2hr; 40min) and Inverness (7 daily; 2hr 10min) stop near the train station.

INFORMATION AND ACTIVITIES

Tourist office 22 Atholl Rd (April–June Mon–Sat 9.30am–5.30pm, Sun 10am–4pm; July & Aug Mon–Sat 9.30am–6.30pm, Sun 9.30am–5.30pm; Sept & Oct Mon–Sat 9.30am–4.30pm, Sun 10am–4pm; reduced hour

WALKS AROUND PITLOCHRY

BEN VRACKIE

Pitlochry is surrounded by good walking country. The biggest lure has to be **Ben Vrackie** (2733ft; OS Explorer map 386), which provides a stunning backdrop for the town, and deserves better than a straight up-and-down walk. However, the climb should only be attempted in settled weather conditions and if you're properly prepared.

The direct route up the hill follows the course of the Moulin burn past the inn of the same name. Alternatively, a longer but much more rewarding circular route heads northwest out of Pitlochry, along the edge of Loch Faskally, then up the River Garry to go through the **Pass of Killiecrankie**. This is looked after by the NTS, which has a visitor centre (see p.406) providing background on the famous battle here. From the NTS centre follow the route past Old Faskally to meet the main track at Loch a'Choire. Alternatively, you can turn back here and loop around Loch Faskally instead.

BLACK SPOUT

A lovely short hill walk from the south end of Pitlochry follows a path through oak forests along the banks of the **Black Spout** burn; when you emerge from the woods it's just a few hundred yards further uphill to the lovely Edradour Distillery (see above).

9

Nov–Feb & March; ☎ 01796 472215). Can sell you a guide to walks in the surrounding area (£1) and also offers an accommodation booking service.

Bike rental For bike rental (£24/day), advice on local cycling routes, as well as general outdoor gear, try Escape Route, 3 Atholl Rd (daily 9am–5.30pm; ☎ 01796 473859, ⓦ escape-route.co.uk).

ACCOMMODATION

★ **Craigatin House and Courtyard** 165 Atholl Rd ☎ 01796 472478, ⓦ craigatinhouse.co.uk. On the northern section of the main road through town, this is an attractive, contemporary B&B with large beds, soothing decor, superb breakfasts and a pretty garden. **£98**

Fonab Castle Hotel Foss Rd, south of the river ☎ 01796 470140, ⓦ fonabcastlehotel.com. Once the headquarters of a power company, this turreted, waterside landmark has now been transformed into a luxury hotel with a spa and panoramic fine-dining restaurant. The interiors, with sparkly Swarovski wall coverings, may be a little bling for some tastes. **£195**

Moulin Hotel 11 Kirkmichael Rd, Moulin, on the outskirts of Pitlochry ☎ 01796 472196, ⓦ moulinhotel.co.uk. Pleasant old travellers' inn with a great bar and restaurant (see below) and its own brewery offering free guided tours (Thurs–Mon noon–3pm). Rooms are swathed in tartan. **£90**

Pitlochry Backpackers Hotel 134 Atholl Rd ☎ 01796 470044, ⓦ pitlochrybackpackershotel.com. Right in the centre of town, this hostel is based in a former hotel, and offers dorms, twin and double rooms, and a communal lounge. Dorms **£17.50**; doubles **£52.50**

EATING AND DRINKING

Moulin Inn 11 Kirkmichael Rd, Moulin, on the outskirts of Pitlochry ☎ 01796 472196, ⓦ moulininn.co.uk. Joined to the hotel of the same name, this restaurant serves decent pub grub such as deep-fried haggis (£7.50) in a cosy, country setting at the foot of Ben Vrackie. Daily noon–9.30pm.

Scottish Deli 96 Atholl Rd ☎ 01796 473322, ⓦ scottish-deli.com. Busy deli with a few seats along one wall, where you can tuck into freshly made rolls, baguettes and ciabattas (from £4.50), with plenty of different fillings to choose from. Mon–Sat 8am–5.30pm, Sun 10am–5pm.

Strathgarry Hotel 113 Atholl Rd ☎ 01796 472469, ⓦ strathgarryhotel.co.uk. You'll find a range of moderately priced bistro food at this hotel on Pitlochry's main drag; expect to pay £6.50 for a bowl of soup and a sandwich. Daily 10am–10pm.

ENTERTAINMENT

Pitlochry Festival Theatre Port na Craig, south side of the river ☎ 01796 484626, ⓦ pitlochry.org.uk. On the southern edge of Pitlochry, just across the river, lies Scotland's renowned "Theatre in the Hills". A variety of productions – mostly mainstream theatre from the resident repertoire company, along with regular music events – are staged in the summer season and on ad hoc dates the rest of the year. Box office daily May–Oct 9am–8pm, Nov–April 9am–5pm.

Blair Atholl

Three miles north of Killiecrankie, the village of **BLAIR ATHOLL** makes for a much quieter and more idiosyncratic stop than Pitlochry. Extravagant Blair Castle makes the place understandably popular with day-trippers, but if you decide to stick around there are plenty of walks and bike rides to enjoy in the surrounding countryside.

Blair Castle

Just off the B8079, midway between the train station and the bridge over the River Tilt • Easter–Oct daily 9.30am–5.30pm (last admission 4.30pm); Nov–March occasional weekends only (see website for details) • Castle and grounds £10.70; grounds only £5.90 • ☎ 01796 481207, ⓦ blair-castle.co.uk

Seat of the Atholl dukedom, whitewashed, turreted **Blair Castle**, surrounded by parkland and dating from 1269, presents an impressive sight as you approach it up the drive. You might even spot a piper, one of the Atholl Highlanders, playing in front of the castle; this select group was retained by the duke as his private army – a unique privilege afforded to him by Queen Victoria, who stayed here in 1844.

Thirty or so rooms display a selection of paintings, antique furniture and plasterwork that is sumptuous in the extreme. Highlights are the soaring **entrance hall**, with every bare inch of wood panelling covered in weapons of some description, and the vast **ballroom**, with its timber roof, antlers and mixture of portraits.

9

Blair Atholl Watermill

Ford Rd • April–Oct daily 9.30am–5pm; milling takes place Wed–Fri • Free • ☏ 01796 481321, ⊕ blairathollwatermill.co.uk

Close to the River Tilt is Blair Atholl's **Watermill**, which dates back to 1613. During the summertime you can wander around and witness the mill in action. Better still is a trip to the pleasant timber-beamed tearoom (see below), where you can enjoy home-baked scones and light lunches (many items are made with the mill's own flour).

INFORMATION AND ACTIVITIES   BLAIR ATHOLL

Atholl Estates Information Centre Close to the bridge over the River Tilt, a 5min walk east of the train station (April–Oct daily 9am–4.45pm; ☏ 01796 481355, ⊕ athollestatesrangerservice.co.uk). Modern ranger station, where you can get details of the extensive network of local walks and bike rides, as well as information on surrounding flora and fauna.

ACCOMMODATION AND EATING

Atholl Arms Hotel On the main road, near the train station ☏ 01796 481205, ⊕ athollarms.co.uk. Grand but reasonably priced, and the best place in town for a drink or a bar meal. The Atholl Highlander meat platter costs £12.95. Bar Mon–Thurs & Sun noon–10.45pm, Fri & Sat noon–11.30pm; food served daily noon–9.30pm. **£90**

★ **Blair Atholl Watermill** Ford Rd ☏ 01796 481321, ⊕ blairathollwatermill.co.uk. Blair Atholl's top spot for tea, tray bakes, toasties and bagels (snacks around £5) in a charming (and still functioning) old watermill. April–Oct daily 9.30am–5pm.

Blair Castle Caravan Park In the grounds of Blair Castle ☏ 01796 481263, ⊕ blaircastlecaravanpark .co.uk. Busy but attractive campsite with laundry facilities, a games room and a shop selling the estate's own sausages. Per pitch **£18**

Loch Tummel

West of Pitlochry, the B8019/B846 makes a memorably scenic, if tortuous, traverse of the shores of **Loch Tummel** and then Loch Rannoch. These two lochs and their adjoining rivers were much changed by the massive hydroelectric schemes built in the 1940s and 1950s, yet this is still a spectacular stretch of countryside and one that deserves leisurely exploration. **Queen's View** at the eastern end of Loch Tummel is an obvious vantage point, looking down the loch to the misty peak of **Schiehallion**; the name comes from the Gaelic meaning "Fairy Mountain".

Schiehallion

Rising cone-like to a peak of 3553ft, **Schiehallion** is a popular, fairly easy and inspiring mountain to climb (3–4hr round trip), with views on a good day to the massed ranks of Highland peaks. The path starts up at Braes of Foss, just off the B846 that links Aberfeldy with Kinloch Rannoch. You'll get a good view of the mountain from the cosy *Loch Tummel Inn*, about halfway along Loch Tummel.

Loch Rannoch and around

Beyond Loch Tummel, marking the eastern end of **Loch Rannoch**, the small community of **Kinloch Rannoch** doesn't see a lot of passing trade – fishermen and hillwalkers are the most common visitors. Otherwise, the only real destination here is Rannoch railway station, a lonely outpost on the Glasgow–Fort William West Highland train line, sixteen miles further on: the road goes no further. Here you can contemplate the bleakness of **Rannoch Moor**, a wide expanse of bog, heather and wind-blown pine trees that stretches right across to the imposing entrance of Glen Coe (see p.404).

ARRIVAL AND DEPARTURE   LOCH RANNOCH AND AROUND

By train The West Highland Railway stops at Rannoch and, a little to the north, Corrour station, which has no road access at all.

Destinations (from Rannoch station) Corrour (3–4 dai

RANNOCH MOOR

9

Rannoch Moor occupies roughly 150 square miles of uninhabited and uninhabitable peat bogs, lochs, heather hillocks, strewn lumps of granite and gnarled Caledonian pines, all of it over one thousand feet above sea level. Perhaps the most striking thing about the moor is its inaccessibility: one road, between Crianlarich and Glen Coe, skirts its western side, while another struggles west from Pitlochry to reach its eastern edge at Rannoch train station. The only regular form of transport here is the **West Highland Railway**, which stops at **Rannoch** and, a little to the north, Corrour, which has no road access at all – though it does have a great café (see below). **Corrour** stole an unlikely scene in the film *Trainspotting* when the four central characters headed here for a taste of the great outdoors; a wooden SYHA hostel is located a mile away on the shores of **Loch Ossian** and is only accessible on foot, making the area a great place for hikers seeking somewhere genuinely off the beaten track. From Rannoch train station, beside which is the isolated *Moor of Rannoch* hotel, it's possible to catch the train to Corrour and walk the nine miles back; it's a longer slog west to the eastern end of Glen Coe, the dramatic peaks of which poke up above the moor's western horizon. Determined hillwalkers will find a clutch of Munros around Corrour, including remote Ben Alder (3765ft), high above the forbidding shores of Loch Ericht.

12min); Fort William (3–4 daily; 1hr); Glasgow Queen Street (3–4 daily; 2hr 50min); London Euston (sleeper service Mon–Fri & Sun daily; 11hr–12hr 40min).

By bus A local bus service (Broons Bus #85) from Kinloch Rannoch provides connections with Rannoch railway station, 16 miles to the west (up to 4 daily; 40min).

ACCOMMODATION AND EATING

LOCH RANNOCH

Macdonald Loch Rannoch Half a mile west of Kinloch Rannoch along the B846 ☎08448 799059, ⓦmacdonaldhotels.co.uk. This large and rather plain hotel has a redeeming lochside location. Guests have access to a leisure complex with an indoor pool and gym. **£83**

RANNOCH MOOR

★**Corrour Station House** Corrour Station ☎01397 732236, ⓦcorrour-station-house-restaurant.co.uk. Fantastically remote café, only reachable by train or on a 20 mile hike. Soups, sandwiches and fine home baking, plus venison burgers, fish and chips and the like for dinner; mains are £10–15. Easter–Oct daily 8.30am–9pm.

★**Moor of Rannoch Hotel** Rannoch Station ☎01882 633238, ⓦmoorofrannoch.co.uk. If it's isolation you want, this is the place to stay; there's no internet access, radio or TV but instead open fires, board games and a big whisky selection. The five comfy en-suite rooms look out over the boggy moorland. Off-road bikes to rent (£18). **£125**

LOCH OSSIAN

SYHA Loch Ossian A 1-mile walk northeast from Corrour's train station, on the shores of Loch Ossian ☎01397 732207, ⓦsyha.org.uk. Only accessible on foot, this is an excellent option for hikers seeking somewhere genuinely off the beaten track. There's a wood-lined self-catering kitchen for making basic meals, but no fridge. Dorms **£20.50**

Northeast Scotland

DUNNOTTAR CASTLE

Northeast Scotland

A large triangle of land thrusting into the North Sea, northeast Scotland consists of the area east of a line drawn roughly from Perth north to the fringe of the Moray Firth at Forres. The region takes in the county of Angus and the city of Dundee to the south and, beyond the Grampian Mountains, the counties of Aberdeenshire and Moray, and the city of Aberdeen. Geographically diverse, the south of the region is comprised predominantly of undulating farmland. However, as you travel further north this gives way to wooded glens, mountains and increasingly rugged terrain, fringed by a dramatic coastline of high cliffs and long sandy beaches.

The long-depressed city of **Dundee** is valiantly trying to shed its post-industrial image with a reinvigorated cultural scene and an impressive waterfront development based around **Discovery**, the ship of Captain Scott ("of the Antarctic") and a new outpost of the V&A. A little way up the Angus coast are the historically important towns of **Arbroath** and **Montrose**, which are linked by an especially inviting stretch of coastline, featuring scarlet cliffs and sweeping bays. Further south towards Dundee, these are replaced by gentler dunes and long sandy beaches, while inland the long fingers of the **Angus glens** – heather-covered hills tumbling down to rushing rivers – are overlooked by the southern peaks of the Grampian Mountains. **Glen Clova** is one of the most popular, along with **Glen Shee**, which attracts many visitors to its ski slopes. Handsome if uneventful market towns such as **Brechin**, **Kirriemuir** and **Blairgowrie** are good bases for visiting the area, and extravagant **Glamis Castle** is well worth a visit.

The northeast was the southern kingdom of the **Picts**, reminders of whom are scattered throughout the region in the form of beautifully carved stones found in fields, churchyards and museums, such as the one at **Meigle**. Remote, self-contained and cut off from the centres of major power in the south, the area never grew particularly prosperous, and a handful of feuding and intermarrying families grew to wield a disproportionate influence, building many of the region's **castles** and religious buildings, and developing and planning its towns.

Aberdeenshire and **Moray** cover a large chunk of the northeast, some 3500 square miles, much of it open and varied country dotted with historic and archeological sights, from eerie prehistoric rings of standing stones to quiet kirkyards and a rash of dramatic castles. Geographically, the counties break down into two distinct areas: the **hinterland**, once barren and now a patchwork of fertile farms, rising towards high mountains, sparkling rivers and gentle valleys; and the **coast**, a classic stretch of rocky cliffs, remote fishing villages and long, sandy beaches.

Many of the most appealing settlements in these counties are along the coast, but while the fishing industry is but a fondly held memory in many parts, a number of the northeast's ports were transformed by the discovery of **oil** in the North Sea in the 1960s – particularly **Aberdeen**, Scotland's third-largest city. It's the region's obvious focal

FISHMONGER, ARBROATH

Highlights

❶ McManus Art Galleries and Museum
Dundee's most impressive Victorian building is the place to come for ceramics, fine art and contemporary photography. **See p.346**

❷ Arbroath smokies A true Scottish delicacy: succulent haddock best eaten when it's still warm from the oak smoker. **See p.351**

❸ Pictish stones Fascinating carved relics of a lost culture, standing alone in fields or protected from the elements in museums such as that at Meigle. **See p.360**

❹ Aberdeen This northeastern city features a gorgeous cityscape carved out of granite, and a dramatic harbour. **See p.362**

❺ Dunnottar Castle Scotland's moodiest clifftop ruin, with centuries of bloody tales to tell and views across the swirling North Sea. **See p.373**

❻ Museum of Scottish Lighthouses Learn about light, lenses and legends at one of the best small museums in the country. **See p.382**

❼ Pennan and Gardenstown Tiny one-street fishing villages on the Aberdeenshire coast: there's no room for any more between the cliff and the sea. **See p.383**

HIGHLIGHTS ARE MARKED ON THE MAP ON PP.342–343

Cullen
Portsoy
Whitehills
Macduff Gardenstown
Banff **Duff House**
Crovie
7 Pennan
B9031
6 Fraserburgh
Cairnbulg
B9033
Inverallochy

River Deveron
A95
A97

Turriff A947
A950
Mintlaw
Peterhead

A948
A952

Cruden
Bay
Bullers of Buchan
A90
Slains Castle

untly
A96
Fyvie

Rhynie

A920

Insch
Bennachie
(1733ft)
Inverurie

Pitmedden
Newburgh
Collieston
Forvie National Nature Reserve

nsden

Alford A944
Craigievar Castle
A980
River Don

River Don

A96

4 Aberdeen

Aboyne

Drum Castle
Crathes Castle
A93
Banchory

River Dee
B974

5 Stonehaven
Dunnottar Castle
RSPB Fowlsheugh Nature Reserve
Catterline

Glenesk Retreat And Folk Museum
Esk
Fasque
Fettercairn
Arbuthnott
Kinneff
Inverbervie

Fettercairn
Edzell
B966

HOWE OF THE MEARNS

A90

Bridgend

FAULT
A90

House of Dun
A935
Brechin
Aberlemno
B9134
Restenneth Priory
B9113

St Cyrus
R. North Esk

Lunan Bay

N O R T H   S E A

St Vigeans
Auchmithie
2 Arbroath

Carnoustie
Monifeth

Orkney & Shetland
N

HIGHLIGHTS

1 McManus Art Galleries and Museum

2 Arbroath smokies

3 Pictish stones

4 Aberdeen

5 Dunnottar Castle

6 Museum of Scottish Lighthouses

7 Pennan and Gardenstown

NORTHEAST SCOTLAND

point, with bold architecture, attractive museums and a lively social scene, and continues to ride a diminishing wave of oil-based prosperity. The city's transport connections make it an undeniably handy base; there's an international **airport**, and **trains** connect the centre with Inverness and major points further south.

From Aberdeen, it's a short hop west to **Deeside**, a fertile yet ruggedly attractive area made famous by the royal family, who have favoured the estate at **Balmoral** as a summer holiday retreat ever since Queen Victoria fell in love with it back in the 1840s. Close by, the villages of **Ballater** and **Braemar** act as a gateway to the spectacular mountain scenery of the **Cairngorms National Park**. To the north lies the meandering **Don Valley**, a quiet area notable for **castles** such as Kildrummy and Corgarff, both of which are appealingly remote. Further north still, the dramatic **coastline** is punctuated by picturesque fishing villages, and there is a handful of engaging sights including **Duff House**, an outpost of the National Galleries of Scotland, and the New Age community at **Findhorn**.

10

GETTING AROUND   NORTHEAST SCOTLAND

By train Trains from Edinburgh and Glasgow connect with Dundee, Aberdeen and other coastal towns, while an inland line from Aberdeen heads northwest to Elgin and on to Inverness.

By bus The region has a reasonably comprehensive scheduled bus service; only in the most remote and mountainous parts does public transport disappear altogether.

By car Northeast Scotland is well served by an extensive road network, with fast links between Dundee and Aberdeen, while the area north and west of Aberdeen is also dissected by a series of efficient routes.

Dundee

At first sight, **DUNDEE** can seem a grim place. In the nineteenth century it was Britain's main processor of jute, the world's most important vegetable fibre after cotton, which earned the city the tag "Juteopolis". The decline of manufacturing wasn't kind to Dundee, and the city's population of 145,000 are still living with its effects. But regeneration is today's big buzzword, with some commentators drawing comparisons with Glasgow's reinvention as a city of culture in the 1980s and 1990s. A major project under way at the time of writing is the construction of the V&A's Museum of Design, a liner-like construction rising on the waterfront. Less apparent is the city's international reputation as a centre of biotechnology, computer game technology and cancer research.

Brief history

Even prior to its Victorian heyday, Dundee was a town of considerable importance. It was here in 1309 that **Robert the Bruce** was proclaimed the lawful King of Scots, and during the Reformation it earned itself a reputation for tolerance, sheltering leading figures such as **George Wishart** and **John Knox**. During the Civil War, the town was destroyed by the Royalists and Cromwell's army. Later, prior to the Battle of Killiecrankie, it was razed to the ground once more by Jacobite **Viscount Dundee**, known in song and folklore as "Bonnie Dundee", who had been granted the place for his services to the Crown by James II.

Dundee picked itself up in the 1800s, its train and harbour links making it a major centre for shipbuilding, whaling and the manufacture of **jute**. This, along with jam and journalism – the three Js which famously defined the city – has all but disappeared, with only local publishing giant D.C. Thomson, publisher of the timelessly popular *Beano* and *Dandy* (among other comics and newspapers), still playing a meaningful role in the city. Look out for the statues of Dundee heroes **Desperate Dan** and **Minnie the Minx**, both from the old *Dandy* comic, given pride of place at the junction of Reform Street and City Square.

10

DUNDEE

& Broughty Ferry

Leuchars

Tay Road Bridge (Toll)

Victoria Dock

City Quay Shopping Centre

Unicorn

V&A Museum of Design

RRS Discovery

Discovery Point

Discovery Quay

Train Station

Seagate Bus Station

Wellgate Shopping Centre

St Paul's Episcopal Cathedral

McManus Art Galleries & Museum

Dundee Travel Shop

Howff Burial Ground

Overgate Shopping Centre

Caird Hall

St Mary's Church

Verdant Works

Avertical World Climbing Centre

University of Dundee

Dundee Repertory Theatre

Dundee Science Centre

DCA

Hertz

Ninewells Hospital & Balgay Hill

Tay Rail Bridge, Spokes Bike Hire & Cineworld

& Airport

PEEP O DAY LANE

VICTORIA ST

PRINCES STREET

BLACKSCROFT

FOUNDRY LANE

EAST DOCK STREET

KING STREET

NELSON ST

VICTORIA ROAD

HILLTOWN

QUEEN'S ST

ALLAN STREET

SEAGATE

COWGATE

TRADES LANE

MARKET GAIT

MURRAYGATE

PANMURE ST

SQUARE

COMMERCIAL ST

ALBERT SQUARE

REFORM STREET

DUDHOPE STREET

BELL STREET

BARRACK ST

CONSTITUTION ROAD

NORTH MARKETGAIT

WEST BELL STREET

WARD ROAD

SOUTH WARD ROAD

NORTH LINDSAY STREET

HIGH STREET

CASTLE ST

EXCHANGE ST

SHORE TERRACE

DOCK ST

NORTHERN BOULEVARD

SOUTHERN BOULEVARD

WEST VICTORIA DOCK RD

SOUTH VICTORIA DOCK RD

UNION ST

CITY SQUARE

EAST MARKETGAIT

WEST MARKETGAIT

OVERGATE LANE

WEST MARKETGAIT

BROWN STREET

DOUGLAS STREET

MILN STREET

GUTHRIE STREET

SESSION STREET

HAWKHILL

HAWK HILL

WEST PORT

SOUTH TAY ST

TAY SQ

NETHERGATE

PARK PLACE

SMALLS WYND

GREENMARKET

RIVERSIDE DRIVE

N

0 — 200 yards

The Tay bridges

The best approach to Dundee is across the modern mile-and-a-half-long **Tay Road Bridge** from Fife. Running parallel a mile upstream is the **Tay Rail Bridge**, opened in 1887 to replace the spindly structure which collapsed in a storm in December 1879 only eighteen months after it was built, killing the crew and 75 passengers on a train passing over the bridge at the time. While the Tay bridges aren't nearly as spectacular as the bridges over the Forth near Edinburgh, they do offer a magnificent panorama of the city on the northern bank of the firth; look out for seals bobbing in the water.

10

St Paul's Episcopal Cathedral

High St, close to the junction with Commercial St • Tues–Sat 11am–3pm; call if you'd like to visit at other times • Free • ☎ 01382 224486

Midway between the Wellgate and Overgate shopping centres is the mottled spire of **St Paul's Episcopal Cathedral**, a rather gaudy Gothic Revival structure designed by George Gilbert Scott, notable for its vivid if sentimental stained glass and floridly gilded high altar. Immediately in front of the cathedral is a statue to one of the city's heroes, **Admiral Duncan of Camperdown**, who defeated a Dutch fleet not far offshore from Dundee during the Napoleonic Wars.

McManus Art Galleries and Museum

Albert Square • Mon–Sat 10am–5pm, Sun 12.30–4.30pm; last entry 15min before closing • Free • ☎ 01382 307200, Ⓦ www.mcmanus.co.uk

The **McManus Art Galleries and Museum**, Dundee's most impressive Victorian structure, is an unmissable stop for art lovers. The **ground-floor rooms** explore the nature of museums, the surrounding natural landscape and the making of modern Dundee, while upstairs there's the splendid **Victoria gallery**, its curved red walls densely hung with an impressive collection of works by masters including Rossetti and Henry Raeburn. The rest of this floor is equally engrossing: Dundee and the World shows an eclectic ethnographic collection; the **20th Century Gallery** showcases work by the Scottish Colourists and others; the **Long Gallery** is lined with historic and modern ceramics; while **Here and Now** displays fine art acquisitions, including contemporary photography. The museum's bright and attractive **café** is also a good pit stop, especially on a sunny day when you can sit on the stone terrace outside.

Verdant Works

West Henderson's Wynd, Blackness • April–Oct Mon–Sat 10am–6pm, Sun 11am–6pm; Nov–March Wed–Sat 10.30am–4.30pm, Sun 11am–4.30pm • £9.25; joint ticket with Discovery Point £16 • ☎ 01382 309060, Ⓦ www.rrsdiscovery.com

An award-winning museum, **Verdant Works** tells the story of **jute**, from its harvesting in India to its arrival in Dundee on clipper ships. The museum, set in an old jute mill, makes a lively attempt to re-create the turn-of-the-twentieth-century factory floor, the highlight being the chance to watch jute being processed on fully operational quarter-size machines originally used for training workers. The excellent guides include one of the last mill workers.

DCA

152 Nethergate • Daily: complex 10am–midnight; galleries 11am–6pm, until 8pm Thurs • Free • ☎ 01382 909900, Ⓦ dca.org.uk

Principal among the city's many arts venues is the hip and exciting **DCA**, or Dundee Contemporary Arts, a stunning five-floor complex that incorporates galleries, a print studio, a classy design shop selling some of the prints made in-house, and an airy café-bar. It's worth visiting for the stimulating temporary and touring exhibitions of contemporary art, as well as an eclectic programme of art-house films and cult classics (see p.350).

Discovery Point

Discovery Quay • April–Oct Mon–Sat 10am–6pm, Sun 11am–6pm; Nov–March Mon–Sat 10am–5pm, Sun 11am–5pm (last entry 1hr before closing) • £9.25, audio-guide £3; joint ticket with Verdant Works £16 • ☎ 01382 309060, ⓦ www.rrsdiscovery.com

Just south of the city centre, in the redeveloped waterfront area, domed **Discovery Point** is an impressive development centring on the Royal Research Ship *Discovery*, which sits dramatically alongside in a dry dock. Something of an icon for Dundee's renaissance, *Discovery* is a three-mast steam-assisted vessel built in Dundee in 1901 to take **Captain Robert Falcon Scott** on his polar expeditions. A combination of brute strength and elegance, it has been beautifully restored, with polished wood panels and brass trimmings giving scant indication of the privations suffered by the crew. In the Antarctic, temperatures on board would plummet to -28°C and turns at having a bath came round every 47 days. Before you step aboard there is a series of interactive displays about the construction of the ship and Scott's journeys, including the chill-inducing "Polarama" about life in Antarctica. Another highlight is Herbert Ponting's classic images of the ship and crew.

10

Unicorn

Victoria Dock • April–Oct daily 10am–5pm; Nov–March Wed–Fri noon–4pm, Sat & Sun 10am–4pm • £5 • ☎ 01382 200900, ⓦ frigateunicorn.org

An endearingly simple wooden frigate built in 1824, **Unicorn** is the oldest British warship still afloat and was in active service up until 1968. Although the interior is sparse, the cannons, the splendid figureheads and the wonderful model of the ship in its fully rigged glory (the real thing would have featured over 23 miles of rope) are fascinating. The ship is moored across from *Discovery* on the other side of the road bridge near the multimillion-pound redevelopment of Victoria Dock (a footpath connects the two ships).

Dundee Law

A 30min walk north of the city centre, or take bus #22 from Commercial St

A mile or so north of town, **Dundee Law** is the plug of an extinct volcano and, at 571ft, the city's highest point. Once the site of a seventh-century defensive hillfort, it's now an impressive **lookout point**, with great views across the whole city and the Tay. The steep (and often windy) climb to the top, which is marked by a monument commemorating both world wars, takes around half an hour from the centre.

Mills Observatory

Balgay Hill, 2 miles west of the centre • April–Sept Tues–Fri 11am–5pm, Sat & Sun 12.30–4pm; Oct–March Mon–Fri 4–10pm, Sat & Sun 2.30–4pm; planetarium show Oct–March every other Fri, plus one Wed/month in summer (see website for details) • Free; planetarium £1 • ☎ 01382 435967, ⓦ leisureandculturedundee.com • Buses #17 and #26 from Nethergate stop on Ancrum Rd, on the edge of Lochee Park

Balgay Hill, Dundee's smaller volcanic outcrop, sits a mile to the west of Dundee Law and is skirted by wooded **Lochee Park**. On its summit sits the **Mills Observatory**, Britain's only full-time public observatory with a resident astronomer. The best time to visit is after dark on winter nights; in summer there's little to be seen through the telescope, but well-explained, quirky exhibits and displays chart the history of space exploration and astronomy, and on sunny days you can play at being a human sundial and take in the fantastic views over the city through little telescopes. From October to March the **planetarium** runs a fortnightly show, while the observatory also has special opening times to coincide with eclipses and other astronomical events.

Broughty Ferry and around

ⓦ cometobroughty.co.uk • Connected to the city by a 20min bus ride; use National Express bus #5 or #17, or Stagecoach Strathtay's #73 and #73a services; all leave from either High St or Seagate in the town centre

Four miles east of Dundee's city centre lies the seaside settlement of **BROUGHTY FERRY**, now engulfed by the city as a reluctant suburb. The ferry referred to in the name was a railway ferry, which transported carriages travelling between Edinburgh and Aberdeen; it was inevitably closed following the building of the first ill-fated Tay Rail Bridge. Comprising an eclectic mix of big villas built by jute barons up on the hillside and small fishermen's cottages along the shoreline, "The Ferry", as it's known, has experienced a recent resurgence in popularity. It's now a pleasant and relaxing spot with some good restaurants and pubs, and both the beach and the castle's "green" (or grounds) are popular run-around spots for kids.

Broughty Castle and Museum

Castle Approach • Mon–Sat 10am–4pm, Sun 12.30–4pm (Oct–March closed Mon) • Free • ☎ 01382 436916

The striking **Broughty Castle and Museum**, right by the seashore, is worth a look, if only to admire its location at the mouth of the River Tay. Constructed in 1496 to protect the estuary, and rebuilt in the nineteenth century, its four floors now house local history and military exhibits and cover the story of Broughty Ferry from 400 million years ago to its development as a fishing village.

Claypotts Castle

Just off the A92 at Claypotts Junction • Limited opening hours – for details call ☎ 01786 431324 • Free

Just north of Broughty Ferry, at the junction of the A92 and B978, the chunky bricks of **Claypotts Castle** constitute one of Scotland's most complete Z-shaped tower houses. Built between 1569 and 1588, its two round towers have stepped defensive projections which support extra rooms, a sixteenth-century architectural practice that makes Claypotts look like it's about to topple over. Note that you can only view the castle from outside.

ARRIVAL AND DEPARTURE
DUNDEE

BY PLANE

Dundee's airport (☎ 01382 662200, ☻ hial.co.uk) is 2 miles west of the city centre. There are no buses into the centre so expect to fork out around £8 for a taxi.
Destinations London City (Mon–Fri 2 daily, 1 on Sat, 1 on Sun; 1hr 25min).

BY TRAIN

Trains arrive at and depart from the station on Riverside Drive, about 300yds south of the city centre, near the river.
Destinations Aberdeen (every 30min; 1hr 15min); Arbroath (every 30min; 20min); Edinburgh (every 30min; 1hr 30min); Glasgow (hourly; 1hr 30min); Montrose (1–2 hourly; 30min).

BY BUS

Long-distance buses operated by Stagecoach Strathtay

(☎ 01382 313700) arrive at the Seagate bus station, a couple of hundred yards east of the centre. For timetables and information contact Traveline Scotland (☎ 08712 002233; ☻ travelinescotland.com).
Destinations Aberdeen (hourly; 2hr 20min); Arbroath (every 30min; 30–50min); Blairgowrie (every 30min–1hr 50min–1hr); Forfar (every 30min; 30min); Glamis (2–5 daily; 35min); Kirriemuir (hourly; 55min); Meigle (hourly; 40min); Montrose (hourly; 1hr).

BY CAR

Car rental Arnold Clark, East Dock St (☎ 01382 59934C ☻ arnoldclark.com); Enterprise, 131 Seagate (☎ 0138; 205040, ☻ enterprise.co.uk); Hertz, 18 West Marketga; (☎ 01382 223711, ☻ hertz.co.uk).

GETTING AROUND

By bus Local buses leave from the high street or from nearby Union St. Dundee Travel Shop at 92 Commercial St (☎ 01382 340006, ☻ nxbus.co.uk/Dundee) sells Daysaver tickets, which provide unlimited bus travel for a day

(£3.70), and hands out information on local bus routes.
By taxi There are taxi ranks on Nethergate, or try Dunde Private Hire (☎ 01382 203020).

INFORMATION

Tourist office Discovery Point, in the building beside the RSS *Discovery* ship (Mon–Sat 11am–4/5pm, Sun 11am–4/5pm; ☎ 01382 527527). The tourist office is

conveniently located just across from the train station.
Website For info on the city's upcoming exhibition shows and events, see ☻ www.dundee.com.

ACTIVITIES

Bike rental Spokes, at 272 Perth Rd (☎ 01382 666644, ⓦ www.spokescycles.net), is the most central option for cycle rental, with bikes for £20/day.

Cycle routes/walking trails At the tourist office you can get route maps for Maritime and Heritage Walking Trails (1–2hr duration; free), which depart from the DCA. There's also a map of a citywide cycle route.

Indoor climbing Avertical World, at 7 Blinshall St (☎ 01382 201901, ⓦ www.averticalworld.co.uk), offers roped climbing and bouldering in an old church west of the centre; 1hr taster sessions cost £20. They're open Mon–Fri noon–10pm, Sat & Sun 10am–7pm (until 5pm Sat & Sun June–Aug).

Football The city has two leading football clubs, Dundee (☎ 01382 889966, ⓦ dundeefc.co.uk) and Dundee United (☎ 01382 833166, ⓦ dundeeunitedfc.co.uk), whose stadiums face each other across Tannadice St in the north of the city.

Monifeith Golf Club 8 Princes St, Monifieth ☎ 01382 532678 Offers two challenging 18-hole courses east of Broughty Ferry.

10

ACCOMMODATION

HOTELS

Apex City Quay Hotel 1 West Victoria Dock Rd ☎ 01382 202404, ⓦ apexhotels.co.uk. Large, sleek and modern hotel that stands out among the new developments of the dockland area, incorporating a spa, swimming pool and restaurant. **£72**

Malmaison 44 Whitehall Crescent ☎ 01382 339715, ⓦ malmaison.com. Part of a flash boutique chain and with gorgeous Victorian features, including a wrought-iron staircase and a grand dome. Handy for the city sights and waterfront. **£65**

Premier Inn Dundee Centre Riverside Drive ☎ 08715 78320, ⓦ premierinn.com. Bland hotel that's part of a nationwide chain, but there's no denying it's well positioned beside Discovery Point and the train station. **£75**

GUESTHOUSES AND B&BS

Aberlaw Guest House 230 Broughty Ferry Rd ☎ 01382 56929, ⓦ aberlaw.co.uk. Well-run guesthouse 1.5 miles from the city centre, with spotlessly clean rooms (including a large family room for £80), and a welcoming owner who knows the local area inside out. **£70**

★ **Duntrune House** Duntrune, 5 miles northeast of town ☎ 01382 350239, ⓦ duntrunehouse.co.uk. Three spacious rooms in one wing of a grand but welcoming country house, built in 1826 and standing in lovely mature gardens five miles northeast of Dundee. **£100**

Fisherman's Tavern 10–16 Fort St, Broughty Ferry ☎ 01382 775941, ⓦ fishermanstavern-broughtyferry .co.uk. Neat contemporary rooms – mostly en suite, and one with facilities for disabled guests – above a cosy, popular traditional pub with a roaring fire and good real ales. **£90**

HOSTEL

Dundee Backpackers Hostel 57 High St ☎ 01382 224646, ⓦ www.hoppo.com. Dundee's only backpackers' hostel, with dorms and private rooms in a warren-like former merchant's house constructed in 1560. Dorms **£17**; doubles/twins **£45**

EATING

The **west end** of Dundee, around the main university campus and Perth Rd, is the best area for eating and drinking; the **city centre** has a few good pubs and one or two decent restaurants tucked away near the Repertory Theatre. **Broughty Ferry** is a pleasant alternative, with a good selection of pubs and restaurants that get particularly busy on summer evenings.

Agacan 113 Perth Rd ☎ 01382 644227. Tiny, moderately priced Turkish restaurant with an unmistakeable colourful exterior, and rough-hewn walls inside; they serve up decent kebabs (lamb doner £11) and stuffed pittas, and also do takeaways. Tues–Thurs 5–9pm, Fri & Sat 5.30–9.30pm.

Castlehill 22 Exchange St ☎ 01382 220008, castlehillrestaurant.co.uk. Probably the most reliable spot for well-sourced, confidently cooked fine Scottish food in the city. The two-course dinner menu costs £30, with dishes including Angus lamb and wild halibut. Daily noon–2.30pm & 5.30–10pm.

Elk Café 118 Nethergate ☎ 01382 228794. A bright and funky city-centre daytime café with a spiral staircase leading to a lower floor. Great for breakfast, coffee and a sandwich/soup lunch from £4, with veggie and gluten-free options. Mon–Sat 8am–6pm.

Metro Brasserie At the Apex City Quay Hotel, 1 West Victoria Dock Rd ☎ 01382 202404, ⓦ apexhotels.co.uk. A style-led, but still pleasant, restaurant space, on the ground floor of the dockland's sleekest hotel, serving imaginative Scottish cuisine like Ayrshire pork with an apple purée and black pudding (£17). Daily noon–2.30pm & 6–9.30pm.

The Playwright 11 South Tay St ☎ 01382 223113, ⓦ theplaywright.co.uk. Swanky, well-staffed restaurant right by the Repertory Theatre, serving indulgent à la carte dishes (think saddle of venison with dauphinoise; £25.95) and cheaper pre-theatre and lunch menus. Mon–Sat noon to roughly midnight, last food orders at 9.30pm.

10

The Sands Restaurant Glass Pavilion, The Esplanade, Broughty Ferry ☎01382 732738, ⓦthesands .restaurant. Dramatic, glass-fronted former bathing shelter with 1930s Art Deco styling, serving delicious home baking, healthy light meals and traditional high tea (4–7pm; £13.95). Daily 9am–9pm.

DRINKING AND NIGHTLIFE

Beer Kitchen 10 South Tay St ☎01382 202070, ⓦthebeerkitchen.co.uk. Run by the Innis & Gun brewery, this is a hipster pub with a great range of beers and fine food on the side, including an excellent weekend brunch: try the Arbroath smokie omelette (£6.50). Mon–Thurs & Sun 11am–midnight, Fri & Sat 10am–1am.

Fisherman's Tavern 10–16 Fort St, Broughty Ferry ☎01382 775941, ⓦfishermanstavern-broughtyferry .co.uk. Just off the shore in a busy traditional cottage, this pub serves a variety of real ales. There's a small garden for when the sun is shining. Daily 11am–midnight/1am.

Ship Inn 121 Fisher St, Broughty Ferry ☎01382 779176, ⓦtheshipinn-broughtyferry.co.uk. A narrow pub with a warm atmosphere and nautical feel, right on the waterfront with good views over the Tay. Does good seafood dishes (crab salad £9.25) and a fine selection of beers. Mon–Sat 11am–midnight, Sun 12.30–midnight.

The Reading Rooms 57 Blackscroft ☎01382 228496, ⓦreadingroomsdundee.com. From rock 'n' roll and disco to soul, blues and punk, you'll find it all here. The schedule (available online) is mostly taken up by DJs and club nights, but live guitar bands play here too. Thurs–Sat 10.30pm–2.30/3.30am.

Trades House Bar 40 Nethergate ☎01382 229494, ⓦtradeshouse-dundee.co.uk. A converted bank fronted with stained-glass windows, which provides a friendly atmosphere for boozing in the heart of the city. Also does pub meals for around £7.50. Daily 10/11am–midnight.

ENTERTAINMENT

Caird Hall City Square ☎01382 434940, ⓦleisure andculturedundee.com/culture/caird-hall. The city's best venue for classical music, including visits by the Royal Scottish National Orchestra and other bigwigs, is Caird Hall, whose bulky frontage dominates City Square. See website for show times.

Cineworld Camperdown Leisure Park ☎08712 002000, ⓦcineworld.co.uk/cinemas/dundee. Nine-screen cinema a fair way out of the centre, which shows mostly blockbuster movies. Take bus #4 from Commercial St to get here. Call for show times.

DCA 152 Nethergate ☎01382 909900, ⓦdca.org.uk. DCA has two comfy auditoria showing an appealing range o foreign and art-house movies alongside some of the more highbrow Hollywood releases. Daily 10am–midnight.

Dundee Repertory Theatre Tay Square ☎01382 223530, ⓦdundeereptheatre.co.uk. This prodigiou venue sits right at the heart of the Cultural Quarter, north o Nethergate. It's an excellent place for indigenousl produced contemporary theatre and the home of the onl permanent repertory company in Scotland. Box offic Mon–Sat 10am–7.30/8pm.

DIRECTORY

Medical facilities Ninewells Hospital (☎01382 660111) is in the west of the city and has an Accident and Emergency department; Dundee Dental Hospital (☎01382 425791); Boots pharmacy, 49–53 High St (☎01382 221756).

Police Scotland's Tayside division is based at West Bell S (☎01382 223200 or ☎101).

Post office 4 Meadowside (Mon–Fri 9am–5.30pm, Sa 9am–12.30pm).

The Angus coast

The predominantly agricultural county of **ANGUS**, east of the A9 and north of the Firth of Tay, holds some of the northeast's greatest scenery and is relatively free of tourists. The coast from **Montrose** to **Arbroath** is especially inviting, with scarlet cliffs and sweeping bays, then, further south towards Dundee, gentler dunes and long sandy beaches.

GETTING AROUND   **THE ANGUS COAS**

By car Two roads link Dundee to Aberdeen and the northeast coast of Scotland. By far the more pleasant option is the slightly longer A92 coast road, which joins the inland A90 at Stonehaven, just south of Aberdeen.

By bus Intercity buses from Dundee to Aberdeen tend to use the A90, passing Forfar on the way.

By train The coast-hugging train line running north fro Dundee is one of the most picturesque in Scotland, passi attractive beaches and impressive cliffs, and stopping the old seaports of Arbroath and Montrose.

Arbroath and around

Since it was settled in the twelfth century, local fishermen have been landing their catches at **ARBROATH**, situated on the Angus coast where it starts to curve in from the North Sea towards the Firth of Tay, about fifteen miles northeast of Dundee. The name of the town stems from Aber Brothock, the burn which runs into the sea here, and although it has a great location, with long sandy beaches and stunning sandstone cliffs on either side of town, as well as an attractive old working harbour, Arbroath – like Dundee – has suffered from car-focused development.

The town's most famous product is the **Arbroath smokie** – line-caught haddock, smoke-cured over smouldering oak chips, and still made here in a number of family-run smokehouses tucked in around the harbour.

10

Signal House Museum

Ladyloan, just west of the dock • Tues–Sat 10am–5pm • Free • ☎ 01241 435329

Down by the harbour, the elegant Regency **Signal House Museum** still stands sentinel, as it has since 1813 when it was built as the shore station for the Bell Rock lighthouse, improbably erected on a reef eleven miles offshore by Robert Stevenson. Bell Rock is the oldest remaining offshore lighthouse in the world. The interior of the house is now given over to some excellent local history displays: a schoolroom, fisherman's cottage and lighthouse kitchen have all been carefully re-created.

Arbroath Abbey

Abbey St, half a mile north of the dock • Daily: April–Sept 9.30am–5.30pm; Oct–March 9.30am–4pm • £5.50; HES • ☎ 01241 878756, www.historicenvironment.scot

By the late eighteenth century, chiefly due to its harbour, Arbroath had become a trading and manufacturing centre, famed for boot-making and sail-making (the *Cutty Sark*'s sails were made here). The town's real glory days, however, came much earlier in the thirteenth century with the completion in 1233 of **Arbroath Abbey**, whose rose-pink sandstone ruins, described by Dr Johnson as "fragments of magnificence", stand on Abbey Street. The abbey was dissolved during the Reformation, and until the nineteenth century, when the first steps were taken to protect the abbey, it was little more than a source of red sandstone for local houses.

However, there's enough left to get a good idea of how vast the place must have been: the semicircular **west doorway** is more or less intact, complete with medieval mouldings, and the **south transept** has a beautiful round window, once lit with a beacon to guide ships. In the early 1950s, the **Stone of Destiny** had a brief sojourn here when it was stolen from London by a group of Scottish nationalists and appeared, wrapped in a Scottish flag, at the High Altar. It was duly returned to Westminster Abbey, where it stayed until its relatively recent move to Edinburgh Castle (see box, p.63).

St Vigeans

Although now little more than a northwestern dormitory of Arbroath, the pristine and peaceful hamlet of **ST VIGEANS** is a fine example of a Pictish site colonized by

THE DECLARATION OF ARBROATH

Arbroath Abbey was the scene of one of the most significant events in Scotland's history when, on April 6, 1320, a group of Scottish barons drew up the **Declaration of Arbroath**, asking the pope to reverse his excommunication of Robert the Bruce and recognize him as king of a Scottish nation independent from England. The wonderfully resonant language of the document still makes for stirring reading: "For so long as one hundred of us remain alive, we will never in any degree be subject to the dominion of the English, since it is not for glory, riches or honour that we do fight, but for freedom alone, which no honest man loses but with his life." It was duly dispatched to Pope John XXII in Avignon, who in 1324 agreed to Robert's claim.

Christians: the church is set defiantly on a pre-Christian mound at the centre of the village. Many **Pictish stones** and fragments, dating back to 842 AD, are housed in the wonderful little museum, including the Drosten Stone, presumed to be a memorial. One side depicts a hunt, laced with an abundance of Pictish symbolism, while the other side bears an intricate Celtic cross.

Auchmithie

10

Four miles north of Arbroath by road or coastal footpath, the clifftop village of **AUCHMITHIE** is the true home of the Arbroath smokie. However, the village didn't have a proper harbour until the nineteenth century – local fishermen, apparently, were carried to their boats by their wives to avoid getting wet feet – so Arbroath became the more important port and laid claim to the delicacy.

ARRIVAL AND DEPARTURE

ARBROATH AND AROUND

By train Trains arrive at the station on Keptie St, less than a 10min walk from the seafront.

Destinations Aberdeen (every 30min; 1hr); Dundee (every 30min; 20min); Montrose (roughly every 30min; 15min).

By bus The bus station is on Catherine St, close to the railway station and within easy walking distance of the tourist information office.

Destinations Aberdeen (hourly; 1hr 45min); Dundee (hourly; 30min); Forfar (hourly; 45min); Montrose (every 30min; 25min).

INFORMATION

Tourist office Fishmarket Quay, in the revamped harbour area (April–Sept Mon–Sat 9.30am–5pm, Sun noon–4pm; Oct Mon–Fri 10am–5pm, Sun noon–4pm; Nov–March Mon–Fri 10am–4pm, Sat 11am–4pm;

☎01241 872609). Look out for the free Arbroath Path Network leaflet, which has a useful map showing coastal walking routes in the area.

ACCOMMODATION

★**Brucefield B&B** Cliffburn Rd ☎01241 875393, ⓦbrucefieldbandb.com. Rooms at this renovated 1920s manor house are as good as those in the region's best hotels, with high-end bathrooms and plush beds. Downstairs there's a sitting room with a free minibar, and outside there are seats overlooking a croquet lawn. **£120**

The Old Vicarage 2 Seaton Rd ☎01241 43047, ⓦtheoldvicaragebandb.co.uk. Simple and friendly, The Old Vicarage has an impressive breakfast table that includes hot Arbroath smokies, a freshly baked loaf of bread and home-made preserves. **£75**

EATING AND DRINKING

But'n'Ben In Auchmithie, 4 miles east of Arbroath ☎01241 877223. One of the best restaurants along this stretch of coast, specializing in delicious, moderately priced seafood. The flavoursome platter of local smoked fish and shellfish costs £19.95. Daily except Tues noon–2pm & 6–9pm.

M&M Spink 10 Marketgate ☎01241 875287. This tiny whitewashed shop is one of the most approachable and atmospheric places to try the famous Arbroath smokie

(£8/kg); chef and cookery writer Rick Stein described the fish here, still warm from the smoke, as "a world-class delicacy". Mon–Sat 8am–5pm, Sun 10am–5pm.

The Old Brewhouse 1 High St, by the harbour wall ☎01241 879945, ⓦoldbrewhousearbroath.co.uk. A convivial and moderately priced restaurant-cum-pub where you can sit down and tuck into Arbroath smokies smothered in melted butter and lemon (£11.25). Daily noon–9pm.

Montrose and around

MONTROSE, a seaport and market town since the thirteenth century, can sometimes smell a little rich, mostly because of its position on the edge of a virtually landlocked two-mile-square lagoon of mud known as the **Basin**. But with the wind in the right direction, the ancient royal burgh of Montrose is a great town to visit, with a pleasant old centre and an interesting museum. The Basin, too, is of interest: flooded and emptied twice daily by the tides, it's a nature reserve for the host of geese, swans and wading birds that frequent the ooze.

If you have time to spare, be sure to check out the town's fabulous golden **seashore**. The beach road, Marine Avenue, across from the town museum, heads down through sand dunes and golf links to car parks fringing the fine, wide beach, which is overlooked by a slender white lighthouse.

Montrose Museum and Art Gallery

Panmure Place, on the western side of Mid Links Park • Tues–Sat 10am–5pm • Free • ☎ 01674 662660, Ⓦ www.angus.gov.uk

Two blocks behind the soaring kirk steeple at the lower end of High Street, the **Montrose Museum and Art Gallery** is one of Scotland's oldest museums, dating from 1842. In the local history section look out for Pictish stones, and the mechanical paper sculpture of the town, with a green train running along the top and yachts sailing by. Outside the museum entrance stands a winsome study of a boy by local sculptor William Lamb.

10

William Lamb Memorial Studio

24 Market St • July to mid-Sept Tues–Sun 2–5pm; at other times ask at the museum • Free • ☎ 01674 662660, Ⓦ www.angus.gov.uk

Scottish sculptor William Lamb (1893–1951) was a superbly talented but largely unheralded artist. His career is all the more impressive because he taught himself to sculpt with his left hand, having suffered a war wound in his right. Much of his work can be seen in the moving **William Lamb Memorial Studio**, including bronze heads of the Queen, Princess Margaret and the Queen Mother. There's another Lamb sculpture, *Whisper*, outside the library on the high street.

Montrose Basin Wildlife Centre

Around a mile west of Montrose on the A92 • March–Oct daily 10.30am–5pm; Nov–Feb Fri–Sun 10.30am–4pm • £4 • ☎ 01674 676336, Ⓦ montrosebasin.org.uk

On the south side of the Basin, a mile or so out of town, the **Montrose Basin Wildlife Centre** has binoculars, high-powered telescopes and remote-control video cameras available for visitors who want to catch a glimpse of wading birds and kingfishers. Family-friendly guided walks also depart from the wildlife centre (see the website for a schedule).

The House of Dun

4 miles west of Montrose off the A935 • Late March to June & Sept–Oct Wed–Sun noon–5pm; July & Aug daily 11am–5pm; last admission 45min before closing • £10.50; NTS • ☎ 01674 810264 • Accessible on the hourly Montrose–Brechin bus service (#30); ask the driver to let you off outside

Across the Basin, four miles west of Montrose, is the Palladian **House of Dun**. Built in 1730 for David Erskine, Laird of Dun, to designs by William Adam, the house was opened to the public in 1989 after extensive restoration, and is crammed full of period furniture and objets d'art. Inside, the ornate relief plasterwork is the most impressive feature, extravagantly emblazoned with Jacobite symbolism. The buildings in the courtyard – a hen house, gamekeeper's workshop and potting shed – have all been renovated, and include a tearoom and a craft shop. There's a Victorian walled garden to explore, as well as formal planting and parkland.

ARRIVAL AND DEPARTURE	MONTROSE AND AROUND
By train The town's train station is by the Basin's edge, a block back from the high street on Western Rd. *Destinations* Aberdeen (every 30min–1hr; 45min); Arbroath (every 30min; 15min); Dundee (every 30min; 20min); Stonehaven (every 30min–1hr; 25min).	**By bus** Most buses stop on the high street, close to Lloyds Pharmacy, or at the railway station. *Destinations* Aberdeen (hourly; 1hr 20min); Brechin (for the House of Dun; hourly; 20min); Dundee (every 30min; 25min); Stonehaven (every 30min; 50min).

ACCOMMODATION AND EATING

36 The Mall The Mall, in the north of town ☎ 01674 673464, Ⓦ 36themall.co.uk. Attractive B&B accommodation with en-suite facilities in every room.

The breakfast menu includes fish smoked in nearby Arbroath. **£80**

The Haven 8 Lower Hall St ☎ 01674 677741,

Ⓦ thehaven-montrose.co.uk. Near the centre, these serviced apartments offer good-value singles and doubles in a clean, three-storey house. Guests have access to a communal kitchen, and are given space in the fridge. **£60**
Roos Leap 2 Trail Drive, by the golf club Ⓣ 01674

672157, Ⓦ roosleap.com. The liveliest (though hardly cosiest) place in Montrose is this sports bar and restaurant offering burgers, steaks and sandwiches from £6.95. Mon–Fri noon–2.30pm & 5–9.30pm, Sat & Sun noon–9.30pm.

10 Strathmore and the Angus glens

Immediately north of Dundee, the low-lying Sidlaw Hills divide the city from the rich agricultural region of **STRATHMORE**, whose string of tidy market towns lies on a fertile strip along the southernmost edge of the heather-covered lower slopes of the Grampian Mountains. These towns act as gateways to the tranquil **ANGUS GLENS**, offering some of the most rugged and majestic landscapes in northeast Scotland. **Glen Clova** in particular is well and truly on the tourist circuit, with the rolling hills and dales attracting hikers, birdwatchers and botanists in the summer, grouse shooters and deer-hunters in autumn, and winter skiers who pray for a bountiful snowfall.

GETTING AROUND   STRATHMORE AND THE ANGUS GLENS

By car The most useful road through the glens is the A93, which cuts through Glen Shee, linking Blairgowrie to Braemar on Deeside (see p.378). It's pretty dramatic stuff,

threading its way over Britain's highest main road, the Cairnwell Pass (2199ft). Public transport in the region is extremely limited.

Brechin

Eight miles west of Montrose, **BRECHIN** is an attractive town whose red-sandstone buildings give it a warm, welcoming feel. The chief attraction is the old **cathedral**, a building that's emboldened some (including the local football team) to proudly describe Brechin – in line with the historic definition – as a fully fledged city.

The Cathedral

Bishop's Close, off the high street • Daily 9am–5pm • Free • Ⓣ 01356 629360

There's been a religious building of sorts here since the arrival of evangelizing Irish missionaries in 900 AD, and the red-sandstone structure of the **cathedral** has become something of a hotchpotch of architectural styles. What you see today dates chiefly from an extensive rebuilding in 1900, with the oldest surviving part of the cathedral being the 106ft-high round tower, one of only two in Scotland. The cathedral's doorway, built 6ft above the ground for protection against Viking raids, has some notable carvings, while inside you can see various Pictish stones, illuminated by the jewel-coloured stained-glass windows.

ARRIVAL AND DEPARTURE   BRECHIN

By bus Brechin is easy to get to and from; bus #30 runs at least once an hour to Montrose, nine miles to the east.

INFORMATION AND TOURS

Tourist office St Ninians Place (April–Oct Mon–Sat 9am–5pm, Sun 10am–5pm; Nov–March Sat 9am–5pm, Sun 10am–5pm; Ⓣ 01356 623050).
Caledonian Railway tours Brechin station Ⓣ 01356

622992, Ⓦ caledonianrailway.com. Trains operate every weekend from June to August, travelling along four miles of track from Brechin to the Bridge of Dun (£6 return). Diesel trains run on Saturdays, steam trains run on Sundays.

ACCOMMODATION

Gramarcy House 6 Airlie St Ⓣ 01356 622240. Bright, spacious and tastefully furnished rooms in a house set back from the main road. There's also a self-catering kitchen area

and the sunny breakfast room with bay windows gets the day off to a good start. Agnes, the owner, is friendly and helpful. **£80**

Edzell and around

Travelling around Angus, you can hardly fail to notice the difference between organic settlements and planned towns that were built by landowners who forcibly rehoused local people in order to keep them under control, especially after the Jacobite uprisings. One of the better examples of the latter, **EDZELL**, five miles north of Brechin on the B966, was cleared and rebuilt with Victorian rectitude a mile to the west of its original site in the 1840s. Through the Dalhousie Arch at the entrance to the village the long, wide and ruler-straight main street is lined with prim nineteenth-century buildings, which now do a roaring trade as genteel teashops and antiques emporia.

The original village (identifiable from the cemetery and surrounding grassy mounds) lay immediately to the west of the wonderfully explorable red-sandstone ruins of Edzell Castle, itself a mile west of the planned village.

10

Edzell Castle

A mile west of Edzell • April–Sept daily 9.30am–5.30pm • £5.50; HES • ☎ 01316 688800, ⊛ historicenvironment.scot

The main part of **Edzell Castle** is a good example of a comfortable tower house, where luxurious living rather than defence became a priority. However, it's the **pleasance garden** overlooked by the castle tower that makes a visit essential, especially in late spring and early to mid-summer. The garden was built by Sir David Lindsay in 1604, at the height of the optimistic Renaissance, and its refinement and extravagance are evident. The walls contain sculpted images of erudition: the Planetary Deities on the east side, the Liberal Arts on the south and, under floods of lobelia, the Cardinal Virtues on the west wall. In the centre of the garden, low-cut box hedges spell out the family mottoes and enclose voluminous beds of roses; in one corner sits a gabled summer house.

The Caterthuns

Four miles southwest of Edzell, lying either side of the lane to Bridgend (which can be reached either by carrying on along the road past the castle or by taking the narrow road at the southern end of Edzell village), are the **Caterthuns**, twin Iron Age hillforts that were probably occupied at different times. The surviving ramparts on the White Caterthun (978ft) – easily reached from the small car park below – are the most impressive; this is thought to be the later fort, occupied by the Picts in the first few centuries AD.

ARRIVAL AND DEPARTURE — EDZELL AND AROUND

By bus Edzell is 5 miles north of Brechin on the B966, and linked to it by buses #21, #29 and #30.

ACCOMMODATION AND EATING

Alexandra Lodge Inveriscandye Rd ☎ 01356 648266, ⊛ alexandralodge.co.uk. Just a short walk east of the high street, this is a friendly B&B located on a quiet street in little Edwardian lodge built in 1907. April–Oct. **£75**

Glenesk Hotel High St ☎ 01356 648319, ⊛ glenesk hotel.com. A 38-room Victorian hotel with sweeping gardens, a golf course and full-size snooker table, plus a pool and spa. The bar has seven hundred whiskies. **£100**

Tuck Inn 44 High St ☎ 01356 648262, ⊛ tuckinnedzell .co.uk. An old-school red-painted restaurant/café, which dishes up filling fodder such as scampi (£9.25), fish and chips and treacle pudding. Eat in or take away. Daily 11am–8pm.

Glen Esk

Just north of Edzell, a fifteen-mile road climbs alongside the River North Esk to form **Glen Esk**, the most easterly of the Angus glen, which, like the others, is sparsely populated. Further up the glen there are some excellent **hiking** routes, including one to Queen Victoria's Well in Glen Mark and another up Mount Keen, Scotland's most easterly Munro. For information on hiking routes around Glen Esk, see ⊛ visitcairngorms.com.

10

Glenesk Retreat and Folk Museum

Tarfside, 10 miles northwest of Edzell • Easter to Nov Mon–Fri 10am–5pm, Sat & Sun 10am–6pm • Free • ☎ 01356 648070, ⓦ gleneskretreat.co.uk

Ten miles along Glen Esk, the excellent **Glenesk Retreat and Folk Museum** brings together records, costumes, photographs, maps and tools from the Angus glens, depicting the often harsh way of life for their inhabitants. Housed adjacent to a former shooting lodge known as The Retreat, built by a retired sea captain in the 1840s, it's run independently and enthusiastically by the local community. The museum's main attraction is its collection of agricultural tools, some of which date from the eighteenth century. There's also a great little café.

ACCOMMODATION   **GLEN ESK**

Glenesk Caravan Park Burn Estate ☎ 01356 648565, ⓦ caravanparkangus.co.uk. 1.5 miles north of the village, you can camp at this small, child-friendly site. Reception daily 9–11am & 4–6pm; April–Oct. Per pitch **£12**

Forfar and around

Around fifteen miles north of Dundee on the A90 lies **FORFAR**, Angus's county town and the ancient capital of the Picts. The town's wide high street is framed by some impressive Victorian architecture and small old-fashioned shops. If you stop here it's worth popping into the quaint bakeries that proudly stock the famous **Forfar bridie**, a semicircular folded pastry-case of mince, onion and seasonings.

Just west of town, a series of glacial lochs peters out at **Forfar Loch**, now surrounded by a pleasant country park with a visitor centre and three-mile nature trail. Further west still is **Glamis Castle** (see p.358), whose ostentatious interiors, carefully sculpted gardens and château-like turrets make it one of Scotland's most fantastical fortresses.

Meffan Institute Museum and Art Gallery

20 West High St • Tues–Sat 10am–5pm • Free • ☎ 01307 476482, ⓦ www.angus.gov.uk

Midway along Forfar's high street, the **Meffan Institute Museum and Art Gallery** exhibits Neolithic, Pictish and Celtic remains and a thoroughly enjoyable collection of replica historical shops and street scenes; the most disturbing examines the town's seventeenth-century passion for witch-hunting, with a taped re-enactment of locals baying for blood.

Restenneth Priory and around

A couple of miles east of Forfar in the middle of farmland are the remains of **Restenneth Priory**, approached along a side road off the B9113 (go beyond the Angus Archives to reach the car park). King Nechtan of the Picts was thought to have established a place of worship here in the eighth century, although the oldest parts of the present structure are from an Augustinian priory erected on the spot around 1100.

A little way south of this, off the B9128, a cairn in the village of **Dunnichen** commemorates a battle at nearby Nechtansmere in 685 in which the Picts unexpectedly defeated a Northumbrian army, thus preventing the Angles from extending their kingdom northwards.

EATING AND DRINKING   **FORFAR AND AROUND**

Goodfellow & Steven 35 Castle St ☎ 01307 460030. If you want to try the local speciality, Forfar bridie, call in at this bakery near the town's municipal building. A steak-filled bridie will set you back a very reasonable £1.55. Daily 8am–4pm.

Tiffins 12 West High St ☎ 01307 461152. The carpet seen better days and the wallpaper's old-fashioned, but the friendly staff make this tearoom a pleasant spot for vanilla slice and a cuppa (£2.60). They also do good sandwiches. Daily 9.30am–4.30pm.

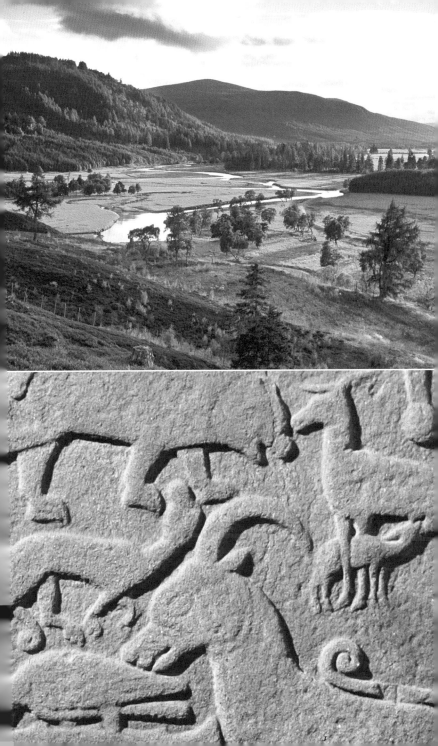

Glamis Castle

Dundee Rd, about 6 miles west of Forfar • March–Oct daily 10am–6pm; last tour 4.30pm • £11 • ☎ 01307 840393, ⓦ glamis-castle
.co.uk • Take Stagecoach bus #20C from West High St in Forfar or Commercial St in Dundee

Pink-sandstone **Glamis Castle**, located a mile north of the picturesque village of **GLAMIS** (pronounced "glahms"), is a wondrously over-the-top, L-shaped five-storey pile set in an extensive landscaped park. It's also one of Scotland's most famous castles: Shakespeare chose it as a central location in *Macbeth*, and its **royal connections** (as the childhood home of the late Queen Mother and birthplace of the late Princess Margaret) make it one of the essential stops on every coach tour of Scotland.

As you approach the castle down the long main drive, a riot of turrets, towers and conical roofs appears fantastically at the end of the sweeping avenue of trees, framed by the Grampian Mountains. Obligatory guided **tours** (50min) take in the fifteenth-century **crypt**, where the 12ft-thick walls enclose a haunted "lost" room, reputed to have been sealed with the red-bearded lord of Glamis and Crawford inside, after he dared to play cards with the Devil one Sabbath. Artist Jacob de Wet was commissioned to produce the frescoes in the family **chapel**, completed in 1688, and his depictions of Christ wearing a hat and St Peter in a pair of glasses have raised eyebrows ever since. **Duncan's Hall**, a fifteenth-century guardroom, is the traditional – but inaccurate – setting for Duncan's murder by Macbeth (it actually took place near Elgin).

Brief history

The bulk of the current castle dates from the fifteenth century, although many of the later additions give it its startling Disneyesque appearance. Glamis began life as a comparatively humble **hunting lodge**, used in the eleventh century by the kings of Scotland. In 1372 King Robert II gave the property to his son-in-law, Sir John Lyon, who built the core of the present building. His descendants, the earls of Kinghorne and Strathmore, have lived here ever since.

Kirriemuir and around

The sandstone town of **KIRRIEMUIR**, known locally as Kirrie, is set on a hill six miles northwest of Forfar on the cusp of glens Clova and Prosen. Despite the influx of hunters up for the "season", it's still a pretty special place, a haphazard confection of narrow closes, twisting wynds and steep braes. The main cluster of streets has all the appeal of an old film set, with its old-fashioned bars, tiled butcher's shop, tartan outlet and haberdasheries, but somehow manages to avoid being contrived and quaint.

Barrie's birthplace

9 Brechin Rd • Mid-March to June Sat–Wed noon–5pm; July & Aug daily 11am–5pm; Sept & Oct Sat–Wed noon–5pm • £6.50; NTS •
☎ 01575 572646

Kirrie was the birthplace of **J.M. Barrie** (born 1860). A local handloom-weaver's son, Barrie first came to notice with his series of novels about "Thrums" – a village based on his home town – and in particular *A Window in Thrums* and his third novel, *The Little Minister*. The story of **Peter Pan**, the little boy who never grew up, was penned by Barrie in 1904 – some say as a response to a strange upbringing dominated by the memory of his older brother, who died in a skating accident at the age of 13. **Barrie's birthplace**, a plain little whitewashed cottage which housed the family's ten children, has a series of small rooms decorated as they would have been during Barrie's childhood, as well as displays about his life and works.

Camera obscura

In the old cricket pavilion above town, just off West Hill Rd • Mon & Thurs–Sun noon–4pm • Donation

One of the few **camera obscuras** still functioning in Scotland, this unexpected treasure is run by the local community, along with a small café. It was donated to the town in

1930 by J.M. Barrie, and offers splendid views of Strathmore and the glens: on a clear day it's possible to see as far as Ben Ledi, almost sixty miles to the west.

| ARRIVAL AND DEPARTURE | KIRRIEMUIR AND AROUND |

By bus The hourly #20 bus runs from Kirriemuir's high street to Forfar (15min) and Dundee (50min).

ACCOMMODATION AND EATING

Muirhouses Farm 2 miles north of town on the way to Cortachy ☎ 01575 573128, ⓦ muirhousesfarm .co.uk. Offering a proper taste of the countryside hereabouts, this is a working cattle farm with bright, plain rooms, which are looked after by friendly owner Susan. Breakfast includes fresh meat from the local butcher. Offers discounts for longer stays. **£78**

Thrums Hotel Bank St ☎ 01575 572758, ⓦ thrumshotel.co.uk. Good central option for lunches and evening meals; the menu includes chicken with black pudding (£9.50). There are also nine en-suite rooms available. Daily noon–2pm & 5–8pm. **£80**

SHOPPING

Star Rock Shop 27–29 The Roods ☎ 01575 572579. Pretty, old-style shop specializing in Scottish confectionery, which first opened in 1833. This is a nice place to try the hard, sweet and milky Scottish candy known as tablet (£2/bag). Tues–Sat 9/10am–5pm.

Glen Clova and around

With its stunning cliffs, heather slopes and valley meadows, **Glen Clova** – which in the north becomes **Glen Doll** – is one of the loveliest of the Angus glens. Although it can get unpleasantly congested in peak season, the area is still remote enough to enable you to leave the crowds with little effort. Wildlife is abundant, with deer on the mountains, wild hares, and even grouse and the occasional buzzard. The meadow flowers on the valley floor and arctic plants (including great splashes of white and purple saxifrage) on the rocks make it a botanist's paradise.

WALKS FROM GLEN DOLL

Ordnance Survey Explorer maps 388 & 387

These **walks** are some of the main routes across the Grampians from the Angus glens to Deeside, many of which follow well-established old drovers' roads. All three either fringe or cross the royal estate of Balmoral, and Prince Charles's favourite mountain – **Lochnagar** – can be seen from all angles. The walks all begin from the car park at the end of the tarred road where Glen Clova meets Glen Doll; all routes should always be approached with care, and you should follow the usual safety precautions.

CAPEL MOUNTH TO BALLATER

15 miles; 7hr

Initially, the path zigzags its way up fierce slopes before levelling out to a moorland plateau, leading to the eastern end of Loch Muick. It then follows the River Muick to Ballater.

CAPEL MOUNTH ROUND-TRIP

15 miles; 8hr

Follows the above route to Loch Muick, doubling back along the loch's southern shore. The dramatic Streak of Lightning path that follows Corrie Chash leads to a ruined stables below Sandy Hillock; the descent passes the waterfall by the bridge at Bachnagairn, where a gentle burn-side track leads back to Glen Doll car park.

JOCK'S ROAD TO BRAEMAR

14 miles; 7hr

A signposted path leads below Cairn Lunkhard and along a wide ridge towards the summit of Crow Craigies (3018ft). From here, the path bumps down to Loch Callater then follows the Callater Burn, eventually hitting the A93 two miles short of Braemar.

10

Clova

The B955 from Dykehead and Kirriemuir divides at the Gella Bridge over the swift-coursing River South Esk. Around six miles north of Gella, the two branches of the road join up once more at the hamlet of **CLOVA**, home to little more than the hearty *Glen Clova Hotel* (see below). An excellent, if fairly strenuous, four-hour walk from behind the old school at the back of the hotel leads up into the mountains and around the lip of **Loch Brandy**.

North from Clova village, the road turns into a rabbit-infested lane coursing along the riverside for four miles to a car park, which makes a useful starting point for numerous superb **walks**. There are no other facilities beyond the village.

10

ACCOMMODATION AND EATING   **GLEN CLOVA AND AROUND**

Glen Clova Hotel Clova, 15 miles north of Kirriemuir, along the B955 ☎ 01575 550350, ⓦ clova.com. Inviting country hotel, which also has its own climbers' bunkhouse and a private fishing loch. The restaurant serves up traditional Scottish food with a twist, such as timbale o haggis, neeps and tatties (mains from £11). Mon–Thurs & Sun noon–7.45pm, Fri & Sat noon–8.45pm. Dorms £17 doubles £90

Glen Prosen

Five miles north of Kirriemuir, the low-key hamlet of **Dykehead** marks the point where **Glen Prosen** and Glen Clova divide. A mile or so up Glen Prosen, you'll find the house where Captain Scott and fellow explorer Doctor Wilson planned their ill-fated trip to Antarctica in 1910–11, with a roadside **stone cairn** commemorating the expedition.

From here on, Glen Prosen remains essentially a quiet wooded backwater, with all the wild and rugged splendour of the other glens but without the crowds. To explore the area thoroughly you need to go on foot, but a good road circuit can be made by crossing the river at the tiny village of **Glenprosen** and returning to Kirriemuir along the western side of the glen via Pearsie. Alternatively, the reasonably easy four-mile **Minister's Path** links Glen Prosen with Clova; it is clearly marked and leaves from near the church in the village.

Meigle Museum

Dundee Rd, Meigle • April–Sept daily 9.30am–5pm • £4.50; HES • ☎ 01828 640612, ⓦ historicenvironment.scot • Hourly bus #57 from Dundee to Perth passes through Meigle

Fifteen miles north of Dundee on the B954 lies the tiny settlement of **Meigle**, home to Scotland's most important collection of early Christian and Pictish **inscribed stones**. Housed in a modest former schoolhouse, the **Meigle Museum** displays 26 pieces dating from the seventh to the tenth centuries, all found in and around the nearby churchyard. The majority are either gravestones that would have lain flat, or cross slabs inscribed with the sign of the cross, which were usually standing. Most impressive is the 7ft-tall great cross slab, said to be the gravestone of Guinevere, wife of King Arthur. The exact purpose of the stones and their enigmatic symbols is obscure, as is the reason why so many of them were found at Meigle. The most likely theory suggests that Meigle was once an important ecclesiastical centre that attracted secular burials of prominent Picts.

Glen Isla and around

Three and a half miles north of Meigle is **Alyth**, near which, legend has it, Guinevere was held captive by Mordred. It's a sleepy village at the south end of **Glen Isla**, which runs parallel to Glen Shee, and is linked to it by the A926. If you decide to stay in the area, your best options for accommodation are in and around **Kirkton of Glenisla**, a small hamlet ten miles north of Alyth.

Reekie Linn

Close to the Bridge of Craigisla, which is a ten-minute drive north of Alyth along the B954, the River Isla narrows and then plunges some 60ft into a deep gorge to produce the classically pretty waterfall of **Reekie Linn**, or "smoking fall", so-called because of the water mist produced when the fall hits a ledge and bounces a further 20ft into a deep pool known as the Black Dub. There's a car park beside the bridge, and the waterfall is a short walk away along the river's edge.

ARRIVAL AND DEPARTURE	GLEN ISLA AND AROUND	**10**

By bus Transport connections into the glen are limited. Alyth is on the main bus routes linking Blairgowrie with Dundee.

ACCOMMODATION

Glenisla Hotel Kirkton of Glenisla ☎01575 582223, ⌨glenisla-hotel.com. Cosy whitewashed hotel, which doubles as a good place for classy home-made bar food and convivial drinking. **£80**

★ **West Freuchies** 1 mile east of Kirkton of Glenisla ☎01575 582716, ⌨glenisla-westfreuchies.co.uk. A comfortable B&B whose first-floor rooms have views over the hills; they make their own bread for breakfast, and you might spot red squirrels in the grounds. There's also self-catering accommodation nearby in a converted mill. Approaching from Alyth, a right-hand turn leads northeast to the B&B (signposted before you reach Kirkton of Glenisla). **£76**

Glen Shee and around

The upper reaches of **Glen Shee**, the most dramatic and best known of the Angus glens, are dominated by its **ski fields**, ranged over four mountains above the Cairnwell mountain pass. The resorts here may not amount to much more than gentle training slopes in comparison with those of the Alps or North America, but they all make for a fun day out for everyone from beginners to experienced skiers. During the season (Dec–March), ski lifts and tows give access to gentle beginners' slopes, while experienced skiers can try the more intimidating Tiger run. In summer it's all a bit sad, although there are some excellent hiking and mountain-biking routes. Active types tend to overnight in Spittal of Glenshee, or twenty miles further south along the A93 in Blairgowrie (see p.362), a small town at the southern end of the glen.

Spittal of Glenshee

The small settlement of **SPITTAL OF GLENSHEE** (the name derives from the same root as "hospital", indicating a refuge), though ideally situated for skiing, has little else to commend it other than the busy Gulabin Lodge Outdoor Centre. From Spittal the road climbs another five miles or so to the ski centre at the crest of the Cairnwell Pass.

ACCOMMODATION AND ACTIVITIES	SPITTAL OF GLENSHEE

Dalmunzie Castle Blairgowrie ☎01250 885224, ⌨dalmunzie.com. A lovely Highland retreat in a magnificent turreted mansion, with first-class dining and over sixty malt whiskies to enjoy by the fireside. The entrance is just south of Gulabin Lodge Outdoor Centre, across the bridge. **£170**

Gulabin Lodge Outdoor Centre Just off the A93 immediately north of Spittal of Glenshee ☎01250 885255, ⌨gulabinoutdoors.co.uk. Snow sports are the big draw here in winter, of course, but staff can also arrange summer activities like archery and rock climbing. Pre-booking advised. There is also clean, basic accommodation in a nineteenth-century manse, with singles, doubles and family rooms all available. **£55**

SKIING IN GLEN SHEE

For information on skiing in Glen Shee contact **Ski Glenshee** (☎01339 741320, ⌨ski-glen shee.co.uk), which also offers ski rental and lessons, as does the **Gulabin Lodge Outdoor Centre** (see above), at the Spittal of Glenshee. For the latest snow and weather conditions, phone Ski Glenshee or check out **VisitScotland's page**: ⌨visitscotland.com/see-do /active/skiing-snowsports.

Blairgowrie

Travelling to Glen Shee from the south, you'll pass through the well-heeled little town of **BLAIRGOWRIE**, set among raspberry fields on the glen's southernmost tip, and a good place to pick up information and plan your activities. Strictly two communities – Blairgowrie and **Rattray**, set on either side of the River Ericht – the town's modest claim to fame is that St Ninian once camped at Wellmeadow, a pleasant grassy triangle in the town centre.

10

Cateran Trail

The **Cateran Trail** is an ambitious, long-distance footpath that starts in Blairgowrie then heads off on a long loop into the glens to the north following some of the drove roads used by caterans, or cattle thieves. It takes four to five days to tramp the 64-mile route, though of course it's possible to walk shorter sections of the way (see the website ⓦcaterantrail.org for more information).

ARRIVAL AND INFORMATION

By bus Blairgowrie is well linked by hourly bus #57 to both Perth (50min) and Dundee (1hr).
Tourist office 26 Wellmeadow (April–June & Sept–Oct Mon–Fri 10am–5pm, Sun 10.30am–3.30pm; July & Aug Mon–Sat 9.30am–5pm, Sun 10.30am–3.30pm; Nov–March Mon–Sat 10am–4pm; ⓣ01250 872960 ⓦperthshire.co.uk). Blairgowrie's friendly tourist office can help with booking accommodation.

ACCOMMODATION AND EATING

Bridge of Cally Hotel 6 miles north of town on the A93 ⓣ01250 886231, ⓦbridgeofcallyhotel.com. A welcoming roadside pub serving simple grub throughout the day (steak and kidney pie £10.50), plus real ale by an open fire. They also have plain rooms. Daily 10am–8.45pm. **£90**
Cargills By the river on Lower Mill St ⓣ01250 876735, ⓦcargillsbistro.com. Popular bistro serving inexpensive formal meals as well as civilized coffee and cakes. The menu includes good vegetarian options such as mushroom risotto (£9). Daily 10.30am–9pm.
Little's 4 Wellmeadow ⓣ01250 875358, ⓦlittlesrestaurant.co.uk. Lovely little restaurant specializing in prettily presented fresh local fish; mussels with cider cost £8.95. Tues–Thurs 4–9pm, Fri & Sat noon–2.30pm & 6–9.30pm.

SHOPPING

Blairgowrie Farm Shop 14–16 Reform St ⓣ01250 876528, ⓦblairgowriefarmshop.co.uk. Jams, vegetables, organic breads and frozen meats are all for sale at this well-stocked deli and farm shop. Mon–Sat 8.30am–5.30pm.

Aberdeen

The third-largest city in Scotland, **ABERDEEN**, commonly known as the "Granite City" lies 120 miles northeast of Edinburgh on the banks of the rivers Dee and Don, smack in the middle of the northeast coast.

Since the 1970s, **oil** has made Aberdeen a wealthy and self-confident place, though heavily dependent on the vagaries of oil prices. The city can sometimes seem to exist only as a departure point for the transient population of some ten to fifteen thousand who live on the 130 oil platforms out at sea. But its **architecture** is stunning – a granite cityscape created in the nineteenth century by three fine architects: Archibald Simpson and John Smith in the early years of the century and, later, A. Marshall Mackenzie. Classical inspiration and Gothic Revival styles predominate, giving grace to a material once thought of as only good enough for tombs and paving stones. In addition, the urban **parks** are some of the most beautiful in Britain.

Getting your bearings is easy enough, as Aberdeen divides neatly into five main areas. The **city centre**, roughly bounded by Broad Street, Union Street, Schoolhill and Union Terrace, features the opulent Marischal College, the colonnaded Art Gallery with its

ABERDEEN

ACCOMMODATION

Aberdeen City Centre Hotel	5
Allan Guest House	13
Butler's Guest House	10
Carmelite	6
Crombie Johnston Halls	2
Dutch Mill	9
Ferryhill House	14
Globe Inn	4
Hilton Garden Inn	1
Malmaison	8
Marcliffe at Pitfodels	12
Skene House	3
Roselea House	11
SYHA Aberdeen	7

● SHOPPING

Books and Beans	3
La Gourmandise	4
The Old Aberdeen Bookshop	2
Tiso	1

● EATING

Blue Moon	12
Books and Beans	4
The Breadmaker	3
Café 52	8
Fusion	5
Howies	11
Kilau Coffee	1
Musa	9
Ninety-Nine Bar & Kitchen	7
Poldino's	6
Rocksalt & Snails	13
Sand Dollar Café	2
Silver Darling	10

■ NIGHTLIFE

Babylon	9
The Blue Lamp	1
The Tunnels	5

■ DRINKING

Brewdog Aberdeen	2
The Grill	8
The Illicit Still	4
Prince of Wales	6
St Machar Bar	3
Slains Castle	7

0   yards   200

10

Beach & Cineworld
Footdee & 10
Duthie Park & Winter Gardens

St Andrews Episcopal Cathedral
Peacock Visual Arts
Mercer Cross
KING ST
Marischal College
The Tolbooth Museum
Provost Skene's House
First Travel Centre
Maritime Museum & Provost Ross's House
St Nicholas Kirk
Aberdeen Art Gallery
Academy Shopping Centre
Belmont Picture House
Triple Kirks
His Majesty's Theatre
Library
St Mary's Catholic Cathedral
Music Hall

REGENT QUAY
VIRGINIA STREET
MARISCHAL STREET
BLAIKIES QUAY
Ferry Terminal
Fish Market
ALBERT QUAY
COMMERCIAL QUAY
JAMESON QUAY
Harbour
TRINITY QUAY
MARKET STREET
PALMERSTON ROAD
N. ESPLANADE W.
SHIPROW
Bus Station
Train Station
GUILD STREET
COLLEGE STREET
BRIDGE STREET
CROWN STREET
MARYWELL STREET
DEE PLACE
SPRINGBANK STREET
DEE STREET
BON ACCORD STREET
SPRINGBANK TERRACE
BON ACCORD STREET
BON ACCORD CRESCENT
LANGSTANE PLACE
HARDGATE
UNION STREET
Golden Square
UNION TERRACE
Union Terrace Gdns.
BELMONT ST
SCHOOLHILL
DENBURN ROAD
BACK WYND
LITTLE BELMONT STREET
THE GREEN
CORRECTION
NETHERKIRKGATE
BROAD STREET
WYND
ROSEMOUNT VIADUCT
SUMMER STREET
SKENE STREET
HUNTLY STREET
CHAPEL STREET
THISTLE STREET
WEST END
ROSE STREET
ALFORD LANE
HOLBURN STREET
JUSTICE MILL LANE

Ringroad & Airport

N

fine collection, the burgeoning nightlife of Belmont Street, and homes that pre-date Aberdeen's nineteenth-century town planning and have been preserved as museums. Union Street leads west to the twin diversions of gentrified shopping and raucous nightlife that defines the **West End**. To the south, the **harbour** still heaves with boats serving the fishing and oil industries, while north of the centre lies attractive **Old Aberdeen**, a village neighbourhood presided over by King's College, St Machar's Cathedral and a stunning new university library. The long sandy **beach** marks Aberdeen's eastern border, just a mile or so from the heart of the city.

Brief history

In the twelfth century, Alexander I noted "Aberdon" as one of his principal towns, and by the thirteenth century it had become a centre for **trade** and fishing, a jumble of timber and wattle houses perched on three small hills, with the castle to the east and St Nicholas Kirk outside the gates to the west.

It was here that **Robert the Bruce** sought refuge during the Scottish Wars of Independence, leading to the garrison of the castle by Edward I and Balliol's supporters. In a night-time raid in 1306, the townspeople attacked the garrison and killed them all, an event commemorated by the city's motto "Bon Accord", the watchword for the night. The victory was not to last, however, and in 1337 Edward III stormed the city, forcing its rebuilding on a grander scale. A century later Bishop Elphinstone founded the Catholic university in the area north of town known today as **Old Aberdeen**, while the rest of the city developed as a mercantile centre and important port.

Industrial and economic expansion led to the Aberdeen New Streets Act in 1800, setting off a hectic half-century of development that almost led to financial disaster. Luckily, the city was rescued by a boom in trade: in the **shipyards** the construction of Aberdeen clippers revolutionized sea transport, giving Britain supremacy in the China tea trade, and in 1882 a group of local businessmen acquired a **steam** tugboat for trawl fishing. Sail gave way to steam, and fisher families flooded in.

By the mid-twentieth century, Aberdeen's traditional industries were in decline, but the discovery of **oil** in the North Sea transformed the place from a depressed port into a boom town. This oil-borne prosperity may have served to mask the thinness of the region's other wealth creators, but it has nonetheless allowed Aberdeen to hold its own as a cultural and academic centre, and as a focus of the northeast's identity.

Union Street

The centre of Aberdeen is dominated by mile-long **Union Street** – still the grandest and most ambitious single thoroughfare in Scotland. The challenge for the early nineteenth-century city planners who conceived the street was the building of the ambitious **Union Street bridge**, spanning two hills and the Denburn gorge. The first attempt, a triple-span design by Glasgow architect David Hamilton, bankrupted the city and collapsed during construction. The famous civil engineer Thomas Telford then proposed the single-arch structure that became an engineering wonder of its age. Since completion in 1805 the bridge has been widened twice, the second time, in 1963, adding a row of shops to the southern side that obscures the dramatic impact of the structure.

Castlegate

Any exploration of the **city centre** should begin at the open, cobbled **Castlegate**, where Aberdeen's long-gone castle once stood. At its centre is the late seventeenth-century **Mercat Cross**, carved with a unique gallery of Stewart sovereigns and topped with a unicorn. Castlegate was once the focus of city life but nowadays seems rather lifeless unless you dart along the easily missed lane to **Peacock Visual Arts** at 21 Castle St (Tues–Sat 9.30am–5.30pm; free; ☎01224 639539, ⓦwww.peacockvisualarts.co.uk), a hub for the northeast's contemporary art scene with a focus on printmaking; they also run live music events.

The Tolbooth Museum

Castle St • July–Sept Tues–Sat 10am–4pm, Sun 12.30–3.30pm • Free • ☎ 01224 621167

As Union Street begins you have to crane your neck to see the towering, turreted spire of the **Town House**, though the steely grey nineteenth-century exterior is in fact a facade behind which lurks the early seventeenth-century **Tolbooth**, one of the city's oldest buildings. A jail for centuries, The Tolbooth now houses **The Tolbooth Museum** of crime and imprisonment, featuring winding narrow stairs leading to cramped cells. The prime grisly exhibit is the blade of the city's seventeenth-century guillotine.

St Andrew's Episcopal Cathedral

King St • May to mid-Sept Tues–Fri 11am–4pm, Sat 10.30am–1pm, Sun for worship • Free • ☎ 01224 640119

The sandstone **St Andrew's Episcopal Cathedral**, where Samuel Seabury, America's first bishop, was ordained in 1784, contrasts with the uniform granite of central Aberdeen. Inside, spartan whiteness is broken by florid gold ceiling bosses representing the (then) 48 states of the USA and 48 local families who remained loyal to the Episcopal Church during the eighteenth-century Penal Laws.

Provost Skene's House

45 Guestrow • Mon–Sat 10am–5pm, closed at the time of writing for renovations • Free • ☎ 01224 641086

Tucked away between Broad Street and Flourmill Lane, **Provost Skene's House** is Aberdeen's oldest-surviving private house, dating from 1545. The house is now a museum, with a costume gallery, archeological exhibits, period rooms and a café-bar. Don't miss the Painted Gallery, where a cycle of beautiful religious tempera paintings from the mid-seventeenth century shows scenes from the life of Christ.

Marischal College

On Broad Street stands Aberdeen's most imposing edifice, and the world's second-largest granite building after the Escorial in Madrid – exuberant **Marischal College**, whose tall, steel-grey pinnacled neo-Gothic facade is in absolute contrast to the hideously utilitarian concrete office blocks opposite. This spectacular building, with all its soaring, surging lines, has been painted and sketched more than any other in Aberdeen, though it's not to everyone's taste – it was once described by an art historian as "a wedding cake covered in indigestible grey icing".

The college was founded in 1593 by the fourth Earl Marischal, and coexisted as a separate Protestant university from Catholic King's, just up the road, for over two centuries. It was long Aberdeen's boast to have as many universities as the whole of England, and it wasn't until 1860 that the two were united as the University of Aberdeen. In 1893, the central tower was more than doubled in height by A. Marshall Mackenzie and the profusion of spirelets added, though the facade, which fronts an earlier quadrangle designed by Archibald Simpson in 1837–41, was not completed until 1906.

St Nicholas Kirk

Just north of Union St • May–Sept Mon–Fri noon–4pm; Oct–April contact church office • Free • ☎ 01224 643494, ⓦ www.kirk-of-st nicholas.org.uk

Between Upperkirkgate and Union Street stands **St Nicholas Kirk**. It's actually two churches in one, with a solid, central bell tower, from where the 48-bell carillon, the

10

largest in Britain, regularly chimes. There's been a church here since 1157 or thereabouts, but as the largest kirk in Scotland it was severely damaged during the Reformation and divided into the West and the East Church, separated today by the transepts and crossing; only the north transept, known as Collinson's aisle, survives from the twelfth century.

The Renaissance-style **West Church**, formerly the nave of St Nicholas, was designed in the mid-eighteenth century by James Gibbs, architect of St Martin in the Fields in London. The **East Church** was rebuilt over the groin-vaulted crypt of the restored fifteenth-century St Mary's Chapel (entered from Correction Wynd), which in the 1600s was a place to imprison witches: you can still see the iron rings to which they were chained.

Aberdeen Art Gallery

Schoolhill • Tues–Sat 10am–5pm, Sun 2–5pm; closed for restoration until winter 2017 • Free • ☎ 0300 020 0293, ⓦ aagm.co.uk

The first-rate **Aberdeen Art Gallery** was purpose-built in 1884 to a Neoclassical design by Scottish architect Alexander Marshall Mackenzie. You enter via the airy **Centre Court**, dominated by Barbara Hepworth's central fountain and thick pillars running down from the upper balcony, each hewn from a different local marble. The walls highlight the policy of acquiring contemporary art, with British work to the fore. The **Side Court** contains *Jungled*, a garish, erotic spin on stained-glass windows by Gilbert and George, and works gifted by the Saatchi collection. The **Memorial Court**, a calming, white-walled circular room under a skylit dome, serves as the city's principal war memorial. It also houses the Lord Provost's book of condolence for the 167 people who died in the 1988 Piper Alpha oil rig disaster. The **upstairs** rooms house the main body of the gallery's painting collection.

Belmont and Little Belmont streets

Opposite the Aberdeen Art Gallery is the city's answer to a Bohemian quarter: cobbled **Belmont** and **Little Belmont** streets feature a number of the city's more interesting bars, shops and restaurants, and **farmers' markets** take place on the last Saturday of each month (9am–5pm).

Union Terrace Gardens and around

West of Belmont Street and Denburn Road, the sunken **Union Terrace Gardens** are a welcome relief from the hubbub of Union Street. From here there are views across to the three domes of the Central Library, St Mark's Church and His Majesty's Theatre, traditionally referred to as "Education, Salvation and Damnation". Outside the theatre itself stands a grandiose gesturing statue of William "Braveheart" Wallace, erected in 1888. The once derelict red-brick spire at the other end of the viaduct tops **Triple Kirks**, which is now at the centre of a new student housing development. Built in 1843 and one of Archibald Simpson's most famous creations, it was Scotland's only example of a single building hosting three churches for three denominations.

The West End

The **West End**, the area around the westernmost part of Union Street, begins more or less at the great granite columns of the city's **Music Hall**, which is currently undergoing a major restoration. A block north is **Golden Square** – a misnomer as the trim houses, pubs and restaurants surrounding the statue of the Duke of Gordon are uniformly grey. The city has invested much in gentrifying the area north of Union Street, resulting in neat cobbles, old-fashioned lamps, a growing restaurant scene and a string of somewhat stuffy designer boutiques around Thistle Street.

Bon Accord Square

To the south of Union Street, wedged between Bon Accord Street and Bon Accord Terrace, **Bon Accord Square** is a typically elegant Aberdeen streetscape. A grassy centre surrounds a huge solid block of granite commemorating **Archibald Simpson**, architect of much of nineteenth-century Aberdeen.

The harbour

Aberdeen's **harbour**, at the mouth of the River Dee, is one of the busiest ports in the country. From the eastern end of Union Street, cobbled Shiprow winds downhill, passing the Maritime Museum on the right-hand side. The cobbles stop on **Market Street**, which runs the length of the harbour with its brightly painted oil-supply vessels, sleek cruise ships and peeling fishing boats.

10

The Maritime Museum and Provost Ross's House

Shiprow • Tues–Sat 10am–5pm, Sun noon–3pm • Free • ☎ 01224 337700, ⓦ aagm.co.uk

On Shiprow, peering towards the harbour through a striking glass facade, is the **Maritime Museum**, which combines a modern, airy museum with the aged labyrinthine corridors of Provost Ross's House. The museum is a thoroughly engrossing, imaginative tribute to Aberdeen's maritime traditions. Just inside the front entrance you'll see a blackboard updated every day with the price of a barrel of crude oil. Suspended above the foyer and visible from five different levels is a spectacular 27ft-high model of an oil rig, which, along with terrific views over the bustling harbour, serves as a constant reminder that Aberdeen's maritime links remain very much alive.

The older industries of herring fishing, whaling, shipbuilding and lighthouse-keeping plus the exploration of the northwest passage also have their place, with well-designed displays and audiovisual presentations, many drawing heavily on personal reminiscences. Passages lead into **Provost Ross's House**, where intricate ships' models and a variety of nautical paintings and drawings are on display.

Footdee

An easy 20min walk from Market St or bus #15 from Union St (near St Nicholas Kirk)

At the north end of Market Street, Trinity Quay runs past industrial yards and down York Street towards **Footdee**, or Fittie, a quaint nineteenth-century fishermen's village of higgledy-piggledy cottages backing onto the sea. Their windows and doors face inwards for protection from storms but also, so they say, to stop the devil sneaking in the back door.

Duthie Park

Polmuir Rd • Daily 8am to 1hr before dusk; Winter Gardens daily: April & Sept–Oct 9.30am–5.30pm, May–Aug 9.30am–7.30pm, Nov–March 9.30am–4.30pm • Free • A 20min walk or 10min bus ride from the centre (#17 or #18 from Union St)

From Market Street it's a short hop to **Duthie Park**, on the banks of the Dee at the end of Polmuir Road. The rose garden here, known as Rose Mountain due to its profusion of blooms, can be stunning in summer, but the real treat is the **Winter Gardens**, a steamy paradise of enormous cacti and exotic plants. By the obelisk, a parterre garden has been installed and outdoor concerts are occasionally held at the restored vintage bandstand. From the northwestern corner of Duthie Park a great cycle and walkway, the **Old Deeside Railway Line**, heads west out of the city past numerous long-gone train stations.

Old Aberdeen

10min ride north of the city centre on bus #20 from Littlejohn St

North of the modern centre and an independent burgh until 1891, tranquil **Old Aberdeen** has maintained a village-like identity. Dominated by King's College and

St Machar's Cathedral, its medieval cobbled streets, wynds and little lanes are beautifully preserved, and the gleaming cube of the new **university library** adds contemporary interest.

King's College Chapel

King's Campus, University of Aberdeen • Mon–Fri 9.30am–3.30pm • Free • ☎ 01224 272137

The southern half of cobbled High Street is overlooked by **King's College Chapel**, the first and finest of the city's college buildings, completed in 1495 with a chunky Renaissance spire. Named in honour of James IV, the chapel's west door is flanked by his coat of arms and that of his queen. It stands on the quadrangle, whose gracious buildings retain a medieval plan but were built much later; those immediately north were designed by Alexander Marshall Mackenzie early in the last century, with the exception of Cromwell Tower at the northeast corner, completed in 1658. The highlights of the interior, which, unusually, has no central aisle, are the ribbed arched wooden ceiling, and the rare and beautiful examples of medieval Scottish woodcarving in the screen and the stalls. A carved wooden pulpit from nearby St Machar's is also here, while outside sits the flamboyant 1911 bronze and marble tomb of Bishop Elphinstone.

St Machar's Cathedral

The Chanonry • Daily: April–Oct 9.30am–4.30pm; Nov–March 10am–4pm • Free • ☎ 01224 485988, ⓦ www.stmachar.com

From King's College, High Street leads a short way north to **St Machar's Cathedral** on the leafy Chanonry, overlooking Seaton Park and the River Don. The site was reputedly founded in 580 AD by Machar, a follower of Columba, when he was sent by the latter to find a grassy platform near the sea, overlooking a river shaped like the crook on a bishop's crozier. This setting fitted the bill perfectly, and the cathedral, a huge fifteenth-century fortified building, became one of the city's first great granite edifices. Inside, the stained-glass windows are a dazzling blaze of colour, and the heraldic oak ceiling above the nave dates from 1520 and shows nearly fifty different coats of arms from Europe's royal houses and Scotland's bishops and nobles.

Seaton Park

A wander through Seaton Park, immediately to the north of St Machar's Cathedral, brings you to the thirteenth-century **Brig o'Balgownie**, which gracefully spans the River Don nearly a mile north of the cathedral. The bridge is best visited at sunset; Byron, who spent much of his childhood in Aberdeen, remembered it as a favourite place.

The beach

To reach the beach, take bus #15 from Union St; to reach the golf links take buses #9 and #13

Aberdeen can surely claim to have the best sandy **beach** of all Britain's large cities. Less than a mile east of Union Street is a great two-mile sweep of clean sand, broken by groynes and lined all along with an esplanade. Further north, most of the beach's hinterland is devoted to golf links.

ARRIVAL AND DEPARTURE   ABERDEEN

BY PLANE

Aberdeen Airport (☎ 08444 816666, ⓦ aberdeen airport.com), seven miles northwest of town, is served by flights from more than fifty UK and European destinations. First Aberdeen bus #27 (£2.70 single; ☎ 01224 650000) and Stagecoach Bluebird bus #727 (£2.90 single; ☎ 01224 597590) run to the city centre

from the airport; a taxi costs around £20.

Destinations Belfast (1 daily, 1hr 10min); Birmingham (Mon–Fri 3 daily, Sat & Sun 1–2 daily; 1hr 30min); Bristol (Mon–Fri & Sun 1–2 daily; 1hr 25min); East Midlands (Mon–Fri 2–3 daily; 1hr 25min); Kirkwall, Orkney (Mon–Fri 3 daily, Sat 2 daily; 50min); London Gatwick (Mon–Fri 2 daily, 1 on Sat; 1hr 40min); London Heathrow (Mon–Sa up to 12 daily; 1hr 30min); London Luton (Mon–Sat 1 daily; 1hr 25min); Manchester (Mon–Fri up to 8 daily, Sat 2 daily; 1hr 20min); Newcastle (Mon–Fri up to 6 daily, Sun 1 daily; 55min); Norwich (Mon–Fri 5 daily, Sat & Sun 1–2 daily); Stornoway (Mon–Fri 1 daily, 55min); Wick (Mon–Fri 2–3 daily; 35min).

BY TRAIN
The main train station is on Guild St, in the centre of the city. There are lockers here for left luggage, which cost £2–4 for 24hr.
Destinations Arbroath (every 30min; 1hr); Dundee (every 30min; 1hr 15min); Edinburgh (roughly hourly; 2hr 25min); Elgin (up to 11 daily; 1hr 30min); Forres (up to 11 daily; 1hr 45min); Glasgow (hourly; 2hr 35min); Inverness (up to 11 daily; 2hr 20min); Inverurie (roughly hourly; 25min); London (3 daily, 1 nightly sleeper service; 7hr, sleeper service 10hr); Montrose (every 30min; 40min); Nairn (up to 11 daily; 1hr 50min); Stonehaven (every 30min; 15min).

BY BUS
The bus terminal is right beside the train station. For information on local and intercity bus times, call Traveline Scotland on ☎08712 002233 or visit ⓦtravelinescotland.com.
Destinations Ballater (hourly; 1hr 45min); Banchory (every 20min–1hr; 55min); Banff (every 30min; 1hr 55min); Braemar (roughly every 2hr; 2hr 5min); Crathie, for Balmoral (roughly every 2hr; 1hr 55min); Cullen (hourly; 2hr 30min); Dundee (hourly; 2hr 20min); Elgin (hourly; 2hr 25min); Forres (hourly; 2hr 55min); Fraserburgh (hourly; 1hr 30min); Inverurie (every 10min; 50min–1hr 20min); Macduff (hourly; 1hr 50min); Peterhead (every 30min; 1hr 15min); Stonehaven (every 15–30min; 35min).

BY CAR
Driving into Aberdeen is easy enough, but as many spaces are designated for local permit-holders it can be tricky (and expensive) to find somewhere central to park.
Car rental Arnold Clark, Girdleness Rd (☎01224 238520, ⓦarnoldclark.com); Budget, Wellheads Drive (☎01224 771777, ⓦbudget.co.uk); Europcar, 16 Broomhill Rd (☎08713 841092, ⓦeuropcar.co.uk); Hertz, at the airport (☎08433 093001, ⓦhertz.com).

BY FERRY
Aberdeen has ferry links to Lerwick in Shetland and Kirkwall in Orkney, with frequent NorthLink services (☎08456 000449, ⓦnorthlinkferries.co.uk) departing from Jamieson's Quay in the harbour.
Destinations Kirkwall, Orkney (Thurs, Sat & Sun, plus Tues in summer; 6hr); Lerwick, Shetland (daily; 10–12hr overnight).

10

GETTING AROUND

Aberdeen's centre is best explored **on foot**, but you might also need to use **buses** – most of which pass along Union St – to reach some sights.

BY BUS
Information and routes Most buses are operated by First (ⓦfirstgroup.com/Aberdeen); the bus station is on Guild St. Useful routes from the centre include the #15 bus to the beach esplanade, and the #20 bus to Old Aberdeen.
Tickets and passes All-day tickets covering city routes aboard any First bus cost £4.70 (£4 after 9.30am on weekdays); weekly passes are £18. If you plan to use the buses a lot, you can buy a First TravelCard in £10 or £20 denominations) from the depot at 395 King St, or the travel centre at 47 Union St, which also hands out transport maps; each time you travel the fare is deducted from the card.
Night buses Late-night services on Friday and Saturday – the last leaving at around 3.15am – cost a flat £3, and head to seven separate destinations on the city's outskirts.

BY TAXI
Taxis operate from ranks throughout the city centre, all of which attract long queues after the pubs and clubs empty at the weekend. If you don't manage to hail one, call Rainbow Taxis (☎01224 878787) or ComCab Aberdeen (☎01224 353535).

INFORMATION

Tourist office 23 Union St, near the junction with Broad St (July & Aug Mon–Sat 9am–6.30pm, Sun 10am–4pm; Sept–June Mon–Sat 9.30am–5pm, Sun 11am–4pm; ☎01224 269180). The tourist office can also provide you with excellent leaflets detailing themed heritage trails around the city, each with a different focus, from maritime history and sculpture to the city's use of granite.
Listings magazine/website Keep your eyes peeled for the free What's On programme published by Aberdeen Performing Arts, which lists upcoming events, art exhibitions and theatre productions. For details of local gigs, try ⓦaberdeen-music.com.

ACTIVITIES

Football The local football team, Aberdeen, struggles to live up to its golden era of the 1980s when then-manager Alex Ferguson brought home league titles and European trophies. Home fixtures take place at Pittodrie Stadium (☎ 08719 831903, ⓦ afc.co.uk), between King St and the beach.

Golf There are good options for golfing around Aberdeen; the municipal Kings Links (☎ 01224 641577, ⓦ kings-links .com) has a driving range and an artificial putting area near the beach.

ACCOMMODATION

10

The emphasis on business trade means **weekday rates** can be considerably more expensive than weekends (the prices quoted here). Even in **low season** the whole city is frequently booked up, so it pays to arrange accommodation a week or more ahead of your arrival.

HOTELS

Aberdeen City Centre Hotel 9 Belmont St ☎ 01224 658406, ⓦ aberdeen-city-centre-gb.book.direct. A smart little place tucked away on pedestrianized Belmont St; the rooms feature spa baths. There are bargain weekend rates and they also have apartments to rent. **£70**

Carmelite Stirling St ☎ 01224 589101, ⓦ carmelitehotels.com. Handily located near the Union Square mall, fusing tradition and modern style in a revamped 1820s hotel. The kitchen serves up a surprisingly modestly priced taste of Scotland. **£69**

Ferryhill House 169 Bon Accord St ☎ 01224 590867, ⓦ ferryhillhousehotel.co.uk. This mansion is set in its own grounds within walking distance of Union St. Offers good-value lunches and a great Malt Room for guests to sample real ales and whisky by a roaring fire. **£80**

Hilton Garden Inn 31 St Andrew St ☎ 01224 451444, ⓦ hiltongardeninn3.hilton.com. Beyond this central building's glass and stone facade are comfy but brashly designed rooms, with deep-red carpets and splashes of gold and black. The hotel also has a small gym and a business centre. **£87**

Malmaison 49–53 Queen's Rd ☎ 08446 930649, ⓦ malmaison.com. Part of the stylish Malmaison chain, with striking contemporary decor and all the latest in hi-tech features, plus a day-spa and a brasserie decorated with Scottish art. **£99**

★**Marcliffe at Pitfodels** North Deeside Rd, Pitfodels ☎ 01224 861000, ⓦ marcliffe.com. Four miles west of the city centre, this 42-room hotel in its own grounds is by far the most luxurious and tasteful option in the Aberdeen area. There's a spa, and a fine restaurant with suitably special dishes. **£150**

Skene House 95 Rosemount Viaduct ☎ 01224 645971, ⓦ skene-house.co.uk. Swish modern serviced apartments in the cultural quarter with a great hotel-style breakfast served. Rooms are spacious and quiet with plain furnishings, and there are self-catering facilities. **£70**

GUESTHOUSES AND B&BS

★**Allan Guest House** 56 Polmuir Rd ☎ 01224 584484, ⓦ allanguesthouse.co.uk. Traditional-style guesthouse not far from Duthie Park and just 5min from the city centre on bus #17. Free wi-fi, DVD library and good breakfasts. **£70**

Butler's Guest House 122 Crown St ☎ 01224 212411, ⓦ butlersguesthouse.com. Central but dated rooms that attract a mix of business travellers and holidaymakers. A cold breakfast is included in the rate, but the cooked option costs £6.50 extra. **£49**

Dutch Mill 7 Queen's Rd ☎ 01224 322555, ⓦ dutchmill .co.uk. Has a range of cosy, business-like rooms a mile west of the city centre. They're all above a bar and restaurant that serves the usual pub staples, from prawn cocktails to gammon steaks. **£125**

Globe Inn 13–15 North Silver St ☎ 01224 624258, ⓦ the-globe-inn.co.uk. Easy-going city-centre inn with seven en-suite rooms above a bar that hosts live jazz and blues on Friday and Saturday. The rate includes a continental breakfast. **£75**

Roselea House 12 Springbank Terrace ☎ 01224 583060, ⓦ www.roseleahouse.co.uk. Welcoming guesthouse in a little stone bungalow near the bus station with accommodation suitable for people with restricted mobility. Floral decor and a friendly welcome. **£55**

HOSTEL AND CAMPUS ACCOMMODATION

Crombie Johnston Halls College Bounds, Old Aberdeen ☎ 01224 273444, ⓦ abdn.ac.uk/summe _accommodation. These private rooms in the city's bes student halls are also in one of the most interesting parts o town. Rooms are available from early July to Sept, thoug there's also some year-round accommodation. Singles **£35** twins **£55**

SYHA Aberdeen 8 Queen's Rd ☎ 01224 646988 ⓦ syha.org.uk. Hostel in a grand stone mansion a mil from the train station, with clean but rather dated dorm and private rooms. A good option for budget-consciou travellers. To get there take bus #11 or #17 from Union S Dorms **£16**; singles **£28**

EATING

CAFÉS

Books and Beans 22 Belmont St ☎01224 646438. As the name suggests, secondhand books go hand in hand here with decent lattes (£2.49), fresh soups and sandwiches. Mon–Sat 7.45am–4.30pm, Sun 9.45am–4pm.

The Breadmaker 50–52 Rosemount Viaduct ☎01224 641520, ⓦthebreadmaker.org.uk. Enjoy a coffee (£1.60) and fresh baking (cakes from £2) in this friendly place that gives people with learning difficulties training and meaningful employment. Mon–Sat 8.30am–5pm.

Kilau Coffee 57 High St ☎01224 485510, ⓦkilaucoffee.wordpress.com. Quirky coffee specialists in Old Aberdeen who also serve salads such as squash, pine nut and halloumi, plus focaccia and so on, as well as excellent cakes; coffee and cake costs £3.50. Mon–Fri 8am–8pm, Sat 10am–5pm.

★Musa 33 Exchange St ☎01224 571771, ⓦmusaaberdeen.com. A good-value art café based in an old church and banana warehouse. The terrific daytime vibe continues into the evening with live music and mains (from £12.90) made using ingredients sourced from small Scottish suppliers. Tues–Sat noon–11pm.

Rocksalt & Snails 40 St Swithin St ☎01224 200012. Like its sister restaurant in Ballater, this branch of *Rocksalt* does a decent job of healthy snacks and panini (£5.95 with salad and crisps). Mon–Fri 8am–5pm, Sat 9am–5pm, Sun 10am–4pm.

Sand Dollar Café 2 Esplanade ☎01224 572288, ⓦsanddollarcafe.com. The cheery interior, decorated with seashells and model lighthouses, makes this the most attractive of the cafés along the beach esplanade. Great for breakfast or brunch (from £7.95), and look out for their jazz nights. Mon–Wed 7.30am–8pm, Thurs–Sun 7.30am–9pm.

RESTAURANTS

Blue Moon 11 Holburn St ☎01224 589977, ⓦbluemoonaberdeen.com. Still the pick of Aberdeen's Indian restaurants, with sleek surroundings and dozens of inventive, moderately priced dishes, such as spiced halibut cooked with white radishes; mains from £8. Mon–Thurs noon–2pm & 5pm–1am, Fri–Sun noon–1am.

Café 52 52 The Green ☎01224 590094, ⓦcafe52 .net. Cosy, bohemian hangout by day that turns into a hip restaurant by night, with cullen skink (£4), game and vegetarian meals among the tasty, reasonably priced options. Mon–Sat noon–midnight, Sun noon–6pm.

★Fusion 10 North Silver St ☎01224 652959, ⓦwww .fusionbarbistro.com. A chic bistro done out in acid colours, where seasonal local produce is the highlight and fish and game feature heavily. Two courses for £24.95. Tues–Sat noon–1am.

Howies 50 Chapel St ☎01224 639500, ⓦhowies .uk.com. Aberdeen outpost of an Edinburgh institution, serving modern Scottish cooking from steamed Shetland mussels (£6.25) to ribeye veal (£24.50). Set meals and house wine are well priced. Mon–Sat noon–2.30pm & 6–10pm.

Ninety-Nine Bar & Kitchen 1 Back Wynd ☎01224 631640, ⓦ99aberdeen.com. Lounge-like bar/ restaurant where, instead of the usual pub food, punters can order US-style burgers and £9.50 chicory-smoked pulled pork. Also does great cocktails. Daily 11am/ noon–midnight/1am.

Poldino's 7 Little Belmont St ☎01224 647777, ⓦpoldinos.co.uk. An Aberdonian Italian institution, combining fine flavours and quality with convivial dining. Classic Italian dishes for around £10. Mon–Sat noon– 2.30pm & 5.30–10.15pm.

Silver Darling Pocra Quay, North Pier ☎01224 576229, ⓦthesilverdarling.co.uk. Attractively located at the harbour in Footdee, beside the lighthouse, this pricey French place specializes in fresh seafood – the pan-fried yellow-fin tuna will cost you £22.50. Mon–Fri noon– 1.45pm & 6.30–9.30pm, Sat 6.30–9.30pm.

DRINKING

Brewdog Aberdeen 17 Gallowgate ☎01224 581459. Hipster-friendly bar that sets itself apart from the crowd, with exposed brickwork, dangly lightbulbs and a cracking selection of Scottish ales (most bottles £4.50). Mon– Thurs noon–midnight, Fri & Sat noon–1am, Sun 2.30pm–midnight.

The Grill 213 Union St ☎01224 573530, ⓦthegrill aberdeen.co.uk. One of the city's older pubs, with a distinctive old-world charm. Sells real ales on tap, dozens of malts (£2.50 and upwards) and hot stovies. Daily 10am–midnight.

The Illicit Still 24 Netherkirkgate, Broad St ☎01224 623123, ⓦillicit-still.co.uk. Follow the stairs down past sneering gargoyles to this subterranean bar with cowhide-covered seats and intimate little booths, where diners tuck into fish and chips, burgers and so on (around £12). Daily 11am–late.

Prince of Wales 7 St Nicholas Lane ☎01224 640597, ⓦprinceofwales-aberdeen.co.uk. Opened in 1850, the quintessential Aberdeen pub has a 20ft-long bar and a flagstone floor. With fine pub grub, renowned real ales and a Sunday evening folk session, it's little wonder that it's often crowded. Mon–Thurs 10am–midnight, Fri & Sat 10am–1am, Sun 11am–midnight.

St Machar Bar 97 High St, Old Aberdeen ☎01224 483079. The medieval quarter's only pub, a poky,

10

10

old-fashioned bar attracting an intriguing mix of King's College students and workers. Mon–Sat 11am–11pm, Sun 12.30pm–6pm.
Slains Castle 14–18 Belmont St ☎01224 631877, ⓦeerie-pubs.co.uk. An old church is the perfect setting

for this Gothic-themed bar, whose cocktail list includes potions named after the seven deadly sins (£4.25). Live bands every Friday. Mon–Thurs 11am–midnight, Fri & Sat 11am–1am, Sun noon–midnight.

NIGHTLIFE

Aberdeen's nightlife is at its liveliest during term time.

CLUB
Babylon 9 Alford Place ☎01224 595001, ⓦpbdevco.com/babylon.html. Popular with an older crowd, *Babylon* bills itself as one of Aberdeen's hippest nightspots. The Gothic-styled interior here reverberates to the latest dance tunes. Fri & Sat 11pm–3am.

LIVE MUSIC VENUES
The Blue Lamp 121 Gallowgate ☎01224 619769. A spacious bar featuring live jazz, usually at weekends,

and a Monday folk session; there's also a much smaller snug for relative peace and quiet. Most acts start at 8pm.
The Tunnels Carnegies Brae ☎01224 619930, ⓦfacebook.com/tunnelsaberdeen. One of the city's most popular live music venues, established within graffitied old tunnels under Union St. Live bands play a different musical genre every evening including reggae, hip-hop, ska and Northern Soul. See website for show times.

ENTERTAINMENT

You can buy tickets for most events at the city's theatres and concert halls from the **box office** beside the Music Hall on Union St (Mon–Sat 9.30am–6pm; ☎01224 641122).

CONCERT HALLS
Aberdeen Exhibition and Conference Centre Off Ellon Rd at Bridge of Don ☎01224 824824, ⓦaecc.co.uk. Huge hall with a mainstream vibe, hosting the biggest touring rock and pop acts as well as family-friendly shows.
Cowdray Hall Schoolhill ☎01224 523700, ⓦaagm.co.uk. Classical music venue at the Aberdeen Art Gallery, often with visiting orchestras playing; occasionally it hosts free lunchtime concerts.
Music Hall Union St ☎01224 632080 or 641122, ⓦwww.musichallaberdeen.com. Currently being restored, but generally they feature big-name comedy and music acts.

THEATRES
ACT Aberdeen 33 King St ☎01224 635208, ⓦact-aberdeen.org.uk. Hosts a variety of theatrical productions, lectures, exhibitions and drama classes. They stage amateur dramatics and music events, as well as a long-established summer arts carnival.

His Majesty's Theatre Rosemount Viaduct ☎01224 641122, ⓦaberdeenperformingarts.com. The city's main theatre resides in a beautiful Edwardian building, and its extensive programme ranges from highbrow drama and opera to pantomime.
Lemon Tree 5 West North St ☎01224 641122, ⓦaberdeenperformingarts.com. The fulcrum of the city's arts scene, with live music, performance art, club nights, spoken word and comedy. The emphasis is on experimental and alternative events.

CINEMAS
Belmont Filmhouse 9 Belmont St ☎08719 025721 ⓦbelmontfilmhouse.com. Art-house cinema (with a comfortable café-bar) showing the more cerebral new releases alongside classic, cult and foreign-language films.
Cineworld Queen's Links Leisure Park, Links Rd ☎08712 002000, ⓦcineworld.co.uk. Huge multiple cinema close to the beachfront that shows all the mainstream releases.

SHOPPING

Books and Beans 22 Belmont St ☎01224 646438, ⓦbooksandbeans.co.uk. This popular café (see p.371) has shelves packed with paperbacks and quiet spaces for reading. Mon–Sat 7.45am–4.30pm, Sun 9.45am–4pm.
La Gourmandise 63 Thistle St ☎01224 625974, ⓦlagourmandise.co.uk. Well-run French patisserie shop

that stocks gorgeous croissants, macaroons, tartlets and iced cakes, as well as freshly baked baguettes. Mon–F 7.30am–6pm, Sat 9am–5pm.
The Old Aberdeen Bookshop 140 Spital ☎01224 65 355, ⓦoldaberdeenbookshop.com. The city's best be for secondhand and antiquarian books, with a specialism academic titles, classics and Scottish literature. Mon–F

11.15am–5.15pm, Sat 11.30am–5pm.
Tiso 1 John St ☎01224 646872, ⊗tiso.com. Well-stocked outdoor shop with separate sections for footwear,

watersports, mountain sports and camping. Mon, Tues, Fri & Sat 9am–6pm, Wed 10am–6pm, Thurs 9am–7.30pm, Sun 10am–5pm.

DIRECTORY

Medical facilities The Royal Infirmary, on Foresterhill, northeast of the town centre, has a 24hr casualty department (☎01224 681818). Boots pharmacy is in the Bon Accord Centre on George St (☎01224 626080).

Police The main police station is on Queen St (☎08456 005700), including the lost property office.
Post office The central office is upstairs in the St Nicholas Centre, between Union St and Upperkirkgate, with other branches at 371 George St and 489 Union St.

10

Stonehaven and around

A pretty, pebble-dashed harbour town linked to Aberdeen by the A90, **STONEHAVEN** is a popular summer getaway. Its location along the sheltered Kincardine coastline certainly adds to the appeal, as does the respected **Stonehaven Folk Festival**, which takes place annually in early July. Less auspiciously, the *Carron Fish Bar* on Allardice Street was the birthplace of a notorious Scottish snack – the deep-fried Mars Bar – in 1995.

The town itself is split into two parts, the picturesque working **harbour area** being most likely to detain you. The old high street, lined with some fine townhouses and civic buildings, connects the harbour and its surrounding **old town** with the late eighteenth-century planned centre on the other side of the River Carron. On New Year's Eve, High Street is the location for the ancient ceremony of **Fireballs**, when locals parade its length swinging metal cages full of burning debris around their heads to ward off evil spirits for the coming year. The **new town** focuses on the market square, overlooked by the dusky-pink granite market hall with its impressive steeple.

Another reason to base yourself in Stonehaven is **Dunnottar Castle**, a stunningly moody ruin perched on jagged cliffs two miles south. The area south and west of this is known as the **Mearns**, an agricultural district of scattered population and gathering hills famous for its links to Scots author Lewis Grassic Gibbon. Unfortunately, public transport into the Mearns is virtually non-existent.

Tolbooth

Old Quay, down by the harbour • April–Sept daily except Tues 1.30–4.30pm • Free • ☎07512 466329

On one side of the harbour, the sixteenth-century **Tolbooth** is Stonehaven's oldest building. Originally built as a storehouse during the construction of Dunnottar Castle (see below), it is now a **museum** of local history and fishing. Above it, rather fittingly, there's a top-notch seafood restaurant (see p.376).

Dunnottar Castle

2 miles south of Stonehaven along the coast • Daily: April–Oct 9am–6pm (last entry 5.30pm); Nov to March 10am–sunset • £6 • ☎01569 762173, ⊗dunnottarcastle.co.uk

Stonehaven's tourist office hands out free walking guides for the scenic amble to **Dunnottar Castle**, one of Scotland's finest ruined castles. This huge ninth-century fortress is set on a three-sided sheer cliff jutting into the sea – a setting striking enough to be chosen as the backdrop for Zeffirelli's film version of *Hamlet*. Once the principal fortress of the northeast, the mainly fifteenth- and sixteenth-century ruins are worth a good root around, and there are many dramatic views out to the crashing sea.

Siege and bloodstained drama splatter the castle's past: in 1297 the whole English Plantagenet garrison was burnt alive here by **William Wallace**, while one of the more gruesome tales from the castle's history tells of the imprisonment and torture of 122 men and 45 women Covenanters in 1685 – an event, as it says on the Covenanters' Stone in the churchyard, "whose dark shadow is for evermore flung athwart the Castled Rock".

Arbuthnott

10

Some five miles inland and south of Dunnottar Castle is the straggling village of ARBUTHNOTT, the home of prolific local author **Lewis Grassic Gibbon** (1901–35), whose romanticized realism perfectly encapsulates the spirit of the agricultural Mearns area. *Sunset Song*, his most famous work, is an essential read for those travelling in this area. He is buried (under his real name of James Leslie Mitchell) in the corner of the little village graveyard, overlooking the forested banks of the Bervie Water off the main road.

Grassic Gibbon Centre

Half a mile northwest of the church, along the B967 • March–Oct daily 10am–4.30pm • £3 • ☎ 01561 361668, ⓦ grassicgibbon.com

The community-run **Grassic Gibbon Centre** and café is a great introduction to the fascinating and self-assured author who died sadly young of peritonitis. In the small exhibition beyond the café you'll find some of his personal effects housed in glass cabinets, plus snippets of information on local history.

ARRIVAL AND DEPARTURE

STONEHAVEN AND AROUND

By train Rail services from Aberdeen (every 30min; 25min) and Montrose (every 30min; 20min) pull in at Stonehaven station, just off Arduthie Rd.

By bus Buses from Aberdeen (several hourly; 35–50min) and Montrose (every 30min; 40min) stop at the southern end of Barclay St, near the junction with Cameron St.

INFORMATION AND TOURS

Tourist office 66 Allardice St, the main street past the square (late March to June & Sept–Oct Mon–Sat 10am–5pm; July & Aug Mon–Sat 10am–6pm, Sun 1–5.30pm; ☎ 01569 762806).

Boat trips From March to October, you can take a private boat trip from Stonehaven's harbour to Dunnottar Castle

(45min return; from £75/person). A much cheaper option is to join one of the weekend tours (March–Aug Sat & Sun 12.30pm & 2.30pm; £18/person), which take in the castle, a local seal colony (best March–May) and the RSPB reserve at Fowlsheugh. To book, contact Ruari at Castle Charter (☎ 07411 010559, ⓦ castlecharter.co.uk).

ACCOMMODATION

★**Arduthie House** Ann St, close to the junction with Margaret St ☎ 01569 762381, ⓦ arduthiehouse.scot. Attractive, arty six-bedroom B&B that has a small gallery/tearoom serving excellent cakes. It's located in a fine stone Georgian villa, with stuccoed fireplaces and stained glass. **£90**

Marine Hotel 9–10 Shorehead ☎ 01569 762155, ⓦ marinehotelstonehaven.co.uk. Smart en-suite rooms equipped with coffee machines and flatscreen TVs, right by the harbour. The bar has a decent selection of Belgian beers and whisky, including single malts from the local area. **£110**

EATING AND DRINKING

Carron Restaurant 20 Cameron St ☎ 01569 760460, ⓦ carron-restaurant.co.uk. The gorgeous Art Deco architecture of this restaurant complements classic, well-made meat and fish dishes (from £15.95); there's a special vegetarian menu, and weekend afternoon tea (£17.50). Wed–Sat noon–2pm & 6–9.30pm, Sun noon–6pm.

Creel Inn Catterline, 4 miles south of Dunnottar Castle ☎ 01569 750254, ⓦ thecreelinn.co.uk. In Catterline, a

clifftop hamlet typical of those along this stretch of coast, the whitewashed *Creel Inn* serves moderately priced seafood and game. Main courses from £12.95. Wed–Fri noon–2pm & 6–9.30pm, Sat noon–2pm & 5–9.30pm, Sun noon–8.30pm.

Maggie Mays 25 Market Square ☎ 01569 760333, ⓦ maggiemaysstonehaven.co.uk. Cosy corner café that does a mean hot chocolate topped with Maltesers, marshmallows and whipped cream for £2.95. For lunch

RIGHT GARDENSTOWN (P.383)

there are burgers, soups and panini. Daily 9am–5pm.

Tolbooth Restaurant Above the Tolbooth museum by the harbour ☎01569 762287, ✆tolbooth-restaurant .co.uk. Moderately expensive but beautifully sited

restaurant, serving fresh Scottish seafood such as hand-dived west coast scallops with pea purée (£23.95). Tues–Sat noon–2pm & 6–9.30pm, Sun noon–3pm & 6–9pm (Oct–Feb closed Sun).

Deeside

10

More commonly known as **ROYAL DEESIDE**, the land stretching west from Aberdeen along the River Dee revels in its connections with the royal family, who have regularly holidayed here, at **Balmoral**, since Queen Victoria bought the estate. Eighty thousand Scots turned out to welcome her on her first visit in 1848. Victoria adored the place and the woods were said to remind Prince Albert of Thuringia, his homeland.

Deeside is undoubtedly handsome in a fierce, craggy, Scottish way, and the royal presence has helped keep a lid on any unattractive mass development. The villages strung along the A93, the main route through the area, are well heeled and have something of an old-fashioned air. Facilities for visitors hereabouts are first class, with a number of bunkhouses and hostels, some decent hotels, and plenty of castles and grounds to snoop around. It's also an excellent area for **outdoor activities**, with hiking routes into both the Grampian and Cairngorm mountains, alongside good mountain biking, horseriding and skiing.

GETTING AROUND   **DEESIDE**

By bus Stagecoach Bluebird buses #201, #202 and #203 from Aberdeen regularly chug along the A93, serving most of the towns on the way to Braemar. Bus #201 from

Aberdeen runs to Crathes (45min), Banchory (50min), Ballater (1hr 45min) and Braemar (2hr 10min), while #202 and #203 stop at Lumphanan and Banchory respectively.

Drum Castle

Near Drumoak, 10 miles west of Aberbeen off the A93 • April–June & Sept Mon & Thurs–Sun 11am–4pm; July & Aug daily 11am–4pm; Garden of Historic Roses April–Oct daily 11am–4.15pm • £12.50; NTS • ☎01330 700334

Squat **Drum Castle** stands in a clearing in the ancient woods of Drum, made up of the splendid pines and oaks that covered this whole area before the shipbuilding industry precipitated mass forest clearance. The castle itself combines a 1619 Jacobean mansion with Victorian extensions and the original, huge thirteenth-century keep, which has been restored and reopened. Given by Robert the Bruce to his armour-bearer, William de Irvine, in 1323 for services rendered at Bannockburn, the castle remained in Irvine hands for 24 generations until the NTS took over in 1976.

The main part of the house is Victorian in character, with grand, antique-filled rooms and lots of family portraits. The finest room is the **library**, within the ancient tower; you'll get an even better sense of the medieval origins of the place by climbing up to the upper levels of the tower, where the battlements offer views out over the forest.

Crathes Castle

Crathes, 2 miles east of Banchory • Jan–March plus Nov & Dec Sat & Sun 10.30am–3.45pm; April–Oct daily 10.30am–4.45pm; last admission 45min before closing • £12.50, including access to the gardens; NTS • ☎01330 844525

Four miles west of Drum Castle and around two miles east of **Banchory** (a small town that acts as a gateway into rural Deeside), **Crathes Castle** is a splendid sixteenth-century granite tower house adorned with flourishes such as overhanging turrets, gargoyles and conical roofs. Its thick walls, narrow windows and tiny rooms loaded with heavy old furniture make Crathes rather claustrophobic, but it's enlivened by some wonderful ceilings painted with lively figures of musicians strumming their instruments; the earliest dates from 1602. The extensive grounds include a Go Ape climbing centre (see opposite)

By bus Stagecoach Bluebird buses #201, #202 and #203 from Aberdeen bus station stop at the entrance to Crathes Estate, as well as at nearby Banchory.

INFORMATION AND ACTIVITIES

Tourist office The nearest tourist office is the museum in Banchory (April–Oct Mon–Sat 10am–5pm; also Sun 1–5pm July & Aug; ☎01330 822000). Staff can provide information on walking and fishing in the area.

Go Ape Zip wires, Tarzan swings, rope ladders and skateboard zip take you through the trees in the grounds of Crathes Castle (☎0845 0949273, ☒goape.co.uk).

10

ACCOMMODATION AND EATING

Milton Brasserie Near the entrance to Crathes Castle ☎01330 844566, ☒miltonbrasserie.com. Smart daytime brasserie just across from Crathes Castle, serving moderately priced à la carte meals such as baked seabass with sizzled ginger (£13). Mon–Fri noon–3pm, Sat & Sun noon–5pm.

Raemoir House Just over 2 miles north of Banchory ☎01330 824884, ☒raemoir.com. Glamorous country-house hotel set in spacious parkland, complete with a decadent drawing room. The best rooms have four-poster beds. **£195**

Tor-Na-Coille Hotel Inchmarlo Rd, Banchory ☎01330 822242, ☒tornacoille.com. Once a retreat for Charlie Chaplin and his family, *Tor-Na-Coille* has a scenic location on the town's southern edge. Some of the smart rooms overlook Banchory Golf Club's rolling fairways. **£85**

Ballater

The neat and ordered town of **BALLATER**, attractively hemmed in by the River Dee and fir-covered mountains, was hard hit by floods in December 2015, and is still in recovery. The town was dragged from obscurity in the nineteenth century when it was discovered that waters from the local Pannanich Wells might be useful in curing scrofula. Deeside water is now back in fashion, though these days it's bottled and sold far and wide as a natural mineral water.

It was in Ballater that Queen Victoria first arrived in Deeside by train from Aberdeen back in 1848; she wouldn't allow a station to be built any closer to Balmoral, eight miles further west. Although the line has long been closed, the town's rather self-important royalism is much in evidence at the restored **train station** in the centre. The local shops that supply Balmoral with groceries and household basics also flaunt their connections, with oversized "By Appointment" crests.

If you prefer to discover the fresh air and natural beauty that Victoria came to love so much, you'll find Ballater an excellent base for local **walks and outdoor activities**. There are numerous hikes from Loch Muik (pronounced "mick"), nine miles southwest of town, including the Capel Mounth drovers' route over the mountains to Glen Doll (see p.359), and a well-worn but strenuous all-day trek up and around Lochnagar (3789ft), the mountain much painted and written about by the current Prince of Wales.

ARRIVAL AND DEPARTURE | **BALLATER**

By bus Buses stop at the northern end of Golf Rd, near the A93.

Destinations Aboyne (hourly; 20min); Banchory (hourly; 40min); Braemar (9 daily; 35min).

INFORMATION AND ACTIVITIES

Tourist office In the renovated former train station on Station Square (daily: July & Aug 10am–6pm; Sept–June 10am–5pm; ☎01339 755306).

Bike rental Good-quality bikes, including mountain bikes

and tandems, can be rented from Cycle Highlands (☎01339 755864, ☒cyclehighlands.com, daily 9am–5pm) from £18/day at 13–15 Victoria Rd.

ACCOMMODATION

Auld Kirk ☎01339 755762, ☒theauldkirk.com. As the name suggests, this pleasingly unorthodox B&B is

based in a renovated church, which features an unmissable rocket-like spire. All of the rooms are

10

upstairs, leaving the ground floor free for a licensed lounge area. £115

Ballater Caravan Park South of Anderson Rd, close to the River Dee ☎ 01339 755727. Large campsite down by the water that mostly attracts touring caravans – tents are welcome too, though, and there are laundry and shower facilities. April–Oct. Per pitch £10

Habitat @ Ballater Bridge Square ☎ 01339 753752, ☢ habitat-at-ballater.com. Excellent, friendly and well-equipped hostel tucked away off the main road. Choose between a bunk bed with its own locker, or one of the private rooms. Dorms £22; doubles £55

No 45 45 Braemar Rd ☎ 01339 755420, ☢ no45.co.uk. Welcoming nineteenth-century house with relatively expensive doubles and twins, all of which are en suite. The bar downstairs is stacked full of whisky and bottled ales, and there's also a restaurant in the large conservatory out the back. £100

EATING AND DRINKING

Barrel Lounge 6 Church Square ☎ 01339 755488. If you fancy a wee dram with the locals, pop into this pub on the main green. There's an open fire and the TV's usually on in the corner. Mon–Wed & Sun 11am–midnight, Thurs–Sat 11am–1am.

Lochnagar Indian Brasserie 2 Church Square ☎ 01339 755611, ☢ lochnagarindian.co.uk. A great location on the green, a warm welcome and excellent aromatic cooking.

Mains from £9.50; book ahead. Daily noon–2pm & 5–11pm.

Riverside Cottage Café Cambus O'May, 2 miles east of Ballater ☎ 01339 755126. A cultured spot serving good coffee, snacks and light meals, as well as superb cakes (around £1.50) and bread from the award-winning Channach Bakery. Also offers Spanish tapas on a Friday and Saturday evening. Daily 10am–5pm, plus Fri & Sat 5.30–9pm (reduced hours in winter).

Balmoral Castle and around

8 miles west of Ballater, off the A93 • April–July daily 10am–5pm • £11.50; audio tour included in admission price (additional £5 deposit required per handset); Land Rover safari £60/person for 3hr (minimum two people) • ☎ 01339 742534, ☢ balmoralcastle.com

Originally a sixteenth-century tower house built for the powerful Gordon family, **Balmoral Castle** has been a royal residence since 1852, when it was converted to the Scottish Baronial mansion that stands today. The royal family traditionally spend their summer holidays here each August, but despite its fame it can be something of a disappointment even for a dedicated royalist. For the three months when the doors are nudged open, the general riffraff are permitted to view only the ballroom, an exhibition room and the grounds. With so little of the castle on view, it's worth making the most of the **grounds** and larger estate by following some of the country walks, heading off on a Land Rover safari or allowing the free audio tour to guide you around.

Opposite the castle's gates on the main road, the otherwise dull granite church of **Crathie**, built in 1895 with the proceeds of a bazaar held at Balmoral, is the royals' local church.

INFORMATION   BALMORAL CASTLE AND AROUND

Tourist office In the car park by the church on the main road (April–Oct daily 10am–5pm; Nov–March Mon–Fri 10am–noon; ☎ 01339 742414).

Braemar and around

West of Balmoral, the road rises to 1100ft above sea level in the upper part of Deeside at the village of **BRAEMAR**, situated where three passes meet and overlooked by an unremarkable **castle**. It's an invigorating, outdoor kind of place, well patronized by committed hikers, but probably best known for its Highland Games, the annual **Braemar Gathering** (see box opposite), on the first Saturday of September.

Linn of Dee

A pleasant diversion from Braemar is to head six miles west to the end of the road and the **Linn of Dee**, where the river plummets savagely through a narrow rock gorge. From here there are countless walks into the surrounding countryside or up into the heart of the Cairngorms (see box, p.425), including the awesome Lairig Ghru pass which cuts all the way through to Strathspey.

DEESIDE AND DONSIDE HIGHLAND GAMES

Royal Deeside is the home of the modern **Highland Games**, which claims descent from gatherings organized by eleventh-century Scottish king Malcolm Canmore to help him recruit the strongest and fittest clansmen for his army. The most famous of the local games is undoubtedly the **Braemar Gathering**, held on the first Saturday in September, which can see crowds of fifteen thousand. Since Queen Victoria's day, successive generations of royals have attended the event, which has become something of an overcrowded, overblown affair. You're not guaranteed to get in if you just turn up; the website (ⓦbraemargathering.org) has details of how to book **tickets** in advance.

Vying for celebrity status in recent years has been the **Lonach Gathering** in nearby Strathdon on Donside, held the weekend before Braemar, where local laird Billy Connolly dispenses drams of whisky to marching village men and has been known to invite some Hollywood chums along – Steve Martin has appeared dressed in kilt and jacket, while in 2010 Robin Williams competed in the punishing hill race.

For a true flavour of the spirit of Highland gatherings, however, try to get to one of the events that take place in other local towns and villages at weekends throughout **July** and **August**, where locals outnumber tourists and the competitions are guaranteed to be hard-fought and entertaining. Local tourist offices and the tourist board website (ⓦaberdeen -grampian.com) should be able to tell you what's happening where.

10

ARRIVAL AND DEPARTURE

By bus Buses from and to Ballater (9 daily; 35min) stop on Auchendryne Square, while long-distance coaches drop

BRAEMAR AND AROUND

package tourists in the car park opposite the *Fife Arms Hotel*.

INFORMATION AND ACTIVITIES

Tourist office In The Mews, in the middle of the village on Mar Rd (daily: April–June & Sept–Oct 9.30am–5pm; July & Aug 9.30am–6pm; Nov–March 9.30am–4.30pm; ☎01339 741600).

Outdoor activities Advice on outdoor activities, as well as ski, mountain-bike and climbing equipment rental, is available from Braemar Mountain Sports (daily 9am–6pm; ⓦbraemarmountainsports.com).

ACCOMMODATION

Braemar Caravan Park Park Half a mile south of the village off Glenshee Rd ☎01339 741373, ⓦbraemar caravanpark.co.uk. Year-round caravan site which also has thirty camping pitches. Can get busy in the summer, so book ahead. Per pitch **£20.50**

★ **Ivy Cottage Guest House** Cluniebank Rd ☎01339 741642, ⓦivycottagebraemar.co.uk. A lovely Victorian home with trim and comfortable rooms, and a view of red

squirrels and birds as you eat your breakfast. They also have two self-catering options, both with wood-burning stoves: a cottage and a bothy/studio (three nights from £185). **£75**

SYHA Braemar Corrie Feragie, 21 Glenshee Rd ☎01339 741659, ⓦsyha.org.uk. SYHA hostel a short stroll from the centre in a former shooting lodge with bike storage facilities and a big communal kitchen. **£16.50**

EATING AND DRINKING

The Gathering Place 9 Invercauld Rd ☎01339 741234. Bistro in the heart of the village selling mouthwatering, Scottish-based cuisine, including a game pie made with ale and red wine (£16.95). Tues–Sat –8.30pm.

Taste Beside the Mar Rd roundabout ☎01339 741425, ⓦtaste-braemar.co.uk. Reliably good coffee shop and moderately priced contemporary restaurant doing home-made, gluten-free soups (served with local bread) for £3.60. Tues–Sat 10am–5pm.

The Don valley

The quiet countryside around the **DON VALLEY**, once renowned for its illegal whisky distilleries and smugglers, lies at the heart of Aberdeenshire's prosperous agricultural region. From Aberdeen, the River Don winds northwest through **Inverurie**, where it takes a sharp turn west to **Alford**, then continues past ruined castles through the **Upper Don valley** and the heather moorlands of the eastern Highlands. This remote and under-visited area is positively littered with ruined castles, Pictish sites, stones and hillforts.

GETTING AROUND   THE DON VALLEY

By car Although public transport connects Aberdeen with Inverurie and Alford, getting any further than this   without a car is all but impossible.

Alford and around

ALFORD (pronounced "aa-ford"), 25 miles west of Aberdeen, only exists at all because it was chosen, in 1859, as the terminus for the Great North Scotland Railway. A fairly grey little town now firmly within the Aberdeen commuter belt, it's still well worth making the trip here for the **Grampian Transport Museum**.

Grampian Transport Museum

Main St • Daily: April–Sept 10am–5pm; Oct 10am–4pm • £9.50 • ☎ 01975 562292, ⓦ gtm.org.uk

The **Grampian Transport Museum** is home to a diverse display of transport through the ages, from old tramcars and pushbikes to modern, ecofriendly cars. Notable exhibits include the Craigevar Express, a strange, three-wheeled steam-driven vehicle developed by the local postman for his rounds, and that famous monument to British eccentricity and ingenuity, the Sinclair C5 motorized tricycle.

Alford Valley railway

Just north of Main St, or a short walk east of the Grampian Transport Museum • April–June & Sept Sat & Sun 12.30pm–4pm; July & Aug daily 12.30pm–4pm • Return trip £4.50 • ☎ 07879 293934, ⓦ alfordvalleyrailway.org.uk

A couple of minutes' walk from the Grampian Transport Museum is the terminus for the **Alford Valley railway**, a narrow-gauge train that runs for about a mile from Alford Station through wooded vales to the wide-open space of **Murray Park**. The return journey takes an hour.

ARRIVAL AND INFORMATION   ALFORD AND AROUND

By bus Stagecoach Bluebird buses #218 and #220 link Aberdeen with Alford (1hr 10min).
Tourist office The Grampian Transport Museum is home   to the helpful tourist office (April–Sept Mon–Sa 9am–5pm, Sun 12.45pm–5pm; ☎ 01975 562650).

Craigievar Castle

6 miles south of Alford on the A980 • Castle April–June & Sept Fri–Tues 11am–4.45pm; July & Aug daily 11am–4.45pm; grounds daily 11am–5.30pm • £12.50; car parking £1; NTS • ☎ 08444 932174

South of Alford, **Craigievar Castle** is a Disneyesque pink confection of turrets, gables, balustrades and cupolas bubbling over from its top three storeys. It was built in 1626 by a Baltic trader known as Willy the Merchant, who evidently allowed his whimsy to run riot here. Inside you can see Jacobean woodwork and original plaster ceilings, whil the grounds hold a Victorian kitchen garden and a Scottish glen garden.

The Upper Don valley

Travelling west from Alford, settlements become noticeably more scattered and remote as the countryside takes on a more open, familiarly Highland appearance. The **Lecht Road**, crossing the area of bleak but wonderfully empty high country to the remote mountain village of Tomintoul (see p.432), passes the Lecht ski centre (see p.432) at 2090ft above sea level, but is frequently impassable in winter due to snow.

Kildrummy Castle and Gardens

Kildrummy, 10 miles west of Alford off the A97 • **Castle** April–Sept daily 9.30am–5.30pm • £4.50; HES • **Gardens** April–Oct daily
noon–5pm • £4.50 • ☎ 01975 571203, ⓦ historicenvironment.scot

Ten miles from Alford stand the impressive ruins of the thirteenth-century **Kildrummy Castle**, where Robert the Bruce sent his wife and children during the Wars of Independence. The castle blacksmith, bribed with as much gold as he could carry, set fire to the place and it fell into English hands. Bruce's immediate family survived, but his brother was executed and the entire garrison hanged, drawn and quartered. Meanwhile, the duplicitous blacksmith was rewarded for his help by having molten gold poured down his throat. The sixth earl of Mar used the castle as the headquarters of the ill-fated Jacobite risings in 1715, but after that Kildrummy became redundant and it fell into disrepair. Beside the ruins, the separate **Kildrummy Castle Gardens** are quite a draw, boasting everything from swathes of azaleas in spring to Himalayan poppies in summer.

10

Lost Gallery

4 miles north of Strathdon • Wed–Mon 11am–5pm • Free • ☎ 019756 51287, ⓦ lostgallery.co.uk

Ten miles west of Kildrummy Castle, the A944 sweeps round into the parish of **Strathdon**, little more than a few buildings scattered along the roadside. Four miles north of here, up a rough track leading into Glen Nochty, lies the unexpected **Lost Gallery**, which shows work by some of Scotland's leading modern artists in a wonderfully remote and tranquil setting; as well as paintings, there are indoor and outdoor sculptures.

Corgarff Castle

Corgarff, 10 miles southwest of Strathdon • April–Sept daily 9.30am–5.30pm; Oct–March Sat & Sun 9.30am–4.30pm • £5.50; HES Free •
☎ 01316 688800

In Corgarff, just off the A939, lies **Corgarff Castle**, an austere and isolated tower house with an unusual star-shaped curtain wall and an eventful history. Built in 1537, it was turned into a barracks by the Hanoverian government in 1748, in the aftermath of Culloden, in order to track down local Jacobite rebels; a century later, English redcoats were stationed here with the unpopular task of trying to control whisky smuggling. Today the place has been restored to resemble its days as a barracks, with stark rooms and rows of hard, uncomfortable beds – authentic touches which also extend to graffiti on the walls and peat smoke permeating the building from a fire on the upper floor.

ACCOMMODATION AND EATING	CORGARFF CASTLE

Allargue Arms Hotel Half a mile north of the castle • ☎ 01975 651410, ⓦ allarguearmshotel.co.uk. The nearest accommodation option to Corgarff Castle, offering simple B&B and good-value bar meals that include a half-pound steak burger (£7). This old wayside inn overlooks the castle and is a cosy base for skiing, fishing or hiking trips. Daily noon–3pm & 7–9pm. **£60**

The northeast coast

The **NORTHEAST COAST** of Scotland from Aberdeen to Inverness has a rugged, sometimes bleak fringe with pleasant if undramatic farmland rolling inland. Still, if the weather is good, it's well worth spending a couple of days meandering through the various little fishing villages and along the miles of deserted, unspoilt beaches. The largest coastal towns are **Peterhead** and **Fraserburgh**, both dominated by sizeable fishing fleets; while neither has much to make a long stay worthwhile, the latter's museum of Scottish Lighthouses is one of the most attractive small museums in Scotland. More appealing to most visitors are the quieter spots along the **Moray coast**, including the charming villages of **Pennan**, **Gardenstown**, **Portsoy** and **Cullen**.

By train Trains are a faster but less frequent option than taking the bus, running every 1–2hr from Aberdeen to Elgin (1hr 30min), Forres (1hr 45min) and Nairn (2hr).

By bus The main towns and villages along this stretch of coast are well served by buses, with hourly services from Aberdeen to Elgin (2hr 30min), Forres (2hr 50min) and Nairn (3hr 15min).

Forvie National Nature Reserve

3 miles north of Newburgh • Visitor centre April–Sept daily 9am–5pm; call for winter hours • Free • ☎ 01358 751330

Fifteen miles north of Aberdeen and 3 miles north of Newburgh, a turning (signposted to Collieston) leads off the main A90 coast road to **Forvie National Nature Reserve**. This area incorporates the Sands of Forvie, one of Britain's largest and least disturbed **dune systems**, which is home to Britain's largest colony of breeding eider duck. There's a small but informative **visitor centre**, from which a network of **trails** winds along the coast and through the dunes, with one leading to the site of a fifteenth-century village buried by the shifting sands.

Cruden Bay

Superb sandy beaches can be found eight miles north of Forvie at **Cruden Bay**, from where a pleasant fifteen-minute walk leads to the huge pink-granite ruin of **Slains Castle**. The ruin itself is not especially interesting – it was over-modernized in the nineteenth century – though its stark clifftop beauty is striking and it claims notoriety as the place that inspired Bram Stoker to write *Dracula*. The best approach is to pull into the Meikle Partans car park on the A975 north of the village and follow the obvious path until you begin to see the ruins.

Bullers of Buchan

Reached by driving one and a half miles north from Cruden Bay along the A975, or walking three precarious miles north from Slains Castle along the cliffs, the **Bullers of Buchan** is a splendid 245ft-deep **sea chasm**, where the ocean gushes in through a natural archway eroded by the sea. This is some of the finest cliff scenery in the country and attracts a huge number of (smelly) nesting seabirds.

Fraserburgh

Just west of a swooping, sandy bay, **FRASERBURGH** is a large and fairly severe-looking place, edged by warehouse-like superstores and farmland. The intriguing **Museum of Scottish Lighthouses** makes a short visit worthwhile, and you'll find good, seafront hotel rooms nearby in the sleepy fishing village of **St Combs**.

Museum of Scottish Lighthouses

Stevenson Rd • May–Sept Mon & Wed–Sun 10am–5pm, Tues noon–5pm; Oct–April Wed–Sun 11am–4pm • £6 • ☎ 01346 511022, ⓦ lighthousemuseum.org.uk

At the northern tip of the town, an eighteenth-century lighthouse protrudes from the top of sixteenth-century **Fraserburgh Castle**. The lighthouse was one of the first to be built in Scotland and is now part of the excellent **Museum of Scottish Lighthouses**, where you can see a collection of huge lenses and prisms gathered from decommissioned lighthouses, and a display on various members of the famous "Lighthouse" Stevenson family. The highlight of the museum is the tour of Kinnaird Head lighthouse itself, preserved as it was when the last keeper left in 1991, with its century-old equipment still in perfect working order. The **tearoom** features sea views and home baking.

By bus Fraserburgh bus station is located on Hanover St.
Destinations Aberdeen (every 30min; 1hr 30min); Banff
(3 daily; 1hr); Macduff (3 daily; 55min).

Tourist office 3 Saltoun Square (April–Sept Mon–Sat
10am–5pm; Oct Mon–Sat 10am–4pm; ☎ 01346 518315;
ⓦ visitfraserburgh.com).

ACCOMMODATION AND EATING

Tufted Duck Hotel Corsekelly Place, St Combs
☎ 01346 582481, ⓦ tuftedduckhotel.co.uk. Large,
family-owned hotel in the village of St Combs, a 10min
drive southeast of Fraserburgh. The building is an ugly
duckling, but the rooms – many of which have

unobstructed sea views – are comfortable and quiet.
The restaurant serves a mix of Scottish and Far Eastern
flavours, with mains from £11.50. Daily noon–2pm &
5–9pm. **£110**

10

Fraserburgh to Gardenstown

The coast road between **Fraserburgh** and **Gardenstown**, fifteen miles to the west, is
particularly attractive: inland there are villages with pretty churches and cottages, while
countless paths lead off it to ruined castles, clifftop walks and lonely beaches.

Pennan

PENNAN is a tiny fishing hamlet that lies just off the B9031 down a steep and
hazardous hill. Consisting of little more than a single row of whitewashed stone
cottages tucked between a cliff and the sea, the village leapt into the limelight when
the British movie *Local Hero* was filmed here in 1982; you can stay at one of the
identifiable landmarks from the film, the *Pennan Inn* (see below).

Crovie

Locals in the tiny but appealing village of **CROVIE** (pronounced "crivie"), on the other
side of Troup Head from Pennan, frequently have their doorsteps washed by the sea.
The Head itself supports over 1500 gannet nests. Wedged in against the steep cliffs,
Crovie is so narrow that its residents have to park their cars at one end of the village
and continue to their houses on foot.

Pennan Inn By the waterfront ☎ 01346 561201,
thepennaninn.co.uk. Crovie's most recognizable
landmark is the handsome whitewashed *Pennan Inn*, a key
location in *Local Hero*. The three en-suite rooms are brightly

painted and cosy. You can also grab a drink or something to
eat in the bar (Thai curry £13.50). Daily noon–2pm &
5–11pm. **£85**

Gardenstown

GARDENSTOWN, a short way west of Crovie, is one of the more attractive villages
along this stretch of coast, with stone cottages huddled around a wave-gnawed bay.
Its considerably larger than Crovie, and supports a small gallery and teashop down by
the harbour.

Macduff

Heading west along the B9031 from Pennan brings you, after ten miles, to **MACDUFF**,
a famous spa town during the nineteenth century that now has a thriving and pleasant
harbour. Macduff and its neighbour Banff are separated by little more than the
beautiful seven-arch bridge over the River Deveron.

By bus Buses from towns and villages along the northeast
last stop on Union Rd or Shore St, both near the harbour.

Destinations Banff (at least hourly; 5min); Cullen via
Portsoy (hourly; 40min); Fraserburgh (1–2 daily; 55min).

Banff and around

10

Roughly the same size as its neighbour, Macduff, **BANFF** has a mix of characterful old buildings and boarded-up shops, which give little clue to the extravagance of Duff House, the town's main attraction. Look out for the historic tollbooth building, and the town's pre-Reformation market cross.

Duff House

Half a mile south of Banff's high street • April–Oct daily 11am–5pm; Nov–March Thurs–Sun 11am–4pm • £7.10; HES • ☎01261 812062, ⓦ duffhouse.org.uk

Built to a design by William Adam in the 1730s, **Duff House** is an elegant four-floor Georgian Baroque house that was originally intended for one of the northeast's richest men, William Braco, who became earl of Fife in 1759. It was clearly built to impress, and could have been even more splendid had Adam been allowed to build curving colonnades either side; Braco's refusal to pay for carved Corinthian columns to be shipped in from Queensferry caused such bitter arguments that the laird never came to live here, and even shut his coach curtains whenever he passed by. Since then, the house has been used variously as a hotel, family home and sanatorium. Today, it's home to a **tearoom** and a **gallery**, with an impressive collection of fine art provided by the National Galleries of Scotland.

Cullen and around

Twelve miles west of Banff is **CULLEN**. Strikingly situated beneath a superb series of arched viaducts, which were built because the earl and countess of Seafield refused to allow the railway to pass through the grounds of Cullen House, the town is made up of two sections: **Seatown**, by the harbour, and the **new town** on the hillside. There's a lovely stretch of sheltered sand by Seatown, where the colourful houses – confusingly numbered according to the order in which they were built – huddle end-on to the sea. The town is perhaps best known as the home of **cullen skink** – a thick soup made from milk (or cream), potato and smoked haddock.

10

Six miles east of Cullen is the quiet village of **PORTSOY**, renowned for its green marble (once shipped to Versailles), and its annual traditional boat festival in early July.

ARRIVAL AND DEPARTURE
CULLEN

By bus Hourly bus #35A connects Cullen with Aberdeen (2hr 35min), arriving at and departing from The Square in the new town.

INFORMATION

Tourist office You can pick up leaflets about local walks at the town's independent tourist office on the main square of the new town (generally June–Aug daily 11am–5pm; 01542 841863), but as it's run by volunteers the opening hours can be sporadic.

ACCOMMODATION

Cullen Harbour Hostel Port Long Rd 01542 841997, cullenharbourholidays.com. Cheap hostel beds are available under exposed wooden rafters in this pretty stone building by the harbour. There's a piano, a well-stocked bookcase and a sociable kitchen. Dorms **£20**

Buckie and Spey Bay

West of Cullen, the scruffy fishing town of **BUCKIE** marks one end of the **Speyside Way** long-distance footpath (see p.430). This follows the coast west for five miles to windy **Spey Bay**, at the mouth of the river of the same name, which can also be reached by a small coastal road from Buckie. It's a remote spot bounded by sea, river and sky. It is sometimes possible to see dolphins feeding if you wander along the long pebbly spit by the mouth of the Spey; this is also a good spot to see otters and birds, including ospreys.

Scottish Dolphin Centre

Spey Bay • April–Oct daily 10.30am–5pm • Free • 01343 820339, uk.whales.org

The main mission of the **Scottish Dolphin Centre** is researching the Moray Firth dolphin population (see p.419). The centre, run by the Whale and Dolphin Conservation Society, houses an exhibition and a café; alongside, the **Tugnet Ice House**, a partially subterranean, thick-walled house with a turf roof used by fishermen in the days before electric refrigeration to store their ice and catches, makes for an atmospheric auditorium in which films of the underwater world are shown.

ACCOMMODATION
BUCKIE AND SPEY BAY

Rosemount B&B 63 East Church St, Buckie 01542 833434, rosemountbb.co.uk. Large B&B in a Victorian townhouse, with a cosy TV room to relax in. Rooms at the front of the house have views across the Firth. **£72**

Elgin

The lively market town of **ELGIN**, a fifteen-mile drive from Buckie, grew up around the river Lossie in the thirteenth century. The centre has mostly kept its medieval street plan, and while the busy main street is choked with chain stores, it does open out onto an old cobbled marketplace with a tangle of wynds and pends on either side.

10

Elgin Cathedral

King St • April–Sept daily 9.30am–5.30pm; Oct–March Mon–Wed, Sat & Sun 9.30am–4.30pm • £5.50; joint ticket with Spynie Palace (see opposite) £7.20; HES • ☎ 01343 547171, ⓦ historicenvironment.scot

On King Street, a few blocks from the tourist office and clearly signposted, is the lovely ruin of **Elgin Cathedral**. Once considered Scotland's most beautiful cathedral, rivalling St Andrews in importance, it's little more than a shell today, though it does retain its original facade. Founded in 1224, the three-towered building was extensively rebuilt after a fire in 1270, and stood as the region's highest religious house until 1390 when the Wolf of Badenoch (illegitimate son of Robert II) burned the place down, along with the rest of the town, in retaliation for having been excommunicated by the Bishop of Moray when he left his wife; the notorious Wolf's tomb is in Dunkeld (see p.330). The cathedral suffered further during the post-Reformation period, when all its valuables were stripped and the building was reduced to a common quarry for the locals. Unusual features include the Pictish cross slab in the middle of the ruins and the cracked gravestones with their memento mori of skulls and crossbones.

Elgin Museum

King St • April–Oct Mon–Fri 10am–5pm, Sat 11am–4pm; Nov–March open on request or if staff are in the building • Free • ☎ 01343 543675, ⓦ elginmuseum.org.uk

At the very top of High Street is one of Britain's oldest museums, the **Elgin Museum**, which has been housed here since 1843. Following a major refurbishment, it has plenty of modern touches, with displays on local history and some weird anthropological artefacts including a shrunken head from Ecuador. In addition, you can see an excellent collection of fossils, some well-explained Pictish relics and a display on the important Birnie hoard of silver Roman dinarii from 197 AD, found nearby.

Glen Moray

Bruceland Rd • Mon–Fri 9am–5pm, Sat 10am–4.30pm (Oct–April closed Sat) • £5 • ☎ 01343 550900, ⓦ glenmoray.com

Elgin is on the edge of whisky country, and while the attractive local distillery, **Glen Moray** isn't part of the official Malt Whisky Trail (see p.431), tours are still available – the distinctive thing here is that your guide is quite likely to be the stillman, mashman or one of the other workers from the distillery floor.

ARRIVAL AND INFORMATION

By train The train station, served by the Aberdeen–Inverness line, is slightly detached from the city centre on the south side of town. All services below run 5–11 times a day.
Destinations Aberdeen (1hr 30min); Forres (15min); Inverness (50min); Nairn (25min).
By bus The bus station is on Alexandra Rd, right in the

town centre.
Destinations Aberdeen (hourly; 2hr 20min); Burghead (hourly; 30min); Duffus (hourly; 15min); Forres (every 30min; 25min); Inverurie (hourly; 1hr 40min); Lossiemouth (every 30min; 20min); Nairn (every 30min; 45min).
Tourist information Elgin Library, Cooper Park (Mon–Fri 10am–8pm, Sat 10am–4pm; ☎ 01343 562608).

ACCOMMODATION

Moraydale Guest House 276 High St ☎ 01343 546381, ⓦ moraydaleguesthouse.com. Grand Victorian B&B with off-road parking and seven top-class rooms, some of which are on the ground floor. There's a sunny conservatory to eat your breakfast in. **£75**
★ **Old Church of Urquhart** Meft Rd, Urquhart, 5 miles

east of town ☎ 01343 843063, ⓦ oldchurch.eu. The *Old Church of Urquhart* is one of the area's most appealing places to stay: an unusual and comfortable B&B in an imaginatively converted church. There's also a self-catering apartment available (£86). **£76**

EATING AND DRINKING

Lido 29 South St ☎ 01343 556464. Neatly styled French restaurant near the high street, with mid-priced

mains (the beef bourguignon is £12.95). There's also good range of appetizers, including grilled asparag

with hollandaise sauce (£5.50). Mon–Sat noon–3pm & 5–11pm.
Scribbles 154 High St ☎01343 542835, ⓦfacebook .com/scribbles.elgin. Rather try-hard interior design, but you'll find very good fruit smoothies (£3), plus reasonable coffees, main meals and pizzas (£8.50). Good for families with kids (crayons provided). Mon–Sat 9am–10pm, Sun noon–10pm.

SHOPPING

Gordon & MacPhail 58 South St ☎01343 545110, ⓦwww.gordonandmacphail.com. You can pick up some great picnic foods at this old-fashioned Aladdin's cave of delicacies; they claim to have the largest selection of whiskies in the world. Mon–Sat 8.30am–5pm.

10

Pluscarden Abbey

6 miles southwest of Elgin • Daily 4.30am–8.30pm • Free • ☎01343 890257, ⓦwww.pluscardenabbey.org

Set in an attractive, verdant valley southwest of Elgin, **Pluscarden Abbey**, looms impressively large in a peaceful clearing off an unmarked road. One of only two abbeys in Scotland with a permanent community of monks, it was founded in 1230 for a French order and, in 1390, became another of the properties burnt by the Wolf of Badenoch (see p.330); recovering from this, it became a priory of the Benedictine Abbey of Dunfermline in 1454 and continued as such until monastic life was suppressed in Scotland in 1560. The abbey's revival began in 1897 when the Catholic antiquarian, John, third Marquess of Bute, started to repair the building. In 1948 his son donated it to a small group of Benedictine monks from Gloucester who established the present community. It is possible to **stay** here on retreat for a few days, taking part in the routines of monastic life; see the website for details.

Lossiemouth

Five miles north of Elgin across the flat land of the Laich of Moray, Elgin's nearest seaside town, **LOSSIEMOUTH** (generally known as Lossie), is a cheery golf-oriented seaside town blessed with lovely sandy beaches; the glorious duney spit of the **East Beach** is reached over a footbridge across the River Lossie from the town park. The town's only blight is the frequent sky-tearing noise of military aircraft from the nearby RAF base.

Spynie Palace

miles south of Lossiemouth off the A941 • April–Sept daily 9.30am–5.30pm; Oct–March Sat & Sun 9.30am–4.30pm • £4.50; joint ticket with Elgin Cathedral £7.20; HES • ☎01343 552255, ⓦhistoricenvironment.scot

Lossiemouth's development as a port came when the nearby waterways of **SPYNIE**, three miles inland, silted up and became useless to the traders of Elgin. Little remains of the settlement except hulking **Spynie Palace**, home of the bishops of Moray from 1107 until 1686. The enormous rectangular David's Tower – visible for miles around – offers stunning views from the top over the Moray Firth and the Spynie Canal.

Burghead

Another of this coastline's tightly packed, stone-built fishing villages, windswept **BURGHEAD**, nine miles northwest of Elgin, was once the site of an important Iron Age fort and the ancient Pictish capital of Moray. Between 1805 and 1809 a fishing village was built on the promontory where the ancient fort had stood, in the course of which some unique Pictish stone carvings known as the **Burghead Bulls** were discovered. One is on display in the **Burghead Visitor Centre** (April–Sept daily noon–4pm; entry by donation; ☎01343 835518), built into the round white lookout tower at the tip of the promontory; others can be seen in the Elgin Museum, the National Museum in Edinburgh and the British Museum in London. The tower offers great views of the Moray Firth, while inside are displays about Pictish times and the dramatic annual fire ceremony known as the **Burning of the Clavie**, one of only a few that still take place in Scotland. A burning tar barrel is carried around the town on January 11 to mark the old calendar's new year, before being rolled into the sea, sparks and embers flying.

ARRIVAL AND DEPARTURE   **BURGHEAD**

By bus Burghead is served by hourly bus #32 from Elgin (30min).

10 Findhorn

A wide sweep of sandy beach stretches five miles around Burghead Bay to **FINDHORN**, a tidy village with some neat fishermen's cottages, a delightful harbour dotted with moored yachts, a small **Heritage Centre** (May & Sept Sat & Sun 2–5pm; June–Aug daily 2–5pm; free; ⊚findhorn-heritage.co.uk) in the village's former salmon-net sheds and grass-roofed ice house, and a couple of good pubs. Like Lossiemouth, however, it's hard to escape the military presence in the area, with **RAF Kinloss**, one of the UK's most important front-line airfields, right on its doorstep.

The Findhorn Foundation

Findhorn is best known for the communal **Findhorn Foundation**, based beside the town's caravan park. Visitors are free to turn up and explore the rambling streets of the foundation, but it's worth trying to take a more informed look by means of a **guided tour** (see opposite). While you're here, don't miss the **Moray Art Centre** (Tues–Fri 10am–5pm, Sat 10am–4pm; free; ☎01309 692426, ⊚morayartcentre.org), on the edge of the Findhorn Foundation but not officially a part of it. The centre, located in a terracotta-hued ecofriendly building, hosts eclectic and imaginative temporary exhibitions and regular (often free) art classes including woodworking and nature photography.

ARRIVAL AND DEPARTURE   **THE FINDHORN FOUNDATION**

By bus You can get here on Stagecoach bus #31 (every 1–2hr) from Forres High St (15min) and Elgin (30min).

FOUNDING FINDHORN

In 1962, with little money and no employment, Eileen and Peter Caddy, their three children and friend Dorothy Maclean, settled on a **caravan site** at Findhorn. Dorothy believed that she had a special relationship with what she called the "devas … the archetypal formative forces of light or energy that underlie all forms in nature – plants, trees, rivers", and from the uncompromising sandy soil they built a remarkable **garden** filled with plants and vegetables, far larger than had ever been seen in the area.

A few of those who came to see the phenomenon stayed to help out and tune into the **spiritual aspect** of daily life at the nascent community. With its emphasis on inner discovery and development, but unattached to any particular doctrine or creed, the **Findhorn Foundation** has today blossomed into a **permanent community** of a few hundred people, with a well-developed series of courses and retreats on subjects ranging from astroshamanic healing to organic gardening, drawing another eight thousand or so visitors each year. The original caravan still stands, surrounded by a whole host of newer timber buildings and eco-homes employing solar power and earth roofs.

The foundation is not without controversy: a community leader once declared that "behind the benign and apparently religious front lies a hard core of New Agers experimenting with hallucinatory techniques marketed as spirituality." Findhorn is also accused of being overly well heeled, and a glance into the shop or a tally of the smart cars parked outside the well appointed eco-houses does give some substance to such a view. However, the community continues to prosper and it is well known around the world. The reputation of the place is such that it attracts visitors both sympathetic and sceptical – and both find something to feed their preconceptions.

INFORMATION AND TOURS

Visitor centre The visitor centre is near the foundation's main entrance (May–Sept Mon–Fri 10am–5pm, Sat & Sun 1–4pm; Oct–April Mon–Fri 10am–5pm; ☎ 01309 690311, ⓦ findhorn.org).

Tours Guided tours (April, Oct & Nov Mon, Wed & Fri 2pm; additional tours May–Sept at 2pm on Sat & Sun) cost £5; you can also guide yourself via a booklet (£5) available at the shop or visitor centre

ACCOMMODATION

The visitor centre can provide you with information on staying within the community, either as part of an introductory "**Experience Week**"(cost based on your income), or simply overnighting. There are a number of **eco-houses** within the area around the Moray Art Centre offering good-value B&B accommodation.

10

Findhorn Bay Holiday Park At the entrance to the foundation ☎ 01309 690203, ⓦ findhornbayholiday park.com. Despite enormous growth, the foundation is still situated on the same land as this caravan and camping park, which has pitches (April–Oct only), stationary caravans (Dec–Oct) and unusual eco-chalets (year-round). Per pitch £22; caravan per week **£525**; chalet per week **£685**

★ **Sunflower** 404 The Field of Dreams ☎ 01309 692080, ⓦ sunflower-findhorn.co.uk. Right in the heart of the community, *Sunflower* is an attractive wooden house with two twin rooms and a single. They serve a good organic breakfast. Single **£40**; twins **£65**

EATING AND DRINKING

Bakehouse 91–92 Findhorn Rd ☎ 01309 691826, ⓦ bakehousecafe.co.uk. In Findhorn village, this moderately priced café sells food freshly prepared on site, from organic local cheeses to divine chocolate brownies (£2). There are picnic benches for alfresco dining. Daily 10am–4pm, with extended hours in summer.

★ **Phoenix Café** At the entrance to the Universal Hall ☎ 01309 690110, ⓦ phoenixshop.co.uk. Be sure to stop off at the community's excellent wholefood café, which serves healthy soups, organic pasties (£3.50), herbal teas and irresistible organic cakes. Daily 10am–5pm.

ENTERTAINMENT

Universal Hall Arts Centre A short walk north of the visitor centre ☎ 01309 691170, ⓦ findhorn.org. Connected to the *Phoenix café* is the Universal Hall Arts Centre, an occasional venue for stand-up comedy, drama, and good touring folk and jazz bands. Most events begin at 7.30/8pm (see website for show times).

The Great Glen and River Spey

GLEN COE

The Great Glen and River Spey

The Great Glen, a major geological fault line cutting diagonally across the Highlands from Fort William to Inverness, is the defining geographic feature of the north of Scotland. A huge rift valley was formed when the northwestern and southeastern sides of the fault slid in opposite directions for more than sixty miles, while the present landscape was shaped by glaciers that only retreated around 8000 BC. The glen is impressive more for its sheer scale than its beauty, but the imposing barrier of loch and mountain means that no one can travel into the northern Highlands without passing through it. With the two major service centres of the Highlands at either end, it makes an obvious and rewarding route between the west and east coasts.

11

Of the **Great Glen**'s four elongated lochs, the most famous is **Loch Ness**, home to the mythical monster; lochs **Oich**, **Lochy** and **Linnhe** (the last of these a sea loch) are less renowned, though no less attractive; all four are linked by the **Caledonian Canal**. The southwestern end of the Great Glen is dominated by the town of **Fort William**, the self-proclaimed "Outdoor Capital of the UK". Situated at the heart of the Lochaber area, it is a utilitarian base, with plenty of places to stay and excellent access to a host of adventure sports. While the town itself is charmless, the surrounding countryside is a magnificent blend of rugged mountain terrain and tranquil sea loch. Dominating the scene to the south is **Ben Nevis**, Britain's highest peak, best approached from scenic Glen Nevis. The most famous and dramatic glen of all, **Glen Coe**, lies on the main A82 road half an hour's drive south of Fort William, the two separated by the coastal inlet of **Loch Leven**. Nowadays the whole area is unashamedly given over to tourism, with Fort William swamped by bus tours throughout the summer, but take a short drive from town and solitude is easy to find.

At the northeastern end of the Great Glen is the capital of the Highlands, **Inverness**, a sprawling city that hugs the northern end of the River Ness, close to the Beauly Firth; it's most often used as a springboard to more remote areas further north. Inevitably, most transport links to the northern Highlands, including Ullapool, Thurso and the Orkney and Shetland islands, pass through Inverness.

Rising high in the heather-clad hills above remote Loch Laggan, forty miles due south of Inverness, the **River Spey**, Scotland's second-longest river, drains northeast towards the Moray Firth through one of the Highlands' most spellbinding valleys. Famous for its ancient forests, salmon fishing and ospreys, the area around the upper section of the river known as **Strathspey** is just as spectacular as the Great Glen to the west. Strathspey is dominated by the **Cairngorms**, Britain's most extensive mountain massif, unique in supporting subarctic tundra on its high plateau.

BOTTLENOSE DOLPHINS, THE MORAY FIRTH

Highlights

West Highland Museum Featuring loot from the Spanish Armada, relics from the Jacobite uprising and the rifle used in the Appin Murder, this little museum in Fort William provides a heady introduction to Highland history. **See p.397**

Glen Coe Spectacular, moody, poignant and full of history – a glorious spot for hiking or simply absorbing the atmosphere. **See p.404**

Glen Affric Head for the hills amid some of Scotland's best-hidden scenery, with ancient Caledonian forests, high peaks and gushing rivers. **See p.412**

Culloden The visitor centre on the site of the last battle on British soil gives a stirring and

unsettling account of the fight, and the subsequent massacre of survivors and civilians. **See p.418**

❺ **Dolphins of the Moray Firth** Europe's most northerly school of bottlenose dolphins can be seen from the shore or on a boat trip. **See p.419**

❻ **The Cairngorms** Scotland's grandest mountain massif, located within Britain's largest national park, where rare plants, wild animals, inspiring vistas and challenging outdoor activities abound. **See p.425**

❼ **Whisky nosing** Take a tutored "nosing" (tasting) on the very premises where the stuff is made and matured. **See p.431**

HIGHLIGHTS ARE MARKED ON THE MAP ON PP.394–395

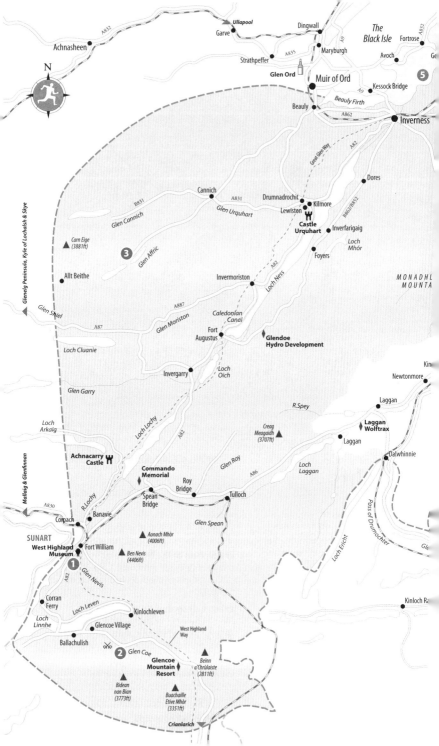

Buckie

0   10
miles

Nairn

Forres

Cawdor

Cawdor Castle

A96

A939

R. Findhorn

4

en

SPEYSIDE

Grantown-on-Spey

Carrbridge

Nethy Bridge

A9

Boat of Garten

Loch Garten

A939

Aviemore

Inverdruie

Loch Morlich

ATHSPEY

Kincraig

Feshiebridge

ch
sh

CAIRNGORM MOUNTAINS

6

Cairn Gorm
(4084ft)

Ben Macdui
(4294ft)

GRAMPIAN MOUNTAINS

Fochabers

Speyside Way

Strathisla

Glen Grant

Keith

Macallan

Cardhu

7

Craigellachie

Glenfiddich

Dufftown

Aberlour

Huntly

A941

River Spey

A95

Ballindalloch

Glenlivet

Carbrach

Rhynie

Lumsden

Tomintoul

**Lecht
Ski Area**

**Kildrummy
Castle**

Kildrummy

Strathdon

Cock
Bridge

River Don

**Craigievar
Castle**

**Corgarff
Castle**

CAIRNGORMS
NATIONAL PARK

River Dee

Aboyne

Crathie

Ballater

Glen Tanar

**Balmoral
Castle**

Braemar

Inverey

Lochnagar
(3789ft)

Mount Keen
(3080ft)

Glendronach Distillery

Glen Clova

Glen Esk

Clova

Spittal of Glenshee

Glen Shee

Glen Prosen

**Blair
Castle**

Blair Atholl

Killecrankie

Kirkton of
Glenisla

A9

HIGHLIGHTS

1 West Highland Museum

2 Glen Coe

3 Glen Affric

4 Culloden

5 Dolphins of the Moray Firth

6 The Cairngorms

7 Whisky nosing

**THE GREAT GLEN AND
RIVER SPEY**

BLOODY TALES BEYOND THE BEAUTY

Although best known for its windswept slopes and glassy lochs, the Great Glen has a turbulent and bloody **history**. Founded in 1655 and named in honour of William III, the town of Fort William was successfully held by government troops during both of the **Jacobite risings**. The country to the southwest, meanwhile, is inextricably associated with Bonnie Prince Charlie's flight after **Culloden** (see p.418). **Glen Coe** is another historic site with a violent past, renowned as much for the infamous massacre of 1692 as for its magnificent scenery.

A string of villages along the river provides useful bases for setting out into the wilder country, principal among them **Aviemore**, a rather ugly straggle of housing and hotel developments which nevertheless has a lively, youthful feel to it. A little way north, **Grantown-on-Spey** is more attractive, with solid Victorian mansions but much less vitality, while smaller settlements such as **Boat of Garten** are quieter.

Downriver, Strathspey gives way to the area known as **Speyside**, famous as the heart of Scotland's malt whisky industry. In addition to the Malt Whisky Trail that leads round a number of well-known distilleries in the vicinity of places such as **Dufftown**, the lesser-known **Speyside Way**, another of Scotland's long-distance footpaths, offers the chance to enjoy the scenery of the region, as well as its whiskies, on foot.

GETTING AROUND
THE GREAT GLEN AND RIVER SPEY

By bus The Great Glen is reasonably well served by buses, with several daily services between Inverness and Fort William. There are also frequent buses connecting Inverness with Aviemore and Grantown-on-Spey. Further north in malt whisky country, services are extremely limited.

By car The main A82 road runs the length of the Great Glen, although relatively high traffic levels mean that it's not a fast or particularly easy route to drive. The A9 and A95 allow for quick hops between towns on the western side of the Cairngorms, but elsewhere within the national park roads are necessarily narrower (and slower).

By boat The traditional and most rewarding way to travel through the Great Glen is by boat: a flotilla of kayaks, small yachts and pleasure vessels takes advantage of the Caledonian Canal and its old wooden locks during the summer.

By bike Well-marked routes make it possible to cycle all the way from Fort William to Inverness. Mountain bikers especially are drawn to the Cairngorms, where there are excellent trails for beginners and experts.

On foot The 79-mile Great Glen Way links Fort William with Inverness, and takes five to six days to walk in full (see box, p.398).

Fort William

With its stunning position on Loch Linnhe, tucked in below the snow-streaked bulk of Ben Nevis, **FORT WILLIAM** (known by the many walkers and climbers who come here as "Fort Bill") should be a gem. Sadly, the anticlimactic end point of the West Highland Way (see box, p.401) has had its waterfront wrecked by ribbon bungalow development and an ill-advised dual carriageway. The main street and the little squares off it are more appealing, though occupied by some decidedly tacky tourist gift shops. Other than its excellent **museum**, the town is short on must-sees, but it's undeniably a convenient base for **outdoor activities** – most notably walking. Several cruises leave from the town pier every day, offering the chance to spot the marine life of Loch Linnhe, which includes seals and seabirds. Shops rent out kayaks and mountain bikes for independent exploration of the surrounding area, and local guides run mountaineering courses (in summer and winter) on the slopes of nearby Munros. Some of the best views of these peaks can be had from **Corpach**, a small village opposite Fort William on the other side of Loch Linnhe, which also has a number of places to stay and several outdoor activities operators.

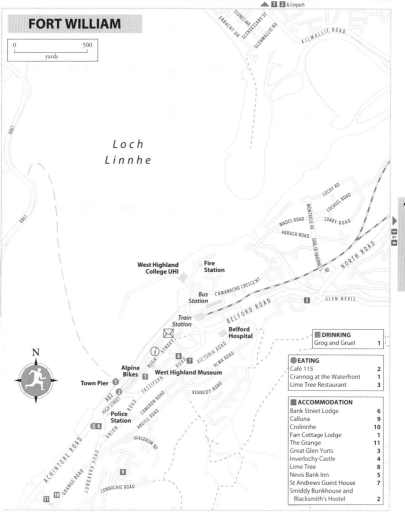

FORT WILLIAM

0   500
        yards

Loch Linnhe

11

West Highland
College UHI

Fire
Station

Bus
Station

CAMANACHD CRESCENT

GLEN NEVIS

5

BELFORD ROAD

Train
Station

Belford
Hospital

N

VICTORIA ROAD

ALMA ROAD

Alpine
Bikes

HIGH STREET

6 **7**

1 West Highland Museum

Town Pier **1**

2

FASSIFERN ROAD

KENNEDY ROAD

Police
Station

3 **8**

CAMERON ROAD

ARGYLL ROAD

GLASDRUM RD

UNION ROAD

ACHINTORE ROAD

GRANGE ROAD

LUNDAVRA ROAD

CONNOCHIE ROAD

11 **10**

9

■ **DRINKING**	
Grog and Gruel	1

● **EATING**	
Café 115	2
Crannog at the Waterfront	1
Lime Tree Restaurant	3

■ **ACCOMMODATION**	
Bank Street Lodge	6
Calluna	9
Crolinnhe	10
Farr Cottage Lodge	1
The Grange	11
Great Glen Yurts	3
Inverlochy Castle	4
Lime Tree	8
Nevis Bank Inn	5
St Andrews Guest House	7
Smiddy Bunkhouse and Blacksmith's Hostel	2

West Highland Museum

Cameron Square, just off the high street • April–Oct Mon–Sat 10am–5pm; March, Nov & Dec Mon–Sat 10am–4pm • Free •
☎ 01397 702169, ⓦ westhighlandmuseum.org.uk

Collections at the splendid and idiosyncratic **West Highland Museum** cover virtually
every aspect of Highland life and the presentation is traditional, but very well done,
making a refreshing change from the state-of-the-art heritage centres popping up across
Scotland. You'll find treasures from the Spanish Armada, quasi-religious relics
associated with Bonnie Prince Charlie and the Jacobite uprising, and the long Spanish
rifle used in the Appin Murder (an event which inspired Robert Louis Stevenson's
Kidnapped). There's even a 550kg slab of aluminium, the stuff that's processed into
silver foil just five miles north of town (you'll see the huge pipes running down the
mountainside), and a section on the World War II commandos, who received their
famously tough training in nearby Lochaber.

The Jacobite Steam Train

At the train station on Station Square • Mid-May to Oct Mon–Fri; mid-June to mid-Sept daily; departs Fort William 10.20am, returns from Mallaig at 2.10pm; additional afternoon service (June–Aug only) departs Fort William 2.30pm, with return at 6.40pm • Return tickets £34 (£58 for first class) • ☎ 08448 504685, ⓦ westcoastrailways.co.uk

Excursions from Fort William include the 84-mile return trip to Mallaig (see p.445) on the **West Highland Railway Line** aboard the **Jacobite Steam Train**. Heading along the shore of Loch Eil to the west coast via historic Glenfinnan (see p.443) and a sinuous Victorian viaduct, the train has stunning views of the water and distant mountains, though these days it's as popular for its role in the *Harry Potter* films. The locomotives used are black and barrel-shaped machines from the 1920s and 1930s tugging younger British Rail carriages from the 1960s.

ARRIVAL AND DEPARTURE   FORT WILLIAM

By train Fort Willilam is one of the stops on the scenic West Highland Railway from Glasgow. The train station is just across the A82 dual carriageway from the north end of the high street.
Destinations Crianlarich (Mon–Sat 4 daily, Sun 3 daily; 1hr 50min); Glasgow Queen Street (Mon–Sat 3 daily, Sun 2 daily; 3hr 50min); London (1 nightly; 12hr); Mallaig (Mon–Sat 4 daily, Sun 3 daily; 1hr 20min).

By bus Intercity coaches from Glasgow and Inverness stop outside the train station on MacFarlane Way.
Destinations Drumnadrochit (9 daily; 1hr 25min); Edinburgh (1 daily; 4hr); Fort Augustus (9 daily; 50min); Glasgow (8 daily; 3hr); Inverness (Mon–Sat 9 daily, 6 on Sun; 2hr); Mallaig (Mon–Fri 3 daily; 1hr 20min); Oban (Mon–Sat 3 daily; 1hr 30min); Portree, Skye (4 daily; 3hr).

GETTING AROUND AND INFORMATION

By bus Fort William itself is small enough to get around on foot, but several accommodation options and activities operators listed below are based in Corpach, three miles along the Mallaig road – it's served by regular bus #45 (every 30min; 20min) from Middle St in Fort William.
Tourist office 15 High St (April & May Mon–Sat 9am–5pm, Sun 10am–5pm; June Mon–Sat 9am–6pm,

Sun 9.30am–5pm; July & Aug Mon–Sat 9am–6.30pm, Sun 9am–6pm; Sept & Oct Mon–Sat 9am–5pm, Sun 10am–4pm; Nov–March Mon–Sat 9am–5pm, Sun 10am–3pm; ☎ 01397 701801, ⓦ visithighlands.com). Busy and very helpful tourist office, which stocks an excellent selection of maps and guide books on exploring the Great Glen. Upstairs you can surf the net (£1/20min).

THE GREAT GLEN WAY AND CYCLE PATH

Ordnance Survey Landranger maps 26, 34 and 41

The enormous cleft of the Great Glen is the most obvious – and by far the flattest – way of traversing northern Scotland from coast to coast. Stretching 79 miles, the **Great Glen Way** long-distance footpath is a relatively undemanding five-to-six-day hike that uses a combination of canal towpath and forest- and hill-tracks between Fort William and Inverness. Accommodation is readily available all the way along the route in campsites, hostels, bunkhouses and B&Bs, though in high season you should book ahead, and if you know you're going to arrive late somewhere it's worth checking that you can still get a meal either where you're staying or somewhere nearby.

There are various **guidebooks** that describe the route, including *The Great Glen Way*, published by Rucksack Readers (£11.99). For the best selection of guides, plus the relevant Ordnance Survey Landranger maps (£8.99 each) head to the tourist office in Fort William. Note, however, that forestry work can see the route diverted at short notice, so it's wise to check the official website (ⓦ outdoorhighlands.co.uk) before setting off.

Cyclists with mountain bikes or hybrids can also use the Great Glen Way, which offers a tranquil alternative to the hazardous A82 (currently the only option for those with road bikes). The route is well signposted and can be pedalled in one long day or two easier days, though of course you can tackle shorter sections. Bikes can be rented at Fort William, Banavie, Drumnadrochit and Inverness.

Whether you're cycling or walking, the suggested **direction** for following the route is from west to east, to take advantage of the prevailing southwesterly wind.

TOURS AND ACTIVITIES

BOAT TOURS

Crannog Cruises Town pier (☎01397 703786, ⓦcrannog.net/cruises). Runs 1hr 30min cruises (£15) from the town pier down Loch Linnhe, where you'll have the chance to spot porpoises and grey seals. Daily trips April–Sept at 10am, noon, 2pm & 4pm, plus evening cruises July & Aug Tues, Thurs & Sun 7.30pm.

Seaventures 3 Kincardine Place (☎01397 701687, ⓦseaventuresscotland.co.uk). Seaventures offers live-aboard charters, plus wildlife cruises (3hr 30min) to nearby islands (June–Aug Mon, Wed & Fri; £30). Departures from the town pier.

MOUNTAIN BIKING

Alpine Bikes 117 High St (☎01397 704008, Nevis Range ☎01397 705825, ⓦtiso.com/alpine). High-spec mountain bikes are available for rent here (from £15/day). Staff know the best routes and can also issue free maps. There's a second branch at the Nevis Range gondola base station (see p.402) – a location that boasts forest rides and a world-championship standard downhill track.

MOUNTAINEERING

Snowgoose Mountain Centre Station Rd, Corpach (☎01397 772467, ⓦhighland-mountain-guides.co.uk). Set beside *Smiddy Bunkhouse* and *Blacksmith's Hostel*, this activity centre offers instruction, rental and residential courses for activities such as mountaineering, ice climbing and dinghy sailing. Sea-kayaking, for example, costs £60 for a full day.

West Coast Mountain Guides (☎01397 719120, ⓦwestcoast-mountainguides.co.uk). Long-established group of experienced guides who run climbing and mountaineering courses throughout the year. A five-day introduction to winter mountaineering costs £500/person. Trips to Skye (and even the Swiss Alps) can also be arranged.

KAYAKING

Rockhopper Unit 17, Annat Industrial Estate, Corpach (☎07739 837344, ⓦrockhopperscotland.co.uk). Get in touch with Rockhopper for sea-kayak coaching, including half-day excursions (£45) and two-day camping trips with meals provided (£195/person).

11

ACCOMMODATION

The town itself isn't the most exciting place to base yourself, but Fort William's plentiful accommodation ranges from large luxury hotels to budget hostels and bunkhouses. Numerous **B&Bs** are also scattered across town, many of them in the suburb of Corpach on the other side of Loch Linnhe, three miles along the Mallaig road (served by regular buses), where you'll also find a couple of good **hostels**; try also nearby Banavie (see p.403).

HOTELS AND B&BS

Crolinnhe 37 Grange Rd ☎01397 703795, ⓦcrolinnhe.co.uk. Beautifully appointed guesthouse overlooking Loch Linnhe, with elegant French furniture in the rooms and attractive landscaped gardens outside. April–Oct. **£130**

★ The Grange Grange Rd ☎01397 705516, ⓦgrangefortwilliam.com. Top-grade accommodation in a striking old stone house, with log fires, views towards Loch Linnhe and luxurious en-suite doubles. Does vegetarian breakfasts on request. April–Oct. **£145**

Inverlochy Castle Torlundy, 3 miles north of the town centre on the A82 ☎01397 702177, ⓦinverlochycastlehotel.co.uk. Built on the site of a thirteenth-century fortress, this is one of Scotland's grandest and most luxurious country-house hotels with fantastic accommodation and Michelin-star food. **£465**

★ Lime Tree Achintore Rd ☎01397 701806, ⓦlimetreefortwilliam.co.uk. A stylish and relaxing option in an old manse, with a great modern restaurant and an excellent contemporary art gallery; they've also got the practicalities covered with a drying room, map room and bike storage. **£140**

Nevis Bank Inn Belford Rd ☎ 01397 705721,

ⓦnevisbankinn.co.uk. The small, functional hotel rooms here are a little on the plain side but they're comfortable and quiet, and the attached restaurant is a convenient place to grab some pasta or a steak. **£138**

St Andrews Guest House Fassifern Rd ☎01397 703038, ⓦstandrewsguesthouse.co.uk. Comfortable and good-value B&B in a turreted former choir school a 5min walk uphill from the high street, featuring various inscriptions and stained-glass windows. **£62**

HOSTELS AND CAMPSITES

Bank Street Lodge Bank St ☎01397 700070, ⓦbankstreetlodge.co.uk. A bright, clean 43-bed hostel, handy for transport options and the town centre. Choose between dorm accommodation and a good range of en-suite rooms. Dorms **£17**; singles **£25**; doubles **£55**

Calluna Connochie Rd ☎01397 700451, ⓦfortwilliamholiday.co.uk. Well-run self-catering and hostel accommodation a 10min walk from the centre of town, configured for individual, family and group stays. Also has on-site laundry facilities and a bouldering wall. The owners can also organize mountaineering trips. Dorms **£15**; doubles **£42**

Farr Cottage Lodge 3.5 miles from Fort William in

Corpach, on the main A830 ☎01397 772315, ⓦfarrcottage.co.uk. Well-equipped, lively place with a range of dorms and double/twin rooms. Offers a multitude of outdoor activities including canyoning and sea-fishing. Dorms £16.50; doubles £34

Great Glen Yurts 3 miles northeast of Fort William off A82 (signposted from Torlundy) ⓦgreatglenyurts.com. Rotund and spacious, these luxury yurts occupy a magnificently peaceful setting with views of Ben Nevis.

There's also a shepherd's hut and wooden cabins, and an open-sided kitchen is great for sociable evening meals. April–Oct. £80

Smiddy Bunkhouse and Blacksmith's Hostel Snowgoose Mountain Centre, Station Rd, Corpach ☎01397 772467, ⓦhighland-mountain-guides.co.uk. Alpine hostel and bunkhouse on the site of an old blacksmith's workshop. It's 4 miles from Ben Nevis at the southwestern end of the Caledonian Canal. Dorms £16

EATING

Café 115 115 High St ☎01397 702500. A decent, cheap and central place to stop for coffee and a snack – a toasted bagel with cheddar and red onion will cost you £3.95. Mon–Sat 10am–4pm.

Crannog at the Waterfront Town pier, just off the bypass on entering Fort William ☎01397 705589, ⓦcrannog.net. Red-roofed restaurant with lochside views and fresh seafood, including Mallaig langoustine,

plus a reasonable wine list. Good lunchtime deals: the two-course lunch is £15. The neighbouring shack sells cullen skink for £3 and oysters for £1.50. Daily noon–2.30pm & 6–9pm.

Lime Tree Restaurant The Old Manse, Achintore Rd ☎01397 701806, ⓦlimetreefortwilliam.co.uk. Serves an excellent selection of contemporary Scottish food. Ardnamurchan venison costs £19.95. Daily 6–9pm.

DRINKING

Grog and Gruel 66 High St ☎01397 705078. Loud and friendly, the downstairs alehouse at *Grog and Gruel* is a good bet for Scottish beer. The upstairs restaurant is more

relaxed, doing mostly Mexican mains, including a spicy "chilli dogs" for £6.95. Mon–Wed & Sun noon–midnight, Thurs–Sat noon–1am.

Around Fort William

Any disappointment you harbour about Fort William town should be offset by the wealth of scenery and activities in its immediate vicinity. Most obvious – on a clear day, at least – is **Ben Nevis** (see box, p.402), the most popular, though hardly the most rewarding, of Scotland's high peaks. The path up leaves from beautiful **Glen Nevis**, also a starting point for some other excellent walks of various lengths and elevations. The mountain abutting Ben Nevis is **Aonach Mhòr**, home of Scotland's most modern ski resort and an internationally renowned honeypot for downhill mountain-bike enthusiasts.

The main road travelling up the Great Glen from Fort William towards Inverness is the A82, ten miles along which is the small settlement of **Spean Bridge**, a good waypoint for getting to various remote and attractive walking areas with several backpacker hostels – in glens **Spean** and **Roy** – found along the A86 trunk road, which links across the central Highlands to the A9 and the Speyside region.

Glen Nevis

A ten-minute drive south of Fort William, **GLEN NEVIS** is among the Highlands' most impressive glens: a classic U-shaped glacial valley hemmed in by steep bracken-covered slopes and swathes of blue-grey scree. With the forbidding mass of Ben Nevis rising steeply to the north, it's not surprising that the valley has served as a location in the films *Rob Roy* and *Braveheart*. Apart from its natural beauty, Glen Nevis is also the starting point for the ascent of **Ben Nevis** (see box, p.402).

A great **low-level walk** (six miles return) runs from the end of the road at the top of Glen Nevis. The good but very rocky path leads through a dramatic gorge with impressive falls and rapids, then opens out into a secret hanging valley, carpeted with wild flowers, with a high waterfall at the far end. If you're really energetic (and properl

THE WEST HIGHLAND WAY

OS Explorer maps 342, 347, 348, 364, 377, 384, 385 & 392

Opened in 1980, the spectacular **West Highland Way** was Scotland's first long-distance footpath, stretching some 96 miles from Milngavie (pronounced "mill-guy"), six miles north of central Glasgow, to Fort William, where it reaches the foot of Ben Nevis, Britain's highest mountain. Today, it is by far the most popular such footpath in Scotland, and while for many the range of scenery, relative ease of walking and nearby facilities make it a classic route, others find it a little too busy in high season, particularly in comparison with the isolation of many other parts of the Highlands.

THE ROUTE

The route follows a combination of ancient **drove roads**, along which Highlanders herded their cattle and sheep to market in the Lowlands, military roads, built by troops to control the Jacobite insurgency in the eighteenth century, old coaching roads and disused railway lines. In addition to the stunning scenery, which is increasingly dramatic as the path heads north, walkers may see some of Scotland's rarer **wildlife**, including red deer, feral goats and, soaring over the highest peaks, golden eagles.

Passing through the Lowlands north of Glasgow, the route runs along the eastern shores of Loch Lomond, over the Highland Boundary Fault Line, then round Crianlarich, crossing open heather moorland across the **Rannoch Moor** wilderness area. It then passes close to **Glen Coe** (see p.404) before reaching **Fort William** (see p.396). Apart from a stretch between Loch Lomond and Bridge of Orchy, when the path is within earshot of the main road, this is wild, remote country: north of Rowardennan on Loch Lomond, the landscape is increasingly exposed, and you should be well prepared for changeable weather.

TACKLING THE ROUTE

Though this is emphatically not the most strenuous of Britain's long-distance walks – it passes between lofty mountain peaks, rather than over them – a moderate degree of **fitness** is required as there are some steep ascents. If you're looking for an added challenge, you could work a climb of **Ben Lomond** or **Ben Nevis** into your schedule. You might choose to walk individual sections of the Way (the eight-mile climb from Glen Coe up the Devil's Staircase is particularly spectacular), but to tackle the whole thing you need to set aside at least **seven days**; avoid a Saturday start from Milngavie and you're less likely to be walking with hordes of people, and there'll be less pressure on accommodation. Most walkers tackle the route from south to north, and manage between ten and fourteen miles a day, staying at hotels, B&Bs and bunkhouses en route. **Camping** is permitted at recognized sites.

INFORMATION

Website ⓦ west-highland-way.co.uk. The route's official website includes further details about the Way and a comprehensive accommodation list. The site also has links to tour companies and transport providers, who can take your luggage from one stopping point to the next.

The West Highland Way Official Guide Includes a foldout map as well as descriptions of the route, with detailed cultural, historical, archeological and wildlife information. It costs £16.99 and is widely available locally.

equipped) you can walk the full twelve miles on over **Rannoch Moor** to **Corrour Station** (see box, p.307), where you can pick up one of four daily trains to take you back to Fort William (50min).

ARRIVAL AND INFORMATION

GLEN NEVIS

By bus Bus #42 runs from the high street in Fort William, past the Glen Nevis Visitor Centre, campsite and SYHA hostel to the Lower Falls car park (3 daily; 25min) almost five miles up the Glen Nevis road.

Glen Nevis Visitor Centre 1.5 miles southeast of Fort William along the Glen Nevis road (daily 8.30am–6pm;

ⓣ 01397 705922); take bus #41 (summer only) from Fort William. Staff here can give good advice on climbing the mountain. It's also worth asking for a copy of the useful leaflet *Ben Nevis: safety information for walking the mountain track.*

11

ASCENT OF BEN NEVIS

Harvey's Ben Nevis Superwalker map (£12.95) is available from Fort William's tourist office and most local bookshops and outdoor stores.

Of all the walks in and around Glen Nevis, the **ascent of Ben Nevis** (4411ft), Britain's highest summit, inevitably attracts the most attention. In high summer the trail teems with hikers – around a hundred thousand trek up to the summit each year. However, this doesn't mean that the mountain should be treated casually. It can snow at the summit any day of the year and people die on the slopes, so make sure that you take the necessary precautions; in winter, of course, the mountain should be left to the experts. The most obvious **route**, a Victorian pony-path up the whaleback south side of the mountain, built to service the observatory that once stood on the top, starts from the helpful **Glen Nevis Visitor Centre** (see p.401). This also sells mountain equipment and last-minute supplies, and is located a mile and a half southeast of Fort William along the Glen Nevis road. Return via the main route or, if the weather is settled and you're confident enough, make a side trip from the wide saddle into the **Allt a'Mhuilinn glen** for spectacular views of the great cliffs on Ben Nevis's north face. Allow a full day (8hr) for the climb and check the weather forecast before setting out (ⓦ bennevisweather.co.uk is useful).

ACCOMMODATION AND EATING

Note that the *Achintee Farm Guest House* and *Ben Nevis Inn* are on the opposite side of the river from the main **Glen Nevis road** from Fort William – drivers should get to these places via the Achintee road from Fort William; coming by bus (see p.397), get off at the Glen Nevis Visitor Centre and take the footbridge over the river.

Achintee Farm Guest House Achintee, across the river from the visitor centre ⓣ01397 702240, ⓦ achinteefarm.com. Friendly B&B with adjoining hostel and a rugged little stone cottage, right by the *Ben Nevis Inn* at the start of the Ben Nevis footpath. Also has drying rooms and wi-fi. Dorms £17; doubles £90

★ **Ben Nevis Inn** Achintee, across the river from the visitor centre ⓣ01397 701227, ⓦ ben-nevis-inn.co.uk. A basic and cosy bunkhouse (booking advised) in the basement of a lively 250-year-old pub at the start of the Ben Nevis footpath. The pub has a terrific atmosphere, and the menu – with ale-battered North Sea haddock for £11.50 – is especially tempting after a day on the mountain. Daily noon–11pm; food served noon–9pm. Dorms £16.50

Glen Nevis Caravan and Camping Park Half a mile past the visitor centre along the Glen Nevis road ⓣ01397 702191, ⓦ glen-nevis.co.uk. Offers a range of lodges and rentable caravans as well as camping pitches. Gorgeous views and facilities include hot showers, a shop and restaurant and wheelchair-accessible bathrooms. Per pitch £9

SYHA Glen Nevis 1 mile past the visitor centre along the Glen Nevis road ⓣ01397 702336, ⓦ syha.org.uk. This friendly hostel is an excellent base for walkers and has full catering, as well as a decent kitchen. It gets very busy in summer, so book ahead. Dorms £15; doubles £27

The Nevis Range

Situated seven miles northeast of Fort William by the A82, on the slopes of **Aonach Mhòr**, one of the high mountains abutting Ben Nevis, the **Nevis Range** is Scotland's highest ski area. The fifteen-minute **gondola trip** (daily: Easter to June, Sept & Oct 10am–5pm; July & Aug 9.30am–6pm; early Nov & late Dec to Easter 9am–sunset; £12.50; ⓦ nevisrange .co.uk/gondola-info.asp) to get here, rising 2000ft, gives an easy approach to some high-level walking as well as spectacular views from the terrace of the self-service restaurant at the top station. There's also a **Discovery Centre** here, providing insights into the mountain's geology and wildlife. The **base station** area in Torlundy, just east of Fort William, also has a café, and there's a high-wire adventure course and nature trail nearby.

ARRIVAL AND INFORMATION   THE NEVIS RANGE

By bus Bus #42 runs year-round from Fort William to the gondola's base station (4 daily Mon–Sat, 2 daily on Sun; 20min).

Tourist information In the Mountain Discovery Centre, located at the top gondola station (June–Aug 9.30am–6pm; Sept & Oct 10am–sunset; ⓣ01397 705825, ⓦ nevis-range.co.uk).

DOWNHILL MOUNTAIN BIKING ON THE NEVIS RANGE

From the top of the Nevis Range gondola station, you can experience a white-knuckle ride down Britain's only World Cup standard **downhill mountain-bike course**, a hair-raising 3km route that's not for the faint-hearted. There are also over 25 miles of waymarked off-road bike routes, known as the Witch's Trails, on the mountainside and in the Leanachan Forest, ranging from gentle paths to cross-country scrambles. At the entrance to the lower gondola station, **Alpine Bikes** (☎01397 705825, ⓦ alpinebikes.com) rents general mountain bikes (from £15) as well as full-suspension ones for the downhill course. The **Nevis Bike School** (☎01397 705825, ⓦ bike.nevisrange.co.uk) runs training courses (2hr 30min; £36/person, minimum three people). Depending on the trail you choose, you may also need to buy a **gondola pass** (£11.50).

Neptune's Staircase

In the suburb of **Banavie**, three miles north of the centre of Fort William along the A830 to Mallaig, the Caledonian Canal (see p.415) climbs 64ft in less than half a mile via a punishing but picturesque series of eight locks known as **Neptune's Staircase**. There are stunning views from here of Ben Nevis and its neighbours, and it's a popular point from which to walk or cycle along the canal towpath.

ARRIVAL AND GETTING AROUND · NEPTUNE'S STAIRCASE

By bus Stagecoach bus #45A runs from Middle St in Fort William to Banavie (every 15–30min; 10min).

Bike rental You can rent a bike (£15/day; ☎01397 772315, ⓦ farrcottage.com) at *Farr Cottage Lodge* in nearby Corpach; from there it's a short ride northeast along the canal towpath to Neptune's Staircase.

ACCOMMODATION AND EATING

Chase the Wild Goose Hostel Locheil Crescent, Banavie ☎01397 772531, ⓦ great-glen-hostel.com. A small, comfortable hostel close to Neptune's Staircase and also handy for the Great Glen Way. Has a barbecue area for use in summer. Dorms **£19**

Eagle Barge Inn Laggan Locks, at the northern end of Loch Lochy ☎07789 858567. If you do choose to cycle along the Caledonian Canal, look out for this unusual pub, where mains like peat-smoked salmon (£17.80) and real ale are offered aboard a wonderful 1920s Dutch barge. Easter–Oct Mon & Thurs–Sun noon–11pm; food served noon–3.30pm & 5.30–8.30pm.

Moorings Hotel Beside the Staircase in Banavie ☎01397 772797, ⓦ moorings-fortwilliam.co.uk. This mid-sized hotel near the canal serves curries and other pub staples in its bar, as well as classy and beautifully presented Scottish dinners (£30 for three courses) in the main restaurant. Bar daily noon–9.30pm; restaurant daily 7–9.30pm. **£125**

★**Treetops** Badabrie, Banavie ☎01397 772496, ⓦ treetopsfortwilliam.co.uk. This modern chalet offers incomparable Ben Nevis and Loch Linnhe views and soothingly cosy rooms. Superb breakfasts (veggie haggis is an option) and warmly welcoming and helpful hosts. **£85**

Spean Bridge and around

Ten miles northeast of Fort William, the village of **SPEAN BRIDGE** marks the junction of the A82 with the A86 from Dalwhinnie and Kingussie (see p.428). If you're here, it's well worth heading a mile out of the village on the A82 towards Inverness to the **Commando Memorial**, a bronze statue depicting a group of soldiers which commemorates the men who trained in the area during World War II. Their story is told in depth at the West Highland Museum in Fort William (see p.397). The statue looks out on an awesome sweep of moor and mountain that takes in the wider Lochaber area and the Ben Nevis massif.

Glen Roy

Three miles east of Spean Bridge, a minor road turns north off the A86 and up **Glen Roy**. Drive a couple of miles along the glen and you'll see the so-called "parallel roads": not roads at all, but ancient beaches at various levels along the valley sides, which mark the shorelines of a loch confined here by a glacial dam in the last Ice Age.

Tulloch and around

East of Roy Bridge along the A86, just before **Tulloch**, the train line and the main road part company. From Tulloch's small railway station, accessible only by a single-track road and served by Caledonian sleeper services from London, trains swing south to pass Loch Treig and cross Rannoch Moor (see box, p.337).

Beyond the turn-off at the Tulloch station, the A86 runs alongside the artificial **Loch Laggan** with the picturesque Ardverikie Castle on its southern shore and the attractive walking area of Creag Meagaidh National Nature Reserve to the north.

ARRIVAL AND DEPARTURE   SPEAN BRIDGE AND AROUND

By bus Buses bound for Spean Bridge depart from Fort William's bus station a couple of times per hour, taking 15–30min to arrive in the centre of the village.

ACCOMMODATION AND EATING

Àite Cruinnichidh 3.5 miles west of Tulloch railway station, just south of A86 ☎ 01397 712315, ⓦ highland -hostel.co.uk. A comfortable wood-lined bunkhouse in a beautiful setting, with good facilities including family rooms and a sauna, as well as local advice for walkers and cyclists. Dorms **£16.50**

Old Pines Hotel and Restaurant A few hundred yards northwest of the Commando Memorial, on the B8004 to Gairlochy ☎ 01397 712324, ⓦ oldpines.co.uk. At this welcoming hotel and restaurant, diners are treated to home-made cooking and locally sourced game and shellfish (the seared scallop starter is £8.50) as well as home baking, pasta and ice cream. Mon & Sun 6.30–9pm, Tues–Sat noon–3pm & 6.30–9pm.

Station Lodge At Tulloch Station ☎ 01397 732333, ⓦ stationlodge.co.uk. The station building at Tulloch is now a friendly and well-equipped hostel that can provide cooked breakfasts (£6), packed lunches (£6) and two-course dinners (£11) with advance notice. Dorms **£18**

Glen Coe and around

Breathtakingly beautiful **GLEN COE** (literally "Valley of Weeping"), sixteen miles south of Fort William on the A82, is a spectacular mountain valley between velvety-green conical peaks, their tops often wreathed in cloud, and their flanks streaked by cascades of rock and scree.

Arriving from the south across the desolate reaches of Rannoch Moor, you're likely to find the start of the glen – with **Buachaille Etive Mhòr** to the south and **Beinn a'Chrùlaiste** to the north – little short of forbidding. By the time you've reached the heart of the glen, with the huge rock buttresses known as the **Three Sisters** on one side and the Anoach Eagach ridge on the other combining to close up the sky, you'll almost certainly want to stop. Added to the compelling emotional mix is the story of the **massacre of Glen Coe** in 1692, the bloody nadir of the long-standing enmity between the clans MacDonald and Campbell.

Beyond the small village of **GLENCOE** at the western end of the glen, the glen itself (a property of the NTS since the 1930s) is virtually uninhabited, and provides outstanding climbing and walking. From **Loch Leven** the main road goes west and over the bridge at Ballachulish en route to Fort William, while at the eastern end of the loch is the slowly reviving settlement of **Kinlochleven**, site of the world's largest indoor ice-climbing centre and a waypoint on the West Highland Way long-distance footpath (see box, p.401).

Brief history

In 1692 Glen Coe was the site of a notorious **massacre**, in which the MacDonalds were victims of an abiding government desire to suppress the clans. Fed up with what they regarded as unacceptable lawlessness, and a groundswell of Jacobitism and Catholicism, the government offered a general pardon to all those who signed an oath of allegiance to William III by January 1, 1692. When clan chief **Alastair**

WALKS AROUND GLEN COE

Ordnance Survey Explorer map 384

Flanked by sheer-sided Munros, **Glen Coe** offers some of the Highlands' most challenging **hiking** routes, with long steep ascents over rough trails and notoriously unpredictable weather conditions that claim lives every year. The walks outlined below number among the glen's less ambitious routes, but still require a map. It's essential that you take the proper precautions, and stick to the paths, both for your own safety and the sake of the landscape, which has become badly eroded in places. For a broader selection of walks, get hold of the Ordnance Survey *Pathfinder Guide: Fort William and Glen Coe Walks* (£11.99).

DEVIL'S STAIRCASE

A good introduction to the splendours of Glen Coe is the half-day hike over the **Devil's Staircase**, which follows part of the old military road that once ran between Fort William and Stirling. The trail, part of the West Highland Way (see box, p.401), starts at the village of **Kinlochleven** and is marked by thistle signs, which lead uphill to the 1804ft pass and down the other side into Glen Coe.

ALLT COIRE GABHAIL

Set right in the heart of the glen, the half-day **Allt Coire Gabhail** hike starts at the car park opposite the distinctive Three Sisters massif on the main A82. This explores the so-called "Lost Valley" where the Clan MacDonald fled and hid their cattle when attacked. Once in the valley, there are superb views of the upper slopes of Bidean nan Bian, Gearr Aonach and Beinn Fhada, which improve as you continue on to its head, another twenty- to thirty-minute walk.

BUACHAILLE ETIVE BEAG

Undoubtedly one of the finest walks in the Glen Coe area that doesn't entail the ascent of a Munro is the **Buachaille Etive Beag** circuit, which follows the textbook glacial valleys of Lairig Eilde and Lairig Gartain, ascending 1968ft in only nine miles of rough trail. Park near the waterfall at **The Study** – the gorge part of the A82 through Glen Coe – and walk up the road until you see a sign pointing south to "Loch Etiveside".

11

MacDonald missed the deadline, a plot was hatched to make an example of "that damnable sept", and **Campbell of Glenlyon** was ordered to billet his soldiers in the homes of the MacDonalds, who for ten days entertained them with traditional Highland hospitality. In the early morning of February 13, the soldiers turned on their hosts, slaying around forty people and causing more than three hundred to flee in a blizzard.

Glencoe Mountain Resort

Half a mile south of the A82 at the foot of the mountain • Jan–Oct Mon–Thurs & Sun 9am–8.30pm, Fri & Sat 9am–10.30pm; Nov & Dec daily 9am–4.30pm • ☎ 01855 851226, ⓦ glencoemountain.co.uk • Chairlift £10; full day's ski/snowboard rental £25

From the **Glencoe Mountain Resort** a chairlift climbs 2400ft to Meall a Bhuiridh, giving fine views over Rannoch Moor and to Ben Nevis. At the base station, there's a simple but pleasant café. Skiing, snowboarding and mountain-biking sessions can all be arranged at this spectacularly located resort too.

Glencoe Village

Tucked between steep mountains, Loch Leven and the grassy banks of the River Coe, **Glencoe Village** is an attractive place to spend a couple of days. There's a good choice of accommodation in the area, and if you fancy a break from walking, the village museum and nearby visitor centre make for pleasant distractions.

Glencoe Folk Museum

Main St • Easter–Aug Mon–Sat 10am–4.30pm (last admission 4pm) • £3 • ☎ 01855 811664, ⓦ glencoemuseum.com

If you have an hour to spare in Glencoe Village, it's worth paying a visit to the delightful heather-roofed **Glencoe Folk Museum**. Various games and activities for kids can be enjoyed within this cosy 1720 croft where items include a chair that reputedly once belonged to Bonnie Prince Charlie. Look out for their special storytelling events and workshops.

NTS visitor centre

1 mile east of Glencoe Village on the A82 • Feb–Easter & Nov–Jan Thurs–Sun 10am–4pm; Easter–Oct daily 9.30am–5.30pm; guided walks Easter & June–Sept (book ahead) • £6.50; guided walks from £5; NTS • ☎ 01855 811307, ⓦ glencoe-nts.org.uk

The attractive and ecofriendly timber **NTS visitor centre** sits in woodland a mile south of Glencoe Village. It has a good exhibition, a film giving a balanced account of the massacre, plus information about the area's natural history and conservation issues, and some entertaining material on rock- and hill-climbing through the years. There's also a cabin area providing information on the local weather and wildlife, and you may be able to join a ranger-led **guided walk** of the surrounding area.

ARRIVAL AND ACTIVITIES

GLEN COE AND AROUND

By bus To get to the NTS visitor centre or chairlift station from Fort William's bus station, hop on one of the Glasgow-bound Scottish Citylink coaches (up to 8 daily; 30–45min). Bus #44 from Fort William also stops at least 10 times a day (3 on Sun) at Glencoe village en route to Kinlochleven.

ACCOMMODATION AND EATING

★**Clachaig Inn** 2.5 miles south of Glencoe Village on the minor road off the A82 ☎ 01855 811252, ⓦ clachaig.com. The liveliest, best-known hotel in the area is a great place to reward your exertions with cask-conditioned ales and heaped platefuls of food (such as venison casserole, £10.95); they also have 23 comfy en-suite rooms. Mon–Thurs & Sun 8am–11pm, Fri 8am–midnight, Sat 8am–11.30pm. __£53__

Glencoe Independent Hostel North of the river ☎ 01855 811906, ⓦ glencoehostel.co.uk. Cheap and excellent independent hostel and bunkhouse in rustic whitewashed buildings, offering free wi-fi, hot showers and a laundry service. Dorms __£13__

Red Squirrel 150m south of the turn-off to Glencoe Independent Hostel ☎ 01855 811256, ⓦ redsquirrel campsite.co.uk. Sylvan year-round campsite, just south of the SYHA hostel on the road to *Clachaig Inn*. Campfires and pets permitted. Per pitch __£11__

Scorry Breac On the north side of the river ☎ 01855 811354, ⓦ scorrybreac.co.uk. Secluded and friendly, a short walk from the centre of Glencoe village, *Scorry Breac* has five affordable en-suite rooms, the best of which have views over the mountains. __£64__

SYHA Glencoe Adjacent to the Glencoe Independent Hostel ☎ 01855 811219, ⓦ syha.org.uk. A basic but decent wood-tiled hostel with a dining area, cosy lounge and well-equipped kitchen. Dorms __£15__

Kinlochleven

At the easternmost end of Loch Leven, the settlement of **KINLOCHLEVEN** is, thanks to its location on the West Highland Way, steadily reviving its fortunes. For many years it was a tourism backwater best known as the site of a huge, unsightly aluminium smelter built in 1904. The tale of the area's industrial past is told in **The Aluminium Story** (same hours as tourist information centre; free), a small series of displays in the same corrugated metal building as the post office and tourist information centre (see opposite). As well as being close to Glen Coe, Kinlochleven stands at the foot of the Mamore hills, popular with Munro-baggers; Fort William is a day's walk away.

The Ice Factor

Leven Rd • Mon, Wed & Fri–Sun 9am–7pm, Tues & Thurs 9am–10pm • 2.5hr ice-climbing course £48 • ☎ 01855 831100, ⓦ ice-factor.co.uk

Kinlochleven's disused aluminium smelter is now the home of an innovative indoor mountaineering centre called **The Ice Factor**. The facility includes the world's largest artificial ice-climbing wall (13.5m) as well as a range of more traditional climbing walls, plus equipment rental, a steam room and sauna. There's a bar upstairs and food is available too.

ARRIVAL AND INFORMATION KINLOCHLEVEN

By bus The hourly #44 bus from Fort William runs to the centre of Kinlochleven (50min), passing Glencoe (35min) en route.

Tourist information In the Aluminium Story building on Linnhe Rd, in the centre of the village (Mon, Tues, Thurs & Fri 9am–12.30pm & 1.30–5.30pm, Wed & Sat 9am–1pm;

☏01855 831021). Staff at the combined post office, museum and information point can give tips on local attractions. Look out for the useful leaflet, published by Kinlochleven Community Trust, which details local walking routes.

ACCOMMODATION AND EATING

Blackwater Hostel Beside the river on Lab Rd ☏01855 831253, ⓦblackwaterhostel.co.uk. A decidedly upmarket hostel, with en-suite dorms and Hobbit-sized two-bed "microlodges" available for rent. You can also camp here. Dorms £16.50; microlodge £35; camping per person £8

Edencoille Guest House Garbhein Rd ☏01855 831358, ⓦkinlochlevenbedandbreakfast.co.uk. There's fine hospitality at this Edwardian-built house where, with notice, they can organize packed lunches, evening meals and guided walking trips. £72

Lochleven Seafood Café 5 miles west of Kinlochleven on the B836 (north side of the loch) ☏01855 821048,

ⓦlochlevenseafoodcafe.co.uk. The best place to eat near Kinlochleven, this is a relaxed restaurant with an attractive outdoor terrace overlooking the loch. Specializes in local shellfish such as whole brown crab cooked in seawater (£12.95). Daily noon–3pm & 6–9pm.

MacDonald Hotel Fort William Rd ☏01855 831539, ⓦmacdonaldhotel.co.uk. This central hotel has ten decent en-suite bedrooms as well as cabins and a campsite, but is best visited for its Bothy Bar, where you can join fellow walkers for fish and chips (£8.90) and other pub meals. Bar Mon–Wed 12.30–11.30pm, Thurs–Sat 12.30pm–12.30am, Sun 12.30–11.15pm. Doubles £90; cabins for 2 £20; camping per person £8

Loch Ness and around

Twenty-three miles long, unfathomably deep, cold and often moody, **LOCH NESS** is bound by rugged heather-clad mountains rising steeply from a wooded shoreline, with attractive glens opening up on either side. Its fame, however, is based overwhelmingly on its legendary inhabitant, Nessie, the "Loch Ness monster" (see box, p.408), who encourages a steady flow of hopeful visitors to the settlements dotted along the loch, in particular **Drumnadrochit**. Nearby, the impressive ruins of **Castle Urquhart** – a favourite monster-spotting location – perch atop a rock on the lochside and attract a deluge of bus parties during the summer. Almost as busy in high season is the village of **Fort Augustus**, at the more scenic southwest tip of Loch Ness, where you can watch queues of boats tackling one of the Caledonian Canal's longest flights of locks. You'll need your own **car** to complete the whole loop around the loch, a journey that includes an impressive stretch between Fort Augustus and the high, hidden Loch Mhòr, overlooked by the imposing Monadhliath range to the south.

Away from the lochside, and seeing a fraction of Loch Ness's visitor numbers, the remote glens of **Urquhart** and **Affric** make an appealing contrast, with Affric in particular boasting narrow, winding roads, gushing streams and hillsides dotted with ancient Caledonian pine forests. The busiest of these glens to the north is the often bleak high country of Glen Moriston, a little to the southeast of Glen Affric, through which the main road between Inverness and Skye passes.

GETTING AROUND LOCH NESS AND AROUND

By bus Using the A82, which runs along the western shore of Loch Ness, buses can travel the entire length of the loch, from Inverness to Fort Augustus. On the eastern side,

however, regular bus services are limited to the stretch between Inverness and Foyers.

By car Although most visitors drive along the tree-lined

11

NESSIE

The world-famous **Loch Ness monster**, affectionately known as **Nessie** (and by serious aficionados as *Nessiteras rhombopteryx*), has been a local celebrity for some time. The first mention of a mystery creature crops up in St Adamnan's seventh-century biography of **St Columba**, who allegedly calmed an aquatic animal that had attacked one of his monks. Present-day interest, however, is probably greater outside Scotland than within the country, and dates from the building of the road along the loch's western shore in the early 1930s. In 1934 the *Daily Mail* published London surgeon **R.K. Wilson**'s sensational photograph of the head and neck of the monster peering up out of the loch, and the hype has hardly diminished since. Recent encounters range from glimpses of ripples by anglers to the famous occasion in 1961 when thirty hotel guests saw a pair of humps break the water's surface and cruise for about half a mile before submerging.

Photographic evidence is showcased in two separate exhibitions located at **Drumnadrochit**, but the most impressive of these exhibits – including the renowned black-and-white movie footage of Nessie's humps moving across the water, and Wilson's original head-and-shoulders shot – have now been exposed as **fakes**. Indeed, in few other places on earth has watching a rather lifeless and often grey expanse of water seemed so compelling, or have floating logs, otters and boat wakes been photographed so often and with such excitement.

Yet while even high-tech sonar surveys carried out over the past two decades have failed to come up with conclusive evidence, it's hard to dismiss Nessie as pure myth. After all, no one yet knows where the unknown layers of silt and mud at the bottom of the loch begin and end: best estimates say the loch is over **750ft deep**, deeper than much of the North Sea, while others point to the possibilities of underwater caves and undiscovered channels connected to the sea. What scientists have found in the cold, murky depths, including pure white eels and rare arctic char, offers fertile grounds for speculation, with different theories declaring Nessie to be a remnant from the dinosaur age, a giant newt or a huge visiting Baltic sturgeon.

11

A82 road on the western side of the loch, the sinuous, single-track B862/B852 (originally a military road built to link Fort Augustus and Fort George) that skirts the eastern shore is quieter and affords far more spectacular views.

Fort Augustus

FORT AUGUSTUS, a tiny, busy village at the scenic southwestern tip of Loch Ness, was named after George II's son, the chubby lad who later became the "Butcher" duke of Cumberland of Culloden fame; it was built as a barracks after the 1715 Jacobite rebellion. Today, it's dominated by comings and goings along the **Caledonian Canal**, which leaves Loch Ness here, and by its large former **Benedictine abbey**, a campus of grey Victorian buildings founded on the site of the original fort in 1876. Until relatively recently this was home to a small but active community of monks, but it has now been converted into luxury flats. There are some good cycling routes locally, notably along the Great Glen cycle route.

ARRIVAL AND DEPARTURE
FORT AUGUSTUS

By bus Frequent buses ply the A82, linking Fort Augustus with Drumnadrochit (35min) and Inverness (1hr) to the north, and Fort William, 30 miles south (1hr).

INFORMATION

Tourist office In the car park north of the canal (April & May Mon–Sat 9.30am–5pm, Sun 10am–4pm; June Mon–Sat 9am–5pm, Sun 10am–4pm; July & Aug Mon–Sat 9am–6pm, Sun 10am–4pm; Sept & Oct Mon–Sat 9.30am–5pm, Sun 10am–3pm; Nov–March daily 10am–3pm; ☎01320 366779). Fort Augustus's very helpful tourist office hands out useful free walking leaflets and stocks maps of the Great Glen Way (see box, p.398). **Caledonian Canal Visitor Centre** Ardchattan House Canalside, by the locks (Easter–Oct daily 10am–1.30pm

FROM TOP MOUNTAIN BIKER, LAGGAN WOLFTRAX (P.429); GLEN AFFRIC (P.412)

2–5.30pm; ☎01320 366493). Houses a small exhibition showing why, when and how the Caledonian Canal was built. Black and white pictures reveal how the canal looked in the nineteenth century, but aside from these (and a dusty old telescope) there's little in the way of proper exhibits.

TOURS AND ACTIVITIES

Boat tours From its berth by the Clansman Centre, near the swing bridge, Cruise Loch Ness sails five miles up Loch Ness (daily; 1hr; £14; ☎01320 366277, ⊛cruiselochness .com), using sonar technology to provide passengers with impressive live 3D imagery of the deep where underwater cave systems, salmon, cannibalistic trout (and, some would speculate, Nessie) are to be found.

Fishing The tourist office can advise you on how to obtain permits to fish the loch or nearby river.

ACCOMMODATION

Corrie Liath Market Hill, half a mile south of the centre along the A82 ☎01320 366409, ⊛corrieliath.co.uk. Small, thoughtfully managed B&B whose comfortable rooms have books and DVDs for guests to enjoy. The garden has a barbecue hut for use in the summertime. £74

Cumberlands Campsite Glendoe Rd, by Stravaigers Lodge ☎01320 366257, ⊛cumberlands-campsite .com. Spacious campsite with good facilities, a 5min walk from the loch and a short stroll from the shops and pubs of Fort Augustus. Per pitch £10

Lovat Arms Hotel On the A82 in the centre of town ☎01456 490000, ⊛thelovat.com. Expensive hotel refurbished along ecofriendly principles and built on the site of the 1718 Kilwhimen Barracks. The hotel's restaurant and brasserie serve inventive (and costly) dishes with a local focus. £65

Morag's Lodge Bunoich Brae, on the Loch Ness side of town ☎01320 366289, ⊛www.moragslodge.com. The atmosphere at this well-equipped hostel – with four- and six-bed dorms – livens up with the daily arrival of backpackers' minibus tours. Dorms £22.50; doubles £54

Stravaigers Lodge Glendoe Rd, a short walk south of the centre ☎01320 366257, ⊛highlandbunkhouse .co.uk. Basic hostel with a mix of twin rooms and cheaper bunk rooms, split between two separate buildings, each with its own kitchen. Dorms £18; twins £46

EATING AND DRINKING

The Lock Inn Canalside, opposite the Caledonian Canal Visitor Centre ☎01320 366302. With attractive wood-panelled interiors and a wider selection of pub meals (such as chicken curry, £11.95), The Lock is a slightly better choice than its neighbour, The Bothy. Daily 11am–11pm; food served noon–3.30pm & 5.30–8.30pm.

The east side of Loch Ness

The tranquil and scenic **east side** of Loch Ness is skirted by General Wade's old military highway, now the B862/B852. From Fort Augustus, the narrow single-track road swings up, away from the lochside through the near-deserted **Stratherrick** valley, which is dotted with tiny lochans. To the east of Fort Augustus you'll pass the massive earth workings of the Glendoe Hydro Development. From here, the road drops down to rejoin the shores of Loch Ness at **FOYERS**, where there are numerous marked forest trails and an impressive waterfall.

Past **Inverfarigaig** – where a road up a beautiful, steep-sided river valley leads east over to Loch Mhor – is the sleepy village of **DORES**, nestled at the northeastern end of Loch Ness, where the whitewashed *Dores Inn* provides a pleasant pit stop.

ARRIVAL AND DEPARTURE   THE EAST SIDE OF LOCH NESS

By bus Local buses run up and down the northeast side of the loch, shuttling visitors from Inverness south to Foyers (Mon–Fri up to 5 daily; 2 on Sat; 45min).

ACCOMMODATION AND EATING

DORES

Dores Inn North of the village centre, by the loch ☎01463 751203, ⊛thedoresinn.co.uk. Only 9 miles southwest of Inverness (and 11 miles north of Foyers), this old lochside pub is popular with Invernessians, who trickle out here on summer evenings for a stroll along the grey pebble beach and some monster spotting. Pancetta-wrapped cod loin costs £15.95. Mon–Thurs 10am–11pm, Fri & Sat 10am–midnight, Sun 10am–10pm.

FOYERS

Foyers House In Upper Foyers, up the track next to Waterfall Café ☎01456 486405. Out of the way, adults-only B&B with fabulous views of the loch from its terrace. Has a self-catering kitchen and dining room. **£50**

Waterfall Café In Upper Foyers, opposite the footpath to the waterfall ☎01456 486233. Previously known as the *Red Squirrel Café*, this friendly teashop still runs a live webcam of red squirrels nesting across the road – and does delicious breakfasts, lunches and baking to boot. April–Oct Mon–Thurs 9am–5pm, Fri & Sat 9am–7pm, Sun 10am–3pm; Nov–March Mon–Thurs 9.30am–4pm, Fri & Sat 9.30am–7pm, Sun 10am–2pm.

Drumnadrochit and around

Situated above a verdant, sheltered bay of Loch Ness fifteen miles southwest of Inverness, **DRUMNADROCHIT** is the southern gateway to remote Glen Affric and the epicentre of Nessie-hype, complete with a rash of tacky souvenir shops and two rival monster exhibitions whose head-to-head scramble for punters has occasionally erupted into acrimonious exchanges, detailed with relish by the local press.

Loch Ness Centre & Exhibition

On the main A82 • Daily: Easter–June & Sept–Oct 9.30am–5pm; July & Aug 9.30am–6pm; Nov–Easter 10am–3.30pm • ☎01456 450573, ⓦlochness.com • £7.95

Of the two major monster hubs in Drumnadrochit (the other being the Nessieland Monster Centre), the **Loch Ness Centre & Exhibition** is the better bet, offering an in-depth rundown of eyewitness accounts and information on various Nessie research projects. It does a good job, mixing "evidence" of the monster's existence with frank appraisals of pictures and sightings that turned out to be hoaxes.

Nessieland Monster Centre

Just west of the Loch Ness Centre & Exhibition on the A831 • Daily: July & Aug 9am–9pm; Sept–June 9am–5pm • £6 • ☎01456 450342, ⓦnessieland.co.uk

Aimed mainly at families, the rather feeble **Nessieland Monster Centre** has an exhibition on monster sightings, a plastic model of Nessie for kids to clamber on, plus its own adventure playground. The wood-panelled and heavily tartanized interior of the adjacent *Loch Ness Lodge Hotel* is said to harbour a resident ghost.

Castle Urquhart

Beside Loch Ness, 2 miles southeast of Drumnadrochit and just off the A82 • Daily: April–Sept 9.30am–6pm; Oct 9.30am–5pm; Nov–March 9.30am–4.30pm • £8.50; HES • ☎01456 450551, ⓦhistoricenvironment.scot

The thirteenth-century ruined lochside **Castle Urquhart** was built as a strategic base to guard the Great Glen. The castle was taken by Edward I of England and later held by Robert the Bruce against Edward III, only to be blown up in 1692 to prevent it from falling to the Jacobites. Today it's one of Scotland's classic picture-postcard ruins, particularly splendid at night when it's floodlit and the crowds have gone. In the small visitor centre, a short film highlights the turbulent history of the castle.

ARRIVAL AND DEPARTURE   DRUMNADROCHIT AND AROUND

By bus Drumnadrochit is served by frequent buses from Inverness (at least hourly; 30min), Fort William (up to 9 daily; 1hr 30min) and Fort Augustus (up to 10 daily; 35min). Buses stop near the post office, on the A82.

INFORMATION AND TOURS

Tourist information In the middle of the main car park in the village (April & May Mon–Sat 9.30am–5pm, Sun 10am–3pm; June Mon–Sat 9am–5pm, Sun 10am–6pm; July & Aug Mon–Sat 9am–6pm, Sun 10am–4pm; Sept & Oct Mon–Sat 9.30am–5pm, Sun 10am–3pm; Nov–March Mon–Sat 9.30am–3.30pm; ☎01456 459086).

Boat tours The sonar-equipped *Nessie Hunter* (☎01456 450395, ⓦloch-ness-cruises.com) runs hourly trips on the loch from 9am to 6pm, from Easter to October. The hour-long cruise costs £15 and can be booked online or at the Nessieland Monster Centre.

11

ACCOMMODATION

Benleva Kilmore Rd, Kilmore ☎01456 450080, ⓦbenleva.co.uk. Small, basic hotel in Kilmore, a 15min walk from the monster centres of Drumnadrochit. The six en-suite rooms have tartan bedspreads and free wi-fi. **£70**

Borlum Farm A mile southeast of central Drumnadrochit, off the A82 ☎01456 450220, ⓦborlum.com. Attractive campsite overlooking the village, with space for caravans and tents. The site is part of a popular riding school offering lessons, rides and treks (from £19.50/hr). Per pitch **£7**

Glenkirk B&B 300m west of Nessieland Monster Centre along the A831 ☎01456 450802, ⓦlochnessbandb.com. Bright, friendly B&B in a former church located just a few minutes' walk from the centre, with simple yet smartly decorated bedrooms. **£85**

Loch Ness Backpackers Lodge Coiltie Farmhouse, Lewiston, 1 mile south of the centre of Drumnadrochit ☎01456 450807, ⓦlochness-backpackers.com. For a cheap bed for the night, head for this immaculate and friendly hostel, which has dorms, private rooms and good facilities including a bar and two lounges. Coming from Drumnadrochit, follow the signs to the left. Dorms **£16**, doubles **£52**

EATING AND DRINKING

11

Benleva Kilmore Rd, Kilmore ☎01456 450080. One of many hotels doing bar food, *Benleva* sets itself apart by using local beer in some of its dishes, including the steak and ale pie with chips and seasonal veg (£10.50). Mon–Thurs noon–midnight, Fri noon–1am, Sat noon–11.45pm, Sun noon–11pm.

Fiddlers' Just south of the village green on the A82 ☎01456 450678, ⓦfiddledrum.co.uk. Busy, friendly bar with plenty of outside seating and, it's claimed, more than five hundred single malt whiskies. The mostly meaty menu has a couple of veggie options too, including a veggie and brie burger (£11.95). Daily 12.30–2.30pm & 6–9.30pm.

Glen Affric

Due west of Drumnadrochit lies a vast area of high peaks, remote glens and few roads. The reason most folk head this way is to explore the picturesque native forests and grand mountains of **Glen Affric**, heaven for walkers, climbers and mountain bikers. Munro-baggers (see p.10) are normally much in evidence, and it's possible to tramp 25 miles all the way through Glen Affric to Shiel Bridge, on the west coast near Kyle of Lochalsh.

Cannich and Loch Affric

The main approach to Glen Affric is through the small settlement of **CANNICH**, thirteen miles west of Drumnadrochit on the A831. Cannich is a quiet and uninspiring village, but it has an excellent campsite where mountain bikes can be rented. From the car park at the head of the single-track road along the glen, ten miles southwest of Cannich, there's a selection of **walks**: the trip around **Loch Affric** will take you a good five hours but allows you to appreciate the glen and its wildlife.

ARRIVAL AND DEPARTURE   GLEN AFFRIC

By bus From July to September, Ross's Minibuses (☎01463 761250, ⓦross-minibuses.co.uk) runs scheduled services to the car park at Glen Affric from Cannich (4 on Mon, Wed & Fri; 30min); Drumnadrochit (3 on Mon, Wed & Fri; 1hr 35min) and Inverness (2 on Mon, Wed & Fri; 2hr 10min). The vehicles will also carry bikes if given advance notice.

INFORMATION AND ACTIVITIES

Tourist information Notice boards are dotted around the glen; the Forestry Commission website (ⓦscotland .forestry.gov.uk/visit/glen-affric) includes an interactive map showing where they're located.

Volunteering For details of volunteer work in Glen Affric helping with restoration of the woodland, get in touch with Trees for Life (ⓦtreesforlife.org.uk).

ACCOMMODATION AND EATING

Bog Cotton Café At Cannich Camping & Caravan Park. The best option for food in Cannich, this welcoming chalet-like café has large windows overlooking the campsite.

Planning a hike? You can buy takeaway sandwiches here for £3 too. Daily 9am–5pm.

Cannich Camping & Caravan Park In the centre

Cannich ☎01456 415364, ⓦhighlandcamping.co.uk. Mountain bikes can be rented (£17/day) at this pretty, shaded campsite, which has good facilities, including wi-fi and a TV room. Per person **£8**

SYHA Glen Affric Allt Beithe, 20 miles southwest of Cannich ☎08452 937373, ⓦsyha.org.uk. Utterly remote, this SYHA hostel near the head of Glen Affric makes a convenient if rudimentary stopover on the 25-mile hike through Glen Affric to Shiel Bridge. A wind turbine and solar panels provide the hostel with electricity, but note that you'll need to bring all your own food. Dorms **£23**; twins **£58**

Inverness

Straddling a nexus of major road and rail routes, **INVERNESS** is the busy hub of the Highlands, and an inevitable port of call if you're exploring the region by public transport. Over a hundred miles from any other major settlement yet with a population rapidly approaching 100,000, Inverness is the only city in the Highlands. Crowned by a pink crenellated **castle** and lavishly decorated with flowers, the city centre still has some hints of its medieval street layout, though unsightly concrete blocks do an efficient job of masking it. Within walking distance of the centre are peaceful spots along by the Ness, leafy parks and friendly B&Bs located in prosperous-looking stone houses.

Brief history

The sheltered harbour and proximity to the open sea made Inverness an important entrepôt and shipbuilding centre during medieval times. **David I**, who first imposed a feudal system on Scotland, erected a castle on the banks of the Ness to oversee maritime trade in the early twelfth century, promoting it to royal burgh status soon after. Bolstered by receipts from the lucrative export of leather, salmon and timber, the town grew to become the kingdom's most prosperous northern outpost, and an obvious target for the marauding Highlanders who plagued this remote border area. A second wave of growth occurred during the eighteenth century as the Highland cattle trade flourished. The arrival of the **Caledonian Canal** and **rail links** with the east and south brought further prosperity, heralding a tourist boom that reached a fashionable zenith in the Victorian era, fostered by the royal family's enthusiasm for all things Scottish.

Inverness Castle

Looming above the city and dominating the horizon is **Inverness Castle**, a predominantly nineteenth-century red-sandstone building perched above the river. The original castle formed the core of the ancient town, which had rapidly developed as a port trading with Europe after its conversion to Christianity by St Columba in the sixth century. Robert the Bruce wrested the castle back from the English during the Wars of Independence, destroying much of the structure in the process, and while held by the Jacobites in both the 1715 and the 1745 rebellions, it was blown up by them to prevent it falling into government hands. Today's edifice houses the **Sheriff Court** and is not open to the general public. However, there are good views down the River Ness and various plaques and statues in the grounds, including a small plinth marking the start of the 73-mile Great Glen Way.

Inverness Museum and Art Gallery

Castle Wynd • Tues–Sat 10am–5pm • Free • ☎01463 237114, ⓦhighlifehighland.com

Below the castle, the revamped **Inverness Museum and Art Gallery** on Castle Wynd offers an insight into the social history of the Highlands, with treasures from the times of the Picts and Vikings, taxidermy exhibits such as "Felicity" the puma, caught in Cannich in 1980, and interactive features including an introduction to the Gaelic language. It also houses the Highland Photographic archive, and has impressive temporary art exhibitions.

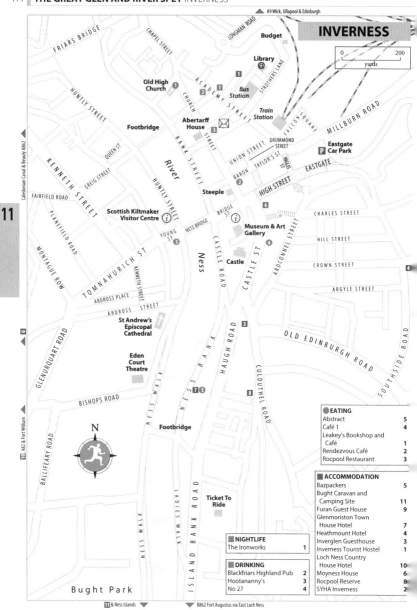

INVERNESS

0   200
yards

A9 Wick, Ullapool & Edinburgh

LONGMAN ROAD

FRIARS BRIDGE

CHAPEL STREET

Budget

Library @

ACADEMY STREET

STROTHERS LANE

Old High Church

CHURCH STREET

Bus Station

Train Station

FALCON SQUARE

MILLBURN ROAD

HUNTLY STREET

Footbridge

Abertarff House

BANK STREET

UNION STREET

DRUMMOND STREET

Eastgate Car Park

QUEEN ST

KENNETH STREET

GREIG STREET

River Ness

HUNTLY STREET

TAYLOR'S ST

BARON

HIGH STREET

INGLIS ST

EASTGATE

FAIRFIELD ROAD

Steeple

BRIDGE ST

CHARLES STREET

PLANEFIELD ROAD

Scottish Kiltmaker Visitor Centre

YOUNG ST

NESS BRIDGE

CASTLE ROAD

Museum & Art Gallery

ARDCONNEL STREET

HILL STREET

MONTAGUE ROW

TOMNAHURICH ST

KENNETH STREET

Castle

CASTLE ST

CROWN STREET

ARGYLE STREET

ARDROSS PLACE

ARDROSS STREET

St Andrew's Episcopal Cathedral

HAUGH ROAD

CULDUTHEL ROAD

OLD EDINBURGH ROAD

SOUTHSIDE ROAD

GLENURQUART ROAD

Eden Court Theatre

NESS WALK

NESS BANK

BISHOPS ROAD

BALLIFEARY ROAD

Footbridge

N

LADIES WALK

Ticket To Ride

ISLAND BANK ROAD

Bught Park

Caledonian Canal & Beauly A862

A82 & Fort William

& Ness Islands

B862 Fort Augustus via East Loch Ness

● EATING

Abstract	5
Café 1	4
Leakey's Bookshop and Café	1
Rendezvous Café	2
Rocpool Restaurant	3

■ ACCOMMODATION

Bazpackers	5
Bught Caravan and Camping Site	11
Furan Guest House	9
Glenmoriston Town House Hotel	7
Heathmount Hotel	4
Inverglen Guesthouse	3
Inverness Tourist Hostel	1
Loch Ness Country House Hotel	10
Moyness House	6
Rocpool Reserve	8
SYHA Inverness	2

■ NIGHTLIFE

| The Ironworks | 1 |

■ DRINKING

Blackfriars Highland Pub	2
Hootananny's	3
No 27	4

Old High Church

Church St, next to Leakey's bookshop • Grounds open to public; church open for Sun services 11.15am • Free • ☎ 01463 250802

The **Old High Church**, founded in 1171 and rebuilt on several occasions since, stands just back from the east bank of the river on Church Street, hemmed in by a walled graveyard. Those Jacobites who survived the massacre of Culloden were brought here and incarcerated prior to their execution in the cemetery.

f you look carefully you may see the bullet holes left on gravestones by the firing
squads.

Scottish Kiltmaker Visitor Centre

In the Highland House of Fraser shop at 4–9 Huntly St, on the river's west bank • Daily 9am–10pm, kilt-making demonstrations daily
am–5pm • £2.50 • ☎ 01463 222781, ⊛ highlandhouseoffraser.com

Entered through the factory shop, the **Scottish Kiltmaker Visitor Centre** is an
imaginative small attraction, complete with the outfits worn by actors for the
Braveheart and *Rob Roy* films, which sets out everything you ever wanted to know
about tartan. There's an interesting seven-minute film shown on the hour, and on
weekdays you can watch various tartan products being made in the workshop. The
finished products are, of course, on sale in the showroom downstairs, along with all
manner of Highland knitwear, woven woollies and classy Harris tweed.

Ness Islands

From **St Andrews Episcopal Cathedral**, on the west bank of the river, you can wander a
mile or so upriver to the peaceful **Ness Islands**, an attractive, informal public park
reached and linked by footbridges. Laid out with mature trees and shrubs, the islands
are the favourite haunt of local anglers.

Caledonian Canal

Half a mile upstream from the Ness Islands park, the River Ness runs close to the
Caledonian Canal, which was designed by Thomas Telford in the early nineteenth
century as a link between the east and west coasts, joining lochs Ness, Oich, Lochy and
Linnhe. Today its main use is recreational, and there are cruises through part of it to
Loch Ness (see p.407), while the towpath provides relaxing walks with good views.

ARRIVAL AND DEPARTURE
INVERNESS

ain station **left-luggage** lockers cost £3–5 for 24hr, depending on size (Mon–Sat 6.40am–7.50pm, Sun 10.40am–6.20pm);
e left-luggage room in the bus station costs £4/item/day (Mon–Sat 8.30am–5.30pm, Sun 9am–5.30pm).

By plane Inverness airport (☎ 01667 464000) is at
Dalcross, seven miles east of the city; from here, bus #11
every 30min, 6am–11pm, 25min; £3.75; ⊛ www
.stagecoachbus.com) goes into town, while a taxi (try
Tartan Taxis on ☎ 01463 222777) costs around £14.
Destinations Belfast (6 weekly; 1hr 5min); Birmingham
Mon–Fri & Sun 1 daily; 1hr 30min); Bristol (1–2 daily; 1hr
5min); Kirkwall (Mon–Sat 1–2 daily; 45min); London
Gatwick (4–5 daily; 1hr 50min); Luton (1 daily; 1hr 20min);
Manchester (Mon–Fri 2 daily, Sat & Sun 1 daily; 1hr 30min);
Stornoway (Mon–Fri 3–4 daily, Sat & Sun 1 daily; 40min).

By train The train station is on Station Square, just off
Academy St, to the northeast of the centre.
Destinations Aberdeen (Mon–Sat 11 daily; 5 on Sun; 2hr
min); Aviemore (Mon–Sat 11 daily, 7 on Sun; 40min);

Edinburgh (Mon–Sat 8 daily, 5 on Sun; 3hr 30min);
Glasgow Queen Street (3–4 daily; 3hr 20min); Kyle of
Lochalsh (Mon–Sat 4 daily, 2 on Sun; 2hr 30min); London
King's Cross (Mon–Fri & Sun 2 daily, 1 on Sat; 8hr–12hr
45min); Thurso (Mon–Sat 2 daily, 1 on Sun; 3hr 45min);
Wick (Mon–Sat 4 daily, 1 on Sun; 4hr 20min).

By bus The main bus hub is just north of the train station,
close to the public library.
Destinations Aberdeen (hourly; 3hr 50min); Aviemore (every
30min; 45min); Drumnadrochit (at least hourly; 30min); Fort
Augustus (up to 9 daily; 1hr); Fort William (up to 9 daily; 2hr);
Glasgow (5 daily; 3hr 25min–4hr); Kyle of Lochalsh (3 daily;
2hr); Nairn (every 20–30min; 45min); Perth (7 daily; 2hr
50min); Portree (3 daily; 3hr 15min); Thurso (Mon–Sat 5 daily,
3 on Sun; 3hr); Ullapool (2–4 daily; 1hr 25min).

GETTING AROUND

Car rental Budget, Railway Terrace, behind the train
station (☎ 01463 713333).
Bike rental Ticket to Ride at The Pavilion, Bellfield Park

(☎ 01463 419160, ⊛ tickettoridehighlands.co.uk), rents
out decent hybrid bikes for £20/day.

11

INFORMATION AND ACTIVITIES

Tourist office The tourist office is in an unsightly 1960s block on Castle Wynd, a 5min walk from the train station (April & May Mon–Sat 9am–5pm, Sun 10am–5pm; June Mon–Sat 9am–6pm, Sun 9.30am–5pm; July & Aug Mon–Sat 9am–6.30pm, Sun 9.30am–6pm; Sept & Oct Mon–Sat 9am–5pm, Sun 10am–4pm; Nov–March Mon–Sat 9am–5pm, Sun 10am–3pm). It stocks a wide range of literature, including free maps of the city and its environs, and the staff can book local accommodation for a £4 fee.

There's also a CalMac ferry booking office in the building (ⓦ calmac.co.uk).

Outdoor equipment Tiso Outdoor Experience at ? Henderson Rd, on the Longman Estate (Mon, Tues, Fri & Sa 9am–6pm, Wed 9.30am–6pm, Thurs 9am–7pm, Su 10am–5pm; ☎01463 729171, ⓦtiso.com), has a larg range of outdoor gear to rent or buy. There's also an indo climbing wall and a path for testing walking boots befor you buy.

TOURS

Inverness bus station is the departure point for a range of **day-tours** and **cruises** to nearby attractions, including Loc Ness, Skye, Orkney and the Moray Firth, where there's a chance to spot dolphins (see box, p.419). Inverness is also one o the few places where transport connections allow you to embark on a major **grand tour** of the Highlands.

The Highlands and Skye For exploring the northwest, ScotRail (☎08457 550033, ⓦscotrail.co.uk) sells a Highland Rover pass (£81.50), offering four days of unlimited travel over eight consecutive days, with many train, ferry and coach routes included. Buy tickets at the train station or online.

Loch Ness Loch Ness cruises typically incorporate a visit to a monster exhibition at Drumnadrochit and Urquhart Castle. Jacobite Cruises, on Dochgarroch Lock at the

northern point of the loch (☎01463 233999, ⓦjacobi* .co.uk), runs a 3.5hr coach trip (£33) to Loch Ness, includin a 30min cruise and admission to the Loch Ness Centre Exhibition (see p.411).

Orkney From June to August, John O' Groats Ferri (☎01955 611353, ⓦwww.jogferry.co.uk) runs day-trip to Orkney (£72), including visits to Kirkwall, Scapa Flo and the Ring of Brodgar. Departures leave daily fro Inverness at 7.15am.

ACCOMMODATION

HOTELS

Glenmoriston Town House Hotel 20 Ness Bank ☎01463 223777, ⓦglenmoristontownhouse.com. A smart contemporary hotel by the riverside just a few minutes' walk from the town centre, with muted decor and a good dining experience on offer at *Abstract* (see opposite). **£154**

Heathmount Hotel Kingsmill Rd ☎01463 235877, ⓦheathmounthotel.com. Reasonably central boutique hotel with blingy but comfortable rooms, some of which have four-poster beds; all come with Sky TV and an iPod dock. **£105**

Loch Ness Country House Hotel Off the A82 Fort William Rd ☎01463 230512, ⓦlochnesscountry househotel.co.uk. Luxurious country-house hotel, three miles southwest of central Inverness. Offers modern Scottish food, fine wines and more than two hundred malts, as well as very comfortable and spacious rooms. **£169**

★**Rocpool Reserve** Culduthel Rd ☎01463 240089, ⓦrocpool.com. Only a 10min walk south of the castle, this acclaimed hotel and restaurant has minimal but luxurious rooms (think white cotton bedsheets, subtle splashes of colour and jacuzzis in the high-end rooms), plus a swanky, French-inspired restaurant. **£253**

B&BS

Furan Guest House 100 Old Edinburgh Rd ☎01463 712094, ⓦfuran.co.uk. Good-value B&B a mile south of

the centre, run by former hoteliers. Has a good choice spotlessly clean rooms and a friendly resident cat. Bo direct for the best rates. **£85**

★**Invernglen Guest House** 7 Abertarff Rd ☎014 716350, ⓦinvernglenguesthouse.co.uk. Supremely co and colourful rooms in a handsome villa. Smoked Scotti salmon is on the breakfast menu, and they run single-d or two-day photography workshops, with trips to near glens and castles (£150 /day). **£95**

★**Moyness House** 6 Bruce Gardens ☎01463 2338 ⓦmoyness.co.uk. Warm, welcoming, upmarket B&B the west side of Inverness, with original Victorian featu (it was built in 1880) and a nice walled garden. **£78**

HOSTELS

Bazpackers 4 Culduthel Rd ☎01463 7176 ⓦbazpackershostel.co.uk. The most cosy and relaxe the city's hostels, with more than thirty beds, includ three doubles and two twins; some dorms are mix Good location in an 1826 townhouse, great views an garden, which is used for barbecues. Dorms **£18**; twi doubles **£50**

Inverness Tourist Hostel 24 Rose St ☎01463 2419 ⓦinvernesshostel.com. Conveniently located hostel n the bus station, with cheery, helpful staff. The downsid that the dorms are a little scruffy, and there's a sligl institutional feel to the place. Dorms **£20**

SYHA Inverness Victoria Drive, off Millburn Rd ☎01463 231771, ⓦsyha.org.uk. Big SYHA hostel with large kitchens and communal areas, plus six-bed family rooms (£138) and cheap singles (£22) in addition to the usual dorms. However, it's almost a mile from the centre, and the building is devoid of character. Dorms <u>£20</u>; twins <u>£46</u>

CAMPSITE

Bught Caravan and Camping Site Bught Park, a mile south of the centre ☎01463 236920, ⓦinverness caravanpark.com. Inverness's main campsite on the west bank of the river near the sports centre. Has good facilities, but it can get very crowded at the height of the season. April–Sept. Per person <u>£10</u>

EATING

Abstract 20 Ness Bank ☎01463 223777, ⓦglenmoriston townhouse.com. This award-winning French restaurant within the *Glenmoriston Town House Hotel* (see opposite) serves stylish French/Mediterranean/Asian fusion food; mains start at around £18. Tues–Sat 6–10pm.

★**Café 1** 75 Castle St ☎01463 226200, ⓦcafe1.net. You'll find contemporary Scottish cooking – like pan-seared venison with oven-roasted fig – in a bistro-style setting here. The restaurant's beef, lamb and pork is reared on a croft 8 miles north of Inverness. The three-course set menu is £32. Mon–Fri noon–2.30pm & 5–9.30pm, Sat 1–3.30pm & 6–9.30pm.

★**Leakey's Bookshop and Café** Church St ☎01463 239947. Prise yourself away from the old books and maps

at this beautiful galleried secondhand bookshop to enjoy a cup of tea, cake or a bowl of soup (£4) at the upstairs café. Mon–Sat 10am–5.30pm.

Rendezvous Café 14a Church St ☎01463 718444. Good coffee and big breakfasts are served inside and out at this modern corner café, which is one of the more relaxed places for coffee and a snack in the city centre (soup £2.80). Mon–Sat 8am–5pm, Sun 9am–4pm.

Rocpool Restaurant 1 Ness Walk ☎01463 717274, ⓦrocpoolrestaurant.com. Another of the city's excellent, smart-ish dining options, with a contemporary setting, attentive staff and deliciously rich food. The escalope of calves' liver with roasted purple figs is £19.95. Mon–Sat noon–2.30pm & 5.45–10pm.

DRINKING AND NIGHTLIFE

Blackfriars Highland Pub 93–95 Academy St ☎01463 233881. Popular pub where you can enjoy folk music most Friday and Saturday nights, plus a selection of real ale, cheap steak and gravy pies (£2.25), and bigger pub meals (food served daily 11am–9pm). Mon–Thurs 11am–midnight, Fri 11am–1am, Sat 11am–12.30am & Sun 12.30pm–11pm.

Hootananny's 67 Church St ☎01463 233651, ⓦhootananyinverness.co.uk. Lively watering hole with homely food (including a butternut squash and chickpea casserole served with cheese scones). Regular live music events, plus on Saturday afternoons there are ceilidhs from

2.30–4.30pm. Mon–Thurs noon–1am, Fri & Sat noon–3am, Sun 6.30pm–midnight.

The Ironworks 122b Academy St ☎0871 789 4173, ⓦironworksvenue.com. Large live music venue with space for a thousand music fans. The place to come for touring bands, stand-up comedy and the occasional club night. See website for events and opening times.

No 27 27 Castle St ☎01463 241999, ⓦnumber27 inverness.uk. Skinny bar/restaurant with a wide range of beers (there's a new guest ale every Sunday) and burgers and pasta dishes for around £9. Mon–Thurs 11am–11pm, Fri & Sat 11am–midnight, Sun 12.30pm–11pm.

DIRECTORY

Internet Inverness Library (Mon & Tues 9am–6.30pm, Wed 10am–6.30pm, Thurs 9am–8pm, Fri 9am–6.30pm, Sat 9am–5pm), near the bus station, offers free internet access (ID required).

Medical facilities The Raigmore Hospital (☎01463

704000) is at Old Perth Rd on the southeastern outskirts of town, close to the A9.

Police 6 Burnett Rd ☎ 01463 228411.

Post office 14–16 Queensgate (Mon & Wed–Sat 9am–5.30pm, Tues 9.30am–5.30pm).

Around Inverness

A string of worthwhile sights punctuates the approach to Inverness along the main route from Aberdeen. The low-key resort of **Nairn**, with its long white-sand beaches and championship golf course, stands within striking distance of several monuments, including whimsical **Cawdor Castle**, best known for its role in Shakespeare's *Macbeth*, and **Fort George**, one of several impressive Hanoverian bastions erected in the wake of the Jacobite rebellion. The infamous battle and ensuing massacre that ended Bonnie

Prince Charlie's uprising took place on the outskirts of Inverness at **Culloden**, where a visitor centre and memorial stones beside a heather-clad moor recall the gruesome events of 1746.

Northeast of Inverness is the **Moray Firth**, one of the UK's best locations for spotting dolphins (see box opposite). Closer to the city, where this inlet merges with the River Ness, is the start of the Beauly Firth, a sheltered sea loch bounded by the Black Isle in the north and the wooded hills of the Aird to the south.

GETTING AROUND

AROUND INVERNESS

By bus The region's main towns are well served by public transport, but to access Cawdor Castle and Fort George outside of the peak summer season (when special tourist routes are briefly opened) you will first need to travel to Nairn and then transfer to a taxi or the local Dial-a-Bus service (☎ 01667 456066).

By car The overloaded A96 links Inverness with Nairn, 16 miles northeast, with quieter minor roads leading off it to Fort George, Cawdor Castle and Culloden. Heading northwest from Inverness, most traffic uses Kessock Bridge (the A9) to cross the Moray Firth; the A862, which skirts the shoreline and the mud flats, offers a slower, more scenic alternative.

Culloden

6 miles east of Inverness off the B9006 • Visitor centre daily: April, May, Sept & Oct 9am–5.30pm; June–Aug 9am–6pm; Nov, Dec, Feb & March 10am–4pm • £11; entrance includes an audio-guide of the site; NTS • ☎ 0844 493 2159, ⊚ nts.org.uk/culloden • Hourly Stagecoach buses run from Falcon Square near Inverness train station to the visitor centre (35min)

The windswept moorland of **CULLODEN** witnessed the last-ever battle on British soil when, on April 16, 1746, the Jacobite cause was finally subdued – a turning point in the history of the Scottish nation. Today, this historic site attracts more than 200,000 visitors annually. Your first stop should be the superb **visitor centre**, which hosts costumed actors and state-of-the-art audiovisual and interactive technology, all employed to tell the tragedy of Culloden through the words, songs and poetic verse of locals and soldiers who experienced it. The *pièce de résistance* is the powerful "battle immersion theatre" where visitors are surrounded by lifelike cinematography and the sounds of the raging, bloody fight.

Every April, on the Saturday closest to the date of the battle, there's a small commemorative service at Culloden. The visitor centre has a reference library and will check for you if you think you have an ancestor who died here.

Brief history

The second Jacobite rebellion began on August 19, 1745, with the raising of the Stuarts' standard at **Glenfinnan** on the west coast (see p.443). Shortly after, Edinburgh fell into Jacobite hands, and Bonnie Prince Charlie began his march on London. The ruling Hanoverians had appointed the ambitious young Duke of Cumberland to command their forces, which included troops from the Lowlands and Highlands. The duke's pursuit, together with bad weather and lack of funds, eventually forced the Jacobite forces – mostly comprised of Highlanders – to retreat north. They ended up a **Culloden**, where, ill fed and exhausted after a pointless night march, they were hopelessly outnumbered by the government forces. The open, flat ground of Culloden Moor was totally unsuitable for the Highlanders' style of courageous but undisciplined fighting, which needed steep hills and lots of cover to provide the element of surprise, and they were routed.

The end of the clan system

After the battle, in which 1500 Highlanders were slaughtered (many of them as they lay wounded in the battlefield), **Bonnie Prince Charlie** fled west to the hills and islands where fiercely loyal Highlanders sheltered and protected him. He eventually escaped to France, leaving his supporters to their fate – and, in effect, ushering in the end of the **clan system**. The clans were disarmed, the wearing of tartan and playing of bagpipes

THE DOLPHINS OF THE MORAY FIRTH

The **Moray Firth**, a great wedge-shaped bay forming the eastern coastline of the Highlands, is one of only three areas of UK waters that support a resident population of **dolphins**. Around two hundred of these beautiful, intelligent marine mammals live in the estuary, the most northerly breeding ground in Europe for this particular species – the bottlenose dolphin (*Tursiops truncatus*) – and you stand a good chance of spotting a few, either from the shore or a boat.

One of the best places in Scotland, if not in Europe, to look for them is **Chanonry Point**, on the Black Isle – a spit of sand protruding into a narrow, deep channel, where converging currents bring fish close to the surface, and thus the dolphins close to shore; a rising tide is the most likely time to see them.

Several companies run dolphin-spotting **boat trips** around the Moray Firth. However, researchers claim that the increased traffic is causing the dolphins unnecessary stress, particularly during the all-important breeding period when passing vessels are thought to force calves underwater for uncomfortably long periods. So if you decide to go on a cruise to see the dolphins, which also sometimes provides the chance of spotting minke whales, porpoises, seals and otters, make sure that the operator is a member of the Dolphin Space Programme's accreditation scheme (Ⓦdolphinspace.org).

BOAT TOURS

Trips with these **accredited operators**, most of which operate between April and October, are especially popular in July and August, so be sure to book them well in advance. To get from Inverness to Avoch (20min) or Cromarty (50min) with public transport, take Stagecoach bus #26 from the bus station (at least hourly); note that not all services run as far as Cromarty, so check before boarding.

Phoenix Boat Trips Inverness Marina (Ⓣ07703 168097, Ⓦdolphin-trips-nairn.co.uk). Runs hour-long trips (£18) from Inverness Marina. When demand warrants it, they also run a 2hr 30min cruise to Fort George (see p.420) and Chanonry Point (£30).

Dolphin Trips Avoch On the northern side of the firth in Avoch (Ⓣ01381 622383, Ⓦdolphintripsavoch .co.uk). Hourly sailings from Avoch's harbour, at the eastern end of the village, with trips lasting an hour (£16).

Ecoventures Victoria Place, Cromarty (Ⓣ01381 600323, Ⓦecoventures.co.uk). Based on the Black Isle, on the northern side of the firth, Ecoventures runs 2hr wildlife cruises (£28) with the chance to spot dolphins, harbour porpoises and grey seals.

11

orbidden, and the chiefs became landlords greedy for higher and higher rents. The attle also unleashed an orgy of violent reprisals on Scotland, as unruly government roops raped and pillaged their way across the region; within a century, the Highland vay of life had changed out of all recognition.

he battlefield

lags mark out the positions of the two armies while simple headstones mark the **lan graves**. The **Field of the English**, for many years unmarked, is a mass grave for he fifty or so government soldiers who died (though as this government force also ncluded Scottish infantry regiments, the term "English" is a pseudo patriotic nisnomer).

Half a mile east of the battlefield, just beyond the crossroads on the main road, is the **umberland Stone**, thought for many years to have been the point from where the uke watched the battle. It is more likely, however, that he was much further forward nd simply used the stone for shelter. Elsewhere, the restored **Leanach cottage** marks he spot where thirty injured Jacobites were burnt alive.

awdor Castle

miles northeast of Inverness off the A96 • May–Oct daily 10am–5.30pm • £10.70; £6 for gardens & nature trails only •
01667 404401, Ⓦcawdorcastle.com • To get here, take a train or bus from Inverness to Nairn (several per hour; 20–45min), then
k up a taxi for the final 6 miles (around £14) – book ahead with Taxi 24/7 Nairn (Ⓣ01667 459595) and a driver will meet you at

the bus station; a cheaper but less reliable option is Nairn's Dial-a-Bus service (☎ 01667 456066), which must be booked by 6pm the day before you wish to travel

The pretty village of **CAWDOR**, eight miles east of Culloden, is the site of **Cawdor Castle**, a setting intimately linked to Shakespeare's *Macbeth*: the fulfilment of the witches' prediction that Macbeth was to become thane of Cawdor sets off his tragic desire to be king. Though visitors arrive here in their droves each summer because of the site's dramatic associations, the castle, which dates from the early fourteenth century, could not possibly have witnessed the grisly eleventh-century events on which the Bard's drama was based. However, the immaculately restored monument – a fairy-tale affair of towers, turrets, hidden passageways, dungeons, gargoyles and crenellations whimsically shooting off from the original keep – is still well worth a visit. Outside is a 1620 walled kitchen garden, a formal flower garden and a rambling 1960s wild garden.

11 Fort George

13 miles northeast of Inverness, near Ardersier • Daily: April–Sept 9.30am–5.30pm; Oct–March 10am–4.30pm • £8.50; HES • ☎ 01667 460232, ⓦ historicenvironment.scot • There are no scheduled bus services to Fort George – as with Cawdor Castle (see above), the best bet is to take a bus or train from Inverness to Nairn, where you can pick up a taxi or local Dial-a-Bus service for the final stretch

Eight miles of undulating coastal farmland separate Cawdor Castle from **Fort George**, an old Hanoverian bastion with walls a mile long, considered by military architectural historians to be one of the finest fortifications in Europe. Crowning a sandy spit that juts into the middle of the Moray Firth, it was built between 1747 and 1769 as a base for George II's army, in case the Highlanders should attempt to rekindle the Jacobite flame. By the time of its completion, however, the uprising had been firmly quashed and the fort has been used ever since as barracks; note the armed sentries at the main entrance and the periodic crack of live gunfire from the nearby firing ranges. The dog cemetery commemorates regimental hounds, and there's a small café.

Walking on the northern, grass-covered casemates, which look out into the estuary, you may be lucky enough to see a school of bottlenose **dolphins** (see box, p.419) swimming in with the tide. This is also a good spot for birdwatching: a colony of kittiwakes occupies the fort's slate rooftops.

Nairn

One of the driest and sunniest places in the whole of Scotland, **NAIRN**, sixteen miles east of Inverness, began its days as a peaceful community of fishermen and farmers. The former spoke Gaelic, the latter English, allowing James VI to boast that a town in his kingdom was so large that people at one end of the main street could not understand those at the other end. Nairn became popular in Victorian times, when the train line offered a convenient link to its revitalizing sea air and mild climate, and today the 11,000-strong population still relies on tourism, with all the ingredients for a traditional seaside holiday – sandy beach, ice-cream shops and fish-and-chip stalls. The town has two championship golf courses, and Thomas Telford's **harbour** is filled with leisure craft rather than fishing boats.

Nairn Museum

Viewfield House, King St • May–Oct Mon–Fri 10am–4.30pm, Sat 10am–1pm (last admission 30min before closing) • £3 • ☎ 01667 456791, ⓦ nairnmuseum.co.uk

The **Nairn Museum** provides a general insight into the history and prehistory of the area: the **Fishertown Room** illustrates the parsimonious and puritanical life of the fishing families, while the weapon-filled **Military Room** includes information on the battles of Culloden and Auldearn.

ARRIVAL AND DEPARTURE

NAIRN

By train Nairn's railway station is just south of the centre, where Chattan Drive meets Cawdor St. Services run every 1–2hr from/to Aberdeen (2hr), Elgin (25min), Forres (10min) and Inverness (20min).

By bus Buses arrive at and depart from a car park on King St, just south of the police station.

Destinations Aberdeen (hourly; 3hr 15min); Elgin (every 30min; 45min); Forres (every 30min; 25min); Inverness (every 20min; 45min).

GETTING AROUND AND INFORMATION

Bike rental Bikes are available from Bike and Buggy at 6a Falconers Lane (☎01667 455416, ⓦbikebugnairn.co.uk) for £15/day.

Tourist information There's a tourist information point within the Nairn Community & Arts Centre on King St

(Mon–Thurs 8.30am–10pm, Fri 8.30am–late, Sat 8.30am–5pm, Sun 9am–1pm & 5–9pm; ☎01667 453476, ⓦnairncommunitycentre.co.uk). Their handy "Welcome to Nairn" map is worth picking up.

ACCOMMODATION AND EATING

Boath House Auldearn, 2 miles east of Nairn ☎01667 454896, ⓦboath-house.com. The most luxurious place to stay in the area, this is a fine Georgian country house set in magnificent gardens, with its own Michelin-starred restaurant that draws upon organic produce and regional dairy, fish and meat suppliers. For an affordable taste of such luxury, book a lunchtime table (three courses for £30). Note that there is only one sitting for dinner. Daily 12.30–2.15pm & 7.30pm. **£295**

★ **Cawdor House** 7 Cawdor St ☎01667 455855,

ⓦcawdorhousenairn.co.uk. A bright and attractive B&B set in a fine 1850s villa, conveniently located between the train station and the main shopping street. Good choice of breakfasts, with vegetarians well catered for. **£76**

The Classroom 1 Cawdor St ☎01667 455999, ⓦtheclassroombistro.com. Nairn's most popular bar/restaurant, serving tasty light bites, lunches and dinners. Try the house salad with sun-blushed tomatoes and chargrilled chicken (£5.75); mains start at £14. Mon–Sat 10am–late, Sun 11am–late.

11

Strathspey

The richly forested area around the River Spey's upper reaches – **STRATHSPEY** – is a magnet for outdoor enthusiasts. Of Strathspey's scattered settlements, **Aviemore** absorbs the largest number of visitors, particularly in midwinter when it metamorphoses into the UK's busiest ski resort. The village struggles to reflect the charm of its surrounding area, but it's a good first stop for information, to sort out somewhere to stay or to find out about nearby outdoor activities, which are likely to seem very enticing after a glimpse of the soaring Cairngorms mountain range or the Glenmore Forest Park, a protected area that's home to one of Scotland's last remaining tracts of ancient Caledonian pinewood.

For summer visitors who'd rather avoid Aviemore, the planned Georgian town of **Grantown-on-Spey** makes a good alternative base. Further upriver, the sedate villages of **Newtonmore** and **Kingussie** are older-established holiday centres, more popular with anglers and grouse hunters than canoeists and climbers. The whole area boasts a wide choice of good-quality accommodation, particularly in the budget market, with various easy-going hostels run by and for outdoor enthusiasts.

Aviemore and around

The once-sleepy village of **AVIEMORE** was first developed as a ski and tourism resort in the mid-1960s and, over the years, fell victim to profiteering developers with scant regard for the needs of the local community. Despite recent attempts to turn things around, it remains a soulless hotchpotch of retail outlets, café-bars and characterless housing developments. That said, Aviemore is undeniably well equipped with services and facilities and is the most convenient base for the Cairngorms.

In summer, the main activities around Aviemore are **walking** (see box, p.424) and **watersports**, and there are great opportunities for pony trekking and fly-fishing (for the latter, the Aviemore tourist office provides a brochure outlining which permits you'll need). For both the adventurous and novice cyclist, the entire region is great for mountain biking; the **Rothiemurchus Estate** has several excellent (and non-technical) way-marked trails running through its extensive lands. Sailing, windsurfing and canoeing are also popular, with a specialist centre at **Loch Insh** providing lessons and loaning out equipment.

Wintertime sees the tourist focus switch away from the lochs and rivers and up towards the surrounding slopes, home to a well-established **ski resort** and the country only **dogsled centre**.

Strathspey Steam Railway

Aviemore Station, Dalfaber Rd • July & Aug three times daily; less regular service at other times • £11.25 return • ☏ 01479 810725, ⓦ strathspeyrailway.co.uk

The main attractions of Aviemore are its outdoor pursuits, though train enthusiasts are also drawn to the restored **Strathspey Steam Railway**, which chugs the short distance between Aviemore and Broomhill, just beyond Boat of Garten village. The return journey takes an hour and a half, with glimpses of the Cairngorm Mountains visible through the trees.

Cairngorm Sleddog Adventure Centre

Moormore Cottage, 3 miles east of Aviemore on the Rothiemurchus Estate • Sledding Oct–April, by appointment • Museum £8; 30min sled experience £60/person; 3hr sleddog safaris £175/person; no under 12s • ☏ 07767 270526, ⓦ sled-dogs.co.uk

Between Loch Morlich and Inverdruie lies the **Cairngorm Sleddog Adventure Centre**, the UK's only sleddog centre. On a pre-booked tour of the centre's museum you can meet the centre's dogs and learn more about the history of sledding. More exhilarating are the centre's highly recommended **sled trips** through the forest on a wheeled or ski-based sled, pulled by around ten dogs.

Cairngorm Ski Area

9 miles southeast of Aviemore • Ski season Dec–April, but varies depending on snowfall • ☏ 01479 861319, ⓦ cairngormmountain.org
Buses from Aviemore wind past Inverdruie, stopping at the Coire Cas car park, near the funicular railway's base station

By Continental European and North American standards it's all on a tiny scale, but occasionally snow and sun coincide at the **Cairngorm Ski Area** to offer beginner and expert alike a great day on the pistes. High above Loch Morlich in Glenmore Forest Park, the ski area is well served by public transport. From the car park at Coire Cas (2150ft), the year-round **funicular railway** is the principal means of getting to the top of the ski slopes.

Base station

Accessed via the Coire Cas car park • Ranger office daily: April–Oct 8.30am–5pm; Nov–March 8.30am–4.30pm • Free

At the Cairngorm Ski Area base station there's a **ranger office** where you can find out about various trails, check the latest weather report and – on fine days between May and October – join guided walks. The "Guided Walk @ The Top" (£20; allow 2hr 30min) involves riding the funicular partway up the mountain, joining a guided walk to the summit, and then taking the funicular back down to the base station. Guided mountain-bike descents of the mountain can also be arranged (from £22.50).

Cairn Gorm Mountain Railway

Leaves from the base station • Daily: May–Oct 10.20am–4.30pm; Nov–April 9am–4.30pm; every 20min; last train up 4pm • £12.50

The Cairngorm Ski Area base station is the departure point for the **Cairn Gorm Mountain Railway**, a two-car funicular system that runs to the top of the ski area.

WALKS AROUND AVIEMORE

Ordnance Survey Explorer maps 402 & 403

Walking of all grades is a highlight of the Aviemore area, though you should heed the usual safety guidelines (see box, p.43). These are particularly important if you want to venture into the subarctic climatic zone of the **Cairngorms**. However, as well as the high mountain trails, there are some lovely and well-signposted low-level walks in the area.

LOCH AN EILEAN

It takes an hour or so to complete the gentle circular walk around pretty Loch an Eilean (with its ruined castle) in the **Rothiemurchus Estate**, beginning at the end of the back road that turns east off the B970 a mile south of Inverdruie. The helpful estate visitor centres at the lochside and by the roadside at Inverdruie provide more information on other woodland trails.

RYVOAN PASS

Another good, shortish (half-day) walk leads along a well-surfaced forestry track from *Glenmore Lodge* (see opposite) up towards the **Ryvoan Pass**, taking in An Lochan Uaine, known as the "Green Loch" and living up to its name, with amazing colours that range from turquoise to slate grey depending on the weather.

MEALL A' BHUACHAILLIE

The **Glenmore Forest Park Visitor Centre** (daily 9am–5pm; ☎01479 861220, ⓦwww .forestry.gov.uk) by the roadside at the turn-off to *Glenmore Lodge* is the starting point for the three-hour return climb of Meall a'Bhuachaillie (2654ft), which offers excellent views and is usually accessible year-round. The centre has information on other trails in this section of the forest too.

A highly controversial £15 million scheme that was bitterly opposed by conservationists, the railway whisks skiers in winter, and tourists throughout the year, along a mile and a half of track to the top station at an altitude of 3600ft, not far from the summit of Cairn Gorm mountain (4085ft). The top station incorporates an exhibition/interpretation area and a café-restaurant from which spectacular views can be had on clear days. Note that there is no access beyond the confines of the top station and its open-air viewing terrace, so unless you're embarking on a winter skiing trip or a guided walk, you'll have to trudge up from the car park at the bottom.

ARRIVAL AND DEPARTURE

AVIEMORE AND AROUND

By train Aviemore's train station is on Grampian Rd, just south of the tourist office.

Destinations Edinburgh (Mon–Sat 12 daily, Sun 6 daily; 3hr); Glasgow (11 daily, Sun 6 daily; 2hr 50min); Inverness (Mon–Sat 11 daily, Sun 7 daily; 40min).

By bus Buses depart from outside the train station.

Destinations Cairngorm ski area (hourly; 30min); Edinburgh (6 daily; 3–4hr); Glasgow (5 daily; 2hr 40min; 3hr 20min); Grantown-on-Spey (Mon–Sat every 30min; 1hr, Sun 4 daily; 30min); Inverness (at least 11 daily; 45min).

GETTING AROUND AND INFORMATION

By bus The most useful local bus route is the #31, which runs hourly from Aviemore to the Cairn Gorm Mountain Railway (see p.422) via Rothiemurchus and Loch Morlich. The #34 service is also handy, running regularly to Grantown (roughly hourly; 40min) via Boat of Garten.

Tourist office 7 The Parade, Grampian Rd (April & May

Mon–Sat 9am–5pm, Sun 10am–5pm; June Mon–S 9am–6pm, Sun 9.30am–5pm; July & Aug Mon–S 9.30am–6.30pm, Sun 9.30am–6pm; Sept–Mar 9am–5pm, Sun 10am–4pm; ☎01479 810930). Offers accommodation booking service and reams of leaflets local attractions.

ACTIVITIES

FISHING

Rothiemurchus Estate Inverdruie (☎01479 810703, ⓦrothiemurchus.com). Has a stocked rainbow

trout-fishing loch, where success is virtually guaranteed A one-hour lesson followed by an hour's fishing cos £45.

HORSERIDING

Alvie Stables 5 miles south of Aviemore, near Kincraig (☎07831 495397, ⓦalvie-estate.co.uk). Family-friendly riding centre set in superb countryside a short drive from Aviemore, offering 30min lessons and longer guided rides (£25/hr).

OUTDOOR TRAINING

National Outdoor Training Centre Glenmore Lodge, 8 miles east of Aviemore (☎01479 861256, ⓦglenmore lodge.org.uk). For a crash course in surviving Scottish winters, you could do worse than try a week at the National Outdoor Training Centre, at the east end of Loch Morlich. This superbly equipped and organized centre (complete with cosy après-ski bar) offers winter and summer courses in hillwalking, mountaineering, alpine ski-mountaineering, avalanche awareness and much more.

SKIING

G2 Outdoor Plot 10, Dalfaber Industrial Estate, Aviemore (☎01479 811008, ⓦg2outdoor.co.uk). The experts at G2 Outdoor will provide one-to-one tuition in the art of telemarking (£120/2hr for 2 people) and back-country skiing. In summer, they also run kayaking and canyoning trips.

Mountain Spirit 98 Grampian Rd (☎01479 811788, ⓦmountainspirit.co.uk). If you want to buy or rent equipment, from ski boots and poles to mountaineering gear, pay a visit to this friendly and well-stocked shop in the centre of Aviemore (daily 9am–5.30pm).

The Ski School In the Day Lodge, near the funicular railway's base station in the Cairngorm Ski Area (☎08455 191191, ⓦtheskischool.co.uk). A good bet for ski/board rental and lessons, not least because of its proximity to the funicular, which whizzes skiers up to the slopes. Courses run mid-Dec to early April.

WATERSPORTS

See also G2 Outdoor in "Skiing", above.

Loch Insh Watersports Centre 6 miles up-valley near Kincraig (☎01540 651272, ⓦlochinsh.com). Offers sailing, windsurfing and canoeing trips and rents mountain bikes (£19/day), as well as boats for fishing. To save visitors travelling back and forth from Aviemore, the centre also offers accommodation.

ACCOMMODATION

HOTELS AND B&BS

Glenmore Lodge 8 miles east of Aviemore ☎01479 861256, ⓦglenmorelodge.org.uk. Specialist outdoor pursuits centre with excellent accommodation in en-suite twin rooms and self-catered lodges – guests can make use of the superb facilities, which include a pool, weights room, sauna and indoor climbing wall. Twins **£80**

Ravenscraig Guest House 141 Grampian Rd ☎01479 810278, ⓦaviemoreonline.com. This welcoming, family-friendly B&B has a handy central location. Single, double and family rooms available, plus a wide choice of breakfast options, including sausages bought from a local butcher. **£80**

HOSTELS AND BUNKHOUSES

Aviemore Bunkhouse Dalfaber Rd, next to the Old Bridge Inn ☎01479 811181, ⓦaviemore -bunkhouse.com. A large modern place beside a cosy pub and walking distance from the station, with six- and eight-bed dorms, plus private rooms. Dorms **£19**; doubles **£50**

SYHA Aviemore 25 Grampian Rd ☎01479 810345, ⓦsyha.org.uk. Aviemore's large SYHA hostel, with its own bike store and drying room, has rather plain rooms but is within easy walking distance of the town centre. Dorms **£17**; singles **£25**; twins **£45**

SYHA Cairngorm Lodge 6.5 miles east of Aviemore,

CAIRNGORMS NATIONAL PARK

The **Cairngorms National Park** (ⓦcairngorms.co.uk) covers almost 1750 square miles and incorporates the Cairngorms massif, the largest mountainscape in the UK and the only sizeable plateau in the country over 2500ft. It's the biggest national park in Britain, and while Aviemore and the surrounding area are regarded as the main point of entry, particularly for those planning outdoor activities, it's also possible to access the park from Perthshire as well as Deeside and Donside in **Aberdeenshire**. Crossing the range is a significant challenge: by road the only connection is the A939 from Tomintoul to Cock Bridge, frequently impassable in winter due to snow, while on foot the only way to avoid the high peaks is to follow the old cattle drovers' route called the **Lairig Ghru**, a very long day's walk between Inverdruie at the edge of Rothiemurchus and the Linn of Dee, near Inverey.

The name Cairngorm comes from the Gaelic An Carm Gorm, meaning "the blue hill" after the blueish-tinged stones found in the area. The park is home to a quarter of Scotland's native woodland and a quarter of the UK's threatened wildlife species; the tracts of ancient **Caledonian forest** at Rothiemurchus (see p.422) are even home to red squirrels.

by Loch Morlich ☎01479 861238, ⓦsyha.org.uk. This SYHA hostel towards the Cairngorms at Loch Morlich is located in an old shooting lodge. Closed Nov & Dec; Jan open weekends only. Dorms **£15**; twins **£34**

CAMPING

Rothiemurchus Caravan Park 2 miles southeast of Aviemore in Coylumbridge ☎01479 812800, ⓦrothiemurchus.net. Relaxed site for tents and caravans, nestled among tall pine trees at Coylumbridge, on the way to Loch Morlich. Per person **£12**

EATING AND DRINKING

★**Mountain Café** 111 Grampian Rd ☎01479 812473, ⓦmountaincafe-aviemore.co.uk. Above the Cairngorm Mountain Sports shop in the centre of town, Kiwi-run *Mountain Café* is reasonably priced, serving an all-day menu of wholesome snacks and freshly prepared meals for around £10. Specializes in wheat- and gluten-free food. Mon, Tues & Thurs 8.30am–5pm, Sat, Sun & Mon 8.30am–5.30pm.

Old Bridge Inn Dalfaber Rd, next to Aviemore Bunkhouse ☎01479 811137. Fire-warmed pub that hosts regular live music sessions and serves up decent

dinners; the menu includes a whole grilled sea bream with new potatoes and dressed leaves for £16. Mon–Thurs & Sun noon–midnight, Fri & Sat noon–1am; food served noon–3pm & 5.30–9pm.

The Winking Owl 123 Grampian Rd ☎01479 812368 ⓦthewinkingowl.co. Lively brewery pub serving draught ales and beers and classy Mediterranean/Scottish food. Mon–Thurs 11am–11pm, Fri & Sat 11am–1am, Sun 12.30–11pm; food served Mon–Sat noon–9.30pm, Sun 12.30–9.30pm.

Carrbridge

Worth considering as an alternative to Aviemore – particularly as a skiing base – **CARRBRIDGE** is a pleasant, quiet village about seven miles to the north. Look out for the spindly Bridge of Carr at the northern end of the village, built in 1717 and still making a graceful stone arch over the River Dulnain.

Landmark Forest Adventure Park

Just off the B9153 at the southern end of the village • Daily: April to mid-July 10am–5/6pm; mid-July to Aug 10am–7pm; Sept–March 10am–5pm • £17.95 • ☎08007 313446, ⓦlandmarkpark.co.uk

The main attraction in Carrbridge is the **Landmark Forest Adventure Park**, which offers families a host of excellent outdoor and indoor activities including forest walks, nature trails, water fun rides and a vertiginous wooden tower with 360-degree views of the surrounding mountains.

ARRIVAL AND DEPARTURE CARRBRIDGE

By train The train station is around half a mile west of the village centre, served by trains from Aviemore (5–6 daily; 10min) and Inverness (4–5 daily; 30min).

By bus Frequent buses (every 1–2hr; 15min) from Aviemore stop at the car park 200m south of the river the B9153.

ACCOMMODATION

MellonPatch Station Rd, roughly halfway between the train station and the Bridge of Carr ☎01479 841592, ⓦmellonpatch.com. Rambling house with good, large

colour-themed rooms and friendly owners. The rate including a full Scottish breakfast, are low for this area – a look out for woodpeckers and red squirrels in the garden. **£**

Boat of Garten

Seven miles northeast of Aviemore, close to the River Spey, sits the attractive village o **BOAT OF GARTEN**, which has a number of good accommodation options. A short driv or pleasant walk away on the other side of the river is the northeastern shore of **Loch Garten**, famous as the nesting site of the osprey, one of Britain's rarest birds.

Abernethy Forest RSPB Reserve

2.5 miles east of Boat of Garten, on the northeastern edge of Loch Garten • Reserve open year-round; visitor centre daily: April–Aug

10am–6pm; 3hr guided walks late May to early Aug Wed 9.30am • £5; guided walks £6 • ☎ 01479 831476, ⓦ rspb.org.uk • To get here from the village, cross the Spey then take the Grantown road; the reserve is signposted to the right

The **Abernethy Forest RSPB Reserve** on the shore of **Loch Garten**, a short drive from the attractive village of Boat of Garten and seven miles northeast of Aviemore, is famous as the nesting site of one of Britain's rarest birds. A little over fifty years ago, the **osprey**, known in North America as the fish hawk, had completely disappeared from the British Isles. Then, in 1954, a single pair of these exquisite white-and-brown raptors mysteriously reappeared and built a nest in a tree half a mile or so from the loch. One year's eggs fell victim to thieves, and thereafter the area became the centre of an effective high-security operation. There are now believed to be up to three hundred pairs nesting across the UK.

The best time to visit is between April and August, when the ospreys return from West Africa and the RSPB opens a **visitor centre**, complete with powerful telescopes and CCTV monitoring of the nest.

ARRIVAL AND GETTING AROUND | BOAT OF GARTEN

11

By train Strathspey Steam Railway trains (July & Aug daily, less frequent at other times) stop at the attractive old station in the centre of Boat of Garten and run to Aviemore (3 daily; 15min) and Broomhill (3 daily; 25min).

By bus Buses from Aviemore run hourly to Boat of Garten (12min), stopping outside the post office on Deshar Rd.

Bike rental You can rent two-wheeled transport from Cairngorm Bike and Hire near the station (daily July & Aug 9.30am–5.30pm; limited hours at other times; ☎ 01479 831745, ⓦ cairngormbikeandhike.co.uk) for £16/day.

ACCOMMODATION AND EATING

Anderson's Deshar Rd, 300m west of the train station ☎ 01479 831466, ⓦ andersonsrestaurant.co.uk. Attractive place for lunch or dinner, serving creative dishes based on local ingredients, like smoked and fresh local fish with samphire cream (£16.95). Daily noon–1.45pm & 6–9.30pm.

Boat Hotel Just across from the train station ☎ 01479 831258, ⓦ boathotel.co.uk. The most elegant place to stay in the village, with fresh, airy bedrooms. The hotel also has a bistro serving its own interpretations of Scottish favourites – from cullen skink to chicken tikka masala. **£110**

★ **Fraoch Lodge** 15 Deshar Rd ☎ 01479 831331, ⓦ scotmountainholidays.com. Excellent hostel providing high-quality home-cooked meals along with good facilities such as a purpose-built drying room. Enthusiastically run by experienced mountaineers, who also offer guided walking holidays. Minimum stay of two nights when booking in advance. Singles **£25**; twins **£50**

★ **Old Ferryman's House** Just east of the village, across the Spey ☎ 01479 831370. A wonderfully simple and homely B&B, with an old-school approach: a wood-burning stove, no TVs, lots of books and delicious evening meals and breakfasts. **£75**

Grantown-on-Spey

Around fifteen miles northeast of Aviemore, the pretty town of **GRANTOWN-ON-SPEY** makes a good alternative base for exploring the Strathspey area. Local life is concentrated around the central square, with its attractive Georgian architecture, but there are plenty of opportunities for hiking and biking in the immediate area.

ARRIVAL AND DEPARTURE | GRANTOWN-ON-SPEY

By bus Buses from Aviemore (roughly hourly; 35min) and Inverness (at least 2 per day Mon–Sat; 1hr 10min) stop on

Grantown-on-Spey's high street.

GETTING AROUND AND INFORMATION

Bike rental You'll find good bikes and decent coffee at BaseCamp Bikes (Mon–Sat 9.30am–5.30pm, Sun 10am–5pm; ☎ 01479 870050, ⓦ basecampmtb.com; £25/day), next door to the Co-op convenience store on the town's main square.

Tourist office 54 High St (April–June, Sept & Oct

Mon–Sat 9.30am–5pm, Sun 10am–3pm; July & Aug Mon–Sat 9am–5.30pm, Sun 10am–4pm; ☎ 01479 872242, ⓦ visitgrantown.co.uk). Grantown's seasonal tourist office has leaflets on local attractions, as well as maps of the area.

ACCOMMODATION

★**Dunallan House** Woodside Avenue ☎01479 872140, ⓦdunallan.com. Large house with big double rooms – all en suite or with private facilities – and comfy, welcoming lounges to relax in. The room on the top floor, with a freestanding bathtub across the landing, is the pick of the bunch. £92

Garth Hotel Castle Rd, at the north end of the town square ☎01479 872 836, ⓦgarthhotel.com. If you're after some reasonably swish accommodation head for the

large seventeenth-century *Garth Hotel*, where the restaurant serves respectable, traditional meat-based dinners. £101

★**Lazy Duck Hostel** Nethy Bridge, 6 miles south of town ☎01479 821642, ⓦlazyduck.co.uk. Tiny, eight-bed hostel with its own sauna, and various idyllic woodland huts (from £75). Makes a peaceful and comfortable retreat, with woodland camping (May–Oct) and great moorland walking on its doorstep. Dorms £19; camping per pitch £15

EATING AND DRINKING

Craig Bar Woodside Avenue ☎01479 872669, ⓦthecraigbar.co.uk. Snug pub full of military aviation memorabilia, from pictures of fighter planes to dangling model aircraft. Warm yourself by the fire with a pint of real ale while you choose some food. The choice is made easy; the jovial landlord only sells pies (£7.75), made with free-range meat. Mon–Fri 5pm–midnight, Sat & Sun 11am–midnight.

The High Street Merchants 74 High St ☎01479 872246, ⓦthehighstreetmerchants.com. An attractive wood-lined café and gallery on the high street serving organic, fairtrade and local food platters including venison salami are around £9, and they also serve pizzas. Tues–Sat 10am–5pm, Sun 10am–4pm.

Kingussie

Twelve miles southwest of Aviemore at the head of the Strathspey Valley, **KINGUSSIE** (pronounced "king-yoos-ee") is a pleasant village best known for the free-to-access ruins of **Ruthven Barracks**, which stand east across the river on a hillock. The best-preserved garrison built to pacify the Highlands after the 1715 rebellion, it makes for great exploring by day and is impressively floodlit at night.

ARRIVAL AND DEPARTURE

KINGUSSIE

By train Kingussie's train station is on Station Rd, just south of the A86.
Destinations Edinburgh (Mon–Sat 7 daily, 5 on Sun; 2hr 40min); Glasgow (Mon–Sat 4 daily, 2 on Sun; 2hr 30min); Inverness (Mon–Sat 12 daily, 7 on Sun; 55min); Newtonmore (Mon–Sat 5 daily, 3 on Sun; 5min).

By bus Buses arrive at and depart from near the *Duke of Gordon Hotel*, on the high street.
Destinations Edinburgh (5 daily; 3hr 30min); Inverness (Mon–Sat 8 daily, 5 on Sun; 1hr); Newtonmore (roughly hourly; 5min).

ACCOMMODATION AND EATING

★**The Cross** North of the centre off Ardbroilach Rd ☎01540 661166, ⓦthecross.co.uk. One of the most appealing places to stay in the whole of Speyside, this relaxed but stylish restaurant with rooms is located in a converted tweed mill on the River Gynack. The restaurant is the most ambitious (and costly) in the area, where a three-course meal carefully crafted from fresh Scottish

ingredients like Shetland lobster and Perthshire lamb cost £55. Daily 7–8.30pm. £110

The Tipsy Laird 68 High St ☎01540 66133 ⓦthetipsylaird.co.uk. No-frills pub on the high street which hosts occasional jam sessions and karaoke night. They have a good selection of malt whiskies and of simple bar food. Daily noon–11pm.

Newtonmore

Kingussie's closest neighbour, **NEWTONMORE**, is also its biggest rival. The two villages, separated by a couple of miles of farmland, both have long-established shinty teams that battle for dominance in the game – a fierce indigenous sport from which ice hockey and golf evolved. Newtonmore itself is notable for its top-notch **folk museum**, and there are plenty of mountain-biking routes in the forests to the south.

Highland Folk Museum

Kingussie Rd • Daily: April–Aug 10.30am–5.30pm; Sept & Oct 11am–4.30pm • Free; donation requested • ☎ 01540 673551,
ⓦ highlandfolk.com

Newtonmore's chief attraction is the fantastically evocative **Highland Folk Museum**. The outdoor site is a living history museum, with reconstructions of a working croft, a water-powered sawmill and a church where recitals on traditional Highland instruments are given. Look out for the costumed Highland Rising Re-enactment in July.

Laggan Wolftrax

8 miles southwest of Newtonmore on the A86, just beyond the junction with the A889 from Dalwhinnie • Free; car parking £3/day •
☎ 01463 791575, ⓦ scotland.forestry.gov.uk

Laggan Wolftrax is a superb, free facility with more than twenty miles of marked **mountain-biking trails** to suit all abilities. The three-mile-long green route is the best place for those starting out, but expert riders might prefer the gruelling black route, which traverses a steep and rocky staircase made up of uneven slabs. You can also walk and do orienteering here.

11

ARRIVAL AND INFORMATION

NEWTONMORE

By train The train station is south of the centre on Station Rd.

Destinations Edinburgh (Mon–Sat 3 daily, 2 on Sun; 2hr 30min); Glasgow (Mon–Sat 2 daily, 1 on Sun; 2hr 20min); Inverness (Mon–Sat 5 daily, 3 on Sun; 55min); Kingussie (Mon–Sat 5 daily, 3 on Sun; 5min).

By bus Buses for Edinburgh and Inverness arrive at and depart from Main St.

Destinations Edinburgh (Mon–Fri 5 daily; 3hr 25min);

Inverness (Mon–Sat 8 daily, 5 on Sun; 1hr 10min); Kingussie (roughly hourly; 5min).

Tourist information For tourist information, including maps of walking trails that pass local waterfalls and forests, try the volunteer-run Wildcat Centre on Main St (June–Aug Mon & Thurs 9.30am–12.30pm, Tues & Sat 9.30am–12.30pm & 2–5pm; Sept–May Mon, Thurs & Sat 9.30am–12.30pm; ☎ 01540 673131).

ACCOMMODATION

★ **Coig Na Shee** Laggan Rd, a 10min walk west of Main St ☎ 01540 670109, ⓦ coignashee.co.uk. A soothingly decorated B&B in an old Edwardian hunting lodge. Bright rooms with free wi-fi and good en-suite facilities. **£75**

The Pottery Bunkhouse 8 miles south of Newtonmore at Laggan Bridge ☎ 01528 544231, ⓦ pottery bunkhouse.co.uk. The most convenient accommodation for Laggan Wolftrax, with an excellent coffee shop, good-value six-bed dorms and a couple of five-person family rooms (£80), and even an outdoor hot tub (extra charge). Dorms **£18** (bedding £4 extra)

Speyside

Strictly speaking, the term **SPEYSIDE** refers to the entire region surrounding the River Spey, but to most people the name is synonymous with the "**whisky triangle**", stretching from just north of Craigellachie, down towards Tomintoul in the south and east to Huntly. Indeed, there are more whisky distilleries and famous brands concentrated in this small area than in any other part of the country.

At the centre of Speyside is the quiet market town of **Dufftown**, full of solid, stone-built workers' houses and dotted with no fewer than nine whisky distilleries. It's one of the best bases for a tour of whisky country, whether you're on the official Malt Whisky Trail or more independent explorations. Fewer visitors take the chance to discover the more remote glens, such as Glenlivet, which push higher up towards the Cairngorm massif, nestled into which is Britain's highest village, **Tomintoul**, situated on the edge of both whisky country and a large expanse of wild uplands. Though not surrounded by distilleries, the market town of **Huntly** has an impressive ruined castle and serves as a useful point of entry if you're coming into the region from the Aberdeenshire side.

THE SPEYSIDE WAY

The **Speyside Way** (Ⓦ speysideway.org), with its beguiling blend of mountain, river, wildlife and whisky, is fast establishing itself as an appealing and less taxing alternative to the popular West Highland and Southern Upland long-distance footpaths. Starting at **Buckie** on the Moray Firth coast (see p.385), it follows the fast-flowing River Spey from its mouth at Spey Bay south to **Aviemore**, with branches linking it to **Dufftown**, Scotland's malt whisky capital, and **Tomintoul** on the remote edge of the Cairngorm mountains. Some 65 miles long without taking on the branch routes, the whole thing is a five- to seven-day expedition, but its proximity to main roads and small villages means that it is excellent for shorter walks or even cycling trips, especially in the heart of **distillery** country between Craigellachie and Glenlivet; the Glenfiddich, Glenlivet, Macallan and Cardhu distilleries, as well as the Speyside Cooperage, lie directly on or a short distance off the route.

GETTING AROUND SPEYSIDE

11

By train The only mainline railway stops in the area are at Keith, twelve miles northeast of Dufftown, and Huntly.

By bus Transport connections are poor through the area, with irregular buses connecting the main villages.

Dufftown

The cheery community of **DUFFTOWN**, founded in 1817 by James Duff, fourth Earl of Fife, proudly proclaims itself "Malt Whisky Capital of the World" for the reason that it produces more of the stuff than any other town in Britain. A more telling statistic, perhaps, is that as a result Dufftown also reportedly raises more capital for the exchequer per head of population than anywhere else in the country. There are seven active distilleries around Dufftown, as well as a cooperage, and an extended stroll around the outskirts of the town gives a good idea of the density of whisky distilling going on, with glimpses of giant warehouses and whiffs of fermenting barley or peat smoke lingering on the breeze. On the edge of town along the A941 is the town's largest working distillery, **Glenfiddich** (see box opposite).

There isn't a great deal to do in the town itself, but it's a useful starting point for orienting yourself towards the whisky trail. Dufftown's four major streets converge on its main square, scene of a lively annual party at Hogmanay when free drams are handed out to revellers.

Whisky Museum

24 Fife St • Mon–Fri 1–4pm • Free • ☎ 01340 821181, Ⓦ keith whisky.dufftown.co.uk

The tiny volunteer-run **Whisky Museum** has a slightly disorganized collection of illicit distilling equipment, most of which has been donated by local distilleries. There are also plenty of old books and photographs to help to give visitors a flavour for the industry's humble beginnings.

Keith & Dufftown Railway

Station Rd • April–Sept Sat & Sun 3 trips daily (June–Aug also on Fri) • £11 return • ☎ 01340 821181, Ⓦ keith-dufftown-railway.co.uk for journey times

Restored by enthusiasts, the old Dufftown train station is now the departure point for the **Keith & Dufftown Railway**, which uses various restored diesel locomotives to chug forty minutes through whisky country to Keith, home of the Strathisla distillery (see box opposite).

ARRIVAL AND INFORMATION DUFFTOWN

By bus Buses from/to Aberlour (Mon–Sat hourly; 10–15min) and Elgin (Mon–Sat hourly; 50min) stop

outside the railway station.

Tourist office The small tourist office, based in t

handsome clocktower at the centre of the square (April–June & Sept Mon–Sat 10am–4pm; July & Aug Mon–Sat 10am–5pm; ☏01340 820501), can offer advice on which distilleries to visit.

ACCOMMODATION

Morven On the main square ☏01340 820507, ⓦmorvendufftown.co.uk. Simple, inexpensive B&B that's conveniently located near the tourist office and the Whisky Museum in the middle of town. The owners offer a small reduction for longer stays. **£45**

Tannochbrae Guest House 22 Fife St ☏01340 820541, ⓦtannochbrae.co.uk. Pleasant and enthusiastically run former provost's house near the main square, with six comfortable en-suite rooms, a lovely restaurant and a well-stocked whisky bar. **£80**

TOURING MALT WHISKY COUNTRY

Speyside is the heart of Scotland's **whisky** industry, and the presence of more than fifty **distilleries** is testimony to a unique combination of clear, clean water, benign climate and gentle upland terrain. Yet for all the advertising-influenced visions of timeless traditions, whisky is a multimillion-pound business dominated by huge corporations, and to many working distilleries visitors are an afterthought, if not a downright nuisance. That said, plenty are located in attractive historic buildings that now go to some lengths to provide an engaging experience for visitors. Mostly this involves a tour around the essential stages in the whisky-making process, though a number of distilleries now offer pricier connoisseur tours with a tutored tasting (or **nosing**, as it's properly called) and in-depth studies of the distiller's art. Some tours have restrictions on children.

There are eight distilleries on the official **Malt Whisky Trail** (ⓦmaltwhiskytrail.com), a clearly signposted seventy-mile meander around the region. These are Benromach, Cardhu, Dallas Dhu Historic Distillery, Glenfiddich, Glen Grant, Glenlivet, Glen Moray and Strathisla. Unless you're seriously interested in whisky, it's best to just pick out a couple that appeal. All offer a guided tour. You could cycle or walk parts of the route, using the Speyside Way (see box opposite). The following is a list of selected highlights from the area (not all are on the official trail).

Glen Grant Rothes ☏01340 832118, ⓦglengrant.com. Makes a well-known, floral whisky aggressively marketed to the younger customer. The highlight here is the attractive Victorian gardens, a mix of well-tended lawns and mixed, mature trees, a tumbling waterfall and a hidden whisky safe. Tours £5 including voucher. April–Oct 9.30am–5pm; Nov–March Mon–Sat 9.30am–5pm, Sun noon–5pm.

Glendronach 8 miles northeast of Huntly ☏01466 730202, ⓦglendronachdistillery.co.uk. Off the official trail, this isolated distillery makes much of the fact that, uniquely, its stills are heated in the traditional method by coal fires. Tours £5. May–Sept daily 10am–4.30pm; Oct–April Mon–Fri 10am–4.30pm.

Glenfiddich On the A941 just north of Dufftown ☏01340 820373, ⓦglenfiddich.com. The biggest and slickest of all the Speyside distilleries, despite the fact that it's still owned by the same Grant family who founded it in 1887. It's a light, sweet whisky packaged in triangular bottles – unusually, the bottling is still done on the premises and is part of the £10 tours (offered in various languages). April–Oct daily 9.30am–4.30pm; Nov–March daily 11am–3pm.

Glenlivet On the B9008 to Tomintoul ⓦuk.theglenlivet.com. A famous name in a lonely hillside setting. This was the first licensed distillery in the Highlands, following the 1823 act that aimed to reduce illicit distilling and smuggling. The Glenlivet 12-year-old malt is a floral, fragrant, medium-bodied whisky. Tours are free. Easter to mid–Nov Mon–Sat 9.30am–4pm, Sun noon–4pm.

Macallan Near Craigellachie ☏00340 871471, ⓦthemacallan.com. Small tours, and a classy whisky aged in sherry casks to give it a rich colour and flavour. Tours £15. Easter–Sept Mon–Sat 9.30am–6pm; Oct–Easter Mon–Fri 9.30am–5pm.

Strathisla Keith ☏01542 783044, ⓦmaltwhiskydistilleries.com. A small, old-fashioned distillery claiming to be Scotland's oldest (1786); it's certainly one of the most attractive, with the River Isla rushing by. Inside there's an old-fashioned mash tun and brass-bound spirit safes. You can arrive here on one of the restored trains of the Keith & Dufftown Railway. Tours £7.50. April–Oct Mon–Sat 9.30am–5pm, Sun noon–5pm.

Speyside Cooperage Craigellachie ☏01340 871108, ⓦspeysidecooperage.co.uk. This cooperage – which produces and repairs the casks used in whisky-making – is the only stop on the official trail that isn't a distillery, and offers fascinating glimpses of a highly skilled and vital part of the industry. Tours £3.50. Mon–Fri 9.30am–5pm.

11

EATING AND DRINKING

Dufftown Glassworks 16 Conval St ☎01340 821534, ⓦ dufftownglassworks.com. This combined café and gallery is a smart place to sit with a coffee and plan your trip around whisky country. The rocky road slices (£2) are scrumptious. Daily 10.30am–5pm.

Taste of Speyside 10 Balverie St, just off the main square ☎01340 820860, ⓦ atasteofspeyside.com. You can sample a range of quality Scottish food at the town's most popular restaurant, where mains include a vegetable crumble made with tomato and basil sauce. You'll pay around £20 for two courses. Tues–Sat noon–2pm & 6–9pm.

SHOPPING

The Whisky Shop 1 Fife St ☎01340 821097, ⓦ whiskyshopdufftown.co.uk. A mind-bogglingly well-stocked shop with over six hundred malts and umpteen beers, produced not just on Speyside but all over Scotland. Mon–Sat 10am–6pm & Sun 10am–5pm.

Tomintoul

Deep into the foothills of the Cairngorms, **TOMINTOUL** (pronounced "*tom*-in-towel") is, at 1150ft, the highest village in the Scottish Highlands, and the northern gateway to the **Lecht Ski Area** (see below). Its long, thin layout is reminiscent of a Wild West frontier town; Queen Victoria wrote that it was "the most tumble-down, poor looking place I ever saw". A spur of the Speyside Way connects Ballindalloch through Glenlivet to Tomintoul, and there are plenty of other terrific walking opportunities in the area, as well as some great routes for mountain biking.

Glenlivet Crown Estate

If you've come this far it's worth exploring the **Glenlivet Crown Estate**, an extensive tract of carefully managed land abutting Tomintoul; information and useful maps about its wildlife (including reindeer) and the numerous paths and bike trails are available from the tourist office or the estate **ranger's office** at the southern end of the long main street.

ARRIVAL AND INFORMATION

TOMINTOUL

By car The only reliable way to reach Tomintoul is by car; from Grantown-on-Spey the A939 snakes east, passing Tomintoul on the way to Ballater.

Tourist office On the central square, the helpful tourist office (April–Oct Mon–Sat 10am–5pm; ☎01309 696261) also acts as the local museum, with mock-ups of an old farm kitchen and a smithie.

Estate ranger's office At the southern end of Main St (Mon–Fri 9am–5pm; ☎01479 870070, ⓦ glenlivetestate .co.uk). The place to come for information on local walks and events.

ACCOMMODATION

As well as the options listed below, it's possible to **camp** beside the Glenlivet Estate ranger's office for free, though there are no facilities here whatsoever.

★ **Argyll Guest House** 7 Main St ☎01807 580766, ⓦ argyletomintoul.co.uk. Six spacious and comfy rooms, and a great breakfast choice including home-made bread and porridge. The hosts give expert advice on local hiking and biking. **£64**

Smuggler's Hostel Main St ☎01807 580364, ⓦ thesmugglershostel.co.uk. Billed as the highest hostel in the Highlands and run by the community, with good facilities including drying sheds, a well-equipped kitchen and spacious communal areas. Dorms **£17**; doubles **£50**

Lecht Ski Area

7 miles southeast of Tomintoul along the A939 • Open year-round • Full-day pass £28; ski rental costs £20/day from the ski school at the base station • For information on skiing and road conditions, call the base station on ☎01975 651440, or check ⓦ lecht.co.uk or ⓦ visitscotland.com/see-do/active/skiing-snowsports

The **Lecht** is the most remote of Scotland's ski areas, but it works hard to make itself appealing with a range of winter and summer activities. While its runs include some gentle beginners' slopes, there's little really challenging for experienced skiers other than a **Snowboard Fun Park**, with specially built jumps and ramps. Snow-making equipment helps extend the snow season beyond January and February, while downhill bike tracks open in the summer (there's no bike rental on site, though).

Huntly

The ancient burgh of **HUNTLY**, ten miles east of Dufftown, has one of the smallest and prettiest, albeit rather skeletal, castles in the area. The town also makes a good base for salmon fishing on the Deveron River, which flows right past the castle, and it is just on the fringe of whisky country, with the isolated **Glendronach Distillery** (see box, p.431) the nearest to town.

Huntly Castle

Half a mile north of town near the river • April–Sept daily 9.30am–5.30pm; Oct–Nov Mon–Wed, Sat & Sun 9.30am–4.30pm • £5.50; HES • ☎ 01466 793191, ⓦ historicenvironment.scot

Huntly Castle, power centre of the Gordon family, sits in a peaceful clearing on the banks of the Deveron River, a ten-minute walk from the town centre down Castle Street. Built over a period of five centuries, it became the headquarters of the Counter-Reformation in Scotland in 1562. During the Civil War the earl of Huntly, who had supported Charles I, was shot against his castle's walls, after which the place was left to fall into ruin.

ARRIVAL AND DEPARTURE

By train Huntly is on the main train route from Aberdeen to Inverness; services run up to 11 times a day from/to Aberdeen (55min), Elgin (35min) and Inverness (1hr 25min). The station is on the east side of town, across the River Bogie.

By bus Hourly buses from/to Aberdeen (1hr 20min), Elgin (1hr) and Inverness (2hr 30min) arrive at and depart from Gordon St in the town centre.

INFORMATION

Tourist office 9a The Square (April–Oct Mon–Sat 10am–5pm, July to mid-Aug also Sun 10am–4pm; ☎ 01466 792255). The friendly tourist office is in the middle of town, on the main square, and can provide information on the best places to go fishing.

ACCOMMODATION

Castle Hotel Marquis Drive ☎ 01466 792696, ⓦ castlehotel.uk.com. The former home of the duke of Gordon is now a classy hotel that stands at the end of a long driveway behind the castle ruins. The best rooms here have four-poster beds and fireplaces, and the on-site restaurant serves indulgent mains like baked guinea fowl for around £17. **£125**

Coynachie Guesthouse Gartly, about 5 miles south of Huntly ☎ 01466 720383, ⓦ coynachieguesthouse.com. Handsome, family-run B&B in the countryside south of Huntly, with three good-sized bedrooms and a cosy breakfast room. **£90**

The north and northwest Highlands

THE WEST HIGHLAND RAILWAY

The north and northwest Highlands

As you drive along a single-track road, with bagpipes blaring on Gaelic radio and only sheep, stags and moody Highland cattle for company, the bleak yet beautiful north and northwest Highlands feels like nowhere else in Britain. Here the weather is as changing as the scenery: a combination of bare mountains, remote glens, dark lochs and tumbling rivers surrounded on three sides by a magnificent coastline. Although the landscape, along with its tranquility and space, is the main attraction, so too is the enduring sense of remoteness; the vast peat bogs in the north are among the most extensive and unspoilt wilderness areas in Europe and some of the west-coast crofting villages can still be reached only by boat.

Different weather conditions and cultural histories give each of the three coastlines a distinct character. For many visitors, the Highlands' **west coast** is the reason to visit Scotland. The Vikings, who ruled the region in the ninth century, called it the "South Land", from which the modern district of Sutherland takes its name. After Culloden, the Clearances emptied most of the inland glens of the far north, and left the population clinging to the coastline, which is the main reason to come. Cut by fjord-like **sea lochs**, it is scalloped by white-sand **beaches** or **waterfalls** in high, shattered cliffs, with **mountains** sweeping up from the shoreline. Weather fronts roll over rapidly, but when the sun shines, the sparkle of the sea, the rich colours in the clear light and the clarity of the views to the Hebrides are pure magic. With exhilarating scenery everywhere you look, this isolated region has historically seen far fewer visitors than the rest of Scotland, but the wiggling single-track roads are slowly getting busier as touring visitors from around the world flock to complete the new **North Coast 500** road trip. The north and northwest Highlands also provide some of the best **cycling**, **walking** and **sea-kayaking** in Britain, superlative trout and salmon **fishing**, and wildlife by the ton. In fact the only issues are the west coast's predictably unpredictable **weather**, and **midges** that drive even the locals to distraction from June to August.

The most visited part of the west coast is the stretch between Kyle of Lochalsh and Ullapool. This is **Wester Ross**, with quintessentially west-coast scenes of beautiful coast set against some of Scotland's most impressive mountains and Skye and the Western Isles on the horizon. The obvious highlights are the mountainscape of **Torridon**, **Gairloch**'s sandy beaches, the botanic gardens at **Inverewe**, and **Ullapool** itself, a bustling fishing town and launch pad for the Outer Hebrides. However, press on north or south and you get a truer sense of the isolation that makes this coast so special. Traversed by few roads, the remote northwest is wild and bleak. Villages in the southwest tend to be more sheltered, but they are separated by some of the most extensive wilderness areas in Britain – lonely peninsulas like **Ardnamurchan**, **Glenelg** or **Knoydart**, a magnificently untamed expanse with no road access and the remotest pub in mainland Britain.

The other coasts receive fewer visitors, and of the two the **north coast** is more popular. Stretching from **Cape Wrath** at the very northwest tip of the mainland to **John O'Groats**, it is even more rugged than the west, its sheer cliffs and white-sand bays bearing the

PASSING PLACE

NORTH COAST 500

Highlights

❶ North Coast 500 Scotland's answer to Route 66 loops around the entire north and northwest Highlands; an unforgettable road trip. **See p.440**

❷ The West Highland Railway Ride the rails of Britain's most scenic train journey from Glasgow to Mallaig via Fort William for scenery that's more spectacular by the mile. **See p.444**

❸ Knoydart It can only be reached by boat or a two-day hike, but thrilling remoteness is not the only reason to visit Britain's last wilderness – there's also its most isolated pub, *The Old Forge*. **See p.446**

❹ Foodie Lochinver The Highlands' foodie capital offers everything from slap-up pies to Michelin-starred cuisine, with some Scottish tapas thrown in for good measure. **See p.462**

❺ Suilven A glimpse of the fantastical sugarloaf outline of this iconic mountain is reason enough to travel to Assynt. **See p.462**

❻ Dunnet Head Come to the true tip of mainland Britain, all remote red cliffs and empty seascapes to Orkney. **See p.471**

❼ Cromarty A lovely mix-and-match of handsome Georgian townhouses and cute cottages all packaged up in a friendly small town on the coast. **See p.473**

HIGHLIGHTS ARE MARKED ON THE MAP ON PP.438–439

THE NORTH & NORTHWEST HIGHLANDS

HIGHLIGHTS

1. North Coast 500
2. The West Highland Railway
3. Knoydart
4. Foodie Lochinver
5. Suilven
6. Dunnet Head
7. Cromarty

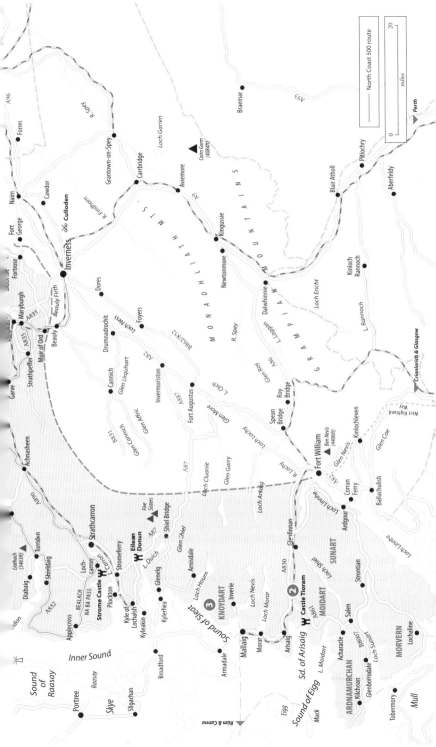

THE NORTH COAST 500

Unveiled in 2014 as "Scotland's answer to Route 66", the **North Coast 500** was created to tempt visitors up to this most remote corner of mainland Scotland, and it seems to be working. While driving or cycling in the north Highlands, you'll be asked "are you doing the North Coast 500" on a daily basis, and you probably are doing at least a stretch of the touring route, even if you didn't know. There are few alternative ways of getting around this part of Scotland, and certainly none more impressive than this route hugging the coastal fringes of the north Highlands.

With Inverness, Applecross, Durness and John O'Groats forming the four cardinal points of the route, pretty much everything in this chapter is covered by the North Coast 500. If you are on a mission to tour the full five hundred miles, try to incorporate **Plockton** and **Cromarty** – and, if time permits, **Skye** – into your itinerary; all short detours from the designated route but highlights of the region. See ⓦ northcoast500.com for more information on the official route.

brunt of frequently fierce Atlantic storms. The only town here is the surfing hub of **Thurso**, jumping-off point for the main ferry service to Orkney.

All of this makes the fertile **east coast** of the Highlands such a surprise. Stretching north from Inverness to the old herring port of **Wick**, it is a place of rolling moors, green fields and woodlands which run down to the sandy beaches of the **Black Isle** and **Cromarty** and **Dornoch firths**. If the west coast is about raw nature, the east is one of human history: **Golspie**'s Sutherland Monument and castle, **Dornoch**'s fourteenth-century sandstone cathedral, relics of the **Picts** and several sites linked to the **Clearances**.

12

GETTING AROUND   THE HIGHLANDS

Getting around the **Highlands**, particularly the remoter parts, can be tricky without your own transport. **Bus services** are sporadic and often cease entirely on Sunday. Most sizeable villages have a petrol station or 24-hour fuel supply (typically card payment only), although these are few and far between in the west and north, so fill up early and be prepared for higher prices. Bear in mind, too, that the Highlands' single-track roads are far from fast; remember to pull in to let drivers behind overtake.

Morvern to Knoydart: the Rough Bounds

Its Gaelic name *Garbh-chiochan* translates as the "**Rough Bounds**", implying a region geographically and spiritually apart, and the southwest corner of the Highlands is indeed remote and sparsely populated. From the empty district of **Morvern** to the isolated **Knoydart** peninsula are lonely mountains and moors, a rocky, indented coast studded with white beaches, and wonderful views to Mull, Skye and other islands. It's scenery that begs you to spend time exploring on foot.

Morvern

Bounded on three sides by sea lochs and in the north by desolate Glen Tarbet, the mountainous **Morvern peninsula** lies at the southwest corner of the Rough Bounds. Many inhabitants of St Kilda were settled here when the island was abandoned (see box, p.513), and the landscape can seem bleak until the coast reveals views to Mull.

Lochaline

Most visitors only travel through the Morvern peninsula to get to **LOCHALINE** (pronounced "loch-*aa*lin") on the **Sound of Mull**, little more than a scattering of houses around a small pier built as a work-for-food scheme during famine in 1846. From here a small ferry chugs to **Fishnish** – the shortest crossing to Mull from the mainland and cheaper than the Oban–Craignure crossing with a car. The town is also the departure point for excellent wreck-diving and snorkelling excursions in the Sound of Mull.

ARRIVAL AND DEPARTURE MORVERN

By bus Shiel Buses (☎ 01967 431272, ⊛ shielbuses.co.uk) runs a service between Morvern and Fort William on Tues, Thurs and Fri (1hr 25min), plus a Sat service from mid-June to early Sept. By request, the bus goes as far as Drimnin (40min on from Lochaline), at the northwest corner of Morvern, for ferries to Tobermory.

By ferry To save the long journey around Loch Eil into the peninsula, a ferry nips across to Ardgour from Corran Ferry,

9 miles south of Fort William, every 20–30min (Mon–Sat 6.30am–9.30pm, Sun 8.45am–9.30pm; 10min). In addition, two services link the peninsula to Mull: a CalMac car ferry (☎ 01854 612358, ⊛ calmac.co.uk) from Lochaline to Fishnish (Mon–Sat 7am–6.35pm, Sun 8.45am–5.45pm; 15min) and a passenger-only private charter service from Drimnin to Tobermory, run by Ardnamurchan Charters (☎ 01972 500208, ⊛ www.west-scotland-marine.com).

ACTIVITIES

Lochaline Dive Centre Lochaline ☎ 01967 421627, ⊛ lochalinedivecentre.co.uk. Based in the village centre, this outfit specializes in underwater archeology on local

wrecks, and provides drift, shallow, scenic and shore dives, and snorkelling excursions. Also offers air filling and cylinder rental, plus a four-star lodge and the *O2 Café*.

EATING

★**Whitehouse Restaurant** Lochaline ☎ 01967 421777, ⊛ thewhitehouserestaurant.co.uk. Arguably the best reason to visit Morvern, this is one of the Highlands' finest restaurants. Simple style belies outstanding modern

European cooking that showcases local meat and seafood like smoked mussels and hand-dived scallops. Best deals at lunch (two courses around £20). Booking essential. Easter–Oct Tues–Sat 11am–9pm.

The Ardnamurchan peninsula

12

The **Ardnamurchan peninsula** is the most westerly point on the British mainland. Once ruled by Norse invaders, the peninsula lost most inhabitants during the Clearances and only a handful of crofting settlements cling to the coastline, making this one of the west coast's backwaters. Yet with its empty beaches and sea vistas, Ardnamurchan is an inspiring place.

A single-track road threads down its length, a superb route with a real sense of transition from ancient mossy oak forest to salt-sprayed moorland as you approach the sea. It's not fast, but this is slow travel at its best, with a huge variety of wildlife and scenery to make walking a pleasure; pick up a locally produced guide from tourist offices and most shops.

Strontian and Salen

Actually part of the near-roadless regions of **Sunart** and **Ardgour**, **STRONTIAN** serves as a gateway base for the peninsula. The village's moment of fame came in 1722, when local lead mines yielded the first-ever traces of **strontium**, which was named after the village. The hamlet of **SALEN**, spread around another sheltered notch on the loch's shore, marks the turn-off for Ardnamurchan Point: from here it's 25 miles of scenic driving beside Loch Sunart – slow and all the better for it. The turf-roofed **Garbh Eilean Wildlife Hide** (free access) five miles west of Strontian is an opportunity to peer for seals, seabirds and the occasional eagle; on Mondays between Easter and October you'll find a knowledgeable ranger on-hand to help spot wildlife.

Ardnamurchan Natural History Visitor Centre

miles west of Glenborrodale • Easter–Oct Mon–Sat 9am–5pm, Sun 10am–4pm • Free • ☎ 01972 500209, ardnamurchannaturalhistorycentre.com

The **Ardnamurchan Natural History Visitor Centre**, a small, child-friendly natural history centre, introduces the flora, fauna and geology of Ardnamurchan. The centre is in a timber "Living Building" designed to allow in wildlife – pine martens nest within the walls, long-eared bats occasionally hang from the rafters and a glass wall descends into a wildlife pond. Otherwise there are the usual wildlife displays and a film, plus cameras trained on whatever's most interesting – the pine martens, perhaps, or a heronry opposite.

Kilchoan and Ardnamurchan Lighthouse

Lighthouse exhibition April–Oct daily 10am–5pm · £5 · **Lighthouse tour** April–Oct daily 11am–4pm · £6 · ☎ 01972 510210,
ⓦ ardnamurchanlighthouse.com

KILCHOAN is Ardnamurchan's main village – a modest crofting settlement which straggles along the Sound of Mull. From here, the road continues to **Ardnamurchan Point**, the most westerly point in mainland Britain, marked by a 118ft-high **lighthouse**. The lighthouse buildings house a small café and an **exhibition** on local history, while tours go up the tower to see the lighting mechanism. Three miles northeast of the lighthouse, **Sanna Bay** is a white-sand beach with unforgettable views of the Small Isles.

ARRIVAL AND DEPARTURE

By bus A single service (Mon–Sat; ☎ 01967 431272) that begins at Fort William (currently 1.25pm) goes via Corran Ferry to reach Strontian (50min) before continuing to Kilchoan (2hr 40min).
By ferry A CalMac (ⓦ calmac.co.uk) car ferry operates

THE ARDNAMURCHAN PENINSULA

between Tobermory (Mull) and Kilchoan (Mon–Sat 7 daily, plus Sun May–Aug 5 daily; 35min).
By car The single-track road from Salen to Ardnamurchan Point is 25 miles long; allow about 1hr 30min in each direction.

INFORMATION AND ACTIVITIES

Strontian tourist office Run by Visit Scotland, on the village green (Easter–Oct daily 10am–4pm; ☎ 01967 402382).
Kilchoan tourist office In the community centre (Mon–Sat: Easter–Oct 9am–5pm; Nov–March 10am–4pm; ☎ 01972 510711, ⓦ ardnamurchan.com).

Ardnamurchan Charters ☎ 01972 500208 ⓦ www.west-scotland-marine.com. Operates wildlife watching trips from Laga Bay, near Acharacle, to observe dolphins, seals, basking sharks, whales and possibly sea eagles. Also run trips around the Isle of Carna (ⓦ carnaconservation.org).

ACCOMMODATION AND EATING

STRONTIAN

Ariundle Centre 1 mile north of Strontian ☎ 01967 402279, ⓦ ariundlecentre.co.uk. This tearoom and bunkhouse is a godsend for walkers and cyclists. Expect inexpensive fresh lunches and dinner such as beef casserole in Glenfinnan ale, and local ales and spirits in the newly fitted bar. Modern bunkhouse has dorms, family rooms and twins, all en suite; it's set among woods a mile from the centre – turn right across Strontian bridge. Food served 8am–10pm. Extra £8 for breakfast at bunkhouse. Dorms **£18**

SALEN

Salen Hotel Salen ☎ 01967 431661, ⓦ salenhotel .co.uk. Less a small hotel than a restaurant with three smart rooms above – tastefully furnished where modern flair meets antiques – and simpler comfy rooms in the cheaper chalet. The restaurant offers a Scottish gastropub menu: pan-seared guinea fowl with Drambuie cream and local seafood for around £8–18. Breakfast by prior

arrangement. Easter–Oct daily 8–9am, 12.30–2.30pm & 5.30–11pm; Nov–Easter Thurs–Sun 8–9am, 12.30–2.30pm & 5.30–8pm. **£70**

GLENBORRODALE

Lochview Tearoom Ardnamurchan Natural History Visitor Centre ☎ 01972 500209, ⓦ ardnamurchannaturalhistorycentre.com. The simple tearoom attached to the visitor centre (see p.441) rustles up excellent home-made soups, scones and cakes. Easter–Oct Mon–Sat 9am–5pm, Sun 10am–4pm.

KILCHOAN

★**Ardnamurchan Campsite** Ormsaigbeg ☎ 01972 510766, ⓦ ardnamurchanstudycentre.co.uk. Cracking views, plus campfires on the beach of a laudably back-to-basics campsite behind the loch – pure magic at sunset and usually spared summer midges by a breeze. Find it past the Ferry Stores. Easter–Sept. Per person **£9**

Acharacle and Glenuig

At the eastern end of Ardnamurchan, just northwest of Salen where the A861 heads north towards the district of Moidart, the main settlement is **ACHARACLE**, a nondescript crofting village set back from **Loch Shiel**. The reason to swing through is **Castle Tioram** (pronounced "cheerum"), one of Scotland's most atmospheric monuments. Perched on a promontory above **Loch Moidart** and accessed via a sandy causeway (its Gaelic name means "dry land"), the thirteenth-century fortress was the seat of the MacDonalds of Clanranald until it was destroyed by their chief in 1715 to prevent it falling into Hanoverian hands. There's no entry into the castle, but for a slice of picture-postcard romantic Scotland, it's hard to beat. It's located three miles north of Acharacle via a side road off the A861.

Keep going north on the A861 and you'll roll through woods to arrive at **GLENUIG**, gathered on a picturesque inlet on the Sound of Arisaig. Barely a hamlet, it makes a fine base for walking, sea-kayaking (see below) – or partying, when the community centre hosts gigs every other Saturday (listings on ⌨glenuig.org.uk).

ARRIVAL AND ACTIVITIES ACHARACLE AND GLENUIG

By bus Buses go from Fort William (Mon–Sat 1–2 daily) to Acharacle (1hr 20min) and Glenuig (1hr 10min).

By boat Loch Shiel Cruises runs trips to Acharacle from Glenfinnan at the head of Loch Shiel (April to early Oct Wed

only; £18 single, £26 return; ☎01687 470322, ⌨highlandcruises.co.uk).

Sea-kayaking The owner of the *Glenuig Inn* (see below) runs half- and full-day trips in the Sound of Arisaig from £55.

ACCOMMODATION AND EATING

Glenuig Inn Glenuig ☎01687 470219, ⌨glenuig.com. A refurbished inn that ticks all boxes: an excellent hostel with single beds, not bunks; modest motel-style rooms in an

annexe; and local beers plus well-priced bar food – lamb kofta kebabs, root vegetable curries and home-made burgers, all around £12. Daily noon–9pm. Dorms **£30**; doubles **£110**

The Road to the Isles

The "Road to the Isles" from Fort William to Mallaig, followed by the West Highland Railway and the winding A830, traverses the mountains and glens of the Rough Bounds before breaking out near **Arisaig** onto a spectacular coast of sheltered inlets, white-sand beaches and wonderful views to the islands of Rùm, Eigg, Muck and Skye. This is a country commonly associated with **Bonnie Prince Charlie**, whose adventures of 1745–46 began on this stretch of coast with his gathering of the clans at **Glenfinnan** and ended here too when he embarked near Arisdale and fled into French exile.

12

Glenfinnan

This sleepy village may be spectacularly sited at the head of Loch Shiel, but it's the local history that draws most visitors to **GLENFINNAN**, since it was here that Bonnie Prince Charlie raised his standard and rallied forces before the ill-fated march on London (see p.418). That said, nowadays just as many visitors come to see the imposing arched viaduct, as crossed by the *Hogwarts Express* in the *Harry Potter* films.

Glenfinnan Monument and Visitor Centre

Centre of the village • Daily April, May, June, Sept & Oct 10am–5pm; July & Aug 9.30am–5pm • £3.50; NTS • ☎0844 493 2221 • ⌨nts.org.uk

The spot where the Young Pretender raised his battle standard on August 19, 1745, is marked by one of Scotland's most iconic structures, **Glenfinnan Monument**, a 60ft column crowned with a Highland clansman in full battle dress, erected as a tribute by Alexander Macdonald of Glenaladale in 1815. It's a beautiful, brooding spot at the head of the loch that's best appreciated from a viewpoint behind the **Visitor Centre**. After admiring the view, pop inside for an account of the '45 uprising through to the rout at Culloden (see p.418).

ARRIVAL AND DEPARTURE GLENFINNAN

By train A direct service links Fort William to Glenfinnan (Mon–Sat 4 daily, Sun 3 daily; 35min).

INFORMATION AND TOURS

Tourist information The Visitor Centre (see above) is a good source of local information, as is the website road-to-the-isles.org.uk.

Loch Shiel Cruises ☎01687 470322, ⌨highland

cruises.co.uk. Runs boat trips to view the superb scenery between April and October. Cruises embark from a jetty near *Glenfinnan House Hotel*, signposted off the main road half a mile west of the monument.

ACCOMMODATION AND EATING

Prince's House Centre of the village, on the A830 ☎01397 722246, ⓦ glenfinnan.co.uk. This seventeenth-century former coaching inn offers homely rooms – the best at the front nod to Highlands tradition – and a warm welcome to match. The fine restaurant offers a seasonal, fresh menu or there's gastropub grub in the bar; expect West Coast salmon, lamb and venison. Mains average £12–16. March–Dec; food served Easter–Sept daily 11am–3pm & 7–10pm. **£120**

Sleeping Car Glenfinnan station ☎01397 722295, ⓦ glenfinnanstationmuseum.co.uk. A 1958 camping coach is now a (very) mini-bunkhouse with three twin compartments (bunk beds), a family compartment for four, plus a kitchen, lounge and bathroom – a memorable if rather cosy place to stay. Linen costs extra. The adjacent *Dining Car* is open for light lunches from April to Sept (daily 10am–5pm; phone ahead for evening meals). The owners also run the neighbouring Station Museum. Per person **£15**

Arisaig

The little coastal village of **ARISAIG** (meaning "the Safe Place" in Gaelic) is an appealingly drowsy place scattered around a sandy bay. The only specific attraction in the village is the **Land, Sea and Islands Visitor Centre** (Easter to mid-Oct Mon–Fri 10am–6pm, Sat 10am–6pm, Sun 2–5pm, mid-Oct to Easter Mon 10am–1pm, Sat 10am–4pm, Sun 2–4pm; donations; ☎01687 450771), a volunteer-run community project with displays on crofting life, local characters and the area's role as a base for Special Operations during World War II. There's also a small research library of wildlife and walks – swot up before walking to a seal colony at nearby **Rhumach**, reached via a single-track lane heading west out of Arisaig.

Stretching for eight miles or so north of Arisaig along the road signposted "Alternative Coastal Route" is a string of stunning white-sand, azure-water **beaches**: summer holiday favourites backed by flowery machair and with views out to Eigg and Rùm. Pretty **Traigh** beach is your spot to collect cowrie shells, but larger and more celebrated is **Camusdarach Beach** a mile or so north, where the beach scenes of the films *Local Hero* and *Highlander* were shot. If it's busy, two intimate beaches lie over the headlands on either side.

ARRIVAL AND DEPARTURE ARISAIG

By train Direct services run from Fort William to Arisaig (3–4 daily; 1hr 5min).

By boat Arisaig Marine (☎01687 450224, ⓦ arisaig.co.uk)

sails from Arisaig marina to Eigg, Rùm and Muck at 11am daily, from late April to late Sept.

ACTIVITIES

Arisaig Sea Kayak Centre ☎07858 214985, ⓦ arisaigseakayakcentre.co.uk. Based at the *Arisaig*

Hotel, this operator offers trips every day in season for a levels (guided day-trips £75). Also offers stand-u

THE WEST HIGHLAND RAILWAY

A fixture in lists of the world's most scenic train journeys, the brilliantly engineered **West Highland Railway** runs from Glasgow to Mallaig via Fort William. The line is in two sections: the southern part travels from **Glasgow** Queen Street station, up the banks of Loch Lomond to **Crianlarich**, then around Beinn Odhar on a horseshoe of viaducts to cross **Rannoch Moor**, where the track had to be laid on a mattress of tree roots, brushwood and thousands of tons of earth and ashes. You're out in the wilds here, the line long having diverged from the road. The route then swings into Glen Roy, passing through the **Monessie Gorge** to enter **Fort William**.

Leg two, from Fort William to Mallaig, is even more spectacular. Shortly after leaving Fort William the railway crosses the Caledonian Canal beside Neptune's Staircase at **Benavie**, before travelling along Locheil and crossing the 21-arch viaduct at **Glenfinnan**, where passengers get to live out *Harry Potter* fantasies. Then it's on to the coast, with views of the Small Isles and Skye before journey's end at **Mallaig**. You can book tickets through ⓦ scotrail .co.uk. Between May and October, this leg of the route is also served by the **Jacobite Steam Train** (ⓦ westcoastrailways.co.uk).

paddle-boarding trips (guided day-trips £75; two-day wild-camp adventure £190).
West Coast Cycles ☎ 07769 901823, ⓦ westcoastcycle

hire.co.uk. Rents mountain bikes by the day (£20) or up to a week. Collect bikes from *Arisaig Hotel*.

ACCOMMODATION AND EATING

★**Camusdarach Campsite** Camusdarach ☎ 01687 450221, ⓦ camusdarach.co.uk. By far the loveliest campsite in the area, its neat fields a pleasing balance of eco-emptiness and modern facilities, all spread behind sands so white they've featured in films. Glamping pods available for those who would rather not brave the elements. Decent takeaway pizzas and proper coffees available. Late March to early Oct. Per pitch £15, per pod £45

noc-na-Faire Back of Keppoch, 1 mile north of Arisaig ☎ 01687 450249, ⓦ cnoc-na-faire.co.uk. Highlands meets Art Deco in a B&B with smart modern-country

rooms of tartan fabrics, stainless steel and blond wood. Sweeping views out to the Small Isles make for a memorable stay. £90

Old Library Lodge and Restaurant Arisaig ☎ 01687 450651, ⓦ oldlibrary.co.uk. The best rooms overlook the bay; those in a garden annexe are modest motel numbers with mod cons like flatscreen TVs and wi-fi. The popular dining room offers Scottish dishes: cullen skink or delicious crab sandwiches for lunch (around £8), venison pie or a superb beer-battered haddock and chips for dinner (average £13). Mid-Feb to Oct noon–2.30pm & 6–9pm. £100

Mallaig

The fate of **MALLAIG**, 47 miles west of Fort William, is to be seen as somewhere to go through, not to. Before the railway arrived in 1901 it consisted of a few cottages. Now in season it's full of visitors as the main embarkation point for ferries to Skye, the Small Isles and Knoydart. Even if not especially pretty, it is a solid town given a workaday honesty by its local **fishing** industry – it once had one of Europe's busiest herring ports and the harbour remains the source of the village's wealth.

Mallaig Heritage Centre

Beside the train station • April, May, June & Oct Mon–Fri 11am–4pm, Sat noon–4pm; July & Aug Mon–Fri 10am–6pm, Sat & Sun noon–4pm, Sept Mon–Fri 10am–4pm, Sat & Sun noon–4pm, Nov–March Mon–Thurs noon–4pm • free • ☎ 01687 462085, ⓦ mallaigheritage.org.uk

Apart from the hubbub of the harbour, the town's only sight is **Mallaig Heritage Centre** – nothing to quicken the pulse but worth a browse for displays on the area's past and information about lifeboats, fishing and the highland galleys that once plied the waters of the Inner Hebrides and descend directly from Viking longships.

ARRIVAL AND DEPARTURE — MALLAIG

BY TRAIN
A direct service arrives from Fort William (Mon–Sat 3–4 daily, Sun 4 daily; 1hr 25min) and Glasgow (Mon–Sat daily; 5hr 30min), via Glenfinnan and Arisaig.

BY BUS
There are regular buses from Fort William to Mallaig via Glenfinnan and Arisaig (Mon–Fri 4 daily, Sat & Sun 1 daily; 1hr 10min).

BY FERRY
To CalMac ticket office (☎ 01687 462403, ⓦ calmac uk) is at the main ferry terminal.

To/from Skye Regular services shuttle between Mallaig

and Armadale (Mon–Sat 8 daily; also mid-May to mid-Sept Sun 6 daily; 30min). Car reservations are essential in peak season.

To/from the Small Isles There are services between Mallaig and Eigg (Mon, Thurs, Sat & Sun 1 daily; 1hr 15min); Rùm (Mon, Wed, Fri, Sat & Sun 1 daily; 1hr 20min); Muck (Tues, Thurs, Fri, Sat & Sun 1 daily; 1hr 40min–2hr); and Canna (Mon, Wed, Fri, Sat & Sun; 1 daily; 2hr 30min).

To/from Knoydart Western Isles Cruises (☎ 01687 462233, ⓦ westernislescruises.co.uk) sails from Mallaig to Inverie (May–Sept Mon–Fri 5 daily, Sat 4 daily, Sun 3 daily; April & Oct Mon–Fri 4 daily, Sat 4 daily, Sun 3 daily; Nov–March Mon–Fri 4 daily, Sat 3 daily, Sun 2 daily; 25min; £18 return).

INFORMATION

Tourist office Beside the harbour (Feb–Oct daily 9am–7pm; Nov–Feb 10am–4pm; ☎ 01687 462883,

ⓔ mallaigvisitorcentre@btconnect.com).

12

ACCOMMODATION

Mallaig Backpackers Main St ☎ 01687 462764, ⓦ mallaigbackpackers.co.uk. There are two mixed dorms, a small kitchen and a lounge in this relaxed, independent modern hostel. "Reception" is in the *Tea Garden* restaurant (see below) opposite the harbour. Dorms £18

Seaview Main St ☎ 01687 462059, ⓦ seaviewguest housemallaig.com. Snug dimensions and surprisingly smart decor – tasteful shades of taupe and grey with a leaning towards modest boutique – set the tone in this central B&B with harbour views from the front March–Oct. £70

EATING

Cornerstone Main St ☎ 01687 462306, ⓦ seafood restaurantmallaig.com. A simple first-floor restaurant that's the locals' choice for classic seafood – expect a daily soup and a menu of fresh fish, simply but excellently prepared and fairly priced at around £11–20. March to mid-Oct daily 8.15–10.30am, noon–2.30pm & 5–9.30pm.

Tea Garden Main St ☎ 01687 462764 ⓦ mallaigbackpackers.co.uk. As central as it gets, with terrace to watch the world go by and a relaxed dining room with a traditional bistro menu of Mallaig kippers, pints of prawns (£12.50) or home-made scones. Mid-March to mid-Nov daily 9am–6pm.

The Knoydart peninsula

Touted as "Britain's last great wilderness", the very thought of the **Knoydart peninsula** stirs the imagination. The fact that it is inaccessible by car is part of the allure – to reach the heart of the peninsula, you either catch a **boat** from Mallaig or **hike** across rugged moorland, sleeping in stone bothies (marked on OS maps). The scenery is superb, flanked by **Loch Nevis** ("Loch of Heaven") and the fjord-like **Loch Hourn** ("Loch of Hell") and three Munros sweeping straight up from the sea. Unsurprisingly, the peninsula has long attracted walkers. But with increasingly comfortable accommodation, it is also gaining a cachet among holiday-makers in search of escapism: a place to slow down for a few days' self-imposed exile from modernity.

Brief history

At the end of the eighteenth century, around a thousand people eked out a living from this inhospitable terrain through crofting and fishing. **Evictions** in 1853 began a dramatic decrease in the population, which continued to dwindle through the twentieth century as a succession of landowners ran the estate as a hunting and shooting playground, prompting a famous land raid in 1948 by a group of crofters known as the "**Seven Men of Knoydart**", who claimed ownership of portions of the estate. Although their bid failed, their cause was invoked when the crofters of Knoydart finally achieved a **community buyout** in 1999. An offer to provide the money from theatre impresario Cameron Mackintosh was rejected because locals were wary of giving up control.

WALKING INTO KNOYDART

Ordnance Survey Explorer maps 413 and 398

There are two main **hiking routes** into Knoydart. The trailhead for the first is **Kinloch Hourn** at the far east end of Loch Hourn (turn south off the A87 six miles west of Invergarry). From Kinloch Hourn, a well-marked path winds around the coast on the south side of Loch Hourn to Barisdale, where there's a year-round bothy and wild camp (bothy (max two nights) £3, campsite £1; ⓦ barisdale.com), before continuing ten miles to Inverie; expect 18–20 hours' walk in total. The second path into Knoydart starts from the west end of **Loch Arkaig**, approaching the peninsula via Glen Dessary. Hardened walkers reckon on knocking off the eighteen-mile journey in one long summer's day. The rest of us should set aside two. Either way, take wet-weather gear, a good map, plenty of food, warm clothes and a good sleeping bag, and leave your name and expected time of arrival with someone when you set off.

Inverie

Most of the peninsula's hundred or so occupants live in the sleepy hamlet of **INVERIE**. Spread along Loch Nevis, it has a pint-sized post office and shop (with wi-fi), a ranger post with tips on local walks and wildlife, a pleasant tearoom and mainland Britain's most remote pub, *The Old Forge*. You're here for the Tolkienesque scenery, for walks and for the thrill of dropping off the radar.

ARRIVAL AND DEPARTURE   THE KNOYDART PENINSULA

By boat Western Isles Cruises (☎01687 462233, ⑩westernislescruises.co.uk) sails from Mallaig to Inverie (May–Sept Mon–Fri 5 daily, Sat 4 daily, Sun 3 daily; April & Oct Mon–Fri 4 daily, Sat 4 daily, Sun 3 daily; Nov–March

Mon–Fri 4 daily, Sat 3 daily, Sun 2 daily; 25min; £18 return).

On foot It's a two-day hike into Knoydart; our box (see opposite) gives details.

INFORMATION AND ACTIVITIES

Tourist information A ranger post (☎01687 462242) beside *The Old Forge* has information on the Knoydart Foundation, and on local history and wildlife. The adjoining shop (with wi-fi) sells walking leaflets plus local goods, from wild venison to woolly blankets.

Mountain biking Two mountain-bike trails – a 1.5-mile red-grade route and a 500yd blue-grade route– loop around Inverie. Knoydart Carbon Cycle rents bikes from the village centre (☎01687 462242, ⑧amie@knoydart.org; £12).

ACCOMMODATION

Most beds are in Inverie, with a growing number of self-catering options (see ⑩knoydart-foundation.com). You can **camp** at Long Beach, east of Inverie centre, for a £4 donation to the Knoydart Foundation – pay the ranger or leave it in an honesty box at the campsite. The turf-roofed compost toilet, mountain water supply and cabin shelter make for a comfortable enough stay. Firewood (£4.50) for use in the fire-pits is available at the campsite, and visitors may be able to use the showers in the *Knoydart Bunkhouse* for a small charge.

Doune Knoydart 6 miles northwest of Inverie (owners collect guests by boat from Mallaig) ☎01687 462667, ⑩doune-knoydart.co.uk. This may be the ultimate Highland getaway, with en-suite doubles in restored pine-clad crofts behind a bay. As well as isolation and views, its lovely owners provide superb cooking (also available for non-guests; call ahead). Minimum three nights. Full board. Easter–Sept. **£170**

The Gathering Inverie ☎01687 460051, ⑩thegatheringknoydart.co.uk. Relaxed sophistication

in a modern, ecofriendly B&B just west of the wharf that feels like self-contained accommodation (the owner lives opposite). Superb views and sensational breakfasts. Bring swimming gear to enjoy the hot tub with a view. **£110**

Knoydart Foundation Bunkhouse Half a mile east of the pier, Inverie ☎01687 462163, ⑩knoydart-foundation.com. The community hostel is on an old farm near Long Beach. Dorms are large, facilities include a kitchen and laundry, and there's internet access in a comfy lounge with a woodburner. A revamp in 2016 freshened the place up. Dorms **£17**

EATING AND DRINKING

Knoydart Pottery & Tearoom Inverie ☎01687 460191. A lovely spot to lose a few hours (or a long wet day): choose from sofas, a long communal table or the outdoor decking with the best loch view in Knoydart. Isla and Rhona serve up breakfast rolls, home-made soups and gluten-free home-baking for around £5–8. Easter–Oct Mon–Fri 9am–5pm, Sat 11am–4pm; Nov–Easter Mon, Wed & Fri 10am–4pm.

★**The Old Forge** Inverie ☎01687 462267. Britain's most isolated pub remains one of Scotland's finer boozers, fuelled by a convivial atmosphere and wonderful sense of remoteness. Generous bar meals feature local seafood – specials are around £16, fish and chips £11.95 – and terrific loch views. The chocolate waffles (£2) are as good as you'd expect from Belgian owners. Nov–Easter daily 4–11pm, Easter–Oct daily noon–1am.

Kyle of Lochalsh and around

Prior to the construction of the Skye Bridge in 1995, the **Kyle of Lochalsh** was Skye's main ferry port, but these days it's mainly used as a terminus for the train route from Inverness. Nearby, the photogenic **Eilean Donan Castle** sits on the glassy shores of **Loch**

Duich. Both are fixtures on the tourist trail, which makes the remote **Glenelg** peninsula to the south side of Loch Duich all the more inspiring. A few miles north of Kyle of Lochalsh, the village of **Plockton** is a lovely spot, with a superb setting on **Loch Carron**, a long inlet which acts as a dividing line between Kyle of Lochalsh and the splendours of Wester Ross to the north.

Kyle of Lochalsh

Truth be told, traffic has little reason to stop in **KYLE OF LOCHALSH**, especially since Skye or Plockton nearby offer more appealing accommodation. One good reason to pause here is the *Seaprobe Atlantis*, the UK's only semi-submersible **glass-bottom boat** (see below).

ARRIVAL AND ACTIVITIES   KYLE OF LOCHALSH

By train It's a glorious journey from Inverness to Kyle of Lochalsh (Mon–Sat 4 daily, Sun 2 daily; 2hr 35min); trains stop at Plockton (15min from Kyle) en route.

By bus Reservations are recommended for all services (☎0870 550 5050, ⓦcitylink.co.uk). Buses stop on the waterfront at the old slipway.

Destinations Fort William (7 daily; 1hr 55min); Glasgow

(5 daily; 5hr 15min); Inverness (8 daily; 2hr); Kyleakin, Skye (6 daily; 5min).

Boat tours The glass-bottom *Seaprobe Atlantis* (☎0147 822716 or ☎0800 980 4846, ⓦseaprobeatlantis.com leads summer trips to protected seal and bird colonies of Seal Island (1hr; £12.99) or over the World War II wreck HMS *Port Napier* (1hr 15min; £15.99).

Loch Duich

12

Skirted on its northern shore by the A87, **Loch Duich** features prominently on the tourist trail: coach tours from all over the world thunder down from **SHIEL BRIDGE** en route to Skye and one of Scotland's most iconic castles, Eilean Donan. Not that it's just the happy hordes who visit: at the end of the loch is Glen Shiel, flanked by the **Five Sisters of Kintail** – a classic tough trek that ticks off three Munros (see box, p.10).

Eilean Donan Castle

Beside A87 near the village of Dornie • Feb–Easter 10am–5pm, Easter–Oct 10am–6pm, Nov–Dec 10am–4pm • £7 • ☎01599 555202, ⓦeileandonancastle.com

After Edinburgh's fortress, **Eilean Donan Castle** has to be the most photographed monument in Scotland. Located on the A87 guarding the confluence of lochs Alsh, Long and Duich, its tower rises on an islet, joined to the shore by a stone bridge and set against a backdrop of mountains. Small wonder it has featured in *Highlander* and the James Bond adventure *The World is Not Enough*. The castle was established in 123? by Alexander II to protect the area from the Vikings but was destroyed during the Jacobite uprising of 1719. It was rebuilt between 1912 and 1932 by a British army officer, John Macrae-Gilstrap, because of the Macrae clan's ancestral links to the area. So, its three floors, including the banqueting hall, the bedrooms and the troops' quarters, are re-creations rather than originals. The Jacobite and clan relics on display are all original. As of 2016, visitors can see one of the few working portcullises in Scotland in action (demonstrations at 10.45am & 2.45pm).

ARRIVAL AND DEPARTURE

By bus Citylink bus #917 (3 daily) stops at Eilean Donan Castle, about halfway between Inverness (1hr 50min) and

Portree (1hr 20min).

ACCOMMODATION AND EATING   LOCH DUICH

Grants at Craigellachie Ratagan, 2 miles south of Shiel Bridge ☎01599 511331, ⓦhousebytheloch.co.uk. You'll find B&B charm and hotel quality in the three modern en-suites plus a suite with kitchenette. The owner's intimate

restaurant (guests only) serves first-class modern Scot dishes like pot-roast pheasant with wild boar, leek tarragon stuffing. Reservations essential. Easter–Oct. £

Ratagan SYHA Hostel Ratagan, 2 miles south of S

Bridge ☎01599 511243, ⍟syha.org.uk. Superbly sited on the loch, with views across to the Five Sisters. Traditional in public areas but dorms are more IKEA-esque. March–Oct. Dorms £19.50; doubles £54

Shielbridge Caravan Park & Campsite Off the A87, just south of Shiel Bridge ☎01599 511221, ⍟shielbridgecaravanpark.co.uk. A minor legend among hikers thanks to its superb location at the west end of Glen Shiel beneath the Five Sisters. Late March to Oct. Per person £6.90

The Glenelg peninsula

Even though summer traffic trickles through for the Kylerhea ferry to Skye, sleepy **Glenelg peninsula** remains a quiet backwater jutting into the Sound of Sleat – one benefit of being on a road to nowhere. Indeed, the peninsula has probably changed little since Gavin Maxwell wrote about it in his otter novel *Ring of Bright Water* and he disguised its pristine coast by calling it "Camusfearnà". The landward approach is equally impressive on a road that switchbacks over the Mam Ratagan Pass (1115ft), rewarding drivers with spectacular views over the **Five Sisters** massif. The main village, **GLENELG**, is an appealingly soporific spot – a row of whitewashed houses, surrounded by trees, that shows little indication of its time as a strategic centre in the 1700s, when a large barracks kept clans in check. The ruins of Bernera Barracks are on the left as you approach the ferry.

Glenelg Brochs

Nearly two miles south of Glenelg, a left turn up Glen Beag leads to the **Glenelg Brochs**, one of the best-preserved Iron Age monuments in Scotland. Its spectacular circular towers – Dun Telve and Dun Troddan – in a sheltered valley are thought to have been erected around two thousand years ago to protect surrounding settlements from raiders.

Arnisdale

A lonely backroad beyond Glenelg village snakes southeast through a scattering of old crofting hamlets, timber forests and views of Skye and Eigg that grow more spectacular at each bend. Eventually you drop down to the shore of Loch Hourn at **ARNISDALE**, actually two hamlets in the bosom of the mountains: **Camusbane**, a traditional crofting settlement ranged behind a pebble beach; and **Corran** a mile further, a minuscule, whitewashed fishing hamlet huddled around a river mouth. Display boards in the latter's **Ceilidh House and Heritage Centre** (always open; free) relate local history, including that of Mansion House between the hamlets, built by Valentine Fleming, father of James Bond author Ian.

ARRIVAL AND DEPARTURE	**THE GLENELG PENINSULA**
By bus MacRae Kintail bus service (Mon–Fri 1 daily; ☎01599 511384) operates from Kyle of Lochalsh to Glenelg (50min; request on boarding) and Arnisdale (1hr 40min; booking essential) via Shiel Bridge.	**By ferry** The six-car Glenelg–Kylerhea turntable ferry (daily: Easter–Oct 10am–6pm; June–Aug till 7pm; ☎01599 522313, ⍟skyeferry.co.uk) shuttles to and from Skye every 20min, taking 5min.

ACCOMMODATION AND EATING	
The Glenelg Inn Glenelg ☎01599 522273, ⍟glenelginn.com. Snug, eclectic, with a fire in the grate and a spectacular lochside setting to boot. Comfortable rooms and a decent gastropub menu that showcases local seafood – fish, crabcakes, mussels (mains average £12) – confirm this is a class act. Occasional live music. Daily Easter–Oct, bar only Nov–Easter Thurs–Sun. £110	**Sheena's Tea Hut** End of the road, Corran ☎01599 522336. Probably Britain's most remote cuppa, and well worth the journey. This charmingly ramshackle corrugated hut, now run by local legend Sheena's daughter, Lorraine, serves up cockle-warming soups, toasties and cakes, plus fish and chips (£6.50). A true one-off. Mon–Fri & Sun 10am–5pm.

Plockton

With its picture-postcard cottages curved behind a tiny harbour and views across Loch Carron to mountains, **PLOCKTON** is one of the most picturesque settlements on the west coast. Until the end of the eighteenth century, Am Ploc, as the settlement was then known, was just another crofting hamlet. Then a local laird transformed it with a prosperous fishery, funding a planned village that was renamed "Plocktown". It's packed in high season with yachties – a popular regatta fills the bay over a fortnight from late July – artsy second-home owners with easels in tow, and visiting families squelching over the seabed at low tide to take a turn around the small island. It may look familiar to first-time visitors – its flower- and palm-filled seafront featured in cult horror film *The Wicker Man*.

ARRIVAL AND DEPARTURE

PLOCKTON

By train Trains from Inverness stop in Plockton (2hr 20min; Mon–Sat 4 daily, Sun 2 daily) before continuing on to Kyle of Lochalsh (15min).

INFORMATION AND ACTIVITIES

Tourist information ⓦ plockton.com.
Calum's Seal Trips ☎ 01599 544306 or ☎ 07761 263828, ⓦ calums-sealtrips.com. Expect "better views than the QE2" aboard this pretty, traditiona cruiser. Perhaps true if you like seals (1hr; £11.50 or free no seals).

ACCOMMODATION

An Caladh 25 Harbour St ☎ 01599 544356, ⓦ plockton .uk.com. Anna and Bob's whitewashed fisherman's cottage is one of the best of Plockton's many B&Bs, with sea views from front rooms – though not en suites in all. **£65**
Duncraig Castle Turn-off midway between Duirnish and Plockton ☎ 01599 544295, ⓦ duncraigcastle.com. On the opposite side of the bay from Plockton village in a truly stunning setting, this grand Baronial pile was undergoing a top-to-bottom renovation on our last visit,

with plans to reopen in spring 2017. **£109**
Plockton Hotel 41 Harbour St ☎ 01599 544274 ⓦ plocktonhotel.co.uk. This friendly, small hotel provide cosy, contemporary-cottage decor in rooms, of which th best come with a view at the front. A four-room annexe c the harbour appeals for its shared kitchen as much as i cheaper rates that still include breakfast. Well-stocked pu downstairs, with a grassy beer garden overlooking the ba Annexe **£90**; doubles **£140**

EATING AND DRINKING

Plockton Inn Innes St ☎ 01599 544222, ⓦ plocktoninn .co.uk. The locals' choice offers excellent lunches like watercress and sweet-potato soup or smoked trout pâté, then a fine evening menu including haggis and clapshot (£9.50) and their famous Plockton prawns (£15.25). Good vegetarian options and music on Tues and Thurs evenings. Daily noon–11.30pm; food served noon– 2.15pm & 6–9pm.

Plockton Shores 30 Harbour St ☎ 01599 54426 Metropolitan-styled café-restaurant that starts the day a relaxed coffee and lunch stop, then shifts up a gear f Modern Scottish dishes like scallops in a lime, ginger ar honey glaze (£15.95). Rotating exhibition of local artwo adorns the walls. Mid-March to Oct Tues–S 9.30am–9pm & Sun noon–9pm, Nov–March Wed–S 10am–8.15pm, Sun noon–2.15pm.

Loch Carron

North of Plockton are the twin sea lochs of **Loch Kishorn**, so deep it was once used as an oil-rig construction site, and **Loch Carron**, which cuts far inland to **STRATHCARRON** a useful rail link between Kyle of Lochalsh and Torridon, but little else.

Attadale Gardens

2.5 miles south of Strathcarron • Easter to mid-Oct Mon–Sat 10am–5.30pm • £6 • ☎ 01520 722603, ⓦ attadalegardens.com

Made up of twenty artistically landscaped acres, **Attadale Gardens** are ranked among Scotland's finest by horticultural aficionados. Fans include the Duke and Duchess of Rothesay (the titles given to Prince Charles and Camilla while on Scottish duties) who paid a royal visit in June 2016 to view the gardens' waterfalls and rhododendrons.

Lochcarron

With supermarkets, cafés, a bank and fuel set along a long whitewashed seafront, **LOCHCARRON** represents a considerable hub hereabouts. While it's of more use than nterest, two crafty sights warrant a pause. A mile north of town on the main road, the **Smithy Community Hub** (Easter–Oct Mon–Sat 10am–5pm), a nineteenth-century smithy and forge, is open erratically in season but has become a focus for local **crafts collectives** selling their wares. More celebrated are the tartans of **Lochcarron Weavers** (☎01520 722212, ✆lochcarron.co.uk). You can see weaving demonstrations (and buy fabrics and clothing) in its workshop two miles south of Lochcarron towards Strome Castle.

ARRIVAL AND INFORMATION   **LOCHCARRON**

By rail Strathcarron is on the splendid Kyle of Lochalsh–Inverness line (Mon–Sat 4 daily, Sun 2 daily): trains run from/to Inverness (1hr 50min) and Kyle (40min).

By bus Timetables are coordinated so that buses meet train arrivals at Strathcarron. Services run to Lochcarron from Shieldaig (Mon–Sat 1 daily; 35min) and Torridon (Mon–Sat 1 daily; 1hr; call ☎01520 722682 to request).

Tourist information Tourist information desk in the Smithy Community Hub (Easter–Oct Mon–Sat 10am–4.30pm, ☎01520 722952).

ACCOMMODATION AND EATING

★ **Kishorn Seafood Bar** Kishorn, 6 miles northwest of Lochcarron ☎01520 733240, ✆kishornseafoodbar.co.uk. A baby blue, lodge-like café often named in the top-ten British seafood restaurants for local and fresh seafood. Come for sharing platters (£30 for two), Skye mussels or just garlic scallops and a croissant (£10). Outdoor seating available. Easter to mid-July & mid-Sept to Nov Sat–Thurs 10am–5pm, Fri 10am–9pm; mid-July to mid-Sept Mon–Sat 10am–9pm, Sun 10am–5pm.

Old Manse Church St, Lochcarron ☎01520 722208, ✆theoldmanselochcarron.com. Floral fabrics, pine furniture and wrought-iron beds – country style rules in the five spacious en-suite rooms of the *Old Manse*, on the road to Strome Castle. Perhaps its real appeal is the location before the loch – £10 extra buys you a room with a view. **£70**

12

Wester Ross

The western seaboard of the old county of Ross-shire, **Wester Ross** is where the west coast ups the ante. Here, all the classic elements of Scotland's **coastal scenery** – craggy mountains, sandy beaches, whitewashed crofting cottages and shimmering island views come together. Settlements such as **Applecross** and the peninsulas north and south of **Gairloch** maintain a simplicity and sense of isolation outside of peak season. There is some tough but wonderful **hiking** in the mountains around **Torridon** and **Coigach**, while **boat trips** and the prolific marine life and birdlife draw nature-lovers. The hub of activity is **Ullapool**, a proper fishing town and ferry port whose modest size ranks as a metropolis in these parts.

The Applecross peninsula

The **Applecross peninsula** sounds bucolic; the English-sounding name is a corruption of the Gaelic *Apor Crosan*, meaning "estuary". Yet the approach from the south – up a glacial U-shaped valley and over the **Bealach na Bà** ("Pass of the Cattle") at 2054ft – is one of the classic drives and cycle pistes of the Highlands. With a sticker-strewn sign at the base warning off large vehicles and learner drivers (heed the advice!), this former drovers' road provides the greatest road ascent in the UK, with a 1:5 gradient and switchbacks worthy of the Alps. Views across the Minch to Raasay and Skye more than compensate – assuming the weather plays ball. The other way in from the north is a beautiful coast road that meanders from Shieldaig on Loch Torridon, past scattered crofting villages and with gorgeous seascapes.

Applecross

The sheltered, fertile coast around **APPLECROSS** village, where an Irish missionary Maelrhuba founded a monastery in 673 AD, is a surprise after experiencing the wilds that surround it. Though popular in peak season, it feels exhilaratingly remote, with little to do but visit the excellent pub, potter along lanes, paddle a kayak or build sandcastles on the beach. A small **Heritage Centre** (April–Oct Mon–Sat noon–4pm; ⓦapplecrossheritage.org.uk) near the site of St Maelrhuba's monastery, and beside Clachan church, showcases local history, and several **waymarked trails** along the shore are great for walking off lunch. Come towards the end of July for the barnstormin' annual Applecross Highland Games.

ARRIVAL AND DEPARTURE   APPLECROSS

By bus The Dial-A-Bus (ⓣ01520 722205) takes passengers from Applecross to Inverness, with stop-offs in Lochcarron, Shieldaig and Kishorn.

INFORMATION AND ACTIVITIES

Tourist information Village websites are ⓦapplecross .info and ⓦapplecross.uk.com. On our last visit, the tourist info point opposite the fuel station was about to close and reopen as a sparkly new café-bistro, with the Applecross Campsite set to become the best place to pick up brochures.

Mountain & Sea Guides ⓣ01520 744394, ⓦapplecross.uk.com/msg. Located by the fuel pumps, this company organizes mountain walking and climbing adventures, plus sea-kayaking, from half-day tasters to overnight wild-camping trips.

ACCOMMODATION AND EATING

Applecross Campsite East of the centre ⓣ01520 744268, ⓦapplecross.uk.com/campsite. A popular, well-run two-field site above the village – the furthest field is the quietest. It also provides basic cabins that sleep four. The Flower Tunnel common area is a splendid spot to while away an afternoon. No fires allowed. March–Oct. Camping per person **£9**; cabins **£45**

★**Applecross Inn** On the waterfront ⓣ01520 744262, ⓦapplecross.uk.com/inn. The heart of the community provides pretty, cottagey en-suites in the eaves, all with sea views. In the lively bar downstairs are Highland ales and freshly prepared classic pasta dishes plus divine seafood like Applecross Bay prawns (£18.50)

and king scallops (£17.50). Outside, the *Applecross Innside Out* food cart serves up quality fish and chips and ice cream during the summer. Reservation recommended in season. Daily noon–11pm; food served noon–9pm. **£130**

The Walled Garden Signposted northeast of the bay ⓣ01520 744440, ⓦapplecrossgarden.co.uk. Head here to enjoy delicious food in the laidback atmosphere of walled Victorian garden. Decent full Scottish breakfast (£10), generous slices of divine home-made cake, with dishes like bouillabaisse stew (£20) and chickpea, feta and spinach parcels (£12) available in the evening. March–Oct daily 8.30am–8.30pm.

Loch Torridon

Loch Torridon marks the northern boundary of the Applecross peninsula and a transition into some awe-inspiring scenery. From the water rise the mountains of **Liathach** and **Beinn Eighe**, shapely hulks of reddish, 750-million-year-old white quartzite. Around fifteen thousand acres of the massif are under the protection of the National Trust for Scotland, which makes this superb walking country, with a trio of Munros to bag.

Shieldaig

Smuggled off the main road on the shore of Loch Torridon, pretty **SHIELDAIG** ("herring bay") is a gentle spot – until the Shieldaig Fete and Rowing Regatta livens things up with some wacky boat races over the first weekend in August. A track winding north up the peninsula from the village makes for an enjoyable stroll. Otherwise, simply enjoy the view to **Shieldaig Island**, managed by the National Trust for Scotland.

Torridon

TORRIDON village, at the east end of the loch, marks where the road heads inland through spectacular Glen Torridon to Kinlochewe (see p.454). The village itself – thirty or so houses and a shop – straggles along the loch beneath the mountains, making it a fine launchpad for hikes. A **Countryside Centre** (daily 10am–5pm; donation requested)

12

☏01445 791221, ⓦnts.org.uk/property/torridon) at the turning into the village provides advice on mountain walks plus information on geology, flora and fauna. Their **Deer Museum** down the road (same hours) has information on the history and management of red deer, which are abundant in the region.

ARRIVAL AND ACTIVITIES   LOCH TORRIDO

By bus The Dial-A-Bus (☏01520 722205) from Strathcarron calls at Shieldaig and Torridon (Mon–Sat 1 daily).

Torridon Activities 1 mile south of turn-off into village ☏01445 791242, ⓦ thetorridon.com/activities. An operator based at the *Torridon Hotel* (see below) provides the full range of local fun: guided walks, gorge

scrambling, coasteering and climbing, plus kayaking an even clay pigeon shooting.

Torridon Sea Tours Shieldaig ☏01520 75535. ⓦ torridonseatours.com. Luxury boat tours reveal th superb scenery and wildlife in the area: morning trip half-day excursions, full-day journeys to Isle of Rona wi seafood lunch, plus a sunset trip with wine and canapés.

ACCOMMODATION AND EATING

SHIELDAIG

Camping area A designated campsite with no facilities but superb views of the loch is above the waterfront near the primary school at the village's north end.

★ **Tigh-an-Eilean** On the waterfront ☏01520 755251, ⓦ tighaneilean.co.uk. Faultless service and utter relaxation in a lovely small hotel on the waterfront with classy country accommodation plus a sensational restaurant (reservation essential); expect the likes of west coast sea bream with a Provençal tomato confit on innovative daily menus (non-residents £45 for three courses). The attached *Shieldaig Bar and Coastal Kitchen* rustles up top-notch bistro dishes like the famous seafood stew (£14.95) and wood-fired pizzas (£8–12). Bar Feb–New Year daily 11am–11pm; food served March–Oct daily 6–9pm. **£140**

TORRIDON

Camping area A wild camp is located beside the turning into the village next to the SYHA hostel. Dishwashing and a shower is in an adjacent public toilet. Beware the midges in summer, though.

SYHA Torridon Start of village, 100yds from turn-off ☏01445 791284, ⓦ syha.org.uk. Though the

Seventies-vintage municipal building is no looker, this hos is spacious and a popular choice with hikers and bike thanks to a location beneath the peaks. Provides the usu kitchen, laundry and drying room, plus very cheap mea daily. Closed three weeks in Jan. Dorms **£20**; doubles **£5**

★ **Torridon Hotel** 1.5 miles southwest of turn-off in village ☏01445 791242, ⓦ thetorridon.com/hotel. T Victorian hunting lodge is one of the west coast's grande stays. Sympathetically styled where boutique mee baronial in public areas and Master rooms; Classics a more up to date, while the new 1887 Suite is pu indulgence. A fine-dining restaurant (£60 for thr courses) is splendidly elegant for daily menus of seasor modern European cuisine, the whisky bar with 350-p malts a delight (tasting session £30). **£245**

Torridon Inn Next to the Torridon Hotel ☏014 791242, ⓦ thetorridon.com/inn. More cyclist- a walker-friendly than the neighbouring *Torridon Ho* (same owners), with neat, modern en-suites. Bar-bis serves regional ales and good gastropub cooking – veg stir-fry, fish and chips or steak-and-ale pie (£9–12). Fe Easter Mon–Sat 8am–9pm, Sun till 5pm; Easter– daily 8am–9pm. **£120**

Loch Maree

About eight miles north of Loch Torridon, **Loch Maree**, dotted with Caledonian-pine covered islands, is one of the area's scenic highlights, best viewed from the A832 road that drops down to its southeastern tip through Glen Docherty; try to time your journey here with early dawn or dusk, when red deer take over the land. At the southeastern end of the loch, the A896 from Torridon meets the A832 from Achnasheen at small **KINLOCHEWE**, a good base if you're heading into the hills.

Beinn Eighe Nature Reserve

The A832 skirts the southern shore of Loch Maree, passing the **Beinn Eighe Nature Reserve**, Britain's oldest national nature reserve, set up in 1951. Parts of the reserve are forested with Caledonian pine, which once covered the whole country, an it is home to pine martens, wildcats, buzzards and golden eagles. A mile north of Kinlochewe, the **Beinn Eighe Visitor Centre** (Easter & May–Oct daily 10am–5pm;

01445 760254, www.nnr-scotland.org.uk/beinn-eighe), on the A832, informs visitors about the rare species and offers several all-ability tours. Two **walks** start from the Coille na Glas-Leitir Trails car park just over a mile north of the visitor centre: a mile-long trail into ancient pine woodland and a 3.5-mile track into the mountains. The visitor centre has excellent free leaflets covering the walks.

ACCOMMODATION AND EATING	LOCH MAREE
Kinlochewe Hotel On A832, centre of village ☎ 01445 760253, kinlochewehotel.co.uk. A traditional hotel dating back to 1850 with a warm welcome and a fantastic line in regional ales and good-value soups and casseroles. Rooms are comfy enough, though en-suites cost another £23. An annexe holds a very basic twelve-bed self-catering bunkhouse, with triple-deck bunks in one room (bedding not included). Doubles **£75**; dorm **£16.50**	**Whistle Stop Café** Torrisdale Rd ☎ 01445 760423. This brightly decorated, refurbed old village hall is always a good stop before or after the hills, serving hearty breakfasts, fresh smoothies and a modern-European bistro menu. Sandwiches and wraps to salads of scallops and bacon (£6–14). A well-placed log-burner guarantees to warm the cockles. Feb–Nov Mon–Sat 9am–6pm.

Gairloch and around

Cheerful and unpretentious, **GAIRLOCH** thrives as a low-key holiday resort, with several sandy beaches for the bucket-and-spade brigade, some good coastal walks within easy reach and an abundance of wildlife cruise operators that pray for passing minke whales. The township is divided into distinct areas spread along Loch Gairloch: to the south, in **Flowerdale Bay**, is Charlestown with the harbour; west, at the turn-off to Melvaig, **Achtercairn** is the centre of Gairloch; and along the north side of the bay is the crofting area of **Strath**. Near the *Old Inn* in Charlestown, the **Sòlas Gallery** (Sept–June Mon–Sat 1–5pm, July & Aug daily 1–5pm; ☎ 01445 712626, solasgallery.co.uk) is worth a stop for its ceramics and watercolours inspired by the Highlands landscapes. A 1.5-mile walk (round trip) tracks the Flowerdale River through a woodland glen to a waterfall.

Gairloch Heritage Museum

On the turn-off from the A832 into Achtercairn • April–Oct Mon–Fri 10am–5pm, Sat 11am–3pm • £4 • ☎ 01445 712287, gairlochheritagemuseum.org

The **Gairloch Heritage Museum** houses eclectic displays of traditional Highland life, from a mock-up crofthouse to one of the largest Fresnel lenses ever constructed, from the nearby Rua Reidh Lighthouse, plus a temporary art exhibition. The archive and library contains a wealth of information on genealogy, local history and Gaelic language (access by appointment). Plans for a change of premises were under way in 2016, so check ahead.

Big Sand and Melvaig

The area's real attraction is its **coastline**. There's a **beach** just north of the harbour in Charlestown, a crescent of pure sand, or a more impressive stretch a few miles around the north side of the bay at **Big Sand** – it's cleaner, quieter and a mite more pebbly. The B8021 terminates at the crofting hamlet of **Melvaig**, where a community-funded replacement for the legendary but now-closed *Melvaig Inn* was in the pipeline on our last visit.

Rua Reidh and around

From Melvaig, a private track heads three miles to **Rua Reidh** (pronounced "roo-a-ray"), where a fully operational lighthouse houses a hostel in its keepers' quarters (see p.456). Although the approaching road is a public right of way, the owners of the lighthouse have taken steps to restrict access. The topic remains a thorny issue among locals, many of whom will insist you can drive, walk or cycle to the lighthouse.

Around the headland lies beautiful **Camas Mòr** beach, from where a marked footpath tracks inland (southeast) beneath a sheer scarp slope, past a string of lochans and ruined crofts to **MIDTOWN** on the east side of the peninsula, four miles north of

Poolewe on the B8057. Allow half a day, though be aware that few buses travel back from Poolewe (check times on ☎01445 712255).

Badachro

On the south side of Loch Gairloch, a single-track lane (built with the Destitution Funds raised during the nineteenth-century potato famine) winds past wooded coves and inlets along the loch to **BADACHRO**, a secluded, former fishing village with a wonderful pub (see opposite). Five miles on, Redpoint has beautiful peach-coloured beaches and marks the trailhead for the wonderful coastal walk to Lower Diabaig.

ARRIVAL AND INFORMATION   GAIRLOCH AND AROUN

By bus Public transport is minimal and requires careful planning. Bus stops for all services are at the *Old Inn*, Charlestown, as well as Achtercairn and Strath.
Destinations Inverness (Mon–Sat 1 daily; also ScotBus June–Sept Mon–Sat 1 daily; 2hr 45min); Poolewe (Mon,

Wed & Sat 1 daily; 15min); Ullapool (Mon, Wed, Thurs & S 1 daily; 1hr 10min).
Tourist information In community centre Gale Centre Achtercairn (Mon–Fri 9.30am–5pm, Sat 10am–4pm, Su 11am–3pm; ☎01445 712071, ⊕galeactionforum.co.uk.

ACTIVITIES

BOAT TRIPS

Gairloch prides itself on wildlife cruises from its harbour. Orcas and minke whales migrate past from late spring to late summer; porpoise and dolphins are common year-round, and seal-spottings near enough guaranteed. All operators are located on the harbour at Charlestown.
Gairloch Marine Life Centre & Cruises Charlestown ☎01445 712636, ⊕porpoise-gairloch.co.uk. Up to three fun and informative trips (10am, 12.30pm & 3pm, Easter–Oct; £20) a day run by the largest operator, which deploys a mini-sub for underwater pictures and a hydrophone to pick up audio. Its visitor centre (Easter–Oct daily 10am–4pm) has displays of local sea life.

Hebridean Whale Cruises Charlestown ☎014 712458, ⊕hebridean-whale-cruises.co.uk. As well in-shore cruises, the longest-established operator ru trips (Easter–Oct; call for winter cruises; from £49.50) in high-speed RIB that allows it to reach further offshore ir the North Minch out to the Shiant Isles off Lewis.

PONY TREKKING

Gairloch Trekking Centre 1 Flowerdale Mai Charlestown ☎07769 838 528, ⊕gairlochtrekki centre.co.uk. Lead-rein rides for young or inexperien riders, plus longer hacks (1hr £22.50; 2hr £46) through pre Highland scenery, between Easter and Oct (closed Thurs).

ACCOMMODATION

GAIRLOCH

Old Inn Signposted off A832, Charlestown ☎01445 712006, ⊕theoldinn.net. Country character abounds in the rooms of this former coaching inn set off the main road beside the Flowerdale River. Expect pretty patchwork-style quilts or tartan headboards in cosy en-suite rooms. **£120**

BIG SAND

Gairloch Sands SYHA On B8021, 2.5 miles west of Gairloch ☎01445 712219, ⊕syha.org.uk. This former hunting lodge is spectacularly sited above the foreshore, with vast views to Skye from its lounge. It dates back to 1880 and rather shows its age. April to late Sept. Dorms **£20**; doubles **£48**
Sands Caravan and Camping On B8021, 3.5 miles west

of Gairloch ☎01445 712152, ⊕sandscaravana camping.co.uk. The best of the area's campsites, with pitc behind the dunes for sea views. Also rents "wigwams" actually Scandi-style cabins for up to five with a fire-Laundry facilities, plus kayak (£25/day) and bike rental (£ day). The cosy on-site *Barn Café* serves evening meals (rese ahead). March–Nov. Per pitch **£18**; wigwams for two **£40**

RUA REIDH

Rua Reidh Lighthouse Rua Reidh ☎01445 7712 ⊕stayatalighthouse.co.uk. Epic seascapes to Hebrides in the only lighthouse hostel on Britain's w coast (see p.455), with homely decorative touches private bathrooms throughout. Breakfasts, packed lun and dinner (£18.50) available. Easter–Oct. **£95**

EATING AND DRINKING

GAIRLOCH

Mountain Coffee Company Achtercairn ☎01445 712316. Here's an unusual find for a small Highlands town – a relaxed café with a global backpacker vibe. Coffees,

mammoth-sized scones and toasted bagels with fresh filli plus a good bookshop on-site and rooms upstairs. Eas Nov daily 9am–6pm; Dec–Easter Mon–Sat 10am–4p
Old Inn Charlestown ☎01445 712006. Flagstone fl

12

and stone walls provide character in a modernized coaching inn. Posh-pub specials such as game casserole (£12.50), plus beers of the on-site microbrewery, provide the sustenance. Mains average £12. Easter–Nov daily 11am–11pm; food served noon–2.30pm & 5–8.30pm.

BADACHRO

★ **Badachro Inn** ☏ 01445 771212. Settle onto the terrace with a plate of pork belly or creel-caught langoustine (£10–13) and this pub by the old harbour is as fine a place as you'll find for a sunny afternoon. Inside are real ales, excellent malts and a fire for chill evenings. Look out for otters at dawn and dusk. April–Oct daily noon–midnight, Sun noon–11pm; Nov–March Wed–Sun same hours; food served weekdays noon–3pm & 6–9pm, Sat & Sun noon–3pm.

Poolewe

It's a short hop over the headland from Gairloch to the sleepy village of **POOLEWE** at the sheltered southern end of Loch Ewe. During World War II, the Arctic convoy embarked from here and the deep-water loch remains one of only three berths for nuclear submarines. One of the area's best **walks** begins nearby, signposted from the lay-by viewpoint on the A832, a mile south. It takes a couple of hours to follow the easy trail across open moorland to the shores of **Loch Maree** (see p.454), then the car park at Slattadale, seven miles southeast of Gairloch. Double-check timetables (☏ 01445 712255), but you should be able to continue along the loch shore to catch the Wester bus from Inverness back to Poolewe from the *Loch Maree Hotel* just after 2pm (Tues, Thurs & Fri only).

Inverewe Gardens

Half a mile north of Poolewe on A832 • **Visitor Centre** daily April, May & Sept 10am–5pm; June–Aug 9.30am–6pm; Oct 10am–5pm; Nov–March 10am–3pm • **Restaurant** April–Oct 10.30am–5pm • £10.50; NTS • ☏ 0844 493 2225, ⌨ nts.org.uk

Most visitors arrive in Poolewe for **Inverewe Gardens**, a subtropical-style oasis of foliage and riotously colourful compared to the wild coast. A network of paths and walkways wanders through more than a dozen gardens featuring exotic plant collections from as far afield as Chile, China, Tasmania and the Himalayas. Free **guided walks** depart from the visitor centre, and the self-service restaurant offers up sandwiches and soups, with hot grub during the height of summer. Visitors can also explore the opulent **Inverewe House**, which opened to the public in 2016 following major conservation works.

12

ARRIVAL AND DEPARTURE

POOLEWE

By bus There's a bus to Poolewe from Gairloch (15min; Mon, Wed & Sat 7.45am; Tues, Thurs, Fri & Sat 7.45pm).

ACCOMMODATION AND EATING

Inverewe Gardens Camping & Caravanning Centre of Poolewe on A832 ☏ 01445 781249, ⌨ campingandcaravanningclub.co.uk. As trim a site as usual from a member of the Camping & Caravanning Club and largely occupied by motorhomes. Facilities are well maintained and a few pitches in a shady corner allow campers to wake up to loch views. Easter–Oct. Per pitch **£30.65**

★ **Pool House Hotel** Centre of Poolewe on A832 ☏ 01445 781272, ⌨ pool-house.co.uk. Once the residence of Inverewe Gardens' Osgood MacKenzie, the Harrison family home remains one of the Highlands' most elegantly opulent small hotels – think rich fabrics, family antiques and art, loch views and a serene sense of calm. Don't be surprised if you struggle to leave the lounge. Easter–Oct. **£250**

Poolewe to Ullapool

At **LAIDE**, nine miles north of Poolewe, the road skirts the shores of **Gruinard Bay**. It's a great drive, offering fabulous views and, at the inner end of the bay, some excellent sandy beaches before you swing east, tracking high above Little Loch Broom, with gorgeous views to mountains opposite – **Badrallach**, seven miles from a left-turn at the head of the loch, is a magical spot to drop off the radar.

Inland, the route joins the A835 at **Braemore Junction**, above the head of Loch Broom. Easily accessible from a lay-by on the A835, the spectacular 160ft **Falls of Measach** plunge through the mile-long **Corrieshalloch Gorge**, formed by glacial meltwaters. After walking for five minutes you'll reach a Victorian suspension bridge that spans the chasm, offering a vertiginous view of the falls and gorge, whose 197ft vertical sides are draped in wych elm, goat willow and bird cherry.

Ullapool

ULLAPOOL, the northwest's principal town, is an appealing place spread across a sheltered arm of land in Loch Broom – a perfect base for exploring the northwest Highlands. Here you'll find all the cultural life of the only town worth the title in the region, with a penchant for barnstorming live music nights and a few excellent restaurants. Founded by the British Fisheries Society at the height of the herring boom in 1788, the grid-plan town remains an important fishing centre, which gives it a salty authenticity despite the hundreds of visitors who pass through in high season, bound north or to catch the **ferry** to Stornoway on Lewis (see p.507).

Ullapool Museum

7–8 West Argyle St • Easter–Oct Mon–Fri 10am–5pm, Sat 10am–4pm • £3.50 • ☎01854 612987, ⓦullapoolmuseum.co.uk

The only conventional attraction in town, the community-run **Ullapool Museum**, in the old parish church, uses photographs and audiovisual displays to provide an insight into crofting, fishing, local weather and emigration. During the Clearances, Ullapool was one of the ports through which evicted crofters left to start new lives abroad – it also has some genealogy resources.

Isle Martin

ⓦislemartin.org

Three miles northwest of Ullapool in Loch Broom, **Isle Martin** was inhabited on and off for a few thousand years – they say it was named after a follower of St Columba who may be under a fifth-century gravestone in the old graveyard – until the last crofting families called it a day in 1949. Gifted to the RSPB in 1999, the four-hundred-acre island is a romantic spot to be a temporary castaway, with beaches, walks and views to the cliffs of Beinn Mhor Coigach and the Summer Isles. Bothy-style accommodation is available in the *Croft House* or bunk rooms in the *Mill House* (both £35). At the time of research no scheduled ferries were running to the island, but the local community was in the process of buying a boat and scheduling a new passenger route. In the meantime, visitors can get over on a

ULLAPOOL

DRINKING	
Ferry Boat Inn	1

EATING	
The Arch Inn	3
The Ceilidh Place	2
West Coast Delicatessen	1

ACCOMMODATION	
Broomfield Holiday Park	5
The Ceilidh Place	3
Point Cottage	6
SYHA Ullapool	2
Tanglewood House	1
West House	4

12

shing boat with advance notice (contact Ullapool's tourist office, below), or via a
IB trip with Seascape Expeditions (£15; see below).

ummer Isles

)uring summer, the *Summer Queen* steamer (May to early Sept Mon–Sat; from £25;
01854 612472, ☏ summerqueen.co.uk) and the RIB-safari operator Seascape
xpeditions (£30; see below), run wildlife cruises and trips to the **Summer Isles**, twelve
iles west of Ullapool, to view seabird colonies, grey seals, dolphins, porpoises and the
ccasional whale. Whether slow and stately or fast and full-on in caves, it's a trip worth
king (weather permitting).

RRIVAL AND INFORMATION   ULLAPOOL

bus Buses stop at the pier, near the ferry dock.
stinations Durness (May–Sept Mon–Sat 1 daily, plus
n 1 daily in July & Aug; 3hr); Inverness (Mon–Sat 3 daily,
n 1 daily; 1hr 30min); D&E bike-carrying bus from
verness (May & June Thurs–Mon, July–Sept Mon–Sat;
r 30min).

ferry CalMac (☏ 01854 612358, ☏ calmac.co.uk) sails
Stornoway, Lewis (Mon–Sat 2 daily, Sun 1 daily; 2hr
min); two extra sailings run on Sun from late June to

early Sept. Seascape Expeditions (☏ 01854 633708, ☏ sea
-scape.co.uk) run trips to Isle Martin and Summer Isles
during the summer.

Tourist office Argyle St (Easter–May & Sept Mon–Sat
9.30am–5pm, Sun 10am–3pm; June–Aug Mon–Sat
9am–6pm, Sun 9.30am–4.30pm; Oct Mon–Sat
9.30am–4.30pm, Sun 10am–3pm; ☏ 01854 612486,
☏ ullapool.com). This friendly, well-run tourist office also
offers an accommodation booking service.

ACCOMMODATION

Ullapool is busy from Easter through until September – **booking in advance** is essential.

HOTELS, GUESTHOUSES AND B&BS

★ **The Ceilidh Place** West Argyle St ☎ 01854 612103, ⓦ theceilidhplace.com. Antique bed frames, old books on vintage cabinets and Roberts Radios add character to rooms of this lovely small hotel, where the mantra is "no TVs, and proud". Some are pepped up with stylish wallpaper, otherwise modern-rustic rules. The lounge and library, with honesty bar, offers sophisticated relaxation. The cheapest rooms share bathrooms. Also manages a bunkhouse (£23, includes linens) directly opposite. £124

Point Cottage West Shore St ☎ 01854 613015, ⓦ pointcottagebandb.co.uk. A seafront former fisherman's cottage with loch views from its two pretty front rooms, finished, like the rear double, in soft natural shades and subtle tartans for a homely atmosphere. Even if you're not staying here, pop by to pick up an ice cream and put a coin in the honesty box. £75

★ **Tanglewood House** 1 mile south off A835 ☎ 01854 612059, ⓦ tanglewoodhouse.co.uk. Charm and character in an extraordinary, curved house full of art and antiques. Rooms are individually furnished; the best (the Green Room) with a terrace to enjoy the position above Loch Broom, is worth its extra £14. Factor in a rocky beach

beneath for a dip and this is a truly memorable stay, May–Oct. £96

West House West Argyle St ☎ 01854 613126, ⓦ westhousebandb.co.uk. A former manse, with all the handsome proportions that suggests, plus charming owners who spoil you with home-made bread and cake. Relaxing modern rooms and a pre-stocked fridge in each room means a continental breakfast at your leisure. All in all a bargain. April–Sept. £60

HOSTEL AND CAMPSITE

Broomfield Holiday Park West Shore St ☎ 01854 612020, ⓦ broomfieldhp.com. Hurrah: a campsite in the centre of town with loch views and space galore at the tip of Ullapool, plus standard facilities and all a short walk from the heart of Ullapool. Easter–Sept. Per pitch £19

SYHA Hostel Shore St ☎ 01854 612254, ⓦ syha.org.uk. Busy hostel bang on the seafront, where prints and murals of seaside scenes help add a cheerful holiday atmosphere. There are dorms of various sizes, doubles, twins, twin lounges, internet access and laundry plus lots of good information about local walks. April–Oct. Dorms £2□ doubles £45

EATING

As well as the decent Scottish pub grub offerings that you would expect of any Highlands town, Ullapool has both an Indian, *Essence of India*, and a Chinese, *The Jade House*. Though neither is likely to win an award any time soon, visitors on longer tours may well be grateful to have something that isn't game or seafood.

CEILIDHS

The **ceilidh** is essentially an informal, homespun kind of entertainment, the word being Gaelic for a "visit". In remote Highland communities, talents and resources were pooled, people gathering to play music, sing, recite poems and dance. The dances themselves are thought to be ancient in origin; the Romans wrote that the Caledonians danced with abandon round swords stuck in the ground, a practice echoed in today's traditional sword dance, where the weapons are crossed on the floor and a quick-stepping dancer skips over and around them.

Highland ceilidhs, fuelled by whisky and largely extemporized, must have been an intoxicating, riotous means of fending off winter gloom. Like much of clan culture, however, the traditions died or were forced underground after the defeat of the Highlanders at **Culloden** and the passing of the 1747 Act of Proscription, which forbade the wearing of the plaid and other expressions of Highland identity.

Ceilidhs were enthusiastically revived in the reign of tartan-fetishist **Queen Victoria**, and in the twentieth century became the preserve of the village hall and hotel ballroom, buoyed to some extent by the popularity of jaunty 1950s TV programmes. More recently, though, the ceilidh has thrown off its dated associations, with places such as *The Ceilidh Place* in Ullapool (see opposite) and the *Taybank Hotel* in Dunkeld (see p.330) restoring some of its spontaneous, infectious fun to a night of Scottish music and dancing.

Whether performed by skilled traditional musicians or in more rollicking form by younger players, ceilidh music is irresistible, and it's common to find all generations gathering. Ceilidh dances look complex. Actually most are reasonably simple and are explained or "called" beforehand by the bandleader. We find a whisky or two earlier helps.

The Arch Inn West Shore St ☎01854 612454. Ullapool's liveliest pub divides between a popular bar and informal restaurant with Scottish-European cooking: starters like sautéed scallops with pickled apple (£7.95) or cullen skink (£5.95), then sirloin steak (£19.95) alongside the usual fish and chips (£10.95). Mon–Thurs 11am–11pm, Fri & Sat 11am–1am, Sun 12.30–11pm; food served noon–2.30pm & 5–9pm.

The Ceilidh Place West Argyle St ☎01854 612103. Barn-like venue remains one of the best in town. After breakfasts, it shifts to a bistro menu – home-made burgers, salads, schnitzels, plus daily specials like risotto and fish casseroles (mains £11.50–20) – and its bar hosts regular live music. Fantastic bookshop attached. Daily 8am–10pm.

West Coast Delicatessen Argyle St ☎01854 613450. Fine food deli serves up proper coffees, home-made houmous and fresh salads, tarts and cakes, plus unmissable "pakora Fridays". For a proper fry-up, the *Tea Store* over the road will do the job. Mon–Sat 8.30am–5pm.

DRINKING

Ullapool has no shortage of decent boozers. The liveliest pub around, the *Arch Inn* (see above), hosts live bands, and live Scottish **folk music** is a feature at *The Ceilidh Place* (see above).

Ferry Boat Inn Shore St ☎01854 612366. Popular with locals with their dogs, the *FBI* remains a choice spot to swig a pint of ale at the lochside (midges permitting) and watch the boats. Live music, and also at sister pub *The Argyle* round the corner. Daily 11am–11pm.

Assynt

If the landscape before Ullapool was impressive, the **Assynt** region just north has an epic, almost cinematic, quality. Marking the transition from Wester Ross into Sutherland, this region is one of the least populated areas in Europe and its landscape consists not of mountain ranges but of extraordinary peaks which rise individually from the moorland. See a mountain like **Suilven** and you understand why the name is said to derive from "A-ssynt", meaning seen from afar, or "ass" – Old Norse for rocky. Certainly, Assynt boasts some of the world's oldest rock formations, and roadside signs highlight the region's geological importance as the **Northwest Highlands Geopark** (☺nwhgeopark.com).

12

Coigach

Coigach is the peninsula immediately north of Loch Broom, accessible via a road off the A835. It's a beautiful drive, squeezing between the northern shore of Loch Lurgainn and mountains like mammoths, including **Cul Beag** (2523ft), craggy **Stac Pollaidh** (2012ft) and the awesome bulk of **Ben More Coigach** (2439ft), southeast, which presides over the area. There's some spectacular coastal scenery too. It's a place to unwind, with gorgeous views of the Summer Isles scattered offshore and signposted trails along coastal moors and mountains. If the steep Ben More Coigach–Sgurr an Fhidhleir horseshoe (7 miles; 7hr) seems too tough, the Culnacraig circuit (5 miles; 5hr) between Achduart and Culnacraig also offers great views. Coigach's main settlement is **ACHILTIBUIE**, a crofting village spread above beaches and rocks. Sunsets here can be astonishing.

Tanera Mor

A mile offshore, **Tanera Mor** is the largest island of the **Summer Isles**. It briefly hit the headlines in March 2016 when its family custodians put it up for sale – a snip at £1.95 million – after a community buyout failed. Presumably the new owner, or owners if the three available plots are bought individually, will continue to allow boat trips (May–Sept Mon–Sat; 9.30am, noon & 2.30pm; £25; ☎07927 920592, ☺summerisles-seatours.co.uk) round the isles to put ashore on Tanera Mor for an hour, allowing visitors to potter up to the post office to buy "Summer Isles" stamps or have a cuppa in a small café by the pier.

ARRIVAL AND INFORMATION

By bus The Scotbus service from Ullapool to Achiltibuie (Mon–Fri 2–3 daily, Sat 1 daily; 1hr 15min) doubles as the school bus, so services are scheduled around the start and end of the school day.

Tourist information Useful websites include ⓦ coigach .com, or ⓦ summer-isles.com for Tanera Mor.

ACCOMMODATION AND EATING

Am Fuaran Bar Althandhu ☎01854 622339, ⓦ amfuaran.co.uk. A lovely pub whatever the exterior suggests, as cosy as a cabin inside – log-burner and all – and with a fine menu of steak-and-ale pies (£14.50), chickpea tagine (£10.25), and scallops in ginger and lemon butter (£7.20). Daily noon–11.45pm; food served 12.30–2.30pm & 6–8.30pm, till 8pm Sun.

★ **Port A Bhaigh Campsite** Althandhu ☎01854 622339, ⓦ portabhaigh.co.uk. Spread behind the beach with mesmerizing sea views to the Summer Isles and excellent facilities that include a laundry, this is as fine a campsite as you'll find in the Highlands. Midges can be horrendous but the *Am Fuaran Bar* is literally over the road. Per pitch £9

Summer Isles Hotel Achiltibuie ☎01854 622282 ⓦ summerisleshotel.co.uk. A stylish hideaway with a superb setting, fresh modern-country decor and lovel simple rooms, most in adjoining annexes. Its restaura (£49 menu; reservation recommended) is no longe Michelin-starred, but seasonal modern British menus sti dazzle with plates such as scallops or langoustine. Th attached former crofters' pub serves up regional ales an a less glitzy bar menu during the day, plus occasiona music in the evenings. Easter–Oct; bar open noon– 11pm; food served in bar noon–3pm, in dining room 6.30–9pm. £140

Lochinver and around

It's hard to think of a more beautiful route than the single-track road that wriggles north from Coigach towards Inverkirkaig. Unremittingly spectacular, the journey is the Highlands in miniature, threading through stunted beech woods, heaving valleys, open moorland and bare rock, past the startling shapes of Cul Beag (2523ft), Cul Mor (2785ft) and the distinctive sugar-loaf **Suilven** (2398ft) until it slaloms along the sea shore to Inverkirkaig, the start of two fantastic walks (see below). **LOCHINVER**, another two miles north, marks the return to civilization. One of the busier fishing harbours in Scotland, the small town (oversized village, really) has a pleasingly down-to-earth atmosphere. Factor in excellent budget and high-end accommodation and an established reputation for food, and it makes a natural base for the area.

Inverkirkaig Falls and Suilven

A car park at the south end of Inverkirkaig, three miles south of Lochinver, marks the start of a **walk** upriver to **Falls of Kirkaig**, itself the start of a long but gentle walk to the base of **Suilven** – its huge sandstone dome is as much of a landmark today as it was for Viking sailors. Serious hikers use the path as an approach to scale the peak (10–12hr), but you can also follow it for an easy five-mile, three-hour (return) ramble, taking in a waterfall and a secluded loch.

ARRIVAL AND INFORMATION

LOCHINVER AND AROUN

By bus Lochinver may be large by local standards, but connections are not great.
Destinations Ullapool (Mon–Sat 2 daily; 1hr).
Tourist information The Assynt Visitor Centre in central Lochinver (Easter to mid-June & Sept–Oct Mon–Sat

10am–4pm; mid-June to Aug Mon–Sat 9.30am–5pm, S 11am–3pm; ☎01571 841073, ⓔ lochinver.org.uk) h displays on geology, wildlife and history and is stuffed w local tourist information, including the booklet *Ass Walking Network* (£2).

ACTIVITIES

Inver Cruises Lochinver harbour ☎ 01571 844406. Runs 90min cruises around Lochinver's coastline (4 daily; £20).

ACCOMMODATION AND EATING

Some of the local accommodation is in a conjoined village, **Baddidarrach**, on the north side of the loch; from Lochinv cross the bridge and turn left.

The Albannach Baddidarrach ☎01571 844407, ⓦthealbannach.co.uk. Lesley Crosfield and Colin Craig's Victorian house provides a stay of exquisite taste and astonishing views over the walled garden to the sea loch and Suilven beyond. Individually decorated rooms vary from romantic to hip, with great bathrooms. The couple also possess Britain's most northerly Michelin star: six-course set menus (dinner included for residents; £75 for non-residents) of modern Scottish food created from local and home-grown ingredients. Their fantastic pub in the village, *The Caberfeidh*, is a good option for anyone who wants to sample their top-quality food at affordable prices. No children under 12. Food served from 6pm: Feb–March Fri–Sun, April–Nov & late Dec Tues–Sun. **£305**

An Cala Café & Bunkhouse Lochinver harbour ☎01571 844598, ⓦcadaleah.co.uk. The former seamen's mission by the harbour houses a cosy hostel and great café serving the likes of battered monkfish scampi (£11.95) or tandoori veggie masala (£9.95). It has fourteen beds in three modern dorms – spotless if a bit tight for space in the six-bed – plus a good kitchen and laundry facilities. Dorms **£22**; doubles **£40**

★**The Caberfeidh** Main St, near bridge ☎01571 844321, ⓦthecaberfeidh.co.uk. Run by the same owners as the Michelin-starred *Albannach*. Small plates and wine by the glass bring the same superb quality but for a fraction of the price; think wild venison meatballs £6.95) and straight-from-the-boat bouillabaisse (£5.95). River views and a roaring fire top this off as one of the Highlands' best dining pubs. Mon 5.30–11pm & Tues–Sun noon–11pm; food served noon–2.30pm & 6–9pm.

Inver Lodge Signed off Main St, Lochinver ☎01571 844496, ⓦinverlodge.com. Refurbishment of a hillside hotel has created a five-star stay, featuring relaxed contemporary decor with a nod to Highlands country style and loch views. The latter are at their best from the restaurant, an outpost of *Chez Roux*, with fresh seafood plus rich French country dishes like confit duck leg; menus start at £44.50. April–Oct daily 6–10pm. **£250**

Lochinver Larder Main St, near bridge ☎01571 844356, ⓦlochinverlarder.co.uk. Sensational home-made pies, including exotics like wild boar and saag paneer, have made it famous, but this fine bistro prepares other food too: think smoked fish linguini, home-made fishcakes (both £13.95) or langoustine in lime, ginger and chilli butter (£20). Takeaway available. Easter–Oct Mon–Sat 10am–7.45pm, Sun 10am–5.30pm; Nov–March daily 10am–4pm.

12

North of Lochinver

There are two routes **north** from Lochinver: the fast A837 along the shore of Loch Assynt (see p.461) to join the A894, or the scenic B869 coast road. Hugging the indented shoreline, the latter offers coastal views, superb **beaches** and high cliff walks. The first village worth a detour is **ACHMELVICH**, four miles northwest of Lochinver, where a tiny bay cradles a white-sand beach lapped by azure water. It's popular (relatively speaking), but there are equally seductive beaches up the coast, including a tiny, hidden cove, **Port Alltan na Bradhan**, a mile north, plus a beautiful strand at **CLACHTOLL** a couple of miles beyond.

Old Man of Stoer

A side road that branches north off the B869 between **STOER** and **CLASHNESSIE** ends abruptly by a lighthouse at **Raffin**. The reason to come is a two-mile stroll along a boggy track to reach the **Old Man of Stoer**, a 197ft rock stack just off the Point of Stoer, the headland's tip, surrounded by sheer cliffs and occasionally scaled by climbers. It's worth a circuit around the south side of the headland to return with a last view of the mountains of Assynt, after which you'll deserve a cuppa in the tea van at the car park (April–Sept Mon–Fri & Sun 11am–5pm, except in high winds and heavy rain).

ACCOMMODATION AND EATING   **NORTH OF LOCHINVER**

Achmelvich Beach SYHA Achmelvich ☎01571 844480, ⓦsyha.org.uk. Although the open-plan lounge-kitchen of this 22-bed hostel in a former school and cottage struggles when full, most people are outside anyway – just yoyds away are the white sands of the beach. Dorms, a family room and private twins are available. Closed mid-Sept to Easter, as well as weekdays Sept & Easter; whole hostel rental available all year. Dorms **£20**; twins **£49.50**

Clachtoll Beach Campsite Clachtoll ☎01571 855377, ⓦclachtollbeachcampsite.co.uk. This simple, neat site at the heart of the crofting village is all about its location right behind one of the most appealing stretches of powder white sand on the west coast. Easter–Sept. Per pitch **£17**

Kylesku and around

Until a road bridge swept over the mouth of lochs Glencoul and Glendhu, **KYLESKU**, 33 miles north of Ullapool, was the embarkation point for a ferry that was the only link from the west Highlands to north Scotland. Off the main road since the bridge's construction in 1984, it's now a beautiful, soporific spot, where interlocking slopes plunge into the deep waters. Marking a last hurrah before the Assynt's sharp sandstone gives way to rounded quartzite, Kylesku is popular with walkers due to its proximity to **Quinag** (2651ft), less a single peak than several peaks reached by a **ridge walk**. The easiest ascent is from a car park on the A894 a few miles south of Kylesku. Also in the area is Britain's highest waterfall, **Eas a Chùal Aluinn** (650ft), at the head of Loch Glencoul. It's five miles return east of a car park two miles south of Kylesku or a full day on a track around the north side of both lochs. Alternatively, boat tours run from the wharf.

ARRIVAL AND ACTIVITIES
KYLESKU AND AROUND

By bus D&E Coaches' (☎01463 222444) summer-only service from Inverness to Durness via Ullapool stops at Kylesku. It can carry bikes with a reservation (May & June Thurs–Mon, July–Sept Mon–Sat).

Destinations Inverness (late May to Sept 1 daily Mon–Sat, plus Sun 1 daily in July & Aug; 4hr); Lochinve (same times; 30min).

Tours Gentle cruises into lochs Glendhu and Glencoul with Kylesku Boat Tours (April–Sept 2 daily; round trip 1h 45min; £25; ☎01971 502231, ⓦkyleskuboattours.com).

ACCOMMODATION AND EATING

Kylesku Hotel Kylesku ☎01971 502231, ⓦkylesku hotel.co.uk. A small hotel of crisp, modern style beside the loch. It provides by far the best food in the area, all sourced locally – from the vegetables to the shellfish. Expect the likes of Kylesku langoustines (£20.95) or hogget curr (£17.50). The smart new wing, "Willy's Hoose", is name after a local – some rooms with private balcony and loc views. Feb–Nov. **£105**

The far northwest coast

The **far northwest coast**, in Sutherland, is too far for some, but those who make the journey will find this captures the stark, elemental beauty of the Highlands like nowhere else. Here, as the geology shifts into ice-scoured pinkish quartzite barely covered by a thin skin of moorland, peaks become more widely spaced and settlements smaller and fewer, linked by twisting roads and shoreside footpaths. Up here, life feels exhilaratingly on the edge of civilization. The flip side is that accommodation and food are sparse; be prepared that places get booked up fast in season and the options are thir on the ground during the winter.

Scourie and around

Ten miles north of Kylesku, **SCOURIE** lies among a landscape marbled with lochs and lochans. This is prime Scottish **fly-fishing** territory; permits (£5–20) are available from the Fishing Tackle Shop in the garage (ⓦscouriefillingstation.uk). There's also some terrific **walking** hereabouts up mountains like Ben Stack (2359ft) – locals yarn that its pyramidal peak inspired a visiting Hollywood executive to create the logo for Paramount Pictures – and a beautiful beach makes it a good choice for families.

Handa Island

Managed by the Scottish Wildlife Trust (ⓦswt.org.uk) • No charge to visit, but donations encouraged • Ferries operate April–Sept Mon–Sat 9am–2pm, every 20–30min (£12.50)

Reason enough to come through Scourie is **Handa Island**, the huge chunk of red Torridon sandstone just offshore. Carpeted with machair and purple heather, the islan is maintained as a **wildlife reserve** by the Scottish Wildlife Trust and supports one of the largest seabird colonies in northwest Europe – razorbills and Britain's largest breeding colony of guillemots on ragged sandstone cliffs during summer, and puffins in clifftop burrows from late May to mid-July.

Ferries shuttle regularly in summer from **Tarbet**, a six-mile drive north of Scourie. When you arrive on Handa Island you will be greeted by a volunteer, who offers an introductory talk on the history and ecology of the island. Allow three hours at least to follow a **footpath** around the island – an easy and enjoyable walk taking in Great Stack, a 361ft rock pillar on the north shore, and fine views across the Minch.

ARRIVAL AND DEPARTURE

SCOURIE AND AROUND

By bus Scourie is on the summer-only bike-carrying Inverness–Durness service of D&E Coaches (☎01463 222444) via Ullapool and Lochinver (May & June Thurs–Mon, July–Sept Mon–Sat). Durness Bus (☎01971 511223) runs from Lairg to Durness, stopping at Scourie (Mon–Fri).
Destinations Durness (Mon–Sat 1 daily; 1hr); Inverness (late May to Sept Mon–Sat 1 daily, plus Sun 1 daily in July & Aug; 4hr 10min); Lochinver (same times; 50min); Ullapool (same times; 1hr 10min).

ACCOMMODATION AND EATING

Scourie Caravan and Camping Park Scourie ☎01971 502060, ⊛scouriecampsitesutherland.com. Spread behind the beach, this well-maintained site provides sea views to go with its flat pitches and tidy amenities block. On-site café-bar, *The Anchorage* (daily May–Sept 8am–10pm), rustles up food and drinks and has a lounge area in case of bad weather. April to early Oct. Per pitch **£16**

Scourie Hotel Scourie ☎01971 502396, ⊛scouriehotel.com. A traditional, family-run coaching inn – fully refurbed in 2015 – whose fishing obsession only adds character. There are taxidermied trout in the wood-panelled cocktail bar, real ales in the public bar, and enormous maps of Scotland in the entrance hall. Themed Highlands headboards are a nice touch in the simple, elegant rooms. Seasonal four-course dining menu for £32, or bar meals like fish and chips from £12. A memorable stay. April–Sept. **£125**

★ **Shorehouse** Tarbet wharf ☎01971 502251. With its views of pristine shore, Handa and the Man of Stoer beyond, this feels like the restaurant at the end of the world. Nautical and airy inside, serving home-made soups and sandwiches, plus mains of salmon, hot mackerel and seafood platters, around £13. Couldn't be much fresher – they catch their own shellfish. Mon–Sat noon–7pm, until 8pm July & Aug.

Kinlochbervie

North of Scourie, the road sweeps through the Highlands at its starkest – rocks piled on rocks, bog and water, and a bare, stony coastline that looks increasingly inhospitable. For some that's a call to adventure: sailor and adventurer John Ridgway established an outdoor school on an isolated sea loch off **Loch Laxford** in the 1960s. The largest settlement here, reached on the B801, is **KINLOCHBERVIE**, where a huge fish market and harbour reveal this as the premier fishing port in the area, reduced in stature since its heyday in the late 1980s, but still serviced by trucks from all over Europe. Otherwise it's a scruffy, utilitarian place, usually visited only as a launchpad for Sandwood Bay (see p.466).

ARRIVAL AND DEPARTURE

KINLOCHBERVIE

By bus Kinlochbervie is on the summer-only Inverness–Durness service of D&E Coaches (☎01463 222444) via Ullapool and Lochinver (May & June Thurs–Mon, July–Sept Mon–Sat).
Destinations Durness (40min); Scourie (30min); Ullapool (1hr 50min).

ACCOMMODATION AND EATING

Old School Restaurant and Rooms Inshegra, 1 mile before Kinlochbervie on B801 ☎01971 521383, ⊛oldschoolklb.co.uk. By far the most comfortable accommodation option in the area, with a handful of rather smart rooms, including a cute separate en-suite single. Guests are treated to good-value evening meals of home cooking: expect haddock chowder, cullen skink, venison casserole or veggie lasagne (£13–16). **£65**

12

Sandwood Bay

A single-track road continues northwest of Kinlochbervie through **OLDSHOREMORE**, an isolated crofters' village above a stunning white-sand beach (a magic spot to wild camp), then on to **BLAIRMORE**, start of the four-mile walk to **Sandwood Bay**. The shell-white **beach** beyond the peat moors is one of the most beautiful in Scotland, flanked by rolling dunes and lashed by gales for much of the year. Vikings beached their longships here over a millennium ago – the name is a corruption of "sand" and "vatn", meaning sand and water. Good luck with them both if you decide to wild camp here.

It's possible to trek overland from Sandwood Bay north to Cape Wrath (see opposite), the northwestern tip of mainland Britain, a full day's walk away. If you're planning to meet the Cape Wrath minibus to Durness (see below), contact them first since it won't run if the weather turns bad.

The north coast

For years, very few visitors would travel the length of Scotland's isolated, wild north coast. Those who did get this far would most likely head for John O'Groats, take a photo, have a cuppa then head back. But these days the north coast has become a destination in its own right. The soaring popularity of the North Coast 500 route (see box, p.440) has brought an influx of tourers – cyclists, drivers, caravans and all – to Scotland's rugged northern shore, and few go home disappointed. This gorgeous stretch of road is backed by steep mountains in the west and by lochs and open rolling grasslands in the east, while between them is mile upon mile of crumbling cliffs, sheer rocky headlands and perfect white beaches that are nearly always deserted except for intrepid surfers who come for the best waves in Scotland. Visit between January and March and there's a chance you might witness the Northern Lights, too.

Wee **Durness** is a good jumping-off point for **Cape Wrath**, the windswept promontory at Scotland's tip which has retained an end-of-the-world mystique lost long ago by John O'Groats. Continuing east, **Tongue** enjoys an attractive setting and a Munro to climb nearby, while **Thurso**, the largest town on the north coast, is acclaimed by surfers. For everyone else it's a gateway to some of Scotland's most populous seabird colonies around **Dunnet Head** and **Duncansby Head**.

Durness and around

Scattered over sheltered sandy coves and grassy clifftops, **DURNESS** is the most northwesterly village on the British mainland, straddling the point where the road swings from peat bogs to the fertile limestone machair of the north coast. The village sits above Sango Sands bay, whose fine beach has made it a modest resort. Beatle **John Lennon** came here as a teenager on family holidays to stay with his Auntie Lizzie (Elizabeth Parkes) – his memories later went into the song *In My Life* and he revisited in 1969 with Yoko. Parkes is buried in the graveyard at Balnakeil, and there is a slightly bizarre memorial to Lennon at the Durness Village Hall which still attracts a trickle of die-hard Beatles fans throughout the year.

Smoo Cave

1 mile east of Durness • Always open • Free

A mile east of the village is **Smoo Cave**, a gaping hole in a limestone cliff created by the sea and a small burn. Tucked at the end of a narrow sea cove, the main chamber is accessible via steps from the car park. The much-hyped rock formations are quite impressive, and if the weather behaves you can take a fantastic twenty-minute trip by rubber dinghy (run on demand Easter–Sept; £4; ☎01971 511704) into two further caverns; after heavy rain a waterfall cascades through the middle of the cavern.

Balnakeil

A mile northwest of Durness, the white sands of **Balnakeil Bay** are stunning in any weather, but especially spectacular when sunny days turn the sea a brilliant Mediterranean turquoise. A path winds north through the dunes behind to reach **Faraid Head** – fine views east to the mouth of Loch Eriboll and west to Cape Wrath make this circuit (3–4hr) the best in the area. While here, drop by the Balnakeil Craft Village, a hippie commune borne out of a disused 1970s military camp.

Cape Wrath

Closer to Iceland than London, the headland takes its name not from stormy seas but from the Norse word *hvarf* ("turning place"), a throwback to the days when Viking warships passed en route to raid the Scottish coast. Yet **Cape Wrath** still exudes a powerful sense of nature in the raw. The British mainland's most northwesterly point – and one of only two capes in the country – is tipped by a Stevenson lighthouse and stands above **Clo Mor cliffs**, the highest sea cliffs in Britain and a prime breeding site for seabirds. On a clear day you'll gaze out to Orkney and the Outer Hebrides.

The surprise is that Cape Wrath is so easily reached on a day-trip from Durness. The journey begins two miles southwest at **Keoldale**. A foot-passenger **ferry** crosses the Kyle of Durness estuary to link with a **minibus** for the fourteen-mile run to Cape Wrath and the *Ozone* café at the lighthouse (open daily year-round; ☎01971 511314). With two to three days to spare, you could catch the ferry then walk a circuit to Sandwood Bay, catching a bus back to Durness from Kinlochbervie. There's a basic free bothy at Kearvaig. Note that the Ministry of Defence maintains Garvie Island (An Garbh-eilean) as an air bombing range and so occasionally closes the road to Cape Wrath. At the time of research the Durness Development Group was raising funds to purchase the 110 acres of land surrounding the lighthouse at Cape Wrath (ⓦdevelopingdurness.org).

12

ARRIVAL AND DEPARTURE

DURNESS AND AROUND

DURNESS

By bus Public transport is sparse; the key service is the D&E Coaches (May & June Thurs–Mon, July–Sept Mon–Sat). It goes from Inverness (4hr 15min) via Ullapool (2hr 25min) and Scourie (1hr 5min) and has a cycle carrier.

CAPE WRATH

By ferry and minibus The foot-passenger ferry from Keoldale runs from April to Sept (in theory daily at 11am, plus June–Aug 9am; £6.50 return; ☎01971 511246, ☎07719 678729); call to confirm tides and Ministry of Defence schedules. It drops you on the opposite bank of the kyle to connect with a minibus to Cape Wrath (£12 return; ☎07742 670196).

INFORMATION AND ACTIVITIES

Tourist office Just east of the centre of Durness (April, May & Oct daily 10am–4.30pm; June–Aug daily 9.30am–5pm; ☎01971 509005, ⓦdurness.org). This helpful tourist office can provide information about walks and cycle tracks, including guided ranger walks. Information on Cape Wrath is at ⓦvisitcapewrath.com.

Golf Durness golf course (☎01971 511364, ⓦdurnessgolfclub.org), the most northwesterly course on mainland Britain, is a nine-hole with two tee-off options per hole to create 18 holes (£20). Closed to visitors Sun morning; equipment rental from clubhouse (from £5).

ACCOMMODATION AND EATING

DURNESS

Lazy Crofter Bunkhouse ☎01971 511202, ⓦvisitdurness.com/bunkhouse. Run year-round by *Mackay's* next door, this is the finest bunkhouse on the north coast, far more appealing than the SYHA hostel by Smoo Cave. Has a snug cabin atmosphere and gets extra marks for individual reading lights in cosy twins and two dorms. The terrace has sea views. Sleeps twenty. Easter–Oct. **£19**

★**Mackay's** ☎01971 511202, ⓦvisitdurness.com /rooms. Handmade and vintage furniture, luxury linen, natural colours and genuine hospitality make this one of the best stays on the north coast. It also manages weekly self-catering options: from a sweet cabin to carbon-negative Croft 103's eco-chic. No dinners, but they compensate for it with superb breakfasts, picnic lunches and afternoon tea, plus nibbles in the evenings. Easter–Oct. **£129**

Sango Sands Oasis ☎01971 511726, ⓦsangosands .com. This flat, spacious site spreads over cliffs above the turquoise waters of its namesake and beside the pub that manages it; now the only place in Durness serving dinner, with hearty bar standards from £10–16.50. Campers get premier pitches, so wake to a vast seascape. Free out of season, though cold-water showers only. April–Oct. Per person £8

BALNAKEIL

Cocoa Mountain Balnakeil Craft Village ☎01971 511233, ⓦcocoamountain.co.uk. "The Best Hot Chocolate", a rich bitter-sweet hot chocolate topped off by white chocolate, is the speciality in the bright modern café of this chocolatier. Sells snacks (£5–7) plus its chocolates and truffles. A treat after time in the wilds. Call out of season and the friendly owner may open up for you. Easter–Oct daily 9am–6pm.

CAPE WRATH

Daill Camping Pods Daill beach ☎01971 511246. Cape Wrath's first non-bothy accommodation offering. A couple of basic camping pods (both doubles) with outdoor kennels for hardy companions. £6 extra for bedding, cooking equipment and crockery. £22

Tongue to Thurso

Vast and empty, the landscape between Tongue and Thurso has considerable drama. It's a bleak moorland intercut with sandy sea lochs and with few inhabitants: tiny **Tongue** is pleasant enough, as is **Bettyhill**, further east. But the real reason to venture this far is the landscape: a dead-end **coast road** west of Tongue; **Ben Hope** (3040ft), the most northerly Munro; or the blanket bog of the **Flow Country** inland.

Tongue and around

Having taken a slow circuitous route around Loch Eriboll and east over the moors of A'Mhoine, you roll finally into the pretty crofting township of **TONGUE**. Dominated from a hillside spur by the ruins of **Castle Varrich** (Caisteal Bharraich), a medieval stronghold of the Mackays (three-mile return walk), the village is strewn above the east shore of the **Kyle of Tongue**, which you can cross either via a causeway or by a longer and more scenic single-track road around its southern side. When the tide recedes, this shallow estuary becomes a mass of golden sand flats, superb on sunny days, with the sharp profiles of **Ben Hope** (3040ft) and **Ben Loyal** (2509ft) looming like twin sentinels to the south, and the Rabbit Islands a short way out to sea. A dead-end road offers views of the islands, plus superb seascapes and scenery as it threads through Talmine towards a beach at **Strathan**; take the left turn to Melness before Tongue causeway.

ACCOMMODATION AND EATING
TONGUE AND AROUND

Ben Loyal Tongue ☎01847 611216. Seafood fresh off the owner's boat is served in a relaxed pub along with favourites such as steak pie or home-made burgers. With decent prices (£9–18 main) and live music most Saturdays, this is the choice of many locals. Daily 11.30am–3pm & 5–11.30pm; food served noon–2.30pm & 6–9pm.

Kyle of Tongue Hostel & Holiday Park East of Kyle of Tongue Bridge ☎01847 611789, ⓦtonguehosteland holidaypark.co.uk. The Duke of Sutherland's old shooting lodge has been repurposed as a large, well-equipped hostel with spacious dorms and family rooms, plus great mountain views. SYHA-affiliated, with plans to expand as caravan park and campsite. Mid-April to Sept. Dorms £19 twins £44

Tongue Hotel Tongue ☎01847 611206, ⓦtonguehot .co.uk. This nineteen-bedroom small hotel marries relaxed modern taste with the architectural heritage of a former ducal hunting lodge. There are antiques in the best rooms, even the odd marble washstand, and spacious proportions throughout. The Superior rooms are worth the extra £20. £120

Bettyhill and around

Twelve miles east of Tongue, **BETTYHILL** is a major crofting village, set among rocky green hills. In Gaelic it was known as *Am Blàran Odhar* ("Little Dun-coloured Field"). The origins of the English name are unknown but it was definitely not named after Elizabeth, Countess of Sutherland, who presided over the Strathnaver Clearances whose sorry tale is told in the town museum. The village is also surrounded on either side by beautiful beaches: **Farr beach**, a splendid crescent of white sand, is behind the museum, while the unbroken arc of **Torrisdale Bay** sweeps west of the town beyond the Naver

---

THE FLOW COUNTRY

A detour inland on the A897 east of Bettyhill towards Helmsdale heads south into the **Flow Country** tundra. The name (pronounced to rhyme with "now") derives from *flói*, an Old Norse word meaning "marshy ground", and this 1544-square-mile expanse of "blanket bog" – the largest in the world, says UNESCO, which has it filed under "possible" on its World Heritage status – is both a valuable carbon sink and a home to a wide variety of birdlife. The RSPB's **Forsinard Flows Visitor Centre** (Easter–Oct daily 9am–5pm; free; ☎01641 571225, ⓦrspb .org.uk/forsinard), at the train station in **FORSINARD**, is the gateway to the so-called Forsinard Flows. Pick up a leaflet then follow the mile-long **Dubh Lochan Trail**. Follow the new boardwalk to the Flows Lookout Tower before walking over flagstones to learn about its blanket bog. En route, you get to see bog asphodel, bogbean, and insect-trapping sundew and butterwort; you've also got a good chance of spotting greenshanks, golden plovers and hen harriers. During the summer, the visitor centre runs **guided walks** through the area to explain the wonders of peat; wellies or walking boots are recommended.

River. Both receive good surf. For more cerebral stuff, the 24-mile **Strathnaver Trail** runs south along the B873 to Altnaharra, past historical sites from the Neolithic, Bronze and Iron Age periods, as well as the remains of crofting villages cleared in the early 1800s. Free printout area guides are available from the museum (donations welcome).

Strathnaver Museum

n the old Farr church, east of the main village • April–Oct Mon–Sat 10am–5pm • £2 • ☎01971 521418, ⓦ strathnavermuseum.org.uk

The volunteer-run **Strathnaver Museum** houses exhibits of ethnological and archeological interest – crofting items including a bizarre fishing buoy made from a dogskin, Pictish stones and a 3800-year-old early Bronze Age beaker – and also narrates the Sutherland Clearances through a short film. Its most famous item is free to view – the **Farr stone**, a ninth-century engraved Pictish gravestone, is in the west end of the graveyard.

ACCOMMODATION AND EATING	**BETTYHILL AND AROUND**
Bettyhill Hotel Main road ☎01641 521202, ⓦbettyhillhotel.com. Recent renovation has spruced things up at this 200-year-old hotel. Twenty spacious, individually furnished rooms, plus a cosy lounge. Bar hosts live, folksy music. On-site *Eilean Neave Restaurant* serves up Scottish dishes, like honey roast duck breast or Scrabster scallops (£12–19). Restaurant 6–9pm. **£80**	**Café at Bettyhill** Beside Strathnaver Museum, east of the main village ☎01641 521742. One of the few options in Bettyhill, this small, simple café is all about home cooking, whether daily specials like fisherman's pie (£8) or filled baked potatoes or cakes. It serves fish and chips year-round at weekends (Fri & Sat 5–7pm). April–Oct Mon–Sat 10.30am–5pm, Fri & Sat 10.30am–4pm & 5–7.30pm.

Thurso

THURSO feels like a metropolis after the wild west. In reality it's a modest administrative service centre, most of whose visitors only pause before catching the ferry to Orkney from its port, **Scrabster**. Yet it makes a good base for the area and is legendary among British **surfers**, drawn to a wave which barrels off a reef just east of the harbour. One of the most powerful waves in Europe, "Thurso East" is not a break for beginners.

The town's name derives from the Norse word *Thorsa*, literally "River of the God Thor", and in Viking times this was a major gateway to the mainland. Later, ships set sail for the Baltic and Scandinavian ports loaded with meal, beef, hides and fish. Much of the town, however, dates from the 1790s, when Sir John Sinclair built a large new extension to the old fishing port. Consequently, Thurso's grid-plan streets have some rather handsome Victorian architecture in local, greyish sandstone, not least the recently refurbished **Thurso Library**, opened in 1862 as the Miller Institute and complete with clocktower and pillared facade. There's little sign of the town's older roots except **Old St Peter's Church** on the High Street, a substantial ruin with origins in the thirteenth century.

12

Caithness Horizons

High St • Mon–Fri 10am–6pm, Sat 10am–5pm, & also May–Aug Sun noon–5pm • Free (donations welcome) • ☎ 01847 896508,
ⓦ caithnesshorizons.co.uk

Caithness Horizons, a local museum in a revamped Victorian town hall, is more modern than any other museum on the north coast. Artefacts relate to the Dounreay Nuclear Power Plant, the Vikings and the Picts, and there is a herbarium collection of local botanist Robert Dick. The centre also has a temporary exhibition gallery, a café and a gift shop.

ARRIVAL AND DEPARTURE   THURSO

By train Trains to Thurso leave from Inverness and go up the east coast via Lairg. The following services are all Mon–Sat 3–4 daily, Sun 1 daily.
Destinations Inverness (3hr 50min); Lairg (2hr 5min); Wick (30min).
By bus Buses depart from the train station, Olrig St and Sir George's St.

Destinations Inverness (4–5 daily; 3hr); John O'Groats (Mon–Fri 6–10 daily, Sat 5 daily; 1hr); Wick (Mon–Fri 8–10 daily; 35min).
By ferry NorthLink ferries (ⓦ northlinkferries.co.uk) operate ferries to Stromness, Orkney (2–3 daily; 2hr 15min), from Scrabster, a mile west of town, linked by buses from the train station.

INFORMATION AND ACTIVITIES

Tourist office Located in the foyer of Caithness Horizons, on the High St (same opening hours; ☎ 01847 893155).

Café Tempest Surf Hire Thurso harbour ☎ 01847 892500. Offers equipment rental, including boards (£20/ day), wetsuits (£20/day), and boots and gloves (£5/day).

ACCOMMODATION

Forss House Hotel 5 miles west of Thurso on A836 ☎ 01847 861201, ⓦ forsshousehotel.co.uk. Built in 1810 as a hunting lodge, this thirteen-bedroom hotel offers an upmarket stay, with a choice of traditional accommodation in the main house or more modern rooms in annexes. The Forss River, which wends through the grounds, offers fine salmon fishing. **£135**

Pennyland House B&B West of Town on A9, ☎ 01847 891194, ⓦ pennylandhouse.co.uk. One of Thurso's newest B&Bs is also the town's best. Rooms are named after golf courses and each has its own character, whether it be a sea view or an eighteenth-century

fireplace. King-size beds, excellent breakfast and en-suites seal the deal. **£90**

Sandra's Backpackers Hostel 24–26 Princes S ☎ 01847 894575, ⓦ sandras-backpackers.co.uk. The only hostel in town is a clean enough, zero-frills but well run 27-bed place. Refurbished in 2015, its small rooms are all en suite. Dorms **£18**; doubles **£42**

Thurso Bay Camping & Caravan Park Scrabste Terrace ☎ 01847 892244, ⓦ thursobaycamping.co.uk Large, trim site a 5min walk west from the town centre As well as views to Dunnet Head and Orkney, it has a on-site diner with free wi-fi and a laundry. April–Sept. Pe pitch **£15.50**

EATING

★**Captain's Galley** Harbour, Scrabster ☎ 01847 894999, ⓦ captainsgalley.co.uk. Fish fresh off the boat is the speciality – unfussy dishes like roast hake with borlotti broth and mussels – on three-course menus (£54) that win awards for sustainability as much as flavour. Also offers takeaway fish and chips of whatever's freshest (Tues–Sat 12.30–6.30pm). Reservations essential. Easter–Oct Thurs–Sat 6.30–10pm.

Le Bistro 2 Traill St ☎ 01847 893737. An eternally popular option in Thurso even though it can feel cramped at peak times. The reason is reliable bistro dishes; fish and chips, Mexican chilli bean crêpes or a smashing cullen skink (mains £11–17). June–Aug Tues–Sat 10am–9pm; Sept–May Tues–Wed 10am–3pm, Thurs–Sat 10am–9pm.

Tempest Surf Café Thurso Harbour ☎ 0184 892500. Home-baking, toasties and home-mac burgers (£5–8) served in a harbourside café with laidback surf-shack vibe: think surf newspaper cutout colourful surfboards and driftwood art on the wal Bring-your-own drinks on Saturday evenings during t' summer (£3 corkage). April–Dec Mon–Fri 10am–6pr Sat 10am–8pm, Sun 10am–4pm; Jan–March dai 10am–4pm.

Y Not Bar and Grill Meadow Lane ☎ 01847 89227 Rock 'n' roll memorabilia, sizzling steaks (£19–25) a stacked burgers for under a tenner in this split-level din and live-music venue (gigs weekends only). Da 8.30am–late.

Dunnet and around

Despite the publicity given to John O'Groats, the most northerly point of mainland Britain is actually **Dunnet Head**, four miles north of the sleepy village of **DUNNET**. Here there's not a great deal to do beyond popping in to Britain's most northerly micro-distillery, the Dunnet Bay Distillers (☎01847 851287, ⓦdunnetbaydistillers. co.uk) – who are to thank for the fantastic Rock Rose gin and Holy Grass vodka. It's an evocative spot up at the Dunnet Head, covered in heather and bog and plummeting in red cliffs at the headland, marked by a Stevenson lighthouse, and with the whole north coast spread out before you from Cape Wrath to Duncansby Head on a clear day.

Dunnet Bay

Just south of Dunnet lies **Dunnet Bay**, a vast, golden beach backed by huge dunes. Surfers come for a smattering of reef breaks plus a beach break that offers shelter for beginners depending on whereabouts on the bay you tuck in. At the northeast end of the bay, the **Seadrift Visitor and Ranger Centre** (May–June & Sept Mon, Tues, Thurs, Fri & Sun 2–5pm; July–Aug from 10.30am; free; ☎01847 821531) holds an exhibition about the fauna of the northwest coast and ecology of its sand dunes. It also stocks information leaflets on local history and nature walks.

Mary-Ann's Cottage

South end of Dunnet • June–Sept daily 2–4.30pm • £3 • ☎01847 851765

Signposted off the through road in Dunnet, **Mary-Ann's Cottage** is a farming croft vacated in 1990 by the then 93-year-old Mary-Ann Calder. Her grandfather built the cottage and today it is maintained as she left it, full of mementoes of the three generations who lived and worked there over 150 years. With its antique rocking chair before a blackened hearth, still with its old metal teapot, and family photos, it's a very intimate portrait of a recent past that already feels distant.

Castle of Mey

miles east of Dunnet • May–July & mid-Aug to Sept daily 10.20am–4pm • £11, gardens & grounds only £6.50 • ☎01847 851473, ⓦcastleofmey.org.uk

The handful of houses that make up the village of Mey whizz past in a moment – yet it was here that the late Queen Mother had her Scottish home. The original **Castle of Mey** was a sixteenth-century Z-plan affair, owned by the earls of Caithness until 1889, and bought in a state of disrepair in 1952, the year the Queen Mother's husband, George VI, died. She spent her summer holidays here each August, which may help explain why it's a modest wee place, unstuffy inside despite the facade that bristles with turrets. The walls are hung with works by local amateur artists and watercolours by Prince Charles (who still visits in late July, when it's closed for two weeks), and personal mementoes of the Queen Mum remain on show – guides are more than happy to explain their significance. The **gardens** outside are a lovely spot for an amble on a sunny day, not least for their views across the Pentland Firth.

ARRIVAL AND DEPARTURE **DUNNET AND AROUND**

By bus Bus #80 between Thurso (stops at train station and Sir John's Sq St) and John O'Groats passes through Dunnet and Mey (Mon–Fri 8–9 daily, Sat 6 daily).

ACCOMMODATION AND EATING

Castle Arms Hotel Mey ☎01847 851244, ⓦcastlearms hotel.co.uk. A simple but comfortable stay almost opposite the castle entrance; all rooms are en suite, family-size suites are good value. The restaurant prepares good pub grub such as local steak and fish and chips (average £12) plus daily specials and decent vegetarian options. April–Oct 6–10pm. **£85**

Dunnet Bay Caravan Club Dunnet Bay ☎01847 721319, ⓦcaravanclub.co.uk. On the plus side are the position behind the dunes – a surfer's paradise when waves are firing – and immaculate facilities. The bad news is it's geared to motorhomes and is expensive due to a £12 surcharge for non-Caravan Club members. March–Oct. Per pitch **£31**

12

John O'Groats and around

Snap-happy tourists, windswept pilgrims and knackered cyclists convene at **JOHN O'GROATS**, the most northeasterly settlement on mainland Britain. Consisting of a car park, a souvenir village and not much else, the place has never quite lived up to its folkloric name, although a recent regeneration project has brought some new life to the place with the opening of a technicoloured seafront hotel and a sparkly new café. There are plenty of prettier places to see the sea in north Scotland, but as one end of the Land's End to John O'Groats tour, there's always a happy flow of people either beginning or ending a life-affirming journey here.

Duncansby Head

Marked by a lonely square-towered lighthouse and spectacular cliffs, **Duncansby Head** is the actual northeastern point of mainland Britain, and offers the edge-of-the-world experience that you might have hoped for at John O'Groats, two miles west. The birdlife here is prolific – fulmars, razorbills, puffins, guillemots and kittiwakes in their thousands – and south of the headland lie spectacular 200ft-high cliffs, cut by sheer-sided clefts known locally as *geos*, and several impressive sea stacks. Ask nicely at the tourist office and somebody might be able to take you on a free guided tour.

ARRIVAL AND INFORMATION   JOHN O'GROATS AND AROUND

By bus John O'Groats has regular bus services from Thurso (Mon–Fri 6–10 daily, Sat 5 daily; 1hr) and Wick (Mon–Fri 7 daily, Sat 5 daily; 50min).

By ferry The John O'Groats passenger ferry (☏ 01955 611353, � jogferry.co.uk) sails to Burwick, Orkney (May–Sept 2–3 daily; 45min). It also offers afternoon cruises around the seabird colonies and stacks of Duncansby Head or the Atlantic grey seal colonies of Stroma (mid-June to Aug daily 2.30pm; 1hr 30min; £18).

Tourist office Beside the main car park (March–Oct daily 9am–5pm; ☏ 01847 851287, ⍵ caithness.org).

ACCOMMODATION AND EATING

Natural Retreats John O'Groats ☏ 01955 698583, ⍵ naturalretreats.com/john-ogroats. A multi-million-pound regeneration has brought a tired old seafront hotel back to life as *The Inn*, with neat self-catering apartments and a brightly coloured, Scandi-style extension to boot. All part of the same Natural Retreats development, there are also 23 high-spec wooden lodges facing out to sea. Their *Shorehouse Café* offers sandwiches, pizzas and the like (£6.50–10) and the only Starbucks coffee for miles, or champagne for those with something to celebrate. Daily Easter–May 9am–5pm, June–Oct 8am–7pm, Nov– Easter 9am–4pm. **£185**

The Black Isle and around

The **east coast** of the Highlands is nowhere near as spectacular as the west, and feels more lowland than highland. Heading north from Inverness, you're soon into the **Black Isle** – not an island at all, but a peninsula whose rolling hills, prosperous farms and deciduous woodland make it more reminiscent of Dorset or Sussex than the Highlands. It probably gained its name because of its mild climate: there's rarely frost, which leaves the fields "black" all winter. Another explanation is that the name derives from the Gaelic word for black, *dubh* – a possible corruption of St Duthus (see p.476).

The Black Isle is littered with **prehistoric sites**, but the main incentive to detour east off the A9 is **Cromarty**, a picturesque fishermen's town that is arguably the highlight of the entire Highlands' east coast. If you're heading this way with your own transport, a string of villages along the south coast are worth a stop en route for a modest cultural fix, while **Chanonry Point** is among the best **dolphin-spotting** sites in Europe. In a lay-by just across the Kessock Bridge from Inverness, the small **Scottish Dolphin Centre** (daily 10.30am–5pm; free; ☏ 01343 820339, ⍵ wdcs.org) provides the chance to observe (and listen to) the creatures, and you can get out into the water with Dolphin Trips Avoch a few miles west (£16; ☏ 01381 620961, ⍵ dolphintripsavoch.co.uk).

Fortrose and Rosemarkie

FORTROSE, ten miles northeast of Inverness, is a quietly elegant village dominated by the beautiful ruins of a once huge, early thirteenth-century **cathedral** (daily 9.30am–5.30pm; free) founded by King David I. It languishes on a pretty green bordered by red-sandstone and colourwashed houses. **ROSEMARKIE** a mile on is equally appealing, with its neat high street of stone houses. On sunny days local families descend on the sandy beach, where a cheap-and-cheerful caff has picnic benches looking out to sea. If you're lucky, you might spot a dolphin in the bay.

Groam House Museum

High St, Rosemarkie • March–Oct Mon–Fri 11am–4.30pm, Sat 2–4.30pm; Nov–early Dec Sat 2–4pm • Free • ☎ 01381 620961, ⓦ groamhouse.org.uk

At the lower end of Rosemarkie's high street, **Groam House Museum** displays fifteen intricately carved **Pictish standing stones** (among them the famous Rosemarkie Cross Slab) dating from as early as the eighth century. It also screens a video that highlights other sites in a region that was a stronghold of Pictish culture – a primer to tempt any history buff into a visit to Portmahomack (p.477). There's also a harp to pluck, and kids can "build their own" digital Rosemarkie Stone and print it out.

ARRIVAL AND DEPARTURE   **FORTROSE AND ROSEMARKIE**

By bus Stagecoach buses #23 and #26 from Inverness to Cromarty stop at both Fortrose and Rosemarkie (Mon–Sat   every 30min, Sun 4 daily; 30–35min).

Cromarty

An appealing jumble of handsome Georgian townhouses and pretty workers' cottages knitted together by a cat's-cradle of lanes, **CROMARTY**, the Black Isle's main settlement, is simply a joy to wander around. An ancient ferry crossing on the pilgrimage trail to Tain, it became a prominent port in 1772, fuelling a period of prosperity that gave Cromarty some of the Highlands' finest Georgian houses. The railways poached that trade in the nineteenth century – a branch line to the town was begun but never completed – but the flip side of stagnation is preservation. Out of town, there's a fine four-mile circular coastal **walk**: leave town to the east on Miller Road and turn right when the lane becomes "The Causeway". For a simpler shoreline walk, turn left here, following the path to the water.

Cromarty Courthouse

Church St • April–Oct Sun–Thurs noon–4pm • free; donations welcome • ☎ 01381 600418, ⓦ cromarty-courthouse.org.uk

The streets are gorgeous, but to help bring Cromarty's past alive try this child-friendly museum in the old **Courthouse**, which tells the history of the courthouse and town using audiovisuals and slightly haunting "talking" mannequins in period costume. You are also issued with an audio handset and a map for an excellent **walking tour** around the town.

Hugh Miller's Birthplace Cottage and Museum

Church St • Late March to Sept daily noon–5pm; Oct Tues, Thurs & Fri noon–5pm • £6.50; NTS • ☎ 01381 600245, ⓦ hughmiller.org

Cromarty's most celebrated son is **Hugh Miller**, a nineteenth-century stonemason turned author, journalist, geologist, folklorist and Free Church campaigner. His thatched cottage **birthplace** has been restored to give an idea of what Cromarty must have been like in his day, with decor that swings between cosy rustic and rather formal Victoriana, and displays that highlight his efforts as a social reformer. Friendly staff and a pretty garden add to the appeal.

ARRIVAL AND DEPARTURE   **CROMARTY**

By bus Stagecoach buses #23 and #26 run from Inverness main bus station (Mon–Sat every 30min, Sun 5 daily; 1hr).

ACTIVITIES

EcoVentures Off Bank St, next to Sutor Creek ☎01381 600323, ⓦecoventures.co.uk. Sails from the harbour in a powerful RIB out through the Sutor stacks to the Moray Firth to see the resident bottlenose dolphins and other wildlife up to three times daily (2hr; £28).

ACCOMMODATION AND EATING

Royal Hotel Marine Terrace ☎01381 600217, ⓦroyalhotel-cromarty.co.uk. On the seafront just behind the harbour, this traditional inn provides fairly bland but perfectly acceptable rooms which overlook the Firth. Superiors provide the most character through a mix and match of antique furnishings and more modern decor. One of two options for a pint in town. Mon–Fri 11am–11pm, Sat & Sun till 1am. **£110**

★ **Sutor Creek** 21 Bank St ☎01381 600855, ⓦsutorcreek.co.uk. A lovely café-restaurant full of laidback seaside charm. It focuses on local and seasonal food, whether light lunches (£6–10) or excellent dinners like Shetland scallops with black pudding. The same ethos carries into wood-fired pizzas, best washed down with Cromarty Brewery beers. On the other side of town, sister restaurant *Couper's Creek* specializes in open sandwiches, coffee and cakes. May–Sept daily noon–9pm; Oct–April Wed 5–9pm & Thurs–Sun 11am–9pm.

Sydney House High St ☎01381 600451, ⓦsydneyhouse.co.uk. Antique wood or iron beds and pretty dressing tables are typical of the furnishings picked up over the years by the owners to lend character to the three en-suites in their smart redbrick house just off High St. The best rooms look out over the rear gardens. **£70**

Strathpeffer

Visitors first came to this leafy Victorian spa town to take the waters. In the 1970s and 1980s they arrived with coach tours to wallow in its faded glamour. Now STRATHPEFFER is restyling itself again as a place for activities in the surrounding hills, with a focus – ironically – on "wellbeing" that sees it return to its origins as a renowned European **health resort**. All manner of guests disembarked from the *Strathpeffer Spa Express* train: George Bernard Shaw, Emmeline Pankhurst (who caused a scandal with a lecture on women's rights) and Franklin and Eleanor Roosevelt on honeymoon.

Renovation has transformed the town's Victorian grand hall into an arts centre and upgraded the adjacent **Upper Pump Room** (April–Sept Mon–Sat 10am–5pm, Sun 1–5pm; donation), where displays narrate the spa town's fascinating history.

For all the appeal of the town's faded grandeur, it's the hills that will make you stay. Within striking distance is **Ben Wyvis**, an approachable Munro usually scaled without complication from **GARBAT**, six miles west of Strathpeffer, in five hours. Another excellent hike in the area is up Cnoc Mor hill, where the Iron Age hillfort of **Knock Farril** affords superb panoramic views to the Cromarty Firth and surrounding mountains.

ARRIVAL AND GETTING AROUND

STRATHPEFFER

By bus Stagecoach bus #27 from Inverness drops passengers in the town square (Mon–Sat 12 daily, Sun 5 daily; 45min).

Bike rental The excellent Square Wheels (☎01997 42100 ⓦsquarewheels.biz; closed Sun & Mon) on the main squar rents out bikes and offers good advice on local trails.

ACCOMMODATION AND EATING

Craigvar The Square ☎01997 421622, ⓦcraigvar.com. Good breakfasts set you up for a day in the hills and a relaxing atmosphere to settle into afterwards. As central as it gets, this B&B provides modern decor that refers to the early Victorian house (love the clawfoot baths) yet includes flatscreen TVs and wi-fi throughout. **£98**

★ **Linnmhor House** Park Rd ☎01997 420072, ⓦlinnmhor-house.co.uk. A relaxing and rather luxurious stay, this B&B boasts the period features of an Edwardian villa in en-suite rooms, all tastefully and sympathetical furnished. The friendly owners dish up superb breakfast and delicious dinners such as coq au vin, seared scallops venison stroganoff, for guests upon request. **£100**

The Pavilion Restaurant Pavilion ☎01997 42012 ⓦstrathpefferpavilion.org/restaurant. Set in th grand Pavilion building, this popular new ventu focuses on seasonal local produce. Come on Wednesda for curry night (£12.50) or Sundays for a superb roa

(£9.95). Wed–Sat 11am–3pm, 5–9pm, Sun noon–4pm.
Red Poppy Main St ☎01997 423332, ⊛redpoppy restaurant.co.uk. Chef Nico Gardes serves up

well-manicured dishes, like venison fillet or roasted sea bass with plum sauce (£13–20) in this bright, modern bistro. The two-course lunch menu (£10) is good value. Tues–Sat 11.30am–9pm, Sun 12.30–4pm.

The Dornoch Firth and around

For centuries, visitors on the pilgrim trail to the **Fearn peninsula** came from the south by ferry from Cromarty. Nowadays the area north of **Dornoch Firth** is linked by the A9, skirting past the quiet town of **Tain**, best known as the home of Glenmorangie whisky, and the neat town of **Dornoch** itself, an unexpected pleasure known for its cathedral and golf courses.

Tain

There's a sense of having arrived somewhere as you swing through the handsome buildings of central **TAIN**. Reputedly Scotland's oldest royal burgh, it was the birthplace of **St Duthus**, an eleventh-century missionary. Many a medieval pilgrim came to venerate his miracle-working relics enshrined first in a sanctuary then in fourteenth-century **St Duthus Collegiate Church**. James IV visited annually, usually fresh from the arms of his mistress, Janet Kennedy, whom he had installed in nearby Moray.

12

Tain Through Time

Tower St • April–Oct Mon–Fri 10am–5pm, June–Aug also Sat & Sun 10am–5pm • £3.50 • ☎01862 894089, ⊛tainmuseum.org.uk

Installed in three buildings of St Duthus church and graveyard, the town museum, **Tain Through Time**, is a good place to gen up on the Fearn peninsula's Pictish past and Tain's pilgrimage history, the latter taking in King James's guilty conscience. The dressing-up box is handy if you have kiddies to entertain, and the ticket price includes an audio **walking tour** of the town (set aside twenty minutes). The same ticket gets you into a neighbouring **museum** with a dry display of Tain silver, alongside clan memorabilia.

Glenmorangie Distillery

On the A9, 1 mile northwest of Tain • Tours June–Aug daily 10am–4pm every 30min, April–May & Sept–Oct Mon–Sat 10am–3pm hourly, Nov–March 10am or 2pm by appointment; shop Mon–Fri 10am–5pm, April–Oct also Sat 10am–4pm, June–Aug also Sun noon–4pm • £7 (book ahead) • ☎01862 892477, ⊛glenmorangie.com

Whatever the history, Tain's most popular attraction is the **Glenmorangie Distillery**. Tours of the whisky distillery and warehouses explain the alchemic process that ferments mashed malt, distils the liquid in Scotland's tallest stills then matures it in oak casks to create a delicate, vanilla-y malt. There's a dram or two to finish, naturally. Die-hard whisky aficionados should consider the more comprehensive tasting session on the Signet Tour (£30).

ARRIVAL AND DEPARTURE   **TAIN**

By train Tain is on the Inverness–Thurso Far North Line (5 daily; Inverness, 1hr 10min; 4 daily Thurso 2hr 35min).

By bus Stagecoach east coast buses from Inverness to Thurso (#X99) stop in Tain (Mon–Sat 3–5 daily, Sun 4 daily; Inverness 50min; Thurso 2hr 15min).

ACCOMMODATION

Golf View House 13 Knockbreck Rd ☎01862 892856, ⊛bedandbreakfasttain.co.uk. Just south of the centre, this former manse offers a lovely B&B stay in its five rooms.

Decor is relaxed contemporary Scottish with a touch of romance and en-suite bathrooms are excellent. Factor in fine views to the Dornoch Firth and full Scottish breakfasts. £80

Portmahomack and around

The fishing village of **PORTMAHOMACK**, strung out around a curving sandy beach, is a surprise after the rolling fields of the **Fearn peninsula** east of Tain. Though all but empty nowadays, this was a heartland of eighth-century Picts before Viking raids became too much.

Tarbat Discovery Centre

Tarbatness Rd • April Mon–Sat 2–5pm; May Mon–Sat 10am–5pm; June–Sept Mon–Sat 10am–5pm, Sun 2–5pm; Oct daily 2–5pm • £3.50 • ☎ 01862 871351, Ⱄ tarbat-discovery.co.uk

Archeological digs in the church at the edge of the village have unearthed sculpted artefacts, including some fine gravestones decorated with Celtic animals or mythical beasts, all well presented in the church as the **Tarbat Discovery Centre**. It marks the first stop on a trail of other Pictish sites south on the peninsula – pick up their handy leaflet to locate other standing stones on the peninsula, including those at Hilton and Shandwick.

Tarbat Ness

North of Portmahomack lies **Tarbat Ness**, a gorse-covered point with one of the tallest lighthouses in Britain at its tip. Come for sea views and a seven-mile stroll (2–3hr round trip). The **walk** heads south from Tarbat Ness for three miles, following a narrow passage between the cliffs and foreshore, to the hamlet of Rockfield. A road leads past fishermen's cottages to Portmahomack to rejoin the road back to the lighthouse.

ARRIVAL AND DEPARTURE
PORTMAHOMACK AND AROUND

By bus Buses from Tain, Lamington St, go east to Portmahomack (Mon–Fri 6 daily; 20min), and to Shandwick, Hill and Fearn (Mon–Fri 7–8 daily, Sat 5 daily).

ACCOMMODATION AND EATING

Caledonian House Bistro by the Sea Main St, Portmahomack ☎ 01862 870169, Ⱄ caledonian-house.co.uk. Lovely bistro-cum-B&B opened in 2015. Exposed bricks, log-burner and pastel blue and white tones in the bistro, decked out with local artwork and serving the likes of Moroccan spiced salmon (£11.70) and Sunday roasts. En-suite rooms have enormous beds, and there are sea views over the breakfast table. Fri–Sun 11am–3pm & 6–10pm, Sun 11am–3pm. **£70**

Dornoch

DORNOCH, a genteel, villagey town eight miles north of Tain, lies on a headland overlooking the **Dornoch Firth**. Blessed with good looks and a sunny climate (by Scottish standards) and surrounded by sand dunes, it has morphed into a modest upmarket resort: all antiques shops and fine accommodation in the historic sandstone centre, a championship **golf course** plus miles of sandy beaches just outside. The town had its fifteen minutes of fame in 2002, when Madonna married Guy Ritchie at nearby **Skibo Castle** and had her son baptized in Dornoch Cathedral.

The Cathedral

Castle St • Visitor times mid-May to mid-Sept Mon–Fri 10am–4pm; services Sun 11am • ☎ 01862 810296

Dating from the twelfth century, Dornoch became a royal burgh in 1628. Pride of place among its oldest buildings grouped around the square is the imposing **Cathedral**, founded in 1224 and built of local sandstone. The original was horribly damaged by marauding Mackays in 1570, and much of what you see today was restored by the Countess of Sutherland in 1835, though the worst of her Victorian excesses were removed in the twentieth century, when the interior stonework was returned to its original state. The stained-glass windows in the north wall were later additions. The counterpart to the cathedral is the fortified sixteenth-century **Bishop's Palace** opposite, now refurbished as a hotel (see p.478).

Historylinks

The Meadows • 10am–4pm: April Thurs & Fri, May & Oct Mon–Fri; June–Sept daily; Nov–March Wed & Thurs • £3 • ☎ 01862 811275, ⓦ historylinks.org.uk

A block behind the Bishop's Palace on the high street, **Historylinks** is a small museum which tells the story of Dornoch, from local saints and the last witch burning in Scotland, which occurred here in 1727, to golfers and Madonna herself, with the usual exhibits, plus three films. Around the village, the signposted Historylinks Trail takes you on a tour around Dornoch's historic sights.

ARRIVAL AND DEPARTURE   DORNOCH

By bus Stagecoach's Inverness–Thurso service (via Helmsdale) stops at Dornoch.

Destinations Inverness (5 daily; 1hr 10min); Thurso (Mon–Sat 4 daily, Sun 3 daily; 1hr 45min).

INFORMATION AND ACTIVITIES

Tourist office Sparkly new tourist information centre in the courthouse building next to the *Dornoch Castle Hotel* (Mon–Fri 9am–6pm, plus Sat June–Aug and Sun July & Aug, same hours; ☎ 01862 810594). Has a section devoted to the North Coast 500 (see box, p.440).
Royal Dornoch Golf Club Golf Rd ☎ 01862 810219,

ⓦ royaldornoch.com. Opened four hundred years ago, this golf club maintains a par 70 Championship links course (£110) rated among the world's best by many golf media, and the easier par 71 Struie course (£40). Booking essential to play. Note that it has a dress code of no T-shirt (except polo shirts).

ACCOMMODATION AND EATING

2 Quail Castle St ☎ 01862 811811, ⓦ 2quail.com. What it lacks in size this three-room B&B makes up in traditional country character and charm. Decor is beautiful, featuring tartan fabrics and paint shades of mossy green and soft mustard, old pine furnishings and oil paintings by local artists. The owner is a chef, so breakfasts are excellent; two- or three-course dinners are available on request. **£100**
Dornoch Castle Hotel Castle St ☎ 01862 810216, ⓦ dornochcastlehotel.com. For a splurge, choose the fabulous historic Deluxe rooms in the turreted tower of the Bishop's Palace. Elsewhere this smart hotel is more modern – spacious Superiors with pillow chocolates and whisky miniatures or comfy but bland garden-facing rooms. The well-stocked bar (particularly for whisky fans) serves up "Highland tapas" (3 small plates for £10), while modern British cuisine

like Highland venison (mains £18–20) is available in *Tc Garden* restaurant. On our last visit, plans were afoot for a in-house whisky microdistillery; watch this space. Bar: dai noon–3pm; Restaurant: 6.30–9pm. **£129**
Luigi's Castle St ☎ 01862 810893. A modern metropolita styled bistro focuses on soups, ciabattas and pizzas during t. day and in the evenings seafood like mussels in red Thai bro Mains £10–18. Lunch daily 11am–2pm; dinner Easter–C Sat & Sun 6.45–9pm, & daily during peak months.
Trevose Cathedral Square ☎ 01862 810269. Centra placed directly opposite the *Dornoch Castle Hotel* but a fraction of the price of its neighbour, this detach nineteenth-century B&B swathed in roses beside t cathedral is all warm golds and creams in its two room decorated with country style. May–Sept. **£66**

North to Wick

North of Dornoch, the A9 hugs the coast for most of the sixty miles to **Wick**, the principal settlement in the far north of the mainland. The most telling landmark in th stretch is the **Sutherland Monument** near Golspie, erected to the first duke of Sutherland, the landowner who oversaw the eviction of thousands of tenants during the Clearances. That bitter memory haunts the small towns and villages of this stretch including **Brora**, **Dunbeath**, **Lybster** and pretty **Helmsdale**. Nonetheless, many of thes settlements went on to flourish through a thriving fishing trade, none more so than Wick, once the busiest herring port in Europe.

Golspie and around

Ten miles north of Dornoch the A9 rolls through the red-sandstone town of **GOLSPIE**. It's a pleasantly bustling if fairly forgettable place, and for most visitors serves only as a gateway to good mountain-bike trails or the grandest castle of this coastline.

Dunrobin Castle

A9, 1 mile north of Golspie • March, April, May, Sept & Oct Mon–Sat 10.30am–4.30pm, Sun noon–4.30pm (no falconry Sun); June–Aug daily 10.30am–5pm (falconry daily) • £11 • ☎ 01408 633177, ⊛ dunrobincastle.co.uk

Mountain-biking aside, the reason to stop in Golspie is to tour the largest house in the Highlands, **Dunrobin Castle**, north of the centre. Modelled on a Loire chateau by Sir Charles Barry, the architect behind London's Houses of Parliament, it is the seat of the Sutherland family, once Europe's biggest landowners with a staggering 1.3 million acres. They were also the driving force behind the Clearances here – it's worth remembering that such extravagance was paid for by evicting thousands of crofters.

Only a tenth of the 189 furnished rooms are visited on tours of the **interior**, as opulent as you'd expect with their fine furniture, paintings (including works by Landseer, Allan Ramsay and Sir Joshua Reynolds), tapestries and objets d'art. Alongside, providing a venue for falconry displays (11.30am & 2pm), the attractive **gardens** are pleasant to wander en route to Dunrobin's **museum**, housed in the former summerhouse and the repository of the Sutherlands' vulgar hunting trophies – heads and horns on the walls plus displays of everything from elephants' toes to rhinos' tails – and ethnographic holiday souvenirs from Africa.

The last extravagance is that the castle has its own **train** station (summer only) on the Inverness–Wick line; no surprise, considering the duke built the railway.

The Sutherland Monument

Approaching Golspie, you can't miss the **monument** to the first duke of Sutherland on the summit of **Beinn a'Bhragaidh** (Ben Bhraggie). The stiff **climb** to the monument (round trip 1hr 30min) provides vast coast views but the steep path is tough going and there's little view until the top. Head up Fountain Road and cross (or park at) Rhives Farm, then pick up signs for the Beinn a'Bhragaidh footpath (BBFP).

12

ARRIVAL AND DEPARTURE

GOLSPIE AND AROUND

By bus Stagecoach's Inverness–Thurso service stops at Golspie.

Destinations Inverness (Mon–Sat 5 daily, Sun 4 daily; 1hr min); Thurso (Mon–Sat 5 daily, Sun 4 daily; 1hr 35min).

By train Dunrobin Castle is a summer stop on the Inverness–Thurso line (April–Oct Mon–Sat 3 daily; 2hr 15min from Inverness, 1hr 35min from Thurso).

ACTIVITIES

Highland Wildcat Trails (⊛ highlandwildcat.com) have information on the area's black-, red- and blue-graded mountain biking trails, including a huge single-track descent from the summit of Ben Bhraggie to sea level. All trails are accessed from the end of Fountain Rd.

ACCOMMODATION AND EATING

Coffee Bothy Fountain Rd ☎ 01408 633022. A cabin-like café popular with bikers and walkers. Fill up on all-day breakfasts, fresh soups and ciabattas beforehand (£4–5), and reward yourself with home baking afterwards. Feb–Dec Mon–Fri 9am–4pm, Sat 9am–4pm.

Granite Villa Fountain Rd ☎ 01408 633146, ⊛ granitevilla.co.uk. Expect country charm and period furnishings in this late Victorian house. Accommodation is spacious and comfortable, all in en suites. Don't miss the home-made honey at breakfast. **£85**

Sleeperzzz Rogart, 8 miles west of Golspie ☎ 01408 641343, ⊛ sleeperzzz.com. Sleep in the quirkiest accommodation for miles around: a first-class railway carriage parked in a siding beside the Inverness–Thurso line; a 1930s showman's caravan; or a Bedford bus. March–Sept. Per person **£17**

Helmsdale

HELMSDALE is one of the largest villages between Golspie and Wick. It's certainly the most picturesque: a tight little grid of streets set above a river-mouth harbour. Romantic novelist Barbara Cartland was a frequent visitor and must have looked as exotic as a flamingo in its grey stone streets. For all its charm, it's a newcomer, founded in the nineteenth century to house the evicted inhabitants of Strath Kildonan, which lies behind it, and which subsequently flourished as a herring port.

Timespan Heritage Centre

Dunrobin St • March–Oct Mon–Sat & Sun 10am–5pm; Nov–Feb Tues 2–4pm, Sat & Sun 10am–3pm • £4 • ☎ 01431 821327, ⓦ timespan.org.uk

Good looks and sleepy ambience aside, the appeal of Helmsdale is the **Timespan Heritage Centre** beside the river. An ambitious venture for a place this size, the modern museum tells the story of Viking raids, crofting in re-created houses, the Kildonan Gold Rush, the Clearances, and fishing through high-tech displays, a movement senso to navigate animations of local yarns, and audio-tours. It also has an art gallery, and a café serving up soups and cakes, with lovely views out to the river.

ARRIVAL AND INFORMATION   HELMSDAL

By train On the Inverness–Thurso line (4 daily; 2hr 35min from Inverness, 1hr 10min from Thurso).
Tourist information Strath Ullie Crafts on the harbour

doubles as a source of tourist information (Mon–S 10am–5.30pm; ☎ 01431 821402). Otherwise, vis ⓦ helmsdale.org.

ACCOMMODATION AND EATING

On our last visit the once-excellent *Bridge Hotel* was still awaiting sale after years of closure. Hopefully a new owner w restore its restaurants and accommodation.

Helmsdale Hostel Stafford St ☎ 01431 821636, ⓦ helmsdalehostel.co.uk. Wee hostel for fourteen guests in two dorms and two rooms, most with single beds. In 2016 host Irene was giving it a complete refurb, set to reopen in 2017. Easter–Sept. Dorms £17; twins £45

La Mirage Dunrobin St ☎ 01431 821615, ⓦ lamirage .org. Not quite "The North's Premier Restaurant" as it

claims, but possibly the most bizarre due to the tastes decor of a former proprietor who styled herself af Barbara Cartland. The menu, although as dated as Ba herself, is solid: fish or scampi and chips, gamm steaks, even chicken Kiev (average £9). For somethi more upmarket, try *Thyme + Plaice* over the ro Daily 11am–9pm.

Lybster and around

Another neat planned village, **LYBSTER** (pronounced "libe-ster") was established at the height of the nineteenth-century herring boom. Two hundred boats once worked out of its picturesque small harbour, a story told in the **Waterlines** heritage centre here (May–Oct daily 11am–5pm; £2.50 donation requested, ☎ 01593 721520) – there are modern displays about the "silver darlings" and the fishermen who pursued them, plu a smokehouse and a café.

Seven miles north of Lybster, the **Grey Cairns of Camster** are the most impressive of the prehistoric burial sites that litter this stretch of coast. Surrounded by moorland, these two enormous reconstructed burial chambers were originally built five thousan years ago with corbelled dry-stone roofs in their hidden chambers. A few miles furthe north on the A99, the 365 uneven **Whaligoe Steps** lead steeply down to a natural harbour surrounded by high cliffs.

Wick

Since it was founded by Vikings as *Vik* (meaning "bay"), **WICK** has lived by the sea. I actually two towns: Wick proper and, south across the river, **Pultneytown**, created by the British Fisheries Society in 1806 to encourage evicted crofters to take up fishing. By the mid-nineteenth century, Wick was the busiest herring port in Europe, with a fleet of more than 1100 boats, exporting fish to Russia, Scandinavia and the West Indian slave plantations. Robert Louis Stevenson (who wrote *Treasure Island* here) described it as "the meanest of man's towns, situated on the baldest of God's bays". The demise of its fishing trade has left Wick down at heel, reduced to a mere transport hub. Yet the huge harbour in Pultneytown and a walk around the surrounding area – scruffy rows of fishermen's cottages, derelict net-mending sheds and stores – gives an insight into the scale of the former fishing trade.

Wick Heritage Centre

Bank Row, Pultneytown • Easter–Oct Mon–Sat 10am–5pm, last entry 3.45pm • £4 • ☎ 01955 605393, ⓦ wickheritage.org

The volunteer-maintained **Wick Heritage Centre** is the best place to evoke the heyday of the fishing boom. Deceptively labyrinthine, it contains a fascinating array of artefacts from the old days, including fully rigged boats, boat models and reconstructed period rooms, plus a superb archive of photographs from the Johnstone Collection captured by three generations of a local family between 1863 and 1975.

Old Pulteney Distillery

Huddart St • May–Sept Mon–Sat 10am–5pm, Oct–April Mon–Fri 10am–4pm; tours at 11am & 2pm or by arrangement (from £7) • ☎ 01955 602371, ⓦ oldpulteney.com

Until city fathers declared Wick dry in the 1920s, fishermen consumed three hundred gallons of whisky a day. The last distillery in town – and second most northerly in Scotland – distils more refined malts nowadays; most are light or medium-bodied, with a hint of sea salt. The tours give a close-up glimpse of a functioning distillery, which is less polished than some of the others in the Highlands and more charming for it. Needless to say, it ends with a dram or full tastings. On our last visit they were about to revamp a large section of the distillery.

12

ARRIVAL AND DEPARTURE   WICK

By plane Wick John O'Groats Airport (☎ 01955 602215, ⓦ wickairport.com), just north of town, has flights to and from Edinburgh (Mon, Wed–Fri & Sun 1 daily; 1hr) and Aberdeen (Mon–Fri 3 daily; 35min) with Flybe/Loganair and Eastern Airways respectively.

By train The train station is immediately south and west of the central bridge. Trains from Inverness (Mon–Sat 4 daily, 4hr 20min) make a long but scenic journey via

Lairg, Helmsdale, then the Flow Country inland.

By bus Local buses depart just south and west of the central bridge. They run to John O'Groats then Thurso; long-distance routes to and from Inverness involve a coordinated change at Dunbeath.

Destinations Inverness (Mon–Sat 6 daily, Sun 4 daily; 3hr); John O'Groats (Mon–Fri 7 daily, Sat 5 daily; 35min); Thurso (Mon–Sat approx hourly, Sun 5 daily; 30–35min).

ACTIVITIES

Caithness Sea Coast ☎ 01955 609200, ⓦ caithness seacoast.co.uk. Harbour cruise (30min; £10) plus longer tours to spot wildlife and admire the high cliffs south (from

£19) in a fast RIB. The operator also runs longer trips to Lybster (3hr; £50), including one-way trips in either direction (£30). All April–Oct.

ACCOMMODATION AND EATING

Bord de l'Eau Market St ☎ 01955 604400. Riverside bistro offers a slice of France. Changing menu of Gaelic and seafood dishes, plus some French classics (£14–20). The best seats are in the airy conservatory. Tues–Sat noon–2.30pm & 6–9pm, dinner only Sun.

Mackays Union St ☎ 01955 602323, ⓦ mackayshotel

.co.uk. Oversized headboards, streamlined oak furnishings and iPod docks make this Wick's prime accommodation option. First- and second-floor rooms are our pick. The acclaimed *No.1 Bistro* serves the likes of lemon-and-garlic roast chicken with Moroccan spices, plus superb fish and chips (mains average £14). Daily 8am–9pm. **£122**

Skye and
the Small
Isles

THE CUILLIN RANGE

13

Skye and the Small Isles

For many visitors the Isle of Skye (An t-Eilean Sgiathanach) is the Highlands in miniature. With its shapely summits and shifting seascapes, its superb hiking routes, wildlife and crofting villages, it crams much of the region's appeal into one manageable island. It even has classic Highlands weather. According to one theory, Skye is named after the Old Norse for "cloud" (*skuy*), earning itself the Gaelic moniker *Eilean a' Cheò* (Island of Mist). Despite unpredictable weather, tourism has been an important part of the economy since the railway reached Kyle of Lochalsh in 1897. The Edwardian bourgeoisie swarmed to its mountains, whose beauty had been proclaimed by the Victorians ever since Sir Walter Scott visited in 1814, arguably the most successful tourism PR campaign in Scottish history. People still come in droves, yet Skye is deceptively large. You'll get the most out of it – and escape the worst crowds – if you explore the remoter parts of the island, and visit outside of the tourist season, which enters full-throttle between June and August.

The Clearances saw an estimated thirty thousand indigenous *Sgiathanachs* (pronounced "ski-anaks") emigrate in the mid-nineteenth century; today, the population is just over nine thousand. Tourism is now by far the island's biggest earner and has attracted hundreds of incomers from the rest of Britain over the last couple of decades, including an increasing quota of artists and first-time B&B owners. Nevertheless, Skye remains the most important centre for **Gaelic culture** and language outside the Western Isles. Over a third of the population is fluent in Gaelic, the Gaelic college on Sleat is the most important in Scotland, and the Free Church maintains a strong presence.

In contrast to the crowds on Skye, the so-called **Small Isles** – the improbably named Rùm, Eigg, Muck and Canna – to the south only receive a trickle of visitors. Each with a population of fewer than a hundred and with its own identity, they are easily accessible by ferry from Mallaig and Arisaig, though limited accommodation means an overnight visit requires planning.

Skye

Skye ranks among Scotland's most visited destinations, with all the summer coach tours that suggests. Yet Scotland's second-largest island also has twenty Munros to bag and year-round hikers and climbers pay homage to the **Cuillin** ridge, whose peaks dominate the island; you'll need experience and determination to explore them. For years, the hiking-and-heather view of Skye was all you'd get, but over the last decade a new generation of islanders, including an influx of younger settlers, has introduced a vibrant arts and crafts scene and revolutionized the food and accommodation on offer. Nowadays, Skye holds its own against anywhere in Scotland. In fact, so sophisticated some of the relaxation on offer that the island is no longer the preserve of hikers and coach tours. The former congregate around Cuillin or the impressive rock formations

WATERFALL, TROTTERNISH

lighlights

Skye Cuillin Countless lochans, twelve
unros, one challenging eight-mile ridge trail
and the mountains are almost as impressive
en on the road to Glenbrittle as up on the trail.
ee p.489

Loch Coruisk Few sights in Scotland prepare
u for the drama of this glacial loch in the
illin – the boat ride there from Elgol just adds
the fun. **See p.490**

Trotternish Take a walk into the bizarre,
keinesque landscapes of the Quiraing or say
llo to the Old Man; this peninsula has some of
ye's most distinctive scenery. **See p.494**

❹ **Food on Skye** Whether you opt for silver
service at Michelin-starred *Kinloch Lodge* (see
p.488), cosy seafront dining at *Loch Bay* (see
p.493) or alfresco lobster and chips at *The Oyster
Shed*, you'll definitely eat well on Skye. **See p.491**

❺ **Isle of Raasay** A glimpse of what Skye might
have been like before the tourists arrived. Hike
to the flat top of Dun Caan and survey the epic
surrounds. **See p.497**

❻ **Isle of Eigg** Sample off-grid island living in
the most compelling of the Small Isles, with
sandy beaches, an easy climb and peace
everywhere. **See p.499**

HIGHLIGHTS ARE MARKED ON THE MAP ON P.486

13

of the **Trotternish** peninsula, the latter **Dunvegan** and its castle or **Portree**, the island's capital, with modest charm and amenities. And if the summer crush really gets too much, there's always the peaceful **Isle of Raasay** off the east coast.

ARRIVAL AND DEPARTURE

SKYE

By car The Skye Bridge sweeps across from Kyle of Lochalsh. If driving, don't underestimate the size of Skye.

Fuel is available 24hr at Broadford, as well as at Portree, Armadale, Dunvegan and Uig.

SKYE & THE SMALL ISLES

N

HIGHLIGHTS

1. Skye Cuillin
2. Loch Coruisk
3. Trotternish
4. Food on Skye
5. Isle of Raasay
6. Isle of Eigg

13

SKYE CRAFTS

Skye has a growing number of independent craft traders, each offering a great opportunity to pick up some unique, high-quality local produce that isn't fudge or whisky. Some give free tours without prior arrangement; the perfect remedy to a rainy day. Here are a few of our favourites:

Isle of Skye Brewing Co Uig harbour ☎ 01470 542477, ⌨ skyeale.com. In 1992 a few Skye locals joked that the only solution to the island's poor standard of beers would be to brew their own. Three years later those same locals set up this brewery, and these days any self-respecting Skye pub has their ales on tap. You can pop into their brewery in Uig to have a taster and pick up a bottle or two. April–Oct daily 10am–6pm.

Skyeskyns Stein ☎ 01470 592237, ⌨ skyeskyns .co.uk. The friendly folk at Scotland's only functioning tannery offer informative, witty tours explaining the whole process of leather making. Upstairs, you can browse the final products, from surprisingly affordable woolly rugs right up to tailored gilets pushing the £1000 mark. Daily April–Oct 9am–6pm, Nov–March 9.30am–5.30pm; last tours 30min before closing.

Skye Weavers Signposted off the B884, 1 mile east of Glendale ☎ 01470 511201, ⌨ skyeweavers.co.uk. Stop by Skye Weavers and you may well catch Roger or Andrea pedalling on their extraordinary bicycle-powered loom. They'll happily talk you through the weaving process, and you can browse their exquisite shawls, scarves and other items in the small shop next door. March–Oct Tues–Sat 10am–6pm.

y ferry From Mallaig, Caledonian MacBrayne (☎ 0800 066 000, ⌨ calmac.co.uk) operates regular car ferries across to rmadale on the Sleat peninsula (Mon–Sat 9–11 daily, Sun –8 daily; 35min). In addition, a tiny community-run car rry called the Glenachulish (☎ 01599 522313, ⌨ skyeferry o.uk) hops across to Kylerhea from Glenelg, south of Kyle of ochalsh (Easter to mid-Oct daily 10am–6pm, June–Aug till m every 20min; 5min). In bad weather CalMac often ncel services, so check before you travel.

y train and ferry or bus Mallaig (departure point for rries to Skye – see above) is served by direct trains from Fort William (3–4 daily; 1hr 20min) and Glasgow Queen St (Mon–Sat 3 daily, Sun 2 daily; 5hr 10min). There are also trains from Inverness to Kyle of Lochalsh (Mon–Sat 3–4 daily, Sun 1–2 daily; 2hr 40min). Stagecoach operate a service from Kyle of Lochalsh, stopping at Kyleakin, Broadford and Elgol (Mon–Fri 3 daily, Sat 1 daily).

Moving on to the Western Isles It's 57 miles from Armadale and 49 miles from Kyleakin to Uig, from where CalMac ferries leave for Tarbert on Harris (2 daily Mon, Tues, Thurs & Sat; 1 daily Wed, Fri & Sun) and Lochmaddy on North Uist (2 daily Mon, Wed & Fri; 1 daily Tues, Thurs, Sat & Sun).

ETTING AROUND AND INFORMATION

y bus Bus services peter out in more remote areas and don't n on Sundays. Skye Dayrider tickets for unlimited one-day avel cost £8.50 (☎ 0871 200 2233, ⌨ stagecoachbus.com).

Tourist information The best tourist office on the island is at Portree (see p.494). A useful website about the island is ⌨ skye.co.uk.

he Sleat peninsula

hanks to the CalMac ferry from Mallaig to **ARMADALE**, many people's introduction Skye is the **Sleat** (pronounced "Slate") peninsula at the southern tip of the island. he irony is that it's unlike almost anywhere else hereabouts – an uncharacteristically rtile area branded "The Garden of Skye". The main attraction is the **Armadale Castle** tate (see below), but at the time of writing plans were in place for a new distillery to en up in the not-too-distant future.

an Donald Skye

A851, 0.5 mile north of Armadale • Late March to Oct daily 9.30am–5.30pm, gardens year-round same hours or till dusk • £8.50 • 01471 844305, ⌨ clandonald.com

randed as **Clan Donald Skye** on account of its former inhabitants, **Armadale Castle**, a ile north of the ferry terminal, is the shell of the neo-Gothic seat of the MacDonald an – the laird moved into the gardeners' cottage when the kelp fertilizer market llapsed in the 1920s. Intended as an account of the clan, its modern **Museum of the es** is actually more interesting for its perspectives on Highland history, with sections the Jacobite period and its aftermath, featuring Bonnie Prince Charlie keepsakes such

13

as his shoe buckles worn in battle at Culloden and a couple of cannonballs fired at the castle by HMS *Dartmouth*, sent by William III. Just as appealing is the castle's forty-acre wooded **garden**, where you can try your hand at archery and clay-pigeon shooting.

Isleornsay

Having retired as Skye's main fishing port, **ISLEORNSAY** (Eilean Iarmain), six miles north of Armadale, is these days just a pretty, secluded village. Come for views: out across the bay to a necklace of seaweed-encrusted rocks and the tidal **Isle of Ornsay**, and behind it all a dramatic panorama of peaks on the mainland.

ARRIVAL AND GETTING AROUND

By ferry Reservations are recommended in peak season (☎0800 066 5000, ⓦcalmac.co.uk) for the Mallaig–Armadale crossing (Mon–Sat 9–11 daily, Sun 6–8 daily; 35min).

By bus All bus services from/to Armadale are via Broadford.

THE SLEAT PENINSULA

Destinations Broadford (Mon–Fri 5 daily, Sat 2 daily; 30min); Portree (Mon–Fri 2 daily; 1hr 20min); Sligachan (Mon–Fri 2 daily; 1hr).

Bike rental You can rent bikes from Armadale Bike (☎07919 278871, ⓦfacebook.com/armadalebikes; £17/day), based at the Skye Ferry Filling Station.

ACTIVITIES

Seafari ☎01471 833316, ⓦseafari.co.uk/skye. Wildlife and scenery trips in a high-speed RIB from Armadale to spot dolphins and minke whales (June–Sept).

ACCOMMODATION AND EATING

Ardvasar Hotel Ardvasar, 0.5 miles south of Armadale ☎01471 844223, ⓦardvasarhotel.com. This pretty little inn – one of the oldest on Skye – has benefited from refurbishment to create comfortable, contemporary accommodation as well as a smart restaurant specializing in local seafood – scallops and crab, plus Speyside beef for around £15. **£130**

★**Eilean Iarmain** Isleornsay ☎01471 833332, ⓦeileaniarmain.co.uk. This small hotel in a whitewashed hamlet is a charmer, romantically furnished in cosy country style: antiques, pretty fabrics, awesome views and not a TV in sight. The restaurant serves fine-dining food such as venison with garlic and white truffle mash (two courses £25), or there's informal eating in the delightful bar (sandwiches from £5). Weekly folk music club every Sunday often runs into the wee hours. Kitchen open Mon–Fri 7am–9.45am, noon–3pm & 5.30–9.30pm, Sat & Sun noon–9.30pm. **£170**

★**Kinloch Lodge** 1 mile north of Isleornsay ☎0147 833333, ⓦkinloch-lodge.co.uk. The island's smartest hot remains the home of Lord and Lady Macdonald of Macdonal and as such is furnished with antiques and clan mementos. M famous is the Michelin-starred food of Marcello Tull molecular tasting menu (from £80) or succinct lunch men showcase super-fresh island ingredients (three courses £33 Expect silver service, and up-to-the-nines clientele. Ther also an on-site spa offering massages from £55. Daily noon 2pm & 6–9pm. Dinner, bed and breakfast **£340**

Skye Forest Garden Entry at ferry terminal, Armada ☎01471 844700, ⓦskyeforestgarden.com. Fiftee pitches, four wooden bothies and a tepee set in a labyrinthi 16-acre woodland campsite. Alongside green credentials, y get eggs from free-range hens, communal campfires and, you're keen, astounding sunrises. The woodland walk, bea cave and otter hide make this a good stop-off for famili Camping per person **£7.50**; bothies/tepee (for two) **£30**

Kyleakin

The **Skye Bridge** that rendered the ferry crossing redundant in 1995 has been a mixed blessing for the old port of **KYLEAKIN** (pronounced "ka*la*kin", with the stress on the second syllable). On the one hand, it's now bypassed; on the other, that leaves its neat centre that bit quieter, even in high season. Bizarrely, it's also evolved into something a backpackers' hangout.

The bridge has been less kind to **Eilean Bàn**, an island from which the bridge leapfro to cross Loch Alsh. From 1968 to 1969, its lighthouse keeper's cottage was briefly the home of Gavin Maxwell, author of *Ring of Bright Water*. The island now serves as a nature reserve and can be visited on tours booked through the Bright Water Visitor Centre (see opposite) in Kyleakin.

ARRIVAL AND INFORMATION

KYLEAKIN

By bus There are buses from and to Kyle of Lochalsh (6 daily; 5min) and Portree via Broadford (6 daily; 55min).

Tourist information Available in the Bright Water Visitor Centre, The Pier (Easter–Sept, generally 10am–4pm but phone for times; ☎ 01599 530040, ⌨ eileanban.org).

ACCOMMODATION AND EATING

Skye Backpackers Kyleakin ☎ 01599 534510, ⌨ skyebackpackers.com. The quirkier and better-equipped of Kyleakin's two hostels. Dorms, doubles, and a couple of stationary hippie caravans out the back offer a basic night's sleep. The Groove Lounge has a log burner and board games. Doubles £52; dorms £19.50; caravan dorm £14

Broadford

Skye's second-largest village, **BROADFORD** (An t-Àth Leathann), strung out along the main road, has a traffic problem and a charm bypass. It is indeed handy for its full quota of facilities – not least a large supermarket and 24-hour fuel – but you won't want to hang around here for too long. Fill the tank, load up the boot with supplies and go explore the island.

ARRIVAL AND INFORMATION

BROADFORD

By bus Broadford is served by local buses from and to Kyle of Lochalsh (Mon–Sat 6–7 daily; 25min), Kyleakin (Mon–Fri 5 daily, Sat 2 daily; 15min) and Portree (Mon–Sat 4–6 daily; 40min).

Tourist information A friendly independent info point is by the 24hr garage and supermarket in the centre (May–Oct Mon–Sat 9.30am–5.30pm, Sun 10am–4pm, April till 4pm; no tel).

ACTIVITIES

Skyak Adventures Lower Breakish ☎ 01471 820002, ⌨ skyakadventures.com. Based outside Broadford at Lower Breakish, this experienced company runs sea-kayaking trips and courses for all abilities.

ACCOMMODATION AND EATING

Café Sia On the A87, Broadford ☎ 01471 822616, ⌨ cafesia.co.uk. The best pizzas on Skye, wood-fired to perfection, and probably one of the best coffees too. Also serves breakfast, and the outdoor deck has views out to the Red Cuillin. Daily 9.30am–9.30pm.

Tigh an Dochais 13 Harrapool ☎ 01471 820022, ⌨ skyebedbreakfast.co.uk. Jaw-dropping views down Broadford Bay through walls of glass are the draw at this striking B&B, although streamlined contemporary style and a calm, grown-up vibe are just as good reasons to check in. March–Nov. £105

The Cuillin and Red Hills

they have razor-edge ridges, the slopes plummet in scree fields and the lonely lochs are imbued with an almost tangible magic. Small wonder that, for many people, the spectacular **Cuillin** range is the sole reason to visit Skye. When – if – the cloud disperses, these spectacular peaks dominate the island. There are three **approaches**: from the south, on foot or by boat from Elgol; from *Sligachan Hotel* to the north; or from Glenbrittle to the west of the mountains. Glen Sligachan is one of the most popular routes as it divides the granite of the round-topped **Red Hills** (sometimes referred to as the Red Cuillin) to the east from the Cuillin themselves – sometimes known as the **Black Cuillin** on account of the colour of their coarse-grained jagged gabbro. With twenty Munros between them, these are mountains to take seriously. There are around five fatalities a year here and many routes are for experienced climbers only. If you're unsure, hire a guide.

Elgol, Loch Coruisk and Glen Sligachan

The road to **ELGOL** (Ealaghol) at the tip of the Strathaird peninsula is one of the most impressive on Skye, swooping into the heart of the Red Hills to culminate in beautiful views of the Small Isles above Elgol pier.

13

WALKING IN THE CUILLIN

Ordnance Survey Explorer map 411

For many walkers and climbers, there's nowhere in Britain to beat **the Cuillin**. The main ridge is just eight miles long, but with its immediate neighbours it is made up of over thirty peaks, twelve of them Munros. Those intent on doing a complete traverse of the Cuillin ridge usually start at **Gars-bheinn**, at the southeastern tip, and finish off at **Sgùrr nan Gillean** (3167ft), descending on the famous *Sligachan Hotel* for a well-earned pint. The entire journey takes a minimum of sixteen hours, which either means a very long day or two days and a bivouac. A period of settled weather is pretty much essential, and only experienced walkers and climbers should attempt it. Take note of all the usual safety precautions and be aware that **compasses** are unreliable in the Cuillin, due to the magnetic nature of the rocks.

If you're based in Glenbrittle, one of the more straightforward walks is the five-mile round trip from the campsite up **Coire Làgan**, to a crystal-cold lochan squeezed in among the sternest of rockfaces. If you simply want to bag one or two of the peaks, several corries provide relatively straightforward approaches to the central Munros. From the SYHA hostel, a path heads west along the southern bank of the stream that tumbles down from the **Coire a' Ghreadaidh**. From the corrie, you can climb up to An Dorus, the obvious gap in the ridge, then ascend **Sgùrr a' Mhadaidh** (3012ft) or **Sgùrr a' Ghreadaidh** (3192ft) to the south. Alternatively, before Coire a' Ghreadaidh, you can head south to the Coir' an Eich, from which you can easily climb **Sgùrr na Banachdaich** (3166ft) via its western ridge. To the south of the youth hostel, the road crosses another stream, with another path along its southern banks. This path heads west past the impressive **Eas Mòr** (Great Waterfall), before heading up to the **Coire na Banachdaich**. The pass above the corrie is the main one over to Loch Coruisk, but also gives access to Sgùrr Dearg, best known for its great view of the **Inaccessible Pinnacle** or "In-Pin" (3235ft) – it doesn't actually live up to the name, but Scotland's most difficult Munro requires good rock-climbing skills. Back at Eas Mòr, paths head off for Coire Làgan, by far the most popular corrie thanks to its steep sides and tiny lochan. If you're unsure about any hike or want help, hire a guide: try Skye Guides (☎01471 822116, ⊛skyeguides.co.uk).

The chief reason for visiting Elgol is to take a boat, whether a wildlife cruise or a trip across Loch Scavaig to visit **Loch Coruisk**. This isolated, glacial loch lies beneath the highest peaks of the Cuillin and is a superb trip, about an hour by boat then up to a half-day ashore. **Walkers** use the boat simply to begin hikes in the Red Hills or over the pass into **Glen Sligachan**. Alternatively, you can walk round the coast to the bay of **Camasunary**, over two miles to the east – a difficult walk that involves a tricky river crossing and negotiating "The Bad Step", an overhanging rock with a 30ft drop to the sea – and head north to Glen Sligachan. Conversely, a time-honoured approach into Glen Sligachan is from the north via the *Sligachan Hotel* (see opposite), a popular hikers' base.

Glenbrittle

Yet another route into the peaks is from **Glenbrittle** on the west side. The valley edges the most spectacular peaks of the **Cuillin**, a semicircle of mountains which rim Loch Coruisk, before it runs to a beach at Loch Brittle. One of the least demanding walks is a five-mile round trip (3hr) from Glenbrittle campsite (see opposite) up Coire Làgan to a lochan squeezed among stern rock faces. An equally good reason to come is the **Fairy Pools**, one of Britain's most celebrated wild swimming destinations. The scenery is superb as the river tumbles beneath peaks – the downside is water temperature of 8–10°C at best, and its popularity is such that in summer months tailbacks of cars have been known to extend for miles along the single-track road. The pools are signposted from Glumagan Na Sithichean car park five miles from the Glenbrittle turn.

By bus Elgol is accessed most easily from Broadford (Mon–Fri 3–5 daily, Sat 2 daily; 40min). Sligachan is a stop on the Portree–Broadford route (Mon–Sat 6–7 daily; Broadford 30min, Portree 15min).

Boat trips From Easter to Oct, two operators offer superb trips from Elgol to Loch Coruisk, taking 1hr each way, with

up to half a day ashore: the *Bella Jane* (daily; £14 single, £26 return; ☎ 01471 866244, �)bellajane.co.uk) and the *Misty Isle* (Mon–Sat; £12.50 single, £26 return; ☎ 01471 866288, �)mistyisleboattrips.co.uk). The owner of *Bella Jane* also runs wildlife-watching and walking trips to the Small Isles in a fast RIB as Aquaxplore (Easter–Oct daily; from £20).

ACCOMMODATION AND EATING

★ **Coruisk House** Elgol ☎ 01471 866330, �)coruisk house.com. A taste of Skye on unfussy super-fresh menus – fillet of cod with Orbost Iron Age pork belly, or roast loin of venison with port and juniper sauce – with two courses around £30. Above are two beautiful cottage rooms of understated luxury: expect dinner, a relaxing night and an awesome breakfast. Perfect. Reservations essential. Daily noon–2pm & 7–10pm. **£130**

Glenbrittle Campsite End of road, Glenbrittle ☎ 01478 640404. With sea views and the beach in front, and mountains behind, this spacious, remote site is the best of both worlds. The bad news is midges. Thousands of them, though they vanish with a breeze. On-site shop and café sells camping essentials and proper coffee. April–Sept. Per person **£9**

Glenbrittle SYHA Glenbrittle ☎ 01478 640278, �)syha .org.uk. Mountain chalet vibe in this recently modernized hostel, with excellent facilities and an open lounge arrangement. Its old wood panelling and leather sofas combine into a sort of rugged Scandi chic. A favourite

among climbers. Offers frozen prepared meals. April–Sept. Dorms **£18**; doubles **£53**

Sligachan Bunkhouse On A87 ☎ 01478 650458, �)sligachanselfcatering.com. There are peaks just beyond the back door from this modern, clean, no-frills bunkhouse adjacent to the *Sligachan Hotel*. Within are large dorm rooms with some of the largest bunks you'll see plus a laundry, a spacious kitchen and a small lounge with a fireplace. Dorms **£20**

Sligachan Hotel and Campsite On A87 ☎ 01478 650204, �)sligachan.co.uk. This long-standing launchpad for hikers is almost embraced beneath Cuillin's peaks. Alongside dated but comfy enough en-suite rooms, it maintains the barn-like *Seumas' Bar* which serves dishes like venison stew or rib of beef with haggis (£10–15), and which is stocked with over 400 whiskies and serves beer from the on-site Cuillin Brewery. A campsite is over the road (no telephone) – the midges in summer are as famous as the view. Hotel: March–Oct; campsite: year-round. **£140**; camping per person **£7.50**

Minginish

If the Cuillin has disappeared into the mist for the day and you have your own transport, you can while away a happy afternoon exploring the nearby **Minginish** peninsula, north of Glen Brittle.

Talisker whisky distillery

Loch Harport, Carbost • April, May & Oct Mon–Sat 9.30am–5pm; June & Sept Mon–Sat 9.30am–5pm, Sun 11am–5pm; July & Aug Mon–Sat 9.30am–5.30pm, Sun 11am–5pm; Nov–March Mon–Fri 10am–4.30pm • Tours from £8, adults only • ☎ 01478 614308

One ideal wet-weather activity is a guided tour of the Talisker whisky distillery, which produces a sweet full-bodied single malt with a whiff of smoke and peat. Skye's only distillery is situated on the shores of Loch Harport at **CARBOST**, not at the village of Talisker itself, which lies on the west coast of Minginish. Proper whisky fanatics will dash out for the excellent Talisker Tasting Tour (£35).

ACCOMMODATION AND EATING | MINGINISH

Old Inn and Waterfront Bunkhouse Carbost ☎ 01478 640205, �)theoldinnskye.co.uk. A chalet-style building and lochside location lend this bunkhouse a cheerful holiday atmosphere. It's managed by the historic *Old Inn* next door, which provides good bar meals – fresh local seafood plus cheaper staples like haggis, neaps and tatties in a whisky cream sauce – for around £10 a main. Also has five well-appointed B&B

rooms. Daily 8am–9pm. Dorms **£20**, doubles **£90**

★ **Oyster Shed** Carbost ☎ 01478 640383, ☎)skye oysterman.co.uk. This artisanal farm shop serves the freshest, best-value seafood you'll find anywhere on Skye. They now even smoke their own salmon, oysters and shellfish. Half lobster and chips (£8.50) or pan-fried scallops in garlic butter (from £6.50). Take away, or eat on the picnic benches overlooking Loch Harport. Daily noon–5pm.

13

Dunvegan

DUNVEGAN (Dùn Bheagain) is something of a letdown after the route there, skirting the bony sea cliffs and stacks of the west coast. Yet it has one of Skye's most famous traditional sights, plus two of the island's more interesting peninsulas, Duirinish and Waternish, in its backyard.

Dunvegan Castle

1 mile north of Dunvegan • Easter to mid-Oct daily 10am–5.30pm • £12, or £10 for gardens only • ☎ 01470 521206,
ⓦ www.dunvegancastle.com

Just north of the village, **Dunvegan Castle** sprawls over a rocky outcrop, sandwiched between the sea and several acres of attractive **gardens**. It's been the seat of the Clan MacLeod since the thirteenth century – and the chief still lives here with his family today – but the present facade is a product of Victorian romanticism. Older architecture remains inside, where you get the usual furniture and oil paintings alongside some more noteworthy items, with tour guides on-hand to bring the history to life. The most intriguing display is the remnants of the **Fairy Flag**, carried back to Skye, they say, by the Gaelic boatmen of King Harald Hardrada after the Battle of Stamford Bridge in 1066. MacLeod tradition states that the flag was the gift of a fairy to protect the clan – as late as World War II, MacLeod pilots carried pictures of it for luck. Seal-spotting boat trips are available from the grounds during the summer (see below).

ARRIVAL AND ACTIVITIES

DUNVEGAN

By bus Dunvegan is served by buses that loop around northern Skye from Portree (Mon–Fri 6 daily, Sat 3 daily; 45min); half of them stop at the castle.

Boat trips Seal-watching trips (mid-April to Se 10am–5pm; £7.50) in a rowing boat embark from a qua beneath Dunvegan Castle's garden.

ACCOMMODATION AND EATING

Jann's Cakes Dunvegan. This tiny place on the high street is a Skye legend for its cakes and home-made chocolates, and also prepares fresh sandwiches and soups, plus hot organic meals like tagine and curries. Not cheap – £5 for a slice of cake or £6 for smoked haddock chowder – but the quality is high. Mon–Sat 10am–5pm, Sun 10am–4pm.

Kinloch Campsite Loch Dunvegan ☎ 01470 521531, ⓦ kinloch-campsite.co.uk. Spreads across the head of Loch Dunvegan just as its name (literally "loch head") suggests, although motorhomes and caravans claim the prime waterfront – campers pitch at the sides and on a low hill. April–Oct. Per person £8

The Old School Dunvegan ☎ 01470 52142 ⓦ oldschoolrestaurant.co.uk. Offers traditional Scotti dishes such as venison haunch with whisky and hon sauce or hake with langoustine bisque (average £15). Ra stone walls add character to a lofty and rather smart dini room. Live traditional music every other Saturday. Easte Dec daily 6–10pm, open for lunch April–Oct.

Roskhill House Roskhill, 3 miles south of Dunveg ☎ 01470 521317, ⓦ roskhillhouse.co.uk. Stone wa crafts and home-made cake bring charm to this crofthouse, whose modern oak furnishings and bed thro over crisp white linen lend understated style to your st Great breakfasts too. £85

The Duirinish peninsula

Much of the **Duirinish peninsula**, west of Dunvegan, is inaccessible to all except walke prepared to scale or skirt the area's twin flat-topped basalt peaks: Healabhal Bheag (1600ft) and Healabhal Mhor (1538ft). The mountains are better known as **MacLeod Tables** – the story goes that the MacLeod chief held a royal feast on the lower of the two for James V.

Colbost Folk Museum

Colbost village • Easter–Oct daily 9.30am–5.30pm • £1.50 • ☎ 01470 521296

Local history plus information about nineteenth-century crofting is told through new cuttings in this restored blackhouse, four miles up the road from Dunvegan. A guide usually on hand to answer questions, and the peat fire is often lit.

ARRIVAL AND INFORMATION

By bus Buses go to Colbost from Portree via Dunvegan (schooldays only; Mon–Fri 2 daily; 1hr 10min).

THE DUIRINISH PENINSULA

Tourist information A useful website on the area is ⓦ glendaleskye.com.

ACCOMMODATION AND EATING

Carter's Rest 8/9 Upper Milovaig, 4 miles west of Colbost ☎ 01470 511272, ⓦ cartersrestskye.co.uk. Little touches like a digital radio impress almost as much as furnishings such as super king beds in this luxury four-star B&B with astonishing coast views. **£110**

★**Red Roof Gallery** Holmisdale, 3 miles west of Colbost ☎ 01470 511766, ⓦ redroofskye.co.uk. This cosy café owned by an artist-musician couple has a loyal fan base for its superb lunches (average £5–8) of local cheese or seafood platters with home-made breads, plus home-baking with great coffee. Occasionally holds intimate live music nights. Sun–Thurs 11am–5pm.

★**Three Chimneys** Colbost ☎ 01470 511258, ⓦ threechimneys.co.uk. An intimate, gourmet restaurant at the vanguard of Skye's foodie revolution. Seven Courses of Skye menus (£90) offer exquisite seafood plus unfussy mains like blackface lamb with rosemary maize. Shorter, cheaper menus also available. Reservations essential. A six-seat kitchen table experience, with tasting menu, costs £110. Six sumptuous rooms are available across the courtyard. Mid-Jan to mid-Dec daily 6.30–9.30pm; also open for lunch in high season. Doubles **£345**

Waternish

Waternish is a backwater by Skye's standards. Though not as spectacular as Duirinish or Trotternish, it provides equally good views over to the Western Isles, and, with fewer visitors, feels appealingly remote. To reach the peninsula, you cross the **Fairy Bridge** Beul-Ath nan Tri Allt or "Ford of the Three Burns"), at the junction of the B886. Legend has it that the fourth MacLeod clan chief was forced to say farewell to his fairy wife here when she had to return to her kind – her parting gift was the Fairy Flag (see opposite). At the end of the road that continues north from Stein is the medieval shell of **Trumpan Church**.

Stein

STEIN, looking out over Loch Bay to the Western Isles, is Waternish's prettiest village, a row of whitewashed cottages built in 1787 by the British Fisheries Society. The place never really took off and was more or less abandoned within a couple of generations. Today it's a little livelier, thanks to its world-class restaurant and historic pub – there are few nicer places on Skye for a pint on a sunny summer evening.

ACCOMMODATION AND EATING

WATERNISH

Loch Bay Seafood Restaurant Stein ☎ 01470 592235, ⓦ lochbay-restaurant.co.uk. Chef Michael Smith, formerly of the *Three Chimneys*, has taken up the mantle at this tiny, romantic dining room. The focus is mainly, but not entirely, on fresh seafood. Choose between the three-course menu (£37.50) or a divine tasting menu (£55). Reservations highly recommended. Easter to mid-Oct Wed–Sun 12.15–1.45pm, Tues–Sat 6.15–8.45pm.

Stein Inn Stein ☎ 01470 592362, ⓦ steininn.co.uk. This eighteenth-century waterfront inn – the oldest on Skye – is as traditional as you would hope. Come for local ales, an impressive array of malts and uncomplicated dishes like beer-battered Mallaig haddock and chips (average £11). Above are five cheerful en-suite rooms with sea views. Mon–Thurs 11am–11pm/midnight, Fri & Sat 11am–midnight/1am; food served Easter–Oct noon–4pm & 6–9pm; Oct–Easter noon–2.30pm & 5.30–8pm. **£77**

Portree

With a population of around 2500, **PORTREE** is something of a metropolis by Skye's standards. That said, the town still has a small-village feel and is one of the most attractive ports in northwest Scotland, its deep, cliff-edged harbour filled with fishing boats and circled by multicoloured houses. Originally known as Kiltaraglen, it takes its current name – some say – from Port Righ (Port of the

13

King), after the state visit James V made in 1540 to assert his authority over the chieftains of Skye.

The focus of activity for many visitors is the **harbour**, with an attractive wharf that dates from the early nineteenth century and a fishing fleet that still lands a modest catch. Looming behind is **The Lump**, a steep and stumpy peninsula on which public hangings once attracted crowds of up to five thousand. The tidy town centre spreads around **Somerled Square**, built in the late eighteenth century as the island's administrative and commercial centre. Rather sadly, it now serves as Portree's bus station and car park.

ARRIVAL AND DEPARTURE   PORTREE

By bus Portree is the hub of all transport on the island and has mainland connections from Glasgow with CityLink.
Destinations Broadford via Sligachan (Mon–Sat 4–6 daily;

50min); Dunvegan (Mon–Sat 3–6 daily; 45min); Glasgow (Mon–Sat 3 daily; 6hr 15min); Glenbrittle (Mon–Sat 2 daily; 50min); Trotternish circuit via Old Man of Storr, Staffin and Uig (Mon–Sat 6 daily; 2hr total circuit).

GETTING AROUND AND INFORMATION

Bike rental Island Cycles, accessed off The Green or above the long-stay car park (Easter–Oct Mon–Sat 9am–5pm, call other months; ☎ 01478 613121).
Tourist office Just off Bridge St (Mon–Sat 9am–5pm,

plus Sun 10am–4pm April–Oct, Mon–Sat till 6pm May–Oct; ☎ 01478 612992). The best tourist office on the island can book accommodation and has internet terminals.

ACCOMMODATION

★**Ben Tianavaig** 5 Bosville Terrace ☎ 01478 612152, ⓦ ben-tianavaig.co.uk. The best B&B in the centre, with a warm welcome from your hosts and four cottagey en-suites that are modern and bright, with unrestricted harbour views from the top-floor rooms. Sociable atmosphere over breakfast, which includes a daily special – such as eggs Benedict – as well as the usual options. Reservations essential. May–Sept. **£75**
Portree SYHA Centre of town, on Bridge Rd ☎ 01478 612 231, ⓦ syha.org.uk. Sparkling new, this SYHA hostel

is one of the best equipped on the island. Some 55 beds across bunk dorms and private doubles with en-suites. Dorms **£24**, doubles **£72**
★**Viewfield House** Signposted off A87 ☎ 01478 612217, ⓦ viewfieldhouse.com. The last word in Scots Baronial style is this pile on the southern edge of town. It's almost eccentric in its Victorian grandeur, all fabulous floral wallpaper, hunting trophies, stuffed polecats and antiques. Rooms are individually furnished; some tranquil, some gloriously over the top. Easter to early Oct. **£170**

EATING AND DRINKING

Café Arriba Quay Brae ☎ 01478 611830, ⓦ cafearriba .co.uk. This local institution packs in the punters, who come for a gossip over coffee or tea served in large china pots as much as the globe-trotting lunch menu of home-made soups, wraps, pastas or creative fast food like wild-boar hot dogs (mains around £10). Good veggie options available. Easter–Oct daily 7am–6pm.
Dolse and Brose Bosville Hotel ☎ 01478 612846, ⓦ bosvillehotel.co.uk. The name translates as "seaweed and oatmeal" and the menu is as varied as this suggests; everything from home-smoked chicken to Moroccan fishcakes, all served in sophisticated, chic surroundings.

The neighbouring *Merchant Bar* is the best boozer in town, serving Skye beers and a wealth of whiskies in an understated, cool space. Bar daily noon–5pm, restaurant serves lunches daily noon–3pm & dinner 6–10pm.
★**Scorrybreac** Bosville Terrace ☎ 01478 612069, ⓦ scorrybreac.com. Just eight tables in what could somebody's front room, but is in fact Skye's most exciting new restaurant. Chef Calum Munro serves the likes coffee-seared venison or smoked haddock with curried egg (2 courses £32.50) in charmingly intimate quarters. No surprises it got a nod from Michelin just months after opening. Feb–Nov daily 6–10pm.

Trotternish

Protruding twenty miles north of Portree, the **Trotternish peninsula** has some of the island's most bizarre scenery, particularly on the east coast, where volcanic basalt has pressed down on softer sandstone and limestone, causing massive landslides. These, in

13

turn, have created sheer cliffs, peppered with outcrops of hard, wizened basalt – pinnacles and pillars that are at their most eccentric in the **Quiraing**, above Staffin Bay, a long arc of beach just north of Staffin village.

Old Man of Storr
6 miles north of Portree along the A855

The most celebrated column of rock on Skye, the **Old Man of Storr** is all that is left after one massive landslip. Huge blocks of stone still occasionally break off the cliff of the Storr (2358ft) above. A half-hour trek from a car park ascends to the pillar, but don't expect to have it to yourself – this is one of the island's signature sights, and will be busy whatever the weather.

Quiraing

Just past Staffin Bay, a single-track road cuts east across the peninsula into the **Quiraing**, a spectacular area of rock pinnacles, sheer cliffs and strange rock formations produced by rock slips. There are two **car parks**: from the first, beside a cemetery, it's a steep half-hour climb to the rocks; from the second, on the saddle, it's a longer but more gentle traverse. Once you're among the rocks, you can make out "The Prison" to your right, and the 131ft "Needle" to your left. "The Table", a sunken platform where locals used to play shinty, lies a further fifteen-minute scramble up the rocks.

Skye Museum of Island Life
On the A855, 2 miles southwest of Duntulm • Easter–Oct Mon–Sat 9.30am–5pm • £2.50 • ☎ 01470 552206, ⊕ skyemuseum.co.uk

It's a short trip from Duntulm to the best of the island's folk museums. Run by a local family, the **Skye Museum of Island Life** – an impressive collection of eight thatched blackhouses decorated with home furnishings and farming tools – provides an insight into a way of life commonplace only a century ago. Behind the museum are the graves of **Flora MacDonald**, heroine during Bonnie Prince Charlie's flight, and her husband. Such was her fame that the original mausoleum fell victim to souvenir hunters and had to be replaced. The Celtic cross headstone is inscribed with a tribute by Dr Johnson, who visited her in 1773: "Her name will be mentioned in history, if courage and fidelity be virtues mentioned with honour."

Uig

Skye's chief ferry port for the Western Isles is **UIG** (Uige; pronounced "oo-ig"), which curves its way round a dramatic, horseshoe bay. In the past most folk would just pass through here, but with the reopening of an excellent pub and a new boutique bunkhouse – plus the chance to pop into the Skye Brewery on the harbour – this is becoming a destination in its own right. Don't miss the lovely, gentle **walk** up Glen Uig, better known as the **Faerie Glen**, a Hobbity landscape of miniature hills at the east end of the bay.

ARRIVAL AND GETTING AROUND   TROTTERNISH

By ferry CalMac (☎ 0800 066 5000, ⊕ calmac.co.uk) sails between Uig and Tarbert on the Isle of Harris (1–2 daily; 1hr 40min).

By bus A circular bus route (service #57A and #57C) loop around the peninsula from Portree via Old Man of Storr, Staffin and Uig (Mon–Sat 6 daily; 2hr total circuit).

ACCOMMODATION AND EATING

★**Cowshed Bunkhouse** Just south of Uig, off the A87 ☎ 07917 536820, ⊕ skyecowshed.co.uk. Skye's first "boutique bunkhouse", with underfloor heating and all, is far closer to chic hotel than banged-up bothy. The relaxed, open-plan living and dining area is kitted out with log-burner and Space Invaders gaming table, and offers panoramic views of

Uig harbour. Sophisticated dorms, and now also has glamping pods on offer. Dorm £16, pod £60

★**Ferry Inn** On the A87, Uig ☎ 01470 5423C Reopened in 2015, this sophisticated, luxury inn has fc en-suite doubles – the front two with bay views – abc one of Skye's best pubs. The long, impressive bar was ma from elm wood salvaged from the Clan Donald estate, and the cask Isle of Skye Brewing Co ales are brewed just a few hundred yards away (see box, p.487). **£150**

Skye Pie Café 3 miles south of Staffin ☎01470 562248, ⚲skyepiecafe.co.uk. Hands down the best pies

on Skye. Innovative combinations like pulled mutton with harissa, apricot and coriander, or classics like apple crumble (all around £5). Upstairs, three spacious, king-sized rooms are decorated in quirky, vintage style. Café open Mon–Fri noon–4pm. **£90**

Isle of Raasay

The hilly, fourteen-mile island of **Raasay** (Ratharsair) sees few visitors. Yet in many ways it's the ultimate Skye escape, with plenty of walks – intimate strolls compared to the wide spaces of Skye – and rich flora and fauna, including golden eagles, snipe, orchids and the unique Raasay vole, not to mention the castaway thrill of a small island. Most visitors come on foot – if you come by car, be aware there's no filling station. The ferry docks in Churchton Bay, near **INVERARISH**, the island's tiny village set within thick woods on the southwest coast. There isn't anywhere to "go" in the village beyond a local shop and post office, although the planned opening of the Isle of Raasay Distillery and visitor centre will surely lure more visitors over to this often overlooked isle.

Dun Caan

Most visitors come to walk into the island's interior – a rugged terrain of sandstone in the south and gneiss in the north. The obvious destination is the flat-top volcanic plug of **Dun Caan** (1456ft) where Boswell "danced a Highland dance" when he visited with Dr Johnson in 1773. The five-mile trail to the top is easy to follow; a splendid trek along the burn through forest behind Inverarish, culminating in epic 360-degree views of Skye and the mainland from the top. The quickest return is down the northwest slope, but you can also get back to the ferry along the path by the southeast shore, passing the abandoned crofters' village of Hallaig. Keep your eyes peeled for roaming eagles overhead and the odd scuttling grouse.

ARRIVAL AND INFORMATION

ISLE OF RAASAY

By ferry The CalMac ferry (Mon–Sat 8–10 daily, Sun 2 daily; 25min; ☎01687 462403, ⚲calmac.co.uk) to Raasay departs from Sconser, 3 miles northeast of

Sligachan Hotel (see p.491).
Tourist information ⚲raasay.com.

ACCOMMODATION AND EATING

Raasay House Short walk from ferry pier ☎01478 650300, ⚲raasay-house.co.uk. The MacLeods' rebuilt manor offers everything from four-star deluxe rooms with balconies and views to the Cuillins to modern bunkrooms. This is also the only place to eat or drink on the island, in

the convivial bar/restaurant (mains £12–18). Among activities on offer (Easter–Oct, weather-dependent other months) are guided walks and canyoning, boat trips (2hr; £8), coasteering, kayaking and sailing. Bike rental available for £15/half day. Dorms **£25**; doubles **£95**

The Small Isles

Seen from southern Skye or the west coast of the Highlands, the **Small Isles** – **Rùm**, **Eigg**, **Muck** and tiny **Canna** – lie scattered in a silver-grey sea like a siren call to adventure. After centuries of being passed between owners, most islands have stabilized into tight-knit communities of crofters. While Muck is still privately owned, Eigg was bought out by its islanders in 1997, ending more than 150 years of property speculation, while other islands have been bequeathed to national agencies: Rùm, by far the largest and most visited of the group, passed to the Nature Conservancy Council (now Scottish Natural Heritage) in 1957; and Canna has been in the hands of the National Trust for Scotland since 1981.

13

Many people come on a day-trip from Mallaig, but the Small Isles deserve longer. They are an opportunity to experience some off-grid island life while walking, birdwatching or simply admiring seascapes. Accommodation requires **forward planning** and public transport on the islands is nonexistent. But regular ferries mean you're not as cut off as the atmosphere suggests. Better still, services link all islands for a happy week of island-hopping.

ARRIVAL AND DEPARTURE   **THE SMALL ISLES**

Be aware that boats are frequently cancelled by bad **weather**, so check forecasts.

By ferry CalMac (☎ 01687 462403, ⓦ calmac.co.uk) sails from Mallaig (late March to mid-Oct daily, otherwise Mon–Sat), although doesn't sail to all islands each day. Long day-trips are possible on Sat. Sheerwater (☎ 01687 450224, ⓦ arisaig.co.uk) sails return trips daily from Arisaig (see p.444 to Eigg (£18), plus Rùm (£20) or Muck (£25) from late April t late Sept. The ride doubles as a wildlife cruise, so, whil enjoyable, is more expensive than travelling with CalMac.

Rùm

After almost a century as the "Forbidden Isle" – the exclusive sporting estate of self-made Lancastrian industrialists the Bulloughs – **Rùm** has opened up. Indeed, since it passed to Scottish Natural Heritage (SNH) in 1957, visitors are positively encouraged. Many come to hike the eight-mile **Rùm Cuillin Ridge Walk**, tracking a crown of peaks that are modest by Skye's standards – the summit of Askival is only 2663ft – but every bit as impressive in looks. And in recent years, crofting land has been released as SNH tries to encourage a community. Most of the island's forty inhabitants live around **KINLOCH** on the east coast, and many are employed by SNH, which runs the island as a National Nature Reserve. SNH have reintroduced native woodland and **white-tailed (sea) eagles**, most of which promptly flew to neighbouring islands. The island is renowned for its **Manx shearwaters**, which nest in burrows on high peaks. You can learn more about the flora and fauna in an unmanned **visitor centre** halfway between the wharf and castle.

The best **beach** is **Kilmory** in the north of the island, a flattish walk on tracks through Kinloch then Kilmory glens (10 miles, 5hr return from Kinloch). Bear in mind that Rùm is the wettest of the Small Isles, and is notorious for midges (see box, p.41) – come prepared.

HIKING IN THE RÙM CUILLIN

Ordnance Survey Explorer map 397

Rùm's **Cuillin** may not be as famous as Skye's, but in fine weather offers equally exhilarating **hiking** possibilities. Whatever route you choose, be sure to take all the usual safety precautions (see box, p.43).

The most popular walk is to traverse most or part of the **Cuillin Ridge**, around a twelve-hour round trip from Kinloch. The most frequent route is via Coire Dubh, then on to the saddle of Bealach Bairc-mheall. From here, you can either climb Barkeval to the west, or go for **Hallival** (2372ft) southeast, which looks daunting but is only a mild scramble. South of Hallival, the ridge is grassy, but the north ridge of **Askival** (2663ft) needs to be taken carefully, sticking to the east side. Askival is the highest mountain on Rùm, and if you're thinking of heading back, or the weather's closing in, Glen Dibidil provides an easy descent.

To continue along the ridge, head west to the double peak of **Trollaval** (or Trallval). The descent to Bealach an Fhuarain is steep, after which it's another scramble to reach the top of **Ainshval** (2562ft). Depending on the time and weather, you can continue along the ridge to **Sgùrr nan Gillean**, descend via Glen Dibidil and take the coastal path back to Kinloch, or skip the Sgùrr and go straight on to the last peak of the ridge, **Ruinsival**.

Kinloch Castle

Kinloch, signposted 15min walk from ferry • March–Oct Mon–Sat 45min guided tours coincide with the ferry • £9 • ☏ 01687 462037

Most day-trippers to Rùm head straight for **Kinloch Castle**, a squat, red-sandstone edifice. Built at huge expense in 1900 – the red sandstone was shipped in from Dumfriesshire and the soil for the gardens from Ayrshire – its interior is sheer Edwardian decadence. It's also appealingly bonkers. From the galleried hall, with its tiger rugs, stags' heads and giant Japanese incense burners, to the Soho snooker table in the Billiard Room, the interior is packed with technical gizmos accumulated by **Sir George Bullough** (1870–1939), the spendthrift son of self-made millionaire, Sir John Bullough, who bought the island as a sporting estate in 1888.

During our last visit only the downstairs of Kinloch Castle was open for the tour. The damp walls, furniture rips and ceiling cracks may add to the ramshackle charm of the place, but you feel that the sooner the £10–15 million restoration fund comes, the better.

ARRIVAL AND INFORMATION

RÙM

By ferry The longest day-trip possibilities from Mallaig are on Rùm (just under 11hr). Note that overnight visitors cannot bring dogs, but day-trippers can. Summer timetables are: Arisaig–Rùm (Tues, Thurs & Sat 1 daily; 1hr 45min–2hr 10min); Canna–Rùm (Mon, Wed, Fri & Sat 1 daily; 55min);

Eigg–Rùm (Mon & Sat 1 daily; 1hr–3hr 30min); Mallaig–Rùm (Mon, Wed, Fri, Sat & Sun 1 daily; 1hr 20min–2hr 30min).

Tourist information There is an unmanned visitor centre on the way from the ferry to Kinloch Castle. Another good source of information is ⓦ isleofrum.com.

ACCOMMODATION AND EATING

Visitors are permitted to **wild camp** and there are two simple **bothies** (three nights maximum) in Dibidil, on the southeast coast, and Guirdil, on the northwest coast. You'll find a shop/post office/off-licence in Kinloch, beside the community hall, which serves **teas** and **snacks** (during summer open 10am–noon on ferry days, and 5–7pm most evenings).

Ivy Cottage Kinloch ☏ 01687 462744, ✉ fliss @isleofrum.com. Delivers loch views from two pleasant en-suite rooms and the conservatory where you have breakfast, plus a relaxed atmosphere in the first B&B on Rùm, in a modern house on the loch in front of the castle. Its young owners prepare dinners for guests (included in the price) and non-residents on request. Bikes to rent, and craft shop next door. **£140**

Kinloch Campsite ☏ 01687 460328. A community-run campsite with an appealing location spread along the shore on the south side of Kinloch Bay. Also on site are four tiny, insulated camping cabins with four beds each. Camping per person **£5**; cabins for two **£20**

Rum Bunkhouse Kinloch ☏ 01687 460318, ⓦ rumbunkhouse.co.uk. This impressive new bunkhouse is the most comfortable option on the island for walking groups who don't want to brave the bothies. Twenty beds (one twin, three four-beds and a six-bed dorm), plus a large living area with sofas and a wood-burning stove. Per person **£23**

Eigg

Eigg – which measures just five miles by three – does little to conceal its volcanic origins. It's made of a basalt plateau, and a great stump of pitchstone lava, known as An Sgùrr, rises in the south. Geology aside, Eigg has an appealingly strong sense of community among its hundred-odd residents. This was given an enormous boost in 1997 when they (alongside the Scottish Wildlife Trust) pulled off the first **buyout** of a Highlands estate, thereby ending Eigg's unhappy history of private ownership, most recently by Keith Schellenberg, an Olympic bobsleigher and motor magnate. The anniversary is celebrated with an all-night **ceilidh** on the weekend nearest June 12. Its other world-first is that its electricity grid is powered entirely by renewable sources.

Galmisdale

Ferries arrive into **Galmisdale Bay**, in the southeast corner of the island. Head up through woods for superb sea views, or track the shore south to see crofting ruins before the Sgùrr cliffs – the remains of Upper and Lower Grulin settlements. If the tide is low you can scramble along the shore into Cathedral Cave or Massacre Cave (**Uamh Fhraing**), where

13

all but one of Eigg's 396 inhabitants died in 1577, suffocated by the MacLeods of Skye, who lit a fire in the cave mouth. Bring a torch and prepare to feel spooked.

An Sgùrr

The largest piece of pitchstone in the UK, **An Sgùrr** (1289ft) is the obvious destination for a hike. Actually, the route up is not as daunting as the cliffs suggest; the path is signposted left from the main road, crossing boggy moor to approach the summit from the north via a saddle (3–4hr return). The rewards are wonderful views to Muck and Rùm.

Cleadale

For an easy stroll, strike out to **CLEADALE**, the main crofting settlement in north Eigg. It's spectacularly sited beneath the island's basalt ridge, **Ben Bhuidhe**, and above a beach known as Camas Sgiotaig, or the **Singing Sands**, because the quartz grains squeak underfoot. The views from here to Rùm, its peaks often cloaked by clouds, are unforgettable.

ARRIVAL AND DEPARTURE

EIGG

By ferry Summer timetables are: Canna–Eigg (Mon & Sat 1 daily; 2hr 10min); Mallaig–Eigg (Mon, Thurs, Sat & Sun 1hr 15min); Muck–Eigg (Thurs 1 daily; 35min); Rùm–Eig (Mon & Sat 1 daily; 1hr–3hr 20min).

GETTING AROUND AND INFORMATION

By minibus or bike A minibus is scheduled around ferries (☏ 01687 482494; £2). Bike rental is available from Eigg Adventures (☏ 01687 347007, ☺ eiggadventures.co.uk; £15/day), based at the harbour. They also offer kayak rental

(call for details) and archery sessions (£12; 50min).
Tourist information The friendly folk at the *An Laimhr* complex will give you all the information you nee Alternatively, visit ☺ isleofeigg.org.

ACCOMMODATION AND EATING

An Laimhrig Harbour. Island ingredients go into homemade soups, quiche, pizza, lamb or venison burgers, plus blackboard specials such as fishcakes – all for under £10. Craft shop and well-stocked mini-supermarket in the same complex. Summer open 10am (Sun 11.30am), evening meals available during peak months, winter open around ferry schedules.

Glebe Barn Galmisdale ☏ 01687 482417, ☺ glebebarn .co.uk. Eigg's hostel on the hill above the harbour has a spacious lounge with awesome coast views and pleasant wee dorm rooms. Better still is the self-contained cottage *Glebe Apartment* – a superb stay for up to five people. April–Oct. Dorms **£20**; twins **£45**; annexe from **£60**

Kildonan House Down a long, unmarked road, north side of Galmisdale Bay ☏ 01687 482446, ☺ kildonan houseeigg.co.uk. A traditional stay in an eighteenth-century farmhouse. Warm and welcoming host Marie offers three pleasingly simple pine-panelled rooms, one

with an en-suite shower, all with sea views and dinne (usually catch-of-the-day) included. **£120**

★ **Lageorna** Cleadale ☏ 01687 460081, ☺ lageorn .com. Beautiful, modern rooms full of contemporary craf – think rustic wooden beds (built on Rùm) and knitte throws – and astonishing views, plus a lovely vinta cottage that sleeps four. The owner also prepares hear dishes such as venison on a bed of spicy puy lenti reservations recommended. Closed over Christmas ar New Year, open by arrangement over winter month Doubles **£100**; cottage **£500**

Sue Holland's Croft Cleadale ☏ 01687 48248 ☺ eiggorganics.co.uk. On an organic croft, this is the or designated campsite and it's a belter, with views a sunsets to inspire poetry. The old cowshed is now a ba bothy for up to four, or for more comfort choose a yurt. S also runs crofting tours and courses on growing vegetabl Camping per person **£5**; bothy and yurt **£45**

Muck

Barely two miles long, tiny **Muck** is the smallest and most southerly of the Small Isles. Low-lying and almost treeless, it is extremely fertile, so has more in common with Co and Tiree (see p.251) than its neighbours. Its name derives from *muc*, the Gaelic for "pig" (or possibly *muc mara*, "sea pig" or porpoise, which are plentiful), and has long caused embarrassment to lairds – they preferred to call it the "Isle of Monk" because i briefly belonged to the medieval church.

PORT MÓR is the hub of all activity, where visitors arrive and just about all of the thirty or so residents live – a tenth of the 320 of the early 1800s. A mile-long road connects Port Mór with the island's main farm, **Gallanach**, which overlooks rocky skerries on the north side. The nicest sandy **beach** is Camas na Cairidh, to the east of Gallanach. For a stiffer challenge, **Beinn Airein** (2hr return), in the southwest corner of the island, is worth climbing, despite being only 450ft above sea level, for a 360-degree panorama of surrounding islands from its summit.

ARRIVAL AND INFORMATION   MUCK

By ferry Summer timetables are: Canna–Muck (Sat 1 daily; 1hr 35min); Eigg–Muck (Thurs, Sat & Sun 1 daily; 45min); Mallaig–Muck (Tues & Thurs–Sun 1 daily; 1hr 30min–2hr).

Tourist information The Craft Shop & Tea Room (see below) doubles as an information point. See also ⓦ isleofmuck.com.

ACCOMMODATION AND EATING

To **wild camp** on the island, check in at The Craft Shop & Tea Room to find out about any areas currently off-limits.

The Craft Shop & Tea Room Port Mór ☎ 01687 462990. The only shop on the island prepares daily soups and sandwiches made from fresh home-baked bread, plus afternoon teas and dinners of fresh shellfish prepared on request. April, May & Sept days & hours vary; June–Aug Mon–Sat 11am–4pm.

Gallanach Lodge Gallanach Bay ☎ 01687 462365, ⓦ gallanachlodge.co.uk. A purpose-built luxury lodge that takes full advantage of a superb position above the

beach to provide fantastic views to Rùm. The style is island boutique – rustic, handmade beds in rooms with hotel-style mod cons. Full board only. **£170**

Isle of Muck Bunkhouse Port Mór ☎ 01687 462042, ⓔ info@isleofmuck.com. Two bunkrooms and two doubles in the island's simple wee hostel, sited near the port. Life revolves around the Raeburn stove in the simple living room and the kitchen. Hardly luxurious but full of character. Extra £5 for bedding. Per person **£20**

Canna

Measuring a mere five miles by one, **Canna** is managed as a **bird sanctuary** by the National Trust for Scotland (NTS). There are no roads, just open moorland stretched over a basalt ridge, and few people now that the population has dwindled to eight. While Canna doesn't receive many visitors by ferry, plenty come by yacht for the best harbour in the Small Isles, a sheltered bay off Canna's main hamlet, **A'Chill**. Notwithstanding walks (see below), you come to Canna for birdlife; this has been a sanctuary since 1938, and 157 species have been recorded, including golden and white-tailed eagles, and Manx shearwaters, razorbills and puffins on cliffs at the western end.

Although less obviously scenic than other Small Isles, the flat(ish) terrain makes for enjoyable **walks**. You can circuit the entire island on a long day (10hr; 12 miles), or from the dock it's about a mile across a grassy plateau to the cliffs on the north shore and Compass Hill, named because its high iron content distorts compasses. A mile west is Carn a'Ghaill, Canna's summit at a heady 688ft.

ARRIVAL AND INFORMATION   CANNA

By ferry Summer timetables are: Eigg–Canna (Mon & Sat; daily; 2hr 20min); Mallaig–Canna (Mon, Wed, Fri & Sun daily, Sat 2 daily; 2hr 30min–3hr 45min); Muck–Canna

(Sat 1 daily; 1hr 35min); Rùm–Canna (Mon & Fri–Sun 1 daily; 1hr 5min).
Tourist information ⓦ theisleofcanna.com.

ACCOMMODATION

With permission from the NTS, you may **wild camp** on Canna, though bring supplies.

Tighard ☎ 01687 462474, ⓦ tighard.co.uk. The Sanday Room is the pick – spacious, traditional and with sweeping sea views – in the only B&B on Canna. Its other two smaller

and simpler twins also enjoy sea views. Friendly hosts Colin and David also offer packed lunch and dinner with prior arrangement. **£120**

The Western Isles

GARENIN (GEARRANNAN)

The Western Isles

Beyond Skye, across the unpredictable waters of the Minch, lie the wild and windy Outer Hebrides, officially known as the Western Isles. A 130-mile-long archipelago stretching from Lewis and Harris in the north to the Uists and Barra in the south, the islands appear as an unbroken chain when viewed from across the Minch, hence their nickname, the Long Isle. In reality there are more than two hundred islands, although only a handful are inhabited, with the total population around 28,000. This is truly a land on the edge, where the turbulent seas of the Atlantic smash up against a geologically complex terrain whose coastline is interrupted by a thousand sheltered bays and sweeping sandy beaches. The islands' interiors are equally dramatic, veering between flat, boggy, treeless peat moor and bare mountaintops soaring high above a host of tiny lakes, or lochans.

The major difference between the Western Isles and much of the Hebrides is that the islands' fragile economy is still mainly concentrated around crofting, fishing and weaving, and the percentage of incomers is low. In fact, the Outer Hebrides remain the heartland of **Gaelic** culture, with the language spoken by the majority of islanders. Its survival is partly thanks to the efforts of the Western Islands Council, the Scottish parliament and the influence of the Church in the region: the Free Church and its various offshoots in Lewis, Harris and North Uist, and the Catholic Church in South Uist and Barra.

Lewis and Harris form two parts of the same island. The interior of the northernmost, **Lewis**, is mostly peat moor, a barren and marshy tract that gives way to the bare peaks of **North Harris**. Across a narrow isthmus lies **South Harris**, with wide beaches of golden sand trimming the Atlantic in full view of the rough boulder-strewn mountains to the east. Across the Sound of Harris, to the south, a string of tiny, flatter isles linked by causeways – **North Uist**, **Benbecula**, **South Uist** – offer breezy beaches, whose fine sands front a narrow band of boggy farmland, which, in turn, is bordered by a lower range of hills to the east. Finally, tiny **Barra** contains all the above landscapes in one small Hebridean package.

In contrast to their wonderful surroundings, villages in the Western Isles are seldom picturesque in themselves, and are usually made up of scattered, relatively modern crofthouses dotted about the elementary road system. The Outer Hebrides' only sizeable settlement is Stornoway, a town which retains a modicum of charm thanks to what's left of its old harbour frontage and traditional and Victorian buildings in the near vicinity. Many visitors, walkers and nature-watchers forsake the main settlements altogether and retreat to secluded cottages, simple hostels and B&Bs.

ARRIVAL AND DEPARTURE   THE WESTERN ISLE

By plane There are scheduled flights from Glasgow, Edinburgh, Inverness and Aberdeen to Stornoway on Lewis, and from Glasgow to Barra and Benbecula. Be warned: weather conditions are notoriously changeable, making flights prone to delay and even cancellation.

By ferry CalMac car ferries run two services daily fro Ullapool to Stornoway; from Uig, on Skye, to Tarbert a Lochmaddy; and from Oban to Barra and Mallaig to Sou Uist daily. The timetables quoted in the text are summ frequencies – check ⦿ calmac.co.uk for the latest a always book ahead.

Gaelic in the Western Isles p.507
St Kilda (Hiort) p.513

Harris tweed p.515
SS Politician p.523

LUSKENTYRE BAY

Highlights

Garenin, Lewis An abandoned crofting village whose thatched blackhouses have been beautifully restored: some are now self-catering cottages, one is a café, and a couple have been left as they were when they were last inhabited. See p.512

Callanish standing stones, Lewis Scotland's finest standing stones have a serene hillside setting on the west coast of the Isle of Lewis. See p.512

St Kilda Permanently inhabited until 1930, now a UNESCO World Heritage Site; getting to this tiny, remote island chain forty miles north-west of North Uist is an adventure in itself. See p.513

❹ Beaches The western seaboard of the Outer Hebrides, particularly on South Harris and the Uists, is strewn with stunning, deserted golden-sand beaches backed by flower-cloaked machair. See p.515

❺ St Clement's Church, Harris Rodel's pre-Reformation church, at the southernmost tip of Harris, boasts the most ornate sculptural decoration in the Outer Hebrides. See p.516

❻ Barra Barra is a great introduction to the Western Isles: a Hebridean island in miniature, with golden sands, crystal-clear rocky bays and mountains of Lewissian gneiss. See p.524

HIGHLIGHTS ARE MARKED ON THE MAP ON P.506

GETTING AROUND

By car and by ferry A series of causeways makes it possible to drive from one end of the Western Isles to the other with just two interruptions – the ferry from Harris to Berneray, and from Eriskay to Barra. If you're going to take the ferry, it's advisable to book in advance.

By bus The islands have a decent bus service, though there are no buses on Sundays.

By bike The wind makes cycling something of a challenge – head south to north to catch the prevailing wind. It's free to take bikes on all ferry services, or if you prefer to rent, there are rental outlets in Barra and Stornoway.

14

Lewis (Leodhas)

Shaped rather like the top of an ice-cream cone, **Lewis** is the largest and most populous of the Western Isles. Nearly half of the island's inhabitants live in the crofting and fishing villages strung out along the northwest coast, between **Callanish** (Calanais) and **Port of Ness** (Port Nis), in one of the country's most densely populated rural areas. On this coast you'll also find the best-preserved **prehistoric remains** – Dun Carloway (Dùn Charlabhaigh) and the Callanish standing stones. The landscape is mostly peat bog – hence the island's Gaelic name, from *leogach* (marshy) – but the shoreline is more dramatic, especially around the Butt of Lewis, the island's northernmost tip. The rest of the island's population live in **Stornoway**, on the east coast, the only real town in the Western Isles. To the south, where Lewis is physically joined with Harris, the land rises to over 1800ft, providing an exhilarating backdrop for the excellent beaches that pepper the isolated western coastline around **Uig**.

Stornoway (Steòrnabhagh)

In these parts, **STORNOWAY** is a buzzing metropolis, with all the trappings of a large town. It's a centre for employment, a social hub for the island and home to the Western Isles Council or **Comhairle nan Eilean Siar**, set up in 1974, which has done so much to promote Gaelic language and culture. Aesthetics are not the town's strong point, and the urban pleasures on offer are limited, but in July Stornoway hosts the **Hebridean Celtic Festival** (⊕hebceltfest.com), a Celtic music festival held in Lews Castle grounds, and An Lanntair arts centre.

For centuries, life in Stornoway focused on its **harbour**, now a shadow of its former commercial self – the nicest section is Cromwell Street Quay, where the remaining fishing fleet ties up for the night. Stornoway's commercial centre, to the east, is little more than a string of unprepossessing shops and bars. The one exception is the old **Town Hall** on South Beach, a splendid Scots Baronial building from 1905, its rooftop peppered with conical towers, above which a central clock tower rises. One block east along South Beach, and looking rather like a modern church, you'll find **An Lanntair** – Gaelic for "lantern" – Stornoway's modern cultural centre (see p.510).

Lews Castle

Across the bay from the town centre • Grounds open 24hr; Museum June–Sept Mon–Sat 10am • Free • ☎ 01851 822750, lews-castle.co.uk

The castellated pomposity that is **Lews Castle** was built by Sir James Matheson in

GAELIC IN THE WESTERN ISLES

All Ordnance Survey maps and many **road signs** are exclusively in **Gaelic**, a difficult language to the English-speaker's eye, with complex pronunciation (see p.599), though the English names sometimes provide a rough pronunciation guide. If you're driving, it's a good idea to pick up a bilingual Western Isles **map**, available at most tourist offices. We've put the English equivalent first in the text, with the Gaelic in parentheses.

14

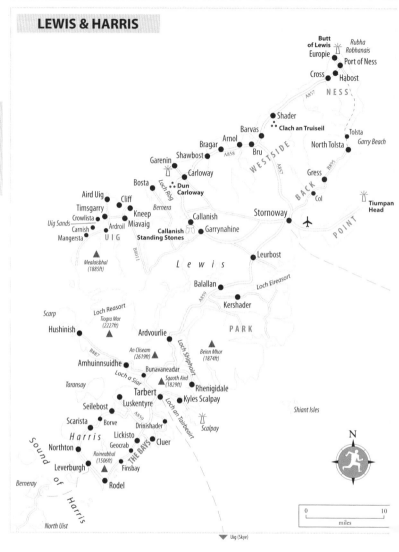

LEWIS & HARRIS

Butt
of Lewis
Europie
Port of Ness
Cross
Habost
Rubha Robhanais
N E S S
Shader
Barvas
Clach an Truiseil
Tolsta
Garry Beach
Bragar
Arnol
North Tolsta
Shawbost
Bru
W E S T S I D E
Garenin
Carloway
Gress
Bosta
Dun Carloway
Loch Roag
B A C K
Col
Tiumpan Head
Aird Uig
Cliff
Bernera
Callanish
Stornoway
Timsgarry
Crowlista
Kneep
Miavaig
Uig Sands
Carnish
Ardroil
Callanish Standing Stones
Garrynahine
Mangersta
U I G
P O I N T
L e w i s
Mealaisbhal (1885ft)
Leurbost
Balallan
Loch Eireasort
Kershader
Scarp
Loch Reasort
Tiorga Mor (2227ft)
P A R K
Hushinish
Ardvourlie
Beinn Mhor (1874ft)
An Cliseam (2619ft)
Loch Shiphort
Amhuinnsuidhe
Bunavaneadar
Sgaoth Aird (1829ft)
Rhenigidale
Taransay
Loch a Siar
Tarbert
Kyles Scalpay
Seilebost
Luskentyre
Loch an Tairbeairt
Shiant Isles
Scarista
Borve
Drinishader
Scalpay
H a r r i s
Lickisto
Geocrab
Cluer
Northton
Roineabhal (1506ft)
T H E   B A Y S
Leverburgh
Finsbay
S o u n d   o f   H a r r i s
Rodel
Berneray
North Uist

N

0 — 10 miles

Uig (Skye)

1863 after resettling the crofters who used to live here. As the former laird's pad, it is seen as a symbol of oppression. However, the building – closed for over 25 years – is currently undergoing a £14 million makeover. Part of the makeover included a new extension to house a state-of-the-art bilingual museum, which is now open, telling the story of the islands' geology, Gaelic culture, struggles of the nineteenth century and the Leverhulme era.

Lews Castle's external attraction is its mature wooded **grounds**, a unique sight on the Western Isles, for which Matheson imported thousands of tons of soil. Hidden among the trees is the **Woodland Centre**, which has a straightforward exhibition on the history of the castle and the island, and a decent café serving soup, salads and cakes.

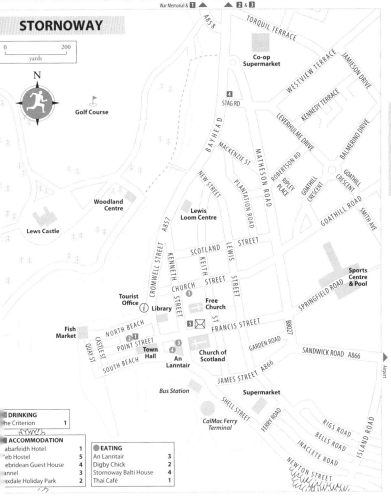

STORNOWAY

War Memorial & **1** ▲ ▲ **2** & **3**

14

DRINKING
The Criterion   1

ACCOMMODATION
...abarfeidh Hotel   1
...eb Hostel   5
...ebridean Guest House   4
...annel   3
...axdale Holiday Park   2

EATING
An Lanntair   3
Digby Chick   2
Stornoway Balti House   4
Thai Café   1

...RIVAL AND DEPARTURE

...plane Stornoway airport (☏ 01851 702256, ⌨ hial
...uk) is 4 miles east of the town centre: the hourly bus
...s 15min (Mon–Sat only), or it's a £5 taxi ride into town.
...ferry Ferries between Stornoway and Ullapool (Mon–
...2–3 daily, Sun 1 daily; 2hr 30min; ☏ 0800 0665000)
...from the octagonal CalMac ferry terminal on South
...ch, near the bus station.
...bus The bus station (☏ 01851 704327) is on South
...ch in the town centre.

...TTING AROUND AND INFORMATION

...ar Car rental is available from Mackinnon Self-Drive, 18
...ete Rd (☏ 01851 702984, ⌨ mackinnonselfdrive.co.uk)

STORNOWAY

Destinations Arnol (Mon–Sat 4–7 daily; 30min);
Barvas (Mon–Sat 4–7 daily; 20min); Callanish (Mon–
Sat 3–6 daily; 32min); Carloway (Mon–Sat 2–6 daily; 45min);
Garenin (Mon–Sat 3–4 daily; 1hr); Great Bernera
(Mon–Sat 4 daily; 1hr); Leverburgh (Mon–Sat 4–5 daily;
2hr); Port of Ness (Mon–Sat 6–8 daily; 1hr); Shawbost
(Mon–Sat 6–9 daily; 45min); Tarbert (Mon–Sat 5 daily;
1hr); Tolsta (Mon–Sat hourly; 40min); Uig (Mon–Sat
4 daily; 1hr–1hr 30min).

from around £25/day – they're based in Stornoway but
will deliver locally for free.

14

By bike Alex Dan's Cycle Centre, 67 Kenneth St (☎01851 704025, ⓦstornowaycyclehire.co.uk; closed Sun), offers bike rental from £20/day to £60/week; panniers and car racks are also available.

Tourist office 26 Cromwell St (April to mid-Sep Mon–Sat 9am–5.45pm; mid-Sept to Oct Mon–Sa 9am–4.45pm; Nov–March Mon–Fri 9am–5pm ☎01851 703088).

ACCOMMODATION

Cabarfeidh Hotel Manor Park ☎01851 702604, ⓦcabarfeidh-hotel.co.uk. Large, reasonably upmarket hotel near Lews Castle with an excellent choice of cooked breakfasts including kippers, pancakes with syrup and the full Scottish fry-up. **£115**

Heb Hostel 25 Kenneth St ☎01851 709889, ⓦhebhostel.co.uk. A clean, centrally located terrace house in salmon pink, converted into a simple hostel, with free breakfast, wi-fi, laundry and kitchen facilities. Run by a friendly resident warden. Per person **£18**

Hebridean Guest House 61 Bayhead St ☎01851 702268, ⓦhebrideanguesthouse.co.uk. Whitewashed property a 5min walk from the harbour and within easy

reach of Lews Castle with a large range of en-suite an tastefully decorated rooms. **£120**

Jannel 5 Stewart Drive ☎01851 705324, ⓦjann -stornoway.co.uk. A short walk from the town centre, th B&B is run by a delightful landlady, and offers fi immaculate en suite rooms. **£79**

Laxdale Holiday Park Laxdale Lane ☎01851 70323 ⓦlaxdaleholidaypark.com. The well-equipped campsi has caravans, a self-catering bungalow, camping huts a a purpose-built bunkhouse, as well as a sheltered spot f tents. It lies a mile or so along the road to Barva Bunkhouse per person **£18**; camping hut **£36**; camping p pitch **£16**

EATING

An Lanntair Kenneth St ☎01851 703307, ⓦlanntair .com. Arts venue with a stylish, modern café-bar-restaurant that serves food all day. Light lunches start at £4 for soup and bread, or, for more substantial eating, they do burgers, fish and chips and pastas from £10. Food served Mon–Sat 10am–8pm.

★Digby Chick 5 Bank St ☎01851 700026, ⓦdigbychick .co.uk. Smart, modern, buzzy little bistro with a real emphasis on using local produce, such as the famous Stornoway black pudding. There are some interesting options on offer here like their Indian-French fusion of salmon with curried bisque, tandoori onions and coconut bonbons, or ordinary battered fish and chips if curry's not your thing. Two-course lunch menu costs £14.50. Mon–Sat noon–2pm & 5.30–9pm.

Stornoway Balti House 24 South Beach ☎018 706116. Family-run restaurant that's been in Stornow for decades. The curries are the real thing and the servic great, but the real boon is that it's open on Sundays. B value are the set menus: lunch £10, dinner £16. Da noon–2pm & 5–11.30pm.

Thai Café 27 Church St ☎01851 701811, ⓦthai-ca -stornoway.co.uk. Despite the name, this is actually restaurant, serving authentic Thai food. The lunchtime p Thai is particularly good value at £5, while evening ma like the spicy Jungle Curry – stir-fried beef and pepp in a spicy cocount gravy – cost around £9. No licence, bring your own bottle (£1 corkage). Mon–Sat noo 2.30pm & 5–11pm.

DRINKING

The Criterion 32 Point St ☎01851 701990. A tiny, authentic no-frills Stornoway pub, where they have regular informal (music) sessions – if nothing's going down, try

nearby *MacNeill's*. Mon–Thurs 11am–11pm, Fri & S 11am–1am.

The road to Ness (Nis)

Northwest of Stornoway, the A857 crosses the vast, barren **peat bog** of the Lewis interic an empty, undulating wilderness riddled with stretch marks formed by peat cuttings an pockmarked with freshwater lochans. The whole area was once covered by forests, but these disappeared long ago, leaving a deposit of peat six feet thick, and still being forme in certain places. For the people of Lewis the peat serves as a valuable energy resource; i pungent smoke is one of the most characteristic smells of the Western Isles.

Twelve miles across the peat bog the road approaches the west coast of Lewis and divides, heading southwest towards Callanish (see p.512), or northeast through **BARVAS** (Barabhas), and a string of bleak and fervently Presbyterian crofting and weaving villages. These scattered settlements have none of the photogenic qualities o Skye's whitewashed villages: the churches are plain and unadorned; the crofters' hous elatively modern and smothered in grey pebbledash rendering or harling; the stone ottages and enclosures of their forebears often lie half-abandoned in the front garden; nd a rusting assortment of discarded cars and vans store peat bags and the like.

Iess (Nis)

ventually, you reach the densely populated settlements that make up the parish of ESS (Nis), at the northern tip of Lewis. Ness has the highest percentage of Gaelic-peakers in the country (75 per cent), but the locals are best known for their annual ulling of young gannets on **Sula Sgeir**, a tiny island forty miles north. The road rminates at **PORT OF NESS** (Port Nis), with its tiny harbour and lovely golden beach. Shortly before you reach Port of Ness, a minor road heads northwest to the hamlet f **EUROPIE** (Eoropaidh) – pronounced "Yor-erpee". By the road junction that leads to e Butt of Lewis stands the simple stone structure of **St Moluag's Church** (Teampull lholuaidh), amid the runrig fields, now acting as sheep runs. Thought to date from e twelfth century, when the islands were still under Norse rule, but restored in 912, the church features a strange south chapel with only a squint window onnecting it to the nave.

From Europie, a narrow road twists to the bleak and blustery northern tip of the and, **Rubha Robhanais** – well known to devotees of the BBC shipping forecast as the utt of Lewis – where a lighthouse sticks up above a series of sheer cliffs and stacks, and alive with kittiwakes, fulmars and cormorants, with skuas and gannets feeding fshore; it's a great place for marine mammal-spotting.

RRIVAL AND DEPARTURE   NESS

bus There's a regular bus service between Stornoway and Port of Ness (Mon–Sat 6–9 daily; 1hr).

CCOMMODATION AND EATING

fé Sonas Port of Ness ☎ 01851 810222. A wholly nticing café from the outside, but things improve when step in and see the views across the bay. Lots of fresh food available here like the lobster bisque and soda ad for £9.50, or opt for a cheese quiche for £8. Mon–Sat 30am–5pm.

e Decca Ness, 2 miles south of the Butt of Lewis hthouse ☎ 01851 810571, ⊕ thedecca.co.uk. First and most a tearoom that also does B&B and a wide repertoire

of meals for £20 if booked in advance. The en-suite rooms are attractive enough and there's a living room for guests with maps of the area, books, games and DVDs. **£90**

Galson Farm South Galson (Gabhsann Bho), 8 miles northeast of Barvas ☎ 01851 850492, ⊕ galsonfarm .co.uk. An attractive converted eighteenth-century farmhouse with two sitting rooms, which offers generous portions of Aga-cooked dinner (for £20), bed and breakfast, and runs a six-bunk hostel close by. Dorms **20**; doubles **£91**

estside (An Toabh Siar)

ading southwest from the crossroads near Barvas (Barabhas) brings you to the stside. The main road lies a mile or so inland from the coast, but several villages ander down towards the sea. At **Arnol** and **Garenin** (Gearrannan) there are utifully preserved blackhouses to explore, and, at **Callanish** (Calanais), the islands' tifiably popular standing stones.

1ol Blackhouse

rnol • April–Sept Mon–Sat 9.30am–5.30pm; Oct–March Mon–Tues & Thurs–Sat 10am–4pm • £4.50 • ☎ 01851 710395

Arnol, the remains of numerous **blackhouses** lie abandoned by the roadside, with e carefully preserved to show exactly how a true blackhouse, or *taigh-dubh*, would e been. The interior is dimly lit and heated by a small peat fire in the central hearth bare earth. Smoke drifts up through the thatch, helping to kill any creepy-crawlies, p out the midges and turn the heathery sods and oat-straw thatch into next year's ilizer. The animals would have slept in the byre, separated only by a low partition, ile potatoes and grain were stored in the adjacent barn.

14

Garenin (Gearrannan)

5a Garenin • May–Sept Mon–Sat 9.30am–5.30pm • £3.50 • ☎ 01851 643416, Ⓦ gearrannan.com

A mile-long road leads north off the A858 to the beautifully remote coastal settlement of **GARENIN** (Gearrannan). Here, in contrast to Arnol, a whole cluster of nine thatched crofters' houses – the last of which was abandoned in 1974 – has been restored and put to a variety of uses. As an ensemble, they give a great impression of what a **Baile Tughaidh**, or blackhouse village, must have been like. The first house is occupied by the ticket office and café. The second house has been restored to its condition at the time of abandonment, so there's electric light, but no running water, lino flooring, but a peat fire and box-beds – and a weaving machine in the byre. The third house has interpretive panels and a touch-screen computer telling the history of the village and the folk who lived there. Several others have been converted into **self-catering** accommodation.

Dun Carloway (Dùn Charlabhaigh)

Signposted off the A858 • Open 24hr • ☎ 01851 710395

Just south of Carloway village, **Dun Carloway** (Dùn Charlabhaigh) perches on top of a conspicuous rocky outcrop overlooking the sea. One of Scotland's best-preserved **brochs**, or fortified towers, its dry-stone circular walls reach a height of more than 30ft on one side. The broch consists of two concentric walls, the inner one perpendicular, the outer one slanting inwards, the two originally fastened together by roughly hewn flagstones, which also served as lookout galleries reached via a narrow stairwell. The only entrance to the roofless inner yard is through a low doorway set beside a crude and cramped guard cell. As at Callanish, there have been all sorts of theories about the purpose of the brochs, which date from between 100 BC and 100 AD; the most likely explanation is that they were built to provide protection from Roman slave-traders.

Callanish (Calanais) standing stones

Stones Open 24hr • Free • **Callanish Visitor Centre** April, May, Sept & Oct Mon–Sat 10am–6pm; June–Aug Mon–Sat 9.30am–8pm; Oct–March Tues–Sat 10am–4pm • £3.50 • ☎ 01851 621422, Ⓦ callanishvisitorcentre.co.uk

Overlooking the sheltered, islet-studded waters of Loch Ròg are the islands' most dramatic prehistoric ruins, the **Callanish standing stones**. These monoliths – nearly fifty slabs of gnarled and finely grained gneiss up to 15ft high – were transported here between 3000 and 1500 BC, but their exact function remains a mystery. No one knows why the ground plan resembles a colossal Celtic cross, why there's a central burial chamber or why many of the stones are aligned with the positions of the sun and the stars. Whatever the purpose of the site, there's certainly no denying the powerful primeval presence, not to mention sheer beauty, of the stones.

A blackhouse adjacent to the main stone circle serves as a tearoom offering limited snacks. On the other side of the stones is the **Callanish Visitor Centre**, which has a slightly longer (though no more imaginative) menu than the blackhouse as well as a small museum on the site, but with so much information on the panels beside the stones there's little reason to visit it. If you want to commune with standing stones in solitude, head for the smaller circles in more natural surroundings a mile or two southeast of Callanish, around Garynahine (Gearraidh na h-Aibhne).

ARRIVAL AND DEPARTURE

WESTSI

By bus A circular bus service connects Callanish, Carloway and Garenin to Stornoway (Mon–Sat 3–6 daily; Callanish 32min, Carloway 45min, Garenin 1hr).

ACCOMMODATION

Eilean Fraoich Campsite Shawbost (Siabost) ☎ 01851 710504, Ⓦ eileanfraoich.co.uk. Located behind the old village church, this pristine, flat, grassy campsite is in complete contrast with the surrounding undulating landscape. The site offers a kitchen with the usual appliances, a dining attached and laundry facilities. April–Oct. Per pitch £12

Leumadair 7a Callanish (Calanais) ☎ 01851 621 Ⓦ leumadair.co.uk. A purpose-built modern guesth with views of the Callanish stones. Owned by a very friendly Lewis couple, who keep birds of prey, hens and pigs and provide three-course dinners for £25 on request. **£86**

Uig (Uuige)

It's a long drive along the B8011 to the remote parish of **UIG**, which suffered badly from the Clearances. The landscape here is hillier and more dramatic than elsewhere, a combination of myriad islets, wild cliff scenery and patches of pristine golden sand.

Timsgarry (Timsgearraidh)

The main road takes you through the narrow canyon of Glen Valtos (Glèann Bhaltois) to **TIMSGARRY** (Timsgearraidh), overlooking **Uig Sands** (Tràigh Uuige), the largest and most prized of all Lewis's golden strands, where the sea goes out for miles at low tide; the best access point is from the cemetery car park in Ardroil (Eadar Dha Fhadhail), a couple of miles south of Timsgarry.

Uig Museum

Uig Community Centre, just off the B8011 at the Aird Uig turn-off • Easter–Sept Mon–Sat noon–5pm • £2 • ☎ 01851 672233

A giant wooden statue of one of the **Lewis Chessmen**, which were found in a local sandbank in 1831, heralds the **Uig Museum** in Timsgarry. Inside, you can see some replicas of the beautifully expressive twelfth-century Viking chess pieces, carved from walrus ivory and whale teeth. As well as putting on some excellent temporary exhibitions, the museum has bygone bits and bobs from old blackhouses; there's also a welcome **tearoom** attached selling soup for £3, rolls for £5 and a selection of cakes.

ARRIVAL AND DEPARTURE   **UIG**

By bus There are regular buses between Stornoway and Uig (Mon–Sat 4 daily; 1hr–1hr 30min).

ACCOMMODATION AND EATING

Ardroil campsite Ardroil (Eadar Dha Fhadhail) ☎ 01851 672248. The location, by one of the most remote and incredible sandy beaches in the Western Isles, is unbeatable. There's a small, recently erected utilities block with showers and sinks plus an electric socket. Nearest shop is a 10min walk. Per person **£2**

Auberge Carnish 5 Carnish (Carnais) ☎ 01851 672459, ⓦ aubergecarnish.co.uk. A new-build clapboard guesthouse on the far side of the stunning Uig Sands. The rooms are spacious and tastefully furnished with unparalleled views over the bay. Open to the public, the restaurant's food – like the owners – is Franco-Hebridean, with two courses for £30.50. Mid-March to mid-Nov daily 6.30–8.30pm. **£130**

Baile na Cille Timsgarry (Timsgearraidh) ☎ 01851 672242, ⓦ bailenacille.co.uk. A chaotic kind of place, run by an eccentric couple who are very welcoming to families and dogs and dish up wonderful set-menu dinners for £30 a head. Mid-April to mid-Sept. **£130**

Kneep campsite Kneep (Cnip) ☎ 01851 6722332. Small campsite beside the wonderful sandy Reef Beach

(Tràigh na Beirghe) and an ideal place to take a kayak (i you have one) to explore the tiny islands nearby. The site i run by the local community and the only facilities are a small unisex toilet block with coin-operated showers (£1 shower). Easter to mid-Sept. Per person **£10**

Suainaval 3 Crowlista (Cradhlastadh) ☎ 0185 672386, ⓦ suainaval.com. The best B&B in the whol area, run by a truly welcoming couple; rooms have pin floors and furnishings and fabulous views over the golde sands of Uig. **£70**

Harris (Na Hearadh)

Harris (from the old Norse for "high land") is much hillier, more dramatic and more immediately appealing than Lewis, its boulder-strewn slopes descending to aquamarine bays of dazzling white sand. Lewis and Harris are, in fact, one island, the "division" embedded in a historical split in the MacLeod clan, lost in the mists of time. For the record, the dividing line comprises Loch Reasort in the west, Loch Seaforth (Loch Shìphoirt) in the east, and the six miles in between. Harris itself is clearly divided by a minuscule isthmus into the wild, inhospitable mountains of **North Harris** and the gentler landscape and sandy shores of **South Harris**.

Tarbert (An Tairbeart)

Sheltered in a green valley on the narrow isthmus, **TARBERT** is the largest place on Harri and a wonderful place to arrive by boat. The port's mountainous backdrop is impressive and the town is attractively laid out on steep terraces sloping up from the dock.

ARRIVAL AND INFORMATION

TARBER

By ferry There are CalMac car ferries to and from Uig on Skye (Mon–Sat 1–2 daily; 1hr 45min).

By bus Tarbert is served by six different bus routes and is reachable from Stornoway and all the nearby coastal settlements.

Destinations Hushinish (schooldays Mon–Fri 2–3 daily; school holidays Tues & Fri 3 daily; 40min); Leverburgh

(Mon–Sat 6–8 daily; 45min–1hr); Leverburgh via the Ba (Mon–Sat 2–4 daily; 1hr); Rhenigdale (by request ☎ 077 159218; Mon–Sat 2–3 daily; 30min); Scalpay (Mon–S 4–6 daily; 20min).

Tourist office Main Square (April–Oct Mon–S 9am–6pm; open to greet the evening ferry; ☎ 018 502011).

ACCOMMODATION

Coel na Mara 7 Direcleit ☎ 01859 502464, ⓦ ceolnamara.com. With your own transport, this secluded B&B, just south of Tarbert, is a good choice. Nicely furnished throughout, with great views over East Loch Tarbert. The smallest and cheapest room doesn't have en-suite facilities. **£90**

Harris Hotel Scott Rd ☎ 01859 502154, ⓦ harrishotel .com. Just a 5min walk from the harbour, this is Tarbert's longest-established and largest hotel. The 23 en-suite

rooms are tastefully furnished, and some have sea view The hotel is also open to the public for food – even o Sunday – with a lunch menu that includes a generc portion of venison burger for £12. **£110**

No. 5 hostel 5 Drinishader (Drinisiadar) ☎ 018 511255, ⓦ number5.biz. A converted cottage, 3 m south of Tarbert, offering bed linen and laundry service alc with canoes, kayaks (£15/half day) and cycles (£15/day) rent. Beds are in dorms, plus one twin. Per person **£21**

EATING AND DRINKING

★ **First Fruits** Pier Rd ☎ 01859 502439. Surprisingly good tearoom housed in an old stone-built cottage that serves real coffee, crumbly scones and light lunches. You can get a sandwich and salad for just £3.50 or a seriously

tasty home-made burger for £5. April & May Mon, We Fri 10.30am–4pm, Thurs & Sat 10.30am–3pm; Jur Sept Mon–Fri 10am–4pm, Sat 10am–3pm.

Isle of Harris Inn Scott Rd ☎ 01859 502566. A liv

ub, across the road from (and owned by) the *Harris Hotel* and chips and pizzas. Mon–Sat 11am–11pm; food ffering an all-you-can-eat buffet for £12 as well as fish served noon–9.30pm.

North Harris (Ceann a Tuath na Hearadh)

f you're coming from Stornoway on the A859, mountainous **North Harris** is a pectacular introduction to Harris, its bulging, pyramidal mountains of gneiss looming ver the dramatic, fjord-like **Loch Seaforth** (Loch Shìphoirt). From **ARDVOURLIE** (Aird ' Mhulaidh), you weave your way over a boulder-strewn saddle between mighty gaoth Aird (1829ft) and An Cliseam or the **Clisham** (2619ft), the highest peak in the Vestern Isles. This bitter terrain, littered with debris left behind by retreating glaciers, ffers but the barest of vegetation, with an occasional cluster of crofters' houses sitting i the shadow of a host of pointed peaks, anywhere between 1000ft and 2500ft high.

CCOMMODATION NORTH HARRIS

henigidale (Reinigeadal) Hostel 4 miles off the 359 ☏ gatliff.org.uk. A member of the Gatliff Hebridean ostels Trust, this well-equipped 27-bed hostel also has mping space outside. It's situated in an isolated coastal mmunity – there's a bus connection (request-only: call

☏ 07769 159218 by 8pm the day before) or else it's a magnificent six-mile (3hr) hike over the rocky landscape from Tarbert: ask at the tourist office for directions. No advance booking and no phone. Per person **£14**

South Harris (Ceann a Deas na Hearadh)

he mountains of **South Harris** are less dramatic than in the north, but the scenery is no ss attractive. There's a choice of routes from Tarbert to the ferry port of **Leverburgh**, hich connects with North Uist: the east coast, known as **The Bays** (Na Baigh), is rugged id seemingly inhospitable, while the **west coast** boasts some of the finest stretches of lden sand in the Western Isles, buffeted by the Atlantic winds. Surprisingly, most people 'e along the harsh eastern coastline rather than the more fertile west side. But not by loice – they were evicted from their original crofts to make way for sheep-grazing.

he west coast

he main road from Tarbert into South Harris snakes its way west for ten miles across ie boulder-strewn interior to reach the most stunning **beach**, the vast golden strand of skentyre Bay (Tràigh Losgaintir), first of a chain of sweeping sands, backed by rich achair, that stretches for nine miles. In good weather, the scenery is particularly

HARRIS TWEED

Far from being a picturesque cottage industry, **Harris tweed** production is vital to the local economy, with a well-organized and unionized workforce. Traditionally, the tweed was made by women to provide clothing for their families, using a 2500-year-old process. Each woman plucked the wool by hand, washed and scoured it, dyeing it with lichen, heather flowers or ragwort, carding (smoothing and straightening the wool, adding butter to grease it), spinning and weaving. Finally the cloth was dipped in urine and "waulked" by a group of women, who beat the cloth on a table to soften it while singing Gaelic waulking songs. Harris tweed was originally made all over the islands, and was known simply as *clò mór* (big cloth).

In the mid-nineteenth century, Catherine Murray, **Countess of Dunmore**, who owned a large part of Harris, started to sell surplus cloth to her aristocratic friends and helped kick-start the modern industry, which still serves as a vital source of employment, though demand (and therefore employment levels) can fluctuate wildly as fashions change. To earn the official **Harris Tweed Authority (HTA)** trademark of the Orb and Maltese Cross – Lady Dunmore's coat of arms – the fabric has to be hand-woven on the Outer Hebrides from pure new Scottish wool, while the manufacturing process must take place in the local mills – currently in Carloway and Shawbost, in Lewis – where the wool is dyed, carded and spun.

impressive, with foaming breakers rolling along the golden sands set against the rounded peaks of the mountains to the north and the islet-studded turquoise sea to the west. A short distance out to sea is the island of **Taransay** (Tarasaigh), which once held a population of nearly a hundred, but was abandoned as recently as 1974. South of Luskentyre lies **Scarista** (Sgarasta), where one of the first of the Hebridean Clearances took place in 1828, when thirty families were evicted and their homes burnt.

14

Seallam!

Northton (Taobh Tuath) • Mon–Sat 10am–5pm • £2.50 • ☎ 01859 520258, ⊛ seallam.com

There's loads of information on local history, geology, flora and fauna at **Seallam!**, a purpose-built heritage centre close to the village of **Northton** (Taobh Tuath), overlooked by the round-topped hill of Chaipabhal at the westernmost tip of South Harris. As well as detailing the area's history of emigration, it's a useful centre for ancestor-hunters, and there's a good section on St Kilda (see box, p.513).

Leverburgh (An t-Ob)

The west coast road trims the island's south shore, eventually reaching the sprawling settlement of **LEVERBURGH** (An t-Ob). Named after Lord Leverhulme, who planned to turn the place into the largest fishing port on the west coast of Scotland in the 1920s, it's the terminal for the CalMac **car ferry** service to Berneray and the Uists across the skerry-strewn Sound of Harris.

Rodel (Roghadal)

A mile or so from Renish Point (Rubha Reanais), the southern tip of Harris, is the old port of **RODEL** (Roghadal), where a smattering of ancient stone houses lies among the hillocks, and the venerable *Rodel Hotel* sits by the old harbour, where the ferry from Skye used to arrive.

St Clement's Church (Tur Chliamainn)

Rodel • Generally open at all times • Free; HES

On top of one of Rodel's grassy humps, with sheep grazing in the graveyard, is **St Clement's Church** (Tur Chliamainn), burial place of the MacLeods of Harris and Dunvegan in Skye. Dating from the 1520s – in other words pre-Reformation, hence the big castellated tower (which you can climb) – the church was restored in 1873 by the Countess of Dunmore. The bare interior is distinguished by its wall tombs, notably that of the founder, Alasdair Crotach, whose heavily weathered effigy lies beneath an intriguing backdrop and canopy of sculpted reliefs depicting vernacular and religious scenes – elemental representations of, among others, a stag hunt, the Holy Trinity, St Michael and the devil, and an angel weighing the souls of the dead. Look out, too, for the *sheila-na-gig* halfway up the south side of the church tower; unusually, she has a brother displaying his genitalia, below a carving of St Clement on the west face.

ARRIVAL AND INFORMATION SOUTH HARR

By ferry There's a daily ferry to and from Berneray, North Uist (1–2 daily in winter, 3–4 daily in summer; 1hr).

By bus There's a regular bus connection along the west coast between Leverburgh and Tarbert (Mon–Sat 6 daily; 45min–1hr), and a less frequent one via the Bays the east coast (Mon–Sat 2–4 daily; 1hr).

ACCOMMODATION AND EATING

THE BAYS

★ **Lickisto Blackhouse Camping** Lickisto (Liceasto) ☎ 01851 530485, ⊛ freewebs.com/vanvon. Beautiful campsite by a rocky bay with a restored blackhouse for the campers' use. A couple of renovated thatched byres house basic washing facilities while the blackhouse is the place to

congregate with other campers by the peat fire. Yurts a available. March–Oct. Yurts **£70**; camping per pitch **£2**

Old School House Finsbay (Fionnsbhagh) ☎ 01 530420, ⊛ theoldschoolhousefinsbay.com. Attrac Victorian former village schoolhouse with three en-s twin rooms. It's run by a very friendly couple who prov

...ood home cooking and generous portions for dinner (£20–30) and breakfast. __£80__

THE WEST COAST

...eul-na-Mara Seilebost ☎01859 550205, ⓦbeulna ...ara.co.uk. This is a perfectly decent B&B run by a local ...ouple, but what makes it particularly special is the ...unning location, overlooking the golden sands of ...uskentyre Bay (Tràigh Losgaintir). __£95__

...airc an t-Srath Borve (Na Buirgh) ☎01859 550386, ...paircant-srath.co.uk. A working crofthouse, tastefully ...rnished with antiques and Harris tweeds, that has a superb ...ew from the dining room, particularly at sunset. Guests can ...cover from a hard day's hiking in the in-house sauna before ...nner – three beautifully prepared courses for £37. __£108__

...: Temple Café Northton (Taobh Tuath) ☎07876 ...0416. Great waterside café in a unique stone and timber ...ilding resembling a hobbit house. They offer tasty deep-...ed pies and quiches that come with a crunchy salad for ...'. There's a good selection of tray bakes and scones too.

April–Sept Tues–Sun 10.30am–5.30pm, Thurs–Fri & Sun 6.30–9pm; Oct–March same hours, Sat & Sun only.

LEVERBURGH

★ **Am Bothan** Ferry Rd ☎01859 520251, ⓦambothan .com. Quirky, bright-red timber-clad bunkhouse that makes for a pretty luxurious, very welcoming hostel close to the ferry. Lovely big kitchen/living room, plus laundry and drying facilities too. Per person __£22.50__

The Anchorage Ferry Terminal ☎01859 520225. Lots of locally sourced seafood on offer in this lively bar/restaurant by the ferry slipway. Considerably more expensive than your average Hebridean eatery (scallops with truffle purée and chorizo for £21.50), but there are cheaper options like roast vegetable fregola for £11.50. Mon–Sat noon–11pm; food served noon–9pm.

Carminish House 1a Strond ☎01859 520400, ⓦcarminish.com. Modern guesthouse with bright, en-suite rooms and a residents' lounge, which has an open fire and some fabulous views over the Sound. __£90__

14

North Uist (Uibhist a Tuath)

...ompared to the mountainous scenery of Harris, **North Uist** – seventeen miles by ...irteen – is much flatter and for some comes as something of an anticlimax. Over half ...e surface area is covered by water, creating a distinctive peaty-brown lochan-studded ...rowned landscape". Most visitors come here for the trout and salmon fishing and the ...eerstalking, both of which (along with poaching) are critical to the island's economy. ...thers come for the prehistoric sites, the birds, the otters, or the sheer peace of this ...indy isle and the solitude of North Uist's vast sandy beaches, which extend – almost ...ithout interruption – along the north and west coast.

...ochmaddy (Loch nam Madadh) and around

...espite being situated on the east coast, some distance away from any beach, the ferry ...ort of **LOCHMADDY** – "Loch of the Dogs" – makes a good base for exploring the ...and. Occupying a narrow, bumpy promontory, overlooked by the brooding ...ountains of North Lee (Lì a Tuath) and South Lee (Lì a Deas) to the southeast, it's ...fficult to believe that this sleepy settlement was a large herring port as far back as the ...venteenth century. While there's not much to see in Lochmaddy itself, there are ...veral prehistoric sites in the surrounding area.

...igh Chearsabhagh

...n–Sat 10am–4pm • £3 • ☎01876 603970, ⓦtaigh-chearsabhagh.org

...e only thing to keep you in Lochmaddy is **Taigh Chearsabhagh**, a converted ...ghteenth-century merchant's house that's now home to a community arts centre ...using a café, post office, shop and museum, which puts on some seriously innovative ...hibitions. Taigh Chearsabhagh was one of the prime movers behind the commissioning ...a series of seven sculptures dotted about the Uists – ask for directions to the ones in ...d around Lochmaddy. The most interesting is the **Both nam Faileas** (Hut of the ...adow), half a mile or so north of Lochmaddy. The hut is an ingenious dry-stone, ...f-roofed camera obscura built by sculptor Chris Drury that projects the nearby land, ...and skyscape onto its back wall – take time to allow your eyes to adjust to the light.

14

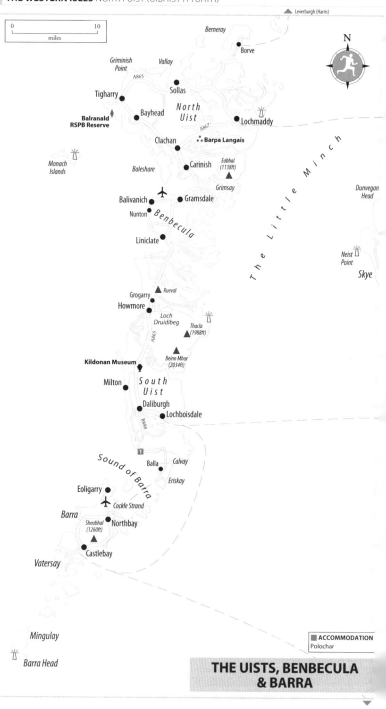

THE UISTS, BENBECULA & BARRA

ARRIVAL AND INFORMATION

By ferry There's a daily ferry from and to Uig, Skye (1–2 daily; 1hr 45min).

By bus A regular bus service runs down the backbone of the Uists to Lochboisdale and Eriskay.

Destinations Balivanich (Mon–Sat 6–8 daily; 30–45min);

LOCHMADDY AND AROUND

Balranald (Mon–Sat 3 daily; 50min); Eriskay (Mon–Sat 3 daily; 2hr 20min); Lochboisdale (Mon–Sat 5–6 daily; 1hr 30min).

Tourist office Pier Road, Lochmaddy (July to mid-Oct Mon–Sat 10am–5pm; also opens to greet the evening ferry; ☎01876 500321).

ACCOMMODATION AND ACTIVITIES

Hamersay House Lochmaddy ☎01876 500700, ⓦhamersayhouse.co.uk. One of the region's more upmarket hotels; stylish and modern inside and out. The in-house brasserie has lots of pricey seafood options like langoustines for £20, while the vegetarian option usually comes for a more economically palatable £13. Daily 6–9pm. **£135**

Uist Outdoor Centre Lochmaddy, 100yds north of the village ☎01876 500480, ⓦuistoutdoorcentre.co.uk. Outdoor centre with hostel accommodation and activities ranging from sea-kayaking to rock climbing for residents and non-residents alike. March to early Dec. Per person **£20**

Berneray (Bhearnaraigh)

Berneray is a low-lying island immediately to the north of North Uist, connected via a causeway that starts some eight miles north of Lochmaddy. Two miles by three, with a population of around 140, the island has a superb three-mile-long sandy **beach** on the west and north coast, backed by rabbit-free dunes and machair.

ARRIVAL AND INFORMATION

By ferry The ferry from Leverburgh on Harris arrives at the very southern tip of Berneray (1–2 daily in winter, 3–4 daily in summer; 1hr).

By bus There's a decent bus connection with Lochmaddy

BERNERAY

(Mon–Sat 5–6 daily; 20min).

Tourist information The community website ⓦisleofberneray.com is a useful source of information.

ACCOMMODATION AND EATING

Berneray Hostel 2 miles north of the ferry port ⓦgatliff.org.uk. The island has a wonderful Gatliff Trust hostel, which occupies a pair of thatched blackhouses in a lovely spot by a beach, beyond the main village. The property is very well equipped and there are plenty of tourist pamphlets and even some binoculars if you fancy doing a

spot of whale watching. No advance booking. Per person **£14**

The Lobster Pot Borve (Borgh) ☎01876 540288. A useful tearoom (and shop) on the main road, near the ferry terminal, serving bog-standard cooked breakfasts, toasties (for around £4) and soup (for £3.60). Mon–Sat 9am–6pm; closes 5.30pm in winter.

Balranald

Seven miles northwest of Clachan is the **Balranald RSPB Reserve**, best known for its **corncrakes**, once common throughout Britain but now among the country's rarest birds. They're good at hiding, so you're unlikely to see one; however, the males' loud "craking" can be heard from May to July throughout the Uists and Barra: one or two usually make a loud noise right outside the RSPB **visitor centre**, from which you can pick up a leaflet outlining a two-hour **walk** along the headland, marked by posts. A wonderful carpet of flowers covers the machair in summer, and there are usually corn buntings and arctic terns inland, and gannets, Manx shearwaters and skuas out to sea. On a clear day you can see the unmistakeable shape of St Kilda (see box, p.513).

ACCOMMODATION

Balranald Hebridean Holidays Balranald ☎01876 510304, ⓦbalranaldhebrideanholidays.com. Lovely campsite by the RSPB reserve, surrounded by fields of wild flowers and close to a sandy beach – as well as the

BALRANALD

usual facilities, there's free wi-fi, a washing machine and tumble drier, and the office sells basic provisions. March–Sept. Per pitch **£11**

Clachan (Clachan na Luib) and around

At **CLACHAN** (Clachan na Luib), by the crossroads with the A867 from Lochmaddy, there's a post office and general store. Offshore, to the southwest, lie two flat, tidal, dune and machair islands, the larger of which is **Baleshare** (Baile Sear), with its fantastic three-mile-long beach, connected by causeway to North Uist.

ACCOMMODATION — CLACHAN AND AROUN▮

★**Bagh Alluin** 21 Baleshare (Baile Sear) ☎01876 580370, ⓦjacvolbeda.co.uk. A secluded, beautifully designed modern B&B with large rooms and fantastic views. Run by a friendly Dutch artist, who can point you in the right direction to see the best of the island's wildlife. **£85**

Langass Lodge Loch Eport, just off the A867 ☎01876 580285, ⓦlangasslodge.co.uk. A former hunting lodge beside a small wood (a very rare sight in the Uists), which has reasonably tasteful, spacious rooms, a bar and restaurant that mostly serves excellent local seafood for

around £25 for the main course. Daily 6–8.30pm. **£115**
★**Moorcroft Holidays** 17 Carinish (Cairinis) ☎0187▮ 580305, ⓦmoorcroftholidays.co.uk. An exposed, b▮ flat and very well-equipped campsite, with sea views; th▮ bunkhouse is pretty luxurious with three twin room▮ lovely wooden floors and furnishings, a modern kitche▮ and a homely living/dining room. If you prefer som▮ privacy they also rent out little "hobbit homes" for up t▮ three people that have a fridge, sink and cooking facilitie▮ April–Oct. Bunkhouse per person **£20**; camping p▮ person **£8**; hobbit home **£40**

EATING AND DRINKING

Claddach Kirkibost Centre Claddach Kirkibost (Cladach Chireboist) ☎01876 580390, ⓦcladdach-kirkibost.org. Community-centre café in a conservatory with sea views, which uses local produce to make soups, sandwiches and simple dishes, even the occasional curry or Tex-Mex dish (£6–7). Mon–Sat 11am–4pm.

Westford Inn Claddach Kirkibost (Cladach Chireboist)

☎01876 580653, ⓦwestfordinn.com. North Uist's on▮ pub – luckily it's a good one – is housed in the eighteent▮ century factor's house. There's a wood-panelled bar p▮ several smaller rooms with real fires in bad weather, Isle▮ Skye Brewing Company ales on tap and pub food un▮ 9pm. Sun–Thurs noon–11pm, Fri noon–midnight, S▮ noon–1am.

Benbecula (Beinn na Faoghla)

Blink and you could miss the pancake-flat island of **Benbecula** (put the stress on the second syllable), sandwiched between Protestant North Uist and Catholic South Uist. Scarred from the postwar presence of the Royal Artillery who once made up half the local population, the only reason to come to **BALIVANICH** (Baile a Mhanaich), Benbecula's grim, grey capital, is if you're flying into or out of **Benbecula airport**, or yo▮ need an ATM or a supermarket.

ARRIVAL AND DEPARTURE — BENBECUL▮

By plane Benbecula Airport (☎01870 602 310, ⓦhial .co.uk/benbecula-airport) is just a 10–15min walk north of Balivanich. The airport serves Glasgow and Stornoway and there's a small café inside the terminal building.
By bus Buses en route to and from South or North Uist stop

outside Balivanich's airport.
Destinations Berneray (Mon–Sat 5–7 daily; 1hr 10m▮ Eriskay (Mon–Sat 5–7 daily; 1hr 30min); Lochboisc▮ (Mon–Sat 7–8 daily; 1hr); Lochmaddy (Mon–Sat ▮ daily; 30min).

ACCOMMODATION AND EATING

Nunton House Hostel Nunton ☎01870 602017, ⓦnuntonhousehostel.com. Four small dorm rooms in the eighteenth-century former clan chief's house, where Bonnie Prince Charlie dressed up in drag before his escape over the sea to Skye. Sadly the prince wouldn't recognize the place these days as all the charm has been modernised out of it, save for the delightful hearth. Per person **£25**

Shell Bay campsite Liniclate (Lionacleit) ☎01▮ 602447. Flat, wind-buffeted, grassy field right nex▮ the main school (and museum) on Benbecula – facili▮ are quite good (including laundry and hot showe▮ though it's not the most romantic of spots. April–Se▮ Per pitch **£14**

Stepping Stone Balivanich (Baile a Mhana▮

☎01870 603377, ⊛steppingstone10.tripod.com. A modern café-restaurant that serves cheap sandwiches and soups at lunchtime for around £3–4 and more varied

dishes in the evening, such as chicken supreme with whisky sauce for £15. Mon–Fri 9am–9pm, Sa 11am–9pm, Sun noon–9pm.

South Uist (Uibhist a Deas)

14

South Uist is the largest and most varied of the southern chain of islands. The west coast boasts some of the region's finest machair and beaches – a necklace of gold and grey sand strung twenty miles from one end to the other – while the east coast features a ridge of high mountains rising to 2034ft at Beinn Mhòr. The Reformation never took a hold in South Uist (or Barra), and the island remains Roman Catholic as is evident from the various roadside shrines. The only blot on South Uist's landscape is the Royal Artillery missile range, which dominates the northwest corner of the island.

The north

The northern half of the island contains the best **mountains** and **beaches**. To climb the mountains, you need a detailed 1:25,000 map, to negotiate the island's maze of lochans; to reach the beaches (or even see them), you have to get off the main road and pass through the old crofters' villages that straggle along the west coast.

One of the best places to reach the sandy shoreline is at **HOWMORE** (Tobha Mòr), a pretty little crofting settlement with a number of restored houses, many still thatched, including one distinctively roofed in brown heather. It's an easy walk from the village church across the flower-strewn machair to the gorgeous beach. In among the crofts are the shattered, lichen-encrusted remains of no fewer than four medieval churches and chapels, and a burial ground now harbouring just a few scattered graves.

ACCOMMODATION

Howmore (Tobha Mòr) hostel Howmore (Tobha Mòr) ⊛gatliff.org.uk. Simple Gatliff Trust hostel occupying a lovely thatched crofthouse near the village church, and just a short walk from the beach. No advance bookings. Per person **£14**

Kinloch Grogarry (Groigearraidh) ☎01870 620316, ⊛kinlochuist.com. A fine, modern B&B sheltered by a little patch of woodland and overlooking freshwater Loch

Druidibeg – run by a very keen angler, who will do three course evening meals for £25. **£98**

Orasay Inn Lochcarnan (Loch a' Charnain) ☎018 610298, ⊛orasayinn.co.uk. A modern purpose-bu hotel and restaurant off the main road with well-ke rooms, some of which have a private decked area. Da noon–2.30pm & 6–8.30pm. **£89**

Lochboisdale (Loch Baghasdail) and around

LOCHBOISDALE occupies a narrow, bumpy promontory on the east coast, but, despite being South Uist's chief settlement and ferry port, has only very limited facilities (there's a bank here, but the nearest supermarket is three miles west in Dalabrog).

Kildonan Museum (Taigh-tasgaidh Chill Donnain)

5 miles south of Howmore • April–Oct daily 10am–5pm • £2 • ☎01878 710343, ⊛kildonanmuseum.co.uk

Reasonably large museum featuring mock-ups of Hebridean kitchens through the ages, two lovely box-beds and an impressive selection of old photos, accompanied by an unsentimental yet poetic text on crofting life in the last two centuries. Pride of place go to the sixteenth-century **Clanranald Stone**, carved with the arms of the clan who ruled over South Uist from 1370 to 1839. The museum café serves sandwiches and home-made cakes, and has a choice of historical videos for those really wet and windy days.

ARRIVAL AND INFORMATION

By ferry One ferry connects Mallaig to Lochboisdale (winter one on Tues & Sat; summer one daily & Sun; 3hr 50min).

By bus There's a regular bus service along the spine road (as they call it) to North Uist (Mon–Sat only).

ACCOMMODATION AND EATING

Heron Point Lochboisdale ☎01878 700073, ☻heron point.co.uk. Homely B&B just a mile up the road from the ferry terminal with four en-suite bedrooms. Efficiently run by a very friendly host who cooks up a wonderful breakfast of smoked salmon and poached eggs. £90

Lochboisdale Hotel Lochboisdale ☎01878 700332, ☻lochboisdale.com. The town's long-established hotel is a convenient place to shelter if you're waiting for a ferry, and it does fish and chips and other typical bar meals for around £10–14. If you are staying over, the accommodation is a bit dated but the rooms are spacious,

LOCHBOISDALE AND AROUND

Destinations Balivanich (Mon–Sat 2–5 daily; 1hr); Berneray (Mon–Sat 1 daily; 2hr 50min); Eriskay (Mon–Sat 4–6 daily; 40min); Lochmaddy (Mon–Sat 1–2 daily; 1hr 30min).

Tourist office Pier Rd (Easter–Oct Mon–Sat 9am–5pm; also open for an hour to meet the ferry; ☎01878 700286).

comfortable and have great views over the harbour. £100

★**Polochar Inn** Polochar (Poll a' Charra) ☎01878 700215, ☻polocharinn.com. One of the best places to hole up in, right on the south coast overlooking the Sound of Barra, and with its own sandy beach close by; the rooms all have sea views, and on the ground floor is a good pub, with attached restaurant dishing up creamy pesto gnocchi for £12 or scallops and black pudding for £22. Mon–Thurs 11am–11pm, Fri & Sat 11am–1am, Sun 12.30–11pm; food served Mon–Sat 12.30–2.30pm & 5.30–9pm, Sun 12.30–8.30pm. £90

14

Eriskay (Eiriosgaigh)

Famous for its patterned jerseys and peculiar breed of pony, originally used for carrying peat and seaweed, the barren, hilly island of **Eriskay** is connected to South Uist by a causeway built in 2001. The island, measuring just over two miles by one, shelters a small fishing community of 150, and makes a great day-trip from South Uist. The island's main beach on the west coast, Prince's Cockle Strand (Coilleag a Phrionnsa), was where **Bonnie Prince Charlie** landed on Scottish soil on July 23, 1745 – the sea bindweed that grows there is said to have sprung from the seeds Charles brought with him from France. The prince, unaccustomed to hardship, spent his first night in a local blackhouse and ate a couple of flounders, though he couldn't take the peat smoke and chose to sleep sitting up rather than endure the damp bed.

ARRIVAL AND DEPARTURE

ERISKAY

By ferry CalMac run a small car ferry between Eriskay and Barra (5 daily except Sun in winter when there's 2; 40min).

By bus There's a regular bus service between Eriskay and Lochboisdale (Mon–Sat 4–6 daily; 40min).

ACCOMMODATION AND EATING

Am Politician Rubha Ban ☎01878 720246. The island's purpose-built pub named after the SS *Politician* (see box below) is unlikely to win any design awards. However, it

offers great views out to sea from its conservatory, where you can dine on scallops with black pudding for £8.50 as well as the usual pub grub options. Easter–Oct Mon–Sat

---

SS POLITICIAN

Eriskay's greatest claim to fame came in 1941 when the 8000-ton **SS Politician** – or "*Polly*" as it's fondly known – sank en route from Liverpool to Jamaica, along with its cargo of bicycle parts, £3 million in Jamaican currency, and 264,000 bottles of whisky, inspiring the book (by Compton Mackenzie) and Ealing comedy *Whisky Galore!* (filmed on Barra in 1948 and released as *Tight Little Island* in the US). The real story was less romantic, especially for the 36 islanders charged with illegal possession by the Customs and Excise officers. Nineteen of the islanders were found guilty and imprisoned in Inverness. The ship's stern used to be seen at low tide northwest of Calvay Island in the Sound of Eriskay until the sea finally swallowed it up. One of the original bottles (and other memorabilia) can be viewed at the pub *Am Politician* (see above).

11.30am–11pm (sometimes later), Sun noon–11pm; Oct–Easter open some weekends 11.30am–11pm; food served noon–7.45pm.

Oir na Mara ☎01878 720216. This plain, modern

bungalow B&B is kept by a true perfectionist; the rooms are spotlessly clean and the bedding is high quality. Tea and home-made cakes are offered to guests on arrival and Eriskay's pub is conveniently nearby for meal times. **£70**

Barra (Barraigh)

14

Four miles wide and eight miles long, **Barra** is the Western Isles in miniature: sandy beaches backed by machair, mountains of Lewissian gneiss, prehistoric ruins, Gaelic culture and a laidback, welcoming population of around 1200. A kind of feudal island state, it was ruled over for centuries, with relative benevolence, by the MacNeils. Unfortunately, the family sold the island in 1838 to Colonel Gordon of Cluny, who had also bought Benbecula, South Uist and Eriskay. The colonel deemed the starving crofters "redundant" and offered to turn Barra into a state penal colony. The government declined, so the colonel called in the police and proceeded with some of the most cruel forced Clearances in the Hebrides. In 1937, the 45th chief of the MacNeil clan bought back most of the island, and in 2003 gifted the estate to the Scottish government.

Castlebay (Bàgh a Chaisteil)

The only settlement of any size is **CASTLEBAY** (Bàgh a Chaisteil), which curves around the barren rocky hills of a wide bay on the south side of the island. It's difficult to imagine, but Castlebay was a herring port of some significance back in the nineteenth century, with hundreds of boats in the harbour and curing and packing factories ashore. Barra's religious allegiance is immediately announced by the large Catholic church, Our Lady, Star of the Sea, which overlooks the bay; to underline the point, there's a Madonna and Child on the slopes of **Sheabhal** (1260ft), the largest peak on Barra and a fairly easy hike from the bay.

Kisimul Castle

April–Sept daily 9.30am–5.30pm • £5.50; HES • ☎01871 810313 • Access by ferry from Castle Slip Landing, Castlebay (call for sailing times), weather permitting

As its name suggests, Castlebay has a castle in its bay, the picturesque medieval islet-fortress of Caisteal Chiosmuil, or **Kisimul Castle**, ancestral home of the MacNeil clan. The castle burnt down in the eighteenth century, but when the 45th MacNeil chief – conveniently enough, a wealthy American and trained architect – bought the island back in 1937, he set about restoring the castle. There's nothing much to see inside, but the whole experience is fun – head down to the slipway at the bottom of Main Street, where the ferryman will take you over.

Dualchas

The Square • March, April & Sept Mon, Wed & Fri 10.30am–4pm; May–Aug Mon–Sat same hours • £2 • ☎01871 810413

The Barra Heritage Centre, known as **Dualchas** (Gaelic for Heritage), is on the road that leads west out of town. It's an unpretentious little museum, housing the odd treasure like the monstrance from St Barr's Church in Northbay. There are lots of old newspapers, photo archives and local memoirs to trawl through, plus a handy café.

The north

In the north, Barra is squeezed between two sandy bays: the dune-backed west side taking the full force of the Atlantic breakers, while the east side boasts the crunchy shell sands of Tràigh Mhòr or **Cockle Strand**. The beach is also famously used as the island's **airport**, with planes landing and taking off according to the tides, since at high tide the beach (and therefore the runway) is covered in water. As its name suggests, the strand also famous for its cockles and cockleshells, the latter being used to make harling (the rendering used on most Scottish houses).

North of the airport is the scattered settlement of **EOLIGARRY** (Eòlaigearraidh), with several sheltered sandy bays. Here, too, is **St Barr's Church** (Cille-Bharra), burial ground of the MacNeils (and author Compton MacKenzie). The ground lies beside the ruins of a medieval church and two chapels, one of which houses several carved medieval gravestones and a replica of an eleventh-century rune-inscribed cross; the original is in the National Museum of Scotland (p.74).

14

ARRIVAL AND GETTING AROUND

BARRA

By plane Barra airport (☎01871 890212, ✆hial.co.uk) has direct flights to and from Glasgow.

By ferry The main ferry terminal on Barra is in Castlebay where the ferry from Oban arrives: from Eriskay, you arrive at an uninhabited spot on the northeast of the island.

Destinations Coll (Wed; 4hr); Eriskay (5 daily, 2 in winter on Sun; 40min); Oban (summer daily, winter Wed & Fri–Mon; 5hr); Tiree (Wed; 2hr 45min).

By bus There's a fairly decent bus service out of Castlebay,

which does the rounds of the island.

Destinations Airport (Mon–Sat 4–7 daily; 30min); Eoligarry (Mon–Sat 3–6 daily; 35min); Eriskay ferry (Mon–Sat 2–5 daily to coincide with ferry timetable; 25min); Vatersay (Mon–Sat 2–3 daily; 20min).

By car or bike Barra Car Hire (☎01871 890313) will deliver cars to either ferry terminal or the airport, and Barra Cycle Hire (☎01871 810846) will do the same with bikes (£15/day).

INFORMATION AND ACTIVITIES

Tourist office Main St, Castlebay (Easter–Oct Mon–Sat 15am–4.45pm, Sat 9am–5pm; June–Aug Sun 11am–3pm; also open to greet the evening ferry; ☎01871 810336).

Sea-kayaking Guided tours available from the *Dunard Hostel* (see below).

ACCOMMODATION

Castlebay Hotel Castlebay ☎01871 810223, ✆castlebay-hotel.co.uk. The Castlebay is the more welcoming of the town's two hotels – a solid Victorian pile, with spectacular views over the bay from the restaurant and some of the rooms. The six rooms vary in price considerably so early booking is essential for the cheapest one. **£90**

Dunard Hostel Castlebay ☎01871 810443, ✆dunardhostel.co.uk. A relaxed, family-run place that has twins, dorm beds and a family room. There's a well-equipped kitchen, a long dining table and a cosy living room with resident cats snoozing by the fire. They also offer a range of guided sea-kayaking trips posted up on the noticeboard (average around £20). Per person **£18**

Heathbank Hotel Northbay (Bagh a Tuath) ☎01871 810266, ✆barrahotel.co.uk. Converted mission church

now home to a comfortable hotel and unpretentious local watering hole and upmarket restaurant. **£120**

Northbay House Northbay (Bagh a Tuath) ☎01871 890255. The old schoolhouse in Northbay, originally built in 1888, is now a B&B run by a friendly couple – breakfast menu includes smoked haddock and poached egg. **£76**

Scurrival campsite 3 Eoligarry (Eòlaigearraidh) ☎01871 890292. This is a lovely, simple site with showers and toilet facilities, overlooking the sea and close to the wide sandy beach of Scurrival (Tràigh Sgurabhal) in the north of the island. April–Oct. Per person **£5**

Tigh-na-Mara Castlebay ☎01871 810304, ✆tighna mara-barra.co.uk. For value and location – just a few minutes from the pier in Castlebay – you can't beat this simple Victorian guesthouse overlooking the sea. **£80**

EATING AND DRINKING

Café Kisimul Castlebay ☎01871 810645, ✆cafekisimul.co.uk. As well as offering Italian comfort food and great music, the *Kisimul* also cooks up the best curry in northwest Scotland (mains £13–18) – try the unique scallop pakora starter for £7.95. Mon–Sat 11am–4pm & 6–9pm, Sun 5.30–9pm.

Castlebay Hotel Castlebay ☎01871 810223,

✆castlebay-hotel.co.uk. The *Castlebay* has a restaurant serving standard pub food like hamburgers for £10 by day and mixed grills in the evening for £17. If you prefer something light, there's always a vegetarian option. The hotel's bar is wisely in the adjacent building as it can get pretty rowdy on certain evenings. Daily noon–2pm & 6–9.30pm.

ENTERTAINMENT AND SPORT

Films are occasionally shown on Saturday evenings at the **local school** – look out for the posters – where there is also a **swimming pool** (Tues–Sun), **library** and **sports centre**, all of which are open to the general public.

Orkney

ST MAGNUS CATHEDRAL, KIRKWALL

Orkney

Orkney is a captivating and fiercely independent archipelago of seventy or so mostly low-lying islands, with a population of around twenty thousand. The locals tend to refer to themselves first as Orcadians, regarding Scotland as a separate entity, and proudly flying their own flag. For an Orcadian, "the Mainland" invariably means the largest island in Orkney rather than the rest of Scotland, and throughout their distinctive history the islands have been linked to lands much further afield, principally Scandinavia.

15

Orkney has excellent coastal walking, abundant birdlife and beautiful white-sand beaches. It has two chief settlements: **Stromness**, an attractive old fishing town on the far southwestern shore, and the capital, **Kirkwall**, at the dividing point between East and West Mainland. Relatively heavily populated and farmed throughout, the Mainland is joined by causeways to a string of southern islands, the largest of which is **South Ronaldsay**. The island of **Hoy**, the second largest in the archipelago, south of Mainland, presents a superbly dramatic landscape, with some of the highest sea cliffs in the country. Hoy, however, is atypical: Orkney's smaller, much quieter **northern islands** are low-lying, fertile outcrops of rock and sand, scattered across the ocean.

ARRIVAL AND DEPARTURE

By plane Flybe (☎ 0371 700 2000, ⓦ flybe.com) operate direct flights to Kirkwall from Inverness, Aberdeen, Edinburgh, Glasgow and Sumburgh in Shetland. Be warned: weather conditions are notoriously changeable, making flights prone to delay and even cancellation.

By ferry NorthLink run car ferries daily from Scrabster (with a shuttle bus from Thurso) to Stromness and less

frequently from Aberdeen and Lerwick (in Shetland) ￼ Kirkwall; Pentland Ferries run daily car ferries from Gills Ba (near John O'Groats) to St Margaret's Hope; and Joh O'Groats Ferries run a small passenger ferry to Burwick. Th timetables in the text are summer frequencies – che online for the latest sailing schedule and always bo ahead.

GETTING AROUND AND TOURS

By plane Loganair (☎ 01856 873457, ⓦ loganair.co.uk) run flights from Kirkwall to most of the outer isles, using an eight-seater plane, with discounted fares to North Ronaldsay and Papa Westray and between the islands if you stay over.

By ferry Getting to the other islands by ferry from the Mainland isn't difficult, but travel between individual islands isn't straightforward. Ask Orkney Ferries (☎ 01856 872044, ⓦ orkneyferries.co.uk) about additional Sunday sailings in summer, which often make useful inter-island connections. Tickets are expensive. Book ahead if you're taking a vehicle.

By bus The bus service on Orkney Mainland is pretty good overall. Except in Stromness and Kirkwall, there are no scheduled bus stops so just stand at a safe, visible spot and

flag the bus down. On the smaller islands, a minib usually meets the ferry and will take you to yo destination. Check ⓦ www.orkney.gov.uk for b timetables.

By bike Cycling is an option if the weather holds, sin there are few steep hills and distances are modest, thou the wind can make it hard going. For Orkney Cycle Hire Stromness, see p.532; for Cycle Orkney in Kirkwall, see p.53

Tours There's a whole range of escorted tours around t Mainland, which are great for those without a vehic Wildabout Orkney (☎ 01856 877737, ⓦ wildaboutorkn .com) offer a variety of tours of the Mainland, w departures from Stromness and Kirkwall, and there ￼ several other companies specializing in particular islan as listed throughout this chapter.

MAES HOWE

Highlights

Maes Howe Orkney's – and Europe's – finest Neolithic chambered tomb, built nearly 5000 years ago. **See p.534**

Skara Brae Older than Stonehenge or the Great Pyramids, Skara Brae is a mesmerizing Neolithic settlement, crammed with domestic detail. **See p.534**

St Magnus Cathedral, Kirkwall Beautiful red-sandstone Romanesque cathedral in miniature, built by the Vikings in the twelfth century. **See p.536**

Tomb of the Eagles Fascinating, privately owned Neolithic chambered tomb on the southeastern tip of South Ronaldsay. **See p.541**

❺ **Scapa Flow Visitor Centre, Hoy** Learn about the wartime history of Orkney's great natural harbour once Britain's chief naval base and site of the scuttling of the German Fleet in 1919. **See p.544**

❻ **Westray** Thriving Orkney island with seabird colonies, sandy beaches, a sixteenth-century ruined castle and a figurine that's one of the earliest representations of the human form found in the UK. **See p.548**

❼ **North Ronaldsay** Orkney's northernmost island features a world-renowned bird observatory, seaweed-eating sheep and Britain's tallest land-based lighthouse. **See p.554**

HIGHLIGHTS ARE MARKED ON THE MAP ON P.530

Stromness

STROMNESS is a quite enchanting port at which to arrive by boat, its picturesque waterfront a procession of tiny sandstone jetties and slate roofs nestling below the green hill of Brinkies Brae. It makes a great introduction to Orkney, and is an excellent base too. Its natural sheltered harbour (known as Hamnavoe) has been used since Viking times, but the town itself only really took off in the eighteenth century when the Hudson's Bay Company made Stromness its main base from which to make the journey across the North Atlantic. Today Stromness remains a

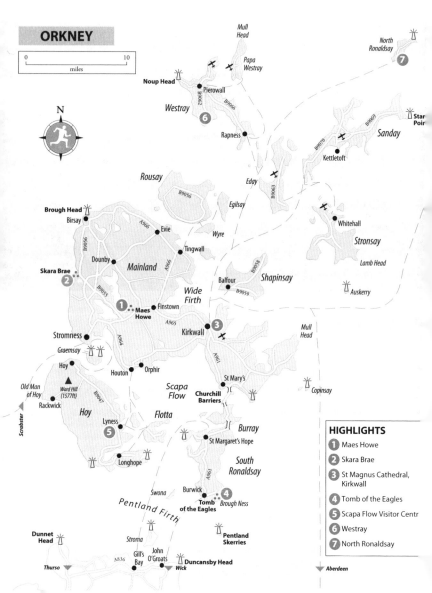

ORKNEY

0 ——————— 10
miles

N

Mull Head

North Ronaldsay

Papa Westray

Noup Head
B9062
Pierowall

Westray

B9066

Rapness

Star Poir

B9069
Sanday

Kettletoft
B9070

Rousay

B9056

Eday

B9063

Egilsay

Wyre

Whitehall

Stronsay

Brough Head
Birsay

A966
Evie

Tingwall

Lamb Head

Skara Brae

Dounby

Mainland

B9056

A966

B9055

Balfour

Shapinsay

B9059

Wide Firth

B9058

Auskerry

Maes Howe

Finstown

A965

Kirkwall

Mull Head

Stromness

A964

Graemsay

Hoy

Houton
Orphir

A961

St Mary's

Copinsay

Old Man of Hoy

Ward Hill (1577ft)

B9047

Rackwick

Hoy

Lyness

Flotta

Scapa Flow

Churchill Barriers

Burray

Scrabster

Longhope

St Margaret's Hope

South Ronaldsay

A961

Swona

Burwick

Tomb of the Eagles

Brough Ness

Pentland Firth

Stroma

Pentland Skerries

Dunnet Head

Gill's Bay

John O'Groats

Duncansby Head

Thurso

A836

Wick

Aberdeen

HIGHLIGHTS

1. Maes Howe
2. Skara Brae
3. St Magnus Cathedral, Kirkwall
4. Tomb of the Eagles
5. Scapa Flow Visitor Centr
6. Westray
7. North Ronaldsay

ORKNEY FESTIVALS

The **Orkney Folk Festival** (Ⓦorkneyfolkfestival.com) is a four-day music festival, held at the end of May and centred on Stromness but with gigs all over the Mainland – it's very popular with locals and visitors alike, so expect tickets to sell out fast. The biggest cultural event, by far, however, is the week-long **St Magnus Festival** (Ⓦstmagnusfestival.com), a superb arts festival held in the middle of June, with events held all over the Mainland and the outer islands. July is peppered with several island regattas and agricultural shows, culminating in the agricultural **County Show** held in Kirkwall in the middle of August.

To find out **what's on** (and the weather forecast), tune in at 7.30am to *Around Orkney* on Radio Orkney (93.7FM), and buy yourself a copy of *The Orcadian*, which comes out on Thursdays (Ⓦorcadian.co.uk).

key fishing port and ferry terminal, and is the focus of the popular four-day **Orkney Folk Festival**, held in May.

15

Unlike Kirkwall, the old town of Stromness still hugs the shoreline, its one and only street, a narrow winding affair still paved with great flagstones and fed by a tight network of alleyways or closes. The central section, which begins at the imposing sandstone *Stromness Hotel*, is known as **Victoria Street**, though in fact it takes on several other names as it threads its way southwards. On the east side of the street the houses are gable-end-on to the waterfront, and originally each one would have had its own pier, from which merchants would trade with passing ships.

Pier Arts Centre

Victoria St • Tues–Sat 10.30am–5pm • Free • ☎ 01856 850209, Ⓦ pierartscentre.com

A warehouse on one of the old jetties on Victoria Street now forms half of the **Pier Arts Centre**; the other half is a modern glass-and-steel structure framing views of the harbour. The gallery has a remarkable permanent collection of twentieth-century British art, including work by Scottish sculptor Eduardo Paolozzi, and, most notably, by members of the Cornish group such as Barbara Hepworth, Ben Nicholson, Terry Frost, Patrick Heron and the self-taught Alfred Wallis. The collection is constantly being added to, with contemporary works by the likes of Anish Kapoor enhancing the original bequest.

Stromness Museum

Alfred St • April–Sept daily 11am–5pm; Oct–March Mon–Sat 11am–3.30pm • £5 • ☎ 01856 850025, Ⓦ orkneycommunities.co.uk /stromnessmuseum

At the junction of Alfred Street and South End stands the **Stromness Museum**, built in 1858. Highlights include an early inflatable boat like the one used by John Rae, the Stromness-born Arctic explorer, and some barnacle-encrusted crockery from the German High Seas Fleet that was sunk in Scapa Flow in 1919 (see box, p.540).

ARRIVAL AND DEPARTURE   **STROMNESS**

By ferry Car ferries operated by NorthLink (☎ 0845/600 0449, Ⓦ northlinkferries.co.uk) arrive in the centre of Stromness from Scrabster (2–3 daily; 1hr 30min), which is connected to nearby Thurso by shuttle bus. The tiny passenger ferry to Moaness Pier on Hoy (via Graemsay), run by Orkney Ferries (☎ 01856 872044, Ⓦ orkneyferries.co.uk), departs from the old harbour in Stromness

(Mon–Fri 4–5 daily, Sat & Sun 2 daily; 25min).

By bus Buses depart from Stromness Ferry Terminal. Call ☎ 01856 873535 or check Ⓦ orkney.gov.uk for timetables. Destinations Houton (Mon–Fri 2 daily; 15min); Kirkwall (Mon–Sat hourly, Sun every 2hr; 30min); Skara Brae (Mon, Thurs & Sat 1 daily; 20min); St Margaret's Hope (hourly; 1hr 5min).

STROMNESS

ACCOMMODATION
Brinkies Guest House	4
Brown's	3
Burnside Farm	2
Hamnavoe Hostel	1
Point of Ness Campsite	5

EATING
Hamnavoe Restaurant	2
Julia's Café and Bistro	1

DRINKING
Ferry Inn	1

Hoy, Graemsay & Scrabster ▼

INFORMATION AND GETTING AROUND

Tourist office Stromness Ferry Terminal houses the tourist office (March–Oct Mon–Sat 10am–3pm, ☎01856 850716, ⓦ visitorkney.com).

By bike Orkney Cycle Hire, 54 Dundas St (☎018⁚ 850255, ⓦ orkneycyclehire.co.uk), rent bikes from £7. a day.

ACCOMMODATION

Brinkies Guest House Innertown ☎01856 851881, ⓦ brinkiesguesthouse.co.uk. A substantial double-bay fronted Victorian guesthouse located a 10min walk up from the town. Rooms enjoy fantastic views and the residents' lounge has loads of reading matter. £70

Brown's 47 Victoria St ☎01856 850661, ⓦ browns orkney.co.uk. A family-run place overseen by the very friendly Mrs Brown and situated right in the centre of town. There are twins, triples and quads as well as regular bunk beds in very small dorms. Dorms £20; doubles £50

Burnside Farm 1 mile north of Stromness on A9 ☎01856 850723, ⓦ burnside-farm.com. A cracki⁚ B&B run by a local couple on a working farm. The vie⁚ are great, and the furnishings and facilities are truly to⁚ notch: en-suite wet-rooms, plus bere bannocks ⁚ breakfast. £80

Hamnavoe Hostel 10a North End Rd ☎01856 8512⁚ ⓦ hamnavoehostel.co.uk. A good 10min walk from ⁚ ferry terminal and no beauty from the outside, but ins⁚ it's all spotlessly clean, welcoming and well equipp⁚ There's a choice of small dorms or singles, some en su⁚ some not. Dorms £20; singles £22

Point of Ness Campsite A mile south of the ferry terminal at Point of Ness ☎01856 873535. Busy council-run campsite in a superb (though extremely exposed) setting, with great views over to Hoy; facilities include a TV lounge and a washing machine. April to Sept. Per pitch £20

EATING

Hamnavoe Restaurant 35 Graham Place ☎01856 850606. Friendly little front-room restaurant, with a real fire burning. The menu concentrates on nicely presented local produce – try the tusk or hake straight off the boats – main courses start at around £15 and booking is essential. May–Sept Tues–Sun only.

Julia's Café and Bistro 20 Ferry Rd ☎01856 850904,

ⓦjuliascafe.co.uk. Daytime café right opposite the ferry terminal, with a sunny conservatory and tables outside if the weather's good enough. It's comfort food for the most part, including a decent home-made fish pie all for under £10. Mon–Sat 9am–5pm, Sun 10am–5pm (longer hours in the summer).

DRINKING

Ferry Inn 10 John St ☎01856 850280, ⓦferryinn.com. Situated opposite the ferry terminal, this is the most popular and welcoming pub in town, serving up classic pub grub as

well as local scallops, Grimbister cheese and spicy Orkney crab cakes (all around £10), washed down with Orkney beer on draught. Daily 7am–midnight; food served until 9pm.

15

West Mainland

The great bulk of the **West Mainland** – west of Kirkwall, that is – is fertile farmland, fenced off into a patchwork of fields used either to produce crops or for cattle-grazing. Fringed by a spectacular western coastline, West Mainland is littered with some of the island's most impressive prehistoric sites, such as the village of **Skara Brae**, the standing **stones of Stenness**, the chambered tomb of **Maes Howe** and the **Broch of Gurness**, as well as one of Orkney's best preserved medieval castles at **Birsay**. Despite the intensive farming, some areas are too barren to cultivate, and the high ground and wild coastline include several interesting **wildlife reserves**.

Stenness

The parish of **Stenness**, northeast of Stromness along the main road to Kirkwall, slopes down from Ward Hill (881ft) to the lochs of Stenness and Harray: the first is tidal, the second is a freshwater trout loch. The two lochs are joined by a short causeway that may well have been a narrow isthmus around 3000 BC, when it stood at the heart of Orkney's most important Neolithic ceremonial complex, centred on the burial chamber of **Maes Howe**.

Stones of Stenness

Guided tours June–Aug Mon, Wed & Thurs 10am • Free; HES • ☎01856 841732, ⓦhistoricenvironment.scot

The most visible part of the complex between lochs Stenness and Harray is the **Stones of Stenness**, originally a circle of twelve rock slabs, now just four, the tallest of which is a real monster at over 16ft, and remarkably slender. A broken tabletop lies within the circle, surrounded by a much-diminished henge (a circular bank of earth and a ditch) with a couple of entrances.

Ring of Brodgar

Guided tours June–Aug daily 1pm • Free; HES • ☎01856 841732, ⓦhistoricenvironment.scot

Less than a mile to the northwest of the Stones of Stenness, past the huge **Watch Stone** which stands beside the road at over 18ft in height, you reach another stone circle, the **Ring of Brodgar**, a much wider circle dramatically sited on raised ground. Here there were originally sixty stones, 27 of which now stand, all wonderfully misshapen, about 7–10ft high; of the henge, only the ditch survives.

Maes Howe

If arriving in your own vehicle, you'll need to book a car park space several days in advance • Daily: April–Sept 9.30am–5pm; July & Aug till 7pm; Oct–March 10am–4pm • £5.50; HES • ☎ 01856 761606, Ⓦ historicenvironment.scot

Maes Howe, one of Europe's most impressive Neolithic burial chambers, lies less than a mile northeast of the Stones of Stenness. Dating from 3000 BC, its excellent state of preservation is partly due to its construction from massive slabs of sandstone weighing up to thirty tons. Visitors must first buy a timed ticket for a guided tour, in advance or direct from Tormiston Mill by the main road, which houses the ticket office, toilets and interpretive display.

You enter the central chamber down a low, long passage, one wall of which is comprised of a single immense stone. Inside, you can stand upright and admire the superb masonry of the lofty corbelled roof. Remarkably, the tomb is aligned so that the rays of the winter solstice sun hit the top of the Barnhouse Stone, half a mile away, and reach right down the passage of Maes Howe to the ledge of one of the three cells in the walls of the tomb. When Maes Howe was opened in 1861, it was virtually empty, thanks to the work of generations of grave-robbers, who had left behind only a handful of human bones. The Vikings, however, left copious runic graffiti, cut into the walls of the main chamber, including phrases such as "many a beautiful woman has stooped in here, however pompous she might be" and the more prosaic "Thor and I bedded Helga".

ARRIVAL AND DEPARTURE

STENNES

By bus Buses from Stromness to Kirkwall (Mon–Sat hourly, Sun every 2hr; 15min) can drop you off at Tormiston

Mill by Maes Howe – under a mile from the Stones Stenness and the same again from the Ring of Brodgar.

ACCOMMODATION AND EATING

★ **Holland House** Harray, 4 miles north of Maes Howe off the A986 ☎ 01856 771400, Ⓦ holland houseorkney.co.uk. A beautiful, solidly built manse filled with artworks. There's a peat fire, and the home cooking, including freshly baked scones for breakfast, is outstanding. **£105**

Merkister Hotel Harray Loch ☎ 01856 771366, Ⓦ merkister.com. Substantial hotel on the north-eastern shore of the Loch of Harray, popular with the locals and visiting anglers. The bar's lively and does reliable, locally sourced dishes such as fish and chips

(around £10) or steak (around £20), but there's restaurant too, offering a wider range of local seafoo (mains £14–20). Food served daily noon–2pm 6–9pm.

Mill of Eyrland 4 miles southwest of Maes Howe o A964 to Orphir ☎ 01856 850136, Ⓦ millofeyrlan .co.uk. Carefully converted former mill by a little strea it's filled to the brim with wonderful antiques and o machinery, as well as all mod cons; and enormo breakfasts at the communal dining table. Free wi-fi patchy in the rooms. **£80**

Skara Brae

Daily: April–Sept 9.30am–5.30pm; Oct–March 10am–4pm • £7.10; HES • ☎ 01856 761606, Ⓦ historicenvironment.scot

The extensive remains of a small Neolithic fishing and farming village, dating from 3000 BC, were discovered at **Skara Brae** in 1850, after a fierce storm ripped off the dunes covering them. The village is amazingly well preserved, its houses huddled together and connected by narrow passages, which would originally have been covere over with turf. The houses themselves comprise a single, spacious living room, filled with domestic detail, including dressers, fireplaces, built-in cupboards, beds and boxes all ingeniously constructed from slabs of stone.

The **visitor centre** houses an excellent **café/restaurant** and an introductory **exhibition** with a few replica finds, and some hands-on stuff for kids. Beyond is a full-scale replic of House 7 (the best-preserved house), complete with a fake wood and skin roof. It's a tad neat and tidy, with fetching uplighting – rather than dark, smoky and smelly – but it gives you the general idea, and makes up for the fact that, at the site itself, yo can only look down on the houses from the outer walls.

In the summer months, your ticket to Skara Brae also covers entry to nearby **Skaill House**, built for Bishop George Graham in the 1620s, but much extended since. The house's prize possession is Captain Cook's dinner service from the *Resolution*; it was delivered after Cook's death when the *Resolution* and the *Discovery* sailed into Stromness in 1780.

ARRIVAL AND DEPARTURE	SKARA BRAE

By bus Services are limited (Mon, Thurs & Sat only), with extra services on schooldays. Alternatively, since it's only 7 miles from Stromness, you could just rent a bike (see p.532).

EATING AND DRINKING

★ Orkney Brewery Quoyloo ☎ 01856 841777, ✆ orkneybrewery.co.uk. The old schoolhouse in Quoyloo has been tastefully converted into a state-of-the-art microbrewery, with tasting tours (£5) and also a great café where local produce is very much to the fore – try the home-made bere bannock burgers – and all dishes are under £10. April–Oct daily 10am–4.30pm.

Birsay and around

Occupying the northwest corner of the Mainland, the parish of **BIRSAY** was the centre of Norse power in Orkney for several centuries before Kirkwall got its cathedral.

Earl's Palace

Birsay is dominated by the imposing sixteenth-century sandstone ruins of the **Earl's Palace**, built by Robert Stewart, Earl of Orkney, using the forced labour of the islanders, who weren't even given food and drink for their work. By all accounts, it was a "sumptuous and stately dwelling", built in four wings around a central courtyard, its upper rooms decorated with painted ceilings and rich furnishings; surrounding the palace were flower and herb gardens, a bowling green and archery butts. The palace lasted barely a century before falling into rack and ruin; the crumbling walls and turrets retain much of their grandeur, although inside there little remaining domestic detail.

Brough of Birsay

Accessible 2hr either side of low tide • Tide times available at Stromness and Kirkwall tourist offices and on Radio Orkney (93.7FM; Mon–7.30–8am)

Over half a mile northwest of Birsay village is the **Brough of Birsay**, a substantial Pictish settlement on a small tidal island. Here there's a small ticket office, where you can see a few artefacts gathered from the site, including an antler pin and a game made from whalebone. The focus of the village was, and still is, the sandstone-built twelfth-century **St Peter's Church** (mid-June to Sept daily 9.30am–5.30pm; £4.50; HES), which is thought to have stood at the centre of a monastic complex; the foundations of a courtyard and outer buildings can be made out to the west. Close by is a large complex of Viking-era buildings, including several houses, a sauna and some sophisticated stone drains.

ARRIVAL AND DEPARTURE	BIRSAY AND AROUND

bus Bus services from Kirkwall (Mon–Sat 2 daily; 30–40min) will get you to Birsay.

ACCOMMODATION AND EATING

Barony Hotel 1 mile east of Birsay ☎ 01856 721327, ✆ baronyhotel.com. Stark hotel overlooking the Loch of Boardhouse. The hotel bar is the only watering hole around the decor in the rooms is a bit dated, but it's clean and comfy enough and the trout from the loch is worth sampling. **£80**

Birsay B&B 1.5 miles east of Birsay ☎ 01856 721495, ✆ birsaybandb.co.uk. Newly built B&B on the hill overlooking the Brough of Birsay – owner Kim is a welcoming host and the rooms are simply furnished and spotlessly clean. **£60**

Birsay Bay Tearoom 500yds south of the Earl's Palace ☎ 01856 721399, ⓦ birsaybaytearoom.co.uk. For light snacks and home-made cake, head for the modern tearoom, at the southern edge of the village, which boasts superb views of the Brough (binoculars provided). May–Sept daily 10.30am–5.30pm; shorter hours in winter.

Birsay Outdoor Centre 1 mile southeast of Birsay at junction of A967 and B9056 ☎ 01856 873517 ext 2415, ⓦ www.orkney.gov.uk. A large council-run hostel with a fully equipped kitchen and a drying room; there's also a campsite alongside. April–Sept. Dorms **£17.50**; per pitch **£20**

Broch of Gurness

Evie • April–Sept daily 9.30am–12.30pm & 1.30–5.30pm • £5.50; HES • ☎ 01856 751414, ⓦ historicenvironment.scot

The best-preserved broch on Orkney is the **Broch of Gurness**, on the north coast, still surrounded by a remarkable complex of later buildings. As at Birsay, the sea has eaten away half the site, but the broch itself, from around 100 BC, still stands, its walls reaching 12ft in places and its inner cells intact. Clustered around the broch, the compact group of homes has survived amazingly well, complete with their original stone shelving and fireplaces. The best view of the site is from the east, where you can make out the "main street" leading towards the broch.

ARRIVAL AND DEPARTURE   **BROCH OF GURNESS**

By bus Bus services from Kirkwall get you to Evie (Mon–Sat 5 daily; 30min), from which it's a 30min walk to the broch.

ACCOMMODATION

Castlehill Evie ☎ 01856 751228, ⓦ castlehillorkney .co.uk. This modern crofthouse under Burgar Hill looks nothing special from the outside but it's well decked out inside, with pleasant wooden furnishings and quality bedding. Great views and top-notch home cooking. **£90**

Howe Bothy Evie ☎ 01856 751449. Choice of a bed in tiny four-bunk hostel in an old cart shed or a little en-suite double with a kitchen in the old cow byre – both beautiful converted by local artist, John Vincent. Use of a boat if you fancy some trout fishing. Dorm **£15**; double **£35**

Kirkwall

Initial impressions of **KIRKWALL**, Orkney's capital, are not always favourable. It has nothing to match the picturesque harbour of Stromness, and its residential sprawl is far less appealing. However, it does have one great redeeming feature – its sandstone **cathedral**, without doubt the finest medieval building in the north of Scotland. In any case, if you're staying any length of time in Orkney you're more or less bound to find yourself in Kirkwall at some point, as the town is home to the islands' better-stocked shops, and it is the ferry terminal for most of Orkney's northern isles.

St Magnus Cathedral

Broad St • Mon–Sat: April–Sept 9am–6pm; Oct–March 9am–1pm & 2–5pm • Free • Guided upper-level tours Tues & Thurs 11am & 2pm £7.75 • ☎ 01856 874894, ⓦ stmagnus.org

Standing at the very heart of Kirkwall, **St Magnus Cathedral** is the town's most compelling sight. This beautiful red-sandstone building was begun in 1137 by the Orkney Earl Rögnvald (aka St Ronald), spurred on by the growing cult surrounding the figure of his uncle Magnus, killed by his cousin Håkon in 1117 (see p.547). When Magnus's body was buried in Birsay, a heavenly light was said to have shone overhead, and his grave soon drew pilgrims. When Rögnvald took over the earldom, he moved the centre of religious and secular power from Birsay to Kirkwall, before he himself was murdered.

Today much of the detail in the soft sandstone has worn away – the capitals around the main doors are reduced to artistically gnarled stumps – but it's still an immensely impressive building. Inside, the atmosphere is surprisingly intimate, the bulky sandstone columns drawing your eye up to the exposed brickwork arches, while

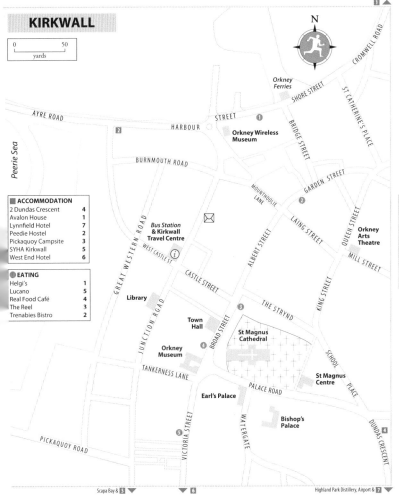

KIRKWALL

ACCOMMODATION
2 Dundas Crescent	4
Avalon House	1
Lynnfield Hotel	7
Peedie Hostel	2
Pickaquoy Campsite	3
SYHA Kirkwall	5
West End Hotel	6

EATING
Helgi's	1
Lucano	5
Real Food Café	4
The Reel	3
Trenabies Bistro	2

Map labels: CROMWELL ROAD, ST CATHERINE'S PLACE, Orkney Ferries, SHORE STREET, AYRE ROAD, STREET, HARBOUR, BRIDGE STREET, Orkney Wireless Museum, Peerie Sea, BURNMOUTH ROAD, GARDEN STREET, MOUNTHOOLIE LANE, Bus Station & Kirkwall Travel Centre, LAING STREET, QUEEN STREET, Orkney Arts Theatre, GREAT WESTERN ROAD, WEST CASTLE ST, ALBERT STREET, MILL STREET, CASTLE STREET, KING STREET, Library, THE STRYND, Town Hall, BROAD STREET, St Magnus Cathedral, SCHOOL PLACE, JUNCTION ROAD, Orkney Museum, TANKERNESS LANE, St Magnus Centre, PALACE ROAD, Earl's Palace, VICTORIA STREET, WATERGATE, Bishop's Palace, DUNDAS CRESCENT, PICKAQUOY ROAD, Scapa Bay &, Highland Park Distillery, Airport &

15

ound the walls is a series of mostly seventeenth-century tombstones, many carved ith a skull and crossbones and other emblems of mortality, alongside chilling scriptions calling on the reader to "remember death waits us all, the hour none ows". In the square pillars on either side of the high altar, the bones of Magnus and gnvald are buried.

n the southeastern corner of the cathedral lies the tomb of the Stromness-born Arctic plorer John Rae, who tried to find Sir John Franklin's expedition; he is depicted eep, dressed in moleskins and furs, his rifle and bible by his side. Beside Rae's tomb Orkney's own Poets' Corner, with memorials to, among others, George Mackay own, Eric Linklater and Edwin Muir.

shop's and Earl's Palaces

ce Rd • April–Oct daily 9.30am–5.30pm • £4.50; HES • ☎ 01856 871918, ⓦ historicenvironment.scot

uth of the cathedral are the ruins of the **Bishop's Palace**, residence of the Bishop of

15

Orkney from the twelfth century. It was here that King Håkon died in 1263 on his return from defeat at the Battle of Largs. Most of what you see, however, dates from the time of Bishop Robert Reid, founder of Edinburgh University, in the mid-sixteenth century. The walls still stand, as does the tall round tower in which the bishop had his private chambers; a narrow spiral staircase takes you to the top for a good view over Kirkwall.

The ticket for the Bishop's Palace covers entry to the neighbouring **Earl's Palace** – better preserved and a lot more fun to explore – built by the infamous Earl Patrick Stewart around 1600 using forced labour. With its grand entrance, fancy oriel windows, dank dungeons, massive fireplaces and magnificent central hall, it has a confident solidity, and is a fine example of Scottish Renaissance architecture. The roof may be missing, but many domestic details remain, including a set of toilets and the stone shelves used by the clerk for his filing. Earl Patrick enjoyed his palace for only a short time before he was imprisoned and charged with treason. The earl might have been acquitted, but he foolishly ordered his son, Robert, to organize an insurrection. Robert held out for four days in the palace against the Earl of Caithness, before being captured, sent to Edinburgh and hanged there, and his father was beheaded at the same place five weeks later.

Orkney Museum

Broad St • Mon–Sat 10.30am–5pm • Free • ☎ 01856 873535

Opposite the cathedral stands the sixteenth-century **Tankerness House**, a former home for the clergy, and now home to the **Orkney Museum**. A couple of rooms have been restored as they would have been in 1820, when it was the Baikie family's private home. The rest houses some of the islands' most treasured finds, among the more unusual of which are a witch's spell box and a lovely whalebone plaque from a Viking boat grave discovered on Sanday.

ARRIVAL AND INFORMATION

By plane Kirkwall Airport (☎ 01856 872421, ⓦ hial.co.uk) is 3 miles southeast of town on the A960; take the hourly bus (15min), or a taxi (£5).

Destinations within Orkney Eday (Mon & Wed 1–2 daily; 10–30min); North Ronaldsay (Mon–Sat 3 daily, 2 on Sun; 20–30min); Papa Westray (Mon–Fri 3 daily, Sat & Sun 2 daily; 15–35min); Sanday (Mon–Fri 2 daily, Sat & Sun 1 daily; 15min); Stronsay (Mon–Fri 2 daily, Sat & Sun 1 daily; 10–25min); Westray (Mon–Fri 2 daily, Sat & Sun 1 daily; 15–25min).

By ferry NorthLink Ferries (☎ 0845 600 0449, ⓦ northlinkferries.co.uk) run services from Shetland (3 weekly; 5hr 30min) and Aberdeen (3–4 weekly; 6hr), and all cruise ships dock at the Hatston terminal, a mile northwest of town; a shuttle bus takes you into Kirkwall (or Stromness if you prefer). Ferries for Orkney's northern isles leave from the town pier in Kirkwall.

Destinations within Orkney Eday (2–3 daily; 1hr 15min– 2hr 25min); North Ronaldsay (Tues & Fri; 2hr 40min); Papa

Westray (Tues & Fri; 2hr 15min); Sanday (2 daily; 1hr 25min); Shapinsay (3–5 daily; 45min); Stronsay (1–3 daily 1hr 40min–2hr); Westray (2–3 daily; 1hr 25min).

By bus ☎ 01856 870555, ⓦ stagecoachbus.com. The bus station is behind the Kirkwall Travel Centre, West Castle St.

Destinations Birsay (Mon–Sat 2 daily; 30–40min); Burwick (2–3 daily; 40min); Evie (Mon–Sat 4–5 daily; 30min); Houton (5–6 daily; 25min); Kirkwall Airport (Mon–Sat every 30min, 10 on Sun; 15min); Skara Brae (June–Aug Mon, Thurs & Sat 1 daily; 50min); St Margaret's Hope (Mon–Sat hourly; 35min); Stromness (Mon–Sat hourly, Sun every 2hr; 30min); Tingwall (Mon–Sat 4–5 daily; 25min).

Tourist office Kirkwall Travel Centre, West Castle St houses the tourist office (daily 9am–5pm; ☎ 01856 872856, ⓦ www.visitorkney.com).

Bike rental Cycle Orkney, Tankerness Lane (☎ 01856 875777, ⓦ cycleorkney.com), rents bikes from £15/day, children's bikes and some electrics available.

ACCOMMODATION

HOTELS AND B&BS

2 Dundas Crescent 2 Dundas Crescent ☎ 01856 874805, ⓦ twodundas.co.uk. Run by an Orcadian couple

and situated just behind the cathedral, this Victorian former manse is grand and tastefully decorated, with spacious rooms and period fittings. **£80**

Avalon House Carness Rd ☎01856 876665, ⓦavalon house.co.uk. Don't judge a B&B by its drab, modern exterior; this is a comfortable, purpose-built guesthouse run efficiently by a very welcoming couple, and situated a pleasant 20min coastal walk from the town centre. **£80**

Lynnfield Hotel Holm Rd ☎01856 872505, ⓦlynnfield.co.uk. Small ten-room hotel in a quiet spot a mile or so out of town near the distillery – the dark wood furnishings make the place seem really quite grand in style and the food is excellent – try the North Ronaldsay mutton, which comes from the island's famous seaweed-eating flock (mains £18–24). **£125**

West End Hotel 14 Main St ☎01856 872368, ⓦwestendkirkwall.co.uk. Orkney's first hospital is now a good old-fashioned hotel located in a quiet street, just a few minutes' walk south of the centre. **£99**

HOSTELS AND CAMPSITES

Peedie Hostel 1 Ayre Houses ☎01856 875477, ⓦkirk wallpeediehostel.com. Centrally located overlooking the old harbour and out to sea, this is a clean and comfortable hostel with just eight beds. Washing machine and tumble dryer available. Dorms **£15**; twin **£30**

Pickaquoy Campsite Ayre Rd ☎01856 879900, ⓦpickaquoy.net. Central and well equipped, since it is behind (and run by) the local leisure centre, but not exactly picturesque. March–Dec. Per pitch **£20**

SYHA Kirkwall Old Scapa Rd ☎01856 872243, ⓦsyha .org.uk. A good 10min walk out of the centre on the road to Orphir – the welcome at this former WWII military base is friendly enough, but it's no beauty outside or in. April–Sept. Dorms **£15**; twins **£40**

15

EATING

Helgi's 14 Harbour St ☎01856 879293, ⓦhelgis.co.uk. Popular modern pub on the harbourfront serving nicely presented bar food, from burger/fish and chips to fajitas (all for around £10). Free wi-fi. Mon–Wed 11am–midnight, Thurs–Sat 11am–1am, Sun 12.30pm–midnight.

Lucano 31 Victoria St ☎01856 875687, ⓦlucano kirkwall.com. Busy, bright, modern, authentic Italian – the family hail from Basilicata – offering 10-inch pizzas, fresh pasta and risotto with an Orcadian angle all for around £10. It's popular so book ahead. Daily 9am–9pm.

Real Food Café 25 Broad St ☎01856 874225, ⓦwww judithglue.com. Cheery cream and sky-blue wood-panelling decor at this small café at the back of Judith Glue's gift shop, opposite the cathedral. Try the Westray crab and bere bannocks (all dishes under £10). June–Sept daily 9am–10pm; shorter hours in the low season.

★**The Reel** 6 Broad St ☎01856 871000, ⓦwrigley andthereel.com. The old customs house near the cathedral is now a fabulous, laidback self-service café, run by the musical Wrigley Sisters, serving great coffee, sandwiches, toasties, panini and cakes, and offering free wi-fi and regular live music (Wed, Thurs & Sat). Mon–Fri 8.30am–6pm, Sat 9am–1am; in summer also Sun 10am–5pm.

Trenabies Bistro Albert St ☎01856 874336, ⓦtrenabiesfairtrade.co.uk. This cosy, old-fashioned café with booths is a classic Kirkwall institution – order Cajun fries and a panino for around £5. Mon–Fri 8.30am–5.30pm, Sat 9am–5.30pm.

ENTERTAINMENT

New Phoenix Cinema Pickaquoy Centre ☎01856 879900, ⓦpickaquoy.net. The "Picky" is a modern leisure centre, but its 1600-seat hall also serves as the town's main large-scale venue for a whole variety of events – it also houses the 250-seat New Phoenix cinema.

Lamb Holm, Burray and South Ronaldsay

Southeast from Kirkwall, the narrow spur of the **East Mainland** juts out into the North Sea and is joined to several smaller islands – the largest of which are **Burray** and **South Ronaldsay** – thanks to the remarkable Churchill Barriers, causeways built as part of the Scapa Flow defences in World War II. As with the West Mainland, the land here is heavily farmed, but it contains fewer of Orkney's famous sights. That said, the **Tomb of the Eagles** is one of the most enjoyable and memorable of Orkney's prehistoric sites.

Lamb Holm: the Italian Chapel

June–Aug daily 9am–6pm; Sept–May shorter hours; Nov–Easter closed Sun • £3

Special camps were built on the uninhabited island of **Lamb Holm** to accommodate the 1700 men involved in building the Churchill Barriers, 1200 of whom were Italian POWs. The camps have long since disappeared, but the Italians left behind the extraordinary **Italian Chapel**, by the main road (A961). This, the so-called "Miracle of Camp 60", must be one of the greatest adaptations ever, made from two Nissen huts, concrete, barbed wire and parts of a rusting blockship. It has a great false facade, and colourful trompe l'oeil decor, lovingly restored by the chapel's original architect, Domenico Chiocchetti, in 1960.

Burray

The largest of the little islands between the Mainland and South Ronaldsay, **Burray** has a population of around 400. The main village expanded in the nineteenth century during the boom years of the herring industry, but was badly affected by th sinking of the blockships during World War I. The two-storey warehouse, built in 1860 in order to cure and pack the herring, has since been converted into the *Sands Hotel* (see below).

15

Orkney Fossil and Heritage Centre

April–Sept daily 10am–5pm • £4.50 • ☏ 01856 731255, ⓦ orkneyfossilcentre.co.uk

Burray's chief attraction is the **Orkney Fossil and Heritage Centre**, housed in a converted farm on the island's main road. The UV "glow room", where the rocks reveal their iridescent colours, is a particular favourite with kids, though be sure to show them the coprolite (fossilized poo) among the main displays, too. Upstairs, there's a lot of wartime memorabilia and a whole section on the Churchill Barriers – kids can practise building their own – while the ground floor has a community-run café.

ARRIVAL AND DEPARTURE   BURRA

By bus Buses from Kirkwall to St Margaret's Hope call in at Burray village shop (Mon–Sat hourly; 30min).

ACCOMMODATION AND EATING

Sands Hotel 14 Main St ☏ 01856 731298, ⓦ thesands hotel.co.uk. An imposing former fish warehouse overlooking Burray harbour – now a hotel with simple pine furnishings and a few original features. The bar menu dishes (all under £10) include herring in oatmeal, and mince and tatties; the restaurant serves up local scallo and black pudding (mains £12–20). Food served Mor Sat noon–2pm & 6–9pm, Sun noon–2pm & 5.3 8.30pm. **£125**

SCAPA FLOW

Apart from a few oil tankers, there's very little activity in the great natural harbour of **Scapa Flow**, yet for the first half of the twentieth century, the Flow served as the main base of the Royal Navy, with more than a hundred warships anchored here at any one time. The coastal defences required to make Scapa Flow safe to use as the country's chief naval headquarters were considerable, and many are still visible all over Orkney, ranging from half-sunk blockships to the causeways known as the Churchill Barriers and the gun batteries that pepper the coastline.

Scapa Flow's most celebrated moment in naval history, however, was when the entire **German High Seas Fleet** was interned here immediately after World War I and then scuttled on the orders of the commanding officer, Admiral von Reuter, on Midsummer's Day 1919 – the greatest loss of shipping in a single day in history. To find out more about Scapa Flow's wartime role, visit the museum on Hoy (see p.544).

Scapa Flow is one of the world's greatest **wreck dive sites**, and Scapa Scuba (☏ 01856 851218, ⓦ scapascuba.co.uk), based in Stromness, offer half a day's taster scuba-diving (from £80). If you don't want to get your feet wet, *Dawn Star II* (☏ 01856 876743, ⓦ orkneyboattrips .co.uk; May–Sept) will give you a history tour above water; tours begin at St Mary's, by the Churchill Barriers (3hr; from £110).

South Ronaldsay

Low-lying **South Ronaldsay** is the largest of the islands linked to the Mainland by the Churchill Barriers. It was traditionally the chief crossing point to the Scottish mainland, as it's only six miles across the Pentland Firth from Caithness. Today, car ferries arrive at St Margaret's Hope, and there's a passenger ferry between John O'Groats and Burwick, on the island's southernmost tip.

St Margaret's Hope

South Ronaldsay's main settlement is **ST MARGARET'S HOPE**, which local tradition says is named after Margaret, Maid of Norway, daughter of the Norwegian king, who is thought to have died here aged eight in 1290. As the granddaughter of Alexander III, Margaret had already been proclaimed queen of Scotland and was en route to marry the future Edward II of England, thereby unifying the two countries. Today, St Margaret's Hope – or "The Hope", as it's known locally – is a quiet, pleasing little gathering of stone-built houses overlooking a sheltered bay.

15

Smiddy Museum

Cromarty Square • May–Aug daily 2–4.30pm • Free • ☎ 01856 831440

The village smithy on Cromarty Square has been turned into a **Smiddy Museum**, which is particularly fun for kids, who enjoy getting hands-on with the old tools, drills and giant bellows. There's also a small exhibition on the annual **Boys' Ploughing Match**, in which local boys compete with miniature hand-held ploughs.

Tomb of the Eagles

Daily: March 10am–noon; April–Sept 9.30am–5.30pm; Oct 9.30am–12.30pm; Nov–Feb by appointment • £7.50 • ☎ 01856 831339, ⏶ tomboftheeagles.co.uk

The chambered cairn at the southeastern corner of South Ronaldsay, known as the **Tomb of the Eagles**, was discovered in 1958 and excavated by local farmer, Ronald Simpson of Liddle. This is a proper hands-on museum, so first off, you get to learn about and handle some of the artefacts in the family's museum of prehistoric finds. Afterwards, you can head out to the nearby Bronze Age **burnt mound**, a Neolithic rubbish dump, and then you can walk a mile or so out to the impressive **chambered cairn** by the cliff's edge, where human remains were found alongside talons and carcasses of sea eagles. To enter the cairn, you must lie on a trolley and pull yourself in using an overhead rope – something guaranteed to put a smile on every visitor's face.

ARRIVAL AND DEPARTURE

SOUTH RONALDSAY

ferry Pentland Ferries (☎ 01856 831226, pentlandferries.co.uk) operates car catamarans from St Margaret's Bay (3–4 daily; 1hr), near John O'Groats (linked by bus to Wick and Thurso). John O'Groats Ferries (☎ 01955 611353, ⏶ jogferry.co.uk) runs a passenger ferry from John O'Groats to Burwick on South Ronaldsay (May–Sept 2–3 daily; 40min). Its departure is timed to connect with the

arrival of the Orkney Bus from Inverness; there's also a free shuttle service from Thurso train station for certain sailings.

By bus There is a regular bus service from Kirkwall to St Margaret's Hope (Mon–Sat hourly; 30min), and a summer-only one to Burwick, which connects with the John O'Groats ferry (May–Sept 2–3 daily; 40min).

ACCOMMODATION AND EATING

ST MARGARET'S HOPE

Bankburn House 0.5 miles south of the Hope on A961 ☎ 01856 831310, ⏶ bankburnhouse.co.uk. Solid Victorian sea captain's house, just outside the Hope, with a variety of rooms, some en suite, some with shared facilities, all with high ceilings and period features. **£52**

The Creel Front Rd ☎ 01856 831284, ⏶ thecreel.co.uk.

There are just three lovely sea-view rooms at this quality B&B, all beautifully furnished with light pinewood fittings. The breakfasts are superb, non-residents can usually drop in for tea and cakes, and evening meals can be arranged too. **£110**

St Margaret's Cottage Church Rd ☎ 01856 831637, ⏶ stmargaretscottage.com. Handsome sandstone house on the edge of The Hope, run by a genuine Orcadian couple, with three rooms available – very handy for the Pentland ferry. **£70**

St Margaret's Hope Backpackers Back Rd ☎01856 831225, ⓦorkneybackpackers.com. Simple hostel, with a number of small rooms with double bunks – singles, doubles and family rooms available. There's a kitchen/lounge and a nice adjacent café with sofas and free wi-fi. Dorms **£16**

Wheems 2 miles southeast of the Hope ☎01856 831556, ⓦwheemsorganic.co.uk. Rambling old crofthouse and organic farm with a couple of wooden bothies, a stone cottage and a yurt for hire, plus a sloping field for camping, with all the usual facilities. Double **£55**; per pitch **£9**

BURWICK

Eastward Guest House 1 mile north of Burwick on the A961 ☎01856 831551, ⓦeastwardhouse.com. In converted former church, this B&B has bags of character reclaimed maplewood flooring, Gothic windows. They also offer guests themed culinary evenings, specializing in Japanese food (ⓦmissingbell.com). **£90**

Skerries Bistro Banks ☎01856 831605, ⓦskerries bistro.co.uk. Ultra-modern bistro, with its own chambered cairn nearby, overlooking the Pentland Firth, offering local fish and king scallops as stea_ (evening mains around £15), plus delicious home-mad_ puddings and cakes. Daytime menu includes bake_ tattie and toasties, too. April–Oct daily except Tu_ eve 11am–5pm & 6–10pm.

Hoy

Hoy, Orkney's second-largest island, rises sharply out of the sea to the southwest of the Mainland. The least typical of the islands, but the most dramatic, its north and west sides are made up of great glacial valleys and mountainous moorland rising to over 1500ft, dropping into the sea off the red-sandstone cliffs of St John's Head, and, to the south, forming the landmark sea stack known as the **Old Man of Hoy**, best accessed from the wild and lonely village of **Rackwick**. Most of Hoy's four hundred residents liv_ on the gentle, fertile land in the southeast, around **Lyness** and **Longhope**. This part of the island is littered with buildings dating from the two world wars, when Scapa Flow was the Royal Navy's main base.

North Hoy

Much of **North Hoy**'s magnificent landscape is made up of rough grasses and heather, which harbour a cluster of arctic plants (a lot of midges) and a healthy population of mountain hares and birdlife. Facilities are minimal, however, with the nearest shop in Longhope (see p.545), and both the villages – Hoy and Rackwick – are absolutely tin_ with very little in the way of transport. If you're walking to Rackwick from Hoy, take the footpath that goes past Sandy Loch and along the large open valley of **Berriedale** (1hr 30min).

Dwarfie Stane

Halfway along the road from Hoy to Rackwick, duckboards head across the heather _ the **Dwarfie Stane**, Orkney's most unusual chambered tomb, cut from a solid block of sandstone and dating back to 3000 BC. Among the copious Victorian graffiti is an inscription on the northern exterior, where Major Mouncey, a former British spy in Persia and a confirmed eccentric who dressed in Persian garb, carved his name backwards in Latin and also carved in Persian the words "I have sat two nights and so learnt patience." Since 2015, however, most of the visitors descending on the Dwarfi_ Stane car park are here to see a young pair of **sea eagles** – the first to nest on Orkney for 142 years – who have chosen a nearby site to attempt to breed.

Rackwick

RACKWICK is an old crofting and fishing village squeezed between towering sandstone cliffs on the west coast. These days only a few of Rackwick's houses are inhabited all ye_

round. A building beside the hostel has a tiny **museum** with a brief rundown of Rackwick's rough history, but for a deeper insight into how folk used to live in these parts, head over to the **Craa Nest**, the oldest crofthouse in the village, just up the path to the Old Man; last occupied in 1940, the place still has its box-beds, barn and kiln intac

The Old Man of Hoy

Despite its isolation, Rackwick has a steady stream of walkers and climbers passing through en route to the **Old Man of Hoy**, a great sandstone stack, 450ft high, perched on an old lava flow that protects it from the erosive power of the sea. It is a popular challenge for rock climbers, and a 1966 ascent, led by Chris Bonington, was the first televised climb in Britain. The well-trodden footpath from Rackwick is an easy three-mile walk (3hr round-trip) – although the great skuas will dive-bomb you durin the nesting season (May–Aug), when the surrounding cliffs provide ideal rocky ledges for thousands of nesting seabirds, including puffins.

15

ARRIVAL AND GETTING AROUND

NORTH HO

By ferry The passenger ferry from Stromness to Moaness Pier, by Hoy village (Mon–Fri 4–6 daily, Sat & Sun 2 daily; 25min; ☎01856 850624) also serves the island of Graemsay en route.

By bus A minibus usually meets the ferry and will take fo over to Rackwick or further afield. A Hoy Hopper bus serv (mid-May to mid-Sept Wed–Fri only; ☎01856 70135 which departs from Kirkwall, also calls at Moaness.

ACCOMMODATION AND EATING

Beneth'ill Café Hoy ☎01856 791119, ⓦbenethillcafe .co.uk. Friendly, simple café, a short walk from Moaness Pier, offering sandwiches and salads in the daytime, along with home-made puddings and proper coffee, and the likes of crab ravioli and local scallops in the evening (mains £10–16). May–Sept Mon 10am–6pm, Tues–Sun 10am–6pm & 6.30–9pm.

Burnside Bothy By beach at Rackwick ☎01856 791316. You can camp in the dry-stone wall field beside this beautiful but basic heather-thatched bothy by the beach – toilets, cold water and a driftwood fire available inside the bothy. Donations welcome.

Hoy Centre 1 mile west of Moaness Pier ☎018 873535 ext 2417. A council-run, SYHA-affiliated hoste an old school. Situated in Hoy village, this place is large a modern, with a well-equipped kitchen, washing a drying facilities and all rooms en suite. Dorms __£20__

Rackwick Outdoor Centre Signposted at entran to village, 0.5 miles north of the beach ☎018 873535 ext 2404. April–Sept. Housed in Rackwick's little former schoolhouse, this simple hostel has eight beds in two rooms and a small kitchen. The cen location in Rackwick village is great. Camping permitt Dorms __£15__

Lyness

Along the sheltered eastern shore of Hoy, high moorland gives way to a gentler environment. Hoy defines the western boundary of Scapa Flow, and **LYNESS** played a major role for the Royal Navy during both world wars. Many of the old wartime buildings have been cleared away over the last few decades, but the harbour and hills around Lyness are still scarred with the scattered remains of concrete structures that once served as hangars and storehouses during World War II, and are now used as barns and cowsheds. Lyness also has a large **naval cemetery**, where many of the victin of the various disasters that have occurred in the Flow now lie, alongside a handful o German graves.

Scapa Flow Visitor Centre and Museum

March, April & Oct Mon–Sat 10am–4.30pm; May–Sept daily 10am–4.30pm • Free • ☎01856 791300, ⓦscapaflow.co

The old oil pump house, standing opposite Lyness ferry terminal, has been turned in the **Scapa Flow Visitor Centre**, giving a fascinating insight into wartime Orkney – eve the **café** has an old NAAFI feel about it. As well as the usual old photos, torpedoes, flags, guns and propellers, there's a paratrooper's folding bicycle, and a whole section devoted to the 1919 scuttling of the German High Seas Fleet and the 1939 sinking he *Royal Oak*. The pump house also retains much of its old equipment used to pump il off tankers into sixteen tanks, and into underground reservoirs cut into the eighbouring hillside.

RRIVAL AND DEPARTURE	**LYNESS**
y ferry The roll-on/roll-off car ferry to/from Houton on he Mainland (Mon–Fri 6 daily, Sat & Sun 2–5 daily; 5min–1hr; ☎ 01856 811397) sometimes calls in at the oil	terminal island of Flotta, and begins and ends its daily schedule at Longhope – if you're taking a vehicle over, you should book in advance.

NTERTAINMENT

able End Theatre 1.5 miles south of Lyness Pier orkneycommunities.co.uk/iohdt. Established in the d North Walls school buildings, this community-run theatre (with its own wind turbine) shows regular films and puts on the occasional theatre piece and gig – check their Facebook page for the latest information.

onghope

15

causeway was built during World War II connecting Hoy with **South Walls** ronounced "Waas"), a fertile tidal island more densely populated with farms and mes than Hoy. Along the north coast is the main settlement of **Longhope**, an important safe anchorage even today.

ackness Martello Tower

ril–Oct daily 9.30am–5.30pm • £4.50 • ☎ 01856 701727, ⊕ historicenvironment.scot

onghope's strategic importance during the Napoleonic Wars is evident at the Point of ackness, where the **Hackness Martello Tower** stands guard over the entrance to the ay, with a matching tower on the opposite promontory of Crockness. Built in 1815, ese two circular sandstone Martello towers are the northernmost in Britain, and rotected merchant ships from American and French privateers. You enter Hackness ower via a steep ladder connected to the upper floor, where nine men and one officer ared the circular room.

RRIVAL AND DEPARTURE	**LONGHOPE**
ferry The roll-on/roll-off car ferry from Houton on the inland to Lyness begins and ends each day at Longhope	– book ahead if you're taking a vehicle over (1 daily, 1hr 20min; ☎ 01856 811397).

CCOMMODATION

d Hall Cottage 2 miles southeast of Longhope 1856 701213, ⊕ oldhallcottage.co.uk. Lovely yr-old converted byre sleeps six at a squeeze and is let on a nightly basis or as B&B; lovely sheltered garden rlooking Scapa Flow. **£60**

omabank Hotel 1.5 miles southeast of Longhope ☎ 01856 701494, ⊕ stromabank.co.uk. This small, unpretentious hotel is housed in the old schoolhouse on the hill above Longhope, with views over the Pentland Firth – there are four en-suite rooms available and the bar serves as the local pub. Bar food available in the evening (closed Thurs). **£80**

hapinsay

t a few miles northeast of Kirkwall, **Shapinsay** is the most accessible of Orkney's rthern isles. A gently undulating grid-plan patchwork of rich farmland, it's a bit like island suburb of Kirkwall, which is clearly visible across the bay.

lfour

pinsay's only village is **BALFOUR**, named after the family who owned the island, rmed the island's agricultural system and rebuilt the village – previously known as

Shoreside – to house their estate workers. The family's grandiose efforts in estate management have left some appealingly eccentric relics around the village. Melodramatic fortifications around the harbour include the huge and ornate **gatehouse**, which now serves as the local pub. There's also a stone-built coal-fired **gasometer**, which once supplied castle and harbour with electricity and, southwest of the pier, the castellated **Douche** or Dishan Tower, a seventeenth-century doocot converted into a Victorian saltwater toilet and shower.

Balfour Castle

Guided tours by appointment • ☎ 01856 711282, ⓦ balfourcastle.co.uk

Shapinsay's chief landmark is **Balfour Castle**, an imposing baronial pile visible as you approach on the ferry and a short walk from the village. Designed by David Bryce, it was completed in 1848 by the Balfour family of Westray, who had made a small fortune in India the previous century. The Balfours died out in 1960 and for the last few years the castle has been used as an exclusive-use holiday or dining retreat.

ARRIVAL AND DEPARTURE   SHAPINSAY

By ferry Shapinsay is an easy day-trip from Kirkwall (3–5 daily; 30min; ☎ 01856 872044).

By bus A Community Bus serves the island (May–Sep; Tues only ☎ 01856 711733).

ACCOMMODATION AND EATING

★ **Hilton Farmhouse** 1 mile northeast of Balfour on B9059 ☎ 01856 711239, ⓦ hiltonorkneyfarmhouse .co.uk. This whitewashed farmhouse has just two sunny, south-facing bedrooms (one of which is en suite), and a restaurant in the conservatory (book ahead) and offers optional full board. £75

The Smithy In the Heritage Centre ☎ 01856 711269,

ⓦ islandcafe.co.uk. Even if you're just coming for the day it's worth popping into the wonderfully cosy licensed café below the heritage centre, which serves a simple menu of toasties, wraps and sandwiches during the day, and does take-away fish and chips and burgers on Fridays (5–7pm). Evening boat charter from Mainland also available. May–Sept, daily 10am–5pm.

Rousay, Egilsay and Wyre

The hilly island of **Rousay** is one of the more accessible northern isles as well as being home to a number of intriguing prehistoric sites. The group of a dozen or so houses above the ferry terminal is the only settlement of any size, but a single road runs around the edge of the island, connecting a string of farms that make use of the more cultivable coastal fringes. Many visitors come on a day-trip, as it's easy enough to reach the main points of archeological interest on the south coast by foot from the ferry terminal.

Rousay's diminutive neighbours, **Egilsay** and **Wyre**, contain a few medieval attractions of their own, which can be visited on a day-trip from Rousay itself, or from the Mainland.

Rousay

Rousay was one of the few parts of Orkney to suffer Highland-style clearances. One laird, Lieutenant General Traill-Burroughs, built a wall to force crofters onto a narrow coastal strip and eventually provoked so much distress and anger that a gunboat had to be sent to restore order. You can learn about the history and wildlife of the island from the well-laid-out display room of the **Rousay Heritage Centre** housed in the back of the ferry waiting room.

Trumland House

Gardens May–Oct daily 10am–5pm • £2 • ☎ 01856 821322

The island's laird, Lieutenant General Traill-Burroughs, built **Trumland House**, the forbidding Jacobean-style pile designed by David Bryce, in the 1870s, hidden in the trees half a mile northwest of the ferry terminal. The house is undergoing much-needed restoration, as are the landscaped **gardens**: the rhododendrons have been pushed back and there are now lovely wooded walks and a walled garden.

The three cairns

The road west from Trumland House runs past a trio of intriguing prehistoric cairns, starting with **Taversoe Tuick**. Dating back to 3500 BC, it's remarkable in that it exploits its sloping site by having two storeys, one entered from the upper side and one from the lower.

A little further west is the **Blackhammar Cairn**, which is entered through the roof via a ladder; the long interior is divided into "stalls" by large flagstones.

Finally, there's the **Knowe of Yarso**, another stalled cairn dating from the same period. It's worth the stiff climb up the hill from the road, if only for the magnificent view. The remains of 29 individuals were found inside, with the skulls neatly arranged around the walls.

Midhowe Cairn

The southwestern side of Rousay is home to the island's most significant and impressive archeological remains. Approached from the east, **Midhowe Cairn** comes as something of a surprise, due to its immense size – it's known as "the great ship of death" and measures nearly 100ft in length – and because it's housed within a stone-walled barn with a corrugated roof. You can't explore the roofless communal burial chamber, dating back to 3500 BC, only look down from the overhead walkway. The central corridor, 25yds long, is partitioned with slabs of rock, with twelve compartments on each side, where the remains of 25 people were discovered in a crouched position with their backs to the wall.

Midhowe Broch

A hundred yards beyond Midhowe Cairn is Rousay's finest archeological site, **Midhowe Broch**, whose compact layout suggests that it was originally built as a sort of fortified family house, surrounded by ditches and ramparts. The interior of the broch, entered through an impressive doorway, is divided into two separate rooms, each with its own hearth, water tank and quernstone, all of which date from the final phase of occupation around 150 AD.

Egilsay

Egilsay, the largest of the low-lying islands close to the eastern shore of Rousay, makes for an easy day-trip. The island is dominated by the ruined twelfth-century **St Magnus Church**, with its distinctive round tower. It's possible that it was built as a shrine to Earl (later St) Magnus, who arranged to meet his cousin Håkon here in 1117, only to be treacherously killed on Håkon's orders by his cook, Lifolf. If the weather's fine, walk the east from the ferry terminal to the coast, where there's a beautiful sandy bay overlooking Eday.

Wyre

Wyre, southwest of Egilsay, opposite Rousay's ferry terminal, is another possible day-trip. It's best known for **Cubbie Roo's Castle**, the "fine stone fort" and "really solid stronghold" mentioned in the *Orkneyinga Saga*, and built around 1150 by local farmer Kolbein Hruga. The outer defences have survived on three sides of the castle, which has a central keep, up to 6ft high, with its central water tank still intact. Close by stands the roofless twelfth-century **St Mary's Chapel**. To learn more about Cubbie Roo or any other aspect of Wyre's history, pop into the **Wyre Heritage Centre** near the chapel.

15

ARRIVAL AND DEPARTURE

By ferry Rousay makes a good day-trip from the Mainland, with car ferries from Tingwall (5–6 daily; 30min), linked to Kirkwall by bus (5 daily; 30min–1hr). Most of the Rousay ferries call in at Egilsay and Wyre, but some are request journeys and must be booked the day before (☎ 01856 751360).

By bus A bus runs every Thursday (7am–7pm; book ahead on ☎ 01856 821360, ⊛ aroundrousay.co.uk/bus). Minibus tours are available on demand (☎ 01856 821234; £32; 5–7hr) from the ferry terminal on Rousay.

ACCOMMODATION AND EATING

ROUSAY

Accommodation and eating options on Rousay are very limited. If you're coming for the day or self-catering, bring your own provisions, as Marion's Shop, the island's main general store, is in the northeastern corner of the island. Free wi-fi is available throughout the island – phone the Manse to get the password (☎ 01856 821229).

The Pier Beside the ferry terminal ☎ 01856 821359, ⊛ pierrestaurantorkney.com. Simple pub serves basic bar meals (all under £10) and Orkney beers, and will serve up lobster or make up some fresh crab sandwiches if you phone in advance. May–Sept Mon, Tues & Thurs 11am–11pm, Wed 11am–6.30pm, Fri & Sat 11am–1am, Sun 11am–7pm; shorter hours in winter.

The Taversoe 3 miles west of ferry terminal ☎ 01856 821325, ⊛ taversoehotel.co.uk. Unpretentious accommodation in four rooms (all with sea views). Serves classic pub meals – fish and chips, scampi or burgers (all under £10). **£80**

Trumland Farm 0.5 miles west of ferry terminal ☎ 01856 821252. This working organic farm has a couple of dorms and a family room – you can also camp here, and they offer bike rental (£8/day). Dorms £14; camping per person £6

Westray

Although exposed to the full force of the Atlantic weather in the far northwest of Orkney, **Westray** shelters one of the most tightly knit, prosperous and independent island communities, with a population of six hundred. Fishing, farming and tourism are the mainstays of the economy. The landscape is very varied, with sea cliffs and a trio of hills in the west, and rich low-lying pastureland and sandy bays elsewhere. However, Westray repays a longer stay, especially as there's lots of good accommodation and the locals are extremely welcoming.

Pierowall

The main village and harbour is **PIEROWALL**, set around a wide bay in the north of the island, eight miles from Rapness ferry terminal on the island's southernmost tip. Pierowall is a place of some considerable size, relatively speaking, with a school, several shops and a bakery (Orkney's only one off the Mainland).

Westray Heritage Centre

May–Sept Mon 11.30am–5pm, Tues–Sat 10am–noon & 2–5pm, Sun 1.30–5pm • £3 • ☎ 01857 677414, ⊛ westrayheritage.co.uk

The village's **Westray Heritage Centre** is a very welcoming wet-weather retreat, and a great place to gen up on (and with any luck catch a glimpse of) the Westray Wife or **Orkney Venus** – the first and finest of a series of remarkable, miniature Neolithic figurines found in the last decade in the dunes to the northwest of Pierowall.

Noltland Castle

Pick up the key, which hangs outside the back door of the nearby farm

The island's most impressive ruin is the colossal sandstone hulk of **Noltland Castle**, which stands above the village. This Z-plan castle, pockmarked with over seventy gun loops, was begun around 1560 by Gilbert Balfour, a shady character from Fife, who was Master of the Household to Mary, Queen of Scots, and was implicated in the murder of her husband Lord Darnley in 1567. Balfour was eventually forced to flee to Sweden, where he was found guilty of plotting to murder the Swedish king and executed in 1576.

Noup Head

The northwestern tip of Westray rises up sharply, culminating in the dramatic sea cliffs of **Noup Head**, particularly spectacular when a westerly swell is up. During the summer months the guano-covered rock ledges are packed with over 100,000 nesting guillemots, razorbills, kittiwakes, fulmars and puffins: a heady sensation of sight, sound and smell. The open ground above the cliffs, grazed by sheep, is superb maritime heath and grassland, carpeted with yellow, white and purple flowers, and a favourite breeding ground for arctic tern and arctic skua.

Castle o'Burrian

The sea cliffs in the southeast of the island around **Stanger Head** are not that spectacular, but it's here that you'll find **Castle o'Burrian**, a sea stack that is the best place on Westray at which to see **puffins** nesting (mid-May to Aug) – there's even a signpost from the main road.

15

ARRIVAL AND GETTING AROUND | WESTRAY

By plane You can fly from Kirkwall (Mon–Fri 2 daily, Sat & Sun 1 daily; 15min) and go on the world's shortest scheduled flight between Westray and Papa Westray (Mon–Sat 1 daily; 2min).

By ferry Westray is served by car ferry from Kirkwall (2–3 daily; 1hr 25min; ☎01856 872044), and there's a passenger ferry between Pierowall (Westray) and Papa Westray (3–6 daily; 25min; ☎01856 677216).

By bus A minibus (May–Sept; at other times phone ☎07789 034289, ⊛westraybusservice.co.uk) meets the ferry and connects with the Papa Westray ferry at Gill Pier in Pierowall; book a seat for the bus on the ferry.

INFORMATION AND TOURS

Tourist information ⊛westraypapawestray.co.uk.

Tours Guided tours of the island by minibus can be arranged with Westraak (☎01857 677777, ⊛westraak .co.uk), who will meet you at the ferry.

ACCOMMODATION AND EATING

The Barn Pierowall ☎01857 677214, ⊛thebarn westray.co.uk. A converted farm hostel at the southern side of Pierowall; it's luxurious inside, with family rooms and twin bunks available, has a small campsite adjacent to and a games room – run by a genuinely friendly Westerly family. Dorms **£22**; camping per pitch **£11**

No. 1 Broughton Pierowall ☎01857 677726, ⊛no1 broughton.co.uk. Top-notch, good-value B&B in a renovated mid-nineteenth-century house with views across the bay, with three en-suite rooms, a lovely conservatory and even a small sauna. **£60**

Pierowall Hotel Pierowall ☎01857 677472, ⊛pierowallhotel.co.uk. The social hub of Pierowall itself is unpretentious and very welcoming – the cheaper rooms have shared facilities. The popular bar has excellent fish and chips, fresh off the boats. **£82**

Papa Westray

Across Papa Sound from Westray is the island of **Papa Westray**, known locally as "Papay". With a population of around ninety, Papay has fought hard to keep itself viable over the last couple of decades, helped by a hefty influx of outsiders. With one of Orkney's best-preserved Neolithic settlements, and a large nesting seabird population, Papay is worth an overnight stay or a day-trip from its big neighbour. The northern tip of the island around **North Hill** (157ft) is an RSPB reserve, and during the breeding season you're asked to keep to the coastal fringe, where razorbill, guillemot, fulmar, kittiwake and puffin nest, particularly around Fowl Craig on the east coast, where you can also view the rare Scottish primrose, which flowers in May and from July to late September. Papay holds a week-long international experimental film, video art, sound art and architecture festival called Papay Gyro Nights (⊛papaygyronights.papawestray.org) around the first full moon in February, plus a more prosaic Fun Weekend in late July.

Holland House

Central point of the island • Farm buildings always open • Free

Papay's visual focus is **Holland House**, occupying the high central point of the island and once seat of the local lairds, the Traill family. Visitors can explore the old farm buildings, including a kiln, a doocot and a horse-powered threshing mill. An old bothy for single male servants has even been restored and made into a small **museum**, filled with bygone bits and bobs, from a wooden flea trap to a box-bed.

Knap of Howar

From Holland House, it's around half a mile to the western shore, where Papay's prime prehistoric site, the **Knap of Howar**, stands overlooking Westray. Dating from around 3500 BC, this Neolithic farm building makes a fair claim to being the oldest standing house in Europe. It's made up of two roofless buildings, linked by a little passageway; one has a hearth and copious stone shelves, and is thought to have been some kind of storehouse.

Old Kelp Store Heritage & Craft Centre

0.5 miles east of the Papay Co-op • Contact Papay Ranger for opening times • ☎ 01856 644224

This stone building down by the old pier was once used for storing kelp, but these days it is home to the **Old Kelp Store Heritage Centre**, a great wet-weather retreat and place to learn about the history of the island. As well as acting as the island's heritage centre, the place also puts on various events from musical evenings to whisky-tasting sessions.

Holm of Papay

Boat trips by arrangement • ☎ 01856 644224 • £25

Papay's Ranger can take **visitors** by boat to the **Holm of Papay**, the little island off the east coast, in order to explore an impressive Neolithic chambered cairn. Visitors enter via a trapdoor in the modern roof to witness the mysterious ancient carvings.

ARRIVAL AND DEPARTURE   PAPA WESTRAY

By plane You can fly direct from Kirkwall to Papa Westray (Mon–Fri 3 daily, Sat & Sun 2 daily; 25min) for around £15 return if you stay overnight. Papay is also connected to Westray by the world's shortest scheduled flight (Mon–Sat 1 daily) – 2min or less with a following wind.

By ferry The passenger ferry from Gill Pier in Pierowall (3–6 daily; 25min; ☎01856 677216) also takes bicycles.

Car ferries On Tuesdays, the car ferry goes from Kirkwall to Papa Westray via North Ronaldsay, taking over four hours; on Fridays, the car ferry from Kirkwall to Westray continues to Papa Westray; at other times, you must catch a bus to connect with the Papa Westray ferry from Pierowall. The bus should be booked ahead, when on the Westray ferry (☎01857 677758); it accepts a limited number of bicycles.

GETTING AROUND AND INFORMATION

Guided tours The Papay Ranger offers Papay Peedie Tours by minibus (☎01857 252028) – full-days with lunch (May–Aug Wed, Thurs & Sat; £40) or half-days (£25) – you can even do it from Kirkwall as a 12hr day-trip. At other times, you can arrange bespoke tours with the Ranger.
Tourist information ⊛ papawestray.co.uk.

ACCOMMODATION AND EATING

Beltane House East side of the island ☎01857 644224, ⊛ papawestray.co.uk. The Papay Co-op offers B&B, a two-room, sixteen-bed hostel (*Papa Westray Hostel*), a place to camp, and a shop, all within the old estate workers' cottages at Beltane, east of Holland House. *Beltane House* runs a self-service café for all island visitors to use and also opens its cupboard" every Saturday night from 9pm, with meals available. Doubles £88; dorms £20; camping/person £8

Eday

A long, thin island, **Eday** shares more characteristics with Rousay and Hoy than with its immediate neighbours, dominated as it is by heather-covered upland, with farmland confined to a narrow strip of coastal ground. However, Eday's hills have proved useful in their own way, providing huge quantities of peat that has been exported to the other treeless northern isles for fuel, and was even, for a time, exported to various whisky distillers. Sparsely inhabited, Eday has no main village as such. The ferry terminal is at the south end of the island, whereas the sights (and most of the amenities) are all in the northern half, about four miles away. The island post office, petrol pump and community shop all cluster in Hammarhill.

Eday Heritage Centre and HMS Otter

April–Oct daily 10am–6pm; Nov–March by appointment • Free • Heritage Centre ☎ 01857 622263; North School ☎ 01857 622225

Eday Heritage Centre, in an old Baptist chapel a mile north of the island's airport, has historical displays on Eday, with information on the island's tidal energy testing centre in the Fall of Warness, as well as a café. Perhaps the most unusual attraction, however, is in the nearby former North School, opposite the island shop, where several internal sections of the Cold War-era **submarine** HMS *Otter* have been reassembled in the old school hall – a truly eerie experience.

Eday Heritage Walk: Mill Loch to Red Head

The clearly marked **Eday Heritage Walk** (4hr 30min return) begins at Mill Loch, which is breeding ground of several pairs of **red-throated divers** where a bird hide overlooks the loch. Clearly visible over the road is the 15ft **Stone of Setter**, Orkney's most distinctive standing stone, weathered into three thick, lichen-encrusted fingers. From here, passing the less spectacular Braeside and Huntersquoy chambered cairns en route, you can climb the hill to reach Eday's finest, the **Vinquoy Chambered Cairn**, which has a similar structure to that of Maes Howe. You can crawl into the tomb through the narrow entrance: a skylight inside lets light into the main, beehive chamber but not into the four side cells. From the cairn, you can continue north to the viewpoint on the summit of **Vinquoy Hill** (248ft), and to the very northernmost tip of the island, where lie the dramatic red-sandstone sea cliffs of **Red Head**, where numerous seabirds nest in summer.

Carrick House

Open by appointment • ☎ 01857 622260

The grandest home on Eday is Carrick House, on the northeast coast. First built by the laird of Eday in 1633, it's best known for its associations with the pirate **John Gow** – on whom Sir Walter Scott's novel *The Pirate* is based – whose ship *The Revenge* ran aground on the Calf of Eday in 1725. He asked for help from the local laird but was taken prisoner in Carrick House, before eventually being sent off to London where he was tortured and executed. The highlight of the tour is the bloodstain on the floor of the living room, where John Gow was detained and stabbed while trying to escape.

ARRIVAL AND INFORMATION   EDAY

By plane You can make a day-trip by plane from Kirkwall to Eday on Wednesdays (1 on Mon, 2 on Wed; 10min).

By ferry Eday is served by regular car ferry from Kirkwall (2–3 daily; 1hr 15min–2hr; ☎ 01856 872044). The ferry terminal is at Backaland pier in the south, although you should be able to get a lift to the north of the island with someone off the ferry if you ask around.

Tourist information ⓦ visiteday.com.

GETTING AROUND AND TOURS

By minibus Eday's minibus (May to mid-Sept Mon, Wed & Fri or by appointment; 2hr 30min; £15; ☎ 01857 622206) will collect you from the ferry, take you on a tour of the island and deposit you wherever you want; every Thursday it will simply take you wherever you wish to go (withou┃ the tour). Eday also has a Ranger service, offering week┃ guided walks – book ahead on ☎ 07964 149155 or chec┃ Eday Scarfs Facebook page.

ACCOMMODATION AND EATING

Roadside Pub Backaland ☎ 01857 622303. Eday's one and only pub is in a pleasant old building overlooking the ferry terminal, and offers B&B in two en-suite rooms and evening meals on request (mains under £10). __£50__
Swenstay Bothy 3 miles southwest of the airport ☎ 01857 622262. Recently renovated, snug, wood-panelled self-catering bothy with flagstone floors and a traditional box-bed – it can be rented out on a night┃ basis. __£50__
SYHA Eday Just south of the airport ☎ 07776 37262┃ ⓦ syha.org.uk. An SYHA-affiliated, community-run hoste┃ situated in an exposed spot – phone ahead as there's n┃ resident warden. Washing machine and dryer, bike rent┃ and free wi-fi, and you can camp there, too. Dorms __£20__

15

Stronsay

A low-lying island, **Stronsay** is strongly agricultural, its interior an almost uninterrupted collage of green pastures. The island features few real sights, but the coastline has enormous appeal: a beguiling combination of sandstone cliffs, interspersed with wide white sands and (in fine weather) turquoise bays. Stronsay (population 350) in the nineteenth century became one of the main Scottish centr┃ for curing herring, until stocks were depleted in the 1930s, and the industry began┃ a long decline.

Whitehall

WHITEHALL, in the north of the island, is the only real village, made up of rows of stone-built fishermen's cottages set between two large piers. Wandering along the tranquil, rather forlorn harbourfront today, it's hard to believe that the village once┃ supported a small army of gutters, coopers, coal merchants, butchers, bakers, sever┃ Italian ice-cream parlours and a cinema. It was said that, on a Sunday, you could walk across the decks of the boats to **Papa Stronsay**, the tiny island that shelters Whitehall from the north. The old Fish Mart by Whitehall pier houses a small **museum** (ask at the adjacent café for access), with a few photos and artefacts from the herring days.

Papa Stronsay

Ferry The island's monks take visitors to the island by boat, by prior arrangement • ☎ 01857 616210, ⓦ papastronsay.com

Clearly visible from the harbour front at Whitehall is the island of **Papa Stronsay**, which is thought originally to have been a **monastic retreat** and later, during the herring boom, was home to no fewer than five fish-curing stations. In 2000, the islan┃ was bought by **Transalpine Redemptorist monks**, who had broken with the Vatican ov┃ celebrating Mass in Latin. They built themselves the Golgotha Monastery, complete with its own creamery; they have since been accepted back into the Roman Catholic Church and renamed the **Sons of the Most Holy Redeemer**.

The island features in the *Orkneyinga Saga* as the place where Earl Rognvald Brusas┃ was murdered by Earl Thorfinn Sigurdsson.

Vat of Kirbuster to Burgh Head

Signposts show the way to Orkney's biggest and most dramatic natural arch, the **Vat of Kirbuster**. Before you reach the arch there's a seaweedy, shallow pool in a ıatural sandstone amphitheatre, where the water is warmed by the sun and kids .nd adults can safely wallow: close by is a rocky inlet for those who prefer colder, nore adventurous swimming. You'll find progressively more nesting seabirds, ncluding a few puffins (mid-May to Aug), as you approach **Burgh Head**, further long the coast.

ɪRRIVAL AND GETTING AROUND — STRONSAY

y plane Flights from Kirkwall (Mon–Fri 2 daily, ɪt & Sun 1 daily; 25min) and from Sanday (Mon–Fri 1 ɪily; 6min).

y ferry Stronsay is served by a regular car ferry service from Kirkwall to Whitehall (1–3 daily; 1hr 40min–2hr; ⓣ01856 872044).

By taxi/car There's no bus service, but D.S. Peace (ⓣ01857 616335) operates taxis and offers car rental.

CCOMMODATION AND EATING

torehouse Whitehall ⓣ01857 616263, ⓦstorehouse ronsay.co.uk. A good alternative to the *Stronsay Hotel* is is welcoming little B&B in Whitehall, with en-suite oms, a guest lounge and full board on request. **£65**

ronsay Fish Mart Whitehall ⓣ01857 616401, stronsayfishmart.uk. The old fish market, by the ferry rminal, has been refurbished as a hostel, a heritage ntre and a cheap and cheerful daytime café serving tea, sandwiches and delicious home-made cakes – check Facebook for the latest opening hours. Free wi-fi available. Dorms **£20**

Stronsay Hotel Whitehall ⓣ01857 616213, ⓦstronsayhotelorkney.co.uk. Stronsay's only hotel, right by the ferry terminal, has modern en-suite rooms, while the hotel bar serves up generous portions of cheap and cheerful pub food. **£80**

ɪanday

espite being the largest of the northern isles, **Sanday** is the least substantial, a great w-lying, drifting dune strung out between several rocky points. The island's veeping aquamarine bays and vast stretches of clean white sand are the finest in rkney, and in dry, clear weather it's a superb place to spend a day or two. The ndy soil is very fertile, and the island remains predominantly agricultural even day, holding its own agricultural show each year in early August. The coastline fers superb walks, with particularly spectacular sand dunes to the south of the st, shallow, tidal bay of **Cata Sand**.

tart Point Lighthouse

essible only during low tide

ıe island has a long history as a shipping hazard, with many wrecks smashed against shores, although the construction of the **Start Point Lighthouse** in 1802 on Sanday's posed eastern tip reduced the risk for seafarers. Shipwrecks were not an unwelcome ht as the island has no peat, and driftwood was the only source of fuel other than w dung – it's even said that the locals used to pray for shipwrecks in church. The ft-high Stevenson lighthouse, from 1870, sports very natty and unusual vertical ıck and white stripes and stands on a tidal island, accessible either side of low tide takes an hour to walk there and back).

uoyness Chambered Cairn

ıday is rich in archeology, with hundreds of sites, the most impressive of which is **oyness Chambered Cairn**, on the fertile peninsula of Els Ness. The tomb, dating m before 2000 BC, has been partially reconstructed, and rises to a height of around ft. The imposing, narrow entrance, flanked by high dry-stone walls, would originally ve been roofed for the whole of the way into the 13ft-long main chamber, where ıes and skulls were discovered in the six small side cells.

ARRIVAL AND DEPARTURE   SANDA\

By plane The airfield is in the centre of the island and there are regular flights to Kirkwall (Mon–Fri 2 daily; Sat & Sun 1 daily; 10min) and a daily connection to Stronsay (Mon–Fri 1 daily; 6min).

By ferry Ferries from Kirkwall to Sanday (2 daily; 1hr

25min) arrive at Loth Pier, at the southern tip of th island.

By bus All sailings are met by the Sanday Bus (☎0185 600438), which will take you to most points on Sanday, bu advance reservation is recommended.

INFORMATION AND TOURS

Tourist information ⓦsanday.co.uk, ⓦsandayorkney .co.uk.

Tours The Sanday Ranger (☎01857 600359,

ⓦsandayranger.org) organizes activities and guided walk throughout the summer, as well as regular Sanday Bu Tours (May–Sept Wed; £35; ☎01857 600438).

ACCOMMODATION AND EATING

Ayre's Rock 6 miles northeast of the ferry terminal ☎01857 600410, ⓦayres-rock-hostel-orkney.com. If you're on a budget, this is a great place to stay: a well-equipped hostel, a couple of caravans and a small campsite (with several wooden camping pods for hire) overlooking the bay, with washing and laundry facilities, a chip shop (every Sat) and bike rental. Caravans **£35**; pods **£20**; dorms **£17.50**; camping per pitch **£10**

Backaskaill Farmhouse 5 miles northeast of ferry terminal ☎01857 600305, ⓦbedandbreakfast sandayorkney.com. Lovely solid stone-built farmhouse overlooking Backaskaill Bay, run by a very welcoming and helpful Manx couple – views over the bay from the

conservatory – full board available on request. **£75**

Belsair Hotel Kettletoft ☎01857 600206. The Belsair one of two pubs in Kettletoft, Sanday's original fishing por Currently under new enthusiastic management, they off decent pub food (fish and chips, burgers and the like f under £10) on a daily basis. Opening hours vary; che ahead.

Braeswick 2 miles north of the ferry terminal ☎018! 600708, ⓦbraeswick.co.uk. Despite the dour exteri this B&B is a good choice, with three very pleasan decorated rooms and a breakfast room with lovely vie over the bay. **£70**

North Ronaldsay

North Ronaldsay – or "North Ron" as it's fondly known – is Orkney's most northerly island, with a population of around fifty. Separated from Sanday by some treacherous waters, it has an outpost atmosphere, brought about by its extreme isolation. Measuring just three miles by one, and rising only 66ft above sea level, the only features to interrupt the flat horizon are **Holland House** – built by the Traill family, wh bought the island in 1727 – and the two lighthouses at **Dennis Head**. North Ronalds has been inhabited for centuries, and continues to be heavily farmed, with **seaweed** playing an important role in the local economy.

Bird Observatory

The island's most frequent visitors are ornithologists, who come to clock the rare migrants that land here briefly on their spring and autumn migrations. The peak tim

NORTH RONALDSAY SHEEP

The island's **sheep** are a unique, tough, goat-like breed, who feed mostly on seaweed, giving their flesh a dark tone and a rich, gamey taste, and making their thick wool highly prized. A high **dry-stone dyke**, running the thirteen miles around the edge of the island, keeps them off the farmland, except during lambing season. North Ronaldsay sheep are also unusual in that they refuse to be rounded up by sheepdogs like ordinary sheep, but scatter far and wide at some considerable speed. Instead, once a year the islanders herd the sheep communally into a series of **dry-stone punds** near Dennis Head, for clipping and dipping, in what is one c the last acts of communal farming practised in Orkney.

f year for migrants are from late March to early June, and from mid-August to early November. However, many breeding species spend the spring and summer here, including gulls, terns, waders, black guillemots, cormorants and even the odd corncrake – the permanent **Bird Observatory**, in the island's southwest corner, can give advice on recent bird sightings.

The Lighthouses and the Wool Mill

Exhibition May–Aug daily 10am–5pm • Free • **Guided tours** by appointment • £6, or £9 with the Mill • ☎ 01857 633297, ☻ northronaldsay.co.uk

The attractive, stone-built **Old Beacon** was first lit in 1789, but the lantern was replaced by the current huge bauble of masonry in 1809. The **New Lighthouse**, designed by Alan Stevenson in 1854 just to the north, is Britain's tallest land-based lighthouse, at over 100ft. There's an exhibition on the lighthouse in one of the keepers' cottages, as well as an exhibition on the history of life on the island and a café. You can also climb the 176 steps to the top of the lighthouse and admire the view – on a clear day you can see Fair Isle, and even Shetland. This can be combined with a tour of the island's **Wool Mill** where they turn the North Ron fleeces into yarn and felt (☻ northronaldsayyarn.co.uk).

15

ARRIVAL
NORTH RONALDSAY

By plane Your best bet is to catch a flight from Kirkwall (Mon–Sat 3 daily, 2 on Sun; 15min): if you stay the night on the island, you're eligible for a bargain £21 return fare.
By ferry The ferry from Kirkwall to North Ronaldsay runs just once a week (usually Fri; 2hr 40min), though there are also summer sailings via Papa Westray (usually Tues; 3hr 10min), and day-trips are possible on occasional Sundays between late May and early September (☎ 01856 872044).

GETTING AROUND

By minibus A minibus usually meets the ferries and planes (☎ 01857 633244) and will take you off to the lighthouse, but phone ahead to make sure.
Bike rental Contact Mark for information on bike rental (☎ 01857 633297, ☻ northronaldsay.co.uk; £8/day).

ACCOMMODATION AND EATING

Bird Observatory ☎ 01857 633200, ☻ nrbo.co .uk. You can stay at the ecofriendly bird observatory, either in an en-suite guest room or in a hostel bunk bed, or you can camp. The *Obscafé* serves decent evening meals (£14 for two courses) – try the mutton, washed down with Dark Island beer. Food served daily noon–2pm & evenings by arrangement. Doubles £65; dorms £18.50; camping per person £5
The Lighthouse ☎ 01857 633297, ☻ northronaldsay .co.uk. Great little café in the old lighthouse keepers' cottages serving snacks and affordable evening meals (by arrangement) – sample one of their North Ronaldsay mutton pies. May–Aug daily 10am–5pm; Sept–April phone ahead.

Shetland

JARLSHOF

Shetland

Shetland is a striking contrast from neighbouring Orkney. While the latter is within sight of the Scottish mainland, the archipelago of Shetland lies beyond the horizon, closer to Bergen in Norway than Edinburgh, and to the Arctic Circle than Manchester. With little fertile ground, Shetlanders have traditionally been crofters, often looking to the sea for an uncertain living in fishing and whaling or the naval and merchant services. The 23,000 islanders tend to refer to themselves as Shetlanders first, and, with the Shetland flag widely displayed, they regard Scotland as a separate entity. As in Orkney, the Mainland is the one in their own archipelago, not the Scottish mainland.

The islands' capital, **Lerwick**, is a busy little port and the only town of any size; many parts of Mainland can be reached from here on a day-trip. **South Mainland**, a narrow finger of land that runs 25 miles from Lerwick to **Sumburgh Head**, is an area rich in archeological remains, including the offshore Iron Age **Mousa Broch** and the ancient settlement of **Jarlshof**. A further 25 miles south of Sumburgh Head is the remote but thriving **Fair Isle**, synonymous with knitwear and exceptional birdlife. The **Westside** of Mainland is sunnier but also more sparsely inhabited, as is **North Mainland**. A mile off the west coast, **Papa Stour** boasts some spectacular caves and stacks; much further out are the distinctive peaks and precipitous cliffs of the remote island of **Foula**. Shetland's three **North Isles** bring Britain to a dramatic, windswept end: **Yell** has the largest population of otters in Scotland; **Fetlar** is home to the rare red-necked phalarope; north of **Unst**, there's nothing until you reach the North Pole.

Weather has a serious influence in these parts. In winter, gales are routine, and even in the summer months it'll often be windy and rainy. The wind-chill factor is not to be taken lightly, and there's often a dampness in the air, even when it's not actually raining. While there are some good spells of dry, sunny weather (often bringing in sea mist) from May to September, it's the **simmer dim**, the twilight which lingers through the small hours at this latitude, which makes Shetland summers so memorable.

ARRIVAL AND DEPARTURE

By plane Flybe (☎ 0371 7002000, ⓦ flybe.com) operate direct flights to Sumburgh airport (ⓦ hial.co.uk), 25 miles south of Lerwick, from Inverness, Aberdeen, Edinburgh, Glasgow and Kirkwall in Orkney, plus summer flights from Bergen in Norway.

By ferry NorthLink runs an overnight car ferry daily fro Aberdeen to Lerwick (12hr 30min), sometimes calling in Kirkwall in Orkney on the way (14hr 30min).

GETTING AROUND AND TOURS

By plane Airtask (☎ 01595 840246, ⓦ airtask.co.uk /shetland) runs flights from Tingwall airport, 5 miles west of Lerwick, to the more remote islands. To reach Tingwall airport, either take the bus from Lerwick bus station (Mon–Fri 5 daily, 1 on Sat; 15min), or there's a dial-a-ride taxi service, which must be booked a day in advance

(☎ 01595 745745).

By ferry The council-run inter-island ferries (☎ 015 743970, ⓦ www.shetland.gov.uk/ferries) are excell and fares are very low.

By bus The bus network (☎ 01595 744868, ⓦ zettr .org.uk) is pretty good in Shetland, with buses fr

MOUSA BROCH

lighlights

Shetland Museum Beautifully designed
odern waterside museum, with imaginative
splays telling the story of Shetland, and a great
fé too. **See p.561**

Traditional music Catch some local music at
e regular informal sessions in Lerwick, or at
e annual Shetland Folk Festival. **See p.564**

Isle of Noss Traffic-free island nature reserve
here you're guaranteed to see seals,
illemots, gannets and puffins. **See p.564**

Mousa Take a short boat trip to this remote
et, which boasts Scotland's finest 2000-year-
d broch and nesting storm petrels. **See p.566**

Jarlshof Crowd-free archeological site

mingling Iron Age, Bronze Age, Pictish, Viking
and medieval settlements. **See p.568**

❻ **Sumburgh Head** Explore Shetland
Mainland's southernmost lighthouse, and then
enjoy the spectacular view out to Fair Isle from
the lighthouse café. **See p.568**

❼ **Fair Isle** Magical little island halfway between
Shetland and Orkney, with a lighthouse at each
end and a world-famous bird observatory in the
middle. **See p.569**

❽ **Hermaness** Run the gauntlet of the
dive-bombing "bonxies" for spectacular views of
nesting seabirds and Muckle Flugga, Britain's
most northerly point. **See p.579**

HIGHLIGHTS ARE MARKED ON THE MAP ON P.560

Lerwick to every corner of Mainland, and even via ferries across to Yell and Unst.

Car rental It's worth considering car rental once on the islands. Bolts Car Hire (☎01950 460777, ⓦboltscarhire.co.uk) and Star Rent-a-Car (☎01950 460444, ⓦstarrentacar.co.uk) have vehicles available at Sumburgh airport and in Lerwick.

Tours There's a range of escorted tours and boat trips around the Mainland, great for those without a vehicle. Specific tours are mentioned throughout the text, but Shetland Wildlife (☎01950 460939, ⓦshetlandwildlife.co.uk) offer a variety of tours and boat trips, while the more adventurous might consider Sea Kayak Shetland (☎01595 840272, ⓦseakayakshetland.co.uk).

SHETLAND

HIGHLIGHTS

1. Shetland Museum
2. Traditional music
3. Isle of Noss
4. Mousa
5. Jarlshof
6. Sumburgh Head
7. Fair Isle
8. Hermaness

Lerwick

The focus of Shetland's commercial life, **LERWICK** is home to a third of the islands' total population. Its sheltered **harbour** is busy with ferries and fishing boats, and oil-rig supply vessels. In summer, the quayside comes alive with visiting yachts, cruise liners, historic vessels such as the *Swan* and the occasional tall ship. Behind the old harbour is the compact town centre, made up of one long main street, Commercial Street; from here, narrow lanes, known as **closses**, rise westwards to the late Victorian new town.

Leir Vik ("muddy bay") was established for the **Dutch** herring fleet in the seventeenth century. Later, it became a year-round **fishing** centre, and whalers called to pick up crews en route to the northern hunting grounds. Business was conducted from the jetties of buildings known as **lodberries**, several of which survive beyond the *Queen's Hotel*. Lerwick expanded in the Victorian era, and the large houses and grand public buildings established then still dominate, notably the **Town Hall**. Another period of rapid growth began during the oil boom of the 1970s, when the farmland to the southwest disappeared under a suburban sprawl and the town's northern approaches became an industrial estate.

Commercial Street

Lerwick's attractive shopping hub is the narrow, winding, flagstone-clad **Commercial Street**, set back one block from the Esplanade. Although the narrow lanes, or closses, that connect the Street to Hillhead are now desirable, it was not so long ago that they were regarded as slum-like dens of iniquity, from which the better-off escaped to the Victorian new town laid out on a grid plan to the west.

Fort Charlotte

Commercial St • Daily dawn to dusk • Free; HES • ⓦ www.historicenvironment.scot

Commercial Street's northern end is marked by the towering walls of **Fort Charlotte**, which once stood directly above the beach. Begun for Charles II in 1665, the fort was attacked and burnt down by the Dutch in August 1673. In the 1780s it was repaired and named in honour of George III's queen. Since then, it's served as a prison and a Royal Navy training centre; it's now open to the public, except when used by the Territorial Army.

Shetland Museum

Hay's Dock • Mon–Sat 10am–5pm, Sun noon–5pm • Free • ☏ 01595 695057, ⓦ shetlandmuseumandarchives.org.uk

Lerwick's chief tourist sight is the **Shetland Museum**, housed in a stylishly modern waterfront building off Commercial Road, half a mile north of the town centre. The permanent exhibition begins in the Lower Gallery, where you'll find replicas of the hoard of Pictish silver found at St Ninian's Isle (see p.568), the Monks Stone, thought to show the arrival of Christianity in Shetland, and a block of butter, tax payment for the king of Norway, found preserved in a peat bog. Kids can try grinding flour with a quernstone and visit a dark "trowie knowe". Among the boats, artistically suspended in the Boat Hall, is a sixareen, once used as a Foula mailboat. The Upper Gallery

SHETLAND PONIES

Shetland is famous for its diminutive **ponies**, but it's still a surprise to find so many of them on the islands. A local ninth-century carving shows a hooded priest riding a very small pony, but traditionally they were used as pack animals, and their tails were essential for making fishing nets. During the Industrial Revolution, Shetland ponies were exported to work in the mines in England, being the only animals small enough to cope with the low galleries. Shetlands then became the playthings of the English upper classes (the Queen Mother was patron of the Shetland Pony Stud-Book Society) and they still enjoy the limelight at the Horse of the Year show.

16

concentrates on the islands' social history, from knitting and whaling to the oil industry. The museum also houses Da Gadderie, which hosts temporary art exhibitions, runs the excellent *Hay's Dock* **café**, puts on events and demonstrations, and shows archive films.

Böd of Gremista

May–Sept Tues–Sat noon–4pm, Thurs noon–7pm · £3 · ☎ 01595 694386, ⦿ shetlandtextilemuseum.com

Just beyond Lerwick's main ferry terminal, a mile and a half north of the town centre, stands the **Böd of Gremista**, the birthplace of **Arthur Anderson** (1792–1868), naval seaman, philanthropist, Shetland's first native MP and founder of Shetland's first newspaper, the *Shetland Journal*. The building has been completely restored and now houses the **Shetland Textile Museum**, which puts on special exhibitions on the heritage of the islands' knitting culture.

ARRIVAL AND DEPARTURE   LERWICK

By plane Flights from outside Shetland land at Sumburgh airport, 25 miles to the south. Flights within Shetland depart from Tingwall airport.

Destinations within Shetland Fair Isle (Mon, Wed & F 2 daily, 1 on Sat; 25min); Foula (Mon & Tues 1 daily, Wed Fri 2 daily; 15min); Out Skerries, calling at Whalsay c

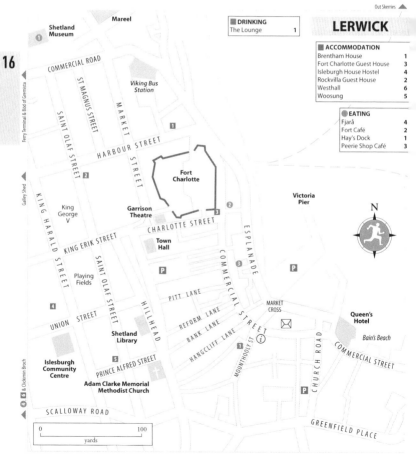

DRINKING
The Lounge   1

LERWICK

ACCOMMODATION
Brentham House	1
Fort Charlotte Guest House	3
Isleburgh House Hostel	4
Rockvilla Guest House	2
Westhall	6
Woosung	5

EATING
Fjarå	4
Fort Café	2
Hay's Dock	1
Peerie Shop Café	3

BÖDS

With only one SYHA hostel in Shetland, it's worth knowing about the islands' unique network of **camping böds** (March–Oct). Traditionally, a böd was a small building beside the shore, where fishermen stored their gear and occasionally slept; the word was also applied to trading posts established by Hanseatic merchants. Today, the tourist board uses the term pretty loosely: the places they run range from stone-built cottages to weatherboarded sail lofts. To stay at a böd, you must **book in advance** with the Shetland Amenity Trust (☎01595 694688, ⓦcamping-bods.com), as there are no live-in wardens. The more basic böds have no cooking facilities or electricity, but all have a solid fuel stove, cold water, toilets and bunk beds with mattresses – those with electricity have a meter, for which you need £1 coins. If you're camping, they're a great way to escape the wind and rain.

quest (Mon & Wed 1 daily, Thurs 2 daily; 20min); Papa our (Tues 2 daily; 10min).

y ferry NorthLink ferries (☎0845 600 0449, ⓦnorthlink rries.co.uk) from Aberdeen (daily; 12hr 30min) and kney (3–4 weekly; 6hr) arrive at Lerwick's ferry terminal, out a mile north of the town centre. Ferries to other ands within Shetland leave from the town harbour.
estinations Bressay (every 30min–1hr; 7min); Fair Isle ternate Thurs; 5hr); Skerries (Tues & Thurs; 2hr 30min).

y bus Buses stop on the Esplanade, close to the old rbour, or at the Viking Bus Station on Commercial Rd,

north of the town centre. Call ☎01595 744868 or visit ⓦzettrans.org.uk for timetables and more information.
Destinations Brae (Mon–Sat 8 daily; 45min); Hamnavoe (2–3 daily; 30min); Hillswick (Mon–Sat 3 daily; 1hr 40min); Laxo (Mon–Sat 2 daily; 40min); Levenwick (Mon–Sat 6–8 daily, 5 on Sun; 30min); Scalloway (Mon–Sat hourly, 4 on Sun; 20min); Sumburgh airport (Mon–Sat 6–7 daily, 5 on Sun; 45min); Tingwall (Mon–Fri 7 daily, Sat 4 daily; 10min); Toft (Mon–Sat 5–6 daily; 50min); Vidlin (Mon–Sat 3 daily; 45min); Voe (Mon–Fri 5 daily, 3 on Sat; 35min); Walls (Mon–Sat 6 daily; 50min).

16

FORMATION

urist office The tourist office is at the Market Cross, mmercial St (April–Oct Mon–Sat 9am–5pm, Sun am–4pm; Nov–March Mon–Sat 9am–4pm; ☎01595 3434, ⓦvisitshetland.com).

Radio station/newspaper For what's on, listen to BBC Radio Shetland, 92.7 FM (Mon–Fri 5.30pm), visit ⓦshetland-music.com, or buy the *Shetland Times* on Fridays (ⓦshetlandtimes.co.uk).

CCOMMODATION

entham House 7 Harbour St ☎01950 460201, brentham.com. Spacious, newly furnished ms in a Victorian, bay-fronted terrace; no reception, and proper breakfast – you pick the keys up from the nese restaurant a couple of doors down. **£75**

rt Charlotte Guest House 1 Charlotte St ☎01595 2140, ⓦfortcharlotte.co.uk. Small guesthouse with at central location (on the south side of the fort), cious rooms and a welcoming host. **£80**

esburgh House Hostel King Harald St ☎01595 5100, ⓦshetland.gov.uk/islesburgh. SYHA-affiliated, cious Victorian hostel offering well-worn but nfortable accommodation, family rooms, a café, free fi and laundry facilities. Dorms **£21**

ckvilla Guest House 88 St Olaf St ☎01595 695804,

ⓦrockvillaguesthouse.com. Recently refurbished guesthouse in one of the handsome Victorian houses in the upper part of town, run by a very hospitable couple, who keep the place spotless and serve up top-notch breakfasts – fast, free wi-fi throughout the building. **£80**

★Westhall Lower Sound ☎01595 694247, ⓦbedandbreakfastlerwick.co.uk. A splendid Victorian mansion, known as the "Sheriff's Hoose", set in its own grounds a mile southwest of town with fabulous views over to Bressay. Rooms are spacious, as is the residents' lounge, the breakfasts are immense and the host is super-friendly. **£110**

Woosung 43 St Olaf St ☎01595 693687, ⓦshetlandvisitor .com/woosung. Family-run B&B, up on the hill above the harbour, run by a very friendly local landlady. The whole place is kept spotlessly clean, but not all rooms are en suite. **£60**

TING

rå Sea Rd ☎01595 697388. Unlikely location (by the Tesco), 15min walk from town, this modern, buzzy tro has been a big hit with the locals – it's right by the reline so the views are great and sandwiches and salads under £10) are imaginative. Booking advised for the

evening when the menu gets more adventurous (mains £10–16). Daily 8am–10pm; food served until 8pm.
Fort Café 2 Commercial St ☎01595 693125. Lerwick's best fish-and-chip shop, situated below Fort Charlotte: takeaway or eat inside in the small café (closes 8pm).

LERWICK'S FESTIVALS

On the last Tuesday in January, Lerwick plays host to **Up Helly-Aa** (ⓦuphellyaa.org), the largest of the winter fire festivals held in Shetland. In late April/early May, the **Shetland Folk Festival** (ⓣ01595 694757, ⓦshetlandfolkfestival.com) features four days of musical mayhem, spread across the archipelago, with everything from local groups to international folk bands; book early as gigs sell out. Held over a week at Mareel, Lerwick, in early August, **Fiddle Frenzy** (ⓣ01595 743843, ⓦshetlandarts.org) shows how fiddling is central to Shetland's musical culture. It's curated by different musicians each year and includes classes for budding fiddlers. The **Shetland Accordion and Fiddle Festival** (ⓣ01595 693162, ⓦshetlandaccordionandfiddle.com) is organized by the local accordion and fiddle club over a long weekend in mid-October. Threatening to eclipse even the Shetland Folk Festival is **Shetland Wool Week** (ⓣ01595 980100, ⓦshetlandwoolweek.com), a week-long celebration of all things knitty in late September/early October.

Mon–Fri 11am–10pm, Sat 11am–9pm, Sun 4–10pm.

★ **Hay's Dock** Shetland Museum, Hay's Dock ⓣ01595 741569, ⓦhaysdock.co.uk. Bright, modern, licensed café-restaurant in the museum, with a great view over the north bay. Sandwiches, bagels and simple lunch dishes, from chowder to burgers, are all around £10; the more adventurous evening menu features local salmon and lamb

dishes (mains £13–20). Mon 10.30am–5pm, Tues–Sa 10.30am–9pm, Sun noon–5pm.

Peerie Shop Café Esplanade ⓣ01595 69281 ⓦpeerieshop.co.uk. Designer shop/gallery/café in an o lodberry (see p.561), with a good range of cakes, soup an sandwiches, and what is probably Britain's northernmo latte. Mon–Sat 9am–6pm.

DRINKING AND ENTERTAINMENT

The Lounge 4 Mounthooly St ⓣ01595 692231. Lerwick's friendliest pub, where local musicians often gather for a session at the weekend. Thursday night is quiz night. Daily 11am–1am.

Mareel North Ness ⓣ01595 745555, ⓦmareel.org. Lerwick's modern cultural complex is the place to come for

films and gigs – and also to sink into one of the leath sofas and enjoy views over the north bay, while tucki into burger and chips, ciabatta sandwiches and sala (until 4pm) or nachos and other bar snacks. Mon–Wed Sun 10am–11pm, Fri & Sat 10am–1am.

Bressay and Noss

Shielding Lerwick from the full force of the North Sea is the island of **Bressay**, dominated at its southern end by the conical Ward Hill (744ft) – "da Wart" – and accessible on an hourly car and passenger ferry from Lerwick (takes 5min). The chief reason for visiting Bressay is the tiny but spectacular island of **Noss**, off the east coast, whose high cliffs support a huge seabird colony in breeding season. If you've time to kill before the ferry back, pop into the **Bressay Heritage Centre**, by the ferry terminal.

Noss

Appropriately enough for an island that slopes gently into the sea at its western end, and plunges vertically 500ft at its eastern end, **Noss** has the dramatic and distinctive outline of a half-sunk ocean liner, while its name means "a point of rock". Inhabited until World War II, it's now a nature reserve and sheep farm, managed by Scottish Natural Heritage, who operate a RIB **ferry** from Bressay.

On the island, the old farmhouse contains a small visitor centre, where the warden will give you a quick briefing and a free map. Nearby is a sandy beach, while behind the haa (laird's house) is a **Pony Pund**, a square stone enclosure built for the breeding of Shetland ponies. The most memorable feature of Noss is its eastern **sea cliffs**, rising to peak at the massive Noup (500ft), from which can be seen vast colonies of cliff-nesting gannets, puffins, guillemots, shags, razorbills and fulmars: one of the highlights of Shetland. As Noss is only a mile or so wide, it's easy enough to walk to the sea cliffs a back (allow 4hr), but make sure you keep close to the coast, since otherwise the great skuas (locally known as "bonxies") may well dive-bomb you.

ARRIVAL AND GETTING AROUND
BRESSAY AND NOSS

By ferry The car ferry to Bressay departs from the town harbour in Lerwick (every 30min–1hr; 7min; ☎01595 743974) and arrives in Maryfield on the west coast. The RIB ferry to Noss (May–Aug daily except Mon & Thurs; £3 return; before setting out phone ☎0800 107 7818, ⓦnature shetland.co.uk) leaves from the east coast, 3 miles from Maryfield – an easy walk or short journey by bike, bus or car.

By bus No direct buses cross Bressay to the Noss ferry, but the bus that meets the Tuesday ferry at 10am from Lerwick will take you part of the way.

Boat trips Shetland Seabird Tours run a 3hr sightseeing boat from Lerwick (May–Oct daily 9.45am & 2.15pm; £45; ☎07767 872260, ⓦshetlandseabirdtours.com), allowing you a sea view of the vast bird colonies.

Scalloway

As you approach **SCALLOWAY** from the east, there's a dramatic view over the town and the islands beyond. Once the capital of Shetland, Scalloway's importance waned during the eighteenth century as Lerwick, just six miles to the east, grew in trading success and status. Nowadays, Scalloway is fairly sleepy, though its harbour remains busy enough, with a small fishing fleet and the North Atlantic Fisheries College (NAFC) on the far side.

Scalloway Castle

the door is locked, get key from Scalloway Museum or Scalloway Hotel • Free; HES • ⓦhistoricenvironment.scot

16

In spite of modern developments nearby, Scalloway is dominated by the imposing shell of **Scalloway Castle**, a classic fortified tower house built with forced labour in 1600 by the infamous Earl Patrick Stewart, and thus seen as a powerful symbol of oppression. Stewart, who'd succeeded to the Lordship of Shetland in 1592, held court here, reputedly increasing his power and wealth by using harsh justice to confiscate assets. He was eventually arrested and imprisoned in 1609 for his aggression toward his fellow landowners; his son, Robert, attempted an insurrection and both were executed in Edinburgh in 1615. The castle fell into disrepair in the following century; what remains is fun to explore.

Scalloway Museum

May–Sept Mon–Sat 11am–4pm, Sun 2–4pm • £3 • ☎01595 880734, ⓦscallowaymuseum.org

The **Scalloway Museum** occupies the old knitwear outlet next to the castle, has a café overlooking the ruin and a couple of Shetland ponies in the next-door field. The displays range from Neolithic finds to the impact of modern aquaculture, and there's a replica wheelhouse and a longship for the kids to play with, but the most interesting section tells the story of the **Shetland Bus** (see box, p.566). There are models of some of the fishing boats that made the trip across the North Sea, a replica of the Lewis guns that were hidden in oil drums aboard the ships and a miniature radio receiver supplied to the Norwegian Resistance.

ARRIVAL AND DEPARTURE
SCALLOWAY

By bus There are regular buses to Scalloway from Lerwick (Mon–Sat hourly, 4 on Sun; 20min) and a less frequent

service from Scalloway to Trondra and Burra (Mon–Sat 2 daily; 20min).

ACCOMMODATION AND EATING

The Cornerstone ☎01595 880346, ⓦthecornerstone bandb.com. Bright, modern café and B&B on the corner of the main street, with five newly refurbished rooms. Café serves breakfast fry-ups until 11.30am, comfort food until

2pm, then scones and cakes after that. Café Mon–Sat 9.30am–5pm, Sun noon–5pm. **£80**
Da Haaf ☎01595 772000, ⓦnafc.uhi.ac.uk/facilities. unpretentious restaurant in the NAFC with views over

Scalloway harbour. Simple, super-fresh grilled fish dishes (£10–15), high-quality fish and chips and tasty home-made puddings (£5–6). Mon–Fri 8.30am–4pm, Fri & Sat 5.30–9pm.

Scalloway Hotel ☎ 01595 880444, ⓦ scallowayhotel.com. Well-established hotel on the harbour front

– ask for a harbour-view room if possible. The hotel restaurant serves up pretty impressive dishes (mains around £20), but you can also eat well in the bar (mains £12–16) – both menus feature lots of local fish and seafood. Food served Mon–Sat noon–3pm & 5–9pm, Sun noon–8pm. **£130**

South Mainland

Shetland's **South Mainland** is a long, thin finger of land, only three or four miles wide but 25 miles long, ending in the cliffs of **Sumburgh Head** and **Fitful Head**. It's a beautiful area with wild undulating landscapes, lots of good green farmland, fabulous views out to sea and the mother of all brochs on the island of **Mousa**, just off the east coast. The most concentrated points of interest are at the southern end of the peninsula, where you'll find a crofting museum, **Jarlshof**, Shetland's most impressive archeological treasure, and the superb new lighthouse visitor centre at Sumburgh Head itself.

Mousa Broch

Day-trip April to mid-Sept Mon, Tues & Thurs 1pm & 4.15pm, Wed & Fri 10am & 1.15pm, Sun 1.30pm & 4.30pm; takes 15min • £16 • **Storm petrel trip** Mid-May to July Wed & Sat 10.30pm; 2hr 30min • £20 • advance booking necessary; ☎ 07901 872339, ⓦ www.mousa.co.uk

Accessible by boat from Sandwick, the island of **Mousa** boasts the most amazingly well-preserved broch in the whole of Scotland. Rising to more than 40ft and looking rather like a Stone Age cooling tower, **Mousa Broch** has a remarkable presence and features in both *Egil's Saga* and the *Orkneyinga Saga*, contemporary chronicles of Norse exploration and settlement. To get to the broch, simply head south from the jetty along the western coastline for about half a mile. The low entrance passage leads through two concentric walls to a central courtyard, divided into separate beehive chambers. Between the walls, a rough (very dark) staircase leads to the top parapet; a torch is provided for visitors.

Thousands of **storm petrels** breed around the broch, only returning to the nests after dark. The ferry runs special late-night trips, setting off in the "simmer dim" twilight. Even if you've no interest in the storm petrels, which appear like bats as they flit about in the half-light, the chance to explore the broch at midnight is worth it alone.

THE SHETLAND BUS

The story of the **Shetland Bus** – the link between Shetland and Norway that helped to sustain the Norwegian Resistance through the years of Nazi occupation – is extraordinary. Under threat of enemy attack, small Norwegian fishing boats ran arms and resistance workers from Shetland into lonely fjords. The trip took 24 hours and on the return journey boats brought back Norwegians wanted by the Gestapo, or volunteers for Norwegian forces fighting with the Allies. For three years, through careful planning, the operation was remarkably successful: cryptic instructions to boats were broadcast by the BBC. Local people knew what was going on, but the secret was well kept. In total, 350 refugees were evacuated, and more than 400 tons of arms, large amounts of explosives and 60 radio transmitters were landed in Norway.

Originally established at **Lunna** in the northeast of the Mainland, the service moved to **Scalloway** in 1942, partly because the village offered good marine engineering facilities at Moore's Shipyard on Main Street, where a plaque records the morale-boosting visit of the Norwegian Crown Prince Olav. Explosives and weapons were stored in the castle, and **Kergord House** in Weisdale was used as a safe house and training centre for intelligence personnel and saboteurs. The hazards, tragedies and elations of the exercise are brilliantly described in David Howarth's book, *The Shetland Bus*; their legacy today is a heartfelt closeness between Shetland and Norway.

St Ninian's Isle

Halfway down South Mainland, a road leads to **Bigton**, on the west coast. From the village, a signposted track heads down to a spectacular sandy causeway, or **tombolo**, connecting **St Ninian's Isle**. The tombolo – a concave strip of shell sand with Atlantic breakers crashing on either side – is usually exposed so you can walk over to the island, where you'll find the ruins of a medieval church.

Crofthouse Museum

May–Sept daily 10am–1pm & 2–5pm • Free • ☎ 01950 460557, ⓦ shetlandheritageassociation.com

Housed in a well-to-do thatched croft in Southvoe, built around 1870, the **Crofthouse Museum** re-creates the feel of crofting life, with a peat fire, traditional box-beds and so forth. Adjacent to the living quarters is the byre for the cows and tatties, and the kiln for drying the grain. Crofting was mostly done by women in Shetland, while the men went out haaf-net fishing for the laird. Down by the nearby burn, there's also a restored thatched horizontal mill.

Old Scatness Broch and Iron Age Village

Mid-May to Aug Fri 10.15am–4.30pm (check ahead) • £5 • ☎ 01595 694688, ⓦ shetlandamenity.org

Extending the airport revealed a vast Iron Age archeological site known as **Old Scatness Broch and Iron Age Village**. At the centre of the site are the remains of an Iron Age broch, surrounded by a settlement of interlocking wheelhouses – so-called because of their circular ground plan – two of which have been either partially or wholly reconstructed.

Jarlshof

Daily: April–Sept 9.30am–5.30pm; Oct–March 9.30am to dusk • £5.50; HES • ☎ 01595 460112, ⓦ historicenvironment.scot

Of all the archeological sites in Shetland, **Jarlshof** is the largest and most impressive. What makes Jarlshof so amazing is the fact that you can walk right into a house built 1600 years ago, which is still intact to above head height. The site is big and confusing, scattered with the ruins of buildings dating from the Bronze Age to the early seventeenth century. The name – misleading, as it is not primarily a Viking site – was coined by Sir Walter Scott, who used the ruins of the Old House in his novel *The Pirate*. However, it was only at the end of the nineteenth century that the Bronze Age, Iron Age and Viking settlements you see now were discovered, after a violent storm ripped off the top layer of turf.

The Bronze Age smithy and Iron Age dwellings nearest the entrance are nothing compared with the cells which cluster around the **broch**, close to the sea. Only half of the original broch survives, and its courtyard is now an Iron Age aisled roundhouse, with stone piers. However, it's difficult to distinguish the broch from the later Pictish **wheelhouses** which now surround it. Still, it's all great fun to explore, as you're free to roam around the cells, checking out the in-built stone shelving, water tanks, beds and so on. Inland lies the maze of grass-topped foundations marking out the **Viking longhouses**, from the ninth century AD. Towering over the whole complex are the ruins of the laird's house, built by Robert Stewart, Earl of Orkney and Lord of Shetland, in the late sixteenth century, and the **Old House of Sumburgh**, built by his son, Earl Patrick.

Sumburgh Head Lighthouse

Daily: Easter–Sept 9.30am–5.30pm • Entry £6, lighthouse tour (Fri–Sun only) £3 • ☎ 01595 694688, ⓦ sumburghhead.com

The Mainland comes to a dramatic end at **Sumburgh Head** (262ft), which rises sharply out of the land only to drop vertically into the sea. The road up to it is the perfect site for watching nesting seabirds such as kittiwakes, fulmars, shags, razorbills and guillemots, as well as gannets diving for fish. This is also the easiest place in Shetland et close to **puffins**: during the nesting season (May to early Aug), you simply need to ook over the western wall, just before you enter the lighthouse complex, to see them arriving at their burrows a few yards below with beakfuls of sand eels.

You can take a guided tour (two at a time) of the clifftop lighthouse, built by Robert Stevenson in 1821, and explore some of the outbuildings, including the reconstructed WWII secret radar hut which helped protect the Royal Navy anchored in Scapa Flow. As well as a visitor centre with an exhibition on the history of the lighthouse, there's a **Marine Life Centre**, with hard-hitting displays on the worrying recent decline in seabird numbers. After roaming the complex, you can settle down and enjoy the sea views from the lighthouse's **café** (daily except Wed 11am–4.30pm).

ARRIVAL AND DEPARTURE · SOUTH MAINLAND

y plane Sumburgh airport, at the southernmost tip of South Mainland, is Shetland's main airport. There's a bus service to Lerwick (Mon–Sat 6–7 daily, 5 on Sun; 45min) or se it's a £25 taxi ride (☏ 01950 460560).

By bus There are regular buses from Lerwick to Levenwick (Mon–Sat 6–8 daily, 5 on Sun; 30min); Sandwick (Mon–Fri 10 daily, 6 on Sat, 5 on Sun; 25min); Sumburgh (Mon–Sat 6–7 daily, 5 on Sun; 45min).

ACCOMMODATION AND EATING

etty Mouat's Cottage Scatness ☏ 01595 694688, ☏ camping-bods.com. Next to an excavated broch and not far from the airport, this stone-built cottage is a camping bod with two bedrooms, hot water, a solid-fuel stove and an electricity meter (£1 coins needed). March–Oct. Dorms **£10**

evenwick Campsite Levenwick ☏ 01950 422320, levenwick.shetland.co.uk. Small, terraced campsite run by the local community with hot showers and laundry facilities, a tennis court and a superb view over the east coast. May–Sept. Per pitch **£8**

Mucklehus Levenwick ☏ 01950 422370, mucklehus.plus.com. A lovely B&B run by a local artist in a former Master Mariner's house built in 1890 near the sandy beach in Levenwick, 18 miles south of Lerwick; the rooms are small, but stylish. **£80**

Setterbrae 2 miles west of Dunrossness ☏ 01950 460468, ☏ setterbrae.co.uk. There's a proper homely feel to this B&B, just a stone's throw from Spiggie Loch – the residents' lounge has lots of books on Shetland and the conservatory has views over the loch. **£80**

Spiggie Hotel Dunrossness ☏ 01950 460409, ☏ thespiggiehotel.co.uk. Hotel with a popular bar serving real ales and a restaurant with great views out to Foula and, if you're lucky, incredible sunsets. Bar meals are priced around £10, or you can have well-presented dishes such as lobster or whatever the local catch is, à la carte in the restaurant (mains £12–18). Food served Mon & Tues 6–10pm, Wed–Sun noon–2.30pm & 6–10pm. **£125**

16

air Isle

Marooned in the sea halfway between Shetland and Orkney, **Fair Isle** is very different from both. The weather reflects its isolated position: you can almost guarantee that it'll be windy, though if you're lucky your visit might coincide with fine weather – what the islanders call "a given day". Fair Isle's population had tumbled from 400 to 44 by the 1950s, at which point evacuation was seriously considered. The laird, **George Waterston**, who'd set up a bird observatory in 1948, passed it into the care of the NTS in 1954 and rejuvenation began. Today, Fair Isle supports a community of around sixty.

The north end of the island rises like a wall, while the Sheep Rock, a sculpted stack of rock and grass on the east side, is another dramatic feature. The croft land and the island's scattered white houses are concentrated in the south. Fair Isle has two **lighthouses**, one at either end of the island, both designed by the Stevenson family and erected in 1892 – the South Lighthouse can be visited by appointment (free; ☏ 01595 760349).

Fair Isle Bird Observatory

April–Oct • Free • ☏ 01595 760258, ☏ fairislebirdobs.co.uk

The most significant building on Fair Isle is the **Bird Observatory** (FIBO), a large building just above the sandy bay of North Haven where the ferry from Shetland arrives, which houses an exhibition on the island past and present. As well as providing accommodation and food to visitors, it's one of the major European centres for ornithology. As a result, the island is a haven for twitchers, who descend on the island whenever a major rarity is spotted; for more casual birders, however, there's also plenty of summer resident birdlife to enjoy. The high-pitched screeching that fills the sky above the airstrip comes from hundreds of arctic terns, and arctic skuas can also be seen here. Those in search of puffins should head for the cliffs around Furse, and to find gannets, aim for the spectacular Stacks of Scroo.

George Waterston Museum

Mon 2–4pm, Wed 10.30am–noon, Fri 2–4pm • Free • ☎ 01595 760244

Fair Isle is known for its **knitting** patterns, still produced with great skill by the local knitwear cooperative. There are samples on display at the **George Waterston Museum**, next to the Methodist Chapel. Particularly memorable are stories of shipwrecks; in 1868 the islanders undertook a heroic rescue of all 465 German emigrants aboard the *Lessing*. More famously, *El Gran Grifon*, part of the retreating Spanish Armada, was lost here in 1588 and three hundred Spanish seamen were washed up on the island. Food was in such short supply that fifty died of starvation before help could be summoned from Shetland.

ARRIVAL AND DEPARTURE

FAIR ISLE

By plane Airtask (☎ 01595 840246, ⊛ airtask.com) flies from Tingwall to Fair Isle (Mon–Sat 1–3 daily) and from Sumburgh (Sat only) for around £85 return.
By ferry The passenger ferry connects Fair Isle with either

Lerwick (alternate Thurs; 4–5hr) or Grutness in Sumburgh (Tues, alternate Thurs & Sat; 3hr); since the boat only takes a limited number of passengers, it's advisable to book in advance (☎ 01595 760363). The crossing can be rough.

ACCOMMODATION AND EATING

If you're staying over, book accommodation in advance and note that camping is not permitted. Although day visitors can get something to eat at the observatory, all accommodation is booked on a full-board basis. There is a shop/post office, Stackhoull Stores, in the south of the island (closed Tues & Sat afternoon, and all day Thurs & Sun).

Fair Isle Bird Observatory Lodge 300yd from the harbour ☎ 01595 760258, ⊛ www.fairislebirdobs .co.uk. Full-board accommodation is available at the modern observatory in en-suite doubles/twins and singles; as the island's social hub, the observatory offers self-service tea and coffee with an honesty box and meals for non-residents by arrangement (breakfast £10, lunch £12, dinner £15). April–Oct. **£140**
South Light House 2 miles south of the airport

☎ 01595 760355, ⊛ southlightfairisle.co.uk. B&B at the southernmost tip of the island, not literally in the lighthouse, but in the adjacent keepers' cottages – note bathrooms are not en suite. **£110**
Upper Leogh 1.5 miles south of the airport ☎ 01595 760248, ⊛ kathycoull.com. You'll be well looked after at this whitewashed crofthouse B&B by spinning and weaving expert, Kathy Coull, who also runs textile courses. **£100**

The Westside

The western Mainland of Shetland – known as the **Westside** – stretches west from Weisdale and Voe to Sandness. Although there are some important archeological remains and wildlife here, the area's greatest appeal lies in its outstanding **coastal scenery** and walks. Cut by several deep voes, the coastline is very varied; aside from dramatic cliffs, there are intimate coves and some fine beaches, as well as the stunning island of **Papa Stour**.

Walls and around

Once an important fishing port, **WALLS** (pronounced *waas*), appealingly set round its harbour, is now a quiet village which comes alive once a year in the middle of August or the Walls Agricultural Show, the biggest farming bash on the island. If you're just passing by, you might like to stop by the **bakery and tearoom**, but Walls also has several good **accommodation** options.

Stanydale Temple

Three miles east of Walls lies the finest Neolithic structure in the Westside, dubbed the **Stanydale Temple** by the archeologist who excavated it because it resembled a temple in Malta. Whatever its true function, it was twice as large as the surrounding oval-shaped houses (now in ruins) and was certainly of great importance, perhaps as some kind of community centre. To reach it, follow the black-and-white poles across the moorland for half a mile from the road.

ARRIVAL AND DEPARTURE   THE WESTSIDE

By bus There's an infrequent bus service between Lerwick and Skeld (Mon–Sat 1–3 daily; 1hr), and between Lerwick and Walls (Mon–Sat 6 daily; 45min), with a feeder service

from Sandness (Mon–Sat 2–3 daily; 45min) – some journeys are dial-a-ride and need to be booked in advance (☎01595 745745).

ACCOMMODATION AND EATING

Bo's B&B 1.5 miles southwest of Walls ☎01595 89258, ⊗bosimmons.wix.com/bosbandb. One double room for B&B in a newly built ecofriendly house, a camping-style bothy and a wooden camping pod for the hardy, situated on the road from Walls to Burrastow. May– Sept. B&B **£70**; bothy **£20**; pods **£10**

Burrastow House 3 miles southwest of Walls ☎01595 809307, ⊗burrastowhouse.co.uk. Beautifully

situated off the beaten track southwest of Walls, parts of the house date back to 1759 and have real character; others are more modern. The cooking is superb and evening meals are available for non-residents, too. **£120**

Voe House Walls ☎01595 694688, ⊗camping-bods .com. This five-bedroom camping böd is Shetland's largest, with its own peat fire. Note that *Voe House*, confusingly, is not in Voe but in Walls. March–Oct. Dorms **£10**

16

Papa Stour

Formed of volcanic lava and ash, the rocky island of **Papa Stour** has been eroded into some of the most impressive coastal scenery in Shetland. In good weather, it makes for a perfect day-trip, but in foul weather or a sea mist it can appear pretty bleak. Its name, meaning "big island of the priests", derives from its early Celtic Christian connections. The land is very fertile, and once supported three hundred inhabitants, but in the early 1970s the population crisis was such that the island had to advertise for incomers – today, the population is back down to single figures. There is no accommodation, but you can wild camp and there are toilets by the ferry terminal.

ARRIVAL AND DEPARTURE   PAPA STOUR

By plane Airtask (☎01595 840246, ⊗airtask.com) flies from Tingwall twice every Tuesday, so a day-trip is feasible (around £70 return).

By ferry The ferry runs from West Burrafirth, 5 miles north

of Walls, to Papa Stour (Wed, Fri & Sat 2 daily; Sun 1 daily; 40min; ☎01955 745804) – book in advance, and reconfirm the day before departure.

WALKING ON PAPA STOUR

Ordnance Survey Explorer map 467

To reach the best of Papa Stour's coastal scenery, head for the west of the island. From **Virda Field** (285ft), the highest point, you can see the treacherous rocks of **Ve Skerries**, where a lighthouse was erected as recently as 1979. The coastline from here southeast to Hamna Voe has some of the island's best stacks, blowholes and natural arches. The most spectacular is **Kirstan's Hole**, a group of partly roofed cleft, extending far inland, where shags nest on precipitous ledges. Look out, too, for red-throated divers, which regularly breed on inland lochs such as Gorda Water.

Foula

At "the edge of the world", **Foula** is the most isolated inhabited island in the British Isles, separated from the nearest point on Shetland by about fourteen miles of often turbulent ocean. Seen from the Mainland, its distinctive mountainous outline is unforgettable. Its western **cliffs**, the second highest in Britain after those of St Kilda, rise to 1220ft at **The Kame**; a clear day offers a panorama stretching from Unst to Fair Isle. On a bad day, the exposure is complete and the cliffs generate turbulent blasts of wind known as "flans", which rip through the hills with tremendous force.

Arriving on Foula, you can't help but be amazed by the sheer size of the island's immense, bare mountains, whose summits are often hidden in cloud, known as "Foula's hat". The gentler eastern slopes provide good crofting land, and plentiful peat, around which the island's population of around forty is scattered. The only road, running along the island's eastern side, is used by Foula's remarkable fleet of clapped-out vehicles.

Foula's name is derived from the Old Norse for "bird island", and it's home to a quarter of a million **birds**. Arctic terns wheel overhead at the airstrip, red-throated divers can usually be seen on the island's smaller lochs, while fulmars, guillemots, razorbills, puffins and gannets cling to the rock ledges. However, it's the island's colony of **great skuas** or "bonxies" that you can't fail to notice, with an estimated 3000 pairs on Foula, making it the largest colony in the world. During the nesting season (May–Aug), they attack anyone who comes near; the best advice is to hold a stick above your head or stick to the road and the coast.

ARRIVAL AND DEPARTURE

By plane Airtask (☎01595 840246, ✆airtask.com) flies from Tingwall (Mon 1 daily, Tues, Wed & Fri 2 daily, 15min); tickets cost around £80 return.

By ferry Be sure to book and reconfirm your journey by ferry (Tues, Thurs & Sat; 2hr; ☎01595 840208, ✆bkmarine.or which departs from Walls (Tues, Sat & alternate Thurs; 2hr) Scalloway (alternate Thurs; 3hr 30min). The ferry arrives Ham, in the middle of Foula's east coast.

INFORMATION AND TOURS

Tourist information Foula has its own resident part-time Ranger, who usually greets new arrivals and offers local advice (mid-April to Oct). It's also possible to arrange for guided walks with a Ranger (Wed & Fri; ☎01595 753236, ✆foulaheritage.org.uk), or you can download self-guided walk leaflets from the website. There's no sh on the island, so bring your own supplies.

Boat trips Day-trips are not possible on the regular fer but Cycharters (☎01595 810887, ✆cycharters.co.uk) boat trips on Wednesdays from Scalloway.

ACCOMMODATION

Leraback Foula ☎01595 753226, ✆www.originart .eu/leraback/leraback.html. The only accommodation on Foula is at this B&B near Ham. It's a simple but very welcoming place to stay; full board only and they'll coll you from the airstrip or pier. **£80**

North Mainland

The **North Mainland**, stretching over thirty miles from the central belt around Lerwick, wilder than much of Shetland, with relentlessly bleak moorland and some rugged and dramatic coastal scenery. It's all but split in two by the isthmus of **Mavis Grind**: to the south lies **Sullom Voe**, Shetland's oil terminal, and **Brae**, the area's largest town; to the north is the remote region of **Northmavine**, boasting some of Shetland's most scenic clif

Voe

If you're travelling north, you'll pass by **VOE**, at the main crossroads of the North Mainland. If you stay on the main road, it's easy to miss the picturesque little port, a tig uddle of homes and workshops down below the road around the pier (and signposted ower Voe). Set at the head of a deep, sheltered sea loch, Voe has a Scandinavian ppearance, helped by the presence of the **Sail Loft**, now a **camping böd** (see below).

CCOMMODATION AND EATING VOE

erhead Restaurant & Bar By the harbour ☎ 01806 ⁼8332. The old butcher's is now a cosy wood-panelled ⁼b with a good bar menu, a longer version of which graces ⁼e upstairs restaurant, featuring local scallops and the odd ⁼tch from the fishing boats (mains £12–18). Mon–Thurs ⁼Sun 11am–10pm, Fri & Sat 11am–1am.

Sail Loft By the harbour ☎ 01595 694688, ⓦ camping -bods.com. Originally a giant storeroom, this enormous böd is situated right by the loch and has hot showers, a kitchen and a solid-fuel fire in the smaller of the two rooms. Bring £1 coins for the electricity meter. March– Oct. Dorms **£10**

⁼unnasting

⁼nnasting is the area to the northeast of Voe, on the east coast. The main town is **⁼DLIN**, departure point for the Out Skerries (see p.576), three miles east of Laxo, the ⁼rry terminal for Whalsay (see p.575).

⁼e Cabin Museum

⁼il–Sept Tues, Thurs, Sat & Sun 1–5pm • Free • ☎ 01806 577232

⁼alfway between Laxo and Vidlin, the B9071 passes **The Cabin Museum**, a modern ⁼rn packed to the rafters with wartime memorabilia collected by the late Andy ⁼bertson. You can try on some of the uniforms and caps or pore over the many ⁼rsonal accounts of the war written by locals.

16

⁼nna

⁼e long thin peninsula of Lunna Ness is pinched in the middle at the tiny remote ⁼tlement of **LUNNA**, a couple of miles northeast of Vidlin. It was here, at **Lunna ⁼ouse**, originally built in 1660, that the Shetland Bus made its headquarters during ⁼orld War II (see box, p.566). Nearby lies the whitewashed **Lunna Kirk**, built in 1753, ⁼ich has a simple tiny interior including a carved hexagonal pulpit. In the graveyard, ⁼eral unidentified Norwegian sailors, torpedoed by the Nazis, are buried.

⁼ae

⁼AE is a sprawling settlement that still has the feel of a frontier town, having expanded ⁼stily in the 1970s to accommodate the workforce for the nearby **Sullom Voe Oil ⁼rminal**, the largest of its kind in Europe. During World War II, Sullom Voe was ⁼me to the Norwegian Air Force and a base for RAF seaplanes.

COMMODATION AND EATING BRAE

⁼usta House ☎ 01806 522506, ⓦ bustahouse.com. ⁼rd's house with stepped gables that sits across the bay ⁼ Brae. Even if you're not staying the night it's worth ⁼ing for afternoon tea in the Long Room, for a stroll ⁼nd the wooded grounds, or for a drink and a meal ⁼ent steak, fish and chips) in the pub-like bar. **£115**

⁼nkie's ☎ 01806 522700, ⓦ frankiesfishandchips ⁼n. Popular fish and chip café with great views over

Busta Voe. As well as fish straight off the boats, you can get king scallops, smoked haddock and mussels. Mon–Sat 9.30am–8pm, Sun noon–8pm.
Westayre ☎ 01806 522368, ⓦ westayre.shetland .co.uk. A modern crofthouse B&B, *Westayre* is in a tranquil position, overlooking a red sandy bay at the very end of the road on the peaceful island of Muckle Roe, linked to the Mainland by a bridge. **£80**

⁼rthmavine

⁼rthmavine, the northwest peninsula of North Mainland, is unquestionably one of ⁼ most picturesque areas of Shetland, with its often rugged scenery, magnificent coastline and wide-open spaces. The peninsula begins a mile west of Brae at **Mavis Grind**, a narrow isthmus at which it's said you can throw a stone from the Atlantic to the North Sea, or at least to Sullom Voe.

Hillswick

HILLSWICK was once a centre for deep-sea or haaf fishing, and later a herring station. In 1900, the North of Scotland, Orkney & Shetland Steam Navigation Company bui the **St Magnus Hotel** to house their customers, importing it in the form of a timber kit from Norway. It still stands overlooking St Magnus Bay, rather magnificently clad in mustard and black timber.

Down by the ancient harbour is **Da Böd**, which was founded by a Hanseatic mercha in 1684, later became Shetland's oldest pub, and is now a seal and wildlife sanctuary and occasional weekend café. The stony beach by the harbour is very sheltered, but th nicest sandiest **beach** is on the west side of the Hillswick isthmus, overlooking Dore Holm, a short walk across the fields from the hotel.

Esha Ness

Just outside Hillswick, a road leads west to the exposed headland of **Esha Ness**, celebrated for its splendid coastline views. Spectacular red-granite **cliffs**, eaten away to form fantastic shapes by the elements, spread out before you as the road climbs away from Hillswick: to the south, out at sea, are the stacks known as **The Drongs**, while in the distance the Westside and Papa Stour are visible. After three miles, you reach Braewick café and campsite, with a great view over the wide bay of Brae Wick, from which several small dead-end roads lead off to the coast.

Tangwick Haa Museum

Easter–Sept daily 11am–5pm • Free • ☎ 01806 503389, ⊚ tangwickhaa.org.uk

One small dead-end road, off the main road, leads south to the **Tangwick Haa Museum**, housed in a seventeenth-century building, which tells the often moving story of this remo corner of Shetland and its role in the dangerous trade of deep-sea fishing and whaling.

Esha Ness Lighthouse

West of Braewick, where the road divides, the northernmost branch ends at **Esha Nes Lighthouse**, a great place to view the red-sandstone cliffs, stacks and blowholes. Bewa of the latter, some of which are hidden far inland. The best example is the **Holes of Scraada**, a partly roofed cleft, half a mile north of the lighthouse, where the sea suddenly appears 300 yards inland from the cliff line. The incredible power of the sea can be seen in the various giant boulder fields above the cliffs: these **storm beaches** ar formed by rocks torn from the cliffs in storms and deposited inland.

ACCOMMODATION AND EATING

NORTHMAVI

HILLSWICK AND AROUND

Almara Urafirth ☎ 01806 503261, ⊚ www.almara .shetland.co.uk. This modern B&B – up on a hill overlooking Ura Firth – serves up a friendly family welcome, big breakfasts and excellent views. **£80**

Da Böd Hillswick ☎ 01806 503348, ⊚ shetlandwildlife sanctuary.com. This eccentric, weekend-only café occupies a rambling ancient building and the proceeds go to the nearby wildlife sanctuary. April–Sept Sat & Sun 11am–5pm.

St Magnus Bay Hotel Hillswick ☎ 01806 503372, ⊚ stmagnusbayhotel.co.uk. Large, distinctive mustard and black hotel with large, high-ceilinged public rooms and rooms ranging from the spacious to the cosy. The

restaurant serves generous and filling portions – Sunday carvery is particularly popular. **£130**

ESHA NESS

Braewick café and campsite Braewick, 4 n northwest of Hillswick ☎ 01806 503345, ⊚ esha .moonfruit.com. Café with great views of the Drongs, se soup, sandwiches and toasties, plus home-made cakes scones; phone to check opening times. The campsite is p exposed but you can always book one of the four wo wigwams if the wind gets too much. Food served 10am–5pm. Wigwams **£48**; camping per pitch **£12**

Johnnie Notions Böd Hamnavoe, 1.5 miles nor

aewick ☎ 01595 694688, ⓦ camping-bods.com. One the few places to stay in Esha Ness, this tiny four-bed böd the birthplace of a pioneer in smallpox inoculation – is in

a remote hamlet of Hamnavoe, north of Braewick. There's no electricity and cold water only, but there is a solid-fuel stove. March–Oct. Dorms **£8**

Whalsay

he island of **Whalsay** (population 1000) is in a world of its own, with a dialect even her Shetlanders struggle to fathom. The islands' fishing crews operate a very ccessful pelagic fleet of immense super-trawlers which can fish far afield in all eathers, catching a wide range of species. The island is extremely fertile, but crofting kes second place to fishing here.

ymbister

he island's chief town is **SYMBISTER**, whose harbour is usually dominated by the esence of several of the island's sophisticated, multi-million-pound purse-netters, me over 180ft long; you'll also see smaller fishing boats and probably a few urareens", which the locals race regularly in the summer months.

er House

1–Sat 9am–1pm & 2–5pm, Sun 2–4pm • Free

ongside the busy harbour is the tiny grey-granite **Pier House**, the key for which ides in the shop opposite. This picturesque little building, with a hoist built into one le, is thought to have been a Hanseatic merchants' store, and contains displays on w the Germans traded salt, tobacco, spirits and cloth for Whalsay's salted, dried fish m medieval times until the eighteenth century.

halsay Heritage Centre

–Sept Wed & Fri–Sun 2–5pm; Oct–May Wed 7–9pm • Free • ☎ 01806 566397, ⓦ whalsayheritage.co.uk

erlooking the town is the imposing Georgian mansion of **Symbister House**, built in ·y granite and boasting a Neoclassical portico. It was built in the 1830s at great expense the laird Robert Bruce, reputedly not because he wanted to live on Whalsay but cause he wanted to deprive his heirs of his fortune. It's now part of the local school, ·ugh you can still see the old doocot behind the house, and various outbuildings in the ·dden Court, one of which houses a **heritage centre** on the history of the island.

RIVAL AND DEPARTURE

WHALSAY

plane There are request-only flights from Tingwall n, Wed & Thurs; ☎ 01595 840246, ⓦ airtask.com), day· are only possible on Thursdays.

ferry Car ferries run regularly to Whalsay from Laxo on

the Mainland (☎ 01806 566259; 30min) – book ahead to take a car. In bad weather, especially southeasterly gales, the service operates from Vidlin instead. Laxo–Symbister (every 45min; 30min).

COMMODATION AND EATING

eve House Symbister ☎ 01595 694688, ·mping-bods.com. The only accommodation on ·lsay is this camping böd in Sodom, on the edge of ·bister. The house has lovely views overlooking Linga ·nd, but is hidden from the road to the Loch of Huxter, ·sk for directions. No electricity or hot water, but a

solid-fuel stove. March–Oct. Dorms **£8**

Oot Ower Lounge and Campsite Huxter ☎ 01595 566658. A family-run pub overlooking the Loch of Huxter – this is pretty much the only place to eat and drink on the island (phone ahead to check they're open and serving food), with fish and chips for £10, and somewhere to camp. Per pitch **£10**

OPPING

·ard Brough, 2 miles northeast of Symbister. The ·try's remotest charity and recycling shop is in Brough.

It has limited opening hours, but is a must if you're in the area. Wed, Thurs & Sat 2–4pm.

Out Skerries

Lying four miles out to sea, off the northeast tip of Whalsay, the **Out Skerries** consist of three low-lying rocky islands, Housay, Bruray and Grunay, the first two linked by a bridge (population 70). That people live here at all is remarkable, and that it's one of Shetland's more robust communities is astonishing, its affluence based on fishing and on salmon farming in a nearby inlet. There are a few prehistoric remains, but the majority of visitors are divers exploring the wreck-strewn coastline, and ornithologists hoping to glimpse rare migrants.

The Skerries' jetty and airstrip are both on the middle island of **Bruray**, which boasts the Skerries' highest point, Bruray Wart (173ft), an easy climb, and home to the islands' ingenious spiral-channel collection system for rainwater, which can become scarce in summer. The easternmost island, **Grunay**, is now uninhabited, though the abandoned lighthouse keepers' cottages on the island's chief hill remain; despite appearances, the Stevenson-designed lighthouse itself sits on the outlying islet of Bound Skerry. The largest of the Skerries, **Housay**, has the most indented and intriguing coastline, to which you should head if the weather's fine.

ARRIVAL AND DEPARTURE

OUT SKERRIES

By plane There are regular flights from Tingwall (Mon, Wed & Thurs), with day-trips possible on Thursdays.
By ferry Ferries to and from Skerries leave from Vidlin on the Mainland (Mon & Fri–Sun; 1hr 30min) and Lerwick (Tues & Thurs; 2hr 30min), but day-trips are only possible from Vidlin (Fri–Sun). Make sure you book your journey by 5pm the previous evening (☎01806 51522) or the ferry might not run. You can take your car over but, with less than a mile of road to drive along, it's not necessary.

ACCOMMODATION

Camping is allowed, with permission. There is a shop, and a shower/toilet block by the pier.

Rocklea ☎01806 515228, ⌨rockleaok.co.uk. The only B&B on the islands is a modern crofthouse on Bruray run by the very welcoming Johnsons, who offer optional board. **£100**

The North Isles

Many visitors never make it out to Shetland's trio of **North Isles**, thinking that they are too remote. This is a shame, as the ferry links are in fact frequent and inexpensive, and the roads fast. Much of the scenery is the familiar Shetland landscape of undulating peat moorland, dramatic coastal cliffs and silent glacial voes. However, the spirit of independence and self-sufficiency in the North Isles is much more keenly felt. **Yell** is best known for its vast otter population, but is otherwise often overlooked. **Fetlar**, the smallest, is home to the rare red-necked phalarope, while **Unst** has the widest appeal, the most northerly land mass in the British Isles, and for its nesting seabird population.

Yell

If you keep to the fast main road, which cuts across the island of Yell, you'll pass a lot of fairly uninspiring peat moorland. Get onto the minor roads, though, and you'll begin to appreciate the island and have more chance of spotting one of Yell's numerous **otters**.

Burravoe

At **BURRAVOE**, in the southeastern corner of Yell, a whitewashed laird's house dating from 1672 houses the **Old Haa Museum** (April–Sept Mon–Thurs & Sat 10am–4pm, Sun 2–5pm; free; ☎01957 702431). Stuffed with artefacts, the museum has lots of material on the history of the local herring and whaling industry and there's a pleasant wood-panelled café on the ground floor. From May to August, you'll find thousands of **seabirds** (including puffins) nesting in the cliffs above Ladies Hole, less than a mile northeast of the village.

Mid Yell and around

The island's largest village, **MID YELL**, has a couple of shops, a pub and a leisure centre with a swimming pool. A mile northwest of the village, on a hill above the main road, stands the spooky, abandoned eighteenth-century **Windhouse**; skeletons were found under the floor and in its wood-panelled walls, and the house is now believed by many to be haunted (its ghost-free lodge is a camping böd; see box, p.563).

ARRIVAL AND TOURS · YELL

By ferry ☎01595 745804, ⓦwww.shetland.gov.uk. Ferries to Ulsta (Yell) from Toft on the Mainland are very frequent (every 30min–1hr; 20min), as are ferries from Gutcher across the Bluemull Sound to Belmont (Unst) and Hamar's Ness (Fetlar) – note it's cash only on the ferries.

By bus An integrated bus and ferry service from Lerwick

goes all the way to Gutcher (Mon–Sat 1 daily; 2hr 10min). On Yell, buses from Ulsta run to Gutcher (Mon–Sat 3–4 daily; 30min).

Guided tours Local otter spotter John Campbell (☎01806 577358, ⓦshetlandotters.com) takes groups of two or three in search of otters (£150 a day for a couple) – book in advance.

ACCOMMODATION AND EATING

The Hilltop Mid Yell ☎01957 702333. Situated in Mid Yell, this pre-fab is the island's chief pub – it's basic, as is the food on offer – but it's the only place to eat out on Yell (everything under £10). Mon–Thurs & Sun 6pm–midnight, Fri & Sat 6pm–1am.

Aywham West Sandwick ☎01957 766256, ⓦquamband wellshetland.co.uk. Large, kit-built Scandinavian-style working croft with sheep, ducks, hens and Shetland

ponies on site. There are wonderful sea views across Yell Sound, and dinner is available for an extra £15 a head. **£70**

Windhouse Lodge camping böd Mid Yell ☎01595 694688, ⓦcamping-bods.com. The Windhouse gatehouse, on the main road near Mid Yell, has a wood- and peat-fired heater and hot showers. Bring £1 coins for the electricity meter. March–Oct. Dorms **£10**

16

Fetlar

Fetlar is the most fertile of the North Isles, much of it grassy moorland and lush green meadows with masses of summer flowers. It's known as "the garden of Shetland", though that's pushing it a bit, as it's still an unforgiving, treeless landscape. **Sir Arthur Nicolson** cleared much of the island's population at forty days' notice to make room for sheep. Today, Fetlar's population of around sixty lives on the southern and eastern sides of the island.

Houbie and around

In the tiny, main settlement, **HOUBIE**, in the centre of the island, there's the **Fetlar Interpretive Centre** (May–Sept Mon–Fri 11am–4pm, Sat & Sun 12.30–4pm; £2; ☎01957 733206, ⓦfetlar.org), a welcoming museum with information on Fetlar's outstanding birdlife and the archeological excavations that took place near Houbie. For a sandy bay in which to relax, the **Sand of Tresta** is less than a mile to the west.

Loch of Funzie

Fetlar is one of very few places in Britain where you'll see the graceful **red-necked phalarope** (late May–early Aug): the birds are unusual in that the female does the courting and then leaves the male in charge of incubation. A hide has been provided overlooking the marshes (or mires) to the east of the **Loch of Funzie** (pronounced "finny"); the loch itself is also a good place at which to spot the phalaropes, and is a regular haunt of red-throated divers.

By ferry Ferries to Fetlar (Mon–Sat 7–9 daily; 25–40min) depart regularly from both Gutcher (Yell) and Belmont (Unst), and dock at Hamar's Ness, three miles northwest of Houbie.
By bus There's a Funzie to Hamar's Ness service (Mon–Sat 3–4 daily), and a dial-a-ride electric minibus service

– to use it you must book your journey the day befor (☏ 01595 745745).
By car If you do have your own vehicle, bear in mind tha there's no petrol station on Fetlar, so fill up before you com across.

ACCOMMODATION AND EATING

Aithbank Böd Aith ☏ 01595 694688, ⓦ camping -bods.com. A cosy wood-panelled cottage, a mile east of Houbie, with two rooms, sleeping a total of seven. Hot water, kitchen, solid-fuel stove. March–Oct. Dorms **£10**
Fetlar Café Houbie ☏ 01957 733227. The island's only café lives inside the island shop/post office in Houbie.

Cooked breakfasts, soup, sandwiches, toasties or a omelette all for £3 or under. Daily 11am–4pm.
Gord Houbie ☏ 01957 733227, ⓔ gordbanc @btinternet.com. The modern house attached to th island shop in Houbie is also a B&B with great sea view from all the rooms. All guests are full board only, and the do meals for non-residents by arrangement. **£100**

Unst

While much of **Unst** is rolling grassland, the coast is more dramatic: a fringe of cliffs relieved by some beautiful sandy beaches. As Britain's most northerly inhabited island, there is a surfeit of "most northerly" sights. Most visitors head straight for Hermaness to see the seabirds and look out over Muckle Flugga and the northernmost tip of Britain, to the North Pole beyond.

Muness Castle

On the south coast of the island, not far from **UYEASOUND**, lie the ruins of **Muness Castle**, a diminutive defensive structure, with matching bulging bastions and corbelle turrets at opposite corners. The castle was built in 1598 by the Scots incomer, Lauren Bruce, stepbrother and chief bullyboy of the infamous Earl Robert Stewart. The inscription above the entrance asks visitors "not to hurt this vark aluayis", but the cast was sacked by Danish pirates in 1627 and never really re-roofed.

Baltasound

Unst's main settlement is **BALTASOUND**, five miles north of Uyeasound; its herring industry used to boost the local population to around 10,000 during the fishing season. As you leave Baltasound, heading north, take a look at **Bobby's bus shelter** (ⓦ unstbusshelter.shetland.co.uk), an eccentric, fully furnished, award-winning Shetland bus shelter on the edge of the town.

Keen of Hamar

The **Keen of Hamar**, east of Baltasound and clearly signposted from the main road, is or of the largest expanses of serpentine debris in Europe and home to an extraordinary arr of plant life. It's worth taking a walk on this barren, exposed, almost lunar landscape that's thought to resemble what most of northern Europe looked like at the end of the last ice age. Armed with a Scottish National Heritage leaflet (kept in a box by the stile), you can identify some of the area's numerous rare and minuscule plants, including Norwegian sandwort, frog orchid, moonwort and the mouse-eared Edmondston's chickweed, which flowers in June and July and is found nowhere else in the world.

Haroldswick

Near the shore, at **HAROLDSWICK**, you'll find the **Unst Boat Haven** (May–Sept Mon–. 11am–4pm, Sun 2–4pm; ☏ 01957 711809; £3), displaying a beautifully presented collection of historic boats along with many tools of the trade and information on fishing. If you want to learn about other aspects of Unst's history, head for the nearb

Unst Heritage Centre (May–Sept Mon–Sat 11am–4pm, Sun 2–4pm; £3; ☎01957 711528), housed in the old school building by the main crossroads, where they also put on have-a-go activities such as spinning, knitting and potting.

Saxa Vord RAF base

Just north of Haroldswick is **SAXA VORD** (also, confusingly, the name of the nearby hill), home to the eyesore former **RAF base**, containing a hotel, restaurant, bar and hostel, and a **chocolate factory** (Mon–Sat 11.30am–5pm, Sun 1–4pm; free; ✆foordschocolates.co.uk), where there's also a basic café and an **exhibition** on the history of the RAF on Unst. The former base is also home to Britain's most northerly brewery, the **Valhalla Brewery**, source of Shetland Ales (visits by appointment; ☎01957 711658, ✆valhallabrewery.co.uk), and **Shetland Reel**, its most northerly gin distillery Tues, Thurs & Sat visits by appointment; ☎01957 711217, ✆shetlandreel.com).

Hermaness Nature Reserve

The road that heads off northwest from Haroldswick leads eventually to the bleak headland of **Hermaness**, home to more than 100,000 nesting seabirds (May–Aug). There's an excellent **visitor centre** in the former lighthouse keepers' shore station, where you can pick up a leaflet showing the marked routes across the reserve. Whatever you do, stick to the path so as to avoid annoying the vast numbers of nesting great skuas. From Hermaness Hill, you can look down over the jagged rocks of the wonderfully named Vesta Skerry, Rumblings, Tipta Skerry and **Muckle Flugga**. There are few more dramatic settings for a lighthouse than Muckle Flugga, and few sites could ever have presented as great a challenge to the builders, who erected it in 1858. Beyond the lighthouse is **Out Stack**, the most northerly bit of Britain. The views from here are marvellous, as is the birdlife; there's a huge gannetry on one of the stacks, and puffins burrow all along the clifftops.

16

ARRIVAL AND TOURS   UNST

ferry Ferries (☎01595 745804) shuttle regularly across Bluemull Sound from Gutcher on Yell over to Belmont on Unst (every 30min–1hr; 10min).

bus An integrated bus and ferry service goes from Lerwick to Baltasound on Unst (Mon–Sat 1–2 daily; 2hr 40min). From Belmont, Unst's ferry terminal, buses run to Baltasound (Mon–Sat 3–4 daily; 15min), Haroldswick (Mon–Sat 3–4 daily; 30min) and Uyeasound (Mon–Sat 3–4 daily; 10min).

Boat trips If your sea legs are better than your walking boots, you can opt to see the great seabird colonies of Hermaness with Muckle Flugga Charters (☎01806 522447, ✆muckleflugga.co.uk), operating out of Baltasound or Burrafirth.

ACCOMMODATION

Gardiesfauld Uyeasound ☎01957 755279, ✆www.gardiesfauld.shetland.co.uk. A large, clean, modern hostel near Uyeasound pier which allows camping, and offers bike rental. April–Sept. Dorms £15; camping per person £6

Prestagaard Uyeasound ☎01957 755234, ✉prestegaard@postmaster.co.uk. This attractive, whitewashed Victorian B&B, with just three rooms, is situated in Uyeasound, and has great sea views – they offer dinner for residents and non-residents, as well as bargain "unserviced" rooms for those who just want a bed for the night. April–Oct. £55

EATING AND DRINKING

Baltasound Hotel Baltasound ☎01957 711334, ✆baltasoundhotel.co.uk. Wherever you stay, it's a good idea to book yourself in for dinner or self-cater – the only other option is the bar food at the *Baltasound Hotel* (mains £12–18). Food served daily 5–8pm.

Skibhoul Café & Stores Baltasound ☎01957 711444. The island's main shop is attached to the local bakery (founded in 1885), has the odd chip supper night and will fill your flask – there's also a self-service café and reading corner in the store. Mon–Sat 9.30am–5.30pm.

Victoria's Vintage Tea Room Haroldswick ☎01957 711885, ✆victoriasvintagetearooms.co.uk. Bone china, patterned bunting and checked tablecloths for a surreal "high tea" experience in this cheerful tearoom close to Unst Boat Haven, with views across the bay. April–Sept Tues–Sat 11am–5pm, Sun 2–5pm.

CELTIC CROSS, KILDALTON

Contexts

History

Scotland's colourful and compelling history looms large, not just for visitors to the country, but for its inhabitants too. Often the nation's history has been defined either by fierce internecine conflict or epic struggles with England, yet from earliest times the influences of Ireland, Scandinavia and Continental Europe have been as important, particularly in aspects of Scotland's creative and cultural development. This has nurtured a sophistication and ambition in Scots that few associate with the land of warring clans and burning castles, peppering the country's story not just with tragic yet romantic heroes, but also notable fighters, innovators and politicians.

Prehistoric Scotland

Scotland, like the rest of prehistoric Britain, was settled by successive waves of peoples arriving from the east. These first inhabitants were **hunter-gatherers**, whose heaps of animal bones and shells have been excavated, among other places, in the caves along the coast near East Wemyss in Fife. Around 4500 BC, **Neolithic farming peoples** from the European mainland began moving into Scotland. To provide themselves with land for their cereal crops and grazing for their livestock, they cleared large areas of upland forest, usually by fire, and in the process created the characteristic moorland landscapes of much of modern Scotland. These early farmers established permanent settlements, some of which, like **Skara Brae** on Orkney, were near the sea, enabling them to supplement their diet by fishing and develop their skills as boat-builders.

Settlement spurred the development of more complex forms of religious belief. The Neolithic peoples built large chambered burial mounds or **cairns**, such as **Maes Howe** in Orkney. This reverence for human remains suggests a belief in some form of afterlife, a concept that the next wave of settlers, the **Beaker people**, certainly believed in. They placed pottery beakers filled with drink in the tombs of their dead to assist the passage of the deceased on their journey to, or their stay in, the next world. They also built the mysterious **stone circles**, thirty of which have been discovered in Scotland, including that of **Callanish** (Calanais) on the Isle of Lewis. The exact function of the circles is still unknown, but many of the stones are aligned with the sun at certain points in its annual cycle, suggesting that the monuments are related to the changing of the seasons.

The Beaker people also brought the **Bronze Age** to Scotland. Bronze, an alloy of copper and tin, was stronger and more flexible than flint, which had long been used for axe-heads and knives. Agricultural needs plus new weaponry resulted in a state of endemic warfare as villagers raided their neighbours to steal livestock and grain. The Bronze Age peoples responded to the danger by developing a range of defences, among them spectacular **hillforts** and **crannogs**, smaller settlements built on artificial islands.

4500 BC	3000 BC	2000 BC	100 BC–100 AD
Neolithic people move to Scotland.	Neolithic township of Skara Brae built.	Callanish standing stones erected on Lewis in the Western Isles.	Fortified Iron Age brochs built across Scotland.

The Celts and the Picts

Conflict in Scotland intensified in the first millennium BC as successive waves of **Celtic** settlers, arriving from the south and using iron, competed for land. These fractious times witnessed the construction of hundreds of **brochs** or fortified towers. Concentrated along the Atlantic coast and in the northern and western isles, the brochs were dry-stone fortifications often over 40ft in height; the best-preserved can be found on the Shetland island of **Mousa**.

At the end of the prehistoric period, immediately before the arrival of the Romans, Scotland was divided among a number of warring Iron Age tribes, who, apart from raiding, were preoccupied with wresting a living from the land, growing barley and oats, rearing sheep, hunting deer and fishing for salmon. The Romans gave them their collective name Picti, or **Picts**, meaning painted people, after their body tattoos.

The Romans

The **Roman conquest** of Britain began in 43 AD. By 80 AD the Roman governor, Agricola, felt secure enough in the south of Britannia (Britain) to begin an invasion of **Caledonia** (Scotland), building a string of forts across the Clyde–Forth line and defeating the Caledonian tribes at the **Battle of Mons Graupius**. The long-term effect of his campaign, however, was slight. Work on a major fort – to be the base for 5000 soldiers – at Inchtuthill, on the Tay, was abandoned and the legions withdrew. In 123 AD **Emperor Hadrian** sealed the frontier against the northern tribes and built **Hadrian's Wall**, which stretched from the Solway Firth to the Tyne and was the first formal division of the island of Britain. Twenty years later, the Romans again ventured north and built the **Antonine Wall** between the Clyde and the Forth. This was manned for about forty years, but the Romans largely gave up their attempt to subjugate the north and instead adopted a policy of containment.

The Romans produced the first **written** accounts of Scotland. Dio Cassius, writing in 197 AD, captures the common Roman contempt of their Pictish neighbours:

They live in huts, go naked and unshod. They mostly have a democratic government, and are much addicted to robbery. They can bear hunger and cold and all manner of hardship; they will retire into their marshes and hold out for days with only their heads above water, and in the forest they will subsist on barks and roots.

The Dark Ages

Following the departure of the Romans, traditionally put at 410 AD, the population of Scotland changed considerably. By 500 the **Picts** occupied the northern isles, and the north and the east as far south as Fife. Today their settlements can be identified by place names with a "Pit" prefix, such as Pitlochry, and by the existence of carved symbol stones like those found at Aberlemno in Angus. To the west, between Dumbarton and Carlisle was a population of **Britons**. Many of the Briton leaders had Roman names, suggesting that they were a Romanized Celtic people, possibly a combination of tribes maintained by the Romans as a buffer between Hadrian's Wall and the northern tribes, and peoples pushed west by the Anglo-Saxon invaders landing on the east coast. Both the Britons and the Picts spoke variations of P-Celtic, from which Welsh, Cornish and Breton developed

43 AD	83	142
The Roman conquest of Britain begins.	The Romans defeat the British tribes at the Battle of Mons Graupius in northeast Scotland.	The Romans build the Antonine Wall between the Firth of Forth and the Firth of Clyde.

THE NORTHERN ISLES

With their sophisticated ships and navigational skills, the **Vikings**, beginning their expansion in the eighth century, soon gained supremacy over the Pictish peoples in Shetland, Orkney, the extreme northeast corner of the mainland and the Western Isles. For the next six centuries the Northern Isles were distinct from the rest of what is now called Scotland, becoming a base for raiding and colonization in Britain and Ireland, and forming links with the Faroes, Iceland, Greenland and, more tenuously, North America. Norse culture flourished, and buildings such as St Magnus Cathedral in Kirkwall, Orkney, give some idea of its energy. However, there were bouts of unrest, and finally Shetland was brought under direct rule from Norway at the end of the twelfth century.

When Norway united with Sweden under the Danish Crown in the fourteenth century, **Norse power** began to wane and Scottish influence to increase. In 1469, a marriage was arranged between Margaret, daughter of the Danish King Christian I, and the future King James III of Scotland. Short of cash for Margaret's dowry, Christian mortgaged Orkney to Scotland in 1468, followed by Shetland in 1469; neither pledge was ever successfully redeemed. The laws, religion and administration of the Northern Isles became Scottish, though their Norse heritage is still very evident in place names, dialect and culture.

On the west coast, to the north and west of the Britons, lived the **Scotti**, Irish-Celtic invaders who eventually gave their name to the whole country. The first Scotti arrived in the Western Isles from Ireland in the fourth century AD, and about a century later their great king, Fergus Mor, moved his base from Antrim to Dunadd, near Lochgilphead, where he founded the kingdom of Dalriada. The Scotti spoke Q-Celtic, the precursor of modern Gaelic. On the east coast, the Germanic **Anglo-Saxons** had sailed north along the coast to settle around Dunbar in East Lothian. The final addition to the ethnic mix was also non-Celtic; from around 800 AD, **Norse** invaders began to arrive, settling mainly in the Northern Isles and the northeast of the mainland.

Many of the Britons had been **Christians** since Roman times and it was a Briton, St Ninian, who conducted the first missionary work among the Picts at the end of the fourth century. Attempts to convert the Picts were resumed in the sixth century by St **Columba**, one of the Gaelic-speaking Scotti, who established the island of **Iona** as a centre of Christian culture, opening the way for many peaceable contacts between the Picts and Scotti. Intermarriage became commonplace and the Scotti king **Kenneth MacAlpine**, who united Dalriada and Pictland in 843 AD, was the son of a Pictish princess. Similarly, MacAlpine's creation of the united kingdom of **Alba**, later known as Scotia, was part of a process of integration rather than outright conquest. Kenneth and his successors gradually expanded their kingdom by marriage and force of arms until, by 1034, almost all of what we now call Scotland was under their rule.

The Middle Ages

The succession of **Malcolm III**, known as Canmore ("Bighead"), in 1057 marked the beginning of a period of fundamental change in Scottish society. Having spent seventeen years at the English court, Malcolm sought to apply to Scotland a range of ideas he had brought back with him. He and his heirs established a secure dynasty based on succession through the male line (as opposed to the female succession

2	**397**	**563**
Romans withdraw from Antonine Wall and retreat behind Hadrian's Wall.	St Ninian establishes the first Christian church north of Hadrian's Wall.	St Columba founds a monastery on Iona and begins to convert the Picts.

practised by the Picts) and introduced **feudalism** into Scotland, a system that was diametrically opposed to the Gaelic system – the followers of a Gaelic king were his kindred, whereas the followers of a feudal king were vassals bought with land. The Canmores, independent of the local nobility, who remained a military threat, also began to reform the **Church**. This development started with **Margaret**, Malcolm III's English wife, who brought Scottish religious practices into line with those of the rest of Europe. **David I** continued the process by importing monks to found a series of monasteries, principally along the border at Kelso, Melrose, Jedburgh and Dryburgh. Similarly, the dynasty founded a series of **royal burghs**, towns such as Edinburgh, Stirling and Berwick, recognized as centres of trade. Their charters usually granted a measure of self-government, and the monarchy hoped this liberality would both encourage loyalty and increase the prosperity of the kingdom. Scotland's Gaelic-speaking clans had little influence within the burghs, and gradually Scots – a northern version of Anglo-Saxon – became the main **language** throughout the Lowlands.

The Wars of Scottish Independence

In 1286 Alexander III died, and a hotly disputed succession gave **Edward I**, King of England, an opportunity to subjugate Scotland. In 1291 Edward presided over a conference where the rival claimants to the Scottish throne presented their cases. Edward chose **John Balliol** over **Robert the Bruce**, his main rival; he obliged Balliol to pay him homage, thus turning Scotland into a vassal kingdom. Bruce refused to accept the decision and in 1295 Balliol renounced his allegiance to Edward and sided with France – beginning what is known as the "**Auld Alliance**". In the ensuing conflict, the Bruce family sided with the English, Balliol was defeated and imprisoned, and Edward seized control of almost all of Scotland.

Edward had shown little mercy during his conquest of Scotland – he had most of the population of Berwick massacred – and his cruelty provoked a truly national resistance. This focused on **William Wallace**, a man of relatively lowly origins who raised an army of peasants, lesser knights and townsmen that was fundamentally different to the armies raised by the nobility. Figures like Balliol, holding lands in England, France and Scotland, were part of an international aristocracy for whom warfare was the means by which they struggled for power. Wallace, by contrast, led proto-nationalist forces determined to expel the English from their country. Probably for that very reason Wallace never received the support of the nobility and, after a bitter ten-year campaign during which he notched up a couple of notable victories over English armies, he was betrayed and executed in London in 1305.

In 1306 Robert the Bruce defied Edward and had himself crowned king of Scotland. Edward died the following year, but the unrest dragged on until 1314, when Bruce decisively defeated a huge English army under Edward II at the **Battle of Bannockburn**. At last Bruce was firmly in control of his kingdom, and in 1320 the Scots asserted their right to independence in a successful petition to the pope, now known as the **Declaration of Arbroath**.

The Stewart dynasty

Following Bruce's death in 1329, the Scottish monarchy gradually declined in influence. The last of the Bruce dynasty died in 1371, to be succeeded by the

843	**1286**	**1296**
Kenneth MacAlpine becomes the first king of the Scots and the Picts.	Death of Alexander III sparks the Wars of Scottish Independence.	Edward I of England invades Scotland.

FLODDEN FIELD

In 1513, possibly the largest Scots army ever to invade England was decimated by the English at **Flodden Field**, just south of the border. The English king Henry VIII had invaded France, and the Scots, under James IV, opted to stand by the Auld Alliance with France and invade England. The Scots army, numbering around 30,000, took several English strongholds before being confronted near Branxton, three miles southeast of Coldstream.

The English artillery was lighter and more manoeuvral, and forced the Scots to come down off their advantageous position on **Branxton Hill**. The heavily armoured Scottish noblemen got stuck in the mud, and their over-long **pikes** and lances proved no match for the English **bills** (like a hooked halberd). English losses were heavy, but the Scots lost as many as 10,000, including the king himself, his son (an archbishop), nine earls, fourteen lords and numerous Highland clan chiefs, all of whom fought at the head of their troops. After the battle, James's blood-stained surcoat was sent to Henry, but his body was denied burial and no one knows what became of it.

If Bannockburn was Scotland's greatest victory over the English, and Bonnie Prince Charlie's last stand at Culloden their most noble defeat, Flodden was simply an unmitigated disaster. It became the subject of numerous songs and ballads and remains a painful memory for Scots even today. The English, meanwhile, have forgotten all about it.

Stewards", hence **Stewarts**, but thereafter a succession of Scottish rulers, culminating with James VI in 1567, came to the throne when still children. The power vacuum was filled by the nobility, whose key members exercised control as Scotland's regents. The more vigorous monarchs of the period, notably **James I**, did their best to curb the power of such families, but their efforts were usually nullified by the next regency. **James IV** might have restored the authority of the Crown, but his invasion of England ended in a terrible defeat for the Scots – and his own death – at the **Battle of Flodden Field**.

The reign of **Mary, Queen of Scots** (1542–67), typified the problems of the Scottish monarchy. Mary came to the throne when just one week old, and immediately the English king, Henry VIII, sought to marry her to his 5-year-old son, Edward. Beginning in 1544, the English launched a series of devastating attacks on Scotland, an episode Sir Walter Scott later called the "Rough Wooing", until, in the face of another English invasion in 1548, the Scots – or at least those not supporting Henry – turned to the "Auld Alliance". The French king proposed marriage between Mary and the Dauphin Francis, promising military assistance against the English. The six-year-old queen sailed for France in 1548, leaving her loyal nobles and their French allies in control. When she returned thirteen years later, following the death of Francis, she had to pick her way through the rival ambitions of her nobility and deal with something entirely new – the religious Reformation.

The Reformation

The **Reformation** in Scotland was a complex social process, whose threads are often hard to unravel. Nevertheless, it is quite clear that, by the end of the sixteenth century, the established Church was held in general contempt. Many of the higher clergy regarded their relationship with the Church purely in economic terms, and forty percent of known illegitimate births were the product of the "celibate" clergy's liaisons.

Another spur to the Scottish Reformation was the identification of Protestantism with anti-French feeling. In 1554 **Mary of Guise**, the French mother of the absent Queen Mary, had become regent, and her habit of appointing Frenchmen to high office was seen as an attempt to subordinate Scotland's interests to those of France. There was considerable resentment, and in 1560, with English military backing, Protestant nobles succeeded in deposing the French regent. When the Scottish Parliament assembled, it asserted the primacy of Protestantism by forbidding the Mass and abolishing the authority of the pope. The nobility proceeded to confiscate two-thirds of Church lands, a huge prize that did much to bolster their new beliefs.

The return of Mary, Queen of Scots

Even without the economic incentives, Protestantism was a highly charged political doctrine. **Luther** had argued that each individual's conscience was capable of discerning God's will. This meant that a hierarchical priesthood, existing to interpret God's will, was unnecessary. This point was made very clearly to Queen Mary by the Protestant reformer **John Knox** at their first meeting on her return in 1561. Subjects, he told her, were not bound to obey an ungodly monarch.

Mary ducked and weaved, trying to avoid an open breach with her Protestant subjects. At the same time, she was engaged in a balancing act between the factions of the Scottish nobility. Her difficulties were exacerbated by her disastrous second marriage to **Lord Darnley**, a cruel and politically inept character, whose jealousy led to his involvement in the murder of Mary's favourite, David Rizzio, who was dragged from the queen's supper room at Holyrood and stabbed 56 times. The incident disturbed the Scottish Protestants, but they were entirely scandalized in 1567 when Darnley himself was murdered and Mary promptly married the **Earl of Bothwell**, widely believed to be the murderer. The Scots rose in rebellion, driving Mary into exile in England at the age of just 25. The queen's illegitimate half-brother, the Earl of Moray, became regent, and her son, the infant James, was left behind to be raised a Protestant prince. Mary, meanwhile, became perceived as such a threat to the English throne that Queen Elizabeth I had her executed in 1587.

Knox could now concentrate on the organization of the reformed Church, or **Kirk**, which he envisaged as a body with power over the daily lives of the people. **Andrew Melville**, another leading reformer, wished to push this theocratic vision further. He proposed the abolition of all traces of the rule of bishops in the Church and that the Kirk should adopt a **Presbyterian** structure, administered by a hierarchy of assemblies, part-elected and part-appointed.

The religious wars

James VI disliked Presbyterianism because its quasi-democratic structure appeared to threaten his authority. He was, however, unable to resist the reformers until, strengthened by his installation as James I of England after Elizabeth's death in 1603, he restored the Scottish bishops in 1610. Raised in Episcopalian England, James's son **Charles I** had little understanding of Scottish reformism. His belief in the Divine Right of Kings was entirely counter to Protestant thought. In 1637 Charles attempted to impose a new prayer book on the Kirk, laying down forms of worship in line with th

1413	**1468**	**1482**
University of St Andrews is founded.	James III marries Margaret of Denmark and receives Orkney and Shetland as part of her dowry.	Berwick-upon-Tweed captu by the English.

High Anglican Church. The reformers denounced these changes as "popery" and organized the **National Covenant**, a religious pledge "to recover the purity and liberty of the Gospel as it was established and professed".

Charles declared all the "**Covenanters**" to be rebels, but when he called a General Assembly of the Kirk, it promptly abolished the episcopacy. Charles pronounced the proceedings illegal, but lack of finance stopped him from mounting an effective military campaign – whereas the Covenanters, well financed by the Kirk, assembled a proficient army under Alexander Leslie. In desperation, Charles summoned the English Parliament, the first for eleven years, hoping it would pay for an army. However, Parliament was much keener to criticize his policies than to raise taxes. In response, Charles declared war on Parliament in 1642.

Until 1650, Scotland was ruled by the Covenanters, and the power of the Presbyterian Kirk grew considerably. Laws were passed establishing schools in every parish and, less usefully, banning trade with Catholic countries. The only effective opposition to the theocratic state came from the **Marquis of Montrose**, who had initially supported the Covenant but lined up with the king when war broke out. His army was drawn from the Highlands and Islands, where the Kirk's influence was weakest. Montrose won several notable victories against the Covenanters, but the reluctance of his troops to stay south of the Highland Line made it impossible to capitalize on these successes, and he was eventually captured and executed in 1650.

The Civil War and the Restoration

Montrose's campaigns, however, were a side show to the **Civil War** being waged further south. Here, the Covenanters and the English Parliamentarians faced the same royal enemy and in 1643 formed an uneasy alliance. There was, however, friction between the allies. Many Parliamentarians, including Cromwell, favoured a looser form of doctrinal control within the state Church than the Presbyterians did. They also suspected the Scots of hankering after the return of the monarchy, a suspicion confirmed when, at the invitation of the earl of Argyll, the future Charles II came back to Scotland in 1650. To regain his Scottish kingdom, Charles was obliged to renounce his father and sign the Covenant, two bitter pills taken to impress the population. In the event, the "Presbyterian restoration" was short-lived. Cromwell invaded, defeated the Scots at Dunbar and forced Charles into exile. Until the Restoration of 1660, Scotland was united with England and governed by even commissioners.

Although the restoration of **Charles II** brought bishops back to the Kirk, they were integrated into an essentially Presbyterian structure of Kirk sessions and presbyteries, and the General Assembly, which had been abolished by Cromwell, was not re-established. More than three hundred clergymen, a third of the Scottish ministry, refused to accept the reinstatement of the bishops and were edged out of the Church and forced to hold open-air services, called **Conventicles**, which Charles attempted to suppress.

Charles II was succeeded by his brother **James VII** (James II of England), whose overt Catholicism caused a Protestant backlash in England. In 1689, he was forced into exile in France and the throne passed to **Mary**, his Protestant daughter, and her Dutch husband, **William of Orange**. In Scotland there was a brief flurry of

13	1560	1587
Scots are defeated by English at the Battle of Flodden Field.	The Scottish Church breaks with the Roman Catholic Church.	Mary, Queen of Scots, is executed on the orders of Queen Elizabeth I.

opposition to William when **Graham of Claverhouse**, known as "Bonnie Dundee", united the Jacobite clans against the government army at the **Battle of Killiekrankie**, just north of Pitlochry. However, the inspirational Claverhouse was killed on the point of victory, the clans dispersed and the threat passed. In Scotland, William and Mary restored the full Presbyterian structure and abolished bishops, though they chose not to restore the political and legal functions of the Kirk, which remained subject to parliamentary control.

The Union

From 1689 to 1697, William was at war with France, a war partly financed by Scottish taxes and partly fought by Scottish soldiers. Yet many Scots, mindful of the Auld Alliance, disapproved of the war and others suffered financially from the disruption to trade with France. There were other economic irritants too, principally the legally sanctioned monopoly that English merchants had over trade with the English colonies. This monopoly inspired the **Darien Scheme**, a plan to establish a Scottish colony in Panama. The colonists set off in 1698, but the scheme proved a miserable failure. The colony collapsed with the loss of £200,000 – an amount equal to half the value

THE HIGHLANDS

The country that was united with England in 1707 contained three distinct cultures: in south and east Scotland, they spoke **Scots**; the local dialect in Shetland, Orkney and the far northeast, though Scots-based, contained elements of **Norn** (Old Norse); while the language of the rest of north and west Scotland, including the Hebrides, was **Gaelic**. These linguistic differences were paralleled by different forms of social organization and customs. The people of north and west Scotland were mostly **pastoralists**, moving their sheep and cattle to Highland pastures in the summer and returning to the glens in the winter. They lived in single-room dwellings, heated by a central peat fire and sometimes shared with livestock, and in hard times they subsisted on cakes made from the blood of their live cattle mixed with oatmeal. **Highlanders** supplemented their meagre income by raiding their clan neighbours and the prosperous Lowlands, whose inhabitants regarded their northern compatriots with a mixture of fear and contempt.

However, the institutions of this society had not existed from time immemorial. This is especially true of the "**clan**", a term that only appears in its modern usage in the sixteenth century. In theory, the clan bound together blood relatives who shared a common ancestor, a concept clearly derived from the ancient Gaelic notion of kinship. But in practice many of the clans were of non-Gaelic origin – such as the Frasers, Sinclairs and Stewarts, all of Anglo-Norman descent – and it was the mythology of a common ancestor, rather than the actuality, that cemented the clans together. Furthermore, clans were often made up of people with a variety of surnames, and there is evidence of individuals changing their names when they swapped allegiances.

It was not until the late seventeenth century that certain **tartans** became associated with particular clans. Previously, Highlanders wore a simple belted plaid wrapped around the body. The detailed codification of the tartan was produced by the Victorians, whose romantic vision of Highland life originated with George IV's visit to Scotland in 1822, when he appeared in an elaborate version of Highland dress, complete with flesh-coloured tights.

1592	1603	1638	1650
Presbyterianism becomes the established religion.	James VI of Scotland becomes James I of England.	National Covenant proclaimed by Scottish Presbyterians.	The Scots Royalist army are defeated at the Battle of Dunbar the English under Oliver Cromwe

f the entire coinage in Scotland – and an angry Scottish Parliament threatened to efuse the king taxes as rioting broke out in the cities.

The situation in Scotland was further complicated by the question of the succession. Mary died without leaving an heir and, on William's death in 1702, the crown passed to her sister **Anne**, who was also childless. The English Parliament secured the Protestant succession by passing the Act of Settlement, naming the Electress Sophia of Hanover as the next in line to the throne. The Act did not, however, apply in Scotland, and the English feared that the Scots would invite James Edward Stewart back from France to be their king. Consequently, Parliament appointed commissioners charged with the consideration of "proper methods towards attaining a union with Scotland".

In response the Scottish Parliament passed the **Act of Security** in 1703, stating that Scotland would not accept a Hanoverian monarch unless they had first received guarantees protecting their religion and their trade.

Nevertheless the Scottish Parliament unexpectedly passed the **Act of Union** by 110 votes to 69 in January 1707. Some historians have explained the vote in terms of bribery and corruption. This certainly played a part (the Duke of Hamilton, for example, switched sides at a key moment and was rewarded with an English dukedom), but there were other factors. Scottish politicians were divided between the Cavaliers Jacobites (supporters of the Stewarts) and Episcopalians – and the Country party, whose Presbyterian members dreaded the return of the Stewarts more than they disliked the Hanoverians. There were commercial considerations too. In 1705 the English Parliament had passed the Alien Act, which threatened to impose penalties on cross-border trade, whereas the Union gave merchants of both countries free access to each other's markets. The Act of Union also guaranteed the Scottish legal system and the Presbyterian Kirk, and offered compensation to those who had lost money in the Darien Scheme.

Under the terms of the Act, both parliaments were to be replaced by a new British Parliament based in London, with the Scots apportioned 45 MPs and 16 peers. There were riots when the terms became known, but no sustained opposition.

The Jacobite risings

When James VII (II) was deposed he fled to France, where he planned the reconquest of his kingdom with the support of the French king. In 1702, James's successor, William, died, and the hopes of the Stewarts passed to James, the "Old Pretender" Pretender in the sense of having pretensions to the throne; Old to distinguish him from his son Charles, the "Young Pretender"). James's followers became known as Jacobites, derived from Jacobus, the Latin equivalent of James. The accession to the Scottish throne of the Hanoverian George I, son of Sophia, Electress of Hanover, marked the **Jacobite uprising of 1715**. Its timing appeared perfect. Scottish opinion was moving against the Union, which had failed to bring Scotland any tangible economic benefits. The English had also been accused of bad faith when, contrary to their pledges, they attempted to impose their legal practices on the Scots. There were also many in England who toasted the "king across the water" and showed no enthusiasm for the new German ruler. In September 1715 the fiercely Jacobite John Erskine, Earl of Mar, raised the Stewart standard at Braemar Castle. Eight days later, he captured

89	1692	1695	1698
uccessful Jacobite sing against am of Orange.	Glencoe massacre: 38 members of the MacDonald clan murdered by anti-Jacobite Campbells.	Bank of Scotland is established.	1200 Scots leave in order to establish a colony in Panama.

Perth, where he gathered an army of more than 10,000 men, drawn mostly from the Episcopalians of northeast Scotland and from the Highlands. Mar's rebellion took the government by surprise. They had only four thousand soldiers in Scotland, under the command of the Duke of Argyll, but Mar dithered and lost the military advantage. The **Battle of Sheriffmuir** in November was indecisive, but by the time the Old Pretender arrived the following month six thousand veteran Dutch troops had reinforced Argyll. The rebellion disintegrated and James slunk back to exile in France in February 1716.

The **Jacobite uprising of 1745**, led by James's dashing son, Charles Edward Stewart (known as "**Bonnie Prince Charlie**"), had little chance of success. The Hanoverians had consolidated their hold on the English throne and Lowland society was uniformly loyalist. Despite early successes which allowed him to march as far south as Derby,

BONNIE PRINCE CHARLIE

Prince Charles Edward Stewart – better known as **Bonnie Prince Charlie** or "The Young Pretender" – was born in 1720 in Rome, where his father, "The Old Pretender", claimant to the British throne (as the son of James VII), was living in exile with his Polish wife. At the age of 25, with no knowledge of Gaelic, an imperfect grasp of English and a strong Catholic faith, the prince set out in disguise for Scotland with two French ships. He arrived on the Hebridean island of **Eriskay** (see p.523) on July 23, 1745, with just seven companions, and was immediately implored to return to France by the clan chiefs, who were singularly unimpressed by his lack of army. Charles was unmoved and went on to raise the royal standard at **Glenfinnan** (see p.443), thus signalling the beginning of the **Jacobite uprising**. He only attracted fewer than half of the potential 20,000 clansmen who could have marched with him, and promises of support from the French and English Jacobites failed to materialize. Nevertheless, after a decisive victory over government forces at the **Battle of Prestonpans**, near Edinburgh, Charles made a spectacular advance into England, getting as far as Derby. London was in a state of panic: its shops were closed and the Bank of England, fearing a run on sterling, slowed withdrawals by paying out in sixpences. But Derby was as far as Charles got. On December 6, threatened by superior forces, the Jacobites decided to retreat to Scotland, against Charles's wishes. Pursued back to Scotland by the Duke of Cumberland, he won one last victory, at Falkirk, before the final disaster at **Culloden** (see p.418) in April 1746.

The prince spent the following five months in hiding, with a price of £30,000 on his head, and literally thousands of government troops searching for him. He certainly endured his fair share of cold and hunger while on the run, but the real price was paid by the Highlanders themselves, who risked their lives (and often paid for it with them) by aiding and abetting the prince. The most famous of these was 23-year-old **Flora MacDonald**, whom Charles first met on South Uist in June 1746. Flora was persuaded to convey Charles "over the sea to Skye", disguised as an Irish servant girl by the name of Betty Burke. She was arrested just seven days after parting with the prince in Portree, and held in the Tower of London until July 1747.

Charles boarded a ship back to France in September 1746, but, despite his promises – "for all that has happened, Madam, I hope we shall meet in St James's yet" – never returned to Scotland, nor did he ever see Flora again. After a string of mistresses, he eventually got married at the age of 52 to the 19-year-old **Princess Louise of Stolberg-Gedern** in an effort to produce a Stewart heir. They had no children, and she fled from his violent drunkenness; in 1788, a none-too-"bonnie" Prince Charles died in the arms of his illegitimate daughter in Rome. Bonnie Prince Charlie became a romantic legend but the real consequence of 1745 was the virtual annihilation of the Highland way of life.

1707	1715	1746	1759
The Act of Union unites the kingdoms of Scotland and England.	Jacobite uprising against the accession of Hanoverian King George I.	Bonnie Prince Charlie's Jacobite army is defeated at the Battle of Culloden.	Scotland's Natio[n] Poet, Rabbie Bu[r] is born in Allowa[y]

Charles was ultimately forced to retreat and finally met his match at the **Battle of Culloden**, near Inverness, in April 1746, the last set-piece battle on British soil. Outnumbered and outgunned, the Jacobites were swept from the field, with more than 1500 men killed or wounded compared to the Duke of Cumberland's 300 or so. After the battle, many of the wounded Jacobites were slaughtered, an atrocity that earned Cumberland the nickname "Butcher".

In the aftermath of the uprising, the wearing of tartan, the bearing of arms and the playing of bagpipes were all banned. Rebel chiefs lost their land and the Highlands were placed under military occupation. Most significantly, the government prohibited the private armies of the chiefs, thereby effectively destroying the clan system.

The Highland Clearances

Once the clan chief was forbidden his own army, he had no need of the large tenantry that had previously been a vital military asset. Conversely, the second half of the eighteenth century saw the Highland population increase dramatically after the introduction of the easy-to-grow and nutritious **potato**. Between 1745 and 1811, the population of the Outer Hebrides, for example, rose from 13,000 to 24,500. The clan chiefs adopted different policies to deal with this. Some encouraged emigration, and as many as six thousand Highlanders left for the Americas between 1800 and 1803. Others developed alternative forms of employment for their tenantry, mainly fishing and gathering kelp (seaweed), while some developed **sheep runs** on the Highland pastures, introducing hardy breeds. But extensive sheep farming proved incompatible with a high peasant population and many landowners decided to clear their estates of tenants, some of whom were forcibly moved to tiny plots of marginal land, where they were to farm as **crofters**.

The pace of these **Highland Clearances** accelerated after the end of the Napoleonic Wars in 1815, when the market price for kelp, fish and cattle declined, leaving sheep as the only profitable Highland product. The most notorious Clearances took place on the estates of the countess of Sutherland, who owned a million acres in northern Scotland. Between 1807 and 1821, around 15,000 people were thrown off her land, often with considerable brutality. As the dispossessed Highlanders scratched a living from the acid soils of tiny crofts, they learnt through bitter experience the limitations of the clan. Famine forced large-scale emigration to America and Canada, leaving the huge uninhabited areas found in the region today.

However, not all landowners acted cruelly or insensitively and many settlements around Scotland, from Inveraray in the west to Portsoy in the northeast, owe their existence to so-called "improving landlords", who invested in infrastructure such as fishing harbours, decent housing and communities of sustainable size. They brought economic prosperity to previously disadvantaged areas. Those left crofting, however, still led a precarious existence, often taking seasonal employment away from home. In 1886, in response to the social unrest, Gladstone's Liberal government passed the **Crofters' Holdings Act**, granting three of the crofters' demands: security of tenure, fair rents to be decided independently and the right to pass on crofts by inheritance. But Gladstone did not increase the amount of land available for crofting and shortage of land remained a major problem until the

62	1843	1846	1886
Beginning of the Highland Clearances.	The Great Disruption: a third of the Church of Scotland leave to form the Free Church of Scotland.	Highland potato famine: 1.7 million Scots emigrate.	Crofters' Holdings Act grants security of tenure in the Highlands and Islands.

Land Settlement Act of 1919 made provision for the creation of new crofts. Nevertheless, the population of the Highlands has continued to decline since then, with many of the region's young people finding life in the city more appealing, and work opportunities there much greater.

Industrialization

Glasgow was the powerhouse of Scotland's **Industrial Revolution**. The passage from Glasgow to the Americas was much shorter than that from rival English ports and a lucrative transatlantic trade in tobacco had developed as early as the seventeenth century. This stimulated Scottish manufacturing, since, under the terms of the Navigation Acts, Americans were not allowed to trade manufactured goods. Scottish-produced linen, paper and wrought iron were exchanged for Virginia tobacco and, when the American War of Independence disrupted trade in the 1770s and 1780s, the Scots successfully turned to trade with the West Indies and, most important of all, to the production of cotton. In 1787, Scotland had only 19 textile mills; by 1840 the were nearly 200.

The growth of the textile industry spurred the development of other industries. In th mid-eighteenth century, the **Carron Ironworks** was founded near Falkirk, producing mainly military munitions. By 1800 it was the largest ironworks in Europe. Scotland' **shipbuilding** industry began as early as 1802, when the steam vessel *Charlotte Dundas* was launched on the Forth and Clyde Canal. The growth of the iron and shipbuilding industries, plus extensive use of steam power, created a massive demand for coal from the coalfields of southern Scotland.

Industrialization led to a concentration of Scotland's **population** in the central Lowlands. In 1840 one-third of the country's industrial workers lived in Lanarkshire, and Glasgow's population grew from 17,000 in the 1740s to more than 200,000 a century later. Such sudden growth created urban overcrowding on a massive scale and as late as 1861, 64 percent of the entire Scottish population lived in one- or two-room houses. For most Clydesiders, "house" meant a couple of small rooms in a grim tenement building, where many of the poorest families were displaced Highlanders a. Irish immigrants; the Irish arrived in Glasgow at the rate of 1000 a week during the potato famine of the 1840s.

By the late nineteenth century a measure of prosperity had emerged from industrialization, and the well-paid Clydeside engineers went to their forges wearing bowler hats and starched collars. They were confident but their optimism was misplaced. Scotland's industries were very much geared to the export market, and aft **World War I** conditions were much changed. During the war, when exports had been curtailed by a combination of U-boat activity and war production, new industries ha developed in India and Japan, and the eastern market for Scottish goods never recovered. The postwar world also witnessed a contraction of world trade, which hit shipbuilding industry very hard and, in turn, damaged the steel and coal industries.

These difficulties were compounded by the financial collapse of the early 1930s, an by 1932 28 percent of the Scottish workforce was unemployed. Some 400,000 Scots emigrated between 1921 and 1931, and those who stayed endured some of the worst social conditions in the British Isles. By the late 1930s, Scotland had the highest infa

1890	1914–18	1928	1939
Forth Rail Bridge opens, spanning the Firth of Forth.	100,000 Scots lose their lives in World War I.	The National Party of Scotland is formed.	The population of Scotland reaches fiv million.

mortality rate in Europe. There was a partial economic recovery in the mid-1930s, but high unemployment remained until the start of **World War II**.

The Labour movement

In the late eighteenth century, conditions for the labouring population varied enormously. Handloom weavers were well paid, whereas the coal miners remained serfs, bought and sold with the pits they worked in. The 1832 **Scottish Reform Act** extended the franchise to include a large proportion of the middle class, and thereafter political radicalism assumed a more distinctive working-class character. During the next thirty years, as Scotland's economy prospered, skilled workers organized themselves into **craft unions**, such as the Amalgamated Society of Engineers, to negotiate improvements for their members within the status quo. Politically, the trade unions gave their allegiance to the Liberal Party, but in 1888 **Keir Hardie** left the Liberals to form the Scottish Socialist Party, later merged with the Independent Labour Party, founded in Bradford in 1893. Scottish socialism as represented by the ILP was ethical rather than Marxist in orientation, owing a great deal to the Kirk background of many of its members. But electoral progress was slow, partly because the Roman Catholic priesthood consistently preached against socialism.

Red Clydeside

In the early years of the twentieth century, two small Marxist groups established themselves on what became known as **Red Clydeside**: the **Socialist Labour Party**, which concentrated on workplace militancy, and the party-political **British Socialist Party**. During World War I local organizers of the SLP gained considerable influence by playing on the fears of the skilled workers, who felt their status was undermined by the employment of unskilled workers. After the war, the influence of the shop stewards culminated in a massive campaign for the forty-hour working week. The strikes and demonstrations of the campaign, including one with 100,000 people (and the Red Flag flying) in St George's Square, Glasgow, panicked the government into sending in troops and tanks. The rank and file had little interest in revolution, however, though many of the activists did go on to become leaders within the newly formed **Communist Party of Great Britain**.

The rise of the Labour Party

The ILP, by then an affiliated part of the socialist **Labour Party**, made its electoral breakthrough in 1922, sending 29 Scottish MPs to Westminster. Their high hopes of social progress and reform were dashed, like trade union militancy, by the 1930s depression. At the 1945 general election, Labour won 40 seats in Scotland and, more recently, the party has dominated Scottish politics. In 1955 the Conservatives had 36 Scottish MPs; by 1997 none at all, though they returned one MP in the 2003 general election and have over a dozen MSPs in the Scottish Parliament.

The ILP MPs of the 1920s combined their socialism with a brand of Scottish nationalism. The Labour Party maintained an official policy of self-government for Scotland, endorsing home rule in 1945 and 1947, but these endorsements were made with less and less enthusiasm. In 1958 Labour abandoned the commitment altogether, adopting a unionist vision of Scotland, much to the chagrin of many Scottish activists.

1939–45	1961	1979	1996
34,000 Scottish soldiers lose their lives in World War II; 6000 civilians die in air raids.	The US deploy Polaris nuclear missiles in Holy Loch.	Scottish referendum for devolution fails to gain required forty percent.	The Stone of Scone is returned to Scotland.

Towards devolution

The **National Party of Scotland** was formed in 1928, its membership mostly drawn from the non-industrial parts of the country. A mixture of practical politicians and left-leaning eccentrics, such as the poet Hugh MacDiarmid, in 1934 it merged with the right-wing Scottish Party to create the **Scottish National Party**. The SNP achieved its electoral breakthrough in 1967 when Winnie Ewing won Hamilton from Labour in a by-election. The following year the SNP won 34 percent of the vote in local government elections, and both the Labour and Conservative parties, wishing to head off the Nationalists, began to work on schemes to give Scotland a measure of self-government, the term **devolution** becoming common currency.

The Scottish referendum

The situation took a dynamic turn in 1974, when Labour were returned to power with a wafer-thin majority. The SNP held seven seats, which gave them considerable political leverage, and meant that devolution was firmly on the agenda. The SNP had also run an excellent election campaign, concentrating on North Sea oil, now being piped ashore in significant quantities. Their two most popular slogans, "England expects ... Scotland's oil" and "Rich Scots or Poor Britons?", seemed to have caught the mood of Scotland.

In 1979 the Labour government, struggling to hold onto office, put its devolution proposals before the Scottish people in a **referendum**. The "yes" vote gained 33 percent, the "no" vote 31 percent – but the required forty percent threshold wasn't reached. Now for the first time, Scottish opinion had shifted away from home rule; the reluctance to embrace it was based on uncertainty about the consequences, concerns about multi-layered government and, in some areas, a fear that the assembly might be dominated by the Clydeside conurbation.

Scotland under Thatcher

The incoming Conservative government of **Margaret Thatcher** set its face against any form of devolution. It argued that the majority of Scots had voted for parties committed to the Union – Labour, the Liberals and themselves – and that only a minority supported the separation advocated by the SNP. At the same time, the government asserted that any form of devolution would lead inevitably to the break-up of the United Kingdom and that the devolution solutions put forward by other parties would result inescapably in separation.

As the Thatcher years rolled on, growing evidence suggested that few Scottish voters accepted either this reasoning or the implication that Scots did not know what was good for them. The Conservatives' support in Scotland was further eroded by their introduction of the deeply unpopular **Poll Tax**, a form of local taxation that took little account of income. The fact that it was imposed in Scotland a year earlier than in England and Wales was the source of further resentment.

Scotland after Devolution

Scotland's first-ever **general election** took place in 1999, using proportional representation (PR) rather than the first-past-the-post system employed in Westminst

1999	2009	2011
Labour win the most seats in Scotland's first-ever general election.	Carol Ann Duffy becomes the first Scottish Poet Laureate.	The Scottish National Party win a majority in the Scottish Parliament.

elections. This meant that, despite winning 39 percent of the vote, Labour had to enter into a coalition with the Liberal Democrats in the 129-seat assembly. The SNP were the second-largest party, with just under 30 percent of the vote. Over the course of two parliamentary terms, the coalition introduced policies to the left of the New Labour programme in Westminster, abolishing tuition fees for Scottish university students and granting state support for the elderly in care.

However, under the commanding leadership of **Alex Salmond**, the nationalists took advantage of voter disenchantment with Labour in both Holyrood and Westminster, becoming the largest party in 2007 (by one seat) and forming a minority administration. Four years later, the SNP won an outright parliamentary majority – something the PR system was designed to prevent – and immediately called a referendum on independence, to be held in 2014. The referendum had an incredible energizing effect on the political scene in Scotland – the debate politicized a whole new generation, and as the campaign went on, the impossible – Scottish independence – began to look possible. Opinion polls in the final weeks before the vote gave the Yes vote a slim majority, but in the end, predictions of economic chaos tipped the balance and the No vote won 55 to 45 – the turnout (85 percent) was a UK record for any election.

Having lost the argument for independence, some predicted the demise of the SNP. Yet despite the resignation of Alex Salmond, the SNP went from strength to strength, with **Nicola Sturgeon**, the extremely popular new leader, leading the party to victory in all but one of the Scottish Westminster constituencies in the 2015 general election – a record never before achieved by any party.

The 2016 Holyrood elections saw Scotland's political landscape change again, leaving SNP just shy of an outright majority, the Conservatives in second place and women leading all three of the country's major political parties. The impact of the 2016 "Brexit" referendum, in which 52 percent of UK voters opted to leave the EU, has yet to be played out. In Scotland, 62 percent voted to remain in the EU, prompting many within the SNP to call for another independence referendum, but so far the polls suggest this has not resulted in a surge of support for Scottish independence.

The Scottish economy

Scotland has benefited from the economic prosperity enjoyed in the UK as a whole, but the decline of heavy industry has been all but total, and **unemployment** has produced profound social problems in parts of Glasgow, Edinburgh and smaller towns. Meanwhile, in Orkney, Shetland and in northeast Scotland, particularly around Aberdeen, the **oil industry** – although well past its boom – continues to underpin an economy which might otherwise have struggled to cope with the uncertainties of agriculture and, especially, **fishing**. In spite of encouraging signs of recent progress, the Highlands and Islands remain an economically fragile area that needs special measures, distance from markets being a fundamental problem. Increasingly, the local environment is seen as a major asset, and the establishment of a system of **National Parks** has gone some way to creating a firm framework in which tourism can develop alongside local communities and the interests of the natural world.

2013	2014	2016
Andy Murray becomes the first Briton to win Wimbledon men's singles title since 1896.	Scotland votes against independence in a referendum.	Scotland votes to remain within the EU, but the UK as a whole votes to leave.

Books

Scottish writing is alive and well and so prolific that it can be difficult to keep up with it. This selection covers both classic and modern, and titles marked with ★ are particularly recommended.

FICTION

★Iain Banks *The Bridge, The Crow Road, Espedair Street, A Song of Stone, The Wasp Factory, Dead Air, The Steep Approach to Garbadale*. Just a few titles by this astonishingly prolific author, who also wrote sci-fi as Iain M. Banks. His work can be funny, pacey, thought-provoking, imaginative and downright disgusting, but it is never dull. His final novel, *The Quarry*, was published posthumously in 2013.

Christopher Brookmyre *One Fine Day In the Middle of the Night, The Sacred Art of Stealing, A Tale Etched in Blood and Hard Black Pencil* and *Bedlam*. All very funny, inventive novels that refuse to be categorized – you'll probably find them in the crime section, but they're as much politico-satirical.

John Buchan *The Complete Richard Hannay*. This single volume includes *The 39 Steps, Greenmantle, Mr Standfast, The Three Hostages* and *The Island of Sheep*. Good gung-ho stories with a great feel for the Scottish landscape. Less well known, but better, are Buchan's historical romances such as *Midwinter*, a Jacobite thriller, and *Witchwood* (Kindle and audio only), a tale of religious strife in the seventeenth century.

Anne Donovan *Hieroglyphics*, her first collection of short stories, and *Budda Da*, her hilarious first novel, were both nominated for major prizes, and rightly so. Her novel *Being Emily* is about growing up in Glasgow.

★Lewis Grassic Gibbon *A Scots Quair*. A landmark trilogy set in northeast Scotland during and after World War I, the events seen through the eyes of Chris Guthrie, torn between her love for the land and her desire to escape a peasant culture.

Alasdair Gray *Lanark: A Life in Four Books*. A postmodern blend of social realism and labyrinthine fantasy. Gray's extraordinary debut as a novelist, featuring his own allegorical illustrations, takes invention and comprehension to their limits.

★Neil M. Gunn *The Silver Darlings*. Probably Gunn's most representative and best-known book, evocatively set on the northeast coast and telling the story of herring fishermen during the great years of the industry.

James Hogg *The Private Memoirs and Confessions of a Justified Sinner*. Complex, dark mid-nineteenth-century novel dealing with possession, myth and folklore, looking at the confession of an Edinburgh murderer from three different points of view.

Jackie Kay *Trumpet*. The protagonist is dead before the novel begins. He was a black Scottish jazz trumpeter, wh[...] left a wife in mourning and a son in deep shock, for t[...] posthumous medical report revealed him to be a woma[...] Kay is also a poet. *Red Dust Road* is a warm and movi[...] memoir of growing up black, gay and adopted in 196[...] Glasgow.

James Kelman *Busconductor Hines*. The wildly fun[...] story of a young Glasgow bus conductor with an intens[...] boring job and a limitless imagination. *How Late it W[...] How Late* is Kelman's Booker Prize-winning and disturb[...] look at life as seen through the eyes of a foul-mouth[...] blind Glaswegian drunk.

★A.L. Kennedy *Looking for the Possible Dance*. T[...] talented writer dissects the difficulties of hum[...] relationships on a personal and wider social level. M[...] recent novels *Original Bliss* and *Paradise* have the same [...] touch, as do her collections of short stories, *Indelible A[...]* and *What Becomes*.

Alexander McCall Smith *44 Scotland Street* and [...] *Sunday Philosophy Club* series. Prolific author of feel-g[...] novels set in middle-class Edinburgh: the *44 Scotland Str[...]* series centres on the occupants of the address and [...] *Sunday Philosophy Club* novels are gentle detective ya[...] with a female amateur sleuth.

Naomi Mitchison *The Bull Calves* is set in 1747 a[...] comments on the terrible after-effects of Jacob[...] rebellion. *Lobster on the Agenda*, written in 1952, clos[...] mirrors contemporary life in Kyntyre where Mitch[...] lived.

★Ian Rankin *The Hanging Garden, The Falls [...] Fleshmarket Close*. Superbly plotted dark stories featu[...] Rebus, the famous maverick police detective who ha[...] the bars of Edinburgh. Made into a TV series and the sub[...] of a guided tour in the city. Rebus retired in *Exit Music*, [...] returned in *Standing in Another Man's Grave*.

Sir Walter Scott *The Waverley Novels*. The books [...] did much to create the romanticized version of Scottish [...] and history.

Muriel Spark *The Prime of Miss Jean Brodie*. Wonde[...] evocation of middle-class Edinburgh life and aspiratio[...]

Robert Louis Stevenson *Dr Jekyll and Mr Hyde, [...] Master of Ballantrae, Weir of Hermiston*. Nineteen[...] century tales of intrigue and adventure.

★Alan Warner *Morvern Callar*. Bleakly humorous s[...] of a supermarket shelf-packer from Oban who finds [...]

byfriend has committed suicide in her kitchen. It'll grip
ou. *The Sopranos* is the story of five teenage convent choir
irls who go to Edinburgh for a competition, full of an
xplosive mixture of adolescent sexuality and naivety. Its
quel, *The Stars in the Bright Sky*, sees them off on holiday.
e Dead Man's Pedal is a teenage boy's rite of passage in
mall-town Scotland in the 1970s.

Irvine Welsh *Irvine Welsh Omnibus*. A compendium

including *Trainspotting*, *The Acid House* and *Marabou Stork
Nightmares*, all of which can also be found as separate
titles. Welsh trawls through the horrors of drug addiction,
sexual fantasy, urban decay and hopeless youth but,
thankfully, his unflinching attention is not without
humour. His latest, *Skagboys*, is a prequel to *Trainspotting*,
and his latest, *A Decent Ride*, is set in the same dark
underworld.

POETRY

bert Burns *Selected Poems*. Scotland's most famous
rd (see box, p.165). Immensely popular all over the
orld, his best-known works are his earlier ones, including
ld Lang Syne and *My Love Is Like A Red, Red Rose*.

ouglas Dunn *New Selected Poems 1964–2000*. A writer
 delicately wrought poetry, ranging from the intensely
vate to poems involved with Scottish issues.

athleen Jamie *The Queen of Sheba*, *Jizzen and The Tree
use*. Although often set in Scotland, her work has a wider
nificance; its tone is strong, almost angry, and its
emes both personal and universal. *Findings* is a prose
urnal of her travels around her native Scotland. In her
est, *The Bonniest Companie*, Jamie set out to write
oem a week during the independence referendum year
2014.

ckie Kay *The Adoption Papers*, *Other Lovers* and *Life
sk*. The current Scottish poet laureate explores being
ck, Scottish and gay and deals with personal
ationships in an accessibly intimate way. *Fiere* is the
etic counterpoint to her memoir *Red Dust Road*.

Liz Lochhead *Bagpipe Muzak*. In a strong
aightforward style, coupled with shrewd observations,
hhead speaks with immediacy on personal
ationships. Some of her best work is in *The Colour of Black
White: Poems (1984–2003)*. *Fugitive Colours* was written
ring her time as Scottish poet laureate (2011–16).

Norman MacCaig *Selected Poems*. Justly celebrated
 its keen observation of the natural world, MacCaig's
k remains intellectually challenging without being
. His poetry, rooted in the Highlands, uses detail to
lore a universal landscape.

gh MacDiarmid *Selected Poems*. Immensely
uential, not least for his nationalist views and use of
ts, MacDiarmid's poetry is richly challenging. His poem

A Drunk Man Looks at a Thistle is acknowledged as a
masterpiece of Scottish literature.

★**George Mackay Brown** *Collected Poems*. Brown's
work is as haunting, beautiful and gritty as the Orkney
islands that inspire it. *Travellers*, published posthumously,
features work either previously unpublished or which had
appeared only in newspapers and periodicals.

Sorley Maclean (Somhairle MacGill-Eain) *From Wood
to Ridge: Collected Poems*. Written in Gaelic, his poems have
been translated in bilingual editions all over the world, and
deal with the sorrows of poverty, war and love.

McMillan and Byrne (eds) *Modern Scottish Women
Poets*. The work of more than a hundred women writers of
the twentieth century, some of whom have sunk into
undeserved obscurity.

Edwin Morgan *New Selected Poems*. A love of words and
their sounds is evident in Morgan's poems, which are
refreshingly varied and often experimental, commenting
on the Scottish scene with shrewdness and humour.

Edwin Muir *Collected Poems*. Muir's idyllic childhood on
Orkney at the turn of the twentieth century remained with
him as a dream of paradise in contrast to his later life in
inhospitable Glasgow. His poems are passionately
concerned with Scotland.

Don Paterson *God's Gift to Women*, *Landing Light* and *Nil
Nil*. The only poet to have won the T.S. Eliot Prize twice, he
is deservedly much respected. *40 Sonnets* is his new and
powerful collection.

Iain Crichton Smith *Collected Poems*. Born on the Isle of
Lewis, Crichton Smith wrote with feeling and sometimes
bitterness, in both Gaelic and English, of the life of the rural
communities, the iniquities of the Free Church, the need to
revive Gaelic culture and the glory of the Scottish
landscape.

HISTORY, POLITICS AND CULTURE

eal Ascherson *Stone Voices*. Intelligent, thought-
voking ponderings on the nature of Scotland and the
d to devolution, interspersed with personal anecdotes.

la Bathurst *The Lighthouse Stevensons*.
aightforward account of the fascinating lives and
azing achievements of Robert Louis Stevenson's family,
 built many of the island lighthouses round Scotland.

n Bell *Scotland's Century – An Autobiography of the*

Nation. Richly illustrated and readable account of the social
history of Scotland, based on radio interviews with people
from all walks of life.

Tom Devine *The Scottish Nation 1700–2000*. The best
post-Union history, from the last Scottish Parliament to the
new one.

Rosemary Goring *Scotland: The Autobiography: 2000
Years of Scottish History by Those Who Saw it Happen.*

Fascinating first-hand accounts from the likes of Tacitus, Mary, Queen of Scots, Oliver Cromwell, Adam Smith, Billy Connolly, as well as ordinary folk.

★**David Howarth** *The Shetland Bus*. Wonderfully detailed story of the espionage and resistance operations carried out from Shetland by British and Norwegian servicemen, written by someone who was directly involved.

Fitzroy Maclean *Bonnie Prince Charlie*. Very readable and more or less definitive biography of Scotland's most romanticized historical figure, written by the "real" James Bond.

Alistair Moffat *Border Reivers*. A vivid account of near 300 years of savage raiding and mayhem which makes ■ look at the now peaceful area with different eyes.

T.C. Smout *A History of the Scottish People 1560–1830* ar *A Century of the Scottish People 1830–1950*. Wide acclaimed books, of particular interest to those keen ■ social history. Smout combines enormous learning with clear and entertaining style.

ART, ARCHITECTURE AND HISTORIC SITES

Jude Burkhauser *Glasgow Girls: Women in Art and Design 1880–1920*. The lively contribution of women to the development of the Glaswegian Art Nouveau movement is recognized in this authoritative account.

Alan Crawford *Charles Rennie Mackintosh*. Part of the World of Art series, describing the major contribution of Scotland's premier architect and designer.

Philip Long and Elizabeth Cumming *The Scottish Colourists 1900–30*. A recognition of the importance of the work of this group of artists; lavishly illustrated.

★**Duncan MacMillan** *Scottish Art 1460–199* Overview of Scottish painting with good sections ■ landscape, portraiture and the Glasgow Boys. *Scotti Art in the 20th Century 1890–2001* offers a detailed lo■ at modern art.

Steven Parissien *Adam Style*. A well-illustrated accou of the birth of the Neoclassical style, named after the t Scottish Adam brothers, Robert and James.

MEMOIRS AND TRAVELOGUES

★**Elizabeth Grant of Rothiemurchus** *Memoirs of a Highland Lady*. Hugely readable recollections written with wit and perception at the turn of the eighteenth century, charting social changes in Edinburgh, London and Speyside.

Hamish Haswell-Smith *The Scottish Islands*. An exhaustive and impressive gazetteer with maps and absorbing information on all the Scottish islands. Filled with attractive sketches and paintings, the book is breathtaking in its thoroughness and lovingly gathered detail.

★**Samuel Johnson and James Boswell** *A Journey to the Western Isles of Scotland* and *The Journal of a Tour to the Hebrides*. Lively accounts of a famous journey around the islands taken by the great lexicographer Dr Samuel Johnson and his biographer and friend James Boswell.

John Lister-Kaye *Song of the Rolling Earth*. The author tells what led him to become a passionate naturalist and turn a derelict Highland estate into a field study cen■ where he encourages others to live in harmony with ■ natural environment. An inspiring story.

George Mackay Brown *Letters from Hamnav* A selection of writings from a weekly column in ■ *Orcadian*, chronicling everyday life in Orkney during ■ early 1970s. Gentle and perceptive.

Alasdair MacLean *Night Falls on Ardnamurchan*. A cla■ story of the life and death of the Highland croft community in which the author grew up.

Robert Louis Stevenson *Edinburgh: Picturesque No* First published in 1879, this is a charming evocation■ Stevenson's birthplace – its moods, curiosities ■ influences on his work.

Betsy Whyte *The Yellow on the Broom*. A fascinat■ glimpse of childhood in a traveller family between ■ wars, both on the road and in council housing for par■ the year to comply with school attendance. *Red Row* and *Wild Honey* continue the story.

Language

Language is a thorny, complex and often highly political issue in Scotland. If you're not from Scotland yourself, you're most likely to be addressed in a variety of English, spoken in a Scottish accent. Even then, you're likely to hear phrases and words that are part of what is known as Scots, now officially recognized as a distinct language in its own right. To a lesser extent, Gaelic, too, remains a living language, particularly in the *Gàidhealtachd* or Gaelic-speaking areas of the northwest Highlands, Western Isles, parts of Skye and a few scattered Hebridean islands. In Orkney and Shetland, the local dialect of Scots contains many words carried over from Norn, the Old Norse language spoken in the northern Isles from the time of the Vikings until the eighteenth century.

Scots

Scots began life as a northern branch of Anglo-Saxon, emerging as a distinct language in the Middle Ages. From the 1370s until the Union in 1707, it was the country's main literary and documentary language. Since the eighteenth century, however, it has been systematically repressed to give preference to English.

Rabbie Burns is the most obvious literary exponent of the Scots language, but there was a revival in the last century led by poets such as Hugh MacDiarmid. Only recently has Scots enjoyed something of a renaissance, getting itself on the Scottish school curriculum in 1996, and achieving official recognition as a distinct language in 1998. Despite these enormous political achievements, many people (rightly or wrongly) still regard Scots as a dialect of English. For more on the Scots language, visit sco.wikipedia.org.

Gaelic

Scottish **Gaelic**, (*Gàidhlig*, pronounced "gallic") is one of the four Celtic languages to survive into the modern age (Welsh, Breton and Irish Gaelic are the other three). Manx, the old language of the Isle of Man, died out early last century, while Cornish was finished as a community language in the eighteenth century. Scottish Gaelic is most closely related to Irish Gaelic and Manx – hardly surprising since Gaelic was introduced to Scotland from Ireland around the third century BC. Some folk still argue that Scottish Gaelic is merely a dialect of its parent language, Irish Gaelic, and indeed the two languages remain more or less mutually intelligible. From the fifth to the twelfth centuries, Gaelic enjoyed an expansionist phase, thanks partly to the backing of the Celtic Church in Iona.

Since then, Gaelic has been in steady decline. Even before Union with England, however, religious ideology and wealth gradually passed into non-Gaelic hands. The royal court was transferred to Edinburgh and an Anglo-Norman legal system was put in place. The Celtic Church was Romanized by the introduction of foreign clergy, and, most important of all, English and Flemish merchants colonized the new trading towns of the east coast. In addition, the pro-English attitudes held by the Covenanters led to strong anti-Gaelic feeling within the Church of Scotland from its inception.

The two abortive Jacobite rebellions of 1715 and 1745 furthered the language's decline, as did the Clearances that took place in the Gaelic-speaking Highlands from the 1770s to the 1850s, which forced thousands to migrate to central Scotland's new industrial belt or emigrate to North America. Although efforts were made to halt the decline in the first half of the nineteenth century, the 1872 Education Act gave no official recognition to Gaelic, and children were severely punished if they were caught speaking the language in school.

The 2011 census put the number of Gaelic-speakers at under 60,000 (just over one percent of the population), the majority of whom live in the **Gàidhealtachd**, though there is thought to be an extended Gaelic community of perhaps 250,000 who have some understanding of the language. Since the 1980s, great efforts have been made to try and save the language, including the introduction of bilingual primary and nursery schools, and a huge increase in the amount of broadcasting time given to Gaelic-language and Gaelic music programmes, and the establishment of highly successful Gaelic colleges such as Sabhal Mòr Ostaig (Ⓦsmo.uhi.ac.uk).

Gaelic grammar and pronunciation

Gaelic is a highly complex tongue, with a fiendish, antiquated **grammar** and, with only eighteen letters, an intimidating system of spelling. **Pronunciation** is easier than it appears at first glance; one general rule to remember is that the stress always falls on the first syllable of a word. The general rule of syntax is that the verb starts the sentence whether it's a question or not, followed by the subject and then the object; adjectives generally follow the word they are describing.

SHORT AND LONG VOWELS

Gaelic has both short and long vowels, the latter being denoted by an acute or grave accent.

a as in c**a**t; before nn and ll, as in c**o**w	**o** as in p**o**t
à as in b**a**r	**ò** like enthr**a**l
e as in p**e**t	**ó** like c**o**w
é like r**ai**n	**u** like sc**oo**t
i as in s**igh**t	**ù** like l**oo**
í like fr**ee**	

VOWEL COMBINATIONS

Gaelic is littered with diphthongs, which, rather like in English, can be pronounced in several different ways depending on the individual word.

ai like c**a**t, or p**e**t; before dh or gh, like str**ee**t	**ei** like m**a**te
ao like the sound in the middle of colonel	**eu** like tr**ai**n, or f**ear**
ea like p**e**t, or c**a**t, and sometimes like m**a**te; before ll or nn like c**o**w	**ia** like f**ear**
	io like f**ear**, or shorter than str**ee**t
èa as in h**ear**	**ua** like w**ooer**

CONSONANTS

The consonants listed below are those that differ substantially from the English.

b at the beginning of a word like the **b** in big; in the middle/end of a word like the **p** in pair

bh at the beginning of a word like the **v** in van; elsewhere it is silent

c as in cat; after a vowel it has aspiration before it

ch always as in lo**ch**, never as in chur**ch**

cn like the **cr** in crowd

d like the **d** in dog, but with the tongue pressed against the back of the upper teeth; at the beginning of a word or before e or i, like the **j** in jam; in the middle or at the end of a word like the **t** in cat; after like the **ch** in church

dh before and after a, o or u is an aspirated **g**, rather like a gargle; before e or i like the **y** in yes; elsewhere silent

fh usually silent; sometimes like the **h** in house

g at the beginning of a word as in get; before e like **y** in yes; in the middle or end of a word like the **ck** sock; after i like the **ch** in loch

gh at the beginning of a word as in get; before or after a

a, o or u rather like a gargle; after i sometimes like the
y in gay, but often silent

after i and sometimes before e like the l in lot;
elsewhere a peculiarly Gaelic sound, produced by
flattening the front of the tongue against the palate

h like the **v** in van

at the beginning of a word as in pet; elsewhere it has
aspiration before it

pronounced as **sht**

s before e or i like the **sh** in ship; otherwise as in
English

sh before a, o or u like the **h** in house; before e like the
ch in loch

t before e or i like the **ch** in church; in the middle or
at the end of a word it has - aspiration before it;
otherwise as in English

th at the beginning of a word, like the **h** in house;
elsewhere, and in the word *thu* (you), silent

AELIC PHRASES, VOCABULARY AND COURSES

e of the best introductory **teach-yourself Gaelic** courses is *Speaking Our Language* by Richard Cox, based on the TV
ries, much of which you can watch on YouTube. If you just want to get better at pronouncing Gaelic words, try *Blas na*
idhlig by Michael Bauer, or for a phrasebook, your best bet is *Everyday Gaelic* by Morag MacNeill. You can also do some
f-learning on the Gaelic section of the BBC website Ⓦ bbc.co.uk.

REETINGS AND BASIC WORDS

s	tha	hotel	taigh-òsda
	chan eil	house	taigh
llo	hallo	story	sgeul
w are you?	ciamar a tha thu?	song	òran
e	tha gu math	music	ceòl
nk you	tapadh leat	book	leabhar
lcome	fàilte	bread	aran
ne in	thig a-staigh	water	uisge
od day	latha math	whisky	uisge beatha
odbye	mar sin leat	post office	post oifis
odnight	oidhche mhath	Edinburgh	Dun Eideann
ers	slàinte	Glasgow	Glaschu
terday	an-dé	America	Ameireaga
ay	an-diugh	Ireland	Eire
orrow	maireach	England	Sasainn
		London	Lunnain

ELIC GEOGRAPHICAL AND PLACE-NAME TERMS

purpose of this list is to help with place-name derivations from Gaelic and with more detailed map reading.

ainn	river	cairn, from càrn	pile of stones
or auch, from achadh	field	camas	bay, harbour
aileach	rock	cnoc	hill
	Scotland	coll or colly, from coille	wood or forest
ach	ridge	corran	a spit or point jutting into
ardan or arden,	a point of land or height		the sea
m àird		corrie, from coire	round hollow in
s	dwelling		mountainside, whirlpool
from allt	stream	craig, from creag	rock, crag
	brake or clump of trees	cruach	bold hill
n	bay	drum, from druim	ridge
or bally, from baile	town, village	dubh	black
och, from bealach	mountain pass	dun or dum, from dùn	fort
	white, fair	eilean	island
	summit	ess, from eas	waterfall
from beag	small	fin, from fionn	white
from beinn	mountain	gair or gare, from geàrr	short
from blàr	field or battlefield	garv, from garbh	rough

geodha	cove	**more, from mór**	large, great
glen, from gleann	valley	**rannoch, from raineach**	bracken
gower or gour,	goat	**ross, from ros**	promontory
from gabhar		**rubha**	promontory
inch, from innis	meadow or island	**sgeir**	sea rock
inver, from inbhir	river mouth	**sgurr**	sharp point
ken or kin, from ceann	head	**sron**	nose, prow or promonto
knock, from cnoc	hill	**strath, from srath**	broad valley
kyle, from caolas	narrow strait	**tarbet, from tairbeart**	isthmus
lag	hollow	**tigh**	house
larach	site of an old ruin	**tir or tyre, from tìr**	land
liath	grey	**torr**	hill, castle
loch	lake	**tràigh**	shore
meall	round hill	**uig**	shelter
mon, from monadh	hill	**uisge**	water

Norn and Norse terms

Between the tenth and seventeenth centuries, the chief language of Orkney and Shetland was Norn, a Scandinavian tongue close to modern Faroese and Icelandic. After the end of Norse rule, and with the transformation of the Church, the law, commerce and education, Norn gradually lost out to Scots and English, eventually petering out completely in the eighteenth century. Today, Orkney and Shetland have their own **dialects**, and individual islands and communities within each group have local variations. The dialects have a Scots base, with some Old Norse words; however, they don't sound strongly Scottish, with the Orkney accent – which has been likened to the Welsh one – especially distinctive. Listed below are some of the words you're most likely to hear, plus some terms that appear in place names, not just in Orkney and Shetland, but also in parts of the Hebrides.

NORN PHRASES AND VOCABULARY

ayre	beach	**mootie**	tiny
bister	farm	**muckle**	large
böd	fisherman's store	**noost**	hollow place where
bruck	rubbish		a boat is drawn up
burra	heath rush	**noup**	steep headland
crö	sheepfold	**peerie/peedie**	small
eela	rod-fishing from	**plantiecrub**	small dry-stone enclos
	small boats	**(or plantiecrö)**	for growing cabbage
ferrylouper	incomer (Orkney)	**quoy**	enclosed, cultivated
fourareen	four-oared boat		common land
foy	party or festival	**roost**	tide race
geo	coastal inlet	**scattald**	common grazing land
haa	laird's house	**scord**	gap or pass in a ridge
hap	hand-knitted shawl		of hills
howe	mound	**setter**	farm
kame	ridge of hills	**shaela**	dark grey
kishie	basket	**sixern/sixareen**	six-oared boat
mool	headland	**soothmoother**	incomer (Shetland)
moorit	brown	**voe**	sea inlet

Glossary

uld Old

airn Baby

en Hill or mountain

lackhouse Thick-walled traditional dwelling

onnie Pretty

othy Primitive cottage, hut or mountain shelter

ae Slope or hill

ig Bridge

och Circular prehistoric stone fort

urn Small stream or brook

re Shelter for cattle; cottage

irn Mound of stones

lMac Caledonian MacBrayne ferry company

ilidh (pronounced "kay-lee") Social gathering involving dancing, drinking, singing and storytelling

ntral belt Central Scotland between the Forth and lyde including Edinburgh and Glasgow

an Extended family

arances Evictions from the Highlands (see p.591)

rbett A mountain between 2500ft and 3000ft high

venanters Supporters of the Presbyterian Church in e seventeenth century

annog Celtic lake or bog dwelling

oft Small plot of farmland with house, common in e Highlands

k A long dagger

lmen Grave chamber

am Literally, one-sixteenth of a fluid ounce. Usually fers to any small measure of whisky

n Fortified mound

h A wide sea inlet or estuary

dhealtachd Gaeldom, Highlands or Gaelic-eaking area

e Personal guide used on hunting or fishing trips

n Deep, narrow mountain valley

ing Limestone and gravel mix used to cover ildings

manay New Year's Eve

ff Meeting place; pub

Historic Environment Scotland, a government-ded heritage organization

bite Supporter of the Stewart claim to the throne, st famously Bonnie Prince Charlie

**Knee-length tartan skirt worn by Highland men

Church

d Landowner; aristocrat

Rounded hill

s Grassy coastal land; coastal golf course

**Lake

Lochan Little loch

Mac/Mc These prefixes in Scottish surnames derive from the Gaelic, meaning "son of". In Scots "Mac" is used for both sexes. In Gaelic "Nic" is used for women: Donnchadh Mac Aoidh is Duncan MacKay, Iseabail Nic Aoidh is Isabel MacKay

Machair Sandy, grassy, lime-rich coastal land, generally used for grazing

Manse Official home of a Presbyterian minister

Mercat Cross lit. Market Cross

Munro A mountain over 3000ft high

Munro-bagging The sport of trying to climb as many Munros as possible

NTS The National Trust for Scotland, a heritage organization

Peel Fortified tower, built to withstand Border raids

Pend Archway or vaulted passage

Presbyterian The form of Church government used in the official (Protestant) Church of Scotland, established by John Knox during the Reformation

RIB Rigid inflatable boat

Runrig A common form of farming in which separate ridges are cultivated by different occupiers under joint agreement

Sassenach Derives from the Gaelic **Sasunnach**, meaning literally "Saxon"; used by Scots to describe the English

Scottish Baronial Style of architecture favoured by the Scottish land-owning class featuring stepped gables and round turrets

Sheila na gig Female fertility symbol, usually a naked woman displaying her vulva

Shinty Stick and ball game played in the Highlands, with similarities to hockey

Smiddy Smithy

SNH Scottish Natural Heritage, a government-funded conservation body

SNP Scottish National Party

Sporran Leather purse worn in front of, or at the side of, a kilt

Tartan Check-patterned woollen cloth

Thane A landowner of high rank; the chief of a clan

Trews Tartan trousers

Wee Small

Wee Frees Followers of the Free Presbyterian or Free Church of Scotland

Wynd Narrow lane

Yett Gate or door

Small print and index

Rough Guide credits

Editors: Greg Dickinson, Melissa Graham, Tim Locke
Layout: Anita Singh
Cartography: Ashutosh Bharti, Richard Marchi
Picture editor: Michelle Bhatia
Proofreader: Jan McCann
Managing editor: Mani Ramaswamy
Assistant editor: Divya Grace Mathew

Production: Jimmy Lao
Editorial assistant: Aimee White
Senior DTP coordinator: Dan May
Cover design: Sarah Stewart-Richardson
Publishing director: Georgina Dee

Publishing information

This eleventh edition published March 2017 by
Rough Guides Ltd,
80 Strand, London WC2R 0RL
4, Community Centre, Panchsheel Park,
New Delhi 110017, India
Distributed by Penguin Random House
Penguin Books Ltd, 80 Strand, London WC2R 0RL
Penguin Group (USA), 345 Hudson Street, NY 10014, USA
Penguin Group (Australia), 250 Camberwell Road,
Camberwell, Victoria 3124, Australia
Penguin Group (NZ), 67 Apollo Drive, Mairangi Bay,
Auckland 1310, New Zealand
Penguin Group (South Africa), Block D, Rosebank Office
Park, 181 Jan Smuts Avenue, Parktown North, Gauteng,
South Africa 2193
Rough Guides is represented in Canada by DK Canada, 320
Front Street West, Suite 1400, Toronto, Ontario M5V 3B6
Printed in Singapore
© Rough Guides 2017
Maps © Rough Guides

All rights reserved. No part of this publication may be
reproduced, stored in or introduced into a retrieval system,
or transmitted in any form, or by any means (electronic,
mechanical, photocopying, recording or otherwise) without
the prior written permission of the copyright owner.
624pp includes index
A catalogue record for this book is available from the
British Library
ISBN: 978-0-24127-103-2
The publishers and authors have done their best to ensure
the accuracy and currency of all the information in **The
Rough Guide to Scotland**, however, they can accept
no responsibility for any loss, injury, or inconvenience
sustained by any traveller as a result of information or
advice contained in the guide.
1 3 5 7 9 8 6 4 2

Help us update

We've gone to a lot of effort to ensure that the eleventh
edition of **The Rough Guide to Scotland** is accurate
and up-to-date. However, things change – places get
"discovered", opening hours are notoriously fickle,
restaurants and rooms raise prices or lower standards. If
you feel we've got it wrong or left something out, we'd like
to know, and if you can remember the address, the price,
the hours, the phone number, so much the better.

Please send your comments with the subject line
"**Rough Guide Scotland Update**" to mail@uk
.roughguides.com. We'll credit all contributions and send a
copy of the next edition (or any other Rough Guide if you
prefer) for the very best emails.
Find travel information, read inspiring features and book
your trip at roughguides.com.

ABOUT THE AUTHORS

Greg Dickinson was let loose from his desk job at Rough Guides to update the Skye, Small Isles and north and northwest Highlands sections of this book. He writes travel features for *The Independent* and ⓦroughguides.com and hosts the Rough Guides podcast.

Brendon Griffin has contributed to, and edited, various Rough Guides including West Africa, Central America, Spain, Portugal, Peru and New York, and has written numerous travel articles for the Rough Guide anthologies *Make the Most of Your Time on Earth* and *Make the Most of Your Time in Britain*. He lives in Edinburgh.

Rob Humphreys has spent some part of every year in Scotland since he was nowt but a lad in rural Yorkshire. One day he hopes to sail round the islands, but in the meantime can be found steering the Puppet Theatre Barge through the waterways of London.

Norm Longley has spent most of his working life in central/eastern Europe – he is the author of the Rough Guides to Slovenia and Romania – but more recently has turned his hand to home shores, contributing to the Scotland, Wales and Ireland guides. He lives in Somerset and can occasionally be seen erecting marquees on The Rec in Bath.

Keith Munro has been a freelance writer since 2010 after a stretch working in London's music industry as a record label manager. A keen traveller, he spent a year in the French Pyrenees before returning to his childhood home of Edinburgh, and has since contribute to *The Rough Guide to France* and other travel related publications.

Helena Smith was lucky to grow up in the Trossachs region of central Scotland and under the Zomba Plateau in Malawi. She is a travel writer and photographer, and blogs about food and community at ⓦeathackney.com.

Acknowledgements

Greg Dickinson: Thanks to Tim Locke for his top notch editing, Leanne Cromie at Bunk Campers for the wheels, Jude Henderson at Visit Scotland for all the help, and to Mani Ramaswamy for commissioning me. Special shout out to my de-facto co-updater Victoria Wainwright for joining me on the adventure; sorry we never saw a puffin.

Rob Humphreys: Thanks to Val for company and for staying in the odd place that will never make it into the guide for good reasons. And thanks to the Wrigley Sisters for a cracking gig in the Hope.

Norm Longley: Norm would like to thank Greg for his first class editing – not to mention his extraordinary patience – in the process of updating this book. Very special thanks are due to Carron Tobin at Rural Dimensions for her

continued, and brilliant, assistance, and Bonnie Wood at the Argyll and the Isles Cooperative in Islay. Thanks are also due to Bridgeen Mullen in Portavadie; David and Jo in Tobermory; Joan and Barry at Corrie House; Alan and Alyson at Dunvalanree in Carradale; Cameron and Lynn at Dunchraigaig House in Kilmartin; Sheila Gilmore at VisitArran; Fiona McPhail at the Tighnabruaich Sailing School; Louisa Davidson at Mount Stuart; Calum Ross in Loch Melfort; David and Ewan at the Ballygrant Inn on Islay; David Ainslie on Seil; Laura McIntyre at the Atlantic Isles Centre on Luing; Fiona Potter in Glasgow; and the at Calmac. Most importantly, thank you to Christian, An Luka and Patrick.

Helena Smith: Helena would like to thank Claire Reid a Angela and Grahame for their hospitality.

Readers' updates

Thanks to all the readers who have taken the time to write in with comments and suggestions (and apologies if we've inadvertently omitted or misspelt anyone's name):

Joanne Archibald, Gert Barlow, Gerry Bell, Naomi Kaye Honova, Peter Jackson, Martyn Rawles, Ben Young.

Photo credits

AWL Images: Alan Copson
Robert Harding Picture Library: Adam Burton
Getty Images: Kathy Collins
Alamy Stock Photo: Ross Gilmore
AWL Images: Doug Pearson (b). **Robert Harding Picture Library:** Julian Elliott (t)
0 Alamy Stock Photo: Andrew Scott-Martin
1 Alamy Stock Photo: Ian Cowe (b); David Nash (c).
etty Images: Mark Sunderland (t)
2 Getty Images: David C Tomlinson
4 Dreamstime.com: Creativehearts
5 Alamy Stock Photo: Simon Grosset (b); Mar notographics (tl). **AWL Images:** Hemis (c). **Getty Images:** ckr Open (tr)
5 Alamy Stock Photo: Mike Booth (tr); Hemis (c); South est Images Scotland (tl). **Getty Images:** Liz Leyden (b)
7 Alamy Stock Photo: David Gowans (b); John Ryan (t)
4 Alamy Stock Photo: Julie Fryer Images (b); Geoff augh (t). **Getty Images:** rabmcbridephotography (c)
9 Alamy Stock Photo: Rob Ford (br); Tim Gainey (tr) nny Williamson (bl). **Dreamstime.com:** Drumist (tl)
9 Alamy Stock Photo: Hugh Harrop (cr); Robert Harding cture Library Ltd (cl); Steven Scott Taylor (b). **Getty ages:** Clare Mansell (t)
Dreamstime.com: William McKelvie (t). **The Three imneys:** Angus Bremner (b)
Alamy Stock Photo: Scottish Viewpoint (b). **Fotolia:** Spiers (t)
Alamy Stock Photo: David Gowans (t); Hemis (b). **tolia:** richsouthwales (c)
Alamy Stock Photo: David Robertson
Alamy Stock Photo: imageBROKER
–51 Getty Images: Alan Copson
Alamy Stock Photo: Jeremy Sutton-Hibbert
Alamy Stock Photo: pictureditor (t); Urbanmyth (b)
5 Alamy Stock Photo: John Peter Photography (tr).
e Royal Circle Bar: (bl)
2–113 Alamy Stock Photo: Wildscape
5 Alamy Stock Photo: Jon Sparks
5–137 Alamy Stock Photo: A.P.S. (UK)
9 Alamy Stock Photo: South West Images Scotland
1 Robert Harding Picture Library: Ashley Cooper
6–157 Getty Images: Peter Chisholm 2010
5–177 Getty Images: Brian Lawrence
9 Getty Images: Ivan Vdovin
5 Alamy Stock Photo: Bill Miller (t). **Corbis:** JAI / Will y (b)
9 Alamy Stock Photo: drew farrell (b); scottish view (t)
–221 Getty Images: Patrick Dieudonne

223 Alamy Stock Photo: Alan Wright
247 Alamy Stock Photo: age fotostock (tl); Alan Payton (b); John Warburton-Lee Photography (tr)
274–275 Getty Images: Jon Arnold Images
277 Alamy Stock Photo: JIM RYCE
291 Alamy Stock Photo: Jon Arnold Images Ltd (t); Jon Arnold Images Ltd (bl); Alan Oliver (br)
303 Getty Images: David Alexander
311 Alamy Stock Photo: John McKenna (br).
Dreamstime.com: Photos1st (t)
318–319 Alamy Stock Photo: Albaimages
321 Alamy Stock Photo: Juergen Schonnop
338–339 Getty Images: Robert Harding World Imagery / Eurasia
341 Alamy Stock Photo: Scottish Viewpoint
357 Alamy Stock Photo: Ancient Art & Architecture Collection Ltd (b). **Robert Harding Picture Library:** Patrick Dieudonne (t)
375 Getty Images: Dennis Barnes
390–391 Robert Harding Picture Library: Alan Majchrowicz
393 Getty Images: Amanda Fletcher
409 Alamy Stock Photo: Ross Gilmore (t). **Getty Images:** Gallo Images (b)
423 Getty Images: Paul Harris
434–435 Corbis: Christophe Boisvieux
437 Alamy Stock Photo: highbrow / Stockimo
453 Getty Images: D W Horner (t). **Robert Harding Picture Library:** John Miller (b)
475 Alamy Stock Photo: David Noton Photography (t)
482–483 4Corners: PhotoFVG / SIME / Fortunato Gatto
485 Getty Images: Sebastian Wasek
495 Alamy Stock Photo: Andy Sutton (t). **Robert Harding Picture Library:** Karl Johaentges (br)
505 Getty Images: Lee Frost
521 Alamy Stock Photo: John Hilton (br). **Dreamstime. com:** Luca Quadrio (t)
529 Alamy Stock Photo: David Lyons
543 Dreamstime.com: John Braid (bl). **The Pier Arts Centre:** Alistair Peebles (br). **Robert Harding Picture Library:** Martin Zwick (t)
556–557 Alamy Stock Photo: Vincent Lowe
559 Alamy Stock Photo: Kevin Schafer
567 Alamy Stock Photo: Dave Donaldson (bl); Kevin Schafer (t); Adam Seward (br)
580 Alamy Stock Photo: DGP_Scotland

Cover: *Portrait of red deer stag, Lochaber, West Highlands* **naturepl.com:** Mark Hamblin

Index

Maps are marked in grey

F

G

M

Map symbols

The symbols below are used on maps throughout the book

――― ― ∙ ―	International boundary	✈	International airport	✉	Post office	/│\\	Hill shading
― ― ―	Chapter boundary	✈	Domestic airport	🍾	Whisky distillery	⌂	Observatory
	Motorway	🅿	Parking	⛷	Skiing	🏛	Abbey
	Major road	○	Train station	⛳	Golf course	🏛	Monastery
	Minor road	ⓣ	Tram stop	〰	Swimming Pool	⚲	Chapel
	Pedestrian road	♦	Point of interest	⩾	Bridge		Building
	Steps	∴	Ruins/archeological site	▲	Peak		Church
― ― ― ―	Footpath	🏛	Stately home	⚡	Viewpoint		Cemetery
― ∙ ― ∙ ―	Railway	♖	Castle	〰	Rocks		Park
― ∙ ― ∙ ―	Ferry route	♣	Museum	🗼	Lighthouse		Forest
	River/coastline	⊤	Gardens	🗻	Waterfall		Beach
	Canal	✂	Battlefield	◖	Cave		Pedestrianized area
―――	Wall	⛺	Campsite	🏛	Cairn(s)		
●‐ ‐ ‐●	Cable car	ⓘ	Tourist office	⊙	Statue		

Listings key

■	Accommodation	
●	Eating	
■	Drinking/nightlife	
●	Shopping	

A ROUGH GUIDE TO
ROUGH GUIDES

ublished in 1982, the first Rough Guide – to Greece was a student scheme that became a publishing henomenon. Mark Ellingham, a recent graduate in nglish from Bristol University, had been travelling in reece the previous summer and couldn't find the right uidebook. With a small group of friends he wrote his wn guide, combining a highly contemporary, ournalistic style with a thoroughly practical pproach to travellers' needs.

he immediate success of the book spawned series that rapidly covered dozens of estinations. And, in addition to impecunious ackpackers, Rough Guides soon acquired a uch broader readership that relished the guides' t and inquisitiveness as much as their thusiastic, critical approach and value-for- oney ethos.

ese days, Rough Guides include commendations from budget to luxury d cover more than 120 destinations ound the globe. Visit Ⓦ roughguides om for travel tips and inspiring features, buy our latest ebooks and plan your xt trip.

Long bus journey? Phone run out of juice?

TEST **YOUR KNOWLEDGE** WITH OUR ROUGH GUIDES TRAVEL QU

1 Denim, the pencil, the stethoscope and the hot-air balloon were all invented in which country?

a. Italy
b. France
c. Germany
d. Switzerland

2 What is the currency of Vietnam?

a. Dong
b. Yuan
c. Baht
d. Kip

3 In which city would you find the Majorelle Garden?

a. Marseille
b. Marrakesh
c. Tunis
d. Malaga

4 What is the busiest airport in the world?

a. London Heathrow
b. Tokyo International
c. Chicago O'Hare
d. Hartsfield-Jackson Atlanta International

5 Which of these countries does not have the equator running through it?

a. Brazil
b. Tanzania
c. Indonesia
d. Colombia

6 Which country has the most UNESCO World Heritage Sites?

a. Mexico
b. France
c. Italy
d. India

7 What is the principal religion of Japa

a. Confucianism
b. Buddhism
c. Jainism
d. Shinto

8 Every July in Sonkajärvi, central Finl contestants gather for the World Championships of which sport?

a. Zorbing
b. Wife-carrying
c. Chess-boxing
d. Extreme ironing

9 What colour are post boxes in Germa

a. Red
b. Green
c. Blue
d. Yellow

10 For three days each April during Song festival in Thailand, people take to th streets to throw what at each other?

a. Water
b. Oranges
c. Tomatoes
d. Underwear

For more quizzes, competitions and inspirational features go to **roughguides.c**

.a / 3:b / 4:d / 5:b / 6:c / 7:d / 8:b / 9:d / 10:a

ROUGH GUIDES

ESCAPE THE EVERYDAY

COLOUR THE WORLD

BEST DAY ON **EARTH**
THE WORLD'S MOST EXTRAORDINARY EXPERIENCES
FROM DAWN TILL AFTER DARK

MAKE THE MOST OF YOUR TIME ON EARTH

ADVENTURE BECKONS
YOU JUST NEED TO KNOW WHERE TO LOOK

roughguides.com